CRITICAL SURVEY

OF

POETRY

Second Revised Edition

Volume 5

James Clarence Mangan - Ezra Pound

Editor, Second Revised Edition
Philip K. Jason
United States Naval Academy

Editor, First Edition, English and Foreign Language Series
Frank N. Magill

SALEM PRESS, INC.
Pasadena, California   Hackensack, New Jersey

Library of Congress Cataloging-in-Publication Data

Critical survey of poetry / Philip K. Jason, editor.—2nd rev. ed.
p. cm.
Combined ed. of: Critical survey of poetry: foreign language series, originally published 1984, Critical survey of poetry: supplement, originally published 1987, and Critical survey of poetry: English language series, rev. ed. published 1992. With new material. Includes bibliographical references and index.
ISBN 1-58765-071-1 (set : alk. paper) — ISBN 1-58765-076-2 (v. 5 : alk. paper) —
1. Poetry—History and criticism—Dictionaries. 2. Poetry—Bio-bibliography. 3. Poets—Biography—Dictionaries. I. Jason, Philip K., 1941 -   .

PN1021 .C7 2002
809.1′003—dc21
2002008536

CONTENTS

COMPLETE LIST OF CONTENTS

VOLUME 1

VOLUME 2

VOLUME 3

VOLUME 4

VOLUME 5

VOLUME 6

VOLUME 7

VOLUME 8

POETRY AROUND THE WORLD

RESEARCH TOOLS

INDEXES

CRITICAL SURVEY

OF

POETRY

JAMES CLARENCE MANGAN

Born: Dublin, Ireland; May 1, 1803
Died: Dublin, Ireland; June 20, 1849

PRINCIPAL POETRY

Poems, by James Clarence Mangan, with Biographical Introduction, by John Mitchel, 1859
Poems of James Clarence Mangan (Many Hitherto Unpublished), 1903 (D. J. O'Donoghue, editor)
Poems, 1996-1999 (4 volumes; Jacques Chuto, editor)

OTHER LITERARY FORMS

James Clarence Mangan is known primarily for his poetry and verse translations from more than twenty different languages, including Gaelic. However, he also wrote and translated witty, humorous prose works, articles, stories and essays, most of which appeared between 1832-1849 in different Irish periodicals, such as the *Comet, Irish Penny Journal, Dublin University Magazine, Vindicator, Nation, Irish Monthly Magazine.* During the last year of his life, Mangan wrote a series of articles called "Sketches and Reminiscences of Irish Writers," published in *The Irishman.*

ACHIEVEMENTS

The biggest distinction any mid-nineteenth century Irish poet could hope to achieve was to be called a national poet. James Clarence Mangan, one of the Young Ireland poets, won this "title" through versatile and prolific poetic production. Although written in English, most of his poetry absorbed distinctly Gaelic patterns and rhythmical structures and effectively revived the tone and imagery of the ancient bardic verse. Mangan's work inspired a whole generation of Irish writers—among them William Butler Yeats and James Joyce—to find their own voice and, thus, continue the process of de-Anglicization of Irish literature and culture, which had been the goal of the first Celtic Revival at the end of the eighteenth century, by means of antiquarian explorations of the ancient Celts' heroic past. Haunted by a sense of cultural inferiority and lost identity caused by the country's colonial dependence on the British Empire, Mangan's poetry responded to the pressing demand in nineteenth century Ireland for a national literature. His authentic, powerful counterimages would help Ireland resist and repair the cultural rupture and discontinuity caused by the colonial intervention.

BIOGRAPHY

Remembered by his contemporaries as a bohemian, James Clarence Mangan was a victim of morbid melancholy, opium, and alcohol. He was prone to painful introspection, which, intensified by his Catholicism, led to frequent withdrawals from friends, family, and society. This, combined with his recurring financial difficulties and physical neglect, resulted in a troubled, though artistically intensive, life and an early death at the age of forty-six.

The poet was born in Dublin, where he spent his whole life. His father gave up his position as a schoolteacher in order to run the grocery business he had inherited through his wife. He sent James to a Jesuit school where the boy started learning Latin, Spanish, French, and Italian—languages that would determine to a great extent the course of his career. A rather eccentric child, he experienced severe difficulties dealing with the "outside" world and withdrew into an eight-year-long state of blindness, allegedly caused by excessive exposure to rain. His relatives found him hard to reach and considered him "mad."

Mangan was fifteen when he became the family's breadwinner—his father had gone bankrupt. The first job he took was at a scrivener's office. It was at this time that he started publishing his first poems in the *Grant's* and *New Ladies'* almanacs and when his mysterious blindness disappeared. Two years later, however, in 1820, an illness and a severe emotional disturbance led to a diagnosis of hypochondriasis. His poetic apprenticeship ended in 1826, but his ill health persisted. By this time, Mangan had moved away from his family and had started publishing nationalistic poetry. He continued earning a meager living by doing clerical work. In 1833, he supported a parliamentary petition for repeal of the Act of Union between Ireland and Britain. His political activism motivated him also to start learning Gaelic and establish close contacts with Gaelic scholars.

In 1834 the *Dublin University Magazine,* Ireland's most prestigious periodical at the time, started accepting

Mangan's poetry for publication. This marked the beginning of a long-term collaboration; in *Dublin University Magazine*, the twenty-two chapters of Mangan's *Anthologia Germanica = German Anthology*, as well as numerous other "translations" from various languages, would appear for the next twelve years. The following few years were also eventful: In 1836 Mangan met Charles Gavan Duffy, the future founder of the nationalist Young Ireland Party and its weekly magazine *The Nation*, both active advocates of physical-force politics as the only means to achieve Irish independence.

Two years later, Mangan was hired by George Petrie, a famous antiquarian, to work at the Ordinance Survey Office. The project involved surveying and remapping the whole of Ireland for the purposes of the British government. This was arguably the most enabling experience in Mangan's life as, on one hand, it strengthened his contacts with Gaelic scholars and, on the other, allowed him to get acquainted with numerous historical sources and manuscripts, and through them, with Ireland's ancient past(s). Touched by concrete visions of the glory of the ancient Celts, Mangan began reworking Eugene O'Curry's prose translations of Irish bardic verse, gaining confidence in the strength of his own artistic voice. These poems, "translations" from the Irish, appeared in the *Irish Penny Journal*, founded in 1840 with the task of popularizing the country's Gaelic past.

Although the late 1830's marked a very fruitful period in Mangan's artistic life, they had detrimental effects on his health, which worsened to such an extent that friends started referring to him as "poor Mangan." They also realized that he had become addicted to opium (later to be substituted by alcohol) in an attempt to deal with his attacks of "intellectual hypochondriacism." He denied the fact, refusing to take an abstinence pledge. His finances worsened when the Ordnance Survey Office was closed in December of 1841. It took Petrie a few months to find Mangan a new job—this time at the Trinity College Library. The poet experienced relative financial stability for a few years but the solitary nature of his work made it hard for him to publish. As biographers point out, his artistic production in *Dublin University Magazine* alone had declined from an average of one hundred pages annually, between 1835 and 1839, to about thirty during each of the following five years.

Having been unemployed for about six months, in 1845 Mangan resumed his job at Trinity Library. It was a half-time position this time, which meant increased financial difficulties for the poet. The years 1845-1846, however, were marked by remarkable creative achievements and the publication in *Nation* of his most passionate nationalistic verse. He declared his readiness, as his biographer Ellen Shannon-Mangan pointed out, "to devote [himself] almost exclusively to the interests of [his] country." Yet, his desire to join openly the physical-force politics led by Duffy was repeatedly thwarted by the latter's refusal to admit Mangan in the Irish Confederation. As the great Famine intensified in Ireland, so did Mangan's bad health. In December of 1847, ill and homeless, he took to drinking again, although he had tried to give it up for a number of years. The remaining year and a half of his life was characterized by bad health and poverty, despite the isolated attempts by few of his friends to help him. Still, Mangan continued to write and publish poetry.

In May, 1849, he contracted cholera. In June, having allegedly recovered from it, he was found dying in a street cellar. He was taken to a hospital, where he died a week later.

ANALYSIS

As an Irish Romantic poet, James Clarence Mangan was aware of a loss of innocence, a feeling central to Romantic subjectivity in general, which was intensified by the poet's attempts to cope with the feeling of being trapped in a present corrupted by Britain's colonial power. The poet's search for an alternative, natural and pure self (individual, cultural, national) was therefore colored by a search for an appropriate medium for its expression. Until the beginning of his ardent nationalism in the mid-1830's, Mangan relied primarily on translation from various European and Middle Eastern languages as a means of escaping his oppressive environment, both personal and social. Through acts of imagination, translation transported him to various, often exotic lands. However, his biographers emphasize repeatedly that Mangan had no knowledge of most of the languages from which he "translated." He often transformed his originals by saturating them, especially Oriental verse and that of the minor German Romantics, with rhetorical and stylistic effects typical for his own nationalistic poetry. When Duffy criticized him once for a rather loose Moorish "translation," Mangan pointed out instead its relevance to the Gaelic Revival, responding in his own witty way: "Well, never mind, it's Tom Moorish."

There were also cases when Mangan attributed his own verse to foreign poets. "Twenty Golden Years Ago," he claimed, was originally a German poem by Selber (German for "himself"). Other works were attributed to a Persian poet by the name of Hafis ("half-his"). It is true that, in the absence of an Irish literary tradition in English, a poet like Mangan had greater chances to support himself by publishing translations from languages with rich and firmly established literary traditions, such as German, or from cultures that were distinctly non-English, such as Turkish, Persian, or even Serbian. Translation, therefore, offered Mangan a means of release from his personal anguish and a means of pulling himself away from English Romanticism, which represented for all Irish the culture of the colonizer. Poems like "Siberia" demonstrate eloquently Mangan's idea of the devastating effects his country's colonial history had had on Irish consciousness. He translated the poem, which originally voiced Freiligrath's impressions of an Icelandic landscape, into a metaphor with distinct political overtones pointing to the inhuman conditions in Ireland during the Famine: "Blight and death alone./ No summer shines." The year was 1846:

> Pain as in a dream,
> When years go by
> Funeral-paced, yet fugitive,
> When man lives, and doth not live,
> Doth not live—nor die.

"O'HUSSEY'S ODE TO THE MAGUIRE"

Mangan never learned enough Gaelic to be able to translate Irish verse. Therefore, he relied primarily on the "translation" strategies he had already acquired. His wide access to old numbers of *Dublin University Magazine* allowed him to benefit from Samuel Ferguson's and other antiquarians' prose translations from the 1820's and 1830's. Mangan's creative imagination and acute ear for melody and rhythm completely transformed them into remarkable pieces of poetry. "O'Hussey's Ode

to the Maguire" serves as a poignant example. Compare the opening stanzas of Ferguson's translation (1834) with Mangan's poem (1846). The speaker is Eochaidh Ó Heodhussa, chief bard of the Maguire Hugh. Hugh, himself, is in the Irish province of Munster, waging war against the colonizing enterprise of Queen Elizabeth I:

> Cold weather I consider this night to be for Hugh!
> A cause of grief is the rigor of its showery drops;
> Alas, insufferable is
> The venom of this night's cold.
>
> Where is my Chief, my master, this bleak night, mavrone!
> O, cold, cold, miserably cold is this bleak night for Hugh,
> Its showery, arrowy, speary sleet pierceth one through
>   and through,
> Pierceth one to the very bone!

Although Mangan preserved the four-line stanza of Ferguson's translation, his poem reveals a psychological intensity not readily audible in Ferguson's version. Partly because each of the poets chose to emphasize different sides of the native Irish character— Ferguson stressed its profound sense of loyalty to a leader, while Mangan singled out its pure, natural force and strength—the two texts convey different political messages. Ferguson, representative of the Anglo-Irish Ascendancy, strives to bring England's attention to the respect and loyalty with which the Old Irish address their leader, a quality the Crown should value in its subjects if the prosperity of both England and Ireland is to be secured. By 1846, however, the physical-force politics as a means to achieve Irish independence had gathered considerable momentum. That is why Mangan's regular *abba* rhyme is opposed to variations in line length and beat, from iambs to dactyls or anapests, to produce a singular explosive power.

"KATHALEEN NY-HOULAHAN"

This poem of 1841 refers to an Irish sovereignty myth, very much like Mangan's most famous poem, "Dark Rosaleen." Ireland is personified as a beautiful young queen ("Ny" is the feminine equivalent of the masculine "O," as in O'Neill), whose beauty and youth fade in sorrow, while waiting for her land and people to be delivered from the distress the enemy has inflicted upon them. Only masculine strength and sacrifice can again transform the "ghostly hag" into a maiden-queen.

Mangan based the poem on a literal translation from the Irish by Eugene O'Curry and, although its immediate context relates to a particular historical event, the eighteenth century Jacobite rebellions, it is beyond doubt that the contemporary readers saw it on another level: the pressing need for decisive action, if Ireland's prosperity was to be restored. In a subtle way, very much as in "Dark Rosaleen," the poem establishes a contrast between a glorious past and a rather bleak present carried across by the conditional in line four below:

> Think her not a ghastly hag, too hideous to be seen,
> Call her not unseemly names, our matchless Kathaleen:
> Young she is, and fair she is, and would be crowned a
> queen,
> Were the king's son at home here with Kathaleen Ny-
> Houlahan!

The poem contains another major theme—homelessness and wondering—introduced and elaborated upon by the framing effect of the first and last quatrains. The implicit comparison between the Irish and God's chosen people justifies the cause of Ireland's independence and renders distinctly optimistic both the end of the poem and the struggle against Britain.

"THE NAMELESS ONE"

Published in 1849, after Mangan's death, this ballad is often interpreted as the poet's farewell to his country. It is worth noting that it was one of James Joyce's favorite poems, and it is not difficult to see why. In the very first stanza, the poet creates a host of images that are distinctly Irish and at the same time transcend the narrow, nationalistic notion of Irishness that Joyce found oppressive: The "song," like the salmon, one of Ireland's ancient symbols, has started its journey to the sea, mature and full of hope. The identity of the singer, his "soul," is no longer to be separated from the "song," his art. The restraining power of history and tradition, language and ideology—the name—means no more. All that matters is the cycle of life itself, encompassing both God (first stanza) and hell (last stanza), birth and death.

OTHER MAJOR WORKS

NONFICTION: *Autobiography,* 1968.

TRANSLATIONS: *Anthologia Germanica = German Anthology: A Series of Translations from the Most Popular of the German Poets,* 1845 (2 volumes); *The Poets and Poetry of Munster: A Selection of Irish Songs by the Poets of the Last Century, with Poetical Translations by James Clarence Mangan,* 1849.

MISCELLANEOUS: *The Prose Writings of James Clarence Mangan,* 1904 (D. J. O'Donoghue, editor).

BIBLIOGRAPHY

Lloyd, David. *Nationalism and Minor Literature: James Clarence Mangan and the Emergence of Irish Cultural Nationalism.* Berkeley: University of California Press, 1987. Mangan's literary production is examined in terms of its "failure" (in the positive sense of "resistance") to comply with imperial narrative models of cultural development. Focus is on the political and cultural effects of colonialism on Irish nationalist ideology and the emerging Irish aesthetic culture.

Shannon-Mangan, Ellen. *James Clarence Mangan: A Biography.* Dublin: Irish Academic Press, 1996. Excellent, detailed study of Mangan's life and works, relying on extensive use of primary materials. Includes short analyses of Mangan's most significant work.

Welch, Robert. "James Clarence Mangan: 'Apples from the Dead Sea Shore.'" In *Irish Poetry from Moore to Yeats.* Irish Literary Studies 5. Totowa, N.J.: Barnes & Noble, 1980. Examines Mangan's literary achievements within the context of the emerging Irish national literature in English. Welch compares Mangan's Romantic nationalism with works of English and German Romantic poets. The chapter contains stylistic and rhetorical analyses of about twenty original poems, translations, and prose works.

Miglena I. Ivanova

ITZIK MANGER

Born: Czernowitz, Bukovina, Austrian Empire (now Chernovtsy, Ukraine); May 28, 1901
Died: Gadera, Israel; February 20, 1969

PRINCIPAL POETRY

Shtern oifn Dakh, 1929

Lamtern in Vint, 1933

Khumish Lider, 1935

Demerung in Shpigl, 1937

Volkens ibern Dakh, 1942

Der Shnyder-gezeln Nota Manger Zingt, 1948

Lid un Balade, 1952

Shtern in Shtoib, 1967

Medresh Itzik, 1951, 1969, 1984 (reprintings of the
    Khumish Lider with later additions)

OTHER LITERARY FORMS

In 1938, Itzik Manger published in the Warsaw Yiddish press his *Noente Geshtaltn* (intimate figures), a
newspaper series of bittersweet, fictionalized portraits of
twenty forerunners of Yiddish poetry: troubadours,
rhyming wedding jesters, itinerant actors and writers of
the nineteenth century and earlier. These popular artists
expressed themselves in Yiddish when it was considered, even by its speakers, a language fit not for literature but for low-class entertainment. They were Manger's first heroes; from their earthy folk style, he learned
the art of simplicity.

Manger's only novel, *Dos Bukh fun Gan-Eden*
(1939; *The Book of Paradise*, 1965), is a fantasy set in
Paradise—a humorous vision of the afterlife in which
familiar human weaknesses and pains persist. In *The
Book of Paradise*, fantasy is the everyday norm, and the
wrinkles are provided by earthly reality: the reality of
human nature and the folkways of the Eastern European
Jewish community. In Manger's novel, Yiddish culture—its folklore, faith, parochialism, and beauty—is
celebrated, satirized, and memorialized. *The Book of
Paradise* was published in Warsaw in August, 1939, and
nearly the entire edition was destroyed at the printer's a
month later by the invading German army. Only a handful of review copies mailed to America survived.

Although Manger's poetry places him in the line of
the English and German Romantics and the French
Symbolists, the cultural movement in which he was personally active was the Yiddish theater. Seeing himself as
the modern heir of the itinerant Yiddish entertainers of
older times, Manger was drawn to the musical theater as
a medium for direct contact with his audience. His un-

usual popularity as a poet brought him the opportunity
to write for several Yiddish theater productions in the
1930's. *Hotzmakh Shpiel*, Manger's adaptation of Abraham Goldfaden's operetta, *Di Kishufmakherin* (the sor-
ceress), was performed in Warsaw in 1936. (Goldfaden
founded the Yiddish theater in the 1870's in Romania,
producing his first musicals in wine cellars and barns.
His troupes played throughout Eastern Europe and in
England in the 1880's and 1890's. In Manger's gallery
of portraits in *Noente Geshtaltn*, Goldfaden appears on
his deathbed, hallucinating scenes.)

Sometime in the 1930's, Manger wrote the lyrics for
the Warsaw musical production of Sholom Aleichem's
novel, *Blondzne Shtern*, 1912 (*Wandering Star*, 1952), a
romance based on the lives of early Romanian Yiddish
actors. In 1935, he wrote the lyrics for the first Yiddish
musical film, *Yidl mitn Fidl* (released 1936; *Yiddle with
His Fiddle*).

Manger's best-known work for the theater is the
tragicomic operetta *Megillah Lider*, published in 1936
but not staged until thirty years later, when it was set
to music by Dov Seltzer and performed in Israel and
on Broadway as *The Megillah of Itzik Manger*. The
first production of Manger's operetta played from 1965
to 1969. It stirred much interest in Manger among the
Yiddish-scorning youth of Israel and led to the Hebrew-
speaking public's discovery of Manger's more serious
poetry. It began to appear in translation in newspapers
and magazines, and, belatedly, Manger became the first
Yiddish writer since Sholom Aleichem to win a wide
readership in Israel.

ACHIEVEMENTS

Itzik Manger's place in the cultural history of the
Jews was officially recognized in 1969 with the first an-
nual awarding of the Manger Prize for Yiddish Litera-
ture. Among the twelve founding members of the Man-
ger Prize Committee were the Hebrew writer S. Y.
Agnon (corecipient of the 1966 Nobel Prize for Litera-
ture); two prime ministers of Israel, Levi Eshkol and
Golda Meir; the then-president of Israel, himself a poet,
Zalman Shazar; and the committee's chairman, Shalom
Rosenfeld, editor in chief of the Tel Aviv daily, *Maariv*.

The committee made public what had been the private sentiment of many readers. Both for the older gen-

eration who knew the poet from prewar years in Europe and for the younger generation who had just discovered him, Manger was an intimate figure, a teacher, muse, and friend. For people whose beliefs in various opposing movements of Judaism and European humanism had failed, Manger's gentle yet hardheaded, sensuous poetry was a spiritual renewal. His poems had the power to evoke feelings and discoveries of religious intensity, but with a light touch, a lighthearted, cheerful acceptance of the evanescence of all meaning. This acceptance made possible, or necessary, Manger's anarchistic eclecticism. His poems assimilated and refined diverse sensibilities and philosophies, from Hasidism to nihilism, from Saint Francis to Friedrich Nietzsche and Sigmund Freud. Manger gleaned from these sources all that answered a human yearning; that which was abstract and therefore susceptible to rigidity and mystification, he sloughed off.

Manger's poetry readings in the 1930's drew audiences of thousands in the major cities of Poland. Local musicians played the tunes they had composed for his words. Not since the days of Sholom Aleichem's public reading tours a generation back had the flowering Yiddish cultural scene experienced such festivity. Within a decade of the publication of Manger's first book, his works were in the curriculum of every grade in the secular Jewish school system of Poland, from kindergarten through secondary school.

Manger's artful mixture of innocence, irony, deviltry, and tenderness charmed away his culture's old, argumentative obsessions with justice and truth, offering instead less instructive but more deeply satisfying ideals: love, beauty, and wisdom. Among poets, these preferences are not new; what is unusual is how far Manger's love strove to outgrow itself, to reconcile the reckless thirst for meaning and beauty with the sober, responsible cultivation of wisdom. His works offered a way to live between beauty and wisdom—between the beauty of sensation, illusion, and faith and the wisdom of memory and detachment.

BIOGRAPHY

Itzik Manger was born in 1901 to Hillel and Khava Voliner Manger, the first of three children close in age. His birthplace was the ethnically Romanian and Jewish city Czernovitz (now Chernovtsy, Ukraine), capital of Bukovina, a province of the Austrian Empire. The city was situated at the intersection of Bukovina, the Russian-ruled Ukraine, and the independent state of Romania; its official language was German. When the Russian army invaded Bukovina in 1914, the Manger family fled to Jassy, capital of the Romanian province of Moldavia, and settled there. The Mangers moved often, going from one single-room apartment or basement to another when the rent was due. Their home served also as the family's tailor shop. "A roof I didn't inherit from my parents," Itzik Manger wrote, "but stars—plenty." They were a happy family. The mother was pious and barely literate, but she knew thousands of Yiddish folk songs.

The future poet, together with his brother and their younger sister, spent childhood summers in the country, in their paternal grandparents' home. Riding through the countryside with his grandfather, Zaida Avremel the wagon driver, revealed wonders of nature and perspective to the boy from the slums. The misty Carpathian Mountains, where the spirit of the Baal Shem Tov, the founder of the Hasidic movement, had roamed seven generations before, haunted Manger, and over the years in his poetry he returned again and again to this setting.

After finishing the traditional Jewish school for boys, Manger was enrolled in a state secondary school in Czernovitz but was expelled in the second semester. This left him time to frequent cafés and wine cellars where Gypsy fiddlers played and to volunteer as a stagehand in the Yiddish theaters of Czernovitz and later Jassy, where he absorbed the folklore of his nineteenth century forerunners.

In Czernovitz, an apprentice-tailor working for Manger's father introduced the boy to the works of Johann Wolfgang von Goethe, Friedrich Schiller, and Heinrich Heine. At thirteen, Manger began writing poetry in German. His teens were an exhilarating time for him and his brother, Nota; together they discovered Rainer Maria Rilke, Friedrich Nietzsche, Paul Verlaine, and "Saint" Baudelaire. (Manger gave that title to only two others: Homer and the Baal Shem Tov.)

Before the late nineteenth century, Yiddish had no tradition of poetry other than primitive folk writings and inspirational polemics. During Manger's childhood and youth, the stories of I. L. Peretz and Sholom Aleichem created a body of modern Yiddish literature. Their example attracted the young writer of German poetry to his mother tongue and its speakers. At fifteen, Manger started to write in Yiddish, wondering whether modern poetry could be written in the language of wagon drivers, Hasidism, peddlers, and uneducated women. His doubts were banished when, in his late teens, he encountered the work of two immigrant Yiddish poets who were writing in New York. The gutsy and delicate lyricism of Moishe Leib Halpern and Mani Leib gave new power to Yiddish and set Manger on his course: He would refine the spirits of his ancient and modern fathers in the language of his mother's lullabies.

During his twenties, Manger was based in Bucharest, where he was active in the Yiddish avant-garde grouped around Eliezer Steinbarg. The group's influences were Russian, French, and German literature mixed with Slavic, Gypsy, and Jewish folklore. The spirit of the group reflected that of the times: Europe was in ferment and the Jews were in turmoil. World War I, the Bolshevik Revolution, and the Russian Civil War broke up what was left, after the mass migration to America, of the old Eastern European Jewish communities. In 1923, the immigration quotas set by the United States Congress closed the "Golden Door," and Jews came in increasing numbers to the large cities of Eastern and Central Europe.

Throughout the nineteenth century and into the twentieth, the religious faith of the Jews had been eroded by contact with the outside world and its liberal ideas. A minority clung zealously to fundamentalism; for the rest, the intensity of the lost faith became converted into various new drives: assimilation, economic and professional ambition, public service, leftist radicalism, political and cultural nationalism, intellectual activity, and art. In the popular Gentile mind, the traditionally despised Jews became the symbol of all the changes that were hitting Europe too fast: inflation, labor conflict, sexual revolution, and radical "modern" ideas of all kinds. Anti-Semitic parties and economic boycotts proliferated in Poland, Romania, Lithuania, and Germany. For the newly "emancipated" Jews, the world seemed to totter between salvation and ruin.

Amid the welter of mass movements promising the Jews a brighter future, Manger, after an adolescent leftist period, raised the unlikely banner of the renewal of Yiddish folk song. "Our wounds need balm," he wrote in a manifesto in his twenties. "All roads lead to Rome and all roads lead to the kingdom of Beauty." Some of the roads taken by Yiddish poets in the 1920's came under his attack. He criticized the radical modernists who were influenced by trends in Germany and the Soviet Union for breaking away from their Jewish roots and experimenting with deliberately unmusical verse. With his brother's meager earnings as a tailor and the occasional support of culture patrons, he traveled throughout the Jewish centers of Romania, Poland, and Lithuania, addressing crowds in outdoor markets, political meetinghouses, and wine cellars, reading poetry and lecturing on Yiddish folklore and Shalom Aleichem's sad humor. For a people whose religion was built on preserving strict dichotomies, Manger dissolved such rigid categories as "old-fashioned or modern," "popular or classical," "secular or sacred." Manger's effect on his audience was described by a poet who grew up in Poland in the 1920's, Avraham Sutzkever, in the autumn, 1958, issue of *Di goldene Keit*, the Israeli Yiddish literary journal that he edited: It was "like a child with a mirror throwing a drop of sun on an old man."

In 1928, Manger moved to Warsaw, the main center of Yiddish life and culture. When his first book, *Shtern oifn Dakh* (stars on the roof), was published in 1929, he instantly became a folk hero, known throughout Eastern Europe. Nourished by an enthusiastic public in Warsaw, he wrote more than half of his lifework there and nearly all of his best. Nevertheless, tired of writers' feuds and of the scandals caused by his penchant for wine, women, and what rabbis called "decadent" poetry, Manger left Warsaw in 1938, traveling to Paris, where there was a colony of expatriate Eastern European Jewish artists and intellectuals. Not much is known of his two years in France. It was there that he wrote his fantasy novel, *The Book of Paradise*, a wistful, gently mocking love letter to the world he had left behind.

As the German army approached Paris in 1940, Manger fled to Algiers, where thousands of legally stateless refugees scrambled for the limited opportunities of transport to safer destinations. The glint in Manger's eye caught the interest of a boat captain and won Manger a space on a boat to Liverpool in late 1940. During the war, Manger managed the German section of a London bookstore owned by Margaret Waterhouse, a great-granddaughter of the poet Percy Bysshe Shelley; she was Manger's companion and nurse for most of his ten years in England. The two months that he spent in a Liverpool hospital upon his arrival from Algiers did not completely cure him of the effects of the hunger and exhaustion he had suffered while fleeing the Nazis, and his poor health was aggravated by his increased drinking in England.

While his people were being massacred in Europe, Manger immersed himself in English and Scottish folklore: "From Herrick to Burns" was his title for an unpublished anthology of English poetry which he did not finish translating into Yiddish. In 1942, Manger's brother, Nota, died on a Soviet collective farm from hunger, exposure, and battle wounds. He had joined the Army of the Red Star as a believer in Socialism.

During his years in England, Manger waited for an American visa. He considered the Yiddish-speaking immigrant community of New York as the closest thing to a home and as the only audience that could support him. In 1951, he left England for Montreal, whose Jewish community had invited him to give a series of readings and lectures during the last months of his wait for an American visa. The enthusiasm with which he was received both in Montreal and, later that year, during a tour making public appearances in American cities, attended by crowds in the thousands, helped to restore his spirits. In 1951, he met and married Genya Nadir, the widow of the Yiddish writer Moishe Nadir. They lived in Brooklyn for the next fifteen years.

New York was a disappointment. It was clear that its Yiddish cultural scene had little future beyond the generation then growing old. Finding a society more open and tolerant than they or their ancestors had ever had, the Jews of America were rushing to assimilate. For most of those who clung to their ethnic roots, the compelling myths and visions were those of a Hebrew future (Zionism) or past (traditional Judaism). Yiddish was the language of the ghetto, whose history Jews wanted to forget. The humanistic renewal of Jewish culture that had been carried on in Yiddish squandered much of its idealism and prestige in leftist ideological squabbling that seemed anachronistic, at best, to

most of the generation that grew up after the Great Depression.

After the passing excitement of his arrival in America, Manger fell into the mood that his poetry had taught others to transcend: bitterness. The little poetry that he wrote in New York had a tired feeling. He managed to antagonize and alienate most of his friends. In the midst of the largest, freest, and richest Jewish community in history, he and his works were neglected. The remnants of the thriving Yiddish cultural scene of prewar Europe had become concentrated in a few neighborhoods of New York, with each writer coveting a share of a shrunken audience. In Israel, the bitterness of the Holocaust survivors was sublimated by the positive determination to build a country. In New York, the bitterness of the non-Zionist Yiddishists spilled out on the only people with whom they had much contact: one another. Manger complained in his letters that he was being boycotted by the Yiddish journals of New York, whose literary editors and their friends were his rivals for the title of the "Last Great Yiddish Poet." As if to belittle his stature as the most popular poet by far in the history of Yiddish, critics in New York referred to him as a mere "balladeer" or "satirist."

Manger, however, lived to see the redemption of the years he had spent facing oblivion. Ironically, it came to him in Israel, the country that had struggled to do away with the history of the Jewish Diaspora—the Diaspora whose language, ethos, and *schleppers* he had celebrated, liberated, enlightened, and exalted. As he lay in Israeli hospitals for the last two and a half years of his life, totally crippled and speechless from a nervous disease but still able to show something of a smile, he heard the news of the nation's rediscovery of his works. On the radio, he heard pop stars and schoolchildren singing his poems, in Hebrew translation, to their old tunes and to new ones as well. He read of the Manger festivals presented by the nation's cultural elite. Three weeks after the return of his power of speech, he died.

ANALYSIS

Using the verse patterns and simple language of traditional Yiddish folk songs, Itzik Manger created a style that brought modern poetic sensibilities to an unsophisticated audience. In style and theme, his poems transform the commonplace into something subtle, wondrous, and beautiful. His subjects are sad—loneliness, disappointment, death, confusion, frustration—but his poems usually evoke smiles.

Manger's voice changes not only from poem to poem but also often within the same poem. With seeming indiscriminateness, he mixes nursery rhymes, gangster jargon, regional Yiddish dialects, classical mythology, traditional prayers, and burlesque theater with the poetic traditions of Europe. His anachronisms have their own integrity, and the same can be said of his irrationalities and contradictory traits in general. Their coming together feels perfectly natural to a reader, like an intuitive click or a rhyme. In the same moment that one of Manger's paradoxes hits the reader, it also resolves itself; it is as if the reader has secretly sensed it already, so that all that is left to do is smile at a crumbled convention.

The poetic clichés that Manger enjoyed using would make a novice blush. He loved the moon and brings it in dozens of times: as a big loaf of bread for a hungry family, a crescent twinkling in Hagar's hair, an earring for Rachel, but usually just as the moon. He went out of his way to use it in rhymes. Equally unoriginal is the form in which he almost always wrote, rhymed quatrains: He meant for his poems to be sung. A list of the poets and other sources he both plagiarized and collaborated with would run as long as the Jewish exile.

BALLADS

Of the many kinds of poems that Manger wrote—ballads, lyric odes, mystical fancies, still lifes, prayers, confessions, ditties, love poems, elegies, children's songs, lullabies, mood reflections, satires, autobiographies, scenes of local color—it is the ballads that have most interested literary critics.

⹁ In his essay "The Ballad: The Vision of Blood," published in 1929, Manger acknowledged that he was influenced by the traditional British ballad of the supernatural. This influence was already apparent in "Ballad of a Streetwalker," his first published poem, which appeared in 1921 in the Bucharest Yiddish journal, *Kultur*, edited by the fabulist-poet Eliezer Steinbarg. The poem anticipates Manger's mature verse, with its emphasis on the primacy of the moment, provocative understatement and paradox, plain speech, twilight blurring of the natural and the supernatural, psychological realism, compassion for characters on the fringe of society, distant, detached

perspectives, and word music. Indeed, of his essential traits, only lightheartedness and folk traditionalism were missing.

"In "The Ballad of the Bridal Veil," published in Manger's first collection, a maiden is spinning thread for her bridal veil. At midnight, when the thread runs out, seven aged women enter, and with the white thread of their hair they weave her a veil. At dawn, they depart, and the maiden turns to the mirror. Her face has turned white.

In the ballads Manger wrote after his twenties, there is a lighter touch, as if he had been released from a spell. While he continued to explore the irrational and to develop his ghostly, grotesque symbolism, he filled his later ballads with incongruous turns of phrase and rhythm, nuances of bittersweet irony, a homey Jewish warmth, and a respect for mundane exigencies as an escape from spiritual tension. He became more resigned to chaos, alienation, cruelty, and perplexity.

"The Ballad of Hanna'leh the Orphan" exemplifies this later style. An orphan girl is visited by her mother's grave. The tears she sheds on the grave, on her mother's instruction, sprout a wonderful husband. With scissors, the daughter snips him apart from the grave, and after she brushes off the worm dangling from his nose, they introduce themselves. As soon as they meet, they go to get married, and the mother's grave waits outside the officiating rabbi's house. On her mother's instruction, the daughter cries again—this time for a baby girl—and one sprouts from the grave. The groom then dismisses his dead mother-in-law, as "we no longer need you." The young family goes off, carrying a thin thread tied to the grave. With unsentimental compassion and delicately eccentric charm, the poet exposes the powerful secret fears and the twisted longings and loves of his heroes. With a folksy Yiddish playfulness that belies the tension latent in the ballad, he makes a dance of the strange collisions and collusions of instinct.

"THE BENT TREE"

A tragic sense pervades Manger's work, yet none of his works is tragedy. In "The Bent Tree," a child looks outside and sees birds flying away for the winter. He decides that he must become a bird. His mother warns him of the dangers, but he insists. Just as he is about to take flight, she rushes to bundle him up against the weather, from head to toe. He lifts his wings, about to fly, but he is now too heavy. All he can do is sing, "I look sadly in my Mama's/ Eyes, without a word./ It was her love that didn't let/ Me become a bird." What in real life is a bitterly tragic conflict is ameliorated in the poem by the enchantingly grotesque and comic action, by the fact that it is the frustrated child who expresses the generously tragic perspective of the final sentence, and by the poet's setting of the lyrics to a lullaby tune, so that they are sung (confessed?) by parents to their children.

RELIGIOUS INFLUENCES

Manger's folkloristic approach to family situations was in the tradition begun in the Book of Genesis, the collection of prose poems about sibling rivalries, marriage problems, and intergenerational relations that is the foundation of Jewish civilization. For adult Jewish men, the traditional course of study has been the interpretation and argumentation of the Talmud, the body of law that developed as an attempt to fix a detailed code of behavior based on the teachings of the Torah (the books of Moses, the first five books of the Old Testament). For Jewish women and children, the path along which the tradition developed has been the study of the Old Testament stories themselves and of the *Midrashim*, legends included in the Talmud, which embellish the original biblical texts. In Manger's religious education, the key influence was his mother, a woman who could read only haltingly and could not write at all. Her knowledge of the Bible came from the *Tsena Urena*, a sixteenth century Yiddish version of the Bible, adapted for women. The book is a rambling narrative of retellings of the original stories according to the *Midrashim*, interwoven with fairy tales, exhortations to piety, household advice, and anecdotes about modern-day heroes (such as Jewish tailors) and villains (such as Christian gentry). The characters in the *Tsena Urena* are portrayed with the quaint reverence of the rabbinic tradition, but with an intimacy and historical naïveté that presents them as if they were members of the reader's family several generations removed.

KHUMISH LIDER

With an imagination whose first literary influence was the *Tsena Urena*, Manger wrote his own *Midrashim*, his *Khumish Lider*, transporting the patriarchs to a nineteenth century Eastern European Jewish setting.

With his wagon driver, Eliezer, Abraham rides with Isaac to the sacrifice:

> "Where are we riding to, Daddy?"
> "To Lashkev, to the Fair."
> "What are you going to buy me, Daddy,
> In Lashkev, at the Fair?"
> "A porcelain toy soldier,
> A trumpet and a drum,
> And some satin for a dress
> For Mama back at home. . . ."

Fully a third of the *Khumish Lider* is about women caught in a man's world: Abishag the Shunamite (five ballads), Bathsheba, Ruth (eight ballads), Dinah, Jephthah's Daughter, and Hagar (three ballads). In one of the last-named ballads, Abraham dismisses his concubine, Hagar, the mother of his son Ishmael, at the instigation of his wife, Sarah. As Hagar packs her things to leave, she pauses to look at a straw summer hat, a silk apron, and some beads that Abraham gave her in better days. She sighs, "'This must be what was meant for us;/ Ishmaelik'l, don't be scared. . . Such were the ways of the Patriarchs/ With their long and pious beards. . . ."

One month after its publication in 1935, the *Khumish Lider* was banned by Agudas Yisroel, the rabbinical council of Poland, as "poison for Jewish children" and "blasphemy against the People, Torah and God of Israel." From another perspective, Manger's accomplishment was to infuse the sacred stories with a sensitivity developed by a people's long and varied experience of living with them—a gift back to its source.

THE HOLOCAUST

For a Yiddish poet, and one who was so intimately attuned to the yearnings of his people, Manger wrote surprisingly little about the Holocaust. He told an interviewer in 1958 that much time would have to pass before hatred of the Germans and their helpers faded enough for artistic objectivity. In his few poetic attempts to face the destruction of his people and culture, he took two approaches: involving Jewish folk motifs and legendary figures in the reality and its aftermath, and bringing the horror down to the small scale of a personal and subjective view. The sad streak that had always run through his poetry grew more pronounced in the 1940's; the tone of some of his poems recalls the pessimism of

Ecclesiastes, though Manger is more gentle. In his poetry, visionary experience prevails over sorrow. In poems that only obliquely show signs of struggle or historical awareness, he ekes enchanting meaning and music out of the quotidian. In the survey of Yiddish literature which appears in *The Jewish People: Past and Present* (an English-language reference work published between 1952 and 1955), Shmuel Niger, the preeminent Yiddish critic, referred to Manger as "a hopeless romantic"—an apt judgment, if taken as an affectionate tribute to the poet's childlike capacity for wonder.

OTHER MAJOR WORKS

LONG FICTION: *Dos Bukh fun Gan-Eden*, 1939 (*The Book of Paradise*, 1965).

PLAYS: *Megillah Lider*, pb. 1936 (libretto; *The Megillah of Itzik Manger*, 1965); *Hotzmakh Shpiel*, pr. 1936.

NONFICTION: *Noente Geshtaltn*, 1938.

MISCELLANEOUS: *Gezamlte Shriftn*, 1961; *Shriftn in Proze*, 1980.

BIBLIOGRAPHY

Davin, Dan. *Closing Times*. New York: Oxford University Press, 1975. A collection of correspondence and reminiscences by several authors including Manger.

Kahn, Yitzhok. *Portraits of Yiddish Writers*. Translated by Joseph Leftwich. New York: Vantage Press, 1979. A collection of biographical essays on Yiddish writers, including Manger.

Roskies, David G. "The Last of the Purim Players: Itzik Manger." *Prooftexts: A Journal of Jewish Literary History* 13, no. 3 (September, 1993): 211-235. A biographical and critical overview of Manger's life and work.

David Maisel (including original translations); bibliography updated by the editors

---

ALESSANDRO MANZONI

Born: Milan, Italy; March 7, 1785
Died: Milan, Italy; May 22, 1873

PRINCIPAL POETRY

"Il trionfo della libertà," 1801
Sermoni, 1801-1804
"A Francesco Lomonaco," 1802
"Ode," 1802-1803
"L'Adda," 1803
"In morte di Carlo Imbonati," 1805-1806
"Urania," 1808-1809
Inni sacri, 1812-1815 (*The Sacred Hymns*, 1904)
"Il cinque maggio," 1821 ("The Napoleonic Ode," 1904)
"Marzo 1821," 1821, 1848

OTHER LITERARY FORMS

Alessandro Manzoni is remembered chiefly for a single work, *I promessi sposi* (1842; *The Betrothed*, 1951)—a revision of the earlier *Gli sposi promessi* (1827; *The Betrothed*, 1828)—his only novel. He was, however, a prolific writer of astonishing range and intellectual depth. Manzoni was a historian, the author of such works as the *Discorso sopra alcuni punti della storia longobardica in Italia* (1822), the *Lettre à Alphonse de Lamartine* (1848), and *La storia della colonna infame* (1842; *The Column of Infamy*, 1964), which accompanied the 1842 edition of *The Betrothed*. He was also a writer of religious and philosophical works, including *Lettre à Victor Cousin* (1829). *Dell'invenzione* (1850) and *Osservazioni sulla morale cattolica* (1819), and a philologist, author of *Sulla lingua italiana* (1850) and *Dell'unità della lingua e dei mezzi di diffonderla* (1868). His bibliography includes many more works, among them volumes of literary criticism such as *Lettera sul romanticismo* (1846) and *Del romanzo storico* (1845), and two historical tragedies, much admired by Johann Wolfgang von Goethe and Charles-Augustin de Sainte-Beuve, *Il conte di Carmagnola* (1820) and *Adelchi* (1822). Finally, his published correspondence, *Epistolario* (1882), makes fascinating reading.

ACHIEVEMENTS

Particularly on the Italian peninsula, Alessandro Manzoni emerged as a dominant figure during his long and extraordinarily productive life. His novel, *The Betrothed*, remains one of the greatest novels of the Western world, not merely of the 1800's but of all time. It is a

Alessandro Manzoni (Library of Congress)

compendium of various novelistic styles and genres, including the historical, in which context the narrative unfolds from a humble beginning concerning two peasants to epic dimensions involving a whole world in moral and physical turmoil. With his tragedy *Adelchi*, which recalls William Shakespeare's *Hamlet* (1600-1601) and *Henry IV* (1597-1598), Manzoni reached the apogee of Christian fatalism in the theater. *The Column of Infamy* is an uncategorizable work which offers psychological insights into the evil of torture; its seventeenth century characterizations reveal a novelist's skill. Finally, as a poet, his fame rests primarily on his religious poetry, *The Sacred Hymns*, an occasional political piece such as "Marzo 1821," and the "historical" ode on Napoleon, "The Napoleonic Ode."

BIOGRAPHY

Alessandro Francesco Tommaso Antonio Manzoni belongs to Lombardy, in whose capital he was born on March 7, 1785. His putative father, Count Pietro, and his mother, Giulia—the daughter of the distinguished jurist and political economist Cesare Beccaria—were incompatible and were legally separated only seven years after Manzoni's birth. Though as a child he studied in various religious schools in and around his native region, and though as a youth he suffered from excessive shyness, he developed strong sympathies with the libertarian ideas of the French Revolution, as the Jacobin flavor of his 1801 poem, "Il trionfo della libertà," clearly indicates. His mother had run off to Paris in 1795 with her new lover, Carlo Imbonati, and the young Manzoni accepted an invitation, ten years later, to join them there. He had traveled in the meantime, but Paris seemed like a shiny goal. While there, he came in contact with many liberal philosophers and politicians, a number of whom (including the historian Claude Fauriel, with whom he formed a lifetime friendship) contributed significantly to his intellectual development and to his experience of the world. He wrote some poetry during these years—"L'Adda," *Sermoni*, and "Urania" (on the civilizing virtues of the arts)—which revealed his lingering classical leanings; he also wrote an elegy in which he began to come into his own as a poet, "In morte di Carlo Imbonati," for his mother's lover, who had died when Manzoni arrived in Paris, and had left him a goodly inheritance.

In 1808, Manzoni married Henriette Blondel, the lovely sixteen-year-old daughter of a Genevese banker, Calvinist by faith. Always attracted to matters of the spirit, Manzoni found Henriette's strong sense of religious devotion a stimulus to regain acquaintance with his original Catholic faith, and it was not long before he underwent a conversion in which several Jansenist clerics played an important role. His wife switched to Catholicism as well, and his mother returned to it after many years. From this point on, back in Lombardy, Manzoni led a long life of semiretirement between Milan and his country retreat in Brusuglio, where he performed a number of agricultural experiments. His conversion inspired him to write a series of religious poems, among them, in 1812-1813, the *Inni sacri:* "La risurrezione," "Il nome di Maria," and "Il natale," followed in

1815 by "La passione" and in 1822 by "La pentecoste" ("Pentecost"). He began *The Betrothed* in 1821, and composed "Il cinque maggio" and "Marzo 1821," his two finest compositions in verse apart from the exceptionally beautiful choruses in *Adelchi*.

With these works, Manzoni's significant poetic period came to an end. What followed was a long list of intellectual works—historical, philosophical, and linguistic—in each of which his scholarly gift for documentation and analysis, to say nothing of his perpetually gentle, serene way of arguing his subjects, made a profound impression on his readers. His novel occupied a good part of his time as well, from 1823, when its first version was published under the title of *Fermo e Lucia*, to 1827, when its next version appeared as *Gli sposi promessi*, and finally to 1842, when the final version, polished in the pure Tuscan idiom and titled *I promessi sposi*, came off the presses. *La storia della colonna infame* accompanied this publication.

Such an apparently serene, productive life was not shielded from sorrow. One of the harshest blows came in 1833 with the death of Manzoni's beloved wife; eight years later, his mother died (his father had died long before). Manzoni remarried, in 1837, but his second wife, Teresa Borri, died in 1861. Of his eleven children, he was survived by only two; even his son-in-law, the well-known author Massimo D'Azeglio, died before him, as did the celebrated theological philosopher Antonio Rosmini, who had been one of the most important intellectual mentors of Manzoni's later years.

Many honors were accorded to Manzoni, though in general he shunned them—indeed, refused them in many instances. Maximilian of Austria, John Henry Newman, and William Ewart Gladstone wanted to be counted among his acquaintances. He turned down the French Legion of Honor, the Grand Duke of Tuscany's Order of Merit, and a deputyship in the Piedmontese Chamber, but he did accept a lifetime pension from King Victor Emanuel II, senatorship in the newly founded Kingdom, and the honorific Roman citizenship. Italians up and down the peninsula looked to him as a national conscience, as he lent his name to several important political actions of his day, and withdrew it symbolically from others: For example, he refused to consider Eugène de Beauharnais for King of Italy (1814),

rejected Austrian honors, and withdrew from participation in Milan's celebrations for the Bourbon Ferdinand I (1838). In 1848, he signed a petition to induce Carlo Alberto to intervene in the north, and in 1860, his vote helped to effect the transfer of the national capital from Florence to Rome.

Little wonder that when he died in Milan on May 22, 1873, of cerebral meningitis, Manzoni was honored by a state funeral and was mourned by all Italy. The occasion inspired Giuseppe Verdi to resume work on his *Messa da requiem*, which was performed, dedicated to Manzoni, one year later to the day. The musical remembrance represents a just tribute.

ANALYSIS

The product of a classical culture, Alessandro Manzoni held the written word in high regard: the fitting expression, the eloquent turn of phrase, the correct vocabulary. Poetry, which emphasized all of these things, was seen as the most fitting genre for artistic utterance. More than this, however, poetry was to be concerned with moral and civic problems rather than indulging itself in languid lyricism and autobiography. Hence, Manzoni's early verses contained barbs against the Church, tyrants, poetasters, the decadent rich, unworthy teachers, and dissolute women. In part, the impetus for this manner came from idealistic pronouncements made during the Napoleonic era (concerning justice, reason, human rights, artistic value, and civic duty) which were never translated into practice, a double standard which easily aroused the indignation of a youthfully vigorous poet.

Although in the background of Manzoni's poetry, besides a list of French authors headed by Voltaire, one finds Alfonso Varano, Giuseppe Parini, Vittorio Alfieri, Ugo Foscolo, and the early revolutionary Vincenzo Monti, the spirit of imitation never guided Manzoni's pen. Conscious of this, in the 1802 sonnet "Alla musa," he bids the deity to show him "new paths."

Manzoni's best poetry exudes a Christian ethos. Hence Goethe's praise, which went beyond Manzoni's "new" poetic manner and his "simplicity of feeling"; Goethe extolled the poet's "boldness of genius, metaphors, transitions," Manzoni's way of being "Christian without fanaticism, Roman Catholic without sanctimoniousness, zealous without hardness." Put otherwise, Manzoni's art was an inspired function of his humanitarianism.

"IL TRIONFO DELLA LIBERTÀ"

Manzoni's first significant piece was his still somewhat classical "Il trionfo della libertà," written after the peace of Lunéville (1801), in four cantos and hendecasyllabic tercets, heavy with references to ancient heroes and myths. Typically pessimistic in approach, the poem at one point considers the figure of the French General Louis-Charles Desaix, who died fighting for the independence of an indifferent land, where he lay a "barbarian . . . foreign corpse." Liberty's "triumph" is limited by the extent of the crimes committed in her name. A similar lament echoes in "A Francesco Lomonaco," a political sonnet chastising Italy for not extolling the heroic martyr for liberty—who, to make matters worse, was even exiled from his native Naples. The true sense of liberty, therefore, cannot be imposed from without; it must grow from within.

Perhaps beauty, instead of liberty, may emerge as the noblest ideal—beauty in a woman of moral and spiritual perfection, "whose sweet mouth conceals a pure smile wherein speaks the soul." This is found in Manzoni's Vergilian "Ode," though late in the poem, he turns incongruously to thoughts of bloodstained Italy. He found it hard to relinquish his youthful pessimism, which also colors a group of four sarcastic poems gathered under the title of *Sermoni:* the Horatian "A Giovan Battista Pagani," the Petronian satire on the enriched plebeian "Panegirico di Trimalcione," the invective against poetasters "Della poesia," and the pungently bitter "love" poem "A Delia." Manzoni blames individuals rather than institutions for a corrupt society in which women become playthings of lust, parlor games mask eroticism, inept poets recite "hard verses," and lovers chase after "incautious virgins"—a society symbolized by rich Trimalchio's vulgar ostentation. A brief attempt to break out of the pessimistic mold, when in 1803 he wrote an idyll on his beloved Lombard river, "L'Adda," found Manzoni this time erring in the direction of stiltedness, bound as he was to classical formulas in composing elegiac verses. The same rigidity appears in his mythologico-philosophical poem of 1808-1809, "Urania," a disquisition on the moral and utilitarian value of poetry, which is

so oratorical that he himself later described it to Fauriel as "hateful."

"IN MORTE DI CARLO IMBONATI"

Manzoni had, however, gone to Paris in 1805, and his best poem of that time, "In morte di Carlo Imbonati," reveals greater detachment and intellectual depth, avoiding the polemical and aggressive manner of his other pieces of the time. The young poet, very devoted to his mother, justifies on the grounds of pure love her cohabitation with Imbonati, defends it against the petty gossip of Milanese society, and places her consort in a paternal role, delivering a Polonius-like counsel to Manzoni, who must be guided by feeling and meditation:

> with little
> be content; never bend your eyes
> from your goal; with things human
> experiment only so much as you need
> to care not for them; never become slave;
> with the base never make peace; never betray
> the holy Truth; nor proffer ever a word
> that applauds vice, or virtue derides.

This poem, along with "A parteneide," was the last of Manzoni's early lyrics; it gave evidence that his invocation to the Muse to find "new ways" was about to be realized. He put aside indignant resentments, violent satire, and rhetorical formulas, and his postconversion poetry bears the imprint of an artist who has gained control both of himself and of his medium. To a friend, Manzoni wrote: "[Verse is] a form which above all likes to express what each one of us can find inside himself, but something no one yet has thought of saying, and which is capable only of rendering those thoughts that develop along with it, and mold themselves on it, as it were, as they are born. . . ."

THE SACRED HYMNS

Manzoni's new mastery is evident in the religious poems gathered under the title *The Sacred Hymns*. Though the collection is uneven, it is informed by a genuine and compelling poetic voice, and its concerns prefigure those of Manzoni's great novel. The civic and moral concerns which animated his early poems are elevated to universal ethical views on society. As Francesco De Sanctis has commented, *The Sacred Hymns* offer an evangelized version of the triad of liberty, equality, and fraternity. Because of their pervasively biblical tone, they may sound more didactic than intended, for in his mature years Manzoni avoided the hortatory manner; he placed revelation above inculcation, and in this he differed from those such as Parini, Alfieri, Foscolo, and Victor Hugo, who believed in the sacerdotal function of the poet.

Fittingly, the first of the *The Sacred Hymns* is called "La risurrezione," six octosyllabic lines capped by a final heptasyllabic line, giving each stanza a liturgical gait, consistent with Christ's victory over sin and death: "Like a strong man exhilarated/ The Lord was reawakened." Occasional faulty imagery and brusque changes of pace, coupled with an inconsistently dramatic representation, mar the genuine sense of *gaudeamus* that the messenger-poet wishes to convey. "Il nome di Maria" (the name of Mary) the second hymn is, by comparison, musically fluent. Three hendecasyllables and one heptasyllable per stanza in alternate rhyme make for compelling sweetness (despite a rather incongruous final image) and comfort in the eternal mother: "In the fears of his dark waking/ The child names You. . . ." In typical fashion, Manzoni is always alive to human miseries, fears, and needs. This spirit underlies the next poem, "Il natale" (the nativity), which responds to the query of what would have happened if Christ had not come:

> . . . the people
> Know not the child who's been born;
> But . . .
> in that humble repose,
> . . . inside that dust inclosed,
> They'll recognize their King.

Manzoni's worldview centers on the key word "humble," and through it the angels rending the night to sing of the holy Nativity acquire inspiring visibility. This final setting of gladsome song contrasts successfully with the opening metaphor of a boulder plunging into a valley. Here again, the poet changes the metrical scheme— seven lines of eight, seven, eight, seven, seven, seven, and six syllables respectively with rhymes of lines two with four, line five with six, and line seven of one stanza with line seven of the next—as he does, too, in the subsequent hymn, "La passione"—octaves composed of two groups of four lines in a syllabic pattern of ten, ten, ten, and nine, rhyming *abacbddc*. More sermonic and therefore less engaging than the rest, the hymn still gathers noticeable power when a choral prayer invokes God's forgiveness for those who trespassed against Jesus:

> Cease now your tremendous anger;
> And . . . may that Blood descend all over them;
> May it be but a rain of mild bathing;
> We all erred . . .

"PENTECOST"

These hymns, however, fade before the beauty of "Pentecost," which was begun in 1817, completed in 1822, and revised in March, 1855. Perhaps because it took him so long to arrive at a final version of this hymn, Manzoni never completed the projected series of twelve. As with the poetry of Saint John of the Cross, the distinction between literature and theology disappears when feeling and meditation blend and when concept translates into image with lyrical intensity:

> Oh Spirit! in supplication
> Before your solemn altars;
> Alone through inauspicious woods;
> Wandering o'er desert seas;
> From Andes chilled to Lebanon,
> From Eire to bristling Haiti;
> Scattered over every shore,
> Through You, singlehearted,
> We implore you
>
> . . . . . .
> Breathe inside the ineffable
> Smiling lips of our children.

The eight- and seven-syllable octaves with a rhyme scheme similar to that of "Il natale" release Italian poetry (with a helping hand from Giacomo Leopardi) from the traditional manner of versification established by Petrarch, Torquato Tasso, and the Arcadians. At the same time, Manzoni strikes a very influential personal note with his unobtrusive pessimism, his reasoned resignation.

"MARZO 1821"

Resignation is a component of Manzonian serenity, his most attractive quality, apparent even in his great political poems, in which it is clear that all nations and all individuals share in the common experience of suffering. "Marzo 1821" (March, 1821; revised 1848), consisting of thirteen eight-line stanzas with a rhyme scheme of *abbcdeec*, was written when the Piedmontese crossed the Ticino River and rushed to the aid of the Lombards, whose insurrection was aimed at Austrian oppression; the poem was dedicated to Theodor Koerner, the German poet-martyr for freedom from Napoleon who had died in the battle of Gadebusch (1813). The ode appeals not only to Italians but also to all civilized nations to rise for freedom. Even so, the oppressor is not challenged with hatred or invective; justice dons the cloak of universal love, as in *Le mie prigioni* (1832; *My Prisons*, 1836), by Manzoni's contemporary Silvio Pellico, who found the same transcending answer to the horrors of the Spielberg dungeons where he had been thrown.

"THE NAPOLEONIC ODE"

Manzoni's finest poem is the historical ode "The Napoleonic Ode," marking the day Napoleon died on St. Helena. These eighteen stanzas of six lines each (with rhymes on lines two and four and a pattern involving the last line of each stanza) elicited the admiration of Goethe, always a great promoter of Manzoni's poetry, and publication in the periodical *Über Kunst und Althertum*. The poem stands above all other European expressions of celebration or criticism of the Emperor because the poet is determined not to pass moral judgment, preferring to let history do the judging on the basis of a central question: "Was his true glory?" Napoleon's life embraced triumph, peril, flight, victory, sovereignty, exile, "Twice low in the dust,/ Twice high on the altar," straddling two centuries and two eras. The warring despot turns into the sorrowing prisoner who remembers in a series of images all of his exhilarations: "A heap of memories!" In the light of such ephemerality, temporal glories appear hollow, and the imposing Emperor has reached the brink of despair, while a superior force looks on, symbolized by the crucifix which "On the deserted bedding/ He placed next to himself." In a string of moving, lyrical, and reflective passages, the historical view modulates into poetic vision, a unique contribution to the literature on Napoleon.

OTHER MAJOR WORKS

LONG FICTION: *I promessi sposi*, 1827, rev. 1840-1842 (*The Betrothed*, 1828, rev. 1951).

PLAYS: *Il conte di Carmagnola*, pb. 1820; *Adelchi*, pr., pb. 1822.

NONFICTION: *Osservazioni sulla morale cattolica*, 1819; *Discorso sopra alcuni punti della storia longobardica in Italia*, 1822; *Lettre à M. C*** sur l'unité de temps et de lieu dans la tragédie*, 1823; *Lettre à Victor Cousin*, 1829; *La storia della colonna infame*, 1842 (*The Column of Infamy*, 1964); *Del romanzo storico*, 1845; *Lettera sul romanticismo*, 1846; *Lettre à Alphonse de Lamartine*, 1848; *Dell'invenzione*, 1850; *Sulla lingua italiana*, 1850; *Dell'unità della lingua e dei mezzi di diffonderla*, 1868; *Lettera intorno al vocabolario*, 1868; *Epistolario*, 1882; *Saggio comparativo su la rivoluzione francese del 1789 e la rivoluzione italiana del 1859*, 1889; *Sentir Messa*, 1923.

BIBLIOGRAPHY

Barricelli, Gian Piero. *Alessandro Manzoni*. Boston: Twayne, 1976. An introductory biography and critical study of selected works by Manzoni. Includes bibliographic references and an index.

Colquhoun, Archibald. *Manzoni and His Times: A Biography of the Author of "The Betrothed" ("I promessi sposi")*. 1954. Reprint. Westport, Conn.: Hyperion Press, 1979. One of the basic resources in English, this biography is by one of the best-known scholars of Italian literature. Illustrated.

Ferlito, Susanna F. "Fear of the Mother's Tongue: Secrecy and Gossip in Manzoni's *I promessi sposi*." *MLN* 113, no. 1 (January, 1998): 30-51. Ferlito discusses how Alessandro Manzoni's representation of the mother-daughter bond in *I promessi sposi* implicitly recognizes and keeps at bay the critical potential of that bond and by extension female alliance among peasants.

_____. *Topographies of Desire: Manzoni, Cultural Practices, and Colonial Scars*. New York: Peter Lang, 2000. Drawing upon a wide range of current disciplinary debates in the fields of comparative politics, anthropology, cultural studies, and comparative literature, this book examines how Manzoni's French and Italian writing produced differences between cultural discourses in a nineteenth-century Europe that was not yet thought of as "naturally" divided between nation-states.

Godt, Clareece G. *The Mobile Spectacle: Variable Perspective in Manzoni's "I promessi sposi."* New York: Peter Lang, 1998. Godt shows how Manzoni consistently represents what the eye sees (landscape, cityscape) and the mind conceives (characters' plans, history) under different and often paradoxical aspects. Its thesis is that the technique of variable perspective has a cognitive function, allowing the novel to "speak" in a timeless manner of reason and folly, goodness and wickedness, human reason and divine grace.

Jean-Pierre Barricelli;
bibliography updated by the editors

MARIE DE FRANCE

Born: Île de France; c. 1150
Died: England(?); c. 1215

PRINCIPAL POETRY
Lais, c. 1167 (English translation, 1911)
Ysopet, after 1170 (*Medieval Fables*, 1983; also known as *Fables*)
Espurgatoire Saint Patriz, 1208-1215 (translation of *Tractatus de purgatorio Sancti Patricii*, attributed to Henry of Saltrey)

OTHER LITERARY FORMS
In addition to the two collections of short narrative poems named above (one of which, the *Fables*, is a translation), Marie de France translated a long poem, the *Espurgatoire Saint Patriz* (1208-1215; *Saint Patrick's Purgatory*). The Latin original, *Tractatus de purgatorio Sancti Patricii* (1208; *Treatise on Saint Patrick's Purgatory*), has been attributed to Henry of Saltrey. Although the particular version Marie translated is no longer extant, virtually all of its lines are to be found in surviving manuscripts. The translation is a faithful one, to which a brief prologue and epilogue (and only a few "asides" or editorial comments) have been added. Because it is a translation and not an original work, its chief interest— if it is properly attributed to Marie de France—is in the

testimony it bears to the poet's thorough knowledge of Latin and to her concern, expressed in the epilogue, that the treatise be accessible to the layperson. The narrative also bears some resemblance in form to the genre of the *roman* (romance), which was becoming increasingly popular in this period. St. Patrick's "purgatory" is a cave on an island in Lough Derg, Donegal, which to this day still draws pilgrims; it was said to have been revealed to St. Patrick in answer to a prayer, and those who enter it hope to witness or experience the sufferings of the souls in purgatory. The treatise translated by Marie describes the adventures of a particular knight, Owein, who entered the cave and was tempted by demons but was saved by invoking the name of Christ. One motif is of particular interest to students of medieval romance: To cross the river of Hell, Owein must resort to a high and dangerously narrow bridge, which widens as soon as he has the courage to start across. Lancelot, the hero of Chrétien de Troyes's romance *Le Chevalier à la charrette* (c. 1170; *The Knight of the Cart*), must cross a similarly narrow bridge in order to rescue the abducted Queen Guinevere; once he has crossed it, the lions who seemed to be guarding the farther end have disappeared. In contrast to most romances, however (and in contrast to Marie's own *Lais*), the *Treatise on Saint Patrick's Purgatory* involves no profane love story; its inspiration is purely religious.

Other works have been attributed to Marie de France. The current scholarly consensus, however, is that none of them is hers, with the possible exception of another translation, *La Vie Seinte Audrée* (c. 1210; *The Life of Saint Audrey*), which would confirm her interest in religious themes.

ACHIEVEMENTS
Marie de France was probably not the first woman to write poetry in the French vernacular. She is, however, the earliest whose name has been recorded. In fact, she is one of the few twelfth century poets, male or female, whose names are known. This is partly because she wished to be remembered; thus, she "signed" her works by naming herself in their opening or closing lines. It is almost certain that she is also the Marie mentioned by a contemporary, Denis Piramus; if so, she was already well-known and "much praised" in the aristocratic cir-

cles of her day, where her lays were often read aloud. (Piramus's further observation that her stories were "not at all true" may even indicate some jealousy of her popularity.)

Marie's originality is harder to gauge, for although she claims to retell "Breton lays," there are no direct parallels to her tales in extant Celtic literature. She gives Celtic names to most characters and places and uses recognizable Celtic motifs (such as the fairy lover, the magic boat, and the hunt for a white animal), but her plots hinge on affairs of the heart, and her characters bear a closer resemblance to those of twelfth century romances than to the heroes and heroines of Celtic folk literature. One critic, Lucien Foulet, has gone so far as to argue that Marie herself invented the genre of the narrative lay. Though scholarly debate in this area is still lively, most would reject Foulet's hypothesis as too extreme; there are courtly lays not by Marie, and even relative dates are difficult to establish for this period. Nevertheless, few modern critics would argue with Foulet's emphasis on the conscious art with which Marie shaped her material, wherever she may have found it. Each of the twelve lays is a carefully constructed whole; the tales are told with great economy of means, yet they include nuances of feeling and of moral character that can be quite delicate. Some critics, notably Edgar Sienaert, have seen a structure in the collection as a whole, and most will grant it a thematic unity, though there is disagreement on the nature and import of this unity. Because of the uncertainty about Marie's originality, nineteenth century critics tended to give her less than her due, but no contemporary scholar will deny that she was one of the major poets of her age.

BIOGRAPHY

Of the life of Marie de France, nothing can be said with certainty; her name is known because she included it in her works, but her identity is otherwise obscure. It is probable that she was born in France, in Île de France (the region of which Paris was the capital), and that she lived much of her life in England. She wrote in the Anglo-Norman dialect of Old French, which was spoken by the ruling class in twelfth century England, and knew English as well (she translated her *Fables* from an English original, now lost). It is unlikely that she would

have identified herself by her place of origin if she had still been living there; moreover, the best manuscripts of her *Lais* and *Fables* were found in England. It is also probable that she was a woman of noble birth, for she had noble patrons and even dedicated her *Lais* to a king; she may also have been a nun, for she knew Latin well (as can be seen from her translation of the *Treatise on Saint Patrick's Purgatory*) and was better educated than most laywomen would have had occasion to be.

Beyond this, all is speculation, and as Philippe Ménard has observed, the very number of proposed identifications indicates the tenuous character of the evidence. An attractive possibility—but only a possibility—is that she was Mary, abbess of Shaftesbury, an illegitimate daughter of Geoffrey Plantagenet and half sister to Henry II of England. This would account for her apparent familiarity with members of noble circles and with the courtly literature of which Henry's queen, Eleanor of Aquitaine, was an important patron.

ANALYSIS

Despite the volume of critical writing on Marie de France, and despite the limpidity of her own style, there is yet no clear scholarly consensus on how the *Lais* should be read. The age of the poems is undoubtedly one source of difficulty: Not only do they belong to a vanished cultural and intellectual milieu, but also much external evidence (such as sources and the means of accurate dating) that might have made their interpretation easier has been lost.

Two further difficulties recur in all discussions of the *Lais*. The first is a question of genre. The genre of the narrative lay is represented in surviving literature by only thirty-odd poems, and these are too diverse to suggest a clear-cut definition. What is more, Marie's own collection of twelve lays contains pieces that are quite disparate in theme and plot structure. The critic must thus seek unifying elements, and while most would agree that the theme of love runs through all the tales like a connecting thread, few agree on Marie's understanding of love or on her intention in portraying it.

The second major difficulty, which individual critics fail to acknowledge but which is evident from a review of the literature, is that the theme of love necessarily evokes subjective responses in readers, even when those readers are scrupulously "objective" critics. This is, of course, a danger in all criticism; it is exacerbated in Marie's case by the dearth of external evidence and by the intimate, almost seductive quality of some of her tales. Though it is important to consider the whole range of such responses, because each may have something to contribute to a full appreciation of the work, the most fruitful lines of research have been a new approach to the issue of genre and various efforts to see the lays in their original cultural and poetic context.

Thanks to important work by Edgar Sienaert, real progress has been made on the genre question; the unique and often puzzling emotional effects of the lays may plausibly be attributed to the ways in which they combine elements of two well-known genres, the fairy tale and the realistic *nouvelle*, or short story. At the same time, the lays have been shown to include didactic, courtly, and religious elements that reflect distinct tendencies of the age in which they were written. Marie is not content merely to entertain or "seduce" her readers; she has much to say about the real world and about the moral choices her characters are called upon to make in it.

MARIE'S CONCEPT OF LOVE

She also puts forward a conception of love that has at least something in common with the courtly love celebrated by her contemporaries the troubadours and trouvères. (Here it may be helpful to recall that Marie may have spent some time at the court of Henry II, whose wife, Eleanor of Aquitaine, was herself a Frenchwoman and the granddaughter of a troubadour.) As Emanuel Mickel has observed, Marie approves of love when it is elevated above concupiscence and self-seeking by a freely given pledge of loyalty. She differs from those courtly authors who celebrate one-sided love; in nearly every lay, the love portrayed is mutual. Though she often depicts such love as triumphing over obstacles, she also acknowledges that it may result in great suffering for the lovers. Her appeals to explicitly Christian values can be unorthodox, and she combines romantic love with Christian charity in unexpected ways, but she does not hesitate to condemn those who betray trusting spouses—or feudal lords or vassals—out of calculated self-interest. The concluding lay of the collection also suggests that romantic love can serve as a bridge to the

more complete love of God. Marie's chief interest, however, is unquestionably in the depiction of mutual romantic attachment and its various outcomes.

If there is still disagreement about Marie's thematic focus, her stylistic gifts are scarcely in doubt. In a reversal of earlier assessments, later critics have seen in her an accomplished storyteller and poet, suiting the length of each tale to its content, using dialogue to great effect, and endowing key objects with symbolic value so that they epitomize the themes of individual tales. The shortest of the tales—"Laüstic" ("The Nightingale") and "Chèvrefeuille" ("The Honeysuckle")—have even been seen as essentially lyric poems, so dominated are they by the central symbols of the nightingale and the honeysuckle entwined with the hazel. Yet even these lays have plots, as Sienaert does well to recall. Though Marie translated her *Fables* from an English original that has been lost, these, too, display poetic and narrative skill (especially in the phrasing of dialogue) that must be attributed, at least in part, to the translator.

THE LAY AS GENRE

Edgar Sienaert's description of the lay as a mixed or intermediary genre is based on the work of folklorists, notably Vladimir Propp and Max Lüthi, who have identified (independently of one another) the basic structure of the European folktale. One of the most striking features of the folktale, or fairy tale (Sienaert's term for the genre is *conte merveilleux:* a tale with a happy ending, in which the "marvelous" is paramount) is that the identities and motivations of characters may be freely altered from one version to another, whereas the plot sequence, and the *roles* characters may fill in it, are rigidly maintained. The mainspring of the fairy-tale plot is not the motivated action of its characters but rather the intrusion of the marvelous, and although the working out of the plot satisfies deep human desires, its conclusion is not attained by human effort but by magic (a potion, a ring) or by a *deus ex machina* (a fairy, a speaking animal). It has long been recognized that there were affinities between the fairy tale and Marie's *Lais*, but these affinities had remained somewhat vague, limited to the happy ending (which does not apply to a number of lays) and an ill-defined "charm." As Sienaert has shown, however, the lays sometimes follow the fairy-tale pattern in which motivation is not linked to plot. Thus, the knight Eliduc, for example, scarcely earns his happiness; it comes to him in spite of the bad faith he has shown his wife and his young lover. At the same time, though, and in the same tales, the motivation of Marie's characters can be essential to the outcome; thus, Eliduc's wife, by her unexampled generosity, makes possible *for her husband* the happy ending he had deserved to forfeit. Sometimes it even happens that a realistically motivated character *forestalls* the expected happy ending, as does the young man in "Les Dues Amanz" ("The Two Lovers"), who refuses to drink the magic potion that would restore his strength. Finally, there are a few stories from which the fairy-tale plot is completely missing. "Equitan" has been compared to a fabliau (a more consistently realistic, generally coarse and cynical, short narrative genre contemporary to the lay) because of its realistic and cautionary plot of betrayal, attempted crime, and punishment; while falling within the scope of the medieval exemplum, or tale with a moral, it resembles the modern short story in linking the outcome to the character and actions of the central figures. Sienaert argues that Marie deliberately placed it second in her collection, after a tale that has many affinities with the fairy tale, to mark the two poles between which her pieces would move.

As will become apparent from a closer look at several lays, this approach to the genre question can be extremely useful. Its chief drawback is its degree of abstraction—it cannot account for the thematic content of the collection.

"LANVAL"

"Lanval" is a good example of a lay using a straightforward fairy-tale plot. Lanval, a "foreign" knight at King Arthur's court, is slighted by the King until a beautiful fairy maiden approaches him, offering both her love and riches if he will keep her existence secret. This he does, until one day the Queen likewise offers him her love, and he reveals the fact that he already loves another, whose least handmaiden surpasses the Queen in beauty and accomplishments. At this, the Queen denounces him to the King as having accosted *her,* nor will the fairy-lover come at his call, since he has revealed her existence. When he is put on trial, however—more for insulting the Queen's beauty than for allegedly accosting her—the fairy relents, first sending her handmaidens and then arriving in person so that all can see the truth of

Lanval's boast. The tale ends as Lanval rides off with her to the otherworldly Avalon, to live happily ever after.

This lay epitomizes a tendency of many of Marie's tales to fuse Celtic folk motifs with the courtly love theme. As Jean Frappier has observed, there is an analogy between the "otherworld" of Celtic mythology, to which the "marvelous" properly belongs, and the privileged condition of courtly lovers, whose experience of love (open only to a small, elect group), gives them a taste of paradise on earth. Avalon thus becomes an allegory for the state of mutual love, where the "foreigner" Lanval finds his true home after rejecting, and being rejected by, the flawed world of Arthur's court (where the king has slighted him and the queen accused him of her own infidelity). As Sienaert would add, however, the motivations of the characters—even of the fairy, who relents in her punishment of Lanval—are fully humanized and linked to the outcome. The lay is thus emotionally satisfying, not only for its fairy-tale ending but also for its vindication of mutual love—though it should also be noted that the "real world" is seen as hostile to that love, which can flourish only in a land of its own. In this respect, "Lanval" is perhaps the most frankly escapist of the lays.

"THE TWO LOVERS"

"The Two Lovers," by contrast, creates the expectation of a fairy-tale ending only to reverse it at the last moment. A widowed king, unwilling to part with his sole daughter, invents a trial in which he thinks no suitor can succeed: To win her hand in marriage, the suitor must carry her to the top of a mountain without pausing to rest. To help a young man whom she favors, the girl sends him to her aunt in Salerno, who provides him with a potion that can restore strength. During the trial, however, the young man feels strong enough to do without the potion; he resists the girl's repeated pleas that he drink it and reaches the summit only to collapse—his heart has given out. The distraught girl spills the potion, which causes medicinal herbs to spring up on the mountainside, and herself dies of grief on the spot, where the two are buried together.

Of all the lays, this one has perhaps evoked the greatest diversity of interpretation. It has been seen as a tragedy, a cautionary tale, even a satire. Here, Sienaert's insights are especially helpful, accounting for the diversity of critical (and emotional) response without explaining it away. The story is indeed tragic insofar as it reverses the carefully created expectation of a happy ending, and it is cautionary insofar as Marie stresses the *démesure* (lack of moderation) that leads to the boy's death. Yet there is also something positive about the ending: After rejecting the magical means to success, the boy accomplishes the feat (though none of his predecessors had come close), and the girl's love, because it equals his, unites them in death. The boy's decision is flawed, as Marie herself observes: "I fear [the potion] will do him little good/ For he had in him no moderation." As Emanuel Mickel points out, the potion is not merely a magical expedient but a symbol of the potential strength and fruition to which the couple's love might have come; thus, the good herbs it causes to flourish on the mountainside might have been the couple's good deeds (as in "Eliduc") or those of their heirs. Nevertheless, it is hard not to sympathize with the boy's desire to prove himself or with the girl's anguished sense of what she has lost. Both characters are brought to vivid life in the scene on the mountain, as Marie endows them with fully human motives.

"EQUITAN"

"Equitan," the "realistic" lay mentioned above, offers yet another perspective on love; it is also one of the most carefully structured of the lays, making expert use of dialogue, symbolism, and irony. Equitan is a king who seems to possess all the knightly virtues. It soon emerges, though, that, like the boy in "The Two Lovers," he has no sense of moderation in love; what is more, he prefers pleasure to his responsibilities and often leaves the administration of justice to his seneschal while he goes hunting—literally and metaphorically, for he is fond of the ladies. (The hunt was frequently used by medieval authors as a metaphor for the pursuit of a woman's favors.) As it happens, the seneschal has a wife who is among the most beautiful women of the realm; hearing her praised, Equitan goes to hunt on the seneschal's lands, succeeds in meeting her, and falls passionately in love with her. Though he recognizes (in a soliloquy) that it means breaking faith with his loyal deputy, the king persuades himself by specious arguments to pursue the woman. At first she objects, but only on the grounds that his rank will make for inequality in their

love; he assures her that—in accordance with the courtly convention-*he* will be her servant and she his lady. As Marie makes plain, this is what literally happens. Urged by his subjects to marry, Equitan refuses, assuring his lover that he would marry her if she were free; she then proposes that they murder her husband, and the king agrees to every detail of her plan. The hunt has become lethal, but this time Equitan is destined to become the quarry. Caught by the seneschal in his lady's arms, Equitan leaps into the boiling bath prepared for the murder. The irony is complete as the seneschal, to whom Equitan had delegated his own judicial responsibilities, proceeds to complete the punishment by throwing his wife in the bath after her lover. As might have been expected, those nineteenth century critics who were chiefly impressed by the "charm" of lays like "Lanval" found "Equitan" shockingly sordid; it seemed, moreover, to give a different and unfavorable account of the courtly love celebrated in many of the lays. Clearly, Marie does not disapprove of courtly love per se. As the ending of "Lanval" indicates, however, it is not always possible to reconcile the state of love—that "otherworld" to which Lanval and his mistress retreat—and the "real world," which makes claims of its own on the lovers. The fidelity of Equitan and his lady might in itself be admirable, but because it is grounded in the *infidelity* of both to the seneschal, it leads them to crime. Because it is also characterized by *démesure*, it also leads to death. In contrast to the *démesure* of the boy in "The Two Lovers," which is excusable because of his youth and which has a dimension that may be considered heroic, the *démesure* of Equitan is a form of slavery to appetite, which is all the more demeaning in the light of Equitan's rank as well as his responsibilities.

As Edgar Sienaert observes, "Equitan" is an extreme case—a worst case, in the *Lais*, where adulterous love is concerned. Marie frequently treats of courtly love that is also adulterous, and she is often sympathetic to the lovers. This is especially true of the three lays "Guigemar," "Yonec," and "The Nightingale," in which the female protagonist is a *mal mariée*—a woman married against her will, usually to a much older man who treats her as his property and shows her no love. Though the protagonist's love for another is portrayed sympathetically in each case, the stories end in very disparate ways: In the most realistic, "The Nightingale," the husband succeeds in separating the lovers by an act of cruelty (killing the bird that gave the wife an excuse to stand at the window from which she could see her lover); in the most fairy-tale-like, "Guigemar," the husband simply disappears from the story as the wife escapes and rejoins her lover in his distant homeland.

"ELIDUC"

The most complex case of adulterous love, however, is that seen in "Eliduc," the longest of the lays and the last in the manuscript that Sienaert takes to reflect Marie's own ordering of the tales. When the story opens, Eliduc has been happily married for some time; he decides to leave home because envious men have slandered him to the Breton king whom he faithfully serves. Crossing to England, he offers his services to the king of Exeter, who is hard-pressed by enemies, and wins a signal victory. The king's daughter, Guilliadun, hearing only good spoken of Eliduc, asks to meet him, and the two fall in love. Though Eliduc restrains himself to the extent that he does not sleep with the girl, he accepts her gifts and kisses and does not tell her of his wife. When his original sovereign, hard-pressed in turn, sends for him, he feels duty-bound to go and refuses to abduct the princess (who wants to go with him) on the grounds that he would be showing disloyalty to her father; yet he promises to return for her when his contract with her father will have expired. He does so—still without telling her of his wife—and during a storm on the channel, she learns the truth from a frightened sailor who thinks Eliduc's adulterous love has caused the storm. At the news, Guilliadun falls in a faint, and, thinking she is dead, Eliduc throws the sailor overboard. The ship reaches land safely, and Eliduc, who cannot yet bring himself to bury the girl, hides her in a chapel on his estate. Worried by his obvious grief, his wife, Guildeluec, has him followed and discovers the girl's body; far from showing envy or hatred, she revives Guilliadun with the aid of a magic herb and says she wishes to enter a convent so that Eliduc can marry the girl. After living for some time in "perfect love," the couple in turn enter religious life, and Guildeluec, now an abbess, welcomes Guilliadun "as her sister."

Once again, Sienaert's observations offer a useful line of approach to this puzzling tale. Like other courtly lovers in the *Lais*, Eliduc would like to keep his love in a world apart, safe from the interference of real life; when the sailor tries to call him back to reality, he blindly kills the man. (It should be noted, however, that the sailor scarcely speaks for Marie; he wants to do away with the innocent Guilliadun.) Unable to resolve his own dilemma, Eliduc is saved by the action of his wife, whose unparalleled generosity takes the place of the magical resolution one would expect in a fairy tale. What this approach cannot account for, however, is the care and the sheer length devoted to the developing love between Eliduc and Guilliadun. If, as Sienaert claims, Guilliadun's swoon represents the impotence of the courtly ethic (and even of a "fairy-tale princess") to deal with the moral dilemmas of the real world, why is such care devoted to the portrayal of her love for Eliduc, and, above all, why does she and not Guildeluec win him back?

Mickel has observed that there is a correspondence between the lengths of individual lays and their plot structures: The shorter lays all end unhappily, whereas the longer ones end with the reunion of the lovers (or, as in "Yonec," with their vindication). Mickel attributes this characteristic to Marie's preference for *faithful* love, which must develop and be tested over time, yet it is Guildeluec who has loved Eliduc longest. Given the care with which Marie describes the growth of the adulterous love (it occupies 431 of 1,184 lines, or more than a third of the poem), it seems hard to avoid the conclusion that Marie meant her audience to be caught up in it. Though Eliduc is clearly acting in bad faith at some level, he never allows this to reach his awareness in his dealings with Guilliadun; he is a confused man, but not a bad one at heart. Because both lovers *are* essentially good, and can see the good in each other, their mutual love (in which they manage to observe some *mésure*) is more than mere concupiscence. This is why it can lead them to a life of shared good works, and ultimately to the love of God. Yet despite the decisive role of Guildeluec's selfless love, and despite the fact that all three protagonists learn to love in her way, it seems wrong to read the entire lay as an exemplum. There is a real difference between romantic and Christian love, and Guildeluec is the first to recognize it. Romantic love must be mutual and cannot be learned; it is, as has been observed, akin to the "marvelous." Thus, Guildeluec makes her decision on the basis of Guilliadun's exquisite beauty, whose power she herself feels. Though Marie admits, in "Equitan," that such love can lead the partners to evil, she prefers stories in which it ennobles them, whether through shared happiness or shared suffering. She is thus both a didactic and a thoroughly courtly poet.

MARIE AS STORYTELLER

Because Marie is a narrative poet, her literary art is primarily that of the storyteller; thus, critical studies have emphasized her choice of significant detail, her use of dialogue, and, above all, her skill in the ordering and pacing of plots. It is important to remember, however, especially if one reads her in a prose translation (and there are no verse translations in English), that she is also a poet, writing in rhymed octosyllabic couplets. Far from interrupting the flow of her narrative, this form contributes to its spare and vigorous quality. In contrast to the romances being written by her contemporaries in the same meter, the lays are anything but digressive. This is especially striking in the shorter lays, where not a line is wasted. *Fables*, though not an original work, deserves to be mentioned in this context because it demonstrates the same skill of compression to an even greater degree: The longer of the fables are of the same length as the shorter of the lays. The moral with which each fable concludes is particularly compressed (between four and eight lines long), and the rhymes are carefully chosen to bring home the point with special force.

IMAGERY AND SYMBOLISM

The other specifically poetic skill Marie displays is in the use of controlling images, which in her narrative context are usually symbolic objects (although she can also use metaphor, as in the tale of Equitan, "the hunter hunted"). Such objects loom especially large in two of the shortest lays, "The Nightingale" and "The Honeysuckle"; in both cases, they are related to the love theme central to the collection. Though the nightingale is on one level a pretext that the woman uses to see her lover, it also symbolizes mutual love as something alive and beautiful. Though the husband can kill it and thus prevent the lovers from seeing each other, he cannot obliterate its memory; thus, the lover, to whom the woman sends the bird's body, has it encased in a jeweled box, which he carries about with him always.

The honeysuckle, which twines itself about the hazel until neither can stand alone, is a related symbol of love as a beautiful living thing. Though the bird and the plant are themselves vulnerable, the fidelity of the lovers in each case holds out a hope that human love may be more durable. In "The Honeysuckle," which describes a meeting between Tristan and Iseult, Tristan himself uses the symbol in this sense. In a passage that is a true lyric fragment (and that may be the message, inscribed on a hazel stick, alerting Iseult to her lover's presence), he exclaims, "Fair love, so it is with us:/ Neither you without me, nor I without you." Deservedly one of Marie's most famous couplets, it captures both her spare, direct style and the ideal of mutual fidelity embodied in so many of her lays.

BIBLIOGRAPHY

Betham, Matilda. *The Lay of Marie*. New York: Woodstock Books, 1996. Betham's interpretation of the *Lais* originally published in 1816. Includes the text of two of the *Lais* and abstracts of the whole collection.

Bruckner, Matilda Tomaryn. "Marie de France." In *French Women Writers*, edited by Eva Martin Sartori and Dorothy Wynne Zimmerman. Lincoln: University of Nebraska Press, 1994. Biographical data include parameters by which Marie's dates and her possible identities are determined. Bruckner discusses the *Lais* by groups according to common elements and draws attention to the poet's use of free indirect discourse to merge her voice with that of her characters. Examples are given from *Fables*, and *Purgatory* is succinctly summarized. A concluding survey of criticism constitutes a helpful bibliography organized by specific areas of investigation.

Burgess, Glyn S. *The "Lais" of Marie de France: Text and Context*. Athens: University of Georgia Press, 1987. The introduction provides an overview of the *Lais* and points out notable features of these narrative poems. Chapter 1 examines the problem of their chronological order, while other chapters, based largely on linguistic considerations, focus on a particular aspect of the stories: women, love, and the medieval chivalric code.

Clifford, Paula. *Marie de France: Lais*. London: Grant and Cutler, 1982. A discussion of the *Lais* based on common traits: aspects of love, fate, and the supernatural. Contains synopses of the stories, historical background on the *lai* and a short examination of the poet's style.

Ferrante, Joan. "The French Courtly Poet Marie de France." In *Medieval Women Writers*, edited by Katharina M. Wilson. Athens: University of Georgia Press, 1984. A brief introduction to the works of Marie de France with concise résumés and special emphasis on the *Lais*. Quotations are in English only. The essay is followed by an English verse translation of one *lai*, "Lanval," and a number of the *Fables*.

McCash, June Hall. "Images of Women in the *Lais* of Marie de France." *Medieval Perspectives* 11 (1996): 96-112. A pellucid study of female characters in their sociological context as presented in the *Lais*, with special attention given to the problem of adulterous behavior and the arranged marriage.

Maréchal, Chantal, ed. *In Quest of Marie de France: A Twelfth-Century Poet*. Lewiston, N.Y.: Edwin Mellen Press, 1992. Contains fifteen articles by established medievalists: three articles on the *Fables*, six general articles on the *Lais*, and six with a narrower focus. Of special interest is the editor's introduction, which offers a chronological approach to critical assessment of Marie through the centuries.

Mickel, Emanuel J., Jr. *Marie de France*. New York: Twayne, 1974. A seminal study of Marie's life and works which presents the various theories of her identity, summarizes and analyzes her three ascribed works, and provides information concerning her sources. Concluding chapters argue the profundity of her concept of love and the effectiveness of her narrative technique.

Sethurman, Jayshree. "Tale-Type and Motif Indexes to the *Fables* of Marie de France." *Le Cygne, Bulletin of the International Marie de France Society* 5 (Spring, 1999): 19-35. A table of folktale types linking Marie's *Fables* to the compilations of universal folktale motifs classified and cataloged by Antti Arne and revised and expanded by Stith Thompson.

Lillian Doherty;
bibliography updated by Judith L. Barban

GIAMBATTISTA MARINO

Born: Naples, Italy; October 18, 1569
Died: Naples, Italy; March 25, 1625

PRINCIPAL POETRY

Le rime, 1602 (*Steps to the Temple*, canto 1 only, 1646)
Il ritratto del serenissimo Don Carlo Emanuello Duca di Savoia, 1608
La lira, 1615
Il tempio, 1615
Epitalami, 1616
La galeria, 1619
Egloghe boscherecce, 1620
La sampogna, 1620
L'Adone, 1623
La Murtoleide, 1626
La strage degli innocenti, 1632 (*The Slaughter of the Innocents*, 1675)
Gerusalemme distrutta, 1633 (unfinished)
L'Anversa liberata, 1956 (unfinished)
Adonis, 1967 (selections from *L'Adone*)

OTHER LITERARY FORMS

Giambattista Marino's voluminous production is almost entirely in poetical form. In 1617, while he was in France, Marino wrote an invective against the enemies of the Catholic Church, *La sferza, invettiva a quattro ministri della iniquitá* (the whip: invective against four ministers of iniquity), which was first published in Paris in 1625. In addition, Marino's copious correspondence, included in *Lettere* (1627) and published in a modern edition, *Epistolario* (1912), is very important, for it provides revealing glimpses of his moral and aesthetic values.

ACHIEVEMENTS

Thematically and stylistically, Giambattista Marino is considered one of the greatest Italian poets of his age and also, perhaps, the most representative man of letters of Baroque Europe. His impact was felt immediately, not only in the various literary circles of Italy but also in France, where he produced his masterpiece, *L'Adone*

(Adonis), and whence his fame spread throughout the Continent. Echoes and imitators of the Marinesque style are indeed to be found everywhere, from the Slavic world (Miklós Zríny, Dživo Bunić-Vucić, Igniat Djordjić, Jan Andrzej Morsztyn) to seventeenth century England (Edward Herbert, Thomas Carew, Andrew Marvell, Richard Crashaw, Samuel Daniel, Edward Sherburne, Thomas Stanley, and so on).

Although Spanish literature of this period was to produce an equally influential figure in Luis de Góngora y Argote (who was to lend his name to Gongorism, an aesthetic current that paralleled Marinism), Spanish poets such as Juan de Tasis, Luis de Carrillo y Sotomayor, and Francisco de Quevedo y Villegas became admirers and imitators of Marino, and Lope de Vega expressed his admiration for the Italian poet by dedicating one of his comedies to him. It was undoubtedly in France, however, where Marino lived for some eight years as a favorite of Queen Marie de Médicis, that his influence was most powerfully felt. Poets as diverse as Antoine-Girard de Saint-Amant, Théophile de Viau, Tristan l'Hermite, Georges de Scudéry, Vincent Voiture, Jean de La Fontaine, Claude de Malleville, and Pierre Le Moyne betray a significant debt to Marino, and it was from France that Marinism radiated all over Europe.

BIOGRAPHY

Giambattista (Giovan Battista) Marino (or Marini, as it is often written), one of seven children, was born in Naples on October 18, 1569, the son of Giovan Francesco Marino. The elder Marino was a lawyer and hoped that his son would follow in his footsteps, but the young Marino was more interested in literary studies than in embracing a legal career. Having disappointed his father, Marino was unceremoniously asked to leave the paternal household, but his reputation as a spirited and bright young poet and man of letters was already sufficient to open to him the doors of several aristocratic houses, and in 1592, he entered the service of Matteo di Capua, Prince of Conca, as a poet and a secretary.

As a young man, Marino led a dissolute life and was twice imprisoned: first in 1598, for having taken part in the rape of a young woman (probably a nun), and again in 1600, for having falsified some documents in order to prepare the escape from prison of his friend, Marc'

Antonio d'Alessandro, who had been condemned to death. Although Marino was freed from prison, he was forced to flee to Rome, where he found protection with the influential Monsignor Melchiorre Crescenzio. In 1601-1602, Marino traveled to Venice to oversee the publication of his first two volumes of *Le rime*, later incorporated in *La lira*. Upon his return to Rome, he found employment with Cardinal Pietro Aldobrandini, the nephew of Pope Clement VIII, and in 1606, after the Pope's death, Marino followed Aldobrandini to his seat at Ravenna.

Enjoying a growing reputation as a poet, Marino accompanied Aldobrandini to Torino in 1608 to attend the marriage of two daughters of Duke Carlo Emanuele I of Savoy, and Marino seized the occasion to write *Il ritratto del serenissimo Don Carlo Emanuello Duca di Savoia* (the portrait of the most serene Don Carlo Emanuele, duke of Savoy), a panegyric in honor of the duke. The duke reciprocated by conferring upon him the order of the knighthood of Saints Maurizio and Lazzaro—the title of "Cavaliere," of which Marino always felt especially proud and which he henceforth always prefixed to his name.

In 1609, the duke's secretary, Gaspare Murtola—himself a poet, jealous of Marino's rapidly rising status at the court of Turin—fired a pistol at Marino, hitting instead another man who was a favorite of the duke. Murtola was condemned to death, but, at Marino's request, the sentence was commuted to exile. In 1611, Marino himself was sent to prison for fourteen months. The charges are not known, but presumably he had offended the duke with some satirical verses. Marino was freed in 1612, and in 1614, he published in Venice the result of years of creative labor: part 3 of *La lira*, later reprinted in a collected edition together with *Le rime* and the *Dicerie sacre* (holy discourses). In 1615, he received permission to go to the royal court in Paris, where he had been invited first by Marguerite de Navarre and then by Marie de Médicis, who had become Queen Regent after the death of her husband, Henry IV.

In Lyon, as soon as he set foot on French territory, Marino published a laudatory poem, *Il tempio* (the temple), in honor of the queen. Marino stayed in Paris, where he became a court favorite, until 1623, enjoying enormous popularity and receiving many honors. While in Paris, he published a volume of ten nuptial odes, *Epitalami* (epithalamia); a collection of six hundred poems celebrating various works of art, real and imagined, *La galeria* (the gallery); a gathering of poems on mythological and bucolic subjects, *La sampogna* (the shepherd's pipe); and finally, in April, 1623, his masterpiece, *L'Adone*, which he dedicated to Louis XIII. Immediately after the publication of the twenty cantos of *L'Adone*—a work more than twice as long as Dante's *La divina commedia* (c. 1320; *The Divine Comedy*) or Torquato Tasso's *Gerusalemme liberata* (1581; *Jerusalem Delivered*, 1600)—Marino, at the very peak of his popularity, decided to return to his native land to savor the triumphs that inevitably would be accorded to him as the greatest living Italian poet. In Rome, he found immediate protection at the household of Cardinal Ludovico Ludovisi, the nephew of Pope Gregory XV; was feted with a banquet held in his honor by the Roman Senate; and was elected prince of the Academy of the Umoristi, of which he had been a member for several years. While in Rome, he witnessed as a special guest the ceremonies for the election of the new pope, Urban VIII (previously Cardinal Maffeo Barberini).

Arriving in May, 1623, in his native Naples, Marino entered the city as a triumphant conqueror. A statue in his honor was unveiled there, and he was welcomed by the Spanish Viceroy and by the various literary academies (the Academy of the Oziosi also made him a prince). In 1624, however, his stay in Naples was marred by the unwelcome news that his *L'Adone* had been placed on the Church's Index. Perhaps tired by his many public appearances and commitments and by the pressure to complete his religious epic, *The Slaughter of the Innocents*, he became ill, initially with a slow fever and then with a painful case of strangury. Before his death on March 25, 1625, he burned many of his sensual and profane writings. By order of the Neapolitan Archbishop Cardinal Decio Carafa, Marino's burial took place during the night.

ANALYSIS

True to the spirit of his time, Giambattista Marino wrote a number of panegyrical poems, among them *Il ritratto del serenissimo Don Carlo Emanuello Duca di Savoia, Il tempio*, and *Epitalami*, a collection of ten very sensual nuptial odes patterned after traditional models, largely mythological in content, and written to celebrate the weddings of various princes and kings. Marino was equally at ease with religious subjects, which he treated with a certain emotional detachment. In 1614, he published *Dicerie sacre*, an important work which included three lengthy and elaborate metaphorical sermons on painting, music, and Heaven, inspired respectively by the "Sindone" (Christ's shroud), the seven last words of Christ, and the orders of Saints Maurizio and Lazzaro. In 1617, while in France, Marino wrote *La sferza, invettiva a quattro ministri della iniquità*, an invective against the enemies of the Catholic Church.

Among Marino's other writings worthy of mention are his pastoral *Egloghe boscherecce* (sylvan eclogues), first published in 1620, although the only extant copies are dated 1627, and the famous *La Murtoleide* (the deeds of Murtola). *La Murtoleide*, published in 1626 but dating back to Marino's Turin period, consists of eighty-one *fischiate* (boos), satirical sonnets written against his rival, the mediocre court poet Gaspare Murtola, who had attacked Marino in a libelous *Abridgement of the Life of Cavalier Marino*. Rather predictably, Murtola retorted by writing a *Marineide* (the deeds of Marino), which consisted of thirty-two *risate* (laughs); he also tried, unsuccessfully, to kill Marino, shooting at him with a pistol.

A well-known tercet that is said to epitomize the quintessence of Marino's poetics is to be found in the thirty-third *fischiata* of *La Murtoleide:* "The goal of the poet is to cause wonder/ (I am speaking about excellent poets and not clumsy ones):/ Those who do not know how to astonish should go to the stables."

Marino also tried his hand at composing serious epic poetry and, great admirer of Tasso that he was, he attempted to deal with two themes much in the Tassian tradition: *Gerusalemme distrutta* (Jerusalem destroyed) and *L'Anversa liberata* (Antwerp delivered). Both of these poems, however, were left unfinished and were published posthumously, the first in 1633 and the second only in 1956.

L'ADONE

Marino's masterpiece, *L'Adone*—an extremely long poem of twenty cantos, first published in Paris in 1623—displays his seemingly unlimited verbal and rhetorical virtuosity as well as his ability to use a surprising array of sources and themes.

Although some of the episodes in *L'Adone* can be traced to Dante, Ariosto, and Tasso, the bulk of the work derives from classical sources, particularly book 10 of Ovid's *Metamorphoses* (c. 8 C.E.). In a sense, *L'Adone* can be seen as a marvelous poetic catalog of a mythological world where the myths and Arcadian adventures of the classical deities, Satyrs, and nymphs are syncretically evoked against a lavishly sensual Baroque setting.

The plot begins unfolding when Cupid, rather ill disposed toward his mother Venus, seeks vengeance by making Adonis—the handsome prince born out of an incestuous relation between Mirrah and her father—arrive in Cyprus and fall in love with the goddess. Readily reciprocating Adonis's love, Venus takes the young prince to her palace and guides him through the Garden of Pleasure, divided into five sections that symbolize the various senses as they are engaged by lovemaking. Afterward, still guided by his pagan, unspiritual "Beatrice," Adonis experiences the pleasures of the mind. Joined by Mercury—clearly reminiscent of Dante's Vergil—Adonis visits Apollo's fountain, symbolizing poetry, and ascends to the first three Ptolemaic spheres, those of the Moon, Mercury, and Venus. There, after some adulatory verses in honor of various royalties, he learns of the most advanced scientific notions and meets some of the most representative figures of the sixteenth century.

Unfortunately, Jealousy informs Mars of Venus's new passion, and Adonis is forced to flee before the enraged god, beginning a long series of adventures. Adonis falls into the hands of the lascivious and wicked fairy Falsirena, who, after unsuccessfully trying to seduce him, transforms him into a parrot and forces him to witness love scenes between Venus and Mars. Following other fantastic encounters, Adonis finally manages to return to Cyprus, where he is elected king of the island and can once more enjoy the favors of the goddess. On a hunt, however, Adonis is killed by a wild boar aroused against him by the disgruntled Falsirena and Mars. The poem ends with Adonis's funeral and with a description of the games held in his honor, as well as with a final series of classical myths dealing with love and death.

In a dazzling display of bravura, Marino's thin treatment of the theme of life, death, and rebirth is overpow-ered by the pageant of sensory delights that he presents to the reader. In a changing world filled with religious upheavals and sociopolitical tensions, Marino's ornate, brilliant display of rhetorical and poetic devices and his unrestrained celebration of life and sensual love offered an escape into the unreal realm of fables and myths. Marino's exuberant affirmation of the *meraviglia* (the astonishing, the marvelous) was judged by later critics as representative of the Baroque at its worst, its most excessive, yet his virtuosity has never been questioned. His masterly use of rhetorical figures remains unsurpassed. Indeed, the abundant use of metaphors by Marino and other Baroque poets went beyond the mere rhetorical exigencies of poetry or even the desire to display exceptional creative ability. Rather, it expressed a deeply felt if unconscious need to interpret their confusing and rapidly changing world.

OTHER MAJOR WORKS

NONFICTION: *Dicerie sacre*, 1614; *La sferza, invettiva a quattro ministri della iniquitá*, wr. 1617, pb. 1625; *Lettere*, 1627 (modern edition, *Epistolario*, 1912).

BIBLIOGRAPHY

Guardiani, Francesco, ed. *The Sense of Marino: Literature, Fine Arts and Music of the Italian Baroque.* New York: Legas, 1994. A critical interpretation of selected poetic works and an introduction the history of Italian poetry of the seventeenth century.

Mirollo, James V. *The Poet of the Marvelous: Giambattista Marino.* New York: Columbia University Press, 1963. A biography of Marino. Includes texts in Italian and English of "La canzone dei baci," "La maddalena di Tiziano," and an extract from "La pastorello."

Segel, Harold B. *The Baroque Poem: A Comparative Survey.* New York: Dutton, 1974. A survey of 150 texts from English, American, Dutch, German, French, Italian, Spanish, Mexican, Portuguese, Polish, Modern Latin, Czech, Croatian, and Russian poetry, in the original languages and accompanying English translations.

Roberto Severino;
bibliography updated by the editors

CHRISTOPHER MARLOWE

Born: Canterbury, England; February 6, 1564
Died: Deptford, England; May 30, 1593

PRINCIPAL POETRY

Hero and Leander, 1598 (completed by George
   Chapman)
"The Passionate Shepherd to His Love," 1599

OTHER LITERARY FORMS

Christopher Marlowe's literary reputation rests primarily on the following plays: *Tamburlaine the Great, Part I* (pr. c. 1587, first octavo edition 1590); *Tamburlaine the Great, Part II* (pr. 1587, first octavo edition 1590); *The Jew of Malta* (pr. c. 1589, first quarto edition 1633); *Edward II* (pr. c. 1592, first quarto edition 1594); *Doctor Faustus* (pr. c. 1588, first quarto edition 1604). Two unfinished plays, *Dido, Queen of Carthage* (pr. c. 1586-1587; with Thomas Nashe) and the fragmentary *The Massacre at Paris* (1593), round out his dramatic canon. He produced two important translations: *Elegies* (1595-1600), which treats three books of Ovid's *Amores* (before 8 C.E.), and Lucan's first book of *Pharsalia* (62 C.E.), first entered in the Stationers' Register as *Lucan's First Book of the Famous Civil War Betwixt Pompey and Caesar* (1593, the earliest extant edition is dated 1600).

ACHIEVEMENTS

His plays established Christopher Marlowe as the foremost of the University Wits, a loosely knit group of young men, by reputation generally wild and rakish, that included Thomas Lodge, Thomas Nashe, George Peele, and the older, perhaps less unruly, John Lyly. Their work largely established the nature of the English drama which would reach its apogee in the work of William Shakespeare. Marlowe shares with Thomas Kyd the honor of developing the English conception of tragedy. Marlowe also developed the rather clumsy blank verse of the day into the flexible vehicle of his "mighty line," using it to flesh out his tragic characters as they fell from greatness. He shares the honor of reshaping the dramatically crude chronicle play into the mature and subtle his-

tory play. His *The Troublesome Raigne and Lamentable Death of Edward the Second* bears comparison with William Shakespeare's *Richard III* (1592-1593) and anticipates Shakespeare's "Henriad."

While Marlowe attracted much casual comment among his contemporaries, serious criticism of his work was rare until the nineteenth century. After the Puritan diatribe of T. Beard in *The Theatre of Gods* [sic] *Judgements* (1597) and W. Vaughn's consideration in *The Golden Grove* (1600), no serious criticism appeared until J. Broughton's article, "Of the Dramatic Writers Who Preceded Shakespeare" (1830). Beginning in 1883, with C. H. Herford and A. Wagner's article "The Sources of Tamburlaine," Marlovian criticism grew at an increasing rate. Two critics initiated the very extensive body of modern scholarship which began in the first decade of the twentieth century: Frederick S. Boas with his edition and commentary of the works (1901), and Brooke with an article, "On the Date of the First Edition of Marlowe's *Edward II*," in *Modern Language Notes* (1909). Boas's contribution culminated in the monumental *Marlowe: A Biographical and Critical Study* (1940). While both writers concentrated on Marlowe's drama, they also began a serious examination of his poetry. From 1910 onward, the volume of criticism has been almost overwhelming. *The New Cambridge Bibliography of English Literature* (1974) cites literally hundreds of books and articles. The annually published *MLA International Bibliography* shows no slackening in scholarly interest.

Marlowe's nondramatic poetry has attracted an impressive, even a disproportionate, amount of critical attention, considering that it consists simply of one lyric poem, known in several versions, and one narrative poem, generally considered to be an 817-line fragment of a longer projected work. Had Marlowe's dramatic work been only middling, it is unlikely that his poetry, excellent as it is, would have been so widely noticed and esteemed. C. F. Tucker Brooke observes in his *The Works of Christopher Marlowe* (1964) that *Hero and Leander,* Marlowe's narrative fragment, was enormously popular with the Elizabethans and that the literature of the period is rich in allusions to the poem. His lyric poem "The Passionate Shepherd to His Love" also enjoyed an early and continuing popularity from its first appearance in *The Passionate Pilgrim* (1599) and *England's Helicon* (1600), two widely circulated collections of English verse. A version of the poem is included in Isaac Walton's *The Compleat Angler, or the Contemplative Man's Recreation* (1653).

While most of the criticism bears on concerns other than the poetry, criticism dealing with *Hero and Leander* and, to a lesser degree, with "The Passionate Shepherd to His Love," is more than respectable in quantity. Interest covers many aspects of the poems: the rhetorical and prosodic forms, with their implications for aesthetics and comedic intent; bibliographic matters dealing with publication history, textual variations, and their implications for questions about authorship; mythological bases and sources; possible autobiographical elements; and moral and ethical values, often centering on sexuality and implied homosexuality. The foregoing list is not exhaustive, and any given study is likely to include several of the aspects while using one of them to illuminate one or more of the others. Marlovian criticism boasts the names of many outstanding modern scholars; a sampling would include J. A. Symonds, T. S. Eliot, U. M. Ellis-Fermor, F. S. Tannenbaum, Mario Praz, J. Q. Adams, M. C. Bradbrook, J. Bakeless, L. Kirschbaum, W. W. Greg, Helen Gardner, F. P. Wilson, C. S. Lewis, and Louis L. Martz.

BIOGRAPHY

Biographical interest in Christopher Marlowe has been keen and perhaps too often controversial. Public records are relatively numerous, considering that he was a sixteenth century Englishman who died before he was thirty years old. His baptism, progress through school and university to the M.A. degree, and the details of his death are documented. Contemporary references to Marlowe and his works are likewise plentiful. The variety of interpretation placed upon this evidence, however, is truly astonishing. What is quite clear is that Marlowe was born into a relatively affluent family of tradesmen in Canterbury. His father was in the shoe trade, possibly as a shoemaker, possibly as an employer of shoemakers. In any case, in January, 1579, Marlowe entered King's School, an institution operating just beyond Canterbury Cathedral. In December, 1580, he enrolled in Corpus Christi College, Cambridge, on a scholarship. In 1584, Marlowe was graduated with a B.A. degree but continued his studies, still on scholarship. Marlowe's attendance was, at least occasionally, irregular, and he was engaged from time to time upon some sort of secret work for the government, the nature of which remains unclear despite much speculation. It involved travel on the Continent; it may have involved spying at home or abroad. When, in 1587, the university determined to withhold the M.A. degree from Marlowe, the Privy Council intervened in the name of the queen and insisted that Marlowe's services to the Crown were sufficient grounds for granting the degree.

Upon leaving Cambridge, Marlowe immediately immersed himself in the political and intellectual life of London, on one hand,

Christopher Marlowe in the only known portrait of him, from around 1585. (Hulton Archive)

in the aristocratic circles of Sir Walter Ralegh and Sir Thomas Walsingham, and on the other, in the bohemianism of the London actors and playwrights. Both groups apparently contributed to the underworld contacts that tavern life and secret government service would suggest. As early as 1588, Robert Greene attacked Marlowe indirectly as an atheist, a charge which reappeared from time to time. In 1589, Marlowe was involved in a brawl with a certain William Bradley which ended with Bradley's death at the hands of one Thomas Watson. Both Marlowe and Watson were jailed temporarily because of the affair, which was finally adjudged to have been a case of self-defense.

By 1592, both *Tamburlaine the Great, Parts I* and *II*, and *Doctor Faustus* had been produced and published. Meanwhile, Marlowe's reputation as a dangerous fellow had grown. In that year, he had been bound over to keep the peace by a brace of frightened constables, and he appears to have been one of the atheist playwrights attacked in Robert Greene's *Groatsworth of Wit Bought with a Million of Repentance* (1592). On May 12, 1593, Marlowe's fellow University Wit, friend, and former roommate, Thomas Kyd, during or shortly after torture, wrote a letter to the Lord Keeper, Sir John Puckering, accusing Marlowe of ownership of papers, found in Kyd's room, which denied the divinity of Christ.

Whether or not Kyd's confession influenced them, the Privy Council issued a warrant for Marlowe's arrest and ordered him to report to them daily. On May 30, Marlowe spent the day at the Bull Inn in Deptford in the disreputable company of the double-agent Robert Poley, and two other possible spies, Nicholas Skeres and Ingram Frizer. The coroner's report indicates that they had walked in the garden during the day and then had eaten supper together. Following a quarrel about the bill, Marlowe is said to have taken Frizer's dagger from his belt and beaten him about the head with it. Frizer managed to grasp Marlowe's arm, reverse the blade, and force it into Marlowe's head. The jury found that the stab wound was the cause of death and declared the death to be instant and accidental.

On the whole, the jury was composed of competent men, the sequence of events plausible, and the jury's conclusion sound. Short, then, of the discovery of more

telling evidence, all theories of a plot of premeditated murder against Marlowe must be taken as only more or less interesting conjectures. Perhaps it was inevitable that the facts about a famous man whose life was both colorful and secretive would excite equally colorful speculation about the facts which lie beyond the official records and public accusations.

ANALYSIS

Christopher Marlowe's lyric poem "The Passionate Shepherd to His Love" is known in several versions of varying length. C. F. Tucker Brooke's 1962 reprint of his 1910 edition of Marlowe's works cites the six-stanza version of *England's Helicon*, with variant readings provided in the notes. Frederick S. Boas, in *Christopher Marlowe: A Biographical and Critical Study*, puts the case for holding that only the first four stanzas are certainly Marlowe's. Fredson Bowers, in the second volume of his monumental *The Complete Works of Christopher Marlowe* (1973), offers a "reconstructed" four-stanza version of the original poem printed alongside the six-stanza version of *England's Helicon*. All versions provide a delightful and innocuous exercise in the pastoral tradition of happy innocent shepherds sporting in a bucolic setting. Simply put, a lover outlines for his sweetheart the beauties and pleasures she can expect if she will live with him and be his love. Nature and the rejoicing shepherds will provide the pair with entertainment, clothing, shelter, and all things fitting to an amorous paradise.

"THE PASSIONATE SHEPHERD TO HIS LOVE"

The stanza is a simple quatrain rhyming in couplets. While it is a fine example of Elizabethan taste for decoration and is very pleasing to the ear, it presents nothing especially clever in its prosody. A few of the couplets are fresh enough in their rhymes, such as "falls/ madrigalls," "kirtle/ Mirtle," and "buds/ studs," but the rest are common enough. The alliteration falls short of being heavy-handed, and it achieves neither clearness nor subtlety. The poem's appeal, then, seems to lie mostly in its evocation of young love playing against an idealized background, its simple language and prosody forming part of its overt innocence.

Sir Walter Ralegh's famous response, "The Nymph's Reply to the Shepherd," also published in *England's*

Helicon, sets all of the cynicism associated with the *carpe diem* poetry of a John Donne or an Andrew Marvell against Marlowe's pose of innocence. Ralegh's shepherdess argues that the world and love are too old to allow her to be seduced by "pretty pleasures." She speaks of aging, of the cold of winter, of the sweet appearance which hides bitterness and approaching death. She scorns his offers of beauty, shelter, and love as things which decay and rot. Were youth, love, and joy eternal, and old age well provided for, then she might love. Both poems are set-pieces and imply nothing except that both poets were makers working within established traditions. The innocence of Marlowe's poem argues nothing about his own personality and much about his ability to project himself imaginatively into a character and a situation. In doing this, he produced a gem, and that is enough.

HERO AND LEANDER

In contrast to the simple, single-leveled "The Passionate Shepherd to His Love," *Hero and Leander* is a more complex, more sophisticated poem. Whatever ultimate plans Marlowe may have had for the completed poem, the two completed sestiads are in the comic mode as they portray the fumbling yearnings and actions of two adolescents faced with passions with which they are totally unprepared to deal. The story of young love, then, is constantly undercut with one sort of comedy or another.

Perhaps the easiest clues to Marlowe's comic intention lie in his choice of epic style and heroic couplets, both of which lend themselves to witty parody because they are traditionally used seriously. The epic tradition allows Marlowe to pay his lovers elaborate, and obviously exaggerated, compliments through the use of epic similes and through comparison with the classical tales of gods and heroes. The heroic couplet allows him to emphasize the fun with variations of the meter and with comic rhymes, generally feminine ones.

The retelling of the famous tale of two ill-fated lovers—whose trysts require Leander to swim across the Hellespont to visit Hero in her tower—begins soberly enough, as a mock-epic should. By the ninth line, however, Marlowe begins a description of Hero's garments which is wildly ornate and exaggerated in style. Her dress, for example, is lined with purple and studded with golden stars; the sleeves are green and are embroidered with a scene of Venus, naked, viewing the slain and bloody Adonis; her veil reaches to the ground and is so realistically decorated with artificial vegetation that men mistake her breath for the odor of flowers and bees search it for honey. The picture, thus far, could pass as an example of Elizabethan taste for the gaudy, and becomes clearly comic only in retrospect.

The twenty-fifth line, however, presents a figure which sets the anticlimactic tone informing the whole piece. Hero's necklace is described as a chain of ordinary pebbles which the beauty of her neck makes shine as diamonds. Later on, her naked beauty causes an artificial dawn in her bedchamber, to Leander's delight. The improbabilities are piled on thickly: Her hands are not subject to burning because sun and wind alike delight in them as playthings; sparrows perch in her shell buskins; Cupid could not help mistaking her for his mother, Venus; and Nature itself resented having been plundered of its rightful beauty by this slip of a girl. Marlowe points up the comedy of the Cupid passage with a feminine rhyme: "But this is true, so like was one the other,/ As he imagined Hero was his mother." He signs the comic intent of the Nature passage with an outrageous conceit and compliment: "Therefore in sign of her treasure suffered wrack,/ Since Hero's time, hath half the world been black." Throughout the two sestiads, similar tactics are employed, including much additional use of comic feminine rhyme (Morpheus/ visit us, cunning/ running, furious/ Prometheus, kist him/ mist him, and yv'ry skin/ lively in) and mocking versions of the epic simile.

The compelling argument for Marlowe's comedic intent, however, lies in this treatment of situation, theme, and character. Boas reflects a view commonly held by critics at the turn of the twentieth century when he argues that Marlowe's purpose was to tell the stories of the lovers, working in as much mythology as possible. He does not see the comedy as anything but incidental, and congratulates Marlowe on rescuing the grossness of Ovidian comedy with "delicate humor." Brooke, also an early twentieth century Marlovian, regards *Hero and Leander* as an essentially original work to be judged independently of George Chapman's continuation of the poem. Brooke treats the poem as an extended example of masterful heroic verse with no hint that such verse could be used here as an adjunct of comedy.

The French critic Michel Poirier comes nearer to Marlowe's comedic intent in his biography, *Christopher Marlowe* (1951, 1968), in which he describes the poem as belonging to the genre of Renaissance hedonism. He sees the poem as a "hymn to sensuality, tastefully done." He too sees the poem as erotic, but argues that it avoids equally ancient crudeness and the rough humor of the medieval fabliaux. Philip Henderson's essay "Christopher Marlowe" (1966) points up the by-then-dominant view by observing that *Hero and Leander* is not only a parody but also a very mischievous one, written by a poet who is so disengaged from his poem that he is able to treat it wittily and with a certain cynicism. John Ingram in *Christopher Marlowe and His Associates* (1970) harks back to an earlier view in claiming that no other Elizabethan poem equals it for purity and beauty. He notes nothing of the ironist at work.

A. L. Rowse, an ingenious if not always convincing literary historian and critic, sees *Hero and Leander*, in *Christopher Marlowe: His Life and Work* (1964), as a sort of rival piece to Shakespeare's *Venus and Adonis*. He goes so far as to suggest that Marlowe and Shakespeare read their poems to each other in a sort of combat of wit. However that may be, Rowse is probably right in seeing the poem as being carefully controlled, in contrast to the view, well-represented by Boas, that the poem is structurally a mere jumble. Rowse sees the poem as organically unified by the careful playing off of this mode and that technique against a variety of others.

In his essay "Marlowe's Humor," included in his most useful book *Marlowe: A Collection of Critical Essays* (1964), Clifford Leech rejects earlier criticism holding that the comic passages were the work of other writers and pits C. S. Lewis's denial, in his *English Literature in the Sixteenth Century* (1954), that *Hero and Leander* contains any humor at all against T. S. Eliot's assertion in *Selected Essays* (1950-1972) that Marlowe was at his best when writing "savage comic humor." Leech's position is that the poem is dominated by a humor at once gentle and delighting, not to say sly. He supports his position with a shrewd analysis of the subtle

effects of tone and verse form. Louis L. Martz, in *Hero and Leander: A Fascimile of the First Edition, London, 1598* (1972), also sees Marlowe's tone as comic and as conveyed through the couplet, and he characterizes the poem as being carefully structured as a triptych, with the Mercury fable, usually viewed as a digression, as the central picture, flanked by tales depicting mortal love. He sees Marlowe's digression as intentional and Ovidian. Martz, as a whole, comes down firmly on the side of those who see the poem as a thoroughgoing comedy.

Philip Henderson keeps to the comedic interpretation but also brings boldly to the fore a factor in the story long recognized but generally treated as minor, incidental, and otherwise unaccountable—that of homosexuality as a theme. In *Christopher Marlowe* (second edition, 1974), he argues that the passage describing Leander's body is "rapturous," but that the element is reduced to farce by Leander's encounter with Neptune as he swims the Hellespont. At the same time, Henderson firmly denies that Rowse's description of Marlowe as a known homosexual has any basis in fact. On balance, Henderson concludes that the critics' urge to find irony and sensational undertones obscures recognition of the beauty properly belonging to *Hero and Leander*, and he notes further that the insistence upon seeing comedy throughout Marlowe's work is a modern one. William Keach, tracing Marlowe's intentions in "Marlowe's Hero as 'Venus' Nun" (*English Literary Renaissance*, Winter, 1972), argues that Marlowe is largely indebted for the "subtleties and complexities" of his poem to hints from his fifth century Greek source, Musaeus. Keach sees both poets as ironists and argues that Hero's activities as a priestess of love who is puritanically virginal are essentially silly.

John Mills, in his study "The Courtship Ritual of Hero and Leander" (*English Literary Renaissance*, Winter, 1972), sees Hero at the opening as a compound of innocence and sexuality, with all the confusions that such a compound can make, both in her own mind and in those of men who observe her. Mills's interest lies, however, not so much in this condition itself as in the web of classical elements and allusions in which it is contained. He argues, in effect, that the poem depends upon an overblown, stereotypical, and mannered attitude toward romantic sex which he compares to Vladimir Nabokov's theory of "poshlust." Mills concludes that Marlowe's "poshlustian comedy" arises out of the actions being played out in a physical and material world of sexuality in such terms that Hero and Leander, and innocent readers, are persuaded that their activities are really spiritual. In another essay, "Sexual Discovery and Renaissance Morality in Marlowe's 'Hero and Leander'" (*Studies in English Literature, 1500-1900*, XII, 1972), published immediately after that of Mills, William P. Walsh argues that Marlowe is ironic in basing the story on love at first sight and making his characters slaves of their irrational passion. His notion is that the lovers themselves, not sexuality, are the objects of humorous comment with which they are not entirely out of sympathy. His development of the theme is detailed and astute, and he points out, in discussing the invented myth of the Destinies' love affair with Mercury, the generally overlooked argument that Marlowe makes for reproduction as the true object of sex, as against pleasure for its own sake. Walsh suggests that the inability of Hero and Leander to see beyond their dream of a sexual paradise at once positions them for the eventual tragic ending traditional to their story, yet keeps them reduced to comic stature in Marlowe's portion of the poem.

In writing *Hero and Leander*, then, Marlowe displayed ingenuity and erudition by telling an ironically comic tale of the mutual wooing and seduction of a pair of inexperienced but lusty young lovers. The telling is intricately and objectively organized and describes a rite of passage which is neither sentimentalized nor especially brutalized. The result is a highly skilled tour de force in the tradition of the Elizabethan maker, cynical enough, perhaps, but confessional or autobiographical only tangentially, if at all. Coupled with "The Passionate Shepherd to His Love," *Hero and Leander* establishes Marlowe's claim to a high place in the select company of those British poets who have produced a slender but superior body of lyric poetry.

OTHER MAJOR WORKS

PLAYS: *Dido, Queen of Carthage*, pr. c. 1586-1587 (with Thomas Nashe); *Tamburlaine the Great, Part I*, pr. c. 1587 (commonly known as *Tamburlaine*); *Tamburlaine the Great, Part II*, pr. 1587; *Doctor Faustus*, pr. c. 1588; *The Jew of Malta*, pr. c. 1589; *Edward II*, pr. c. 1592; *The Massacre at Paris*, pr. 1593.

TRANSLATIONS: *Elegies*, 1595-1600 (of Ovid's *Amores*); *Pharsalia*, 1600 (of Lucan's *Pharsalia*).

MISCELLANEOUS: *The Works of Christopher Marlowe*, 1910, 1962 (C. F. Tucker Brooke, editor); *The Works and Life of Christopher Marlowe*, 1930-1933, 1966 (R. H. Case, editor); *The Complete Works of Christopher Marlowe*, 1973 (Fredson Bowers, editor).

BIBLIOGRAPHY

Bakeless, John. *The Tragicall History of Christopher Marlowe*. 2 vols. Cambridge, Mass.: Harvard University Press, 1942. In this massive study, Bakeless incorporates the efforts of such earlier important Marlowe biographers as Leslie Hotson (1925), C. F. Tucker Brooke (1930), and Mark Eccles (1934). The work remains valuable because of its thoroughness, and Bakeless's interpretations have been only slightly superseded by discoveries of later scholars.

Bloom, Harold, ed. *Christopher Marlowe: Modern Critical Views*. New York: Chelsea House, 1986. This volume consists of thirteen selections, mainly excerpts of previously published books that are landmarks in Marlowe criticism. Analyses of six plays and *Hero and Leander* are uniformly authoritative. Of special interest is Lawrence Danson's essay on Marlovian skepticism, which provides an excellent perspective on the playwright-poet's career as a whole. The bibliography at the end of the volume includes most of the major critical studies of Marlowe.

Hopkins, Lisa. *Christopher Marlowe: A Literary Life*. New York: Palgrave, 2000. Hopkins situates the works of Marlowe within the context of his literary career. Areas covered include: Marlowe's preference for foreign settings and his unusually accurate depictions of them; the importance of his scholarly background; his consistent portrayal of family groups as fissured and troubled; the challenge that his works posed to contemporary orthodoxies about religion, sexuality, and government; and the long and sometimes spectacular afterlife of his works and of his literary reputation as a whole.

Leech, Clifford. *Christopher Marlowe: Poet for the Stage*. Edited by Anne Lancashire. New York: AMS

Press, 1986. Consisting partly of revisions of previously published articles, this posthumous book is especially important for its lucid analyses of *Doctor Faustus* and *Edward II*. Leech sees Marlowe's tragic heroes as ultimately solitary victims. His treatment of *Hero and Leander* is an admiring response to the poet's comic skills.

Levin, Harry. *The Overreacher: A Study of Christopher Marlowe*. Cambridge, Mass.: Harvard University Press, 1952. A critical as well as a biographical study, this landmark book is excellent on both the nondramatic works and the plays. Levin develops the thesis that central to Marlowe's work is the confrontation between the ideals of human beings and their realization that they have inherent limitations, which Levin sees as the essence of Marlovian tragedy.

Pincuss, Gerald. *Christopher Marlowe*. New York: Frederick Ungar, 1975. This brief illustrated book is a good introduction to Marlowe and the theater for which he wrote. Begins with a chronology of the playwright's life and concludes with a representative bibliography adequate for all but the most advanced scholar.

Simkin, Stevie. *A Preface to Marlowe*. New York: Longman, 2000. Provides comprehensive and full analysis of all Marlowe's dramatic and non-dramatic works, brings the texts to life, and emphasizes the performance aspects of the texts. A controversial and challenging reading which reopens debates about Marlowe's status as a radical figure and as a subversive playwright.

Steane, J. B. *Marlowe: A Critical Study*. Cambridge, England: Cambridge University Press, 1964. After reviewing the facts and theories of Marlowe's life, Steane devotes individual chapters to the plays and poems (the latter including not only *Hero and Leander* but also Marlowe's translations of Lucan and Ovid). The sections on the plays are noteworthy primarily because of the analyses of Marlowe's poetic style and Steane's thesis that the changing style reveals how Marlowe became increasingly pessimistic and unstable during his brief life and career.

B. G. Knepper;
bibliography updated by the editors

Harry Martinson

Born: Jämshög, Sweden; May 6, 1904
Died: Stockholm, Sweden; February 11, 1978

Principal poetry
Spökskepp, 1929
Nomad, 1931
Natur, 1934
Passad, 1945
Cikada, 1953
Aniara: En revy om människan i tid och rum, 1956 (*Aniara: A Review of Man in Time and Space*, 1963)
Gräsen i Thule, 1958
Vagnen, 1960
Dikter om ljus och mörker, 1971
Tuvor, 1973
Wild Bouquet, 1985

Other literary forms
    In addition to his poetry, Harry Martinson published impressionistic travelogues as well as two autobiographical childhood recollections and a novel. They are all centered on the major symbol in his work, the "world nomad," the restless traveler, and form one coherent poetic *Bildungsroman* in which initial bitterness over strong social handicaps and anguish at a world without love are superseded by the protagonist's—that is, the poet's—search for tenderness and acceptance. Martinson's later essay collections—sketches, meditations, and prose poems—in which concrete nature observation is blended with philosophical speculation, mark a departure from the autobiographical realm. Yet Martinson insists on drawing parallels between life in nature and human life. This approach leads him to a scathing criticism of modern civilization in the Rousseauian tradition, climaxing in his reports from Finland's Winter War of 1939-1940 against Russia.

Achievements
    The immediate and acclaimed breakthrough that Harry Martinson experienced with his collection *Nomad* was unique in Swedish literature. The critics unani-

mously agreed in acknowledging an unusually gifted writer who combined sharp intellect and concise power of observation with an almost visionary ability to perceive a cosmic unity behind the fragmentation of modern thought, qualities which Martinson's later writings have confirmed.

In Swedish literary history, Martinson belongs chronologically to the 1930's. For a time, he joined the group of young radical poets who rejected morality and modern civilization as too inhibiting in favor of an unrestricted worship of spontaneity and instinctive forces in life. Yet, in spite of his contributions to the anthology *Fem unga* (1929), Martinson is only in part related to the nature of that decade's D. H. Lawrence—inspired vitalism and primitivism. Nor does he belong to the exclusive and self-centered school of T. S. Eliot—inspired modernists of the 1940's. Already during his lifetime, he was accepted as a classicist, a classicist distinguished through linguistic imagination and a highly developed associative and myth-creating imagination. Also notable is his continuous endeavor to search for coherence in a chaotic world and—for the sake of troubled humanity— to warn against abusing the achievements of modern technology.

It is, however, impossible to place Martinson in a specific school or trend. Indeed, after his epic poem *Aniara*, a tremendous critical and public success, he emerged as one of the most independent yet compassionate humanists in twentieth century Scandinavian literature. In 1959, when *Aniara* premiered as an opera, with libretto by another prolific Swedish poet, Erik Lindegren, and music by Karl-Birger Blomdahl, it received international recognition. In 1949, Martinson was elected to the Swedish Academy as its first self-taught proletarian writer; in 1954, he received an honorary doctorate from the University of Gothenburg; and, in 1974, he shared, together with Eyvind Johnson, the Nobel Prize in Literature.

BIOGRAPHY

Harry Edmund Martinson was born on May 6, 1904, in Jämshög in the southeastern province of Blekinge, Sweden. His father, a captain in the merchant marines and later an unsuccessful businessman, died when Martinson was five. One year later, his mother emi-

Harry Martinson, Nobel laureate in literature for 1974. (© The Nobel Foundation)

grated to the United States, leaving her seven children to be cared for by the local parish. As a child, Martinson escaped from harsh reality into nature and into a fantasy world nourished by his reading (in particular the works of Jack London), and he dreamed of going to sea. He spent two years as a vagabond throughout Sweden and Norway before going to sea as a stoker and deckhand. He spent the next six years on fourteen different vessels, with extended periods in India and South America, before he finally returned to Sweden, having contracted tuberculosis.

The year 1929 proved to be a turning point in Martinson's life. He made his literary debut and also married the writer Moa Martinson, beginning a stimulating partnership which lasted until 1940. During the early 1930's, Martinson was tempted to pursue a career as a professional artist. His favorite subjects were factory workers, the jungle, and underwater scenes executed in a colorful and naïve style. In August, 1934, he participated in the Soviet Writers' Congress in Moscow, an experience which disillusioned the former Communist sympathizer. The outbreak of World War II was seen by him as the result of the "civilization of violence." In 1939, after Finland was attacked by the Soviet Union, Martinson joined the Finnish side as a volunteer. He wrote a book about his experiences, partly a glorification of rural Finland and its deep-rooted traditions as well as the country's courageous battle against the war machine from the east, partly direct reportage from the front, the "unequivocal idiot-roaring grenade reality." In 1942, Martinson married Ingrid Lindcrantz and settled in Stockholm, where he died on February 11, 1978.

ANALYSIS

From the very outset, it was Harry Martinson's intention to change the world. He embodied this intention in his utopian figure of the altruistic "world nomad" who represents humanity's search for a better world. The nomadic concept must be understood both concretely, in a geographical sense, and symbolically, as a journey into the realms of fantasy, dream, and the ideal future. Thus, dynamism and a moral intent emerged as the two basic qualities which were to characterize everything he wrote.

Martinson's own life as a sailor was the obvious point of departure for this expansion, which in his earliest poems is mainly depicted as daydreaming without specific direction: "Our thoughts are seabirds and they always fly away from us." They were written at sea on paper bags, Rudyard Kipling and Robert Burns being their models. Nevertheless, these texts, in particular those written with a free rhythmical and rhymeless structure, are characterized by a unique melodious softness and a ballad-like flow hitherto unknown in Swedish literature. In addition, Martinson's own experiences abroad add a quality of reliability and concreteness, which also became a personal trademark of his later writing.

Other literary models, Walt Whitman and Edgar Lee Masters, are noticeable in Martinson's contributions to the anthology *Fem unga*. Yet his poetry increasingly relies on memories from his childhood and impressions from the world of nature and of the sea, guided by the poet's vivid associative power: "Out at sea you feel a spring or summer only like a breeze./ The drifting Florida seaweed sometimes blossoms in the summer,/ and on a spring night a spoonbill stork flies towards Holland." Yet a simultaneous striving for brevity and concentration, influenced by the Old Norse Eddic poetry, occasionally leads to a syntactic complexity and obscurity of thought. These characteristics are particularly present in his third collection, *Natur*, in which some of his most successful texts take on a surrealist quality inspired by Vladimir Mayakovski and contemporary art.

FOCUS ON HUMANITY

Martinson, in his progression from concrete detail to an almost mystical experience of a pantheistic unity, never loses sight of humankind in his writing. Satire can be found in "Rhapsody," the portrayal of a scientist who hunts for birds with a machine gun while at the same time recording bird songs. Usually—and in particular in the volumes *Passad* and *Aniara*—Martinson focuses on humanity in general, treating it in conjunction with the travel motif. In *Passad*, he creates a grandiose vision of the fundamental division of Western civilization pictured in the two travelers, Ulysses and Robinson Crusoe. One is the humanist and poet, the other the empiricist and scientist, and Martinson sees modern man's tragedy in the fact that these two personalities have not been synthesized. The trade wind, the "passad," becomes the symbol of the search for such a unity and harmony, which can only be discovered within oneself: "But new and wise explorers I have met/ have pointed inward . . . and I have listened to them/ and sensed/ a new trade wind." A fictional representative of Martinson's worldview is the persona of Li Kan, introduced in *Passad*, evincing Martinson's preoccupation with Chinese poetry and Asian philosophy, Taoism in particular. Li Kan's media are terse, almost aphoristic maxims, in which a tone of resignation and melancholy counterbalances Martinson's otherwise optimistic message of universal harmony.

ANIARA

Achieving this harmony becomes increasingly problematic in Martinson's works in the period after 1950. This was a time in which his cosmic expansion and escaping dreams offered little consolation, a time over-

shadowed by nuclear bombs, wars, and political up-
risings. Initially expressed in twenty-nine poems or
songs, included in the collection *Cikada*, this misan-
thropy comes to its full expression in the verse epic
Aniara, expanded to 103 songs. For years, Martinson
had taken a keen interest in mathematics, physics, and
astronomy. This expertise now formed the background
for his account of the giant spaceship *Aniara*, which
in the year 9000 takes off with eight thousand evacu-
ees from planet Earth following a nuclear catastrophe.
The passengers seek consolation from the Mima, a supercomputer, which shows pictures from the earth and
from other planets. Soon, however, the journey is no
longer one of discovery but of horrible certainty, a travel
toward ultimate extinction. After twenty-four years in
space, the passengers die and the *Aniara*, now a giant
sarcophagus, continues on its way out of the galaxy. The
Aniara is meant to be an image of civilization, and the
characters aboard, prisoners indeed, represent a world
steadily departing further from humanity toward still
greater technological, impersonal sterility. Life aboard
the spaceship offers a cross section of contemporary society, its different aspects and attitudes. Yet Martinson
goes beyond the social and political realm to an analysis
of man's moral and spiritual decay. Thus, the *Aniara* becomes an image of man and his doomed situation as he
desperately attempts to avert catastrophe through artistic
expression, rituals, and idolatry. Against this ship of
fools, Martinson contrasts an ideal life of simplicity and
harmony with nature as portrayed in an exquisite scene
from the forests of Finnish Karelia. A beam of hope is lit
through the various female characters, who together
strive for nothing less than the Platonic ideals of truth,
beauty, and goodness: "The eternal mystery of the fir-
mament/ and the miracle of the celestial mechanics/ are
laws but not the Gospel. Charity sprouts in the ground
of life."

The style of *Aniara* is remarkable. Martinson's associative technique allows him to create a futuristic language composed of a flow of literary allusions ranging
from the Bible to contemporary popular songs, hidden
quotes, as well as a unique terminology based on self-
coined technical words. With *Aniara*, Martinson created
the only epic in Swedish literature of any significant artistic value.

Subsequently, Martinson returned to a simpler poetic
form closer to that of his earlier works. In collections of
lucid and artless poetry, he protests the exploitation and
destruction of nature and continues to reject today's lifestyle marred by commercialism, superficiality, and rootlessness.

It is important to remember that Martinson's view
of nature is strictly unsentimental and anti-idyllic. His
skepticism is not aimed at technology per se but at humankind's inability to cope with its advances and to
make it subservient to humanity. Instead, the products of
civilization are threatening humankind's dreams and
imagination—the airplane is being used to drop bombs
on civilians, and the radio has become an instrument for
political propaganda. Hence also Martinson's prevailing
hope that humankind can avoid the fate of the *Aniara*
and its passengers, a hope that in some poems takes on a
metaphysical dimension: "We have a foreboding that
what we call space . . . / is spirit, eternal spirit, untouch-
able,/ that we have lost ourselves in the sea of the spirit."

Martinson's vision is wider than that of any modern
Swedish poet. His visionary and mystical approach is
counterbalanced by the clarity and simplicity of his poems about childhood and nature; his sophisticated analyses of modern technology are counterbalanced by an
intuitive delving into the fantasies and hopes of the human mind. He has created an entirely new poetic language and imagery, inspired by modern technology and
the pictorial arts, the boldness of which makes him a
modernist in the forefront of his art. At the same time,
his humanist message establishes bonds that reach back
to a long historical tradition.

OTHER MAJOR WORKS

LONG FICTION: *Vägen till Klockrike*, 1948 (*The
Road*, 1955).

PLAYS: *Lotsen fran Moluckas*, pb. 1938; *Tre knivar
från Wei*, pb. 1964.

NONFICTION: *Det enkla och det svåra*, 1939; *Resor
utan mål*, 1932; *Kap Farvål*, 1933 (*Cape Farewell*,
1934); *Nässlorna blomma*, 1935 (*Flowering Nettle*,
1936, autobiography); *Vägen ut*, 1936 (autobiography); *Svärmare och harkrank*, 1937; *Midsommar-
dalen*, 1938; *Verklighet till döds*, 1940; *Utsikt från en
grästuva*, 1963.

BIBLIOGRAPHY

Martinson, Harry. *Flowering Nettle.* Translated by Naomi Walford. London: Cresset Press, 1936. Martinson's autobiography covers only the first half of his
life but offers valuable insight into his writing.

Rossel, Sven H. *A History of Scandinavian Literature,
1870-1980.* Translated by Anne C. Ulmer. Minneapolis: University of Minnesota Press, 1982. History
and criticism of Scandinavian literature including
selected works by Martinson. Includes an index and
bibliographic references.

Sandelin, Stefan. *Harry Martinson, Nässlorna blomma.*
Hull, England: University of Hull, 1987. A critical
assessment of Martinson's autobiography.

Smith, Scott Andrew. "The Role of the Emersonian
'Poet' in Harry Martinson's *Aniara: A Review of
Man in Time and Space.*" *Extrapolation* 39, no. 4
(Winter, 1998): 324-337. Smith contends that Martinson's *Aniara: A Review of Man in Time and Space*
appears to be both a text with a clear connection to
the science-fiction genre and one that bridges the
gap between the poetic of that genre and the poetic
of a more classical work like Emerson's "The Poet."

Steene, Birgitta. "The Role of the Mima: A Note on
Martinson's *Aniara.*" In *Scandinavian Studies: Essays Presented to Dr. Henry G. Leach,* edited by
Carl F. Bayerschmidt and Erik J. Friis. Seattle: University of Washington Press, 1965. A critical essay
dealing with the Mima, the supercomputer aboard
the Aniara spacecraft, in Martinson's *Aniara.*

*Sven H. Rossel;
bibliography updated by the editors*

ANDREW MARVELL

Born: Winestead-in-Holderness, England; March 31,
1621
Died: London, England; August 18, 1678

PRINCIPAL POETRY

*The First Anniversary of the Government Under
His Highness the Lord Protector,* 1655
Miscellaneous Poems, 1681
Complete Poetry, 1968

OTHER LITERARY FORMS

In 1672, with the publication of *The Rehearsal
Transpros'd,* Andrew Marvell became a pamphleteer. In
this animadversion on the works of Samuel Parker,
Marvell vigorously supported King Charles II's stand in
favor of religious toleration. No other work by Marvell
was so widely received in his lifetime as this urbane,
witty, slashing satire. According to Marvell's contemporary Gilbert Burnet, "From the King down to the trades-
man, his books were read with great pleasure." Parker's
counterattack quickly engendered Marvell's second
pamphlet, *The Rehearsal Transpros'd: The Second Part*
(1673). *Mr. Smirke: Or, The Divine in Mode* (1676), was
Marvell's defense of Herbert Croft, the Bishop of Here-
ford, against Dr. Francis Turner's pamphlet attack. His
next pamphlet, *An Account of the Growth of Popery and
Arbitrary Government in England* (1677), resulted in
the government's offering a reward for the identity of the
author. *Remarks upon a Late Disingenuous Discourse*
was published posthumously in 1678. Some three hundred letters are also extant and available in Margoliouth's edition, as well as in those of Captain Edward
Thompson and Alexander B. Grosart.

ACHIEVEMENTS

In his own century and for some time afterward, Andrew Marvell's reputation rested much more on his
prose pamphlets, a few political poems, and his political
activities, than on his achievement as a lyric poet. Most
of his poems, including all of the lyrics, remained unpublished until the posthumous edition of 1681. By then
the Metaphysical mode was no longer in fashion, and
the book of Marvell's poems seems to have been desired
more for its excellent engraved portrait of the politician
and pamphleteer than for anything else. Appreciation of
Marvell's poetry was increased by Charles Lamb's essay of 1818, but it remained sporadic until after the publication of T. S. Eliot's essay on the occasion of the ter-
centenary of Marvell's birth in 1921. Except for a
quantity of imitations of his verse satires, some of which
were attributed to him, his influence on other poets was
slight. By far his widest poetic audience is in the present

day. He has had a modest influence on some twentieth century writers, such as Marianne Moore.

Today Marvell is recognized as a lyric poet of the first rank, although how uniformly excellent his poems are, individually or collectively, remains a subject of debate. Certainly the quality is somewhat irregular. Nevertheless, with a rather small corpus he has been awarded at least three apt distinctions. That three-quarters of his work is in eight-syllable form and much of it is brilliant has earned him the title "master of the octosyllabic." A few fine poems on a difficult subject have caused him to be called "Cromwell's poet." Finally, while his work includes civic, pastoral, and georgic material, he is, more than any other poet in English, the "garden poet."

BIOGRAPHY

Andrew Marvell was born on March 31, 1621, at Winestead-in-Holderness, Yorkshire. He was the fourth child and only surviving son of Andrew Marvell, Sr., a clergyman. In late 1624, the Reverend Marvell became lecturer at Holy Trinity Church in Hull, to which the family moved. The poet grew up there and was for the rest of his life associated with Hull, representing the city in Parliament for the last eighteen years of his life. On December 14, 1633, the young Marvell entered Trinity College, Cambridge. In 1637 Marvell was converted by Jesuits and ran away to London, whence his father retrieved him and returned him to Cambridge. Sometime in 1641 Marvell left Cambridge, having received the B.A. degree but without completing the requirements for the M.A.

Marvell may then have spent some time working in the commercial house of his brother-in-law, Edmund Popple, in Hull. His activities during the turbulent 1640's are not well recorded, but it is known that during that period he spent four years abroad, learning Dutch, French, Italian, and Spanish. He studied the gentlemanly art of fencing in Spain, and in Rome he paid a visit to the impoverished English Catholic priest, Flecknoe, whom John Dryden would make the butt of a satiric poem. Engaged in this Grand Tour, Marvell seems to have avoided any direct part in the English Civil War. Marvell returned to England in the late 1640's, publishing a congratulatory poem (probably written in 1647) for a volume of Richard Lovelace's verse in 1649, and contributing one poem to a volume lamenting the death of the young Lord Hastings in June, 1649. From 1650 to 1652 Marvell was tutor to Mary Fairfax, daughter of the parliamentary general, Lord Fairfax, whose resignation in June, 1650, left Cromwell dominant. That same month, Marvell must have composed "An Horatian Ode upon Cromwell's Return from Ireland," in which he applauds Cromwell's activities up to that point and anticipates his success in the coming campaign against the Scots. Because the poem also shows great sympathy and regard for the late King Charles in the brief passage dealing with his execution, a good deal of critical attention has been paid to the question of whether Marvell's praise of Cromwell is genuine, ironic, or intended to create an image toward which it might be hoped that the real Cromwell would gravitate. Marvell is elsewhere so prone to see more than one side of a question that it does not really seem remarkable that he may have recognized good qualities in both King Charles and Cromwell. "Upon Appleton House" and "Upon the Hill and Grove at Billborow," which describe two Fairfax estates, must be presumed to date from Marvell's days with the Fairfaxes; it is likely that a number of the lyrics, including "The Garden" and the Mower poems, also date from that period.

In 1653 Marvell left the Fairfax employ and sought, through John Milton, a position with the Commonwealth government. When his association with Milton began is uncertain, but it is known that they became and remained very close friends. In September, 1657, Marvell received a government post, becoming Latin Secretary, sharing (with Milton) responsibility for correspondence with foreign governments. He retained this post until the dissolution of the Commonwealth government. During the Cromwell years, Marvell wrote a number of poems in praise of Cromwell. These include "An Horatian Ode upon Cromwell's Return from Ireland," *The First Anniversary of the Government Under His Highness the Lord Protector*, 1655, and "A Poem upon the Death of His Late Highness the Lord Protector." Although Cromwell and his son, and perhaps close associates, presumably saw these poems, they seem not to have been widely circulated. Only *The First Anniversary of the Government Under His Highness the Lord Protector* was printed, and that anonymously.

Andrew Marvell (Library of Congress)

witty book quickly went through multiple editions. Parker strongly counterattacked with a new pamphlet, causing Marvell (despite an anonymous threat to cut his throat) to reply with *The Rehearsal Transpros'd: The Second Part*. Parker did not reply further. Marvell's last three pamphlets are of considerably less importance. *Mr. Smirke: Or, The Divine in Mode* used with less success and for a less crucial cause the techniques of the two parts of *The Rehearsal Transpros'd*. Next, *An Account of the Growth of Popery and Arbitrary Government in England* evoked the government offer of a reward for the name of the author, who died before action was taken on an informer's report. The title of this work precisely indicates the concerns that Marvell voiced in it, suggesting that leading government figures were involved in a plot to make England Catholic again. By 1674, Marvell himself was involved in clandestine activities as a member of a pro-Dutch "fifth column," apparently operating under the name of "Mr. Thomas"

In 1659 the Corporation of Hull chose Marvell to represent them in Parliament. He remained a member for the rest of his life, being twice reelected. He seems to have made the transition to the Restoration of Charles II with relative ease, and from his position in Parliament joined other friends of Milton in protecting that poet from serious harm under the new regime. During this period Marvell's satiric talents blossomed. His satiric verse included three "advice to a painter" poems parodying a poem by Edmund Waller and lampooning various influential persons and their policies. More important by far were his prose pamphlets, especially the first, *The Rehearsal Transpros'd*. This was an attack on the pamphlets of Samuel Parker, a rising Church of England divine, who strongly supported conformity and had tangled in print with the nonconformists, especially John Owen. The question of toleration versus conformity was a very important one in the politics of 1672, with Charles II, for his own reasons, trying to put through a policy of toleration. Marvell's powerful and

and making secret trips to Holland. Marvell's death, on August 18, 1678, was the result of his physician's treatment of a fever and not, as was suspected by some, a political murder. His last pamphlet, *Remarks upon a Late Disingenuous Discourse* is his least readable work and is of little importance.

ANALYSIS

Andrew Marvell is firmly established today in the ranks of the Metaphysical poets, and there is no question that much of his work clearly displays the qualities appropriate to such a position. He reveals a kinship with the Metaphysical poets through his ingenious use of extended logic, even when dealing with emotions; his yoking of very dissimilar things, of the mundane (even profane) with the sublime, of large with small and far with near; and his analytic quality. His use of puns, often woven into intricate groups, may be added to the list. Like John Donne and the other Metaphysical poets, Marvell shapes his rhythm with careful attention to his meaning.

Marvell's admiration for Donne shows not only in having written some strongly Donne-like poetry ("On a Drop of Dew," "Young Love," and parts of "Upon Appleton House," for example), but in his gratuitously full use of one of Donne's poems in a pamphlet written late in Marvell's life. It might be added that Marvell's prose works, especially his most successful, show the same Metaphysical qualities.

Where Donne's best-known poetry (as well as Marvell's most Donne-like work) resembles puzzles from which attentive reading gradually extracts greater clarity, a similar approach to Marvell's best and most "Marvellian" passages (for example, "a green thought in a green Shade") causes them not to become more clear so much as more dazzling. Marvell has been called "many-sided," "ambiguous," "amphibian," "elusive," and "inconclusive." He is. He has been said to have a vision that is "complex," "double," or "ironic." He does.

Marvell's work often shows a remarkable ability to make opposites interdependent, to create a *concordia discors*. Such is the relationship of Cromwell and King Charles in "An Horatian Ode upon Cromwell's Return from Ireland," and of retirement and action in "Upon Appleton House" and "The Garden." Sometimes, no less remarkably, he achieves moments of what can only be called "fusion," as in the "annihilation of all that's made" in "The Garden," or in the last few lines of "To His Coy Mistress." He will at times surprisingly mix levity and gravity, as in "To His Coy Mistress" and parts of "Upon Appleton House." His use of qualifiers is unusual ("none, *I think*," or "*If* these the times").

Marvell employed decasyllabics for his last two Cromwell poems, inventing a stanza combining lines of eight and six syllables for the first. Three fourths of his work was in octosyllabics, however, and he has been rightly called the "master of the octosyllabic."

"To His Coy Mistress"

Certainly the most widely anthologized and best known of Marvell's poems is "To His Coy Mistress." It is not only a seduction poem, but also a *deduction* poem, in which the theme of *carpe diem* is presented as a syllogism: (1) If there were world enough and time, the lady's coyness would not be a crime; (2) There is not world enough and time; (3) therefore, this coyness may or may not be a crime. Marvell must have been aware

that his poem depended upon flawed logic; he may have meant it to be ironically typical of the desperate reasoning employed by would-be seducers.

In the first section of the poem, the speaker describes the vast amounts of time ("An age at least to every part") and space (from the Ganges to the Humber) he would devote to his love if he could. This apparently gracious statement of patience is then juxtaposed with the striking image of "Time's wingéd chariot hurrying near" and the resultant "Deserts of vast eternity." "Deserts," meaning "unpeopled places," is emphasized by the shift of the stress to the first syllable of the line. There follows the arresting depiction of the drawbacks of postmortem chastity, with worms "trying" the lady's "long-preserved virginity," as her "quaint honor" turns to dust.

Imagery of corruption was not unusual in *carpe diem* poems, and it also occurs (the memento mori theme) in visual arts of the period; Marvell's lines are, however, remarkably explicit and must have been devised to shock and disgust. The passage represents, as Rosalie Colie notes in "*My Ecchoing Song*" (1970), "sound psychology" in frightening the lady into the comfort of her lover's arms, an event that the next two lines suggest may indeed have occurred at this point, as the speaker rescues himself from the danger of excessive morbidity with the urbanely ironic comment, "The grave's a fine and private place,/ But none, I think, do there embrace." This makes the transition to the last section of the poem, wherein the speaker, having shown that however limitless time and space may intrinsically be, they are to mortals very limited, offers his solution. The answer is to take energetic action. The formerly coy mistress, now described (either in hope or in fact) as having a "willing soul" with "instant fires," is invited to join the speaker in "one ball" of strength and sweetness, which will tear "thorough the iron gates of life." This third section of the poem is an addition not typical of *carpe diem* poems, which usually suggest rather than delineate the consummation. The amorous couple, the speaker indicates, should enthusiastically embrace the inevitable and each other. Like the elder Fairfaxes in "Upon Appleton House," they should "make Destiny their choice" and devour time rather than waiting for time to consume them. In its three sections, "To His Coy Mistress" presents first a cheerful and generous offering of limitless time and space, then a chilling reminder that human life is very limited, and finally a frenzied but extraordinarily powerful invitation to break through and transcend all limits.

"THE GARDEN"

If "To His Coy Mistress" makes the case for action versus hesitation, "The Garden," the best-known hortensial work of the "garden poet," considers the question of action versus contemplation. Like much of Marvell's work, it employs a rich texture of wordplay and classical and Christian allusions. It is a retirement poem, in which the speaker begins by celebrating his withdrawal from the busy world of human endeavor. This theme is one rich in tradition, and would have been attractive during the uncertain and dangerous times in which Marvell lived. In this poem, however, the speaker retires not merely from the world of men, but, in a moment of ultimate retirement, from the world of material things. As the poet contemplates the garden, his mind and his soul momentarily transcend the material plane.

In the first stanza, the speaker comments on the folly of seeking human glory. Men "vainly" ("from vanity," and also "in vain") "amaze" themselves (surprise themselves/trap themselves in a maze) in their efforts to achieve honors (represented by the palm, oak, and bay leaves used in classical victors' wreaths). Even the best such victory represents success in only one area of endeavor, for which the victor receives the decoration of a wreath woven from a single species, a wreath which in its singleness "upbraids" (braids up/rebukes) his "toyles" (coils of hair/efforts). In contrast, repose is rewarded by "all flowers and all trees." Addressing Quiet and Innocence personified, the speaker uses a typically Marvellian qualifier when he says that their sacred plants "if here below,/ Only among the plants will grow," suggesting that quiet and innocence may be really unobtainable on Earth. The solitude experienced by the lone visitor among the plants of the garden is nevertheless worth seeking, for, in comparison, "Society is all but rude"—society is nearly "coarse," or (an inversion and a pun) society is almost "rustic." The next three stanzas describe the physical, sensual values that the garden offers in contrast to those of the world. As the "society" of the garden is superior to that of men, so the sensuality of the garden is more intense than that of

men: "No white or red was ever seen/ So amorous as this lovely green" (the colors of fleshly passion are less "amorous" than the green of the garden), and the beauties of the trees exceed those of any woman. The gods Apollo and Pan knew this, the speaker says, since they pursued the nymphs Daphne and Syrinx, not for their womanly charms, but in order to obtain their more desirable dendritic forms.

In the fifth stanza the speaker reaches a height of sensual ecstasy as the various garden fruits literally thrust themselves upon him, in what Rosalie Colie rightly calls a "climactic experience." It is powerfully sexual, yet the speaker is alone and in the garden, as Adam once was in Eden. And then the speaker, "stumbling" and "Insnared," falls, reminding the reader of the Fall in Eden. Marvell's speaker, however, is still alone and still—indeed, more than ever—in the garden. The next two stanzas describe what is occurring "Meanwhile" on the mental and spiritual planes. The mind withdraws from the lesser pleasures of the body to seek its own kind of happiness. Within the mind, an interior paradise, are the images of all things in the physical world, just as the sea was thought to contain creatures corresponding to all terrestrial species. Yet the mind, unlike the sea, can create, imaginatively, "Far other worlds and other seas," transcending the mundane, and "Annihilating all that's made/ To a green thought in a green shade," an image that R. I. V. Hodge in *Foreshortened Time* (1978) calls "arguably the most intriguing image in Marvell's poetry or in the whole of the seventeenth century." Many explications have been offered for this couplet; the central notion seems to be that through the action of the mind in creating the far other worlds and seas, the physical world ("all that's made") is compacted, or by contrast appears to be compacted, into a single thought. It is, however, a "green" thought—a living, fertile thought which is the source, through the action of the mind, of the transcendent worlds and seas. Indeed, perhaps the thinker himself has almost been annihilated; "in a green shade" could indicate not only that the thinker is shaded by the trees, but also that he *is* (for the moment) a shade, an insubstantial shadow of his physical self. The green thought is, perhaps, the Platonic pure *idea* of garden from which all gardens derive. It could be suggested that this is the true garden of the poem.

In stanza seven, the soul leaves the body in a flight indicative of its later, final flight to heaven. In the next stanza the garden is compared explicitly to Eden—not merely Eden before the Fall, but Eden before Eve. Three times, in successive couplets, the speaker states that Paradise enjoyed alone is preferable to Paradise shared. Such praise of solitude can hardly be exceeded, even in the considerable Christian literature on the subject, and perhaps Marvell, relying on his readers' knowledge that Adam had after all requested Eve's company, expected his readers to identify this stanza as a momentary effusion, not shared by the poet himself, on the part of the poem's persona. The reader is reminded, at least, that mortals in the fallen world can only approximate paradisical ecstasy, not achieve it, until they leave this world for a better one. The speaker, now quite recalled from his ecstasy, observes "this dial new." The term may indicate a literal floral sundial, in which small plots of different plants marked the hours around a circle; it clearly and more importantly indicates the entire renewed postlapsarian world, under the mercy of God the "skillful gardener," who provides the "milder sun" (the Son, Christ, God's mercy). The bee, who is industrious rather than contemplative, "computes its time [thyme] as well as we!" This is a typically Marvellian paradox. The bee's industry is reminiscent of the negatively viewed "incessant labors" of the men in the first stanza; the bee, however, is performing wholesome activity in the garden, reckoned with flowers. The situation is analogous to that of the speaker in stanza five who fell, but did not Fall, remaining in the garden.

The poem's persona at first rejected the world of action for the garden's solitude and the contemplative exercise thereby made possible. Contemplation has led to physical, then to mental, then to spiritual ecstasy, but the ecstatic moment is limited because the speaker, dwelling in a world that remains thoroughly fallen, is not yet "prepared for longer flight." Refreshed by his experience and noting that the "dial" is *new*, the speaker can accept the action of the bee and recognize action, as well as contemplation, as an appropriate part of human existence.

"UPON APPLETON HOUSE"

Another poem dealing with the question of withdrawal versus action is "Upon Appleton House," which clearly raises the issue of involvement in the English Civil War and subsequent disturbances. The poem falls into two halves, each depicting both action and retirement, and builds toward a resolution in the form of Lord Fairfax's daughter Mary, who was under Marvell's tutelage. A genre of the time was the "country house" poem, in which a country estate was described, and its inhabitants and their way of life thereby praised. "Upon Appleton House" begins in this manner, with the first nine stanzas devoted to the house itself. Employing a variety of conceits, Marvell finds the modest size and decoration of the structure preferable to the overblown grandeur of other houses. It is on a human scale, with "short but admirable Lines" that "In ev'ry Figure equal Man." Nevertheless, it is less modest than its owner, Lord Fairfax. When he arrives, the house sweats, and from its square hall sprouts a "Spherical" cupola, outdoing the proverbially impossible task of squaring the circle.

A source of building material for the house was the ancient nunnery whose ruins were still evident, wherein had dwelt the nuns whose order had in former times owned the estate. By recounting a historical episode connected with the nunnery, Marvell shows how it is also a source of the estate's present occupants. An ancestral Fairfax had wooed the "blooming Virgin" Isabel Thwaites, "Fair beyond measure" and an heiress. She was induced to enter the nunnery at Appleton, from which she could ultimately be extracted only by a Fairfacian raid. This tale, told in stanzas eleven to thirty-five, falls into two distinct parts. The first (stanzas eleven to twenty-eight) is essentially a nun's eloquent invitation to Isabel to withdraw to the secluded life of the cloister. The joys of this "holy leisure," behind walls that "restrain the World without," are attractively and enthusiastically described, though Marvell would not wish to portray otherwise so Catholic an institution. The passage wherein Isabel is compared to the Virgin Mary, and the later picture of the nuns "in bed,/ As pearls together billeted,/ All night embracing arm in arm," may be meant to raise doubts in the reader's mind that would be confirmed when he is told that "The nuns smooth tongue has suckt her in." After debating what to do, the betrothed Fairfax decides to remove her from the nunnery by force. In a rather burlesque episode, the nuns, whose "loud'st cannon were their lungs," are dispossessed of their prize and, in the next stanza, which flashes forward to the Dissolution, of their nunnery.

Action in this case has been far superior to withdrawal. It leads ultimately, however, to another withdrawal, that of Sir Thomas Fairfax, son of the celebrated couple. After a heroic military career he retired to Appleton House, but the flower beds there, which he shaped like the bastions of a fort, show that he was incapable of retiring fully. Stanzas thirty-six to forty describe the flower-fort, wherein flower-cannons discharge salutes of scent and the bee stands sentinel. There follows (stanzas forty-one to forty-five) a lamentation by the poet over the present unhappy state of England, "The garden of the world ere while," and praise of Fairfax, "Who, had it pleasèd him and God," could have prevented it. In this first half of the poem, then, Marvell has first described the house as an illustration of the greatness of its owner, then shown the virtue of action over withdrawal, then indicated that a man of great action can never fully retire. Finally, he has shown regretful acceptance of Fairfax's retirement, with the clear statement that England suffers without ameliorative action on someone's part. In the second half of the poem the same ideas will be reiterated and enhanced, except in the last part the focus will be not on Fairfax but on his daughter Mary ("Maria"), whose embodiment of the values of retirement and action will effect a resolution.

From the flower fort, the speaker can look down over the meadow (stanzas forty-six to sixty) onto the public world of action. It is a world capable of topsy-turvy, this "Abyss" of a meadow, from which it is a wonder that men rise alive. Men (seen from the hill) look like grasshoppers, but grasshoppers (perched on the tall grass) "are Gyants there." Cows look like beauty spots or fleas, and when the land is flooded, "Boats can over bridges sail" and "Fishes do the stables scale." It is a dangerous world, where the Mowers "massacre the grass," which is very tall, and the rail (humbly close to the ground) is accidentally killed: "Lowness is unsafe as hight,/ And chance o'retakes what scapeth spight." The earlier lamentation over England's condition in stanzas forty-one to forty-three invites the reader, if invitation were needed, to read this section as an allegory of England, although it may be carrying the allegory too far to see the hapless rail as

Charles I, as has been suggested. The mowers who cause the carnage, leaving the field like a battlefield "quilted ore" with piles of hay that look like bodies, are not evil. As they dance in triumph, their smell is fragrant and their kisses are as sweet as the hay. Marvell compares the meadow at the outset with stage scenery, constantly changing. Describing a series of scenes as the hay is harvested and piled and the cattle set loose in the field to crop the last few inches of grass, he ends with a flood. The flood is caused by the opening of sluices up-river, but the reader is meant to think of the biblical Flood.

Taking refuge from the drowned world, the speaker "imbarks" (embarks/encloses in bark) himself in the "green, yet growing ark" of an adjacent wood. The trees are as tightly woven together as are the families of Fairfax and Vere (Fairfax's wife's family). From without, the wood seems absolutely solid, but inside it is "passable" and "loose." The nightingale, a bird of solitude, sings here, and "highest oakes stoop down to hear,/ And listning elders prick the ear." The nightingale may represent Mary Fairfax, twelve years old when Marvell became her tutor, in which case the "Elders" would be her parents. At any rate, while the song of solitude is attractive, the "Sadder" sound of the stockdoves, whose necks bear "Nuptial Rings," is more pleasing. This indication, even within the wood, that private withdrawal may not be desirable, prepares for the later part of the poem, when Mary herself appears. In a lengthy section very reminiscent of "The Garden," the speaker revels in the delights and the security of the wood, a place "where the world no certain shot/ Can make, or me it toucheth not." He wishes never to leave the wood, and requests, in a passage that reminds many readers of Christ's crucifixion, that the vines and brambles fetter him and the "courteous Briars nail [him] through."

Noticing that the flood has subsided, he finds the meadow equally attractive. It is "newly washt," with "no serpent new." The "wanton harmless folds" of the river attract the speaker, who abandons himself to the pleasures of angling, achieving in stanza eighty-one such harmony with the landscape that it is difficult to distinguish between him and it. The sedge surrounds his temples, his side is a riverbank, and his "sliding foot" may remind the reader of the "Fountains sliding foot" in "The Garden." The sudden arrival of Maria, however, extracts him from this reverie by means of an odd inversion wherein she, the pupil, reminds the presumably adult speaker of his responsibility. Calling himself a "trifling Youth," he hastily hides his fishing gear.

Essentially the rest of the poem is devoted to praise of Maria, a creature neither of withdrawal nor of action, but a fusion of both. Among the imagery giving her awesome power are echoes of the Last Judgment: She has "judicious" eyes, she "already is the Law," and by her the world is "wholly vitrifi'd." Nature collects itself in silence, and the sun blushingly conceals himself. As the halcyon, flying "betwixt the day and night," paralyzes nature and turns it blue, so Maria gives her surroundings the stillness of glass and imbues them with her (their) qualities: "Tis She that to these Gardens gave/ That wondrous beauty which they have," and so also with the woods, meadow, and river. Intelligent (learning languages in order to gain wisdom, which is "Heavens Dialect"), without vanity, and raised in the "Domestick Heaven" of Appleton House, she is not the new branch that a male heir would be on the "Farfacian oak." Instead, she is a sprig of mistletoe that will one day be severed "for some universal good." Presumably this will be her marriage, which will be of considerable political importance. The product of the seclusion of Appleton House, she is thus the ideal person to take action to affect the world at large; in her the apparent opposites of withdrawal and action are harmoniously fused.

The final stanza of the poem features a pattern of conceits reminiscent of the first stanza, and compares the fishermen carrying their boats to tortoises, echoing the tortoise in stanza two. The fishermen are "rational amphibii," amphibians who can think; but they are also thinkers who can operate in two mediums: Human beings need both contemplation and action. This concord of opposites, which is more powerful than compromise and is presented with reason and wit, represents those characteristics central to Marvell's work.

OTHER MAJOR WORKS

NONFICTION: *The Rehearsal Transpros'd*, 1672; *The Rehearsal Transpros'd: The Second Part*, 1673 (for modern editions of the two preceding entries, see *The Rehearsal Transpros'd and The Rehearsal Transpros'd: The Second Part*, 1971; D. I. B. Smith, editor);

Mr. Smirke: Or, The Divine in Mode, 1676; *An Account of the Growth of Popery and Arbitrary Government in England*, 1677; *Remarks upon a Late Disingenuous Discourse*, 1678.

MISCELLANEOUS: *The Poems and Letters of Andrew Marvell*, 1927, 1952, 1971 (H. Margoliouth, editor).

BIBLIOGRAPHY

Chernaik, Warren L. *The Poet's Time: Politics and Religion in the Work of Andrew Marvell*. Cambridge, England: Cambridge University Press, 1983. For Chernaik, Marvell is a poet-prophet whose political ideas are consistent, militant, and rooted in his religion. His readings of "Upon Appleton House" and "An Horatian Ode upon Cromwell's Return from Ireland" are extensive and perceptive. He also discusses Marvell's later (post-1666) satiric poetry and his political polemics.

Hunt, John Dixon. *Andrew Marvell: His Life and Writings*. Ithaca, N.Y.: Cornell University Press, 1978. Hunt's intent is to provide a context against which some of Marvell's major poems ("Upon Appleton House," "An Horatian Ode Upon Cromwell's Return from Ireland," and "Last Instructions to a Painter") can be read. Since Hunt's focus is artistic, the book is profusely illustrated. Includes a one-page chronology of Marvell's life and sixty-six engravings and emblems.

Klause, John. *The Unfortunate Fall: Theodicy and the Moral Imagination of Andrew Marvell*. Hamden, Conn.: Archon Books, 1983. Klause finds "lingering preoccupations" rather than consistent viewpoints in Marvell's writing. In his extensive analyses of the Cromwell poems, "The Garden," and "Upon Appleton House," Klause finds Marvell "adapting" to political realities. Complemented by an extensive bibliography of primary and secondary sources.

Murray, Nicholas. *World Enough and Time: The Life of Andrew Marvell*. New York: St. Martin's Press, 2000. Even with the information uncovered in the three decades since the last biography of Marvell was written, little is known about long stretches of Marvell's career. Murray's narrative takes full advantage of what is available and provides a clear portrait of Marvell and his life in the Cromwell era and the Restoration.

Ray, Robert H. *An Andrew Marvell Companion.* New York: Garland, 1998. A comprehensive reference guide to the life and works of the poet and political satirist. Useful to any reader of Marvell, especially any who require information that is usually not easily accessible to the nonspecialist. Includes a chronology of the poet's life and works, a bibliography, and suggestions for further research.

Rees, Christine. *The Judgment of Marvell.* London: Pinter, 1989. Rees argues that Marvell's poetry concerns choice or the impossibility of choosing, and his choices involve the life of pleasure, as well as those of action and contemplation. Using this threefold division, she offers extensive commentary on approximately twenty-five well-known poems.

Stocker, Margarita. *Apocalyptic Marvell: The Second Coming in Seventeenth Century Poetry.* Athens: Ohio University Press, 1986. Stocker's book offers a corrective view of Marvell, a poet committed to an apocalyptic ideology that informs all of his poems. Contains lengthy analyses of Marvell's major poems such as "An Horation Ode Upon Cromwell's Return from Ireland," "Upon Appleton House," and "To His Coy Mistress," as well as the often overlooked "The Unfortunate Lover." Supplemented by an extensive bibliography.

C. Herbert Gilliland;
bibliography updated by the editors

JOHN MASEFIELD

Born: Ledbury, Herefordshire, England; June 1, 1878
Died: Near Abingdon, Berkshire, England; May 12, 1967

PRINCIPAL POETRY

Salt-Water Ballads, 1902
Ballads, 1903
The Everlasting Mercy, 1911
The Widow in the Bye Street, 1912

The Story of a Round-House and Other Poems, 1912
Dauber: A Poem, 1913
The Daffodil Fields, 1913
Philip the King and Other Poems, 1914
Good Friday and Other Poems, 1916
Sonnets and Poems, 1916
Lollington Downs and Other Poems, 1917
The Cold Cotswolds, 1917
Rosas, 1918
A Poem and Two Plays, 1919
Reynard the Fox: Or, The Ghost Heath Run, 1919
Enslaved and Other Poems, 1920
Right Royal, 1920
King Cole, 1921
The Dream, 1922
Sonnets of Good Cheer to the Lena Ashwell Players, 1926
Midsummer Night and Other Tales in Verse, 1928
South and East, 1929
The Wanderer of Liverpool, 1930 (poems and essay)
Minnie Maylow's Story and Other Tales and Scenes, 1931
A Tale of Troy, 1932
A Letter from Pontus and Other Verse, 1936
Ode to Harvard, 1937
Some Verses to Some Germans, 1939
Guatama the Enlightened and Other Verse, 1941
Natalie Masie and Pavilastukay: Two Tales in Verse, 1942
Wonderings (Between One and Six Years), 1943
I Want! I Want!, 1944
On the Hill, 1949
Poems, 1953
The Bluebells and Other Verse, 1961
Old Raiger and Other Verse, 1961
In Glad Thanksgiving, 1967

OTHER LITERARY FORMS

John Masefield wrote books of poems and verse plays, prose plays, novels, and other prose works, including histories.

ACHIEVEMENTS

John Masefield's poetry appealed to a very wide audience. His first book of verse, *Salt-Water Ballads,* sold out in six months, and his narrative poems were very popular. *The Everlasting Mercy* was a sensation in his day. Some of his lyric poems, including "Sea Fever," have become standards of English poetry. He received many honorary degrees, including those from Oxford and Cambridge. In 1930, he was elected to membership in the American Academy of Arts and Letters, and he was president of the Society of Authors in 1937. In 1961, he was made a Companion of Literature by the Royal Society of Literature, and also in that year he won the William Foyle Poetry Prize. In 1964, the National Book League gave him a prize for writers older than sixty-five.

BIOGRAPHY

John Masefield was born June 1, 1878, in Ledbury, Herefordshire. His very early years were happy ones, although the children in the family spent their time with their nurse and saw little of their parents; they saw their mother only between teatime and bedtime at six o'clock. She died a few weeks after giving birth to a sixth child when John was six-and-a-half years old. Their grandparents died a year after their mother, and the family, in reduced circumstances, moved into the grandparents' home. John occasionally visited his godmother, wrote his first poems when he was about ten, and went to boarding school. His father died at age forty-nine after suffering from mental disorders. Taking over as guardians, his aunt and uncle suggested that John be trained to go to sea in the merchant marine. Although he wanted to write or paint, he decided to pursue seafaring because the son of a governess whom he had liked enjoyed being a cadet on the school ship H.M.S. *Conway.*

Masefield joined that ship when he was thirteen and left it when he was sixteen, having learned a good deal of mathematics and navigation. He became an apprentice on a four-masted cargo barque sailing for Chile, which did not touch land for three months. During the voyage, he had some trouble with seasickness and experienced the fury of Cape Horn storms. He was released from service after he became seriously ill with sunstroke and a possible nervous breakdown. After a hospital stay in Valparaiso, he went home. His aunt nagged him into going to sea again; but he deserted

ship in New York, causing his uncle to cut him off financially.

The seventeen-year-old Masefield could not find work in that depression year; thus, he and an acquaintance became vagrants, getting occasional work on farms and sleeping out, an experience that gave him great empathy for the down-and-out. After some months, he returned to New York City, living in Greenwich Village, almost starving but writing poetry. He finally obtained work with long hours at a bar and then moved to Yonkers to work in a carpet factory, reading the English poets in his spare time. At nineteen, he was suffering from tuberculosis and malaria. He returned to England (earning his way back on a ship) hoping to be a writer there. Poor and sick, he obtained a clerk's position in a London bank, which he held for three years. He regained his health, became reconciled with his aunt and uncle, and was especially close to his sisters. He managed to meet William Butler Yeats and to become part of the Yeats circle. In 1901, he became exhibition secretary for an art show in Wolverhampton. His poems were being pub-

John Masefield (AP/Wide World Photos)

lished regularly in magazines, and his first book of verse, *Salt-Water Ballads*, was very popular.

When he met Constance de la Cherois Crommelin, she was thirty-five and he was twenty-three, but despite the difference in their ages, they were married in 1903, after Masefield had obtained an editorial position. They took a house in Greenwich; then John left Constance and his baby daughter Judith for a nighttime editorial position in Manchester. He wrote articles and reviews and worked seven days a week for the publisher; yet, he still managed to write plays, one of which, written in 1907, was produced. (Curiously, also, one of his stories was pirated for the stage.)

About the time that his son Lewis was born, Masefield became infatuated briefly with Elizabeth Robins, an American actress and author who became a veritable goddess to him. He called her "mother" and wrote to her, sometimes many times a day. After she withdrew from his life, he had a burst of creativity that produced *The Everlasting Mercy*, a long narrative poem that caused a great stir.

After settling into a country house in Lollington, he became a Red Cross worker in a French hospital during World War I. In 1915, he visited Gallipoli for the Red Cross, and, in 1916, he traveled to the United States on a lecture tour, but also with the intention of enlisting Americans' sympathy with Britain in the war: He had been in touch with British intelligence. He also organized theatricals and verse reciting contests in his area.

When Masefield's wife Constance was recovering from an operation for a brain tumor, the family moved to the Cotswolds; later they lived in a village near Dorchester, called Clifton Hampden, in the upper valley of the Thames. Masefield died in 1967, after refusing to have his leg amputated when he developed gangrene from an infected toenail. He was cremated, as he had wished, and his ashes were deposited in the Poets' Corner in Westminster Abbey.

ANALYSIS

John Masefield's difficulties in life—his early poverty, ill health, and arduous labors—caused him to develop a reflective attitude toward the world. While he is often thought of as a writer of rollicking sea and narrative poems, his poetry is usually concerned in some way with the tragedy of human life; it is seldom simply humorous. He seemed to value most highly his more formal philosophical poems, although his lighter pieces have been the most popular. Many of these poems seem simple because he chose to speak in the vernacular about common experiences. His own experiences, however, gave him great empathy with the down trodden, and he deliberately chose to treat such matters, as he points out in "Consecration." He will not speak of the great, he says, but of the lowly and scorned; and he ends the poem with a heartfelt "Amen."

Masefield's poems about the life of the common sailor are firmly rooted in the ballad tradition. He makes use of a dramatic speaker as he skillfully interweaves narrative and lyrical material. A number of such poems deal with death at sea; some treat the subject lightly, in a manner of a sea chantey, but the harsh realities underlie the touches of humor. In "The Turn of the Tide" and "Cape-Horn Gospel I," the soul or ghost wants to continue working on the ship after death. Masefield's most famous work, "Sea Fever," is about these two realities, the harshness and the appeal of life at sea. The title suggests a disease; the sea can be a kind of addiction. Masefield's refrain repeatedly emphasized that the speaker "must go down to the seas again," while alliteration effectively evokes the rhythms of wheel and wind and sail. The speaker responds to a call; he has no choice in the matter. The life is like that of the vagrant gypsy, or, not so explicitly, like the gull's and the whale's. The life of the sea fascinates, but it is also lonely, gray, and painful. The middle stanza of the three, however, contains none of these negative images, suggesting that the very heart of the matter is the delight in the movement of the ship. In the last stanza, the wind no longer pleasantly makes the white clouds fly; it is as sharp as a "whetted knife." From this life the speaker, in the last two lines, desires two things: "quiet sleep and a sweet dream when the long trick's over." The sea journey is suddenly the journey of life, with a final sleep at the end. According to the glossary that Masefield supplied for the *Salt-Water Ballads*, a trick is "the ordinary two-hour spell at the wheel or on the lookout," but the "long trick" suddenly suggests the trip itself and life itself, for Masefield has transformed the realistic situation into a symbolic one with a single word.

"CARGOES"

"Cargoes" is a different type of sea poem, without a speaker or story line. Three ships are described briefly, each in one short stanza. Masefield here is an imagist presenting only the pictures, with no explicit connections between them and no commentary on them. The inclusion of the last freighter, the British coaster, seems ironic, since it is less attractive than the ships of the past; it is actually dirty and sails in less attractive seas. Including it may also seem ironic because of its cargo: such humble items as coal and tin trays. It can scarcely be compared with the quinquereme from Nineveh with its glamorous apes and ivory, or with the Spanish galleon with its jewels and gold; yet it is the modern representative of a tradition that goes back to the ancients. A third irony is that it actually exists, whereas the others are gone, though, of course, it too will become a thing of the past. Here, Masefield makes skillful use of meter and stanza form, the unusual number of spondees imparting a feeling of strength, reinforced by the periodic use of two short lines rather than a single long one. Masefield made light of objections that a ship from Nineveh was not plausible because Nineveh was two hundred miles inland. As Constance Babington Smith notes in *John Masefield: A Life* (1978), he responded to a question of an Eton boy: "I can only suggest that a Ninevean syndicate must have chartered the ship; even so it was odd." The first line of the poem is musical in its repetition of sounds, including the *n*, short *i*, and *v*. It is not improbable that the poet chose Nineveh for its alliterative and evocative qualities.

As the modern freighter in "Cargoes" is less distinguished than its antecedents, the modern city in "London Town" is less pleasant than the country and the small town. Masefield is speaking in his own voice here, for in the last line he speaks of the land in which he was bred, and the countryside described is his homeland. The poet alternates stanzas in praise of London with stanzas in praise of the country, but all those in praise of London end with a defect or a deficiency, with a varied refrain in favor of leaving the place. In two of these stanzas, the deficiency is given in only a half line of contrast, as in the statement that the world is busy there, while the mind grows "crafty." The alternate stan-

zas praise the countryside without reservation and are prefaced with a joyous song like "Then hey" or "So hey." The poem is joyous in the delight of the poet in returning to the world of nature, but the criticism of the city is sobering. In the last stanza about London, it hardly matters that the tunes, books, and plays are excellent if "wretchedly fare the most there and merrily fare the few." The city is a tragic place, for beneath its artifice there is misery and poverty. The irony is somewhat like that of Masefield's long narrative poem *Reynard the Fox: Or, The Ghost Heath Run*, in which the hunters seek an exciting diversion, while the fox is only trying desperately to survive.

THE EVERLASTING MERCY

Masefield's homeland, described in the country scenes in "London Town" and other poems, includes the Malvern Hills mentioned at the beginning of the fourteenth century poem *The Vision of William, Concerning Piers the Plowman,* and the influence of that work is apparent in Masefield's long narrative poem *The Everlasting Mercy.* Masefield had resolved to write about the lowly, and some of the lowly are anything but perfect. Saul Kane bit through his father's hand and went to jail nineteen times, but he tells the reader in a monologue that is part soliloquy and part public attestation that he regrets breaking his mother's heart. He says, "Now, friends, observe and look upon me" to see evidence of the Lord's pity; it is an address to the reader that is reminiscent of the medieval religious lyrics in which Christ tells the reader to look at how his side bleeds or in which the Blessed Virgin invites the reader to weep with her. The effect is that the figure, whether it be Christ or Saul Kane, becomes a static moral picture. It is short-lived here, however, as Saul plunges into his story of a poaching-rights argument, boxing, and celebration.

The otherworldly passages in the poem are instrumental in Saul's religious conversion to a different way of life, the first of them being Saul's remembrance on his way to the celebration of how the bell ringer had seen spirits dancing around the church at Christmas. The whole eerie scene becomes vivid to him, and he prays when he thinks of Judgment Day. After the party, he leans out the window and is tempted by the devil to throw himself down, even as Christ was tempted. He decides not to kill himself and feels exalted; he wants to excoriate the righteous, who would secretly like to be whores and sots and who "make hell for all the odd/ All the lonely ones of God." After this realization, he runs through the town and rings the fire bell. After he speaks out to the squire's parson for his actions toward the poor, he is upbraided by the mother of a lost child whom he had befriended; when she summons the mystical imagery of the Book of Revelation, he shrinks away. After he insults a Quaker woman who visits the bar and she leaves, exhorting him, he suddenly feels, in a mystical passage about tide, sun, moon, and bells ringing for someone coming home, that he has been converted. Feeling that he was born to "brother" everyone, he sees everything symbolically, from mole to plowman, and says that Christ will plow at the "bitter roots" of his heart.

First Christ and then Saul become plowmen, a transformation reminiscent of *Piers Plowman*. At the end of the work, where the meter changes from iambic tetrameter to a more lyrical trimeter, he seems to have awakened to the beauty of nature. The poem is enhanced by its many ironies, such as that Saul should experience the world of the spirit while he is drunk, and that Saul, of all people, could become a patient plowman and a Christlike figure. Some of the names in the story are symbolic: certainly Saul and Miss Bourne, the Quaker, and possibly Saul's last name, Kane (Cain). Although Saul is not exactly Everyman, his life in its aimlessness, belligerence, and unhappiness embodies a tragic pattern of human existence that is not uncommon. Masefield was not religious in the traditional sense, but he seems to have believed in reincarnation and to have been fascinated by religion, a number of his works being on religious themes. This poem was a sensation in its time; it was considered shocking for its direct language and crudity. J. M. Barrie, however, described it in the *Daily Chronicle* of November 29, 1912, as "incomparably the best literature of the year."

"CLM"

Because his story poems, sea poems, and songs are so vivid, Masefield's more subdued philosophical poems have been generally neglected. "CLM," a tragic work about women and motherhood, was written during his wife's second pregnancy, when he was romantically involved with Elizabeth Robins, whom he called "mother." The letters of the poem's title stand for the name of Masefield's actual mother. Speaking of his prenatal life, the poet sees the fetus as common earth and as a leech. Pregnancy is "months of birth," and birth itself is hell. His present life involves the death of "some of her," some cells he received from her; thus, the subject of death is first raised in connection with his own life. Not until the second stanza does the reader become aware that the speaker's mother is dead. Both the womb and the grave are dark.

There is a cluster of images associated with his desire to see her again, together with the uncertain nature of such an encounter: gates of the grave, knocking, "dusty" doors, her "dusty" beauty, and passersby in the street. He feels that he has not repaid his debt of life to her and to other women, and he uses the images of men triumphing over women, trampling on their rights and lusting after them, to convey men's selfishness and their subjugation of women. At the end of the poem, in an ironic and tragic reversal of his desire to see his mother again, he tells the grave to stay shut so that he will not be shamed. The shut grave image stands in strong contrast to the image of its opening earlier in the poem.

DAUBER

Much of Masefield's more philosophical poetry was concerned with beauty. Some of his ideas on this theme were embodied in the narrative poem *Dauber,* in which a young artist becomes a sailor because he wants to paint ships and sea life as they have never been painted before. His insensitive shipmates, however, destroy his paintings. When he dies in a fall from the yardarm during a storm, his last words are, "It will go on." Ironically, he is mourned not as an artist but as a fine sailor-to-be.

BEAUTY AND DEATH

The worship of beauty and the linking of beauty and tragedy in human life were recurrent themes in Masefield's sonnets. Beauty exists in nature and within the individual, despite the reality of death, and beauty exists in a life to come. Beauty and death are related, for, as he says in one sonnet, the life that was is "Pasture to living beauty." The beautiful may die, but Beauty will go on. The personified Beauty of many of his sonnets seems to be an amalgam of the goddess Nature, the world soul of Platonic philosophy, God, the Beatrice of

Dante, and the women in the poet's life. "On Growing Old" asks Beauty to be with him as he sits amidst the imagery of age and death: an old dog, his own coldness by the fire, the yellow leaves of a book, the embers. The word "her" indicates that Beauty possesses the seas and cornland where he is no longer able to go. Comparing himself to a beggar in the Strand, he asks Beauty for gifts—ironically, not youth, but wisdom and passion, which he compares to bread and to rain in a dry summer. They are necessities in the closing darkness of old age and death, for with them "Even the night will blossom as the rose."

Masefield, then, was a more philosophical poet than is generally realized. Beauty was a kind of goddess in his work, and a kind of quest as well; he was fascinated by the interrelationship of beauty with tragedy and death. It was also no accident that he chose to retell in his verse the tragic tales of Troy, of Arthur, and of Tristan and Isolt, for he dealt in many of his poems with the tragedies and ironies of human life.

OTHER MAJOR WORKS

LONG FICTION: *Captain Margaret*, 1908; *Multitude and Solitude*, 1909; *Last Endeavour*, 1910; *The Taking of Helen*, 1923; *Sard Harker*, 1924; *Odtaa*, 1926; *The Hawbucks*, 1929; *The Bird of Dawning*, 1933; *Basilissa*, 1940.

SHORT FICTION: *A Mainsail Haul*, 1905; *A Tarpaulin Muster*, 1907.

PLAYS: *The Campden Wonder*, pr. 1907 (one act); *The Tragedy of Nan*, pr. 1908; *Mrs. Harrison*, pb. 1909; *The Tragedy of Nan and Other Plays*, pb. 1909; *The Tragedy of Pompey the Great*, pr., pb. 1910; *The Witch*, pr. 1911 (adaptation of a Norwegian play); *Philip the King*, pr. 1914 (one act); *The Faithful*, pr., pb. 1915; *The Sweeps of Ninety-eight*, pr. pb. 1916; *Good Friday: A Dramatic Poem*, pb. 1916; *The Locked Chest*, pb. 1916 (one act); *Esther*, pr. 1921 (adaptation of Jean Racine's play); *Melloney Holtspur: Or, The Pangs of Love*, pb. 1922; *A King's Daughter: A Tragedy in Verse*, pr. 1923; *Tristan and Isolt: A Play in Verse*, pr. 1923; *The Trial of Jesus*, pb. 1925; *The Coming of Christ*, pr., pb. 1928; *Easter: A Play for Singers*, pr. 1929; *End and Beginning*, pb. 1933; *The Play of St. George*, pb. 1948.

NONFICTION: *Sea Life in Nelson's Time*, 1905; *On the Spanish Main*, 1906; *Shakespeare*, 1911; *Gallipoli*, 1916; *Chaucer*, 1931; *The Nine Days' Wonder*, 1941; *So Long to Learn*, 1952; *Grace Before Ploughing*, 1966.

CHILDREN'S LITERATURE: *Martin Hyde*, 1910; *Jim Davis*, 1911; *The Midnight Folk*, 1927; *The Box of Delights*, 1935.

MISCELLANEOUS: *A Book of Both Sorts: Selections from the Verse and Prose*, 1947.

BIBLIOGRAPHY

Binding, Paul. *An Endless Quiet Valley: A Reappraisal of John Masefield*. Herefordshire, England: Logaston Press, 1998. A critical study of Masefield's works. Includes an index.

Drew, Fraser. *John Masefield's England*. Cranbury, N.J.: Associated University Presses, 1973. This volume is a thematic study of Masefield's portrayal of English life and customs. Drew maintains that this is the key to Masefield's work. His celebration of England was the continuation, not the reversal, of his early stress on the common man. His interest in English life included seamanship and fox-hunting. Useful comparisons with Rudyard Kipling, Joseph Conrad, and others are included.

Dwyer, June. *John Masefield*. New York: Frederick Ungar, 1987. A very simply written, short but comprehensive introductory study. Discussions of the novels and plays, as well as the poems are included. Dwyer maintains that Masefield in part abandoned his rough, common style for a more refined voice as he gained popularity. She attempts a psychological analysis of the verses, endeavoring to show Masefield's loneliness beneath his public persona of national triumph.

Hamilton, W. H. *John Masefield: A Critical Study*. New York: Macmillan, 1922. An influential study, this work celebrates Masefield for his narrative poems, especially *Reynard the Fox*. Hamilton contends that the novels are much less successful. In almost all of his work, Masefield stresses the value of England. He was deeply patriotic, although he abhorred war. The author criticizes Masefield's overemphasis on productivity: This often led him to write inferior work. An amusing chapter collects parodies of Masefield's work.

Knight, G. Wilson. "Masefield and Spiritualism." In *Mansions of the Spirit: Essays in Literature and Religion*, edited by G. A. Panichas. New York: Hawthorne Books, 1967. Knight, one of the greatest twentieth century Shakespearean critics, applies his thematic style of criticism to Masefield. The sea should not be taken only literally in the poems and plays but also as a symbol of the spiritual. Knight maintains that Masefield's poems often express the conviction that man can become acquainted with spiritual powers of various sorts. Knight stresses the recurring use of words and phrases which illustrate this stance. He rates Masefield as one of the great poets of the twentieth century.

Lamont, Corliss. *Remembering John Masefield*. Cranbury, N.J.: Associated University Presses, 1971. Lamont, an American philosopher, was a friend of Masefield for more than forty years. He includes valuable selections from Masefield's letters, expressing Masefield's distaste for modern poetry. The true and noble, in Masefield's view, is the proper object of poetry. World Wars I and II have diverted poets from the proper path. Lamont maintains that Masefield's poems express a coherent philosophy, a suggestion Masefield rejects. The work includes a tribute to Masefield by Robert Graves and a memoir by the poet's daughter.

Spark, Muriel. *John Masefield*. Rev. ed. London: Hutchinson, 1992. A biography and critical study of selected works. Includes bibliographic references.

Sternlicht, Sanford. *John Masefield*. Boston: Twayne, 1977. This excellent survey stresses the long narrative poems. The author contends that *The Everlasting Mercy* is Masefield's greatest achievement. Through his rough, vital style, Masefield paved the way for other twentieth century poets to write in a realistic way about the seamier side of life. Masefield himself strongly defended traditional morality. Sternlicht attributes the decline in Masefield's critical reputation to his "old-fashioned" views and his aversion to experiment in verse.

Rosemary Ascherl;
bibliography updated by the editors

EDGAR LEE MASTERS

Born: Garnett, Kansas; August 23, 1868
Died: Melrose Park, Pennsylvania; March 5, 1950

PRINCIPAL POETRY
  A Book of Verses, 1898
  The Blood of the Prophets, 1905
  Songs and Sonnets, 1910
  Songs and Sonnets, Second Series, 1912
  Spoon River Anthology, 1915
  Songs and Satires, 1916
  The Great Valley, 1916
  Toward the Gulf, 1918
  Starved Rock, 1919
  Domesday Book, 1920
  The Open Sea, 1921
  The New Spoon River, 1924
  Selected Poems, 1925
  The Fate of the Jury: An Epilogue to Domesday Book, 1929
  Lichee Nuts, 1930
  The Serpent in the Wilderness, 1933
  Invisible Landscapes, 1935
  The Golden Fleece of California, 1936
  Poems of People, 1936
  The New World, 1937
  More People, 1939
  Illinois Poem, 1941
  Along the Illinois, 1942
  The Harmony of Deeper Music: Posthumous Poems, 1976

OTHER LITERARY FORMS
    Edgar Lee Masters's prolific output included seven early unproduced plays (all published before *Spoon River Anthology*), four verse dramas, two later volumes of plays, and many volumes of prose.

ACHIEVEMENTS
    Edgar Lee Masters's long and varied career was distinguished by prolific productivity and a versatile display of poetic talent; he tried almost every poetic form, from classical imitation to verse drama to epic, and he

Edgar Lee Masters (© Bettmann/Corbis)

handled them all with seeming ease and technical finesse. The sheer bulk of his writing—well over fifty books in his long lifetime—necessarily resulted in repetitiveness, unevenness, and frequent superficiality; and at his worst his poetry is mere magazine verse. Yet, his undeniable talent had early support from such noted critics and writers as Amy Lowell, John Cowper Powys, Ezra Pound, William Marion Reedy, Harriet Monroe, Harry Hansen, Louis Untermeyer, and Percy H. Boynton; and, at his best, his work surmounts changing fashions in poetic taste and even his own occasional lapses in style, technique, and taste.

Masters was long considered a one-book author. That book, *Spoon River Anthology*, was immensely popular in his lifetime—it went through some seven editions before he died. Given the immense praise, almost amounting to adulation, accorded the book upon its publication, it was small wonder that his reputation thereafter began its long, slow decline; none of his subsequent books had either the popular or the critical appeal that it

did. However, Masters won a Frost Medal (1942), a Shelley Memorial Award (1943), and an Academy of American Poets Fellowship (1946).

Much of Masters's importance as a poet, no doubt, derives from his ability to appeal to both the ordinary reader and the scholar, the same trait found in such contemporaries of Masters as Robert Frost, Edwin Arlington Robinson, and Robinson Jeffers and in later poets such as James Wright. This diverse readership has led to Masters's being accorded a certain place in studies of American poetry and the Chicago Renaissance, but rarely have these studies amounted to anything like genuine analysis. Even though he failed to maintain his popular acclaim after *Spoon River Anthology*, selections from that book continue to be included in virtually every anthology of American literature and to be taught to succeeding generations of students.

BIOGRAPHY

Although he was born in Kansas, Edgar Lee Masters is the quintessential Illinois poet, having moved there as an infant and remained there, first in small Sangamon valley towns and later in Chicago, until he was fifty-five years old. Masters's mother was interested in literature, music, and the church, and his father was a successful attorney and politician, twin emphases that also served to dominate Masters throughout his life. Largely self-taught, he spent one year at Knox College, where he studied German, Greek, and law. In 1892, the year after he was admitted to the Illinois bar, he moved to Chicago, working first as a bill collector for the electric company, while attempting to get established in law, and writing verse pseudonymously for several Chicago newspapers. He spent the following twenty-five years as a successful attorney in Chicago, eight of those years in partnership with Clarence Darrow. The first of his many books appeared pseudonymously in 1898; by 1915, when *Spoon River Anthology* was published, he had published several other collections of poetry and unproduced plays and had come to the attention of the British critic John Cowper Powys, who cited Masters as one of three significant new American poets.

For several years, Masters had been contributing verse to the St. Louis *Mirror*, a weekly edited and published by William Marion Reedy. In 1913, Reedy had introduced Masters to J. W. MacKail's translations published as *Select Epigrams from the Greek Anthology* (1928), and Masters's subsequent first-person free-verse epitaphs of ordinary small-town characters became the work known as *Spoon River Anthology*. The success of the book led Masters to relinquish his law practice in 1923 and move to New York City, where he spent most of the rest of his life. His life in New York was marked on the one hand by ready access to the publishing world and, on the other, by numerous affairs; married twice, Masters also had many love affairs, at least fifteen of which are indexed in his autobiography. From 1931 to 1944, he lived in the Hotel Chelsea in New York, a traditional residence for writers, and then in various convalescent homes until shortly before his death in such a home in a Philadelphia suburb.

ANALYSIS

Edgar Lee Masters had written hundreds of undistinguished or mediocre poems before *Spoon River Anthology*; most of these were typical of the time, derivative and rigidly imitative of European models and metrical forms; not surprisingly, these early poems, even when published in book form (as his first four collections were), were generally ignored. Masters's discovery of *Select Epigrams from the Greek Anthology* and its great influence on his own subsequent work in *Spoon River Anthology* even led him to an ironic touch of self-criticism, as when his character Petit the Poet, speaking from the grave as do the other inhabitants of Spoon River's cemetery, expresses the remorse at his placing so much emphasis on "little iambics" while remaining oblivious to all the important events in the world around him. Masters's accomplishment in this collection was so profound in its originality and its willingness to venture into new patterns that he could scarcely help offering such a reflective comment on his earlier work.

SPOON RIVER ANTHOLOGY

What Masters accomplished in the book for which he is best known was little short of a revolution, although in retrospect a revolution of which he was merely one of the principals. Masters had befriended the young Carl Sandburg and helped him get his *Chicago Poems* published in 1916, and Masters, influenced by William Marion Reedy, gradually realized and expressed in vari-

ous early critical statements that American poetry had to try to offer a distinctively American perspective, not merely to lie buried under layers of technically precise but moribund verse. Both Sandburg and Masters, along with their fellow Midwesterner Vachel Lindsay, were part of this concerted move to free native verse from the constraints of more formal poetry, even though the preponderance of educated and critical opinion opposed and belittled their efforts.

Hence, Masters's accomplishment in *Spoon River Anthology*, based as it was on "realism"—simplicity of language and form, taking ordinary persons for subjects, a commonsensical attitude toward experience, and much of Walt Whitman's celebration of America—resulted in an original work that was immensely popular. Masters's happy ability to combine realistic, plain subject matter with a mystical celebration of both the natural world and the small Midwestern town was unique and, ironically, at the same time a poetic dead end. Masters once observed that World War I meant the end of the world he depicted in *Spoon River Anthology*, partly because the innocence and simplicity he described was no longer possible, and partly because even more revolutionary poetic influences, such as that of T. S. Eliot, were at work. While popular audiences continued to purchase *Spoon River Anthology* and Masters's later books, it was obvious that the world out of which that book came and virtually ceased to exist.

Spoon River Anthology is a collection of 244 dramatic monologues—mostly in free verse—by a host of people of all social and occupational levels speaking from their graves in the Spoon River cemetery. Masters faithfully describes their sense of frustration with the dreary, limited, and consistently unfulfilled lives they had lived. Though the book seemed, to some of its initial readers, unnecessarily defeatist and even obscene, especially as the "genteel tradition" attempted to fight what was already a lost cause for literary propriety, Masters was able to develop what he had attempted, an awakening of "the American vision [and] love of liberty." The sheer honesty of his portrayals thus necessarily shocked some sensitive souls. The speakers, unhindered by the propriety forced upon them in life, speak freely of their frustrations with small-town life, sentiments similar in quality to those subsequently expressed by Sherwood

Anderson in *Winesburg, Ohio* (1919) and by Sinclair Lewis in *Main Street* (1920). Critics evaluating *Spoon River Anthology*, ironically, spent far more time disputing whether the first-person portraits were "poetry" than in considering the extent to which the criticisms were valid. Master's indebtedness to Walt Whitman (and to Ralph Waldo Emerson) was recognized, especially in his rejection of rigid verse forms, but there seemed to be little understanding of Masters's intent or ironic perspective.

THE NEW SPOON RIVER

The 244 first-person portraits—and the 321 portraits in the less successful sequel, *The New Spoon River*—represent virtually all the professions and classes of people in a "typical" small American town, especially a Middle-Western small town. A mere catalog would indicate that these speakers were teachers, druggists, bankers, housewives, soldiers, laborers, dentists, carpenters, prostitutes, lawyers, and so on. While some of these assorted personages aspired to ambitions and careers clearly out of reach for their time, talent, and place, almost all of them felt frustrated; very few seem to possess the innate "greatness" that would enable them to sense a larger vision in their lives that would someday take them far from and above their humble origins. For the most part, their limited abilities, petty perspectives, and stilted ambitions suggest that neither in life nor in death could they have completely escaped the village.

HUMAN PORTRAITS

Yet Masters did not depict these people as consistently evil, idle, imbecilic, corrupt, or depraved; rather, his objectivity and honesty did not allow him to take sides in presenting their stories; he impersonally depicts both good and evil, even in the same person. Without some passing of judgment, the collection was certain to offend the established genteel view of the day that required moral certitude to be praised and evil to be punished. In no sense are Masters's "bad" characters dealt with more harshly than his "good" ones. Indeed, the sheer objectivity with which he views his characters enables them to offer their own comments on their lives, thus reflecting evil or virtue in their own words, not through authorial intrusion. Hence, as satire, the volume is excellent, although it is far from an incessantly pessimistic assemblage of worthless defectives. Even Amy

Lowell, one of Masters's first sympathetic readers, found the book depressing—a "long chronical of rapes, seductions, liaisons, and perversions"—thus suggesting that the sophisticated reader too could miss Masters's intention to "awaken the American vision" and "love of liberty."

FOOLS AND FAILURES

In reality, Masters's plan in *Spoon River Anthology* is deliberately and carefully structured; as Masters said, he put "the fools, the drunkards, and the failures . . . first, the people of one-birth minds [in] second place, and the heroes and enlightened spirits . . . last, a sort of *Divine Comedy*. . . ." Though many of the speakers do tell the truth about themselves without self-consciousness, some are completely hypocritical, and others are unaware of the implications of what they say about themselves. A. D. Blood, for example, is a town official noted for both his pomposity and his hypocrisy; Masters offers his own unspoken commentary on Blood's puritanic life by telling of a "worthless" young couple's lovemaking each night on Blood's tombstone. Editor Whedon, who in life "pervert[ed] truth" for "cunning ends," lies in death "where the sewage flows from the village,/ And the empty cans and garbage are dumped,/ And abortions are hidden."

Some of the unfortunates were victims of well-meaning but unrealistic patriotism, as in the cases of Harry Wilmans and Knolwt Hoheimer; the latter asks of the words on his tombstone, "Pro Patria," "What do they mean, anyway?" Margaret Fuller Slack is, as her first two names suggest, a frontier feminist who had to decide "Should it be celibacy, matrimony or unchastity?" and who, after rearing eight children, found too little time to write and to become as "great as George Eliot": She died from lockjaw after washing her baby's clothes and says, at the end of her speech, "Sex is the curse of life!"

FAVORABLE PORTRAITS

The favorable portraits, although fewer in number, are generally effective and touching. Anne Rutledge, Lincoln's first love, who died before they could marry, tells poignantly of how Lincoln was changed and marked by the loss. Lucinda Matlock, one of the most effective of the poems, tells how she was able to find fulfillment in the small town and in marriage; she asks,

> What is this I hear of sorrow and weariness,
> Anger, discontent and drooping hopes?
> Degenerate sons and daughters,
> Life is too strong for you—
> It takes life to love life.

The kind of life that destroyed weaker souls was one in which she exulted and gloried.

Tennessee Chaflin Shope, who had been "the laughing-stock of the village," especially ridiculed by the "people of good sense" such as a clergyman, reacted to the ridicule by asserting the "sovereignty of [his] soul"; before Mary Baker Eddy had even begun "what she called science," he had "mastered the 'Bhagavad Gita,'/ And cured [his] soul." Jonathan Swift Somers, Spoon River's poet laureate, says in his monologue that after a person has done all that he can to control his life and destiny, his soul might catch fire, enabling him to see the evil of the world clearly; at such a time, that person should be thankful that "Life does not fiddle," that is, meddle with or cheat him. What makes Somers's epitaph especially noteworthy is the fact that Masters appended a portion of Somer's unfinished epic, "The Spooniad," in which the poet ostensibly offers a dramatic portrayal of the conflict between the liberals and the old guard in Spoon River; in "The Spooniad," Masters perfectly imitates the rhythms and diction of a classical epic, but with the point of showing how the town's early history culminated in A. D. Blood's murder. Even though much of *Spoon River Anthology* can be said to reflect Masters's cynicism, his favorable portraits, even more than the unfavorable ones, illustrate the extent to which a few select speakers can see above the mundane pettiness in small-town life and sense the extent to which their lives have great intrinsic value.

NAÏVE IDEALISM

The excesses of naïve idealism, of course, can easily be seen in those monologues spoken by unsophisticated villagers; yet this is also the case with those who have some awareness of the larger world. Archibald Higbie, in the monologue bearing his name, admits that he "loathed" and "was ashamed" of Spoon River and that he had escaped its influence as he traveled through Europe, pursuing his gifts as an artist. Since Spoon River had "no culture," its residual influence could

only bring Higbie shame. Yet his work, ostensibly of Apollo, still contained the visage of Lincoln, and all he could do, "weighted down with western soil," was to pray for "another/ Birth," one "with all of Spoon River/ Rooted out of [his] soul." A similar inordinate emphasis on the "ideal" that existed far from the village, especially in the form of European art from a "simpler" day, can be found in "Caroline Branson": The speaker, after lamenting the loss of another's love, says, not unlike Emily Dickinson, that "only heaven" knows the secret of the "nuptial chamber under the soil"; she too asks for "another trial" and concludes by beseeching, "Save me, Shelley!"

These miniature autobiographies or "autoepitaphs," then, offer candid reflections by ordinary folk who tell frankly what kinds of persons they were and how they lived. Though the majority have lived "lives of quiet desperation," bitter, thwarted existences in a drab little village, Masters does suggest by his careful linking of narrative to narrative and general movement from despair to hope that such an existence does not necessarily lead to self-pity and posthumous despondency, but can—in the words of "Fiddler Jones"—lead to "a thousand memories,/ And not a single regret."

DOMESDAY BOOK AND THE FATE OF THE JURY

None of Masters's later volumes had either the popularity or the critical acclaim of *Spoon River Anthology*. Among the more memorable later volumes are *Domesday Book* and its sequel, *The Fate of the Jury*. *Domesday Book* has often been compared to Robert Browning's *The Ring and the Book* (1868-1869) in that both long poems present a variety of witnesses to a murder as a means of leading the reader to a recognition of the multiplicity of truth; it has also been compared with Theodore Dreiser's *An American Tragedy* (1925). The story, a simple one, is of Barrett Bays, a rabbit hunter, who finds the corpse of a woman on the Illinois River shore near Starved Rock; he sees that the victim is Elenor Murray, his one-time lover. The subsequent coroner's inquest clears Bays of any guilt in the matter, but the coroner, William Merival, is not satisfied. The reader gradually learns that the victim, a "free spirit" who had worked as a nurse in France during the war and whose relationships have led to the breakup of at least one marriage, was a far more complicated person than anyone in the town realized. Merival assembles a coroner's jury and subpoenas various witnesses. Most of *Domesday Book* comprises statements by these witnesses, including the victim's parents, a teacher, a priest, a piano teacher, a physician, and even the sheriff and the governor. Since each one has only a partial glimpse of the young woman, the resultant composite amounts to a skillful picture of a small town as well as of the deceased. Granted, Masters did extend the verse narrative to too great a length, and granted, too, he was repetitious—inevitable when such partial sources of information are cited. The free verse of *Spoon River Anthology* was replaced by blank verse that seemed to many readers and reviewers a monotonous, infelicitous choice. *Domesday Book* remains better in its parts than in the whole, and Masters's attempt to go beyond anything he had attempted previously can today be praised more for the effort and the vision than for the sheer poetic pleasure and drama he was able to create.

The Fate of the Jury, by contrast, is less than half as long as *Domesday Book*, and it picks up where the earlier book ended. In the later book, Masters allows the jurors and the coroner himself to speak about the case: One juror is a suicide; another (an editor) speaks while on his deathbed; a clergyman disappears after talking with the coroner; and the coroner himself, whose story is the frame for the book, eventually marries a young window as relief from the pathos and pressure of the prolonged case; unfortunately, there is mental illness in the widow's family, and shortly after the two are married she goes insane and dies. Thus, the "fate" of the jury—as well as of the coroner and the original victim—is a pathetic, possibly even tragic, decline into even further despair.

Domesday Book and *The Fate of the Jury* suffer from prolixity, stylistic roughness, and pretentious, empty rhetoric. Still, Masters's admitted gift for characterization and for a dramatic, realistic rendering of small-town life in all its squalor and inconsistency is well served by the two books, even though they suffer when compared to better examples of the genre such as Stephen Vincent Benét's *John Brown's Body* (1928) and Edwin Arlington Robinson's *Cavender's House* (1929). Masters wrote some half-dozen later dramatic poems, but none of them achieved even the limited fame and success of *Domes-*

day Book and its sequel. The use of a narrative framework composed of courtroom testimony was natural enough for Masters, who so effectively combined the law with poetry, but the richness of the characterization, as in *Spoon River Anthology*, remains his greatest accomplishment, as well as constituting the single most important parallel with Browning, whose name is so often invoked in relation to Masters. This skillful use of characterization, again in common with courtroom practice, was especially effective when contrasting testimony offered tangential perspective on the truth, with no single speaker or witness having more than a small part of the whole truth. Each speaker in *Domesday Book* and its sequel clearly felt that he or she had the "truth" about the events under investigation; but the primary truth that is revealed is less about the victim than about the speaker.

Though Masters the poet sometimes falters, Masters the psychologist remains a superlative student of character motivation; nevertheless, his achievement is just now beginning to be appreciated. As craftsmanlike and formally successful as many of his lyrics may be, it is likely that his ultimate reputation will rest primarily on his free-verse dramatic monologues and two longer blank-verse dramatic narratives. While he tried virtually every poetic form and technique and wrote on a vast array of topics, all of which resulted in repetitiveness, unevenness, and superficiality, his best work transcends mere changes in literary taste and fashion; it is probable that his ultimate rank will be considerably higher than that which he enjoyed during the first half of the twentieth century.

OTHER MAJOR WORKS

LONG FICTION: *Mitch Miller*, 1920; *Children of the Market Place*, 1922; *The Nuptial Flight*, 1923; *Skeeters Kirby*, 1923; *Mirage*, 1924; *Kit O'Brien*, 1927; *The Tide of Time*, 1937.

PLAYS: *Althea*, pb. 1907; *The Trifler*, pb. 1908; *The Leaves of the Tree*, pb. 1909; *Eileen*, pb. 1910; *The Locket*, pb. 1910; *The Bread of Idleness*, pb. 1911; *Lee: A Dramatic Poem*, pb. 1926; *Jack Kelso*, pb. 1928; *Gettysburg, Manila, Acoma*, pb. 1930; *Godbey*, pb. 1931; *Dramatic Duologues*, pb. 1934; *Richmond*, pb. 1934.

NONFICTION: *Levy Mayer and the New Industrial Era*, 1927; *Lincoln, the Man*, 1931; *The Tale of Chicago*, 1933; *Vachel Lindsay: A Poet in America*, 1935; *Across Spoon River*, 1936; *Walt Whitman*, 1937; *Mark Twain, a Portrait*, 1938; *The Sangamon*, 1942.

BIBLIOGRAPHY

Flanagan, John. *Edgar Lee Masters: The Spoon River Poet and His Critics*. Metuchen, N.J.: Scarecrow Press, 1974. Flanagan describes the reception of Masters's work by American and European critics and stresses the importance of relatively neglected works by Masters, including his *Domesday Book* and his biography of Abraham Lincoln.

Hallwas, John E., and Dennis J. Reader, eds. *The Vision of This Land: Studies of Vachel Lindsay, Edgar Lee Masters, and Carl Sandburg*. Macomb: Western Illinois University Press, 1976. This volume of essays explores the works of three major poets from Illinois. Edgar Lee Masters practiced law for forty years. Charles Burgess's essay examines legal arguments in his poetry, and Herb Russell discusses his literary career in the years immediately after the publication of his *Spoon River Anthology* in 1915.

Masters, Hardin Wallace. *Edgar Lee Masters: A Biographical Sketchbook About a Famous American Author*. Rutherford, N.J.: Fairleigh Dickinson University Press, 1978. This book contains numerous reflections on Edgar Lee Masters by his son. Hardin Masters presents a sympathetic view of his father's poetry, but he does indicate that Edgar Lee Masters was a vain and often insensitive father and husband. Includes a thorough list of the more than fifty books written by Masters.

Primeau, Ronald. *Beyond Spoon River: The Legacy of Edgar Lee Masters*. Austin: University of Texas Press, 1981. Primeau makes extensive use of Masters's 1936 autobiography *Across Spoon River* in order to demonstrate the extensive influence of major writers such as Ralph Waldo Emerson, Johann Wolfgang von Goethe, and Percy Bysshe Shelley on Masters. Primeau argues persuasively that Masters's poetry written after his *Spoon River Anthology* does not merit the relative oblivion into which it has fallen.

Russell, Herbert K. *Edgar Lee Masters: A Biography*. Urbana: University of Illinois Press, 2001. The first book-length biography of Masters, with bibliographical references and an index.

Vatron, Michael. *America's Literary Revolt*. Freeport, N.Y.: Books for Libraries Press, 1969. Vatron proposes that we read the poetry of Vachel Lindsay, Edgar Lee Masters, and Carl Sandburg as expressions of "political Populism." Although this interpretation is somewhat forced, it does remind us of the historical and political context in which their poetry was written.

Paul Schlueter;
bibliography updated by the editors

MATSUO BASHŌ

Born: Ueno, Iga Province, Japan; 1644
Died: Ōsaka, Japan; October 12, 1694

PRINCIPAL POETRY

Sarumino, 1691 (*Monkey's Raincoat*, 1973)
Haikai shichibu-shū, no date

OTHER LITERARY FORMS

The literary works of Matsuo Bashō are difficult to classify, even for those acquainted with Japanese literary history. Bashō is popularly known as the greatest of all *haiku* poets, although the literary form was not defined and named until two hundred years after his death. Modern collections labeled "Bashō's *haiku*" are generally bits and pieces taken from his travel journals and *renku* (linked poems). In a sense, all Bashō's literary works are broader and more complex than the seventeen-syllable *haiku* for which he is remembered. The seven major anthologies of his school, listed above, contain *hokku* (opening verses) and *renku* composed by Bashō and his disciples, as well as an occasional prose piece. Besides *hokku* and *renku*, Bashō is known for his *haibun*, a combination of terse prose and seventeen-syllable *hokku* generally describing his pilgrimages to famous sites in Japan. His best-known travel journals include *Nozarashi kikō* (1687; *The Records of a Weather-Exposed Skeleton*, 1966), *Oku no hosomichi* (1694; *The Narrow Road to the Deep North*, 1933), *Oi no kobumi* (1709; *The Records of a Travel-Worn Satchel*, 1966), and *Sarashina kikō* (1704; *A Visit to Sarashina Village*, 1957). Bashō's conversations on poetry were preserved by disciples, and his surviving letters, numbering more than a hundred, are treasured today.

ACHIEVEMENTS

Matsuo Bashō is the favorite poet of Japan and one of the only poets of Asia whose verses are known popularly in the West. It is paradoxical that this complex poet whose profundity continues to tease the minds of Japan's greatest literary critics is read and recited by schoolchildren in many lands. Although technically he never wrote a *haiku*, Bashō serves as a model for many children, East and West, writing their first verses as *haiku*. The wedding of simplicity and profundity which characterizes Bashō's work provides a true measure of his stature as a poet.

The continuing popularity of Bashō in his homeland, a country where laymen pride themselves on being aesthetic critics, is itself an extraordinary tribute to his work. Japanese still make pilgrimages to the stone monuments marking the stopping places on his journeys. Many recite his verses when they hear a frog splash, smell plum blossoms on a mountain trail, or hear a cicada's shrill voice. Thanks in no small part to his work, the average citizen of Japan still writes poetry, hangs scrolls containing verse, and reads the poetry column in Japan's daily newspapers.

In an age when aristocrats were the arbiters of taste, setting the complex rules for the writing of *waka* and *renga*, the chief poetic forms of Japan, Bashō devoted himself to *haikai*, an informal style of poetry celebrating the seasons of nature and the round of ordinary life among peasants and merchants. Without Bashō, *haikai* was in danger of sliding into slavish imitation of aristocratic canons or of degenerating into a display of vulgarity, coarse humor, and puns. Bashō democratized literature in Japan, and through literature he helped democratize Japanese aesthetics. Bringing to bear his own sensitivity to the nature mysticism of Chinese Daoism and the radical sacramentalization of the ordinary in Zen

Buddhism, he created a poetry of breadth and depth for the Japanese populace. As he observes in one of his *hokku:* "The beginning of art:/ Songs sung by those planting rice/ In the back country."

More specifically, Bashō's achievements in literature led to the maturing of three forms: the *hokku*, the *haikai no renga* (informal linked verse, and the *haibun*. Devoting a lifetime of effort to *hokku*, those seventeen-syllable verses intended as openings for linked poems, Bashō prepared the form for its modern independence as *haiku*. Working tirelessly with disciples in Japan's cities and countryside, Bashō infused a sense of the shared spirit of poetry that led to Japan's greatest *renku*, perhaps the high point of *za no geijutsu* (group art) in the history of world literature. Finally, his mastery of the combination of prose and poetry in travel journals set a new standard for the form the Japanese call *haibun*.

Describing himself in one of his *haibun, The Records of a Travel-Worn Satchel*, Bashō suggested a further unity, the unity of all arts when sounded to their depths, and the unity of art with nature, a philosophy that has given Japan its unique character:

> Finally, this poet, incapable as he is, has bound himself to the thin line of poetry. One and the same thread runs through the *waka* of Saigyō, *renga* of Sōgi, paintings of Sesshū, and tea ceremony of Riky. What the arts hold in common is a devotion to nature and companionship with the four seasons.

BIOGRAPHY

Centuries of warfare among the lords and samurai of Japan's chief clans came to an end when Tokugawa Ieyasu established a military dictatorship, the Shogunate, about 1600. With a Tokugawa shogun established in the thriving merchant city of Edo (modern-day Tokyo) and a ceremonial imperial court in ancient Kyoto, Japan officially closed its doors to the outside world in 1638. Such was the setting in which Matsuo Bashō was born in 1644 at Ueno in Iga province, only thirty miles from the imperial palace in Kyoto and two hundred miles from the powerful shogun in Edo.

Bashō was one of several children born to Matsuo Yozaemon, a minor samurai nominally in the service of the Tōdō family that ruled the Ueno area. Bashō's father had limited means and probably provided for his family by farming and giving lessons in calligraphy. At about age twelve, perhaps the year his father died, Bashō entered the service of the Tōdō family as a study companion to one of the Tōdō heirs, Yoshitada, a youth two years his senior with a bent toward poetry. A genuine friendship with Yoshitada encouraged young Bashō in the study of poetry and gave him access to one of the leading teachers of the day, Kitamura Kigin (1624-1705). When Yoshitada died suddenly in 1666, Bashō, only twenty-two years of age, lost both a friend and a patron. He apparently remained in the area of Ueno and Kyoto, devoting himself to poetry in the *haikai* style of the Teitoku school favored by his teacher Kigin. Pursuing a career as a poet, by 1672 he had published at his own expense *Kai-ōi* (seashell game), a collection of humorous verses by local poets which he matched and commented upon as poet-teacher. Some scholars believe that during this period, Bashō entered a relationship with a woman later known by her religious name, Jutei, and perhaps fathered children by her, but other scholars have dismissed this as pure speculation.

In 1672, at age twenty-eight, Bashō established himself in the bustling city of Edo, where his reputation as *haikai* poet and teacher increased. In 1680, he published *Tōsei montei dokugin nijū kasen* (twenty *kasen* by Tōsei's pupils), a collection of thirty-six-link *renku*. That year, he settled in a hut on the outskirts of Edo, next to which one of his disciples planted a *bashō*. In time, the poet's residence became known as the *Bashō-an* (banana-plant hut), and his students began to address him as "Master Bashō." Thus was born the nickname by which he was known for the rest of his life.

Bashō's early poetry was influenced by the Teitoku or Teimon style of *haikai*, using clever literary allusions and wordplay. In Edo, he came under the influence of the Danrin school, which explored greater freedom in theme and diction and demonstrated genuine interest in the life of the merchants and laborers of Edo. By about 1681, his own style, called *shōfū*, had begun to emerge, as evidenced in his *hokku* describing a crow on a withered branch in autumn twilight. Bashō also began practicing meditation under the direction of a Zen priest, Butchō (1642-1715).

In the fall of 1684, Bashō put on the robes of a Buddhist priest and began a series of pilgrimages over the roads and rugged mountain trails of Japan in order to perfect the new ideal of his art, *sabi* (solitariness). The final twelve years of his life were given largely to strenuous travel, the perfecting of the *haibun*-style travel journal, and sessions with disciples along the way who responded to his teaching and joined him in the art of *haikai no renga*, the linking of verses to produce *renku*. By 1686, he had written his most famous verse, describing the contrast of an old pond and a frog's splash, and by 1689, he had taken the difficult inland journey that led to the height of *haibun* art, *The Narrow Road to the Deep North*. Near the end of his life, to the chagrin of some of his disciples, Bashō had begun to advocate a new principle for the writing of *haikai*: *karumi* (lightness), a focus on the ordinary and unadorned.

During a final trip to Ueno and Ōsaka to preach *karumi* and to patch up a quarrel among his disciples, Bashō's strength failed and an old illness flared up; he dictated a final verse from his deathbed: "Ill on the journey/ My dreams going round and round/ Over withered fields."

ANALYSIS

At a time when many *haikai* poets wrote hundreds of verses during a single night's linked-poetry session, Matsuo Bashō's lifetime accumulation of barely a thousand seventeen-syllable *hokku* is indicative of the seriousness with which he took his art. Constantly struggling with each of these verses, Bashō established a standard of craftsmanship and profundity that would later lead to *hokku*'s independent status as *haiku*.

The *hokku* often singled out as Bashō's first masterpiece is his crow verse of 1681: "On a withered branch/ A crow settles itself down—/ Autumn evening." The stark tableau of a black branch against the darkened sky is broken by the sudden movement of a crow alighting. Here, timelessness and the momentary meet, and as they merge, the wider and deeper cycle of nature's seasonal pattern is revealed. The darkness of branch, crow, and autumn nightfall interpenetrate, suggesting the Japanese aesthetic qualities called *wabi* (poverty) and *sabi* (solitude).

THEMES

What the poet has not said is as significant as his choice of theme. The traditional aristocratic themes of

Japanese court poetry, the scented love notes, koto music, and tear-drenched sleeves of *waka* are absent. Bashō reaches back to the themes and cadences of the great Tang Dynasty poets of China, Du Fu and Li Bo, to lend universality to his verse. The monochromes of the great Chan masters are suggested by the black branch and crow, and perhaps the *hokku* itself suggests the Chinese poetic topic, "shivering crow in leafless tree." The merging of all in the mystery of darkness suggests Bashō's reading preferences: Daoism's Zhuangzi (Chuang-tzu) and Japan's poet-priests Saigyō and Sōgi. The rhythm and repetition of sounds, lost in English translation, witness Bashō's careful craftsmanship: *kare* (withered), *karasu* (crow), *akino-kure* (autumn evening).

FROG VERSES

One of Bashō's Edo disciples, Senka, compiled a *haikai* matching of verses on the subject "frog" in 1686, *Kawazu awase* (frog contest). Bashō provided the opening verse, or *hokku*, the most famous of all his works: "An age-old pond—/ A frog leaps into it/ Splash goes the water." The presence of *kawazu* (frog), a *kigo* (season word), tells the reader that it is spring. The poet sees the still surface of a murky pond, probably an ancient pond edged by rocks and reeds designed centuries earlier by some Zen priest as a setting for a temple. A sudden splash shatters the stillness of the pond, and in that disruption a new awareness of the eternal is sealed on the consciousness. Asian philosophy's yin-yang complementarity is revealed in the relation of stillness to sound, and the Daoist theme of a void from which momentary forms of life emerge and to which they return is celebrated. The consummate demonstration of just how much can be suggested in a few words constitutes Bashō's principal contribution to the *hokku* and suggests the Orient's "one-corner philosophy": Sensitivity to the smallest creature or the briefest moment within the cycle of nature provides a gateway to the motion and meaning of the entire universe. In the words of Zen Buddhism, "The mountains, trees, and grasses are the Buddha."

ZEN AND DAOISM

Bashō's training in Zen Buddhist meditation and his donning the robes of a Buddhist priest for his travels might suggest that the key concept of Buddhism, *sunyata* (emptiness), would find expression in his verses. It is significant that many of Bashō's *hokku* focus not on a presence but rather upon an "absence," a creative emptiness that suggests "pure potentiality." He writes of a skylark "clinging to nothing at all," of Mount Fuji "disappearing in mist," of flowers "without names," and of "a road empty of travelers." The Daoist void and Buddhist emptiness are expressed in the aesthetic quality Japanese call *yūgen* (mysterious vagueness), a quality of the *hokku* akin to the vacant spaces in a Zen scroll painting.

KARUMI

In 1693, just a year before his death, Bashō "shut his gate" for a time, refusing all visitors. When he opened the gate again to his disciples, he began teaching a further development of *haikai* poetry, the principle of *karumi* (lightness). Even close disciples had misgivings and uncertainties about this principle to which the poet devoted his final year. Moving beyond *wabi, sabi*, and *yūgen*, Bashō sought a return to some primal simplicity in the ordinariness of life, simplicity beyond both technical excellence and poetic response to the past. He wrote of a "sick wild duck/ falling in the cold of night," of "salted fish" in a street market, of a "white-haired/ graveyard visit," a "motionless cloud," and "autumn chill." The experience of eternity was no longer simply intensified by the momentary; for Bashō, it had become incarnate in the unadorned ordinariness of life.

THE ART OF HAIKAI

Modern interest in Bashō's art has generally focused on the *hokku*. Bashō himself, however, believed the art of *haikai* was to be found less in isolated verses than in cooperative effort of a like-minded school of poets involved in "sequence composition," and apparently he felt his greatest achievements occurred in this area: "Among my disciples many are as gifted as I am in writing *hokku*. But this old man knows the true spirit of *haikai*." The art of *haikai*, or *haikai no renga*, is so foreign to Western experience that appreciation of its merits and of Bashō's contribution is especially difficult.

The *waka* was the chief poetic form of the Japanese from prehistory through the thirteenth century. The special possession of the aristocracy at court, short *waka* called *tanka* were sometimes created by two persons, one composing the upper seventeen syllables and another responding with the lower fourteen. When *tanka* rules became too confining, some poets began to compose *renga* (linked verses) of a *haikai* (informal) or *mushin* (frivolous) sort. *Renga* soon became adopted by the court and developed its own *ushin* (serious) rules, and so by the sixteenth century a *haikai no renga* movement sought to democratize the form again.

Bashō, an artist of *haikai no renga*, sought to keep the form open to creative contact with everyday life, yet sought also to transcend common wordplay and vulgarities. His cooperative poetic efforts with four Nagoya merchants in *Fuyu no hi* (a winter's day) and with sixteen disciples in a hundred-verse sequence called *Hatsu kaishi* (*First Manuscript Page*), culminating in a series of thirty-six-link *renku* collected in *Monkey's Raincoat*. Using the rules regarding season sequences and moon and flower verses with freedom yet sensitivity, he advocated linking alternate seventeen-syllable and fourteen-syllable verses through the principle of *nioi* (fragrance), a vague but effective sense of atmosphere and mood conveyed by one poet and verse to another.

"IN THE CITY"

A *renku* in thirty-six verses titled "Ichinaka wa" ("In the City") appears in *Monkey's Raincoat*. Its opening verse (*hokku*) is by the poet Bonchō, who introduces the "heavy odor of things" in the city and uses the seasonal words "summer moon." Bashō responds with the answering verse (*waki*), describing voices in the night at "gate after gate." They repeat, "It is hot, so hot." From there, a third poet shifts the scene to a rice paddy, Bonchō continues with a verse describing a farmer's "smoked sardine" meal, and Bashō adds a link that pictures himself as a visitor to this poor farm neighborhood, where "they don't even recognize money." Within the next half dozen verses, a young girl's religious experience is described, the season shifts to winter, and Bashō introduces an aged peasant who "can only suck the bones of fish." Sounds and word associations linking one verse to another are so subtle that even experienced *haikai* poets disagree in their analysis, though not in their high evaluation of the *renku*.

Perhaps the greatest facet of Bashō's art, linked poetry written cooperatively through a shared "fragrance," is largely closed to the Western reader, though a good *renku* translation and commentary may be of some aid. Those familiar with Western chamber music may detect similarities, as themes pass from one player to another, exciting changes in tempo and mood are introduced, and one instrument modulates to support the contribution of another.

THE NARROW ROAD TO THE DEEP NORTH

Finally, it should be noted that some critics view neither the *hokku* nor the *haikai no renga* as the height of Bashō's art. They would view his travel journals, culminating in *The Narrow Road to the Deep North*, as the epitome of his creative efforts.

In *The Narrow Road to the Deep North*, widely regarded as one of the finest works in all Japanese literature, the pilgrim-poet seeks to mature his art by hiking to those sites of beauty and history that inspired Saigyō and other poet-priests of the past. Taking arduous trails both to the inner country of Japan and the inner reaches of his own art, Bashō weaves prose and poetry into a record of a pilgrimage of the Japanese spirit as it responds to the history and beauty of the homeland. The famous opening declares that "moon and sun are eternal travelers," and bids the reader to join in the journey. Bashō describes famous sites and views at Matsushima, Hiraizumi, and Kisagata, pausing to muse over ruined castles and ancient battlefields:

> The summer grasses—
> For courageous warriors
> The aftermath of dreams.

In a land ruled by powerful military shoguns who had closed Japan to all outside contacts, such musings in the spirit of the great T'ang poets of China made this travel journal an act of courage and a proclamation that art cannot be confined by political borders. Allusions to Chinese poetry and philosophy, Japanese history and aesthetics, are woven together in such a complex tapestry that, once again, the Western reader is in need of a superior translation and a helpful commentary, but the treasures to be discovered are worth the effort.

Bashō, the poet whose verses are loved by children yet challenge the best efforts of mature scholars, spent his life in pilgrimage for his art and died on the road. In *The Narrow Road to the Deep North*, he sums up the relevance of his wanderings in a few simple words, identifying his readers as pilgrims, too: "For each day is a journey, and the journey itself is home."

OTHER MAJOR WORKS

NONFICTION: *Nozarashi kikō*, 1687 (travel; *The Records of a Weather-Exposed Skeleton*, 1966); *Oku no hosomichi*, 1694 (travel; *The Narrow Road to the Deep North*, 1933); *Sarashina kikō*, 1704 (travel; *A Visit to Sarashina Village*, 1966); *Oi no kobumi*, 1709 (travel; *The Records of a Travel-Worn Satchel*, 1966).

BIBLIOGRAPHY

Aitken, Robert. *A Zen Wave: Bashō's Haiku and Zen.* New York: Weatherhill, 1978. One of the few studies of Bashō by a Western *roshi*, or master teacher of Zen. This overview evaluates the poet's work in the context of Zen philosophy, offering the claim that Bashō's haiku transcend mere nature poetry and instead serve as a way of presenting fundamental religious truths about mind, nature, and cosmos.

Hamill, Sam, trans. *The Essential Bashō.* Boston: Shambhala, 1999. The introduction to this work represents Bashō as a consummate writer. In this work, religious issues are significantly downplayed. Instead Hamill presents his subject as a poetic and philosophical wanderer: someone engaged in a lifelong process of literary experimentation and discovery. Particularly fascinating is the overview of Bashō's transformation from a highly derivative stylist to a powerfully original poet.

Shirane, Haruo. *Traces of Dreams: Landscape, Cultural Memory, and the Poetry of Bashō.* Stanford, Calif.: Stanford University Press, 1998. This work puts the poet into the position of cultural conservationist, arguing that Bashō's poems drew upon deeply held concepts of nature.

Ueda, Makoto. *Bashō and His Interpreters: Selected Hokku with Commentary.* Stanford, Calif.: Stanford University Press, 1992. This work is a chronologically organized anthology of Bashō's poems, each accompanied by the original Japanese text (transliterated into Western characters) and literal translations. Although it offers little new insight into Bashō's life or interpretations of his work, this volume does demonstrate the tremendous influence of translation on the written word.

_____. *Matsuo Bashō.* New York: Twayne, 1970. This study offers a brief biography as well as gen-eral perspectives on the author's major works. In addition to the expected focus on haiku, this study treats Bashō's *renku* (long collaboratively written poems) and prose works.

Cliff Edwards;
bibliography updated by Michael R. Meyers

WILLIAM MATTHEWS

Born: Cincinnati, Ohio; November 11, 1942
Died: New York, New York; November 12, 1997

PRINCIPAL POETRY

Broken Syllables, 1969
Ruining the New Road, 1970
The Cloud, 1971
The Waste Carpet, 1972
Sleek for the Long Flight, 1972
An Oar in the Old Water, 1973
Sticks and Stones, 1975
Rising and Falling, 1979
Flood, 1982
A Happy Childhood, 1984
Foreseeable Futures, 1987
Blues If You Want, 1989
Selected Poems and Translations, 1969-1991, 1992
Time and Money: New Poems, 1995
After All: Last Poems, 1998

OTHER LITERARY FORMS

Curiosities (1989) is a collection of nineteen essays, ranging from personal reflections on William Matthews's travels in Italy to critical commentaries and reviews of the works of various fellow poets. In *The Poetry Blues: Essays and Interviews* (2001), Matthews speaks of his love of jazz music, language, poetry, and art. The posthumous volume, edited by Sebastian Matthews and Stanley Plumly, includes an autobiographical essay. With Mary Feeney he has translated several volumes of poems from the French by Jean Follain, and he also translated *The Mortal City: One Hundred Epigrams of Martial* (1995).

ACHIEVEMENTS

A prolific poet and a master of the "deep" or surreal image, in the mode of James Wright and Robert Bly, William Matthews has attracted consistent critical acclaim from fellow poets, from the publication of his first full-length collection, *Ruining the New Road*, in 1970, but widespread recognition escaped him until the 1990's. He received a fellowship from the National Endowment for the Arts in 1974, following publication of his second book of poems, and a Guggenheim Fellowship after his fourth book appeared, in 1979. In 1988 he spent a month at the Villa Serbonelli on a grant from the Rockefeller Foundation. In the years just before his early death, he received more significant recognitions. *Time and Money* won the National Book Critics Circle award, and in 1997 Matthews won the Ruth Lilly Poetry Prize. Noted for his often-aphoristic wit and for his ability to bridge the "inner" and "outer" dimensions of the human condition, Matthews ranged easily among Brahms, basketball, blues, and his own backyard.

BIOGRAPHY

"I used to have a morning paper route, played baseball and basketball, had a dog named Spot. Troy, Ohio." So William Matthews writes in his autobiographical essay "Moving Around" (1976). Troy is a town of approximately twenty thousand located about seventy miles north of Cincinnati, where he was born in 1942. When Matthews's father left his job with the Soil Conservation Service for a position with a student exchange program, the family moved back to Cincinnati. This move altered Matthews's small-town view of the world at a crucial age of his life (about twelve). He visited Europe with his family and thereafter remained an avid traveler.

Sent to a boarding school in the Berkshire Hills of Massachusetts, he began writing poems, though he was not to become a serious poet until after his undergraduate days at Yale University, where he received his B.A. in 1965. Having married while at Yale, he moved to the University of North Carolina in Chapel Hill, where the couple's two sons (William and Sebastian) were born and where he did graduate work, receiving his master's degree in 1966. Also at North Carolina he started the literary magazine *Lillabulero*, which ran between 1966 and 1974, and was codirector of Lillabulero Press.

After a year as instructor in the English department at Wells College (1968-1969), Matthews taught at Cornell University, where his first full-length collection, *Ruining the New Road*, was published in 1970, to be followed two years later by *Sleek for the Long Flight*. Following his divorce in 1974, Matthews moved to the University of Colorado, where he taught for a year. Between 1976 and 1980 he served as a member of the panel on literature for the National Endowment for the Arts, on the board of directors of the Associated Writing Programs, and as an advising editor for L'Épervier Press.

Between 1978 and 1983 Matthews taught as full professor and director of creative writing at the University of Washington. After that he became an editor for the Atlantic Monthly Press. Remarried, he settled in New York City where he taught at the City University of New York and directed the creative writing program. He also served a term as president of the Poetry Society of America. Matthews died in New York City in 1997, the day after his fifty-fifth birthday.

William Matthews (© Star Black)

ANALYSIS

In his poems and essays, William Matthews refers frequently to poets as diverse as Horace and Richard Hugo, Wallace Stevens and W. H. Auden, Elizabeth Bishop and Galway Kinnell. Yet the allusions are not limited to other poets. Novelists such as Vladimir Nabokov and Russell Banks are part of that world, and European writers of various periods populate it: Victor Hugo, Gustave Flaubert, Gabriele D'Annunzio, Vergil. Still, such a strictly literary "Who's Who" would give a reader a false impression of Matthews's range. The list would have to include Ted Williams, Jack Nicklaus, and Archie Moore, and it would encompass musicians as various as Wolfgang Amadeus Mozart and Bob Marley, though the emphasis would definitely be on jazz and blues (Janis Joplin, Bessie Smith, Dexter Gordon, Stan Getz). Sigmund Freud also makes frequent appearances in Matthews's work. Perhaps it is indicative of his world that in a poem titled "Self-Knowledge" one encounters him reading Horace while listening to a Bud Powell tape.

RUINING THE NEW ROAD

What is elusive in Matthews's poems is more difficult to account for than the range of his reference or allusion. In the prefatory poem to his first full-length collection, *Ruining the New Road*, Matthews teases his audience with the suggestion that "the search party" does not involve an actual lost child, but that poet and reader are "deep in symbolic woods": "The search is that of art." No sooner does he offer that premise, however, than he insists, "There was a real lost child./ I don't want to swaddle it/ in metaphor." Even as he proclaims what he does not want to do, he does it; not only is the infinitive "to swaddle" metaphoric but it is also "loaded" for any reader of the King James version of the New Testament. His definition of his stance as a writer is as applicable to his later poems as it was to his earlier efforts: "I'm just a journalist/ who can't believe in objectivity." To make such a statement in the poem is to "digress," as he admits, from the poem's supposed subject, so he concludes by informing the reader, "The child was still/ alive. Admit you're glad."

Especially in the first three collections, Matthews seems to be at some pains to contrive a surreal metaphoric base, as in "Cuckold": "You can hear the silverware/ catching its eager breath/ inside the sleeping drawer." Early, too, he established himself as a virtuoso of the simile—both simple, "We twist away like a released balloon" ("Moving"), and complex, "In sleep we issue from the earth/ like prayers the nuns have swallowed/ but can't keep down" ("Der Doppelgänger"). The poems of his first book are often quite spare, and the lines tend to be rather short.

SLEEK FOR THE LONG FLIGHT AND STICKS AND STONES

In *Sleek for the Long Flight* and *Sticks and Stones*, Matthews was to carry this minimalist impulse to nearly the ultimate point, producing three one-line poems, while at the same time exploring the prose poem. His unusual blending of the inner, dreamlike world of the surreal and the outer, quotidian world of the domestic is evident in various ways throughout the long, narrow-lined "The Cat," which begins with "a hail of claws" as the cat lands "in your lap." Matthews greets the cat with playful, Homeric epithets: "Fishbreath, Wind-/ minion." What is most striking, however, is how Matthews moves from a domestic simile, "One night you lay your book/ down like the clothes/ your mother wanted/ you to wear tomorrow," to a surreal metaphor, "The cat exhales the moon." One moment the speaker can be quite direct: "This is the only cat/ I have ever loved." In the next lines, however, he moves to the whimsical, "This cat has written/ in tongue-ink/ the poem you are reading now," and then angles toward the profound: "the poem scratching/ at the gate of silence."

One remarkable poem from *Sleek for the Long Flight* is "Stone," dedicated to fellow poet Charles Simic, which begins with wordplay: "The creek has made its bed/ and wants to lie in it." Matthews delights in moments such as these, in which language seems to deconstruct itself. His best poems are always densely textured; that is, they are not only thoughtful or provocative or profound but also metaphorically rich and musical.

Sticks and Stones, published in a limited edition of six hundred copies by a small press, is a transitional collection. Its most ambitious effort is "The Waste Carpet," a four-page satire on the ecological "apocalypse" which gets quite playful: "Three Edsels forage in the southeast corner,/ a trio of ironical bishops."

RISING AND FALLING

In his next three collections, however, Matthews was back to major key: *Rising and Falling*, *Flood*, and *A*

Happy Childhood. "Memory," Matthews writes in "Moving Again," the second poem of *Rising and Falling*, "is our root system." The poem opens with one of his patentable similes: "At night the mountains look like huge/ dim hens." Now divorced, he sees his sons infrequently: "If I lived with my sons/ all year I'd be less sentimental/ about them." This mingling of the surreal metaphoric element with the mundane statement typifies Matthews's most effective poems. From the top of the mesa, the speaker imagines, he and his sons look down on their new home. Matthews weaves an assonantal long *i* through the lines:

> The thin air
> warps in the melting light
> like the aura before a migraine.
> The boys are tired. A tiny magpie
> fluffs into a pine far below
> and farther down in the valley
> of child support and lights
> people are opening drawers.

An imagined resident opens a drawer and finds a forgotten telephone number. The elusive quality of this ending is not really clarified by comments Matthews offers about two names in the poem (Nicky and Verna) in his essay "Moving Around."

The image of rising and falling permeates the collection of that title, involving activities from climbing a hill to music, basketball, snorkeling, and the sexual act. The poems of *Rising and Falling*, which remains among the strongest of Matthews's collections, also revolve around death, and the juxtaposition of the highly erotic "Isla Mujeres" (isle of women) and "Living Among the Dead" is surely no coincidence. "It was when I learned to read," Matthews writes, "that I began always/ to live among the dead." It is easy to love the dead, he argues, because they are perfected, complete, but "to love a child is to turn/ away from the patient dead." One of his most startling similes comes from this poem: "My sons and I are like some wine/ the dead have already bottled."

FLOOD

The confrontation of death is more immediate in "Bystanders," a narrative poem from *Flood*, in which a fatal accident on a snowy hill draws onlookers together, helpless in the face of inevitability. What is most re-

markable about this poem is the extreme understatement, its flat narration: "A woman wiped blood from his crushed/ face with a Tampax, though he was dead,/ and we stood in the field and stuttered." Matthews simply presents the event, drawing only the subtlest of conclusions: "So we began to ravel from the stunned/ calm thing we had become/ by not dying." Against this quiet metaphor he places the noise of the cleanup; the "staunch/ clank" of the snowplow's chains.

A HAPPY CHILDHOOD

Because he understands language and because he loves words well, Matthews dares trust neither language nor words. This attitude toward language, which is now associated with deconstruction, is especially evident in such poems from *A Happy Childhood* as "Good," a series of eight ten-line poems which opens the collection. The poems are an exercise in form, for no two of them possess the same stanzaic arrangement. The opening poem, for example, which reflects on a friend who was an only child, is arranged in tercets with the seventh line set up alone. The next one, a love poem of sorts, in which the speaker mentions the loss of his "stolen good," is also set up in tercets, but with the last line apart from the others. The third poem in the series (and they do not seem really to constitute a "sequence") opens with the single, "floating" line and involves a change in point of view from first to third person: "Romantic, you could call him." Yet, the poem's subject resembles Matthews himself: "He walks the balance beam/ of his obsession like a triumphant/ drunk passing a police test." In the second tercet he likens the persona to a man in love with "a woman fools would find plain" (presumably "the muse").

In the fourth poem of the series he alternates couplets and tercets in commenting on the "good lie" of art. In the next poem, which is divided into two five-line stanzas, he tortures the word "good" through the satiric comments of the eighteenth century founder of Methodism, John Wesley, who argued that "'my good man' means 'good for his debts,'/ and not for nothing." Returning to the first person in the sixth poem of the series, Matthews probes himself "to the very bone," for which he digs "like a dog, good dog." The body of that poem yields rather playfully to the spirit in the next, which is written in the third person: "The body's dirty/ windows are flung open, and the spirit squints// out frankly." (This enjambment of the line across a stanza break is fairly common in Matthews's poems, and it creates an odd tension: the free flow of line against the imposition of stanza.) The concluding poem of the series, arranged in couplets, reintroduces the first-person speaker, who expresses his gratitude to those who have influenced his poems and freed them so that "they go their own strange ways."

This series, then, becomes a sort of *ars poetica*, touching on most of Matthews's poetic concerns, either directly or indirectly. The counterpoint series, "Bad," appears several pages later in the book, and Matthews also pairs up such poems as "Manic" and "Depressive," "Fat" and "On a Diet," "Right" and "Wrong." He also arranges strings of adjectival titles—for example, "Charming," "Restless," "Masterful." In fact, although the lengthy title poem of the book concludes, "Who knows if he's happy or not?" *A Happy Childhood* is Matthews's most playful collection, reminding the reader that the letter *J* in his "Poet's Alphabet" stands not only for "jazz" but also for "jokes" and "for how much jokes are about language." Among Matthews's jokes is his decision to end the book with the poem "Wrong."

FORESEEABLE FUTURES

Foreseeable Futures and *Blues If You Want* frequently turn on the subjects of music and poetry, though any comment on "subjects" in Matthews's work should take account of his essay "Dull Subjects," in which he observes that the subject matter of a poem is often only its point of departure, the raw material that is to be transformed. Thirty of the thirty-six poems in *Foreseeable Futures* are composed in fifteen lines set up as five tercets, strongly enjambed so that form and line seem constantly to be testing each other. In "By Heart," Matthews poses a familiar question: "Which came first, style or content?" The rather scholarly historical stance, the history of jazz in this case, combined with the inclination to offer up just such a question, reveals much about Matthews's poetic voice. Throughout his work he assumes the distance not only of the journalist but also of the intellectual, and the wit that follows the question above is part of that stance: "To this trick/ question Drs. Xtl and Yrf and Professor Zyzgg/ have given honorable gray hours." Even as he teases the academics here,

Matthews cannot resist joining them, even though his definition of style, which follows, is "poetic" (metaphorical): "Style is that rind// of the soul we can persuade to die with us."

BLUES IF YOU WANT

Yet the world of Matthews's poems has not become "academic" in the often-pejorative sense of the term. It remains typical of his books that one can move from reference to the philosopher and poet George Santayana in one poem to the strikingly dramatic "Caddies Day, the Country Club, a Small Town in Ohio" in the next. Perhaps Matthews's best poems are those such as "It Don't Mean a Thing If It Ain't Got That Swing," from *Blues If You Want*. This five-page poem moves from the following sort of passage:

> A grackle unrolls like a carpet of sandpaper
> its brash lament. A car with an ulcerated
> muffler stutters past. Inside, the girl has on
> those panties, the pale color of key lime pie . . .

to the following:

> and thus what we lazily call "form"
> in poetry,
> let's say, is Language's desperate
>
> attempt to wrench from print
> the voluble body it gave away
> in order to be read.

These passages manifest everything from Matthews's often-startling similes and metaphors and his erotic touch to his indulgence of the cerebral. As Matthews says in "Poet's Alphabet": "Human consciousness is so composed that we can't have experience without a commentary on it. This makes us both silly and interesting. . . . It makes us want to make poems."

TIME AND MONEY AND AFTER ALL

Matthews's volumes of the 1990's, *Time and Money* and the posthumously published *After All*, continue to demonstrate this fine poet's masterly style, his joy in formal play, and the tonic, liberating irony through which his good sense reached a growing number of readers.

In *Time and Money*, Matthews continues to write about what interests him (domestic life, music, food, poetry) in order to find out why it interests him. He ponders the elusiveness of the past, the tricks of time, and the peculiarities of memory. He comments on the parameters of modern life—time and money—and notes drolly "the longer you think about/ either, the stupider you get,// while dinner grows tepid and stale." His muse, Charles Mingus, makes appearances, including "Mingus in Diaspora," in which Mingus is an angry, outspoken genius and, for Matthews, a hero.

In his last collection before his death, *After All: Last Poems*, dark undertones—death, urban paranoia, illness—find a prominent place. The opening poem, "Mingus in Shadow," focuses on the "whittled" body and the rage that "got eaten cell by cell," in a graphic detail of the death of famed bassist and composer Charles Mingus. "A Serene Heart at the Movies," begins, "She strode to her car and turned the key and/ a peony of bomb bloomed all at once." In "People Like Us" an apartment dweller envisions desperate have-nots "surging up the stain/ and up the fee escapes." In "The Shooting" a street confrontation escalates into homicide. Here rage is semingly rampant and death is a slow burn or a hair trigger. "Dire Cure," the longest poem of the book, focuses on his wife's cancer. "A children's/ cancer (doesn't that possessive break/ your heart?) had possessed her," he writes in a poem that witnesses his wife's struggle and eventual conquer of the illness. Life being eroded by disease or shattered by sudden violence forms a core nexus of this collection.

Yet, *After All* also explores and humorously celebrates everyday occurrences such as the antics of a cat or the delectable absurdities of euphemisms. "Sooey Generous," is a mock-epic extolling pigs, while "Promiscuous" and "Oxymorons" highlight a lexicographer's fondness for words, their improbable pairings, and the way in which their roots persist behind accrued meanings. Travel poems, such as "Le Quatre Saisons, Montreal, 1979," and snapshots of place, such as New York's Upper West Side, round out the mix.

OTHER MAJOR WORKS

NONFICTION: *Curiosities*, 1989; *The Poetry Blues: Essays and Interviews*, 2001.

TRANSLATIONS: *Removed from Time*, 1972 (of Jean Follain; with Mary Feeney); *A World Rich in Anniversaries: Prose Poems*, 1979 (of Follain; with

Feeney); *The Mortal City: One Hundred Epigrams of Martial*, 1995.

BIBLIOGRAPHY

Christophersen, Bill. "Late Night Music." *Poetry* 174, no. 2 (May, 1999): 99-107. Christophersen pays homage to Matthews in his lengthy, detailed review of the posthumous collection *After All: Last Poems*. Noting the "sardonic and self-mocking" persona that Matthews often employs, Christophersen calls attention both to the dark tones of these late poems and to the frequent leavening of lighter verse with the "lexicographer's fondness for words." Matthews is likened to "a jazzman on a typewriter keyboard, whose music, as the night wore on, just got bluesier." The review begins with a career overview.

Marowski, Daniel G., ed. "William Matthews." In *Contemporary Literary Criticism* 40. Detroit: Gale Research, 1986: 318-325. This selection of reviews from literary journals and newspapers provides useful secondary material on Matthews's work.

Matthews, William. "Talking About Poetry with William Matthews." *Ohio Review* 13 (Spring, 1972): 32-51. Of interest for information on Matthews's first two collections, *Ruining the New Road* and *Sleek for the Long Flight*.

Ron McFarland,
updated by Philip K. Jason and Sarah Hilbert

VLADIMIR MAYAKOVSKY

Born: Bagdadi, Georgia, Russian Empire (Mayakovsky, Georgia); July 19, 1893
Died: Moscow, U.S.S.R.; April 14, 1930

PRINCIPAL POETRY
Ya, 1913
Oblako v shtanakh, 1915 (*A Cloud in Pants*, 1945)
Chelovek, 1916
Fleita-pozvonochnik, 1916 (*The Backbone Flute*, 1960)
150,000,000, 1920 (English translation, 1949)

Pro eto, 1923 (*About That*, 1965)

Vladimir Ilich Lenin, 1924 (English translation, 1939)

Khorosho!, 1927 (*Fine!*, 1939)

Vo ves' golos, 1930 (*At the Top of My Voice*, 1940)

Polnoe sobranie sochinenii, 1955-1961 (13 volumes)

Mayakovsky: Poems, 1965

Poems, 1972

OTHER LITERARY FORMS

Vladimir Mayakovsky was primarily a poet, but he also wrote several plays, some prose works, and numerous propaganda pieces. His first play, *Vladimir Mayakovsky: Tragediya (pr. 1913; Vladimir Mayakovsky: A Tragedy*, 1968), displayed the characteristics that would become associated with him throughout his career: audacity, bombastic exuberance, a predilection for hyperbole, an undercurrent of pessimism, and, above all, an uncontrollable egotism (underscored by the title). In *Misteriya-buff* (pr., pb. 1918, revised pr., pb. 1921; *Mystery-bouffe*, 1933), subtitled "A Heroic, Epic and Satiric Presentation of Our Epoch," which Helen Muchnic has termed "a cartoon version of Marxist history," Mayakovsky presents the events of World War I as a class struggle between the Clean (the bourgeoisie) and the Unclean (the proletariat). His best two plays, written in the last years of his life, contain sharp satirical attacks on Soviet society. *Klop* (pr., pb. 1929; *The Bedbug*, 1931) depicts a proletarian in the 1920's who forsakes his class by showing bourgeois tendencies. He perishes in the fire during his tumultuous wedding. Resurrected after fifty years, he finds himself forsaken in turn by the future Soviet society. Mayakovsky's warnings about the possibly pernicious direction of the development of Soviet society fell on deaf ears, as did his attacks on Soviet bureaucracy in his last major work, *Banya* (pr., pb. 1930; *The Bathhouse*, 1963). Both plays were complete failures when they were performed in the last year of the author's life. Among the best plays in Soviet literature, they met with greater approval three decades later.

ACHIEVEMENTS

Perhaps Vladimir Mayakovsky's greatest achievement as a poet was his incarnation of the revolutionary spirit in Russian literature. He was indeed *the* poet of the

Vladimir Mayakovsky

Russian Revolution: Right or wrong, he was able to instill the revolutionary spirit into his poetry and to pass it over to his readers. His hold on their fancy and admiration is still alive today. As a member of the Futurist movement, which he helped to organize in Russia, he brought new life into poetry by providing a viable alternative to Symbolism, which had been the dominant force in Russian poetry in the preceding two decades. Mayakovsky effected many innovations by following trends in other national literatures, thus bringing Russian poetry closer to the mainstream of world literature. He could not speak or read any foreign language, but he was always keenly interested in other literatures. His inimitable free verse set a standard for decades. He made the language of the street acceptable to the newly developing taste of both readers and critics, thus appealing to a wide audience despite his excesses. He has had many followers among poets, but none of them has been able to approximate his greatness.

BIOGRAPHY

Vladimir Vladimirovich Mayakovsky was born on July 19, 1893, in Bagdadi (a small town that was later renamed after him), where his father was a forester. From his early childhood, he showed himself to be independent and strong-willed. Although he was not a very good student, he possessed a remarkable memory for facts and long passages from poetry and other books. His childhood and early youth passed amid social unrest and rebellions. Because his entire family leaned toward the revolutionaries, Mayakovsky, too, participated in workers' demonstrations, giving his father's guns to the rebels, reading Socialist literature, and preparing himself for a lifelong revolutionary activism.

In 1906, after the death of Mayakovsky's father, the family moved to Moscow, where Mayakovsky entered high school and continued his association with the revolutionaries. He was accepted by the Communist Party when he was only fourteen and was arrested three times for his underground work. The last time, he was kept in jail eleven months, during which he read voraciously, becoming familiar with the classics of Russian literature for the first time. After his release, he decided to go back to school rather than devote all of his time to political activity. Because of his activism, however, he was allowed to enroll only in an art school, where he fostered his natural talent for drawing and painting. There, he met David Burlyuk, an artist and poet who encouraged him not only in his artistic endeavors but also as a poet, after Mayakovsky's timid beginnings. Together they formed the backbone of the Russian Futurists, a group that had some affinities with Filippo Marinetti's Futurism, although Russian Futurism originated independently from the Italian movement. In 1912, the Russian Futurists issued a manifesto, appropriately titled "Poshchechina obshchestvennomu vkusu" ("A Slap in the Face of the Public Taste"), which included a poem by Mayakovsky. He spent the years before the Russian Revolution writing and publishing poetry, making scandal-provoking public appearances, continuing his revolutionary activity, and impressing everyone with his powerful voice and imposing physique, especially the police. He was not called into the czarist army because of his political unreliability, but during the Revolution, as well as in its aftermath, he helped the cause by drawing posters and writing captions for them and composing slogans, marching songs, and propaganda leaflets.

After the Revolution, however, Mayakovsky began to voice his dissatisfaction with Soviet policies and to fight the burgeoning bureaucracy, which remained his greatest enemy for the rest of his life. He especially disliked the seeming betrayal of revolutionary ideals on the part of the new Soviet establishment. He fell in love with Lili Brik, the wife of his close friend, the critic Osip Brik. He traveled abroad often, including a four-month-long trip to the United States, to which he reacted both favorably and critically. During his visit to Paris, he fell in love with a young Russian émigré woman. His efforts to persuade her to return with him to the Soviet Union were fruitless. This failure, along with other disappointments, led to periods of depression. He had become one of the leading poets in Soviet literature and the poet of the Russian Revolution, yet he and the circle centered on the journal *LEF* (founded by Mayakovsky in 1923) fought protracted and bitter battles with the literary establishment.

LEF, an acronym standing for *Levy front iskusstva* (left front of art), was an independent movement of avant-garde artists and writers organized under Mayakovsky's leadership. As Soviet cultural policy, initially supportive of the avant-garde, turned more conservative, LEF was suppressed, and its eponymous journal was forced to cease publication. In January of 1930, an exhibition which Mayakovsky organized to celebrate his twenty years of writing and graphic work was boycotted by Soviet cultural officials and fellow writers. His increasing dissatisfaction with the regime, his repeated failures in love, a prolonged throat illness, the failure of his plays, and a deep-seated disposition toward self-destruction, which he had often expressed in the past, caused him to commit suicide in his Moscow apartment on April 14, 1930. His death stunned the nation but also provoked harsh criticism of his act. A few years later, however, he received his due as a poet and as a revolutionary, a recognition that is increasing with time.

ANALYSIS

Vladimir Mayakovsky's poetry can be divided into three general categories. In the first group are the poems with political themes, often written on ephemeral occasions as everyday political exigencies demanded. These poems represent the weakest and indeed some of the silliest verses in his opus and are, for the most part, forgotten. The second group contains his serious revolutionary poems, in which he expressed his loyalty to the Revolution as a way of life and as "the holy washerwoman [who] will wash away all filth from the face of the earth with her soap." There are some excellent poems in this group, for they reflect Mayakovsky's undying faith in, and need for, an absolute which would give him strength to live and create, an absolute which he found in Communism. Undoubtedly the best poems from the aesthetic point of view, however, are those from the third group, in which Mayakovsky writes about himself and his innermost feelings. These poems, which are more revealing of his true personality than all the loudly proclaimed utterances which made him famous, are the most likely to endure.

Mayakovsky's development as a poet parallels closely his life experiences. As he was growing into a fiery young revolutionary, his early poetry reflected his ebullience and combative spirit. His first poems, contained in Futurist publications, revealed his intoxication with the enormous power of words, a spirit which informs his entire oeuvre. The Futurist movement offered Mayakovsky a suitable platform from which to shout his messages. Indeed, it is difficult to say whether he joined Futurism for its tenets or Futurism embraced his volcanic energy, both as a poet and an activist, for its own purposes. The Futurists conceived of art as a social force and of the artist as a spokesperson for his age. To this end, new avenues of expression had to be found in the form of a "trans-sense" language in which words are based not so much on their meaning as on sounds and form.

YA AND A CLOUD IN PANTS

Much of Futurist dogma found in Mayakovsky an eager practitioner and an articulate spokesman. His first serious work, a collection of four poems under the title *Ya*, already shows his intentions of "thrusting the dagger of desperate words/ into the swollen pulp of the sky." His most important prerevolutionary work, the long poem *A Cloud in Pants*, begins as a lamentation about an unanswered love but later turns into a treatise on social

ills, punctuated forcefully with slogans such as "Down with your love!" "Down with your art!" "Down with your social order!" "Down with your religion!" Such pugnacity corresponds closely to the irreverent rejection of the status quo in the Futurist manifesto "A Slap in the Face of the Public Taste":

> The past is stifling. The Academy and Pushkin are incomprehensible hieroglyphs. We must throw Pushkin, Dostoevsky, Tolstoy, etc. from the boat of modernity.

The title of the poem reveals Mayakovsky's predilection for a striking metaphor: The cloud symbolizes the poet flying high above everything, while the trousers bring him down to Earth.

150,000,000

The poems Mayakovsky wrote during the Revolution bear more or less the same trademarks. The most characteristic of them, *150,000,000*, was inspired by the American intervention in the Russian Civil War on the side of anti-Bolsheviks. It was published anonymously (the ruse did not work, though), as if 150 million Soviet citizens had written it. The central theme, the struggle between the East and the West, is depicted in a typically Mayakovskian fashion. The East is personified by Ivan (the most common Russian name), who has 150 million heads and whose arms are as long as the Neva River. The West is represented by President Woodrow Wilson, who wears a hat in the form of the Eiffel Tower. Undoubtedly the poet believed that the more grotesque the expression, the more effective the message. He sets the tone at the very beginning:

> 150,000,000 are the makers of this poem.
> Its rhythm is a bullet.
> Its rhyme is fire sweeping from building to building.
> 150,000,000 speak with my lips.
> This edition is printed
> with human steps
> on the paper of city squares.

The protagonist of the poem is in reality the masses, as in another work of this time, the play *Mystery-bouffe*, and in many other works by Mayakovsky. This tendency of the poet to lose himself behind the anonymity of collectivism runs alongside an equally strong tendency to place himself in the center of the universe and to have an inflated opinion of himself, as shown in "An Extraordinary Adventure," where he invites the sun to a tea as an equally important partner in the process of creativity.

SUPPORTING THE REVOLUTION

After the Revolution, Mayakovsky continued to help the regime establish itself, to contribute to the new literature in his country, and to feud with other literary groups. With the introduction of the New Economic Policy (NEP), however, which allowed a return to a modified, small-scale capitalism, Mayakovsky was among many supporters of the Revolution who felt that the ideals for which so much had been sacrificed were being betrayed. His opposition was somewhat muted; instead of attacking directly, he found a surrogate in the ever-growing bureaucracy. He also detected a resurgence of bourgeois and philistine habits, even among the party members and supporters of the regime, who, "callousing their behinds from five-year sittings,/ shiny-hard as washbasin toilets," worried more about their raises and ball attire than about society's welfare. In the poem "In Re Conferences," he lashes out at the new malaise in the Russian society—incessant conferences, actually an excuse to evade work. At the same time, in "Order No. 2 to the Army of the Arts," he exhorts artists to "give us a new form of art." When Lenin died in 1924, Mayakovsky wrote a long poem eulogizing the great leader, using this opportunity to reaffirm his loyalty to pure Communism as personified by Lenin.

ABOUT THAT

During this period, along with poetry on political themes, Mayakovsky wrote poems of an excruciatingly personal nature. The best illustration of this dichotomy in his personality, and one of the most dramatic and disturbing love poems in world literature, *About That*, reveals the poet's unhappiness in his love affair with Lili Brik. More important, however, it lays bare his "agony of isolation, a spiritual isolation," in the words of Helen Muchnic. Belaboring the nature of love, which he does on numerous occasions, the poet is forced to conclude that he is destined to suffer defeat after defeat in love, for reasons he cannot understand. He calls for help, he considers suicide, and he feels abandoned by all, even by those who are closest to

him. In retrospect, one can see in these expressions of loneliness and despair signs of what was to come several years later.

BEYOND THE SOVIET UNION

For the time being, however, Mayakovsky found enough strength to continue his various activities and skirmishes with many enemies. A fateful decision was put off during his several trips abroad in the mid-1920's. In poems resulting from these journeys, he was remarkably objective about the world outside the Soviet Union, although he never failed to mention his pride in being a Soviet citizen. In addition to predictable criticism of the evils of capitalist societies, he expressed his awe before the technical achievements of Western urban centers:

> Here
> stood Mayakovsky,
> stood
> composing verse, syllable by syllable.
> I stare
> as an Eskimo gapes at a train,
> I seize on it
> as a tick fastens to an ear.
> Brooklyn Bridge—
> yes . . .
> That's quite a thing!

It was easy for Mayakovsky to voice such unrestrained praise for the "wonders" of the modern world, for he always believed that the urban life was the only way of life worth living.

The trips abroad, however, troubled Mayakovsky more than he acknowledged. In addition to another unhappy love affair, with the beautiful young Russian émigré Tatyana Yakovleva, he was disturbed by his firsthand experience of the West. After his return, he wrote several poems affirming his loyalty to the Soviet regime in a manner suggesting that he was trying to convince himself of his orthodoxy. It is difficult to ascertain, however, whether Mayakovsky was fully aware at this time of the depth of his obsequiousness and, if he was, why he wrote that way. Several years later, in *At the Top of My Voice*, which was written only three months before his suicide, he would admit the true nature of his submission: "But I/

subdued/ myself,/ setting my heel/ on the throat/ of my own song."

FINE!

Another long poem, *Fine!*, written to celebrate the tenth anniversary of the October Revolution, shows not only Mayakovsky's compulsive optimism but also the signs that his poetic power was diminishing: "Life/ was really/ never/ so good!" he exclaims unabashedly.

> In the cottages
> —farmer lads
> Bushy-beards
> cabbages.
> Dad's rest
> by the hearth.
> All of them
> crafty.
> Plough the earth,
> make
> poetry.

Such idyllic gushing may have reflected truthfully the poet's feelings and observations in 1927, but it is remarkable that only a year or two later he would unleash in his plays a scathing criticism of the same land where "gladness gushes." It is more likely that Mayakovsky wanted to believe what he had written or, more tragically, that he was writing in compliance with an order for a certain kind of poem.

DEPRESSION AND SUICIDE

Mayakovsky's suicide in 1930 showed that everything was not all right, either in his personal life or in his country. Although the act surprised many people, even some professing to have been very close to him, keen observers had felt that Mayakovsky was riddled with morbid pessimism throughout his mature life, his loud rhetoric notwithstanding. Indeed, one could go as far back as 1913 to find, in his very first poem, words such as these: "I am so lonely as the only eye/ of a man on his way to the blind." As early as 1916, in *The Backbone Flute*, he wondered whether he should end his life with a bullet. On another occasion at about that time, in "Chelovek" ("Man"), he stated bluntly:

> The heart yearns for a bullet
> while
> the throat raves of a razor

> . . . The soul shivers;
> she's caught in ice,
> and there's no escape for her.

In a poem discussed earlier, *About That*, he debates with himself whether he should follow the example of a member of the Communist Youth League who had committed suicide. In his last completed poem, *At the Top of My Voice*, he addresses his "most respected comrades of posterity" to explain what he had wanted to achieve in poetry, not trusting contemporary literary critics and historians to tell the truth. Among the incomplete poems found in his apartment after his death, there was a quatrain that may have been intended by Mayakovsky as a suicide note:

> And, as they say, the incident is closed.
> Love's boat has smashed against the daily grind.
> Now you and I are quits. Why bother then
> to balance mutual sorrows, pains, and hurts.

The word "love" in the second line was changed to "life" by Mayakovsky in a handwritten version of this stanza.

Whatever the reasons for his suicide, Mayakovsky's death brought to an end a promising career that symbolized for a long time the birth of the new spirit in Russian literature. The eminant literary critic Roman Jakobson saw in his death the work of an entire generation that had squandered its poets. Boris Pasternak brought into focus a virtue of many Soviet writers, both well known and unsung, when he speculated that Mayakovsky "shot himself out of pride because he had condemned something in himself or around himself with which his self-respect could not be reconciled." Placing the heavy hand of officialdom on the memory of the poet who had spent half of his life fighting insensitive officials, Joseph Stalin praised him belatedly: "Mayakovsky was and remains the best and most talented poet of our Soviet epoch. Indifference to his memory and his work is a crime."

VERSIFICATION AND NEOLOGISMS

The work of this great poet will survive both his human weaknesses and the vagaries of the time and place in which he had to create. Although Mayakovsky was not the first in Russian poetry to use free verse, he wrote it with a verve unequaled before or after him. He rhymes sparingly and unconventionally. He seldom divides verses into stanzas; instead, he breaks them into units according to their inner rhythm, producing a cascading effect.

Another strong feature of Mayakovsky's verse is the abundant use of neologisms; there is an entire dictionary of expressions created by him. Mayakovsky also used slang with abandon, deeming any expression acceptable if it suited his purpose; he is credited with bringing the language of the street into Russian poetry. The sound of his verse is richly textured—indeed, his poems are better heard than read.

When this richness of style is added to his original approach to poetry and to his thought-provoking subject matter, the picture of Mayakovsky as one of the most important and exciting poets of the twentieth century is complete.

OTHER MAJOR WORKS

PLAYS: *Vladimir Mayakovsky: Tragediya*, pr. 1913 (*Vladimir Mayakovsky: A Tragedy*, 1968); *Misteriya-buff*, pr., pb. 1918, revised pr., pb. 1921 (*Mystery-bouffe*, 1933); *Chempionat vsemirnoy klassovoy borby*, pr. 1920 (*The Championship of the Universal Class*, 1973); *A chto y esli? Pervomayskiye grezy v burzhuaznom kresle*, pr. 1920; *Pyeska pro popov, koi ne pobnimayut, prazdnik chto takoye*, pr. 1921; *Kak kto provodit vremya, prazdniki prazdnuya*, pr. 1922; *Radio-Oktyabr*, pr. 1926 (with Osip Brik); *Klop*, pr., pb. 1929 (*The Bedbug*, 1931); *Banya*, pr., pb. 1930 (*The Bathhouse*, 1963); *Moskva gorit*, pr. 1930 (*Moscow Is Burning*, 1973); *The Complete Plays*, pb. 1968.

SCREENPLAYS: *Ne dlya deneg rodivshiisya*, 1918 (adaptation of Jack London's novel *Martin Eden*); *Baryyshyna i khuligan*, 1918; *Serdtse kino*, 1926; *Dekadyuvkov i Oktyabryukhov*, 1928.

NONFICTION: "Kak rabotaet respublika demokraticheskaya," 1922; *Kak delat' stikhi?*, 1926 (*How Are Verses Made?*, 1970).

BIBLIOGRAPHY

Aizlewood, Robin. *Two Essays on Maiakovskii's Verse*. London: University College London Press, 2000. Two short studies of selected poetic works by Mayakovsky.

Brown, Edward J. *Mayakovsky: A Poet in the Revolution*. Princeton, N.J.: Princeton University Press, 1973. Discussion of Mayakovsky in his times and in relationship to the artists, poets, critics, and revolutionaries of the day, including Vladimir Ilich Lenin and Joseph Stalin. Shows how Mayakovsky's work was shaped by events of his life and discusses his relationship to the Soviet state and Communist Party.

Cavanaugh, Clare. "Whitman, Mayakovsky, and the Body Politic." In *Rereading Russian Poetry*, edited by Stephanie Sandler. New Haven, Conn.: Yale University Press, 1999. Discusses the influence of the American poet Walt Whitman on Mayakovsky, and the ways in which Mayakovsky sought to overcome this influence or to displace Whitman as a poet of the people and of self-celebration. This fresh, postmodern perspective emphasizes the body and sexuality in the work of Mayakovsky, in terms both literal and symbolic.

Russell, Robert. "Mayakovsky's *The Bedbug* and *The Bathhouse*." In *Russian Drama of the Revolutionary Period*. Totowa, N.J.: Barnes and Noble, 1988. This chapter discusses the plays *The Bedbug* and *The Bathhouse* as satiric pictures of Soviet life but also explores the way they illustrate Mayakovsky's characteristic obsession with the future, especially in terms of utopian images. Sees the plays as an important contribution to world drama.

Stapanian, Juliette R. *Mayakovsky's Cubo-Futurist Vision*. Houston, Tex.: Rice University, 1986. Examines Mayakovsky from the perspective of the artistic movements of cubism and futurism. Places Mayakovsky not simply within the social and political revolutionary movements of his day but also within the aesthetics of literary and artistic modernism.

Woroszylski, Wiktor. *The Life of Mayakovsky*. New York: Orion Press, 1970. Life of Mayakovsky as told through a variety of records, testimonies, and recollections, which are then arranged in accordance with the author's understanding of their place in Mayakovsky's life. Recollections include that of Boris Pasternak, Ilya Ehrenberg, Lily Brik, and Ivan Bunin. Copious illustrations. Also includes passages from Mayakovsky's poetry.

Vasa D. Mihailovich;
bibliography updated by Margaret Boe Birns

PETER MEINKE

Born: Brooklyn, New York; December 29, 1932

PRINCIPAL POETRY
  Lines from Neuchatel, 1974
  The Night Train and the Golden Bird, 1977
  The Rat Poems, 1978
  Trying to Surprise God, 1981
  Underneath the Lantern, 1986
  Night Watch on the Chesapeake, 1987
  Far from Home, 1988
  Liquid Paper: New and Selected Poems, 1991
  Scars, 1996
  Campocorto, 1996
  Zinc Fingers, 2000

OTHER LITERARY FORMS

Known primarily as a poet, Peter Meinke has also published a collection of short stories titled *The Piano Tuner* (1986), which won the Flannery O'Connor Award. Two volumes of children's verse, *The Legend of Larry the Lizard* (1968) and *Very Seldom Animals* (1970), were his earliest published poetry collections. A critical study, *Howard Nemerov*, appeared in 1968. Meinke also published a handbook for reading and writing poems, *The Shape of Poetry: A Practical Guide to Writing Poetry*, in 1999.

ACHIEVEMENTS

Peter Meinke has earned a reputation as one of the United States' foremost poets of the late twentieth century. Since the appearance of his first full collection in 1977, Meinke has skillfully balanced a variety of approaches, from free verse to traditional patterns—sonnets, sestinas, and villanelles as well as more arcane Continental forms. Meinke's poems have been praised for their clarity and accessibility; by turns witty, darkly absorbing, wry, and philosophical, they resonate with readers often perplexed or browbeaten by contemporary American poetry. As Judith Hemschemeyer says, "Meinke is a skilled craftsman. He is especially adept at building to a strong ending or the ending that shies the poem into an unexpected, but perfect place."

His many awards include the Olivet Prize, the Paumanok Award, three prizes from the Poetry Society of America, two National Endowment for the Arts Fellowships in Poetry, and the Provincetown Workshop Master Artist's Fellowship. He won the Sow's Ear Chapbook Competition for *Campocorto* and the 2001 SEBA Book Award from the Southeast Booksellers' Association for his collection *Zinc Fingers*.

BIOGRAPHY

Born in Brooklyn, New York, the son of a salesman, Peter Meinke attended Hamilton College in Clinton, New York, earning his B.A. in 1955. After serving in the U.S. Army from 1955 to 1957, he attended the University of Michigan, earning his M.A. in 1961, and the University of Minnesota, receiving his Ph.D. in literature in 1965. He taught English at a New Jersey high school and at Hamline University in St. Paul, Minnesota, before beginning a long tenure at Presbyterian College (now Eckerd College) in St. Petersburg, Florida, where he directed the writing workshop until his retirement in 1993. After that time, he has been writer-in-residence at the University of Hawaii; at Austin Peay State University in Clarksville, Tennessee; and at the University of North Carolina at Greensboro. He has also served as Thurber journalist-in-residence at the James Thurber House in Columbus, Ohio.

ANALYSIS

One quality that critics and reviewers have often praised in Peter Meinke's poetry is its wisdom. Edward Field applauds the "literary sanity" of Meinke's voice, the poems spoken by "a lovable, beleaguered man trying to make sense of a difficult world." For all the self-deprecating humor and technical flair, there is "a little of the Ancient Mariner in the tenacity and urgency with which Peter Meinke addresses his readers," according to Ted Kooser. Meinke's poems "get hold of us by the coat lapels and when they release us we are delighted, shaken, and considerably wiser." He writes, says Alicia Ostriker, "beneath a banner of wisdom."

LINES FROM NEUCHATEL

While many, if not most, writers use foreign travel to reinvigorate their work or to force themselves out of habitual perspectives, Meinke seems to have begun his career by such means. The poems in his chapbook *Lines from Neuchatel* focus on Swiss landscapes and the displacements in sensibility and language that come with being in a country not one's own. The speaker in most of the poems—presumably Meinke himself—is often self-conscious about his literary vocation and his nationality. In "Café du Pont" he is shamed by a cleaning woman's comment, "La vie est difficile, monsieur" (life is difficult, sir) as she mops the floor around his desk while he sits "feeling stupid staring at my typewriter." Later in the same poem he catches a glimpse of himself as perhaps just one more "ugly American" in Europe (albeit on a writing fellowship) when Michel, whose wife has left him for a U.S. military man, observes that Americans always seem to have plenty of money. The speaker responds, "I try to look poor./ We *are* poor./ So why don't I work, *eh m'sieu*?"

Elsewhere in *Lines from Neuchatel*, Meinke senses the estrangement from life that art can often inadvertently encourage. He puzzles, for example, over historical coincidences such as eating a gourmet meal in the room where the doomed journalist Jean-Paul Marat was born, and considers how in their Alpine hotel he and his family can enjoy the scenery, almost forgetting "the brooding darkness of America,/ of all countries, the violence/ of which we formed a part." These early free-verse poems, often unconventionally or inconsistently punctuated, tend toward surrealism; snatches of nursery rhyme and childlike sound effects ("ouah ouah ouah" and "boomboomboom") mix effectively with Dadaist images: "where Freud forever sucks Napoleon's fingers" and "the albino dwarf chewing on chicken bones."

THE NIGHT TRAIN AND THE GOLDEN BIRD

This surrealist tendency continues in somewhat muted form in Meinke's first full-length collection, *The Night Train and the Golden Bird*, a title that itself indicates the poet's interest in the subconscious and the often dreamlike qualities of poetic meaning. In "The Poet to His Tongue" the protagonist—in this case decidedly not Meinke himself—remembers how from his cancerous tongue "words burned like houses" and "a sentence filled a room with dead birds." He decides to keep the tongue in a bottle of Jim Beam on his desk and comes to believe he can hear a music coming from it, "a

strain/ unnatural and familiar" that he finally admits might be merely drifting over from the beer joint across the street.

This juxtaposition of the strange with the commonplace continues through the volume. "Chicken Unlimited" recounts the ambitions of a fast-food carton; "The Monkey's Paw" borrows the O. Henry short-story title to imagine reunions between battlefield dead and their loved ones. A love poem, "Surfaces," concludes with lines reminiscent of the Zen poems of the 1960's:

> This is how I feel about you:
> suppose
> on the surface of a rippling pool
> the moon shone clearly reflected
> like a yellow rose
> then
> if a cloud floated over it
> > I would hate the sky.

Even in this volume there are signs of Meinke's growing interest in more traditional poetic forms. He arranges the poem "Because" in three stanzas of seven lines each, repeating the sentence pattern in each stanza as well. A hint of end rhyme appears early in the poem with such words as "lovely" and "tendency" and in the assonance of "possessed" and "breath." Meinke concludes the poem with an exact rhyme—"pain" with "stain"—that acoustically sums up the poem's argument about the false temptations death extends to the suffering, downtrodden, and vulnerable. "Elegy for a Diver" is the earliest example of strict form in Meinke's work, using rime-royal stanzas in part 1 and rhymed tetrameter couplets in part 2. The prosody matches the late diver's athletic precision, the opening line ("Jackknife swandive gainer twist") reappearing in its entirety in subsequent stanzas.

TRYING TO SURPRISE GOD AND
UNDERNEATH THE LANTERN

The poems in *Trying to Surprise God* and *Underneath the Lantern* reveal Meinke gradually becoming more interested in the way poems can be formally shaped to express the most deeply felt experiences. "Robert Frost in Warsaw" finds Meinke pondering how "the human heart can neither forfeit/ nor accept responsibilities." He identifies here with his American predecessor, whose poems seem to "proclaim ambiguous affirmation/ in the dark." Meinke's own work in this period follows the earlier poet in at least two ways. Both a psychic darkness and a stricter attention to form characterize Meinke's poems here. At times the despair is cultural, as in "Supermarket" or "Sonnet on the Death of the Man Who Invented Plastic Roses," both poems gamely battling late twentieth century consumerist ennui with a dose of whimsy. In other poems, such as "The Death of the Pilot Whales" or "Mendel's Laws," Meinke probes for the connections between humanity and nature, between the workings of the cosmos and those of the heart.

Though favoring the sonnet at this point in his career, Meinke proves himself unpredictable and wry as ever in "Myrtle the Turtle" (a prose poem delivered in a pitch-perfect Brooklyn accent) and in "Advice to My Son," which has become perhaps his most anthologized poem. "The trick is, to live your days/ as if each one may be your last," he announces, and he continues to advise in loosely measured but closely rhymed lines ending with a set of admonitions that blend urgency and resignation, sincerity and a knowing irony:

> speak truth to one man,
> work with another;
> and always serve bread with your wine.

> But, son,
> always serve wine.

From such fatherly counsel Meinke turns to family lore, drawing portraits of uncles and aunts from his childhood in Flatbush. In various ways these figures reveal a stubborn streak or a cracked take on life that the poet still admires. In "Aunt Mary" he recalls their singing voices carrying out the window and onto the street, where passersby would slow and pause for moment, recognizing in those voices a "knowledge untranslatable and true," the note Meinke often strikes in his poems. In "Aunt Gertrud" the title character "read travel books so hard/ she felt she actually had gone," a lesson in the imagination's tenacity. (A similar lesson could be found in her charmingly mangled English: "*Vell, you're vunce only young, ain't it?*") Perhaps every family has its feckless Uncle Jim: "on the train to Reno to get divorced/ so

he could marry again/ he met another woman and woke up in California."

NIGHT WATCH ON THE CHESAPEAKE AND LIQUID PAPER

Nostalgic without being saccharine (having sentiment but not sentimentality, as Frost once put it), the poems looking back on his Brooklyn childhood are offered as Meinke's testament to memory's house, that "ideal realm" rebuilt in language. His poems after that have continued their dark ruminations on human behavior and their explorations or adaptations of formal structures. The pseudo-sonnet "Rage" (from *Night Watch on the Chesapeake*) likens the chill of winter to the bitterness of personal disappointment, the emotion proving more lasting and "more/ murderous than this weather." His "Atomic Pantoum" employs the interlocking stanzas of this French traditional form to describe the terrible chain reaction when the "plutonium trigger" is pulled. Yet even as he contemplates the physical and emotional changes of late middle age ("Fifty on Fifty," "Growing Deaf") Meinke can startle with sudden humor. "Progress" shows the poet still chipper in the "New Poems" section of *Liquid Paper:*

> Down a new road
> at last we come.
> Our code: *Libido*
> *ergo sum.*

In the poignant title piece of Meinke's 1991 volume of new and selected poems, *Liquid Paper*, he writes: "If I were God/ I'd authorize Celestial Liquid Paper/ every seven years to whiten our mistakes." As if partially making good on this claim, in his two subsequent collections Meinke eliminates periods and commas from his poems. To some readers this will appear as mere affectation, a tic or experiment from a poet in the waning years of his career. Others may applaud the technique, finding a greater immediacy of expression. The general effect, in any case, is an increased attention on the reader's part to the relationships between words and phrases that are no longer easily parsed by conventional punctuation. Are the resulting gaps versions of the "Scars" alluded to in one title, or are they open spaces to be filled more creatively?

SCARS AND ZINC FINGERS

Whatever the reasons behind this move, the poems otherwise maintain an adherence to formal patterns. Rhymed quatrains, tercets, and couplets are in ample supply in both *Scars* and *Zinc Fingers*. The sestina and the villanelle make appearances, as does "concrete poetry," whose shape on the page bears some analogy to the subject of the poem ("A Hot Day in June"). Meinke arranges both *Scars* and *Zinc Fingers* in interesting ways. In the former, the section titled "Scars" dwells on family rifts ("Ice") or draws character studies in pathos if not outright tragedy ("Noreen"). The section that follows, "Stitches," is devoted to love poems and to moments of grace or renewal. The latter volume brings together alphabetically by title nearly seventy poems, creating some serendipitous combinations or juxtapositions: a poem called "Coal" alongside one titled "Coffee"; "Kissing" next to "Letting Go"; poems about barroom philosophers, pickpockets, poets, and professors, which form a richly ironic sequence. Meinke's command of form and his ready wit have obviously extended beyond the requirements of a particular poem and into the construction of a volume as a whole.

OTHER MAJOR WORKS

SHORT FICTION: *The Piano Tuner*, 1986.

NONFICTION: *Howard Nemerov*, 1968; *The Shape of Poetry: A Practical Guide to Writing Poetry*, 1999.

CHILDREN'S LITERATURE: *The Legend of Larry the Lizard*, 1968; *Very Seldom Animals*, 1970.

BIBLIOGRAPHY

Byrd, Gregory. "Aesthetics at the Southernmost Point: Towards a Definition of Florida Poetry." *The Mississippi Quarterly* 52, no. 2 (Spring, 1999): 287-298. Although Meinke is a transplant to Florida, not a native, Byrd says it is "just as accurate to call him a Florida poet as it is a Southern poet or a New England poet." Meinke is hard to pigeonhole regionally, as his writing reveals influences of the North and the South.

Meinke, Peter. "Essay on 'Zinc Fingers.'" *The Literary Review* 44, no. 1 (Fall, 2000): 507-509. This is an account of the origin of the title poem from Meinke's collection. It involves a clear discussion of the process through several drafts, including such matters as syllabics, rhyme, and other devices of sound in the poem.

_____. "An Interview with Peter Meinke." Interview by James Plath. *Clockwatch Review* 7 (1990/1991). Explores the relationship between fiction and poetry. Meinke's own writing habits in each genre are discussed at length. Good remarks on specific short stories.

_____. *The Shape of Poetry: A Practical Guide to Writing and Reading Poetry*. Boston: Writer, 1999. A useful overview of Meinke's ideas and attitudes toward poetic form and its relationship to subject and meaning. Much of the book is culled from columns the poet wrote for *The Writer* in the 1990's, including "What Makes Good Poetry?" and "Poems and Meaning."

Solomon, Andy. "Meinke Sheds Light Through Small Windows." *St. Petersburg Times*, August 27, 2000. Considers Meinke's "billowing national reputation" in light of the poet's use of local subject matter. Solomon finds Meinke's greatest strength in his ability to "forge that lightning connection" between ordinary things and the universal truths of human existence. ·

James Scruton

HERMAN MELVILLE

Born: New York, New York; August 1, 1819
Died: New York, New York; September 28, 1891

PRINCIPAL POETRY

Battle-Pieces and Aspects of the War, 1866
Clarel: A Poem and Pilgrimage in the Holy Land, 1876
John Marr and Other Sailors, 1888
Timoleon, 1891
The Works of Herman Melville, 1922-1924 (volumes 15 and 16).

OTHER LITERARY FORMS

Herman Melville is best known for his novels, which include *Moby Dick: Or, The Whale* (1851), *The Confidence Man: His Masquerade* (1857), and *Billy Budd, Foretopman* (1924). During his lifetime he also published a collection of short stories and sketches titled *The Piazza Tales* (1856), as well as ten other short stories in various popular magazines. In addition to his novels and short stories, Melville contributed numerous essays, poems, and reviews to literary journals; the most famous of these is surely his review of Nathaniel Hawthorne's *Mosses from an Old Manse* (1846), published as "Hawthorne and His Mosses." In this review Melville indicates that his reading of Hawthorne altered the course of his literary growth. Since his death, several of Melville's journals, kept during such journeys as those to England and Israel, have appeared in print, as has *The Letters of Herman Melville* (1960, Merrill R. Davis and William H. Gilman, editors).

ACHIEVEMENTS

During his lifetime, Herman Melville's public literary achievements were lamentably few. It is only in the last several decades of the twentieth century that his work received just recognition as the product, in the words of Howard P. Vincent (the principal editor of Melville's poems), of America's "most powerful literary genius." Few readers of Melville's novels are aware that he is also a poet of no little talent. In modern times critics generally acknowledge Melville and Walt Whitman as the two best poets of the Civil War. Besides his 1866 *Battle-Pieces and Aspects of the War*, however, Melville, like Whitman, wrote many other poems. In his edition of Melville's poems, Robert Penn Warren states that he agrees with Randall Jarrell's judgment that Melville, Emily Dickinson, and Whitman are the best poets of nineteenth century America. Increased interest in Melville's poetry seems to confirm this judgment.

BIOGRAPHY

Herman Melville was born in New York City on August 1, 1819, into a family of some affluence. His father, Allan Melville, was a prosperous importer, and his mother, Maria Gansevoort, was of the wealthy and distinguished Albany Gansevoorts. When Herman was

eleven, however, his father's business failed and the family entered a period of irreversible decline; Allan Melville died two years later, hopelessly mad. Several of Melville's biographers maintain that the younger Melville carried the stigma of his father's predicament with him the rest of his life, always fearing that either failure or inherited madness would overtake him. Certainly he failed many times to appeal as a writer to a popular audience, and his wife at one time contemplated leaving him because of his alleged insanity. Now, long after his death, Melville has achieved an appreciative audience, and his "insanity" may well be judged the by-product of restive genius.

Following his father's death, Melville worked at numerous odd jobs, such as bank clerk, teacher, and, of course, ordinary seaman. His first tenure at sea occurred in 1839 when he shipped aboard the *St. Lawrence*, a merchant ship sailing between New York and Liverpool. Two years later he embarked upon his South Sea island adventures, joining the crew of the *Acushnet*, a whaling vessel bound for the South Seas out of the harbor of New Bedford, Massachusetts. He returned home in 1844 and began writing about these adventures, producing the immensely successful *Typee: A Peep at Polynesian Life*, his first novel, in 1846. Shortly thereafter he married Elizabeth Shaw, published his second, slightly less successful novel, *Omoo: A Narrative of Adventure in the South Seas* (1847), and settled down in New York into a life of relatively pleasant domesticity.

Following these early successes, Melville soon discovered that both his reputation and his financial rewards as an author were falling rapidly. Critics found *Mardi, and a Voyage Thither* (1849) inscrutable, *Redburn: His First Voyage* (1849) and *White-Jacket Or, The World in a Man-of-War* (1850) promising improvements, but *Moby Dick* and *Pierre Or, The Ambiguities* (1852) immoral books. Nevertheless, along with Richard Henry Dana's *Two Years Before the Mast* (1840), *White-Jacket* did much to influence making American maritime laws more humane; the cruel practice of flogging, for example, became outlawed by an act of Congress. With the failures of *Moby Dick* and *Pierre*, Melville began to consider poetry. He had tried his hand at writing verse at least as early as *Mardi*, which contains twenty-two poems, and again in *Moby Dick* with two more. After trying three more works of prose, *Israel Potter: His Fifty Years of Exile* (1855), *The Piazza Tales* (which enjoyed a measure of success), and *The Confidence Man: His Masquerade* (a dismal failure), Melville seems to have turned all his literary talent to the writing of poetry.

For the remainder of his career, from 1857 until about 1886, when he appears to have begun work on *Billy Budd, Foretopman*, his last novel, Melville wrote only poetry. According to Sidney Kaplan, one of the contemporary editors of *Battle-Pieces and Aspects of the War*, Melville began to chronicle systematically the events of the war in poetry, to become *the* poet of the Civil War. For this purpose he made a deliberate study of prosody and poetic theory. Like his last several novels, *Battle-Pieces and Aspects of the War* was a failure at the bookstores. Melville, who had by this time received an appointment as a district inspector of customs for the New York harbor, remained undaunted (though not uninjured) by an unappreciative public, and began work,

probably in 1867, on his longest poetic work, *Clarel: A Poem and Pilgrimage in the Holy Land*. This poem, running to more than eighteen thousand lines and largely based on Melville's own pilgrimage to Israel in 1856-1857, was printed privately with the financial assistance of his uncle, Peter Gansevoort. The other two volumes of his poetry, *John Marr and Other Sailors* and *Timoleon*, were also privately printed in limited editions of twenty-five copies, which were probably distributed only to interested family and friends. The novel *Billy Budd, Foretopman* remained in manuscript at Melville's death in 1891 and did not appear in print until 1924.

The notices of Melville's death were condescending at best and some were unabashedly disrespectful, expressing surprise and consternation at learning that he had not already died some years before. It was not until the appearance of Raymond Weaver's biography, *Herman Melville: Mariner and Mystic* (1921), that Melville was rediscovered. Since that time, his reputation has consistently and deservedly improved, and he is recognized by all serious readers of literature as one of America's greatest prose writers and poets.

ANALYSIS

As he does in his novels, Herman Melville, in his poems, pursues his personal struggle to discover some degree of certainty in a world in which such a task was becoming increasingly difficult. For the Deists of the eighteenth century, God had receded to the role of watchmaker who, after the machine-like world was constructed, left it to run its course. In the nineteenth century, with the impact of historical criticism of the Bible and of Charles Darwin's theory of evolution, God seemed to have disappeared altogether. Such awareness, however, was confined to the most perceptive thinkers; the masses of people put off such challenges for a later day. Melville was one of those thinkers who refused to put off an intellectual or spiritual challenge which came his way. He was for his time a seer, a prophet. It is probably for this reason that Melville, while speaking with an ever clearer voice today, found himself

Herman Melville (Library of Congress)

misunderstood and finally unheard in his own time. Melville's personal struggle has become that of our time.

Melville sought to reconcile the antinomies of existence. Since the advent of the Christian era, the most serious of these contraries, life and death, could easily be reconciled by the promise of eternal happiness—for the faithful, that is, although one of eternal torture and hell-fire for unbelievers. By Melville's time, the promise of an afterlife had become less certain, and, to some, improbable and even naïve. This is the kind of conflict which preoccupied Melville, and which he confronted with courage and commitment.

BATTLE-PIECES AND ASPECTS OF THE WAR

Melville's first book of poems, *Battle-Pieces and Aspects of the War*, was harshly criticized for its unconventional metrics. One reviewer, writing for *The Round Table* on September 15, 1866, asserted that the poet displayed a "disregard of the laws of verse" and that he "ha[d] but little sense of melody, and almost no sense of proportion." Educated readers of the mid-nineteenth century still expected both to see and to hear regular patterns of rhyme and rhythm—not the irregular, experimental patterns of Whitman, Dickinson, and Melville. As in the better poetry of Whitman and Dickinson, however, irregularities of rhythm and rhyme, when they occur in Melville's better poems, do indeed "seem an echo to the sense" (from Alexander Pope's *An Essay on Criticism*, 1711). Perhaps what is true of Melville's ideas is true of his sound patterns; just as twentieth century minds are required to grasp Melville's penetrating analysis of human estrangement from time-honored but time-worn ideas of God, so modern ears are necessary to connect sound with sense in his poetry.

"MISGIVINGS"

The second poem of *Battle-Pieces and Aspects of the War*, "Misgivings," embodies most of Melville's major themes, as well as displays his formal innovations. The poem, fourteen lines long, suggests the sonnet form; but it exhibits several radical departures from traditional sonnet structure. Instead of fourteen lines of fairly regular iambic pentameter, Melville has two seven-line stanzas. The first five lines of the first stanza are in iambic tetrameter with only one anapest to vary the pattern; line six adopts the familiar iambic pentameter of the sonnet.

The final line of the first stanza, however, contains two anapests and two amphimacers, so six lines of the first stanza retain a four-stress rhythm. The second stanza is another matter. Only the first three lines are iambic tetrameter, with a trochee, two spondees, and an anapest for variation. The fourth line is composed in iambic trimeter with a spondee, but the next two lines expand swiftly, by use of monosyllabic and disyllabic words, into perfectly regular iambic pentameters, leading to the slower concluding alexandrine (iambic hexameter), which contains three anapests. The rhyme scheme is *ababacc* for each stanza, except for the fifth line of stanza two, which does not rhyme with any other line in the poem.

Although Melville's formal innovations struck many of his readers as disagreeable, unpoetic, even clumsy, they are strictly functional. The sound pattern in "Misgivings" complements, with consummate artistry, the poem's meaning. The poem opens as "ocean-clouds" are observed sweeping over "inland hills" during "late autumn brown"; these clouds of huge expanse bring with them destructive storms which fill "the sodden valley" with "horror." The pathetic fallacy developed in the first three lines, that an inanimate valley may be filled with terror, prepares the reader for the fourth line's arresting observation, as well as for its abstract significance. The destructive storm, which comes in dreary autumn, is to be followed by the frozen, paralyzing (even deadly) winter, striking terror in the hearts of the valley's inhabitants, even causing "the spire" to fall "crashing in the town."

That very concrete image, a crashing spire, may first suggest the destruction of a church or of religion. The spire crashes in a town, however, suggesting a further association of the spire with societal order. The poet seems to suggest, then, that the very fabric of his country's civilization is vulnerable to the destructiveness of this storm. The splitting of the Union in 1860 seemed to promise just such destruction. The poet next laments that such promised devastation may be explained metaphorically as "The tempest bursting from the waste of Time/ On the world's fairest hope linked with man's foulest crime."

This couplet echoes Melville's reading of at least two of William Shakespeare's plays, *Macbeth* (1606) and

The Tempest (1611). The action of *The Tempest* comes bursting on the stage as the play opens with a storm of its own, the result of a waste of Time. Prospero, denied his rightful dukedom of Milan for twelve years, has eked out a meager existence on a remote Mediterranean island far from Milan; seizing the opportunity that fate has suddenly provided him, he manages to reassemble the offending parties by having his servant Ariel create the illusion of a storm; he finally attains the justice denied him during these twelve years, this great waste of Time. The second line of the couplet recalls the "fair is foul and foul is fair" motif in *Macbeth*. That which seems fair, Macbeth's hospitality toward King Duncan, is in fact most foul, for Macbeth plots and carries out Duncan's murder. In Melville's poem, "the world's fairest hope," the United States, the modern world's first experiment in democracy, has actively legitimized, from its birth, "man's foulest crime," slavery. For the eighty-four years since Independence, Americans have squandered time by committing a crime they have declared, in principle at least, to be barbarous and unspeakably cruel. The land of the free has enforced and even legislated slavery, freedom's exact opposite.

The metrical architecture of this crucial "Time-crime" couplet is astonishing. The first five lines establish the mood and set the scene for disaster. Religion, civilization, and even nature herself, as in *Macbeth* and *The Tempest*, all seem to herald the speed of doom. The swift pace of these five lines is slowed, however, first by the increase of an extra foot in the "Time" line and then by a much more complicated process in the final line of the stanza. Such a slowing is indeed appropriate, for the poet has commented that this scene moves him to "muse upon my country's ills." Although the sixth line contains five feet and the seventh only four, the last line is lengthened by two anapests which introduce two amphimacers, in each of which the first and last syllables receive primary stress: "fairest hope" and "foulest crime." So the four-foot line actually contains six primary stresses, creating an effect of gravity. Indeed, the poems' subject is most grave. Finally, the precision of "Time-crime" need only be stated, for surely slavery has been Time's crime.

The poem's suggestion that Nature herself also participates in this crime is now stated in the first line of the next stanza: "Nature's dark side is heeded now." Recognizing Melville's dependence on Calvinism's claim that all men are innately depraved ("In Adam's fall/ We sinned all"), one is led to conclude that the "Nature" that Melville names here is that of man's essential depravity, although Melville did not restrict himself to metaphors drawn from Christianity. He drew on other religious traditions as well, particularly on Zoroastrianism, a Near Eastern faith which posits the existence of a good god of light, Ahura Mazda, and one of evil darkness, Ahriman (Angra Mainyu), who struggle for the souls of men. Melville introduced Zoroastrianism into his works when in *Moby Dick* he made Ahab's mysterious servant Fedallah a Parsee, a current term for an adherent of Zoroastrianism. The line "Nature's dark side is heeded now" may just as likely suggest the cosmic struggle between the gods of light and darkness in which the god of darkness now has the upper hand. Certainly the participation of nature in the storm indicates that the struggle here is one of cosmic or exterior proportions and not merely one of interior conscience.

In the following line Melville observes parenthetically "(Ah! optimist—cheer disheartened flown)." In *The Mystery of Iniquity: Melville as Poet, 1857-1891* (1972), William H. Shurr calls this line "an unequivocal statement of Melville's . . . antitranscendentalist polemic." Certainly in a world which heeds "Nature's dark side," there can be little room for transcendental optimism, and the spondee which opens the line would seem to place emphasis on that optimism. The line concludes, however, with the phrase "disheartened flown." The next two lines, made up of monosyllabics and disyllabics, now move swiftly toward the conclusion. The first of these two lines maintains the tetrameter rhythm of the stanza's initial two lines; the next, or fourth, line, however, has four primary stresses but only three feet.

This tetrameter line followed by a trimeter seems to mock first the adults in the town and then those of the country for not having foreseen the inevitable doom of death and destruction: "A child may read the moody brow/ Of yon black mountain lone." The image of a "black mountain" could refer, as some have suggested, to the black race preparing both to liberate themselves and to be liberated. Considering Melville's use of Zoroastrianism, however, the phrase seems to duplicate the terrible evil suggested in the first line of the stanza by the spondaic phrase, "dark side." Something else a bit more subtle is happening here, however, and this subtlety shows Melville at his best as a sound-technician.

The diphthong in "mountain" and the voiced vowel in "lone" set up a pattern which carries over into the following, regularly pentameter line: "With shouts the torrents down the gorges go." While the diphthong of "mountain" appears again in "shouts" and "down," the voiced vowel of "lone" recurs in "torrents," "gorges," and finally in the nonrhyming verb "go." This line is the only one of the poem which does not rhyme; it is lengthened by a foot; and it assonates with the preceding line. All these factors bring emphasis to bear on this line. The next line gives a clue why: "And storms are formed behind the storm we feel." Note the continued assonance of the voiced vowel in "lone" now appearing in "storms," "formed," and "storm." Melville also skillfully retains the liquid *r* in five of these "lone" assonating syllables: "torrents," "gorges," "storms," "formed," and "storm."

Recalling the sweeping storm which opens the poem, the emphasis called for here is very artfully accomplished and should now become apparent. The "storm" is not merely a metaphor from Nature which "we feel"; it has now become an actual storm stirred by men. The storm's metaphorical torrents are, in fact, the shouts of real men, and the poem moves to this apocalyptic conclusion: "The hemlock shakes in the rafter, the oak in the driving keel."

Now since the poison of the hemlock has finally done its work on the rafters of the human soul, the very oak or strength of the steering body, the ship of state, trembles at the horror of the storm. As was suggested in the image of the town's crashing spire, the very fabric of civilization shakes at the discovery of its own evil. This sonnet, then, draws a picture which is perfectly consistent with Melville's worldview in his novels and in many other poems. Melville feels the responsibility to admonish the world of its threatened doom. When our world of "seem" is the exact opposite of the way we perceive it, then our continued existence is indeed imperiled.

"Shiloh, a Requiem"

"Shiloh, a Requiem" relates some of the results of the country's disgorging. The poem is a lament for the shocking loss of life (and "the waste of Time") which

one of the bloodiest conflicts of the Civil War has brought on the country. The poem opens on a cloudy day following the battle of April 6 and 7, 1862. The bursts of cannon and tortured shouts are completely absent now as "Skimming lightly, wheeling still,/ The swallows fly low/ Over the field." As in "Misgivings," Melville is here an artist of sound; for the light skimming and wheeling of the birds echo the passage of bullets through the unresisting air. "Skimming lightly, wheeling *still*," Melville had said; the echoes of the bullets continue to remain haunting visitors to this battlefield which is a national monument. Ironically the poet notes that the men who died here were "Foemen at morn, but friends at eve," and he continues with this succinct observation: "What like a bullet can undeceive!" Such a warning speaks to any culture of any time.

Clarel

Clarel, his long narrative of a spiritual journey, has no images as immediate as those of *Battle-Pieces and Aspects of the War*'s sweeping storms and dying foemen; rather, in the ten years separating the two works Melville has become more philosophical and contemplative. This tone certainly prevails in *Clarel*'s "Epilogue," as the poem's opening lines indicate. The poet asks in a brief question of sweeping scope: "If Luther's day expand to Darwin's year,/ Shall that exclude the hope—foreclose the fear?" Expressing some measure of impatience with the debate suggested by such a question, the poet asserts: "The running battle of the star and clod/ Shall run forever—if there be no God." Finally he advises Clarel to "keep thy heart yet but ill resigned/ . . . thy heart, the issues there but mind."

In the final analysis, Melville seems to be saying, the heart offers the greatest certainty in an uncertain world; indeed, even "Science the feud can only aggravate." If one relies on the heart, however, "Emerge thou mayst from the last whelming sea,/ And prove that death but routs life into victory." These are noble lines. Robert Penn Warren labels them an affirmation. One must note carefully, however, that the statement is conditional: "Emerge thou *mayst*." Melville is still unwilling to subscribe to any dogma, whether religious or scientific (whether of Luther or of Darwin), but he can find solace in his knowledge of the human heart and in the power of human feeling. As for the certainty for which Clarel has made his pilgrimage, the poet's position appears to be finally that of an optimistic agnostic. In other words, Melville seems not to have excluded the hope (to paraphrase from the opening couplet) for some sort of benevolent release from pain and realization of a glorious afterlife, but, at the same time, neither has he embraced such a hope as an absolute certainty.

"THE AEOLIAN HARP"

A later poem from *John Marr and Other Sailors* recaptures some of the skepticism of *Clarel*, as well as the pessimism of *Battle-Pieces and Aspects of the War*. "The Aeolian Harp" relates how the haunting tones of a wind harp cause the poet to conjure up "A picture stamped in memory's mint" of a dismasted, waterlogged wreck which floats aimlessly about but which consequently drifts "Torpid in dumb ambuscade" as a constant threat to the destruction of another unprepared vessel. What is of particular interest here is not the symbolism of Melville's indifferent and unfeeling demon of disaster (another Moby Dick?) but the poet's allusion once again to Shakespeare's *The Tempest*. He compares the vision evoked by the wind harp's "wailing" with the sort of illusions Ariel creates in the play. The wind harp's illusion is ". . . less a strain ideal/ Than Ariel's rendering of the Real." This reference to Ariel is particularly apropos in this poem, for the storm that Shakespeare's Ariel brews forces Ferdinand, Alonso, Gonzalo, Antonio, and others to Prospero's island domain and is replete with terrifying corposants, thunderclaps, and trembling waves. So convincing is Ariel's play that these Neapolitans abandon ship and swim to Prospero's island for safety. The illusion recalled in Melville's poem promises no safety for the hapless victims of this ship, which crashes heedlessly into any unfortunate enough to cross its treacherous course.

Finally, the poet concludes: "Well the harp of Ariel wails/ Thoughts that tongue can tell no word of!" So horrible is this "picture stamped in memory's mint" that the relating of it requires the impetus of the haunting wind harp, now become wholly Ariel's harp. Thus Melville reveals the power of the poet's imagination. Perhaps because his century viewed man's relationship to God and the world in harsher terms, he demanded a poetic world more austere and even more forbidding than the world of Shakespeare's *The Tempest*.

HOPE, HUMOR, AND ART

Melville is not, however, always so severe. The later poems of *Battle-Pieces and Aspects of the War*, for example, are enthusiastically patriotic and finally positive. The poem "Malvern Hill," celebrating the victory of Union forces at Malvern Hill in Virginia on July 1, 1862, concludes with these hopeful lines: "Wag the world how it will,/ Leaves must be green in Spring." His poem "Falstaff's Lament over Prince Hal Become Henry V" is a delightfully humorous portrait of Shakespeare's rejected father-figure, Sir John Falstaff. The discarded old man drowns his sorrow in sack or wine: "Come drawer [tapster], more sack here!" The comic old gentleman shrewdly observes, however, that "now intuitions/ Shall wither to codes." Prince Hal, now become King Henry V, tosses aside the virtues of spontaneity for the rules and responsibilities of a crown.

Melville's predicament as a poet is something like that of the English prince; having come to be a full-fledged poet in his middle age, surely he came to the genre carrying few illusions about the vicissitudes of a world where Darwinism and critical analysis of traditional Christianity challenged established faith. Melville's poetry is inevitably sobering and grave, yet his quest for some degree of certainty, to reconcile a world of opposites, led him to write poetry which is vibrant, sensitive, and sonorous. In one of his last poems, "Art," Melville emphatically declares that, in the poet's poem, opposites "must mate,/ And fuse with Jacob's mystic heart/ To wrestle with the angel—Art."

OTHER MAJOR WORKS

LONG FICTION: *Typee: A Peep at Polynesian Life*, 1846; *Omoo: A Narrative of Adventure in the South Seas*, 1847; *Mardi, and a Voyage Thither*, 1849; *Redburn: His First Voyage*, 1849; *White-Jacket: Or, The World in a Man-of-War*, 1850; *Moby Dick: Or, The Whale*, 1851; *Pierre: Or, The Ambiguities*, 1852; *Israel Potter: His Fifty Years of Exile*, 1855; *The Confidence Man: His Masquerade*, 1857; *Billy Budd, Foretopman*, 1924.

SHORT FICTION: *The Piazza Tales*, 1856; *The Apple-Tree Table and Other Sketches*, 1922.

NONFICTION: *Journal up the Straits*, 1935; *Journal of a Visit to London and the Continent*, 1948; *The*

Letters of Herman Melville (1960, Merrill R. Davis and William H. Gilman, editors).

BIBLIOGRAPHY

Bloom, Harold, ed. *Herman Melville: Modern Critical Interpretations*. New York: Chelsea House, 1986. In his helpful introduction, Bloom discusses the importance of the thirteen articles presented. Major critics interpret Melville's themes, forms, symbolism, and comedy in *Moby Dick*, the tales, *Billy Budd, Foretopman*, and other works. Includes a useful chronology, a bibliography, and an index.

Branch, Watson G., ed. *Melville: The Critical Heritage*. London: Routledge & Kegan Paul, 1974. Brings together the records of the nineteenth century's critical reception of Melville in reviews, essays, and other documents, all of which help readers understand the uneven reception of Melville's genius: Until 1938, he was not considered appropriate for university studies, yet now he is recognized as a great American writer. An index accompanies the text.

Chase, Richard, ed. *Melville: A Collection of Critical Essays*. Englewood Cliffs, N.J.: Prentice-Hall, 1962. Eleven articles illuminate Melville's novels, stories, and writing style. Major twentieth century critics included here are D. H. Lawrence, Alfred Kazin, Robert Penn Warren, and F. O. Matthiessen. The critics cover the relation of novelistic, romantic, and epic elements in his work. His poetic development is traced and his place in the American literary tradition is debated.

Dimock, Wai-chee. *Empire for Liberty: Melville and the Poetics of Individualism*. Princeton, N.J.: Princeton University Press, 1989. Dimock's literary analysis uses metaphors of space, dominance, and fate to show Melville's vision of the human soul. The isolated self builds "thick walls" and "interior spaciousness" (Moby Dick himself) to pursue freedom and to resist the downward pull of doom. Indian-hating in the American "empire" takes on metaphysical dimensions in this difficult but rewarding study. Includes notes and an index.

Hardwick, Elizabeth. *Herman Melville*. New York: Viking, 2000. A short biographical study that hits all the high points and some low ones in Melville's life, from his early seagoing expeditions to his settling down in middle age and finally his languishing in his job as a New York customs inspector.

Miller, Edwin Haviland. *Melville*. New York: George Braziller, 1975. Melville is a difficult subject for biographers because he did not reveal himself intimately in letters, diaries, or journals. Therefore his books and accounts of him by others are where the inner man is found. Using these sources, Miller writes a fascinating and illuminating account. Two plates and fifteen half-plates, a select bibliography, and an index assist the reader.

Renker, Elizabeth. *Strike Through the Mask: Herman Melville and the Scene of Writing*. Baltimore: The Johns Hopkins University Press, 1996. Argues that Melville was obsessed with the difficulties of the material act of writing, as reflected in his repeated themes and leitmotifs, such as the face or mask. His depression, violent nature, and wife abuse are reflected in his writing. Notes, list of works cited, index.

Rollyson, Carl E., and Lisa Paddock. *Herman Melville A to Z: The Essential Reference to His Life and Work*. New York: Checkmark Books, 2001. A comprehensive and encyclopedic coverage of Melville's life, works, and times in 675 detailed entries.

*John C. Shields;
bibliography updated by the editors*

SAMUEL MENASHE

Born: New York, New York; September 16, 1925

PRINCIPAL POETRY
The Many Named Beloved, 1961
No Jerusalem But This, 1971
Fringe of Fire, 1973
To Open, 1974
Collected Poems, 1986
The Niche Narrows: New and Selected Poems, 2000

OTHER LITERARY FORMS
    Samuel Menashe is known primarily for his poetry.

ACHIEVEMENTS

Samuel Menashe has won critical recognition for being one of the most individual and daring poets of his time. Eschewing all the poetic fashions of his day, Menashe writes a tightly chiseled verse that nevertheless is full of visionary experience and intensity. Poets and critics as diverse as Hugh Kenner, Donald Davie, and Kathleen Raine have called attention to Menashe as a demanding and exemplary poet. Menashe has achieved more popularity in Great Britain than in America, perhaps because his sense of a personal sacredness is more in tune with the English poetic tradition than with the more public celebration associated with poets such as Walt Whitman. To an unusual degree, Menashe has created a demanding, radically personal body of poetry that speaks to essential issues of human experience and belief.

BIOGRAPHY

Samuel Menashe was born in New York City, the child of Jewish immigrants. His early exposure to Yiddish and Spanish was crucial in bestowing upon him the sensitivity to linguistic nuance evident in the care he lavishes upon every word in his poems. Menashe especially attributes his verbal gifts to the influence of his mother, who was multilingual. He served in the United States Army during and after World War II and studied at the Sorbonne in Paris, writing a doctoral thesis on poetic experience and gaining an advanced degree.

Menashe has traveled widely in Europe and the Near East and, despite the local settings of his poetry, is quite cosmopolitan as a writer, possessing an awareness of many literatures and cultures. He is an impressive and eloquent reciter of verse who captivates audiences when he reads aloud from his own work and that of his favorite poets. In 1996, his work was included in *Penquin Modern Poets 6 (London)*.

ANALYSIS

The poetry of Samuel Menashe is very distinctive. His poems are all quite short and seem as if they are trying to grasp the essence of their subject in the most simple and fundamental way. Although the length of his poems entitles him to be styled a minimalist, their concerns are not at all minimal; rather, they are all-embracing, al-

most transcendent in their scope. Menashe's poems are easy to comprehend on their surface. Puzzling out the intended meaning of the poems is not particularly challenging for the reader. The richness of Menashe's poems lies in the way their embroidery and orchestration of language illuminate the tenderness and wisdom of his thought.

Menashe has been influenced by many different poets. In the bareness and austerity of his language he recalls twentieth century poets in the modernist tradition, particularly those of the Objectivist school such as George Oppen, Louis Zukofsky, and Charles Reznikoff—most of whom, like Menashe, were of Jewish descent. Unlike these poets, however, Menashe is less interested in the object in itself than in the highly subjective range of human emotions and spirituality. Thus Menashe also has a completely different set of ancestors. His very personal sense of beauty and glory recalls the Bible as well as such maverick religious poets as William Blake, Emily Dickinson, and Gerard Manley Hopkins, who all, like Menashe, excelled in imbuing very short forms with mystery and spirituality.

THE MANY NAMED BELOVED

This latter tradition is most overt in the poems in Menashe's first volume, *The Many Named Beloved*. These poems are the longest and most ornate in Menashe's canon, although still brief and compact compared to the works of most other poets. Some of the most successful poems in the collection are small narratives or parables. A good example is "Promised Land." In this poem, the speaker stands "at the edge/ of a world/ beyond my eyes/ beautiful." Like the biblical Moses, the speaker never manages to enter the promised land he contemplates. Unlike his scriptural predecessor, however, he does not truly yearn to enter this paradise. He realizes that beauty is most vivid when it cannot quite be attained.

Alluding to a Jewish tradition that knows exile and estrangement far more vividly than it knows fulfillment and consummation, the poem concludes, "The river/ We cannot cross/ Flows forever." To cross the river would be to end the exile, to find a definite salvation. The "cannot" in the above clause implies that humankind by nature is forbidden to cross this river, which in some ways is the border between mortality and immortality. Yet there are more subtle reverberations to the "cannot."

These become clear when the whole line is read. "Flows forever" gives an impression of permanence and continuity, not loss or despair. The poem implies that the river is kept flowing by the very way in which its existence allows exile to be maintained. The river's activity is ultimately positive rather than negative, in keeping alive human aspirations and never letting them become resolved into a settled, final state. This is why exile is, in Menashe's phrase, "green with hope" and not green with envy.

In this poem and in others, Menashe uses religious terms and images. Yet he is not a believer in formal religion; unlike some modern poets such as T. S. Eliot, he is not interested in religion as dogma, doctrine, or ritual. Rather, he is excited by the hope and by the poetic magic that religion at times expresses.

No Jerusalem But This

The poems in *No Jerusalem But This* mark a new phase in Menashe's career. There is far less "high" language in these poems. Menashe is less reliant on visionary rhetoric and more content to let his poems speak on their own terms. From this point onward, no comparisons with other poets are relevant; Menashe's career becomes a solitary journey. This solitary emphasis can be seen in the poem that includes the collection's title line. This is probably Menashe's most important and memorable poem. "The Shrine Whose Shape I Am" is a kind of hymn, but it is not the sort that could be included in any religious ceremony. This shrine is not a conventional object of worship or reverence, but rather the speaker's body itself.

Menashe, though, is very canny in that he is not proposing any pagan cult of the body. Instead, he focuses on how the body marks the boundaries of the self and its world. The body for Menashe signifies not earth or blood but the spirit of life itself. This spirit is symbolized in the early lines of the poem by fire. "Flames skirt my skin," the speaker says, as he describes his form as having a "fringe of fire."

The poem goes on to state, "There is no Jerusalem but this." There is no reason to look for Jerusalem, the holy city, in Heaven, where religious thinkers have often placed it. Nor is any Jerusalem on earth—whether the actual Jerusalem which, when the poem was written, had only recently been made part of the new state of Israel or any other site said to be a sacred abode—sufficient in the view of the poem to express human spirituality fully. If there is no Jerusalem either in Heaven or on earth, then Jerusalem must be within the self or body. Yet Menashe is not saying that Jerusalem definitely does exist within the self or body, only that if there is a Jerusalem at all that is where one would find it. This limitation of Jerusalem to the human form is not at all a reduction. This Jerusalem is as wondrous and evocative as any heavenly or earthly city. It is "breathed in flesh by shameless love." The speaker's belief is as vivid as that of any biblical figure: "Like David I bless myself/ with all my might." There is no sense that the speaker's spiritual condition is impoverished when compared to the past.

Still, all is not bliss. The tragedies as well as the triumphs associated with other Jerusalems are also present in this one. The speaker finds that he cannot share the certainty that he attributes to previous ages. "I know that many hills were holy once," he states. "But now in the level lands to live/ Zion ground down must become marrow." In the absence of any larger belief, the physical husk of human skin and bones must sustain any hopes for transcendence. Yet these hopes are, by nature, ephemeral. Menashe is sensitive to the frailty of bone as well as the pulse and color of flesh. The human body is inevitably subject to time and decay. Thus the speaker, in living Jerusalem within his own body, in a way is bound to reenact, or more truly act in his own way, the suffering of Jesus. "And through death's domain I go/ Making my own procession." Each human life holds the pathos and the dignity to be found in larger shapes within traditional religion. Menashe lovingly conveys the connections between human hopes for a higher world and the way these hopes are played out in, and by, the course of an individual life.

"Sheep Meadow"

Poems of this sort, filled with rich, interior reflection, are not the only type to be found in this volume. There are some excellent poems with a natural setting. These poems may seem surprising from a poet of Menashe's visionary intensity, but they are like his other verse in that his eye is never on the setting as such. Instead, he focuses on the metaphorical potential of that setting. In "Sheep Meadow" Menashe conveys a delicate but very accurate sense of this famous green stretch of New York's Central Park, here glimpsed in winter, when it is usually least noticed. Menashe is so much a poet of his beloved New York City that this park scene is as close to pure "nature" as he tends to get. Yet the poem magnificently captures a personal sense of the atmosphere of the place.

He opens by comparing speaking French on the Sheep Meadow to "a very rich hour/ of the Duke of Berry," the allusion being to the well-known medieval illustrated manuscript. By making this comparison, Menashe instantly transforms what would otherwise have been a nondescript, perhaps even banal, scene into one rife with imaginative possibility. He does this, moreover, without ruining the spontaneity of the scene by a heavy-handed reference to high culture. The medieval reference is made offhandedly and naturally, not with an air of pomposity or pretension. From this imaginative base the poem glides strategically into its actual setting. Menashe depicts the snowy meadow "hedged by trees/ on the south side/ where the towers/ of the city rise." The Sheep Meadow is a locus of stillness and peace within the fantastically complex and aggravated edifices of a great metropolis. Its calm and quietness stand out even more within such surroundings than they would if the field lay in the open country. The calm of the Sheep Meadow is not a careless calm but a deliberate and meditative one. It can serve as a resting place for "one of those hours/ in early afternoon/ where nothing happens/ but time makes room." The off-rhyme between "noon" and "room" is emblematic of the close and comfortable but never completely static or placid relationship between nature and the human mind that the poem portrays. Even though nothing dramatic or striking occurs during this sojourn of reverie in the meadow, the serene near-stillness is worthy of notice, because it does not answer to the usual mandate of time. The awareness that time is passing typically leads one to believe that unless something dramatic happens an hour is unimportant. The poem suggests, however, that this equation should be altered. By saying that "time makes room" for this sort of reflective thought, the poem leads the reader to consider whether the spaces in which thought lingers outside the strict limits of time may ultimately evade the logic of day-by-day necessity that reigns outside the

park. The poem starts out with an image, goes into the description of a place, and concludes with a finely honed evocation of a mood.

TO OPEN

In Menashe's *To Open*, as well as the poems that were uncollected until the appearance of *Collected Poems* in 1986, the poet maintains the general type and tone of his verse. Yet in these poems his technique becomes even more refined and masterful. Just as in the shift from the first to the second volume an emphasis on emotional depth and idiosyncratic reverence replaced one on rhetorical grandeur, so does the course of Menashe's poetry after the second volume exhibit less of a stress on subject matter and more of a focus on linguistic concreteness and complexity. The poems become still shorter. Yet even in those of only two or three lines there is as much intricacy as most poets would put into far longer forms. A fine example is "Tears." This poem is so brief that its entire length could be conveyed in one sentence. "Without tears/ The eyes die/ Of dryness—/ You must cry/ To water/ The eye." This miniature container holds enormous conceptual and linguistic depth and skill.

Tears are traditionally far more often the by-product of poetry than its subject. Even when poems take tears as their subject, as in Alfred, Lord Tennyson's "Tears, Idle Tears," they are at least ostensibly supposed to be lamented, not celebrated. Menashe's poem implies, however, that tears are ultimately beneficial. Without tears, the eye would die of dryness. This is to say, without the emotional release of crying the eye would be imprisoned in a cold self-sufficiency, incapable of knowing or feeling any experience outside it. Tears, although apparently an expression of pain, in fact serve to demonstrate a sentimental attachment on the part of the human eye (and mind) to phenomena that are not inherently part of it. As usual, Menashe's content is a wise aphorism strategically designed to counter conventional wisdom.

Yet content is not the only factor here. The very words in which the content is expressed redouble the force of their meaning. Menashe's language is meant not only to sound striking and beautiful but also actually to affect the meaning that is conveyed through it. In fact, it can even be said that the language assists in constructing this meaning. The dominant rhyme in the poem is, in terms of sound, a long *i*, usually expressed visually by the letter *y*. The repetition of this rhyme binds the words together in one phonetic unit of meaning. Yet by more often than not standing at the end of a line (for example, "die," "cry," "eye"), the *y* sound protrudes out of each line just as tears protrude out of the eye. Like the tears, the *y* sound is crucial in communicating feeling and meaning from one isolated unit (whether a mind or a poetic line) to another. Menashe here masterfully combines a large philosophical and emotional sweep with a meticulous concern for the smallest and most closely wrought hint of verbal meaning. He holds in balance the big and the little, the macrocosmic and the microscopic, in order to create an inimitable, superbly controlled piece of poetry.

A similar triumph of closely wrought language is "Waves." In the first stanza, the waves are described: "Waves crest, waver, fall." The monosyllabic, consonant-filled phrases give the impression of hardness and exactitude. Yet they also convey the air of objects that are full of unrest, not at repose with one another. This tension is resolved in the following and final stanza, "Masts sway/ at anchor/ over the bay." The inclusion of the two-syllable word "anchor" conveys a sense of expansive firmness that truly does anchor the language, while the rhyme between "sway" and "bay" mimics the anchor's limitation of the motion represented by swaying as the masts rest in alert peace on the bay. Once again, the language and the scene that it depicts go hand in hand. As with all Menashe's poems, the amount of rewarding labor expended on the part of both reader and writer goes far deeper than the mere appearance of a few words on the page.

THE NICHE NARROWS

For Menashe, every short poem represents a new start, and each poem is written as if the poet's life depended on it. In his omnibus volume *The Niche Narrows*, Menashe's later poems continue his curious mixture of asceticism and transcendence while seeming opt for a slightly more emotive diction and tone. Menashe will certainly never be classified as an expansive poet. As he says in an interview for *Contemporary Authors*, "Those who like my work call it concise or economical. Those who dislike it call it slight."

"Family Silver" takes of themes of art compensating for worldly loss reminiscent of the poetry of Seamus Heaney or Elizabeth Bishop.

> That spoon fell out
> Of my mother's mouth
> Before I was born,
> But I was endowed
> With a tuning fork.

The poet's family was poor—lacking the "silver spoon," referred to with the obliquity of "that spoon"—but fate made up for it by giving the poet his poetic gift, figured in the musical analogy of a tuning fork. It is important to note that is "fate" rather than "God," even though the verb "endowed" recalls phrases like that from the Declaration of Independence, "endowed by their Creator with unalienable rights. . . ." Menashe clearly believes in a spiritual level of existence, but the relevance of a personal God to his value system is far less apparent, even though in "Hallelujah" he uses Psalm 149 as a concluding epigraph and refers to a solitary "Maker." As evident as Menashe's continuing questioning of the soul's destiny is his verbal dexterity, which continues to conjure small patterns that delight the responsive reader. For instance, there is an *o* in the concluding word of each line, and the *ou* in both "out" and "mouth" and the *or* in both "born" and "fork" verge on constituting a submerged rhyme. Also, the use of a comma after "born," rather than the full stop of a period or the half-stop of a semicolon, means that the punctuation operates as a kind of hinge, swinging the tone of the poem from the bleak pessimism of the first three lines to the assertive optimism of the last two.

As Menashe entered his seventies, questions of age and mortality became even more prominent in his verse. Menashe never exactly wrote as a "young" poet; his first book was published when he was thirty-six, and the subjects of his verse had far more to do with playing out life's ultimate concerns than in surveying its peripheral hopes. In the later poems in *The Niche Narrows*, however, death and decay become overriding themes. In "The Niche," for instance, which gives its title to the volume, "the niche narrows" until the poet's bones "disclose him." Disclosure here is part decomposure, but it is also deliverance from the flesh, a kind of spiritual release. In other words, as the niche narrows, the intensity of the light may sharpen.

"What to Expect" explores the paradox that "Each breath you take/ is breathtaking." Every breath is wonderful, and one should cherish and delight in every moment because it brings the amazing gifts of life and percipience. Every breath also, however, takes away breath, as we only have a certain amount of breath within us. Lines like this are not merely aphorisms or adages. They are poetic assertions embedded within a speaking voice that yet is oriented toward the serenity of the poem as a constructed object. The coexistence of beauty and oblivion is seen in "Sunset in Central Park," in which, as the sun disappears, its double reflection—upon the windows of New York skyscrapers and then bounced off onto the surface of a lake in the park—burns most gloriously in its third-hand vanishing, not its primary appearance.

Even when the conclusions are somber, though, the tone is not. Moreover, some of the later poems have a kind of heedless exuberance to them. In "The Spright of Delight," a poem dedicated to Menashe's longtime supporter Kathleen Raine,

> The spright of delight
> springs, summersaults
> vaults out of sight
> riding, self-spun
> Weight overcome.

Note that Menashe coins the neologistic spelling "summersaults" instead of the normal "somersaults," the new coinage expressing the freedom of movement and spirit associated with the carefree purity of a summer day. The repetition of the letter *g* in various combinations of placements and sound patterns gives the poem an integrity that is visual as well as verbal. Menashe manages to confine the gossamer spirit of unbridled relaxation within a short poem. His mixture of verbal lucidity and astonishing implication will continue to augment the admiration it his work has already received.

BIBLIOGRAPHY

Ahearn, Barry. "Poetry and Synthesis: The Art of Samuel Menashe." *Twentieth Century Literature* 42, no. 2 (Summer, 1996): 294. A biographical profile of Menashe and a critical analysis of selections from his work.

Birkerts, Sven. Review of *Collected Poems. Partisan Review* 54 (Fall, 1987): 649-650. Birkerts, one of the leading practical critics of poetry, describes Menashe as a "poet of subtle breath stops and fine detail" who produces "calibrated minims" in which rhyme and construction are paramount.

Davie, Donald. "The Poetry of Samuel Menashe." In *The Poet in the Imaginary Museum*. New York: Persea Books, 1977. One of the longest and most in-depth discussions of Menashe's work. Davie, a distinguished poet and one of Menashe's main critical champions, gives an invaluable survey of both Menashe's work and his temperament, providing a representative sample of his most important poems. Davie is especially valuable on the linguistic and religious aspects of Menashe's poetry.

Heller, Michael. Review of *Collected Poems. The New York Times*, March 8, 1987, p. 32. In the most prominent review of Menashe's *Collected Poems*. Heller, himself a noted poet whose verse possesses qualities similar to Menashe's, sees Menashe's poetry as the work of a "lapidarian" and discusses the formal techniques of his rhymes. Heller aptly observes how even Menashe's most "disarmingly simple" poems possess "uncanny force."

Nicholas Birns, updated by Birns

GEORGE MEREDITH

Born: Portsmouth, England; February 12, 1828
Died: Flint Cottage, near Box Hill, Surrey, England; May 18, 1909

PRINCIPAL POETRY
Poems, 1851
Modern Love and Poems of the English Roadside, 1862
Poems and Lyrics of the Joy of Earth, 1883
Ballads and Poems of Tragic Life, 1887

A Reading of Earth, 1888
Poems: The Empty Purse, 1892
Odes in Contribution to the Song of French History,
    1898
A Reading of Life, 1901
Last Poems, 1909
The Poetical Works of George Meredith, 1912 (3
    volumes)

OTHER LITERARY FORMS

George Meredith wrote more than one dozen novels, including *The Ordeal of Richard Feverel* (1859), *The Egoist* (1879), and *Diana of the Crossways* (1885). His novels attack egoism, or excessive self-importance, and sentimentality, or unfounded pride in fine sensibility. The characters and situations presented in Meredith's novels are fictions, but they are often drawn, sometimes closely, from real people and actual incidents. Meredith's novels have been praised for their descriptions of society and their characterizations, especially of women, and criticized for their excessive elaboration of incident and background and for their highly artificial style, which many readers find both tedious and distracting. Meredith, whose novels explore a vein of comedy marked by rueful self-recognition, articulated his ideas on comedy in *On the Idea of Comedy and the Uses of the Comic Spirit* (1877).

ACHIEVEMENTS

For much of George Meredith's career, his audience was small but select. Reviews of his work were mixed, yet he received praise from writers as varied as Alfred, Lord Tennyson, Robert Browning, Algernon Charles Swinburne, Thomas Hardy, and Robert Louis Stevenson. With the publication of *Diana of the Crossways* in 1885, Meredith's popular reception blossomed. His last years were full of honor. In 1892, on the death of Tennyson, he was elected president of the Society of Authors. Ten years later he was made vice president of the London Library. He was honored several times in his last years by leading figures of the literary world. In 1905 Meredith received the Order of Merit.

BIOGRAPHY

George Meredith was the son and grandson of tailors of modest means whose good looks, social graces, and personal proclivities enabled them to move in higher social circles than most tradespeople did. When Meredith was about eighteen, he became a clerk to a solicitor who introduced him to a circle of writers and artists. Through his friend Edward Peacock, the son of novelist and poet Thomas Love Peacock, Meredith met Mary Peacock Nicolls, a widow six years older than he. She was beautiful, witty, sophisticated, and artistic, and Meredith fell passionately in love with her. He had his good looks to offer her, along with the promise of his talent—and poverty. He proposed, and she refused him several times. Finally, in 1849 they were married.

They had a son, Arthur, but the marriage was stormy. They were both strong-minded, and they were stressed by poverty. Mary was volatile and independent. After seven years the marriage was failing, although the couple kept up appearances. Then she initiated an affair with Meredith's friend

George Meredith (Library of Congress)

the artist Henry Wallis, with whom she had a child. She abandoned her husband and Arthur to go with Wallis to Capri, Italy, in 1858. Soon Wallis abandoned her, and she returned to England in ill health. After she left him, Meredith never saw her again. She lived in poverty, loneliness, and misery until her death in 1861. Some of the emotion of his courtship is reflected in Meredith's "Love in the Valley" and *The Ordeal of Richard Feverel*, and the breakup of the marriage informs "Modern Love," although none of these works should be regarded as reliable autobiography.

Because Meredith's publications did not meet with great popular success, he supported Arthur and himself for a time as a political journalist, writing dutifully for a paper more conservative than he. In 1862 he became a reader for the publishers Chapman and Hall, considering a great many manuscripts, inevitably rejecting some that went on to be great successes for other publishers but also giving important early encouragement to such writers as Thomas Hardy, Olive Schreiner, and George Gissing. He continued with Chapman and Hall until 1894.

Meredith was physically vigorous for much of his life and a great walker, both in frequent short rambles and in longer walking tours. He enjoyed strong friendships. On September 20, 1864, he married Marie Vulliamy. This marriage led to an estrangement between Meredith and his son, but it was a stable and happy union until Marie's death in 1885.

Meredith continued to work actively through the turn of the twentieth century. As he aged, his health declined, but his temperament mellowed. Although many of the friends of his youth and middle age predeceased him, a new generation of friends supported him. On May 18, 1909, after a short illness, he died, widely revered and much honored.

ANALYSIS

George Meredith, a gifted conversationalist, once provoked playwright F. C. Burnand to exclaim, "Damn you, George, why won't you write the way you talk?" Meredith would not. In an age of conscious stylists, he was one of the most mannered, in both prose and poetry. He wrote a great deal of poetry, much of it flawed by strained, awkward, and overly elaborate figures of

speech. His poems are sometimes frustratingly indirect in expression. The grammar of his lines can be extremely convoluted, often for the sake of rhyme. Many of his poems are rhythmically monotonous, and many are quite didactic. Meredith also wrote excellent poetry, however, pleasurable and rewarding to many readers, who may make happy discoveries, particularly among his lyrics. Among his most rewarding poems are "Love in the Valley," "Lucifer in Starlight," and "Modern Love."

"LOVE IN THE VALLEY"

"Love in the Valley" is a much-admired long lyric, first published in 1851 and very extensively revised in 1878. The finished poem consists of twenty-six eight-line stanzas. The poem's pentameter lines have a fluid, seemingly spontaneous rhythm, sometimes mimetic and consistently effective.

The poem's narrator alternately celebrates the beauty, innocence, and freedom of his beloved and describes the rural valley which is her home. The descriptions of the valley are vivid and detailed, presenting images of moonlight, dusk, and dawn; of birds and the sky; of vegetation green and golden. The descriptions of the woman, "Pure from the night, and splendid for the day," are less specific but no less intense. To the censorious, the woman is not faultless; to the narrator of the poem, she is innocent, sensual, changeable, and elusive.

The poem develops in a series of mirror images: A swallow's wings are mirrored in the water, and the woman's mother "tends her before the laughing mirror." Throughout the poem the subject is mirrored metaphorically in nature, as nature is mirrored in her. When the lovers embrace, the narrator says, "our souls were in our names"—that is, each soul was mirrored in the name of the other.

In the last stanza the narrator says, "heaven is my need"—a heaven that is mirrored, by love, in the valley and in the woman. The poem is full of swift, elusive, mutable things: shy squirrels, swooping swallows and owls, winking minnows, the changing sky throughout the day, the cycle of the seasons, and the woman herself, "this wild thing." In all this change, there is constancy; whatever the time of day, whatever the season, the valley—with all its swift, elusive creatures—is still itself. For all her changeableness, the beloved is still herself. In transience is treasured, timeless truth.

"THE LARK ASCENDING"

"The Lark Ascending" (1883) is a poem of 120 lines. The generally regular iambic tetrameter lines rhyme in couplets. The poem describes and reflects on the prolonged and soaring song of the skylark, which sings as it flies, often so high that it is lost to the eye and can be followed only by the ear.

The first long stanza (sixty-four lines) describes the outpouring in song of a skylark at sunrise. The stanza is one long sentence, perhaps imitating the song it describes. Poets, notably Percy Bysshe Shelley, have found in the skylark's song an emblem of spiritual transcendence. Meredith, too, makes it a symbol. In the second stanza, he says that the swallow carries Earth with it and voices Earth in its song. In the third stanza Meredith says that though humankind can hear the song, people lack the voice for such singing, spoiled as they are by the "taint of personality." In the last stanza he corrects himself: Some people, through their life's struggles and self-forgetfulness, have souls great enough to be embodied in the skylark's song of transcendence.

The idea that Meredith struggled to express in "The Lark Ascending" is also expressed, more simply and more clearly, in "Song in the Songless" (1901), eight lines of alternating tetrameter and dimeter: "They have no song, the sedges dry/ And still they sing," the poem begins, and it concludes: "There is but sound of sedges dry/ In me they sing." In this eloquent lyric, the speaker, transcending age, inarticulateness, and personality, is united with nature.

"LUCIFER IN STARLIGHT"

"Lucifer in Starlight," one of Meredith's most widely read poems, is one of twenty-five sonnets Meredith published in 1883. Lucifer is the Prince of Darkness with the name of Light, and the poem plays throughout on imagery of light and dark: Lucifer's shadow on the arctic snow and stars against the dark sky. The poem is Miltonic in its protagonist, its diction, its imagery, and its stately rhythm appropriate to ponderous flight. Significantly, however, the cosmology of Meredith's poem is modern; rolling Earth is no longer the fixed center of the universe.

The imagery of the octave is easily visualizable and highly effective. The sestet, at first reading, is also readily comprehensible, although on reflection it may be less successful. The metaphors shift quickly from "the brain of heaven" to "the army of unalterable law," and neither metaphor is really visual. Nonetheless, the reader can grasp Meredith's point.

Prince Lucifer, the proud rebel, stands against order, which is embodied in military organization and the regular movement of the stars, in reason, in law, and, presumably, in the hierarchy which gives him his title. Lucifer is, in fact, an egoist. He is defeated in this poem not by the tangible force that cost him the scars he wears but by the force of an abstract idea. He surrenders not to God but to "unalterable law"—if unalterable, then presumably as immune to the will of God (whomever or whatever that might be) as to any initiatives of the proud rebel. Meredith, like other late Victorians, abandoned Christianity for the indistinctly defined religion of Science. The strictly prescribed form of the sonnet is highly appropriate to this poem's subject, linking both poet and reader to the order it expresses, embodies, and imposes.

"MODERN LOVE"

"Modern Love" (1862), Meredith's most highly regarded poem, consists of fifty sixteen-line stanzas, which Meredith called sonnets. This sixteen-line form is more flexible than traditional sonnet forms, and Meredith's sonnet sequence differs from others in the detailed and coherent narrative that links the individual sonnets.

"Modern Love" tells the story of a failing marriage, partly through a third-person narrator but largely from the point of view of the husband. The sequence opens with the couple's estrangement. The wife has taken a new lover, and the husband, still in love with his wife as she was, vacillates between jealousy and physical desire for her. He recognizes her misery as they maintain the façade of marriage, yet he cannot bring himself to show her pity. To feed his wounded ego, he initiates a flirtation of his own, an affair which is eventually consummated but unrewarding. Husband and wife painfully attempt to reconcile. The wife does finally believe that she has won back her husband's love, but she commits suicide to leave her husband free to pursue his new love—which, ironically, he does not really want to do.

Among the most memorable sonnets in the sequence are the first, depicting the couple lying uncommunicative in their bed, "each wishing for the sword that severs all"; the thirteenth, in which Nature, who plays "for Seasons, not Eternities," brings both the growth and death of love; the forty-seventh, with its evocative nature imagery; and the last, with its sensitive and remarkably objective analysis of the process by which love dies.

"Modern Love" does not moralize. Many Victorians found this a shocking failure, but later generations have found that what the poem accomplishes instead is much more meaningful. "Modern Love" is remarkable for its subtly modulated presentation of conflicting emotions and for its unsparingly honest expression of the husband's motives, evasions, and perceptions.

OTHER MAJOR WORKS

LONG FICTION: *The Saving of Shagpat*, 1855; *Farina*, 1857; *The Ordeal of Richard Feverel*, 1859; *Evan Harrington*, 1861; *Emilia in England*, 1864; *Rhoda Fleming*, 1865; *Vittoria*, 1867; *The Adventures of Harry Richmond*, 1871; *Beauchamp's Career*, 1874-1875 (serial); *The Egoist*, 1879; *The Tragic Comedians*, 1880; *Diana of the Crossways*, 1885; *One of Our Conquerors*, 1891; *Lord Ormont and His Aminta*, 1894; *The Amazing Marriage*, 1895; *Celt and Saxon*, 1910.

SHORT FICTION: *The Case of General Ople and Lady Camper*, 1890; *The Tale of Chloe*, 1890.

NONFICTION: *On the Idea of Comedy and the Uses of the Comic Spirit*, 1877; *The Letters of George Meredith*, 1970 (C. L. Cline, editor).

BIBLIOGRAPHY

Heimstra, Anne. "Reconstructing Milton's Satan: Meredith's 'Lucifer in Starlight.'" *Victorian Poetry* 30 (Summer, 1992): 122-133. Explores at length Meredith's debt in this poem to Milton's portrayal of Satan in *Paradise Lost* and goes on to analyze the implications of Meredith's wording and imagery.

Kozicki, Henry. "The 'Unholy Battle' with the Other in George Meredith's 'Modern Love.'" *Papers on Language and Literature* 23 (Spring, 1987): 140-160. Begins with a reference to Norman Kelvin's analysis of the battle imagery in "Modern Love" in *A Troubled Eden: Nature and Society in the Works of George Meredith* and continues with a summary of the criticism dealing with conflict in "Modern Love." Kozicki then discusses the poem in detail.

His references to the suppressed version of Sonnet 10 are especially interesting.

Lucas, John. "Meredith as Poet." In *Meredith Now: Some Critical Essays*, edited by Ian Fletcher. London: Routledge & Kegan Paul, 1971. Lucas begins with a frank analysis of Meredith's faults as a poet. "In an age of careful craftsmen, Meredith stands out as extraordinarily slipshod, not so much by design as through indifference," he says, and argues to support this thesis. He goes on, however, to a detailed exploration of "Modern Love," which he calls Meredith's "one undoubted major triumph," focusing on the poem's subtly drawn record of its protagonist's psychological vacillations.

Muendel, Renate. *George Meredith*. Boston: Twayne, 1986. A brief account of Meredith's life, a discussion of his poetry, and an extensive analysis of his fiction. Includes an extensive annotated bibliography.

Sassoon, Siegfried. *Meredith*. London: Constable, 1948. Chiefly useful for the sympathetic picture it draws of the social and cultural milieu in which Meredith lived and worked. The author is the famed war poet of World War I.

Stevenson, Lionel. *The Ordeal of George Meredith*. New York: Scribner's, 1953. The definitive critical bibliography. Stevenson's detailed interpretations of Meredith's character and of his poetry and fiction are thoughtful and convincing.

David W. Cole

WILLIAM MEREDITH

Born: New York, New York; January 9, 1919

PRINCIPAL POETRY

Love Letter from an Impossible Land, 1944

Ships and Other Figures, 1948

The Open Sea and Other Poems, 1958

The Bottle Imp, 1958

Alcools: Poems, 1898-1913, 1964

The Wreck of the Thresher and Other Poems, 1964

Earth Walk: New and Selected Poems, 1970

Hazard, the Painter, 1975
The Cheer, 1980
Partial Accounts: New and Selected Poems, 1987
Effort at Speech: New and Selected Poems, 1997

OTHER LITERARY FORMS

William Meredith worked as the opera critic for *Hudson Review* from 1955 to 1956. He wrote the libretto, based on a Robert Louis Stevenson story, for Peter Whiton's opera *The Bottle Imp,* which was produced in 1958. Meredith edited and introduced a selected edition of Percy Bysshe Shelley's poetry (1962); in 1968, along with Mackie L. Jarrell, he edited and introduced *Eighteenth Century English Minor Poets.* He translated Guillaume Apollinaire's poetry in a work that appeared in 1964 as *Alcools: Poems, 1898-1913.* In 1986 a volume of Bulgarian poetry, edited and introduced by Meredith, was published. His first nonfiction book, *Poems Are Hard to Read,* was published in 1991. In addition, he has written a variety of reviews and essays.

ACHIEVEMENTS

William Meredith's place in the New England literary tradition and twentieth century American poetry is secure. Early in his career his poetry was highly imitative and academic. He eschewed experimentation, and he maintained a reticence and control that constricted his development and caused some to dismiss his understated, formal style as not engaging. Starting with the appearance of his *Ships and Other Figures* in 1948, however, Meredith moved consistently toward a less academic style and a more immediate voice. Since then, his importance to American poetry has steadily increased.

Meredith's superlative accomplishments have been widely praised by his peers. He is the recipient of several honors, including the Yale Younger Poets Award, three annual prizes awarded by *Poetry,* the Loines Prize, the Van Wyck Brooks Award, two Rockefeller Foundation grants, a National Endowment for the Arts grant, the International VAPTSAROV Prize for Literature, the Pulitzer Prize for Poetry, and an American Academy of Poets Award. Meredith has been a Guggenheim Fellow, a Ford Foundation Fellow, and a Woodrow Wilson Fellow at Princeton University. *Effort of Speech: New and Se-*

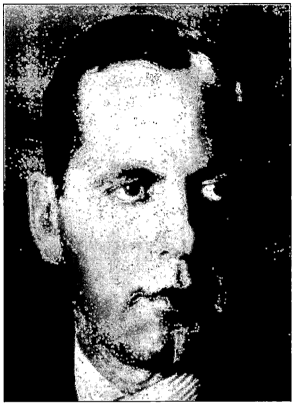

William Meredith

lected Poems won the National Book Award for Poetry in 1997. Connecticut College has recognized his contribution to its institution in two ways: In 1988 he received an honorary doctoral degree, and in 1996 he won the Connecticut College Medal and the William Meredith Endowed Professorship was created. In 1998 he received another honorary doctoral degree, this time from The American University in Bulgaria. He is a member of the American Academy and National Institute of Arts and Letters (for which he has served as secretary) and chancellor of the Academy of American Poets. In addition, Meredith served as consultant in poetry to the Library of Congress from 1978 to 1980. In 1994 and 1995, Meredith's poems were recorded for the Archive of Recorded Poetry and Literature.

BIOGRAPHY

William Morris Meredith was born on January 9, 1919, in New York City and spent his childhood in Darien, Connecticut. He attended the Lenox School in

Massachusetts and then Princeton University, where he received a B.A. and was graduated magna cum laude in 1940. Until 1941 he worked as a copy boy, then reporter, for *The New York Times*. During World War II, Meredith was first a private in the United States Army Air Corps, then a Navy pilot. In 1944, *Love Letter from an Impossible Land* was published while Meredith was a lieutenant. After the war, he became a Woodrow Wilson Fellow, then an instructor in English and a resident fellow in creative writing at Princeton University. *Ships and Other Figures*, published by Princeton University in 1948, is largely a product of his time at this university. During the Korean War he served as a carrier pilot, was promoted to lieutenant commander, and received two Air Medals.

Meredith's association with Connecticut College began in 1955 and continued, with a few interruptions for visiting professorships, until 1983, when he retired following a severe stroke that required months of rehabilitation. Meredith has composed a significant body of creative work. Moreover, he has written in other genres, has been afforded many honors, and has taught at a variety of institutions, including the University of Hawaii, Middlebury College, Bread Loaf, and Carnegie-Mellon University. He has served as a member of the Connecticut Commission of the Arts and as director of the Humanities Upward Bound Project for Connecticut College.

ANALYSIS

William Meredith's interest in exploring ways to order human existence in the face of chaos has remained his principal thematic concern. Although the complexity of this thematic focus has deepened, the subtle shift in Meredith's thematic vision, according to Guy Rotella, has to do with "the degree of confidence he feels in any of the methods and results," along with his understanding of "the threats to its successful completion and to the maintenance of its gains." Meredith's disciplined and at times austere approach to this dilemma can be deceptively straightforward. He is a sophisticated poet who with his precise and elegant voice finds, frequently within small and otherwise unnoticed domestic and natural events, the sublime. His moral quest for personal, public, and artistic order, even while acknowledging humankind's tendency toward disorder, is a steadfast source of amazement and poetic inspiration.

LOVE LETTER FROM AN IMPOSSIBLE LAND

Published in 1944 as part of the Yale Series of Younger Poets, *Love Letter from an Impossible Land* is one of Meredith's apprentice works, a collection of poems (a few written while Meredith was still an undergraduate) that is highly imitative. This work displays a willing commitment to traditional form, meter, and rhyme. Meredith's academic style mirrors the work of many poets, including Matthew Arnold, William Butler Yeats, and W. H. Auden, as well as the Metaphysical poets of the seventeenth century. Although these poems are products of war, they do not impugn its moral validity. Meredith views the many negative results of war—chaos, despair, and death—with a discriminating eye as he attempts to ascertain meaning and purpose in a world that appears to be self-destructing. Several poems here are predictable studies in form, the ultimate purpose appearing to be maintaining the form in question rather than permitting any organic expansion of theme. Others show a willingness to debate spiritual issues, a directness of thought (Meredith's restraint and impersonal tone hinder this), and a use of colloquial diction.

Although many poems in this volume, especially those that adhere to a prescribed form, are not as successful as those that transcend traditional boundaries, this is not to say that all the poems that fall into the imitative category fail. Employing the form of a sonnet and an impersonal voice, "In Memoriam of Stratton Christensen" subtly inquires about the meaning of Stratton Christensen's death. The speaker states, "Your death is a puzzler that will tease them on," refusing to admit that the young airman's loss of life can be totally understood.

By far the most successful poems in this collection are those that stray from academic formalism, employing a more immediate voice and striking imagery. "Love Letter from an Impossible Land," "June: Dutch Harbor," and "Notes for an Elegy" are poems that could have been written by an experienced hand. In these poems, Meredith allows a more mature voice to emerge. In "Notes for an Elegy," the comforting tones usually supplied by an elegy vanish as the speaker attempts to comprehend another airman's death, a death not met during battle. The speaker claims that death is "a fair price" for the power of flight, which he equates with freedom. After discussing the aviator's death and the hope that God will "lift [him] gently," the speaker concludes, "The morning came up foolish with pink clouds/ To say that God counts ours a cunning time,/ Our losses part of an old secret, somehow not loss." Ambiguity persists (for example, in the words "cunning" and "secret"), as death retains an inscrutable aura. The airman's death may not be as significant or easily explained as the speaker desires, yet he searches for signs that will counteract what appears to be a random and tragic event.

SHIPS AND OTHER FIGURES

Written while Meredith was a Woodrow Wilson Fellow at Princeton University, his second volume, *Ships and Other Figures*, is another uneven collection of mostly benign, imitative poetry. The urgency displayed by several war poems in *Love Letter from an Impossible Land* has disappeared. The immediacy of death, which Meredith vividly confronts in his first collection, is muted in this book. Henry Taylor suggests that "one feels the absence of peril in these poems, the safety of academe." Meredith's fascination with fixed forms, order, and how order can reflect and contain what is created dominates these poems, hindering their immediacy and thematic development. Frequently the speaker's voice is lost in the poet's unflagging determination to perform within the confines of a particular form or in a cultivated flatness of voice that at times is bereft of passion or sincerity.

"Carrier," one of Meredith's war poems, succeeds in capturing some of the introspective urgency found in his earlier war poems. The carrier is personified as "huge and peacock vain," a mother who watches "her sprung creatures" as they fly away and "disappear." The airmen who fly from her deck must view her, upon return from a mission, as a safe haven where they can recoup their energies for other missions. Nevertheless, the danger of battle is distant in the poem. The speaker states that there is "far-off dying" with which the personified ship and the crew must contend, but the poem ends without bringing the deadly uncertainty of battle to the reader.

One of the more engrossing poems in this collection (which is revised and retitled in *Partial Accounts: New and Selected Poems*) is "Homeric Simile." The pitch of an air battle is likened to the developmental section of a composition for string quartet. The poem begins with a bomber on a night mission. The threat of "the hostile terrain" below the aircraft is real; the people manning the bomber sense the possibility of death as the navigator leads them to the target. What seems to be a logically staged event becomes chaotic, and the artificial order shatters. Fire and smoke appear below; tracers and searchlights rise to meet the aircraft; friends in other airplanes are killed. Yet the momentary confusion of battle gives way to a musical performance in which "the calm intelligent strings do their duty." The battle is compared to a group of instruments working toward a clear, unified end. The dissonance the instruments have encountered during developmental sections of the composition ultimately concludes in triadic harmony "after uncertain passage." Order eventually returns to the airmen's and the musicians' worlds. Meredith's urge to find order and meaning, even in the face of chaos and death, supersedes, and in some way legitimizes, the horrors of a war.

THE OPEN SEA AND OTHER POEMS

Ten years passed before Meredith's third volume of poetry was published. In many respects *The Open Sea and Other Poems* can be viewed as his first mature collection. Meredith's penchant for order survives, yet he adds another dimension by questioning the conditions of order and meaning. The poems here are intellectually superior to and more sophisticated than his previous work. The volume contains poems that still adhere to fixed forms and display technical and artistic skill; however, Meredith also displays a willingness to experiment with these forms. Richard Howard writes, "This third book insists on the autonomy of art, and with it of form." "The Open Sea" (a sestina), "Sonnet on Rare Animals," and "The Illiterate" (a Petrarchan sonnet) display Meredith's graceful concern with form but do not overshadow or stifle his artistic desire to express thoughts about possession and loss. "The Chinese Banyan," set in iambic trimeter, evinces a newfound willingness to go beyond mere acceptance of a prescribed order. His tone is at times playful and deceptively commonplace, as in "Bachelor" and "Thoughts on One's Head (IN PLASTER, WITH A BRONZE WASH)." When he demonstrates the most control over his lines, as in "Rus in

Urbe," the preciseness of the language impinges on the subject matter of the poem. The carefully pruned garden can produce fruit, which implies that well-measured lines might offer meaning rather than contrived artifice. Occasionally Meredith falters, as in "In Memory of Donald A. Stauffer," and his poems begin to sound like work found in his second volume. Even a poem such as "To a Western Bard Still a Whoop and a Holler Away from English Poetry," which is a sincere yet misguided attempt in quatrains to express Meredith's dissatisfaction with the experimentation of Allen Ginsberg and the Beats, falls flat.

The beautiful sestina "Notre Dame de Chartres" is an excellent example of how a more mature Meredith limns humankind's attempt to order chaos through art and find a hint of salvation and meaning within that order. Meredith's tone is relaxed as he explores the urge to order. When the faithful find the "Sancta Camisa" (holy shirt) after fire has destroyed the first church and town, they raise a far greater church, "the vast basilica," which will house the shirt in royal fashion. Yet it is "faith that burned / Bright and erroneous" that creates the architectural marvel. The inclusion of the word "erroneous" suggests that the manifestation of order, in this case the cathedral, arises from a loving faith that somehow is tainted and perhaps even false. Yet the final stanza suggests that despite the speaker's obvious reservations, he finds some validity in the order created by "the blessed shirt," which "spoke to the stone that slept in the groin of France."

THE WRECK OF THE THRESHER AND OTHER POEMS

The publication of *The Wreck of the Thresher and Other Poems* in 1964 marked Meredith's entry into the ranks of important contemporary poets. Gone is the occasionally overbearing concern with fixed form and the infringement of institutional authority. The poems found here are more personal (although never confessional) and less academic, using a voice that is sometimes reminiscent of the better poems in *Love Letter from an Impossible Land*. Meredith's friendships with both Robert Frost and John Berryman, which developed between the publication of *The Open Sea and Other Poems* and this volume, are evident in his use of colloquial language, his narrative technique, and his wry humor. Frost's influ-

ence is perhaps best illustrated in "Roots," in which Mrs. Lemmington reflects on her past, her mortality, and her ultimate return to the earth. Her fascination with roots as inversions of branches and leaves is a metaphorical and biological fusion of the historical past and future with the present. As with Frost, the tree (as well as the sea in Meredith's case) becomes a contemplative symbol.

Again, Meredith is concerned with order in a world that is fraught with disorder and chaos. Death is the arbitrary destroyer of any ordering done by humankind, whether on a grand scale or in the quiet confines of one's home. In "On Falling Asleep to Birdsong" the speaker, who is near sleep, hears the lone call of a whippoorwill. Rather than finding solace in the call, which must be very familiar, the speaker thinks about his parents and his own mortality. Convinced that "this is a question of will," he dreams of nightingales, and this thought leads him to Ovid's story of the rape of Philomela. Unable to break free of his own mortality, the speaker hears the whippoorwill's call again and understands its implication of courage in the face of disorder and mortality.

The poem "The Wreck of the *Thresher*" represents Meredith at his most eloquent. This poem is a probing, if somewhat dramatic, elegy inspired by the *Thresher* disaster of 1963, in which the nuclear submarine's crew perished. The limits of technology, which is an extension of the human urge to order, are addressed, as are the mystery of human existence and nature's capacity to assimilate human grief. The speaker concedes that all attempts to create order are regularly threatened, that safety, especially the safety of technology, is mostly imagined, and that destruction haunts all human activity. He admits that "the bottom here is too far down for our sounding;/ The ocean was salt before we crawled to tears." The mysteries of the sea and death remain unfathomable. Although the speaker acknowledges the fragility of any attempt to order, especially where the sea is involved, he also leaves the reader with a sense that without the perpetual and valorous urge to invent and reinvent order, only disorder, chaos, and death are left.

EARTH WALK

Earth Walk: New and Selected Poems contains fifty-three poems, fourteen of which are new works. Meredith's selection of his previous work is heavily weighted toward *The Open Sea and Other Poems* and *The Wreck of the Thresher and Other Poems*. His introduction reveals an awareness that the poems in his two latter volumes are more accomplished and that those selected "engage mysteries I still pluck at the hems of." Meredith's choices also emphasize his near obsession with human ordering; these poems tend to examine and approve humankind's attempt to stave off despair by creating order. The new poems in this volume are straightforward, utilizing an assortment of points of view and a cultivated innocence that at times startles and deceives. Meredith does not abandon the fixed form, but his formal poems tend to be less hampered than many of his earlier attempts. His tone is both conversational and immediate. Many poems are open and narrative in nature without heavy use of rhyme, as in "In Memory of Robert Frost." The numerous gains made in earlier volumes are reaffirmed and strengthened here. The poem "Earth Walk" is a fine example of the new flexibility in Meredith's style. The poem's freedom with point of view, the irregular rhyme, the brief, almost playful allusions to space technology and mortality, and the wry, casual humor illustrate his ability to move beyond his original confines and to explore earth's riddles freely.

In "Winter Verse for His Sister" Meredith utilizes a contemplative tone as the speaker, a thinly disguised Meredith, practices for death by going "to that other house/ Where our parents did most of their dying,/ Embracing and not embracing their conditions." The natural world appears to be indifferent, above the questions being asked or at least "noncommittal," as the speaker fruitlessly tries to discover some meaning in life and death—something Meredith grudgingly must leave unresolved.

Another poem that tackles nature's mysteries is "Walter Jenks' Bath," in which a young African American contemplates the meaning of atoms and how they compose matter. The boy's conclusion is best illustrated by the last few lines of the poem: "Even if I died the parts would go on spinning,/ Alone, like far stars, not knowing it." Meredith's spirit is present in this young man's realization that there is a viable connection between the particles that compose his body and those of the universe. Within this connection, however extemporaneous, the boy imagines an inclusive, orderly system.

HAZARD, THE PAINTER

Hazard, the Painter is a slim volume containing only sixteen poems, all of which are somewhat autobiographical. In his opening note to the reader, Meredith states, "Resemblances between the life and character of Hazard and those of the author are not disclaimed but are fewer than the author would like." The poems focus on the life of a less-than-important middle-aged American painter who is a witness to his own slow decay as well as a country "in late imperial decline." Meredith does not attempt to present Hazard as a complete individual; the poems are an incomplete portrait of his tenuous and at times disordered life. Most events examined in this volume are small domestic occurrences, rituals that make up everyday life; there are also satirical meditations on existence and hesitant reflections on death. The colloquial spontaneity of these poems, an influence of Berryman more than Frost, can be ingratiating. Beneath the surface of Hazard's daily perambulations and interior monologues, Meredith is at work, taking a hard look at the United States in the 1970's. The disintegration Hazard discovers is a direct threat to his concept of order and meaning.

In "Hazard Faces a Sunday in the Decline," the painter yearns for a vanished civility as he presides over his family's dinner table. He is comfortable in the material sense and cautiously optimistic, yet he recognizes his culture's deterioration as well as his family's failings. He accepts the challenge before him (although he can never succeed in imposing his personal order upon the world) and reflects, "Someone has fed us and blessed us," but adds, "with the manners of bohemia. Among barbarians,/ a lot is expected of us, ceremony-wise./ We rise to that expectation." In "Hazard's Optimism" he grapples with his own shortcomings as well as "morale in a morbid time." He has been working on one painting for two years. Much of his time is spent daydreaming, not at his canvas. His lack of success with his painting is emblematic of humankind's ultimate failure to give a lasting order to existence. Yet his attempt to bring temporary order to life through his art, in the face of decay and death, is all-important. The struggle permits Hazard, and others who challenge disorder, a small portion of dignity.

Hazard's concerns about America are most evident in "Nixon's the One." As Hazard tries to remove

McGovern-Shriver stickers from his cars after the Democratic Party's loss in the 1972 presidential race, he muses, "Who were all those cheering on the gray glass/ screen last night, loving their violent darling,/ America, whom they had married to money?" His poignant, rather estranged acknowledgment "that his nation has bitterly misspoken itself" is disheartening. In Hazard's mind, the country has become a vast desert of consumerism, greedily oblivious to a senseless war as long as profits continue to materialize.

Hazard senses that life and death are controlled by random forces. Nature cannot be permanently ordered by humankind. In "Squire Hazard Walks" he casually ruminates on death and how "the cat will be disassembled/ in his own time by underground technicians." Yet any attempt to draw a personal analogy is stymied by Hazard as his "thought turns chicken." The life-sustaining order that he so desperately needs comes in the last poem, "Winter: He Shapes Up." Meredith returns symbolically to the quatrain and to slant rhymes. Hazard is painting again, "gnawed by a vision of rightness." He reasons that life, whether it be public or private, can be measured only by "a few things made by men,/ a galaxy made well." This is all that is afforded humankind. Hazard realizes that in the face of chaos, he must paint, attempt to nurture order, and endure, even though he sees the incongruous realities before him.

THE CHEER

The Cheer contains thirty-five poems that are highly reflective of Meredith's primary thematic interest. Some of the poems are formal, but much of the work found in this volume is informal, and some leans toward experimentation, as in "Give and Take." Meredith's thematic interests are well seasoned by his acceptance, or at least recognition, of the painful limits and possibilities of human existence, as shown in "Examples of Created Systems." There is never a suggestion, however, that the individual should acquiesce and accept decay and disorder. Again, Meredith finds value in the heroic posture of resistance. He says in the opening piece, "The Cheer," that "words addressing evil won't turn evil back/ but they can give heart./ The cheer is hidden in the right words." Despair is not the answer: "Against evil, between evils, lovely words are right." The poet brings cheer, and not a small amount of hope, to a world that sits perilously close to despair, chaos, and death.

As an icebreaker works to clear a path through the ice on the river at mid-night in "Winter on the River," the temporary relief and order the vessel brings symbolize the prescribed formula against the harsh realities of this world. Humankind's dependence on nature, which constantly intrudes on the human will to create and order, is evident as the icebreaker moves past the speaker and the ice-making cold reclaims the river. Antithetical states are constantly observed and analyzed in Meredith's poetry. To defeat or at least to delay the inevitable negative state is a formidable task.

"Two Masks Unearthed in Bulgaria" and "Homage to Paul Mellon, I. M. Pei, Their Gallery, and Washington City" show how creativity (not only in the artistic sense) can defy mortality by producing meaningful constructs that act as bridges between generations and centuries. Even though a specific creation is made within a certain time frame, it can transcend temporality because it employs materials that connect it to the past and the future. Such a realization permits the creative mind to continue in the face of chaos, because it implies continuity, a way to bring thoughts of order and meaning to bear on ever-present decay.

Several poems in this volume view mortality with a discerning eye. In "Trelawny's Dream," Edward John Trelawny struggles with his part in his friend Percy Bysshe Shelley's death. Speaking from middle age, Trelawny has spent most of his life attempting to understand the meaning of the tragedy and assuage his feelings of guilt. Trelawny's attempt to find meaning in the deadly tragedy, the loss of a great poet and his companions, is his way of bringing order to an event that defies explanation. The inexplicable randomness of death is what Trelawny is facing; he states, "Though I am still a strong swimmer/ I can feel this channel widen as I swim." Although Trelawny must ultimately fail, his heroic attempt to find meaning gives his troubled life dignity and purpose.

PARTIAL ACCOUNTS

Meredith's *Partial Accounts* is a retrospective collection of nearly fifty years of writing. Of the 104 poems included in the volume, only eleven are new. The recent material is very much in tune with his mature work and his thematic concerns. Meredith refuses to yield to confessionalism and other poetic trends; this collection is modest and illustrates his lifelong desire, which is documented in "What I Remember the Writers Telling Me When I Was Young," to use a polished reticence to tackle the sublime. The title of the book suggests that something positive has been accomplished, yet there is still much to do. Meredith's understanding of existence and the ramifications of life's tendency toward chaos would never permit him to make a greater claim. Philosophical closure, even if attractive, is not permitted in a world that resists order and defies explanation with its randomness. The poet remains quite optimistic in the face of the bleak reality confronting everyday life. Again, Meredith sees the poet's role as one that brings good cheer, a little comfort, hope, and a temporary refutation of disorder. "The Jain Bird Hospital in Delhi" focuses on the Jains' small acts of compassion to injured birds as evidence of humanity's potential for caring and an undeniable connection between humankind and nature.

Another poem that represents what Meredith has worked so many years to say is "Among Ourselves," which looks at the way people seem to court stories of suffering and disaster but never relish their personal tales of happiness and success. After the guests have departed, the speaker asks, "Why do we never recount that,/ friends? And our lives,/ what about them? Our sweet, deliberate lives?" Meredith's determination to spread good cheer rather than support the bleaker, mortal side of existence is understandable, yet he has been criticized for his imperturbability.

One of the more important new poems in this collection is "The American Living-Room: A Tract." The quiet, personal, and self-critical voice Meredith employs in this poem quickly brings the reader into the speaker's confidence. The speaker states, "Ideally, you should be in your own/ when you read this." After a diatribe on individualism and on how fortunate Americans are to have enough rooms to label one the living room when many people have nothing, he comments that the living room is used for living but is also a repository of absurdity and clutter. The occupant can be identified by the room's contents: "To others/ this room is what your scent is to a dog./ You can't know it or help it." The final stanza moves away from the nature of living rooms to the nature of poetry: "With us in America, a person who has a printed poem/ is likely to have a living room." Poetry "has somehow gone along/ with the privileges of the nation/ it intends to change, to dispossess of material demons." Meredith's outcry against American materialism—which, in a way, fuels the reader's ability to purchase his book—is only temporary, for he has a modest request. His poem (and indeed all of his poetry) "would like nothing better/ than to be added to the dear clutter here." Again, Meredith calls his readers to look beyond the difficulties of life and be thankful, and he hopes they will accept his poetry into the clutter of their lives, where it might, if only for a brief time, offer a renewal of spirit and a modicum of order.

EFFORT AT SPEECH

In 1983, at the age of sixty-four, William Meredith suffered a stroke that left him with expressive aphasia, which means that he was not able to use language to say or write exactly what he wanted to say. "I know it!" he will utter with force, "but *I* can't say the words!" His struggle and feelings of betrayal by his body are captured in his aptly titled collection *Effort at Speech*. The title poem, written in the 1960's, is dedicated to poet Muriel Rukeyser.

The collection's voice is that of a tired heart, of a life well lived with, at times, quiet suffering. The earlier poems—starting with selections from *Love Letter from an Impossible Land* and continuing through *The Wreck of the Thresher and Other Poems*—showcase Meredith's precise meter and perfectly tuned end-rhyme, making them subtly powerful. In the poems inspired by the poet's service at sea during World War II, devastation comes on the hushed waves of sonnets:

> This is a stuff that cannot come to rest
> For it owns ties to heaven and to the ground;
> While there are achings in the lodestone flesh
> Still will the quick move out and the dead move down.

The poems in the book's latter half (1970-1987) find formalism surrendering some ground to free verse as Meredith attempts to ease the pains of aging—"But the clock goes off, If you have a dog/ It wags, if you get up now you'll be less/ Late"—and the absence of such fallen comrades as Robert Frost, Robert Lowell, W. H. Auden, and John Berryman.

OTHER MAJOR WORKS

EDITED TEXTS: *Shelley*, 1962; *Eighteenth Century English Minor Poets*, 1968 (with Mackie L. Jarrell); *Poets of Bulgaria*, 1986 (John Balaban, translator).

NONFICTIONS: *Poems Are Hard to Read*, 1991.

BIBLIOGRAPHY

Howard, Richard. "William Meredith: 'All of a Piece and Clever and at Some Level, True.'" In *Alone with America: Essays on the Art of Poetry in the United States Since 1950*. New York: Atheneum, 1980. An enlightening if brief study of Meredith's work through *Hazard, the Painter.* Howard's concern with Meredith's quest for "order and delight," using a style that "is partly evasive and sly, party loving and solicitous," is informed and scholarly.

Ludwig, Richard M. "The Muted Lyrics of William Meredith." *Princeton University Library Chronicle* 25 (Autumn, 1963): 73-85. An early and essential critical study of Meredith's first three volumes of poetry. The article includes other writers' comments about Meredith, a biographical sketch, and a comprehensive list of early Meredith publications.

Meredith, William. "The Frost Tradition: A Conversation with William Meredith." Interview by Gregory Fitz Gerald and Paul Ferguson. *Southwest Review* 57 (Spring, 1972): 108-117. This interview, originally produced for television, provides a brief look at Meredith's thoughts and influences. The questions cover a wide range of topics, including his World War II poetry, much of his work up to *Earth Walk*, the importance of Frost and others, the translating of Apollinaire's poetry, and Meredith's fascination with form.

Rotella, Guy. *Three Contemporary Poets of New England: William Meredith, Philip Booth, and Peter Davison*. Boston: Twayne, 1983. Among the most thorough and important analyses of Meredith's poetry available. The text includes biographical notes and a detailed bibliography. Rotella places Meredith firmly in the New England tradition, concluding that he is an important twentieth century poet who is not strictly "an unreconstructed academic formalist," as some critics claim, but a poet who "still seeks hopefully for an ordered life and art, for meaning and value, to affirm and to praise."

Taylor, Henry. "'In Charge of Morale in a Morbid Time': The Poetry of William Meredith." *Hollins Critic* 16 (February, 1979): 1-15. One of the more probing investigations of Meredith's poetry through *Hazard, the Painter.* Taylor sees Meredith's voice, beginning with *The Wreck of the Thresher and Other Poems*, as civilized and "engaged in encounters of inexhaustible interest." Taylor views his frequent use of form as "method, not a barrier."

· *Robert Bateman,*
updated by Sarah Hilbert

JAMES MERRILL

Born: New York, New York; March 3, 1926
Died: Tucson, Arizona; February 6, 1995

PRINCIPAL POETRY

First Poems, 1951
The Country of a Thousand Years of Peace and Other Poems, 1959, revised 1970
Water Street, 1962
Nights and Days, 1966
The Fire Screen, 1969
Braving the Elements, 1972
Divine Comedies, 1976
Mirabell: Books of Number, 1978
Scripts for the Pageant, 1980
The Changing Light at Sandover, 1982
From the First Nine: Poems, 1946-1976, 1982
Late Settings, 1985
The Inner Room, 1988
A Scattering of Salts, 1995
Collected Poems, James Merrill, 2001

OTHER LITERARY FORMS

James Merrill was known mainly as a poet, but he also produced novels, essays, and plays. Two years before his death, his memoir *A Different Person: A Memoir* appeared.

ACHIEVEMENTS

James Merrill was a major voice in American poetry after 1967, when he won his first National Book Award for *Nights and Days*. His 1972 collection *Braving the Elements* won the Bollingen Prize in Poetry, and *Divine Comedies* won the Pulitzer Prize four years later. He was awarded another National Book Award for *Mirabell: Books of Number. The Changing Light at Sandover,* which combines *Divine Comedies, Mirabell,* and *Scripts for the Pageant* with a coda, won the National Book Critics Circle Award. In 1988 the Bobbitt National Prize for Poetry was awarded for *The Inner Room.* Known as a lyric poet and recognized as a master of traditional poetic forms, Merrill stood among the first rank of poets in the United States.

BIOGRAPHY

James Ingram Merrill was born in New York City to Charles Merrill, an extremely powerful and successful stockbroker and founder of the firm that became Merrill Lynch. His mother, Hellen Ingram Merrill, was Charles Merrill's second wife. When James was twelve years old, his parents were divorced. His father married a third time, and that marriage also ended in divorce.

Merrill was graduated in 1947 from Amherst College, where he wrote a senior thesis on Marcel Proust. He served in the U.S. Army at the end of World War II, from 1944 to 1945. For fifteen years, beginning in 1959, he spent part of each year at his home in Greece. He traveled widely in other countries but made his primary home in Stonington, Connecticut.

ANALYSIS

James Merrill's poetry is lyrical, and most of it was written in traditional forms. He was, indeed, a master of the lyric; his ingenious rhymes and subtle utilization of the envelope quatrain (one of his favorite forms), the sonnet, and other forms are almost overwhelming. Helen Vendler, one of the country's best-known critics, called his lyrical gift "ravishing." The poems in his first six books were mostly short ones, but with the publication of *Divine Comedies* he began writing a series of long narrative poems that he brought together in *The Changing Light at Sandover.* Since then a considerable amount of critical attention has been given to this novel in verse. Merrill's concerns include the family, love, change and metamorphosis, the appeal of opposites, and the differences and similarities of imagination and reality. In many poems these concerns are almost inextricably intertwined. Themes from one book appear again in subsequent volumes, as do characters, sometimes commenting on the former work. His methods include humor, especially the humor of irony and of puns, the quoting or paraphrasing of the work of other writers, various narrative techniques, and one technique that might be called philosophical—the construction of a new order for the universe. Informing both his themes and his methods is his immense sense of play.

FIRST POEMS AND THE COUNTRY OF A THOUSAND YEARS OF PEACE

Merrill's *First Poems* includes "Transfigured Bird," four variations on a theme from childhood. Critics have assumed that the child in the poem is Merrill himself. This poem indicates a number of things about the child:

James Merrill

his sense of isolation, his loneliness, and, most important, his discovery that things are often not what they seem at first glance. This book and the one that followed it eight years later, *The Country of a Thousand Years of Peace*, both include poems about love, but the poet's carefully controlled forms and reticent language seem to evade the expression of feelings. For this reason, many critics found Merrill's early work cold and viewed his poetic technique as a mask that seemed to hide his emotions. As W. H. Auden had done, Merrill addressed his love poems to an anonymous "you," thus disguising his homosexuality. This reticence seemed to be particularly handicapping because Merrill chose not to explore the world of current events or the world of ideas, where emotion would not be essential. His personal subject matter seemed to cry out for feeling. This second volume includes Merrill's first poem about the world of the Ouija board—a world that would assume major significance in the later work, but which he dismisses at this point.

WATER STREET

Water Street represents a major change. In this volume the narrator's voice becomes identifiable as that of Merrill himself. For the first time poems that are clearly confessional are included; yet they are confessional only in that they begin to utilize material that is perhaps neurotic, distressing, or humiliating and anguish-filled. Merrill was not one of the confessional poets who spill their lives and feelings wantonly. Having always valued good manners, he did not violate them here; he wrote with restraint, but with power and feeling. In fact, the last stanza in the book is a kind of introduction to the new way he would treat his material. "If I am host at last," he writes, "it is of little more than my own past./ May others be at home in it." Thus he begins to push aside the mask.

Memories of childhood and loneliness are still evident, as in "A Vision of a Garden," in which Merrill shows the reader the picture of a solitary little boy who draws a face with his finger on a winter-frosted window. This poem, while beginning with the child, ends with the adult who has found a lover "whose words whose looks alone undo/ such frosts." There are poems about the family, too, and in this volume Merrill plunges deeper into both family and romantic relationships.

NIGHTS AND DAYS

In his third book, *Nights and Days*, which won the National Book Award, he includes a series of seven sonnets, exploring his feelings about his parents. Although violence and anger are masked, powerful emotion is communicated when he writes that in his father's blue gaze he can see "the soul eclipsed by twin black pupils, sex/ and business; time was money in those days." Although the chief character of the book's final poem is a woman (who in one scene wears makeup that turns her face into a clown's mask), the poem's title, "Days of 1964," alludes to the titles used by C. P. Cavafy for poems about homosexual liaisons. In this volume Merrill moves closer to expressing his true feelings.

THE FIRE SCREEN

Judith Moffett writes of Merrill's next book, *The Fire Screen*, that it does not seem to advance the work. On the other hand, Stephen Yenser finds that in it the narrative impulse predominates, and that in use of anecdote and character "Kostas Tympakianakis" points toward Merrill's later long narratives. In almost every collection Merrill includes at least one poem that concerns family; in this volume, it is "Mornings in a New House," which includes the lines that give the volume its title. He shows a cold man in a new house in front of its fireplace. He thinks about the fire screen stitched in crewel by his mother when she was a child. The screen, depicting giant birds and flowery trees, is a kind of embroidery made from lustrous threads, but threads that have been crossed, recrossed, and knotted—not unlike, perhaps, the relationships between mother and child. Love is a theme of several of these poems, but it is artfully veiled. In the volume's first poem, "Lorelei," the narrator speaks of an unnamed loved one, saying that each steppingstone has stranded "you." Next Merrill's typical opposites appear, and he changes, saying, "Does not. Not yet. Not here./ Is it a crossing? Is there no way back?"

BRAVING THE ELEMENTS

Merrill's next book, *Braving the Elements*, is significant in several ways. First, it is replete with puns and numerous other wordplays, as his previous books were, but they are even more evident and delightful here. He uses these methods in "The Emerald," another poem about both family and love. In this poem his mother gives him an emerald ring that his father had given her when his son was born. It is for his future wife, she says. Although the poem says that he does not tell his mother, he is telling the reader that he is homosexual, that he will not marry and father children.

> I do not tell her, it would sound theatrical,
> *Indeed this green room's mine, my very life.*
> *We are each other's; there will be no wife;*
> *The little feet that patter here are metrical.*

In the final poem in the book, the last four words, arranged in a cross pattern, illustrate Merrill's persisting love for antithesis. The words, to be read first down and then across, are "Nought/ Sought/ Waste Erased." They cancel one another out in one sense, but in another sense, if nothing is looked for, then the time one might have spent looking is not erased at all, but is available for other purposes. Still, it may be wasted because nothing worthwhile was tried. Merrill would have it both ways.

Although Merrill frequently used narrative elements in his poems, and in fact wrote two novels, in this volume he presents one of his most significant narratives. "Days of 1935" combines his concern with family, his childhood loneliness, and his narrative imagination. The little rich boy who has appeared in many previous poems knows about the Lindbergh kidnapping and in his fancy constructs his own kidnappers, Floyd and Jean, who seem extremely interesting, however sinister. In the end, however, although they have snatched him out of his ordinary life and transported him into their illicit one, they let his parents take him back. He is abandoned to his mother's "Grade/ A controls" and his father's provisions, the latter implying that the father was more likely to give gifts than time or love. This pattern of rescue and return is one that will repeat itself in his grown-up love affairs—the excitement of the early interest and then the desertion. Merrill draws this parallel clearly in another poem in this volume, "Days of 1971," in which he defines love:

> Proust's Law (are you listening?) is twofold:
> (a) What least thing our self-love longs for most
> Others instinctively withhold;
> (b) Only when time has slain desire
> Is his wish granted to a smiling ghost
> Neither harmed nor warmed, now, by the fire.

DIVINE COMEDIES

One of Merrill's most significant books, *Divine Comedies* was published in 1976; it contains "The Book of Ephraim," a long narrative poem that was to become part 1 of the trilogy *The Changing Light at Sandover*. Judith Moffett says of it, "This suspension bridge joining the body of Merrill's earlier poetry to his *Sandover* trilogy may well be ultimately adjudged his finest single piece of writing." This long poem, essentially the beginning of a journey of discovery about the nature of God, grew out of the experience Merrill and his friend and lover, David Jackson, had over a period of years with a Ouija board. The two had shared houses since 1955 in Stonington, Connecticut; Athens, Greece; and Key West, Florida.

Soon after they had moved into their Stonington house, the two were whiling away an evening at the Ouija board when something extraordinary began to happen. The cup that they were using for a pointer began to spin furiously and spelled out letter after letter, which Merrill began copying down as rapidly as possible. They were being visited by a familiar from the spirit world, one Ephraim, who explained that he was a homosexual Greek Jew who had become a servant of the Roman Emperor Tiberius. The first story line in the book has to do with the relationship between JM (Merrill) and DJ (Jackson) and their relationship to the garrulous, humorous, but not altogether reliable Ephraim. One of Ephraim's major teachings is that God is imagination. Ephraim serves as an instructor to the two younger men about the science of the soul after death.

The second line in the plot involves characters from a novel that Merrill was writing and whose manuscript he lost in a taxi in Georgia. These characters are Eros, a person who seems to resemble Ephraim; Sergei Markovich, who may incorporate characteristics of Merrill; a Mrs. Rosamund Smith; Leon Cade, a Vietnam War veteran who has suffered some horrifying experiences in the war; and others. The third line has to do with the writing of the poem. Both JM and DJ comment on what Ephraim tells them, express doubts, and have reservations. Later, other characters appear, including Hans Lodeizen, a young Dutch poet who died of leukemia in 1950; Maya Deren, an avant-garde dancer and filmmaker who was a friend of both JM and DJ; and the poet W. H. Auden, who had recently died.

Besides opening up the exploration of the question of the nature of God, this poem continues Merrill's interest in the nature of love. In fact, as Merrill approached middle age, he found that "we've wanted/ Consuming passions; these refine instead . . . Yield such regret and wit as MERRILY/ GLOW ON when limbs licked blazing past recall/ Are banked where interest is minimal." This poem is full of typical Merrill wordplays and, though focused on an otherworldly chronicle, still evidences Merrill's concern with family. Details about JM and DJ's everyday life and worries are included with the more esoteric and metaphysical work. The poem describes David Jackson's aged parents living in the West, still "at each other's gnarled,/ Loveless mercy." It speaks as well of Merrill's father, who

> in his last illness complained
> Of the effect of medication on
> His real self—today Bluebeard, tomorrow
> Babbitt. Young chameleon, I used to
> Ask how on earth one got sufficiently
> imbued with otherness. And now I see.

This passage again illustrates Merrill's opposites, and his fascination with illusion and reality.

MIRABELL

Mirabell, which becomes part 2 of the Sandover trilogy, is unlike "The Book of Ephraim," in several ways. In "The Book of Ephraim," Merrill wrote the story; in this second part, and again in part 3, the spirits dictate the material. After Ephraim's book was finished, one day in 1976 Merrill and Jackson were engaged in what they considered would be a friendly chat with the spirits. Instead, some strange, dreadful powers intruded and ordered Merrill to write "poems of science," because, they insisted, the work was not finished yet. After accepting their dictates, Merrill and Jackson found themselves giving hours every day to the Ouija board. Merrill spent additional hours transcribing and trying to make sense of the voluminous messages, and eventually gave them both a poetic shape and a narrative structure. What resulted is a mythology to account for the new science that has discovered black holes and other astronomical anomalies, as well as the mysteries of the cell and physi-

cal chemistry. This is an intriguing reversal of the world's other genesis mythologies in that all of those were prescientific, whereas this mythology provides stories to explain the scientifically known. In the beginning Merrill was uneasy because he did not have control of the material and resented that "it's all by someone else." Moreover, both Merrill and Jackson were uncomfortable with some of the things the spiritual messengers told them, especially their insistence on determinism and elitism. Nevertheless, Merrill eventually came to look forward to the enormous work of each day; he told Helen Vendler in an interview published in 1979, "I woke up day after day beaming with anticipation."

The spirits provide the myths to explain God Biology, who is referred to thereafter as God B. These spirits who begin *Mirabell* are bats. They have numbers for names and are metaphorically the rebellious angels; they are also antimatter itself, as well as the negative electrical charge within the atom. Other characters arrive also—many of them, fortunately, more benevolent. Auden has a large role, as does JM and DJ's old friend Maria Mitsotaki. These two act, in a certain sense, as surrogate parents for JM and DJ, Auden addressing them as "my boys" and Maria calling them "mes enfants." These two characters have several other functions as well. Auden suggests poetic techniques to JM when the poet is struggling for an adequate form. Furthermore, he is at first the most skeptical of all the students. This works very well, because Auden had a skeptical, inquiring nature, yet his eventual adoption of the traditional Anglican faith is well known. His voice can thus lend authenticity to the bizarre proceedings. Maria, unlike Auden, was not a public figure; she was a Greek friend of JM and DJ. She serves as both a mother figure and an example of life's strange unknowns: They discover that her death was not natural but instead a suicide. Later they also learn that her brilliant mind is really that of one of the Five Immortals.

In part 3 other friends, four angels, the Nine Muses, two numbered familiars, and other characters also appear. *Mirabell* is the most dense of the three parts and includes a great many explanations that have a certain tedium. The last two books continue the exploration of the nature of God but concentrate much more on humankind's relationship with nature. The spiritual teachers are appalled at overpopulation and at massive destruction of nature's riches. All of this is lightened by Merrill's puns, spoonerisms, and other kinds of wordplay, and by comments from JM and DJ on what they are being told.

SCRIPTS FOR THE PAGEANT

Scripts for the Pageant became part 3 of the trilogy, and in it JM and DJ discover that the *Mirabell* spirits were not completely informed and hence told them some things that were wrong. It also introduces God B's twin, Psyche/Chaos/Mother Nature. It contains further disturbing revelations. The two learned in "The Book of Ephraim" that the first law is survive and the second is no accidents; now they are instructed about "V Work," the only work that really counts. Further, the spirit guides insist that humans sinned when they discovered how to split the atom and that a kind of apocalypse is coming. The four major characters, drawn together by their strange lessons, puzzle over the happenings. The final stanza of "Samos," the canzone that introduces the last part of *Scripts for the Pageant*, addresses their mutual confusion.

> Samos. We keep trying to make sense
> Of what we can. Not souls of the first water—
> Although we've put on airs, and taken fire—
> We shall be dust of quite another land
> Before the seeds here planted come to light.

This passage is full of puns and wordplay, but it also illustrates the familial feeling of the four students, JM, DJ, Auden, and Maria.

In fact, when it is time for Maria to take her leave to be born again in Bombay, her last speech is of friendship and love. She says that her old life had too few attachments, and then, anticipating her new life, says, "yet if loving's 88/ percent is chemical I anticipate/ forming some strong new bonds." There is more than a comment on love here; there is also a punning reference to the fact that Maria is to be reborn as a biochemist. Numerous changes have also occurred in this volume, but one of the most startling has to do with Maria. In the "NO" section the readers learn that she is really Plato.

THE CHANGING LIGHT AT SANDOVER

When *The Changing Light at Sandover* appeared, Merrill added a coda both to give a sense of closure to the entire work and to keep the process going. At the end of *Scripts for the Pageant* the poem insists on swirling up, to hear God B one last time. The coda involves returns and also the possibility of new beginnings. Many of the pronouncements in *Mirabell* were as grim as Old Testament prophecy. Perhaps a case could be made for *Scripts for the Pageant*'s making subtle correspondences with the first four books of the New Testament. The coda then may correspond to the New Testament's Book of Acts. The correspondence between the visions of Saint John in Revelation and some of the revelations in this account must not be discounted either.

The Changing Light at Sandover is Merrill's most notable achievement. It will surely be read and studied for years, and it places him among that elite group of poets who have also dared to write their metaphysical visions: William Butler Yeats, William Blake, John Milton, and Dante. It is not surprising that a poet who was a master of poetic forms would turn his hand (or his psyche) to a system. While the systems of Blake, Milton, and Dante were concerned primarily with humanity's relation to God, and Yeats's work was partially concerned with this connection, Merrill's work is more concerned with humans' relationship to the earth on which they live. That this relationship has far-reaching and even theological implications should be no surprise.

It must be noted, however, that although the critic could study the system for its theology, the entire premise—in fact, the machinery that brings the "revelations"—is based on play. One plays with a Ouija board; it is a kind of game. This spirit of play permeates the entire work and is evident especially in the varieties of humor. Some of this is the humor of irony; some of it comes from puns, to which Merrill was addicted; some of it comes from other kinds of wordplay. The entire work merits study for its wordplay alone. One of Merrill's most effective techniques was using a word and meaning more than one of its meanings—frequently several of them at once. This technique was used by Marianne Moore, who introduced some of her best ideas into her work this way. A study of the roots of the words Merrill carefully chose yields further clues to the depth of his humor (and his thinking as well).

Throughout Merrill's work, family relations, the nature of love, changes, and the differences between appearance and reality occupied his attention. He began by writing poems that were relatively short but branched out into the long narrative poem, which gave him the room to let his imagination range across the whole universe and throughout history (and even prehistory) and to launch sorties into the world of ideas. There is no doubt that the writing of *The Changing Light at Sandover* changed and enlarged his work remarkably.

LATE SETTINGS

The year in which *The Changing Light at Sandover* appeared also saw the publication of *From the First Nine*, a selection from Merrill's first nine books of poetry. *Late Settings*, published in 1985, includes some fragments that had been cut from the final *The Changing Light at Sandover*. "From the Cutting-Room Floor" includes bits starring William Carlos Williams, Marianne Moore, and Gertrude Stein, who appears as hostess of *Meet the Press in Heaven*, interviewing Elvis Presley. The understated humor of these pieces is delightful.

The two most important poems in this volume, however, are "Clearing the Title," which has to do with new beginnings, and "Santorini: Stopping the Leak." The latter makes a number of references to persons and places seen in *The Changing Light at Sandover*. The narrator finds himself in the night kicking off his bedclothes, and the sheets flap "like bats in negative"—surely akin to the bats in *Mirabell*. He also passes a chapel to Saint Michael, who was one of the important characters in *Scripts for the Pageant*. Also, the narrator has had X rays to remove a plantar wart on his foot, but as readers know from *The Changing Light at Sandover*, too many X rays can burn up the soul. Now he finds that he has a small ghost-leak in the "footsole."

THE INNER ROOM

The Inner Room reveals a new twist in Merrill's poetic technique. He had seldom used prose poems, but this volume contains a series of them in a section titled "Prose of Departure." Because these poems describe a trip to Japan, they include a number of haiku. The Japanese influence is further evident in that the poems echo Matsuo Bashō's travel journals. The most significant part of this book, however, is the brief play *The Image Maker*. The chief character in this play is a *santero*, a carver and repairer of saint statues in a Caribbean village. He is obviously a maker in the Aristotelian sense.

He and his society practice Santería, a Latin American religion that combines Christian concepts with Yoruba lore from West African religions. In Santería the saints have double characters, their beneficent Christian side and an opposite side that belongs to a pagan deity, Chango, who is violent and chaotic. Merrill's work has always been concerned with doubleness, and this situation provides him with an opportunity to explore it. Although the *santero* has the skill to shape the saints' figures and dress, their inner lives belong equally to good and evil. Thus the maker can provide a symbol but has no control over the actions resulting from his creations. When the *santero* is called away from his combined home and workplace by the voice of the damaged Saint Barbara, who imitates the voice of his sickly and whining mother, the *santos* come to life and their wild and evil selves prevail. Francisco kills the pet dove, and Barbara sets fire to a wall calendar, thus destroying all the holy days. When the *santero* returns, he cleans up the mess, then appeases Chango with cigar smoke and a ceremony, and returns to his work of repairing Barbara.

Merrill here continues some of the concepts from *The Changing Light at Sandover*. Just as the familiars from another world had insisted, the creative artist of any kind does not have control over the effects of creation. God B and Mother Nature lament this fact in *The Changing Light at Sandover*. Although not knowing how a created work will turn out has negative aspects, it can have positive aspects as well. The discovery in the work not only may affect the work but also can have profound effects on the maker. Merrill says, "Writing his or her poems changes a poet, over the years, in ways that perhaps time or society by themselves couldn't."

Moreover, the artist does not know when he or she begins how the product will turn out. The artist is often surprised, because the materials for the work discover their possibilities as the process proceeds. This play affirms the "V Work" and provides, as well, a miniature of one of the major concepts of *The Changing Light at Sandover*—the multifaceted nature of human beings. In a simple yet profound way, it demonstrates that cleaning up is one of the virtues and explores once again the complex relationship between reality and illusion.

There is no doubt that the Sandover trilogy affected Merrill's work. This does not mean that the subsequent poems are lesser. It may mean that as his work took new turns, the later work was glossed by *The Changing Light at Sandover* rather than the reverse. Merrill's work is of major importance for its poetic technique, for his brilliant use of language, and for the quality of the imagination he displays. Moreover, his exploration of metaphysical concerns that are universal and timeless puts it among works of important thought.

A SCATTERING OF SALTS

A Scattering of Salts, published in 1995 after Merrill's death, was the last book he saw through production. Although Merrill had written about death before, those poems in this final collection that address mortality, fragility, aging, and the passage of time acquire particular irony and poignancy. Still, as readers of Merrill might expect, even in the most serious and sometimes bitter poems, humor—jokes, wordplay, topical allusions—nearly always forms a part of the poet's scheme.

The book's title offers insight into its perspective. Merrill makes use of most of the familiar proverbial or biblical references to salt in a number of these poems. The first poem, "A Downward Look," plays on the image of salts in a bath wherein one sees the "sky." The last poem in the collection, suitably called "An Upward Look," refers to the superstition of keeping Satan at a distance by scattering salt on the ground, to the tradition of tossing a pinch of spilled salt over one's shoulder in order to avoid bad luck, and to the biblical expression "salt of the earth." Yet whereas "A Downward Look" sounds a cheerful note (a baby's hand is among the last images), "An Upward Look" is about burial—and, perhaps, a kind of resurrection.

Between these two complementary poems are other works of varying length about themes that always surface in Merrill's poetry. Some poems which feature members of his family (for instance, the touching "My Father's Irish Setters" and "164 East 72nd Street"), in others humor dominates ("Scrapping the Computer"), and in still others, the meaning of life itself is the subject in one way or another ("Tony: Ending the Life"). Merrill nearly allows the book to end on a note of profound bitterness. His "Self Portrait in Tyvek (TM) Windbreaker" energetically, and often comically, excoriates politicians, cheap sex, lazy parents, false camaraderie, and

"Ecosaints" as well as those who have defiled nature. The collection ends, however, without bitterness: The last three lines of Merrill's last poem, "An Upward Look," must be read as signs of hope:

> First the grave dissolving into dawn
> then the crucial recrystallizing
> from inmost depths of clear dark blue.

OTHER MAJOR WORKS

LONG FICTION: *The Seraglio*, 1957; *The (Diblos) Notebook*, 1965.

PLAYS: *The Bait*, pr. 1953; *The Immortal Husband*, pr. 1955; *The Image Maker*, pr., pb. 1986.

NONFICTION: *Recitative*, 1986; *A Different Person: A Memoir*, 1993.

BIBLIOGRAPHY

Adams, Don. *James Merrill's Poetic Quest*. Westport, Conn.: Greenwood Press, 1997. A comprehensive look at Merrill's often difficult symbolism. Adams sees Merrill's life as a "quest to save his life through his art" and considers specific works in this light. Provides a close reading of *The Changing Light at Sandover*.

Bloom, Harold, ed. *James Merrill*. Modern Critical Views Series. New York: Chelsea House, 1986. Harold Bloom's introduction to this collection of essays is especially valuable. There is a chronology and an index.

Labrie, Ross. *James Merrill*. Boston: Twayne, 1982. This volume in the Twayne's United States Authors series is the first full-length study of Merrill's poems, fiction, and plays. Contains separate chapters on Merrill's life and art, his plays, his fiction, and his poems of the 1940's and 1950's, and a chapter that analyzes the *Divine Comedies*. Includes an interesting section on Merrill's view of art. Supplemented by a two-page chronology of the poet's life, notes and references, a select bibliography, and an index. Suitable for all students.

Lehman, David, and Charles Berger, eds. *James Merrill: Essays in Criticism*. Ithaca, N.Y.: Cornell University Press, 1982. This volume collects a number of essays on Merrill's work. Especially useful are David Lehman's "Elemental Bravery: The Unity of James Merrill's Poetry," Willard Spiegelman's "Breaking the Mirror: Interruption in Merrill's Trilogy," and David Jackson's "Lending a Hand." This volume has an index, notes, and a bibliography.

Materer, Timothy. *James Merrill's Apocalypse*. Ithaca, N.Y.: Cornell University Press, 2000. Covers Merrill's entire career and focuses on the poet's preoccupation with the violence that threatens us in reality. Materer deals with Merrill's novels as well as the poetry, making use of the Washington University collection of Merrill's papers. Places the moral and religious themes found in *The Changing Light at Sandover* in context with the tradition of apocalyptic literature and with Merrill's earlier poetry and prose. Notes, index.

Moffett, Judith. *James Merrill: An Introduction to the Poetry*. New York: Columbia University Press, 1984. Moffett traces Merrill's themes of childhood, family, love, and masking, and the influences on his work of Proust and opera. She uses a chronological method, beginning with his first book, privately published by his father when Merrill was only sixteen. She admires Merrill's work but is critical of passages that she finds too obscure. This volume is an easy-to-read entry into Merrill's work. The text is supplemented by notes, a good selected bibliography, and an index.

Polito, Robert. *A Reader's Guide to James Merrill's "The Changing Light at Sandover."* Foreword by James Merrill. Ann Arbor: University of Michigan Press, 1994. Polito's purpose is to make Merrill's work more accessible by unifying, in an alphabetical reference, characters and events that appear in widely separated passages or under different names in the trilogy. This guide functions as an annotated index with cross-references to related terms. An additional section collects appraisals of the poem from critics and other poets, and an afterword examines the ways the poem treats the themes of surface appearances and hidden realities.

Vendler, Helen. "James Merrill." In *Part of Nature, Part of Us: Modern American Poets*. Cambridge, Mass.: Harvard University Press, 1980. The section on Merrill provides informative commentary on *Braving the Elements, Divine Comedies*, and *Mirabell: Books of Number*. Vendler says that in *Braving the Elements* Merrill finally found a use for all of his many talents, including his fondness for narrative and his gift for euphony. Includes a foreword by Vendler and a bibliography of books discussed.

Von Hallberg, Robert. "James Merrill: Revealing by Obscuring." In *American Poetry and Culture, 1945-1980*. Cambridge, Mass.: Harvard University Press, 1985. Von Hallberg asserts that much of Merrill's style—his elegance, good manners, and literary language—comes from his position as part of the American upper class. He addresses Merrill's subversion of his own texts and briefly argues that *The Changing Light at Sandover* was written at least partly out of consideration for David Jackson, his companion.

Yenser, Stephen. *The Consuming Myth: The Work of James Merrill*. Cambridge, Mass.: Harvard University Press, 1987. This study emphasizes Merrill's proclivity for seeing duality while still being aware of the interconnectedness of things. This book is more detailed and complex than Moffett's and addresses in greater depth Merrill's literary references. The text is supplemented by an index, extensive notes, a useful list of Merrill's works, and photographs.

Ann Struthers,
updated by Gordon Walters

THOMAS MERTON

Born: Prades, France; January 31, 1915
Died: Bangkok, Thailand; December 10, 1968

PRINCIPAL POETRY

Thirty Poems, 1944
A Man in the Divided Sea, 1946
Figures for an Apocalypse, 1947
The Tears of the Blind Lions, 1949

The Strange Islands, 1957
Selected Poems, 1959, 1967
Original Child Bomb, 1962
Emblems of a Season of Fury, 1963
Cables to the Ace, 1968
The Geography of Lograire, 1969
The Collected Poems, 1977

OTHER LITERARY FORMS

Better known for his nonfiction prose than his poetry, Thomas Merton wrote an autobiography, *The Seven Storey Mountain* (1948); four journals, *The Secular Journal* (1959), *The Sign of Jonas* (1953), *Conjectures of a Guilty Bystander* (1966), and *The Asian Journal of Thomas Merton* (1973); and numerous books of theology and devotion, including *Seasons of Celebration* (1950), *No Man Is an Island* (1955), and *Contemplative Prayer* (1969). His other works include an early novel, published posthumously, *My Argument with the Gestapo* (1969); translations of church fathers, including *Clement of Alexandria* (1962) and *The Wisdom of the Desert* (1960); and several works about Eastern religion: *The Way of Chuang Tzu* (1965), *Mystics and Zen Masters* (1967), and *Zen and the Birds of Appetite* (1968). Merton published numerous articles on a similar range of topics in periodicals such as *Commonweal, The Catholic Worker, The American Benedictine Review, Jubilee*, and *The Sewanee Review*. A selection of his photographs and calligraphy has been published by John Howard Griffin in *A Hidden Wholeness* (1970). Merton's literary essays, introductions, and related materials are collected in *The Literary Essays of Thomas Merton* (1981).

ACHIEVEMENTS

A teacher of English literature turned Cistercian monk, Thomas Merton bridges two worlds, bringing his considerable skill as a prose stylist to his religious works and turning Catholic dogma into poetry. He has been acclaimed by many critics, with some justification, as the most important religious writer of the mid-twentieth century—a superlative that is, of course, impossible to establish. One thing, however, is certain: Neither as influential or skillful a poet as T. S. Eliot or W. H. Auden, nor as important a theologian as Karl

Barth or Dietrich Bonhoeffer, Merton is impressive in both areas; among his contemporaries, only C. S. Lewis can rival him. Beyond this there is Merton's importance as an antiparadigm for modern society. His life and writings reveal a mind unwilling to rest in any of the easy philosophies of twentieth century Western culture.

BIOGRAPHY

Thomas Merton was born near Prades, France, in the Pyrenees, on January 31, 1915. His father, Owen Merton, a post-Impressionist painter of some note, was a New Zealander who met his American wife, Ruth, while both were art students in Paris. Because of the dangers of World War I, Merton's family soon moved across the Atlantic to Douglastown, Long Island, to be near his maternal grandparents. There his brother John Paul was born in 1918 and shortly afterward, in 1921, his mother died of stomach cancer. While the younger brother remained in America with his grandparents, young Merton's father took him to Bermuda, France, and England in order to find fit subjects to paint. The stay in France was one of the formative influences on Merton's life, for there he was deeply moved by the "medieval" aspects of French village life, including the Catholic churches that he saw but never entered.

After his removal to England, Merton began his serious education by matriculating at Oakham School in Rutland in 1929. Almost immediately after this, his father contracted brain cancer and died in 1930 after a period of invalidism. This death left the fifteen-year-old Merton orphaned, yet, because of a settlement from his grandfather, financially secure. Only minimally supervised by his grandparents across the Atlantic and a guardian in London, Merton spent his adolescence and early twenties in increasing commitment to two things—literature and dissipation.

He started off on a disastrous walking tour of Germany during one of the academic holidays at Oakham and came back with an infection that developed into a near-fatal case of blood poisoning. In 1936 he matriculated at Clare College, Cambridge, where he began a year of dissipation unusual even for college freshmen, one of the few sober moments of which, it seems, was the winter holiday which he spent touring Rome and visiting the many impressive churches there. On the recommendation of his guardian, he left Cambridge at the end of the school year, realizing that he was wasting his time there. He left England and took up residence with his grandparents on Long Island and matriculated at Columbia University.

At Columbia he was accepted into a circle of literary-minded undergraduates including several who were later successful as writers and editors—Edward Rice, Robert Lax, and Robert Giroux. This relationship led him to channel some of his restless energy into several of Columbia's student publications—forming a habit of regular and prolific writing that never left him. With his friends, he discovered the teaching of Mark Van Doren—a circumstance that convinced Merton to major in English and write a master's thesis under Van Doren, titled "Nature and Art in William Blake" (1939). His conversion to Catholicism was a process of which the external causes are more difficult to identify than those of his conversion to writing. Among the discernible influences, however, were his enrollment in a course in Scholastic philosophy under visiting professor (later Father) Daniel Walsh, his discovery of the theological writings of Jacques Maritain, his study of the "mysticism" of Blake, and his reading of the journals of Gerard Manley Hopkins. On November 16, 1938, he was baptized a Catholic.

Soon after Merton's conversion two important things happened. First, he began to write poetry, and, second, he began to entertain ideas of devoting himself totally to God by entering one of the religious orders, deciding finally on the Franciscans. He was conditionally accepted, but just days before entering the novitiate, he compulsively confessed doubts about his former way of life to the Franciscan priest who was arranging his vocation. He was consequently turned down as unstable.

Disconsolate, he accepted a position teaching English at the Franciscan St. Bonaventure's University in Olean, New York, as a means of living as close to the monastic life as he could manage as a layman—reciting the Breviary daily and writing religious verse. During this time, dissatisfaction still plagued him; he had gradually given up his dissipations, but life at a Franciscan school in upstate New York seemed too easy—not the total dedication to God that he desired. Two alternate vocations presented themselves to him: joining, in voluntary poverty, the Friendship House in Harlem, a Catholic social agency run by Catherine de Hueck Doherty, or entering the Gethsemani Monastery near Louisville, Kentucky, the Cistercian Abbey he visited for a retreat during Holy Week of 1941. The decision was a difficult one, but the attraction of a contemplative life won, and he entered Gethsemani on December 10, 1941, only three days after the United States' entry into World War II.

For a period of time in the late 1940's, Merton considered leaving the Cistercians for the eremitical life of the Order of the Carthusians. He finally perceived this as a temptation, and by the time he progressed through the novitiate, vows, minor clerical orders, and finally the priesthood in 1949, the desire had left him. As soon as he entered Gethsemani, his superiors recognized his abilities as a writer, commissioning him to write books on various monastic topics and especially encouraging his poetry. His four volumes of poetry published in the 1940's attest both his talent and the initial encouragement of his superiors.

Thomas Merton (Library of Congress)

Merton, however, saw his vocation as a writer totally opposed to that as a monk, preferring the humble anonymity of silence to the clatter of the typewriter. In short, he wrote under obedience to his Abbot. The irony of this situation should not escape anyone who reads the poet whose influence over Merton's personal and poetic life is greater than any other—Hopkins. Hopkins, like Merton, an undergraduate convert to Catholicism given to journal writing and poetry, was denied permission to compose verse by his superiors in the Jesuit order. Merton solved his dilemma with a compromise, finding that writing books on theology was actually helping rather than hindering his contemplative tendencies but receiving permission to stop writing poetry. Consequently, he published no volumes of poetry between 1949 and 1957—the period that was his most prolific for prose.

The last period of Merton's life, the decade before his death in 1968, is in many ways the most complex. It is characterized by his sudden and prolific rededication to poetry, his increasing reinvolvement in the world through his social criticism and interest in the Civil Rights movement, his commitment to the ecumenism and monastic renewal mandated by Vatican II, his increasing interest in Asian religions, and, finally, his retreat in 1965 to a secluded hermitage on the grounds of Gethsemani Abbey where he could devote himself to a life of total prayer and contemplation which incorporated practices both Catholic and Zen. At this stage, he also took up calligraphy and photography as Zen disciplines. This growing love of Asian religions and ideas led him to leave Gethsemani in the fall of 1968 for an Asian trip to speak at several religious conferences and, more important, to learn at first hand of Hinduism, Sufism, and Buddhism. He visited the Dalai Lama and other religious leaders in India, Sri Lanka, and Thailand, kept a journal, and wrote several poems about his experiences. On December 10, 1968, twenty-seven years to the day after his entry into the monastic life, he delivered a paper in Bangkok, Thailand, to a religious conference; he retired to his room that afternoon and, because of faulty wiring in a large electric fan, died accidentally of electric shock. He left in manuscript a considerable body of work, both poetry and prose—much of which has been published posthumously.

ANALYSIS

As a prose writer who published more than forty volumes of autobiography and theology, Thomas Merton is surprisingly homogenous, dealing with the same themes and subjects, presenting the same insights from slightly different perspectives. Even his books on Asian religions develop Eastern refinements on insights he had already developed from a Western point of view— inner peace and how to achieve it. His poetry, however, is amazingly diverse. In *The Collected Poems*, a volume of more than a thousand pages, echoes can be heard of a widely diverse group of literary figures who attracted his interest: John Donne, T. S. Eliot, James Joyce, Richard Crashaw, Gerard Manley Hopkins, William Blake, George Herbert, Andrew Marvell, Hart Crane, Ezra Pound, William Carlos Williams, and the Provençal troubadours.

This list, however, is not an indication that Merton was a slavishly derivative poet; its diversity alone indicates that part of his creativity was his ability to assimilate so much material. Yet he does more than assimilate; the vast difference between his first volume of verse, *Thirty Poems*, and his last, *The Geography of Lograire*, bespeaks a mind both open to new experiences and able to re-create itself poetically. Unlike many other poets, Merton has more than one thing to say, and much of the aesthetic enjoyment of reading his work is hearing him discover a voice suitable to his subjects.

THIRTY POEMS

Thirty Poems contains poems that Merton wrote during his secular years after his conversion to Catholicism and during his first years as a novice at Gethsemani. The thirty short poems are composed in a lyric mode, mainly on religious themes. Some of them are travel poems ("Song for Our Lady of Cobre," "Night Train," "Aubade: Lake Erie"), while most reflect cessation of motion in the dual stability of place ("The Trappist Abbey: Matins") and liturgy ("The Communion," "The Holy Sacrament of the Altar"). The thirty poems chart a journey away from a dangerous world toward a monastic retreat—Merton's physical and mental journey recorded in *The Seven Storey Mountain*—"The Flight into Egypt," to borrow the title of one of them. Merton's rejection of the world is evident in such poems as "Dirge for the Proud World," "Lent in a Year of War," and the poignant lament, "For My Brother: Reported Missing in Action, 1943."

In *Thirty Poems*, as in much of Merton's early poetry, Hopkins is a strong influence. Merton had even begun a doctoral thesis at Columbia on Hopkins—a project terminated by his monastic vocation. Not only does Merton owe much of his general religious imagery to Hopkins in *Thirty Poems*; he also owes the title and subject matter of "The Blessed Virgin Compared to a Window" to Hopkins's "The Blessed Virgin Mary Compared to the Air We Breathe."

A MAN IN THE DIVIDED SEA

A Man in the Divided Sea, Merton's second volume of poetry, written simultaneously with his first and dedicated to Mary, queen of poets, is a longer continuation of *Thirty Poems*. The themes of travel ("Tropics," "Calypso's Island," "The Ohio River—Louisville"), rest ("A Letter to My Friends on Entering the Monastery," "After the Night Office—Gethsemani Abbey," "The Trappist Cemetery—Gethsemani"), and retreat from the world ("Poem: 1939," "Dirge for a Town in France," "Ode to the Present Century") function in the same way. This longer, richer volume contains themes missing in the earlier one, notably the sacramental view of nature, in which the woods, fields, and hills around Merton's Abbey become a mystical path running parallel to the liturgical one. Poems such as "April," "Advent" (a poem about winter nights), and "Trappists, Working" (a poem about laboring in the fields) take their place in *A Man in the Divided Sea* beside poems such as "The Candlemas Procession" and "Song for the Blessed Sacrament."

The depth of Merton's reading also becomes evident in this volume, for there are poems on subjects from Greek myths, poetic treatments of several saints, and aubades in imitation of the Provençal troubadours. Merton, like many of his poetic generation, imitates T. S. Eliot: "April" and "Ash Wednesday" owe titles, imagery, and prosody to the Eliot of *The Waste Land* (1922). More important than these influences is that of the seventeenth century Metaphysical poets. Merton admits in his autobiography that Andrew Marvell's rhymed octosyllabic couplets shaped, to a large extent, his early poetry, and one can still hear echoes of Marvell in *A Man in the Divided Sea*, even if Merton chose not to publish many of his rhymed poems. "An Invocation to St. Lucy" has its

forerunner in a poem of Marvell's greater predecessor, John Donne ("A Nocturnal upon St. Lucy's Day"), and some of the sensual Catholic imagery found in Richard Crashaw emerges in "The Biography." "Transformation: For the Sacred Heart" owes its subject and some oddities of phrasing to George Herbert, while an occasional psalm paraphrase in Merton has its equivalent in Herbert and other seventeenth century poets.

FIGURES FOR AN APOCALYPSE

"Figures for an Apocalypse," the title poem of Merton's third volume, is his first published attempt at a long poem—a type to which he became increasingly committed. It is a poem in eight sections roughly paralleling the biblical book of the Apocalypse but modernizing it drastically. The seriousness of subject matter is tempered by some passages of exuberant satire, especially Section III, subtitled "Advice to my Friends Robert Lax and Edward Rice, to get away while they still can." Section VI, "In the Ruins of New York," is notable for its view of that city blooming into flowers and grasses after the apocalypse cleanses it.

The rest of *Figures for an Apocalypse* consists of short, lyric poems in the mode of Merton's two earlier volumes dealing with the same themes. "Canticle for the Blessed Virgin" and "Duns Scotus" are Hopkinsian, as are the frequent nature poems—"Landscape: Wheatfields," "Evening: Zero Weather," "Winter Afternoon," and "Spring: Monastery Farm." "Natural History" is, perhaps, Merton's most derivative poem, for in it he even adopts some of Hopkins's syntactical oddities, including the ungrammatical omission of relative pronouns. This exuberant imitation of poets he liked could have led Merton into slavishness, except for an equally exuberant tendency to mix the seemingly unmixable. "Spring: Monastery Farm," for example, combines Hopkins's nature with complex astronomical imagery drawn from Donne's "Good Friday, 1613." "Duns Scotus," similarly, is derived from Hopkins's "Duns Scotus's Oxford," but its syntax and some of its imagery echo not Hopkins but the William Blake of "The Tyger." As one might expect, Blake, the subject of Merton's master's thesis and a poet whose mysticism opened a spiritual door to Merton, also leaves his mark on Merton's poetry. The surprising fact, however, is that Blake's influence is not discernible until *Figures for an Apoca-*

lypse. Blake's influence grows, while that of Hopkins diminishes in Merton's later poetry.

THE TEARS OF THE BLIND LIONS

Two small volumes, *The Tears of the Blind Lions* and *The Strange Islands*, are transitional, indicating the direction of Merton's later poetry while retaining some of the influences and themes of his earlier work. Dedicated to Jacques Maritain, the French lay theologian and philosopher whose books helped lead Merton to conversion and who later became his personal friend, *The Tears of the Blind Lions* is the last volume of poems that Merton published before his eight-year cessation of poetic composition in the 1950's. It no longer includes poems of travel and of retreat from the world; even the liturgical poems are mostly gone; the volume is sustained by poems about saints and some fine nature poems such as "On a Day in August" and "In the Rain and the Sun." Hopkins's hold on Merton is apparent in these two poems and also in "Song" and "Hymn for the Feast of Duns Scotus." The abandonment of his favorite early themes, however, is significant, for in the 1950's Merton gradually repudiated the idea that a monk is someone who retreats from the world in favor of its opposite—that a monk is an ordinary man of the world who cannot escape his responsibilities to it. Merton's interest in civil rights and disarmament began about that time, but he had not yet found a poetic voice for it.

THE STRANGE ISLANDS

Dedicated to his teacher and friend Mark Van Doren and Van Doren's wife, Dorothy, *The Strange Islands* is the transitional volume on the other side of Merton's poetic hiatus. It represents the initial stage of Merton's shift from the short, lyrical poems of his early years to his long, complex, satirical last poems. The volume is divided into three parts: the first, which consists of short poems mixed with several of medium length; the second, which is a long drama in both verse and prose titled "The Tower of Babel"; and the third, which is composed of short lyrics. One can still hear Hopkins in "The Annunciation" and some notable nature poems such as "Spring Storm," but the predominant mood is satiric, not only in "The Tower of Babel" but also in poems such as "Sports Without Blood—a Letter to Dylan Thomas." Merton's habit of including prose passages in his poems, beginning with "The Tower of Babel" and continuing in

his later volumes, is evidence of the increasing influence of modernism on his verse, although it is also reminiscent of Blake's *The Marriage of Heaven and Hell* (1790).

ORIGINAL CHILD BOMB AND
EMBLEMS OF A SEASON OF FURY

Original Child Bomb, Emblems of a Season of Fury, and *Cables to the Ace* in different ways represent Merton's new style. *Original Child Bomb* consists of a single long prose poem, satiric in tone, which arranges the details surrounding the explosion of the first atomic bomb. The first poetic treatment of Merton's social and political concerns, it is an eloquent statement.

Emblems of a Season of Fury is primarily a volume of poems about people. Saints such as Macarius the Elder, Macarius the Younger, and Fulbert, and philosophers such as Averroës and Lee Ying are juxtaposed with Ernest Hemingway and James Thurber. There is a strongly satirical mood not only in such juxtaposition but also in many of the individual poems, such as "An Elegy for Five Old Ladies." Some reflect Merton's social and political concerns ("And the Children of Birmingham," "Chant to Be Used in Processions Around a Site with Furnaces"), and many, such as *Original Child Bomb*, are prose poems.

CABLES TO THE ACE AND
THE GEOGRAPHY OF LOGRAIRE

Dedicated to Robert Lax, *Cables to the Ace* is a long poem in eighty-eight sections, with prologue and epilogue, and alternates verse with prose poetry. Its tone is satiric: Quotations from Shakespeare, William Wordsworth, and Meister Eckhardt and allusions to James Joyce's *Finnegans Wake* (1939) are juxtaposed with references to the Vietnam War and Zen.

Merton was still working on *The Geography of Lograire* when he died, leaving the longest of his poems unfinished. Epic in scope and modern in mode, its antecedents were Hart Crane's *The Bridge* (1930), William Carlos Williams's *Paterson* (1946-1958), and especially Ezra Pound's *Cantos* (1925-1972). Its development is paratactic: Autobiographical allusions, references to anthropological studies, and obscure historical matters interweave to develop Merton's twin themes of the blindness of Western culture and the desperation of the cultures it has oppressed. Divided into four sections, "South," "North," "East," and "West," the poem juxtaposes the words of oppressed groups such as the Mayas, English Ranters, Kanakas, and Sioux with the words of their oppressors. The wide but specialized knowledge that the poem requires, together with its broken syntax, makes this Merton's most difficult poem. In the opinion of many critics, however, it is his most rewarding.

The Collected Poems

In addition to his separately published volumes of poetry, Merton's *The Collected Poems* includes unpublished early poetry, humorous verse, concrete poems, fragments, French poems, and, most important, his translations from French, Spanish, Latin, Portuguese, Chinese, Greek, and Persian. Merton's interest in concrete poetry can be traced to Herbert as well as to modern practitioners of that genre; a particularly interesting one is a rectangle constructed out of the Latin *Natura abhoret vacuum* (Nature abhors a vacuum) in which the *u*'s in the last word expand in various ways to fill out several lines. Notable among the translations are the numerous poems of Chuang Tzu, the early Daoist (especially "Cutting up an Ox"), and the seven poems of Raissa Maritain, including her moving "Chagall."

Other major works

LONG FICTION: *My Argument with the Gestapo*, 1969.

NONFICTION: *Cistercian Contemplatives*, 1948; *The Seven Storey Mountain*, 1948; *What Is Contemplation?*, 1948; *Exile Ends in Glory*, 1948; *The Waters of Siloe*, 1949; *Seeds of Contemplation*, 1949; *What Are These Wounds?*, 1950; *Seasons of Celebration*, 1950; *The Ascent to Truth*, 1951; *A Balanced Life of Prayer*, 1951; *The Sign of Jonas*, 1953; *No Man Is an Island*, 1955; *The Living Bread*, 1956; *The Silent Life*, 1957; *Silence in Heaven*, 1957; *Thoughts in Solitude*, 1958; *The Secular Journal*, 1959; *Disputed Questions*, 1960; *New Seeds of Contemplation*, 1961; *The Behavior of Titans*, 1961; *The New Man*, 1962; *Life and Holiness*, 1963; *Raids on the Unspeakable*, 1964; *The Way of Chuang Tzu*, 1965; *Conjectures of a Guilty Bystander*, 1966; *Mystics and Zen Masters*, 1967; *Zen and the Birds of Appetite*, 1968; *Faith and Violence*, 1968; *Contemplative Prayer*, 1969; *The Climate of Monastic Prayer*, 1969; *Opening the Bible*, 1970; *Contemplation in a World of Action*, 1971; *The Asian Journal of Thomas Merton*, 1973; *The Literary Essays of Thomas Merton*, 1981.

TRANSLATIONS: *The Wisdom of the Desert*, 1960 (of the church fathers); *Clement of Alexandria*, 1962 (of Clement of Alexandria)

MISCELLANEOUS: *The Merton Reader*, 1962; *A Hidden Wholeness*, 1970 (photographs and calligraphy).

BIBLIOGRAPHY

Cooper, David A. *Thomas Merton's Art of Denial: The Evolution of a Radical Humanist*. Athens: University of Georgia Press, 1989. This work is an excellent study of the congruence of contemplative thought and social criticism in the writings of Merton. Cooper stresses both the unity and the evolution in Merton's reflections on his commitment to spiritual values and his role as a social critic.

Cunningham, Lawrence. *Thomas Merton and the Monastic Vision*. Grand Rapids, Mich.: W. B. Eerdmans, 1999. The details of Merton's spiritual development and monastic life are explored. Cunningham follows the trajectory of the poet's life after his entrance into Kentucky's Abbey of Gethsemani in 1941. Merton continued to grapple with the issues of the century, including the antiwar and Civil Rights movements.

Hart, Patrick, ed. *Thomas Merton, Monk: A Monastic Tribute*. New York: Sheed & Ward, 1974. A thoughtful assessment of Merton's significance as a writer by fellow monks who knew him well. The essays by Jean Le Clerc, Thérèse Lentfoehr, and James Fox stress the originality of his writings on monasticism and spiritual renewal.

Inchausti, Robert. *Thomas Merton's American Prophecy*. Albany: State University of New York Press, 1998. Both a critical biography of Merton and cultural criticism of the 1960's. Inchausti places the poet's work within its historical context and shows how Merton's rejection of both radical and conservative points of view allowed him to produce a profound analysis of contemporary civilization.

Kramer, Victor A. *Thomas Merton: Monk and Artist*. Kalamazoo, Mich.: Cistercian, 1984. The eighth chapter, "Experimental Poetry," analyzes the links between poetry and contemplative thought in Merton's last two books of poetry, *Cables to the Ace* and *The Geography of Lograire*. Contains an annotated bibliography of studies on Merton.

Labrie, Ross. *The Art of Thomas Merton*. Fort Worth: Texas Christian University Press, 1979. This thoughtful book examines Merton's stylistic creativity and analyzes well the impressive blend of prose and verse poems in *Cables to the Ace*. Labrie argues persuasively that Merton was a major lyric poet.

Mott, Michael. *The Seven Mountains of Thomas Merton*. Boston: Houghton Mifflin, 1984. This volume is an essential introduction to the life and works of Merton, an authorized and well-researched biography, from Merton's birth in France in 1915 until his death in Thailand in 1968. Mott interviewed several people who knew Merton personally. Contains a thorough list of primary and secondary sources, as well as an index.

Robert E. Boenig;
bibliography updated by the editors

W. S. MERWIN

Born: New York, New York; September 30, 1927

PRINCIPAL POETRY
A Mask for Janus, 1952
The Dancing Bears, 1954
Green with Beasts, 1956
The Drunk in the Furnace, 1960
The Moving Target, 1963
The Lice, 1967
Animae, 1969
The Carrier of Ladders, 1970
Writings to an Unfinished Accompaniment, 1973
The First Four Books of Poems, 1975
The Compass Flower, 1977
Feathers from the Hill, 1978
Finding the Islands, 1982
Opening the Hand, 1983

The Rain in the Trees, 1988
Koa, 1988
Selected Poems, 1988
The Second Four Books of Poems, 1993
Travels, 1993
The Vixen, 1996
Flower and Hand: Poems, 1977-1983, 1997
The Folding Cliffs: A Narrative, 1998
The River Sound: Poems, 1999
The Pupil, 2001

OTHER LITERARY FORMS

A talented translator, W. S. Merwin has translated numerous works including *The Poem of the Cid* (1959), Persius's *Satires* (1961), *The Song of Roland* (1963), *Voices*, by Antonio Porchia (1969, 1988), *Transparence of the World: Poems*, by Jean Follain (1969), Dante's *Purgatorio* (2000), and poetry by Pablo Neruda and Osip Mandelstam. He has also written plays: *Rumpelstiltskin*, produced by the British Broadcasting Corporation (BBC) in 1951; *Pageant of Cain*, produced by BBC Third Programme in 1952; *Huckleberry Finn*, produced by BBC television, 1953. *Darkling Child* was produced in London by Arts Theatre in 1956, *Favor Island* was produced by Poet's Theatre in Cambridge, Massachusetts, in 1957, and *The Gilded West* was produced in 1961 in Coventry, England, by the Belgrade Theatre. Merwin's prose work includes *The Miner's Pale Children* (1970), *Houses and Travellers* (1977), a memoir of childhood titled *Unframed Originals* (1982), *Regions of Memory: Uncollected Prose, 1949-1982* (1987), edited by Cary Nelson; and *The Lost Upland* (1992).

ACHIEVEMENTS

Merwin received early recognition for his poetry with the selection of *A Mask for Janus* as the 1952 Yale Series of Younger Poets Award winner, and he went on to receive many grants, fellowships, and awards. He received a *Kenyon Review* fellowship in 1954; the American Academy Grant, 1957; an Arts Council of Great Britain bursary, 1957; a Rabinowitz Research Fellowship, 1961; the Bess Hokin Prize, 1962; a Ford Foundation Grant, 1964; the Chapelbrook Award, 1966; the Harriet Monroe Memorial Prize (*Poetry*, Chicago),

1967; a PEN Translation Prize for *Selected Translations, 1948-1968*, 1969; a Rockefeller grant, 1969; a Pulitzer Prize for *The Carrier of Ladders*, 1971; the Academy of American Poets Fellowship, 1973; the Shelley Memorial Award, 1974; a National Endowment for the Arts Grant, 1978; and a Bollingen Prize, 1979. In 1987 Merwin received the Governor's Award for Literature of the State of Hawaii. He is a member of the American Academy. In the 1990's, he was awarded the Lenore Marshall Poetry Prize (for *Travels*), the 1994 Tanning Prize, and the 1998 Lilly Poetry Prize. In 1999, Merwin was selected to share the duties of poet laureate of the United States with poets Rita Dove and Louise Glück.

Biography

William Stanley Merwin was born in New York City on September 30, 1927, and grew up in Union City, New Jersey (where his father was a Presbyterian minister), and in Scranton, Pennsylvania. From his own account, his parents were strict and rather cheerless. His earliest poems, written as a child, were austere hymns for his father. He received his bachelor's degree in English from Princeton University, New Jersey, in 1947. While at Princeton, he was befriended by the critic R. P. Blackmur and became very interested in the work of Ezra Pound. Like Pound, he was a student of romance languages and began to value translation as a means of remaking poetry in English. As a student he even grew a beard in imitation of Pound's and eventually went to visit Pound at St. Elizabeths Hospital. In 1949 he followed Pound's example and left the United States to become an expatriate. His sojourn was to last some seven years. From 1949 to 1951 he worked as a tutor in France and Portugal. In 1950 he lived in Mallorca, Spain, where he was tutor to Robert Graves's son, William. Graves's interest in myth became one important influence on the younger poet. After that he made his living for several years by translating from French, Spanish, Latin, and Portuguese. From 1951 through 1953 he worked as translator for the BBC's Third Programme. In 1954 he was married to Diana Whalley. During 1956 and 1957 Merwin was playwright-in-residence for the Poets' Theatre in Cambridge, Massachusetts, and in 1962 he served as poetry editor for *The Nation*. He was an asso-

W. S. Merwin (© Dido Merwin)

ciate at the Théâtre de la Cité in Lyons, France, during 1964-1965. In 1971 he won the Pulitzer Prize for his collection *The Carrier of Ladders*.

In 1978, Merwin and his wife, Paula, made their home in Hawaii. Since then, Merwin has made Hawaii the base from which he makes journeys to the great cities of the mainland United States to lecture and give readings. He frequently writes for *The New Yorker* while continuing to live in Hawaii on eighteen acres near the forested village of Haiku on the Hana coast. He has also turned into an ecological advocate, lending his support to the Hawaii's environmental movement.

Analysis

The achievement of W. S. Merwin is both impressive and distinctive. His body of work encompasses a wide range of literary genres and includes poetry, plays, translations, and prose. His development as a poet has spanned great literary distances, from the early formalism of *A Mask for Janus* to the spare, simple language and openness of the verse form he refined in *The Lice*. His poetry has often displayed a prosaic, almost conversational quality, as in "Questions to Tourists Stopped by a Pine-apple Field," from *Opening the Hand*.

Although Merwin himself has carefully avoided making in-depth comments or pronouncements about his poetry and has not engaged in the often fussy critical debate that has shadowed his career, his work continues to show evidence that the exploration of the power and enigmatic nature of language is one of his great concerns. His many remarkable translations have perhaps been a stimulating influence on his own innovations of poetic form. In moving away from the rather mannered style of his early verse with its reliance on myth, rhyme, and punctuation to a poetry of silence and absence, Merwin, according to Sandra McPherson, began "researching the erasures of the universe."

Beginning with his first book of poetry, *A Mask for Janus*, W. S. Merwin has explored how language structures and creates experience. He has also been devoted to myth, or mythmaking, as a way of making sense of experience. While experimenting with language and myth, he has examined the possibilities of developing poetic forms suited to expressing what language can reveal about the mind and existence. In his search, Merwin has had rich resources to draw from, such as the other languages of his many translations and his firm grounding in earlier poetic traditions. His background led him first to master orthodox forms and later to move beyond them.

His devotion to poetry and his life as a wandering poet have given him a folk hero's aura. Being of the generation that began writing in the 1940's and 1950's, he had his poetic roots in more classically influenced, technically controlled verse forms. His disaffection with the formal poetic styles of his predecessors was shared by other poets of his generation such as James Wright and Robert Bly. What he had to say required new ways of communicating, new vessels that would journey toward new realms of perception. By immersing himself in the literature of other cultures, both as a student of languages and as a translator, Merwin has been able to bring a sense of the archetypal source of all poetic expression to his work. His ability to look at a tree and describe the space between its leaves may be unique among contemporary poets. Merwin has referred to his poems as houses that he makes out of virtually anything

and everything he can find. These houses made of words are places where the reader can enter and experience "the echo of everything that has ever/ been spoken."

A MASK FOR JANUS

Published in 1952, *A Mask for Janus* used myth and traditional prosodic forms to explore such themes as the birth-death cycle and the isolated self. In "Meng Tzu's Song," the speaker meditates on concerns of identity and solitude:

> How can I know, now forty
> Years have shuffled my shoulders,
> Whether my mind is steady
> Or quakes as the wind stirs?

At first reading, this poem has the flavor of a translation. Ed Folsom, writing in *W. S. Merwin: Essays on the Poetry* (1987), notes that while the verse in *A Mask for Janus* was seen by some critics as an example of traditional craftsmanship, it was also stiff at times, wordy, and overwrought. In recalling and using the structures and tonalities of a more formal poetry, however, Merwin was able to develop his mastery of those elements and earn his release from them.

THE DANCING BEARS

Merwin continued his use of myth and the narrative form in *The Dancing Bears*. In "East of the Sun and West of the Moon," Merwin uses the myth of Psyche and Cupid to explore the problem of identity. Through language that is often elegant and precisely shaped into neat thirteen-line stanzas, he offers clues to the enigma of inner and outer reality. In what may be read as a clarifying statement, Merwin reveals his belief that "all metaphor . . . is magic," and "all magic is but metaphor." Here, he employs his magic to explore the hidden realms of being.

THE DRUNK IN THE FURNACE

The preoccupation with myth and a formal, poetic style followed in his next two works, *Green with Beasts* and *The Drunk in the Furnace*. Yet there is also a strange new energy working as Merwin begins moving away from Greco-Roman myths and toward the creation of his own.

In "The *Portland* Going Out" (*The Drunk in the Furnace*), the apparent randomness of the disaster that strikes a passing ship recalls to the poet the mystery of life and death and thus of existence itself. The *Portland* had passed close by the poet's ship on its way out of the harbor to an ill-fated rendezvous with a storm, where it put "all of disaster between us: a gulf/ Beyond reckoning." This glimpse into the abyss works ironically as a reaffirmation of life.

There are several other poems in this collection that revolve around images of the sea. Alice N. Benston, writing in *Poets in Progress* (1962), calls the sea the "perfect symbol for Merwin." The duality inherent in the sea as both life-giver and symbol of nature's indifference to humanity provides Merwin with a metaphor for the unknown.

The poems in *The Drunk in the Furnace* take some other new and significant directions. For example, several examine the poet's youth and the family members who helped shape his early experiences. These poems are not reverential but sober, almost bitter reflections on his memories of "faded rooms," his grandfather left alone to die in a nursing home, and his grandmother's failure to see her worst sins as she reminisces about her life. The sarcastic tone of "Grandfather in the Old Men's Home" seems directed at the society in which Merwin was brought up—a society that he would later reject.

The family poems in *The Drunk in the Furnace* and others such as "Home for Thanksgiving" and "A Letter from Gussie" in *The Moving Target* allowed Merwin to explore his past further before turning away to begin a new journey. It is as if these poems generate and voice his realization and declaration that he will no longer be bound by the expectations of the culture into which he was born. Nor will he recognize any longer the restraints of the poetic forms that served as his early models.

THE LICE

The new style toward which Merwin was moving in *The Moving Target* emerges more fully realized in *The Lice*. Here he abandons narrative, adopts open forms, and eliminates punctuation:

> The nights disappear like bruises but nothing is healed
> The dead go away like bruises
> The blood vanishes into the poisoned farmlands
> Pain the horizon
> Remains

With *The Lice*, in effect, Merwin leaves the shore, lifts off the launching pad, and enters a new realm where the poem becomes the vessel for voyages toward "nameless stars." While numerous critics have pointed to the overall negativism and pessimism of *The Lice*, hope is undeniably evident in the very act of poetic discovery, as Merwin sheds his skin and emerges as something born not only "to survive," but indeed "to live."

In *The Lice* lie keys to an understanding of the work that will follow. The stark, even dumbfounding silences in a poem such as "December Among the Vanished"—in which "the old snow gets up and moves taking its/ Birds with it"—attract Merwin away from a world that seems to be in the process of self-destruction and toward a new, strange sensibility. A new spareness, a new simplicity and immediacy inform these poems. Gone are the earlier elaborate, formal structures. According to Ed Folsom and Cary Nelson in their introduction to *W. S. Merwin: Essays on the Poetry*, Merwin had begun to lose, at this stage, his faith in language and for a time was not even sure he could write words to articulate experience. In an interview with Edward Hirsch in 1987, Merwin explained how he came to distrust language, believing that experience cannot be articulated.

The Lice also reveals a new, more serious concern with the deadly corrosiveness of politics and the wanton destruction of the environment by greedy corporations. Behind the poet's initial anger and numbing frustration over mass environmental destruction, however, is a recognition of the potential for other responses to the earth's tragedy. He listens carefully, trying to hear the hidden voices in nature. These voices, and the voices emanating from his inner self, offer the possibility of discovering new consciousness—new poems—as long as he does not allow his anger to deafen him or the state of the world to distract him.

In listening for these other voices, the poet remains open to the discovery not only of the world but also of himself. In "For a Coming Extinction," he asks the reader to join voices with "the sea cows the Great Auks the gorillas" and, using the speech of innocents, to testify to the inherent significance of all life.

THE CARRIER OF LADDERS

A new tone emerges in Merwin's poetry in *The Carrier of Ladders*, which was awarded the Pulitzer Prize in

1971. The tone is one of rebirth and reaffirmation. Thus far he has stared into the dark night of his disillusionment with a world corrupted by human beings and has seen only his own reflection. However much he regrets the alienation that such a vision brought forth, he realizes at this stage that to live and create he must seek the renewal of his own spirit.

To do so, the poet will have to step into the darkness, the unknown, and accept both what is there and what is not there. In "Words from a Totem Animal" (*The Carrier of Ladders*), Merwin writes,

> My eyes are waiting for me
> in the dusk
> they are still closed
> they have been waiting a long time
> and I am feeling my way toward them

The language and form of *The Carrier of Ladders* are perfectly suited to the poet's task of trying to see things with new eyes. This poetry is less judgmental and more open to the experiences of being alive. The simplicity of the diction, and the clear, fresh immediacy of tone draw the reader into the poems. There the poet waits, "standing in dry air" and "for no reason"—praying simply that his words may be clear.

NATURE

During the 1970's, Merwin continued his search for oneness with nature and the knowledge of self such a quest promises. The childlike innocence achieved in the poems of *The Carrier of Ladders* continues to characterize much of the poetry in *Writings to an Unfinished Accompaniment*, *The Compass Flower*, and *Finding the Islands*. Scattered throughout these books are references to the sea, fish, owls, dogs, cows, stones, mountains, clouds, the moon, and the stars. In "Gift" (*Writings to an Unfinished Accompaniment*), Merwin comes to realize that the revelation he seeks must be found through trust in what is given to him. An almost mystical stillness resides in these poems, as if one could hear the "sound of inner stone."

OPENING THE HAND

With *Opening the Hand*, Merwin looks outward toward more familiar landscapes and situations and fixes his hermetic gaze upon them. In a poem about the death of his father, told as through a dream, the poet halluci-

nates images that seem to haunt him like ominous premonitions. His concern with ecology is also evident in this collection. In "Shaving Without a Mirror," he seems to be waking up from a night outdoors, listening for forest voices. The awe he feels, and his urge to surrender to the experience of being alone in the wilderness, confirms his sense of the interrelatedness of all things, a sense that first emerged in *The Lice*.

"What Is Modern" (*Opening the Hand*) is a poem charged with irony. Merwin comments on the American culture's ridiculous preoccupation with defining modernity. An undeniable sense of humor and a refreshing looseness characterize the poem: "is the first/ tree that comes/ to mind modern/ does it have modern leaves." While grounded in the particular, the recognizable and commonplace, the poetry of *Opening the Hand* still achieves the same obsidian polish of earlier poems whose spare diction and muteness gave an ethereal rather than concrete quality to things.

THE RAIN IN THE TREES

The Rain in the Trees combines many of the qualities in the work of the 1960's and 1970's, while continuing Merwin's experiments in style and form. The subjects include his family, nature, travel, John Keats, language, the Statue of Liberty, Hawaii, and love. In such diversity of subjects come surprise and freshness. The poems mirror his wanderings and his restlessness in pursuit of the ineffable.

In "Empty Water," Merwin uses incantatory speech to invoke the spirit of a toad whose eyes were "fashioned of the most/ precious of metals." He chants for the toad's return:

> come back
> believer in shade
> believer in silence and elegance
> believer in ferns
> believer in patience
> believer in the rain

A joy in the primal unity and the inherent beauty of all life is evident throughout *The Rain in the Trees*. In "Waking to the Rain," the poet wakes from a dream "of harmony" to find rain falling on the house, creating the one sound that reveals the silence that surrounds him.

TRAVELS

Travels shows Merwin continuing to experiment with syllabic lines and formal structures of his own devising. As the title suggests, the themes are varied, as are the locales. Meditations on his parents are among the most successful poems collected here, but what seem most fresh are the narratives that deal with historical figures: "Rimbaud's Piano," "The Blind Seer of Ambon," and "The Real World of Manuel Cordova" are likely to become classics of this kind of poem.

THE VIXEN

The Vixen, with its uniformity of style, can be read almost as a book-length poem. At once lyrical, narrative, and meditative, these pieces portray the landscapes and the people of the region in southwest France that Merwin knows so well and that are the subject of his prose book, *The Lost Upland*. Merwin's long, unpunctuated breaths of sinuous syntax wrap around line ends, twisting corners of thought and emotion in mesmerizing ways. Many of these pieces are quite short, and, though separately titled, they blend into one another to form a large, richly embroidered tapestry of sensation and a prayer-like celebration of interaction with place.

THE FOLDING CLIFFS

More clearly designed as a book-length poem, *The Folding Cliffs* is a sustained historical narrative about the exploitation of nineteenth century Hawaii. It is a major act of homage to that place that has been Merwin's home for more than two decades. Though many poems in his earlier collections deal with damage to Hawaii's ecosystems and to its culture, this poem serves as a capstone to Merwin's efforts. It is another in his ongoing testimonies to the experience of loss.

THE RIVER SOUND

Loss remains a theme, as well, in *The River Sound*, a fascinating if somewhat demanding collection that demonstrates Merwin's great vitality as he moves into old age. Stylistically, it is more varied that any of Merwin's other collections, as if, having tried it all, he can now pull from his long experience whatever suits the matter at hand. While most of the poems here are short, there are three long ones that center and focus the book. "Testimony," with its 229 eight-line stanzas rhyming (though not mechanically) *ababbcbc*, is an ambitious memoir in verse, ranging back over key experiences and people in

Merwin's life. "Lament for the Makers," set in fifty-two tidy couplet quatrains, is his tribute to fellow poets now gone. "Suite in the Key of Forgetting" is more associative, conjuring various states of absence and loss.

THE PUPIL

Hawaii and memories of his boyhood on the Atlantic coast take a back seat in his 2001 collection, *The Pupil*. Instead he turns his poetic eye to to astronomy and the night sky, which allow for reflections on mortality, transience, and the void, delivered in Merwin's familiar fluid sentences. One poem remembers "the year of the well of darkness/ overflowing with no/ moon and no stars"; others portray "the darkness thinking the light" or "the white moments that had traveled so long." Other disparate themes are explored, including government-sponsored torture of bears in Pakistan and 1998's homophobic beating death of Matthew Shepherd in Wyoming.

OTHER MAJOR WORKS

PLAYS: *Rumpelstiltskin*, pr: 1951 (radio play); *Pageant of Cain*, pr: 1952 (radio play); *Huckleberry Finn*, pr: 1953 (teleplay); *Darkling Child*, pr: 1956; *Favor Island*, pr: 1957; *The Gilded Nest*, pr: 1961.

NONFICTION: *The Miner's Pale Children*, 1970; *Houses and Travellers*, 1977; *Unframed Originals*, 1982. *Regions of Memory: Uncollected Prose, 1949-1982*, 1987 (Cary Nelson, editor); *The Lost Upland*, 1992.

TRANSLATIONS: *The Poem of the Cid*, 1959; *Satires*, 1961 (of Persius); *Spanish Ballads*, 1961; *The Song of Roland*, 1963; *Selected Translations, 1948-1968*, 1968; *Twenty Love Poems and a Song of Despair*, 1969 (of Pablo Neruda); *Products of the Perfected Civilization: Selected Writings of Chamfort*, 1969; *Voices*, 1969, 1988 (of Antonio Porchia); *Transparence of the World: Poems*, 1969 (of Jean Follain); *Asian Figures*, 1973; *Selected Poems*, 1973 (of Osip Mandelstam; with Clarence Brown); *Iphigenia at Aulis*, 1978 (with George E. Dimock, Jr.); *Selected Translations, 1968-1978*, 1979; *Four French Plays*, 1985; *From the Spanish Morning*, 1985; *Vertical Poetry*, 1988; *Sun at Midnight*, by Muso Soseki, 1989 (with Soiku Shigematsu); *Purgatorio*, 2000 (of Dante).

BIBLIOGRAPHY

Byers, Thomas B. *What I Cannot Say: Self, Word, and World in Whitman, Stevens, and Merwin.* Urbana: University of Illinois Press, 1989. Byers's chapter on Merwin, "W. S. Merwin: A Description of Darkness," focuses primarily on *The Lice* and attempts to define Merwin's place in the American poetic tradition descended from Ralph Waldo Emerson and Walt Whitman. According to Byers, Merwin sees, as Stevens did, the self as inevitably isolated, even though his poetics recognize the need to see oneself as related to other people and other things in order to become more ecologically aware. Includes notes, a bibliography, and an index.

Christhilf, Mark. *W. S. Merwin, the Mythmaker.* Columbia: University of Missouri Press, 1986. Christhilf discusses Merwin's contributions to the postmodernist movement (with *The Moving Target*) and his assumed role of mythmaker, noting that the poet became ambivalent toward this role in the 1980's. In a useful discussion, Christhilf traces the mythmaking concern in American poetry across four decades.

Davis, Cheri. *W. S. Merwin.* Boston: Twayne, 1981. This study makes the poetry and prose of Merwin accessible to the reader new to his work. While well aware of the variety in Merwin's writing, Davis attempts to reveal what gives it unity. She examines his attitudes toward language and silence, his concern for animals and ecology, and his beliefs about poetry and nothingness. Chapters 1 through 5 look at his books of poetry from *A Mask for Janus* through *The Compass Flower.* Chapter 6 discusses the prose poetry of *The Miner's Pale Children* and *Houses and Travellers.*

Frazier, Jane. *From Origin to Ecology: Nature and the Poetry of W. S. Merwin.* Madison, N.J.: Fairleigh Dickinson University Press, 1999. An anlysis of images of nature in Merwin's poetry. Includes bibliographical references and an index.

Hix, H. L. *Understanding W. S. Merwin.* Columbia: University of South Carolina Press, 1997. Hix argues that despite its reputation for difficulty, Merwin's verse is clear and direct. Close readings of Merwin's verse reveal the emergence of such dominant themes as apocalypse, ecology, society, and place—which incorporates all the others.

Merwin, W. S. "The Art of Poetry: XXXVII." Interview by Edward Hirsch. *Paris Review* 101 (1987): 57-81. Merwin recollects his childhood fascination with Indians and his nightmares that the whole world had become cities. The entire interview reflects his strong environmental concerns. He also talks about literary influences: John Berryman; R. P. Blackmur, his teacher; and Ezra Pound on medieval poetry and the importance of the ear in poetry.

Nelson, Cary, and Ed Folsom, eds. *W. S. Merwin: Essays on the Poetry.* Urbana: University of Illinois Press, 1987. The editors provide a good introductory essay, comparing Merwin to Pound (both students of romance languages), William Carlos Williams, and Wallace Stevens. William H. Rueckert's notes are a help to readers of *The Lice,* and Folsom discusses Merwin's change in style beginning with *The Compass Flower.* Includes comprehensive bibliographies, full notes, and a thorough index.

Scigaj, Leonard M. *Sustainable Poetry: Four American Ecopoets.* Lexington: University Press of Kentucky, 1999. The chapter on Merwin traces how the poet's initial "poetics of absence" has slowly transformed "into an ecological poetics of wakefulness." Scigaj connects Merwin's growing understanding of stressed ecosystems to his aesthetic experimentation.

Francis Poole,
updated by Philip K. Jason and Sarah Hilbert

HENRI MICHAUX

Born: Namur, Belgium; May 24, 1899
Died: Paris, France; October 17, 1984

PRINCIPAL POETRY
Fables des origines, 1923
Les Rêves et la jambe, 1923
Qui je fus, 1927
Écuador: Journal de voyage, 1929 (includes essays and diary; *Ecuador: A Travel Journal,* 1970)
Mes propriétés, 1929

Un Certain M. Plume, 1930

Un Barbare en Asie, 1933 (includes essays and diary; *A Barbarian in Asia*, 1949)

La Nuit remue, 1935

Lointain intérieure, 1938

Plume: Précédé de Lointain intérieur, 1938

Peintures, 1939

Arbres des tropiques, 1942 (includes drawings)

Je vous écris d'un pays lointain, 1942 (*I Am Writing to You from a Far-Off Country*)

Exorcismes, 1943 (includes drawings)

L'Espace du dedans, 1944 (*Selected Writings: The Space Within*, 1951)

Épreuves, exorcismes, 1940-1944, 1945

Peintures et dessins, 1946 (expanded version of *Peintures*; includes drawings)

Nous deux encore, 1948

La Vie dans les plis, 1949

Mouvements, 1951 (includes drawings)

Face aux verrous, 1954

Paix dans les brisements, 1959 (includes drawings)

Poems, 1967

Selected Writings of Henri Michaux, 1968

Émergences-Résurgences, 1972 (*Emergences-Resurgences*, 2000; includes writings and drawings)

Chemins cherchés, chemins perdue, transgressions, 1982

OTHER LITERARY FORMS

Apart from his verse and prose poetry, Henri Michaux has written travelogues, essays, drama, and fiction. He is, however, equally well known as a painter. Often merging forms and genres, Michaux's works traverse the boundaries of real and imaginary worlds, moving from outer to inner space with a constant focus on visual impressions while analyzing the experience. Michaux's writing cannot be divorced from the visual arts, and several of his foremost collections are combinations of original drawings (gouaches, water-colors, inks, acrylics) and texts. The poems are not merely accompanied by illustrations; rather, the two are simultaneous expressions of analogous themes.

Michaux also wrote a one-act play, *Le Drame des constructeurs* (pb. 1930, pr. 1937; the builder's drama), which again reflects his interest in the visual arts. The set-

ting is a lunatic asylum where various inmates, named A, B, C, D, E, F, G, and H, play "construction" games. Their guards can be seen in the background; every time one appears, the "builders" disperse. Law and order, Michaux implies, destroy imagination and deprive man of his ability to exist. Furthermore, the character "God" is aligned with the lunatics, whom he absolves and liberates. Ironically, the inmates continue their imaginary building, the guards remain, and nothing changes.

Yet another literary form that Michaux expertly handles is the aphorism. In *Tranches de savoir* (1950; slices of knowledge), 234 aphorisms, short-circuited proverbs, are posited. These brief phrases, in the French tradition of François La Rochefoucauld, are both sinister and amusing, for they scramble traditional sayings and reflect the themes and clichés found throughout literature. One can easily discover Molière, Jean de La Fontaine, and Charles Baudelaire reworked and answered across time and space in succinct one-line summaries of the human condition.

Michaux is especially well known for his introspective, scientific, and informative prose accounts of his experiences with mescaline and other hallucinogenic drugs. His period of drug usage lasted sixteen years (from 1955 to 1971) and produced five major essays: *Misérable miracle, la mescaline* (1956; *Miserable Miracle, Mescaline*, 1963), *L'Infini turbulent* (1957; *Infinite Turbulence*, 1975), *Connaissance par les gouffres* (1961; *Light Through Darkness*, 1963), *Vents et poussières* (1962; winds and dust), and *Les Grandes Épreuves de l'esprit et les innombrables petites* (1966; *The Major Ordeals of the Mind and the Countless Minor Ones*, 1974). What distinguishes Michaux's investigations from those of the historical line of French writers who have created while under the influence of drugs is his objectivity. While he appreciates the liberating effect of hallucinogens, he found them to be more revelatory than creative. His prose accounts are not "automatic writings," in the tradition of the Surrealists, but reasoned, after-the-fact analyses of the feelings of fragmentation, alienation, energy, and elasticity of the persona.

ACHIEVEMENTS

Henri Michaux's achievements integrate both his literary and his artistic worlds. The poetry collection *Qui je fus*, Michaux's first work published in France, received considerable critical acclaim. Although he began painting in the mid-1920's, his first book of drawings and paintings did not appear until 1936. During the next several years, Michaux became a presence in the French world of art, and his premiere exposition of paintings and gouaches was held in the Galerie Pierre in Paris in 1938. In 1941, André Gide published, in booklet form, the controversial panegyric *Découvrons Henri Michaux*, which revealed the modernity and complexity of Michaux's creative process. In 1948, the Galerie René Drouin exhibited Michaux's first collection of wash drawings and, in 1954, his premiere exposition of ink designs. In 1960, he received the Einaudi Award in Venice.

Michaux turned to yet another medium in 1963 and created, with Eric Duvivier, a film titled *Images du monde visionaire*. The Musée National d'Art Moderne de Paris honored Michaux with a grand retrospective of his works in 1965; in the same year, he was featured by Geneviève Bonnefoi and Jacques Veinat in the film *Henri Michaux ou l'espace du dedans*. Also in 1965, Michaux was voted to receive the Grand Prix National des Lettres, which he decided not to accept. Both to acknowledge his literary works and to honor his refusal, the committee then chose not to award the prize that year. In 1966, a special issue of the journal *L'Herne* was dedicated to Michaux, and in 1976, the Fondation Maeght mounted another major retrospective exhibition of Michaux's drawings.

BIOGRAPHY

Henri-Eugène-Guislain Michaux's life, like his works, was cosmopolitan. He was born in Namur, Belgium, on May 24, 1899, and was reared in Brussels. Because of his delicate health and obstinate temperament, he was sent to a boarding school in Putte-Grasheide. After five years in the country, which was for him a time of solitude and refusal of societal norms, Michaux returned to Brussels in 1911 for the remainder of his formal education. He was graduated from his *lycée* in 1916, but because of the German Occupation, he could not immediately enroll in a university. During this period, Michaux studied literature voraciously, learning about the lives of the saints and discovering the writings of

mystics such as Jan van Ruysbroeck, Leo Tolstoy, and Fyodor Dostoevski. Refusing to believe that literature alone held the key to the essence of life, Michaux, in 1919, enrolled in medical school, but he later abandoned his studies there as well.

At the age of twenty-one, Michaux embarked upon the first of a series of voyages that greatly influenced his life and writing. He first became a sailor on a five-masted schooner at Boulogne-sur-Mer; then he joined the crew of the ten-ton *Victorieux* at Rotterdam. He explored the civilizations bordering the Atlantic, including the United States and South America. Michaux stayed in Marseilles, France, for a year, then returned to Brussels, where his first volumes–*Fables des origines* (fables on origins) and *Les Rêves et la jambe* (dreams and the leg)—were published. He was, however, dissatisfied with life in Belgium, particularly with his family's view of his "failure," and had already moved to Paris when the two works appeared.

The Parisian artistic scene of the 1920's had a tremendous impact on Michaux. Introduced to the Surrealists and to plastic art—primarily the paintings of Paul Klee, Max Ernst, and Giorgio de Chirico—he became interested in design. As early as 1927, he experimented with his own ideograms (*signes*), a mixing of the literary (the alphabet) and the plastic arts. Furthermore, the publication of *Qui je fus* in 1927 marked his break with parental and cultural authority. He traveled to South America with the poet Alfredo Gangotena and spent a year in Quito, Ecuador. In 1929, both of Michaux's parents died, and he journeyed to Turkey, Italy, and North Africa in an effort to erase the remaining psychological influences of both his homeland and his family. The year 1930 marks the appearance of Michaux's best-known fictional character, the humorous and pointedly emotionless Plume.

From 1930 to 1939, Michaux traveled extensively: to India, Ceylon (Sri Lanka), Malaya, Indonesia, China, Korea, Japan, Portugal, Uruguay, and Brazil. These were also years of important literary production, and they included Michaux's first painting exhibition. During World War II, Michaux continued to write and draw. He experimented with various artistic techniques (watercolor and gouache) and published several volumes with original artwork. In order to escape the German

Occupation of Paris, Michaux moved to Saint-Antonin and then to Lavandou, where he married in 1941.

His well-known anthology *Selected Writings: The Space Within* was published in 1944 during a time of personal tragedy. Michaux's brother had recently died, and his wife contracted tuberculosis. Throughout 1947, Michaux traveled in order to help his wife convalesce, but in 1948, she died from burns received in a terrible accident. Despair moved him to compose the haunting *Nous deux encore* (still the two of us), and in the following years, he published several significant literary collections. There was also at that time a dramatic change in Michaux's creative direction. Removed from all family ties, he returned to his point of departure, the alphabet-sign. He wrote less and painted much more. The album *Mouvements* demonstrates his increased devotion to design and his personal voyage from one art form to another.

In 1955, Michaux became a naturalized French citizen. When, in 1957, he lost the use of his right hand, he trained himself to use his left hand to paint; he also embarked upon a new travel experience—the systematic use of hallucinogens to explore the inner self. The result of this experimentation was a series of essays devoted to the clinical analysis of drug-induced activity. It is important to note that during these same years, Michaux received international plaudits for his painting, and he revised and republished his major literary collections. He died in Paris on October 17, 1984, at the age of eighty-five.

ANALYSIS

Few modern French poets have equaled the range and scope of Henri Michaux. Often contrasted with René Char, who represents a positive vision of and affirmation of the creative force, Michaux is known for his humor, his destructive power that renders all generic and structural barriers useless, and his ongoing investigation of the inner self and rejection of the outer world's conventions. Michaux's poetry transcends national boundaries and defies specific literary schools. His strong belief in the will makes his poetic images strong and intense. Yet Michaux is also an enigma, an ethereal go-between from one world to the next. It is through this paradox—attack countered by whimsy, delicacy balanced by audacity, the pen in tandem with the brush—that each of Michaux's poems comes alive.

This paradox in Michaux's writing is displayed in his use of traditionally nonpoetic literary forms—artistic commentary, drama, travelogue, proverb, and essay—as a background for his poetry. Flux, rhythm, alliteration, litany, and repetition of sounds and words may be found in any Michaux text. Furthermore, all Michaux's creations are self-referential and could never be considered objective nonfiction.

ECUADOR: A TRAVEL JOURNAL

Michaux's travelogues are a poetic voyage through both real and imaginary countries and creatures. *Ecuador: A Travel Journal* is the unique journal of Michaux's travels through South America and is not to be mistaken for a traditional guidebook. Rather, it is about Michaux's own self-discovery, a first-person narration that skips from vague, sensory perception to the specific notations of a diary, incorporating twenty-two free-verse poems, several prose essays, and entries recorded by hour and day. The importance of *Ecuador*, however, lies not in what Michaux sees and does, in the conventional approach to travel literature, or in the novel approach to traditional literary exoticism, but, instead, in Michaux's explorations of his self in an effort to expand his knowledge and feeling.

A BARBARIAN IN ASIA

Similarly, *A Barbarian in Asia* reveals a subjective view of Michaux's travels in the Far East. Here, Western man is revealed to be a barbarian—ignorant and unschooled, especially when faced with the refinement of Eastern civilization. In a series of short poetic essays, a "naïve" Michaux examines not "facts" but "style, gestures, accent, appearance, and reflexes" and also discovers that the Chinese originated the ideogram, his particular obsession.

IMAGINARY COUNTRIES

Michaux has also created in his poetry/travelogue form extensive accounts of imaginary countries and characters, the best of which—*Voyage en Grande Garabagne* (1936; trip to Great Garabagne), *Au pays de la magie* (1941; in the land of magic), and *Ici, Poddema* (1946; here, Poddema)—are grouped together in the collection *Ailleurs* (1948; elsewhere). Great Garabagne is a complete civilization; it has tribes, distinct geographical locations, and social and religious customs. In these accounts, Michaux is not concerned with Utopian visions but with a reordering of reality.

He continues in the same vein with the *Portrait des Meidosems* (1948), in which are presented personages whom Malcolm Bowie, in his 1973 study, *Henri Michaux*, has accurately defined as "me-images": shifting, self-propelled forms living in a world of continual flux.

I AM WRITING TO YOU FROM A FAR-OFF COUNTRY

In another form of imaginary travelogue, *I Am Writing to You from a Far-Off Country*, Michaux wrote twelve prose-poem segments, supposedly from a feminine writer to a desired partner, thus creating both the author and the reader of the text, who interjects his own commentary. While the faraway country does not exist, its sea, waves, and unusual fauna seem real because they are described personally and because the writer is trying to persuade her companion to meet her on this imagined plane of existence. This preoccupation with travel between real and make-believe worlds permeates all Michaux's works.

THE PLUME PERSONA

In his travelogues, as in all of his works, Michaux refuses to imitate the world, preferring to turn it upside down. His first fictional character, Plume (whose name means both "feather" and "pen"), is indeed a lightweight, often pathetic, creature. His form varies from text to text; he has no firm characteristics and little awareness of the world around him. As a representative of modern man, Plume symbolizes the desperate and suffering yet resilient and matter-of-fact person existing in the bleak, often hostile, world of reality. Plume is the antithesis of Michaux's ideal; he is a victim who does not intervene, a dupe. Michaux uses humor in the Plume prose poems both to distort and to give relief. Plume cannot laugh—or at least, he does not—but the reader laughs at Plume, enjoys mocking him, and anticipates his destruction with glee.

"A TRACTABLE MAN"

In "Un Homme paisible" ("A Tractable Man"), Plume awakens to a series of disasters. The first time, he cannot find the walls of his room because ants have eaten them. Unperturbed, he falls back to sleep until his wife screams that the house has been stolen. Plume expresses disinterest and dozes off. Shortly afterward, he thinks that he hears a train, but again sleep overtakes him. When he awakens, he is very cold, covered with blood, and surrounded by various pieces of his wife. Expressing mild displeasure that the train passed by so quickly, he once more falls asleep and is abruptly disturbed by the voice of a judge who cannot decipher the mystery of Plume's apathy. Plume does not offer a defense, and when the judge plans Plume's execution for the following day, Plume pleads ignorance of the whole affair, excuses himself, and goes back to bed.

Michaux makes it clear that Plume richly deserves to be judged, condemned, and punished for not taking an active part in life. Each time Plume falls asleep, he repeats the Fall of Man, but Plume's sin is far worse, because he refuses to act. Michaux's use of the past tense in this poem expresses pessimism; man was born into a state of guilt (sleep), so he accepts his condemnation (falls back to sleep). Michaux calls upon the reader to attack Plume, to make fun of him—in short, not to identify with Plume's "peaceful" behavior but, instead, to take charge of life. One can feel no pity for the condemned man who has faced life with total passivity. The reader's laughter signifies his recognition of the absurdity of life and his alienation from Plume's apathy. Michaux encourages man to struggle, to fight for existence, even though it may be a futile battle with a hostile and absurd world.

"MY KING"

The theme of resistance and the attitude of scorn for man's paralysis are reiterated in the prose poem "Mon Roi" ("My King"), in the collection *La Nuit remue* (night on the move). Night, a time of apparitions and hallucinations, is the traditional period of sleep (bitterly attacked in the Plume pieces) and is a static and noncombative time for man: Man is defeated at night. Michaux wishes to stir him to motion, to agitate him, to force him to participate. In the poem, it is during the night that an unnamed first-person narrator attacks a character he calls "my King," the figure of a super proprietor who is unique and powerful. The narrator strangles and shakes the King, laughs in his face, throws him on the ground, slaps him, and kicks him. Yet the King does not move, his blue visage returns to normal, and every night he returns to the chamber of the narrator. The King is always seemingly victorious, but he cannot exist without a subject, while his subject, who is also a victim, cannot rid himself of the King. Like Albert Camus's Sisyphus, the narrator can acquire dignity and purpose only when in continual motion and revolt.

Michaux uses the present tense in "My King" to indicate that man's struggle never ends. This is the human condition wherein liberty is both necessary and impossible; the battle itself is what counts. Michaux's violent style, his use of the shock technique, and his refusal to reproduce the real constitute his call to action, his attack on society, and his indictment of man, who contains within him two spirits: one, domineering and parasitic; the other, impotent and inert, a mere spectator of life. Man must not be resigned to this dilemma, Michaux asserts, for the only promise of salvation is in action.

"Clown"

The poem "Clown" (in the collection *Peintures*) is a brilliant summary of Michaux's poetic vision. A clown is a fool, a jester who paints on a ridiculous face, the caricature of a human being. What amuses the spectator about a clown, as he performs his zany antics, is the viewer's own superiority to the buffoon's mishaps, clumsiness, and inability to cope with the world. The clown exists in an absurd universe. He trips, he fumbles, he uncovers the unexpected, he pops in and out of boxes too small to contain human beings. His ludicrous nature, the "laughable," is dependent upon a reaction from the viewer; likewise, the spectator's appreciation and self-importance rest on the existence of the clown, his victim. Man's laughter is therefore grotesque. On the other hand, the clown is not known as an individual but as a force. He is free in that he breaks with convention and logical order, going about the "expected" in his own way. Clowns make life more bearable by the creative energy of their destruction. Michaux's clown states that he will "chop off, upset, break, topple and purge" the "miserable modesty, miserable dichotomy" of his shackles.

Michaux's use of future tense in this poem is extremely important. In addition to lending urgency and a sense of power, it underscores the intolerable present and the interdependency of clown and audience. The jester must rid himself of his "worthy fellow-beings," his

"look-alikes," in order to find the essence of a new and incredible freshness and purity (*rosée*). The sound of the word *rosée*, however, reveals a layer of deep pessimism and sets the tone for the ambiguous conclusion of the poem. A *rosé* is also a wine, potent as well as a cross between red and white, suggesting the very duality that the clown hopes to escape. Furthermore, Michaux indicates that the final revelation is *nul* (void) *et ras* (and blank) *et risible* (and ludicrous, laughable). After finally marshaling the strength and determination to discover what he might attain, the clown may find nothing but a vacuum—the final laugh.

Other major works

FICTIONAL TRAVELOGUES: *Ailleurs*, 1948 (includes *Voyage en Grande Garabagne*, 1936; *Au pays de la magie*, 1941; and *Ici, Poddema*, 1946); *Portrait des Meidosems*, 1948.

PLAY: *Le Drame des constructeurs*, pb. 1930 (one act).

NONFICTION: *Un Barbare en Asie*, 1933 (travel journal and poetry; *A Barbarian in Asia*, 1949); *Entre centre et absence*, 1936 (writings, drawings, and paintings); *Passages, 1937-1950*, 1950 (collected articles); *Tranches de savoir*, 1950 (aphorisms); *Misérable miracle, la mescaline*, 1956 (*Miserable Miracle, Mescaline*, 1963); *L'Infini turbulent*, 1957 (*Infinite Turbulence*, 1975); *Connaissance par les gouffres*, 1961 (*Light Through Darkness*, 1963); *Vents et poussiéres*, 1962; *Les Grandes Épreuves de l'esprit et les innombrables petites*, 1966 (autobiographical essays; *The Major Ordeals of the Mind and the Countless Minor Ones*, 1974).

MISCELLANEOUS: *L'Espace du dedans*, 1944 (*Selected Writings: The Space Within*, 1951); *Selected Writings of Henri Michaux*, 1968; *Darkness Moves: An Henri Michaux Anthology, 1927-1984*, 1994.

Bibliography

Bowie, Malcolm. *Henri Michaux*. Oxford, England: Clarendon Press, 1973. A critical study of Michaux's literary works. Includes bibliographic references.

Broome, Peter. *Henri Michaux*. London: Athlone Press, 1977. A short critical assessment of the works of Michaux. Includes and index and bibliography.

Hellerstein, Nina S. "Calligraphy, Identity: Scriptural Exploration as Cultural Adventure." *Symposium* 45, no. 1 (Spring, 1991): 329. A critical comparison of the works of Paul Claudel and Henri Michaux traces each writer's fascination with Chinese and Japanese writing systems.

Kawakami, Akane. "Barbarian Travels: Textual Positions in *Un Barbare en Asie*." *Modern Language Review* 95, no. 4 (October, 2000): 978-991. *Un Barbare en Asie* is not so much a collection of Henri Michaux's views on Asia as the trace of his passage through it. There is a complex relationship between Michaux and these Asian cultures which requires a more subtle explanatory model that the dualistic one of hegemony.

La Charité, Virginia A. *Henri Michaux*. Boston: Twayne, 1977. An introductory biography and critical study of selected works by Michaux. Includes bibliographic references.

Katherine C. Kurk;
bibliography updated by the editors

Michelangelo (Library of Congress)

MICHELANGELO

Born: Caprese, Italy; March 6, 1475
Died: Rome, Italy; February 18, 1564

PRINCIPAL POETRY

Rime di Michelagnolo Buonarroti, 1623
Le Rime di Michelangelo Buonarroti, 1863 (Cesare Guasti, editor)
The Sonnets of Michel Angelo, 1878
Sonnets of Michel Angelo, 1905
Rime di Michelangelo Buonarroti, 1960
The Complete Poems of Michelangelo, 1960
Michelangelo: Self-Portrait, 1963

OTHER LITERARY FORMS

"The visions of the painter are perpetuated in the vault; the cares of the man in his letters," E. H. Ramsden declares in the introduction to her edition of English translations of Michelangelo's letters (*The Letters of Michelangelo*, 1963). The renowned painter and sculptor, creator of the statue of David and the epic paintings of the Sistine Chapel's ceiling, also left a literary legacy. Along with his poetry, he wrote some five hundred letters which, though never intended as publishable literature, are a rich source of psychological and biographical material. Michelangelo's letters are largely concerned with money, contracts, the difficulties of dealing with popes, family quarrels and obligations, real estate deals and speculations, politics (very obliquely referred to), premonitions, and setting his worthless brothers up in business. Rarely, if ever, does he discuss the art which was his sole reason for existence. When he completed the paintings in the Sistine Chapel after four years of hard labor, all he wrote to his father was:

I have finished the chapel I have been painting; the Pope is very well satisfied. But other things have not turned out for me as I'd hoped. For this I blame the times, which are very unfavorable to our art. . . .

ACHIEVEMENTS

By all accounts, Michelangelo reigned as the most important and most gifted sculptor of the Renaissance. When his *Pietà*, commissioned for Saint Peter's and carved when Michelangelo was barely twenty, was unveiled, it caused a great flurry of excitement, and when his *David* was presented less than a decade later, there was little doubt that his work would define the standards for the highest period of the Italian Renaissance. Throughout his life, he was sought after by both the Papacy and the patriarchs of Florence, not only for his talents as a sculptor but also for his gifts as an architect and a military engineer.

His allegiance always to his art, Michelangelo was able to produce commissioned works as great as the Sistine Chapel or the Medici tombs without falling prey to the political rivalries between Rome and Florence—a feat in itself, attesting the esteem in which he was held by the ruling class. Four centuries after his death, Michelangelo is revered by popular opinion; his most famous works, especially the *Pietà* of Saint Peter's Basilica, the *David*, and the Sistine Chapel, draw tens of thousands of people every year, and are among the most popular tourist attractions in Europe. In addition, critics have reevaluated Michelangelo's poetry, establishing its merit not simply as a sidelight to his sculpture but as an innovative and important body of work in its own right.

BIOGRAPHY

Michelangelo di Lodovico Buonarroti Simoni's attainments as a poet can be understood, both thematically and aesthetically, only against the background of the artist's life in the service of six popes of the Italian Renaissance and his colossal achievements in all the visual arts—sculpture, painting, and architecture.

Brought to Florence from Caprese while still an infant, Michelangelo was sent to nurse with a stonecutter's wife in Settignano, where, he later liked to say, he imbibed marble dust with his wet-nurse's milk. When he was still a child, his mother died, leaving her husband, Lodovico, with five young sons. Lodovico remarried in 1485, and about that time, Michelangelo returned to Florence to live in the Santa Croce quarter with his father, stepmother, four brothers, and an uncle. Of the brothers, only Buonarroto, two years younger

than Michelangelo, married and left progeny. The eldest brother, Leonardo, became a Dominican monk; the youngest brothers, Giovansimone and Sigismondo, passed their lives in trade, soldiering, and farming. Undoubtedly the untimely death of his mother and the overwhelmingly male household in which the artist spent his early years are important clues to certain aspects of Michelangelo's personality. He never married, asserting that his art was sufficient mistress for him; his nudes are characterized by a blurring of distinctly male and female attributes, a projection of a race whose physiognomy and physiology would seem to partake of the qualities of both sexes. Similar qualities are manifest in his poetry.

Michelangelo's correspondence with his father and brothers reveals the artist's deep, almost morbid attachment to his family, despite the fact that comprehension of, or even interest in, Michelangelo's art was entirely lacking on their part. Throughout their lives, his father and brothers looked upon Michelangelo only as a source of income or as a counselor in their various projects. Although in his letters Michelangelo frequently refers to his financial affairs, he never discusses art with his family, and rarely indeed with anyone else.

As a boy, Michelangelo cared little for the traditional Latin and Humanist studies; his inclination to draw led his father, despite his scorn for art, to enroll him (on April 1, 1488) as a student apprentice in the workshop of Domenico Ghirlandaio, then the most popular painter in Florence. A year later, however, Michelangelo left that master to study in the Medici gardens near San Marco, where Lorenzo the Magnificent had gathered a collection of ancient statues and had assigned Bertoldo di Giovanni, a follower of Donatello, to train young men in sculpture. A faun's head (now lost) that Michelangelo had freely copied from a classic fragment attracted Lorenzo's attention, and Michelangelo, then fifteen years old, was taken to live almost as a son in the Medici Palace, first with Lorenzo de' Medici, then briefly with his son Piero. It was during these impressionable years that the youthful artist absorbed the Neoplatonic ideas of Lorenzo's famous circle of Humanists, Poliziano, Marsilio Ficino, and Giovanni Pico della Mirandola. Undoubtedly, Michelangelo's notion of reality as an essence underlying, or contained within, an enveloping substance was derived from conversations he heard in Lorenzo's "academy." The sculptural art of "taking away"—that is, revealing the figure already contained within the block—is analogous to ascending the Platonic ladder to a preexistent Form. At Poliziano's suggestion, the young sculptor carved a relief, the *Battle of the Centaurs*, that showed indications of his mastery of the nude as the ideal vehicle of expression. The Neoplatonism which Michelangelo absorbed in the Medici Palace is one of the major themes of his poetry, especially the contrast between carnal and ideal love.

After the death of Lorenzo the Magnificent on April 8, 1492, his unworthy son Piero showed little interest in Michelangelo's genius, assigning the sculptor such tasks as making a snowman. Subsequently, fearing the imminent invasion of the French under Charles VIII and the threatened fall of the Medici, Michelangelo and two companions fled to Venice and then returned to Bologna. Several times during the artist's life, unpredictable flights of this kind occurred, resulting apparently from nameless fears.

Michelangelo remained in Bologna from the fall of 1494 until the beginning of 1495 as a guest of Gianfrancesco Aldovrandi, a wealthy merchant, to whom Michelangelo read Dante, Petrarch, and other Tuscan poets. During his lifetime, Michelangelo had the reputation of being a profound scholar of Dante's *La divina commedia* (c. 1320; *The Divine Comedy*). A harsh exaltation informs the work of both Tuscans, and in Michelangelo's own poetry, the intellectual power of Dante is matched, if not his graceful style and fertile imagery.

In 1495, Michelangelo returned to Florence, where he carved in marble a *San Giovannino* and a *Sleeping Cupid* (both lost). The Cupid was such a skillful imitation of classical sculpture that it was sold to a Roman art dealer, who in turn sold the counterfeit as an authentic antique to Cardinal Raffaello Riario. Discovering the deception, the cardinal summoned Michelangelo to Rome in June, 1496, thinking to order other works from the astonishing young talent. Although the cardinal's patronage ultimately proved unrewarding, Michelangelo remained in Rome for five fruitful years. During this period he completed a *Bacchus* in marble for the

Roman banker Jacopo Galli and the *Pietà* that is now in Saint Peter's Basilica for the French Cardinal Jean Villiers de la Groslaye. This first sojourn in Rome resulted in great fame for the youthful sculptor. Sharply revealed in his *Bacchus* and *Pietà* at this time are two of the main contrasting themes which served Michelangelo all of his life: pagan exaltation of the nude male figure and love-pity for the Christ. Both of these works, however, in their combination of naturalistic detail, high finish, and rather cold classical beauty, still hark back to the earlier fifteenth century Florentine sculptors. A comparison of this *Pietà* with a *Pietà* from his last years shows how far the artist moved from this early, vigorous naturalism to an abstract spiritualization of form and material.

Three months before Michelangelo signed his contract for the *Pietà*, Girolamo Savonarola was burned at the stake (May 23, 1498) after his condemnation by the Borgia Pope Alexander VI. The martyrdom of the Dominican deeply affected Michelangelo, who continued to read Savonarola's sermons throughout his life. The prophetic nature of the friar was probably also a factor that led the artist to assiduous reading of the Old Testament. Nevertheless, the years of Savonarola's domination had been unfavorable to art, and it was perhaps the more propitious atmosphere that had come about in Florence, as well as the repeated urgings of his father, that drew Michelangelo back to his native city. When Michelangelo returned from Rome in 1501, he was already a famous sculptor. He was deluged with commissions, most notably for the gigantic *David*, a fourteen-foot nude extracted from a single, awkwardly shaped block of Carrara marble (1501-1504).

This colossal *David* was, both in dimension and conception, Michelangelo's first truly heroic work. The frowning hero is the first expression of the *terribilità* for which the sculptor later became so famous. In the disproportionate right hand and the strained position of the left hand holding the sling bag at the shoulder, the artist was already moving away from the more literal naturalism of his earlier work. The huge hand is an apotheosis of *la man che ubbidisce all' intelletto*—"the hand that serves the intellect." The fierce frown plays an odd counterpoint against the relaxed pose, a typical Michelangelo equilibrium between contrary forces, a coexistence of contrarieties frequently found also in his poetry.

In 1505, Pope Julius II summoned Michelangelo to Rome, assigning him the task of creating the pope's mausoleum. The project, which involved over forty life-size figures, seemingly lacked any trace of religious spirit, and would have been a suitable secular glorification of the worldliness of the Renaissance papacy.

The intention was to place the mausoleum in the new apse then being constructed in the old basilica of Saint Peter's. The project threatened to dwarf the existing church and thus suggested to Julius the idea of reconstructing the entire basilica on a new, immense scale. It may therefore be said that the colossal dimensions of Michelangelo's plans for the tomb were an indirect cause of the construction of the new Saint Peter's. The fickleness of the pope and his failure to pay Michelangelo for the expense of carting the marble, as well as a nameless presentiment that his life was in jeopardy, caused the hypersensitive artist to depart unexpectedly for Florence on April 17, 1506, the day before the laying of the cornerstone of the new Saint Peter's. Followed in vain by messengers and threats from the pope, who sent three peremptory briefs to the Signory of Florence, Michelangelo fiercely refused to return to Rome. Several violent sonnets addressed to Pope Julius probably date from this period. Eventually Michelangelo was persuaded to attempt a reconciliation. In November, 1506, Michelangelo, "with a rope around my neck" (the traditional symbol of submission), came to Julius at Bologna, which the old pope, marching at the head of his troops, had just reconquered from the local tyrant, Giovanni Bentivoglio. In a stormy meeting, Julius pardoned Michelangelo and assigned him a new task; to cast a huge bronze statue of the pope to be set over the main portal of San Petronio in Bologna.

The bronze finished, Michelangelo returned home, planning to complete many assignments; Julius, however, summoned him again to Rome. Michelangelo sought in vain to free himself from the pope's insistence that Michelangelo fresco the vault of the Sistine Chapel instead of resuming work on the tomb. Again, the Florentine found himself engaged in a craft which he did not consider his own. Nevertheless, once Michelangelo undertook the assignment, he set to work with typical fury

and confidence, resolved to surpass all other achievements in the art of fresco. Six assistants whom he had summoned from Florence were soon dismissed by the fiercely individualistic artist. Except for some manual help in preparing the plaster grounds, and perhaps in painting some portions of the architectural setting, the entire stupendous task of decorating a barrel vault 128 feet long and forty-five-feet wide, sixty-eight feet from the pavement, together with lunettes over twelve windows, was carried out by Michelangelo alone. From May 10, 1508, until October, 1512, with some interruptions, he worked on a special scaffolding, painting at great personal discomfort with the brush over his head "dripping a rich pavement" on his chest:

> I've already grown a goiter from this toil,
> as water swells the cats in Lombardy
> or any other country they might be,
> forcing my belly to hang under my chin.
> My beard to heaven . . .

And after describing the grotesque distortions his body must assume, painting the vault sixty-eight feet above the pavement, the poet-artist cries out:

> Therefore, fallacious, strange
> the judgment carried in the mind must fly,
> for from a twisted gun one shoots awry.
> My dead picture defend
> now, Giovanni, and also my honor,
> for I'm in no good place, nor I a painter.

Eventually the huge surface was covered with a vast panorama comprehending the story of Genesis up to the Flood and three episodes from the life of Noah. The choice of subject was Michelangelo's own, but it harmonized with the themes treated in the fifteenth century lateral-panel frescoes already in the chapel, which dealt with parallel episodes in the lives of Moses and Christ. Undoubtedly the most awesome pictorial achievement of the High Renaissance, the Sistine Chapel ceiling is the fullest expression of Michelangelo's genius in employing the human form and face in their manifold attitudes and attributes. The Sistine ceiling balances pictures from the Old Testament and nude Greek youths, pre-Christian prophets and pagan sibyls, pagan Humanism and orthodox Christianity.

Michelangelo, however, had never ceased to think of resuming work on Julius's mausoleum. Even during the creation of the most stupendous piece of painting in Western art, he had signed his letters "Michelangelo, sculptor in Rome." He had already arranged for the purchase, later concluded, of a house in Rome on the Macel de' Corvi near the area of the Trajan Forum, where he could collect and work the marble. On February 21, 1513, however, Pope Julius died, and then began that which biographer Asconio Condivi called "the tragedy of the tomb": the litigation with Julius's heirs, the abandonment of Michelangelo's first grand idea, the successive diminutions of the project to the present mediocrity in San Pietro in Vincoli. This much-reduced version has as its chief attraction Michelangelo's sculpture *Moses*. In the menacing *Moses*, with its hyperbolic beard and strained posture, left foot drawn back, the *terribilità* of the artist reached volcanic expression. Michelangelo was inspired more often by the heroes, prophets, and judgmental Jehovah of the Jews than by the Gospels. Only in the drawings and poems of his extreme old age does the Crucifixion appear as a theme.

In 1516, while Michelangelo was at Carrara gathering marble for the mausoleum, he had to return to Rome, where Pope Leo X (elected March, 1513) ordered him to construct and decorate with statues the facade of San Lorenzo in Florence. Thus, the artist again found himself deflected from the vast project on which he had set his heart, and once again he found himself in the service of the Medici. Leo, indeed, had known Michelangelo as a boy when they had sat together, almost as brothers, at the table of Lorenzo, Leo X's father. The pope was exactly Michelangelo's age, forty-one years old, a pleasure-loving man famous for his remark: "Let us enjoy the Papacy, since God has given it to us." Although he commissioned Michelangelo on the basis of competitive drawings and models, the contract was soon broken. Probably Leo found the sweeter and softer-natured Raphael more to his liking than the litigious and austere sculptor. At any rate, Michelangelo produced more during his tempestuous relationship with the "terrible" Julius than with the epicurean Leo.

In 1527, Rome was sacked by the Emperor Charles V. At the news, the Florentines once again evicted the Medici (May 17, 1527) and restored the Republic. In July of the next year, Michelangelo's favorite brother, Buonarroto, died in his arms of the plague, and the cares of the widowed family fell on the sculptor's shoulders. When the armies of Clement VII and the reconciled Charles V moved against the city, Michelangelo was named magistrate of the Committee of Nine of the Florentine Militia and, a few months later, he was appointed governor and procurator general of the city's fortifications. Almost against his will, he participated in the defense of his city, executing missions of a military character at Pisa, Livorno, and Ferrara and fortifying the hill at San Miniato.

After the fall of Florence (August 2, 1530), the Medici returned. Pardoned by Clement VII, the artist continued working on the Medici tombs while attending to other assignments heaped on him by the Pope. Then, distrusting Duke Alexander, the new Medici ruler of Florence, and desirous of concluding work on the tomb of Julius according to the last contract, Michelangelo returned to Rome to his house at Macel de' Corvi. He alternated his Rome sojourn with long stays at Florence, where he was needed for work on the library and the tombs. This was the period of his fervent friendships with the young Tommaso Cavalieri at Rome and the young Febo di Poggio at Florence. Many of Michelangelo's most beautiful poems are addressed to Cavalieri. In 1531, Michelangelo's father died at the age of ninety, prompting a touching poem of filial affection.

With the deaths of his favorite brother and father, his native city under a ruler unsympathetic to him, and feeling the urgency to free himself of what had become the incubus of the Julius mausoleum, the artist left Florence in September, 1534, never to return. Michelangelo arrived in Rome two days before the death of Clement VII. The new pope, Paul III, did not hesitate to assign work to the master, forcing him once again to reduce the part that still remained to be executed on the tomb.

Paul set Michelangelo immediately to work on the project of painting in fresco *The Last Judgment* on the wall of the Sistine Chapel (1534-1541). Thus, after having evoked on the vault the beginning of the universe, the artist depicted its end. The violence and disequilibrium of this swirl of nude bodies rising from the grave to Paradise, or descending to Hell, spiraling around a central figure of Christ the Judge, a Christ with the body of a Heracles and the face of an Apollo, is in startling contrast to the luminous, floating balance of the ceiling. The abundant and violent nudity, the athletic Christ, the angels without wings, all stirred violent condemnation during the artist's lifetime and resulted in subsequent painting of loincloths over most of the nudities, in the first instance by Michelangelo's pupil Daniele da Volterra, who thereby won for himself the nickname Il Brachettone (the breeches maker).

Some critics see in *The Last Judgment* a reflection in plastic terms of the crisis of Reformation and Counter-Reformation set off by Martin Luther's theses. Certainly, the artist, who grew increasingly religious with the years, was deeply troubled by the civil war in the body of Christianity. He was an intimate member of a reform Catholic movement centering on the poet Vittoria Colonna, whom the artist had met in 1536 and with whom he maintained a passionate platonic relationship until her death in 1547. He made many drawings for Vittoria Colonna, with whom he also exchanged poetry and discussed theological questions, some of which are expressed in intricate and ambiguous verse.

While working on *The Last Judgment*, Michelangelo had been named in 1535 architect, sculptor, and painter of the Apostolic Palace, wherein from 1541 to 1550, he frescoed the Pauline Chapel with the *Conversion of St. Paul* and the *Crucifixion of St. Peter*, thus completing his last paintings at the age of seventy-five. In 1547, Michelangelo was named architect of Saint Peter's. From then on, he was primarily involved with architecture: The disturbances and disequilibrium that still raged within the artist's soul found plastic expression in the broken pediments, recessed columns, blind niches, and frequently grotesque, abstract architectural forms.

Michelangelo's appointment as architect of Saint Peter's was reconfirmed by Julius III (1552), Paul IV (1555), and finally Pius IV (1559). Michelangelo resisted the insistent demands of the Medici Cosimo I that he return to Florence. More than eighty years old, Michelangelo was obsessed above all with the desire to push ahead the construction of Saint Peter's.

During these last years, the artist's thoughts dwelt constantly upon the theme of death. It is probable that many of his finest sonnets and the last great drawings of the Crucifixion were executed during this time. After his seventy-fifth year, Michelangelo began work on the tragic *Pietà* now in the Duomo of Florence, in which the artist portrays himself as Nicodemus, the Pharisee who came to Jesus by night and raised troubled questions: "How can these things be?" According to biographer Giorgio Vasari, his contemporary, the work was intended for Michelangelo's own tomb.

At the end, Michelangelo seems to have broken through his suffering, gone beyond it into that tranquil yet tragic realm of his last two *Pietà* sculptures. The Rondanini *Pietà* leaps out of the Renaissance entirely, in two directions, one might say. The slender verticality—Mother and Son merged—looks back to the column statues of Gothic portals and forward to the abstraction of Constantin Brancusi's *Bird in Space*—an almost macabre reduction of tragedy to pure essence.

ANALYSIS

Michelangelo's tomb in Santa Croce symbolizes his titanic achievements as a sculptor, painter, and architect. Curiously, the fourth crown of laurel is missing, despite the fact that he is currently recognized as the greatest Italian lyric poet of the sixteenth century.

Michelangelo himself refused to take seriously the verses that (especially from his sixtieth year on) he was forever scribbling and revising on the backs of letters, on sheets of drawings, or any other odd scraps of paper at hand. After all, he was not the only artist of his day who wrote poetry. The Renaissance ideal was *l'uomo universale*, the universal man, not the specialist.

Thus, the fact that Michelangelo wrote poetry is not surprising; what is surprising is the extraordinary quality of the best of his work. His contemporaries recognized it. The poems circulated in manuscript; a number of his madrigals were set to music by celebrated Italian and foreign composers, including Jakob Arcadelt; and in 1546, the Humanist Benedetto Varchi lectured on one of Michelangelo's sonnets before the Academy of Florence. Michelangelo was even persuaded to gather a selection of his verses for publication.

The unforeseen death of his friend, the banker Luigi del Riccio, who had been the patron for such a collection, dissuaded the artist from continuing the project. As it turned out, the poems were not published until 1623 in a corrupt edition misedited by Michelangelo's great-nephew, a Florentine academician. Fearful for his great ancestor's reputation, the younger Michelangelo committed mayhem on the text, bowdlerizing anything remotely questionable, turning masculine into feminine, making elegant what was rough, and rewriting images. Not until Cesare Guasti's great edition of 1863 did a responsible text appear. Individual poems have been translated by such well-known English and American poets and writers as William Wordsworth, Robert Southey, Henry Wadsworth Longfellow, Ralph Waldo Emerson, George Santayana, and Robert Bridges.

SONNETS, MADRIGALS, FRAGMENTS

The poetic works comprise 343 pieces—everything from sonnets and madrigals to fragments. Many of them appear to be a personal journal; others, such as the fifty epitaphs written at Riccio's request to commemorate the death of his nephew, serve some social purpose. The bulk of the verses seem to be the musings of an old man, although some love poems, full of conventional mannerisms, probably are earlier. All dating of the poems is speculative, deductive, but the assumption that very little of the earliest poetry has survived is supported by the fact that in 1518 the artist, in a burst of ire, burned many of his poems and drawings.

Michelangelo was particularly fond of the sonnet. Within its small space, as from a constricted block of marble, he hammered out harsh Dantesque lines that profoundly express his agony of spirit, now and again lightened by bursts of rough humor. Recurrent themes are the war of himself against himself; repentance for a nameless guilt; art as a symbol of the relationship of God to man; exalted platonic love; and a religious exaltation of death as liberation.

SPEAKING THINGS

Despite frequent obscurities and abstract knotted metaphors, Michelangelo's poetry is striking for its ultimate confessional power, a nakedness of soul akin to his nudes in the visual arts. "Be silent! Enough of pallid violets and liquid crystals and sleek beasts," the poet Francesco Berni, a contemporary of Michelangelo, cries out in exasperation against the facile Petrarchan warblers of the time. "He speaks things, and you speak words." Berni struck to the core: "Ei dice cose . . ." ("He speaks things"), and in this, Michelangelo is rare not only among Italian poets. His lines seem to struggle out of the matrix of language as his "prisoners" struggle out of the rock. Seldom mellifluous, frequently imageless (or making use of conventional conceits), Michelangelo's verse derives its power from a texture of language that seems to be reproducing the very contours of thought itself: its spurts, its exaltations, its hesitations, its withdrawals. Sometimes ungrammatical, these strained, hammered lines are undoubtedly those of a sculptor. The combination of idealism, harshness, and crude jest reminds Italian readers of Dante. English readers, however, will be reminded of John Donne; there is the same love of paradox, the same coexistence of contraries, the same conflict between sensuality and austerity, the same mannered and overextended conceits, the same war of self against self: "Vorrei voler, Signor, quel ch'io non voglio . . ." ("I would want to want, O Lord, what I do not want . . .").

LOVE AND DANTE

Just as in Michelangelo's sculpture (and in the painted sculpture which is the vault of the Sistine Chapel) *terribilità* coexists with melancholy resignation, so in these poems all the varieties of love—of God, of man, of woman, of art, of country—are celebrated in a grappling of ardor and ashes, the power to do anything frozen at the brink of a desire to do nothing.

Michelangelo was nourished on Dante, whose poetry he knew intimately; indeed, among his contemporaries, he was extolled as a Dante scholar. In Donato Giannotti's *Dialogues* on Dante, the artist figures as a major protagonist. Yet if Michelangelo's spirit vibrated to that of his fellow Florentine, Dante, the forms and imagery of his verse were derived from the fashionable neo-Petrarchianism of the first half of the sixteenth century. The result is that Dantesque vigor and Michelangelesque spiritual suffering sometimes burst the fragile and stereotyped Petrarchan container. When these elements are in balance, the poetic achievement is of the very first order.

NEUROSES OF DESIRE

Michelangelo's poems are those of a man deeply ill at ease with himself and with his world, and it is this tension which makes them seem so neurotically modern. Like a salamander, Michelangelo is always living in flame; like a phoenix, he is always being reborn from the ashes of his suffering: "A single torment outweighs a thousand pleasures." Indeed, there is something masochistic, passive, feminine in many of his curious images. Like gold or silver, the poet's desire must be melted by the fires of love, and then poured into him "through such narrow spaces" to fill his void. As a goldsmith or silversmith must break the form to extract the work, so he must be broken and tortured in order to draw forth the perfect beauty of his lady. In another poem, one whose effectiveness is destroyed by its exaggerations, love enters through the eyes like a bunch of sour grapes forced into a narrow-necked bottle, and swelling within, is unable to escape.

THE CRUCIBLE OF SUFFERING

Elsewhere, Michelangelo compares himself to a block of stone which, being smashed, reveals its inner sparks, and then, pulverized and re-formed, is firebaked to a longer life.

> So in love with the stone, in which it lies,
> Is fire, that, soon drawn forth, with its quick blaze
> It binds it, burns it, breaks it, and in new guise
> It makes it live in some immortal place.
> And that same stone, when baked, can brave and face
> All seasons, and acquires a higher price,
> Just like a soul that soars to blesséd days
> After the flames that cleanse while they chastise.
> Thus, if it is my fate that I soon must
> Be dissolved by this fire that hides in me,
> My new life shall be vast and manifold.
> Therefore, if I am now but smoke and dust,
> Cleansed by this flame, eternal I shall be:
> No iron chisel carves me—one of gold.

The imagery of the first six lines, relating to the preparation of a ground for fresco-painting, is typically masochistic: Suffering, being smashed, pulverized, is a necessary condition for the creation and rewards of art. In swift transition, the poet goes on to compare such purgation to the ascension of souls from Purgatory to Heaven and immediately returns to his central metaphor: Suffering enriches. Suffering is the fiery furnace for the creation of the most precious values.

The initial quatrain of another sonnet expresses with remarkable concision Michelangelo's entire Neoplatonic aesthetic and throws light on his technique of stone carving as well:

> The greatest artist has no single concept
> Which a rough marble block does not contain
> Already in its core; *that* can attain
> Only the hand that serves the intellect

Just as Plato's transcendental forms or ideas exist before their specific manifestations on earth, so the statue, fully formed, exists within the block of marble; there, it awaits the liberating hand of the artist, who finds it by stripping away the excess (*superchio*). Such a liberating hand does not function merely by instinct: It is guided to its goal by intelligence (*la man che ubbidisce all' intelletto*). Thus, the artist is a dis-coverer in the strictest etymological sense of the word.

What is so fascinating is that Michelangelo is always the same artist, whether he is twisting an idea or twisting David's right wrist, whether he is trying to fit all of the ancestors of Christ into a spandrel of the Sistine Chapel or trying to fit too much concept into too little language. Just as the last great *Pietàs* and drawings have almost been dematerialized in the effort to render pure Idea, so in many of Michelangelo's poems language is being smashed, distorted, pulverized, almost as if the artist were trying to dispense with it.

The same poet addressed punning lines to a courtesan named Mancina, "Left-Handed"; lashed out at the bellicose Pope Julius, who was more devoted to the cult of Mars than to the Prince of Peace; and wrote stupendous sonnets to Night, whose dominions may be warred against by a single firefly; at the last, he held out his hands to Christ, longing for death to liberate him as he himself had liberated the perfect forms sleeping within the stone:

> Painting nor sculpturing no more will allay
> The soul turned toward the divine love
> Which opened to us its arms upon the cross.

OTHER MAJOR WORKS

NONFICTION: *I, Michelangelo, Sculptor: An Autobiography Through Letters*, 1962; *The Letters of Michelangelo*, 1963; *Complete Poems and Selected Letters of Michelangelo*, 1963.

MISCELLANEOUS: *Complete Poems and Selected Letters of Michelangelo*, 1963.

BIBLIOGRAPHY

Altizer, Alma B. *Self and Symbolism in the Poetry of Michelangelo, John Donne, and Agrippa d'Aubigne.* The Hague: Martinus Nijhoff, 1973. Study of "expressive mode" of Michelangelo's poetry in treatment of archetypal themes of "alienation, ecstasy, death, rebirth." Notes evolutions from rhetoric to symbolism and in transformations of self as active participant in poetic creation.

Barolsky, Paul. *The Faun in the Garden.* University Park: Pennsylvania State University Press, 1994. Barolsky's "analysis of poetic imagination" deeply relates Michelangelo's poetry to his artistic works and his contemporary biographies. He used all three to weave a fabrication of his "self" as creator and man.

Cambon, Glauco. *Michelangelo's Poetry: Fury of Form.* Princeton, N.J.: Princeton University Press, 1985. Formally analyzes poems as exhibitions of Michelangelo's idiosyncratic "mannerist excess" that are no less highly crafted than his sculptures.

Clements, R. J. *The Poetry of Michelangelo.* New York: New York University Press, 1965. This is a thematic approach to the poetry by one steeped in both the artistic and poetic sides of Michelangelo. Excellent introduction, though lacking chronological sense. It suffers from frequent use of only English translations and these drawn from numerous sources.

Hallock, Ann Hayes. *Michelangelo the Poet.* Palo Alto, Calif.: Page-Ficklin, 1978. Hallock presents a reading and contextualizing of the *Rime*, emphasizing his "drive toward the essential." She uncovers elements of this in his use of language and "nuclei" (themes) of *patria*, family, friends, soul, and life and death. Often complicated language and no English translations.

Ryan, Christopher. *The Poetry of Michelangelo: An Introduction.* Madison, N.J.: Fairleigh Dickinson University Press, 1998. This introduction to the poet and poems emphasizes the individual works and the corpus itself, as it attempts to clarify the intricacies of both. Ryan lays the works out chronologically, in stages, providing relevant historical and biographical background. Translations are the author's.

Sidney Alexander;
bibliography updated by Joseph P. Byrne

ADAM MICKIEWICZ

Born: Zaosie, Lithuania; December 24, 1798
Died: Burgas, Turkey; November 26, 1855

PRINCIPAL POETRY

Ballady i romanse, 1822
Dziady, parts 2, 4, 1823, and 3, 1832 (*Forefathers' Eve*, parts 2, 4, 1925, and 3, 1944-1946)
Grażyna, 1823 (English translation, 1940)
Sonety, 1826
Sonety krymskie, 1826 (*Sonnets from the Crimea*, 1917)
"Farys," 1828 ("Faris," 1831)
Konrad Wallenrod, 1828 (English translation, 1883, 1925)
Pan Tadeusz: Czyli, Ostatni Zajazd na litwie historia Szlachecka zr. 1811 i 1812 we dwunastu ksiegach wierszem, 1834 (*Pan Tadeusz: Or, The Last Foray in Lithuania, a Tale of Gentlefolk in 1811 and 1812, in Twelve Books in Verse*, 1917)
Poems by Adam Mickiewicz, 1944
Selected Poetry and Prose, 1955
Selected Poems, 1956
The Sun of Liberty, 1998

OTHER LITERARY FORMS

In the last twenty years of his life, Adam Mickiewicz, the national bard and prophet of Poland, wrote only a handful of poems, turning instead to religious and political works and to literary criticism. The messianic fervor of Mickiewicz's prose is exemplified by *Ksiegi narodu polskiego i pielgrzymstwa polskiego* (1832; *The Books of the Polish Nation and of the Polish Pilgrims*, 1833, 1925), a tract written in a quasi-biblical style. Mickiewicz's lectures given at the Collège de France in Paris, where from 1840 to 1844 he held the first chair of Slavic literature, fill several volumes of his complete works.

ACHIEVEMENTS

Adam Mickiewicz embodied in his work the soul of the Polish people. Through his poetry, he symbolized the land, history, and customs of Poland. Starting as a classicist and then quickly becoming a Romantic, he portrayed the everyday life of the Polish people and, at the same time, gave voice to visions and prophecies. His poems, written to be understood by the common man, brought him instant popular acclaim but also exposed him to attacks from many critics, who condemned his Romanticism and his provincial idioms.

The first volume of Mickiewicz's poetry was published in Wilno in an edition of five hundred copies. It contained ballads and romances, genres of poetry then unknown in Poland, and portrayed the common people in a simple but eloquent manner. A second volume followed in 1823, containing *Grażyna*, a tale in verse, and parts 2 and 4 of a fragmentary fantastic drama, *Forefathers' Eve*. With the publication of these works, followed by the narrative poem *Konrad Wallenrod*, set in medieval Lithuania, Mickiewicz became the founder of the Romantic movement in Polish literature. During his greatest creative period, in the years from 1832 to 1834, Mickiewicz published part 3 of *Forefathers' Eve*, which seethed with the eternal hatred felt by the Poles for their Russian conquerors. With its publication, Mickiewicz became a national defender, proclaiming that Poland was the Christ among nations, crucified for the sins of others. Like a prophet, he predicted that Poland would rise again. *Pan Tadeusz*, Mickiewicz's masterpiece, was also written during this period. An epic poem in twelve books depicting Polish life in Lithuania in 1811 and 1812, it is the greatest work of Polish literature and perhaps the finest narrative poem in nineteenth century European literature. Devoid of hatred or mysticism, it warmly and realistically depicts the Polish land and people and embodies a firm faith in their future.

BIOGRAPHY

Adam Mickiewicz was born on December 24, 1798, on the farmstead of Zaosie, near Nowogródek, a small town in Lithuania. After the Tartars' savage destruction of Kiev in 1240, the area previously known as Byelorussia and the Ukraine were annexed by the warlike Grand Duchy of Lithuania. In four centuries, however, the Lithuanian gentry was almost completely Polonized, and after the union with the Polish Crown in 1386, Lithuania's territory was greatly reduced. In the district of

Nowogródek, while the gentry was predominantly Polish (old immigrants from Mazovia), the peasants were Byelorussian. Mickiewicz's father, Mikolaj, was a lawyer and a small landowner. His mother, Barbara Majewska, né Orzeszko, was also from the middle gentry. Both families had a strong military tradition.

It is noteworthy that Mickiewicz, the national bard of Poland, the ardent patriot who gave such superb literary expression to the life and aspirations of the Polish people, never even saw Poland proper nor her cultural centers, Warsaw and Krakow. Moreover, during his lifetime, Poland did not exist as a sovereign state, for Mickiewicz was born after the so-called Final Partition of 1795, when Poland was divided among Russia, Prussia, and Austria-Hungary.

Mickiewicz, one of five sons, started his education at home and then continued at the Dominican parochial school in Nowogródek. Later, he studied philology at the University of Wilno, where he excelled in Latin and Polish literature. He was greatly influenced by a liberal historian, Joachim Lelewel, who later became a leader in the Insurrection of 1830-1831. At the university, Mickiewicz was one of the six founders of the Philomathian Society, a secret society that emphasized Polish patriotism and tried to influence public affairs. After spending a short time in Kowno as a district teacher of Greek and Latin, Polish literature, and history, Mickiewicz returned to Wilno, where he maintained close relations with his friends in the Philomathian Society. In 1823, Mickiewicz and several of his friends were arrested by the Russian authorities for plotting to spread "senseless Polish nationalism" and were confined in the Basilian Monastery in Wilno, which had been converted to a prison. After their trial on November 6, 1824, Mickiewicz and his friend Jan Sobolewski were sent to St. Petersburg to work in an office.

In 1819, before his imprisonment and deportation, Mickiewicz met and fell in love with Maryla Wereszczaka, the daughter of a wealthy landowner. Maryla, however, complying with the wishes of her family, refused to marry Mickiewicz, who was only a poor student, and married the rich Count Puttkamer instead. Partially inspired by his unrequited love for Maryla, Mickiewicz turned to writing Romantic poetry and, with the publication of two small volumes of poetry in 1822 and 1823, became the founder of the Romantic school in Poland. His earlier writing shows the influence of the pseudo-classical style then prevalent in Poland.

Mickiewicz stayed in Russia almost four years and wrote his *Sonety* and *Sonnets from the Crimea* there as well as *Konrad Wallenrod* and "Faris," an Arabian tale. He lived in St. Petersburg, Odessa, and Moscow, where he was warmly accepted into literary circles, befriended by Alexander Pushkin and others, and made a welcome guest in the literary salon of Princess Zenaida Volkonsky (herself an accomplished poet, whom Pushkin called "tsarina of muses and beauty"). He often improvised there, gaining the admiration of Pushkin, who called him "Mickiewicz, inspired from above."

In 1829, Mickiewicz secured permission to leave Russia and lived for a time in Switzerland and then in Rome. The Polish Insurrection broke out in 1830, and Mickiewicz tried in vain to join the revolutionists in August, 1831. After the defeat of the Insurrection, Mickiewicz settled in Paris, where he spent most of his remaining years. In 1834, he married Celina Szymanowski, the youngest daughter of Maria Szymanowski, a famous concert pianist, whom he had met while still in Russia. The marriage was unhappy because of her mental illness, and her early death left Mickiewicz with several small children. During this period, he wrote part 3 of *Forefathers' Eve*, a mystical and symbolic dramatic treatment of his imprisonment at Wilno by the Russian authorities. The poem embodied the anti-Russian feeling of the Polish people and intensified their hatred of their oppressor. Mickiewicz's next poem was his masterpiece, *Pan Tadeusz*, which glorifies the rustic life of the Polish gentry in picturesque Lithuanian Byelorussia and praises the Napoleonic invasion of Russia as symbolic of Poland's hope for liberation ("God is with Napoléon, Napoléon is with us"). *Pan Tadeusz* is a true national epic.

After the publication of his masterpiece, Mickiewicz fell under the influence of Andrzej Towiański, a charismatic figure who preached that a new period in Christianity was at hand and that he himself was its prophet. Unconditionally accepting Towiański's claims, Mickiewicz was compelled to give up his professorship at the Collège de France when he used his position to advance the doctrines of Towiański's sect. Mickiewicz spent his last years working for Polish independence and aiding fellow exiles. In 1855, following the outbreak in the previous year of the Crimean War, which he hailed as a prelude to the liberation of Poland, Mickiewicz went to Constantinople. He contracted cholera and died on November 26, 1855. His body was first sent to Paris; in 1890, it was brought to Wawel Castle in Krakow, where it now rests with Tadeusz Kościuszko and the Polish kings.

ANALYSIS

The Romantic movement had unique features in Poland, where it did not begin until the 1820's, some thirty years later than in England and Germany. The most prominent literary figure of Romanticism in Poland was Adam Mickiewicz, whose poetry grew out of his formative years in Lithuanian Byelorussia. Mickiewicz wrote poems that had universal as well as regional and national significance. A poet of genius, he raised Polish literature to a high level among Slavic literatures and to a prominent place in world literature.

Although he was in many respects the quintessential Romantic poet, Mickiewicz eludes categorization. There is a strong classical strain running throughout his oeuvre, evident in the clarity of his diction and the precision of his images. He combined meticulous observation of the familiar world with an evocation of spiritual realms and supernatural experience. His concerns as a poet went beyond poetry, reflecting a responsibility to his beloved, oppressed Poland and to humanity at large. As he was a spokesman in exile for Polish freedom, so he remains a spokesman for all of those who share his hatred of tyranny.

FROM CLASSICISM TO ROMANTICISM

Mickiewicz's work in philology at the University of Wilno instilled in him the values of eighteenth century classicism. Accordingly, his first significant poem, "Oda do mlodości" ("Ode to Youth"), reflected the tradition of the Enlightenment, but it also contained some of the pathos of Romanticism. In the ballad "Romantyczność" ("The Romantic"), this pathos becomes the dominant tone. The poem concerns a woman who is mocked and regarded as insane because, in despair, she talks to the ghost of her beloved. Mickiewicz treats her sympathetically, concluding: "Faith and love are more discerning/

Than lenses or learning." Revealing a Slavic preference for faith and feeling rather than Western rationalism, Mickiewicz returned to these youthful ideas in his later, more complex works.

Mickiewicz's shift toward a thoroughgoing Romanticism was influenced by his reading of Italian, German, and English literature, by his study of early Lithuanian history, and by his love for Maryla Wereszczaka. With his first two volumes of poetry Mickiewicz raised the stature of Polish poetry. His first volume contained short poems, mainly a group of fourteen "ballads and romances" prefaced with a survey of world literature. "The Romantic," the programmatic poem of the Polish Romantic movement, expresses his faith in the influence of the spirit world on man.

FOREFATHERS' EVE, PARTS 1, 2, AND 4

The second volume of Mickiewicz's poems contained the second and fourth parts of the incomplete fantastic drama, *Forefathers' Eve*; a short poem, "The Vampire," connected with that drama; and a short tale in verse, *Grażyna*. The genre of the fantastic drama was in fashion at the time. *Forefathers' Eve*, complete with ghosts and demons, was based on a folk rite that involved serving a meal to the spirits of the departed on All Souls' Day. Part 2 of *Forefathers' Eve* (the first part of the poem to be written) is an idealization of this rite, in which Mickiewicz probably had participated as a boy in Lithuanian Byelorussia. He explained that "Forefathers' Eve" is the name of a ceremony celebrated by the common folk in memory of their ancestors in many parts of Byelorussia, Lithuania, Prussia, and Courland. The ceremony, once called "the Feast of the Goat," originated in pagan times and was frowned upon by the Church.

In the first part of *Forefathers' Eve*, for which he only completed a sketch, Mickiewicz appears in the guise of Gustav, a name taken from *Valérie* (1803), a sentimental novel by Baroness von Krüdener. Gustav kills himself, disappointed in his love for Maryla. In a revised version of part 2 of *Forefathers' Eve*, Mickiewicz added a section expressing his love for Maryla. He depicts Maryla as a "shepherdess in mourning dress" whose lover, Gustav, has died for her. His spirit appears and gazes on the shepherdess and then follows her as she is led out of a chapel. In the fourth part of the poem his ghost appears at the house of a priest and delivers passionate, sorrowful monologues, pouring out his sad tale of disillusioned love while casting reproaches upon Maryla. He recommends to the priest the rites of "Forefathers' Eve" and finally reenacts his own suicide. Gustav is Mickiewicz's version of the self-dramatizing Romantic hero, but he is also a tragic hero in the Aristotelian sense, since he is defeated by a mistake in judgment—his overwhelming love for a person who proves to be unworthy.

GRAŻYNA

Mickiewicz wrote *Grażyna*, an impersonal narrative poem, at about the same time he wrote the highly personal and passionate *Forefathers' Eve*. *Grażyna* resembles the tales or "novels" in verse characteristic of the Romantic movement in Western Europe but lacks the supernatural elements and the exoticism which distinguish such works. The poem concerns the Lithuanians' struggle in the fourteenth century against the German Knights of the Cross. Mickiewicz was inspired by the ruins of a castle near Nowogródek, by his study of early Lithuanian history, and by his reading of Torquato Tasso, Sir Walter Scott, and Lord Byron. In the narrative, the Lithuanian prince, Litavor, plans to join the Teutonic Knights against Duke Witold. These traitorous intentions are foiled by Grażyna, Litavor's brave and patriotic wife. Dressed in her husband's armor, she leads the Lithuanian knights in battle against the Teutons instead of accepting their help against her compatriots. Mickiewicz modeled his heroine on Tasso's Clorinda and Erminia, although the type goes back to Vergil's Camilla and ultimately to the Greek tales of the Amazons. This stately narrative reveals Mickiewicz's extraordinary gift for vivid characterization, even though the poet himself did not attach much importance to the work.

SONNETS FROM THE CRIMEA

At the end of 1826, Mickiewicz published his first cycle of sonnets, the so-called "love sonnets." There were few Polish models in the sonnet form, and he turned for a model to the Petrarchan sonnet, with its elaborate rhyme scheme and rigid structure. His second cycle of sonnets, *Sonnets from the Crimea*, was vastly different in thought and feeling and was met with hostile criticism from Mickiewicz's classically minded contemporaries.

While in Russia, Mickiewicz had made a trip of nearly two months through the Crimea, and it was this journey which produced the eighteen poems that constitute the *Sonnets from the Crimea*. He made the trip with, among others, Karolina Sobański, with whom he had an ardent love affair; critics have speculated that the three sonnets "Good Morning," "Good Night," and "Good Evening" reflect their relationship. With his *Sonnets from the Crimea*, Mickiewicz introduced to Polish literature the Romantic poetry of the steppe, the sea, and the mountains, as well as the Oriental elements of European Romanticism, represented by Byron and Thomas Moore in England and by Pushkin in Russia. The sonnets express an attitude toward nature that is characteristically Romantic and at the same time "modern": Nature is valued for its own sake as well as for its symbolic reflection of the poet's psychological states. The sonnets are further distinguished by their exotic vocabulary, the fruit of Mickiewicz's study of Persian and Arabic poetry, mainly in French translation. (Near Eastern and Oriental literature was popular throughout Europe toward the end of the eighteenth century.) The rigid structure demanded by the sonnet form enabled Mickiewicz to communicate his psychological experiences with utmost conciseness, and these poems are among his finest.

KONRAD WALLENROD

Mickiewicz had conceived the idea of his next major work, *Konrad Wallenrod*, while in Moscow in 1825. Like *Grażyna*, the poem is set in medieval Lithuania during the conflict between the Lithuanians and the Knights of the Cross. *Konrad Wallenrod* is both longer and more powerful than *Grażyna*, however, and, although the poet modified and altered history to some extent, it is mainly based on actual historical events; Mickiewicz himself described the work as "a story taken from the history of Lithuania and Prussia." A tale in verse in the Byronic style, the poem relates the tragedy of a Lithuanian who is forced by fate to become a Teutonic Knight. The hero, in an effort to save his people from annihilation, sacrifices all that is dear to him, including his own honor. Mickiewicz changed the historical Wallenrod, an ineffective Grand Master of the Knights of the Cross, to a Lithuanian who, captured as a youth, has been reared by the Germans and then gains influence and authority over the Teutonic Knights in order to destroy them. To cap-

ture the aura of intrigue, Mickiewicz studied Machiavelli and read Friedrich Schiller's *Die Verschwörung des Fiesco zu Genua* (1783; *Fiesco: Or, The Genoese Conspiracy*, 1796). The poem reverts to the somber and Romantic atmosphere which Mickiewicz had temporarily abandoned in his sonnets; it is Byronic in type, and Mickiewicz evidently used *The Corsair* (1814) and *Lara* (1814) for inspiration. Mickiewicz's Wallenrod, however, differs markedly from the Byronic hero: Above all, he is a patriot, rather than a mysterious outsider. Indeed, so clear is the political allegory which underlies *Konrad Wallenrod* that it is surprising that the Russian censors allowed the poem to be published.

"FARIS"

In St. Petersburg in 1828, Mickiewicz wrote "Faris," a poem depicting an Arab horseman's extravagant ride through the desert. Mickiewicz had developed an interest in Arabic poetry through his contact with the Oriental peoples in the south of Russia. The Arabic word *faris* means "horseman" or "knight." Mickiewicz's special affection for the poem is often attributed to its story of a proud, strong will that triumphs over great obstacles; perhaps Mickiewicz saw himself in this light.

FOREFATHERS' EVE, PART 3

Mickiewicz wrote his greatest works, part 3 of *Forefathers' Eve* and *Pan Tadeusz*, in a brief period from 1832 to 1834. Part 3 of *Forefathers' Eve* is only loosely connected with parts 2 and 4, published almost ten years earlier. It is the longest, the most enigmatic, and certainly the most famous of the three parts. The poet went back for his subject matter to his Wilno days in 1823, when the Russian authorities arrested him and other members of the Philomathians. Using his personal experience in the Romantic manner, Mickiewicz sought to justify the actions of a loving God in allowing a devout Roman Catholic country such as Poland to be partitioned by three cruel neighbors, each "on a lower moral level than their victim."

While in Rome, Mickiewicz had been intrigued by Aeschyulus's tragedy *Prometheus Bound* (fifth century B.C.E.), with its presentation of the Titan who rebels against Zeus in the name of love for humanity, and Aeschylus's influence is apparent in part 3 of *Forefathers' Eve*. The story of Prometheus attracted many Romantic writers, including Perry Bysshe Shelley and Johann

Wolfgang von Goethe. Mickiewicz, who had considered writing his own poetic drama about Prometheus, may have been influenced by these authors as well in composing the third part of *Forefathers' Eve*.

Part 3 of *Forefathers' Eve* consists of a prologue, nine scenes, and a final sequence of six long poems about Russia. This sequence, titled "Ustcp" ("Digression"), constitutes a second act or epilogue. In the prologue, Maryla's lover, Gustav, a young prisoner, is seen in his cell in the Basilian Monastery, watched over by good and evil spirits. He takes the name Konrad, suggesting an affinity with Konrad Wallenrod. The first scene, a description of the life of the student prisoners, is followed by the improvisation—the foundation of the whole drama—in which Konrad arrogantly challenges God's justice, charging Him with an absence of feeling or love in spite of his strength and great intellect. Konrad declares that he himself is greater than God, since he loves his nation and desires her happiness. The improvisation and the following scenes reflect the fulfillment of Mickiewicz's previous plan of writing a tragedy with the Prometheus theme adapted to a Christian setting. Konrad's arrogant pride, although inspired by love for Poland and a sense of divinity within himself, is blasphemous. Father Peter, who represents mystic humility just as Konrad represents mystic pride, receives in a vision an understanding of the source of Konrad's torment—the problem of the fate of Poland, an innocent victim crushed by cruel foreign powers. He sees Poland as the Christ among nations, who, crucified by Prussia, Russia, and Austria, will rise again. The promised hero who will bring about the resurrection of Poland is probably Mickiewicz himself, although in the work there is reference only to a hero whose name is "Forty and Four." With this notion that Poland is the Christ among nations, Mickiewicz became the founder of Polish messianism, a mystic faith which helped to define "Polishness" for generations and which is not without influence in Poland even today.

PAN TADEUSZ

In November, 1832, Mickiewicz began work on *Pan Tadeusz*, a narrative poem that was to become his masterpiece. He worked on the poem until February, 1834. *Pan Tadeusz*, a stately epic of 9,712 lines, is a story of the Polish gentry. The poem's twelve books present the whole of Polish society in Lithuanian Byelorussia during a highly significant period of history, the time of Napoleon's campaign in Russia, in 1811-1812, a time when Polish society appeared to have achieved a temporary harmony, stability, and order. Mickiewicz stresses the value of ritual, order, and ceremony, and his characters are courteous, modest, and patriotic.

The subtitle of *Pan Tadeusz—The Last Foray in Lithuania, a Tale of Gentlefolk in 1811 and 1812, in Twelve Books in Verse*—is significant: Mickiewicz's use of the word "tale" may indicate, as some critics have argued, that *Pan Tadeusz* is not an epic or narrative poem at all, although it is connected to these genres, but a blending together of a number of genres to achieve the poet's artistic purpose in a truly Romantic style. The word "last" in the subtitle implies the disappearance of a traditional way of life, as exemplified in the "foray" or ritualistic execution of justice. Mickiewicz's two main themes, the recapture of the past and the conflict between reality and appearance, are classic themes in Western literature, and the poem thus attains a certain universality in spite of its intense concern with a specific cultural and historical tradition.

The plot concerns Tadeusz, an impressionable young man recently graduated from the university; his love for Zosia; and a feud over a castle between the Soplicas and the Horeszkos: Tadeusz is a Soplica, while Zosia is a Horeszko (a premise which recalls William Shakespeare's *Romeo and Juliet*, c. 1596). To add to the conflict, the father of Tadeusz has killed Zosia's grandfather. The plot becomes more involved later in the work when an emissary of Napoleon turns out to be Tadeusz's father disguised as a monk, Father Robak. (In constructing his plot, Mickiewicz was influenced by Sir Walter Scott.) Mickiewicz chose for his setting rural Lithuanian Byelorussia, the land of his childhood, to which he longed to return. The real hero of the poem is Jacek Soplica, who wants to marry Eva, the daughter of an aristocrat, the Pantler Horeszko. When he is rejected, Jacek kills the Pantler in a fit of anger, under circumstances that falsely suggest collusion with the Russians. Jacek spends the rest of his life humbly serving his country. He becomes a monk and works as a political agent urging Poles to join Napoleon in his campaign against Russia and so to contribute to the restoration of

Poland in an indirect manner. Mickiewicz united in Jacek the conflicting motives of pride and humility, represented in part 3 of *Forefathers' Eve* by Konrad and Father Peter. In *Pan Tadeusz*, Mickiewicz is no longer a prophet and teacher, appearing rather as a kindly, genial man who is proud of the glorious past of his country and has faith in her future. He is once more the jovial companion of his Wilno days and no longer the leader of Polish exiles who were haunted by their own misfortunes and those of Poland. He is a realist who sees the faults of his countrymen but still loves them.

It is difficult to believe that part 3 of *Forefathers' Eve* and *Pan Tadeusz* were written by the same poet within a period of two years. In the latter, the poet is moved by childlike wonder: He sees beauty in even the most commonplace scenes in Poland, such as a young girl feeding poultry in a farmyard. The period about which he was writing embodied the whole life of Old Poland—its people, its customs, and its traditions. While the action of *Pan Tadeusz* develops in the country among rural people, set against a background of vibrant descriptions of nature and animals, all classes of the gentry are described, including the wealthy, the aristocratic, the middle class, and the poor gentry, and there are representatives of a number of old offices, such as chamberlain, *voyevoda*, pantler, cupbearer, seneschal, judge, and notary. In addition, there are representatives of other classes and nationalities, including the peasants (rather incompletely presented, however), a Jew, and various Russians.

In *Pan Tadeusz*, Mickiewicz describes nature in a manner that has never been equaled in Polish literature. He paints verbal pictures of the forest, meadows, and ponds at different times of the day and night in different lights and in myriad colors; he describes sunrises and sunsets, and the world of plants and animals, all with acute perception. Mickiewicz also meticulously describes a mansion, a castle, a cottage of the provincial gentry, an inn, hunting parties, the picking of mushrooms, feasts, quarrels, duels, and a battle—an extraordinary range of settings and experiences.

The masterpiece of Polish literature, *Pan Tadeusz* is regarded by many as the finest narrative poem of the nineteenth century. "The smile of Mickiewicz" reflected in the kindly humor of the poem, the radiant descriptions,

and the dramatic truth of the characters, all contribute to its excellence. *Pan Tadeusz* is known and loved throughout Poland, by peasants as well as university professors. With this masterpiece, Mickiewicz reached the summit of his literary career. It is unfortunate that the total effect of the poem, which is derived from a close interaction of diction, style, and word associations, the portrayal of marvelously drawn characters, the presentation of setting, and the creation of a dynamic atmosphere, cannot be conveyed in all of its beauty in translation.

OTHER MAJOR WORKS

NONFICTION: *Ksiegi narodu polskiego i pielgrzymstwa polskiego*, 1832 (*The Books of the Polish Nation and of the Polish Pilgrims*, 1833, 1925); *Pierwsze wieki historyi polskiej*, 1837; *Wyklady Lozanskie*, 1839-1840; *Literatura slowianska*, 1840-1844 (4 volumes).

BIBLIOGRAPHY

Filipowicz, Halina. "Performing Bodies, Performing Mickiewicz: Drama as Problem in Performance Studies." *Slavic and East European Journal* 43, no. 1 (Spring, 1999): 1-18. Filipowicz examines Adam Mickiewicz's "Lekcja XVI" as a piece at the interstices of theater and performance art.

Gross, Irena Grudzinska. "How Polish Is Polishness: About Mickiewicz's *Grażyna*." *East European Politics and Societies* 14, no. 1 (Winter, 2000): 1-11. Mickiewicz has been enshrined as an icon, his work classic and his vibrant presence is felt strongly in Polish culture. Gross examines Mickiewicz's poem *Grażyna* and the nationalism in it.

Kohn, Hans. *Pan-Slavism: Its History and Ideology*. 2d ed. New York: Vintage Books, 1960. Provides a historical background for the works of Mickiewicz.

Kridl, Manfred. *A Survey of Polish Literature and Culture*. New York: Columbia University Press, 1956. History and criticism of Polish literature including the works of Mickiewicz.

Welsh, David. *Adam Mickiewicz*. New York: Twayne, 1966. An introductory biography and critical study of selected works by Mickiewicz.

John P. Pauls and La Verne Pauls;
bibliography updated by the editors

CHRISTOPHER MIDDLETON

Born: Truro, Cornwall, England; June 10, 1926

PRINCIPAL POETRY

Poems, 1944
Nocturne in Eden: Poems, 1945
The Vision of the Drowned Man, 1949
Torse Three: Poems, 1949-1961, 1962
Nonsequences/Selfpoems, 1965
Our Flowers and Nice Bones, 1969
The Lonely Suppers of W. V. Balloon, 1975
Pataxanadu and Other Prose, 1977
Carminalenia, 1980
Woden Dog, 1981
111 Poems, 1983
Serpentine, 1985
Two Horse Wagon Going By, 1987
Selected Writings, 1989
The Balcony Tree, 1992
Intimate Chronicles, 1996
The Word Pavilion and Selected Poems, 2001

OTHER LITERARY FORMS

In addition to collections of poetry and short prose, Christopher Middleton has published an impressive number of translations, edited volumes, and critical essays. His translations from German cover a wide variety of genres, including poems by Johann Wolfgang von Goethe, Friedrich Hölderlin, Eduard Mörike, Hugo von Hofmannsthal, Georg Trakl, Paul Celan, Günter Grass, and others. He has also translated Friedrich Nietzsche's letters and such major works of modern German prose as Robert Walser's *The Walk and Other Stories* (1957) and *Jakob von Gunten* (1969), Christa Wolf's autobiographical novel *The Quest for Christa T.* (1970), and Elias Canetti's critical study of Kafka's letters to his fiancé, *Kafka's Other Trial: Or, The Letters to Felice* (1974).

Middleton has also edited or coedited several anthologies of verse and prose in translation: *No Hatred and No Flag, Twentieth Century War Poems* (1958), which was published a year later in German as *Ohne Hass und Fahne*; *Modern German Poetry, 1910-1960: An Anthol-*ogy *with Verse Translations* (1962, with Michael Hamburger); *German Writing Today* (1967); and *Jackdaw Jiving: Selected Essays on Poetry and Translation* (1998). He has also published German translations of his own works, including two pieces from *Pataxanadu and Other Prose*, "The Pocket Elephants" (1969; *Der Taschenelefant*) and "Getting Grandmother to Market" (1970; *Wie wir Grossmutter zum Markt bringen*). He is also the author of a libretto for a comic opera, *The Metropolitans* (1964, music by Hans Vogt).

Middleton's critical essays have appeared in numerous journals, and many have been collected in *Bolshevism in Art and Other Expository Writings* (1978) and *The Pursuit of the Kingfisher* (1983).

ACHIEVEMENTS

Christopher Middleton's main achievement is that of a mediator among the disparate worlds of poetry, translation, and academic scholarship. He frequently includes translations in his volumes of poetry and regards the act of translation as a preeminently poetic endeavor, while his critical works appear as the natural by-products of

Christopher Middleton

his familiarity with the history and the direct practice of literature.

Middleton has gained wide recognition as a translator, which is to say that he is recognized for his absence, for not being obtrusively present in the works he reproduces in English. Good translators are always difficult to recognize: On the one hand, they are denied the glory of the first creator of the text (after all, the translator's words are not "his own"), while on the other hand, those bilingual readers best able to appreciate the merits of a translation are precisely the same readers who have no need of one, since they can always read the work in the original. Middleton's many translations, together with his essays on translation, stand as major contributions to a difficult, challenging, and often underestimated art.

Middleton's combined efforts in poetry and translations have attracted much critical attention and honors. He was awarded the Sir Geoffrey Faber Memorial Prize for Poetry in 1963, and a selection of his works was anthologized that same year in *Penguin Modern Poets Four*. He accepted a Guggenheim Fellowship in 1974-1975, served as a National Endowment for the Humanities fellow in 1980, and won the Schlegel-Tieck Translation Prize in 1986 and the Max-Geilinger-Stiftung Prize for translations in 1987-1988. He was nominated for a Neustadt Prize in 1992.

BIOGRAPHY

John Christopher Middleton was born on June 10, 1926, in Truro, Cornwall, where his father was organist at the cathedral. The family soon moved to Ely, and in 1930 they moved on to Cambridge, where his father later became a senior lecturer in music. Middleton's early childhood atmosphere of cathedrals and music was followed by a series of boarding schools in idyllic pastoral settings, where he took up classical studies. He began to write poems at the age of sixteen. Although he later rebelled against the security of his childhood, he acknowledges that it was "a source for ideas of order." "Ideas of order" became very important for the young Royal Air Force (R.A.F.) aircraftsman-interpreter (later sergeant-interpreter) arriving among the ruins of Germany just at the end of World War II. Middleton remained in the R.A.F. until 1948, then returned by way

of southern France to Oxford, where he read German and French and received his B.A. in 1951. He was lecturer in English at the University of Zurich, Switzerland, from 1952 to 1955, during which time he completed his Oxford Ph.D. thesis on the works of Hermann Hesse. In 1953 he married Mary Freer. From 1955 to 1965 he was senior lecturer at King's College, the University of London, except for one year, 1961-1962, when he was visiting professor at the University of Texas at Austin. This brief introduction to the American Southwest marked a crucial turning point in Middleton's career, and Texas joined London and the South of France as a recurring geographical locus for his poems. In 1966 he returned to the University of Texas, where, for more than three decades, he has served as professor of German literature.

ANALYSIS

Christopher Middleton's poems may be understood as poetic tributes to the recurrent possibilities of order. Typically, he subjects an emblem of a conventional and preexistent order (a classical or political theme, a work of art, a still-life on a breakfast table) to linguistic changes which disorder and reorder the given elements in such a way that what emerges is a new and provisional order that contains and signals its own explosive instability. In other words, the poet does not claim to uncover the "real" significance of anything; and the uniqueness of Middleton's poetry-of-process lies at least partly in the fact that the changes that take place in his poems always seem somehow slightly accidental, not fully under control, perhaps not even fully the responsibility of the poet. To lay claim to such control and responsibility would be to defeat the very point of the procedure by undermining the surprising freedom that comes with the startling rediscovery of things long thought familiar. This helps to explain Middleton's evident lack of interest in "inspiration," or the creation of order *ex nihilo*; he chooses rather to subject the available material of an imperfectly ordered world to sensational transformations, performing a trick that, as one critic put it, "makes the things hover in the air like a mirage." For Middleton, creation is recreational re-creation, and his poems have much in common both with translations and with collages. By merging classical elements (images of order) with modernist techniques (procedures of disorder), Middleton is able to avoid both the chill stasis of a sterile classicism and the self-defeating absurdity of an all-too-radical modernism; in his sensitive hands, old forms of order become as disquieting as the marble torsos of Giorgio de Chirico or René Magritte, or as radiant as Paul Cézanne's weighty apples.

Reviewers are often quick to mention Middleton's open allegiance to the traditions of European modernism, and they often praise his accuracy of detail, together with his "fine sense of the absurd." They frequently notice a certain obliquity—not to say obscurity—in Middleton's approach; one reviewer observed that Middleton "handles his insights with great finesse, but always from a distance as though with tweezers." In a similar vein, others have regretted in his works "the quick change from style to style," "the absence of any unifying personal pressure," and "something constrictingly intellectual." These problems are often regarded as endemic to a self-conscious postmodernism. In fact, these same poetic peccadilloes of flexibility and distance would be praised as virtues in a translator, while "intellectual" references to what one critic called "the *disjecta membra* of a scholar's workshop" can be seen simply as the natural expression of a *modus vivendi* operating between the creative and the professional life. In short, Middleton views poetry as a form of translation, translation as a form of creation, and both as legitimate and important subjects and objects for academic study. In a world plagued with divided loyalties and petty territorial rivalries, this example is indeed a major achievement.

Middleton's modernized classicism is evident even in the titles of most of his volumes of poetry, titles which he always takes care to explain. *Nonsequences/Selfpoems* is chosen for its echoes of nonsenses and consequences, and because "the poems are always consequent-nonsequent." Such self-negating hyphenated compounds are posted in Middleton's explanations like warning signs; he mentions elsewhere the "lucky-unlucky" publication of his first two volumes of poetry, or his preference for a "stark-ambiguous" style. The title of *Pataxanadu and Other Prose* blends Samuel Taylor Coleridge's exotic dream-poem with Alfred Jarry's "pataphysics," the "science of imaginary solutions." *Carminalenia* merges two words from a

line of Propertius to convey both a literal Latin sense of "Softsongs" and, as Middleton notes, a latent suggestion of something "criminal."

The world of Middleton's poems is steeped in a kind of all-pervasive "or-elseness," and his most rewarding works are those in which this quality is directly enlisted in the service of the poem's patterned destruction-and-transfiguration. The latent "or-elseness" of a given work is also opened up by translation, which uncovers new possibilities of order in the mediating language. Middleton has described the task of the poet and translator as a matter of "astonishing speech into incandescence," but it is this same incandescence of unstable matter that also astonishes the poet into speech.

TORSE THREE

The title *Torse Three* refers to one of the meanings of the word "torse," a certain kind of geometrical surface; its etymological cousins include "torsion," "tortuous," and "torture." The final twist in this collection is a poem about order, the fifth and last of "Five Psalms for Common Man," which may be taken as Middleton's most direct statement about the subject. Here the first definitive assertion—"Order imagined against fear is not order"—breaks the logical rule of identity, as "order" quickly becomes plural, a dialectic of order and disorder: "Out of a rumbling of hollows an order is born/ to negate another existing order of fear." A few lines later, the Psalmist sings that "Another order of fear is chaos," while throughout the poem, things either happen or they do not happen: Fear "only negates or does not negate existing order," while "images of chaos . . . accord or do not accord." Out of this logical-sounding but ambiguous tangle emerges the final statement: "The orders revolve as improvisations against fear,/ changed images of chaos. Without fear, nothing." Thus the circle of transformation is complete: Order against fear cannot be order, but without "orders of fear" (or chaos—which has no plural) there can be no order at all. Other writers have described this dilemma in terms of the creator's struggle against entropy; but Middleton seems to suggest that order is only the obverse of entropy, undifferentiation momentarily disguised.

NONSEQUENCES/SELFPOEMS

Nonsequences/Selfpoems introduces the "Texan theme" into Middleton's work, where it immediately takes up permanent residence. Images of politics—of social order—also occupy more territory here than in *Torse Three*, as Middleton develops methods for integrating political material into his vision of the poet's dangerous game. In "Difficulties of a Revisionist," a political extension is added to the notion of the poet as translator or maker of kaleidoscopic collages:

> All day fighting for a poem. Fighting against what?
> And for what? What? being its own danger, wants
> to get rescued, but from its rescuer?

Which side is the poet to be on in the struggle for a new revisionary vision, if the poem—its own danger—is struggling to be saved from its poet? Danger lurks also in the poem titled "Dangers of Waking," in which the "reports and messages" brought by children to the recumbent narrator are progressively magnified into the nightmare news of barbed wire, prison cells, and "the killing of this or that/ man, thousand, or million." This poem appears rather late in the volume, and serves as a counterbalance to an earlier description of "Navajo Children" accepting lollipops from tourists in Canyon de Chelly, Arizona.

Repressions past and future stalk the pages of *Nonsequences/Selfpoems,* which shows Middleton at his bleakest. Even the more pastoral and private images of order appear as if at the mercy of angry mobs just over the distant horizon. The natural-unnatural world harbors savages and phantoms: Cats crunch the head bones of mice, the Cyclops's broken eye clings like a slug on a carrot, houses are haunted by shaggy monsters and street-crossings by "this unknown thing." All the poet's combinatory gifts are helpless to rectify or mitigate the horrors of the past; "January 1919" begins with one of Middleton's bitterest lines—"What if I know, Liebknecht, who shot you dead"—and ends with an appeal to "Look upon our children, they are mutilated." In the final poem, "An Englishman in Texas," the poet presents himself as a kind of sky-struck survivor eager to shed the shreds of past identity in order to exist fully in the present; this last nonsequence voices his wish to "drop character,/ its greed for old presences, its dirt" in order to "move once,/ free, of himself, into some few things."

OUR FLOWERS AND NICE BONES

Our Flowers and Nice Bones, Middleton's next volume of poetry, takes its title from a letter by Kurt Schwitters and represents Middleton's most sustained Dadaistic sortie into such experimental forms as concrete poetry, "found" poems, and works in which sound is invited to take precedence over sense. The poet's quest for order seeks its method either in the visual effect of letters on the page ("Birth of Venus," "Milk Sonnet") or in the shock of finding an unintentional poem ready-made, or a poetic possibility in the merging of two or more such "finds" (such as "Found Poem with Grafts," a true poetic collage). He also organizes poems in terms of sound, either by inventing a mock language of suggestive nonsense (like the Teutonic Latin Finneganese of "Lausdeo Teutonicus" or the Mexican yodeling of "Armadillo Cello Solo") or by taking existing words through transformations based on their sounds (as in the jazzy bass be-bop of "Ballade in B").

One of the most interesting applications of this technique occurs in "Computer's Karl Marx," since the substitution of sound for sense also serves as a means of parodying the monotonous jargon of Marxist orthodoxy. The poem's epigraph is a quotation from Nikolai Bukharin about "the reorganization of production relations." Taking the words "production relations" as a source of raw sound-material for the manufacture of other words of Latin origin, Middleton reorganizes vowels and consonant clusters to produce such transmogrified tonal echoes as "conscript prostitutes/ rusticate prelates." Another poem in this collection, "Pavlovic Variations," offers additional insight into Middleton's attitude toward translation. As one learns from a postscript, the title of the poem comes not from Pavlov—as readers trained to respond to allusions will immediately have assumed—but from a Yugoslavian poet named Miodrag Pavlović. The opening section of the poem is Middleton's English rendering of a German translation of one of Pavlović's works, whose classical landscapes and political themes are then explored and developed in five subsequent variations. Middleton's poetic techniques have been compared with those of visual artists and with the Impressionists in particular; but in *Our Flowers and Nice Bones* he borrows systems of order—whether at the level of individual letters, syllables, words, or themes—at least equally from the world of music.

THE LONELY SUPPERS OF W. V. BALLOON

The Lonely Suppers of W. V. Balloon is the most accomplished of Middleton's books of verse, beginning even with the unidentified hovering balloon depicted on the dust jacket, an elaborately equipped bubble of a globe with a suspended Spanish galleon for a gondola, complete with cannon and banners, and dangling ballast of birdcage and wine cask. In this collection Middleton is at his best, displaying a rare and sensitive mixture of whimsy and provocation, game and threat, entirely accurate as if by accident. One of the most beautiful poems in the volume, "A Cart with Apples," shows Middleton's poetry-of-process at its most masterful. The poem paints a simple still life of an apple cart standing in a field of roses; but through the transforming play of attributes, of fullness and roundness, shadows and primary colors (blue, rose, and yellow), every object—cart, apples, field, and all their interwoven shadows—comes to share in the full, round, colorful reality of every other object until the image achieves a vivid shimmering density worthy of Cézanne.

This is cubist poetry, enriching its objects with layers of perspective while preserving the essence of their unity. Unlike paintings, poems accumulate their being in linear time, but here the quality of the light shifting from stanza to stanza is a poetic reflection of Claude Monet's attempt to capture the shifting colors absorbed and reflected by the facade of the Rouen Cathedral. "A Cart with Apples" offers a vision so much a part of the idea of southern France that one recognizes it without having seen it, just as one knows that the setting is southern France although it is never actually mentioned. Something of the quality of Mediterranean light is captured here with simple words and a lucid technique that clearly reflects Middleton's ideas about the transformational nature of order.

The title poem in this volume, "The Lonely Suppers of W. V. Balloon," is another magical still life: a Texas evening, a bottle of wine on the table ("seadark wine," an inversion of the "winedark sea" of Homer's *Odyssey*), and a thunderstorm raging outside. It is a poem about, among other things, gratitude: "Thank the thunderstorm," the poet says, because "Here we sit, love . . .

and believe/ What floated past the window was Balloon's lasso,/ His anchor was the lightning." Thus, through the intercessionary charm of a word as weird as "balloon," the Englishman conjures up a moment of deep peace with the desert phantoms, so that what passes in the dark is not a noose, but a lasso, and even the flash of lightning can be an image of steadfastness.

Yet Balloon's world is not without its dangers, as is suggested by "Briefcase History," a case history of the poet's briefcase done in the style of Guillaume Apollinaire. The briefcase, made from scavenged war materials, is celebrated as a trusted veteran and friend. Nevertheless, the poem ends with an ominous twist— game or threat?—as the poet suddenly tells the travel-worn container of so many mementoes: "you have never contained an explosive device/ never have you contained an explosive device/ yet."

PATAXANADU AND OTHER PROSE

While both *Our Flowers and Nice Bones* and *The Lonely Suppers of W. V. Balloon* contain examples of prose poetry, Middleton's next collection, *Pataxanadu and Other Prose*, consists entirely of short prose parables, enigmas, and fragments in the tradition of Franz Kafka and Jorge Luis Borges. These prose sketches frequently echo themes from earlier poems, though here newly subjected to the quasi-logical rules of prose and to its mimetic possibilities. Most of the narrators of these prose sketches see themselves as isolated historians writing with a sense of duty and urgency about political or familial situations. The assumptions underlying their specific attitudes are revealed only between the lines, as the dreamlike merges with the matter-of-fact and classical motifs mix with visions of a totalitarian future. The confessional order imposed by eyewitness testimony is here locked in soft-spoken but deadly combat with the disorder of randomness or the false order of political oppression.

Unlike most of the pieces, the five title sketches in *Pataxanadu and Other Prose* are generated through a system of lexical substitutions originally developed by Raymond Queneau, which Middleton applies to passages from Sir Thomas Malory, Sir Thomas Urquhart's translation of François Rabelais, Jonathan Swift, Herman Melville, and Charles Doughty. In a sense, these are prose equivalents of the "found" poems in *Our Flowers and Nice Bones*, but here their "finding" involves the deliberate systematic distortion of the original text—a method answering Arthur Rimbaud's call for the "systematic disruption of all the senses"—and the results are remarkably droll (Melville's mates, Starbuck, Stubb, and Flask, are "translated" into Stealbudget, Stuff, and Flaunt).

Pataxanadu and Other Prose also comes with its own key in the form of a review by Middleton's anagrammatical avatar, Doctor Philden Smither, of an imaginary monograph by a certain Professor Erwin Ignaz Steintrommler on the historical significance of short prose. Professor Steintrommler's Germanic pedantry is gently spoofed: He argues, for example, that since all users of language necessarily lie, "the shorter the prose is, the less will be the likelihood of falsification"—a position that leads logically to silence as the supreme form of truth. Steintrommler's examples are all "real," however, ranging from Aesop's fables to Daniil Kharms and Kenneth Patchen, and they offer a valuable reminder of the richness of the tradition of short prose, one which has yet to be fully recognized as a distinct and important genre.

CARMINALENIA

Carminalenia is sparser and sparer than Middleton's previous volumes. Familiar themes recur, and there is also a translation of Apollinaire's "The Palace of Thunder," but the obliquity of many of the poems, the privacy of their references and the mystery of their connections, makes this easily one of the least accessible of all Middleton's works. This privacy extends to the appended notes, where Middleton compares a poem to the experience of diving through a shoal of fish. Middleton's homage to the privacy of his illuminations recalls the style of Wallace Stevens, which finds an obvious echo in the poem titled "A Very Small Hotel Room in the Key of T." Middleton continues to raise questions about the limits of generic frontiers when he titles one blank-verse piece "The Prose of Walking Back to China." In a prose poem titled "Or Else," the poet uses the title phrase as a refrain to retract every statement as soon as it is uttered in favor of an alternative version, itself immediately supplanted by yet another version, and so on. This is another classic example of Middleton's method of composition based on the principle that

order is always self-destructing, that it exists only as a perpetual urge to order; once frozen and taken for granted, it becomes a lie, a target.

THE BALCONY TREE

Middleton's characteristic British sensibility and lack of inspirational moments continued to permeate his collection *The Balcony Tree*. His recording of everyday events—a couple parting at a train station, walking the dog, a new neighbor—take on a reserved quality, and his British spellings and uniform-length stanzas keep his poems proper in every sense. The "proper" in these poems thus continues the inaccessibility, found in the poems of *Carminalenia*. Old-fashioned Bristish grammar seems incongruous with the poems' commonplace themes:

> But into you I leaned
> And felt a trembling go
> From all my body out
> Into your sudden sleep

he says, recalling a tender moment.

Nine surreal prose pieces that form the book's final section are more approachable. Intimate and vividly detailed, these ironic accounts seem lifted from a historical chamber of horrors: the funeral of a clown during Russian-Polish strife in 1920, soldiers in 1939 encamped by the sea, the importance that Turkish peasants attach to sleeping on their roofs. Both less formal and more imaginative, these closing works accomplish what the poems of the collection strain to achieve, turning minor events into harbingers.

OTHER MAJOR WORKS

PLAY: *The Metropolitans*, pb. 1964 (libretto).

NONFICTION: *Bolshevism in Art and Other Expository Writings*, 1978; *The Pursuit of the Kingfisher: Essays*, 1983; *Jackdaw Jiving: Selected Essays on Poetry and Translation*, 1998; *In the Mirror of the Eighth King*, 1999.

TRANSLATIONS: *The Walk and Other Stories*, 1957 (of Robert Walser); *Selected Poems* (of Günter Grass; with Michael Hamburger); *The Poet's Vocation: Selections from the Letters of Hölderlin, Rimbaud, and Hart Crane*, 1967; *Jakob von Gunten*, 1969 (of Walser's novel); *Poems*, 1969 (of Grass); *Selected Letters*, 1969 (of Friedrich Nietzsche); *The Quest for*

Christa T., 1970 (of Christa Wolf's novel); *Selected Poems*, 1972 (of Paul Celan); *Kafka's Other Trial: Or, The Letters to Felice*, 1974 (of Elias Canetti); *In the Egg and Other Poems*, 1977 (of Grass); *Balzac's Horse and Other Stories*, 1988; *Andalusian Poems*, 1993; (with Leticia Garza-Falcón); *Elegies and Other Poems*, 2000 (of Lars Gustafsson's poetry); *Faint Harps and Silver Voices: Selected Translations*, 2000.

EDITED TEXTS: *No Hatred and No Flag: Twentieth Century War Poems*, 1958 (pb. in German as *Ohne Hass und Fahne*, 1959); *Modern German Poetry, 1910-1960: An Anthology with Verse Translations*, 1962 (with Michael Hamburger); *German Writing Today*, 1967.

BIBLIOGRAPHY
Bête Noire (Spring, 1991). A special issue of this British literary magazine, focusing on Christopher Middleton.

May, Hal, and James G. Lesniak, eds. "Christopher Middleton." In *Contemporary Authors New Revision Series*. Vol. 29. Detroit: Gale Research, 1990. A biographical sketch with a chronological overview of Middleton's work. Includes a primary bibliography and references to secondary sources.

Young, Alan. "Christopher Middleton." In *Poets of Great Britain and Since 1960*, edited by Vincent B. Sherry, Jr. Vol. 40 in *Dictionary of Literary Biography*. Detroit: Gale Research, 1985. A thorough and sympathetic account by one of Middleton's best critics. Young stresses Middleton's challenge to the reigning assumptions of contemporary British poetry; he sees Romantic as well as high modernist elements in Middleton's work. Includes a primary bibliography and references to secondary sources.

Gene M. Moore

JOSEPHINE MILES

Born: Chicago, Illinois; June 11, 1911
Died: Berkeley, California; May 12, 1985

PRINCIPAL POETRY
Lines at Intersection, 1939
Poems on Several Occasions, 1941
Local Measures, 1946
Prefabrications, 1955
Poems, 1930-1960, 1960
Civil Poems, 1966
Kinds of Affection, 1967
Saving the Bay, 1967
Fields of Learning, 1968
To All Appearances: Poems New and Selected, 1974
Coming to Terms: Poems, 1979
Collected Poems, 1930-1983, 1983

OTHER LITERARY FORMS
In addition to her many volumes of poetry, Josephine Miles wrote more than a dozen books developing her theories of poetry and applying these theories to particular poets and eras. Among the most widely read of these works are *Eras and Modes in English Poetry* (1957, revised 1964) and *Style and Proportion: The Language of Prose and Poetry* (1967, revised 1984). These books are detailed structural analyses of English poetry and prose; all of Miles's criticism expounds her theory that the structure of language changes to reflect the spirit of the time that the language expresses. Her one play, *House and Home*, was first performed in 1960 and was published in *First Stage* in 1965.

ACHIEVEMENTS
Josephine Miles's contribution to American poetry is valuable and unusual. She combined poetry of political commitment with sound scholarship and theory to produce a body of work that is at the same time of the tower and of the streets. Her work is a challenge both to the poet/propagandist and to the "art for art's sake" poet.

Miles's many awards and honors include Shelley Memorial Award in 1936, the Phelan Memorial Award in 1937, a Guggenheim Award in 1948, the Oscar Blumenthal Prize in 1959, an American Council of Learned Societies Fellowship in 1965, a National Endowment for the Arts grant in 1967, and an American Academy of Poets Fellowship in 1978. She received the Lenore Marshall Poetry Prize in 1984 for *Collected Poems, 1930-1983*. Although her critical works have been to some extent superseded, Miles's poetry has guaranteed for her a lasting place in twentieth century American literature.

BIOGRAPHY

Josephine Louise Miles was born on June 11, 1911, to Reginald and Josephine Miles, a Chicago couple. When she was still an infant, Miles was diagnosed as having rheumatoid arthritis, a disease which plagued her all of her life. When she was five, her father, who was in the insurance business, moved the family to Southern California, hoping that the climate there would be beneficial to his daughter's condition. The family moved back to Evanston, Illinois, for a time, but Miles had identified California as her spiritual home. The family eventually settled down in Los Angeles, and Miles, after finishing at Los Angeles High School, attended the University of California, Los Angeles. After receiving her B.A. in 1932, she enrolled in graduate school at the University of California at Berkeley. She completed her M.A. in 1934 and her Ph.D. in 1938.

Although she had written poems since childhood, it was during her graduate school years that she first began to publish seriously and to gain recognition. Her first poems were published in an anthology, *Trial Balances* (1935), and this work earned for her two awards. Her first book, *Lines at Intersection*, appeared in 1939 and contains the best poems of her graduate school period.

In 1940, Miles began teaching at Berkeley as an instructor, and she remained there for the rest of her life. In 1947, she was the first woman to be tenured by Berkeley's English department, and in 1952 she was made a full professor. Miles never married, devoting her life to teaching, research, and poetry; during her years at Berkeley, she published more than two dozen books, in addition to numerous articles and reviews. She retired in 1978 and was given the status of Distinguished Professor Emerita. She died in Berkeley of pneumonia on May 12, 1985.

ANALYSIS

Josephine Miles's poetry reflects both her political involvement in liberal causes and her intense concern with the sounds and structures of English. Over the decades of her writing, the poems became less formal

and closed as their political content increased. Her topics shifted from minute observations of daily activities to analysis of the poet's role in the chaotic contemporary world. Nevertheless, even her most strident political poems show careful craftsmanship and attention to sound.

Miles's first published poems are tightly structured and intellectually dense. Her often-anthologized "On Inhabiting an Orange," published in the anthology *Trial Balances* in 1935, precedes her first collection. "All our roads go nowhere," the poem begins. "Maps are curled/ To keep the pavement definitely/ On the world." Because of these conditions, people's plans for "metric advance" must "lapse into arcs in deference/ to circumstance." The poem develops its single metaphor with clarity and sureness, using common metaphysical geometric images to provide the pleasure afforded by this kind of poetry. It is not surprising that her first work received two awards, the Shelley Memorial Award (1936) and the Phelan Memorial Award (1937).

LINES AT INTERSECTION

Her first collection, *Lines at Intersection*, is a series of poems of everyday events arranged by time of day—morning poems, noon poems, evening poems. The individual works are mostly formal in structure, but they are more impressionistic than the early poems, and their music is subtler. These poems incorporate such devices as internal rhymes, unusual metrical patterns, Dickinsonian slant rhymes, and incremental repetition. The poems are personal but not intimate, providing new perspective on such familiar things as the morning paper, the door-to-door salesman, baseball games, and theater performances. A few of the poems still show her preoccupation with mathematics and geometry, while others foretell one of her future concerns: the world of business, which was to become a major metaphor for the contemporary world. *Lines at Intersection* was well received, with favorable reviews in *Poetry* and elsewhere.

POEMS ON SEVERAL OCCASIONS

Miles's second collection, *Poems on Several Occasions*, shows a marked divergence from her earlier work in content. These poems, too, are arranged by time of day, and they also represent the life cycle from birth to death; moreover, these poems use the same stylistic devices as those of her earlier collection. This group, however, begins to define Miles's social commitments. By this time, Miles was becoming more aware of the inequalities, injustices, and false promises of contemporary America. Her titles show her new perspective: "Market Report on Cotton Gray Goods," "Committee Report on Smoke Abatement in Residential Area," "Committee Decision on Pecans for Asylum." The America in these poems is as unattractive as that of Allen Ginsberg in the 1950's and 1960's, and often for the same reasons. Business transactions take the place of personal contact, and there is a vast gap between what society would provide and what people want and need. Yet the poems are by and large wistful and do not actively suggest interference with the processes of oppression.

LOCAL MEASURES

Local Measures marks a change in style: These poems are more conversational and irregular than Miles's earlier works. Their subjects include daily observations, social topics, and the relation of art to life. More of these poems are free verse or highly individualized forms. Dancing and motion pictures are analogues to poetry; the collection, written while Miles was working on her analysis of poetic forms in different periods of history, reflects her own search for a form appropriate to herself and her time. The mutual reflection of art and life is a theme approached again and again, as in "Redemption." Films, dances, even the jewelry that appears in these poems show Miles's attempts to define and thus master the process of creation.

PREFABRICATIONS

Prefabrications combines her concerns for art and the social world. This rich and varied collection of sixty poems demonstrates the sense of community and continuity she was developing in the poetic theory on which she was working at the same time. Some of these poems, such as "The Plastic Glass," express the belief that the essentially human transcends the shabbiness and emptiness of life's surfaces. Others, such as "The Student," seek a source or definition of that humaneness, often using metaphors and images that are accessible to all but particularly compelling to academics. Indeed, in this and other poems in the collection, the academic life itself becomes a metaphor of the teaching-learning dialogue with the world. Some of the poems are about art. "Two

Kinds of Trouble," a long poem, compares the social structures that made it hard for Michelangelo to communicate his vision with the problems of contemporary artists—a different kind of trouble.

POEMS, 1930-1960

Miles's *Poems, 1930-1960* included selections from all of her earlier books and a new group of poems, "Neighbors and Constellations," for the most part negative assessments of the possibility of meaningful intercourse among members of the human community. These poems, however, marked a turning point in her attitude, and the next collections showed a more active involvement in causes combined with a belief in the possibility of success.

CIVIL POEMS AND KINDS OF AFFECTION

Civil Poems and *Kinds of Affection* show that Miles was in and of Berkeley in the 1960's. These two collections center on pollution, poverty, destruction of beauty for purposes of greed, experimentation with animals, gun control, the war, the bomb, technology. An index to these poems would please nostalgia buffs, but the poems are less calls to action than expressions of the notion that social involvements are in fact ways of loving, or "kinds of affection." Among references to Dag Hammarskjöld, Molotov cocktails, and other hallmarks of the time, Miles returns again and again to the subject of commonality, the sharing underneath that survives all divisions.

FIELDS OF LEARNING

Fields of Learning does not diverge greatly from the previous two collections, but it includes more science and slightly less politics. The world of these poems is filled with deoxyribonucleic acid, free neutrons, and gravitational electromagnetic fields. Yet despite their heavy freight of theoretical physics and technology, these poems are still accessible. They communicate a sense of human potential that exists not because of, but in spite of, technological advancement.

TO ALL APPEARANCES

To All Appearances, while still political, is in many respects a return to earlier themes. Many of these are quiet poems of family and friendship. Their form is (usually) free verse, but in content the work is often reminiscent of *Local Measures*. One of the most memorable of the group is "Conception," which begins:

> Death did not come to my mother
> Like an old friend.
> She was a mother, and she must
> Conceive him.

The poem elaborates on its controlling metaphor, as do some of Miles's earliest poems, but here the appeal is as much emotional as it is intellectual. In general, these poems seem more direct than her earlier work. She uses "I" often in poems of reflection on her experiences inside and outside the university community.

COMING TO TERMS

Miles's last major collection (exclusive of her *Collected Poems, 1930-1983*) was *Coming to Terms* in 1979. This powerful collection gathers together the many strands of her lifelong preoccupations and weaves them into a single fabric. These are poems of social and aesthetic interest, asking the broadest questions and providing penetrating answers. The critics received the work with highest praise; Miles's last years were filled with honors and awards. More than one reviewer found the long poem "Center" to be Miles's strongest work. The poem poses the question "What are we here for?"—"we" being poets, creators, and humane visionaries. Her answer, not unlike that of the God in Johann Wolfgang von Goethe's *Faust*, is that we are here to make the best mistakes:

> Give us to err
> Grandly as possible in this complete
> Complex of structure, risk a soul
> Nobly in north light, in cello tone . . .

The result of such risk and error is a re-vision, a new perspective from which to view the possible. Human creativity in all of its forms becomes a medium "To take, as a building, as a fiction, takes us,/ Into another frame of space/ Where we can ponder, celebrate, and reshape." Miles's late view of poetry as process, or becoming, is similar to Wallace Stevens's final aesthetic. In this poem, Miles shows her own adjustment of vision, from the downward glance at the fatal curve of Earth in "On Inhabiting an Orange" to the upward and outward vistas of the possible from "the center."

COLLECTED POEMS, 1930-1983

Collected Poems, 1930-1983 gives an overall view of Miles's development and includes her last poems, for the most part scenes of Berkeley and of the university. (She lived only about a year after the appearance of this volume, which was popular as well as critically acclaimed, and she was awarded *The Nation*'s Leonore Marshall Poetry Prize in 1983.) Her careful craftsmanship and metrical felicity can be appreciated in this final publication, a well-edited work which illustrates the range of her poetic gift. Her "search for a common language" antedated Adrienne Rich's better-known one and combined some of the same ingredients. This collection shows how her hopes for community within human society paralleled her search for what she called "commonality" in language. Her intellectually and emotionally persuasive metaphors, her subtle music, and the potency and optimism of her later work make Miles a significant contributor to twentieth century American poetry.

OTHER MAJOR WORKS

PLAY: *House and Home*, pr. 1960.

NONFICTION: *Wordsworth and the Vocabulary of Emotion*, 1942; *Pathetic Fallacy in the Nineteenth Century: A Study of a Changing Relationship Between Object and Emotion*, 1942; *Major Adjectives in English Poetry from Wyatt to Auden*, 1946; *The Primary Language of Poetry in the 1640's*, 1948; *The Primary Language of Poetry in the 1740's and 1840's*, 1950; *The Primary Language of Poetry in the 1940's*, 1951; *The Continuity of Poetic Language: Studies in English Poetry from the 1540's to the 1940's*, 1951 (includes preceding 3 volumes); *Eras and Modes in English Poetry*, 1957, revised 1964; *Renaissance, Eighteenth-Century, and Modern Language in English Poetry: A Tabular View*, 1960; *Ralph Waldo Emerson*, 1964; *Style and Proportion: The Language of Prose and Poetry*, 1967, revised 1984; *Poetry and Change: Donne, Milton, Wordsworth, and the Equilibrium of the Present*, 1974; *Working Out Ideas: Predication and Other Uses of Language*, 1979; *Josephine Miles, Teaching Poet: An Oral Biography*, 1993.

BIBLIOGRAPHY

Beloof, Robert. "Distances and Surfaces." *Prairie Schooner* 32 (Winter, 1958/1959): 276-284. This fine, readable article examines Miles's poetry in terms of poetic strategies. Beloof's analysis is detailed, thematic, and logical.

Chase, Karen. Review of *Collected Poems, 1930-1983*, by Josephine Miles. *World Literature Today* 58 (Summer, 1984): 423. A very favorable review of Miles's career. Excerpts from selected poems are briefly discussed to reveal Miles's versatility.

Guillory, Daniel L. Review of *Collected Poems, 1930-1983*, by Josephine Miles. *Choice* 24 (March, 1984): 978. Guillory suggests a favorable comparison could be made between the poetry of Miles and the poetry of William Carlos Williams. Important themes in Miles's poetry are listed, as well as a thematic and chronological progression.

Miles, Josephine. *Josephine Miles, Teaching Poet: An Oral Biography*. Edited by Marjorie Larney. Berkeley, Calif.: Acacia Books, 1993. A short biographical work that provides invaluable details of Miles's life and thoughts from interviews with the poet by Ruth Teiser and Catherine Harroun.

Smith, Lawrence R. "Josephine Miles: Metaphysician of the Irrational." *Pebble* 18/19/20 (1979): 22-35. An insightful article examining some of the major symbols and themes in Miles's poetry. Careful attention is given to many of Miles's poems.

Janet McCann;
bibliography updated by the editors

EDNA ST. VINCENT MILLAY

Born: Rockland Maine; February 22, 1892
Died: Austerlitz, New York; October 19, 1950

PRINCIPAL POETRY
Renascence and Other Poems, 1917
A Few Figs from Thistles, 1920
Second April, 1921
The Harp-Weaver and Other Poems, 1923
The Buck in the Snow and Other Poems, 1928
Edna St. Vincent Millay's Poems Selected for Young People, 1929

Fatal Interview, 1931
Wine from These Grapes, 1934
Conversation at Midnight, 1937
Huntsman, What Quarry?, 1939
Make Bright the Arrows, 1940
There Are No Islands Any More, 1940
Invocation to the Muses, 1941
Collected Sonnets, 1941
The Murder of Lidice, 1942
Collected Lyrics, 1943
Poem and Prayer for an Invading Army, 1944
Mine the Harvest, 1954
Collected Poems, 1956

OTHER LITERARY FORMS

Edna St. Vincent Millay was known during her early career for her verse plays, the most successful being the first, *Aria da Capo*, first produced in 1919 and published in 1921, followed by *The Lamp and the Bell* and *Two Slatterns and a King*, also published in 1921, and *The Princess Marries the Page* (written during her student years at Vassar), published in 1932. Her reputation as a writer of verse for the stage was such that she was invited to write the libretto for a Deems Taylor opera commissioned by the Metropolitan Opera Company of New York. The result of her collaboration with Taylor was a successful presentation of *The King's Henchman* (1927), a variation of the Tristan story. Millay tried to rework the material of the opera libretto into a drama but finally condemned the result as hopelessly contaminated; she was never able to rid it of the influence of the libretto.

Conversation at Midnight and *The Murder of Lidice* are sometimes classified as plays, the former receiving performance after Millay's death and the latter being written for wartime radio broadcast after the Nazis destroyed the Czechoslovakian town of Lidice and slaughtered its male inhabitants. *The Murder of Lidice* cannot be considered as more than hastily written propaganda at best, and *Conversation at Midnight* suffers if one looks for the conflict and engagement of drama in it. Millay conceded after its completion that it was not really a play but a series of poems with a fixed setting.

In addition to working with dramatic forms, Millay, in the beginning years of her career, wrote topical com-

mentaries for the New York weekly *Vanity Fair* under
the pseudonym Nancy Boyd; they were collected in a
1924 volume as *Distressing Dialogues*, the title used by
the magazine as the pieces appeared. Although these
early essays helped to support the young poet, Millay
was never willing to have them published under her
name. She was, however, proud of her collaboration
with George Dillon on *The Flowers of Evil* (1936), a
translation of Charles Baudelaire's *Les Fleurs du mal*
(1857), although scholars find more of Millay in the
translations than the original may warrant. Millay's letters have been collected and published.

ACHIEVEMENTS

Edna St. Vincent Millay's meteoric rise as a popular
poet seems to have been, in part, a product of her times
and the independent style of life that she represented.
This fact may account for the later critical dismissal of
her work. Millay's poetry is, in many ways, conventional in its formal aspects, often showing strict attention

Edna St. Vincent Millay (Library of Congress)

to rhyme and traditional metrical patterns. Her nineteenth century literary forebears were Alfred, Lord Tennyson and A. E. Housman. She showed no interest in the
experimental work being done by T. S. Eliot, Ezra
Pound, and others of her generation. In her strong allegiance to the lyric, to traditional verse forms, and to conventional diction, she guaranteed that she would not take
her place in the mainstream of influential twentieth century poets, although she was very much aware of contemporary currents. Once her initial popularity waned,
Millay's work was judged to be something of a sport in a
century in which the breaking of forms was thought to
be the best representation of the breaking of traditional
views of the world.

Ironically, much of Millay's early popularity came
from her image as a rebel and nonconformist—a representative of emancipated Greenwich Village culture, a
perfect example of the liberated woman of the 1920's.
This reputation was primarily promoted by the publication of *A Few Figs from Thistles*, a collection of flippant
and audacious poems which seemed a manifesto for the
new woman and her independent, nontraditional attitude
toward modern life. The image of the short-lived candle
burning at both ends and giving its lovely light forged an
identity for Millay that her serious poems could never
alter, and the proverbial candle seems in retrospect almost an ironic paradigm for Millay's own poetic career.

In spite of Millay's waning popularity in the last decades of her life and the harsh judgment of critics who
were suspicious of her early widespread popularity, Millay's poetic accomplishment is considerable. She was
awarded the Pulitzer Prize in 1923 for *The Ballad of Harp
Weaver and Other Poems* and the Frost Medal in 1943.

Millay is very much an American poet in her eclecticism. As a champion of the individual and of freedom
from tyranny of any kind, she deserves a place in the
American tradition beside poets as widely divergent as
Walt Whitman and Archibald MacLeish. As a poet willing to insist on the validity and strength of real emotion
and thought in women and on their individuality in relationships, Millay replaced hitherto largely convention-
bound material with fresh insights. In her frank introspection and exploration of psychological states, she
opened the way for the modern confessional poets who
followed her.

Biography

Although Edna St. Vincent Millay is not usually thought of as a New England poet, she was born in Maine and spent the first twenty years of her life there, most of them in Camden, where her mother moved with her three young girls after a divorce in 1900. Millay and her sisters were encouraged to develop their musical and poetic talents and to read widely in the classics and in English and American literature. Millay's mother supported the family by working as a nurse, and from her example, Millay learned early the independence and self-reliance which were to influence her poetry. She learned to value and trust her personal voice, leading many of her readers to search her poems for the details of her personal life that they were thought to reveal.

With the aid of a patron, Millay was able to attend Vassar College the year after the publication of "Renascence," the beginning of her public career as a poet. After graduation from Vassar, Millay moved to New York and, living in poverty, began her association with Greenwich Village and the Provincetown Players. This period of five or six years before her marriage provides the backdrop against which Millay is remembered and with which she is identified, although it represents a very small portion of her life. It was during this period that her famous friendships and love affairs with Floyd Dell, Arthur Fricke, and Edmund Wilson, among others, began, and during which the Provincetown Players produced *Aria da Capo*. She won fame and national popularity with the publication of *A Few Figs from Thistles* in 1920. After several years in Europe, marked by the beginning of the bad health that was to plague her for the rest of her life, Millay returned to the United States and in 1923 became the first woman to win a Pulitzer Prize for poetry. In the same year, she married a Dutch importer who gave up his business to provide a stable environment for her—on a farm at Austerlitz, New York, and in an island home off the coast of Maine.

Taking an active part in the general outcry of American intellectuals and artists against the death sentencing of Nicola Sacco and Bartolomeo Vanzetti, Millay called on the governor of Massachusetts and wrote public statements and several poems, including "Justice Denied in Massachusetts." She was arrested along with others keeping vigil at the time of the execution. In this, as in

everything she did, Millay acted with total conviction and unflinching courage—qualities which give strength to her poems, although these same unabashed qualities set her apart in an age that increasingly demanded ironic distance as a prerequisite for serious verse.

Millay received several honorary doctorates and was elected to both the National Institute of Arts and Letters and the American Academy of Arts and Letters. By the end of the 1930's, however, after publication of *Conversation at Midnight*, her reputation had suffered a serious decline, a decline accelerated by the work that she published too hurriedly in the service of wartime propaganda: *Make Bright the Arrows* and *The Murder of Lidice* represent the lowest ebb in her reputation as a serious poet. In the summer of 1944, she suffered a severe nervous breakdown accompanied by serious "writer's block" that lasted for more than two years. Just as she was beginning to take up her work again in 1949, her husband died suddenly. The shock resulted in hospitalization again. She returned later that year alone to her farm in Steepletop, New York, where she died of heart failure a little more than a year after her husband's death. A volume of new poems, *Mine the Harvest*, was published in 1954 and her *Collected Poems* in 1956.

Analysis

The theme of individual liberty and the frank acknowledgment of emotion are ever-present in Edna St. Vincent Millay's poems. She speaks as clearly for a democracy of persons, in whatever relationship, as Walt Whitman does and with no hint of snobbery or elitism. She values the simple and common in nature; the reader never finds her straining after exotic effects. Millay is a realist in her expectations, and she refuses conventional romantic attitudes—a refusal which often results in the ironic tone of some of her love poems. It is not surprising that she acknowledged her fondness for Andrew Marvell, the poet of "The Passionate Shepherd to His Love" and "The Nymph's Reply."

Millay's volumes of poetry contain no "major" poems which have entered the canon of literature in the way in which those of Robert Frost, T. S. Eliot, or William Butler Yeats have. Her early volume, *Renascence*, with its title poem written before she entered Vassar, may hold little interest for contemporary readers, although it was highly praised by Harriet Monroe, the editor of *Poetry* magazine. Much of the strength of the other volumes lies in the sustained effect of sonnet sequences and collections of lyrics. There is evidence of growth, however uneven, in Millay's development as a poet, as her work moves from the devil-may-care irony and unabashed emotion of the early poems to a more considered and mature production.

The one form in which Millay excelled is the sonnet, both Shakespearean and Petrarchan. She has been described as a transitional poet, and this is nowhere better born out than in her control of a conventional and circumscribed form in which she was equally comfortable with traditional or modern subject matter and attitudes.

"EUCLID ALONE HAS LOOKED ON BEAUTY BARE"

"Euclid Alone Has Looked on Beauty Bare," published in *The Harp-Weaver and Other Poems*, is an accomplished classical Petrarchan sonnet written early in Millay's career. It takes as its subject the holy, dazzling beauty of pure form or idea available only to the Greek mathematician, Euclid, who perceived a pure beauty which has not been matched by the prattling of subsequent generations seeking imitations of beauty clothed in human form. The octave ends with a command to let the geese gabble and hiss (an allusion both to the use of geese as watchdogs in ancient times and to those who mistakenly cry out that they have sighted Beauty). The sestet presents a vivid description of the blinding and terrible light that Euclid bore when he "looked on Beauty bare," suggesting that lesser men are fortunate that they have not seen Beauty whole, as it would be too much for them to bear. (In the sestet, the word "bare" has become an adjective of personification as well as one carrying its original meaning of "pure," "unadorned.") Lesser men are lucky if they have even once heard Beauty's sandal on a distant rock; those seekers after Beauty who are not Euclids are doubly fortunate to have heard only a distant echo of Beauty's step, for they could not have borne the blinding intensity of Euclid's vision.

This sonnet is seemingly simple and straightforward. It is more complex than it first appears, however, for by the poet's own personification of Beauty (now clothed, in sandals at least), she acknowledges herself to be one of those lesser mortals who followed Euclid. She ironi-

cally accepts her own conventional restrictions. Euclid's vision is of "light anatomized," not of Beauty in the traditional, personified female form.

FATAL INTERVIEW

Fatal Interview, the chronicling of a love affair from inception through intense passion to sad conclusion, represents Millay's longest sustained sonnet sequence. The book's title comes from John Donne's sixteenth elegy in a series about a tragic affair, beginning, "By one first strange and fatal interview." Although the sonnets do not evince the full range of intense emotion that one might expect, Millay manages to treat her subject with the objectivity, control, and irony that mark her love poems as the products of the modern woman, freed from the stereotype of woman as the passive, overwhelmed love object. The passions of love and sexual ecstasy find their way into these poems, but always present too is an awareness of the fleeting nature of even the most passionate relationships and a refusal to accept a bondage that involves the loss of individual integrity. She knows that love can be "stung to death by gnats."

"Well, I have lost you; and I lost you fairly" is the initial line of sonnet 47, and there is a pride expressed in losing well on the speaker's own terms. Nights of weeping she will not deny, but day finds her dry-eyed and fully operative in the world that goes on after love is lost. A more slyly played relationship or one of lesser intensity might have preserved the relationship through another summer, but at too high a cost for lovers who have experienced so much intensity and honesty. The price in "words I value highly" is one that Millay as poet and woman will not, cannot, pay. "Well, I have lost you" is simple and straightforward; a sign of control over pain and grief. Sonnet 30 and others preceding it have made it clear that Millay's realism, her defense against the grief of loss, is a reaction inherent in her philosophical stance in the world; this fact, however, does not lessen the real poignancy of the sonnet. These are the statements of a highly intelligent and sensitive woman who suffers because of the awareness that never leaves her. In "Love is not all: it is not meat nor drink" (sonnet 30) the speaker is conscious that men have died for lack of love even though it is not technically one of the physical necessities of life such as food, drink, and shelter. The sonnet accepts love as a dear necessity for life, but there is in the concluding lines the nagging realization that if it were necessary, she might sell this love for peace, or these passionate memories for food. Although at this moment she is inclined to think she would not, the acknowledgment of the possibility clearly marks the distance between Millay's poem and Elizabeth Barrett Browning's "How do I love thee?" In a more flippant early lyric titled "Thursday," the gulf between Millay and the more conventional Browning is absolute and unbridgeable.

"THE BALLAD OF THE HARP-WEAVER"

Among Millay's poems for her mother, "The Ballad of the Harp-Weaver" and "In the Grave No Flower" are two which display careful simplicity and controlled depth of feeling. "The Ballad of the Harp-Weaver" was criticized by Edmund Wilson for being slight, superficial, and sentimental. He characterized it as a poem for a woman's magazine. The poem is more effective than Wilson suggested and wholly appropriate to its subject: the rich gifts of the spirit given to a child by a mother who, in her poverty, cannot provide the material food and clothing that her child needs. The ballad form controls the simple narrative of the parable, and if the reader accepts the perfect union of form and subject that Millay achieves, the poem is more than a modest success.

"IN THE GRAVE NO FLOWER"

"In the Grave No Flower" names with loving specificity common weeds that, by their rank fecundity and stubborn resistance to the plow, inherit the earth, in contrast to the barren grave where there is and can be no flower. This lyric demonstrates Millay's control of intense grief, heightened by her ability to express it with devastating simplicity. The reader has only to compare "In the Grave No Flower" to the early "Elegy Before Death," written on the death of a close friend, to see the distance that Millay has come in her growth as a poet.

"MENSES"

Millay's best poems may be love sonnets or lyrics of passion or elegy (even "The Buck in the Snow" is an elegy of sorts), but as a poet she is willing to risk the most ordinary of subjects. A poem called simply "Menses," although not one of her best, is an interesting example of the risk-taking that marked Millay both in her personal and in her poetic life. This poem celebrates the settled relationship, the accommodations made between two people out of the love and understanding which comes with adjustments to the most unglamorous cycles of life.

The occasion of the poem is a surface duel between a man and a woman who is undergoing the emotional upheaval associated with her monthly menstrual cycle. The poem is, for the most part, an interior dramatic monologue spoken by the man ("to himself, being aware how it is with her"), who turns aside an incipient quarrel, having "learned/ More things than one in our few years together." Millay's risk-taking in this poem is found with her decision to give to the man the voice in this special situation, and with the woman, driven by physical forces, half-awaiting the relief his understanding will bring her. A simple rendering of the symbiotic daily relationship of two people, this poem is deeply meaningful and, in its own way, as spectacular and surprising as a moment of passion might be in one of Millay's love sonnets.

Millay's poetic subjects thus range more widely than her reputation suggests, for the complexity of her poetry has been obscured by the personal image created during the early years of her career. She is not only the poet whose candle consumes itself and the night and "gives a lovely light!"; she is an accomplished poet of a wide range of complex emotions, themes, and forms.

OTHER MAJOR WORKS

PLAYS: *Aria da Capo*, pr. 1919; *The Lamp and the Bell*, pb. 1921; *Two Slatterns and a King*, pb. 1921; *The King's Henchman*, pr. 1927 (opera libretto); *The Princess Marries the Page*, pb. 1932.

NONFICTION: *Distressing Dialogues*, 1924 (as Nancy Boyd); *Letters*, 1952.

TRANSLATION: *The Flowers of Evil*, 1936 (of Charles Baudelaire).

BIBLIOGRAPHY

Brittin, Norman A. *Edna St. Vincent Millay*. Rev. ed. Boston: Twayne, 1982. Brittin has rewritten his 1967 biography of Millay (he uses the name "Vincent" as her friends and family called her, in the earlier edition), providing more discussion of her prose works and less space to the biography. He brings out her feminist ideas and her relation to the poetic movement of High Modernism. The chronology and useful annotated bibliography have a few new items, but not many. An essential reference.

Cheney, Anne. *Millay in Greenwich Village.* University: University of Alabama Press, 1975. A map of the Greenwich Village section of Manhattan accompanies the introduction to this study of Millay's village years, from 1918 to 1925. The men in her life at that time—Floyd Dell, Edmund Wilson, Arthur Fricke, and the man she married, Eugen Boissevain—are discussed in a chapter devoted to each, with an analysis of the poems dated in the period of each romance. Ten pages of photographs of Millay and New York document this important period in American literary history. Includes notes, a bibliography, and an index.

Drake, William. *The First Wave: Women Poets in America, 1915-1945.* New York: Collier Books, 1987. Drake captures the essential meaning to women poets in the period between the two world wars of the rising movement for female independence, the Freudian backlash to that movement, and the effect of a wave of anticommunism on the critical reception of women poets. Millay's place in this story is well documented and argued, including her avoidance of the psychoanalytical trap and her need for nurturing but not stifling care. A full page photo shows Millay and Lola Ridge being arrested for protesting the Sacco-Vanzetti case. Contains excellent notes, a bibliography, and an index.

Freedman, Diane P., ed. *Millay at One Hundred: A Critical Reappraisal.* Carbondale: Southern Illinois University Press, 1995. A collection of essays by critics of poetry and women's writing that reinterpret the themes of Millay's poetry. Includes bibliographical references and an index.

Gould, Jean. *The Poet and Her Book.* New York: Dodd, Mead, 1969. In seventeen chapters, Gould retells Millay's life from sources oral and written. Many fascinating anecdotes reveal Millay's personality in her childhood, her adolescent and college years, her travels, and her marriage. Readers learn about her friends, her illnesses, and her publishing history. This book is useful for a nonpolitical understanding of her strengths and weaknesses. Sixteen pages of photographs accompany the text.

Sheean, Vincent. *The Indigo Bunting: A Memoir of Edna St. Vincent Millay.* New York: Harper, 1951. The title refers to a small North American bird that sings when other birds are still. So Sheean characterized Millay, his friend for many years. This intimate close-up shows the extent of Millay's culture, her knowledge of Latin literary classics, and music and art history. Her personal fascination shines through these pages of recollections.

Thesing, William B. ed. *Critical Essays on Edna St. Vincent Millay.* New York: Maxwell Macmillan International, 1993. A comprehensive collection of both early reviews and modern scholarly essays. Includes a substantial introduction by the editor and a fictional interview of Millay by Arthur Davison Ficke.

Donna Gerstenberger;
bibliography updated by the editors

VASSAR MILLER

Born: Houston, Texas; July 19, 1924
Died: Houston, Texas; October 31, 1998

PRINCIPAL POETRY
Adam's Footprint, 1956
Wage War on Silence, 1960
My Bones Being Wiser, 1963
Onions and Roses, 1968
If I Could Sleep Deeply Enough, 1974
Small Change, 1976
Approaching Nada, 1977
Selected and New Poems: 1950-1980, 1981
Struggling to Swim on Concrete, 1984
If I Had Wheels or Love: Collected Poems of Vassar Miller, 1991

OTHER LITERARY FORMS
Despite This Flesh: The Disabled in Stories and Poems (1985), poems and stories on the nature of physical disability and its sufferings by various writers, was edited by Vassar Miller.

Vassar Miller

ACHIEVEMENTS

Considered by many to be the best poet to have emerged from Texas, Vassar Miller was widely hailed at the publication of her second book of poems, *Wage War on Silence*, which was nominated for the Pulitzer Prize in 1961. Several of her other books won awards from the Texas Institute of Letters. In 1982, she shared with the poet William Barney the poet laureateship of Texas. Her poetry is noted for its formal craftsmanship, its distinct precision of language and rhyme in traditional form, and its account of a life of loneliness and suffering from cerebral palsy and of a strong faith in Christianity expressed with erotic passion.

BIOGRAPHY

Vassar Miller was born and reared in Houston, Texas, the daughter of a successful real estate developer whose family house, on Vassar Street, is the scene of many of her poems on childhood and on the anguish of coping with chronic illness and debilitation. Her father had early encouraged her by giving her a typewriter and coaching her first efforts at poetry; some of her poems

give harrowing glimpses into the despair of a child whose mother physically rejected her. Miller attended the University of Houston for her B.S. and M.A. degrees; she wrote her master's thesis on mysticism in the poetry of Edgar Arlington Robinson. For a time, she taught in a private school in Houston and was a participant in such literary conferences as the Bread Loaf Writers' Conference in Vermont in 1968 and the Southwest Writers' conferences of 1973 and 1983, held at the University of Houston.

Illness discouraged her from teaching, but for years she was a familiar figure in her neighborhood streets, propelling her three-wheeled bicycle, until a local ordinance restricted its use. Miller is revered in Texas as a voice of resilient faith whose work eschews the major trends of modern poetry but is rich in the values of the Anglo-American tradition, both in candor and in tempered self-reliance.

ANALYSIS

Though Vassar Miller is a poet whose range of techniques is limited, the forms within which she works are brought to mastery and high finish. These forms frame her tale of suffering love and of spirit tested by a life of pain and profound introspection. Her earliest poetry springs from her close study of the New England poet Edwin Arlington Robinson, an exacting formalist whose elegant short poems recounted the bitter lives and emotional corruption of villagers in his imaginary Maine town of Tilbury. Miller's graduate thesis on Robinson worries out the thread of faith and hope running through Robinson's poetry, which he composed at a time when New England had ceased to be an important economic region of the United States and its citizens had resigned themselves to lives of failure and cynical resentment. Her study zeroed in on his portrayals of trapped individuals and how they dealt with their plight, either by suicide or drunkenness or by tapping some inner resource of faith.

ADAM'S FOOTPRINT

Adam's Footprint, which collects her earliest poetry, explores her world of pain, physical and emotional, in compact stanzas of eight lines with neat envelope or alternating rhyme schemes. One may detect in them the echo of hymns, based loosely on ballad measure but here straightened out into full eight- and ten-syllable lines. In an interview published in *Heart's Invention: On the Poetry of Vassar Miller* (1988, edited by Stephen Ford-Brown), Miller described her childhood notebooks as "filled with miserable imitations of equally miserable hymns." Later, she would turn to Emily Dickinson and master a variable, minimalist lyric of excruciating pointedness. Nevertheless, the hymn would remain a base measure of her rhythmic imagination, as it did for Dickinson herself. Both writers are to be credited with having composed secular literary hymns in which sensuous, erotic longings have their place in religious meditation.

Adam's Footprint develops carefully a series of metaphors of the body through feet and coordinated motions, as Miller describes her experiences as a handicapped child. In the title poem, she compares her infirmity to being outcast, an exile like Adam, whose footprint marks the path others of misfortune must follow. Even here, however, Miller carefully avoids self-pity; the poem's scrupulous artistry is the adequate sublimation of her pains. The real ballet of elegant motions occurs in the mind, in the artist's skillful execution of her words even as she cries out against her freakish disability. Another poem, "Spastic Child," laments another child's inability to speak, in a poem lushly confident to express his pain for him. The artist of these poems is the alter ego of the crippled infant, a second, idealized self technically projected out of the subject's own suffering intellect.

The sonnet, one of Miller's favorite forms, is a perfect vehicle for the argumentative lyric she writes in *Adam's Footprint*, with its eight-line assertion or question and its six-line rebuttal. In "The Magnitude of Zero," Adam is the first child, here called the "first citizen," "whom earth splays huge upon my nothing's rack." Verbs such as "trudge," "quail," and "splays" underscore the labored movements of the subject. "The Final Hunger" begins, "Hurl down the nerve-gnarled body," as the reader follows her to painful sleep in another very forceful sonnet. Miller is equally adept at the Petrarchan and the Shakespearean sonnet forms. "Beside a Deathbed," in the Shakespearean mode, closes on a feminine, two-syllabled rhyme, lying,/dying, a small flourish of her technical mastery.

Miller's poetry took a new direction in Texas writing; the tradition of verse in the Southwest is dominated by female poets whose subjects included inspirational thoughts, moral homilies, studies of the landscape, and overall expressions of Christian faith and calm endurance. Miller's probing lyrics delve deep into a world of error and torment, failure and unrequited erotic longings. Though other women had hinted of their dissatisfactions with life on the ranch and in the small prairie towns, Miller's poetry is overtly stark, even brutal in its portrayal of a life of toil and loneliness.

WAGE WAR ON SILENCE

It was perhaps coincidence that Miller should come of age just as the confessional poets were publishing their own first works on similar themes, although with far more intensity. Her second book, *Wage War on Silence*, bore some resemblance to the poems of Robert Lowell, Sylvia Plath, and Anne Sexton, who make up the core of the confessional movement of the 1960's and whose poems dissect their own witheringly painful lives in the public arena of literature. Miller became associated with the women writers of the movement and doubtless benefited by the connection. Her favorite among them was Sexton, to whom she later dedicated one of her poems. In fact, Miller's literary associations all take her back to New England, from Dickinson to Robinson and contemporary writers, among whom she found a parallel preoccupation with the inner life, a subject often avoided by other Texas poets.

"Without Ceremony," a Shakespearean sonnet with the "turn" or riposte saved for the final closing couplet, is an impassioned prayer for mercy addressed to Father Pain, the Word "in whom our wordiness dissolves/ When we have not a prayer except ourselves." Piety, on one hand, rejects artfulness in prayer but, on the other, is proffered with immaculately textured artifice. Unresolved in Miller's poetry is this double standard, this conflict between a pure, unrehearsed experience of her faith and the demands of art. The poems insist upon the reality of their emotions and settings but frame them within the ordered, compact structure of verses. Part of the power of such writing lies in its tension between conflicting attitudes: a singeing, violent emotion and the limpid formality of its expression. Like the poet Denise Levertov, who admires Miller's writing, Miller insists on the most exacting measures for poetry that describes the chaos of modern life. Both poets reject the mode of spontaneous composition as unfit for true poetry.

Songs abound in *Wage War on Silence*; some, such as "Love Song for the Future," are in the racing rhythms of trochaic meter, where the beat falls on the first syllable of the foot and pushes the language along in a quick, dancing motion, as in John Donne's line "Go and catch a falling star." Miller's opening lines are "To our ruined vineyards come,/ Little foxes, for your share." The rhyme scheme is *ababcdcd*, a lacing pattern that enhances the quickness and neatness of the language. The theme of the poem is the dying wilderness, the animal kingdom Saint Francis of Assisi loved, which is doomed by a "world of steel," the town and city. Innocence of all kinds perishes as the landscape is urbanized and the adult world of commerce and greed takes over.

Though not a regional poet in the conventional sense of local-color anecdotes and reminiscences of the land, Miller is subtly regional in her metaphorical landscapes; the wilderness is her own emotional life, but it stands equally for the disappearance of ranch land and wild meadow in urban Texas, for the sprawl of cities such as those her own father helped to develop into megalopolises. Concrete and steel are her images for alienation and loss; childhood is the moist grass and the garden where she recalls a few fond memories of her father and of her still pliant body. The city is the stiffening ground of painful adulthood, and by that indirect means she copies the changes of her region.

"So you are what we name,/ And what we name we love," she writes in the first stanza of "For a Christening," in a six-syllable line that is soothing, melodious, and songlike, crafting a hymn to innocence as a child is baptized. "Each man's sorrow is an absolute" is the noble opening of "The Common Core," which gives grim solace to those who suffer, in a patterned verse like the "songs of experience" William Blake wrote for children. There is much injured innocence in Miller's world, where she often takes on the persona of a child confiding its pains to adult readers.

In another striking lyric, "Defense Rests," she tells the reader cunningly that "Love/ is too much for the heart to bear/ alone." The poem weaves together eros and faith, sexual longing and religious commitment, and

ends by appealing to Christ for comfort of her earthly needs, since he alone in her religion has both suffered and known the love of others, including Mary Magdalene and John the Baptist. Such open confessions of need coupled with powerful religious devotion recall seventeenth century religious verse, the sometimes torrid poetry of John Donne, Henry Vaughan, Richard Crashaw, and Thomas Traherne, among whom passionate prayer mixed with erotic imagery is, if not the norm, the common thread that prompted T. S. Eliot to praise their "undissociated sensibility." Miller restores some of that wholeness of passion when she combines soul and self in the same passage.

My Bones Being Wiser

My Bones Being Wiser, published in 1963, shows increasing maturity in the writing. The forms are not so rigidly enforced, and the language has become more fluid and open, while at the same time sparer in its music. "The leaves blow speaking/ green, lithe words/ in no man's language," begins the poem "Precision," with its deft touch, its suggestive language bordering on dream imagery. The naïve voice perceives talking trees and animate nature, as imagination goes beyond mere selfhood and encompasses the immediate surroundings of her world. This is the "wisdom" of the title, the surer grasp of meaning in her experience. Even the sonnets are more delicate and reflective, as in "Reverent Impiety," with its caustic premise, "I will not fast, for I have fasted longer/ Than forty days" in a life of agonizing debility. The dominant influence of these poems is the taciturn energy of Dickinson, whom Miller closely approximates with stunning lines of her own, though not with Dickinson's reckless daring. "Though you elude my leash of love," she chides her longed-for lover in "Complaint," her rapture is boundless "like the damned."

When one combs such books by Miller, it is not plot one notices but the separate poems on each page. Plot may exist in the slow shift of subject from early life and first passion to these smoother, more mature reflections on unfulfilled longing. Miller's publishers are often asked to sort through the manuscripts she sends and to make books out of them, rather than to depend on her for final arrangement of the work. Fortunately for Miller, her books have found conscientious editors who have discovered a usable thread of narrative running through her poems. Yet one would be mistaken to make too much of how the poems unwind a tale or yield some hidden premise in their relations to one another. Her books record the slow passing of days and years, slight shifts in faith and perspective on the world. The poem, however, is the real focus of experience, as it records a sudden fascination with a word or vowel, a delicate experiment in a new rhythm, a use of slang or even a curse word, or a new metaphor to be worked into a villanelle or sonnet.

ONIONS AND ROSES AND IF I COULD SLEEP DEEPLY ENOUGH

Noticeable in *Onions and Roses* and *If I Could Sleep Deeply Enough* is the theme of middle age taking hold throughout the poetry. The poet is writing from her mid-forties to the age of fifty, and the reader can detect how elegy and lament are increasingly foregrounded in these books. Sleep is no longer a restful escape from the day's pain, but deepens its meaning as a figure of death. The formalism has relaxed; sonnets and regular stanzaic lyrics flank free-verse compositions, a form in which to posit misgivings and doubts in her faith, wrestlings with the Lord, and her acerbic wit or crankiness. The open lyric allows her to experiment with even tighter concision, in brief poems of eight or nine lines, as in "In a Land of Indistinct Seasons," with its spare image of a "crystal pane" where someone has "let the summer out/ and the autumn in." Even here, Miller eschews that other dictate of modern poetry, thought as process or ambiguity. Her language is honed, refined, reduced to a compactness of result, finished and enclosed in its precise certainty of expression.

APPROACHING NADA

Approaching Nada, a brief sequence of lyric meditations, written over a three-day period in March, 1977, while the poet was on a trip to Phoenix, Arizona, tests the limits of her imagination and faith in what many consider her greatest poem. Written in irregular, eight-syllable lines of mainly trochaic meter, a muscular rhythm for driving home one's thoughts, *Approaching Nada* allows the reader to feel the willfulness of her argument as she confronts her lifelong belief in God. The *nada* of the poem is Spanish for "nothing," and the surrounding desert of Phoenix confirms the absence

of things rather than supporting her vision. "Many words do not compose the Word," she admits, but "Somewhere between silence and ceremony springs the Word." Here as nowhere before Miller expands her sense of faith and religion to include a world of vision across all faiths, a sense of God running through Native American, Quaker, Catholic, Protestant, and beyond. God here is the collective longing for spiritual comfort. God is the Nothing, the spirit beyond imagination or words, present in everything but without substance or human conception. The recognition of the spirit's Nothingness raises her religious views to the mystical insight that no religion or spiritual way can take possession of God; spirit resides in the human condition in spite of one's individual ways.

> These poets of the Nada
> obeyed Him. So poets, mystics of
> the bruising thing
> climb up bloody concretes
> to leave nailed high
> white pieces of themselves.

The poet is, as Abbé Bremond wrote, *un mystique manqué*, a failed visionary who

> like the mouse will scuttle
> clean to the border
> of the ineffable,
> then scurry back
> with tidbits of the Vision.

To approach Nada, or the nothing, is to release the illusions of godliness one has cherished and to accept with finality the ineffability of spirit, its transparent presence in the void.

STRUGGLING TO SWIM ON CONCRETE AND IF I HAD WHEELS OR LOVE

Struggling to Swim on Concrete opens with an impassioned sonnet, "Admission," addressed to her father, whom she loved best of all men. "You were my absolute, if such there lives/ Within the prison of the relatives." This and her work collected in *If I Had Wheels or Love* mark a slow shift back to closed form as the dominant mode of her verse, with the sonnet and tercet stanza the dominant forms. A few poems, such as "Whitewash of Houston," a somewhat long tirade against the squalid life of Houston, are prosy and open, but mainly the poet is back to song, to iambic pentameter lines of delicate music such as the opening of "Assertion," "I am no scholar in the ways of love," and "I have been out of the weather of love," in "Seasonal Change." In "Affinity," Miller pays homage to another influence on her life and thought, the great religious short-story writer Flannery O'Connor, who also suffered a lifelong debilitating illness while she wrote. "Had disease and early death not shut/ your door, you might have left the family pew,/ thumbing your nose at every holy 'Tut!'"

The "uncollected poems" that close *If I Had Wheels or Love* are her starkest examinations of the meaning of death, her own and others. In several of these poems, she bids farewell to deceased friends and tries to foresee her own end, while in others she continues her flirtations with potential lovers as the other extreme of her resilient spirit. "You, smiling friend," she writes in "Love Song," a Petrarchan sonnet, "say only that you like me,/ And that, at least for now, is quite enough." She returns to Adam's exile, her metaphor for the loneliness of her own invalid childhood, in "Fiat," which opens, "Eden is closed forever, if it was/ Opened to us at anytime." In one of her loveliest lyrics, "Rivers," she turns to her region directly to write "Rio de Brazos de Dios" on the long, winding river that drops down into the Gulf of Mexico at Freeport:

> river of rest and rescues,
> bear me with lullabies,
> safe to the arms of Jesus.

OTHER MAJOR WORKS

EDITED TEXT: *Despite This Flesh: The Disabled in Stories and Poems*, 1985.

BIBLIOGRAPHY

Christensen, Paul. *West of the American Dream: An Encounter with Texas*. College Station: Texas A&M University Press, 2001. In exploring the land and people of his adopted state of Texas, Christensen assesses the origins of modern poetry and presents three portraits of modern Texas artists and poets—Vassar Miller, Charles Gordone, and Ricardo Sánchez—to show twentieth century poetic evolution in Texas.

Ford-Brown, Steven, ed. *Heart's Invention: On the Poetry of Vassar Miller*. Houston: Ford-Brown, 1988. The first collection of essays on the poetry and life of Vassar Miller contains eight essays by other poets and literary critics, and an interview by Karla Hammond. Themes include the regional aspects of Miller's poetry and the role of religion in her work, the stylistic influences of contemporary poets, and the use of Miller's intricate metrical structures as a metaphor of physical perfection despite her severe disability.

Griffin, Shaun. "A Genius Obscured." *Sojourners* 29, no. 3 (May/June, 2000): 50. Griffin pays tribute to Miller with a profile of her as a poet, self-taught theologian, and disability advocate.

Kellner, Bruce. "Vassar Miller, Swimming on Concrete." *Literature and Medicine* 19, no. 2 (Fall, 2000). In this memoir, Kellner recounts his twenty-five-year friendship with Miller, during which he was her correspondent, intimate friend, explicator, and occasional partner in poetry readings.

Rosenthal, Peggy. "Knowing in the Bones: The Poetry of Vassar Miller." *The Christian Century* 114, no. 17 (May 21-May 28, 1997): 533-538. Miller's explicitly religious poetry is examined. Argues that when Jesus is the subject of Miller's poetry, her intensely personal, deeply lived spiritual awareness is manifested.

Paul Christensen;
bibliography updated by the editors

CZESŁAW MIŁOSZ

Born: Šeteiniai, Lithuania; June 30, 1911

PRINCIPAL POETRY

Poemat o czasie zastygłym, 1933
Trzy zimy, 1936
Wiersze, 1940 (as J. Syruć)
Ocalenie, 1945
Światło dzienne, 1953
Traktat poetycki, 1957 (*A Treatise on Poetry*, 2001)

Król Popiel i inne wiersze, 1962

Gucio zaczarowany, 1964

Wiersze, 1967

Miasto bez imienia, 1969 (*Selected Poems*, 1973)

Gdzie wschodzi słońce i kędy zapada, 1974

Utwory poetyckie, 1976

Bells in Winter, 1978

Poezje, 1981

Hymn o perle, 1982

The Separate Notebooks, 1984

Nieobjęta ziemia, 1984 (*Unattainable Earth*, 1986)

The Collected Poems, 1931-1987, 1988

Provinces, 1991

Facing the River: New Poems, 1995

Piesek przydrozny, 1997 (*Road-side Dog*, 1998)

Wiersze wybrane, 1996

Winter Dialogue: Poems, 1997

Poezje wybrane—Selected Poems, 1998

To, 2000

OTHER LITERARY FORMS

Although it was Czesław Miłosz's poetry that earned for him the 1980 Nobel Prize in Literature, his work in other genres is widely known among the international reading public. One of his most important nonfiction works is the autobiographical volume *Rodzinna Europa* (1959; *Native Realm: A Search for Self-Definition*, 1968). Unlike most autobiographies, this volume emphasizes the social and political background of the author's life at the expense of personal detail. For example, Miłosz makes but two passing references to his wife in the course of the entire work. Despite such lacunae, it is a work of the utmost personal candor and is indispensable for anyone endeavoring to fathom Miłosz's poetic intent. Similarly helpful is the novel *Dolina Issy* (1955; *The Issa Valley*, 1981), the plot of which focuses on a young boy's rites of passage in rural Lithuania during and after World War I. An understanding of the Manichaean metaphysics which inform this work as well as *Native Realm* is fundamental to a reading of Miłosz's poetry.

In an earlier novel, *Zdobycie władzy* (1953; *The Seizure of Power*, 1955), Miłosz presented a series of narrative sketches dealing with the suppression of the insurrection in Warsaw by the Germans in 1944, the Red Army's subsequent advance through Poland, and the eventual seizure of power by pro-Soviet Polish officials. Miłosz also analyzed Communist totalitarianism in a work of nonfiction, *Zniewolony umysł* (1953; *The Captive Mind*, 1953). A large part of this book is devoted to the fate of four writers in Communist Poland and provides a moving account of their gradual descent into spiritual slavery under the yoke of Stalinist oppression. Although Miłosz designates these men only by abstract labels—Alpha, the Moralist; Beta, the Disappointed Lover; Gamma, the Slave of History; and Delta, the Troubadour—their real identities are easily surmised by anyone familiar with postwar Polish literature.

Some of Miłosz's nonfictional works were originally written in English, notably *The History of Polish Literature* (1969, enlarged 1983). A large section of this volume is devoted to contemporary literature, and it is in-

Czesław Miłosz, Nobel laureate in literature for 1980. (© The Nobel Foundation)

structive to read Miłosz's critical evaluation of his own stature as a Polish poet. Another valuable work originally published in English is *The Witness of Poetry* (1983), which gathers Miłosz's Charles Eliot Norton lectures, given at Harvard University during the 1981-1982 academic year. Throughout these lectures, Miłosz argues that poetry should be "a passionate pursuit of the real."

More than half of the essays contained in *Emperor of the Earth: Modes of Eccentric Vision* (1977) are also written in English. Most of the pieces in this collection are devoted to Polish and Russian writers with whom the author shares a spiritual affinity. Among the essays included are two chapters from Miłosz's monograph on Stanisław Brzozowski, *Człowiek wśród skorpionów* (1962; man among scorpions), which was published on the occasion of the fiftieth anniversary of the death of this controversial Polish writer. (These two chapters were translated by the author himself, as were some of the other essays that were originally written in Polish.) The "Emperor of the Earth" referred to in the title is a character in a Russian work of science fiction who poses as a benefactor of humankind but who in reality is the Antichrist, a wolf in sheep's clothing. Miłosz thus underscores his belief that a religion of humanity often paves the way for totalitarian rule. If there is any thematic unity among the disparate essays included in *Emperor of the Earth*, it is to be found in the author's long-standing fascination with the problem of evil.

Miłosz has also published two important collections of essays and what he calls a "spiritual autobiography," *Ziemia Ulro* (1977; *The Land of Ulro*, 1984). In these volumes, Miłosz is inclined toward historical speculation and takes a deeply pessimistic view of contemporary society. The title *The Land of Ulro* is derived from the poetry of William Blake, where Ulro represents the dehumanized world created by materialistic science. Just as the inhabitants of Blake's Ulro are destined one day to experience a spiritual awakening, so Miłosz is hopeful regarding man's ultimate redemption.

Kontynenty (1958; continents) is a collection of works in various genres, including poems, literary essays, diary excerpts, and translations of poetry from several lan-

guages. Later, Miłosz published a similar potpourri, *Ogród nauk* (1979; the garden of knowledge). This volume is divided into three parts: The first section consists of essays; the second part presents verse translations (with commentary) of French, Yiddish, English, and Lithuanian poetry; and the third and final subdivision contains a translation of the biblical Ecclesiastes together with a stylistic analysis of biblical discourse and its relevance to the modern age.

In the 1990's and 2000's collections of Miłosz's prose, letters, poetry, and fiction continued to appear. The breadth of knowledge exhibited in these collections, as well as in his other works of nonfiction, clearly establishes Miłosz as one of the leading polymaths of his time.

ACHIEVEMENTS

Prior to receiving the 1980 Nobel Prize in Literature, Czesław Miłosz had already won a number of other prestigious awards and honors. When his novel *The Seizure of Power* was published in France in 1953 under the title *La prise du pouvoir*, he received the Prix Littéraire Européen (jointly with German novelist Werner Warsinsky). In 1974, the Polish PEN Club in Warsaw honored him with an award for his poetry translations. He was also granted a Guggenheim Fellowship in 1976 for his work as both poet and translator. He received honorary doctorates from the University of Michigan in 1977 and from Catholic University in Lublin, Poland, in 1981, when he finally returned to his native country after thirty years. In 1978, he was selected as the fifth recipient of the biennial Neustadt International Prize for Literature by a panel of judges assembled under the auspices of the editorial board of *World Literature Today* (formerly called *Books Abroad*). Miłosz accepted the award in public ceremonies held at the University of Oklahoma on April 7, 1978.

In a written tribute to his candidate for the 1978 Neustadt Prize, Joseph Brodsky, the eminent Soviet émigré writer and Nobel laureate, declared that he had no hesitation whatsoever in identifying Miłosz as one of the greatest poets of his time, perhaps the greatest. It should be acknowledged at the outset that Miłosz's preeminence as a poet in no way stems from any technical innovations to be found in his poetry. Miłosz is actually quite indifferent toward avant-garde speculation pertaining to aesthetic form, and the greatness of his poetry lies in its content. His own life has been so full of incident that the question of form appears almost to have resolved itself under the pressure of events. Historical circumstances have placed Miłosz at the center of the political and intellectual turmoil of his time, and the most remarkable aspect of Miłosz's poetry is that, despite his having experienced first hand the depths of humankind's depravity in the form of Nazi barbarism and Soviet tyranny, it still affirms the beauty of this world and the value of life.

In addition to making his own original contribution to the poetic literature of his native Poland, Miłosz has been very active in translating works from other languages into Polish. His most important translations from French include the poetry of his cousin Oscar de L. Miłosz and that of Charles Baudelaire. In 1958, while in exile in Paris, Miłosz edited and translated selected writings of Simone Weil from French into Polish. Having taught himself English in Warsaw during the war years, he later put his talents to good use by translating works of English-language poets such as Walt Whitman, Carl Sandburg, and T. S. Eliot. It was Miłosz, in fact, who produced the first Polish version of Eliot's *The Waste Land* (1922) in 1946. In order to promote the fortunes of contemporary poets from Poland, Miłosz has, moreover, translated from Polish into English. For this purpose, he issued an anthology in 1965 titled *Postwar Polish Poetry* (revised 1983). He has also been engaged in producing English versions of many of his own poems, working either independently or in collaboration with his students and fellow poets. Working from the original Greek and Hebrew, he has rendered the Gospel According to St. Mark, the book of Ecclesiastes, and the Psalms into Polish, with the goal of translating the entire Bible into a Polish that is modern yet elevated, sharply distinct from the debased journalistic style of many modern translations of the Bible.

One of Miłosz's most impressive achievements is that he has continued to produce outstanding new work after the age of eighty. In 1997 he published two volumes of a memoir, *Abecadlo Milosza (1997; Miłosz's ABC's*, 2001), written in a distinctively Polish genre called *abecadlo*, an alphabetical arrangement of entries

on people, places, and events from an individual's life. His collection of aphorisms, anecdotes, musings, and observations, *Road-side Dog*, won the 1998 Polish Nike Literary Prize.

BIOGRAPHY

Czesław Miłosz was born to Aleksandr and Weronika (né Kunat) Miłosz in Šeteiniai, which is located in the Kédainiai province of Lithuania. This area of Europe is a place where Polish, Lithuanian, and German blood intermingled over the centuries, and the ancestry of Miłosz himself is a mixed one. It can, however, be established through legal documents that his father's ancestors had been speakers of Polish since the sixteenth century. Nevertheless, Miłosz has great pride in his Lithuanian origins and even takes perverse pleasure from the fact that Lithuania was the last country in Europe to adopt Christianity. The lateness of this conversion, which occurred in the year 1386, permitted the survival of pagan attitudes toward nature on the part of the peasantry, and the influence of this pagan heritage can be detected in much of Miłosz's poetry as well as in his novel *The Issa Valley* 1981.

Like much of Poland itself, Lithuania was part of czarist Russia's empire at the time of Miłosz's birth. Miłosz's father, a civil engineer by profession, made a yearlong trip to Siberia in 1913 under government contract and was accompanied by his wife and son. Shortly after their return home, when World War I broke out, his father was drafted into the Russian army as a military engineer and once again took his family to Russia, where they remained for the duration of the conflict. In these years, Miłosz imbibed Russian to such a degree that proficiency in that language became second nature to him and never deserted him in subsequent years.

After the Bolsheviks seized power in Russia, the Miłosz family returned to the newly independent Baltic states for a few years but finally decided to settle down in the city of Wilno. This city, although once the capital of ancient Lithuania, had long been a predominantly Polish-speaking municipality and was then incorporated into a fully restored Poland. In Wilno, Miłosz entered a Roman Catholic high school at the age of ten. There, he received exceptionally thorough training in religion, science, and the humanities over the course of eight years. It was also there that Miłosz received his first exposure to the Gnostic and Manichaean heresies that were to profoundly alter his outlook on life. Nothing in his homelife could be said to have inspired the religious rebelliousness which he manifested in high school. His father was actually indifferent toward any form of worship, and his mother, although a devout Catholic, was quite tolerant of other faiths. Miłosz's religious revolt, however, stopped far short of atheism, for he lived in a state of constant wonder at the mystery of life and kept expecting an epiphany to occur at any moment.

In 1929, Miłosz matriculated as a law student at the King Stefan Batory University in Wilno and soon published his first poems in its literary review, *Alma Mater Vilnensis*. Here, he also became affiliated with a group of young poets who referred to themselves as żagary (brushwood) and who subsequently founded a journal bearing the same name. While still a student, Miłosz published a slim volume of verse called *Poemat o czasie zastygłym* (a poem on congealed time), for which he received the poetry award from the Polish Writers Union in 1934. In the same year, Miłosz obtained a master's degree in law from the University of Wilno as well as a fellowship in literature from the Polish government, enabling him to study in Paris during the years of 1934 and 1935.

Miłosz had already been in France on one prior occasion when he and two other students from the University made an excursion to Western Europe in the summer of 1931. One of the highlights of that junket was his meeting with Oscar de L. Miłosz (1877-1939), a cousin of his from Lithuania and a highly accomplished poet in the French language. As a result of Miłosz's obtaining his fellowship, the two cousins were able to see each other often, and the older man exerted a profound influence on his young relative from Poland. Oscar de L. Miłosz especially enjoyed indulging in prophetic visions of a catastrophe that was about to befall Europe. His cousin's prophecies struck a responsive chord in Miłosz, whose own psychological state was somewhat chaotic at this time. When Miłosz returned to Poland after his fellowship year in France, he published a collection of poems titled *Trzy zimy* (three winters), in which the theme of personal and universal catastrophe is expressed. Oscar

de L. Miłosz also helped to shape his young cousin's views on the craft of poetry and fostered his commitment to a poetry anchored in religion, philosophy, and politics.

Miłosz went on to obtain employment with the Polish Radio Corporation at its station in Wilno. He was eventually ousted from his post as programmer because of pressure exerted by local rightist groups, who considered him to be a dangerous left-winger if not an actual Communist. Although Soviet-style Communism never attracted Miłosz, his attitude toward Marxist dialectical and historical materialism was a decidedly favorable one at that time. It is also true that Miłosz did little to conceal his intense dislike for the reactionary politicians who controlled Poland after the death of Marshal Pilsudski in 1935. Fortunately, a sympathetic director of Polish Radio in Warsaw offered him a comparable post in that city, and, after touring Italy in 1937, Miłosz settled down to a successful administrative career in broadcasting. This phase in Miłosz's life came to an abrupt halt when the Germans attacked Poland on September 1, 1939. Miłosz put on a uniform in time to join units of the Polish armed forces in a retreat to the eastern part of the country. This region was soon to come under Soviet occupation as a result of an invasion by the Red Army that was initiated on September 17, 1939, and Miłosz eventually returned to Wilno.

Wilno had changed drastically since Miłosz had seen it last, for the Soviets chose to award the city to Lithuania as a gesture of goodwill shortly after capturing it. The Soviets, however, gradually increased their control over Lithuania and finally coerced it into becoming a Soviet Socialist Republic in the summer of 1940. When Lithuania was officially annexed to the Soviet Union, Miłosz concluded that its servitude would, in all likelihood, prove to be permanent, and he resolved to return to Warsaw. At great personal peril, Miłosz made several border crossings to get back to the part of Poland which the Germans had designated as the Government General.

Despite the horrendous conditions in Warsaw, Miłosz continued to write poetry and clandestinely published a new volume of verse called *Wiersze* (poems) in 1940 under the pseudonym J. Syruć. This was probably the first literary work to be printed in occupied Warsaw. It was run off on a ditto machine and laboriously sewn together by Janina Dluska, whom Miłosz married in 1944 and by whom he was subsequently to become the father of two sons. When the Germans decided to rearrange the holdings of Warsaw's three largest libraries, Miłosz managed to get himself hired as a laborer loading and transporting the packing cases, and he spent the next few years engaged in this interminable project. Some form of opposition to the German occupiers was a moral imperative, and he soon became active as a writer in the Resistance movement. In 1942, Miłosz edited a clandestine anthology of anti-Nazi poetry that appeared under the title *Pieśń niepodlegla* (the independent song) and also provided the underground press with a translation of Jacques Maritain's anticollaborationist treatise *À travers le désastre* (1941). Almost as an act of defiance toward the German oppressors, Miłosz began an intensive study of the English language and derived spiritual sustenance from reading poems such as T. S. Eliot's *The Waste Land*. Eliot's poem surely must have made appropriate reading at the time of such tragedies as the Warsaw Ghetto uprising in the spring of 1943.

A revolt against the Germans on a much grander scale occurred in the latter half of 1944 as the Red Army reached the outskirts of the Polish capital. The underground Home Army, whose hierarchy was controlled by the London based government-in-exile, sought to take charge in Warsaw prior to the arrival of the Russian forces and launched an attack on the Germans stationed within the city. Not surprisingly, the Russian response to the insurrection was to cease all military activity against the Germans on the Warsaw front, and the Home Army was left to its own resources to do battle with the vastly superior Nazi forces. Miłosz himself was not a member of the Home Army because he had no desire to see the restoration of the political establishment that had governed Poland before World War II. Then, as now, he considered the rising to be an act of folly. The bitter struggle lasted more than two months and cost more than two hundred thousand Polish lives. After the surrender of the Home Army, the Germans forced the evacuation of the surviving populace and then systematically destroyed the city, block by block. Caught completely unawares by the outbreak of the rising. Miłosz and his wife were seized by the Germans as they attempted to leave Warsaw, but after a brief period of detention in a makeshift camp, they were released through the intercession of friends. Thereafter, they were to spend the next few months wandering about as refugees until the Red Army completed its annihilation of the German forces and Poland was at last liberated after more than five years of Nazi rule.

Since Warsaw had been almost totally destroyed, the center of literary activity in Poland had gravitated to Cracow, and it was there in 1945 that a collection of Miłosz's wartime poetry was issued in a volume titled *Ocalenie* (rescue). This work was one of the very first books to be published in postwar Poland. Because of his prominence as a poet, Miłosz was selected for service in the diplomatic corps and was posted as a cultural attaché at the Polish Embassy in Washington, D.C., from 1946 to 1950. He then was transferred to Paris, where he was appointed First Secretary for Cultural Affairs. In 1951, shortly after the practice of Socialist Realism became mandatory for all Polish writers, he decided to break with the home government in Warsaw and to start life anew by working as a free-lance writer in France. The next decade proved to be remarkably productive for Miłosz. His reasons for breaking with the Warsaw regime were fully set forth in the nonfictional study *The Captive Mind* as well as in the political novel *The Seizure of Power.* At the same time, he continued to create poetry of the highest order. His novel *The Issa Valley* also dates from this period, as does his long poem *A Treatise on Poetry.*

In recognition of these literary accomplishments, Miłosz was invited to lecture on Polish literature at the University of California at Berkeley during the academic year 1960-1961. In 1961, he decided to settle in Berkeley after he was offered tenure as a professor of Slavic languages and literatures. He became a naturalized American citizen in 1970 and eventually retired from active teaching in 1978 with the rank of professor emeritus. Just as he retained his creativity during his years in exile as a freelance writer in Paris, so too did Miłosz manage to maintain his literary productivity within an academic environment in the United States. Fully one-third of the works included in the edition of Miłosz's *Utwory poetyckie* (collected poems), which was printed under the aegis of the Michigan Slavic Publications in 1976, were written in the United States. His lifetime achievement as a poet finally received due acknowledgment when he was selected as the winner of the Nobel Prize in Literature in 1980.

In June, 1981, Miłosz returned to Poland for the first time since his self-imposed exile in 1951. The Polish government, still under communism, now claimed him, although his Nobel Prize acceptance speech was published only after the anticommunist sentiments were edited out. Polish presses were now able to publish his poetry, at last making it available in Polish to his native people, many of whom had never heard of their newly crowned national bard. With the declaration of martial law in December, 1981, however, his work was again banned by the government, although some of it remained available in *samizdat*, or underground, publications. Upon his return to America, Miłosz began a series of lectures as the Charles Eliot Norton professor at Harvard University for the academic year 1981-1982. These lectures were later published in *The Witness of Poetry*.

Miłosz has been incredibly prolific in his twilight years, publishing several collections of poetry, essays, and criticism: As he entered his nineties, Miłosz continued to publish. His wife Janka died in 1986 after a ten-year battle with Alzheimer's disease. Miłosz married again, dividing his time between Berkeley and Cracow.

ANALYSIS

The principal group of Polish poets in the period between the two world wars was known by the name "Skamander," after the title of its official literary organ. The Skamander group consisted of a number of poets with very disparate styles and diverse interests, and its members included such renowned literary figures as Julian Tuwim, Kazimierz Wierzyński, Jarosław Iwaszkiewicz, Antoni Słonimski, and Jan Lechoń. Since the Skamanderites were viewed as belonging to the literary establishment, younger poets formed movements of their own in opposition. A group now designated as the First Vanguard was centered in the city of Cracow during the 1920's and derived much of its aesthetic program from the ideas propounded by the Futurists in Italy. Around 1930, many new literary groups sprang up in various parts of Poland, and these groups are today known

collectively as the Second Vanguard. Building on the formal innovations of the First Vanguard, its members generally sought to intensify the social and political dimensions of poetry.

POEMAT O CZASIE ZASTYGŁYM

The żagary group of poets, to which Czesław Miłosz belonged while a student at the University of Wilno, was part of the Second Vanguard. Because of the apocalyptic premonitions expressed in their poetry, the Wilno group soon came to be labeled "catastrophists." Miłosz's first published book, *Poemat o czasie zastygłym*, represents a youthful attempt to write civic poetry and is often marred by inflated political rhetoric as well as by avant-garde experimentation in both language and form. Apparently, Miłosz himself recognizes its overall shortcomings, since he chose to exclude the work from the edition of his collected poems published at Ann Arbor in 1976.

TRZY ZIMY

His next work, *Trzy zimy*, is largely free from the defects of the previous one and constitutes a decided advance in Miłosz's development as a poet. Despite his continued reliance on elliptical imagery, these poems frequently attain a classical dignity of tone. This quality is even present when Miłosz gives vent to forebodings of personal and universal catastrophe. One of his finest poems in this vein is called "Do ksiedza Ch." (to Father Ch.) and is passionate and restrained at the same time. Here, after describing a world being destroyed by natural calamities as a result of man's sinfulness, Miłosz ends his poem on a note of reconciliation. Shared suffering will, he says, reunite longtime antagonists, and the last pagans will be baptized in the cathedral-like abyss.

OCALENIE

Such premonitions of catastrophe turned into reality after the outbreak of World War II. The poems that Miłosz wrote during the war years in Poland were gathered together and published in 1945 under the title *Ocalenie*. Among the works in this collection are two outstanding poems that deal with the destruction of the Warsaw Ghetto. The first is "Campo di Fiori" and begins with a description of this famous square in modern-day Rome. The poet recalls that Giordano Bruno was burned at the stake on that very spot before a crowd that resumed its normal activities even before the flames were completely extinguished. The scene then shifts to

Warsaw, where the crowds also carry on with mundane matters on a beautiful Sunday evening even while the ghetto is ablaze. The loneliness of the Jewish resistance fighters is then likened to the solitary fate suffered by Bruno. The poet, however, resolves to bear witness to the tragedy and to record the deeds of those dying alone, forgotten by the world.

The second poem is called "Biedny chrześcijanin patrzy na getto" ("A Poor Christian Looks at the Ghetto"). Here, the poet watches as bees and ants swarm over the ruins of the Ghetto. He then spots a tunnel being bored by a mole, whose swollen eyelids remind him of those of a biblical patriarch. Guilt overwhelms the poet as he wonders if in the next world the patriarch will accuse him of being an accomplice of the merchants of death. This guilt is less that of a survivor than of one who regrets that he was unable to help a fellow human being in his hour of need.

Many other poems in the collection focus on purely personal themes, but it is in his role as a national bard that Miłosz is most impressive. Although Miłosz's poetic style is generally modern in character, the reader frequently encounters traces of the diction and phraseology associated with great Romantic poets such as Adam Mickiewicz, Juliusz Słowacki, and Cyprian Norwid. Any avant-garde preoccupation with finding new modes of linguistic expression could only have appeared trivial in the light of the horrendous events that overwhelmed the poet and his nation during the war years.

ŚWIATŁO DZIENNE

While in exile in France during the years 1951 to 1960, Miłosz published two important volumes of verse: *Światło dzienne* (daylight) and *A Treatise on Poetry*. In the first of these works, the poet dwells on political grievances of various sorts. One of the best of these political poems is titled "Dziecie Europy" ("A Child of Europe"). After a bitterly ironic opening section in which the poet reminds those who managed to live through the war how often they sacrificed their honor as the price of survival, he goes on to ridicule the belief in historical materialism and implies that the doctrine of the inevitability of socialism rests more on the use of force against all classes of society than on the laws of history. To those who are compelled to live in a Communist state, he offers a counsel of despair: If you wish to survive, do not love other people or the cultural heritage of Europe too dearly.

A TREATISE ON POETRY

In his *A Treatise on Poetry*, Miłosz surveys the development of Polish poetry in the twentieth century and discusses the role of the poet in an age of crisis. A work of about twelve hundred lines, it is unrhymed, except for a few rhymed insertions, and employs a metrical line of eleven syllables with a caesura after the fifth syllable. The meter is quite familiar to Polish readers because of its previous appearance in major literary works by Mickiewicz and Słowacki. Even so, Miłosz's style here is classical rather than Romantic. A dissertation of this kind that employs verse has, to be sure, a number of contemporary counterparts, such as W. H. Auden's *New Year Letter* (1941) and Karl Shapiro's *Essay on Rime* (1945), but the genre had not been used in Polish literature since the Renaissance. *A Treatise on Poetry* is, therefore, considered to be in the nature of an innovation in Miłosz's homeland. For this and other reasons, it is ranked very highly among the poetical works in Miłosz's oeuvre.

KRÓL POPIEL I INNE WIERSZE

The publication of Miłosz's *Król Popiel i inne wiersze* (King Popiel and other poems) in 1962 was closely followed by a second volume of verse titled *Gucio zaczarowany* (Bobo's metamorphosis) two years later. In both works, all formal features associated with poetry are minimized. Stanza, rhyme, and regular meter tend to disappear, and the poet veers toward free verse. The title poem in the first work tells the story of Popiel, a mythical king from the time of Polish prehistory who was said to have been devoured by mice on his island fortress in the center of a large lake. In recounting this legend, Miłosz makes the reader aware of the narrow mode of existence that must have been the lot of Popiel and his kingly successors, for whom possession of territory and material objects was of overriding importance and to whom all cosmological speculation was alien. The pettiness of Popiel's end mirrors the pettiness of his thought.

GUCIO ZACZAROWANY

Much longer and much more complex is "Gucio zaczarowany" ("Bobo's Metamorphosis"), the title poem of the subsequent collection. Miłosz, with the assistance of Richard Lourie, has himself translated the work into

English and is thus responsible for its current title; a more literal rendition of the original Polish would be "enchanted Gucio." (Gucio is one of the diminutive forms of the name Gustaw.) The poem itself has eight sections; in the seventh, an individual called Bobo (Gucio) is transformed into a fly for a few hours. As a result of this experience, Bobo often has difficulty adopting a purely human perspective on matters. All of the other sections of the poem likewise involve the problem of reconciling various perspectives. In the final section, the poet explores the psychological tensions that arise between a man and a woman as they mutually recognize the impossibility of penetrating the private universe of another person's mind. In place of understanding, they have no recourse but to posit humanity and tenderness. The dialectical tension in this poem, and its resolution, is quite typical of Miłosz's cast of mind, for he intuitively looks at the world in terms of contrary categories such as stasis and motion or universal and particular. Similarly, in many of his poems, a sense of apocalypse is juxtaposed to a feeling of happiness.

MIASTO BEZ IMIENIA

In *Miasto bez imienia* (city without a name), a collection of verse published in 1969 and translated in the 1973 collection *Selected Poems*, Miłosz does much to clarify his view of poetry in the works titled "Ars poetica?" ("Ars Poetica?") and "Rady" ("Counsels"). The opening lines of "Ars Poetica?" are used by the author to proclaim his desire to create a literary form that transcends the claims of either poetry or prose. Nothing short of this, he declares, is capable of satisfying the demoniac forces within the poet which inspire the content of his work. There can, however, be no assurance that the *daimon* will be an angel, for a host of Orphic voices compete for possession of a poet's psyche. Over the years, so many invisible guests enter a poet's mind that Miłosz likens it to a city of demons and reminds the reader how difficult it is for anyone who writes poetry to remain only one person. Still, he personally eschews the morbid and expresses his disdain for confessional poetry of the psychiatric variety. Miłosz is committed to the kind of poetry that helps humankind to bear its pain and misery, and he underscores this belief in "Counsels." Younger poets are hereby cautioned against propagating doctrines of despair. This earth, Miłosz insists, is not a

madman's dream, nor is it a stupid tale full of sound and fury. He himself concedes that this is a world wherein justice seldom triumphs and tyrants often prosper. Nevertheless, Miłosz argues that the earth merits a bit of affection if only because of the beauties it contains.

Neither in "Counsels" nor elsewhere in his poetical oeuvre does Miłosz ever hold God to be the cause of the misfortunes that man inflicts upon man, and he likewise absolves the deity of responsibility for any of the other evils that befall human beings in this world. His conception of God has much in common with that to be found in the writings of the Gnostics and Manichaeans, for which he first developed a partiality while still a high school student in Wilno. Hence, Miłosz is frequently tempted to view God as a perfect being who is completely divorced from all forms of matter and who is, therefore, not responsible for the creation of the material universe. In that light, everything that has a temporal existence can be said to be under the control of a Demiurge opposed to God. Miłosz does, however, advise his readers not to assume a divine perspective in which man's earthly tribulations are to be seen as inconsequential. In "Do Robinsona Jeffersa" ("To Robinson Jeffers"), a poem included in his essay collection *Widzenia nad zatoka San Francisco* (1969; *Views from San Francisco Bay*, 1982), Miłosz objects to the way in which Jeffers, in some of his poetry, demotes the stature of man by contrasting his pettiness with the immensity of nature. Miłosz prefers to remain true to his Slavic and Baltic heritage, in which nature is anthropomorphized, rather than to adopt an inhuman view of the universe such as the one propounded by Jeffers.

GDZIE WSCHODZI SŁOŃCE I KĘDY ZAPADA

The free-verse style of *Gdzie wschodzi słońce i kędy zapada* (from where the sun rises to where it sets) sometimes borders on prose. The author, in fact, freely juxtaposes passages of verse and prose in the title poem, an explicitly autobiographical work that is almost fifty pages long. In the seven sections of this poem, Miłosz moves between past and present in a spirit of free association and contemplates the nature of an inexplicable fate that has brought him from a wooden town in Lithuania to a city on the Pacific coast of the United States. True to his dialectical frame of mind, Miłosz's attitudes alternate between forebodings of death and affirmation of life.

"Dzwony w zimie" ("Bells in Winter"), the final section, contrasts the Wilno of his youth, where he was usually awakened by the pealing of church bells, with the city of San Francisco, whose towers he views daily across the bay in the winter of his life. The entire poem is an attempt to bridge the gap between his expectations as a youth in Poland and the realities of his old age in America.You

"YOU WHO HAVE WRONGED"

Bridge-building in the reverse direction occurred when Polish workers belonging to the Solidarity movement selected some lines from one of Miłosz's poems to serve as an inscription on the monument erected outside the shipyards in Gdańsk for the purpose of commemorating the strikers who died during demonstrations against the government in 1970. These lines are taken from the poem "Który skrzywdziłeś" ("You Who Have Wronged"), included in the collection *Światło dzienne*, and run as follows:

> You, who have wronged a simple man,
> Bursting into laughter at his suffering . . .
> Do not feel safe. The poet remembers.
> You may kill him—a new one will be born.
> Deeds and talks will be recorded.

For a poet in exile, it must have been a source of profound satisfaction to learn that his words had been chosen by his countrymen to express their own longing for a free and independent Poland. Verse that previously had been circulated clandestinely in *samizdat* form could now be read by everyone on a public square in broad daylight.

"LA BELLE ÉPOQUE"

Like the other long serial poems, "La Belle Époque" from "New Poems, 1985-1987," which appears at the end of *The Collected Poems, 1931-1987*, mixes verse and prose, speaks in multiple voices, and moves freely in time, along the way pointing out the intersections of personal fate with history. The poem returns over its seven sections to a few central characters. The poet's father and the beautiful teenage Ela seem to represent for the poet the inevitable human tendency toward empathy and connection; he identifies so closely with each that he feels he "becomes" them. Yet such feeling is terrifyingly fragile in the face of catastrophe, whether natural catas-

trophes or the everyday catastrophe of human mortality. Miłosz relates with necessary, quiet detachment, for instance, the fact of the execution of Valuev and Peterson, train passengers engaged in a debate over mortality, each feverishly in pursuit of his own truth. The poem's final section asserts the fragility of not only the individual human, but the entire *belle époque* and its nearsighted optimism with the sinking of the Titanic.

"SIX LECTURES IN VERSE"

"La Belle Epoque," with its harsh pessimism, is not the conclusion to "New Poems." Rather, in the last poem, "Six Lectures in Verse," with characteristic insight, Miłosz goes beyond the contradiction of mortality to a new recognition: that the facts of history and mortality are forgotten in that moment when sensuous reality is far more present and more "real" than any concept we have of it.

FACING THE RIVER

From the mid-1980's to the mid-1990's Miłosz's poetry underwent a profound change. The poem "Realism," in the 1995 collection *Facing the River*, gives some indication of the source and direction of his poetic goals. Admitting that the language humans use to tame nature's random molecules fails to capture eternal essences or ontological reality, Miłosz still insists on a realm of objectivity embodied in the still life. Abstractionism and pure subjectivity are not the final prison for the triumph of the ego, and Miłosz recalls Arthur Schopenhauer's praise of Dutch painting for creating a "will-less knowing" that transcends egoism through "direct[ing] such purely objective perception to the most insignificant of objects." So Miłosz proceeds in "Realism" from the still life to the idea of losing himself in a landscape:

> Therefore I enter those landscapes
> Under cloudy sky from which a ray
> Shoots out, and in the middle of dark plains
> A spot of brightness glows. Or the shore
> With huts, boats, and on yellowish ice
> Tiny figures skating. All this
> Is here eternally, just because once it was.

"THE GARDEN OF EARTHLY DELIGHTS: HELL"

This is remarkable because the preceding poem, "The Garden of Earthly Delights: Hell," completes the series of meditations—written more than a decade earlier and published in *Unattainable Earth*—on Hieronymous Bosch's terrifying painting of the same title. In moving from the scene of worldly hell to the Dutch still life and landscape, Miłosz conveys his desire to move beyond the tragic and egocentric to the sensuous, yet peaceful and eternal.

"The Garden of Earthly Delights: Hell" is, in fact, one of the most frightening poems in this, the most hell-haunted of all of Miłosz's work. This is the "missing panel" of Miłosz's meditation on Bosch's painting, "The Garden of Earthly Delights." Sensitive to such details in the painting as "a harp/ With a poor damned man entwined in its strings," one feels Miłosz's own painful skepticism of the worth of a life in art. Here he takes one of the most painful jabs at his own endless pursuit of the real as hiding fear of death:

> Thus it's possible to conjecture that mankind exists
> To provision and populate Hell,
> The name of which is duration. As to the rest,
> Heavens, abysses, orbiting worlds, they just flicker a
>   moment.
> Time in Hell does not want to stop. It's fear and
>   boredom together
> (Which, after all, happens) And we, frivolous,
> Always in pursuit and always with hope,
> Fleeting, just like our dances and dresses,
> Let us beg to be spared from entering
> A permanent condition.

This is the ironic version of what he says in "Capri": "If I accomplished anything, it was only when I, a pious boy, chased after the disguises of the lost Reality." The question for Miłosz is when the "chasing" stops that carried him forward in time, out of his past, and now back into his past. Where is the final reality beneath "dresses" and "disguises," metaphors for the changing forms of history and of his own art?

OTHER MAJOR WORKS

LONG FICTION: *Zdobycie władzy*, 1953 (*The Seizure of Power*, 1955); *Dolina Issy*, 1955 (*The Issa Valley*, 1981).

SHORT FICTION: *Road-side Dog*, 1998.

NONFICTION: *Zniewolony umysł*, 1953 (criticism; *The Captive Mind*, 1953); *Kontynenty*, 1958; *Rod-*

zinna Europa, 1959 (autobiography; *Native Realm: A Search for Self-Definition*, 1968); *Człowiek wśród skorpionów*, 1962 (criticism); *Widzenia nad zatoką San Francisco*, 1969 (*Views from San Francisco Bay*, 1982); *The History of Polish Literature*, 1969, enlarged 1983; *Prywatne obowiązki*, 1972; *Emperor of the Earth: Modes of Eccentric Vision*, 1977; *Ziemia Ulro*, 1977 (*The Land of Ulro*, 1984); *Ogród nauk*, 1979; *Nobel Lecture*, 1981; *Świadectwo poezji*, 1983 (criticism; *The Witness of Poetry*, 1983); *Zaczynając od moich ulic*, 1985 (*Beginning with My Streets: Essays and Recollections*, 1991); *Rok myśliwego*, 1990 (*A Year of the Hunter*, 1994); *Abecadło Milosza*, 1997 (*Miłosz's ABCs*, 2001); *Striving Towards Being: The Letters of Thomas Merton and Czeslaw Miłosz*, 1997; *Zycie na wyspach*, 1997; *To Begin Where I Am: The Selected Prose of Czesław Miłosz*, 2001.

EDITED TEXTS: *Pieśń niepoldlegla*, 1942; *Postwar Polish Poetry: An Anthology*, 1965, revised 1983; *With the Skin: Poems of Aleksander Wat*, 1989; *A Book of Luminous Things: An International Anthology of Poetry*, 1996.

BIBLIOGRAPHY

Czarnecka, Ewa, and Aleksander Fiut. *Conversations with Czesław Miłosz*. Translated by Richard Lourie. New York: Harcourt, 1987. Incredibly eclectic and illuminating set of interviews divided into three parts. Part 1 explores Miłosz's childhood through mature adulthood biographically, part 2 delves more into specific poetry and prose works, and part 3 looks at Miłosz's philosophical influences and perspectives on theology, reality, and poetry. It is especially interesting to hear Miłosz's interpretations of his own poems.

Dudek, Jolanta. *Europejskie korzenie poezji Czesława Miłosza*. Cracow: Ksiegarnia Akademicka, 1995. Explores the poetic, philosophical, and religious influences of Miłosz's mature poetry, focusing on the long poem *Gdzie wschodzi słońce i kędy zapada*. Draws connections in the poem to William Blake, William Butler Yeats, and James Joyce. In Polish, with a short summary in English.

Fiut, Aleksander. *The Eternal Moment: The Poetry of Czesław Miłosz*. Translated by Theodosia S. Robertson. Berkeley: University of California Press, 1990. A comprehensive examination of the artistic and philosophical dimensions of Miłosz's oeuvre. Fiut analyzes the poet's search for the essence of human nature, his reflection on the erosion of the Christian imagination, and his effort toward an anthropocentric vision of the world.

Ironwood 18 (Fall, 1981). Special Miłosz issue. Published a year after Miłosz received the Nobel Prize, this issue's self-proclaimed purpose was to "help Americans absorb and assimilate his work." Offers a broad range of responses to Miłosz's work from his American and Polish contemporaries, many well-known and admired poets themselves, such as Robert Hass, Zbigniew Herbert, and Stanisław Barańczak.

Levine, Madeline G. *Contemporary Polish Poetry, 1925-1975*. Boston: Twayne, 1981. Situates Miłosz among a selection of modern Polish poets as a poet who "addresses the crucial problems of the twentieth century." While the article specifically on Miłosz is not particularly in-depth, it does offer a useful chronological overview of some important works and their relation to their historical context.

Malinowska, Barbara. *Dynamics of Being, Space, and Time in the Poetry of Czesław Miłosz and John Ashbery*. New York: P. Lang, 2000. A discussion of poetic visions of reality in the works of two contemporary hyper-realistic poets. In its final synthesis, the study proposes the comprehensive concept of ontological transcendence as a model to analyze multidimensional contemporary poetry. Includes bibliographical references.

Mozejko, Edward, ed. *Between Anxiety and Hope: The Poetry and Writing of Czesław Miłosz*. Edmonton: University of Alberta Press, 1988. Although these seven articles by accomplished poets and scholars are not focused around any one theme, some topics that dominate are catastrophism and the concept of reality in Miłosz's poetry and his place in Polish literature. Also shows Miłosz's ties with Canada in an article comparing his artistic attitudes to those of Canadian poets and an appendix describing his visits to Canada.

Nathan, Leonard, and Arthur Quinn. *The Poet's Work: An Introduction to Czesław Miłosz*. Cambridge, Mass.: Harvard University Press, 1991. The first book by an American to serve, as Stanisław Barańczak puts it in the foreword, as a "detailed and fully reliable introduction . . . to the body of Miłosz's writings." This work by two of Miłosz's Berkeley colleagues (Nathan was also a co-translator with Miłosz of many of his most challenging poems) benefits from the authors' lengthy discussions of the texts with the poet himself.

Victor Anthony Rudowski,
updated by Tasha Haas and Robert Faggen

JOHN MILTON

Born: London, England; December 9, 1608
Died: London, England; November 8, 1674

PRINCIPAL POETRY
Poems of Mr. John Milton, 1645
Paradise Lost, 1667, 1674
Paradise Regained, 1671
Samson Agonistes, 1671
The Poetical Works, 1952-1955

OTHER LITERARY FORMS

Although John Milton's poetry represents only about one-fifth of his total literary production, the prose works are more obscure, largely because he wrote in genres that no longer appeal to a large audience. Milton's prose is usually read today for what it reveals about his biography and his thought. His most prominent theme was liberty—religious, domestic, and civil. The following examples are notable: five antiprelatical tracts (1641-1642); four tracts justifying divorce (1643-1645); and five pamphlets defending the English Puritan cause against the monarchists (1649-1654). The tract *Of Education* (1644) and the classical oration upholding freedom of the press, *Areopagitica* (1644), are the most familiar titles among the prose works. The remaining titles consist largely of academic exercises, letters, additional pamphlets, works of history, and treatises. Milton left in manuscript at his death a Latin treatise on religion, *De doctrina Christiana libri duo Posthumi* (1825), a work which provides valuable clarification of his religious beliefs.

ACHIEVEMENTS

By common agreement, literary historians have ranked John Milton second among English poets. He wrote during the English Renaissance, when authors were attempting to develop a national literature in the vernacular. In this endeavor they had exceedingly rich sources to draw upon: the classics, many recently translated, which provided both genres and themes; the Judeo-Christian tradition, an area of broad interest and intensive study following the Reformation; and national sources—historical, folk, mythical; and literature from the Continent, particularly Italy and France. By the time Milton began writing, William Shakespeare and his contemporaries had created a national drama that surpassed that of other nations, and Ben Jonson had adapted such classical lyric genres as the ode and the epigram to English verse. As yet no poet had succeeded in creating an epic poem based upon a classical model, a task which the age considered the highest achievement of the creative mind.

It remained for Milton to undertake this formidable task, one for which he was well prepared. Among English poets of the first rank he was the most deeply and broadly learned—in classical languages and literature and in works of the Judeo-Christian tradition. From early life, he considered poetry to be a true vocation, and his development as a poet suggests that he emulated Vergil and Edmund Spenser, beginning with lyric genres and progressing by degrees to the epic. Milton's strongest inclination as a poet was to produce a synthesis of classical and Christian elements, a blend which critics have labeled his Christian humanism.

Milton contributed poems of lasting value and interest to English literature in both major and minor genres. He stressed the importance of the individual will by making his most common theme that of the soul in ethical conflict—the wayfaring, warfaring Christian. He developed a style peculiarly "Miltonic." In the verses which Milton would have seen as fitting his ideal of "simple, sensuous, passionate," Matthew Arnold discovered "touchstones," or examples of the sublime in poetry. Finally, he adopted the blank verse of English drama as a vehicle for the long poem on a serious theme.

BIOGRAPHY

John Milton was born into an upper-middle-class family in London, his father being a scrivener with real estate interests, sufficiently affluent to assure Milton that he did not have to follow a profession in order to live. John Milton the elder, who achieved recognition in his own right as a composer and musician, encouraged his son in his studies and enrolled him in St. Paul's School, then a quality day school in London. When he entered

John Milton (Library of Congress)

Christ's College, Cambridge, at sixteen, Milton had an excellent grounding in Latin and Greek.

Even though he was once suspended from Cambridge, he was a serious and successful student, taking two degrees (B.A., 1629; M.A., 1632). While at Christ's College, he wrote a significant amount of lyric poetry, and he altered his original intention of being ordained. Leaving Cambridge in 1632, he returned to his father's estates at Horton and, later, Hammersmith, remaining there until 1638. Although he continued to write poetry, his essential purpose appears to have been further systematic study of classical and Renaissance literature, history, and philosophy.

Approaching thirty, he set out in 1638 to tour France, Switzerland, and Italy, a journey which lasted fifteen months and enabled him to glean impressions of European nature, art, and architecture that later enriched his poetry. During the tour he also visited such learned men as Hugo Grotius and Giovanni Diodati and attended the meetings of learned societies.

Returning to England upon the outbreak of civil war in 1639, he became engaged in the pamphlet war against the bishops. For a period of about fifteen years, Milton turned his primary attention to the writing of polemic prose, which he regarded as promoting the cause of liberty. His poetic output was small, consisting of a few sonnets and lyrics and translations from the Psalms. For a brief time he became a schoolmaster, though his school enrolled only a handful of students, two of whom were Milton's nephews. His marriage to Mary Powell in 1642 lasted until her death following childbirth in 1652; a second marriage ended with the poignant death of Katharine Woodcock in 1658. His work as a controversialist brought his merit to the attention of the government of Oliver Cromwell, and he was appointed secretary of foreign tongues to the Council of State in 1649. He was totally blind by 1652 and had to dictate his correspondence and creative work.

By the late 1650's, he began composing *Paradise Lost*; his three major poetic works occupied the remaining years of his life. As the Restoration approached, he tried in vain to stem the tide by writing more antimonarchial and anticlerical pamphlets. During the years following the Restoration, he lived quietly in London with his third wife, Elizabeth Minshull, receiving friends

and composing and revising his poems. He was much troubled by gout and died of its complications in 1674.

ANALYSIS

The greater part of John Milton's lyric poetry was written during his residences at Cambridge (1625-1632) and at Horton-Hammersmith (1632-1638). The work of the Cambridge period includes numerous occasional poems in English and conventionally allusive Latin epigrams and elegies. These early lyrics may owe something to Milton's "Prolusions," which are academic exercises on a set theme with predictable lines of argument, ornamented with numerous classical allusions. Such prose assignments may well have contributed to Milton's rich style and his firm sense of genre.

The poems cover a wide variety of topics: the death of bishops, of an infant, of the university carrier; the anniversary of the Gunpowder Plot; and religious topics. In "At a Vacation Exercise," written before he was twenty, Milton intimates that he will use his native language for "some graver subject" than the one which the hundred-line lyric develops. His lyric "On Shakespeare," included with the commendatory poems in the second folio (1632), had a theme of special interest to the young Milton, the fame that comes to a poet. In this lyric, as in others, the style and diction indicate a debt to Edmund Spenser.

"ON THE MORNING OF CHRIST'S NATIVITY"

Among the poems written during the Cambridge period, the ode "On the Morning of Christ's Nativity" (1629) remains the most significant, perhaps the best nativity hymn in English poetry. The verses depict Christ as a triumphant redeemer—sovereign over nature, baneful to demons, and warmly human. In a rhyme-royal proem (four stanzas), Milton establishes the occasion and setting, and then celebrates the Nativity in thirty-seven stanzas, each being of eight verses, varying in length and rhyming *aabccbdd*. The hymn has three structural divisions: Stanzas 1-7 portray the peace of nature and the civilized world at the time of Christ's birth; stanzas 8-15 celebrate the promise of Christ for the future, with images of music and harmony; stanzas 16-37 foretell the results of Christ's birth for the near future, the cessation of oracles and the collapse of pagan religions. Milton associates Christ with Pan and Hercules, freely drawing upon classical mythology and reading it as Christian allegory; at the same time, he follows a different Christian tradition by equating the pagan gods with devils. The ode is remarkable for its exuberant metrical movement and its rich imagery of light and harmony.

"L'ALLEGRO" AND "IL PENSEROSO"

Two of Milton's best-known lyrics, "L'Allegro" and "Il Penseroso," cannot be dated with certainty, though they are usually assigned to the period 1629-1632. "L'Allegro" celebrates the pleasures of the mirthful man, while "Il Penseroso" celebrates those of the contemplative man, whose joyous mood may be tinged with melancholy. These companion poems, both written in iambic tetrameter, employ a similar structure. "L'Allegro" begins in early morning and concludes in the evening; its companion begins in the evening and ends with morning. The speaker in each poem moves through a series of settings, and both poems express the delight and pleasure to be derived from nature and art, their chief appeal being to the senses of sight and sound.

A MASKE PRESENTED AT LUDLOW CASTLE

The poems of the Horton-Hammersmith period demonstrate the growth of Milton's poetic power and give promise of further development, in *Comus* (1634; as *A Maske Presented at Ludlow Castle,* 1637) and "Lycidas" (1637) being the most notable. A masque is a brief dramatic entertainment, characterized by a simple plot and conflict, usually presented by amateurs and employing elaborate costumes, fanciful situations, song, dance, and highly poetic passages. The poem represents Milton's first important use of blank verse and his first significant work on the theme of temptation. The mythical Comus, inhabits a wood and entices travelers there to taste his liquor, which transforms them into monstrous shapes and makes them his followers. Milton's heroine, the Lady, becomes separated from her brothers in this wood and is tempted by Comus but refuses. Although he can force her to sit immobile in a chair, he can attain no power over her mind or will. The brothers, assisted by the guardian spirit Thyrsis, arrive on the scene, drive Comus away, and secure her release through the aid of the water nymph Sabrina. Thereupon the two brothers and the Lady are presented to their parents. The theme of temptation enables Milton to celebrate the power of

the human will to resist evil, a central theme of his major poems. In *Comus* the temptation occurs in a natural setting, almost a pastoral milieu; in later works the setting and character are altered to present the theme in greater complexity.

"LYCIDAS"

The occasion of Milton's pastoral elegy "Lycidas" was the death of Milton's fellow student at Cambridge, Edward King, who drowned in the Irish Sea in 1637. At the time of his death he had a career as a clergyman open before him. Milton follows the conventions of the pastoral elegy, King being treated as a shepherd whose songs have ended and for whom all nature mourns. The invocation of the muse, rhetorical questions, the fixing of blame, the procession of mourners, the catalog of flowers—all of these conventional elements find a place. The traditional elegiac pattern of statement of loss, reconciliation, and looking toward the future is also followed in "Lycidas." Milton uses the convention of allegory in pastoral poetry to meditate on fame and to attack abuses within the Church. The elegy employs a complex rhythm and rhyme pattern which is indebted to the Italian *canzone*.

Over a period of approximately thirty years, Milton wrote twenty-three sonnets, among them some of the most memorable lyrics in English. As with other genres, he made contributions to the form, in this instance both thematic and stylistic. Although the first six sonnets, five of them in Italian, are conventional in style, the English sonnets that follow mark new directions that influenced the history of the sonnet form. The first sonnets were love poems, and most early English sonnets were written in the tradition of Francis Petrarch's sequence to Laura. William Shakespeare and John Donne had left influential poems on the themes of friendship and religion. To Milton the sonnet became a poem written not in sequence but on an occasion of personal or public significance—on his twenty-third birthday, on his blindness, on the death of his wife, on the massacre in Piedmont, on the public reception of his divorce tracts. While many of the sonnets reflect Milton's strong religious and moral convictions, they are not, strictly speaking, religious poems.

From the standpoint of style, he broke the traditional quatrain division and introduced an inverted Latinate syntax which allowed freedom in the placement of modifiers. The result was numerous enjambments and an alteration of the pauses within the lines of the sonnet. As in his longer poems, Milton juxtaposes Latinate diction and syntax with simple English diction and meter, creating a powerful tension. These stylistic innovations and the rich allusive texture that Milton brings to the sonnet combine to make the sonnets seem more restricted and concentrated than those of the Elizabethan period. When, a century after Milton, the pre-Romantics revived the sonnet as a lyric form, the predecessor whose work they emulated was Milton.

PARADISE LOST

Although he had been planning to write an epic poem for nearly forty years before *Paradise Lost* was published in 1667, Milton did not seriously begin the composition before the period 1655-1657, when he was approaching fifty years of age. He had thought of an epic based upon either British history or a biblical theme; when the time came, he chose the biblical theme and developed it on the grandest scale possible. From a Christian perspective, he set out to narrate all important events in the temporal and spiritual history of humankind, to answer all important questions, to tell what one poet called "the story of all things." Not content to narrate the fall of man from grace, Milton included in his statement of the theme, as announced in the prologue to Book I, man's restoration and his ability to gain immortality. The theology of *Paradise Lost* is essentially orthodox Protestant, although a few unusual theological views were discovered after students of Milton closely examined the epic in the light of his treatise on theology, *De doctrina Christiana libri duo Posthumi.*

Milton adheres to numerous epic conventions established by Homer and Vergil, his classical predecessors in the form: action set in various realms, divine and human characters, a stated theme, invocation of the muse, epic games, epic similes, warfare, speeches, dreams, catalogs, roll calls, elevated style, and twelve books (or multiples of twelve). A remarkable departure from the practice of earlier epic poets, as T. J. B. Spencer has pointed out, is that numerous minor epic conventions, particularly those concerning warfare and conflict, are more often associated with the demoniac than with the human or the divine. Milton specifically rejects warfare as a subject unworthy of the epic, preferring to celebrate the suffering hero who endures adversity for the sake of conscience and right. In a mythical perspective, Christ represents the hero of Milton's epic, for he is the character who acts, who creates and restores. Yet, Adam receives more attention in the poem and undergoes a change of fortune; for humankind, Milton's readers, he becomes the hero.

As Northrop Frye pointed out, it is instructive to examine *Paradise Lost* as a myth, even though Milton believed that he was narrating events that actually took place—some poetic license and elaboration being permitted. The mythical structure of the epic is cyclic, involving actions primarily of the Deity (constructive) and Satan (destructive). The earliest point in the narrative is the occasion for Satan's revolt, the recognition of Christ as Son of God before the assembled angels in Heaven. Following a three-day war in Heaven, Satan and millions of followers are cast out; and God creates the universe and the human order to restore spiritual beings to vacant places in Heaven. This purpose is challenged by Satan, who journeys to earth to tempt man and bring about his fall. Although Satan achieves his objective, God repairs the loss by giving man the law and redeeming him, enabling man to regain the opportunity of entering Heaven after Judgment Day.

Since Milton follows the epic convention of beginning *in medias res*, the narrative is not presented chronologically. Instead, after stating the theme, Milton begins the first book with Satan and his followers in the depths of hell. Although the poetic structure of *Paradise Lost* may be approached in various ways, the most common is to divide the epic into three major parts or movements, with four related books in each: I-IV; V-VIII; IX-XII. Books I-IV introduce the theme, settings, lines of narrative development, characters (divine, demoniac, human), and motivation. In Book I Satan and Beëlzebub are found suffering in hell, a place which Milton describes as holding a multitude of torments. They resolve never to submit but to continue their vain attempt against God through guile. Rousing his followers, Satan has them build an enormous palace, Pandemonium, as the site of a council of war (Book II). After Moloch, Mammon, Belial, and Beëlzebub have proposed plans of action to the council, the plan of Satan, as presented by

Beëlzebub, is accepted—that they attempt to thwart God's plan by subverting another world and its beings, a mission which Satan volunteers to perform. He sets out to travel through chaos to earth, while his followers divert themselves with epic games.

In Book III the setting is changed to Heaven, where another council takes place. God the Father, presiding over the assembled angels, informs them of Satan's mission, predicts its success, explains the necessity for a redeemer, and accepts Christ's voluntary sacrifice to save humankind. The council in Heaven (III, vv. 80-415) provides the essential theological basis for the poem, clarifying the redemptive theology of Christianity as Milton understood it. This done, Milton returns to Satan, who deceives the angels stationed by God for man's protection and travels to the peak of Mount Niphates overlooking the Garden of Eden. The fourth book introduces the human characters, Adam and Eve, whom Milton describes as ideal human types, living in an idyllic setting. Even Satan finds the creation of God beautiful, though the beauty does not deter him from his destructive plan. Instead, he approaches Eve in the form of a toad and creates in her mind a troubling dream, until the angels appointed to watch over the Garden discover him and drive him out.

Books V-VIII, the middle books of *Paradise Lost*, contribute to the narrative in at least three important ways: They enable Milton to show God's concern for man by sending the angel Raphael to instruct Adam of the danger represented by Satan, the function which George Williamson has described as "the education of Adam." They permit him to provide exposition through an account of the war in Heaven and of the creation. Finally, they enable him to prepare the reader to accept as credible the fall of perfect beings whose only duty was to obey a plain and direct command of God. Book V opens with Eve narrating her dream to Adam, the dream created by Satan, in which an angel tempts her to disobey God's command and eat of the forbidden tree. The dream follows closely the actual temptation sequence in Book IX and so foreshadows the more complex temptation that follows. Adam reassures her that dreams imply no guilt, and the angel Raphael arrives to begin his explanation of the revolt of Satan. In Book VI the angel narrates the three-day war in Heaven. James H.

Hanford has shown that in the narrative Milton describes the types of combat then known—single warriors battling for victory, classic battle formations, artillery, and, finally, an elemental kind of strife like that of the Titans, in which the angels rend up hills to hurl them at their opposition. On the third day Christ appears to drive Satan and his host out of Heaven.

The seventh book provides an account of the creation of the universe and all living things by Christ, who forms the whole from chaos, bringing order and harmony. To Milton the creation is consciously and intentionally harmonious and hierarchical. In Book VIII, Adam explains what he can recall about his own creation and asks Raphael questions about astronomy. When he acknowledges to the angel that he sometimes inclines to Eve's view because her wisdom seems superior, Raphael warns him not to abandon his responsibility as her guide, emphasizing the importance of hierarchy.

The final group of books includes an account of man's fall (IX), its immediate aftermath (X), and the long-term consequences (XI-XII), the final two books representing the education of fallen Adam. In Book IX, Satan returns to the Garden under cover of darkness and enters the body of the serpent. The serpent approaches Eve, who has persuaded Adam to let her work apart, and tempts her to disobey God through promises of greater power. When she returns to Adam, he understands what has happened, and at her invitation eats the forbidden fruit, not because he has been deceived but because he wishes to share Eve's fate. The immediate results include inordinate and ungovernable passions in both and disorder in nature. In Book X, Christ appears in the Garden to pass sentence on man, but his words hold out hope of triumph over Satan. As he is returning to hell, Satan meets the allegorical figures Sin and Death, who are paving a broad way to link hell and the earth. His triumph before his followers in hell is eclipsed when they are transformed into serpents which greedily approach apple trees growing outside the great hall, only to discover the fruit to be bitter ashes. Meanwhile, Adam and Eve have understood that God's will must prevail and have begun to take some hope in the promise given them by the Savior.

In Book XI, the archangel Michael is sent by God to explain to Adam the effects of sin upon his descendants, so that Adam can understand and accept God's plan for humankind. Adam sees the effects of sin, understanding the cause of disease, death, and erroneous choices among men. He witnesses the flood that destroys the world and acknowledges it as just. In Book XII, Michael narrates the bringing of the law through Moses, the birth of Christ, the establishment of the Church, and the history of Christianity until Judgment Day. Having understood the entire scope of human history, Adam gratefully accepts God's plan for the restoration of humanity, and he and Eve depart from the Garden, having lost the original paradise but having gained the ability to attain a "paradise within."

For the exalted theme of *Paradise Lost*, Milton achieves an appropriately elevated style which appeals primarily to the ear, creating the "organ tones" for which it is celebrated. He chose blank verse because he believed it to be the closest equivalent in English meter to the epic verse of the classics; yet the stylistic unit is not the line but rather the sentence, and, at times, the verse paragraph. The more prominent stylistic qualities include the following: Latinate diction and syntax ("the vast profundity obscure"), frequent inversions, words either archaic or used in unfamiliar senses, collocations of proper names, epic similes, compound epithets, compression, and, most prominently, the schemes of repetition—the most frequent being polyptoton, antimetabole, and chiasmus.

The style reveals a weaving of related images and a richly allusive texture that can be grasped only after repeated readings. Christopher Ricks has shown, for example, that references to the "hands" of Adam and Eve recur in poignantly significant contexts, creating a cumulative effect with one image. When Milton uses a biblical name, as Ricks notes, he often "transliterates," that is, provides the literal equivalent in English. Thus, when Satan is named, "adversary" may appear immediately thereafter; "pleasant" occurs in passages that mention Eden—as if to remind the reader that names embody meanings of which he is unaware. Further, reading mythology as allegory, Milton freely associates mythical characters with biblical counterparts—Proserpine with Eve, Deucalion with Noah, Ceres with Christ. Finally, the reader learns to interpret biblical characters typologically, as Milton did, where characters in the Old

Testament anticipate the New—Adam, Noah, and Moses, for example, all being types of Christ. Through these poetic techniques, Milton achieves a style so complex that its interest and appeal can never be exhausted.

PARADISE REGAINED

Milton's brief epic *Paradise Regained*, written in blank verse and published with *Samson Agonistes* in 1671, represents a sequel to *Paradise Lost*, its hero Christ being a second Adam who overcomes temptation that is much more extensive than that experienced by Adam. Milton makes several assumptions about the temptation of Christ in his source, Luke 4:1-14, an account of events which occurred before the beginning of Christ's ministry: First, Christ does not fully understand either his mission or the role of the Messiah; second, he can be genuinely tempted; third, his withstanding temptation assures his success in the role of redeemer. To Milton, the Book of Job represented the ideal model for the brief epic; it appears that no other poem in English or in the classics influenced the form significantly.

The temptations of Christ, narrated in the four books of the poem, offer easy access to those things which Satan supposes a hero of his kind would want. At the beginning of the narrative, Christ has been fasting in the desert for forty days following his baptism, an event which had attracted Satan's interest. Satan had heard God's recognition of Christ following the ceremony and had supposed that Christ might be the offspring of Adam destined to bruise his head. Resolving to subject Christ to temptations, Satan approaches him in disguise and invites him to turn stones into bread in order to allay his hunger. After Christ's refusal, Satan next offers a banquet, also refused because Christ recognizes the giver as evil. When Satan realizes that Christ cannot be tempted by ordinary means, he concludes that he is indeed someone extraordinary and appeals to Christ's supposed ambition by offering first wealth, then the Parthian kingdom, then Rome, and, later, all kingdoms of the world in return to fealty to Satan. In rejecting these offers, Christ reveals that his kingdom is not of the world. Undeterred, Satan offers all the learning—philosophy, poetry, history—of Athens, declined by Christ as unnecessary to him and inferior to that of the Hebrews.

Satan raises a storm in the desert in the hope of terrifying Christ and transports him through the air to the pinnacle of the Temple, where he urges Christ to cast himself down and be rescued from death by God. When Christ replies, "Tempt not the Lord thy God," Satan recognizes his divine nature and falls himself, leaving Christ in the protection of angels who minister to him.

Biographer Barbara Lewalski has pointed out that the temptations in *Paradise Regained* are designed to reveal Christ's roles as priest, prophet, and king. The prophet in the wilderness denies himself, the king acknowledges no kingdom of this world, and the priest rejects the false and unnecessary learning for the true.

SAMSON AGONISTES

For his only tragedy, *Samson Agonistes*, Milton adapts a Greek model of the genre to a biblical episode, the story of Samson, as found in Judges XIII-XVI. The title signifies Samson the wrestler or athlete; Milton's hero represents a type of Christ from the Old Testament, though Samson, unlike Christ, falls from favor and undergoes a series of temptations before being restored. Since Milton wrote the tragedy in verse (1,758 lines in blank verse) and since he clearly states that he did not intend the work for the stage, it is usually studied as a dramatic poem.

Samson Agonistes, said to be the English tragedy which most closely follows the Greek model, employs numerous Greek conventions. It takes place on the final day of the hero's life and follows the unities of time, place, and action. Milton divides the major episodes of the play not by acts but by the choral odes, as in Greek drama. The chorus performs its usual functions—providing exposition, advising the hero, announcing arrivals, and interpreting for the audience.

The tragedy opens with a despairing Samson, blind and enslaved to work in a Philistine mill, being visited on a holiday by a group of his countrymen, who form the chorus. Samson blames himself for the loss of God's favor because he revealed the secret of his strength to his wife Dalila, who betrayed him to the Philistines. The men of Dan announce the arrival of Samson's father Manoa, who is negotiating with the Philistines for his son's release, a prospect which brings Samson little comfort, since he believes that idleness will only increase his sense of guilt. Manoa's effort, however, invites Samson to choose a life of ease and rest much unlike the life he has known, and this he rejects. Dalila

arrives and informs Samson that she now wishes that he would return to her and renew their marriage. Her suggestion only arouses his anger, and she leaves, satisfied that she will enjoy fame among her own people. The next visitor is the Philistine champion Harapha, a giant who has come to challenge Samson to prove his strength once again through physical combat; but Harapha discreetly leaves after Samson defies him. This meeting renews Samson's understanding that his strength derives from God, yet it suggests to him that single combat is no longer his role.

A Philistine officer arrives to command Samson to attend the celebration in Dagon's temple in order to divert the audience with feats of strength. At first Samson scornfully refuses the command as impious and idolatrous, but, after an inward prompting, changes his mind and accompanies the officer to the temple. As the Chorus and Manoa await Samson's return, they hear a fearful noise, and a messenger arrives to announce that Samson has destroyed the temple and has perished in the destruction, along with thousands of Philistines. The chorus recognizes that Samson has been restored to God's favor and has acted in accordance with divine will.

As in his other major works, Milton in *Samson Agonistes* expands and modifies his source while remaining faithful to its original meaning and spirit. The effort of Manoa to obtain Samson's release, the appearance of Dalila during his imprisonment, and the character of Harapha are all Milton's additions. They enable him to interpret the character of Samson as more complex than the biblical character and to show him undergoing a series of temptations. Although the poetic voice is less intrusive in *Samson Agonistes* than in the epics, Milton, as Hanford has pointed out, identifies rather closely with the blind hero of the tragedy.

MORAL SUBLIMITY

There can be little doubt that religion, as Milton understood it, stands as the major theme of his poetry. The protagonists of his four greatest poetic works—the Lady in *Comus*, Adam in *Paradise Lost*, Christ in *Paradise Regained*, and Samson in *Samson Agonistes*—undergo an elaborate temptation (or a series of temptations) and either triumph or come to terms with failure. Critics recognize that Milton does not excel in characterization, one reason being that his characters are subordinate to his narrative and thematic purposes. Nor does Milton possess a gift for humor or comedy; his infrequent efforts in those directions usually appear heavy-handed.

His religious perspective is Protestant, with greater emphasis upon the will than was common for his time. Milton's view of salvation would have been called "Arminian" during the seventeenth century—that is, Christ provided for the salvation of all who willingly accepted him. To Milton this assumption takes on classical overtones derived perhaps from Aristotle and Ovid, among others. In kind of Aristotelian teleology, he assumes that one right choice makes a second easier, and thus man through the proper exercise of his will moves toward the perfection of human nature. Conversely, a wrong choice makes subsequent right choices more difficult and may lead to the degradation of human nature.

In his poetry Milton seeks to celebrate right choices and to guide readers in their own choices. His poetry of the will and of ethical conflict is expressed in literary genres of lasting interest and in a style so sublime and so rich in poetic meaning that one discovers new beauties with each successive reading.

OTHER MAJOR WORKS

PLAY: *Comus*, pr. 1634 (pb. 1637 as *A Maske Presented at Ludlow Castle*).

NONFICTION: *Of Reformation Touching Church Discipline in England*, 1641; *Of Prelatical Episcopacy*, 1641; *Animadversions upon the Remonstrant's Defence Against Smectymnuus*, 1641; *The Reason of Church-Government Urg'd Against Prelaty*, 1642; *An Apology Against a Pamphlet . . .* , 1642; *The Doctrine and Discipline of Divorce*, 1643; *Of Education*, 1644; *The Judgement of Martin Bucer Concerning Divorce*, 1644; *Areopagitica*, 1644; *Tetrachordon*, 1645; *Colasterion*, 1645; *The Tenure of Kings and Magistrates*, 1649; *Eikonoklastes*, 1649; *Pro Populo Anglicano Defensio*, 1651; *Pro Populo Anglicano Defensio Secunda*, 1654; *Pro Se Defensio*, 1655; *A Treatise of Civil Power in Ecclesiastical Causes*, 1659; *Considerations Touching the Likeliest Means to Remove Hirelings Out of the Church*, 1659; *The Readie and Easie Way to Establish a Free Common-*

wealth, 1660; *The History of Britain*, 1670; *Of True Religion, Heresy, Schism, and Toleration*, 1673; *De doctrina Christiana libri duo Posthumi*, 1825; *Complete Prose Works of John Milton*, 1953-1982 (8 volumes).

MISCELLANEOUS: *Works*, 1931-1938 (18 volumes).

BIBLIOGRAPHY

Bloom, Harold, ed. *John Milton*. New York: Chelsea House, 1986. Contains a selection of some of the best Milton criticism from the last thirty years. Includes a bibliography and an index.

Bradford, Richard. *The Complete Critical Guide to John Milton*. New York: Routledge, 2001. An accessible, comprehensive guide to Milton for students. Bradford brings Milton to life in an overview of his life and work and provides a summation of the main critical issues surrounding his work. Includes bibliographical references and an index.

Broadbent, John Barclay, ed. *John Milton: Introductions*. Cambridge, England: Cambridge University Press, 1973. Still one of the best introductions to the work of Milton. Twelve chapters cover his life and times, his poetic formation, his science, his theology, and his art and music. Suggestions for resources and further reading are offered in each chapter. Contains an index.

Danielson, Dennis R. *Milton's Good God: A Study in Literary Theodicy*. New York: Cambridge University Press, 1982. To some extent, this is a reexamination of William Empson's thesis in his *Milton's God*, but mainly it is an analysis of Milton's theology and how it is related poetically to the task he set himself in *Paradise Lost*. Supplemented by a select bibliography and an index.

Fish, Stanley. *How Milton Works*. Cambridge, Mass.: Harvard University Press, 2001. The preeminent and controversial Milton scholar offers a magnum opus in which he argues that all of Milton's work can be seen from the poet's firm belief that the value of his (or any) work lay in its author's commitment to divine truth, not in the tools and devices—plot, narrative, representation—of his aesthetic craft. *Library Journal* noted, "What students of Milton and readers of literary criticism will find refreshing is the low volume of jargon and poststructuralist lit-speak in this solidly argued work."

Hunter, G. K. *Paradise Lost*. Boston: Allen & Unwin, 1980. The great advantage of this short study is its ability to make the poem enjoyable. It suggests ways of reading the text that still take full account of Milton's art, complexities, and contradictions. Contains a bibliography and an index.

Jordan, Matthew. *Milton and Modernity: Subjectivity in Paradise Lost*. New York: St. Martin's Press, 2000. Sees Milton's works as essentially revolutionary, necessarily understood in a context of the author's belief in individual human freedom. Bibliographical references, index.

Lewalski, Barbara Kiefer. *The Life of John Milton: A Critical Biography*. Malden, Mass.: Blackwell Publishers, 2000. A detailed account of Milton's life and career. Lewalski, named honored scholar by the Milton Society of America, provides a close analysis of Milton's prose and poetry and shows his development of a revolutionary prophetic voice. Includes bibliographical references and an index.

Martz, Louis L. *Poet of Exile: A Study of Milton's Poetry*. New Haven, Conn.: Yale University Press, 1980. Sixteen chapters center on *Paradise Lost* as a poem of exile. Two separate sections cover the rest of the poetry, and a fourth section looks closely at the interaction with Ovid in *Paradise Lost* in terms of heroic and pastoral love. Contains appendices and an index.

Milner, Andrew. *John Milton and the English Revolution: A Study in the Sociology of Literature*. Totowa, N.J.: Barnes & Noble Books, 1981. Written from a Marxist perspective, it sets Milton's major poems in the world of the defeat of a rationalist world vision as expressed in Independency and the subsequent need to reorder that vision after the Restoration. It takes particular issue with Christopher Hill and is part of a wider historical debate. Contains notes, a bibliography, and an index.

Ricks, Christopher. *Milton's Grand Style*. Oxford, England: Clarendon Press, 1963. Ricks examines Milton's epic style in *Paradise Lost*, well aware of the controversy surrounding it. In a scholarly manner, he shows that many of the criticisms are unfounded

and that Milton's verse possesses both sublimity and flexibility. Includes indexes.

Silver, Victoria. *Imperfect Sense: The Predicament of Milton's Irony*. Princeton, N.J.: Princeton University Press, 2001. Silver engages the central question of Milton readers: Why do we hate Milton's God? She argues that Milton deliberately presents a repugnant deity, one divided from himself, in an effort to reveal the human experience of a divided or self-contradictory universe driven by our own, ironically limited, vantage.

Stanley Archer;
bibliography updated by the editors

GABRIELA MISTRAL

Lucila Godoy Alcayaga
Born: Vicuña, Chile; April 7, 1889
Died: Hempstead, New York; January 10, 1957

PRINCIPAL POETRY
  Desolación, 1922
  Ternura, 1924, enlarged 1945
  Tala, 1938
  Antología, 1941
  Lagar, 1954
  Selected Poems of Gabriela Mistral, 1957
  Poesías completas, 1958
  Poema de Chile, 1967

OTHER LITERARY FORMS
  Although the poems published in Gabriela Mistral's three main collections are the principal source for her recognition, she was active until her death as a contributor of prose to newspapers and journals throughout Latin America. She also wrote for newspapers whenever she was abroad, and her translated articles appeared frequently in the local press. The quality of this extensive and continuous journalistic effort is not consistent, though Mistral's prose style has been recognized for its personal accent and spontaneity. Her articles were ex-

tremely varied in theme. Much of what she wrote supported principles espoused in her poetry. Though less introspective, the prose, like the poetry, relates closely to the author's life and derives from episodes which left a profound mark upon her. It is combative, direct, and abrupt while revealing her sincerity and ceaseless search for truth and justice.

ACHIEVEMENTS

Latin America's most honored woman poet, Gabriela Mistral was awarded the 1945 Nobel Prize in Literature. The first Latin-American writer to be so honored, she was selected as the most characteristic voice of a rich literature which had until then been denied that coveted award. The intrinsic merits of her work, described as lyricism inspired by vigorous emotion, were representative of the idealism of the Hispanic American world.

Mistral's popularity was keen throughout her adult life, during which she received the National Award for Chilean Literature and honorary doctorates from the University of Florence, the University of Chile, the University of California, and Columbia University.

Neither a disciple of Rubén Darío nor a contributor to the poetic revolution of the vanguard movements (though there are elements of both in her work), Mistral maintained independence from literary groups, preferring to consider herself an outsider. Nevertheless, her personal effort was a ceaseless labor toward unity, in which she pressed her genius into the service of brotherhood among nations, responsibility in professional activity, regard for future generations, appreciation for native American culture, effective education, love for the weak and oppressed, and a yearning for social justice.

All of these endeavors are rooted in the principal sentiment of Mistral's poetry—her unsatisfied desire for motherhood. This emotion is in Mistral both a feminine instinct and a religious yearning for fulfillment. She elevates her great feminine anguish to the heights of art; this is her originality.

BIOGRAPHY

Gabriela Mistral was born Lucila Godoy Alcayaga, the child of Chilean parents of Spanish heritage, proba-

Gabriela Mistral (AP/Wide World Photos)

bly mixed with Indian ancestry. She was said to be part Basque, owing to her mother's last name, and part Jewish, only because her paternal grandmother possessed a Bible and schooled the eager child in its verses. The poet accepted this presumed inheritance, attributing to herself the energy of the Basque, the tenacity of the Jew, and the melancholy of the Indian. When she was three years old, her father left home and never returned. The task of rearing Mistral was shared by her mother and her half sister, Emelina. Both women were teachers and provided the child with primary instruction and a thirst for additional knowledge. Timid and reserved, the young girl had few friends. During her last year of primary instruction, she was falsely accused of wasting classroom materials. Unable to defend herself against this accusation and further victimized when classmates threw stones at her, she was sent home and was taught by Emelina. This first encounter with injustice and human cruelty left a profound impression on the future poet, who became determined to speak out for the rights of the defenseless, the humble, and the poor.

The family moved to La Serena on Chile's coast in 1901. Three years later, the fourteen-year-old Mistral's prose began to appear in local periodicals. These writings seemed somewhat revolutionary in a provincial town and probably accounted for the poet's admission to, and then expulsion from, the normal school. Undeterred, the family continued tutoring her while she finished her studies. In 1905, she began to work as a teacher's assistant. For the next five years, she taught in the primary grades, while nurturing her early work as a writer. This initial poetry possessed a melancholy flavor in tune with poets with whom she was familiar. Certified as an educator in 1910, she began a career as a high school teacher that took her throughout her native country. All during her life she would characterize herself as a simple rural teacher, and she liked to be remembered as such, more than as a diplomat or a poet. She taught for more than twenty years, assuming the role of spiritual guide for many who approached her. Near the end of her career as an educator, Chile named her Teacher of the Nation. A good portion of her literary work, which has an educational motive, is directed toward young people. Behind the writer is the teacher who desires to encourage moral and spiritual awareness and aesthetic sensitivity.

With the publication of her first book in 1922, the poet's literary name, Gabriela Mistral, definitively replaced her birth name. The name Gabriela was chosen for the archangel Gabriel, one who brings good tidings, and Mistral was chosen for the dry wind that blows in the Mediterranean area of Provence. Also in 1922, Mistral left Chile for Mexico, where she had been invited by José Vasconcelos, secretary of education in Mexico, to participate in a national program of educational reform. Intending at first to stay for six months, she remained in Mexico for two years. This sabbatical began a lifetime of travel during which the poet occupied diplomatic posts, represented her country in international and cultural gatherings, and participated in numerous intellectual endeavors.

In 1932, Mistral became a member of the consular corps of the Chilean government, fulfilling various diplomatic assignments in Spain, Portugal, France, Brazil, and the United States. At the same time, she continued a life of writing and intellectual pursuits. She taught Latin American literature at the University of Puerto Rico and at several institutions in the United States. In 1953, she became the Chilean delegate to the United Nations, where she served until poor health forced her to retire.

ANALYSIS

Through a poetry that is at times deliberately crude and prosaic, Gabriela Mistral distinguished herself as an artist of tenderness and compassion. Her themes are nourished by her personal sorrow, which she ably elevates to the realm of the universal. Maternity, children, love, God, the fight against instinct, the soul of things, are voiced in anguish and in reverence by this most feminine of poets, whose vigor belies her femininity and whose high concept of morality is always present but never militant.

Mistral's three major collections of poems, *Desolación, Tala*, and *Lagar*, were published at sixteen-year intervals. They contain a selection of poems from among the many that the poet produced in newspapers during the intervening years. Each volume comprises material that was written at different times and under changing circumstances; thus, a strict topical unity is not to be expected. Each volume was published in response to an external stimulus which affected the life of the poet.

DESOLACIÓN

Desolación was compiled through the initiative of Federico de Onís, professor of Spanish at Columbia University and founder of the Hispanic Institute. Professor Onís had selected the poet's work as the theme for a lecture which he gave at the institute in 1921. The participants, primarily Spanish teachers from the United States, were deeply impressed by the depth and beauty of this vigorous new voice in Hispanic American poetry, and when they discovered that the poet had not yet published a book, Onís insisted on publishing the collection under the auspices of the Hispanic Institute.

The unity of the book is the body of moving, impassioned poems which were inspired by two painful experiences in the life of the youthful poet. While a teacher in La Cantera, Mistral became romantically involved with an employee of the railroad company, but, because of bitter differences, they ended the relationship. When the young man later committed suicide for reasons unrelated to his association with the poet, Mistral was deeply affected. Several years later, she met a young poet from Santiago with whom she fell passionately in love. When he rejected her in favor of someone from Santiago's wealthy elite, Mistral was crushed. Shortly thereafter, she requested a transfer to Punta Arenas in Chile's inhospitable southland.

Inasmuch as the poems inspired by these devastating episodes do not appear in chronological order, one reads them as if the poet were relating the history of a single painful love. With great lyrical strength, she expresses the awakening of love, the joy and self-consciousness, the boldness, timidity, hope, humiliation, and jealousy. The poems which deal with suicide of the beloved reveal the poet's anguish and her petition to God concerning his salvation. She wonders about his afterlife, and expresses her loneliness, remorse, and obsession to be with him still. The poet is pained and in torment, yet in her vigor she displays jealousy, revenge, and hate, all of which are employed to combat the demanding powers of an enslaving, fateful love. God is petitioned in her own behalf as well. The agony is tempered at intervals by tenderness, her disillusionment nurtured by hope, her pain anointed with pleasure, and the hunger for death soothed by a reverence for life. In her moments of rapture there is sorrow and loneliness, identified with the agony of Christ, from whom the poet seeks rest and peace in his presence.

The language of these poems is natural, simple, and direct. It is the realism of one who has lived close to the earth, who eschews delicate subtleties in favor of frankness. Mistral's love is expressed with passion and wrath; her words are coarse, bordering on crudity. This is chaste poetry, nevertheless, inasmuch as its fundamental longing for motherhood and the spiritual yearning for God reject the possibility of eroticism or immodesty.

Mistral lifts her spirit up though it is weighed down in anguish. It is suffering which does not destroy, but brings the spirit to life. The lyrical roots of *Desolación* are not a product of imagination: They are a lived tragedy. When Mistral begins to regard her lost youth, foreseeing the seal of fate in her sterility, condemned to perpetual loneliness, she raises a prolonged, sharp moan. Her entire being protests, argues, and begs at the same time. Overcome, the poet mourns her desolation, her martyrdom in not being able to be the mother of a child from the man she loved. This maternal yearning is not simply the impulse toward the preservation of the race. It is the tender cry of one who loves, who lives in agony over the loss of that which is closest to the ultimate joy of her soul.

Mistral's poetry employs a great variety of verse forms. She freely used sonnets, tercets, quatrains, the five-line stanza, sextains, ballads, and other forms, with little regard for the conventional patterns. She favored the Alexandrine, the hendecasyllabic line, and the nine-syllable line, which gradually became her preferred form; the latter seems to blend well with the slow pace of much of her poetry. The poems in *Desolación* do not follow classical models. Mistral toys with new rhymes, in which her consonants are imperfect or are interspersed with assonances. The artist has been accused of an inability to deal properly with metric forms. It is true that she lacked a musical sense. Her images, too, are frequently grotesque, too close to death and violence. Together with poems of rough, unpolished form in *Desolación*, there are others which are flawless in construction. Mistral reworked many of her poems repeatedly, the result generally being a refinement, although at times it was a disappointment. Her major objective was the power of the word rather than the meter of the lines.

Mistral concludes *Desolación* with the request that God forgive her for this bitter book, imploring men who consider life as sweetness to pardon her also. She promises in the future to leave her pain behind and to sing words of hope and love for others.

TALA

Tala fulfilled this promise sixteen years later. She compiled these poems as a concrete gesture to relieve the suffering of the children of Spain who had been uprooted from their homes during the Spanish Civil War (1936-1939). Mistral was disappointed and ashamed that Latin America had not appeared to share her grief for the plight of these homeless children, and the proceeds from the sale of this volume alleviated the difficulties in the children's camps. The title of the book refers to the felling of trees and applies to both the poems themselves and the purpose for which the author compiled them. The limbs are cut from the living trunk and offered as a gift, a part of oneself, a creation. From within the poet who has made her offering, there remains the assumption of the growth of a new forest. *Tala* has its pain (with allusions to the death of the poet's mother), but this volume is more serene than its predecessor. Mistral controls her emotions to a degree, and happiness, hope, and peace flow in her songs. *Tala* speaks of the beauties of America, as the poet humanizes, spiritualizes, and orders the creatures of the continent around the presence of man. Mistral gathers all things together, animate and inanimate, nourishes them like children, and sings of them in love, wonder, thanksgiving, and happiness. Far from America, she has felt the nostalgia of the foreigner for home, and she desires to stimulate the youth of her native soil to complete the tasks that are ahead.

Mistral sees Hispanic America as one great people. She employs the sun and the Andes Mountains as elements which bind the nations geographically, and she calls for a similar spiritual kinship. She believed that governments should be born of the needs of nations; they should emphasize education, love, respect for manual labor, and identification with the lower classes. Like José Vasconcelos, she believed that American man has a mission to discover new zones of the spirit which harmonize with the new civilization in which he lives. The poet treats this subject with great enthusiasm, declaring also that there is much in the indigenous past which merits inclusion in the present. She invokes the preColumbian past with nostalgia, feeling remorse for the loss of the Indian's inheritance and his acceptance of destiny.

The maternal longing of the poet is the mainspring of Mistral's many lullabies and verses for children that appear in this and other volumes. The other constant, implicitly present in all the poems of *Tala*, is God. She approaches God along paths of suffering, self-discipline, and a deep understanding of the needs of her fellow people. In God, she seeks peace from her suffering, comfort in her loneliness, and perfection. Her ability to humanize all things grows from her desire to find God everywhere. Thus these objects and the wonder derived from them infuse the religious into the poet's creation. Her metaphors and images derive from the contemplation of nature and its relationship with the divine. More objective than the poetry of *Desolación*, this work retains its personal, lyrical quality.

TERNURA

Ternura (tenderness) is a collection of Mistral's children's poems. First published in 1924, it consisted of the children's verses that had appeared in *Desolación*. The 1945 edition added more poems for children which the author had written up to that date. The principal emotion is depicted in the title. The poet sings lullabies, rounds, and games, following traditional Spanish verse forms, especially the ballad. The poems generally teach a moral lesson, such as love and respect for others, development of one's sense of right and beauty, reverence for nature, country, and the creations of God. In Mistral's later children's verses, she sought to create a distinctly American atmosphere. Her vocabulary and background reflect regional and local material, drawing generously from Indian culture and beliefs.

The unique relationship between mother and child is felt in Mistral's soft, unhurried lullabies, in which the mother tenderly gives herself to the peace of her offspring, softly engendering in the child a reverence for the Earth and all of its creatures. She expresses the inner wounds of her heart, but in a tender fashion which does not disturb her baby. The only father in these verses is God, who becomes the source toward whom the yearning mother directs the child.

LAGAR

Lagar (wine press) was published less than three years before Mistral's death. Together with the lack of world peace, the years brought new personal tragedies in the suicide of two of Mistral's closest friends and the devastating suicide of her nephew, Juan Miguel Godoy, whom she had reared like a son. Her health declined, and she became preoccupied with thoughts of death. Restless, Mistral moved frequently during this period. *Lagar* tells of the imprint of these experiences on her soul. The wine press of life and death, ever draining her heart, has left her weak and exhausted. In theme, *Lagar* refers back to *Desolación*, though Mistral no longer regards death with the anger of her frustrated youth. She bids it come in silence in its own due time. She is more confident of herself, eliminating the prose glosses which accompanied earlier collections. Her simple, prosaic verses are austere and purified. They beckon to the world beyond the grave in a poetic atmosphere which is as spiritual as it is concrete. Fantasy, hallucination, and dreams all contribute to an ethereal environment governed by imagination and memory.

Like Mistral's other published collections, *Lagar* lacks topical harmony. Mistral delights the reader with playful songs, revels in her creativity, and feels at one with God; yet the pain and weariness of the ever-draining wine press constitute the dominant mood.

The suicide of her nephew, at seventeen, again brought to Mistral's poetry the agony, the terrible emptiness, and the liberation available only when one has renounced earthly life. The young Juan Miguel had been the poet's constant companion, sensitive and helping, the strongest motive for Mistral's own bond with life. With the passing of this last close relative, the poet's will to live became associated more with life beyond the grave than with earthly cares.

Other verses demonstrate the poet's concern with the effects of war. Mistral protests against injustice and identifies with those who suffer through no fault of their own. Religion, not according to a prescribed dogma but rather in a sense of spiritual communication between the living and the dead, along with the ever-present identification with nature, continue as important themes. In *Lagar*, the fusion of these two motifs is more complete than in the poet's earlier work. Nature is viewed in a spiritual sense. There appears a need to be in contact with the earth and the simplicity of its teaching in order to maintain spiritual harmony with the divine. This thought comforts the poet, who searches for a spiritual state of knowledge and intelligence. By preceding her nouns with the first-person possessive, she assumes a personal stance not found in her work before, as if she were participating more completely in the process of creation. Indeed, she begins to overuse the adjective, not so much to describe physical attributes as to personify the inanimate and to engender a mood. The mood thus created generally drains or destroys. Past participles used as adjectives (burned, crushed, pierced) fortify this effort, thus strengthening the theme of the title and suggesting the travail of life on earth as parallel to the crushing of grapes in the wine press.

POEMA DE CHILE

During her last years, Mistral worked intensely on correcting and organizing her numerous unedited and incomplete compositions. Her posthumous *Poema de Chile* is a collection of poems united by one theme, her native country, in which she carries on an imaginary dialogue with a child, "my little one," showing him the geography and the flora and fauna of Chile as they travel together.

BIBLIOGRAPHY

Arce de Vázquez, Margot. *Gabriela Mistral: The Poet and Her Work*. Translated by Helene Masslo Anderson. Ann Arbor, Mich.: UMI Out-of-Print Books on Demand, 1990. Biography and critical study of Mistral and her work. Includes bibliographical references.

Castleman, William J. *Beauty and the Mission of the Teacher: The Life of Gabriela Mistral of Chile, Teacher, Poetess, Friend of the Helpless, Nobel Laureate*. Smithtown, N.Y.: Exposition Press, 1982. A biography of Mistral and her life as a teacher, poet, and diplomat. Includes a bibliography of Mistral's writing.

Marchant, Elizabeth. *Critical Acts: Latin American Women and Cultural Criticism*. Gainesville: University Press of Florida, 1999. This refreshing reevaluation of Latin American women writers during the first half of the twentieth century recognizes their overlooked contributions to the public sphere. The critic reconsiders some representative poems, focusing on the dichotomy between Mistral's theories and practices and the female intellectual's alienation from the public sphere. While Mistral refused a traditional societal role for herself, she advocated it for her readership. This literary and psychological study also examines and compares the writings of Victoria Ocampo and Lúcia Miguel Pereira to that of Mistral.

Alfred W. Jensen;
bibliography updated by Carole A. Champagne

KENJI MIYAZAWA

Born: Hanamaki, Japan; August 27, 1896
Died: Hanamaki, Japan; September 21, 1933

PRINCIPAL POETRY

Haru to shura, 1924 (*Spring and Asura*, 1973)
The Back Country, 1957

OTHER LITERARY FORMS

In addition to a substantial body of free verse and many *tanka* poems (the *tanka* is a fixed form of thirty-one syllables in five lines), Kenji Miyazawa wrote children's stories, often in a fantastic vein. He also wrote a limited number of essays, the most important one of which outlines his ideas for an agrarian art. The children's stories have proved popular in Japan, and some of them are available along with the major poems in English translation. It should also be noted that Miyazawa drafted and reworked his poems in a series of workbooks over the course of his creative life; while the notebooks are not publications in a formal sense, they might be considered part of the Miyazawa canon. In any case, they are commonly utilized by scholars investigating the sources of the poet's art.

ACHIEVEMENTS

A poet of unique gifts, Kenji Miyazawa spent his relatively brief life in almost total obscurity. Living in a primitive rural area, writing virtually as a form of religious practice, Miyazawa published only one volume of stories and one of poetry during his life. Neither work attracted attention at the time of its publication.

Shortly after Miyazawa's death, however, his work began to be noticed. His utilization of scientific, religious, and foreign terms became familiar, and the striking images and energy of his verses seemed exciting alongside the generally restrained modes of Japanese poetic expression.

Most surprising of all, Miyazawa started to attain the prominence and affection he still enjoys among the general public. Almost any literate Japanese would know one poem that he jotted down in his notebook late in life. Sketching the portrait of Miyazawa's ideal selfless person, the poem begins with the lines, "Neither to wind yielding/ Nor to rain."

Miyazawa began composing *tanka* poems while still a middle school student. His principal works are in free verse, however, and these he composed mostly during the decade of the 1920's. Throughout these years,

various forms of modernism—Futurism and Surrealism, for example—were being introduced to Japan, and certain native poets experimented with these new styles of writing. Miyazawa, however, worked in total isolation from such developments. This is not to say that his work is *sui generis* in any absolute sense. Assuredly a religious poet, Miyazawa worked out a cosmology for certain of his poems which, according to one Western scholar, resembles in a general way the private cosmologies of such poets as William Blake and William Butler Yeats.

BIOGRAPHY

Kenji Miyazawa was born on August 27, 1896, in the town of Hanamaki in the northern prefecture of Iwate. Iwate has a cool climate, and the farmers of the region led a precarious existence. Miyazawa's father ran a pawnshop, a business which prospered in part because of the poverty of the local farmers.

As the oldest son, Miyazawa would normally have succeeded his father as head of the family business. Uneasy at the thought of living off the poverty of others, however, Miyazawa neglected the task of preparing himself to succeed his father in the family business. Instead, he immersed himself in the study of philosophy and religion. An exemplary student in grade school, Miyazawa's record became worse from year to year in middle school as he pursued his own intellectual interests. Some of this independence is also discernible in occasional escapades during his youth, one of which led to his expulsion from the school dormitory.

By 1915, Miyazawa had decided to find work outside the family business. In this year, he entered the Morioka College of Agriculture and Forestry. Along with his studies in such areas as chemistry and soils, Kenji formulated various plans for his future, plans whereby he could utilize his knowledge to contribute to the amelioration of the harsh conditions of rural life. For a time he even hoped to turn the resources of the family business to some new venture that might be of general economic benefit—producing industrial chemicals from the soil of the area, for example.

A new dimension was added to Miyazawa's differences with his father during these years. Initially he had followed his father's religious preference as a believer in the Jōdo Shin sect of Buddhism. Eventually, however, Kenji decided that ultimate truth resided in the militant Nichiren sect, especially in its intense devotion to the Lotus Sutra. In January, 1921, he took the extraordinary step of fleeing the family home in Hanamaki in order to join a Buddhist organization in Tokyo known as the State Pillar Society. Miyazawa returned home late that same year, partly because of the serious illness of his younger sister Toshiko, partly to take a teaching position at the two-year Hienuki Agricultural School.

Toshiko died in November, 1922, an event which the poet commemorated in a number of impressive elegies. Miyazawa continued to teach until March, 1926. In his spare time, he took his students for long treks in the countryside, writing incessantly in the notebooks which he took on these excursions. The poet made his first and only attempt at publishing his work in 1924. In addition to a volume of children's stories, he brought out at his own expense a volume of sketches in free verse, *Spring and Asura*.

Miyazawa gave up teaching from a sense of guilt. How could he accept a regular wage, no matter how small, when the average farmer was often destitute? Miyazawa decided, thus, to become a farmer himself. A bachelor his entire life, he lived by himself raising vegetables for his own table and several small cash crops in addition. Using the knowledge he had acquired over the years, he attempted to serve as an informal adviser to the farm community. In addition, he tried to instill in the rural populace a desire for culture.

Miyazawa had never possessed a strong constitution. He was ill on a number of occasions, and around 1928 unmistakable signs of tuberculosis began to appear. During the final years of his life, Miyazawa seems to have lost his creative urge—or, perhaps, sensing the imminence of death, he simply tried to rework the poems he had already written. The poet spent his last two years, from 1931 to 1933, as an invalid at the family home in Hanamaki. He and his father put aside their religious differences as death came closer for the son. Just before he died, on September 21, 1933, Miyazawa pointed toward a bookshelf and remarked that his unpublished manuscripts lying there had been produced out of a delusion.

ANALYSIS

Like the American poet and physician William Carlos Williams, Kenji Miyazawa absorbed himself in ceaseless service to other people, whether his students or the local farmers. Like the American, Miyazawa, too, would jot down poems in the spare moments available to him. Unlike Williams, however, Miyazawa never seems to have considered a poem finished. With only one volume of poems published in his lifetime, Miyazawa worked steadily at revising and reworking his drafts. Three different sets of poems are titled *Spring and Asura*, a fact which suggests a common ground for a number of seemingly disparate works.

SPRING AND ASURA

The first volume of *Spring and Asura* contains a poem similarly titled, a crucial poem which describes the poet caught up in intense visions of his own making. The persona narrates the vision from the viewpoint of an asura, that is, a being which ranks between humans and beasts in the six realms of existence in the Buddhist cosmology. (The six realms are devas, humans, asuras or demons, beasts, hungry ghosts, and dwellers in hell.) Despite the Buddhist references, the world of this asura is one of the poet's own making. A close study of Miyazawa's visionary poems by the American scholar Sarah Strong has uncovered a structure of levels—from a kind of Vacuum at the highest level (with the possibility of other worlds beyond) to the realm of the Western Marshes at the lowest. In between are various levels, with the Radiant Sea of Sky being the most complicated. The asura of Miyazawa's poems rushes about in this universe, finding "ecstasy" and "brightness" at the upper levels while encountering "unpleasantness" and "darkness" toward the bottom. This "structure," it must be noted, is not an immediately obvious feature of the poem. Indeed, to the untutored reader, many of Miyazawa's poems will seem mystifying and kaleidoscopic. For many, the effect of reading such works will surely be dizzying.

Miyazawa's visionary poems are difficult, but the poet has inserted passages which point the way to understanding. Preceding the Japanese text of "Spring and Asura," for example, he has entered these words in English which indicate the nature of the work to follow: "mental sketch modified." The initial volume of *Spring and Asura* also has an introductory poem or "Proem" preceding the title poem of the collection. In "Proem," Miyazawa includes lines and phrases that appear to point quite definitely at his intentions. For example, the poet says that the sketch to follow represents the workings of his imagination over the past twenty-two months. His way of putting the matter may be unusual (each piece on paper is a "chain of shadow and light," linked together "with mineral ink"), but the difficulty is more with the oddity of expression than with the meaning.

ELEGIES FOR TOSHIKO

Another set of poems by Miyazawa, the famous elegies composed upon the death of his sister Toshiko, also shows the imaginative energy of the poet. In this instance, however, the persona tends to stay within the normal and identifiable bounds of nature. The poet races outdoors to collect snow for comforting his dying sister or, after her death, wanders far beyond the region of the home in search of her whereabouts. The reader, however, knows exactly where the action is occurring. Bound to a specific and easily identifiable situation, these works seem more accessible than the aforementioned works from *Spring and Asura*.

Miyazawa's elegies on Toshiko exhibit an idiosyncrasy of vocabulary and image equal to that of *Spring and Asura*. In contrast to the thematic uniqueness of this visionary poem, however, the elegies actually fit into a venerable tradition of Japanese poetry. Indeed, the elegy goes back to almost the beginnings of Japanese poetry in the eighth century collection known as the *Manyōshū* (collection of myriad leaves; English translation, 1940). Admittedly, the grief expressed by Miyazawa over the death of his sister seems more private and concentrated than the emotion found in certain *Manyōshū* elegies—in the partly ritualistic works by Kakinomoto no Hitomaro, which mourn the deaths of the high nobility, to mention a celebrated example. At the same time, Miyazawa follows Hitomaro and other elegists of the *Manyōshū* in his search for a trace of the deceased in nature and in his refusal to be satisfied with encountering anything less than the actual person.

DIDACTIC POEMS

If Miyazawa had written only visionary and elegiac poems, he probably would not have attained popularity except as a writer of children's tales. At the very least, his frequent use of foreign terms, whether Chinese or Sanskrit, German or Esperanto, would have made the poetry difficult for the average reader. Aside from the poems in which Miyazawa addresses his private concerns, however, certain works reflect the desire to instruct the common people. In the most celebrated of these didactic works—invariably printed as recorded in a notebook, that is, in the *katakana* syllabary understandable even to a beginning schoolchild—the poet sketches a portrait of the ideal person he wishes to be. That person lives a life of extreme frugality and of selfless devotion to others. Like the bodhissattva of Buddhist doctrine, Miyazawa's ideal person is totally compassionate—caring for the sick, alleviating hunger, patching up quarrels, and carrying out other works of charity.

"DROUGHT AND ZAZEN"

Miyazawa was very much involved in the everyday life of the common people. This, in conjunction with his high ideals, occasionally elicited from him at least a partly satiric response. A work in this vein, titled "Kanbatsu to zazen" ("Drought and Zazen"), seems to belittle the Zen practice of meditation—either for ignoring a pressing practical problem or for deluding its adherents into a false sense of religion's sphere of efficacy. The poem begins by describing some frogs as a Zen chorus anxiously trying to solve those perplexing puzzles known as koans. After this comic opening, Miyazawa depicts himself intently calculating the sequential phases through which the rice seedlings must pass before ripening. The contrast between religious petition on one hand and this primitive sort of scientific calculation on the other is very striking.

LIGHTER POEMS

To claim that Miyazawa is satirizing Zen or Zazen in this poem might well be an overstatement. If satire is at work, it is certainly good-humored. In fact, the light-hearted side of the poet needs special emphasis in view of the fact that his central works, especially a poem such as "Spring and Asura" and the elegies on Toshiko, are so somber and brooding.

On occasion, the poet will enjoy a lighter moment by himself—when, for example, in a poem titled "Shigoto" ("Work") he momentarily worries about the manure he threw from a cart and left on a hillside. More often, he will jest with the farmers and peasants of the region. In one poem, he pokes fun at a farmer named Hosuke for getting upset when a manure-carrying horse proves unruly; in another instance, he counsels a hardworking farmer to leave off bundling rice at midnight for the sake of the weary wife who is doing her best to assist him. In most of these works, the poet seems a carefree observer and counselor. Since Miyazawa is normally a somber poet, though, and the farmers, even in his lighthearted poems, are always hard at work, one might surmise that the poet regarded humor principally as a way for the farmer to cope with his burdens.

In any event, this playful side of Miyazawa is present in many different poems. Sometimes, the poet simply observes an appealing scene. His poem on an Ayrshire bull is a good example. The animal, seen at night against the light of a pulp factory, enjoys itself by rubbing its horns in the grass and butting a fence. At other times, Miyazawa seems to play with language in an extravagant manner. A certain horse in another poem is said to "rot like a potato" and "feel the bright sun's juice." A second horse meets a dire fate by running into a high-voltage wire in its stable, the funeral taking place with the human mourners shedding "clods of tears" upon the "lolling head" of the dead animal. Hosuke's manure horse engages in some impressive acrobatics, rearing up with "scarlet eyes" on one occasion as if to "rake in blue velvet, the spring sky."

The poem on the Ayrshire bull depicts a casual encounter, the sort of event that happens often in Miyazawa's playful poems about people. Running into an acquaintance, the poet engages this other in a little drama. These poems, most of them brief, present simple emotions and often contain some deft humor. Certain works employ the same techniques but pursue more ambitious aims. Among them is a fascinating piece titled "Shita de wakareta sakki no hito" ("The Man I Parted from, Below"). The man in question is a somewhat disembodied image which remains in the memory of the poet after the meeting to which the title alludes has taken place. Defined mainly as a smoker, the man has been leading a horse somewhere, possibly to another group of horses visible in the distance. At least this thought occurs to the poet as he surveys the scene before him and composes his appreciation of it. Certain of Miyazawa's typical concerns manifest themselves in the course of the work—

the identification and naming of places, for example, or the sense of things happening in a kind of space-time continuum. Occasionally, an odd turn of phrase, too, reminds the reader of the poet's identity—the "aquamarine legs of winds," for example, or the highlands spread out "like ten or more playing cards." The horses on those highlands originally looked to the poet like "shining red ants." Such language, hardly startling to the Miyazawa aficionado, helps to elevate parts of the poem above mere plain description.

Indeed, "The Man I Parted from, Below" might seem tame alongside the coruscating images of "Spring and Asura" and the vibrating language of "Proem." The poem has certain compensations, however, even as a somewhat atypical work of Miyazawa. It shows that the poet could be at home in the calmer modes of Japanese lyricism, that he could deftly lay out a pattern of relationships involving himself, nature, and his fellowmen.

Having parted from the poet, the smoker is now observed together with his horse moving off toward the distant herd. Though abandoned by the smoker as surely as he had once been by Toshiko, Miyazawa does not seem bereft in this poem. All about him are the familiar mountains and valleys for which, at this moment, he feels an "oddly helpless love." All the men in the poem—the keeper of the distant herd, the man with his sole horse, and the poet, too—seem related to one another, and to the animals as well, by their mere presence in the scene. Slightly idiosyncratic, moderately optimistic, entirely understandable, "The Man I Parted from, Below" shows the poet submitting his vision to the requirements of realism on a human scale.

OTHER MAJOR WORKS

SHORT FICTION: *Ginga tetsudo no yoru*, 1922 (*Night of the Milky Way Railway*, 1991); *Chūmon no ōi ryōriten*, 1924; *Winds and Wildcat Places*, 1967; *Winds from Afar*, 1972; "*Night Train to the Stars and Other Stories*," 1987; *Once and Forever: The Tales of Kenji Miyazawa*, 1993.

MISCELLANEOUS: *Miyazawa Kenji zenshū*, 1967-1968 (12 volumes); *Kohon Miyazawa kenji zenshū*, 1973-1977 (15 volumes); *A Future of Ice: Poems and Stories of a Japanese Buddhist*, 1989.

BIBLIOGRAPHY

Bester, John. Foreword to *Once and Forever: The Tales of Kenji Miyazawa*. Tokyo: Kodansha International, 1993. The preeminent translator of Miyazawa provides insights into the poet and his poetics.

Keene, Donald. *World Within Walls*. New York: Holt, Rinehart and Winston, 1976. A continuation of Keene's history of Japanese literature until 1867, this volume offers useful analyses of poets and poetry in all styles.

Mori, Masaki. *Epic Grandeur: Toward a Comparative Poetics of the Epic*. Albany: State University of New York Press, 1997. Argues that the epic genre can be discerned in the twentieth century in works promoting peace as opposed to war. Considers Miyazawa's *Night on the Galaxy Railroad* as a "transitional epic."

Rimer, J. Thomas. *A Reader's Guide to Japanese Literature*. Tokyo: Kodansha International, 1988. With Keene's works, the best general guide to Japanese literature of the English-speaking audience.

Ueda, Makoto. *Modern Japanese Poets and the Nature of Literature*. Stanford, Calif.: Stanford University Press, 1983. Summaries of modern Japanese poets, including Miyazawa.

Watson, Burton. Introduction to *Spring and Asura*. Chicago: Chicago Review Press, 1973. An overview of Miyazawa's work.

James O'Brien;
bibliography updated by the editors

N. SCOTT MOMADAY

Born: Lawton, Oklahoma; February 27, 1934

PRINCIPAL POETRY

Angle of Geese and Other Poems, 1974
The Gourd Dancer, 1976

OTHER LITERARY FORMS

Although he prefers to call himself a poet, N. Scott Momaday is best known for his novel, *House Made of Dawn*, which won the Pulitzer Prize for fiction the year following its publication in 1968; a second novel, *The Ancient Child*, appeared in 1989. Other important prose works are autobiographical. *The Journey of Tai-me*, privately published in 1967, became part of *The Way to Rainy Mountain*, an exploration of personal and cultural history, which came out in 1969. A second autobiographical book, *The Names: A Memoir*, appeared in 1976. Momaday's weekly column for *Viva*, the Sunday magazine of the Santa Fe *New Mexican*, should also be included among autobiographical forms. The text that Momaday wrote to accompany David Muench's photographs in *Colorado: Summer, Fall, Winter, Spring* (1973) reasserts his persistent sense of affinity for particular landscapes. An early essay, "The Morality of Indian Hating" (*Ramparts*, 1964), reflects an interest that Momaday has continued to explore in essays, prefaces, and speeches: an examination of the Native American people in their relationship to themselves and to the invading European culture. Momaday's vision of nature owes much to his study of American Romantic literature.

ACHIEVEMENTS

N. Scott Momaday's most impressive achievement has been to demonstrate the possibility, viability, and value of Native American literature. When *House Made of Dawn* won the Pulitzer Prize in 1969, at least one critic presumed that its author was the first Native American to write a novel. Although that critic discovered that many novels had been published by Native Americans, their works remain neglected. Writers such as Oliver La Farge had adapted Amerindian themes, and from time to time collections of tales and of poems in translation made by ethnologists had appeared. It has been Momaday, however, who has brought impeccable academic as well as tribal credentials to the writer's task and produced a body of work that has merited critical praise and scholarly attention. Although his work is not popular with either the general public or the academic critics, both groups acknowledge its importance. The achievement is twofold. A specifically Native American tradition in American literature, exemplified by authors such as Gerald Vizenor, Leslie Silko, Louise Erdrich, and James Welch, is now recognized. Second, traditional native literary forms, as Momaday and other authors incorporate them into their writings, have greatly enriched the whole of American literature.

BIOGRAPHY

Six months after his birth in February, 1934, Navarre Scott Momaday was solemnly given the Kiowa name *Tsoai-talee* (Rock-Tree Boy) by Pohd-lohk, his step-grandfather. A year later, the Momadays moved from Oklahoma to New Mexico, and from 1936 to 1943 they lived in various places on the Navajo reservation: Shiprock, New Mexico, and Tuba City and Chinle, Arizona. Although there were stays in Oklahoma, Kentucky, and Louisiana, the reservation was home. After three years near the Army Air Base at Hobbs, New Mexico, the family moved in 1946 to the pueblo of Jemez, New Mexico, where Momaday's parents taught in the day school. Momaday lived at Jemez until his last year of high school, when he attended Augusta Military School in Virginia, from which he was graduated in 1952.

Studies occupied the next eleven years. After attending the University of New Mexico and Virginia Law School, Momaday was graduated from the University of New Mexico in 1958. Following a year of teaching at Dulce, on the Apache reservation, he entered Stanford University as a creative writing fellow. He received his Ph.D. degree in 1963, and in the following years taught at the University of California in Santa Barbara and in Berkeley, at Stanford, at New Mexico State University, and at the University of Arizona. It was in 1965, after the death of his grandmother, that Momaday made the journey north from Oklahoma to South Dakota that was to inspire *The Way to Rainy Mountain*. Shortly afterward, a Guggenheim award enabled him to spend a year at Amherst, Massachusetts, where he studied the work of Emily Dickinson. In 1969, the Gourd Dance Society of the Kiowas, to which his father had belonged, initiated Momaday as a member. Interrupting his years of teaching at American universities, Momaday spent several months in Moscow in 1975 as the first Fulbright lecturer in American literature in the Soviet Union. Momaday became a teacher of literature and creative writing at the University of Arizona, living in Tucson with his wife and daughters.

ANALYSIS

Two themes predominate in all of N. Scott Momaday's work, both poetry and prose. First, he celebrates material, sensory existence. The writer lovingly examines nature and the artifacts of human life, from the smallest creature to the most vast panorama. Whether describing a ghost town in Colorado or the coming of rain to a Southwestern desert, he is concerned to express the perceptual and emotional experience of physical life with eloquence and precision. The prose is often lush; the poetry can be spare, but exceedingly resonant.

A second preoccupation is with imagination, that power of mind that transforms and illumines the perceptible world and endows it with meaning. Momaday sees language as the primary vehicle for this transformation and affirms again and again the elemental importance of words. Collective imagination working upon natural existence creates culture, and in his examination of the contrasts and interweavings of the cultures of his experience, Momaday explores them as products of the human imagination. In an early essay, he speaks of two Kiowa legends, which he then shows to be emblematic of Ki-

N. Scott Momaday (© Thomas Victor)

owa thought and history and of the Kiowas' response to their history. In the same essay, he points to the metaphorical language of a non-Indian historian whose imagery betrays his fundamental bias and underlies a whole theory of civilization versus savagery.

Momaday's prose works—his essays, autobiographies, and fiction—treat the dynamic of the two elements—sensory life and the power of imagination—discursively and sometimes analytically. His poetry, on the other hand, focuses most often on the fundamental meeting of nature and imagination in the act of perception itself. This is a consummately introspective procedure, and the poetry collected in *The Gourd Dancer* demonstrates a loving attentiveness to the natural world as it impinges on the mind.

The number of Momaday's published poems is small—The Gourd Dancer contains fewer than fifty—and he has spoken of the slowness of writing. Nevertheless, the poems derive from a wide variety of traditions, from the eighteenth century epigram to Whitmanian self-celebration to Native American ceremonial lyrics. They consist of free verse, metrical verse, prose-poems, and syllabic verse. Throughout Momaday's poems, in those reflecting his time in the Soviet Union, astronauts' lunar explorations, a vision of planetary holocaust, reflections on landscape—and in his prose works as well—there is woven this theme of the relationship between material reality and the signifying imagination.

"BEFORE AN OLD PAINTING OF THE CRUCIFIXION"

The subtlest and most complex of Momaday's poems is probably that titled "Before an Old Painting of the Crucifixion." The poem is a meditation on being and nothingness. The painted scene evokes in the speaker an imaginative reconstruction of the death of Jesus as a historical event, and he muses on the despair that comes with his recognition of nonbeing. The painting also calls to mind the sea, and memory evokes a recent vision of nature. Nature, however, holds ultimate emptiness for the speaker, whose consciousness of death permits him to see the void beyond death and alienates him from the merely natural process of dying. No inherent significance resides in natural life, and mere imagination remains the only (largely unavailing) defense against the inconsequent passage of time.

It is a profoundly pessimistic poem, and one with a specifically European, post-Cartesian formulation. Momaday has a great admiration for Emily Dickinson, and he has quoted her poem beginning "Farther in summer than the birds" as a realization of this alienation from nature, along with the anguish that such knowledge brings. This perception of man and nature, he believes, is also contrary to the vision of nature in Native American thought. Traditional Indian philosophy regards man as part of nature, indivisible from its processes and kin to all its creatures.

The poem titled "Angle of Geese" draws implicitly on this cultural tradition. This poem had its genesis in a particular event, the death of a friend's child, and it also alludes to a geese-hunting trip Momaday went on as a young adolescent. The goose in the poem is not mere meaningless nature, however, but ancestral, and the poem implies a usable wisdom in nature and affirms human continuity with all forms of life.

The development of Momaday's use of traditional materials can be traced through the poems that appear in his novel, *House Made of Dawn*, and in the two autobiographical works, *The Way to Rainy Mountain* and *The Names*. In general, he moves from using traditional texts to inclusion of material learned at first hand to personal and family traditions and incorporation of general elements of form and content.

The Kiowas' sacred mountain (Devil's Tower in South Dakota) is named *tsoai*, "Rock-Tree," and *talee*, added to it, makes "Rock-Tree Boy," Momaday's Kiowa name. In *The Names*, Momaday extends the process of personal mythologizing begun in *The Way to Rainy Mountain* by inventing an episode in which his great-grandmother's husband, Pohd-lohk, presents him to the family, relates to him the history of the people, and finally gives him the name Tsoai-talee.

"THE DELIGHT SONG OF TSOAI-TALEE"

In "The Delight Song of Tsoai-talee," appearing in his first collection, *Angle of Geese and Other Poems*, Momaday draws on Indian traditions and on the nineteenth century American Romanticism that he has admired particularly in Frederick Goddard Tuckerman and Emily Dickinson. The first-person emphasis, as well as the catalog of items in the natural world, call to mind the second song that Benally sings in *House Made of Dawn*.

Unlike the Navajo song, however, in which each item has a specific meaning in a highly complex religious symbology, Momaday's poem reflects more than anything else Walt Whitman's expansive identification of his own persona with emotionally felt nature. *The Names* carries other echoes of this Whitmanian exuberance, notably in the epilogue with its imaginary journey across the land.

PLAINVIEW POEMS

The one poem that does appear in *The Names*, however, is written in pentameter couplets and echoes Wallace Stevens in its image and themes. This poem is printed in *The Gourd Dancer* as the first in a set of four poems on the imaginary "Plainview." Taken together, the four Plainview poems reflect the scope of Momaday's fascination with differing cultural perspectives and traditions. The punning title introduces the multiple themes of place and perception. Plainview is a location on the Midwestern landscape of which Momaday has written frequently with both familiarity and reverence. The vastness of space implies infinity at the same time that it emphasizes the particularity of objects perceived. Plainview also refers to sight, for whatever is in "plain view" should be visible, whole and unambiguous. In this sense the title is ironic, since in fact four Plainviews are given, each from a different perspective.

"Plainview: 1" is an explicit study in the act of perception. The speaker places himself in relation to the object of vision—the eleven magpies—and records the metamorphoses of shape and light he observes as wind and clouds pass over the grass. The same sense of underlying emptiness prevails here as in the earlier poem, "Before an Old Painting of the Crucifixion," and finally the speaker decides that the birds themselves are an illusion. The poem suggests a theme elaborated in the other three: that landscape itself is the product of imagination.

"Plainview: 2" makes use of specifically Native American themes and forms. The speaker's vision of the old Indian, drunk and pathetic, stands in contrast to the old man's nostalgic vision of his horse. The incantatory repetition and the celebration of the horse reflect native tradition. This version of what is in "plain view" stresses the irony of that title in the disparity between the visibly vulgar and the invisible beauty that lives in imagination and recollection.

"Plainview: 3" is simply a triple set of metaphors comparing the rising sun with a string of glass beads, a drift of pollen, and a prairie fire. Once again the reader is asked to examine the process of perception, this time in the comparison of visual images. The brief poem recalls Imagist works.

Finally, "Plainview: 4" mixes modes, oral and written, prose and poetry. History comes to life in the landscape as the speaker muses on the woman he often dreamed of, a white woman who had been a Kiowa captive. The haunting excerpts from traditional frontier ballads, heard only in the mind's ear as the speaker contemplates the abandoned house, bear out Momaday's comments on the importance of oral tradition to cultural continuity. The poem invokes history and tragedy, but finally both are as evanescent as the magpies in the first poem of the set. Only the wind whistles through the empty house.

THE WAY TO RAINY MOUNTAIN

The Way to Rainy Mountain is more complex than *The Names*, more highly wrought, less conventionally autobiographical. In structure and theme it fuses most successfully the introspective European viewpoint and the communal vision of the oral tradition. Momaday's recollections and anecdotes begin to take their place in legend and lore, and history metamorphoses into myth. He frames his prose narratives with two poems, "Headwaters" and "Rainy Mountain Cemetery," which begin and end the book.

The two poems use conventional meter and rhyme yet echo the traditional Kiowa materials as Momaday interprets them in the text. In "Headwaters" the speaker stands at noon on the plains, meditating on the hidden vitality and even violence immanent in the silent landscape. Only the moss on the hollow log suggests the marshland that is there and the waters swelling out of the land. The waters themselves point to a deeper, archaic source of primitive life forces, as the author's exploration in the chapters that follow takes him to the sources of his family, his people, and his definition of human life. The poem's title refers to one of the geographical objects of Momaday's journey—the ancestral home of the Kiowas at the headwaters of the Yellowstone River. The image of the insect at the mouth of the log recalls the Kiowa creation myth of the people's

emergence through a hollow log; this image of a figure within a circle reappears at the end of the introduction in Momaday's recollection of the sight of a cricket
outlined against the moon "like a fossil" and immediately following the drawing by Momaday's father, Al
Momaday. The image is a talisman for the centripetal
nature of the journey as one that reaches within for self-
knowledge.

"Rainy Mountain Cemetery" the poem that closes
the book, refers to both the starting point and the goal
of Momaday's journey. The pilgrimage began with
Momaday's visit to his grandmother's grave, where he
was inspired to visit the places that she had seen more
perfectly in the mind's eye, as she recollected the historical migration of the Kiowa people. The poem is the
speaker's graveside meditation on her, although, in keeping with Kiowa tradition, her name remains unspoken.
The speaker reflects on the silence and, implicitly, on the
nothingness which is all that remains after death. The
name on the stone, he says, is no more than the stone's
name, and the word "stone" ends both the first and last
lines of the poem, setting an off-rhyme against the first
and third lines of the second stanza. The only unrhymed
line ends in the word "name." The poem reiterates
Momaday's preoccupation with the power of language,
stated most explicitly in the often-quoted passage from
section VIII in which he asserts the creative power of
language and links it to Kiowa traditions of naming. In
"Rainy Mountain Cemetery," then, silence is nonexis-
tence, and the name on the tombstone nothing but a
shadow—the absence of light. The poem concludes the
metamorphosis that the book has both documented and
achieved: The physical has been transformed into myth.
The physical world, vibrant on every page, is transformed to words and lives beyond itself in the imagination. The same is true for the life of the people and that
of the individual. This, Momaday says, is the human
miracle: the creation of self through imagination by
means of words.

THE VISUAL ARTS

Between the publication of *The Names* in 1976
and the appearance of his second novel, *The Ancient
Child*, in 1989, Momaday was in much demand as
a lecturer and interview subject. During the period
he published several important essays, including an

introduction to Native American literature for a new
literary history of the United States. Although he continued to write poetry, no new collections were published.

At this time, Momaday worked more intensively on
another interest, graphic arts, exhibiting prints, drawings, and paintings in several shows. Momaday's work
in visual arts intersects with his sense of language and
poetry, as the title of one essay, "Landscape with Words
in the Foreground," suggests. A series of drawings of
shields embodies the connection. The shield motif
recalls the cover design that Al Momaday, the poet's
father, made for *The Way to Rainy Mountain*. Momaday's drawings include words, usually texts from his
prose poems or retellings of traditional stories, as elements in the graphic presentation. Two of these shield
pictures are reproduced in Charles Woodard's *Ancestral Voice: Conversations with N. Scott Momaday* (1989).
The move toward mixing and integrating visual and
verbal modes began in Momaday's publications with
his drawings for *The Gourd Dancer*; the shield series emphasizes the modernist tendency in Momaday's
work that was implicit earlier in the collage structure and mixed media of *The Way to Rainy Mountain*.
The shield drawings combining picture and text as a
graphic element suggest the work of modernists such
as Pablo Picasso and the Italian Futurists, whose work,
like Momaday's, also grew out of the Symbolist and
post-Symbolist tradition of nineteenth century Romanticism.

Fourteen years in the making, Momaday's second
novel, *The Ancient Child*, reflects his preoccupation
with his dual creative identity as poet and painter. The
novel's protagonist, Locke Setman, is an accomplished,
successful painter, a cosmopolitan man of the world at
home in the great cities of Europe and America. But he
is dissatisfied, suffering from a malaise of the spirit. His
spiritual guide and mentor is Grey, a young Navajo
woman who resembles Emily Dickinson (she wears
white in her dreams and spends much time putting together books of her poems). Both Grey and Locke
Setman are alter egos for Momaday, with clear parallels
in his own life and intellectual development: The poems
Grey writes are Momaday's poems from *The Gourd
Dancer*. The ending of this uneven novel is extremely

ambiguous: The protagonist, like his counterpart, the bear-boy of the ancient legend, leaves the articulate, language-centered life of human beings. His eventual return is uncertain.

IN THE BEAR'S HOUSE

Momaday's 1999 mixed-media book, *In the Bear's House*, weds all of his artistic interests, combining painting, poetry, prose, and an extended dramatic dialogue between Yahweh (or "Big Mystery") and Urset, the Native American ur-bear. All explore aspects of Kiowa bear mythology, a theme long dear to Momaday's heart. Momaday uses the figure of the bear as a vehicle to investigate the interrelationship of wildness and humanity, the tensions of hunter and hunted, the seamlessness of dreaming and storytelling. The strength of this work may lie in Momaday's organization around one powerful theme approached through a variety of artistic genres rather than limiting himself to a single medium—prose, poetry, or paint.

OTHER MAJOR WORKS

LONG FICTION: *House Made of Dawn*, 1968; *The Ancient Child*, 1989.

NONFICTION: "The Morality of Indian Hating," 1964; *The Journey of Tai-me*, 1967 (memoir; revised as *The Way to Rainy Mountain*, 1969); "The Man Made of Words," 1970; *Colorado: Summer, Fall, Winter, Spring*, 1973 (with David Muench); *The Names: A Memoir*, 1976; *Ancestral Voice: Conversations with N. Scott Momaday*, 1989 (with Charles L. Woodard).

CHILDREN'S LITERATURE: *Circle of Wonder: A Native American Christmas Story*, 1994.

EDITED TEXT: *The Complete Poems of Frederick Goddard Tuckerman*, 1965.

MISCELLANEOUS: *In the Presence of the Sun: Stories and Poems, 1961-1991*, 1992; *The Man Made of Words: Essays, Stories, and Passages*, 1998; *In the Bear's House*, 1999.

BIBLIOGRAPHY

Isernhagen, Hartwig. *Momaday, Vizenor, Armstrong: Conversations on American Indian Writing*. Norman: University of Oklahoma Press, 1999. The interviews that are the basis of this book were conducted during the summer of 1994. Isernhagen questions the three authors about their roles as creators, critics, and mentors and balances "interculturality" with traditions unique to Native American cultures. He includes the full list of his question set in a separate section.

Mason, Kenneth C. *Ancestral Voice: Conversations with N. Scott Momaday*. Interviews by Charles L. Woodard. Lincoln: University of Nebraska Press, 1989. The longest published interview with Momaday, the book transcribes hours of conversation in 1986-1987. Topics range from Momaday's sense of "bear power" and a "blood knowledge" of prehistoric migrations to his appreciation for Shakespeare and Dickinson to his sojourns in the Soviet Union. Included are reproductions of twenty-three of Momaday's prints and drawings.

_____. "Beautyway: The Poetry of N. Scott Momaday." *South Dakota Review* 18, no. 2 (1980): 61-83. Mason treats *The Gourd Dancer* as a unified work; he traces thematic progression through the three parts and offers close readings of poems in each section.

_____. *Conversations with N. Scott Momaday*. Edited by Matthias Schubnell. Jackson: University Press of Mississippi, 1997. A collection of interviews from 1970 to 1993 containing Momaday's views on the place of the Indian in American literature and society, his theory of language and the imagination, the influences on his artistic and academic development, and his comments on specific works he has written.

Roemer, Kenneth J. *Approaches to Teaching "The Way to Rainy Mountain."* New York: Modern Language Association, 1990. The brief first part introduces a bibliography/filmography on Momaday of special use to teachers. The second, major portion collects seventeen essays dealing with background contexts, forms and themes, and teaching the book in writing and in literature courses. An interview with a Kiowa elder closes the discussions.

Scarberry-Garcia, Susan. *Landmarks of Healing: A Study of "House Made of Dawn."* Albuquerque: University of New Mexico Press, 1990. This first monograph on *House Made of Dawn* examines analogues and sources in published translations and studies of Navajo chants and myths.

Schubnell, Matthias. *N. Scott Momaday: The Cultural and Literary Background.* Norman: University of Oklahoma Press, 1985. A comprehensive account of Momaday's life and work to 1985, this study focuses particularly on Momaday's intellectual debt to European traditions including Romanticism and symbolism. The book includes an extensive bibliography and a long chapter on the poetry.

Trimble, Martha Scott. *N. Scott Momaday.* Boise, Idaho: Boise State College, 1973. The first monograph on Momaday and his work, this pamphlet introduces major themes through publication of *The Way to Rainy Mountain* and *Angle of Geese and Other Poems.*

Velie, Alan R. *Four American Indian Literary Masters.* Norman: University of Oklahoma Press, 1982. The chapter on Momaday's poetry contains detailed explication of "Angle of Geese," "The Bear," "Buteo Regalis," as well as discussion of "Before an Old Painting of the Crucifixion" and "The Fear of Bo-Talee." Velie concentrates on post-Symbolist theory and the influence of Yvor Winters and Frederick Goddard Tuckerman.

Helen Jaskoski,
updated by Leslie Ellen Jones

JOHN MONTAGUE

Born: Brooklyn, New York; February 28, 1929

PRINCIPAL POETRY

Forms of Exile, 1958
Poisoned Lands and Other Poems, 1961 (revised as *Poisoned Lands,* 1977)
A Chosen Light, 1967
Tides, 1970
The Rough Field, 1972, revised 1989
A Slow Dance, 1975
The Great Cloak, 1978
Selected Poems, 1982
The Dead Kingdom, 1984
Mount Eagle, 1988
New Selected Poems, 1989
About Love, 1993
Time in Armagh, 1993
Collected Poems, 1995
Chain Letter, 1997
Smashing the Piano, 1999

OTHER LITERARY FORMS

John Montague has published short stories, a novella, a memoir, a collection of his essays, several volumes of poems translated into English (some in collaboration with others), and several anthologies of Irish literature.

ACHIEVEMENTS

John Montague is one of the preeminent poets writing in English in the past several decades, perhaps best known for his poems about the Troubles (past and present) in Ireland and about personal relationships. Among his many awards and prizes are the Butler and O'Shaughnessy Awards, from the Irish American Cultural Institute; the Bartlett Award from the Poetry Society of Great Britain; a Guggenheim Fellowship; the Hughes Award; the American Ireland Fund Literary Award; honorary degrees from the State University of New York and University College, Cork; and a Festschrift, *Hill Field,* in honor of his sixtieth birthday. A signal honor was being named, and serving as, the first Ireland Professor of Poetry (1998-2001).

BIOGRAPHY

John Patrick Montague was born in Brooklyn of Irish parents in 1929. His father, James Terence Montague, had gone there for employment in 1925, joining a brother who ran a speakeasy. James's wife, Mary (Molly) Carney, and their two sons joined him in 1928; John, the third son, was produced by this reunion. In 1933 the three brothers were sent to County Tyrone in Northern Ireland, the older two moving in with Carney relatives in Fintona, the youngest staying with two unmarried Montague aunts in Garvaghey. John's mother returned to Ireland in 1936, settling in Fintona (his father did not return until 1952).

Montague was reared apart from his mother and brothers, though he spent some holidays with them. He excelled at local schools, developed a stammer that would persist through his life, and won a scholarship to a boarding school in Armagh. He spent summer holidays during World War II with cousins in the South of Ireland. Having enrolled at University College, Dublin, he received a B.A. in history and English in 1949. He traveled in Austria, Italy, and France; in 1952 he received his M.A. in Anglo-Irish literature.

Montague traveled to the United States in 1953, spending a year at Yale University, a summer at Indiana University, and a year in the University of Iowa Writers' Workshop, where he received a master of fine arts degree in 1955. There he met Madeleine de Brauer, his future first wife. They were married in her native France before returning to Dublin in 1956.

He worked for the Irish tourist board for three years (1956-1959), became associated with Liam Miller's Dolmen Press, helped found Claddagh Records, and published his first book of poems before moving to Paris in 1961, where for two years he was correspondent for the *Irish Times*. He lived in Paris during most of the 1960's, but also in the United States (teaching during 1964-1965 at the University of California, Berkeley) and Ireland. His first marriage ended in divorce; in 1972 he was married to Evelyn Robson, like his first wife a French woman.

They settled in Cork, where Montague taught at University College, Cork (1972-1988) and where they reared their daughters, Oonagh (born 1973) and Sibyl (born 1979). For much of the 1990's Montague spent a semester each year in residence as distinguished professor in the New York State Writers Institute at Albany. He separated from his second wife. He and his new partner, American-born novelist Elizabeth Wassell, made their home at Ballydehob, County Cork, Ireland.

ANALYSIS

The main subjects of John Montague's poetry are Ireland, his family, and love. He writes about people and places he knew growing up in County Tyrone, about sectarian strife in Ulster and its historical sources, and about relatives, especially his parents, seeking to understand them and his relationships with them. He has examined love from all angles: from outside and within, as

desired and feared, found and lost, remembered in joy and pain.

FORMS OF EXILE

If Ireland, family, and love are Montague's main subjects, his main theme is loss, a theme clearly seen in his poems about exile, a topic he has explored thoroughly. The title of his first book of poems, *Forms of Exile*, points to this preoccupation. "Emigrants," the shortest of its poems, confronts a major fact of Irish life since the 1840's: economic exile. Its "sad faced" subjects could be Montague's own parents, bound for Brooklyn.

"Soliloquy on a Southern Strand" looks at another sort of exile. After many years in Australia, an Irish priest reflects disconsolately on what has become of his life. He feels cut off from Ireland, alienated from the young people around him on the beach, discouraged about his vocation. In "A Footnote on Monasticism: Dingle Peninsula," Montague thinks about "the hermits, lonely dispossessed ones," who once lived on the peninsula. He feels a degree of kinship with these "people

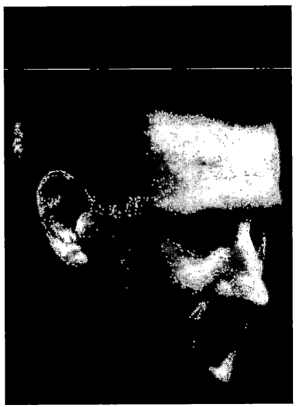

John Montague (© John Vickers)

hurt into solitude/ By loss of love." Dispossession, another form of exile, and "loss of love" appear in this early poem to be equivalent.

More than half the poems in *Forms of Exile* allude to religious belief and practice, a subject seldom mentioned in Montague's later books. Clearly, despite his sympathy for the Irish priest in Australian exile and his qualified empathy with the Dingle hermits, Montague is distancing himself from the more parochial aspects of Irish Catholicism. "Rome, Anno Santo" looks unsympathetically at "the ignorant Irish on pilgrimage." "Incantation in Time of Peace" expresses doubt whether prayer can prevent the coming of "a yet more ominous day" in Ireland.

"Cultural Center" (later retitled "Musée Imaginaire") contemplates artworks from different cultures in a museum, each representing a civilization's values. Among them, commanding the speaker's attention and that of a nun in the museum, is a "minatory" Catalan crucifix. The "rigid figure" on the cross, its "sharp body twisted all awry," bespeaks a religion harsh but undeniably real. At the nun's waist swings a miniature crucifix: "a minute harmless god of silver plate," as "inoffensive . . . and mild" as the nun herself. Given these "conflicting modes" of imaging Catholic Christianity, clearly Montague prefers the strength and authenticity of the "lean, accusing Catalan crucifix"; yet his misgivings about the values it represents are obvious.

Although love would develop into one of Montague's chief subjects, there is more fear than love in *Forms of Exile*. When love does appear, it is merely observed, not actually experienced: in "Irish Street Scene, with Lovers," for example, and "Song of the Lonely Bachelor."

"The Sean Bhean Vocht" introduces an old woman who, symbolically, is Ireland personified, a repository of "local history" and "racial memory." "As a child I was frightened by her," Montague says, but it is not entirely clear what has replaced fear: fascination, respect, perhaps a hint of affection. Montague's ambiguity in this regard suggests that he has only begun to work through his feelings toward Ireland.

POISONED LANDS AND OTHER POEMS

Poisoned Lands and Other Poems overlaps with *Forms of Exile:* 40 percent of its poems appeared in the earlier

book. In its new poems, Montague continues to write about Ireland, reflecting on his relation to it and its relation to the world. Several of these poems attempt to shape and understand childhood memories. "The Water Carrier" describes the chore of fetching water with precisely rendered details, then stops short. "Recovering the scene," Montague says, "I had hoped to stylize it,/ Like the portrait of an Egyptian water-carrier:/ Yet halt, entranced by slight but memoried life." Realizing that he cannot be that detached from memory, he concludes,

> I sometimes come to take the water there,
> Not as return or refuge, but some pure thing,
> Some living source, half-imagined and half-real
>
> Pulses in the fictive water that I feel.

Memory itself is that "fictive water," a resource on which to draw.

"Like Dolmens Round my Childhood, the Old People" evokes the lives of country neighbors. As megalithic structures dot the Irish countryside, mysterious and yet matter-of-factly present, so these figures populate the landscape of the poet's memory. "For years they trespassed on my dreams," he says, "until once, in a standing circle of stones,/ I felt their shadow pass// Into that dark permanence of ancient forms." He has commemorated the old people without sentimentality and made peace with their memories.

The outside world began to impinge on his local world when he was a schoolboy, as he recalls in "Auschwitz, Mon Amour" (later retitled "A Welcoming Party"). Newsreel images of concentration-camp survivors brought home to him the irrelevance of Ireland's "parochial brand of innocence." Having learned something about evil in the wider world, he has yet to comprehend what he has seen. For now, there is nothing to do but return to school and toss a football. The "Irish dimension" of his childhood, he says, came from being "always at the periphery of incident."

In poems such as "Auschwitz, Mon Amour" and the sarcastic "Regionalism, or Portrait of the Artist as a Model Farmer," Montague's disaffection with Irish provincialism gives him an exile's sensibility, in the tradition of one of his masters, James Joyce. "Prodigal Son" reflects on his annual visits to Ulster: It is a nice place to visit, but he would not want to live there. (Montague is well aware that the self-selected exile of the artist has little in common with exile imposed by economic circumstance, such as he alludes to in the opening poem of *Poisoned Lands and Other Poems*, "Murphy in Manchester.")

Within the new poems in this collection, the subject of religion all but disappears. Love is alluded to occasionally, mostly in passing; yet the volume does include Montague's first full-fledged love poem, "Pastorals." It is a dialogue between two lovers, a cynic who sees love as but the "movement of unlawful limbs/ In a marriage of two whims" and an idealist who views it as a sanctuary where "hearts long bruised . . . can trace/ Redeeming patterns of experience."

A CHOSEN LIGHT

The first section of *A Chosen Light* is a gathering of love poems. "Country Matters" and "Virgo Hibernica" recall love unspoken; the inhibiting shyness of adolescence. The latter acknowledges "the gravitational pull/ of love," but the former concludes that "the word of love is/ Hardest to say."

"All Legendary Obstacles" memorializes the reunion of separated lovers. A number of subsequent poems in the section draw upon less ecstatic (less "legendary") experiences, including the strains within a marriage. "Loving Reflections," for example, moves in its three parts from tenderness to an angry argument to grim determination to hold on to the relationship.

Montague begins to explore family connections seriously in *A Chosen Light*, particularly in "The Country Fiddler" and "The Cage." His uncle and godfather John Montague, for whom he was named, had been a country fiddler, but his "rural art [was] silenced in the discord of Brooklyn," and he died in American exile. His nephew, born there, became his uncle's "unexpected successor" when sent to Ireland at age four to live. Montague also sees his craft, poetry, as "succession" to his uncle's "rural craft" of music.

In "The Cage" Montague calls his father "the least happy/ man I have known," who drank himself to "brute oblivion." When he finally returned to Ireland in 1952, after twenty-seven years in Brooklyn, he and his son were briefly reunited; by then, however, the son was but an occasional visitor to Tyrone and would soon head for the United States himself. Mingled in the poem are Montague's conflicting feelings toward his father: pity, revulsion, respect, affection.

"The Road's End" grew out of one of Montague's visits home. He retraces childhood steps, noting changes: overgrown thorns, a disused well, abandoned homes. "Like shards/ Of a lost culture," he says, "the slopes/ Are strewn with cabins, emptied/ In my lifetime." His sense of loss is strong.

TIDES

In *Tides*, only two poems allude to Montague's blood kin, "Last Journey" and "Omagh Hospital," and both move from their specific subjects to the larger world of Northern Ireland. The former is subtitled "i.m. James Montague," but salutes Ulster's, as well as his father's, memory, citing the "placenames that sigh/ like a pressed melodeon/ across this forgotten/ Northern landscape." In "Omagh Hospital," Montague's dying Aunt Brigid pleads to be taken home, but he pictures her house, "shaken by traffic/ until a fault runs/ from roof to base." The house that has become uninhabitable is not only the family home but the whole province, rent by a grievous "fault."

Tides has an increased proportion, and a stunning variety, of love poems. The first two of the book's five sections concentrate on the darker side of love. "Premonition" and "The Pale Light" provide horrific, nightmare images. "Summer Storm" scales down to the more prosaic hell of a couple arguing, Montague returning here to his theme of love gone sour. "Special Delivery," in which "the worm of delight/ . . . turns to/ feed upon itself," reinforces this theme. The two poems in these sections that actually celebrate love are those that, at first glance, might seem least capable of doing so: "The Wild Dog Rose" and "The Hag of Beare." "The Wild Dog Rose" focuses on a haggish woman who has lived a solitary life of few expectations and fewer pleasures. Her one encounter with a man was a terrifying attempted rape. Yet love is not absent from this apparently loveless life: The poem ends with a glimpse of transcendent, absolutely selfless love. The poem elicits not pity for the old woman but admiration for her great heart. In "The Hag of Beare," another crone comes to a higher love, at the end of a life utterly different from that briefly sketched in "The Wild Dog Rose." Having known all fleshly pleasures, now denied by age and infirmity, the

Hag of Beare expresses her willingness to welcome "the Son of Mary," like so many men before, "under my roof-tree."

The middle section of *Tides* introduces a frankly erotic note into Montague's love poetry. "A Dream of July" celebrates "Ceres, corn goddess," whose "abundant body is/ Compounded of honey/ & gold," and similar imagery of honey and gold can be found in "The Same Gesture" and "Love, a Greeting" (as earlier it was found in "Virgo Hibernica"). Love here is primarily physical, exuberant, largely unassociated with responsibilities, and—as in the title poem, "Tracks"—without commitment.

THE ROUGH FIELD

Poems in Montague's first two books of poems are not randomly arranged, but a greater degree of order obtains in books three and four, which group poems into thematically related sections. Moreover, in *Tides*, the fourth book, sea imagery, often metaphorical, helps unify the volume as a whole. Montague's fifth book, *The Rough Field*, is more highly organized still. Though it contains a number of individual poems capable of standing on their own (eight appeared in previous Montague books), in fact it is one long poem composed of many parts.

Montague began work on *The Rough Field* in the early 1960's, concluding it a decade later, after a new outbreak of sectarian violence struck Ulster. Montague says that he began with "a kind of vision . . . of my home area, the unhappiness of its historical destiny." Violent confrontations in Belfast and Derry gave added point to the project and contributed materials that Montague incorporated into the completed work: "the emerging order/ of the poem invaded," as he says in part 9, "by cries, protestations/ a people's pain."

"Rough Field" translates the name of the townland, Garvaghey, where Montague grew up: "Rough Field in the Gaelic and rightly named/ . . . Harsh landscape that haunts me." He weaves together family stories, incidents from his childhood, and episodes from Irish history since the sixteenth century. The book is populated by members of his family, people from Tyrone whom he knew growing up, and historical figures from Hugh O'Neill (1545-1616) to Bernadette Devlin (born 1947). It evokes the landscape and dwells on the place-names

of Tyrone, and of Ulster in general, sites of ancient or recent historical significance. Interspersed among Montague's poems, often with ironic effect, are a variety of "found" texts: excerpts from historical documents, memoirs, letters, newspapers, and the like. The "conversation" among the various voices in *The Rough Field* (Montague's several voices and these "found" voices) contributes to the book's multilayered complexity.

Its complexity notwithstanding, the book is unified by its steady focus on one place (and the continuity of its problems) as well as by recurring images—the rough field, houses, swans—and recurring concerns: home, inheritance, exile; memory; dreams; loneliness; things lost; things broken, shaken, scattered, shattered, including buildings, families, lives, dreams, tradition, a culture, a province. *The Rough Field* is further unified by successfully linking the personal, the familial, the regional, the national, and the global, Montague's Garvaghey becoming a microcosm of "the rough field/ of the universe." Finally, it is unified by successfully linking past and present: generation joined to generation ("This bitterness/ I inherit from my father"), century to century (contemporary exile in the United States and the seventeenth century "Flight of the Earls"). *The Rough Field*, treating a serious theme with artistry and authority, is widely considered Montague's greatest work.

A SLOW DANCE

A Slow Dance is a rich mixture, its five sections linked by recurring images: warmth and cold and, especially, dance. The slow dance, Montague has said, is the "dance of death and life," and this volume reveals a heightened sense of both mortality and vitality.

Section 1 takes the reader "back to our origins"—individually to the womb, collectively to primordial cave—and there the dance of life and death begins. "The humid pull/ of the earth" is immediate; the dance begins "in . . . isolation" but ends in complete identification with the natural world, human "breath mingling with the exhalations of the earth." The section collapses time and dissolves distinctions between civilizations, so that legendary poet-king Sweeny coexists with Saint Patrick, and (in "For the Hillmother") the Christian Litany of the Blessed Virgin provides the form for a pagan invocation to nature as the source of life. The section is about life, with death only hinted at.

Section 2 opens with a birth, but in "Courtyard in Winter," the poet meditates on the suicide of a friend. Montague grieves that he could not "ease the single hurt/ That edged her towards her death," but he does not give in to guilt or despair. Rather, "I still affirm/ That nothing dies, that even from/ Such bitter failure memory grows." Much of the rest of the section consists of lyrical evocations of nature, of which "Windharp" is perhaps the best known.

The opening section collapses time and telescopes civilizations in the service of life; the third does the same in the service of death, "The Cave of Night" substituting for the womb/cave. Ancient Celtic blood sacrifice is juxtaposed to armed struggle in Belfast. Killing with sword and rifle, the slaughtering of a pig in a farmyard and of soldiers on a battlefield, are essentially the same in this hellish section, ruled over by the "Black Widow goddess." The section ends, fittingly, with a poem called "Coldness."

The reader turns with relief in the fourth section to the warmer world of family. Problems here—parents unable to live together, a child denied "the warm circle" of its mother's company—are problems that can be comprehended, sometimes even dealt with. Loneliness is here (it is never far in Montague's poetry), but "human warmth" is, too.

The final section of *A Slow Dance* is Montague's eulogy for his friend the composer Séan Ó Riada. The "slowly failing fire" dies out, and the book ends with a cry of anguish:

> a lament so total
> it mourns no one
> but the globe itself
> turning in the endless halls
>
> of space.

The book, which begins by celebrating "The whole world/ turning in wet/ and silence," thus ends lamenting the same turning world. The "globe itself/ turning" enacts the "slow dance" of life and death.

THE GREAT CLOAK

The Great Cloak focuses on love—no poems here are about growing up, family, or Ireland. Montague examines the breakup of one marriage, the beginning of

another, and the interval between. The poems are short (averaging about half the length of those in *A Slow Dance*), uncomplicated, accessible. Their imagery is predominantly visual (attentive to the play of light and shadow) and tactile (hands touching, caressing).

In the first section, sexual encounters are brief respites from loneliness. Loneliness and worse—nothingness, the void—seem implicit in the ominous image that closes the section: "profound night/ like a black swan/ goes pluming past."

The second section, less self-absorbed, sadly sifts through the fragments of a broken marriage. It is an inventory of losses. "Darkness" finds Montague trying to understand his estranged wife's feelings, and in four other poems he goes so far as to speak with her voice: "I sing your pain/ as best I can," he says, in his own voice. The longest and best poem in the book, "Herbert Street Revisited," returns to the Dublin street where, newly wed, Montague and his wife made their first home. It is a generous-spirited celebration of the love they shared.

"Anchor," title of the last section, expresses a wish; the new relationship Montague explores here seems less fixed, less certain, than the title suggests. "Walking Late," for example, ends with the couple circling "uncertainly/ towards a home." Only in "Protest," which records the birth of their child, and the handful of poems that follow it does the tone of voice become confident enough to warrant the section's title.

SELECTED POEMS

Montague's *Selected Poems* draws from all of his previous books of poems and includes a few that would appear later in *The Dead Kingdom* or *Mount Eagle*. Some poems, particularly early ones, show substantive revisions, and the order in which they appear is not always that of the earlier books.

THE DEAD KINGDOM

Like *The Rough Field*, *The Dead Kingdom* is a single long poem—an arrangement of shorter poems, ten of which appeared in previous books. Unlike *The Rough Field*, *The Dead Kingdom* has a narrative line. It begins when news arrives in Cork that Montague's mother has died. "The 'thread' or plot," Montague has written, "is the long drive North" to attend her funeral.

The drive north takes Montague through the Midlands, calling up bitter-sweet memories of summers in

County Longford. More than half the poems in the book's first two (of five) sections connect with "this neutral realm." "Abbeylara" affectionately recalls summers with Carney relatives, but now they are dead, their house abandoned, their carefully tended garden gone wild. The small piece of land to which they gave order is "reverting to first chaos/ as if they had never been."

Two poems in section 1 meditate on transience itself. In "Process," "time's gullet devouring" all that people value becomes an abyss of "fuming oblivion," across which one can but cast "swaying ropeladders" such as "love or friendship,/ an absorbing discipline." "Gone" recalls things great and small that have been "hustled into oblivion" and stoically salutes "the goddess Mutability,/ dark Lady of Process,/ our devouring Queen." Terms such as "chaos," "oblivion," and "the void" spatter the first half of the book, and the metaphor of "time's gullet" and the "devouring Queen" is reinforced by multiple references to appetite, feeding, and digestive organs.

In section 3, the border of Northern Ireland revives thoughts of violent conflicts there. Weather and mood alike turn cold and dark as the poet returns to the "bloody ground" where he was raised. More despairing than in *The Rough Field*, Montague can but "sing a song for the broken/ towns of old Tyrone" and "for the people,/ so grimly holding on." He calls his wish for "an end to sectarianism" a "forlorn hope."

As in *A Slow Dance*, the almost unrelieved gloom of section 3 gives way to the warmer (even when painful) images of family in section 4. In a series of flashbacks Montague reviews his parents' lives, together and apart (a photograph of the young couple introduces the section).

Music has woven its way through all Montague's books, but none of them is as filled with music as *The Dead Kingdom*, which invokes everything from popular songs ("Kathleen Mavourneen," "Paddy Reilly") to Mary Mulvey's music box and "the sound/ of bells in monastic/ sites." Montague himself calls for song in several poems (for example, "sing a song for/ things that are gone"). The principal singer, however, is his father, teaching his son the words to "Ragtime Cowboy Joe"; singing "Molly Bawn" to his own Molly, after his long-delayed return to Ireland; lending his "broken tenor" to

Christmas carols in Midnight Mass. Montague understands that, back in Brooklyn, his "father's songs/ couldn't sweeten the lack of money" that had contributed to the family's fragmentation. Yet Montague recognizes that "the healing harmony/ of music" had been his father's rope ladder across oblivion, and he regrets that his mother's funeral is "without music or song" to "ease the living" and "sweeten our burden."

Montague continues to examine the subject of exile in its various forms, under its various names: "emigration," "transportation," "diaspora," "dispossession." At last, his mother dead, he brings himself to mention the form of exile he himself has experienced most painfully: being rejected by his mother in childhood. "You gave me away," he says to her posthumously ("The Locket"), "to be fostered/ in Garvaghey" ("A Muddy Cup"), "to be fostered/ wherever charity could afford." This, he says, was the "primal hurt," to be "an unwanted child": "All roads wind backwards to it" ("A Flowering Absence").

"It is hard to work so close to the bone," Montague has said of these poems about his mother. After a lifetime of excavating the strata of his life, Montague has finally reached emotional bedrock. To have been "fostered" is to have been exiled most radically. Yet "The Locket," "a last song/ for the lady who has gone," ends with a "mysterious blessing": The poet learns, after his mother's death, that the locket she had always worn contained an old photograph of "a child in Brooklyn."

His responsibilities in Tyrone finished, Montague turns his attention to the living woman in his life

> I place my hopes
> beside yours, Evelyn,
> frail rope-ladders
> across fuming oblivion

and heads "back across the/ length of Ireland, home."

MOUNT EAGLE

Mount Eagle is neither arranged as a coherent whole, like *The Rough Field* and *The Dead Kingdom*, nor organized into distinct sections, like *A Chosen Light, Tides, A Slow Dance,* and *The Great Cloak*. Rather, like Montague's first two books, *Forms of Exile* and *Poisoned Lands and Other Poems*, it is something of a miscellany, though its poems are generally arranged by subject. The volume includes a quartet of poems related to the Troubles in Northern Ireland, each rendering a sharply etched vignette. There is a late harvest of childhood memories, usually recalled, not for their own sake, but for a connection Montague wishes to draw with something in later life. "The Leap," for example, draws an analogy between daring jumps years before across the Garvaghey River and, referring to his second marriage, a new "taking off . . . into the uncertain dark." Four poems are culled from a father's affectionate observation of his young daughter's investigations of their world. Only one poem alludes to Montague's father, and then in passing; none mentions his mother.

Perhaps a third of the poems could be classified under the general heading of "love." "Fair Head" recalls an early, unconsummated love; several other poems, more characteristically, commemorate consummations. "The Well-Beloved" muses on the process by which smitten lovers, each idealizing the other, descend into married life, and wonders what it takes to "redeem the ordinary." The startling "Sheela na Gig," inspired by the grotesquely sexual female figures carved on medieval Irish churches, synopsizes male human behavior in terms of "banishment" from "the first home" at birth and then a lifetime of trying "to return to that [anatomical] first darkness." Birth, too, is banishment: the first experience of exile.

The most interesting development in *Mount Eagle* is its attention to nature. "Springs" expresses the ecologically correct wish to "erase/ from this cluttered earth/ our foul disgrace." "Peninsula" is a much more appealing celebration of "Dame Nature's self-/ delighting richness." Several poems draw upon Native American nature myths, including the title poem, wherein an eagle trades its freedom to disappear into, and become "the spirit of," a mountain. The poem seems to encode Montague's own intent to dedicate himself to a new sort of poetry: less subject to the buffeting of life's winds, perhaps less confessional, more abstract. (Montague has privately acknowledged that "Mount Eagle" is a homonym for his own name.) The last seven poems in *Mount Eagle*, which include "Luggala" and "The Hill of Silence," reflect this new direction in his work.

ABOUT LOVE

Montague followed *Mount Eagle* with another collection of selected poems, *New Selected Poems*. Some-

what different selections in this published-in-Ireland volume distinguish it from the 1982 *Selected Poems*, published in the United States. The next collection, *About Love*, is a generous compilation of Montague's love poems, all but three of them previously published (about a third of them drawn from *The Great Cloak*). The variety of the poems is remarkable. They examine love of many kinds, at many stages, and in diverse moods; they examine love coolly and in heat (cerebrally and passionately), with regret and gratitude, bitterness and bemusement, longing and contentment. Mostly, they celebrate love, although that emotion is often shaded with darker feelings: jealousy, guilt, loneliness. The book amounts to a learned treatise on love, Montague's anatomy of love.

TIME IN ARMAGH

This small, well-focused collection recalls its author's years at boarding school (St. Patrick's College, Armagh), from 1941 until 1946. World War II is a presence in five of the volume's twenty-six poems, but its emphasis is on "the harshness of our schooling," as Montague says in the preface. The harshness is evident in the physical violence administered both by the priests who ran the school (seven poems, as well as the book's epigraph from Juvenal, allude to canes or beatings) and by fellow students. The harshness is also evident in the absence of tenderness or love. Although there are moments of humor and even of nostalgia in the volume, the prevailing feelings are anger and bitterness, undimmed after half a century. In his preface, Montague compares his school years with those that James Joyce recorded in *A Portrait of the Artist as a Young Man* (1916). When he writes about the beatings administered by the priests at St. Patrick's, most notably in "Guide" and the title poem, "Time in Armagh," Montague's language echoes that of the pandybat scene in Joyce's novel.

COLLECTED POEMS

This magisterial assemblage collects more than three hundred poems, the best work of the first forty years of Montague's output. It is divided into three sections. The first, a bit more than half the book, consists of the three great volumes from the 1970's and 1980's, all symphonically orchestrated (each conceived of as a single, integrated work): *The Rough Field, The Great Cloak,* and *The Dead Kingdom.* The second section, constituting nearly 40 percent of the book, contains poems from

Forms of Exile, Poisoned Lands and Other Poems, A Chosen Light, Tides, A Slow Dance, and *Mount Eagle*. Section 3, less than 10 percent of the book, contains poems from *Time in Armagh* and the previously uncollected long poem "Border Sick Call" (1995). Montague has revised some poems, omitted some poems, and included a few poems translated from the Irish and originally published in *A Fair House: Versions of Irish Poetry* (1973).

SMASHING THE PIANO

Few poets in old age write with undiminished power. William Butler Yeats was one; John Montague is another. *Smashing the Piano* is a smashing follow-up to his *Collected Poems*: not merely a curtain call but a real encore. The collection contains forty-one poems, but, since several of these are sequences of lyrics (individually titled and each capable of standing alone), by another way of reckoning the collection contains sixty-five poems.

Unavoidably, many of the poems in this gathering reintroduce themes and characters introduced in earlier books. The opening half dozen poems, for example, recall figures and incidents from a County Tyrone childhood: Aunt Winifred ("Paths"), Aunt Brigid ("Still Life, with Aunt Brigid"), children who died young ("Kindertotenlieder"). This group segues naturally into a sequence about Montague's own children, "Prayers for My Daughters." The title is deliberately Yeatsian, but the tender domesticity of these poems owes nothing to Yeats.

A sequence of short love poems, "Dark Rooms," recalls many of Montague's earlier love poems, but "Postscript," the sixth of the seven lyrics in the sequence, introduces a new situation: An old poet, having been supplanted by "another, younger man," struggles to contain his rage in the constraining form of a poem—such as this one, more regularly rhymed than most Montague poems. Other poems also demonstrate that this volume is the work of advanced years, most notably "Talking with Victor Hugo in Old Age." The untitled brief poem that serves as the volume's epigraph connects youth and age in a wholly suitable way:

> Fierce lyric truth,
> Sought since youth,
> Grace my ageing

> As you did my growing,
> Till time engraves
> My final face.

A number of poems scattered through *Smashing the Piano* seem to be extensions of the impulse, seen in *Mount Eagle*, to write about nature: "Starspill" even refers to "Mount Eagle." "Between" is a gorgeous meditation on the yin and yang of nature as observed in the Gap, where County Waterford and County Tipperary meet.

The longest sequence in the collection, the eight-part "Civil Wars," reengages political themes that Montague has dealt with memorably before. There are updates here, however: memorializing hunger striker Bobby Sands, excoriating British prime minister Margaret Thatcher, speaking of "the unspeakable" Omagh bombing, respectfully addressing (in conclusion) his own father, once politicized, now dead. "Your faith I envy," he tells his father, though

> Your fierce politics I decry.
> May we sing together
> someday, Sunny Jim,
> over what you might
> still call the final shoot-out:
> for me, saving your absence,
> a healing agreement.

Though in this collection there is the usual great range of subjects and feelings characteristic of Montague's best books of poems, this one is marked with unwonted serenity. This should not be mistaken for a sign of diminished inspiration or power; it is an added, and most welcome, quality: a late blossoming, a late blessing.

OTHER MAJOR WORKS

LONG FICTION: *The Lost Notebook*, 1987.

SHORT FICTION: *Death of a Chieftain and Other Stories*, 1964 (revised as *An Occasion of Sin: Stories*, 1992); *A Love Present and Other Stories*, 1997.

NONFICTION: *The Figure in the Cave and Other Essays*, 1989; *Myth, History, and Literary Tradition*, 1989 (with Thomas Kinsella and Brendan Kennelly); *Company: A Chosen Life*, 2001.

TRANSLATIONS: *A Fair House: Versions of Irish Poetry*, 1973 (from Irish); *November: A Choice of*

Translations from André Frénaud, 1977 (with Evelyn Robson); *Selected Poems*, 1994 (of Francis Ponge; with C. K. Williams and Margaret Guiton); *Carnac*, 1999 (of Eugène Guillevic).

EDITED TEXTS: *The Dolmen Miscellany of Irish Writing*, 1962; *The Faber Book of Irish Verse*, 1972 (subsequently *The Book of Irish Verse*); *Bitter Harvest: An Anthology of Contemporary Irish Verse*, 1989.

MISCELLANEOUS: *Born in Brooklyn: John Montague's America*, 1991 (poetry, short fiction, and nonfiction).

BIBLIOGRAPHY

Irish University Review: A Journal of Irish Studies 19 (Spring, 1989). This "John Montague Issue," edited by Christopher Murray, includes an interview with Montague, seven articles on his work, an autobiographical essay by Montague ("The Figure in the Cave"), and Thomas Dillon Redshaw's checklist of Montague's books.

Kersnowski, Frank. *John Montague*. Lewisburg, Pa.: Bucknell University Press, 1975. The first book-length study of Montague's work (actually a slim monograph), this work surveys his career through *The Rough Field*. Its chief value may be its readings of individual poems and stories.

_____. "The Ulster Muse." Review of *Collected Poems*, by John Montague. *Sewanee Review* 106, no. 2 (Spring, 1998): 369-373. Kersnowski provides a critical assessment of the poetic works in the collection.

Montague, John. *Company: A Chosen Life*. London: Duckworth, 2001. This first volume of Montague's memoirs, focusing mainly on the 1950's and 1960's, provides entertaining and often illuminating accounts of his encounters with Samuel Beckett, Brendan Behan, Theodore Roethke, and many other writers, artists, and other interesting people. The book's most memorable portrait, however, is that which emerges indirectly of the author himself. The warmth, wit, intelligence, generosity, and humor of his sensibility inform the book.

_____. *The Figure in the Cave and Other Essays*. Edited by Antoinette Quinn. Syracuse, N.Y.: Syracuse University Press, 1989. This is the essential source for information about Montague's life, especially in the first four (very autobiographical) essays and in the detailed chronology of his life at the end.

Redshaw, Thomas Dillon, ed. *Hill Field: Poems and Memoirs for John Montague on His Sixtieth Birthday, 28 February 1989*. Minneapolis: Coffee House Press, 1989. Ten brief memoirs offer glimpses into various phases of the first sixty years of Montague's life.

_____. *Well Dreams: Essays on John Montague*. Omaha, Nebr.: Creighton University Press, 2002. Eighteen essays examine successive aspects of Montague's career. Redshaw's "The Books of John Montague, 1958-2000: A Descriptive Checklist" is an authoritative and essential resource. This is easily the most substantial work published on Montague's work to date.

Richard Bizot

EUGENIO MONTALE

Born: Genoa, Italy; October 12, 1896
Died: Milan, Italy; September 12, 1981

PRINCIPAL POETRY

Ossi di seppia, 1925 (partial translation, *The Bones of Cuttlefish*, 1983; full translation, *Cuttlefish Bones*, 1992)
Le occasioni, 1939 (*The Occasions*, 1987)
La bufera e altro, 1956 (*The Storm and Other Poems*, 1978)
Poems by Eugenio Montale, 1959
Satura, 1962 (partial translation in *New Poems*, 1976; full translation, *Satura: Five Poems*, 1969)
Eugenio Montale: Poesie/Poems, 1965
Selected Poems, 1965
Provisional Conclusions: A Selection of the Poetry of Eugenio Montale, 1970
Diario del '71 e del '72, 1973 (partial translation in *New Poems*, 1976)

New Poems: A Selection from "Satura" and "Diario del '71 e del '72," 1976
Quaderno di quattro anni, 1977 (*It Depends: A Poet's Notebook,* 1980)
L'opera in versi, 1980
Collected Poems, 1920-1954, 1998

OTHER LITERARY FORMS

In addition to his several volumes of verse collected by R. Bettarini and G. Contini in a critical edition, *L'opera in versi,* Eugenio Montale wrote the obliquely autobiographical short stories of *Farfalla di Dinard* (1956; *Butterfly of Dinard,* 1971). His critical essays on literature were collected by G. Zampa in *Sulla poesia* (1976; on poetry) and those on broadly cultural or social topics in *Auto da fé* (1966). To them should be added the travelogues and interviews of *Fuori di casa* (1969; abroad), which arose from the practice of journalism, and the musical reviews posthumously reprinted in book form: *Prime alla Scala* (1981; premieres at La Scala), edited by G. Lavezzi. The revealing intellectual diary of 1917, *Quaderno genovese* (wr. 1917, pb. 1983), also deserves mention.

ACHIEVEMENTS

Eugenio Montale won the Premio dell'Antico Fattore (1932), the Premio Manzotto (1956), Italy's Dante Medal (1959), the Feltrinelli Prize from the Accademia dei Lincei (1963, 1964), Paris's Calouite Bulbenkian Prize (1971), and honorary degrees from the Universities of Milan, Rome, Cambridge, Basel, and Nice. In 1967, he was named senator of the Italian Republic. In 1975, he won the coveted Nobel Prize in Literature.

BIOGRAPHY

The youngest of five siblings, Eugenio Montale was born in Genoa on October 12, 1896, to Giuseppina Ricci and Domingo Montale, a well-to-do businessman who shared with two first cousins the ownership and management of a firm for the importation of turpentine and other chemicals. Poor health forced Montale to withdraw from school as a ninth-grader; henceforth, only his insatiable curiosity for books and the unfailing assistance of his sister Marianne—a philosophy student—were to sustain him in the pursuit of a broad culture,

Eugenio Montale, Nobel laureate in literature for 1975. (© The Nobel Foundation)

ranging from Italian, French, and English literature to modern philosophy. Entering the family firm or a bank, as his brothers did, was out of the question from the start for the dreamy adolescent, who, sharing with his family a great love for opera, soon began to train for baritone singing with Ernesto Sivori. This fine teacher's death in 1916 put an end to Montale's plans for an operatic career but not to his lifelong interest in musical theater. In 1917, Montale joined the army and soon was serving as an infantry officer on the Trentino front against the Austrians.

During the years immediately following World War I, Montale's contributions to literary journals and the limited if solid success of *Cuttlefish Bones* were not enough to earn a living, and in 1927, he moved to Florence, where he found work first with Bemporad, a publishing firm, and then as curator of the Vieusseux rare books library in the employ of the city administration. He was to lose that congenial position in 1938 for political reasons, but he remained in Florence through the war years as a freelance translator and an acknowledged leader of the literary scene until, in 1948, he moved to Milan as contributing editor to the leading daily *Il corriere della sera.* Long before he received the 1975 Nobel Prize in Literature, he was made a senator for life by the president of the Italian Republic. The death in 1963 of his wife, Drusilla Tanzi, affected him deeply, as the "Xenia" sequence in *Satura* shows; from then on, the old poet was entrusted to the devoted care of their housekeeper, Gina Tiossi. Much earlier, two other women had left a durable imprint on his art: a visiting American scholar in the 1930's (who became the unnamed angelic figure of many poems in *The Occasions* and the Clizia of *The Storm and Other Poems*) and, in the late 1940's and early 1950's, an Italian poetess (who inspired the "Volpe," or "Vixen," poems in *The Storm and Other Poems*). Montale's funeral in mid-September, 1981, was attended by the Italian chief of state and many other prominent figures of public and artistic life.

ANALYSIS

Emerging from the welter of experiments and iconoclasms that had marked the decade before World War I, Eugenio Montale's intense lyrics set the tone for the interwar period in Italian poetry. Giuseppe Ungaretti's verse, jotted down in the Carso trenches and first published in 1916, had already pointed the way to a new poetics of elliptical imagery, inward essentialness, modern diction, and deconstructed meter which had distilled Futurist exuberance into noiseless immediacy. Montale's first collection, *Cuttlefish Bones,* discovered the untapped possibilities of a venerable tradition, which, purged of academic sclerosis and vatic posturing or bombast, could best articulate the dilemmas, the self-criticism, and the yearning for authentic values that variously haunted so many of the war's survivors. The starkness of style of this first book sharpened into thinly veiled prophetic denunciation with Montale's next collection, *The Occasions,* which registered the gathering of a new storm. In his third collection, *The Storm and Other Poems,* Montale responded to World War II and its aftermath in an unfashionable vein of visionary lyri-

cism. His books of the 1970's, from *Satura* on, approach the threshold of prosiness, in keeping with the prevalently satirical and gnomic bent of his later years. The Nobel laureate of 1975 became the poetic conscience of the generation that had groped for truth in the dark times between two world wars; he showed that the best way for a writer to be modern was not to discard a tradition which went all the way back to Dante but instead (in Ezra Pound's words) to "make it new."

CUTTLEFISH BONES

Cuttlefish Bones displays simultaneously the alert richness of youth and maturity's searching control. Scrupulous attention to the formal resources of the word, far from foundering into aesthetic complacency, bespeaks an ingrained commitment to cognitive values, and since there can be no final certainty about these values, the persona wavering between sudden contemplative rapture and unappeased doubt transcends the merely autobiographical level to become as memorable a spokesman for the modern human condition as T. S. Eliot's Prufrock or Ezra Pound's Mauberley. It was no accident that the author of *Cuttlefish Bones* should eventually become a friend of Pound (politics apart) and try his hand at translating one short section of *Hugh Selwyn Mauberley* (1920) as well as three of Eliot's "Ariel Poems," while Eliot, for his part, published "Arsenio," chronologically the last poem of *Cuttlefish Bones,* in a 1928 issue of *The Criterion.* "Arsenio," the most lucidly despondent and subtly modulated monologue in *Cuttlefish Bones* (the poem first appeared in the collection's third edition), was translated by Mario Praz, and it was Praz who, two decades later, identified certain formal and thematic affinities between Eugenio Montale's and Eliot's poetry.

The affinities are there, if one but thinks of the wastelandish component in Montale's style and worldview, but they should not overshadow the differences and, above all, Montale's independence from the Eliotic paradigm. Montale's poetics of dryness, which found an early embodiment in "Meriggiare pallido e assorto" ("The Wall"), stems from the Dantesque leanings first recognized by Glauco Cambon in 1956 and openly confirmed by the poet himself many years later.

In "The Wall," written several years before the publication of *The Waste Land* (1922), Montale's characteristic tone is already evident:

> . . . e andando nel sole che abbaglia
> sentire con triste meraviglia
> comè tutta la vita e il suo travaglio
> in questo seguitare una muraglia
> che ha in cima cocci aguzzi di bottiglia.
> (. . . and walking on under the blinding sun
> to feel with sad amazement
> how all of life's painful endeavor is
> in this perpetual going along a wall
> that carries on its top sharp bottle shards.)

The familiar sight of such walls protecting gardens and orchards in the northern Italian upland countryside has elicited an unmistakable emblem of the burdensome human condition which the stoic Montalian persona repeatedly faces. The emblem, whether in the same form or in the guise of cognate imagery, pervades Montale's poetry. In one of *Cuttlefish Bones*'s most cryptic and tensest lyrics, "Crisalide" ("Chrysalis"), it reaches its symbolic acme: "e noi andremo innanzi senza smuovere/ un sasso solo della gran muraglia" ("and we shall go right on without dislodging/ even a single stone of the huge wall"). Perhaps, the poem continues, we humans shall never meet on our way "la libertà, il miracolo,/ il fatto che non era necessario!" ("freedom, miracle,/ the fact that was not shackled by necessity!").

That cry of the heart and of the whole mind against the seeming barrier that reality opposes to man's need for knowledge and deliverance voices the central concern of the Montalean persona and propels his utterance beyond whatever seductions the lavish landscape of sensuous experience may offer. "The mind investigates, harmonizes, disjoins," as Montale writes in "I limoni" ("The Lemon Trees"), the first poem of *Cuttlefish Bones* after the epigraph lyric; it is a question of finding "a mistake of Nature,/ the dead point of the world, the loose chain-ring,/ the thread to be unravelled" which will finally "place us in the midst of a truth." Remarkably, and understandably, the search for truth can take place only as an attempt to disrupt the opaque compactness of existence. The revolt against closure, the distrust of intellectual systems that claim to explain everything, marks Montale's imagery and thought from beginning to end and accounts for his interest in Émile Boutroux's contingentist thought, which openly challenged the still prevalent determinist philosophies of science.

Montale is a thinking poet, a "poet on the edge" in Rebecca West's apt words; he cannot take phenomenal reality for granted but must forever question it. Denial is his concomitant gesture. With Arthur Schopenhauer (and Giacomo Leopardi), Montale at times sees and feels existence as sheer suffering. The "pain of living" can be escaped only in a kind of Buddhist "divine indifference," the privilege of the noon-haloed statue in the garden, of the floating cloud, of the high-soaring hawk—or else, acme of negations, in the Nirvanic ecstasy of the sunflower "impazzito di luce" (maddened with the light). The "glory of outspread noon" rules over Liguria's seething sea and rocky, olive-tree-studded slopes, a fierce beauty not to be forgotten by the war-tried persona who revisits the landscape of his childhood.

It was an Eden, now lost forever, as stated in "Fine dell'infanzia" (end of childhood). Here the persona, confronting the numinous turbulences and calms of the Mediterranean, rehearses what had been his initiation to poetry and self-knowledge, in self-differentiation from, and reimmersion in, the godlike native element. Alternatively, he contemplates, in the person of the lithe swimmer Esterina ("Falsetto"), the momentary bliss that immersion in the welcoming bosom of her "divine friend" can bestow, though the contemplator himself remains "on dry land," apart from that alien joy. The "Mediterraneo" ("Mediterranean") series at the center of the book has been faulted by some critics (Gianfranco Contini, Silvio Ramat, and the author himself) as a relapse into suspect exuberance from the terse spareness achieved by "Ossi di seppia" ("Cuttlefish Bones"), the eponymous series that precedes "Mediterranean" in the collection. "Mediterranean," however, with its nearly Whitmanesque expansiveness, counterpoints the systole of "Cuttlefish Bones" and thus makes the entire book pulsate with a vitality of its own.

THE OCCASIONS

When that vitality subsides into the mournfulness of "Arsenio" (a piece added to the third edition of *Cuttlefish Bones* in 1928), the stage is set for the next cycle of poems, *The Occasions*, which disappointed a friendly critic, Pietro Pancrazi; in Pancrazi's opinion, Montale with this new book had turned to abstruse "metaphysical" poetry instead of staying with the "physical" concreteness of *Cuttlefish Bones*. Actually, what occurred was no involution but a deepening of style and vision into the kind of clipped writing that can evoke an innermost reality from the barest outline of factual detail. The relative colorfulness of the sunstruck earlier book yields to a gray monochrome. The diction becomes even more conversational, the tone more low-key yet amenable to sudden soarings in elliptical concentration, and metric patterns tend to disintegrate as far as stanza form goes, even if the lines as such stay mostly within the regular cast of the hendecasyllable and alternative shorter verse types. *The Occasions*, accordingly, evinces a less literary and more penetrating voice than its predecessor, from which it nevertheless takes seminal motifs. The epistemological urge turns from the cosmic to the personal and historical, political sphere, facing the precariousness of individual existence to denounce (in guarded yet ultimately transparent allegory) the evils of Nazi and Fascist totalitarianism, the threat of impending war. Liuba, in "A Liuba che parte" ("For Liuba, Leaving"), is a Jewess forced to flee persecution, carrying her household gods (a cat in a hatbox) like a diminutive Noah's Ark that will tide her over the flood of "the blind times." In "Dora Markus," the title figure, an Austrian Jewess whose very "sweetness is a storm," recalling "migratory birds that crash into a lighthouse," withstands time's (and the times') ordeal by the mere strength of her womanly amulets, while it gets "later, ever later"; in the teeth of Nazism's "ferocious faith," she refuses to "surrender/ voice, legend or destiny." An unnamed girl from Liguria who died young (a poem of the last years will identify her as Annetta) haunts the persona's memory in "La casa dei doganieri" ("The Shorewatcher's House"), where she will never return, while "the compass spins crazily at random" and "there is no reckoning the dice's throw." The persona's interlocutor in "Barche sulla Marna" ("Boats on the Marne") shares with him a peaceful Sunday on that French river which nevertheless conjures in his mind the fateful meandering of human history away from the dreamed possibility of a just, serene, and happy life on earth.

In another holiday setting, the English bank holiday in "Eastbourne," the persona strolling on the beach descries dark omens; "evil is winning, the wheel will never stop," and perhaps not even the countervailing force of love, which holds the world together, will manage to stem the tide. It is a force coming from, and oriented toward, his absent beloved, who thereby acquires mythic, not to say god(dess)like, status; the stirring hyperbole recalls Dante's myth of Beatrice in a different, if equally apocalyptic, context. No less apocalyptically, the same transfigured lady from the Atlantic's other shore battles the forces of obscurantism on a chessboard which clearly figures forth the contemporary world under the gathering storm ("Nuove stanze"), and she dawns on the persona's mind to exorcize those forces in "Elegia de Pico Farnese" (elegy for Pico Farnese) and in "Palio" (Palio at Siena), where the clamoring crowd and the wheeling horses in the folk event of worldwide renown evoke the mass hysteria and the apparent ineluctability of sinister political developments in the late 1930's.

At the heart of *The Occasions*, the Beatrice-like American woman dominates the twenty "motets" addressed to her by a modern troubadour who effortlessly renews the medieval worship of Eros in the very act of confronting a bleak modern reality. Descanting on the vicissitudes of love from afar, Montale attains a poignancy attuned to the contrapuntal polyphony of Orlando di Lasso, Giovanni Pierluigi da Palestrina, Carlo Gesualdo:

> Un ronzìo lungo viene dall'aperto.
> Strazia com'unghia ai vetri. Cerco il segno
> smarrito, il pegno solo ch'ebbi in grazia
> da te.
> E l'infernoè certo.
> (A long whir comes from the outside.
> It grates like a nail on windowpanes. I seek the sign
> lost, the one pledge I had as a grace
> from you.
> And hell is certain.)

Even though, as Montale later saw fit to reveal, this particular motet and the two following ones were inspired by another lady (a Peruvian visitor) and not by the one whom he was to call Clizia, the Ovidian girl metamorphosed into a sunflower in *The Storm and Other Poems*, it serves as a perfect opening to the whole series, with which it thematically and tonally coalesces.

THE STORM AND OTHER POEMS

The "I-thou" rhetorical stance, the repudiation of the irrational times, and the persistent conversation with absent Clizia across the ocean—all these obviously link *The Occasions* to *The Storm and Other Poems*, which at the same time shows new developments in style and theme. The first part of this book, with the title "Finisterre," had been published in Lugano, Switzerland, by Bernasconi in 1943, and one climactic poem, "Primavera hitleriana" ("The Hitler Spring"), protesting Hitler's official visit to Florence in 1938, could not appear in print before the end of the war. "Finisterre" pushes emblematic allusiveness to a truly hermetic point, covertly indicating the war unleashed by the Axis powers. The diction is melodiously stylized, there is a tendency toward legato as opposed to the earlier staccato and related percussive alliterations, and the very fact that three of the poems happen to be sonnets (albeit treated with deft sprezzatura) signals an unprecedented Petrarchan leaning—openly avowed by the author in "Intenzioni, intervista immaginaria" (intentions, an imaginary interview) of 1946, a poem later reprinted in *Sulla poesia*. These "Finisterre" lyrics are germane to the coeval translation of three sonnets by William Shakespeare, to be found in *It Depends: A Poet's Notebook*.

Family memories, a moving poem to Montale's wife (who was briefly hospitalized during the last days of the battle for Florence in August, 1944), and a series of madrigals to the poetically gifted lady addressed under the code name of "la Volpe" (the Vixen), contribute to the uniqueness of *The Storm and Other Poems*, a book also characterized by the frequent naming of God (a novelty in Montale) and by the joyous vitality that the poems to the Vixen and the breathtaking dithyramb "L'anguilla" ("The Eel"), ostensibly addressed to Clizia, hymnically convey. The two poems in the last section, "Conclusioni provvisorie" ("Provisional Conclusions"), provide a dark antiphon by casting a saturnine eye on the disappointing postwar world, where the dominant mass ideologies of Stalinism and Christian Democracy ("red" and "black clerics") seem equally unacceptable to the devotee of a humanist faith in the dignity of man. The impending extinction of Western civilization is allegorized in a "shadowy Lucifer," though the persona still clings to his dream of love for Clizia.

SATURA

Satura (the Latin title means "satire" but also connotes a medley of offerings) picks up those somber clues in a prosaic register which would persist down to the last of Montale's books. A Lucifer-like god darkens by his very absence the allegorized historical scene of "Botta e risposta I" (thrust and riposte I), where the persona, reviewing what preceded and followed the latest catastrophe, decries the fact that Italy's liberation by the Allied armies failed to bring about a permanent cleansing of the Augean stables, public life being now repulsively shapeless. A bracing antiphon to that depressing message and tone rings out in "Xenia," and much else in *Satura*—especially "Angelo Nero" (black angel)—shows Montale's old mettle, even in the new, exceedingly deflated style. The books of the 1970's comment discursively on public issues or private events and memories, and if an aggressively flat chattiness seems at times to take over, the epigrams and some satirical pieces have a sharpness of their own. All in all, these last collections constitute the uneven aftermath of the great poetry that had reached its lyric climax in *The Storm and Other Poems*.

OTHER MAJOR WORKS

NONFICTION: *Quaderno genovese*, wr. 1917, pb. 1983; *Farfalla di Dinard*, 1956 (short articles, prose poems, memoirs; *The Butterfly of Dinard*, 1970); *Auto da fé*, 1966; *Fuori di casa*, 1969; *Nel nostro tempo*, 1972 (*Poet in Our Time*, 1976); *Sulla poesia*, 1976; *Prime alla Scala*, 1981; *The Second Life of Art*, 1982.

BIBLIOGRAPHY

Almansi, Guido, and Bruce Merry. *Eugenio Montale: The Private Language of Poetry*. Edinburgh, Scotland: Edinburgh University Press, 1977. A short critical study of Montale's major works. Includes bibliographic references and an index.

Cambon, Glauco. *Eugenio Montale*. New York: Columbia University Press, 1972. An introductory critical essay on the work of Montale with a selected bibliography.

_____. *Eugenio Montale's Poetry: A Dream in Reason's Presence*. Princeton, N.J.: Princeton University Press, 1982. A critical assessment of Montale's career as a poet. Includes bibliographical references and indexes.

Cary, Joseph. *Three Modern Italian Poets*. Chicago: University of Chicago Press, 1993. Cary presents striking biographical portraits and provides an understanding of the works of Umberto Saba, Giuseppe Ungaretti, and Eugenio Montale. In addition, Cary guides us through the first few, difficult decades of twentieth century Italy. Includes chronological tables, bibliography.

Galassi, Jonathan, trans. *Collected Poems, 1920-1954*, by Eugenio Montale. 1998. Bilingual ed. New York: Farrar, Straus and Giroux, 2000. President of the Academy of American Poets Galassi presents useful notes along with his translations of some of the most important of Montale's poems from *Cuttlefish Bones*, *The Occasions*, and *The Storm and Other Poems*.

Huffman, Claire Licari. *Montale and the Occasions of Poetry*. Princeton, N.J.: Princeton University Press, 1983. A collection of the author's essays and lectures about Montale's life and works. Includes bibliographical references and index.

West, Rebecca. *Eugenio Montale: Poet on the Edge*. Cambridge, Mass.: Harvard University Press, 1981. The well-known novelist's critical interpretations of some of Montale's major works. Bibliographic references and an index.

Glauco Cambon;
bibliography updated by the editors

MARIANNE MOORE

Born: Kirkwood, Missouri; November 15, 1887
Died: New York, New York; February 5, 1972

PRINCIPAL POETRY
  Poems, 1921
  Observations, 1924
  Selected Poems, 1935
  The Pangolin and Other Verse, 1936
  What Are Years, 1941
  Nevertheless, 1944
  Collected Poems, 1951
  Like a Bulwark, 1956
  O to Be a Dragon, 1959

Tell Me, Tell Me, 1966
The Complete Poems of Marianne Moore, 1967, 1981

OTHER LITERARY FORMS

Marianne Moore left a voluminous correspondence with literary figures in America and England. She also wrote occasional reviews and lectured on campuses and at poetry centers. This work, too, shows her imaginative daring, the "idiosyncrasy and technique" that she valued. A sampling of her prose as well as of her verse was published as *A Marianne Moore Reader* (1961). A selection of essays, *Predilections*, appeared in 1955.

The words "collected" and "complete" in a title may promise more than the book delivers; in Moore's case, the contents are only those examples of her work that she wished to keep in circulation. Because she frequently revised extensively, a genuinely complete edition must be variorum. The best available selection is *The Complete Poems of Marianne Moore*. Most of Moore's manuscripts and correspondence, as well as a collection of her furnishings and personal items, are housed in the museum of the Philip H. and A. S. W. Rosenbach Foundation, Philadelphia. *The Complete Prose of Marianne Moore* (1986) includes all of Moore's published prose work, from her early stories to her mature essays and reviews; as editor of *The Dial* from 1921 to 1929, and later, as her poetic reputation grew, she had the opportunity to write on a broad range of twentieth century poets and fiction writers.

ACHIEVEMENTS

If she had lived longer she would have sympathized with the aims, if not with the more fervid rhetoric, of the revived feminist movement, but in her day Marianne Moore sought recognition without regard to gender. Her daring paid off, since her work impresses most critics, male or female, as that of a major figure among poets of modernism; she is considered to be an artist on a par with Wallace Stevens, William Carlos Williams, and Ezra Pound.

Praised by Eliot as "one of those few who have done the language some service," Moore quickly made a reputation among other poets. She won the Dial Award in 1924, and in 1925 was the object of discussion in five consecutive issues of *The Dial*. Her work, however, long

Marianne Moore (Library of Congress)

the poetic self that had begun in a reticence that approached diffidence, that had armored itself as much against temptation from within as against threat from without, had burst through its early encasements to take on the role of moralist and even of sociopolitical adviser. A degree of tolerance for the self and the world perhaps made her choices easier, although it did not always benefit her art.

Moore seems to have had an inborn disdain for the self-indulgent. After a girlhood in Missouri and Pennsylvania and an education at Bryn Mawr College, she taught commercial subjects at the United States Indian School in Carlisle, Pennsylvania, for three and a half years while perfecting her art as a poet. Her verse began to appear in *The Egoist* (London), *Poetry*, and other journals of the new poetry. By 1918, she had settled in Manhattan and become a member of the literary circle that included William Carlos Williams, Wallace Stevens, and Alfred Kreymborg. Her first volume, *Poems* (1921), was brought out in London. The period of the Dial Award was followed by her appointment in 1925 as an editor—soon to be editor-in-chief—of *The Dial*. She guided the journal through its heyday as the premier American periodical of literature and the arts. The work excited her, demonstrated her firm taste, and made her acquainted with most of the prominent writers of the time. After *The Dial* was discontinued in 1928, Moore never again worked at a salaried job. Although she earned occasional small checks for verse and reviews, her career as a writer, according to Driver, was subsidized by the former backers of *The Dial*. In the same year that the publication ended, Moore and her mother—a close adviser until her death in 1947—moved to Brooklyn, where the poet's brother John, a Navy chaplain, was stationed.

Useful though it was, the period with *The Dial* was an interruption. Moore had published *Observations* (1924) before going to work on the journal; her next book, *Selected Poems*, did not appear until 1935. This volume reprinted several pieces from earlier books and also

remained little known to the public. The "beauty" that she sought was the product of an individualistic decorum, a discipline of self and art that yielded the quality she admired in the poem "The Monkey Puzzle" (*Selected Poems*, 1935) as "porcupinequilled, complicated starkness." The quilled and stark imagery is slow to attract admirers other than the *cognoscenti*, but by the 1950's her work was receiving wide recognition.

She had, indeed, a year of wonder in 1952, receiving the National Book Award, the Bollingen Prize, and the Pulitzer Prize. Since that time, some of her poems have appeared in every reasonably comprehensive anthology of modern verse. Either the 1935 or the 1967 version of "Poetry" is almost always included. Other choices vary: "The Pangolin," "What Are Years?," "Virginia Britannia," and "A Grave" are among those poems most frequently anthologized.

BIOGRAPHY

The relaxation in Marianne Moore's later verse and the rise of public acclaim demonstrate that late in her life some more recent work from magazines. The slim *The Pangolin and Other Verse* appeared in 1936. Moore lived quietly for the next two decades, publishing additional thin volumes. In the 1950's, the growing acceptance of modernism and the approval indicated by her numerous awards helped bring public attention; she became, indeed, something of a celebrity. Doubtless interest was furthered by her darting and witty conversation with interviewers, as well as her shrewd adoption of a three-cornered hat as a badge of eccentricity. It became routine to see a photo story in *Life* magazine on Moore's trip to the zoo, to read of her as unofficial hostess for the mayor of New York, and to find *The New Yorker* printing the hilarious exchange of letters that resulted from the request in 1955 that she think up names for a new model from Ford. (The final choice—not one of her suggestions—was "Edsel.") When in 1965 she left her Brooklyn apartment for one in Manhattan, the move was recorded on the front page of *The New York Times.*

Yet Moore could never be accused of self-importance. She enjoyed attention, but was wary—"I am often taken advantage of," she said—and continued to work at essays, reviews, and poetry. In some of her late verse she is sententious or playful. In other pieces she continues to focus on an object, a "thing" that provides her with observable fact that she can carpenter into an aesthetic stairway, a means of rising to discovery. Readers will frequently find in the work of her early and middle decades, and sometimes even in her late poems, the delight, the quilled beauty that is her legacy.

ANALYSIS

In Marianne Moore's best work the imagined and the perceived are interdependent; she merges the two to create her usefully idiosyncratic reality. Often she finds in her universe suggestions of ethical principle. When she integrates statement of principle with sufficient circumstance, she makes the presentation seem not merely a lesson but also a fundamental component of the aesthetic structure of her world.

That "we"—speakers of English, one supposes—have not successfully integrated the world of imagination with that of the senses is part of the closing observation in her best-known poem, the 1935 version of "Poetry." This piece unfortunately has been the victim

of ill-advised revision. Its argument was clear in the 1921 printing; after publishing a much-altered version in her 1924 book, Moore in 1935 returned to the 1921 version. The 1935 printing, however, introduced an ambiguity that illustrates how much may depend on so supposedly trivial a device as a punctuation mark.

The 1935 version, the one that became well-known, opens with a first line that seems to dismiss poetry as "all this fiddle." This is best taken as a bit of rueful humor about Moore's own dedication, since she clearly was in no way contemptuous of her art. The poetry she likes is that which contains the "genuine," a quality that she shows by example and then by assertion to be equivalent to "useful." In what is perhaps a caution against the dangers of her own frequent practice of working from pictures or written descriptions rather than from firsthand experience, she remarks that the too "derivative" may become "unintelligible," and adds that people do not admire "what they cannot understand." In the 1921 version, a period followed "understand," making it clear that the next several examples that the poem gives are included in the "phenomena" mentioned in line 18. After "understand" in the 1935 version, Moore puts a colon, seeming to indicate that the content of the following lines is to be taken as examples of objects that, because they are unintelligible, are not admired. This material, however, consists of several notations of the sort of exact reality that Moore likes to use—a "tireless" wolf, a "twitching critic"—and lines 16 to 18 accept the usefulness of such detail by declaring that, together with other matter, all such "phenomena" are important.

The reader not deterred by the apparent contradiction will next find a warning that mere specification of "phenomena" does not make art, followed by the observation that real poetry is not yet with "us," that it will arise only when poets become "literalists of the imagination" who produce "imaginary gardens with real toads in them." This much-discussed phrase is a careful statement of her own intention: to disclose the universe ("imaginary gardens") suggested by the objects perceived by the senses (such as "real toads"). The ending remark is that "in the meantime" the reader will have to be satisfied with one or the other of the two components of true art: raw material in "all its rawness" and "the genuine." The real poet, it appears, will be the one who merges these elements.

"Poetry" is uncharacteristically broad in its interests. Moore's usual stance in her early work is that of one on guard against threat, controlling and armoring the self. She sees humankind as living in danger, as though over an abyss, an emptiness largely composed of people's ignorance of purpose or significances, together with a suggestion that the universe, insofar as it may heed humankind at all, is indifferent or hostile. One must be rock-hard, alert, wary. In "The Fish" (*Poems*) she portrays the dark colorations, the lack of hiding places, the "iron edge" of the forces that impel life-forms into seemingly chaotic motion. Yet these life-forms represent the intelligence, the consciousness of an enduring cliff of reality and of spirit that withstands all "abuse" and "accident." The view is ultimately optimistic; but the optimism is sparse, the opponent determined, grim, almost victorious. The sense of threat, of a necessary caution in attempts to profit from or even to understand the oceanic indifference that surrounds man, is emphasized in "A Grave" (*Observations*). Here the "sea," the abyss of, perhaps, the universe, society, or self-indulgence, offers the incautious nothing but a grave; it subdues the rapacious with its own superior rapacity; it lies under all activity of man and bird and shell, and, though men may at times create a harmony that seems to deny its power, in the end it extinguishes all that is "dropped," that thoughtlessly stumbles into it.

One protection is decorum, a discipline that keeps focus on the essential, that avoids all gluttony and greed. Moore frequently celebrates objects, creatures, and places that exemplify this spare rectitude. Thus, she presents as an appropriate home for man the town that has an abundance of delights but no excess, the town of "The Steeple-Jack" (*Selected Poems*). The excess that Moore criticizes is that of the artifice that is too clever, too luxuriant in ornament and ingenuity. In "The Jerboa" (*Selected Poems*), stanzas headed "Too Much" condemn the wealth of Egyptian courtiers who accumulated luxuries while poverty and drought afflicted the common people; stanzas headed "Abundance" celebrate the true wealth of the jerboa, the self-sufficient rodent that, unlike the pharaoh's over indulged mongoose, knows a natural "rest" in its desert home. In such early poems, Moore finds in the relatively uncomplicated lives of animals, usually exotic ones that have no traditional symbolism in the English-speaking world, and occasionally in examples from the worlds of flora and of human craftsmanship, the delight that arises from the primary values she recommends. These are the values that make for survival in a world of hard requirements: honesty in function and behavior, modest simplicity in bearing, and courage.

STYLE

The combination of discipline and excitement, of decorum and ardor, is supported by Moore's style. Instead of using the accentual-syllabic measure that determines the length of lines in most poetry in English—a repetitive arrangement of stressed syllables which gives verse a sound quite different from prose—Moore counts syllables. This gives her the freedom to use the syntax normal to prose. Her syntax is at times exotic, but this results from her fondness for ellipses and abrupt juxtapositions that require of the reader some of the dexterity of her own perception. The syllabic measure enables her to use feminine rhyme, which puts the stress on syllables other than those that rhyme. She commonly parallels line lengths from stanza to stanza. In "The Jerboa," for example, the first and second lines of each stanza have five syllables, the third lines each have six, the fourth lines have eleven, and similar parallelism is maintained throughout. She also indents to put together those lines which rhyme. Internal correspondences of sound are frequent. Despite this workmanship, however, the effects are almost entirely visual: Read aloud, a Moore poem sounds like thoughtful prose. Yet the suggestion of verse is there; and it is strengthened by Moore's obvious delight in accumulating specific, colorful detail. Fastidious, seemingly reticent, avoiding the glaring and the grotesque, gaining impact by conveying the sense of tightly controlled, unsentimental emotion, the style suggests possibilities for a verse that English has not yet fully exploited.

THEMES

The theme of most of Moore's early work is summed up in "An Octopus" (*Selected Poems*) as "relentless accuracy." Although in the poetry that she published in mid-career she continues to emphasize need for discipline and heroic behavior, she begins to relent a bit, to add to her exposition an emphasis on love and spiritual grace. She always gives particulars, grounding cautionary generalization firmly in sensory reality. She no longer limits her typical poem to one "thing," one animal or object, however, and she more often considers directly the human behavior that is the underlying subject.

THE PANGOLIN AND OTHER VERSE

The broadening of range shows in the great poem "The Pangolin" (*The Pangolin and Other Verse*), an admiration of the interrelationships of grace as that quality is seen in the observed features of the animal, the architecture and stone ornamentation of a cathedral, and the behavior of men when "kindly" toward one another. In such "splendour" Moore finds a suggestion of the spiritual. The poem is a marvelous interweaving of delighted observations of the animal, appreciative examination of the cathedral, recognition of man's "vileness" but also of his "excellence," and intimation, by question and by assertion of renewal, of the existence of a grace beyond the mundane.

Other poems from *The Pangolin and Other Verse* show similar acceptance of a world beyond the self. Intricate and skillful interweaving of detail and unobtrusive comment makes "Virginia Britannia" a celebration of the possibilities of the American continent, leading to the question: "How could man ignore and destroy?" In "Smooth Gnarled Crape Myrtle"—the title hints at paradox—the poet ends with a rueful "Alas!" for humankind, the creatures who in artifice honor the peace, plenty, and wisdom, the friendship and love, that they do not in fact allow to direct their behavior. In "Spenser's Ireland" (*What Are Years*), a gentler humor accepts certain peculiarities as native to the Irish (among whom the poet lists herself), even while the poem renews Moore's frequent assertion that one is never really free until or unless one is "captive" to a "supreme belief."

"WHAT ARE YEARS?"

The poem "What Are Years?" is Moore's most direct presentation of her values. Perhaps too direct for some tastes, it appeals to others by its accessibility. After noting that people cannot understand the nature of their guilt or innocence, but that all are "naked" to the dangers of existence, the speaker moves on to define courage as "resolute doubt," the strength of spirit to remain strong even when defeated. The chief exponent of such strength is the one who "accedes to mortality," who accepts the fact of death and yet struggles to live, keeps returning to the struggle even though imprisoned in a world of mor-

tality. An ambiguous "So" begins the last stanza: One who feels strongly, who is intensely aware of mortality, "behaves," keeps the ego disciplined. The pattern is that of the caged bird who, though captive, continues to sing. Despite his lack of "satisfaction," presumably of desire for flight and freedom, he knows "joy," the spiritual strength to go on living and to triumph over circumstance. This joyous discipline, it appears, "is" mortality, is knowledge of death, yet also "is" eternity, awareness of something beyond the mortal.

"NEVERTHELESS"

Survival calls, above all, for fortitude, the quality honored in "Nevertheless" (*Nevertheless*). Here the speaker's admiring delight in the way plant life manages to survive, not by withdrawing but by reaching out, by extending its growth, leads to the observation that to achieve "victory" one cannot be merely passive; one must "go/ to it." Two of Moore's most delightful poems are "A Carriage from Sweden," applauding the "unannoying/ romance" of the decorative yet functional cart that the speaker has seen in a museum; and "The Mind Is an Enchanting Thing," celebrating the play of the human mind that is both "trued" by belief and complex enough to experience "conscientious inconsistency."

"IN DISTRUST OF MERITS"

"In Distrust of Merits" praises the sacrifices of Allied soldiers in World War II; the speaker contrasts hate and love, declares that the worst of enemies is the self, and, vowing never to hate people of other skin colors or religions, decries the error of hate and egocentrism. The speaker then backs up: Presumably those who love are "not competent" to make such vows until they have replaced with "life" the scene of death that has resulted from their neglect of others. The guilt is shared by everyone, for wars are "inward." The speaker must learn to live for the beauty that arises from patient (that is, thoughtful and loving) action, not as the "dust," the human being who lives in arrogance.

THE 1950'S

Moore wrote no long poems. Although in her work of the 1950's she appears to have moved away from reticence, she still often prefers to attribute declarative or striking statements to someone else: Few poets have been as given to the indirect, sometimes oblique, view of experience afforded by use of quotations, photographs, and other products of someone else's observation. Moore likes to approach at second hand, so to speak, to comment on and to expand the significance that she finds suggested or confirmed by others. Most such material she takes from her reading, but in some cases one may suspect that she puts quotation marks around a phrase of her own that she wants to hold up for inspection without seeming to impose herself on the reader. This fondness for operating at one remove from the subject is one reason that she would find work as a translator congenial.

SELECTED FABLES OF LA FONTAINE

It is not surprising to note that in 1945, after W. H. Auden proposed to a publisher that she translate the *Fables choisies, mises en vers* (1668-1694) of the French poet Jean de La Fontaine, she began what became an eight-year labor of translation, amounting to two and a half times as much verse as she printed in the *Collected Poems* (1951).

Moore's approach is not the literal translation often demanded by the language teacher, but it remains closer to the original than do most of the translations of, for example, Ezra Pound or Robert Lowell. She was attracted to the task because of La Fontaine's craftsmanship and, one may assume, because his skeptical, world-weary examples of competitive behavior in a sophisticated world of affairs provided vicarious experience of a world with which Moore had little direct contact. Hugh Kenner praised her for discovering "a badly needed idiom, urbane without slickness and brisk without imprecision"; and Donald Hall found that her versions have a "fire of visual imagery" that is lacking in the originals. Laurence Stapleton observed that, good as they are, *Selected Fables of La Fontaine* took her on "a detour from her own best work."

Whatever her hopes that *Selected Fables of La Fontaine* might expand her scope, Moore's last three volumes continue to explore her familiar themes: resistance to threat and intrusion, admiration for the disciplined and delightful. She adds, however, much of what used to be called "occasional" verse, prompted by some event of the moment.

LIKE A BULWARK

The poems of *Like a Bulwark* show these late tendencies. The title poem admires one "firmed" by the assault of fate, leaned and strengthened by his sturdy resistance. Delight in a certain complexity in existence appears in "Then the Ermine": In a quotation that Moore may have devised, she describes the ermine's color as "ebony violet." In "The Sycamore," this pleasure in the parti-colored expands to glorification of "anything in motley." Too often overlooked is "Apparition of Splendor," wherein works of art, the forests of the earth, and traditional fairy tales all contribute to celebrate the courage of the porcupine, which defends itself without aggression. Observation of particulars in skating, tennis, dancing, music, canoeing, pomology, and painting lead in "Style" to an exclamation of joy as the speaker rapturously contemplates artistry wherever it occurs.

CHRISTIAN IMAGES

Several poems make direct use of Christian tradition, although their intention is not to argue specific doctrine but to use this tradition as a vehicle for values. In "Rosemary," Moore represents beauty and love as enwreathed to form "a kind of Christmas-tree," a celebration of Christ's birth. "Blessed Is the Man" may be viewed as a version of the beatitudes, Moore's metrical objections to the intemperate and her praise of the "unaccommodating" man who has faith in the unseen.

TELL ME, TELL ME

In some poems of *Tell Me, Tell Me*, Moore's last book made up primarily of new poems, ardor is as warm as ever. "Arthur Mitchell," a brief admiration of a dancer, shapes its stanzas to imitate the twirl of the performer. The closing imagery of "Sun" (a poem first published in 1916) implies comparison of the power of the sun—standing, one deduces, for courage of spirit—to a work of spiritual art, a gorgeously wrought hourglass. The poem is almost a prayer: The speaker appeals to "Sun" to eradicate the "hostility" found in "this meeting-place of surging enmity," this world, or, even, one's own soul.

The reprinting of "Sun" implies a continuity of thought and feeling. Moore seems, however, to have been conscious of a lessening of her powers. "The Mind, Intractable Thing" is, despite its seemingly playful title, a saddening poem when compared with the sprightly dance of feeling in the earlier "The Mind Is an Enchanting Thing." In the late poem, the speaker still exclaims over her subject, but the details are autumnal, the delight colored by near despair as she complains that the "mind" does not help her, that she does not know how to "deal with" terror and wordcraft. One need not take the poem too literally for, as the several good poems in the volume show, Moore retained great abilities to the end of her life.

CRITICAL RECEPTION

Following the discovery in the 1960's that Moore's work was not, after all, impenetrable, book-length studies are accumulating, and the school anthologies that give most Americans the only experience they have with good poetry regularly print some of her poems. The proselike surface of her art is now understood to be supported by a skill with diction and metrics that, as she put it, is "galvanized against inertia." Most poet-critics have continued to be admiring. Randall Jarrell declared that Moore discovered "a new sort of subject" and "a new sort of connection and structure for it," and John Ashbery speculated that she would eventually be ranked as the best American modernist poet.

Moore has had detractors, of course. In her early years such traditionalists as Louis Untermeyer and Margaret Anderson denigrated her work because it does not have the marked rhythm and heightened language that their Romantic taste demanded. Somewhat later, such middle-of-the-road critics as Oscar Cargill and Babette Deutsch gave her writing only carefully qualified praise. Feminists have struggled to accommodate Moore in their systems. Emily Stipes Watts declared that her reputation was "evaporating" because she followed what are in Watts's view masculine standards. Helen Vendler and Bonnie Costello admire her greatly and are rather possessive about her as a fellow member of what they see as their beleaguered gender, but they are bothered by male critics' applause, suspicious that such praise is only another tactic for putting a woman on a pedestal. Moore's work will survive the obtuse and the silly. Quilled beauty may put off the timid, but it will nevertheless prevail, because by its rigor, grace, and artistry, it achieves aesthetic triumph.

OTHER MAJOR WORKS

PLAY: *The Absentee*, pb. 1962.

NONFICTION: *Predilections*, 1955; *Selected Letters*, 1998.

TRANSLATION: *Selected Fables of La Fontaine*, 1955.

MISCELLANEOUS: *A Marianne Moore Reader*, 1961; *The Complete Prose of Marianne Moore*, 1986.

BIBLIOGRAPHY

Costello, Bonnie. *Marianne Moore: Imaginary Possessions*. Cambridge, Mass.: Harvard University Press, 1981. Having studied the notebooks, clippings, pamphlets, and books from which Moore's many quotations are derived, Costello provides a guide to understanding Moore's poetry. Each chapter discusses a poetic element: symbols, images, poems on poetry, and three of Moore's critical essays and forms. Two poems, "Pangolin" and "Plumet Basilisk," receive a lengthy analysis. Notes and an index accompany the text.

Hadas, Pamela White. *Marianne Moore: Poet of Affection*. Syracuse, N.Y.: Syracuse University Press, 1977. Hadas brings out the human qualities in the objects and animals that are often the subjects of Moore's poems. She shows how Moore bridges the scientific knowledge of animals and the human fields of music, art, and language. Five chapters deal with the biography, poetic style, fascination with animals, self-defensiveness, and vision of heroism in the poet's life and art. This useful book helps to make difficult poems more understandable and ends with notes, a bibliography, and an index.

Joyce, Elisabeth W. *Cultural Critique and Abstraction: Marianne Moore and the Avant-Garde*. London: Associated University Presses, 1998. A critical assessment of Moore's work and her association with the avant-garde. Includes bibliographical references and index.

Molesworth, Charles. *Marianne Moore: A Literary Life*. New York: Atheneum, 1990. Access to Moore's letters to her mother and brother provided Molesworth with valuable biographical material. The book is organized by the places where Moore lived: first Missouri, then Pennsylvania, and finally Brooklyn and Manhattan in New York City. The story of Moore's life revealed here shows how carefully she made decisions about each step she took. She lived a long life as both a major poet and a beloved American personality. Sixteen pages of photographs, notes, and an index complete the work.

Moore, Marianne. *Selected Letters*. Edited by Bonnie Costello, Celeste Goodridge, and Cristanne Miller. New York: Penguin Books, 1998. Moore was an inveterate letter writer; she sometimes wrote up to fifty letters a day to her brother and a variety of other writers and artists. The letters, chosen by the editors from about thirty thousand that survive, are the crème de la crème. Moore's writing describes both the quotidian events of her life and her deepest insecurities about her writing and provides insight into contemporary events.

Stamy, Cynthia. *Marianne Moore and China: Orientalism and a Writing of America*. Oxford: Oxford University Press, 1999. Criticism and interpretation of Moore's poetry. Bibliography, index.

Stapleton, Laurence. *Marianne Moore: The Poet's Advance*. Princeton, N.J.: Princeton University Press, 1978. Stapleton chronicles the continuity of Moore's "courageous act of self-exploration" in a detailed examination of her poems, essays, and translations. A chapter devoted to her translation of Jean de La Fontaine's animal fables indicates the sure understanding of French seventeenth century salon life that allowed Moore to bring the poems to life in English. Includes notes and an index.

Tomlinson, Charles, ed. *Marianne Moore: A Collection of Critical Essays*. Englewood Cliffs, N.J.: Prentice-Hall, 1969. Twenty-one articles by leading critics and poets are grouped in five sections: an interview with Moore; early comments by Ezra Pound, T. S. Eliot, and others; later comments by Wallace Stevens, William Carlos Williams, Randall Jarrell, and Kenneth Burke; the Jean de La Fontaine translations; and articles from the 1960's.

Vendler, Helen. "On Marianne Moore." *The New Yorker* 54 (October 16, 1978): 168-194. Drawing on the Tomlinson and Stapleton books, Vendler offers her provocative insights into Moore's character and poems. "Marriage" is discussed, and the assessment of Moore's male critics who have tended to belittle her achievement helps to form a more accurate view of her work.

Bernard F. Engel;
bibliography updated by the editors

CHRISTIAN MORGENSTERN

Born: Munich, Germany; May 6, 1871
Died: Meran, Austro-Hungarian Empire
 (now Merano, Italy); March 31, 1914

PRINCIPAL POETRY
In Phanta's Schloss, 1895
Horatius travestitus, 1897
Auf vielen Wegen, 1897
Ich und die Welt, 1897
Ein Sommer, 1900
Und aber ründet sich ein Kranz, 1902
Galgenlieder, 1905 (*The Gallows Songs*, 1963)
Melancholie: Neue Gedichte, 1906
Palmström, 1910
Einkehr, 1910
Ich und Du: Sonette, Ritornelle, Lieder, 1911
Wir fanden einen Pfad, 1914
Palma Kunkel, 1916
Stufen, 1918
Der Gingganz, 1918
Epigramme und Sprüche, 1919
Klein Irmchen, 1921
*Mensch Wanderer: Gedichte aus den Jahren 1887-
 1914*, 1927
The Moon Sheep, 1953
The Daynight Lamp and Other Poems, 1973
Gesammmelte Werke in einem Band, 1974
Lullabies, Lyrics, and Gallows Songs, 1995

OTHER LITERARY FORMS
 Christian Morgenstern was an active translator of Scandinavian literature. Among his translations are August Strindberg's *Inferno* (1897) in 1898; a large number of plays and poems for the German edition of Henrik Ibsen's work; and Knut Hamsun's *Aftenrøde* (1898) in 1904 as *Abendröte*, and his *Livets spil* (1896) in 1910 as *Spiel des Lebens*. Morgenstern also translated the works of Frederick the Great. There are two editions of his letters, *Ein Leben in Briefen* (1952) and *Alles um des Menschen willen* (1962). Otherwise, Morgenstern is known chiefly for his poems.

ACHIEVEMENTS

Christian Morgenstern began to write serious and humorous verse while still in school. By 1894, he was contributing to various magazines, and in the following years he began to travel extensively. In 1903, he became a reader for publisher Bruno Cassirer and edited *Das Theater*. The serious side of his nature was stimulated by the lectures of Rudolf Steiner, and in 1909, he became a member of the Anthroposophical Society. The German Schiller Society made him the recipient of an honorary stipend in 1912, and in November, 1913, he was honored at a Morgenstern festival in Stuttgart.

BIOGRAPHY

Christian Morgenstern was born just as the Franco-Prussian War ended, and he died shortly before the outbreak of World War I. His life span covers a long interval of peace in the history of modern Germany. The lack of external political problems may have been responsible in part for his attention to that which ailed the country from within, particularly the crass materialism he perceived and the callousness of the upper class with regard to the plight of the worker.

Morgenstern was the only child of Carl Ernst Morgenstern, a landscape painter, and his wife Charlotte, né Schertel. Both parents came from artists' families. Because of the frequent changes of residence necessitated by his father's profession, Morgenstern's education was erratic. He changed schools frequently and sometimes received private tutoring. After the death of his mother in 1881 of tuberculosis—a disease from which he also suffered, requiring frequent sanatorium visits—he was sent to his uncle's family in Hamburg. This arrangement proved to be unsuitable, and when his father married again, Morgenstern was sent to a boarding school in Landshut. The strict, oppressive environment there, which included corporal punishment, was unbearable for him, and his bitter complaints to his father resulted in his removal from the school after two years. In March, 1884, he joined his parents in Breslau and attended a local *Gymnasium* for four years. Although Morgenstern's schooling was not a positive experience, he began to write poetry and became acquainted with the philosophy of Arthur Schopenhauer and medieval German mystics such as Meister Eckhart and Johannes Tauler. Shortly be-

fore entering a military academy in 1889, he met Friedrich Kayssler, who became an actor and Morgenstern's best and lifelong friend. It quickly became obvious that Morgenstern was not suited for the military life; in 1890, he entered the *Gymnasium* in Sorau and, after his graduation in 1892, he became a student of economics and political science at the University of Breslau. The following two years brought some personal upheavals that culminated in his estrangement from his father. In the summer of 1893, his tubercular condition became more severe, requiring an extensive period of rest. He began reading Friedrich Nietzsche, to whose mother he sent his first book of poetry. Meanwhile, his father had divorced his second wife, remarried, and refused to finance his son's further schooling. In the spring of 1894, Morgenstern left for Berlin.

Newly independent, Morgenstern was briefly employed at the National Gallery. He then began to contribute to a number of different journals, among them the *Neue Deutsche Rundschau* and *Der Kunstwart*. For the latter magazine, he wrote theater reviews. This activity brought him in contact with Max Reinhardt, the famous theatrical producer, who became one of Morgenstern's friends. In 1895, his first volume of poetry, *In Phanta's Schloss*, was published. Morgenstern characterized it as humorous and fantastic, but it contains lyrics with mythological and mystical elements engulfed in pathos. Even as a sixteen-year-old, he had written a poem on reincarnation, and during the winter of 1896-1897, he had several dreams that he transformed into a cycle of lyric poems. They became part of *Auf vielen Wegen*. Between 1897 and 1903, Morgenstern translated a large number of plays and poems by Henrik Ibsen, whom he met in 1898 on a journey to Oslo. Morgenstern always had a sense of urgency about his work—a conviction that his time was limited. He traveled extensively to Scandinavia, Switzerland, Italy, and within Germany, always writing, always battling his deteriorating health. While vacationing in Dreikirchen in the Tirol, in 1908 he met Margareta Gosebruch von Liechtenstern, to whom he became engaged in the same year and whom he married in 1910.

At this point in his life, Morgenstern was seriously ill and had to spend considerable time in hospitals and sanatoriums. After learning of the spiritualist and occultist research being done by Rudolf Steiner, the couple attended his lecture in January, 1909, on Leo Tolstoy and Andrew Carnegie. Steiner had written studies on Johann Wolfgang von Goethe and Nietzsche as well as on mysticism in Christianity. After having outlined his philosophy in *Philosophie der Freiheit* (1894; *Philosophy of Freedom*, 1964) and in his *Theosophie* (1904; *Theosophy*, 1954), he published a work in 1909 outlining his method of attaining a knowledge of the occult. Morgenstern became a member of his Anthroposophical Society in May, 1909, and attended Steiner's lectures in Oslo, Budapest, Kassel, and Munich. During the last years of his life, Morgenstern's longing for communication with a world beyond that of his present existence took shape in a number of poems of a meditative nature. Two weeks before his death, he determined that the last collection of his lyrics was to be called *Wir fanden einen Pfad* (we found a path). After being removed from a sanatorium in Gries to private quarters in Untermais, Morgenstern died on March 31, 1914.

ANALYSIS

Morgenstern himself considered his serious lyrics paramount in his poetic oeuvre, although he is best known for his humorous poems. He has been compared to contemporaries such as Stefan George, Hugo von Hofmannsthal, and Rainer Maria Rilke, with whom he shared a sense of poetic mission and a certain melodiousness of verse. Morgenstern's poetry is considerably less complicated both linguistically and metaphorically than Rilke's, although it expresses emotion sincerely. Only a few of his serious poems have been translated into English, and German audiences were more receptive to his grotesque humor than to the expressions of his religious convictions or metaphysical thought. Although Morgenstern considered his light and provocative verse to be *Beiwerke* (minor efforts), it is in this area that he anticipated trends that were later exploited more extensively in Dadaism and concrete poetry. He experimented with visually and acoustically innovative techniques, presented a satirical view of a philistine society in his verse, and playfully created new and sometimes nonsensical word constellations that appear to mock both the advocates of a *poésie pure* and the efforts of those who, thirty years after his death, attempted a reconstruction of his poetry with ciphers and absolute metaphors. Satire,

religious fervor, humor, and mysticism found in Morgenstern an expressive spirit.

THE GALLOWS SONGS

Christian Morgenstern's frivolous verse is the foundation of his fame, notwithstanding his protestations. His most popular collection was *The Gallows Songs*, which ran through fourteen editions in his lifetime and by 1937 had sold 290,000 copies. Critics persisted in reading hidden meanings into these witty lyrics, so that he felt compelled to render mock explanations in *Über die Galgenlieder* (1921; about the gallows songs). The first group of these whimsical lyrics were composed when Morgenstern was in his twenties. On the occasion of an outing with some friends, they arrived at a place referred to as Gallows Hill. Being in a bantering mood, they founded the "Club of the Gallows Gang," Morgenstern contributing some frivolous poems that another of the group later set to music. These poems obviously attest Morgenstern's lighter side, and no attempt should be made to imbue them with a depth that they do not have and that was not intended, yet it will not detract from the reader's pleasure if the spirit of innovation and the subtle humor that pervade them are pointed out.

Morgenstern's raw material is the sound, the structure, the form, and the idiomatic usage of the German language. The nineteenth century saw an abundance of grammarians and linguists who attempted to regulate and explain linguistic phenomena and to limit expression to precisely defined and carefully governed modes of communication. Morgenstern perceived this approach to be hopelessly dull, "middle-class safe," and philistine. A degree of arbitrariness is an essential element of language, and he proceeded to point this out by confusing the complacent and satirizing the pedants. He accomplished this on the semantic, grammatical, and formal levels in his poems. In "Gruselett" ("Scariboo"), he created what has come to be known as a nonsense poem:

> The Winglewangle phlutters
> through widowadowood,
> the crimson Fingoor splutters
> and scary screaks the Scrood.

By arranging essentially meaningless words according to a familiar syntactical pattern within the sentence and by adding a number of adjectives and verbs that stimulate lexical memory, Morgenstern coerces the reader into believing that he has grasped the sense of what has been said. It must be pointed out here that most of the translations of Morgenstern's poems have not been literal and have frequently deviated greatly from the original in order to preserve a semblance of the poet's intention (the use of puns, untranslatable idioms, grammatical constructions not found in English, and so on).

"THE BANSHEE"

Proper inflection, punctuation, and use of tense also come under attack by Morgenstern, who freely admitted that his teachers had bored and embittered him. His poem "Der Werwolf" ("The Banshee") reflects the eagerness, gratitude, and eventual disillusionment of the pupil, as well as the futility and uselessness of that which is taught by smug grammarians. When the banshee requests of an entombed teacher, "Inflect me, pray," the teacher responds:

> "The banSHEE, in the subject's place;
> the banHERS, the possessive case.
> The banHER, next, is what they call
> objective case—and that is all."

The banshee, delighted at first, then asks how to form the plural of "banshee":

> "While 'bans' are frequent," he advised,
> "a 'she' cannot be pluralized."
> The banshee, rising clammily,
> wailed: "What about my family?"
> Then, being not a learned creature,
> said humbly "Thanks" and left the teacher.

The teacher's wisdom is depicted as severely limited and out of touch with reality. His linguistic expertise extends only to abstractions.

"AMONG TENSES" AND "KORF'S CLOCK"

Time, that element which is "money" to the businessperson and is "of the essence" to the philistine, is only relative to Morgenstern. He satirizes the preoccupation of humanity with the temporal in several ways, one of them grammatical. In the poem "Unter Zeiten" ("Among Tenses"), past and future are on equal terms in the present: "Perfect and Past/ drank to a friendship to last./ They toasted the Future tense/ (which makes sense)./ Futureperf and Plu/ nodded too." The clock, the

object that enslaves humanity because it measures every minute and every hour and restlessly reminds us that "time flies" (*tempus fugit*), is reinvented to improve on the fatal flaw. "Die Korfsche Uhr" ("Korf's Clock") not only deprives time of its sovereignty but also recalls those people who, while still existing in the present, seem to live forever in the past:

> When it's two—it's also ten;
> when it's three—it's also nine.
> You just look at it, and then
> time gets never out of line,
>
> . . . .
> time itself is nullified.

A counterpart to Korf's clock, and one with yet greater flexibility and sophistication, is Palmström's clock ("Palmströms Uhr"): it heeds requests and slows or quickens its pace according to the individual's wishes. It "will never/ stick to petty rules, however," and is "a clockwork with a heart." For those who are incurably enslaved by time and who permit it to upset their equilibrium grievously, Morgenstern suggests a cure: Since time is not a matter of reality but merely of habit, it is useful to read tomorrow's paper to find out about the resolution of today's conflicts.

"THE FUNNELS" AND "FISH'S LULLABY"

Morgenstern's visual verse is a forerunner of concrete poetry. It expresses graphically in the poem what is described linguistically in the choice of words. Max Knight translates the poem "Die Trichter" ("The Funnels") in the singular:

> A funnel ambles through the night.
> Within its body, moonbeams white
> converge as they
> descend upon
> its forest
> pathway
> and
> so
> on

The funnel in effect becomes its own pathfinder as it streamlines the moonlight through its neck and directs it like a flashlight on the dark path. Although this poem is meant to be humorous, it contains an element of Morgenstern's own undaunted search for cosmic (divine) direction and communication, which is very evident in his serious poetry. As a final example of Morgenstern's humorous verse, the visual poem "Fisches Nachtgesang" ("Fish's Lullaby"), may suffice:

```
          -
        ~ ~
        - - -
      ~ ~ ~ ~
        - - -
      ~ ~ ~ ~
        - - -
      ~ ~ ~ ~
        - - -
      ~ ~ ~ ~
        - - -
        ~ ~
          -
```

Fish, as mute creatures, can express lyrical sentiments only wordlessly, by rhythmically opening and closing their mouths. The unverbalized song is formally recorded by Morgenstern as a series of dashes that leave the content to the imagination of the reader.

"THE EIGHTEEN-YEAR-OLD" AND "EVOLUTION"

A large part of Morgenstern's work is serious prose, much of it dealing with profound matters, such as the search for truth, and with humanity's position in the universe and in relation to God. Not only did Morgenstern write deeply religious verse in the Christian tradition, but also he developed poems involving the concepts of pantheism and reincarnation. Although his basic philosophical tenets may not have changed significantly, a change in style, a greater facility and fluency in writing, is evident in a comparison of portions of his early with his late work. This may be perceived in the opening stanzas of two poems dealing with reincarnation, one of which, "Der Achtzehnjährige" ("The Eighteen-Year-Old"), was written in 1889, while the other, "Evolution," was written shortly before Morgenstern's death. "The Eighteen-Year-Old" begins:

> How often may I already have wandered before
> on this earthly sphere of sorrow,
> how often may I have changed
> the substance, the form of life's clothing?

The formal aspects of this poem in the German are scrupulously observed: iambic meter with four feet, regular *abab* rhyme scheme. The first two strophes posit the fundamental question (rhetorically), and the last one answers it with the metaphor of the ever-changing waves of the sea. The finality of the answer is sententious. Despite the use of enjambment, the poem grinds along with the deadening regularity that is one of the pitfalls of iambic meter, and it does so because the metric stress coincides almost perfectly with the syllabic emphasis of the words.

Thus, the prosodic perfection becomes somnolent and detrimental to the poem's overall effect. The single place (in the second stanza) in which the word "order" is reversed for the sake of the rhyme causes the verse to sound contrived and strange. It may be argued that the monotony of the verse is intentional, thereby underscoring the repetitiousness of life, death, and rebirth inherent in the concept of reincarnation. While such a theory is certainly plausible, other early poems by Morgenstern with different topics show a similar emphasis on the regularity of rhyme and meter and thereby reveal the style to be a sign of poetic immaturity and inexperience.

The difference between "The Eighteen-Year-Old" and the poem "Evolution" is striking. The latter begins:

> Barely that that, which once separated itself from Thee,
> recognized itself in its special entity,
> it immediately longs to return to its element.

The excessive pathos and the sententiousness that characterized the first poem are missing here. The certainty, too, is absent: There are no answers in "Evolution," only ambiguity, longing, and the realization that this yearning cannot yet find fulfillment. The easy solutions of youth have mellowed into a peaceful submission, a quiet recognition and acceptance of the inevitable unfolding of individual and collective destiny. The formal presentation is also different. Although the poem in its entirety retains a formal meter (iambic pentameter) and a regular rhyme scheme (*aba bcb c*), there is a natural flow of rhythm akin to that inherent in prose: The monotony of the iambs is broken by the deliberate placement of semantically significant syllables on metrically unstressed ones, and vice versa. The interlocking rhymes facilitate the smooth flow of verse, and the third strophe is not a glib retort but a reduction, a one-line confrontation with an unfathomable phenomenon.

Morgenstern's serious poetry is not without beauty and merit, although it has been neglected both by the reading public and by the critics. There is a certain dogmatism, a religious and mystical undercurrent inherent in it that limits its appeal and precludes the kind of universal acceptability that, for example, the lyrics of Rainer Maria Rilke possess. Morgenstern's lighter verse, which exemplifies the cheerful side of his personality, not only requires less empathy from the reader, but it also stimulates the reader's intellect without engaging the personal prejudices that he might have. It is an art worthy of pursuit.

OTHER MAJOR WORKS

NONFICTION: *Ein Leben in Briefen*, 1952; *Alles um des Menschen willen*, 1962.

TRANSLATIONS: *Inferno*, 1898 (of August Strindberg's novel); *Abendröte*, 1904 (of Knut Hamsun's play *Aftenrøde*); *Spiel des Lebens*, 1910 (of Hamsun's play *Livets spil*).

MISCELLANEOUS: *Über die Galgenlieder*, 1921.

BIBLIOGRAPHY

Bauer, Michael. *Christian Morgensterns Leben und Werk.* Munich: R. Piper, 1941. The standard biography, illustrated. In German.

Forster, Leonard. *Poetry of Significant Nonsense.* Cambridge, England: Cambridge University Press, 1962. A brief treatment of Morgenstern in the context of Dada and nonsense verse.

Hofacker, Erich P. *Christian Morgenstern*, 1978. Boston: Twayne. A good English-language introduction to Morgenstern's life and works.

Knight, Max, trans. Introduction to *The Daynight Lamp and Other Poems*, by Christian Morgenstern. Boston: Houghton Mifflin, 1973. The translator's introduction to this slim collection casts light on Morgenstern's poetics.

Mazur, Ronald. *The Late Lyric Poetry of Christian Morgenstern*, 1975. A rare treatment in English.

Helene M. Kastinger Riley;
bibliography updated by the editors

WILLIAM MORRIS

Born: Walthamstow, England; March 24, 1834
Died: London, England; October 3, 1896

PRINCIPAL POETRY

The Defence of Guenevere and Other Poems, 1858
The Life and Death of Jason, 1867
The Earthly Paradise, 1868-1870
Love Is Enough: Or, The Freeing of Pharamond, 1872
The Story of Sigurd the Volsung and the Fall of the Nibelungs, 1876
Chants for Socialists, 1884, 1885
The Pilgrims of Hope, 1885-1886
Poems by the Way, 1891

OTHER LITERARY FORMS

William Morris's first publication was a series of short prose romances and a review of Robert Browning's *Men and Women* (1855) in *The Oxford and Cambridge Magazine* (1856). Except for his translations of several Icelandic sagas and his journal of two expeditions to Iceland (1871, 1873), Morris wrote no significant prose until 1877, when he began his career as a public lecturer. Some of his lectures were published as pamphlets; those he considered the more important were collected in *Hopes and Fears for Art* (1882) and *Signs of Change* (1888). Other lectures appear in *The Collected Works of William Morris* (1910-1915, May Morris, editor); *William Morris: Artist, Writer, Socialist* (1936; May Morris, editor); and *The Unpublished Lectures of William Morris* (1969; Eugene D. LeMire, editor). During this period he also contributed to the Socialist journal *Commonweal*, which he edited from 1885 until 1890 and in which he published two utopian dream-visions: *A Dream of John Ball* (1888) and *News from Nowhere* (1891). *Icelandic Journals* are an important supplement to the Norse stories in *The Earthly Paradise* and *The Story of Sigurd the Volsung and the Fall of the Nibelungs* and, less directly, to *Love Is Enough*, written the year after his first visit to Iceland. His Socialist prose, both fiction and nonfiction, provides a necessary context for the *Chants for Socialists* and *The*

Pilgrims of Hope, and should be of interest to anyone concerned with the relationship between the aesthetic earthly paradise of his poetry and the political earthly paradise of his socialism.

Morris's Utopian fiction is closely related to the series of prose romances he wrote during the last dozen years of his life: *A Tale of the House of the Wolfings* (1888), *The Roots of the Mountains* (1890), *The Story of the Glittering Plain* (1891), *The Wood Beyond the World* (1894), *The Well at the World's End* (1896), *The Water of the Wondrous Isles* (1897), and *The Sundering Flood* (1897). It is in these works that the thematic concerns of his earlier poetry reach their final development.

A selection of Morris's letters appears in *The Letters of William Morris to His Family and Friends* (1950; Philip Henderson, editor). The complete edition of his letters, edited by Norman Kelvin, has been published under the title *The Collected Letters of William Morris* (1984-1987).

ACHIEVEMENTS

With the publication of *The Earthly Paradise* by 1870, William Morris was acknowledged a major poet and, two decades later, considered the logical successor to Alfred, Lord Tennyson as England's poet laureate. His strength as a poet lies in his grasp of human psychology and his inventiveness with narrative forms. The dramatic monologues of *The Defence of Guenevere and Other Poems* are remarkable for their daring psychosexual realism, and, both for this reason and because they are short enough to anthologize, they have come to be the poetry for which Morris is most widely known. The longer narrative poems that followed, *The Life and Death of Jason* and *The Earthly Paradise*, experiment with techniques of distancing and so forgo the dramatic immediacy of his earliest work; however, they continue Morris's exploration of sexuality and broaden it into a profound analysis of the relationship between erotic desire and the creative impulse.

The complexly structured *Love Is Enough* and the epic *The Story of Sigurd the Volsung and the Fall of the Nibelungs*, which Morris considered his poetic masterpiece, furthered his experiments with narration. Along with his prose fiction, his longer poems constitute a major exploration of narrative technique.

Today, Morris's poetry has been partially overshadowed by his essays and prose fiction and by his accomplishments as a designer, typographer, and political activist. Instead of displacing Morris's achievement as a poet, however, his other work should be judged with it as part of a total effort to transform the thought and lifestyle of Victorian England. Precisely because his interests extended beyond poetry, Morris exemplifies the bond between poetry and other forms of artistic and political expression.

BIOGRAPHY

William Morris was born on March 24, 1834, in the village of Walthamstow, a few miles northeast of London. His father was a well-to-do broker who maintained a household characterized by old-fashioned self-sufficiency. Morris's early life was centered in his family, who encouraged his tastes for literature and medievalism. At the University of Oxford, which he entered in 1853, he developed close ties with Edward Burne-Jones, and a group of friends ("the Brotherhood") who shared

William Morris (Library of Congress)

these interests. The year after Morris left Oxford, the Brotherhood undertook the publication of *The Oxford and Cambridge Magazine*, which Morris financed and, for a while, edited, and to which he was a regular contributor. In the same year, he articled himself to the architect G. E. Street, but, following the example of Burne-Jones, who had determined to become an artist, he gave up architecture after a few months in Street's office and became a disciple of the Pre-Raphaelite painter Dante Gabriel Rossetti.

Under the spell of Rossetti, Morris joined in the artist's project to paint scenes from Sir Thomas Malory's *Le Morte d'Arthur* (c. 1469, 1485) on the interior walls of the Oxford Union. Lingering in the congenial atmosphere of the university, he wrote most of the poems he later published in *The Defence of Guenevere and Other Poems*, and paid court to Jane Burden, a hauntingly beautiful woman whom Rossetti had persuaded to sit for him as a model. Morris and Jane Burden were married in 1859 and established themselves at Red House, near Upton, ten miles south of London. The house, of considerable architectural interest, had been designed for them by Morris's friend Philip Webb. Morris himself took an active role in planning the interiors of Red House, and this concern led to the establishment of a firm—Morris, Marshall, Faulkner and Company (later, Morris and Company)—dedicated to the improvement of British interior design. The firm produced stained glass, wood carving, metalwork, furniture, wallpaper, fabrics, and carpets, and in time exercised a significant role in modifying Victorian tastes.

The period of Red House, during which his daughters Jane (Jenny) and Mary (May) were born, was the happiest in Morris's married life. In response to the growing business of the firm, however, he moved back to London in 1865, and with this move began Jane Morris's gradual estrangement from her husband and her involvement with Rossetti—a relationship about which little is certain but much has been said. Morris's disappointment with his marriage is reflected in *The Earthly Paradise*, which he had begun at Red House but completed in the years after his return to London.

Search for a weekend and vacation home led Morris to Kelmscott Manor in a distant corner of Oxfordshire, a house he leased in 1871 and with which he was soon strongly identified. In the same year, he took the first of his two expeditions to Iceland—an outgrowth of the study of Icelandic language and literature which he had begun in 1868 and which was to exert a formative influence on his subsequent writing.

Although the 1870's saw the publication of *The Story of Sigurd the Volsung and the Fall of the Nibelungs* and a major reorganization of the firm, the decade is more strongly marked as the beginning of Morris's political activism. His original concerns were foreign policy and the destruction of historical buildings in the name of "restoration." Soon, though, he had also begun lecturing on the theory of design and manufacture. These efforts to influence public policy confronted Morris with the intransigence of the political and economic establishments, and this experience, along with the influence of John Ruskin, whose writings Morris had admired since his days as an Oxford undergraduate, led him to socialism.

In the 1880's Morris became one of the central figures in the British Socialist movement. He edited the journal *Commonweal*; he traveled and lectured up and down the country; he fought, risking his own imprisonment, for the Socialists' freedom of speech; he set forth his notion of an ideal society in the Marxist romances that remain his most widely read books: *A Dream of John Ball* and *News from Nowhere*.

Ultimately, dissension within the Socialist League and his own general fatigue led to a partial withdrawal from political activities in the 1890's. It was during these last years of his life that Morris established the Kelmscott Press and published a number of books, for which he designed the type, layout, and binding. It was also during this period that he returned to the themes of his earlier writing in a series of prose romances that found a popular audience during the 1970's and 1980's. Morris died on October 3, 1896, and was buried in Kelmscott churchyard.

ANALYSIS

Like other Victorian poets, William Morris is best understood in relationship to the Romantic poets whose work preceded his. Like Alfred, Lord Tennyson and Robert Browning, he sought an alternative to the Romantic preoccupation with self by writing in literary forms from which the self of the poet was distanced or removed. Unlike Tennyson and Browning, but in part through their example, he had discovered such forms by the time of his first collection of verse. Excluding himself from his poetry, however, was not enough; Morris went on to find and test ways of replacing the self with a collective consciousness. It is this effort that gives shape and purpose to his literary career.

THE DEFENCE OF GUENEVERE
AND OTHER POEMS

Tennyson and Browning had found congenial settings for many of their important poems in classical Greece or Rome, Arthurian England, or the Italian Renaissance. Morris set his earliest poems in the Middle Ages, and this setting freed him, at least partially, from the restraints of his times and allowed him to express emotional and intellectual states for which there were no Victorian equivalents. The violence and sexuality of *The Defence of Guenevere and Other Poems* would have been difficult or impossible to treat in poems dealing with contemporary England. Moreover, the poems are spoken either by dramatized personas or by the anonymous voice of the traditional song or ballad. Thus, the contemporary poet is excluded from the text and thereby relieved of the need to moralize or interpret its subject by Victorian standards.

The contents of *The Defence of Guenevere and Other Poems* fall into three categories: poems based on Arthurian materials, poems based on Jean Froissart's *Chronicles* (1373-1410) of the Anglo-French wars of the fourteenth century, and poems linked not by their common source but by their strong, often hallucinatory symbolism.

The title poem exemplifies the first group. In it, Guenevere uses an extended autobiographical apology to forestall the knights who are about to execute her as an adultress. Because it is a dramatic monologue, the central ambiguity of the poem remains unresolved: Is Guenevere really a repentant victim of circumstances, or is her speech simply a ploy to gain time? It is, of course, both. If she is a victim—if she allowed herself to be led into marriage with a man she did not love—then her victimization signals the same weakness, the same passive sensuality, that precipitated her infidelity. Yet her confession of weakness is itself a seduction of her accusers. In a world determined by sexual desire, her passivity be-comes a form of strength. By absenting himself from the poem, Morris allows these contradictory interpretations to interact and thus, in effect, to complicate its meaning. The Guinevere of *Idylls of the King* (1859-1885) is an expression of Tennyson's need to confirm Victorian sexual morality. Morris's Guenevere, in contrast, calls the relevance of moral order itself into question. Ultimately, Lancelot will come to her rescue, and that, in the end, is all that matters.

The Froissartian poems dramatize characters with a real, although usually minor, place in history. They give the lie to the accusation that Morris sentimentalized the Middle Ages. In poems such as "The Haystack in the Floods," "Sir Peter Harpdon's End," and "Concerning Geoffrey Teste Noire," the slow English defeat in the last years of the Hundred Years' War is portrayed with grim realism. In the first and shortest of the three poems, the lovers Jehane and Robert have been taken in ambush and Jehane offered the choice of becoming the lover of an enemy and so saving Robert's life—or at least postponing his death—or refusing and thus bringing about Robert's immediate murder and her own trial by water as a witch. Instead of brooding over her dilemma, she falls asleep, leaning against the wet haystack beside which they had been ambushed. After an hour, she awakens, speaks a quiet "I will not," and sees her lover decapitated and his head beaten to pieces. Again, the power of the poem lies in the absence of authorial comment. Nothing stands between the reader and Jehane's purely instinctual response. Overwhelmed by circumstances, her consciousness is reduced to a sequence of images, culminating in "the long bright blade without a flaw" with which Robert is executed; and the poem is all the more intense for this refusal to verbalize her emotional state.

In the third group of poems, Morris's concentration on imagery results in a poetry comparable to that of the French Symbolists. (Like the Symbolists, Morris at this point in his career was strongly influenced by Edgar Allan Poe.) Poems such as "The Wind" and "The Blue Closet" are richly evocative but elude precise decipherment. The first depicts a speaker who is psychotic; the second, based on a painting by Dante Gabriel Rossetti, uses deliberate inconclusiveness to suggest a deteriorating consciousness. The longest of the fantasy poems,

"Rapunzel," offers a more positive account of the psychosexual development of its protagonist prince from youth to maturity and seems to foreshadow Morris's later concern for the relationship between art and the erotic drives; any interpretation of the poem, however, is bound to be tenuous.

THE LIFE AND DEATH OF JASON AND THE EARTHLY PARADISE

The success of these early poems in confronting the reader with states of passionate intensity has made it difficult for some critics to understand Morris's decision to write in a very different style in the narrative poetry of the 1860's. If the immediacy of *The Defence of Guenevere and Other Poems* is missing in *The Life and Death of Jason* and *The Earthly Paradise*, though, the shift in style is in no sense a falling off. The manner of the earlier poems would not have worked in a longer narrative. Intensity can be sustained only so long; in time, it becomes unbearable or ludicrous. Moreover, the dramatic monologues and dialogues of *The Defence of Guenevere and Other Poems*, rich in psychological complexity, limit the role of the reader to that of an observer. The poems that followed reflect Morris's growing concern with the full nature of the experience of art; hence, the storyteller, since his role is now a matter of consequence, must be restored to a position of importance.

The storytellers of *The Life and Death of Jason* and *The Earthly Paradise* are not, however, merely extensions of William Morris. Storytelling in *The Earthly Paradise* is complex; the basic assumption of the two works is clear in the simpler narrative of *The Life and Death of Jason*. Morris's subject is classical; his models, however, are not the primary Homeric epic but the imitative secondary epic of Apollonius of Rhodes, his chief source for the materials of the poem, and, explicitly in the invocation to Book XVII, the medieval poet Geoffrey Chaucer. Thus, *The Life and Death of Jason* is not a direct imitation of a classical narrative, but the imitation of an imitation. The chief result of this device is to distance the storyteller from his story. It is no longer *his* story. Rather, it belongs to tradition. It is his task in the present to retell the tale, not to use it as a mode of self-expression, and, given the emphasized distance from the original narrative, the possibility of self-expression is limited. It is the story itself that dictates narrative structure and determines closure—not the narrator's sense that he has had his say. "Another story now my tongue must tell," the poet announces as, having completed his narrative of "the Winning of the Golden Fleece," he undertakes his account of the events that occurred to Jason ten years after his return to Argos. Similarly, when this final episode is completed and capped with the death of Jason, the poem concludes with the assurance that "now is all that ancient story told."

In its original form, *The Life and Death of Jason* was to have been a much shorter poem, "The Deeds of Jason," within the narrative frame of *The Earthly Paradise*. Despite its independent publication, the poem is best understood in that context. *The Earthly Paradise* is an enormous work—more than four times the length of *Idylls of the King* and almost twice as long as Browning's *The Ring and the Book* (1868-1869). The poem consists of a prologue ("The Wanderers") and a related series of narrative interludes framing twenty-four stories drawn from classical and Germanic sources and arranged according to the cycle of the year, from March to February, with two stories for each month. In addition to this narrative frame, the poem begins with an apology and ends with an epilogue, and prefaces each month's storytelling with a twenty-one-line lyric appropriate to the season, all in a first-person voice that may be identified with Morris. If the poet is present in these occasional verses, it is only as an accretion; and this deliberately adventitious role emphasizes his dissociation from the narratives themselves.

The Wanderers are fourteenth century Vikings who flee a plague-stricken Norway in search of a fabled Earthly Paradise—a land of immortal life and happiness—across the Atlantic. After a lifetime of disappointed expectations, they reach an island "midmost the beating of the steely sea," to which long ago Grecian colonists had been sent and where, cut off from the outside world, classical civilization has flourished long into the Christian era. The Wanderers, now old men, decide to remain here and, along with the Greek elders, agree to pass the time telling stories drawn from their two traditions. The obvious lesson of this narrative frame is that the quest for a geographical earthly paradise is vain, and that timelessness and beauty, if they exist at all, are to be found in art. Yet the art available to the storytellers, like that of *The Life and Death of Jason*, is carefully limited in its effects. It is not directly self-expressive. It is, at best, a temporary illusion. For the space of the storytelling, its auditors may forget their cares, but the sequence of stories itself—from spring to winter—reminds the reader that they are only a respite, never a real escape from the relentless movement of time and decay. Thus, *The Earthly Paradise* is less a celebration of the power of art than a study of the limits of artistic experience. Its most telling literary analogues are not the medieval frame narratives from which it takes its general structure, but John Keats's "Ode to a Nightingale" and "Ode on a Grecian Urn"—Romantic poems in which the nature of art is probed and tested.

The Wanderers' quest suggests a model of the artist's career. Like the protagonist of another Romantic poem about art, Percy Bysshe Shelley's *Alastor* (1816), they seek a real equivalent to the figments of their imagination—and, since their quest is in part motivated by artistic accounts of an earthly paradise, by the imaginative vision embodied in traditional art and oral storytelling, the failure of this quest teaches them the fundamental irreconcilability of the imagination and the natural world. It is therefore a necessary discipline that prepares them to accept the more limited notion of art that enables them to tell the tales of *The Earthly Paradise*. As such, their geographical quest corresponds to the stage of early Romanticism characteristic of many Victorian writers. (The story of their adventures is, fittingly, Romantic autobiography: The only first-person narrative available to them is the account of their own failure.)

In contrast, the Argonauts of *The Life and Death of Jason*, the classical tale originally to have followed immediately after the Wanderers' prologue, are motivated by two realizable aims—seizing the Golden Fleece and returning safely with it to Argos. The classical counterparts of the Wanderers exemplify, in other words, a classical reasonableness in setting goals for themselves. Yet Jason, having accomplished all this, ends his life dissatisfied. His heroic deeds brought to pass, he is left sitting aimlessly on the sand by the rotting hulk of his ship, at length to be crushed in sleep by its falling stem. The Wanderers are able to transform their failure into successful art and so give form and meaning to their lives.

Jason, without art, is trapped in memories he is powerless to reshape to the purposes of old age.

This notion of art as strictly limited yet necessary is present in the opening lines of the apology. Morris, referring to himself as "the idle singer of an empty day," compares his work first to the Christmastide illusion of a wizard who made the spring, summer, and fall appear through windows on three sides of a room, "While still, unheard, but in its wonted way,/ Piped the drear wind of that December day"; then, to "a shadowy isle of bliss" like that which the Wanderers come upon "Midmost the beating of the steely sea." These images argue that the full power of art is realized only when its limitations are perceived. The wizard's spell is powerful because his audience never loses awareness of the winter it temporarily displaces; the island is blissful precisely because it holds its own against the sea. The Camelot of Tennyson's *Idylls of the King* is, like the Wanderers' storytelling, a city "built to music." Its relationship to the real world is always ambiguous, however, and it is this ambiguity that spawns the doubt that destroys Arthur's kingdom. For ambiguity, Morris substitutes a tension between the recognized claims of the actual and those of the imaginary, through which each heightens, by contrast, the experience of the other. Art, by giving up its claims to replace actuality, thus subtly pervades and enhances the real world—just as the "lesser arts" of Morris and Company were able to exert an influence over day-to-day life unavailable to the "fine arts" of Victorian England.

In keeping with the project, the twenty-four narratives of *The Earthly Paradise* are generally familiar in subject and simple in narrative style. Certain of the stories, however—in particular, those in the second half of the collection—violate this rule, perhaps reflecting the strains of Morris's personal life, perhaps his impatience with simplicity itself. Both in length and in tone, "The Lovers of Gudrun" (November), which Morris based on the Icelandic Laxdaela Saga, seems to break out of its narrative frame.

Two overlapping groups of stories, those dealing with erotic quests and those dealing with artists, appear to have particularly caught Morris's imagination: "The Story of Cupid and Psyche" (May), "Pygmalion and the Image" (August), "The Land East of the Sun and

West of the Moon" (September), "The Man Who Never Laughed Again" (October), and "The Hill of Venus" (February). Eros, for Morris, may be sublimated in art or idealized love, but its basic nature as irrational drive is never forgotten. Each of these stories recapitulates, in its own way, the journey and disillusionment of the Wanderers. The protagonists of the first three eventually find fulfillment of their desires, but only after a nadir of despair in which all hope for the recovery of imaginative life is lost. Put to the test, the man who never laughs again is unable to resist the claims of the imagination and is destroyed by the strength of his own desire. In Morris's version of the Tannhäuser legend, Walter's acceptance of the limits of art—here, the erotic fantasy world of the Venusberg—leaves him in a nightmare limbo of "hopeless" joys and "horrors passing hell." Significantly, in this, the final story in the collection, the tension between the imaginary and the actual has itself become a source of frustration. Just as his empathic recreation of the figures on the Grecian Urn leads Keats to "A burning forehead, and a parching tongue," Morris's storytelling returns full circle to the painful self-consciousness he had originally sought to banish. The earthly paradise afforded by narrative art can, it turns out, provide just the opposite of an escape from the pains of desire.

LOVE IS ENOUGH

This discovery lies behind *Love Is Enough*, the most complex and in some ways most personally revealing of Morris's longer poems. Written after his 1871 journey to Iceland, it is the first of his literary works to reflect his firsthand experience of the scenery and ambience of the North. The core plot is a version of the erotic quests of *The Earthly Paradise*, but carried to an unexpected conclusion. Pharamond deserts his kingdom in search of Azalais, a maiden in a Northern valley about whom he has dreamed obsessively. Years and much hardship later, he finds her and they are united. He then leaves her, however, to return to his old kingdom, now under a new ruler. The poem ends with Pharamond contemplating the changes that have taken place and deciding to return to—yet still apart from—Azalais. This fable is presented as a masque celebrating the wedding of an Emperor and Empress who, along with the peasant couple Giles and Joan, and the mayor, who functions as a mas-

ter of ceremonies, comment on the story. Within the masque, Love acts as a commentator on, and at times agent in, the fable; a series of lyric poems ("The Music") add yet another interpretative dimension to Pharamond's quest.

While these framing devices invite comparison with *The Earthly Paradise*, they are not merely a more complicated attempt to distance Morris—and the reader—from his central romantic narrative. Instead, they signal Morris's new concern for the role of the audience. *The Earthly Paradise* deflects attention from the story to the act of storytelling; *Love Is Enough* deflects it from the story to the act of story-receiving. The audience witnessing the masque is carefully chosen to represent the nobility, the bourgeoisie, and the working class. Each group's response is different; each uses art for its own purposes; each perceives the story of Pharamond in a somewhat different context. Together, they make up a composite cultural response. Further, it is important to note that this response includes an awareness of the performance of the work. The actor and actress who play the parts of Pharamond and Azalais are the subject of audience discussion. The point, however, is not that the audience is conscious of theatrical artifice—in the way that the listeners to the tales in *The Earthly Paradise* are conscious that what they are hearing is literary artifice. Rather, awareness of the human participants in the masque gives art a grounding in actuality: The story of Pharamond is more "real" because "real" human beings perform it. The truth of art, Morris suggests, lies not in its imitation of life but in its integration with human experience.

It follows from this view that the artist who seeks this integration must concern himself with the lives of his audience and with the kind of life in which art is most vital. Although the Emperor and Empress are developed as romantic figures, it is Giles and Joan who are granted the fullest experience of the masque. Their range of response is unhindered by a sense of public role; at the end of the performance, they propose to invite the actor and actress home with them to "crown the joyance of today," thus completing the integration of art and life; significantly, they have the last word in the poem. It would seem that the peasant couple represent the consciousness toward which Pharamond himself grows in the course of his life. The subtitle of the poem, "The Freeing of Pharamond," refers to his freedom first from the role of king and, finally, from the role of romantic quester. He must forgo the need for dominance either as a ruler or as a heroic lover if he is to find happiness with Azalais. For this reason *Love Is Enough* represents an important stage in Morris's development as a social revolutionary. Yet it is revolutionary in theme only, not in tone. The dominant feeling of the poem is pain, and the figure of Love who controls the action of the masque is markedly sadistic. Here, more than anywhere else in the longer poems, Morris's own erotic frustration seems to determine the ambience of the narrative.

THE STORY OF SIGURD THE VOLSUNG AND THE FALL OF THE NIBELUNGS

The link between a revolutionary consciousness and eros marks *Love Is Enough* as a turning point in Morris's literary career. It follows from the poem that Morris was beginning to recognize a conflict between his intentions as an artist and the limitations of his bourgeois audience. This conflict is pronounced in *The Story of Sigurd the Volsung and the Fall of the Nibelungs*, for Morris's epic is a poem written for a sensibility markedly different from that of the late Victorian reading public.

As early as 1870, Morris had been fascinated by the *Volsunga Saga*, a prose translation of which he had published in that year. What struck him about the Icelandic poem was its artless understatement—"All tenderness is shown without the use of a tender word, all misery and despair without a word of raving, complete beauty without ornament." It is, as a result, "something which is above all art." If the powerful effects that Morris admires in the saga do not have verbal equivalents in the text, then they must be outside it, in the reader's supplying what has gone unsaid. Appropriately, the poet of such work is anonymous—"some twelfth century Icelander, living the hardest and rudest of lives," whose work is more a collection of material than an original composition. Thus, the reader not only is forced to supply the emotional force of the poem but also is given no identifiable narrator on whom to rely.

Further, because Victorian conventions represent an inappropriate supplement to his work, Morris wrote the poem in language that discourages a response based on contemporary assumptions of behavior and morality. He relies heavily on an often archaic Anglo-Saxon vocabulary that forces the reader to perceive the text as embodying an alien mode of expression. The poem makes little effort to engage the modern reader, and for that reason it may seem difficult to read. Only when one has adapted oneself to its style does the poem's power become apparent.

Even its narrative form is un-Victorian. If the structure of a novel organized according to the developmental pattern of human life defines what his contemporaries expected from the plot of an extended narrative, then Morris chose a story that ignores this expectation. His central figure, Sigurd, does not appear until the second of the poem's four books and is killed before the end of the third. In the course of the poem various characters— Sigurd, Regin, Brynhild, Gudrun—come into prominence and then pass away. Morris uses imagery and symbolism to suggest organic wholeness, but these devices do not obscure the lack of novelistic unity fundamental to *The Story of Sigurd the Volsung and the Fall of the Nibelungs*. Instead of a narrative organized around the development of individual character, it traces the collective fate of a people. The reader, to respond to this subject, must be able to identify structure with a collectivity rather than with an individual life; it is for this reason that the poem is closely related to Morris's later Marxist writings.

Although *The Story of Sigurd the Volsung and the Fall of the Nibelungs* effectively ended the major phase of Morris's poetic career, it was not a dead end. After 1876, his chief energies shifted from writing poetry to changing society so that such poems could be read. When he returned to imaginative literature, it was with the recognition that the audience he was seeking could be reached best by prose. The archaic language and collective consciousness of *The Story of Sigurd the Volsung and the Fall of the Nibelungs*, however, reappear in *A Tale of the House of the Wolfings* and the romances that followed.

LATER POETRY

Except for his translations of *The Odyssey of Homer* and *The Tale of Beowulf* and for a few of the short pieces collected in *Poems by the Way*, the only verse that Morris published in the last twenty years of his life was directly related to his efforts to popularize socialism. The subject of his *Chants for Socialists*, which appeared in Socialist journals and pamphlets during the mid-1880's, is clear from titles such as "The Voice of Toil," "No Master," "All for the Cause," and "The March of the Workers." The power of such poetry may have passed with its historical occasion; however, that Morris could write verse that caught the imagination of the common man was no mean accomplishment.

The Pilgrims of Hope is a fictional narrative, the concluding sections of which are based on the 1871 Paris Commune. As Karl Marx did, Morris saw the events in France as a stage in the overthrow of bourgeois culture, and for this reason his portrait of the Communards is biased and perhaps sentimentalized. Moreover, the poem, which appeared serially in *Commonweal*, was hastily written, and it was only after Morris was well into it that he seems to have hit upon the theme that would bring it to a conclusion. Despite its lapses, however, *The Pilgrims of Hope* is successful in its realistic portrait of working-class London and urban socialism. It also suggests some of Morris's own problems in justifying his status as a businessman with his socioeconomic beliefs. Yet, just as *Love Is Enough* links eros and revolution, the later poem connects Marxism with a love triangle made up of the protagonist, his wife, and a socialist comrade. Indeed, their decision to go together to Paris and fight for the Commune is less strongly felt as a commitment to socialism than as an—explicitly suicidal—resolution of the tensions in their relationship. Not only does the medium of the poem return Morris to the erotic concerns of his earlier poetry; that return itself argues that, beneath his commitment to social action, those concerns remained unresolved—a view confirmed by the prose romances of the 1890's, in which he returned to the theme of the erotic quest, now envisioned not simply as an act of the individual protagonist, but as a component of the social history of a people.

Seen in isolation, Morris's career as a poet is inconclusive; seen in terms of his work as a whole, its pattern of development becomes clear. If, like Tennyson and Browning, Morris sought to free his poetry of Romantic self-consciousness, his alternative was more radical than theirs. Typically, the Romantic poem confronts the reader with the self of the poet—in William Wordsworth's terms, "a man speaking to men"—whose presence de-

mands a very personal response. Tennyson, Browning, and the Morris of *The Defence of Guenevere and Other Poems* replace the self of the poet with a collection of other selves. These alternative figures may no longer speak with the authority of the poet, but the relationship between reader and poem is basically the same: One responds to the poem as one responds to a fellow human being, either directly, in the dramatic monologues, or at second hand, in narrative verse. In the poetry he wrote after *The Defence of Guenevere and Other Poems*, Morris rejects this model. *The Earthly Paradise* removes even the art of storytelling from the world of the reader. The complicated structure of *Love Is Enough* "frees" not only Pharamond but also the reader from identification with a model of individual development. *The Story of Sigurd the Volsung and the Fall of the Nibelungs* replaces individual selves with a collectivity—the language and narrative conventions of Victorian England with alien speech and storytelling. If these poems are difficult to judge by literary standards derived from the work of other poets—if they do not fit the reader's notion of what a Victorian poem is supposed to be—this should remind us that Morris, not only in politics but also in poetry, was a revolutionary.

OTHER MAJOR WORKS

LONG FICTION: *A Dream of John Ball*, 1888; *A Tale of the House of the Wolfings*, 1888; *The Roots of the Mountains*, 1890; *The Story of the Glittering Plain*, 1891; *News from Nowhere*, 1891; *The Wood Beyond the World*, 1894; *The Well at the World's End*, 1896; *The Water of the Wondrous Isles*, 1897; *The Sundering Flood*, 1897.

NONFICTION: *Hopes and Fears for Art*, 1882; *Signs of Change*, 1888; *William Morris: Artist, Writer, Socialist*, 1936 (May Morris, editor); *The Letters of William Morris to His Family and Friends*, 1950 (Philip Henderson, editor); *The Unpublished Lectures of William Morris*, 1969 (Eugene D. LeMire, editor); *The Collected Letters of William Morris*, 1984-1987 (4 volumes; Norman Kelvin, editor).

TRANSLATIONS: *The Aeneids of Virgil*, 1875; *The Odyssey of Homer*, 1887; *The Tale of Beowulf*, 1895.

MISCELLANEOUS: *The Collected Works of William Morris*, 1910-1915 (May Morris, editor).

BIBLIOGRAPHY

Burdick, John. *William Morris: Redesigning the World.* New York: Todtri, 1997. This biography, illustrated both color and black-and-white photographs, examines the full range of Morris's talents: as designer, activist, businessman, poet, and prose writer.

Coote, Stephen. *William Morris: His Life and Work.* Stroud: Alan Sutton, 1996. This biography considers not only the full range of Morris's broad achievements but also his personal relationships. Bibliography, index.

Faulkner, Peter. *Against the Age: An Introduction to William Morris.* London: Allen & Unwin, 1980. This readable introduction to Morris, with frequent quotations from his writings and contemporary criticism of his work, stresses the continuing relevance of Morris's ideas for modern readers. The six chapters are arranged according to the stages of his life, each one introduced by an excerpt from a letter Morris wrote summarizing his own life. A selected list of primary and secondary sources and an index are included.

Harvey, Charles. *Art, Enterprise, and Ethics: The Life and Works of William Morris.* Portland, Oreg.: Frank Cass, 1996. A life that focuses on Morris as businessman with reference to previous biographies, origins of his family's wealth, his experiences abroad, and the ethical basis for his business. Bibliographical references, index.

Kirchhoff, Frederick. *William Morris.* Boston: Twayne, 1979. This book provides an overview of Morris's literary achievements, viewing them as "his central mode of self-discovery and expression." Kirchhoff stresses the interdependence of theory, experience, and emotion, and of folk art and sophisticated literary traditions in Morris's work. Includes a chronology, a select bibliography, and an index.

Le Quesne, A. L., et al. *Victorian Thinkers: Carlyle, Ruskin, Arnold, Morris.* New York: Oxford University Press, 1993. The philosophies of Morris are usefully presented in the context of his times and the major contemporary philosophers in cultural, literary, and arts criticism.

Lindsay, Jack. *Willam Morris: His Life and Work.* New York: Taplinger, 1979. In this important full-scale biography, Lindsay builds on the work of earlier biographers, with emphasis on the changes throughout Morris's life, along with the enduring influences of his childhood experience. A bibliography and an index are included.

MacCarthy, Fiona. *William Morris: A Life for Our Time.* London: Faber and Faber, 1994. Brings all aspects of Morris's childhood, personal life, political career, literary pursuits, and design innovations to bear on an understanding of the man and his achievements.

McGann, Jerome J. *Black Riders: The Visible Language of Modernism.* Princeton, N.J.: Princeton University Press, 1993. The focus here is on Morris's poetry and its relation to his printing and graphic design, along with their mutual influence on modernism in British and American poetry. The nineteenth century's value of the physical look of books brought import to the look of printed words and the meaning conveyed by that appearance.

Oberg, Charlotte H. *A Pagan Prophet: William Morris.* Charlottesville: University Press of Virginia, 1978. Oberg explores the paradoxes throughout the works of this "enigmatic Victorian" and then examines the unity in his poetry and prose fiction, which, she asserts, must be read as a living whole. Includes an index and illustrations.

Salmon, Nicholas. *The William Morris Chronology.* Bristol: Thoemmes Press, 1996. This substantial reference (292 pages) contains more than two thousand entries, providing a nearly daily account of the life, along with stories and anecdotes told by contemporaries. A unique guide to Morris's life and career. Bibliography.

Silver, Carole. *The Romance of William Morris.* Athens: Ohio University Press, 1982. Silver focuses on Morris's use of romance in this book-length study because "interwoven in the poems and romances Morris wrote throughout his life are the strands of all his other thought." Seven chapters trace the patterns in Morris's romances through his career. Illustrations, a bibliography, and an index are included.

Thompson, Paul. *The Work of William Morris.* 3d ed. New York: Oxford University Press, 1993. Illustrated in both color and black and white, the standard concise introduction to Morris's life.

Tompkins, J. M. S. *William Morris: An Approach to the Poetry*. London: Cecil Woolf, 1988. Tompkins fills in the gaps in previous criticism of Morris's writings by discussing the narrative poems in detail, paying attention to the sources of the tales and the links with Morris's daily life. Includes an index.

Victorian Studies 13 (Fall/Winter, 1975). This special double issue includes a reassessment of Morris in William E. Fredeman's introduction, and D. G. Rossetti's playlet on the death of William "Topsy" Morris. Six of the thirteen articles focus on Morris's poetry, including Hartley S. Spatt's essay on Morris's general theme of the transcendence of social history through an individual perspective on the past. Three articles discuss unpublished works. Color as well as black-and-white plates are included.

Frederick Kirchhoff;
bibliography updated by the editors

Howard Moss

HOWARD MOSS

Born: New York, New York; January 22, 1922
Died: New York, New York; September 16, 1987

PRINCIPAL POETRY

The Wound and the Weather, 1946
The Toy Fair, 1954
A Swimmer in the Air, 1957
A Winter Come, A Summer Gone: Poems, 1946-1960, 1960
Finding Them Lost and Other Poems, 1965
Second Nature, 1968
Selected Poems, 1971
Chekhov, 1972
Travel: A Window, 1973
Buried City, 1975
A Swim off the Rocks, 1976
Tigers and Other Lilies, 1977
Notes from the Castle, 1979
Rules of Sleep, 1984
New Selected Poetry, 1985

OTHER LITERARY FORMS

Like many other contemporary poets, Howard Moss experimented with drama. His play *The Folding Green* was first performed in 1954 by the Poets' Theatre in Cambridge, Massachusetts, and again, in 1965, in a workshop production by the Playwrights' Unit of Theater 1965. *The Oedipus Mah-Jongg Scandal* was performed in 1968 by the Cooperative Theatre Club, Inc., in New York. A third play, *The Palace at 4 A.M.*, was given a staged reading by the Playwrights' Unit in New York. Both *The Palace at 4 A.M.* and *The Folding Green* were published in 1980. In addition to drama, Moss published a critical study, *The Magic Lantern of Marcel Proust* (1962), and three collections of criticism: *Writing Against Time: Critical Essays and Reviews* (1969), *Whatever Is Moving* (1981), and *Minor Monuments: Selected Essays* (1986); the last discusses the work of writers ranging from Gustave Flaubert to Anton Chekhov to Katherine Anne Porter. In 1974, he published *Instant Lives*, satirical biographies illustrated by Edward Gorey. Moss was also editor of: *Keats* (1959), *The Nonsense Books of Edward Lear* (1964), *The Poet's Story* (1973), and *New York: Poems* (1980).

ACHIEVEMENTS

Although widely respected for his poetry, Howard Moss is perhaps better known for having been the poetry editor of *The New Yorker*. After 1950, when he assumed that post, his careful editorial judgment and clearheaded vision helped to construct the environment of taste, wit, and sensibility in which many of the well-known poets writing in the English language today developed and matured. Moss opened the pages of *The New Yorker* to a rich and diverse flow of poetic talent: John Updike and David Ray, Elizabeth Bishop and Mark Strand, David Wagoner and Donald Justice, W. H. Merwin and Dave Smith, Philip Levine and Charles Simic. The list is long and impressive and could be extended almost indefinitely. Moss is one of a handful of influential editors and craftsmen who helped give shape and direction to the flow of poetry in the twentieth and twenty-first centuries.

Moss's poetry is characterized by a lucid, often ironic voice; by evocative images; and by sure, sensitive, rhythmical language. His major concerns remained almost unchanged after they were first voiced in *The Wound and the Weather*: the passage of time, the paradox of change and permanence, the acceptance of loss and gain (of friends, of beauty, of love, of life). His own influences seem clearly marked: Wallace Stevens (visible in Moss's wordplay and in his sometimes extravagant language) and W. H. Auden (noted chiefly in Moss's carefully controlled music and in his ironic wit).

As a critic, Moss varied in his approach—from detailed New Critical textual analysis to purely subjective response. "I distrust," he said, "all theses and theories about writing, and dislike the idea of 'schools' of writing, both in the traditional and in the educational sense."

Moss received *Poetry*'s Janet Sewall David Award in 1944, the Brandeis Creative Award in 1962, an Avery Hopwood Award in 1963, a grant from the National Institute of Arts and Letters in 1968, a National Book Award for Poetry in 1972 (for *Selected Poems*), the Brandeis University Citation in Poetry in 1983, another National Endowment for the Arts Award in 1984, an Academy of American Poets fellowship in 1986 for "distinguished poetic achievement," and the Lenore Marshall Poetry Prize in 1986. In 1957 and 1964, he was a judge for the National Book Awards.

Widely respected both as a critic and as a craftsman, Moss provided his contemporaries with a level of accomplishment difficult to surpass. Perhaps his dominant strength was his single vision: his dependence upon intellect rather than emotion. That vision of art enabled him to keep the welter of life "just under control."

BIOGRAPHY

Howard Moss was the son of David and Sonya (Schrag) Moss. When he was still a young child, his grandfather and grandmother were brought over from "the old country"—Lithuania. As a consequence, Moss writes, "I grew up in a middle-class community but was really under the care of my two grandparents, who were of another flavor unmistakably." In spite of this background, Moss was one of an increasing number of contemporary poets identified with the city and with urban life. Much of his poetry concerns itself with the metropolis—with New York City—both its moments of beauty and its moments of bleakness.

After attending public school and high school in Belle Harbor, New York, Moss studied at the University of Michigan from 1939 to 1940, then transferred to the University of Wisconsin, where he received his B.A. degree in 1944. Other formal education included a summer at Harvard University in 1942 and postgraduate work at Columbia University in 1946.

After college, Moss worked for one year (1944) for *Time* magazine as a copyboy and, later, as a book reviewer. Following a short period with the Office of War Information, he was an English instructor at Vassar College for two years, served one year as fiction editor of *Junior Bazaar*, and, finally, joined the editorial staff of *The New Yorker* in 1948. He was poetry editor for the magazine until his death in 1987 at the age of sixty-five.

ANALYSIS

One of the definitions of a poem, Howard Moss wrote, is that it "keeps the welter of life, the threat of disorientation, just under control. . . ." This sense of uneasy balance—of order poised at the edge of chaos—informs Moss's editorial, critical, and poetic judgment.

As an editor, Moss established himself as one of the influential figures in American letters during the second half of the twentieth century. His strength as an editor derived primarily from his single vision of art: a dependence upon wit and intellect rather than upon spontaneity and emotion. He once said, "Though I respect and sometimes envy spontaneity in writing, I revise my work a great deal." The poems that appeared in *The New Yorker* during Moss's tenure as poetry editor reveal how clearly Moss transmitted his own vision of poetry to other poets.

As a critic, Moss's interests were far-ranging—from Proust to John Keats to William Shakespeare to Jean Stafford. In his major work of criticism, *The Magic Lantern of Marcel Proust*, Moss organized the structure and content of Proust's *À la recherche du temps perdu* (1913-1927; *Remembrance of Things Past*, 1922-1931) around four metaphysical concepts: gardens, windows, parties, and steeples. Although the book received mixed reviews, Moss was praised for his vivid and lucid writing. The pieces collected in *Whatever Is Moving* continued to illustrate Moss's wide range of critical interests: Walt Whitman, Robert Frost, Anton Chekhov, Elizabeth Bishop. In "The First Line," Moss presents a perceptive and original investigation into the different ways poets have used first lines to launch a poem.

EARLY COLLECTIONS

As a poet, Moss's reputation grew slowly but steadily over a long and productive period, beginning in 1944, when he received the Janet Sewall David Award from *Poetry*. One criticism of his first collection, *The Wound and the Weather*, was that the poems relied heavily upon abstraction. He was recognized, however, for his skill with language, his consistency of metaphor, and his adherence to formal and traditional structures and values. *The Wound and the Weather* adumbrated many of Moss's continuing concerns: the urban setting, the preoccupation with loss, the awareness of time. The next two collections, *The Toy Fair* and *A Swimmer in the Air*, showed Moss's progress as a poet in both technique and subject matter. Howard Nemerov called *The Toy Fair* "one of the most accomplished collections of lyric poetry since the war" (*Atlantic Monthly*, September, 1954).

A WINTER COME, A SUMMER GONE

In his fourth book, *A Winter Come, A Summer Gone*, Moss presented, in addition to fourteen new poems, a selection of the best work from his three previous volumes—poems embodying those characteristics which have come to be associated with his poetry. The two title poems, "A Winter Come" and "A Summer Gone," are excellent examples. Both poems have the same formal structure: ten stanzas of eight lines each, shaped by an iambic pentameter rhythm, with a basically regular rhyme scheme. In each, the voice is that of the first person singular; it is a predominantly lyric voice but muted with what Moss has called, in another context, a "delicious undertone" of regret, "the way nostalgia can be redeeming or the sadness of fall pleasurable."

In "A Winter Come," the first eight stanzas sketch brief, telling vignettes of the winter season: the windblown leaves, the stiffened boughs, the landscape blurred with snow, the insubstantial clouds of breath on winter air, footprints of birds on "a scroll of white," frozen waterfalls, snow-covered statues. The next-to-last stanza, with its metaphor of fire as "the end of words," turns the poem on the axis of ambiguity: "By ambiguity/ We make of flame a word that flame can burn,/ And of love a stillness." The last stanza returns the poem to its now reshaped locus of winter and the bittersweet truth that "icy wind makes young blood sweet/ In joining joy, which age can never have./ And that is what all old men know of love."

In "A Summer Gone," the first two stanzas create a vivid image of the late summer seaside: "stilts/ Of slipshod timber," spiral shells, "now empty of their hosts." The next three stanzas directly address the listener, asserting, finally, "Those beautiful outsides, those thin-skinned maps/ Are part of love. Or all of it, perhaps." Stanzas VI, VII, and VIII offer metaphors of loss—loss of sight, of sound, of touch. The two final stanzas turn back to the loss of summer and look ahead to "Sad fall," colored by a thousand dyings. As in "A Winter Come," the last image is that of love: "The view/ To take is but another wintry one,/ To wait for the new nestings of the sun."

THE 1960'S

In the 1960's, Moss both widened his range of poetic techniques and probed more deeply into his constant theme of loss and deprivation. *Finding Them Lost and Other Poems* received widespread critical acceptance. Moss said in an interview for *The New York Quarterly* that he was trying in this collection to change from his "usual methods." Particularly successful examples of this change were a group of poems called "Lifelines"— "attempts to get certain people I knew down on paper." In *Second Nature*, Moss essayed, in poems such as "Sands" and "Front Street," a more conversational line, approaching free verse. The sure choice of language and the ever-increasing concreteness of image, however, remained characteristic strengths of his poetry. The *Selected Poems* pulled together the strongest of his earlier verse, complemented by seven previously uncollected poems. The collection, a National Book Award winner, illustrated Moss's increasing understanding of his craft and validated his own definition of poetry as that form which "focuses, compresses, intensifies."

BURIED CITY

Buried City reinforced Moss's stature as a poet and revealed again the depth and range of his major concerns. The images here are those of the city: In the title poem, an archaeologist from some future time examines the ruins of New York City. Two subsequent volumes, *A Swim off the Rocks* and *Tigers and Other Lilies*, turn in different directions. The former is a volume of light verse, ranging from the surreal to satiric wordplay. *Tigers and Other Lilies* is a book of poems for children— poems about plants with animals in their names.

NOTES FROM THE CASTLE

Moss's 1979 collection, *Notes from the Castle*, reaffirmed the lucid voice, the sensitive music, and the evocative images that distinguish his poetry. Moss's one constant was his commitment to the intellect to make sense of the world. In these poems, it is the mind that speaks—wisely and memorably—elegiac words: of gravel, of stars, of ideas. In "Gravel," there is the yearning to be "made separate/ Or to be part/ Of some great thing . . . / To be made solid." In "Stars," there is the haunting image of the speaker reaching up "to pluck the stars like words to make/ A line, a phrase, a stanza, a whole poem." In "Elegy for My Sister," one image encapsulates all the others: "What are ideas but architecture/ Taking nature to heart and sustaining/ Inviolable forms." Although the tendency to abstraction remains, Moss moves more and more toward the concrete image. Even when the abstract occurs, the poet frequently redeems it through the use of startling language and unusual contexts.

RULES OF SLEEP

Rules of Sleep, Moss's last collection of new poetry, continues his concern with time and loss as well as his uncommon use of commonplace settings or subjects. The speaker of a meditation on Albert Einstein, for example, is Einstein's old bathrobe. Moss's penchant for urban surroundings (and his use of contemporary speech) is exemplified by a poem set in Miami Beach in which a street is "strung out on lights." There is anxiety in the poems' reflections on mortality—"the chill of what is about to happen"—but there is also a wit and calmness that keeps the fear at bay: "Everything permanent," Moss writes, "is due for a surprise."

OTHER MAJOR WORKS

PLAYS: *The Folding Green*, pr. 1954; *The Oedipus Mah-Jongg Scandal*, pr. 1968; *The Palace at 4 A.M.*, pr. 1972.

NONFICTION: *The Magic Lantern of Marcel Proust*, 1962; *Writing Against Time: Critical Essays and Reviews*, 1969; *Instant Lives*, 1974; *Whatever Is Moving*, 1981; *Minor Monuments: Selected Essays*, 1986.

EDITED TEXTS: *Keats*, 1959; *The Nonsense Books of Edward Lear*, 1964; *The Poet's Story*, 1973; *New York: Poems*, 1980.

BIBLIOGRAPHY

Gioia, Dana. "The Difficult Case of Howard Moss." *The Antioch Review* 45 (Winter, 1987): 98-109. Although this is primarily a review of Moss's *New Selected Poetry*, it also surveys the poet's life, poetry, and career as poetry editor for *The New Yorker.* Gioia acknowledges that Moss's career at *The New Yorker* had a largely negative impact on his poetry by robbing it of serious and sustained critical evaluations and admirably corrects this oversight.

Howard, Richard. *Alone with America*. New York: Atheneum, 1980. The chapter on Moss reviews his work and illustrates the qualities that set him apart from "the many others who are merely suave or serviceable." Among these qualities are his rhythms, his use of conceits and puns, and his contrasts of human and universal order. Howard writes in a lean style and includes passages from major Moss works to illustrate his key points.

Leiter, Robert. "Howard Moss: An Interview." *The American Poetry Review* 13 (September/October, 1984): 27-31. Leiter's important interview provides essential information about and by Moss, including his experience as a professor at Vassar College and as a poetry editor at *The New Yorker.* Moss discusses the mechanics of poetry editing, composition, and structure, and in the process reveals the criteria he uses in writing and editing his own work.

Malkoff, Karl. *Crowell's Handbook of Contemporary American Poetry.* New York: Thomas Y. Crowell, 1973. A succinct and informative overview of Moss and his poetic technique, which includes a description of Moss's stylistic evolution illustrated with a contrast between "Elegy for My Father" and "Arsenic." Malkoff suggests the poet's work is best reviewed using the methods of New Criticism and provides the reader with a select bibliography.

St. John, David. "Scripts and Water, Rules and Riches." *The Antioch Review* 43 (Summer, 1985): 309-319. St. John asserts that Moss wrote "some of the most powerful and moving poems of the last ten years." He argues his case by citing a variety of Moss's works, including *Rules of Sleep, Buried City,* and *Notes from the Castle.* The beauty, emotion, and musical quality of Moss's works are illustrated with extensive passages from these and other poems.

Robert C. Jones

LISEL MUELLER

Born: Hamburg, Germany; February 8, 1924

PRINCIPAL POETRY

Dependencies, 1965
The Private Life, 1976
Voices from the Forest, 1977
The Need to Hold Still, 1980
Second Language, 1986
Waving from Shore, 1989
Alive Together: New and Selected Poems, 1996

OTHER LITERARY FORMS

Drawing upon her native language, Lisel Mueller has translated several works by German women, including *Selected Later Poems of Marie Luise Kaschnitz* (1980); *Whether or Not* (1984), a short prose collection by Kaschnitz; a novel by W. Anna Migutsch, *Three Daughters* (1987); and *Circe's Mountain* (1990), also by Kaschnitz.

Throughout her career, Mueller has also written critical articles and reviews for the magazine *Poetry* and for the *Chicago Daily News.* Her essay "Midwestern Poetry: Goodbye to All That" appears in a collection of essays *Voyages to the Inland Sea I* (1971), edited by John Judson. Also, a brief essay titled "Parentage and Good Luck" appears in *Where We Stand: Women Poets and the Literary Tradition* (1993), edited by Sharon Bryan.

ACHIEVEMENTS

Although Lisel Mueller began writing poetry in college, she did not turn to serious writing of poetry for several more years. Her first volume of poems, *Dependencies,* was published in 1965. This volume is often regarded as excessively literary, but the lead poem, "The Blind Leading the Blind," is frequently anthologized. Mueller's second full volume of poetry, *The Private Life,* won the Lamont Poetry Prize in 1975. Mueller was awarded the 1981 National Book Award for Poetry for *The Need to Hold Still.* Finally, she was awarded the Pulitzer Prize in poetry for *Alive Together.*

BIOGRAPHY

Lisel Mueller was born in Hamburg, Germany, to Fritz C. Neumann and Illse Burmester Neumann, both teachers. Leaving her grandparents behind, her immediate family fled Nazi Germany in 1939 and settled in Evansville, Indiana. Mueller was blessed with a set of parents who were, according to Mueller, "wholly and blessedly gender-blind." Mueller characterizes her mother as "feminine in the sense that she was warm, outgoing, and impulsive, but she was totally ignorant of 'feminine wiles,' such as manipulation of, and deference to, men." It was only when Mueller moved to Evansville, Indiana, at the age of fifteen that she discovered the more traditional roles of women and gender discrimination.

In 1943, Lisel Neumann married Paul Mueller, an editor, and they had two daughters, Lucy and Jenny. Although Mueller would dabble in poetry while in college, preparing for a social-work career, she began to write serious poetry only after the death of her mother in 1953. Many years later she explains, in her poem "When I Am Asked," why she began writing poetry: On a beautiful June day shortly after her mother died, Mueller discovered that she had to place her grief "in the mouth of language,/ the only thing that would grieve with me."

Mueller has worked as an instructor of creative writing at Elmhurst College, Goddard College, and the Warren Wilson M.F.A. Program for Writers. She is a self-taught poet, strongly influenced by the New Critics, including T. S. Eliot, Cleanth Brooks, I. A. Richards, and John Crowe Ransom. Mueller greatly admires Wallace Stevens; although she does not believe that she writes anything like Stevens, she does allude frequently to his poems in her own work. Mueller also developed her critical skills and her awareness of contemporary poetry by writing reviews for the *Chicago Daily News*. Perhaps most important, Mueller has drawn upon her life experiences as a mother and spouse for the material of her poems.

Mueller remained almost exclusively in the Midwest after her arrival in the United States, and it is a midwestern landscape that appears most often in her poetry. Yet she has never been simply midwestern in her thoughts or outlook. Of the Midwest she says,

> I am more at home here than anywhere. At the same time I am not a native; I see the culture and myself in it, through a scrim, with European eyes, and my poetry accommodates a bias toward historical determinism, no doubt the burdensome heritage of a twentieth century native German.

ANALYSIS

Lisel Mueller's poetry is unassuming, spare, and solidly grounded in history, both public and private. Without the banners of feminism or other celebrated causes,

Pulitzer Prize-winning poet Lisel Mueller at her home in Lake Forest, Illinois, in 1997.
(AP/Wide World Photos)

Mueller has quietly and steadily recorded her impressions of life in America. Her perspective is unique, marked as it is by her immigration experience at the age of fifteen and the loss of her grandparents to the horrors of Nazi Germany. She writes of life events that are the causes for quiet celebration—a long, happy marriage, the birth and lives of her children, and the inevitable process of growing old.

DEPENDENCIES

Looking back, Mueller was not happy with most of the poems that she wrote in *Dependencies*. She said that they "seem overly decorated, too metaphorical." Most critics agree that these poems are overly literary, but this is only a mark of the New Critics that Mueller studied so closely. The lead poem, "The Blind Leading the Blind," presents the theme of interdependencies between human beings, a theme that appears often in her poetry. In this poem, Mueller uses a cave metaphor, reminiscent of Plato's cave parable, to represent the journey of two companions through major life events. The speaker, presumably female, is the guide, and she speaks with the natural authority of one who has "been here before." She knows where the ground is rock, where it is mud, where there are turn-offs. Yet she reiterates her need for the other, the fact that "there are two of us here" in this cave, or on this journey through life.

Another important theme brought forth in this work is the continuity between generations of Mueller's family. She writes of her pregnancy, a means of allowing the continuation of her and her spouse's love. The birth of her child becomes part of healing the grief of her mother's death; Mueller realizes that her own ability to love her daughter is a direct result of the love that she first experienced from her mother.

THE PRIVATE LIFE

Many critics agree that in Mueller's next full volume of poetry, *The Private Life*, she reveals her most characteristic voice and themes. In an interview with Stan Sanvel Rubin and William Heyen, Mueller identifies two important "springs" for her poetry: her domestic life with her husband and daughters, and the Vietnam War, which she says made her "think of the interdependency, certainly in our age, of the public and private life." However, Mueller seldom alludes directly to the Vietnam War. The public life of World War II remains a greater immediate interest to her because of its more direct impact upon her family of origin.

"My Grandmother's Gold Pin" begins as a charming explanation from a mother to a daughter about why the mother wears a particular pin so often. Each fleur-de-lis reminds the mother-speaker of objects in her grandparents' home, their mannerisms, the music. When the mother comes to the center pearl in the pin, she is bitterly reminded of her grandparents' death by starvation in an animal shed. Through this poem, Mueller illustrates that there can be no neat, clean separation between the public and private, past and present. The mother tells her daughter that this private memento, the pin, is

all I have left of an age when people believed the heart was
an organ of goodness, and light stronger than darkness,
that death came to you in your proper time:
An age when the dream of Man nearly came true.

The value of silence, the space beyond language or our immediate perceptions, is also an important theme introduced in *The Private Life*. "What the Dog Perhaps Hears" is a playful musing on all that people do not hear—the growth of a child, the unfurling of a snake, the birth of a baby bird pushing its way out of the shell. The final line "and we heard nothing when the world changed," reminds us that so much takes place beyond the perception of the five senses.

The poem "The Private Life" begins with a flat statement: "What happens, happens in silence." Things that happen in silence include what goes on inside of other people's heads, the death of an aspen in an ice storm, the rot of fruit at the market. The poet seems weary of words, especially the screaming headlines of the daily news. More important things are happening outside language: "in a red blood cell,/ a curl in the brain,/ in the ignorant ovum."

THE NEED TO HOLD STILL

In this winner of the 1981 National Book Award for Poetry, Mueller continues to explore the limitations of language and the continuity between past and present. She chooses to speak more often in the voices of others and begins to distance herself from her more youthful self. In "Talking to Helen," Mueller speaks to Helen Keller, imagining the absence of both sight and sound in the sequence of perceptions that led to Keller's realization of what the word "water" means. Yet, in many ways, Keller's perceptions, limited as they were to the tactile world, may have been superior to the poet's own perceptions. Keller's "world was imagination/ all possible worlds, while mine/ shrinks with the speed of speed."

In "The Triumph of Life: Mary Shelley," Mueller speaks in the voice of the nineteenth century novelist and author of *Frankenstein* Mary Shelley, a woman with an enviably feminist upbringing. Shelly's father "taught [her] to think/ to value mind over body,/ to refuse even the airiest cage." Yet "None of this kept [Shelley] from bearing/ four children and losing three/ by the time [she] was twenty-two." Mueller reminds her readers through this poem that feminism is possible only through medical science. Mary Shelley remained a victim of biology and fate. However, the contemporary age is hardly superior with its demystification of the female body and of the heart:

You don't speak of the heart
in your letters, your sharp-eyed poems
You speak about your bodies

as though they had no mystery,
no caves, no sudden turnings.

Shelley also refuses the role of the prophet, claiming, "But I only wanted to write/ a tale to tremble by." It is only by accident that her tale predicted the potential horrors of human genetic engineering. Shelley was concerned only with the business of living and knowing what she could about her own life.

In the poem "The Need to Hold Still," Mueller begins to explore the process of aging. Here, she uses winter weeds as a metaphor for the aging woman, who is, like the weeds, "among the thin/ the trampled on/ the inarticulate." As a woman ages, she becomes less visible and demands less from life; she notices "that gray and brown/ are colors/ she disappears into// that her body/ has stopped asking/ for anything except calm." However, aging has its compensations. There is less need to cling or to try to wring the "last drop of juice." Dignity, design, cleanness of line all remain in the winter weeds as well as the aging woman.

SECOND LANGUAGE, WAVING FROM SHORE, AND ALIVE TOGETHER

A theme that unites these three volumes of poetry is the process of sorting through what is necessary, what is important, what to keep, what to leave behind—a process more typical of one's later years. In "Necessities," Mueller examines what is necessary on her continued journey toward old age and death. One thing that is necessary is "a map of the world." This map includes both the public and the private; it is the map with the landscape of our childhood, the place where we first made love, the roads that we did and did not take, "the private alps no one knows that we have climbed." Other necessities include "the illusion of progress," "answers to questions," and "evidence that we matter." It does not matter that people do not really progress, or that the answers may be wrong, or that the things people interpret as "evidence that we matter" may only be quirks of fate. The important thing is that humans momentarily believe, at least long enough to relieve their anxieties.

Mueller continues to grieve the loss of her parents throughout her life. In "Voyager" (*Second Language*), Mueller expresses the need for the "impossible photograph," the one that would show the world the father that she remembered from her younger years. She must somehow come to terms with "the hardest knowledge:/ that no one will remember you/ when your daughters are gone." Similarly, in "Missing the Dead" (*Waving from Shore*), Mueller wishes that she had more tangible evidence of her parents' existence. She wishes that they had been musicians who left behind their musical scores or that she could believe that their bodies were transformed into stars that she could point to so that others might see "how they shimmer,/ how they keep getting brighter/ as we keep moving toward each other."

Several poems from these three volumes deal directly with Mueller's coming to terms with her own eventual death. In "Poem for My Birthday" (in *Waving from Shore*), old age has brought Mueller to the point where she is no longer "the heroine of [her] bad dreams." She has left behind "the melodramas/ of betrayal and narrow escapes." She is no longer the one who takes foolish risks like "the one/ who swims too far out to sea." Rather, she has become "the one who waves from shore," a minor player in her own life. Mueller asks, "Does that mean I have solved my life?" In many ways, the answer to the question is affirmative. Language has its limitations, but the poet's access to her own language stores has become more limited. In "Aphasia," she observes that the world "no longer/ offers itself to [her]/ as an infinite dictionary." However, this aging process that Mueller presents is far from a picture of grim, unrelenting diminishment. In "Monet Refuses the Operation," the speaker (artist Claude Monet) refuses to believe that his way of seeing is simply "an aberration/ caused by old age, an affliction." He responds to the doctors:

> I tell you it has taken me all my life
> to arrive at the vision of gas lamps as angels,
> to soften and blur and finally banish
> the edges you regret I don't see.

As Monet's speech illustrates, the old can often "see" the interconnectedness of things in a way that the young can seldom "see."

Mueller refuses to romanticize her own death or even the power of her own achievements beyond death. This vision is a difficult one to achieve; perhaps it takes someone who has lived at least half of his or her own life to understand it.

OTHER MAJOR WORKS

TRANSLATIONS: *Selected Later Poems of Marie Luise Kaschnitz*, 1980 *Whether or Not*, 1984 (of Kaschnitz); *Three Daughters*, 1987 (of W. Anna Mitgutsch); *Circe's Mountain* (of Kaschnitz).

BIBLIOGRAPHY

Bryan, Sharon, ed. *Stand: Women Poets and the Literary Tradition*. New York: W. W. Norton, 1993. Mueller's essay "Parentage and Good Luck" appears in this collection and casts much light on the poet's life and concerns.

Rubin, Stan Sanvel, and William Heyen. "'The Steady Interior Hum': A Conversation with Lisel Mueller." In *The Post-Confessionals: Conversations with American Poets of the Eighties*, edited by Earl G. Ingersoll, Judith Kitchen, and Stan Sanvel Rubin. New York: Associated University Presses, 1989. Mueller discusses her beginnings as a poet, the changes in her poetry between the first and second published volume, and her European heritage.

Solyn, Paul. "Lisel Mueller and the Idea of Midwestern Poetry." In *Regionalism and the Female Imagination: A Collection of Essays*, edited by Emily Toth. New York: Human Sciences Press, 1985. Solyn takes issue with many points that Mueller makes in "Midwestern Poetry: Goodbye to All That." Solyn is particularly disturbed by Mueller's separation of rural and urban midwestern poets. Mueller does not believe that urban poets from large midwestern cities are distinctly different from other urban poets.

Nancy E. Sherrod

PAUL MULDOON

Born: County Armagh, Northern Ireland; June 20, 1951

PRINCIPAL POETRY

Knowing My Place, 1971
New Weather, 1973
Spirit of Dawn, 1975
Mules, 1977
Names and Addresses, 1978
Immram, 1980
Why Brownlee Left, 1980
Out of Siberia, 1982
Quoof, 1983
The Wishbone, 1984
Mules, and Early Poems, 1985
Selected Poems, 1968-1983, 1986
Selected Poems, 1968-1986, 1987
Meeting the British, 1987
Madoc: A Mystery, 1990
The Annals of Chile, 1994
The Prince of the Quotidian, 1994
Six Honest Serving Men, 1995
New Selected Poems, 1996
Hay, 1998
Kerry Slides, 1998
Poems, 1968-1998, 2001

OTHER LITERARY FORMS

Unlike many other contemporary Irish poets, Paul Muldoon is, generally speaking, content to let his verse speak for him exclusively. Hence his production of articles and reviews is small and not very helpful in coming to terms with his poetry. His most notable contribution to Irish literary culture has been his idiosyncratic, and in some quarters controversial, editing of *The Faber Book of Contemporary Irish Verse* (1986). Muldoon has also published translations of a small number of poems by the important contemporary Irish-language poet Nuala Ni Dhomhnaill. The distinctive character of Muldoon's own verse invites the conclusion that translating is much closer to his imaginative inclinations than editing is. He has also edited *The Scrake of Dawn: Poems by Young People from Northern Ireland* (1979), *The Essential Byron* (1989), and *To Ireland, I: The Clarendon Lectures in English Literature 1998* (2000).

ACHIEVEMENTS

Despite the regular appearance of book-length collections and his increasingly familiar presence internationally, particularly in the United States, Paul Muldoon's status remains somewhat overshadowed by that of older, more celebrated poets from Northern Ireland.

In addition, Muldoon's fluency and inventiveness have been constants since the publication of his precocious volume *New Weather* in 1973. As a result, it has been easier to take pleasure in his method than to chart the development of his aesthetic and thematic concerns. It is possible that the poet himself has experienced some of this sense of occlusion and that this has accounted, at least in part, for his increasing tendency to write unfashionably long poems. The publication of the book-length poem *Madoc* in 1990—a work that in many senses is a typically quirky yet not wholly unexpected product of the longer poems in *Why Brownlee Left*, *Quoof*, and *Meeting the British*—provides a pretext for an interim report on the attainments, challenges, and difficulties of the most original Irish poet to emerge since the 1930's.

While the critical jury may still be out as to the overall significance of Muldoon's work, there is no doubt that it already signifies an impressive departure not only from that of his immediate predecessors among Northern Irish poets (such as Seamus Heaney, John Montague, and Michael Longley) but also from the conception of Irish poet as cultural watchdog and keeper of the national conscience, promoted and embodied by the founding father of modern Irish poetry, William Butler Yeats.

Certainly the number of awards Muldoon has received suggests a critical acceptance of his work. Some of the accolades he has received include the Eric Gregory Prize (1972), the Sir Geoffrey Faber Memorial Award (1994), the T. S. Eliot Prize (1994), the American Academy of Arts Award in Literature (1996), and the *Irish Times* Literature Prize (1997).

BIOGRAPHY

Paul Muldoon was born on June 20, 1951, in the remote rural community of The Fews, County Armagh, Northern Ireland. Shortly afterward, his family moved to the no less remote area of The Moy, County Tyrone. The poet, therefore, comes from a background that is similar is many external respects to that of the poets of Northern Ireland, such as Seamus Heaney and John Montague, who have done much to put that part of the world on the literary map. This point is relevant in view of how different Muldoon's response to his background has been from that of his illustrious near-contemporaries.

After secondary education at St. Patrick's College, Armagh, Muldoon read English at Queen's University, Belfast, and was graduated with a B.A. in 1971. Like many writers from Northern Ireland, particularly those of an older generation, he worked as a talks producer for the Northern Ireland regional service of the British Broadcasting Corporation in Belfast. He resigned this position in 1986 and began working as a visiting professor in a number of American universities. He has taught at Columbia University, the University of California, the University of Massachusetts, and in 1990, he began teaching at Princeton University. In 1993, he became director of creative writing at that school, and in 1999 he was elected professor of poetry at Oxford, succeeding James Fenton.

ANALYSIS

Although direct environmental influences on the growth of the imagination are impossible to prove, it does seem relevant to point out that Muldoon's coming to consciousness coincided with the disintegrative threats to the social fabric of his native province. These threats of violence to civilians and forces of law and order alike, to property and the general communal infrastructure of Northern Ireland, date from 1969, when Muldoon was a freshman at Queen's University, Belfast. The threats have been both carried out and resisted. Disintegration of families, neighborhoods, and institutions has occurred, yet those entities continue to survive. Codes of self-protective speech have arisen, and things are no longer necessarily what they seem on the surface. It would be fanciful to argue that such characteristics of the poet's outer world are precisely what Muldoon's poetry reproduces, since, to begin with, such an argument overlooks the inevitable significance of form in his work. At the same time, however, there is such a degree of unpredictability, play, and opacity in his poetry that it is tempting to consider it an attractive, exuberant, puzzling, and blessedly harmless parallel universe to that of bombers and demagogues.

This does not mean that Muldoon has not addressed poems to the trials and tribulations of the Northern Ireland of his adult life. Poems such as "Anseo" in *Why*

Brownlee Left (*anseo* is the Irish word for "here," meaning "present" in the poem), "The Sightseers" in *Quoof*, and the arresting and unnerving title poem of *Meeting the British*—to name well-known instances—confront in ways that are not particularly euphemistic the euphemistically named Troubles. Yet it is equally, if not more, revealing of Muldoon that he would name a collection of poems for "our family word/ for the hot water bottle" (*Quoof*), particularly since the reader has only the poet's word for it that this is what *quoof* actually means. More than any other Irish poet of his generation, perhaps, Muldoon demands to be taken first and foremost, and if possible exclusively, at his word.

Muldoon's slightly surreal, slightly whimsical, very subjective, and very oblique view of his material—his almost perverse conception of what constitutes "material" itself—sits at a seemingly crazy but refreshing angle to the modern Irish poetic tradition. Concerned more with the making of verses than with the making of statements, his work is airy, reckless, private, and provocative. Many of his poems are as much teases as they are texts in the predictable sense. Yet they can also be seen as indebted to a more intriguing tradition of Irish poetry than that inaugurated by Yeats. Muldoon's implicit rejection of the public, vatic role of the poet, his frequent absorption in the minutiae of the natural world, his deployment of fragmented narrative, his use of pastiche, his finding himself equally at ease with foreign or domestic themes, his playfulness, and the challenge of his cunning superficiality have—among numerous other devices and resources—provided a valuable counterpoint to the more solemn, preoccupied, and fundamentally historicist poetry of his Northern Irish elders.

NEW WEATHER

The title *New Weather* has become over time a helpful phrase to describe the surprising novelty of Muldoon's poetry and its place in the canon of modern Irish verse. The poem in which the phrase "new weather" occurs, "Wind and Tree," is in one sense not a particularly representative Muldoon work, with its talk of love and its unironic, somewhat sheepishly attention-claiming "I." The poem's elaborate metaphorical conceit of lovers being injured as trees are by wind heralds one of the most conspicuous elements in Muldoon's distinc-

tive art, his generally shape-changing propensity, of which metaphor is a primary feature. "Wind and Tree" also provides the revealing lines, "Most of the world is centred/ About ourselves," often availed of by readers struggling for a foothold in some of the poet's less hospitable works.

Much more instructive of things to come in Muldoon's work is the poem "Hedgehog," for the economy and distinctively contemporary quality of its imagery ("The snail moves like a/ Hovercraft, held up by a/ Rubber cushion of itself"), the outrageousness of its conceits (the hedgehog is referred to as "the god/ Under this crown of thorns"), and the possibility that the poem overall is a metaphor for communal and interpersonal division and defensiveness both in Northern Ireland and beyond. As the line in "Our Lady of Ardboe," from *Mules*, has it, "Who's to know what's knowable?"

MULES

By the time of the publication of *Mules* the question of knowability in Muldoon's work was not strictly rhetorical—or, to be Muldoonish about it, was strictly rhetorical, meaning that it was built into the nature of the poem, rather than occurring every so often as a detachable line from a given poem. The mysterious "Lunch with Pancho Villa," and the very novelty of an Irish poet's having something to write under such a title, is not merely a witty imaginative adventure, expressive of the poet's range and restlessness. In addition, the poem interrogates in a tone that is all the more incisive for lacking solemnity the consequences of violence and questions whether the poet's duty is to respond to what the world contains or to the contents of his own imagination.

"CUBA"

One answer to this question—a question that may be used as a means of investigating Muldoon's increasingly complex mapping of his subjectivity—may be found in "Cuba," from *Why Brownlee Left*. Here a remembrance of family life and common usages, both domestic (a father's predictable anger) and communal (an erring daughter goes to Confession), is located in the context of the Cuban Missile Crisis of 1962, revealing the quirky, intimate, and reassuringly unresolved and unmechanical manner in which personal and public history overlap. This poem, ostensibly a simple narrative elaborating a vignette of memory, is a delicate essay in remoteness and intimacy, last things and initial experiences, innocence and eschatology. The poem's open rhythm (often captured by Muldoon through direct speech) leaves the reader in no doubt that the poet stands for the tender insignificances of the human realm rather than a melodramatic characterization of the machinations of history.

"Why Brownlee Left"

A comparable sense of openness, of life as new beginnings and deliberately unfinished business, is provided by the title poem of *Why Brownlee Left*, in which the material achieves significance by—as the title implies—being neither a question nor an answer. Who Brownlee is seems irrelevant. The emphasis is on what has remained "a mystery even now." The point is the leaving, the possibility of pastures new, lyrically recapitulated by the absconder's horses at the end of the poem, "gazing into the future."

"Immrama"

Perhaps Brownlee wanted to be able to say, like the narrator in "Immrama," from the same collection, "I, too, have trailed my father's spirit"—even if the trail leads to an inconclusive and implausible end for both father and son. Conclusion is less important than continuity. Analogously, Muldoon's work suggests that a poem's happening—the multifarious activities of the words contained by and excited within a prosodic framework (itself various and informal, though necessarily final)—is of more consequence than the poem's meaning. At an elementary level, which the reader dare not overlook, perhaps the happening is more lifelike, by virtue of its free play and variety, its sometimes outrageous rhymes and syncopated rhythms, than the meaning. Though quest as a motif has been present in Muldoon's work from the outset—"Identities" in *New Weather* begins "When I reached the sea/I fell in with another who had just come/ From the interior"—it becomes more pronounced in the collections after *Why Brownlee Left*. The unusual title "Immrama" draws attention to this fact, as presumably it is meant to. It is the plural form of *immram*, the name in Irish for the genre of medieval Irish romances (including tales of travel to the other world) and a word that in the singular provides the title of Muldoon's first important long poem, which also appears in *Why Brownlee Left*.

In "Immrama," Muldoon releases the possibilities latent or implied not only in the quirky lyrics of *Why Brownlee Left* but also in his overall body of work. Using narrative in order to subvert it—a strategy familiar from, for example, "Good Friday, 1971, Driving Westward" in *New Weather*—Muldoon brings the reader through a somewhat phantasmagorical, surreal adventure that pantomimes the style of hard-boiled detective fiction. Set in Los Angeles, the story itself is too erratic and effervescent to summarize. As the title of the poem is intended to suggest, however, the material maps out a territory that is rich and strange, which may be the landscape of dream or of vision or the objective manifestation of the psychic character of quest. Lest the reader be merely exhausted by the extent of the poem's literary high jinks—"I shimmied about the cavernous lobby./ Mr. and Mrs. Alfred Tennyson/ Were ahead of me through the revolving door./ She tipped the bell-hop five dollars"—there are important themes, such as identity, fabulation, and rootlessness, and an alert meditation on the hybrid nature of writing as an imaginative process, of which "Immrama" is a helpful rehearsal.

"The More a Man Has the More a Man Wants"

Much more allusive, spectacular, and demanding is Muldoon's next adventure in the long poem "The More a Man Has the More a Man Wants," from *Quoof*. Here, an increasingly prominent interest on the poet's part in the lore and legends of Native American traditional literature comes influentially into play. In particular, the various legends of jokers and shape-changers, particularly those of Winnebago literature, are availed of, not in the sense of overt borrowings or new translations but with a respect for and fascination with their spirit. Muldoon is not the first poet to pay homage to these mythical figures. The English poet laureate Ted Hughes employed them in one of his most celebrated works, *Crow* (1970, revised 1972). The results are so different, however, that it is tempting to think of "The More a Man Has the More a Man Wants" as Muldoon's response to the senior poet.

The subject of the poem is change. As in the case of "Immrama," scenes shift with confusing rapidity, and the inherent transience and adaptability of the persona is once again a central, enabling concern. The thematic mixture is far richer, however, in "The More a Man Has the More a Man Wants." In particular, the nature of change is not confined to Muldoon's familiar deployments, such as travel, quest, and dream. Violence as an agent of change is also explored and its consequences confronted. Here again, a certain amount of frustration will be experienced by the reader, largely because the poem, though promising to be a narrative, becomes a variety of open-minded narrative options, while the integration of the material takes place by virtue of the reader's ability to explore the possibilities of congruence within the widely diversified settings and perspectives. Sheer verve, inventiveness, unpredictability, and impenitent originality make "The More a Man Has the More a Man Wants" the poem that most fully illustrates the scope of Muldoon's ambitious aesthetic energies, through which all that is solid—including, perhaps particularly, the legacy of history—is transformed into airy, insubstantial, but memorable surfaces.

MADOC

Any claim for the centrality of "The More a Man Has the More a Man Wants" must be made in the awareness of Muldoon's book-length poem *Madoc*. This poem is in effect prefaced by a handful of lyrics recognizably in the mode of, say, those in *Quoof*, among which is the superb elegy "Cauliflowers" (the incongruousness of the title is a typical Muldoon maneuver). "Madoc" itself, however, consists of a sequence of rather impenetrable lyrics, all of which are headed by the name of a philosopher. Subtitled *A Mystery*, it is certainly a baffling poem. Once again, the assertion and denial of narrative are fundamental to the poet's procedures.

The source of the poem is a work of the same name written by the English Romantic poet Robert Southey, drawing in a manner vaguely reminiscent of Sir Walter Scott on the heroic legends of one of Great Britain's marginal peoples, in this case the Welsh. Muldoon, without adapting Southey's theme or prosody, seems to have adapted, in a satirical vein, Southey's method. His *Madoc* looks back to an adventure in which Southey was involved—namely, the establishment of a pantisocratic community on the banks of the Susquehanna River in

Pennsylvania. The inspiration for this ill-fated scheme was the major English Romantic poet Samuel Taylor Coleridge. Casting his own mind back over the historic, not to mention romantic, dream of community, Muldoon reproduces his own puzzlement with such a project, articulating not the self-deceiving confidence of Coleridge's thought (and, by invoking the names of philosophers, of thought generally) but the fact that so little that is clear remains of what such thought asserted. In turn, or rather concurrently, a disquisition on the knowability of the world, a surreal satire on the inevitable insubstantiality of ideals, and a narrative poem whose most submerged feature is its storytelling, *Madoc* is clearly Muldoon's most sustained and substantial work, though most readers will find it easier to admire than it is to enjoy or decipher.

"INCANTATA"

Muldoon's reputation for mischief making, obfuscation, and intellectual pyrotechnics can lead the reader to forget that he is also a poet of considerable lyric skill and occasionally deep feeling. "Incantata," from *The Annals of Chile*, is written in memory of Mary Farl Powers, a former lover, who died of cancer in 1992. It is loaded, as usual, with recondite material, but somehow gets out from under its wittiness to reveal, if often in a sideways gesture, his feeling for Powers, often in the context of her work as an artist:

> I saw you again tonight, in your jump-suit, thin as a rake,
> your hand moving in such a deliberate arc
> as you ground a lithographic stone
> that your hand and the stone blurred to one
> and your face blurred into the face of your mother.

The form of the poem (an eight-line stanza) is taken from Abraham Cowley, the seventeenth century Royalist poet. Muldoon quietly traces the history of the affair, sometimes sadly and sometimes with comic gusto, as in their encounter with a priest who objected to their living together outside marriage. "Who came enquiring about our 'status', of the hedge-clippers/ I somehow had to hand, of him running like the clappers." Through the superfluity of references, the feeling rings true:

> . . . the day your father came to call, of your leaving
>   your sick-room
> in what can only have been a state of delirium,

of how you simply wouldn't relent
from your vision . . .
that fate governs everything . . .

It is a poem that disproves the complaint that Muldoon is often "too clever by half" while, at the same time, showing how clever he is.

"ANONYMOUS: MYSELF AND PANGUAR"

"Anonymous: Myself and Panguar," from *Hay*, shows how relaxed and direct Muldoon can be if the subject is right. In this poem about the poet and his cat, Panguar, the idea is to compare his cat's search for mice with his own search for the right word:

> much as Panguar goes after mice
> I go hunting for the precise
>
> word.

The poem is light, simple, and without show of the virtuoso flashiness that Muldoon possesses:

> Panguar going in for the kill
> with all his customary skill
> while I, sharp-witted, swift and sure,
> shed light on what had seemed obscure.

He may be teasing with the last line, aware, as he is, of the criticism of his sometime obscurity.

OTHER MAJOR WORKS

PLAYS: *Shining Brow*, pr. 1993 (libretto); *Six Honest Serving Men*, pb. 1995; *Bandanna*, pb. 1999 (libretto).

NONFICTION: *To Ireland, I,* 2000.

CHILDREN'S LITERATURE: *The Last Thesaurus,* 1995; *The Noctuary of Narcissus Batt,* 1997.

TRANSLATIONS: *The Astrakhan Cloak: Poems in Irish by Nuala Ni Dhomhnail,* 1993; *The Birds,* 1999 (of Aristophanes' play).

EDITED TEXTS: *The Scrake of Dawn: Poems by Young People from Northern Ireland,* 1979; *The Faber Book of Contemporary Irish Verse,* 1986; *The Essential Byron,* 1989; *The Faber Book of Beasts,* 1997; *Bandanna: An Opera in Two Acts and a Prologue,* 1999.

BIBLIOGRAPHY

Birkets, Sven. "Paul Muldoon." In *The Electric Life: Essays on Modern Poetry.* New York: Morrow, 1989. An assessment of the poet's relationship to his contemporaries on the international scene. Muldoon's originality is identified and appreciated. The provision of a wider context for his work reveals its scope and interest. In particular, Muldoon's distinctive verbal deftness receives alert attention.

Goodby, John. "'Armageddon, Armagh-geddon': Language and Crisis in the Poetry of Paul Muldoon." In *Anglo-Irish and Irish Literature: Aspects of Language and Culture,* edited by Birgit Bramsback and Martin Croghan. Uppsala, Sweden: Uppsala University Press, 1988. The title comes from Muldoon's poetic sequence "Armageddon." In using the name to pun on the poet's birthplace, the author draws attention to Muldoon's verbal dexterity. His dismantling and reassembling of language is reviewed. These practices are also related to Muldoon's background.

Johnston, Dillon, *Irish Poetry After Joyce.* Notre Dame, Ind.: University of Notre Dame Press, 1985. Chapter 6 locates Muldoon in two related ways. His connection to his immediate contemporaries is characterized. In addition, his individual voice is appraised in the overall context of modern Irish poetry. A valuable critique.

Kendall, Tim. *Paul Muldoon.* Bridgend, Wales: Seren, 1996. One of the first full-length studies of Muldoon with individual chapters on all the books up to and including *The Annals of Chile.* A sensible, intelligent reading of the poems in the context of his entire career.

Robinson, Peter. "Muldoon's Humour." In *Politics and the Rhetoric of Poetry: Perspectives on Modern Anglo-Irish Poetry.* Amsterdam: Rodolpi, 1995. The question of how to use humor in serious poems, and otherwise, is examined in the light of Muldoon's reputation for wit.

Wills, Claire. *Reading Paul Muldoon.* Newcastle: Bloodaxe Books, 1998. Wills's sensible comments are considerable help in clarifying Muldoon's more difficult texts.

George O'Brien,
updated by Charles H. Pullen

DAVID MURA

Born: Great Lakes, Illinois; June 17, 1952

PRINCIPAL POETRY
  After We Lost Our Way, 1989
  Listening, 1992
  The Colors of Desire, 1995

OTHER LITERARY FORMS

David Mura is the author of *A Male Grief: Notes on Pornography and Addiction* (1987). His poems and essays have been published in *The Nation, The New Republic, New England Review, Utne Reader, Quarry*, and *American Poetry Review*, among other journals. His two memoirs, *Turning Japanese: Memoirs of a Sansei* (1991) and *Where the Body Meets Memory: An Odyssey of Race, Sexuality, and Identity* (1995), provide an intimate glimpse of the author's struggles to come to terms with his heritage and his sexuality. His vivid descriptions of places and people captivate the reader, though some may be repelled by his obsession with sex and pornography. Discovering his Japanese identity forms the core of *Turning Japanese*, and *Where the Body Meets Memory* is an account of his addictions, what he deems their genesis, and his struggle to come out of the depths of self-hatred.

Mura is also a noted performance artist. He wrote and performed in *Relocations: Images from a Japanese American* (1990), *Silence and Desire* (1994; with Tom Rose, Kim Hines, and Maria Cheng), and *Internment Voices* (1997; with Esther Suzuki). In 1994, with Alex Pate, he helped create the multimedia performance piece *Secret Colors*, about the lives of men of color and relations between Asian Americans and African Americans, which was later adapted for television for the Public Broadcasting System.

ACHIEVEMENTS

David Mura is known for his outspoken discussion of the interconnection between race and sexuality, a predominant theme in all his literary works. He has won several honors for his poetry and nonfiction works. He was awarded the Fanny Fay Wood Memorial

Prize by the American Academy of Poets in 1977. He was the U.S./Japan Creative Artist Fellow in 1984 and was awarded the National Endowment for the Arts Literature Fellowship in 1985. He won the Creative Nonfiction Prize from Milkweed in 1985 and the Discovery/*The Nation* Award in 1987. In 1988 he was the winner of National Poetry Series Contest and in 1990 was awarded the Pushcart Prize. *Turning Japanese* received the Josephine Miles Book Award from the Oakland, California, chapter of PEN in 1991 and was cited as by *The New York Times* as a Notable Book of the Year. It has been translated into Japanese and Dutch. He won a Lila Wallace-*Reader's Digest* Writer's Award in 1995 and has received several other fellowships and grants.

BIOGRAPHY

David Mura was born in Great Lakes, Illinois, in 1952 to Tom K. and Tesuko Mura. Mura's grandfather, like many other men of his generation, lost his business after President Franklin Roosevelt issued Executive Order 9066 after the bombing of Pearl Harbor, which forced the relocation of Japanese residing on the West Coast to hastily created camps. The internment left indelible marks on the lives of the Nisei, the second-generation Japanese Americans. Seeing the disintegration of the lives of their parents, who had been denied any rights and had been treated as traitors, the Nisei often turned their energies to becoming assimilated in the mainstream and proving their loyalty to the American way of life at the expense of their own heritage. By the time David was born, his father had shortened his family name Uyemura to Mura and converted to Christianity so he could meld into the mainstream. David grew up in comfortable circumstances in a prosperous section of the city.

Mura's childhood was typical of all Sansei, or third-generation Japanese Americans. The oldest of four children, he was expected to excel in academics and extramural activities. However, his childhood and adolescence were not very happy: Like many children of minority families who quickly become Americanized in their behavior and thinking, he chafed under his father's autocratic ways and felt that denying his Japanese roots would grant him acceptance at the majority white school he attended. He was a respected athlete and a good student, but he assumed the persona of a loud, obnoxious person in order to avoid the stereotype of the successful, timid Asian scholar. He went to Grinnell College in Iowa for his undergraduate work. Moving away from home did not free him from his repressed anger, and in 1974, his decision to pursue graduate work in literature at the University of Minnesota, instead of going to law school, did not improve his relationship with his parents, especially his father, who wanted him to pursue a respectable, money-making profession. Mura provides a detailed account of this period of his life in *Where the Body Meets Memory*. He met his future wife, two years his junior, at Grinnell.

The next few years were filled with turmoil as he struggled to deal with identity issues. Being accepted as an honorary white, he found, did not help: He found that the culture around him either ignored members of his race or conveniently categorized the individuals among popular stereotypes. He attributed his behavior—dabbling with drugs and alcohol, indulging in promiscuity, and being unable to sustain relationships—to low self-esteem generated by the racial situation. To some extent, his behavior was typical of many liberal youths of the late 1960's and early 1970's, who protested not only the war in Vietnam but also all forms of societal controls. At the insistence of his girlfriend, who by now had finished medical school, Mura went into therapy to overcome his obsessions, addictions, and ensuing depression. His marriage, a year spent in Japan on a fellowship, the birth of his children, his gradual success in his career, and his acceptance of his parents, all helped him over time to shed his insecurities and to assume his role as a husband, parent, and an American proud to reclaim his Japanese heritage. He settled in Minneapolis with his family and became an active member of the Asian American Renaissance, an arts organization.

ANALYSIS

The recurring themes in David Mura's poems are alienation, racism experienced by minorities (particularly by Japanese Americans), the betrayal of the Issei (first-generation Japanese Americans) by the United States government, life in the internment camps, and the overreaching power of the loss of sexual identity. The collec-

tions *After We Lost Our Way* and *The Colors of Desire* reveal his preoccupation with these themes.

AFTER WE LOST OUR WAY

After We Lost Our Way has four sections. The first section, composed of ten poems, deals with Mura's parents, grandparents, the survivors of the atomic bombing of Hiroshima, life in U.S. internment camps, and the manner in which Japanese Americans endured the hardships and indignities in silence. The second section is about Pier Paolo Pasolini (1922-1975), an Italian writer and director persecuted because of his sexual orientation and decadent ways. Sections 3 and 4, consisting of twelve poems, return to personal themes again.

Two poems, "These Years Are Obscure, Their Chronicle Uncertain" and "Hope Without Hope," touch on Mura's purpose in writing. In the first poem, he talks of the oppressed of the world and how their history is often forgotten. His role, he believes, is to keep the memory of the past alive. The second poem recognizes the seeming futility of these efforts to capture the truth as "History rolls on, lie by lie." Many of the poems in this book attempt to record the forgotten segments in the lives of Japanese Americans.

"Grandfather and Grandmother in Love" and "Suite for Grandfather and Grandmother Uyemura: Relocation" capture the imagined serene life of Mura's grandparents before the "betrayal." Though burdened by "blight and bad debts," *otoo-san* and *okaa-san* (grandfather and grandmother) manage to maintain their loving relationship. "The Hibakusha's Letter" has a survivor of the atomic bomb paint her bleak life. She mourns a world gone and her inability to conceive, yet finds occasional moments of happiness. "Letters from Poston Relocation Camp," addressed to a sister in Tokyo, dwells upon the desolate life in the camps, the loss of the speaker's greenhouse and the home she was forced to leave, and a reference to a dream foreshadowing the aftermath of the atomic bomb.

Another poem, "An Argument: On 1942," depicts the mother's refusal to talk about her life in the relocation camps, dismissing it as something that needs to be forgotten: "it was so long ago—how useless it seems. . . ." She understands the need of her writer son to probe but reiterates her stand: "why can't you glean/ how far we've come." "A Nisei Picnic: From an Album" pictures the uncle who was wounded in the war and came back to find that he could not rent an apartment. The speaker finds it baffling that the family still would not talk about their camp experiences and fall back on the philosophy expressed in the saying *Shikatta ga nai* (it cannot be helped).

All these poems use several poetic forms ranging from free verse to blank verse, liberal use of alliteration and assonance, and often internal rhymes. Variations of the length of lines enable Mura to convey thoughts briskly or in a slow, meditative tone.

THE COLORS OF DESIRE

Fifteen poems in this collection are primarily about Mura's struggle to accept his heritage, and seven of these depict his infidelities and obsessions. Mura does not spare himself and paints his life, his love affairs, and his addiction to pornography with stark, almost brutal honesty. One of the most effective techniques he employs is the juxtaposition of disparate scenes.

For instance, in the poem "The Colors of Desire," he begins with a depiction of "Photograph of a Lynching (circa 1930)." The scene melds into his father's riding the bus on a weekend pass from his camp in Arkansas. He is invited to sit in the front; at the same time, the African Americans in the back ask him to join them. This subtle juxtaposition of the two incidents suggests more than the words reveal. By allowing an Asian man to sit in the front, the whites are giving him an honorary status, but in view of his internment, the emptiness of the gesture becomes obvious. Then again, the father's decision to ignore those at the back clearly indicates that he has cast his lot with those in power.

The next section jumps ahead to fifteen years later, when David is a boy of six and witnesses his father's resigned acceptance of unprovoked racial slurs hurled at him. The scene then shifts to the father's beating of the boy for getting into a fight with his younger brother. Not much is overtly said, but it is clear that Mura sees the connection between the suppressed helpless anger of the adult and the violence inflicted on the vulnerable. The next scene, six years later, shows the adolescent boy discovering *Playboy* magazines in his father's closet, the beginning of a love affair with pornography. Obviously, Mura is suggesting a link between his parents' handling of the situation and his subsequent problems. However,

to be fair, he interjects the father's response as well. The father dismisses the episode and asks the son why he cannot recall the good times they shared, "Is nothing in your life your own volition?/ The past isn't just a box full of horrors."

Some of the most moving poems in the collection are about Mura's grandparents and their generation. "Issei Strawberry" portrays an Issei who toils in the strawberry fields. He has a good harvest, yet his heart is full of sorrow, for the laws of the country do not allow him to own his land. The deed of the land is in the name of his minor sons; citizens by birth, they are gradually moving into the mainstream, leaving the parents behind. "Issei: Song of the First Years in America" takes the women's perspective of the hardships they endure. Most came as picture brides and found their grooms very different from the men they had envisioned. The speaker thinks of the backbreaking labor, the expectations of the husband that she will give him sons, take care of him and his children, and ask nothing in return and realizes it is enough to break the spirit of anyone. The poem captures vividly the loneliness and despair of these women.

Several of the other poems in *The Colors of Desire* deal with the speaker's obsession with pornography and his inability to sustain a faithful relationship with the woman who lived with him. His characterization of his various affairs, the long poem "The Affair," giving his and her versions of the relationship, becomes tiresome after a while. However, the poem "Gardens We Have Left," composed of seven sections, juxtaposes scenes of domesticity: the father fixing dinner with his child assisting him, his thoughts wandering from the future of this biracial child, the irony of the union of a descendant of the Mayflower family and a Japanese, his relationship with his father, his wife, and his identity, to, finally, his acceptance of the present with its limitations. What could have turned into a piece of mawkish sentimentality becomes a carefully crafted panorama of a thirty-nine-year-old man's journey in life.

OTHER MAJOR WORKS

NONFICTION: *A Male Grief: Notes on Pornography and Addiction*, 1987; *Turning Japanese: Memoirs of a Sansei*, 1991; *Where the Body Meets Memory: An Odyssey of Race, Sexuality, and Identity*, 1995.

PERFORMANCE ART: *Relocations: Images from a Japanese American*, 1990; *Silence and Desire*, 1994 (Tom Rose, Kim Hines, and Maria Cheng); *Secret Colors*, 1994 (with Alex Pate); *Internment Voices*, 1997 (with Esther Suzuki).

BIBLIOGRAPHY

Gidmark, Jill B. "David Mura: Tearing Down the Door." *Asian America: Journal of Culture and the Arts* 2 (Winter, 1993): 120-129. Gidmark discusses how Mura's cultural and sexual identity defines the themes of his major works.

Mura, David. Interview by Bill Moyers. In *The Language of Life: A Festival of Poets*. New York: Doubleday, 1995. Mura sheds light on the technique in his poetry and how he achieves the effects through a judicious choice of words and tone. He describes his poetry as existing between two poles: "the tension between the moment of the aesthetic and the beautiful . . . and the process of history which is often brutal and unjust." Poetry allows him to "combine and compress" the complexity of his experience to enable him to understand his past and his relationship to the present.

_____. Interview by Lee Rossi. *Onthebus* 2, no. 2 (Summer/Fall, 1990): 263-273. Mura comments on the Asian American literary renaissance and his treatment of the Japanese American experience. His choice of Japanese American themes he sees as a natural outcome of the Black Power movement, the women's movement, antiwar movements, and the Civil Rights movement. Mura emphasizes that he does not see himself as an interpreter of the Japanese American experience but simply as a recorder of the experience. His writing is an attempt to keep alive the voices that were silenced.

Zhou, Xiaojing. "David Mura's Poetics of Identity." *MELUS* 23, no. 3 (Fall, 1998): 145-166. Zhou places Mura's poetry in the context of his development as a poet. Mura believes that he has to devise new ways to capture the minority experience. Zhou demonstrates how Mura accomplishes his goal by the use of monologues, mimicry, and ingenious vocabulary.

_____. "Race, Sexuality, and Representation in David Mura's *The Colors of Desire*." *Journal of Asian American Studies* 1, no. 3 (October, 1998): 245-267. Zhou points out that the intersection of race, gender, and culture in minority literature is a comparatively new area of discussion. Mura's *The Colors of Desire*, she contends, reflects a significant development among Asian Americans and their growing consciousness of the complex relationship between race and sexuality.

Leela Kapai

LES A. MURRAY

Born: Nabiac, New South Wales, Australia; October 17, 1938

PRINCIPAL POETRY

The Ilex Tree, 1965 (with Geoffrey Lehmann)
The Weatherboard Cathedral, 1969
Poems Against Economics, 1972
Lunch and Counter Lunch, 1974
Selected Poems: The Vernacular Republic, 1976
Ethnic Radio, 1977
The Boys Who Stole the Funeral, 1979
The Vernacular Republic: Poems, 1961-1981, 1982
Equanimities, 1982
The People's Otherworld, 1983
The Daylight Moon, 1987
The Vernacular Republic: Poems, 1961-1983, 1988
The Idyll Wheel, 1989
Dog Fox Field, 1990
The Rabbiter's Bounty: Collected Poems, 1991
Translations from the Natural World, 1992
Subhuman Redneck Poems, 1996
Fredy Neptune: A Novel in Verse, 1998
Conscious and Verbal, 1999
Learning Human: Selected Poems, 2000

OTHER LITERARY FORMS

Les A. Murray has collected several volumes of prose pieces, primarily reviews and articles: *The Peasant Mandarin: Prose Pieces* (1978), *Persistence in Folly* (1984), *Blocks and Tackles: Articles and Essays* (1990),

The Paperbark Tree: Selected Prose (1992), and *A Working Forest: Selected Prose* (1997). Of particular interest in the second book is the essay "The Human Hair-Thread," in which Murray discusses his own thought and the influence Aboriginal culture has had on it.

ACHIEVEMENTS

Les A. Murray is considered not only Australia's major poet but also one of the finest poets of his generation writing in English. His following is an international one, and the uniqueness and power of his poetic voice have caught the ear of many of his fellow poets throughout the world: He has been hailed by Joseph Brodsky, Peter Porter, Mark Strand, and others. He is a prolific and ambitious writer, always willing to try new and unusual techniques but equally at home in the traditional forms of verse, of which he seems to have an easy and lively mastery.

Murray has received numerous awards and prizes, including the Grace Leven Prize (in 1965, with Geoffrey J. Lehmann, and also in 1980 and 1990), the Cook Bi-Centenary Prize for Poetry (1970), Austalian National Book Council Award (1974, with others; 1985, 1992), the C. J. Dennis Memorial Prize (1976), the Mattara Prize (with others, 1981), the New South Wales Premier's Prize for the best book of verse (1983-1984), the Australian Literature Society Gold Medal (1984), the Fellowship of Australian Writers Medal (1984), the Canada-Australia Prize (1985), Australian National Poetry Award (1988), the Australian Book Council's Bicentennial Prize for Poetry (1988), Officer in the Order of Australia (1988), the New South Wales Premier's Prize for Poetry (1993), the Victoria Premier's Prize for Poetry (1993), the European Petrarch Award (1995), and the United Kingdom's prestigious T. S. Eliot Prize (1996). Murray won the Queen's Gold Medal for Poetry in 1999.

BIOGRAPHY

Leslie Allan Murray was born at Nabiac, on the rural north coast of New South Wales, and brought up on a dairy farm in nearby Bunyah, a locale that often figures as the subject or backdrop for his poems. He attended school in the town of Taree and then, in 1957, went to the University of Sydney, where he stayed until 1960.

Between 1959 and 1960, he served in the Royal Australian Naval Reserve. He and Valerie Morelli were married in 1962 (they would have several children), and Murray worked as a translator at the Australian National University in Canberra from 1963 to 1967. After a year in Europe, he returned to Sydney, was graduated from the University of Sydney in 1969, and worked at a number of transient jobs before going to Canberra again, where he took a position in the Prime Minister's Department in the Economic Development Branch.

Moving back to Sydney and refusing to work any longer in, for him, meaningless employment, Murray, in his own words, "Came Out as a flagrant full-time poet in 1971." He thereafter supported himself solely on the basis of his literary work. In addition to the books he published and those he edited, Murray wrote book reviews, contributed to newspapers and magazines, advised the publishing firm Angus and Robertson, and gave poetry readings throughout Australia and abroad. Between 1973 and 1979, he served as editor of *Poetry Australia*.

Murray lived in Sydney until 1986 and then moved to a farm in Bunyah, near his boyhood home, with Valerie and the youngest of his five children. His celebrity expanded when he became the subject of a televised documentary in 1991, and he continued to win awards. Then, in the mid-1990's, diabetes, depression, a liver infection led in 1996, to a collapse. After two surgeries and weeks in the hospital, he emerged in time to take note that he had won the United Kingdom's prestigious T. S. Eliot Award, arguably the most important award for poetry that nation bestows. He was too weak to travel to England to accept the award, but he did recover, his literary powers undiminished. His subsequent volumes confirmed his status as the most important voice in Australian poetry.

ANALYSIS

Readers of Les A. Murray's poetry are often attracted by the coherence of the thematic concerns that reappear consistently in his work and that are presented lucidly and imaginatively. Moreover, the stylistic features of his verse, though varied, have themselves cohered into an identifiable style uniquely his own and flexible enough to allow for the wide range of his poetic interests. Broadly, these interests may be grouped under categories of the religious and spiritual, the societal and cultural, the historical and familial, the linguistic and poetic. Murray has strong opinions about many issues facing contemporary society, and his poetry often bespeaks them.

In their most reductive form, these issues would require consideration of such propositions as: Western man must rediscover a core of religious values and recover certain traditional modes of being; society should embrace a more democratic egalitarianism, avoiding the twin perils of elitism and false ideology; Aboriginal attitudes regarding nature and the environment need to be better understood by white Australians and to some extent adopted; Australia itself represents an island of hope in the world, as a place where many of the divisive features undermining modern society might be finally reconciled.

"DRIVING THROUGH SAWMILL TOWNS"

In an early poem, "Driving Through Sawmill Towns," Murray renders the remoteness and tedium of life in the rural towns, those "bare hamlets built of boards," where "nothing happens" and "the houses watch each other." The evocative detail, the careful diction, the sense of quiet control convey both an appreciation of this as a way of life and an acknowledgment that it is a lonely and even desperate existence. A woman gazes at a mountain "in wonderment,/ looking for a city," and men sit by the stove after tea, "rolling a dead match/ between their fingers/ thinking of the future." It is a place one only drives through, not a place in which one wishes to live. In that sense, this poem contrasts with others in which the country life appears more salubrious, as in "Noonday Axeman" or "Spring Hail," where isolation is not necessarily loneliness.

"THE BULADELAH-TAREE HOLIDAY SONG CYCLE"

Murray's most famous poem of rural Australia is also the one most indebted to Aboriginal sources, "The Buladelah-Taree Holiday Song Cycle." It is a long poem, in thirteen sections, based in part on a translation by R. M. Berndt of "The Moon-Bone Song," a ritual poem of Arnhem Land Aborigines which Murray claims "may well be the greatest poem ever composed in Australia." His poem is an attempt to use an Aboriginal mode and structure to "celebrate my own spirit country," a stretch

of land on the north coast between the two towns of Buladelah and Taree, where he grew up and lives as an adult and where many holiday vacationers go in the summer to enjoy the beaches and the countryside.

In the same way that the Aborigines celebrate their unity as a people and their harmony with the land, Murray sees the returning vacationers, many of whom have family ties to the area, as a cyclic affirmation of ancestral values and a joyous communing with nature. In his vision, each new generation rediscovers the spiritual significance of commonplace things, as people come to possess the land imaginatively. Each section of the poem presents an aspect of this summer ritual, from the preparations made by the local inhabitants to the journey from Sydney along the Pacific Highway (represented as a glowing snake) to all the adventures, experiences, and tensions that go with a summer holiday. The poem ends with a linking of the region with the heavens above, as the Southern Cross constellation looks down upon "the Holiday."

The poem is unique in its successful wedding of an Aboriginal poetic structure with the matter of white Australian culture; in particular, Murray's use of place-names and capitalization seems to give mythic status to the events and locations of the poem, analogous to the Aborigine's sense of a "spirit of place."

THE BOYS WHO STOLE THE FUNERAL

In 1979, Murray published *The Boys Who Stole the Funeral*, a verse novel consisting of 140 sonnets of considerable variety. This unusual poem picked up many of the concerns and opinions prevalent in the earlier work and fashioned them into a narrative, both effective as poetry and affective as a story. In this work, two young Sydney men, Kevin Forbutt and Cameron Reeby, steal from a funeral parlor the body of Kevin's great-uncle, Clarrie Dunn (a "digger," or World War I veteran), in order to take him back home to the country where the old man had asked to be buried. Clarrie's relations having refused to pay for or honor this request, the boys have taken it upon themselves. In doing this, they set out on a journey of self-discovery as well.

Such familiar Murray themes as the value of community and respect for the ordinary man are underscored repeatedly in the poem, as when the two boys get to Dark's Plain, Clarrie's old home, and are assisted by people there with the burial and with evading the police who have come to arrest them. The novel later culminates with the shooting of Cameron by a policeman. The shocked and distraught Kevin flees into the bush, falls ill, drops into a coma, and has a vision of two figures from Aboriginal legend, Njimbin and Birroogun. In this vision, the central event of the novel, Kevin is put through an initiation where his soul is healed by the symbolic "crystal of Crystals," and where he is instructed by Njimbin and Birroogun (whose name modulates to Berrigan, connoting a blend of white and black Australians) in the mysteries of the spirit. Kevin is offered the Common Dish from which to eat, the vessel of common human joys and sufferings by which most people in the world are nourished. As an act of solidarity with common humanity, Kevin takes it and eats and then wakes from his comatose vision. Having been in effect reborn, he returns to live at Dark's Plain, to "keep faith" with the rural "battlers" who are the spiritual inheritors of the land.

The poem as a whole is a virtuoso performance, displaying Murray's ability to handle the complex interplay of form, narrative, and character. He holds the reader's attention and, once again, interweaves Aboriginal material in a convincing way.

THE VERNACULAR REPUBLIC

One of Murray's preoccupations is with the notion of the vernacular; indeed, when he calls his selected poems *The Vernacular Republic*, he is reflecting upon the colloquial nature of his language and simultaneously reflecting a passionate concern which the world of his poems addresses: the need for Australia to fuse its three cultures, urban, rural, and Aboriginal. Murray's vision for Australia is for a culture of convergence, where the sophisticated city dwellers, the more traditional rural folk, and the indigenous blacks can all come together to forge a society in harmony with the continent. In this, he is close to the position of the Jindyworobaks, a literary movement of the 1930's and 1940's that emphasized the uniqueness of the Australian environment and sought to align itself with Aboriginal culture.

Although not as narrowly nationalistic as that earlier group, Murray does see a need to avoid repeating the mistakes of Europe and America and to develop in accordance with the character and values of Australia itself, not in submission to alien and imported fashions or ideologies. For him, Australia has the possibility of becoming truly egalitarian, a place of justice and virtue for the common man, a place where what is traditional is recognizably Australian. This, for Murray, includes a certain dry sense of humor and an appreciation of an unhurried mode of living, which may be primarily a rural manner but nevertheless seems a national characteristic.

"THE QUALITY OF SPRAWL"

His poem "The Quality of Sprawl" is a good example. "Sprawl," in this poem, is defined through the course of eight stanzas as a way of being, at once nonchalant ("the rococo of being your own still centre"), laid-back ("Sprawl leans on things"), generous ("driving a hitchhiker that extra hundred miles home"), unpretentious ("the quality/ of the man who cut down his Rolls-Royce/ into a farm utility truck"), classless (someone "asleep in his neighbours' best bed in spurs and oilskins"), unflappable ("Reprimanded and dismissed/ it listens with a grin and one boot up on the rail/ of possibility"), and so on. It is also defined by what it is not: "It is never lighting cigars with ten-dollar notes"; "Sprawl almost never says Why Not? with palms comically raised"; "nor can it be dressed for." Murray presents it as a very attractive quality indeed, but, characteristically, he is aware of the negative element, the price one sometimes has to pay for independence of mind. "It may have to leave the Earth," he says, but then he gently undercuts his own hyperbole: "Being roughly Christian, it scratches the other cheek/ and thinks it unlikely." While not exactly turning the other cheek in Christian fashion, he does conclude with the mild warning: . . . people have been shot for sprawl."

Sprawl, then, is the opposite of the uptight, aggressive, overly sophisticated self-consciousness that Murray sees around him and that he considers foreign and inappropriate for Australia—a place, perhaps, where Mark Twain's Huck Finn might have been at home. While "sprawl" may appear a public attitude and manner, it rests upon a more essential inward feature, which Murray terms "equanimity," in a poem of that title.

"EQUANIMITY"

"Equanimity" is a poem that draws together several strands of Murray's work: His populist, bardic stance mingles with a more purely prophetic strain. Here, his democratic vistas are underwritten by a transcendental authority, based upon a personal and even sacramental experience. That experience, which he calls "equanimity," is like an influx of quiet power, an exaltation of the spirit grounded in love. "There is only love," he says; "human order has at heart/ an equanimity. Quite different from inertia," a place "where all are, in short, off the high comparative horse/ of their identity." This is the place at which people join together in a "people's otherworld," a vernacular republic of the spirit that allows for a "continuous recovering moment." It is an effortless effort, reminiscent of a Buddhist or Kantian disinterestedness: "Through the peace beneath effort/ (even within effort: quiet air between the bars of our attention)/ comes unpurchased lifelong plenishment."

Yet, foremost for Murray, this is a Christian quality; it is at the very heart of Christ's teachings and is the place from which he taught: "Christ spoke to people most often on this level/ especially when they chattered about kingship and the Romans;/ all holiness speaks from it." To experience such equanimity would be tantamount to experiencing holiness itself, and that is precisely the sort of graceful redemption Murray seeks to convey. There can be nothing programmatic about such an attitude, but no program of reform, be it social, political, or cultural, can possibly succeed without it. That, for Murray, is the basis upon which all else proceeds, including his own poetry. For Murray, writing is like playing upon an instrument, finding out just what it can do and learning how to do it. His poems have an energy and inventiveness that reveal a delight in the resources of language and a conviction that what needs to be said can be communicated through the adequacies of poetry.

BLOCKS AND TACKLES

Murray's faith in the redemptive possibilities of poetry was sorely tested during the 1980's, when it became increasingly clear to him that the production of literature in Australia was tied to a commercial system fundamentally at odds with the spirit of poetry, and that the academic and critical establishment that controlled the terms under which literature was to be studied and understood was itself run by a "cabal" of "elites," notable for their

"moral cowardice." In response there was a discernible retrenchment in Murray's poetry and prose, a willingness to accept his embattled position in the cultural field as a necessary corollary to his role as a virtual poet-prophet to his people. In the essays collected in *Blocks and Tackles*, Murray became more assertive about the sacramental and mysterious qualities of poetry. As he writes in "Poems and Poesies":

> Poetry models the fullness of life, and also gives its objects presence. Like prayer, it pulls all the motions of our life and being into a concentrated true attentiveness to which God might speak. "Here am I, Lord," as Samuel says in his book of the Bible. It is the plane or mirror of intuitions.

DOG FOX FIELD

In the poems published in *Dog Fox Field*, however, the poet attends more often to his function as social critic, particularly in his denunciations of "relegation," the denial of the full humanity of others. In a poem titled "To the Soviet Americans," a working-class man (here the abstract object of much false Marxist piety) ironically declares:

> Watch out for the ones in jeans
> who'll stop you smoking and stop you working:
> I call them the Soviet Americans.

The tone of these poems is often stern and unyielding, written in an age in which one finds "self pity and hard drugs everywhere." Yet, this hardened voice does continue to yield up poems of sympathetic feeling, as if, once protected from the incursions of a hostile world, there is ample room for the common enjoyments of a shared living:

> Never despise those
> who fear an order vaster than reason, more charming
>   than prose:
> surely are those who unknowingly chime with the noblest
> and love and are loved by whom they rhyme with best.
> So let your river be current and torrent and klong
> as far and intricate as your love is long. . . .

SUBHUMAN REDNECK POEMS

The title of this collection, which won for Murray the 1996 T. S. Eliot Prize, indicates Murray's unrepentant determination to diminish the idea of poetry as the exclusive purview of the intellectual elite. The book is as outspokenly angry and tonally excessive as anything he has produced, and, on occasion, goes a bit too far in expressing his disillusion with the new Australia:

> Ethnics who praise their home ground
> while on it are called jingo chauvinists.
> All's permitted, though, when they migrate;
> the least adaptable are the purest then,
> the narrowest the most multicultural.

His politics swing sometimes crazily into conservatism, and there is a sense that he is not always free of a kind of ungenerous rant.

The book, however, contains several lovely lyrics. Murray's gift for this kind of work is often ignored in the sound and fury of his politically engaged poems. "The Warm Rain" brandishes

> palm trees like mops,
> its borders swell over the continent . . .
> Fruit bumps lawns, and every country dam
>
> brews under bubbles . . .

Murray's eye for detail and witty transformation of such into poetic image is quite charming in "Dead Trees in a Dam":

> Castle scaffolding tall in moat,
> the dead trees in the dam
> flower each morning with birds.

Once away from argument, the poetic juices run magnificently riot:

> . . . it may be a misty candelabrum
> of egrets lambent . . .
>
> .   .   .   .
>
> Odd mornings, it's been all bloodflag
> and rifle green: a stopped-motion shrapnel
> of kingparrots. . . .

FREDY NEPTUNE

Murray's "novel in verse" follows the life of an itinerant World War I sailor/soldier of German ancestry across two hundred pages. The narrative, through unlikely adventures and plot twists, follows Fredy's attempts to return home after having been kidnapped and forced onto a German battleship. He experiences both moral outrage and physical disability in response to the atrocities of war—the burning of Armenian women, for example, causes him to lose his sense of touch. The theme of survival in a chaotic world reaches its climax when, upon finally making his way back home, Fredy discovers that war has destroyed his homeland and he must re-enlist. The language in which Fredy's picaresque experiences are related—full of Australian, blue-collar slang and hit-and-miss rhymes that work to reflect the lunacy of Fredy's experiences—garnered glowing reviews from critics.

CONSCIOUS AND VERBAL

The title of this collection echoes the Australian press reports when the nation's celebrated poet, after three weeks in a coma, awoke. He eventually recovered, and this collection was one of the results. Murray renders his experience here in "Travels with John Hunter," named after the hospital where the poet worked his way back to health. The poems in this collection examine God as a presence in nature, the Australian character, racism and Murray's outraged stance against it, and other typical Murray themes. Also characteristic of Murray are his moral pronouncements, his deploring "that monster called the Twentieth Century," and his didacticism. In "The Instrument," for example, he answers the question of why he writes poetry by stating simply that one must "[work] always beyond/ your own intelligence." Although critics gave the volume mixed reviews, these poems remain a fitting tribute to Murray's reawakening.

OTHER MAJOR WORKS

NONFICTION: *The Peasant Mandarin: Prose Pieces*, 1978; *Persistence in Folly*, 1984; *The Australian Year*, 1985 (photographs by Peter Solness); *Blocks and Tackles: Articles and Essays*, 1990; *The Paperbark Tree: Selected Prose*, 1992; *A Working Forest: Selected Prose*, 1997.

EDITED TEXT: *The New Oxford Book of Australian Verse*, 1986, enlarged 1992; *Anthology of Australian Religious Verse*, 1986; *Fivefathers: Five Australian Poets of the Pre-Academic Era*, 1994.

MISCELLANEOUS: *Killing the Black Dog: Essays and Poems*, 1997.

BIBLIOGRAPHY

Birkerts, Sven. "The Rococo of His Own Still Center." *Parnassus* 15, no. 2 (1989): 31-48. A serious and sympathetic appreciation of Murray's poetry by a prominent critic. Birkerts highlights those poems most appropriate for inclusion in the Murray "canon," showing a keen sense of what Murray's poetic project entails. Among the first thorough treatments of Murray's poetry in the United States, this is an accessible and useful introduction.

Murray, Les A.. "An Interview with Les Murray." *The American Poetry Review* 15 (March/April, 1986): 28-36. This interview by Carole Oles, which is lively, wide-ranging, and informative, focuses on many of Murray's central concerns. A good introduction to the way in which Murray himself sees his own poetic project, it contains some useful background information on Australian literary politics and movements.

_____. "Les Murray in Conversation." *PN-Review* 6LL (July/August, 1996): 29-36. The distinguished English poet and critic Willilam Scammell is particularly good at bringing out the critical and aesthetic best in the loquacious Murray.

Taylor, Andrew. "The Past Imperfect of Les A. Murray." In *Reading Australian Poetry*. St. Lucia: University of Queensland Press, 1987. Taylor, an Australian poet and critic himself, examines Murray's sense of time and suggests that the absence of the female in the poetry is a result of the early death of Murray's mother. This essay is part of a "deconstructive" reading of Australian poetry.

Walcott, Derek. "Crocodile Dandy." *The New Republic* 6 (February, 1989): 25-28. This is a generous review by one important poet of another. Walcott makes a case for the international stature of Murray, looking at his extraordinary verbal facility and mastery of form. The sacramental quality of Murray's poetry is noted, and comparisons are made to such authors as Walt Whitman, Dylan Thomas, and Rudyard Kipling.

William, Barbara. *In Other Words: Interviews with Australian Poets*. Amsterdam: Rodolpi, 1998. Murray in conversation and in the context of poets in his own country.

Paul Kane, updated by
Charles H. Pullen and Christina J. Moose

CAROL MUSKE

Born: St. Paul, Minnesota; December 17, 1945

PRINCIPAL POETRY

Camouflage, 1975
Skylight, 1981
Wyndmere, 1985
Applause, 1989
Red Trousseau, 1993
An Octave Above Thunder: New and Selected Poems, 1997

OTHER LITERARY FORMS

As Carol Muske Dukes, the poet has published the novels *Dear Digby* (1989), *Saving St. Germ* (1993), and *Life After Death* (2001), as well as a collection of critical essays, *Women and Poetry: Truth, Autobiography, and the Shape of the Self* (1997).

ACHIEVEMENTS

Carol Muske's work has earned many awards, including a John Simon Guggenheim Fellowship, an Ingram-Merrill grant, a National Endowment of the Arts poetry fellowship, and the Alice Fay di Castagnola Prize from the Poetry Society of America. Widely anthologized, her poetry has won several Pushcart Prizes as well as the Dylan Thomas Award. Muske also received a Witter Bynner Fellowship from the Library of Congress and became a fellow at the Los Angeles Institute for the Humanities.

BIOGRAPHY

Carol Anne Muske's roots are firmly planted in the Great Plains. Wyndmere, which forms the title of one collection of poetry, is found in North Dakota, where her grandfather was a wheat farmer. Although her mother won a scholarship for college, her family was too poor to send her. Instead, she married. While raising a family, she maintained a love for poetry, which she passed on to her daughter. Muske has written about her mother's memorizing of poems and of her reciting them from time to time.

After earning her bachelor of arts degree from Creighton, in Nebraska, and her master of arts from California

State University at San Francisco, she went to Europe, where she performed in a Paris production of *Hair.* When she returned to New York, she taught at Columbia University, exploring the sense of conflict and dislocation she felt as a writer and a woman. Riker's Island Prison, where she taught, provided a physical symbol of enclosed places that are controlled by men. Earning a National Endowment of the Arts grant enabled her to establish a program, "Art Without Walls," in the prison.

In 1981, Muske went to live in Italy on a Guggenheim Fellowship. She met actor David Dukes, whom she would marry in 1983, having divorced her first husband, Edward Healton. Under the name Carol Muske Dukes, she began focusing on writing and publishing fiction. In 2000, her husband suddenly died after suffering a heart attack. She has a son and a daughter.

Muske has taught in the graduate writing programs at Columbia University, the Iowa Writers' Workshop, the University of California at Irvine, the University of Virginia, and the University of Southern California in Los Angeles.

ANALYSIS

Much of the critical acclaim which Carol Muske's poetry has merited comes from the vivid language with which she explores family experiences. Although a feminist perspective flows throughout her poems, the ideas that are discussed are not limited to one point of view.

CAMOUFLAGE

Published in 1975, this collection announced many of the themes that would emerge in Muske's work. Many of the poems, such as "Swansong" and "Rendezvous with a Harp," are autobiographical. Muske's strength is such that she is able to elevate the specific details beyond the merely personal. "Swansong," for example, speaks of a woman who taught ballet to children. She was quite in demand until a cab ran over her toe, ending her career. Totally dedicated to her work, she gave all she had, even after she could no longer dance:

> She often wept, sipping brandy,
> nodding when the needle stuck
> on a crack in *Romeo and Juliet.*
> Those days we stood on ceremony.

> Mute sisters of the dance, we froze
> holding second position till six
> when the mothers came.

The young girls cannot understand the demands of one's art or the sacrifices which it requires. The ballet teacher can no longer "speak" in the same way—that is, through dance. For their part, the children have not yet learned to speak.

Likewise, "Rendezvous with a Harp" demonstrates the extremes to which an artist is willing to go for the sake of the art. The player and the harp are almost at odds, in a kind of artistic struggle for dominance. The harp insists on its own selfhood, flying ahead of her as she plays.

SKYLIGHT

Muske's next collection continued her examination of the nature of art and the role of the artist. Within these familiar themes, Muske interweaves the male-female relationship, in all its complicated variety. "The Painter's Daughter" sets the tone, telling the reader that "It's a kind of blindness." Beginning by cataloging the painter's use of images that he has used before in his work, the poet suggests that such limitation dulls the senses of the artist.

The poet says that she knows "the murder in a painter's eye/ as he reaches for red." The painter is her father, who has incorporated her face into his work, teaching her to see the world as he does:

> *The ventriloquism of color,* he said.
> Purple and green bleeding through white.
> The plum split in the skeleton's hand.
> *See through the suspension,* he said
> and I see snow fences, the red skull of sun.

The poet reveals, at the end, that she has been revisiting a photograph, a tactic that tricks the reader, who, all along, participated in the present-time of the reflection. The photograph continues to mislead those who see it:

> Imagine my cries in the center of that sight.

> Though it appears we are carefree,
> in the photograph we look sleepy—

> just like any father and daughter
> our watching the sun go down.

The tension between what the daughter perceives in her own right and what the father wants her to see will bring about the end of the hierarchic nature of their relationship. Even parenthood culminates in a peer relationship between parent and the adult child.

WYNDMERE

Poems in this volume spring from the conceit of "wind-mother," the meaning of the title. Indeed, many of the images in this collection center on the mother-child bond, as fragile and unfathomable as it can be. The poem "Wyndmere, Windemere" brings this idea to the surface:

> In the wind, on the back step,
> you spoke the words of poets
> who got it right again and again,
>
> in a world so wrong,
> it measures only loss
> in those crosses of thin air.
> In the blowdown and ascent
>
> of the separator, the mother,
> whose face catches once,
> then turns from me, again and again.

The face of the mother is the first the baby learns, the first loss the child comes to fear.

The poems in this collection speak of friends, lovers, and family as they experience life's various enigmas. "China White" is a friend who was raped. Muske's rendering of that event avoids the sensational while maintaining the force of the emotional, rendering of the effect of assault on the victim. The poem "We Drive Through Tyndall's Theory of Sight" draws a parallel between Tyndall's idea that "impurities in the air allow us to see light" and the poet's recognition that she is in love. The birth of Anna Cameron, in "Sounding," provides the reader with a sense of the vulnerability and helplessness which the new mother feels, as well as the sense of power which comes to her as she holds her newborn.

APPLAUSE

Many of the poems in *Applause* reflect the poet's challenge to find and experience beauty in the face of life's pain. Muske suggests that the writer—indeed, any artist—has no choice if the artist is to remain true to the

calling. In the poem "After Care," a mortician speaks of the care that he takes in preparing a body for viewing, "after nobody/ feels sorry for anybody anymore." There is power in such care:

> I feel I've done what no one else
> has with love—I've made the dead
> for once, return it—

Sardonic in his reflections, the mortician maintains a dry distance from the horror that surrounds him every day. The reader is at once repulsed and amazed at such a man as his "hands work/ for an effect we remember/ long past compassion." The reader does not want to continue to look at this man yet is irrevocably drawn to him. Muske would suggest that such is the stance that the poet takes in the face of personal and public suffering.

The title poem, "Applause," is a long work dedicated to the writer Paul Monette, who died of AIDS. Certainly if there is an emblematic disease which has caused fear on one hand and heartbreak on the other, AIDS is that disease. Monette spoke openly about his struggle with the disease at a time when secrecy about his being gay would have been expected. This poem is less a lament for his impending death than it is a celebration of his life; consequently, the last section stuns with its beauty:

> . . . Applauding applause. One day a while
> before he died, you came over with him. Annie was
>   napping
> in her crib and he touched her head and said
> sleep well honey. I wanted to cheer him for going on
> like that, for blessing my child when he knew he was
>   dying—

Not only does the world continue after the death of family and friends; the poet suggests that they would not have it any other way. In fact, to keep memory alive, the dead require that the living continue.

RED TROUSSEAU

The color red operates as a leitmotif in this collection. Blood is red, especially in "Frog Pond" ("Here's a fat man rattling a blood red/ genie in a pickle jar"), a poem delving into the nature of a girl's coming to understand herself as female. However, the title poem, "Red Trousseau," offers perhaps the most fully developed use of red. The poem posits a woman who is being tried for the capital crime of witchcraft, for which she will be burned at the stake. The poem appears in numbered sections, and each section explores the intricacies of the woman in the face of the man whose love betrayed her. His face became:

> . . . a glass of red wine,
> the simplest, thoughtless vessel, that was it,
> wasn't it, held up, like this, an offering?

As her accusers number the accounts of her practice of witchcraft, the poet interrupts the narrative to reflect on her own questions about the woman's guilt, admitting that the poet never felt sympathy for the woman. Muske suggests a kind of enjoyment that the woman experienced:

> I suspected her mind of collaboration,
> apperceptive ecstasy, the flames wrapped
> about her like a red trousseau, yes,
> the dream of immolation.

The poet wants to know, actually needs to know, if at any point in the burning the woman could have willed herself to say, in her defense, "I am worth saving." The trousseau is decidedly a sexual image, akin to fantasy, as if the woman believed that such a death made her desirable. Muske is not suggesting that the woman is at fault here. Instead, she implies that the societal constructs were such that the woman could not conceive of such a thing.

AN OCTAVE ABOVE THUNDER

This collection pulls together the strongest of the poems from Muske's books, as well as beginning with a selection of new poems. Starting the book with "Like This," Muske alerts the reader that, although the world is not composed as one would have it, nevertheless it is too early to begin a song about its end. Poets have the peculiar task to reflect, not the end of the world, but the fact that it refuses to die. Previous poems have testified to the horror of illness and death, of broken relationships; however, such poems have also affirmed the existence of beauty in the midst of all that. The poet provides images that give the reader a sense of the imaginable.

Speaking of a troubled young man whose antisocial tendencies terrorize other students, Muske describes him as a perceptive poet when his images compare a spray of bullet holes to the fantail of a peacock:

> . . . But look, he sees what we die

> from not seeing—how different beauty opens
> its different eyes. The expanse unfolds,
> many-eyed, iridescent, it holds. Unbroken,
> salutes you. The fiery gaze turns gold.

Muske returns to the imagery of immolation that she developed in previous poems. The challenge of the poet is to be willing to risk for the sake of giving voice to every experience, every perception which comes.

OTHER MAJOR WORKS

LONG FICTION: *Dear Digby*, 1989 (as Carol Muske Dukes); *Saving St. Germ*, 1993 (as Dukes); *Life After Death*, 2001 (as Dukes).

NONFICTION: *Women and Poetry: Truth, Autobiography, and the Shape of the Self*, 1997.

BIBLIOGRAPHY

Gathman, Roger. "Carol Muske-Dukes: The Cruel Poetries of Life." *Publishers Weekly* 248, no. 25 (June 18, 2001): 52. This comprehensive interview develops a consideration of Muske's biographical influences and her work as teacher and writer. It also discusses the themes that have shaped her work, as well as how her characters are often at odds with the prevailing societal norms.

Gilbert, Sandra M. "Family Values." *Poetry* 164, no. 1 (April, 1994): 39-53. In this review of *Red Trousseau*, Gilbert expresses the view that, while some of the narrative line is difficult to follow, the book is strong in its use of language. The images are strong, with natural energy.

Gould, Jean. "Carol Muske." In *Modern American Women Poets*. New York: Dodd, Mead, 1984. The writer presents a thorough biography of Muske. The poems are referenced as they reveal aspects of the biography. The review focuses on the emergence of the poet.

Kizer, Carolyn. "Motherhood, Magic, and Lavender." *The New York Times Book Review*, November 3, 1985, p. 13. Primarily an analysis of *Wyndmere*. The reviewer feels that the language is this collection is not as dazzling as in Muske's previous collection. Discusses the symbols common in Muske's work.

McFadden, Kevin. "In the Mood with Carol Muske." Meridian: The Semi-Annual from the University *of Virginia*, 1999. www.engl.virginia.edu/meridian/muske.html. An interview with Muske that explores the influences on her work, from Sylvia from Plath, John Berryman, and Gerard Manley Hopkins to Rainer Maria Rilke and Ovid, among many others. Muske's personal life consists of being wife, mother, professor, writer, and owner of a house and pets. Such a life works its way into her work.

Muratori, Fred. Review of *An Octave Above Thunder. Library Journal* 122 (October 1, 1997): 86. The reviewer discusses this collection as an overview of the entire body of the poet's work, finding that Muske has undergone a broadening of her philosophical views as they are expressed in her poetry. He speaks of the influence of feminism and political awareness as well as analysis and meditation.

Santos, Sherod. Review of *Skylight. Western Humanities Review* 36, no. 1 (Spring, 1982): 54-58. Focuses on the positive aspects of the poems, specifically the relationships between men and women. The poems elicit a wide range of emotion from their speaker, as well as from the reader. The reviewer discusses several poems in depth, analyzing form and word choice.

Seaman, Donna. Review of *Red Trousseau. Booklist* 89, no. 9 (January 1, 1993): 790. A very positive review of this collection, touching on language and imagistic dexterity.

Martha Modena Vertreace-Doody

ALFRED DE MUSSET

Born: Paris, France; December 11, 1810
Died: Paris, France; May 2, 1857

PRINCIPAL POETRY

Contes d'Espagne et d'Italie, 1829 (*Tales of Spain and Italy*, 1905)
Un Spectacle dans un fauteuil, 1833 (first series, 2 volumes; *A Performance in an Armchair*, 1905)
Rolla, 1833 (English translation, 1905)

Poésies complètes, 1840 (*Complete Poetry*, 1905)
Poésies nouvelles, 1852 (*New Poetic Works*; definitive ed. in *The Complete Writings*)
Premières Poésies, 1854 (*First Poetic Works*; definitive edition in *The Complete Writings*, 1905)

OTHER LITERARY FORMS

Alfred de Musset's prose *contes* and *nouvelles* have sustained an appreciative audience, but it is his lyric verse and, above all, his dramas that truly endure. As Phillipe Van Tieghem has observed, Musset's theater is an admirable synthesis of the neoclassical tastes of seventeenth as well as eighteenth century theater with the passion and variety of Romantic trends. This synthesis also characterizes the best of Musset's verse.

ACHIEVEMENTS

Henry James called Alfred de Musset "one of the first poets" of his day, a judgment which many modern critics would dispute. Although neither innovative nor influential, Musset's verse achieves a distinctive personal voice. In his foreword to a recent French revaluation of Musset and his works, Yves Lainey muses that no one has replaced Musset as the supreme poet of love, and Lainey poses the loaded question of whether it is possible to lose one's taste for reading Musset. This query can be answered by only a consideration of the handful of Musset's poems which, both in the original French and in translation, maintain their vitality.

BIOGRAPHY

Born in Paris on December 11, 1810, Louis Charles Alfred de Musset lived the role of the Romantic artist with a self-destructive passion. His family traced itself back to the twelfth century, numbering among its ancestors the great Renaissance poet Joachim du Bellay. Musset spent his childhood in an atmosphere of belles-lettres. His father not only was responsible for an edition of the works of Jean-Jacques Rousseau but also wrote a critical and biographical study of Rousseau. Musset's mother held a salon attended by some of the noted literary figures of the day, and it was in this milieu that Musset took his first, faltering steps in verse.

Two important notes in the ground bass of Musset's life were sounded in the poet's youth—his emotional

Alfred de Musset (Hulton Archive)

hypersensitivity and his dependency on his brother Paul. The latter, in his biography of Musset, has recorded an anecdote demonstrating both characteristics. A gun which Musset was handling accidentally fired a shot that narrowly missed Paul; perhaps as a result, Musset was stricken with a high fever. Indeed, "brain fever," as it was known in the nineteenth century, plagued the poet throughout his life.

Musset achieved literary celebrity with his first volume of verse, *Tales of Spain and Italy*. In the following decade, he produced a great number of plays, a fair body of poetry, and a variety of work in other forms as well. In 1833, he began a stormy liaison with the novelist George Sand (who was then thirty years old to Musset's twenty-three). Both Musset and Sand wrote novels based on the affair: Musset's *La Confession d'un enfant du siècle* (1836; *The Confession of a Child of the Century*, 1892) and Sand's *Elle et lui* (1859; *She and He*, 1902); the latter prompted a rebuttal from Paul de Musset, the novel *Lui et elle* (1859; he and she). Alfred de Musset's liaison with Sand was only the most

notorious of a number of love affairs in which he was involved. Among them, one of the most important was his relationship with the great tragic actress Rachel (Elisa Felix), who nourished his love for the neoclassical masterpieces of French, particularly the works of Jean Racine.

Musset's production dropped sharply in the 1840's and the 1850's, though he enjoyed several theatrical successes and was elected to the Académie Française. The last years of his life were marred by alcoholism. Musset died in Paris on May 2, 1857.

ANALYSIS

Alfred de Musset's passion for neoclassical literature and femmes fatales offers a useful guide to his lyric poetry; in addition, to anyone with an essentially Anglo-American background in literature, the career of Lord Byron might offer a passport into that of Musset. Indeed, the neoclassical strain in the works of Musset is very like that in Byron. Both made solid contributions to a Romantic trend that they despised. In their best work, they looked to Greco-Roman classicism and French neoclassicism for their models. Musset's aesthetic, like Byron's, was neither Romantic nor neoclassical; rather, elements of the two were counterpoised in a balanced tension. Musset also resembles Byron in his posing and attitudinizing before what he regarded as the "infernal feminine." Both men took personal delight and gained poetic capital from the pains they suffered at the hands of a rather impressive number of women. Although both poets were masters of satire, neither indulged in didacticism—political or religious.

Although Musset later denied any direct influence from Byron, his first two collections of poetry are filled with Byronic elements. *Tales of Spain and Italy* and *A Performance in an Armchair*, after their initial publication, were later authoritatively compiled in *First Poetic Works*. Beyond their biographical importance as juvenilia, these poems are of only slight significance.

By the standards of a Byron or a Hugo, Musset's output was quite small; moreover, his most ambitious poems, such as *Rolla*, have fallen by the wayside. Musset the poet worked best in miniature, when he could keep his Romantic and his neoclassical impulses in perfect balance.

"MAY NIGHT"

Musset's growing mastery of poetic form became evident in "La Nuit de mai" (1835; "May Night"), composed in the year of his final separation from George Sand, the year in which he came under the more benevolent influence of a Madame Jaubert. In this work, Musset's persona, the poet, has suffered from a love affair—presumably based on that of Musset and Sand. "May Night," which found its definitive place in the collection titled *New Poetic Works*, is the most frequently anthologized representative of Musset's less restrained Romantic side. Even this undeniably passionate work, however, is not without a certain restraint. The dialogue form permits the poet to maintain a certain distance from the personal subject matter, although such control is not sustained throughout the poem. Musset's failure to maintain aesthetic control of his material is reflected in the form of the verse: As the poem progresses, the caesura is often lost, and lines alternate randomly between ten and twelve syllables.

When the Muse first speaks to the poet, he cannot hear her; he can only sense her by hazy and indirect manifestations, which anticipate the mysterious auras pervading the Symbolist dramas of Maurice Maeterlinck. In his second speech, the poet bursts into a series of questions, seeking to unveil the secret behind the uncanny phenomena which surround him. Only in her third speech is the Muse able to penetrate the poet's torpid senses, reminding him of a bitter experience. The poet has only recently had his first sorrowful encounter with a woman; in the words of the Muse, "still a youth, you were dying of love." This youthful passion and sorrow, acted upon by the same Spring which is transforming the landscape, forms the substance of which the poet's divine ecstasy is made: "the wine of youth ferments tonight in the veins of God."

In the Muse's fourth speech, Musset adopts the rhetorical flamboyance which the critic Henri Peyre has identified as characteristic of French Romanticism. Many of the lines, sometimes for five lines running, begin with a first-person-plural verb formulation (such as *chanterons-nous*). The rich images range from legendary Greece to Rome, from medieval to modern France. One important image in this veritable barrage is that of a hunter in the Middle Ages, who, after killing a deer, cuts out its still-

beating heart and throws it to the dogs. The image, emblematic of the poet's act of self-immolation, prepares the way for the culminating symbol of self-immolation in the Muse's fifth speech.

The Muse, in this her final address, continues what has been fully established as the central theme of "May Night": that poetry grows from its creator's active confrontation of his human hurts. As the Muse says, "Nothing makes us so great as a great sorrow." Although in his final speech, which closes the poem, the poet rejects the Muse's advice and dismisses any poetry he might create as mere writing "on the sand," the existence of the poem itself demonstrates that Musset, as opposed to his persona, felt otherwise and followed the bidding of the Muse. Musset's creativity was encouraged, not thwarted, by his encounters with women.

"A WASTED EVENING"

Equal to the influence exercised by George Sand and Madame Jaubert on Musset's lyric creativity was that of the celebrated actress Rachel. "Une Soirée perdue" ("A Wasted Evening") is a meditation centering upon a performance of Molière's *Le Misanthrope* (1667; *The Misanthrope*, 1714), referred to in the poem by the name of its protagonist, Alceste, at the Théâtre-Français, better known now as the Comédie-Française. Musset clearly had been aggravated by the poor attendance at the performance.

"A Wasted Evening" is a pastiche—but in the best sense of the word—of Molière's Alexandrines. In the main, the poem might be termed a critical dialogue between a persona who represents the popular taste of the day and another representing Musset's own views. The first ten lines of the poem are given to the representative of the crowd, who observes that the play, after all, "was only Molière." This great playwright, judged by the melodramatic standards of the well-made play of the mid-nineteenth century, is a "great bungler" who seems unable "to serve a concluding scene cooked to perfection." Here, Musset's irony is a bit heavy-handed; the poet has changed his usual rapier for a broadsword.

In the eleventh line, the poet offers his rebuttal: "I, however, listened to this simple harmony/ And hear how common sense can make genius speak." In these lines, the neoclassical concepts of "simple harmony" and "common sense" have been joined with the Romantic notion of "genius." As if reverting to the fashionable view, the second speaker asks rhetorically if mere admiration for this play suffices. His reply is clearly in the Romantic camp, if on his own terms: He says that it is enough to attend this performance "in order to hear in the depths of the soul a cry of nature." He catches sight of a young woman whose intense absorption in the performance is clear proof of the play's entrancing qualities. He describes her by way of a synecdoche, speaking of her white neck and black hair, which he then compares with ebony encased in ivory. It is no accident that this image echoes lines of the neoclassical, if transitional, poet, André Chenier.

In the next stanza, Musset's spokesman calls for a return to neoclassical art, with its paradoxical capacity to combine frankness with subtlety. This he sees as the necessary replacement for the "muddy stage" of Victor Hugo and Alexandre Dumas, *fils*. The next stanza continues in the same vein: The poet calls upon the satirical spirit of Molière, "master of us all," appealing for a renewed attack on inferior art and on the society which sponsors it.

In the last stanza, however, the speaker abruptly dismisses his dream of artistic triumph as "a foolish fancy." He then notices the young woman—now veiled—and follows her unconsciously, only to see her "disappear on the threshold of her home." The artistry with which Musset gradually introduces the young woman recalls the subtle clarity that he admires in French neoclassical literature. The woman is a symbol for the concrete beauty that distracts the poet from his public aspirations:

> "Alas! my dear friend, that is the story of my life.
> While my soul was seeking its will,
> my body had its own and followed beauty;
> and when I awoke from this reverie,
> there only remained for me the sweet image."

"ON A DEAD WOMAN"

"Sur une morte" ("On a Dead Woman"), which deals out its wit with greater subtlety than does "A Wasted Evening," is unique in its combination of a rich lyricism of rhythm and imagery with a spirit of pure invective; only Catullus might offer a parallel. Here, Musset does not denigrate the object of his satirical attack; rather, he

makes it clear that she is a formidable woman—clearly worthy of his wrathful energies. Musset makes her strength eminently clear in the opening stanza: She is compared to the impressively muscled virago called *Night* that Michelangelo sculpted on the tomb of Giuliano de' Medici. If the woman in question is beautiful, says the poet, then Michelangelo's *Night* "can be fair."

It is known that the poem was directed at the Princess Christine Trivulce de Begiojoso, whose great crime was to have resisted Musset's advances. In short, she was a strong woman—so strong, in fact, that in 1849, long after the poem had appeared, she wrote, with *her* pride undamaged, a gracious letter complimenting Musset on one of his plays that had recently been performed.

In the next three stanzas, the poet continues the attack by impugning the princess's salient traits: Her Christian charity and piety are viewed as hypocrisy; her intellectual aspirations, as the pretensions of a bluestocking. These stanzas are impressive, above all, for the concrete precision of their imagery. The princess's act of giving alms is reduced to the mere motion of "the hand casually opening and giving" and to "gold" given "without pity." Similarly, her intelligent conversation is presented as "the empty noise of a sweetly modulated voice," which in turn is compared to a "babbling brook." Most devastating of all, one can only consider her prayers to be such "if two fair eyes, now fixed earthward, now raised heavenward, can be called prayers." Here again, the feeling is inescapable: Such well-loaded siege guns suggest an impressive target.

"On a Dead Woman" crystallizes all the characteristic qualities of Musset's poetry. Typically, the poem was inspired by an encounter with a woman. Although motivated by a powerful emotion (here, anger), the poem is marked by a restraint that recalls the icy control of the neoclassicists.

OTHER MAJOR WORKS

LONG FICTION: *La Confession d'un enfant du siècle*, 1836 (*The Confession of a Child of the Century*, 1892).

SHORT FICTION: *Les Deux Maîtresses*, 1837; *Emmeline*, 1837; *Le Fils du Titien*, 1838; *Frédéric et Bernerette*, 1838; *Margot*, 1838; *Histoire d'un merle blanc*, 1842; *Pierre et Camille*, 1843; *Le Secret de Javotte*, 1844; *Les Frères Van Buck*, 1844; *Mimi Pinson*, 1845; *La Mouche*, 1854.

PLAYS: *La Nuit vénitienne: Ou, Les Noces de Laurette*, pr. 1830 (*The Venetian Night: Or, Laurette's Wedding*, 1905); *La Coupe et les lèvres*, pb. 1833; *À quoi rêvent les jeunes filles*, pb. 1833; *André del Sarto*, pb. 1833; *Les Caprices de Marianne*, pb. 1833 (*The Follies of Marianne*, 1905); *Fantasio*, pb. 1834 (English translation, 1853); *On ne badine pas avec l'amour*, pb. 1834 (*No Trifling with Love*, 1890); *Lorenzaccio*, pb. 1834 (English translation, 1905); *Un Spectacle dans un fauteuil*, pb. 1834 (second series, 2 volumes); *La Quenouille de Barbarine*, pb. 1835, revised 1851, pr. 1882 (*Barbarine*, 1890); *Le Chandelier*, pb. 1835 (*The Chandelier*, 1903); *Il ne faut jurer de rien*, pb. 1836; *Un Caprice*, pb. 1837 (*A Caprice*, 1847); *Il faut qu'une porte soit ouverte ou fermée*, pb. 1845 (*A Door Must Be Either Open or Shut*, 1890); *L'Habit vert*, pr., pb. 1849 (with Émile Augier); *Louison*, pr., pb. 1849 (English translation, 1905); *On ne saurait penser à tout*, pr. 1849; *Carmosine*, pb. 1850 (English translation, 1865); *Bettine*, pr., pb. 1851 (English translation, 1905); *L'Âne et le ruisseau*, wr. 1855, pb. 1860; *Comedies*, pb. 1890; *A Comedy and Two Proverbs*, pb. 1955; *Seven Plays*, pb. 1962.

TRANSLATION: *L'Anglais Mangeur d'opium*, 1828 (of Thomas de Quincey's *Confessions of an English Opium Eater*, 1821).

MISCELLANEOUS: *The Complete Writings*, 1905 (10 volumes).

BIBLIOGRAPHY

Levin, Susan M. *The Romantic Art of Confession: De Quincey, Musset, Sand, Lamb, Hogg, Frémy, Soulié, Janin.* Columbia, S.C.: Camden House, 1998. A critical study of eight writers and their use of the confessional form. Includes bibliographical references and index.

Peyre, Henri. "Alfred de Musset and the 'Mal du Siècle.'" In *What Is Romanticism?*, translated by Roda Roberts. University: University of Alabama Press, 1977. A summary of Musset's role in the Romantic movement in France.

Rees, M. A. *Alfred de Musset.* New York: Twayne, 1971. An introductory biography and critical interpretation of Musset's work. Includes a bibliography.

Sices, David, ed. *Comedies and Proverbs*, by Alfred de Musset. Baltimore: Johns Hopkins University Press, 1994. Although this edition of seven of Musset's comedies focuses on his drama, Sices's commentary provides insight into the poet as well.

Rodney Farnsworth

N

OGDEN NASH

Born: Rye, New York; August 19, 1902
Died: Baltimore, Maryland; May 19, 1971

PRINCIPAL POETRY
Hard Lines, 1931
Free Wheeling, 1931
Happy Days, 1933
The Primrose Path, 1935
The Bad Parents' Garden of Verse, 1936
I'm a Stranger Here Myself, 1938
The Face Is Familiar, 1940
Good Intentions, 1942
Many Long Years Ago, 1945
Versus, 1949
Family Reunion, 1950
The Private Dining Room, 1953
You Can't Get There from Here, 1957
Everyone but Thee and Me, 1962
Marriage Lines: Notes of a Student Husband, 1964
The Animal Garden, 1965
Santa Go Home: A Case History for Parents, 1967
The Cruise of the Aardvark, 1967
There's Always Another Windmill, 1968
Bed Riddance: A Posy for the Indisposed, 1970
The Old Dog Barks Backwards, 1972
I Wouldn't Have Missed It: Selected Poems, 1972

OTHER LITERARY FORMS
Ogden Nash's staple was the short comic poem. He wrote hundreds of them and collected them in more than twenty books. He also wrote essays for *The New Yorker* and other magazines, and he collaborated with friends on a variety of enterprises, contributing to several screenplays for Hollywood and two Broadway musicals. His daughters seem to have given him ideas for children's fiction, but he wrote for boys as often as he did for girls, and his most famous fiction, *Custard the Dragon* (1959), is pure fantasy. After he died, his older daughter collected the letters he had written to her and other family members during the last three decades of his life, *Loving Letters from Ogden Nash: A Family Album* (1990). These letters show him to have been as honest in private life as he was candid in print. Still other readers continue to collaborate with Nash as illustrators of his poems.

ACHIEVEMENTS
During his lifetime, Ogden Nash was one of America's best-loved humorists. Educated adults and precocious children quoted Nash much as their parents and grandparents had quoted Mark Twain, to give a distinctly American perspective on life, love, and English language. He was in many ways his own creation, for he invariably wrote in the persona of a middle-aged, middle-class American of middle income: a husband and father, a friend and neighbor, optimistic about life in general but pessimistic about the social and economic forces at work in the twentieth century. His tone was invariably urbane yet avuncular and slightly daft. Though often imitated he was never duplicated, and his books usually sold very well. Indeed, he was so successful commercially that grudging purists claimed his light verse was not poetry at all. Other readers agreed with the poet laureate Archibald MacLeish, who claimed, in the preface to the posthumously published *I Wouldn't Have Missed It: Selected Poems* (1972), that Nash was a true poet and a master of American English. Though he never won a major literary award, he was elected to the National Institute of Arts and Letters in 1950 and the American Academy of Arts and Sciences in 1965.

BIOGRAPHY
Frederic Ogden Nash was born in a suburb of New York and was raised in various East Coast cities where his father's business moved. He completed high school in Newport, Rhode Island, and spent a year at Harvard before financial pressures drove him to seek work. He held a series of jobs in New York—teaching, selling, and writing advertising copy—before landing a job in publishing with the firm of Doubleday. He began writing humorous poems in 1929, contributing them to the daily newspaper column written by Franklin P. Adams.

Nash's light humor was a tonic for hard times, as the United States entered a decade of economic depression. In 1930, he sold his first poem to *The New Yorker*, a verse comment on the war on "smut" recently waged by a senator named Smoot. Senator Smoot came from Utah (commonly abbreviated Ut.), but the endless stream of rhymes came from Nash. Soon he was a regular contributor to *The New Yorker*, where he appeared alongside great humorists such as James Thurber and S. J. Perelman. He was paid the princely sum of one dollar a line for his verses. Before long he was ready to collect a treasury of Nash; he wanted to call it a "trashery of Nashery," but his publishers found a more conventional title for this highly unconventional writer.

Nash married in 1931, after having published a first volume of poetry, and enjoyed a happy family life as the father of two loving daughters. After a second volume appeared, he left his job in publishing to devote his time to writing. Thereafter he commanded top dollar for his occasional poems, which appeared in such magazines as *Cosmopolitan*, *Harper's*, *Life*, and *The Saturday Evening Post*. He also made frequent appearances on radio and television. As he and the century approached middle age, he realized that he spoke for a large number of Americans. His fame brought him contracts to edit anthologies and allowed him to help out struggling poets. However, he realized with some bitterness that he was a victim of his own success, always commissioned to write more "Nashery," and would never become a "major" poet.

To the end, Nash remained a typical American: a proud grandparent; a world traveler by rail and ship, though never by air; and a reluctant user of medical services. He kept up with the new names in modern culture and wrote a poem on the existential philosophy of Jean-Paul Sartre for *The New Yorker* when he was nearing his own end ("One Man's Opium," 1970). He died from a massive stroke after surgery in 1971.

ANALYSIS

Ogden Nash admired the acerbic couplets of Dorothy Parker, including her famous remark that "Men seldom make passes/ At girls who wear glasses." His early contributions to *The New Yorker* were "Random Reflections" in verse, including the oft-quoted lines on "Ice-

Breaking": "Candy/ Is dandy/ But liquor/ Is quicker." His sentences could be gnomic, like this one or its successor, "Pot/ Is not." More often, they would tumble headlong in search of a rhyme, often violating standard syntax and spelling to get the rhyme. He claimed to have learned his technique from reading bad poetry; in particular he mentioned Julia A. Moore (1847-1920), known as the Sweet Singer of Michigan after the title poem of her most enduring book. Mark Twain claimed that Moore had "the touch that makes an intentionally humorous episode pathetic and an intentionally pathetic one funny." Nash's humor was intentional, unlike Moore's; he claimed to have "intentionally maltreated and manhandled every known rule of grammar, spelling, and prosody," but his rhythms and rhymes were just as bad.

"SPRING COMES TO MURRAY HILL"

Nash's first published poem, in 1929, shows his technique fully formed. The poem consists of fourteen lines, in seven rhymed couplets, and each of the rhymes is a stretch. In the fourth line, Nash turns the noun "gargle" into "goggerel" to rhyme with "doggerel," which seems

Ogden Nash (Hulton Archive)

an apt characterization of the writing. The speaker is Nash himself, an office worker on Madison Avenue whose mind wanders during a bout of spring fever. There is no real point to the wandering, which takes him from Missouri to Massachusetts and from his chiropodist to John the Baptist, who becomes the "Bobodist." There is only the vague wish for freedom, symbolized by the "wings of a bird." By the illogic of rhyme, the "bird" can take the speaker to Second Avenue and even to "Third."

"MORE ABOUT PEOPLE"

Nash began writing for publication when the United States was entering the Great Depression. Although he wrote for a magazine that targeted New York's affluent social set, he became increasingly aware of the gap between the rich and the poor. A contribution from 1930, "More About People," shows his awareness that "work is wonderful medicine" for anyone in danger of starvation. Seeking a rhyme for "medicine," he runs through a list of employers, "Firestone and Ford and Edison," using the well-known names to evoke successful people. Nevertheless, he sides with the employed rather than with the employers. The poem continues through eight couplets, ending with "a nasty quirk": "if you don't want to work you have to work to earn enough money so that you won't have to work."

"A NECESSARY DIRGE"

Nash loved to play the curmudgeon and could rail about everything from billboards to parsnips, but he was always able to put life in perspective. "A Necessary Dirge" (1935) is a reflection on the perversity of "man's fate" in ten rhyming couplets. For example, "How easy for those who do not bulge/ Not to indulge." Nash combines the universal and the particular, the Lexington Avenue express subway train and the hero's quest. He would like to raise the big question of theodicy: He would like to ask God why there is suffering in the world. Yet he accepts his fate, "to be irked," and advises readers to take the "irking with insouciant urbanity." Humorous poetry can also be wise, as this poem shows.

"ASK DADDY, HE WON'T KNOW"

As his family grew, Nash's poems extended to all aspects of domestic life. Looking forward to the rituals of homework in a 1942 poem, "Ask Daddy, He Won't Know," the speaker dreads the impending discovery that yesterday's genius—the boy whose "scholarship was fa-

mous"—will become tomorrow's "ignoramus," unable to answer questions about geometry and geography. The speaker is proud of his children but admits that he is "overwhelmed by their erudite banter." Of course, the poem is ironic; Nash commands all sorts of random information, even if it tends to stay "just back of the tip of my tongue." The real ignoramuses, by implication, are the young who assume that he knows nothing, and not just Nash's young. "Try to explain that to your young," he says to the reader.

VERSUS

Nash's first volume of poetry after World War II was full of paradoxes. Its very title suggests that the poet is adversarial in nature, going against the prosaic order of things. His verses on subjects from bridge to birthday cake are also statements "versus" unthinking acceptance of things as they are. He is well aware of his poetic tradition; he knows that William Wordsworth said, "The Child is father of the Man" (in "My Heart Leaps Up," 1802); however, he knows enough about children that he would like to add, "But not for quite a while." His poem on the subject, titled "Lines to Be Embroidered on a Bib," employs the verse form known as the clerihew; it takes the names of famous writers and thinkers and makes rhymes with them with the sort of witty precision that W. H. Auden would master.

Nash jokes about the squabbles between a big dog and a little dog in a poem whose title, "Two Dogs Have I," alludes to Sonnet 144 of William Shakespeare. The dust-jacket blurb notes that British readers had found the philosophical side of Nash that Americans often miss, and it quotes *The Times* of London on the "Democritean streak which entitles him to the respect due to a philosopher, albeit a laughing one." Indeed, much as the ancient Greek philosopher Democritus opined on the full and the void, Nash turns the old adage "Nature abhors a vacuum" into a personal reflection on the housing crisis in "Nature Abhors a Vacancy." No matter if one misses the occasional allusion: There are gags for all.

THERE'S ALWAYS ANOTHER WINDMILL

Amid the postwar optimism, Nash found much to grumble about but few publishers who wanted his grumblings. He turned to lighter subjects, like animals, and to familiar verse forms like the limerick. When he took on unpopular causes, he adapted a quixotic tone, hence the title of his late volume *There's Always Another Windmill* (1968). Included here is "The Nonbiography of a Nobody," a darkly confessional poem which finds only "one compensation for being a minor literary figure": "There's little there for the ghouls to feed on." The volume has its bright moments, including a series of limericks written as a tribute to Edward Lear (1812-1888), the self-styled inventor of "nonsense verse" and the main popularizer of the limerick. It concludes with "The Sunset Years of Samuel Shy," a Nash persona who claims to be a master, "But not of my fate."

OTHER MAJOR WORKS

PLAYS: *Four Prominent So and So's*, pb. 1934; *One Touch of Venus*, pr. 1943, pb. 1944 (with S. J. Perelman and Kurt Weill); *Two's Company*, pr. 1952, pb. 1978.

SCREENPLAYS: *The Firefly*, 1937; *The Shining Hair*, 1938 (with Jane Murfin); *The Feminine Touch*, 1941 (with George Oppenheimer and Edmund L. Hartmann).

NONFICTION: *Loving Letters from Ogden Nash: A Family Album*, 1990.

CHILDREN'S LITERATURE: *The Cricket of Carador*, 1925 (with Joseph Alger); *Parents Keep Out: Elderly Poems for Youngerly Readers*, 1951; *The Boy Who Laughed at Santa Claus*, 1957; *The Christmas That Almost Wasn't*, 1957; *Custard the Dragon*, 1959; *A Boy Is a Boy*, 1960; Scrooge *Rides Again*, 1960; *Custard the Dragon and the Wicked Knight*, 1961; *Girls Are Silly*, 1962; *A Boy and His Room*, 1963; *The Adventures of Isabel*, 1963; *The Untold Adventures of Santa Claus*, 1964; *The Mysterious Ouphe*, 1965.

EDITED TEXTS: *P. G. Wodehouse: Nothing but Wodehouse*, 1932; *The Moon Is Shining Bright as Day: An Anthology of Good-Humored Verse*, 1953; *I Couldn't Stop Laughing: Stories Selected and Introduced by Ogden Nash*, 1957; *Everybody Ought to Know: Verses Selected and Introduced by Ogden Nash*, 1961.

MISCELLANEOUS: *Under Water with Ogden Nash*, 1997.

BIBLIOGRAPHY

Axford, Lavonne B. *An Index to the Poems of Ogden Nash*. Metuchen, N.J.: Scarecrow, 1972. Nash's one-liners are easy to remember but devilishly hard to track down unless you have access to this helpful guide. Though not a concordance, this guide includes most key words in Nash's titles.

Crandall, George W., ed. *Ogden Nash: A Descriptive Bibliography*. Metuchen, N.J.: Scarecrow, 1990. Gives complete publishing details of Nash's many books, through all their printings. Helpful for identifying occasional pieces not cited in Axford's index.

Kermode, Frank. "Maturing Late or Simply Rotting Early?" *The Spectator*, September 24, 1994, p. 36-37. A major British critic discusses Nash's appeal to a new generation of readers. Kermode is able to catch the literary allusions in Nash's collected poems and dignifies Nash with a careful reading.

Smith, Linell Nash, ed. *Loving Letters from Ogden Nash: A Family Album*. Boston: Little, Brown, 1990. Edited by Nash's eldest daughter, this volume contains letters to family members written during the poet's last forty years. Nash emerges as a thoroughly decent man with a distinctive take on life in the twentieth century. New words from Europe (such as *maître d'* for "head waiter") mark the opposite of progress, in Nash's opinion. Inventions like the airplane are not improvements either; indeed, "two Wrights made a wrong."

Stuart, David. *The Life and Rhymes of Ogden Nash*. Lanham, Md.: Madison Books, 2000. A critical biography, illustrated with photos from the Nash papers at the University of Texas in Austin. Includes verses about Nash by contemporary reviewers imitating his style and previously unpublished verses by such friends as Dorothy Parker and E. B. White.

Thomas Willard

THOMAS NASHE

Born: Lowestoft, Surrey, England; November, 1567
Died: Yarmouth(?), England; 1601

PRINCIPAL POETRY

Pierce Peniless, His Supplication to the Divell, 1592 (prose and poetry)

Strange News of the Intercepting of Certain Letters,
   1592 (prose and poetry; also known as *The Four
   Letters Confuted*)
Summer's Last Will and Testament, 1592 (play and
   poetry)
*The Unfortunate Traveller: Or, The Life of Jack Wil-
   ton*, 1594 (prose and poetry)
The Choise of Valentines, 1899

OTHER LITERARY FORMS

Almost all that Thomas Nashe wrote was published
in pamphlet form. With the exception of a long poem
(*The Choise of Valentines*), several sonnets and songs,
and at least two dramas (*Summer's Last Will and Testament*, pr. 1592, and *The Isle of Dogs*, pr. 1597), all of his
work was prose. His prose works include *The Anatomie
of Absurditie* (1589); *An Almond for a Parrat* (1590);
a preface to Sir Philip Sidney's *Astrophel and Stella*
(1591); *Pierce Peniless, His Supplication to the Divell*;
Strange News of the Intercepting of Certain Letters;
Christ's Tears over Jerusalem (1593); *The Terrors of the
Night* (1594); *The Unfortunate Traveller: Or, The Life of
Jack Wilton; Have with You to Saffron-Walden* (1596);
and *Nashe's Lenten Stuffe* (1599).

ACHIEVEMENTS

Thomas Nashe was more a journalist than an artist, if
the definition of artist is one who follows the Aristotelian principles of using life as a source from which one
creates a story with a beginning, middle, and end. Nashe
informed and entertained his sixteenth century audience
in the same way that a journalist pleases the public today. He was known in his time not as a poet or a drama-
tist, although he wrote both poetry and plays. He was
known as the worthy opponent of the scholar Gabriel
Harvey, as one who with lively rhetoric, biting invective,
and soaring wit destroyed every argument the pompous
Harvey could muster. He was also known to Elizabethans as the chief defender of the Anglican Church
against the attack of the Puritans in the Martin Marprelate controversy. The magnificent invective found in
the speeches of William Shakespeare's Falstaff, Prince
Hal, and (more especially) Kent was almost certainly
derived from the vituperation Nashe hurled at his adversaries.

Among modern students of literature, Nashe is remembered for his most unusual work, the picaresque
novel of adventure, *The Unfortunate Traveller: Or, The
Life of Jack Wilton*. It is the story of a young page who,
after serving in the army of Henry VIII, travels to Europe to find means of earning a living. The underworld
realism that Nashe presents in his descriptions of Jack
Wilton's escapades has earned him a reputation for being something other than a hurler of invective. The book
is not a unified work of art; its characters, other than
Jack himself, are not particularly memorable. Its descriptions of the harshest elements of human life, such
as disease, hunger, torture, rape, and murder, place it in
stark contrast to the sweet absurdities of romance; it thus
shows the way to the modern novel.

BIOGRAPHY

Thomas Nashe was born in November, 1567, the
son of William Nashe, a minister in Lowestoft, Suf-
folk. Since no record exists of William's being a university graduate, it can be assumed that he was probably
a stipendiary curate in Lowestoft, not a vicar. Although
the title pages of *Pierce Peniless* and of *Strange News of
the Intercepting of Certain Letters* refer to "Thomas
Nashe, Gentleman," Nashe himself denied that he was
of gentle birth. From his earliest years, indeed, he disliked the propensity he found in middle-class Englishmen to pretend to be something other than what they
were.

In 1573, Nashe's father was granted the living in
West Harling, Norfolk, where young Thomas probably
spent his early years. Nothing is known of Nashe's basic education except that it was sufficient to allow him
to enter St. John's College, Cambridge, in October,
1582. In March, 1586, he received his bachelor of arts
degree and enrolled immediately to work toward the
master of arts degree. In 1588, however, he left Cambridge without the degree. Perhaps financial difficulties
forced him to leave the university, for his father had
died the year before, in 1587. Without financial support
from home, Nashe likely would not have been able to
continue his education; probably his college, dominated
as it was by Puritans, would not look with favor in the
form of financial assistance upon the satirical young
Nashe, who supported the pursuit of humanistic studies

over the more narrow Puritan theology then in vogue at Cambridge.

Whatever his reasons for leaving Cambridge, Nashe certainly had not the economic means to remain idle long. He followed the lead of two other Cambridge graduates who, armed with no wealth but their wits, turned to literature as a means of earning a livelihood. Both Robert Greene and Christopher Marlowe had gone to London to write and both had found moderate success. Nashe may have been acquainted with both men at Cambridge, but he certainly knew them both in London. Like Nashe, both loved poetry and detested Puritans. In the same year that he left Cambridge, he published *The Anatomie of Absurditie*, a work of inexperience and brashness.

A young writer of pamphlets in London had few opportunities to earn a living by his work. He was generally paid a flat amount for his manuscript, usually two pounds. If a pamphlet were well-received by the public, the patron to whom it was dedicated might be so flattered that he or she might feel disposed to grant the author a stipend to continue his work. Nashe's *The Anatomie of Absurditie*, dedicated to Sir Charles Blount, was, however, of so little literary merit that Nashe probably received no more than his original author's fee.

Nashe dedicated no more works to Sir Charles; but because he did need patrons, he dedicated later works to a variety of people in a position to offer him assistance. Finally, after the dedication of *The Unfortunate Traveller* to Henry Wriothesley, the earl of Southampton, Nashe decided that patrons were more trouble than they were worth. Hating hypocrisy in others and finding himself forced into hypocrisy in order to be paid for his work, Nashe turned to writing only for his readers and depended upon them to reward his efforts.

Perhaps what gave Nashe his biggest literary boost was the famous Martin Marprelate controversy. Nashe's part in the verbal battle was limited to the pamphlet *An Almond for a Parrat*, but the style and the vigorous prose of Martin could not help influencing Nashe. Although he was hostile to Martin's Puritanical ideas, Nashe must nevertheless have learned much from the formidable prose of his Puritan adversary, for he attacks Martin with the same devices and force of language that the Puritan propagandist used.

Thomas Nashe (Hulton Archive)

Nashe's entry into the Martin Marprelate controversy brought with it rewards beyond what he might have hoped. Gabriel Harvey wrote disparagingly of Nashe's part in the controversy, thus starting a new fight: the Nashe-Harvey controversy. It was in this battle of wits that Nashe found his place as a writer. Here the verbal street-fighter had the great good fortune to be attacked by a man of reputation who was inferior in wit and writing ability to Nashe. Harvey's reputation never recovered from Nashe's fierce invective. Beginning with a slap at Harvey in his preface to Greene's *A Quip for an Upstart Courtier* (1592) and ending with *Have with You to Saffron-Walden*, Nashe earned a good reputation and a fair living from his anti-Harvey prose.

All of his previous writings were practice for *The Unfortunate Traveller*, published in 1594. A kind of pamphlet itself, but longer and more complex, the work was not particularly popular during his lifetime, but today it is his best-known work.

Nashe was hounded from London in 1597 when the authorities decided that *The Isle of Dogs*, a play he had begun, and which Ben Jonson had finished, was "seditious." Jonson was jailed and Nashe sought, but the famous pamphleteer had fled to Yarmouth, in Norfolk. By 1598, he was back in London, where *Nashe's Lenten Stuffe* was entered in the Stationers' Register.

After *Nashe's Lenten Stuffe*, Nashe wrote no more, and in 1601 history records a reference to his death.

ANALYSIS

Thomas Nashe the satirical pamphleteer, who was wont to use language as a cudgel in a broad prose style, seldom disciplined himself to the more delicate work of writing poetry. Both his temperament and his pocketbook directed him to the freer and more profitable form of pamphlet prose. It is this prose that made his reputation, but Nashe did write poems, mostly lyrical in the manner of his time. No originator in poetic style, Nashe followed the lead of such worthy predecessors as Geoffrey Chaucer, the earl of Surrey, Edmund Spenser, and Christopher Marlowe.

Nashe's interest in poetry was not slight. In typical Renaissance fashion, he believed poetry to be the highest form of moral philosophy. Following Sidney, he insisted that the best poetry is based upon scholarship and devotion to detail. Not only does poetry, in his perception, encourage virtue and discourage vice, but also it "cleanses" the language of barbarisms and makes the "vulgar sort" in London adopt a more pleasing manner of speech. Because he loved good poetry and saw the moral and aesthetic value of it, Nashe condemned the "balladmongers," who abused the ears and sensitivities of the gentlefolk of England. To him, the ballad writers were "common pamfletters" whose lack of learning and lust for money were responsible for littering the streets with the garbage of their ballads—a strange reaction for a man who was himself a notable writer of pamphlets. For the learned poetry of Western culture, Nashe had the highest appreciation.

Nashe's own poetic efforts are often placed in the context of his prose works, as if he were setting jewels among the coarser material, as did George Gascoigne, Thomas Lodge, Robert Greene, Thomas Deloney, and others. *Pierce Peniless*, "The Four Letters Confuted," and *The Unfortunate Traveller* all have poems sprinkled here and there. The play *Summers Last Will and Testament*, itself written in quite acceptable blank verse, has several lyrics of some interest scattered throughout.

Nashe's shorter poetic efforts are almost equally divided between sonnets and lyrical poems. The longer *The Choise of Valentines* is a narrative in the erotic style of Ovid.

SONNETS

Nashe's sonnets are six in number, two of which may be said to be parodies of the form. Each is placed within a longer work, where its individual purpose is relevant to the themes of that work. Most of the sonnets are in the English form, containing three quatrains and a concluding couplet. Following the lead of the earl of Surrey (who is, indeed, the putative author of the two sonnets to Geraldine in *The Unfortunate Traveller*), Nashe uses a concluding couplet in each of his sonnets, including "To the Right Honorable the lord S.," which in other respects (as in the division into octave and sestet rhyming *abbaabba, cdcdee*) is closer to the Italian form.

In his first sonnet, "Perusing yesternight, with idle eyes," Nashe pauses at the end of *Pierce Peniless* to praise the lord Amyntas, whom Edmund Spenser had neglected in *The Faerie Queene* (1590-1596). In "Perusing yesternight, with idle eyes," the famous poem by Spenser, Nashe had turned to the end of the poem to find sonnets addressed to "sundry Nobles." Nashe uses the three quatrains to rehearse the problem: He read the poem, found the sonnets addressed to the nobles, and wondered why Spenser had left out "thy memory." In an excellent use of the concluding couplet in this form, he decides that Spenser must have omitted praise of Amyntas because "few words could not cōprise thy fame."

If "Perusing yesternight, with idle eyes" is in the tradition of using the sonnet to praise, Nashe's second sonnet, "Were there no warres," is not. Concluding his prose attack on Gabriel Harvey in "The Four Letters Confuted," this sonnet looks forward to John Milton rather than backward to Petrarch. Here Nashe promises Harvey constant warfare. Harvey had suggested that he would like to call off the battle, but in so doing he had delivered a few verbal blows to Nashe. To the request for a truce, Nashe responds with a poetic "no!" Again using the three quatrains to deliver his message, the poet calls for "Vncessant warres with waspes and droanes," announces that revenge is an endless muse, and says that he will gain his reputation by attacking "this duns." His couplet effectively concludes by promising that his next work will be of an extraordinary type.

The next two sonnets may be thought of as parodies of the Petrarchan style and of the medieval romance generally. Nashe, like his creation Jack Wilton, had little use for the unrealistic in love, war, or any aspect of life. The exaggerated praise of women in the Petrarchan tradition sounded as false to him as it did to Shakespeare and to the later writers of anti-Petrarchan verse. Both "If I must die" and "Faire roome, the presence of sweet beauty's pride," found in *The Unfortunate Traveller*, are supposedly written by the lovesick Surrey to his absent love, Geraldine. Both poems are close enough to the real Surrey's own sonnets to ring true, but just ridiculous enough to be seen clearly as parodies.

The first is addressed to the woman Diamante, whom Surrey mistakes for Geraldine. The dying Surrey requests that his mistress suck out his breath, stab him with her tongue, crush him with her embrace, burn him with her eyes, and strangle him with her hair. In "Faire roome, the presence of sweet beauty's pride," Surrey, having visited Geraldine's room in Florence, addresses the room. He will worship the room, with which neither the chambers of heaven nor lightning can compare. No one, he concludes, can see heaven unless he meditates on the room.

Such romantic nonsense held no attraction for Jack or for Nashe. Jack makes fun of "suchlike rhymes" which lovers use to "assault" women: "A holy requiem to their souls that think to woo women with riddles." Jack, a much more realistic man, wins the favor of Diamonte with a plain table.

The final two sonnets are also anti-Petrarchan in content. Addressed to a would-be patron to whom he dedicated *The Choise of Valentines*, both "To the Right Honorable the lord S." and "Thus hath my penne presum'd to please" ask pardon for presuming to address an overtly pornographic poem to a "sweete flower of matchless poetrie." In the octave of the former, Nashe excuses himself by declaring that he merely writes about what men really do. In the sestet, he proudly asserts that everyone can write Petrarchan love poems, full of "complaints and praises." No one, however, has written successfully of "loves pleasures" in his time—except, the implication is, him.

LYRICS

Nashe's earliest two lyrics, although they are very different in content, are each in four stanzas of six lines of iambic pentameter. The rhyme in each case is *ababcc*. The later songs, those in *Summers Last Will and Testament*, are in couplets and (in one case) tercets. Except for "Song: Spring, the sweete spring," all the lyrics are laments.

The most personal of the lyrics is "Why ist damnation," printed on the first page of Nashe's famous pamphlet *Pierce Peniless*. Trying to gain prosperity and failing, Nashe "resolved in verse to paint forth my passion." In a logical progression, the poet first considers suicide ("Why ist damnation to dispaire and die") but decides against it for his soul's safety. He then determines that in England wit and scholarship are useless. He asks God's forgiveness for his low mood, but despairs because he has no friends. Finally, he bids adieu to England as "unkinde, where skill is nothing woorth."

"All Soul, no earthly flesh," Nashe's second lyric, is more like the anti-Petrarchan sonnets that Nashe has the earl of Surrey write in *The Unfortunate Traveller* than it is like the other lyrics. Full of exaggerated comparisons (Geraldine is "pure soul," "pure gold"), comic images (his spirit will perch upon "hir silver breasts"), and conventional conceits (stars, sun, and dew take their worth from her), the poem is as far from Nashe as John Lyly's *Euphues, the Anatomy of Wit* (1579) is.

In *Summers Last Will and Testament*, Nashe includes four major lyrics and several minor ones. Some of the lyrics are cheery "Song: Spring, the sweete spring," "Song: Trip and goe," and "Song: Merry, merry, merry," for example. The general mood of the poems is sad, however, as the subject of the whole work would dictate: the death of summer. In watching summer die, readers, like Gerard Manley Hopkins's Margaret, see themselves. "Song: Fayre Summer droops" is a conventional lament on the passing of summer. Written in heroic couplets, the poem uses alliteration successfully in the last stanza to bring the song to a solid conclusion. "Song: Autumn Hath all the Summer's Fruitfull Treasure," also in heroic couplets, continues the theme of lament with lines using effective repetition ("Short dayes, sharpe dayes, long nights come on a pace"). Here, Nashe turns more directly to what was perhaps his central theme in the longer work: man's weakness in face of natural elements. The refrain, repeated at the end of each of the two stanzas, is "From winter, plague, & pestilence, good Lord, deliver us."

It was surely fear of the plague and of man's frailty in general that led Nashe to write the best of his lyrics, "Song: Adieu, farewell earths blisse," sung to the dying Summer by Will Summer. Nashe recognizes in the refrain which follows each of the six stanzas that he is sick, he must die, and he prays: "Lord, have mercy on us."

In a logical development, Nashe first introduces the theme of *Everyman:* "Fond are lifes lustful ioyes." In succeeding stanzas he develops each of the "lustfull ioyes" in turn. "Rich men" are warned not to trust in their wealth, "Beauty" is revealed as transitory, "Strength" is pictured surrendering to the grave, and "Wit" is useless to dissuade Hell's executioner. In a very specific, orderly manner and in spare iambic trimeter lines, Nashe presents man's death-lament and prayer for mercy. One stanza will show the strength of the whole poem:

> Beauty is but a flowre,
> Which wrinckles will deuoure,
> Brightnesse falls from the ayre,
> Queenes have died yong and faire,
> Dust hath closed Helens eye.
> I am sick, I must dye:
> Lord, have mercy on vs.

THE CHOISE OF VALENTINES

Nashe's last poem is by far his longest. *The Choise of Valentines* is an erotic narrative poem in heroic couplets running to more than three hundred lines. With the kind of specificity that one would expect from the author of *The Unfortunate Traveller,* Nashe tells of the visit of the young man Tomalin to a brothel in search of his valentine, "gentle mistris Francis." Tomalin's detailed exploration of the woman's anatomical charms, his unexpected loss of sexual potency, and her announced preference for a dildo all combine to present an Ovidian erotic-mythological poem of the type popular in Elizabethan England. Nashe's poem must, however, be set off from Shakespeare's *Venus and Adonis* (1593) and Marlowe's *Hero and Leander* (1598), which emphasize

the mythological more than the erotic. Nashe clearly emphasizes the erotic, almost to the exclusion of the mythological. Why not? he seems to say in the dedicatory sonnet accompanying the poem: Ovid was his guide, and "Ouids wanton Muse did not offend."

Nowhere, with the exception of the excellent "Song: Adieu, farewell earths blisse," does Nashe rise to the heights of his greatest contemporaries, Spenser, Sidney, Marlowe, and Shakespeare. In that poem, in the sonnet "Were there no warres," and in perhaps one or two other poems his Muse is sufficiently shaken into consciousness by the poet's interest in the subject. The remainder of Nashe's poetry is the work of an excellent craftsman who is playing with form and language.

OTHER MAJOR WORKS

LONG FICTION: *The Unfortunate Traveller: Or, The Life of Jack Wilton,* 1594 (prose and poetry).

PLAYS: *Dido, Queen of Carthage,* pr. c. 1586-1587 (with Christopher Marlowe); *Summer's Last Will and Testament,* pr. 1592; *The Isle of Dogs,* pr. 1597 (with Ben Jonson; no longer extant).

NONFICTION: preface to Robert Greene's *Menaphon,* 1589; *The Anatomie of Absurditie,* 1589; *An Almond for a Parrat,* 1590; preface to Sir Philip Sidney's *Astrophel and Stella,* 1591; *Pierce Peniless, His Supplication to the Divell,* 1592 (prose and poetry); preface to Greene's *A Quip for an Upstart Courtier,* 1592; *Strange News of the Intercepting of Certain Letters,* 1592 (prose and poetry; also known as *The Four Letters Confuted*); *Christ's Tears over Jerusalem,* 1593; *The Terrors of the Night,* 1594; *Have with You to Saffron-Walden,* 1596; *Nashe's Lenten Stuffe,* 1599.

BIBLIOGRAPHY

Helgerson, Richard. *The Elizabethan Prodigals.* Berkeley: University of California Press, 1977. Nashe and his colleagues Christopher Marlowe, Thomas Kyd, George Peele, Robert Greene, and Thomas Lodge, all with university training, formed a group of literary bohemians in London. Helgerson catalogs their escapades and relates them to their lives, which were adventurous, barbarous, and impoverished in turn. The index cross-references topics well.

Hibbard, G. R. *Thomas Nashe: A Critical Introduction.* Cambridge, Mass.: Harvard University Press, 1962. Hibbard basically tells the story of Nashe's life, giving passing attention to his poems and writings and to his theories about literature and life. Contains an index and an appendix.

Hilliard, Stephen S. *The Singularity of Thomas Nashe.* Lincoln: University of Nebraska Press, 1986. Hilliard takes a fresh look at Nashe's life and writing, discovering the distinctive qualities of his wit and style and showing how they transformed both poetry and prose. A good index ties topics together, and the bibliography provides a good source for further research.

Holbrook, Peter. *Literature and Degree in Renaissance England: Nashe, Bourgeois Tragedy, Shakespeare.* Cranbury, N.J.: Associated University Presses, 1994. A historical study of political and social views in sixteenth century England. Includes bibliographical references and index.

Muir, Kenneth. *Introduction to Elizabethan Literature.* New York: Random House, 1967. This excellent single-volume guide to the period has good standard comments on Nashe and his place in Elizabethan poetry. Muir is a sound scholar with profound insights into the period. The bibliography is dated, but the full notes provide good supplementary material.

Nicholl, Charles. *A Cup of News: The Life of Thomas Nashe.* London: Routledge & Kegan Paul, 1984. This scholarly biography sets a high standard. In addition to substantial discussions of Nashe's life and writings, Nicholl includes illustrations of portraits and scenes, as well as reproductions of relevant documents. He is particularly illuminating about the poetry. The notes, bibliography, and index are all excellent.

Nielson, James. *Unread Herrings: Thomas Nashe and the Prosaics of the Real.* New York: P. Lang, 1993. A critical study of selected works by Nashe. Includes bibliographical references.

Ostriker, Alicia, and Leslie Dunn. "The Lyric." In *English Poetry and Prose, 1540-1674,* edited by Christopher Ricks. New York: Peter Bedrick Books, 1986. This compound essay, with sections on poetry and on song lyrics, is in accordance with a practical division first initiated in the Elizabethan period. Nashe's connections with both are covered, although he is considered an incidental figure. The select bibliography lists most of the major sources.

Rhodes, Neil. *Elizabethan Grotesque.* London: Routledge & Kegan Paul, 1980. Collects a fascinating set of amusing and bizarre stories from a notably roguish period. Nashe and his fellow wits come into sight regularly. This entertaining book of literary gossip re-creates Nashe's lifestyle effectively. The notes make browsing easy.

Eugene P. Wright;
bibliography updated by the editors

JOHN G. NEIHARDT

Born: Sharpsburg, Illinois; January 8, 1881
Died: Lincoln, Nebraska; November 3, 1973

PRINCIPAL POETRY
The Divine Enchantment, 1900
The Wind God's Wooing, 1904
A Bundle of Myrrh, 1907
Man Song, 1909
The Stranger at the Gate, 1912
The Song of Hugh Glass, 1915
The Song of Three Friends, 1919
The Song of the Indian Wars, 1925
The Song of the Messiah, 1935
The Song of Jed Smith, 1941
A Cycle of the West, 1949 (includes the previous five titles)

OTHER LITERARY FORMS
John G. Neihardt's range is extensive. During a seventy-five-year literary career, he wrote at least 3,027 poems, plays, novels, stories, essays, articles, reviews, and histories, as well as a two-volume autobiography. Most of Neihardt's prose fiction was written before 1912. His short stories about fur trappers and Native Americans gathered in *The Lonesome Trail* (1907) and

Indian Tales and Others (1926) are often excellent. His early novels are less successful, but *Black Elk Speaks* (1932) and his last novel, *When the Tree Flowered* (1951), are considered masterpieces of the literature on Native Americans and have been translated into many languages.

In addition, Neihardt excelled in nonfiction: *The River and I* (1910) chronicles his outdoor adventure down the Missouri River, *The Splendid Wayfaring* (1920) provides a history of fur expeditions, and *Poetic Values* (1925) outlines Neihardt's philosophy of poetry developed during an editorial career of almost forty years.

ACHIEVEMENTS

For many, John G. Neihardt is the premier Western poet; he is also a primary midwestern literary critic and authority on the Plains Indians. In 1917, he received his first honorary doctorate from the University of Nebraska, and his epics were subsequently printed in school editions to acquaint Nebraska's students with their heritage. In 1921, he was celebrated as the poet laureate of Nebraska; he was awarded the Gold Scroll Medal of Honor in 1935 and the American Writers Award for Poetry in 1936.

International recognition came in 1959 in Lindau, Germany, when Neihardt was made a fellow of the International Institute of Arts and Letters. He was honored as the Plains State poet laureate in 1968, and at the time of his death, there was a bill before Congress to appoint him poet laureate of the United States. Although he received all these honors graciously, his goal was to do for the prairies what Homer had done for Ilium.

BIOGRAPHY

John Gneisenau Neihardt was born January 8, 1881, in a two-room rented farmhouse near Sharpsburg, Illinois. Later, his family moved into a one-room sod house in Kansas. Neihardt grew up on the edge of the frontier, gathering buffalo chips for fuel, as the great herds had vanished only a few years earlier.

Two experiences deeply impressed the young Neihardt: the sight of the Missouri River in flood, and a fever-induced, mystical dream in which he vividly experienced flight. These two powerful experiences turned him toward poetry. He continued to gather raw materials

from his closeness to nature's beauty and power and through his lifelong contact with Plains Indians, fur trappers, migrant workers, and cowboys.

Neihardt went directly from elementary school to Nebraska Normal School. Then after harvesting beets, pulling weeds, and teaching in a Nebraska country school, he set out on a hobo journey to Kansas City, Missouri, all the while revising his first book of poems, *The Divine Enchantment*.

Next Neihardt worked as an editor for the *Omaha Daily News* and began to establish a fellowship with the Omaha Indians, whose tribal chant rhythms are directly reflected in *The Wind God's Wooing*. His collected lyric poems in *A Bundle of Myrrh* became an immediate success and brought him an offer to finance a solo adventure down the Missouri River in a homemade boat, documented in *The River and I*. Also, this volume of poetry reached New Yorker Mona Martinson, who was studying sculpture in Paris, and after a brief courtship by mail, she and Neihardt were married in Oklahoma.

In 1910, Neihardt joined the literary staff of *The New York Times*, and he subsequently served as editor for the Minneapolis *Journal*, *The Kansas City Journal*, and *The Saint Louis Post-Dispatch*. During his editorial career, he continued to write, producing several short stories, four verse plays, and two novels, *The Dawn Builder* (1911) and *Life's Lure* (1914). In 1932, at thirty-one, with his reputation secure, Neihardt began work on his epic, *A Cycle of the West*. Twenty-nine years later, he completed this heroic cycle on the adventures of the American fur trade.

Neihardt's best friend among the Sioux was Black Elk, the tribe's last surviving priest. The poet became the shaman's spiritual son and absorbed the Lakota mysticism which became part of Neihardt's most popular prose work, *Black Elk Speaks*.

In 1942, Neihardt worked in Chicago slums with street gangs while waiting for a vacancy in the Bureau of Indian Affairs. In 1948, he purchased Skyrim Farm in Missouri and became poet in residence at the University of Missouri, Columbia, teaching literary criticism and a class called Epic America. When he died at ninety-two, he was in the process of writing *Patterns and Coincidences* (1978), a second volume to his autobiography, *All Is but a Beginning* (1972).

ANALYSIS

THE DIVINE ENCHANTMENT

With his pockets filled with poetry of Alfred, Lord Tennyson and Robert Browning, pulling weeds for a living, John G. Niehardt composed his first major work. *The Divine Enchantment* is a long narrative poem inspired by his readings in Hindu mysticism. It received some favorable reviews, but most of the five hundred copies of the first and only edition ended in his stove as needed fuel. Niehardt later gave these same ideas theoretical expression in *Poetic Values* (1925). Throughout his life, he sustained a mystical view that all parts of life are an interconnected expression of the life force, and his associations with the Sioux would reveal new facets of this harmonious unity.

A BUNDLE OF MYRRH

Neihardt published thirty-one love lyrics in his first successful book of poetry, *A Bundle of Myrrh*. In his 1965 prefatory note, he indicated that this volume represented the beginning of a spiritually progressive sequence with its "experiences of groping youth." The reviewers were enthusiastic, and even though this is apprentice work, there are indications of the powers of the future poet. "Recognition" is the outpouring of a lover who sees lovers of the past in himself and his beloved:

> O I have found
> At last the one I lost so long ago
> In Thessaly.

Here the poet claims a link to the great poets of antiquity. In many of his works, Neihardt insists upon the unity of all time and human experience. With Ralph Waldo Emerson and Henry David Thoreau, he celebrated a transcendent organic tradition and, like T. S. Eliot, felt that a writer should not write only with his own times in mind, but in the light of the whole tradition of literature from Homer forward.

"Let Me Live Out My Years," the most popular poem in this volume, exemplifies the heroic resolve of Tennyson's Ulysses:

> Let me live out my years in heat of blood!
> Let me die drunken with the dreamer's wine!
> Let me not see this soul-house built of mud
> Go toppling to the dust—a vacant shrine!

Here is a memorable expression of Neihardt's love of adventure, of living life on an epic scale, and of not settling for a faded or mechanical life: "Give me high noon," the poet shouts, displaying the fire and idealism of adolescence.

MAN SONG

Neihardt's 1909 volume *Man Song* contains twenty-seven lyrics that examine various aspects of manhood, including the contemplative life and struggles with the dehumanizing world of labor ("Lonesome in Town" and "Song of the Turbine Wheel"). "A Vision of Woman" is a mature love song, a long meditation in blank verse, more conversational and more philosophical than the earlier love lyrics.

THE STRANGER AT THE GATE

After expressing youthful rapture and then the joys of matrimony in his two previous collections of lyrics, Neihardt, in *The Stranger at the Gate* (1912), celebrates in twenty-one lyrics the mystery of new life at the birth of his first child. Some reviewers felt the poems were unabashedly sentimental, while others found their spiritual insights worthy of careful study.

The long poem *The Poet's Town*, included in *The Stranger at the Gate*, explores the poet's relationship to society and community, which for Neihardt at this time was the provincial midwestern town of Bancroft, Nebraska. He decries the poet's poor reception by the greedy philistines in the town:

> None of your dream-stuffs, Fellow,
> Looter of Samarkand!
> Gold is heavy and yellow,
> And value is weighed in the hand!

He also explores other themes: an acceptance of the genteel poverty of a poet, the heroic ideals found in Greece and Rome, nature's great organic power, the degradation and futility of the business ethic, and the development of a cosmic consciousness.

After this apprenticeship in lyric poetry, as well as a brief attempt at dramatic verse, Neihardt was a mature poet with developed views and a clear goal. He then set out to spend his next thirty years writing his epic cycle of songs on the West.

A CYCLE OF THE WEST

Neihardt's extended national epic celebrates important figures of the American fur trade and of the American Indian wars. It consists of five songs composed over twenty-nine years and totaling more than sixteen thousand lines. The five songs merge in a unified work around a central theme: the conflict over the Missouri River Valley from 1822 to the 1890 Battle of Wounded Knee, which marks the end of Sioux resistance.

Neihardt chose the heroic couplet to help underscore his topic's universal significance. He also modeled his poetry after other heroic epics, noting in *The River and I* that the story of the American fur traders had such literary potential, it made the Trojan War look like a Punch and Judy show.

The Song of Three Friends, though composed second, begins the cycle with Will Carpenter, Mike Fink, and Frank Talbeau starting up the Missouri River in 1822 with a beaver-trapping expedition. These comrades end up destroying one another's potential over what starts as a rivalry for a chief's half-breed daughter. The descriptive passages are powerful because, as Neihardt notes in his 1948 introduction, "If I write of hot-winds and grasshoppers, of prairie fires and blizzards, . . . of brooding heat and thunderstorms in vast lands, I knew them early."

The second book of the cycle is *The Song of Hugh Glass*, based on the historical trek of an old trapper who survives because he knows the ways of the wilderness. Left to die by the others after being mauled by a grizzly, Glass is filled with a desire for revenge. He crawls for miles, endures starvation, thirst, near drowning, and freezing to track his betrayers. However, instead of a brutal revenge, he chooses to nobly forgive. Much like the Ancient Mariner, Glass is brought back to his better self by the vision of a ghostly brother:

> Stripped of his clothes, Hugh let his body drink
> At every thirsting pore. Through trunk and limb
> The elemental blessing solaced him;

The Song of Jed Smith, though last to be completed, presents the third song of the cycle. This story is told by three first-person narrators, all trapper friends of Smith. Also, while the first two songs center on the larger-than-life, but brutish, figures of Mike Fink and Hugh Glass, Jed Smith represents a more perfect flowering of the frontiersman. He is an awe-inspiring hero, a frontier saint, finding water in the desert, trail-blazing the unknown.

The Song of the Indian Wars begins in 1865 with the period of migration; it focuses on the last great contest for the bison lands between the Plains Indians and the superior technology of the invading white race. The Sioux cannot understand the white people's lust for land and gold, for their faith assumes a sacred unity with the earth and its resources.

Since Neihardt intended his cycle to show a progress in spirit, in this song he turns from the mere indomitable physical prowess celebrated in the earlier songs to the spiritual triumph of the Sioux, even in the midst of their defeat. After his victory at the Battle of the Little Bighorn, Crazy Horse is hounded into starvation and surrender. The last section of this song, "The Death of Crazy Horse," was Neihardt's most popular work and was most often requested at his recitations. Here the landscape and animals reflect the agony of the tragic hero as Crazy Horse surrenders for the sake of his people. He

> loosed the bonnet from his head
> And cast it down. "I come for peace," he said;
> "Now let my people eat." And that was all.

The last moments of the brave young man are dignified and noble, his language simple and straightforward.

The Song of the Messiah, the fifth and last song of the cycle, records the conquered people, whose time for heroic deeds is over. The beavers, the buffalo, and the mighty hunters are gone; all that remains of these native people is their spirit. Although the whites appear to have mastered the continent, the poet indicates that he still needs to attend to his spiritual self if he is to be whole.

The reduced Sioux people turn to the Ghost Dance religion, which offers nonviolence and a mystical link to ancestors, but this desire for rebirth is doomed; the song ends with the massacre at Wounded Knee. As the leader Sitanka dies, he has a vision of the soldier who smashes his skull:

> . . . And he knew
> The shining face, unutterably dear!
> All tenderness, it hovered, bending near,
>
> .   .   .   .
> . . . He strove to rise in vain,
> To cry "My brother!"
> > > > And the shattered brain
> Went out.

Although the white solders seem to have won, they have not yet understood the harmony of the flowering tree or the sacred hoop's mystery of universal brotherhood and transcendental unity.

OTHER MAJOR WORKS

LONG FICTION: *The Dawn Builder*, 1911; *Life's Lure*, 1914; *Black Elk Speaks*, 1932; *When the Tree Flowered*, 1951.

SHORT FICTION: *The Lonesome Trail*, 1907; *Indian Tales and Others*, 1926.

PLAYS: *Death of Agrippina*, pb. 1913; *Two Mothers*, pb. 1921.

NONFICTION: *The River and I*, 1910; *The Splendid Wayfaring*, 1920; *Poetic Values*, 1925; *All Is but a Beginning*, 1972; *Luminous Sanity*, 1973 (John Thomas Richards, editor); *Patterns and Coincidences*, 1978.

BIBLIOGRAPHY

Aly, Lucile F. *John G. Neihardt: A Critical Biography.* Amsterdam: Rodopi, 1977. The most complete biography of Neihardt, factual and well-documented, although it lacks an index.

Deloria, Vine, Jr., ed. *A Sender of Words: Essays in Memory of John G. Neihardt.* Chicago: Howe Brothers, 1984. A collection of essays honoring Neihardt, contributed by Dee Brown (author of *Bury My Heart at Wounded Knee*, 1970), as well as by editors, historians, professors, anthropologists, singers, actors, political commentators, and theologians. The range of contributors and their topics testifies to the universal appeal and the expansive application of Neihardt's work.

Lee, Fred L. *John G. Neihardt: The Man and His Western Writings.* Kansas City, Mo.: Trail Guide Press, 1974. A friend's brief account of Neihardt's life; Lee, an expert on writings about the American West, also examines Neihardt's work in light of that tradition.

Lind, L. R. "The Great American Epic." *Classical and Modern Literature: A Quarterly* 17, no. 1 (Fall, 1996): 7. Examines North and South American long poems which convey traditional beliefs and customs fundamental to specific American cultures; Neihardt's *A Cycle of the West* is examined among other twentieth century North and South American poets.

Richards, John Thomas. *Rawhide Laureate: John G. Neihardt.* Metuchen, N.J.: Scarecrow Press, 1983. An annotated bibliography of the works of Neihardt. Also includes a complete listing of Neihardt's articles, essays, reviews, and literary criticism, as well as recordings and films of the poet, books and dissertations on his life and work, and public and private collections of Neihardtania.

_____. *A Voice Against the Wind: John G. Neihardt as Critic and Reviewer.* Oregon, Wis.: New Frontiers Foundation, 1986. Covers Neihardt's career as a professional critic, reviewer, and editor; outlines his views on Western literary tradition and examines his critical philosophy, which ultimately became the graduate course he taught at the University of Missouri.

Whitney, Blair. *John G. Neihardt.* Boston: G. K. Hall, 1976. Contains biographical and critical material, especially focusing on the rugged, frontier aspects of both the man and his work.

Marie J. K. Brenner

HOWARD NEMEROV

Born: New York, New York; March 1, 1920
Died: Universal City, Missouri; July 5, 1991

PRINCIPAL POETRY

The Image and the Law, 1947
Guide to the Ruins, 1950
The Salt Garden, 1955
Mirrors and Windows, 1958
The Next Room of the Dream: Poems and Two Plays, 1962
The Blue Swallows, 1967
Gnomes and Occasions, 1973
The Western Approaches: Poems 1973-75, 1975
The Collected Poems of Howard Nemerov, 1977
Sentences, 1980
Inside the Onion, 1984
War Stories: Poems About Long Ago and Now, 1987
Trying Conclusions: New and Selected Poems, 1961-1991, 1992

OTHER LITERARY FORMS

Though known primarily for his poetry, Howard Nemerov wrote novels–*The Melodramatists* (1949), *Federigo: Or, The Power of Love* (1954), and *The Homecoming Game* (1957)—and short stories, collected in *A Commodity of Dreams and Other Stories* (1959) and *Stories, Fables, and Other Diversions* (1971). Two verse dramas, *Endor* and *Cain*, are included with his collection *The Next Room of the Dream*. His criticism and reflections on the making of poetry are to be found in various volumes: *Poetry and Fiction: Essays* (1963), *Reflexions on Poetry and Poetics* (1972), *Figures of Thought: Speculations on the Meaning of Poetry and Other Essays* (1978), *New and Selected Essays* (1985), and *The Oak in the Acorn: On "Remembrance of Things Past" and on Teaching Proust, Who Will Never Learn* (1987). *Journal of the Fictive Life* is a series of candid autobiographical meditations.

ACHIEVEMENTS

As a poet, novelist, critic, and teacher, Howard Nemerov was a man of letters in the eighteenth century tradition. He was identified with no particular school of poetry. In the pamphlet *Howard Nemerov* (1968), Peter Meinke says that Nemerov's work explores the dilemma of "the existential, science-oriented (or science-displaced) liberal mind of the twentieth century."

Almost every available award came to Nemerov; his honors included the Bowdoin Prize from Harvard University (1940), a *Kenyon Review* fellowship in fiction (1955), a National Institute of Arts and Letters Grant (1961), a Guggenheim Fellowship (1968-1969), an Academy of American Poets fellowship (1970), the Pulitzer Prize and National Book Award (1978), the Bollingen Prize from Yale University (1981), the Aiken Taylor Award for Modern Poetry (1987), and the presidential National Medal of Art (1987). He served as a poetry consultant to the Library of Congress and as the United States poet laureate from 1988 to 1990. The National Institute of Arts and Letters, the American Academy of Arts and Sciences, and Alpha of Massachusetts all claimed him as a member.

Nemerov was the poet of the modern person. His deep division of temperament and his interest in science illustrated the fragmentation and scientific bent of the twentieth century. His sense of the tragic nature of the human condition and his spiritual questing with no subsequent answers reflected the twentieth century search for meaning. Although his poetry has a decidedly religious quality, Nemerov appeared to resolve his spiritual questions by honoring life's mystery rather than by adopting specific beliefs.

BIOGRAPHY

Howard Nemerov was born in New York City on March 1, 1920, to David and Gertrude (Russek) Nemerov. His wealthy parents were also cultivated and saw to it that their son was well educated. They sent him first to the exclusive private Fieldston Preparatory School, where he distinguished himself as both scholar and athlete. Nemerov then entered Harvard University, where he began to write poetry, essays, and fiction. In his junior year, he won the Bowdoin Prize for an essay on Thomas Mann. Nemerov was graduated in 1937 and immediately entered the Royal Air Force Coast Command as an aviator, based in England. Subsequently, he joined the Eighth United States Army Air Force, which was based in Lincolnshire. On January 26, 1944, Nemerov was married to Margaret (Peggy) Russell (a union that

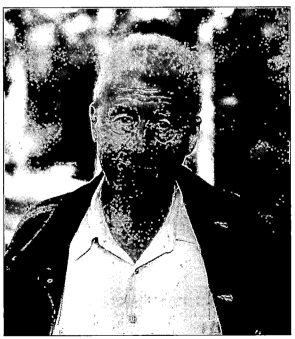

Howard Nemerov (© Miriam Berkley)

produced three sons, David, Alexander, and Jeremy Seth). In 1945, when he was discharged as a first lieutenant from the Air Force, the Nemerovs moved to New York City to settle into civilian life.

During this time, Nemerov chose, against his father's will, to become a poet. This was an anguished decision, for tradition decreed that, as the only son, he should carry on the family business. As a "Jewish Puritan of the middle class," Nemerov felt keenly the separation from custom. In his *Journal of the Fictive Life* (1965), he credits his emphasis on work to a "guilty acknowledgment that I became a writer very much against the will of my father."

Since poetry customarily brings more pleasure than money, Nemerov left New York after a year to join the faculty at Hamilton College in Clinton, New York. In 1948, he became a member of the English department of Bennington College and taught there until, in 1966, he went to Brandeis University in Massachusetts. During his stay at Brandeis, Nemerov also held interim teaching appointments. He left Brandeis in 1969 to become the Hurst Professor of Literature at Washington University in St. Louis. He became Washington University's Edward Mallinckrodt Distinguished University Professor of English in 1976. He completed a writer-in-residency at the University of Missouri at Kansas City in April, 1991, shortly before his death from cancer in July.

ANALYSIS

Howard Nemerov's poetry revolves about the theme of the absurd place of humankind within the large drama of time. It also illustrates his divided temperament, about which he wrote in *Journal of the Fictive Life*, "I must attempt to bring together the opposed elements of my character represented by poetry and fiction." These conflicts—the romantic-realist, the skeptic-believer, the scientist-poet—reflect the fragmentation and angst of modern existence. He did not employ scientific terms in a sentimental manner in his poetry but included nebulae, particles, and light-years as true poetic subjects, not simply metaphors for human concerns. Nemerov was a Renaissance man in his breadth and an eighteenth century man of letters in his satire, wit, and respect for form. His spiritual questions and his refusal of any orthodoxy, whether religious or artistic, made him a twentieth century existentialist.

Like any great figure, however, Nemerov defied categorization. He lived his life in and for literature in an age that values, as he wrote in his *Journal of the Fictive Life*, "patient, minute analysis"; he gave himself to "the wholeness of things," "the great primary human drama" in a time when some consider that loving the human story is "unsophisticated, parochial, maybe even sinful."

Many writers reach a plateau; Howard Nemerov kept growing. In his evolution, he became less bitter and more loving. As he became more complex, his language grew simpler, elegantly expressing his subtle mind and his ultimate sadness at the tragic position of humanity in the universe. Nemerov's divided nature shows in his poetry's empiricism and acceptance of objective reality and his subjective, poetic self that searched, perhaps futilely, for a definite Word of God.

THE IMAGE AND THE LAW AND GUIDE TO THE RUINS

Nemerov's first three poetry collections, *The Image and the Law*, *Guide to the Ruins*, and *The Salt Garden*, demonstrate his growth from a somewhat derivative writer to a mature poet with a distinctive voice. *The Image and the Law* is based on his dual vision, what he called "poetry of the eye" (the image) and "poetry of the mind" (the law). He tries to illustrate the "everpresent dispute between the two ways of looking at the world." *The Image and the Law*, as a first book, was competent, but was criticized for lack of unity and for being derivative. Critics found too many echoes of T. S. Eliot, W. H. Auden, William Butler Yeats, and Wallace Stevens—admittedly Nemerov's models.

Nemerov's second book, *Guide to the Ruins*, drew the same complaint, as did *The Salt Garden*. The latter collection, however, was recognized as exhibiting the beginning of his "most characteristic voice, a quiet intelligent voice brooding lyrically on the strange beauty and tragic loneliness of life," as Peter Meinke has described it.

In *The Image and the Law* and *Guide to the Ruins*, not only is Nemerov practicing what he has learned from Yeats, Eliot, and others, but he also starts to purge himself of war-won realizations. Although *The Image and the Law* deals mainly with the city, war, and death, it also contains religious imagery and wit. His poems wail, like an Old Testament lament—"I have become a gate/ To the ruined city, dry" ("Lot's Wife"). The poems in *The Image and the Law* exhibit ironic detachment as well as seriousness, for to Nemerov "the serious and the funny are one." The dualism in the poems is suggested in the title.

Guide to the Ruins has a broader scope than his first collection and reveals artistic growth. The "ruins" are those created in World War II, although the war is not actually over. Again, there is duality in the poems; the poet feels trapped between art-faith and science-reality, but sides with neither wholeheartedly. His tension between the two produces a Dostoevskian religious agony that visits Christianity, but consistently returns to Judaism. Several poems in *Guide to the Ruins* unite war and religion into a pessimism that will become more evident in later works. Paradoxically, and typical of his dualistic vision, he celebrates life not only in spite of war but also because of it.

THE SALT GARDEN

The Salt Garden, while still exhibiting some derivation, exhibits not only the poet's own voice but also a "center," that center being Nemerov's interest in nature. True to his double vision, he contrasts "brutal" nature with "decent" humankind. The link between the two is found in liquids such as ocean and blood, which combine into humankind's "salt dream," the call of the subconscious toward wildness. The poems in *The Salt Garden* range from a decent, rational man's reflection on his garden to the nightmarish, Freudian dream "The Scales of the Eyes." A brilliant combination of the "civilized" and the "wild" is found in "I Only Am Escaped Alone to Tell Thee." By degrees, this poem shows the submerged anguish of a prosperous nineteenth century woman. The whalebone stays of her corset are a central image, leading to other images of sea, mirrors, and light, until "the black flukes of agony/ Beat at the air till the light blows out." *The Salt Garden* treats not only humanity, "brutal" nature, and the link between the two, but death as a part of "time's ruining stream." Water, sea, and blood are beyond moral categories; they are the substance of life. In this respect, according to Julia Bartholomay in *The Shield of Perseus: The Vision and Imagination of Howard Nemerov* (1972), Nemerov's perspective is biblical. Water is creative and purifying; it "sanctifies that which it permeates and recreates, for all objects are but fleeting forms on the changing surface of eternity."

MIRRORS AND WINDOWS

Nemerov's interest in nature, which is first evident in *The Salt Garden*, continues in *The Next Room of the Dream, Mirrors and Windows*, and *The Blue Swallows*. Nature, in these poems, has objective reality; it is never merely a projection of human concerns. Like Robert Frost, Nemerov not only describes nature as something "other" than himself but also brings philosophical issues into his nature poems. In *Mirrors and Windows*, Nemerov indicates that poetry helps make life bearable by stopping it in a frame (poem). It sheds no light upon the meaning of life or death; it only reveals life's beauty or terror.

THE NEXT ROOM OF THE DREAM

The Next Room of the Dream, a collection of poems and two verse plays, illustrates Nemerov's decision to stay close to what he calls in *Journal of the Fictive Life* the "great primary human drama." His plays *Cain* and *Endor*, based on biblical themes, illustrate his humanitarianism as well as his quest for ultimate truth. This quest is ironically expressed in "Santa Claus," which begins, "Somewhere on his travels the strange Child/ Picked up with this overstuffed confidence man," and ends, "At Easter, he's anonymous again,/ Just one of the crowd lunching on Calvary."

Nemerov's plays, however, provide no spiritual resolution to man's questions. Stanley Knock in *The Christian Century* comments, "Nemerov succeeds only in revealing the devastating emptiness of contemporary beliefs." The poem "Nothing Will Yield" sums up Nemerov's perception of human helplessness in the face of reality; even art is no solution, although poets will continue to speak "holy language" in the face of despair. In *The Next Room of the Dream*, the poems become simpler, with more precise natural descriptions and more obvious compassion for humankind.

Nemerov's dark vision mellows in his later work. In two later collections of poetry, *Gnomes and Occasions* and *Sentences*, the emphasis is spiritual, the tone elegiac. In *The Western Approaches: Poems, 1973-75*, the topics range from speculation about fate ("The Western

Approaches") to the sterility of space travel ("The Backward Look").

THE BLUE SWALLOWS

The Blue Swallows, published twenty years after his first collection, indicates further growth in Nemerov's technique and development of his philosophy of "minimal affirmation." In this book, Nemerov's paradoxical view of humanity as both helpless and indomitable is expressed in images of gulls and swallows that circle around this world, only to find it illusory and strange. His duality is expressed in symbols of physics and theology, again underlining the division between science-reality and art-faith. According to his philosophy of minimal affirmation, human beings may be crushed, but they rise "again and again," as in the end of "Beyond the Pleasure Principle." The final emphasis of the poem is simultaneously on the absurdity of life and death and the inexplicable resilience of humankind. "Beyond the Pleasure Principle" expresses the central theme of *The Blue Swallows*, a theme that was to remain constant in Nemerov's works until his later years.

"RUNES"

Critics have commented profusely on Nemerov's witty pessimism and urbane helplessness. Though Bartholomay acknowledges Nemerov's dualistic nature, she finds other meanings in his poems besides wit and hopelessness. She sees Nemerov as a witty sophisticate who responds to life bitterly, yet she also points out his capacity to be "philosophical, subjective, lyrical, or even mystical."

To support this contention she calls attention to "Runes," considered by many to be Nemerov's finest poem. Mutability is the theme of "Runes," but with a recognition of the mystery of life. The poem expresses pessimism but avoids nihilism, attacking the emptiness of modern life while affirming "the stillness in moving things." "Runes" is religious in that it is concerned with the mystery of creation and finds resolution in total submission to life's riddle.

The major artistic triumph of "Runes" is the integration of external and internal through which its paradox is resolved. This unity is achieved through the brilliant treatment of three reflexive images: two objective images—water and seed—and a subjective image—thought itself. "Runes" is perhaps the most complete

expression of Nemerov's philosophy of minimal affirmation. In it Nemerov returns to the mystery of creation, in which he finds the beginnings of art. Imagination is reality's agent, revealing "the divine shadow of nature's signature on all things."

GNOMES AND OCCASIONS

Gnomes and Occasions consists of epigrams, riddles, meditations, and reflections, all poems that stress origins and ends. They have the epigrammatic style of wisdom literature—pithy, sage, and provocative. The language is rife with references to the Bible, priests, grace, and God, as well as nature. There are also the characteristic wit, irony, and doubt, as expressed in "Creation Myth on a Moebius Band":

> This world's just mad enough to have been made
> By the Being his beings into Being prayed.

Nemerov's interest in nature is also apparent in this book, in poems such as "Late Butterflies" and "The Rent in the Screen," a lyric dedicated to science writer Loren Eiseley. Nemerov's sharp observations of nature are here transformed into melancholy, sometimes irony. "The Rent in the Screen" ends by commenting on the lives of moths and men, "How brief a dream." Compassion for the fate of butterflies in winter ends with the dry "We take our pity/ Back in the house,/ The warm indoors."

THE COLLECTED POEMS OF HOWARD NEMEROV

The publication of Nemerov's *The Collected Poems of Howard Nemerov* in 1977 led to a critical revaluation of Nemerov's work. This collection (which includes all of his poetry written through 1977) exhibits "a gradual intensifying of a unified perspective," according to critic Phoebe Pettingell. The effect of *The Collected Poems of Howard Nemerov* is to delineate the depth and breadth of Nemerov's insights. Throughout the volume certain questions recur—questions having to do with the nature of reality and the role of poetry in revealing the world's appearances and sometimes, perhaps, what lies beyond appearances.

SENTENCES

Despite the increasingly religious quality of his language, Nemerov, as usual, does not make specific religious statements. It is poetry, if anything, that comes closest to being an intercessor between God and man, and this link is the theme of *Sentences*. Here Nemerov applies his belief that "in the highest range the theory of poetry would be the theory of the Incarnation, which seeks to explain how the Word became Flesh." In a letter to Robert D. Harvey, he wrote,

> Poetry is a kind of spiritual exercise,
> a (generally doomed but stoical) attempt
> to pray one's humanity back into the universe;
> and conversely an attempt to read, to derive anew,
> one's humanity from nature . . . In the darkness
> of this search, patience and good humour are
> useful qualities. Also: the serious and the funny
> are one. The purpose of poetry is to persuade,
> fool or compel God into speaking.

Indeed, the main theme of *Sentences* is the coherence art gives to life's randomness. In accordance with his theory of connecting through the power of art, the book is divided into sections titled "Beneath," "Above," and "Beyond"; these sections correspond to sex and power (beneath), metaphysics and poetry (above), and human destiny (beyond). The first section is ironic, the middle is speculative, and the last is moving. Critics generally disliked the first part of *Sentences*, but applauded the other two sections.

INSIDE THE ONION AND WAR STORIES

After *Sentences*, Nemerov published another stunning poetry collection, *Inside the Onion*. The title wryly implies his subjective-objective, romantic-realist nature. In this book Nemerov blends the homely and the humorous into poems that avoid the dramatic and highlight the commonplace, making it arresting.

War Stories contains forty-six poems grouped into three parts: "The War in the Streets," "The War in the Air," and "The War in the Heavens." This volume is Nemerov at his metaphysical best, grounding his spiritual musings in everyday experience. His interest in science and modern events is linked to literature—for example, the advent of Halley's Comet is hailed in the language of the speech in the Anglo-Saxon epic *Beowulf* that compares man's life to a swallow's brief flight through a mead hall. These poems range from an elegy for a student to explorations of subtle psychological insights to profound spiritual observations: "Though God

be dead, he lived so far away/ His sourceless light continues to fall on us" ("The Celestial Emperor").

OTHER MAJOR WORKS

LONG FICTION: *The Melodramatists*, 1949; *Federigo: Or, The Power of Love*, 1954; *The Homecoming Game*, 1957.

SHORT FICTION: *A Commodity of Dreams and Other Stories*, 1959; *Stories, Fables, and Other Diversions*, 1971.

NONFICTION: *Poetry and Fiction: Essays*, 1963; *Journal of the Fictive Life*, 1965; *Reflexions on Poetry and Poetics*, 1972; *Figures of Thought: Speculations on the Meaning of Poetry and Other Essays*, 1978; *New and Selected Essays*, 1985; *The Oak in the Acorn: On "Remembrance of Things Past" and on Teaching Proust, Who Will Never Learn*, 1987.

EDITED TEXT: *Poets on Poetry*, 1965.

MISCELLANEOUS: *A Howard Nemerov Reader*, 1991.

BIBLIOGRAPHY

Bartholomay, Julia A. *The Shield of Perseus: The Vision and Imagination of Howard Nemerov*. Gainesville: University of Florida Press, 1972. This book discusses Nemerov's use of multivalent images and other poetic techniques, and his poetry's recurrent themes. There is detailed information about the poet drawn from his letters and conversations. For the reader seeking a hypothesis about Nemerov's "religious" outlook and a careful examination of his artistic techniques, this book is an excellent source.

Knock, Stanley F., Jr. "Renewal of Illusion." *The Christian Century*. January 16, 1962, 85-86. In this review of Nemerov's verse drama *Endor*, Knock shows how Nemerov transports an Old Testament story into the context of existentialism and the Cold War. Rather than "see ourselves as others see us," as Robert Burns advised, Nemerov finds hope not in the stripping of illusion, but in its renewal.

Meinke, Peter. *Howard Nemerov*. Minneapolis: University of Minnesota Press, 1968. One of the most comprehensive books on Nemerov insofar as general knowledge is concerned. It covers not only biographical data but also the effect some life incidents had on his work. There are brief comments on Nemerov's major works. These volumes also trace Nemerov's rise to literary prominence, for the reviews indicate his artistic growth and public acceptance.

Potts, Donna L. *Howard Nemerov and Objective Idealism: The Influence of Owen Barfield.* Columbia: University of Missouri Press, 1994. Potts contends that Nemerov was profoundly influenced by the objective idealism of British philosopher Barfield. Includes excerpts from the thirty years of correspondence between the two and selections of Nemerov's poetry.

Mary Hanford Bruce;
bibliography updated by the editors

PABLO NERUDA

Neftalí Ricardo Reyes Basoalto
Born: Parral, Chile; July 12, 1904
Died: Santiago, Chile; September 23, 1973

PRINCIPAL POETRY

Crepusculario, 1923

Veinte poemas de amor y una canción desesperada, 1924 (*Twenty Love Poems and a Song of Despair*, 1969)

Tentativa del hombre infinito, 1926

El hondero entusiasta, 1933

Residencia en la tierra, 1933, 1935, 1947 (3 volumes; *Residence on Earth and Other Poems*, 1946, 1973)

España en el corazón, 1937 (*Spain in the Heart*, 1946)

Alturas de Macchu Picchu, 1948 (*The Heights of Macchu Picchu*, 1966)

Canto general, 1950

Los versos del capitán, 1952 (*The Captain's Verses*, 1972)

Odas elementales, 1954 (*The Elemental Odes*, 1961)

Las uvas y el viento, 1954

Nuevas odas elementales, 1956

Tercer libro de odas, 1957

Estravagario, 1958 (*Extravagaria*, 1972)

Cien sonetos de amor, 1959 (*One Hundred Love Sonnets*, 1986)

Navegaciones y regresos, 1959

Canción de gesta, 1960 (*Song of Protest*, 1976)

Cantos ceremoniales, 1961

Las piedras de Chile, 1961 (*The Stones of Chile*, 1986)

Plenos poderes, 1962 (*Fully Empowered*, 1975)

Memorial de Isla Negra, 1964 (5 volumes; *Isla Negra: A Notebook*, 1981)

Arte de pájaros, 1966 (*Art of Birds*, 1985)

Una casa en la arena, 1966

La barcarola, 1967

Las manos del día, 1968

Aún, 1969 (*Still Another Day*, 1984)

Fin de mundo, 1969

La espada encendida, 1970

Las piedras del cielo, 1970 (*Stones of the Sky*, 1987)

Selected Poems, 1970

Geografía infructuosa, 1972

New Poems (1968-1970), 1972

Incitación al Nixonicidio y alabanza de la revolución chilena, 1973 (*Incitement to Nixonicide and Praise of the Chilean Revolution*, 1979; also as *A Call for the Destruction of Nixon and Praise for the Chilean Revolution*, 1980)

El mar y las campanas, 1973 (*The Sea and the Bells*, 1988)

La rosa separada, 1973 (*The Separate Rose*, 1985)

El corazón amarillo, 1974 (*The Yellow Heart*, 1990)

Defectos escogidos, 1974

Elegía, 1974

Pablo Neruda: Five Decades, a Selection (Poems, 1925-1970), 1974

2000, 1974 (English translation, 1992)

Jardín de invierno, 1974 (*Winter Garden*, 1986)

Libro de las preguntas, 1974 (*The Book of Questions*, 1991)

El mal y el malo, 1974

El río invisible: Poesía y prosa de juventud, 1980

OTHER LITERARY FORMS

Pablo Neruda was an essayist, translator, playwright, and novelist as well as a poet. His memoirs, *Confieso que he vivido: Memorias* (1974; *Memoirs*, 1977), are a lyric evocation of his entire life, its final pages written after the coup that overthrew Salvador Allende. Neruda's translations include works by Rainer Maria Rilke, William Shakespeare, and William Blake. The volume *Para nacer he nacido* (1978; *Passions and Impressions*, 1983) includes prose poems, travel impressions, and the speech that Neruda delivered on his acceptance of the Nobel Prize. He has written a novel, *El habitante y su esperanza* (1926); a poetic drama, *Fulgor y muerte de Joaquín Murieta* (pb. 1967; *Splendor and Death of Joaquin Murieta*, 1972); and essays on Shakespeare, Carlo Levi, Vladimir Mayakovsky, Paul Éluard, and Federico García Lorca, as well as several works of political concern.

ACHIEVEMENTS

Winner of the Nobel Prize in 1971, Pablo Neruda is one of the most widely read poets in the world today. His most popular book, *Twenty Love Poems and a Song of Despair*, has more than a million copies in print and,

Pablo Neruda (Library of Congress)

like much of his work, has been translated from Spanish into more than twenty languages. Neruda was so prolific a writer that nine of his collections of poems have been published posthumously.

Neruda's goal was to liberate Spanish poetry from the literary strictures of the nineteenth century and bring it into the twentieth century by returning verse to its popular sources. In *Memoirs*, written just before his death, Neruda congratulates himself for having made poetry a respected profession through his discovery that his own aspirations are representative of those shared by men and women on three continents. Writing on the rugged coast of southern Chile, Neruda found passion and beauty in the harshness of a world that hardens its inhabitants, strengthening but sometimes silencing them. His purpose was to give his fellowmen the voice they too often lacked.

BIOGRAPHY

Pablo Neruda was born Neftalí Ricardo Reyes Basoalto in the frontier town of Parral in the southern part of Chile on July 12, 1904. His mother died of tuberculosis a few days after his birth, and Neruda lived with his stepmother and father, a railroad conductor, in a tenement house with two other families. Hard work and an early introduction to literature and to the mysteries of manhood distinguished his first seventeen years. In school, the famous Chilean educator and poet Gabriela Mistral, herself a Nobel Prize winner, introduced the young Neruda to the great nineteenth century Russian novelists. In the fall of his sixteenth year, while he was assisting in the wheat harvest, a woman whom he was later unable to identify first introduced the young man to sex. A wide-ranging, voracious appetite for books and the wonders of love are memories to which Neruda continually returns in his work, as well as to the harsh Chilean landscape and the problems of survival that confronted his countrymen.

His father's determination that Neruda should have a profession took the young poet to Santiago, where he intended to study French literature at the university. He had learned French and English in Temuco from his neighbors, many of whom were immigrants. His affiliation as contributor to the journal *Claridad* with the politically active student group, Federación de Estudiantes, and the attractions of life in a large city, where Neruda quickly made friends with many influential people, served to expand his original plans. While living with the widow of a German novelist, Neruda tried repeatedly to gain access to the offices of the Ministry of External Affairs, hoping to obtain a diplomatic post in Europe. More important, he had begun to write his first serious poetry during his evenings alone in a boardinghouse at 513 Maruri Street.

Neruda's hatred of political oppression became firmly established when the students of a right-wing group attacked the officers of *Claridad* and the Santiago police freed the attackers and arrested the editors, one of whom died in jail. Thus, after a year and a half in Santiago, Neruda abandoned his university career and dramatically declared himself a poet and political activist, taking the pen name Pablo Neruda from the Czech writer Jan Neruda (1834-1891) in order to conceal his activities from his father.

In 1923, in order to publish his first book of poems, *Crepusculario*, Neruda sold his furniture and borrowed money from his friends; favorable critical reviews validated his decision. The similarity of his verse to that of the Uruguayan poet Sabat Erscaty forced Neruda to turn from inspirational and philosophical themes back to a more intimate poetry based on personal experience. The result in 1924 was *Twenty Love Poems and a Song of Despair*, Neruda's most popular book, in which he sings of the joy and pain of casual affairs with a student from Santiago and the girl he left in Temuco.

Neruda's abandonment of his university career to write for *Claridad* coincided with his moving to Valparaíso. The port city immediately won his favor. He had not abandoned his goal of a diplomatic post, and finally, through the influence of the Bianchi family, he succeeded in meeting the Minister of External Affairs, who was persuaded to allow Neruda to pick his post. Neruda chose the one city available about which he knew nothing: Rangoon, Burma, then a province of India.

After a short stay in Burma, Neruda obtained a new post in Ceylon, setting the pattern of his life for the next twenty-five years. During this period, Neruda was abroad most of the time, usually under the auspices of the Chilean government—although on occasion he would flee government arrest. Returning to Chile from the Far East, he was quickly off to Argentina, then to Spain (during the Spanish Civil War), then to France, where he had stopped en route to Rangoon and to which he returned a number of times. During the early years of World War II, Neruda held a diplomatic post in Mexico; he resigned in 1943 to return to Chile, where he became active in politics as a member of the Chilean Communist Party.

Neruda's Communist sympathies (which had their origin in the Spanish Civil War) hardened into an uncritical acceptance of Stalinism, ill accorded with his genuine populist sentiments. He became a frequent visitor to the Eastern bloc in the 1950's and 1960's, even serving on the committee that met annually in Moscow to award the Lenin Peace Prize, which he himself had won in 1950.

From 1960 until his death in 1973, Neruda worked tirelessly, publishing sixteen books of poetry and giving conferences in Venezuela (1959), Eastern Europe (1960), Cuba (1960), the United States (1961, 1966, and 1972), Italy and France (1962), England (1965), Finland (1965), and the Soviet Union (1967). He was named president of the Chilean Writers Association, correspondent of the department of romance languages of Yale University, doctor *honoris causa* at Oxford, and Nobel Prize winner in 1971. In 1969, he was nominated for the presidency of Chile; he rejected the nomination in favor of Salvador Allende, who named Neruda ambassador to France. Neruda's health, however, and his concern about a civil war in Chile, precipitated his return in 1973. His efforts to prevent a *coup d'état* proved fruitless, and Neruda died a few days after Allende. He had just finished his *Memoirs*, writing that he enjoyed a tranquil conscience and a restless intelligence, a contentment derived from having made poetry a profession from which he could earn an honest living. He had lived, he said, as "an omnivore of sentiments, beings, books, happenings and battles." He would "consume the earth and drink the sea."

ANALYSIS

Pablo Neruda stated in a prologue to one of four editions of *Caballo verde*, a literary review he had founded in 1935 with Manuel Altalaguirre, that the poetry he was seeking would contain the confused impurities that people leave on their tools as they wear them down with the sweat of their hands. He would make poems like buildings, permeated with smoke and garlic and flooded inside and out with the air of men and women who seem always present. Neruda advocated an impure poetry whose subject might be hatred, love, ugliness, or beauty. He sought to bring verse back from the exclusive conclave of select minorities to the turmoil from which words draw their vitality.

CREPUSCULARIO

Neruda's work is divided into three discernible periods, the turning points being the Spanish Civil War and his return to Chile in 1952 after three years of forced exile. During the first phase of his work, from 1923 to 1936, Neruda published six rather experimental collections of verse in which he achieved the poetic strength that carried him through four more decades and more than twenty books. He published *Crepusculario* himself in 1923 while a student at the University of Santiago. *Crepusculario* is a cautious collection of poems reflecting his reading of French poetry. Like the Latin American *Modernistas* who preceded him, he consciously adhered to classical forms and sought the ephemeral effects of musicality and color. The poem that perhaps best captures the message indicated by the title of the book is very brief: "My soul is an empty carousel in the evening light." All the poems in *Crepusculario* express Neruda's ennui and reveal his experimentation with the secondary qualities of language, its potential for the effects of music, painting, and sculpture.

There are several interesting indications of Neruda's future development in *Crepusculario* that distinguish it from similar derivative works. Neruda eventually came to see poetry as work, a profession no less than carpentry, brick masonry, or politics; this conception of poetry is anticipated in the poem "Inicial," in which he writes: "I have gone under Helios who watches me bleeding/ laboring in silence in my absent gardens." Further, in *Crepusculario*, Neruda occasionally breaks logical barriers in a manner that anticipates much of his later Surrealistic verse: "I close and close my lips but in trembling roses/ my voice comes untied, like water in the fountain." Nevertheless, *Crepusculario* is also characterized by a respect for tradition and a humorous familiarity with the sacred which Neruda later abandoned, only to rediscover them again in the third phase of his career, after 1952: "And the 'Our Father' gets lost in the middle of the night/ runs naked across his green lands/ and trembling with pleasure dives into the sea." Linked with this respect for his own traditions is an adulation of European culture, which he also abandoned in his second phase; Neruda did not, however, regain a regard for Western European culture in his mature years, rejecting it in favor of his own American authenticity: "When you are old, my darling (Ronsard has already told you) / you will recall the verses I spoke to you."

In *Crepusculario*, the first stirrings of Neruda's particular contribution to Spanish poetry are evident—themes that in the early twentieth century were considered unpoetic, such as the ugliness of industrialized cities and the drudgery of bureaucracies. These intrusions of objective reality were the seeds from which his strongest poetry would grow; they reveal Neruda's capacity to empathize with the material world and give it a voice.

TWENTY LOVE POEMS AND A SONG OF DESPAIR

One year after the publication of *Crepusculario*, the collection *Twenty Love Poems and a Song of Despair* appeared. It would become the most widely read collection of poems in the Spanish-speaking world. In it, Neruda charts the course of a love affair from passionate attraction to despair and indifference. In these poems, Neruda sees the whole world in terms of the beloved:

> The vastness of pine groves, the sound of beating wings,
> the slow interplay of lights, a solitary bell,
> the evening falling into your eyes, my darling, and in you
> the earth sings.
> Love shadows and timbres your voice in the dying echoing
> afternoon
> just as in those deep hours I have seen
> the field's wheat bend in the mouth of the wind.

Throughout these twenty poems, Neruda's intensity and directness of statement universalize his private experiences, establishing another constant in his work: the effort to create a community of feeling through the expression of common, universal experience.

TENTATIVA DEL HOMBRE INFINITO

In 1926, Neruda published *Tentativa del hombre infinito* (venture of infinite man), his most interesting work from a technical point of view. In this book-length poem, Neruda employed the "automatic writing" espoused by the Surrealists. The poem celebrates Neruda's discovery of the city at night and tests the capacity of his poetic idiom to sound the depths of his subconscious. Ignoring the conventions of sentence structure, syntax, and logic, Neruda fuses form and content.

The poem opens in the third person with a description of the poet asleep in the city of Santiago. It returns to the same image of the sleeping man and the hearth fires of the city three times, changing person from third to second to first, creating a circular or helical structure. The imagery defies conventional associations: "the moon blue spider creeps floods/ an emissary you were moving happily in the afternoon that was falling/ the dusk rolled in extinguishing flowers."

In the opening passages, Neruda explores the realm between wakefulness and sleep, addressing the night as his lover: "take my heart, cross it with your vast pulleys of silence/ when you surround sleep's animals, it's at your feet/ waiting to depart because you place it face to face with/ you, night of black helixes." In this realm between motive and act, Neruda's language refuses to acknowledge distinctions of tense: "a twenty-year-old holds to the frenetic reins, it is that he wanted to follow the night." Also, the limits that words draw between concepts disappear, and thoughts blend like watercolors: "star delayed between the heavy night the days with tall sails."

The poem is a voyage of exploration that leads to a number of discoveries. The poet discovers his own desperation: "the night like wine enters the tunnel/ savage wind, miner of the heavens, let's wail together." He discovers the vastness of the other: "in front of the inaccessible there passes by for you a limitless presence." He discovers his freedom: "prow, mast, leaf in the storm, an abandonment without hope of return impels you/ you show the way like crosses the dead." Most important, he discovers wonder: "the wind leaving its egg strikes my back/ great ships of glowing coals twist their green sails/ planets spin like bobbins." The abstract becomes concrete and hence tractable: "the heart of the world folds and stretches/ with the will of a column and the cold fury of feathers." He discovers his joy: "Hurricane night, my happiness bites your ink/ and exasperated, I hold

back my heart which dances/ a dancer astonished in the heavy tides which make the dawn rise."

When the poet finds his beloved, he begins to acquire a more logical grasp of objective reality, but when he realizes that he is still dreaming, his joy becomes despair. He gradually awakens; his senses are assaulted by the smell of the timber of his house and the sound of rain falling, and he gazes through the windows at the sky. Interestingly, his dream visions do not abandon him at once but continue to determine his perceptions:

> birds appear like letters in the depths of the sky
> the dawn appears like the peelings of fruit
> the day is made of fire
> the sea is full of green rags which articulate I am the sea
> I am alone in a windowless room
> snails cover the walk
> and time is squared and immobile.

In this experimental work, Neruda mastered the art of tapping his subconscious for associative imagery. Although he never returned to the pure Surrealism of *Tentativa del hombre infinito*, it is the union of strikingly original and often surreal imagery with earthly realism that gives Neruda's mature poetry its distinctive character.

RESIDENCE ON EARTH

In the poems of *Residence on Earth*, Neruda first achieved that mature voice, free of any derivative qualities. One of the greatest poems in this collection, "Galope muerto" ("Dead Gallop"), was written in the same year as *Tentativa del hombre infinito*, 1925, although it was not published in book form until 1933. "Dead Gallop" sets the tone for the collection, in which Neruda repeatedly expresses a passionate desire to assimilate new experiences: "Everything is so fast, so living/ yet immobile, like a mad pulley spinning on itself." Many of the poems in *Residence on Earth* begin in the same manner, recording those peripheral and secondary sensations which reside on the fringe of consciousness. They work toward the same end, resolving the new into understandable terms. As the poems come into focus, the reader participates in the poet's assimilation of his new world. For example, the significance of his vague memories of saying goodbye to a girl whom he had left in Chile gradually becomes clear in one poem:

Dusty glances fallen to earth
or silent leaves which bury themselves.
Lightless metal in the void
and the suddenly dead day's departure.
On high hands the butterfly shines
its flight's light has no end.
You kept the light's wake of broken things
which the abandoned sun in the afternoon throws at the
    church steps.

Here, one can see Neruda's gift for surreal imagery without the programmatic irrationality and dislocation of the Surrealists.

In *Residence on Earth*, too, there are magnificent catalogs in the manner of Walt Whitman: "the angel of sleep—the wind moving the wheat, the whistle of a train, a warm place in a bed, the opaque sound of a shadow which falls like a ray of light into infinity, a repetition of distances, a wine of uncertain vintage, the dusty passage of lowing cows."

Like Whitman, Neruda in *Residence on Earth* opens Spanish poetry to the song of himself: "my symmetrical statue of twinned legs, rises to the stars each morning/ my exile's mouth bites meat and grapes/ my male arms and tattooed chest/ in which the hair penetrates like wire, my white face made for the sun's depth." He presents uncompromising statements of human sensuality; he descends into himself, discovers his authenticity, and begins to build a poetic vision that, although impure, is genuinely human. He manages in these sometimes brutal poems to reconcile the forces of destruction and creation that he had witnessed in India in the material world of buildings, work, people, food, weather, himself, and time.

Although Neruda never achieved a systematic and internally consistent poetic vision, the balance between resignation and celebration that informs *Residence on Earth* suggests a philosophical acceptance of the world. "Tres cantos materiales" ("Three Material Songs"), "Entrada a la madera" ("Entrance to Wood"), "Apoges del apio" ("Apogee of Celery"), and "Estatuto del vino" ("Ordinance of Wine") were a breakthrough in this respect. In "Entrance to Wood," the poet gives voice to wood, which, though living, is material rather than spiritual. Neruda's discovery of matter is a revelation. He introduces himself into this living, material world as one

commencing a funereal journey, carrying his sorrows with him in order to give this world the voice it lacks. His identification with matter alters his language so that the substantives become verbs: "Let us make fire, silence, and noise,/ let us burn, hush and bells."

In "Apogee of Celery," the poet personifies a humble vegetable, as he does later in *The Elemental Odes*. Neruda simply looks closely and with his imagination and humor reveals a personality—how the growth of celery reflects the flight of doves and the brilliance of lightning. In Spanish folklore, celery has humorous though obscene connotations which Neruda unflinchingly incorporates into his poem. The resultant images are bizarre yet perfectly descriptive. Celery tastes like lightning bugs. It knows wonderful secrets of the sea, whence it originates, but perversely insists on being eaten before revealing them.

Popular wisdom also finds its way into the poem "Ordinance of Wine." Neruda's discovery of the wonders of matter and of everyday experience led him to describe the Bacchanalian rites of drunkenness as laws, the inevitable steps of intoxication. In the classical tradition, Neruda compares wine to a pagan god: It opens the door on the melancholy gatherings of the dishonored and disheartened and drops its honey on the tables at the day's edge; in winter, it seeks refuge in bars; it transforms the world of the discouraged and overpowers them so that they sing, spend money freely, and accept the coarseness of one another's company joyfully. The celebrants' laughter turns to weeping over personal tragedies and past happiness, and their tears turn to anger when something falls, breaks, and abruptly ends the magic. Wine the angel turns into a winged Harpy taking flight, spilling the wine, which seeps through the ground in search of the mouths of the dead. Wine's statutes have thus been obeyed, and the visiting god departs.

In "Ordinance of Wine," "Apogee of Celery," and "Entrance to Wood," Neruda reestablished communion between man and the material world in which he lives and works. Since work was the destiny of most of his readers, Neruda directed much of his poetry to this reconciliation between the elemental and the social, seeking to reintroduce wonder into the world of the alienated worker.

Neruda was writing the last poems of *Residence on Earth* in Madrid when the Spanish Civil War erupted. The catastrophe delayed the publication of the last book of the trilogy by twelve years. More important, the war confirmed Neruda's stance as a defender of oppressed peoples, of the poor. Suddenly, Neruda stopped singing the song of himself and began to direct his verse against the Nationalists besieging Madrid. The war inspired the collection of poems *Spain in the Heart*, a work as popular in Eastern Europe as is *Twenty Love Poems and a Song of Despair* in the West. These poems, such as Neruda's 1942 "Oda a Stalingrad" ("Ode to Stalingrad"), were finally published as part of *Residence on Earth*. They were written from the defensive point of view of countries fighting against the threat of Fascism. In them, the lyric element almost disappears before the onslaught of Neruda's political passion. Indeed, from 1937 to 1947, Neruda's poetry served the greater purpose of political activism and polemics:

> You probably want to know: And where are the lilies?
> the metaphysics covered with poppies?
> And the rain which often struck
> his words filling them
> with holes and birds?
> I'm going to tell you what has happened.
> I lived in a neighborhood in Madrid
> My house was called
> the House of Flowers . . .
> And one evening everything was on fire
> . . . Bandits with planes and with Moors
> bandits with rings and duchesses
> bandits with black friars giving blessings
> came through the sky to kill children.

More than ten years had to pass before Neruda could reaffirm his art above political propaganda.

CANTO GENERAL

During the 1940's, Neruda worked by plan on his epic history of Latin America, *Canto general*. Beginning with a description of the geography, the flora, and the fauna of the continent, the book progresses from sketches of the heroes of the Inca and Aztec empires through descriptions of conquistadores, the heroes of the Wars of Independence, to the dictators and foreign adventurers in twentieth century Latin America. Neruda interprets the history of the continent as a struggle toward autonomy carried on by many different peoples who have suffered from one kind of oppression or another since the beginnings of their recorded history.

THE CAPTAIN'S VERSES

Neruda, however, did not disappear entirely from his work during these years. He published anonymously *The Captain's Verses* to celebrate falling in love with the woman with whom he would spend the rest of his life, Matilde Urrutia. Unlike his previous women, Matilde shared Neruda's origins among the poor of southern Chile as well as his aspirations. These poems are tender, passionate, and direct, free of the despair, melancholy, and disillusionment of *Twenty Love Poems and a Song of Despair* and of *Residence on Earth*.

LAS UVAS Y EL VIENTO

While working in exile for the European Peace Party, Neruda recorded in his book *Las uvas y el viento* (the grapes and the wind) impressions of new friends and places, of conferences and renewed commitments made during his travels through Hungary, Poland, and Czechoslovakia. Neruda warmly remembers Prague, Berlin, Moscow, Capri, Madame Sun Yat-sen, Ilya Ehrenburg, Paul Éluard, Pablo Picasso, and the Turkish poet Nazim Hikmet. The most interesting works in the collection recreate Neruda's return to cities from which he had been absent for more than thirty years.

THE ELEMENTAL ODES

Neruda's travels through the East assured his fame. His fiftieth year signaled his return to Chile in order to fulfill the demand for his work which issued from three continents. In 1954, he built his house on Isla Negra with Matilde Urrutia and published the first of three remarkable collections, *The Elemental Odes*, followed by *Nuevas odas elementales* (new elemental odes) and *Tercer libro de odas* (third book of odes). In these books, Neruda returned to the discoveries made in the "Material Songs" of *Residence on Earth*. In the odes, Neruda's poetry again gained ascendancy over politics, although Neruda never ignored his political responsibilities.

The elemental odes reflect no immediately apparent political concern other than to renew and fulfill the search for an impure poetry responsive to the wonder of the everyday world. Neruda writes that earlier poets, himself included, now cause him to laugh because they never see beyond themselves. Poetry traditionally deals only with poets' own feelings and experiences; those of other men and women hardly ever find expression in poetry. The personality of objects, of the material world, never finds a singer, except among writers such as Neruda, who are also workers. Neruda's new purpose is to maintain his anonymity, because now "there are no mysterious shadows/ everyone speaks to me about their families, their work, and what wonderful things they do!"

In the elemental odes, Neruda learns to accept and celebrate the common gift of happiness, "as necessary as the earth, as sustaining as hearth fires, as pure as bread, as musical as water." He urges men to recognize the gifts they already possess. He sings of such humble things as eel stew, in which the flavors of the Chilean land and sea mix to make a paradise for the palate. Against those who envy his work and its unpretentious message of common humanity, Neruda responds that a simple poetry open to common people will live after him because it is as unafraid and healthy as a milkmaid in whose laughter there are enough teeth to ruin the hopes of the envious.

Indeed, the language of the elemental odes is very simple and direct, but, because Neruda writes these poems in such brief, internally rhyming lines, he draws attention to the natural beauty of his Spanish, the measured rhythm of clauses, the symmetry of sentence structure, and the solid virtues of an everyday vocabulary. In the tradition of classical Spanish realism, the elemental odes require neither the magic of verbal pyrotechnics nor incursions into the subconscious to achieve a fullness of poetic vision.

EXTRAVAGARIA AND LATER WORK

After the collection *Extravagaria*—in which Neruda redirected his attention inward again, resolving questions of his own mortality and the prospect of never again seeing places and people dear to him—the poet's production doubled to the rate of two lengthy books of poems every year. In response partly to the demand for his work, partly to his increased passion for writing, Neruda's books during the last decade of his life were often carefully planned and systematic. *Navegaciones y regresos* (navigations and returns) alternates a recounting of his travels with odes inspired by remarkable people, places, and events. *Cien sonetos de amor* collects one hundred rough-hewn sonnets of love to Matilde

Urrutia. *Isla Negra* is an autobiography in verse. *Arte de pájaros* is a poetic ornithological guide to Chile. *Las piedras de Chile, Cantos ceremoniales* (ceremonial songs)*, Fully Empowered*, and *Una casa en la arena* (a house in the sand) are all-inclusive, totally unsystematic collections unified by Neruda's bold style, a style that wanders aimlessly and confidently like a powerful river cutting designs in stone. *Las manos del día* (the hands of the day) and *La espada encendida* (the sword ignited), written between 1968 and 1970, attest Neruda's responsiveness to new threats against freedom. *Geografía infructuosa* (unfruitful geography) signals Neruda's return again to contemplate the rugged coast of Chile. As Neruda remarks in his *Memoirs* concerning his last decade of work, he gradually developed into a poet with the primitive style characteristic of the monolithic sculptures of Oceania: "I began with the refinements of Praxiteles and end with the massive ruggedness of the statues of Easter Island."

OTHER MAJOR WORKS

LONG FICTION: *El habitante y su esperanza*, 1926.

PLAYS: *Romeo y Juliet*, pb. 1964 (translation of William Shakespeare); *Fulgor y muerte de Joaquín Murieta*, pb. 1967 (*Splendor and Death of Joaquin Murieta*, 1972).

NONFICTION: *Anillos*, 1926 (with Tomás Lago); *Viajes*, 1955; *Comiendo en Hungría*, 1968; *Confieso que he vivido: Memorias*, 1974 (*Memoirs*, 1977); *Cartas de amor*, 1974 (letters); *Lo mejor de Anatole France*, 1976; *Para nacer he nacido*, 1978 (*Passions and Impressions*, 1983); *Cartas a Laura*, 1978 (letters); *Correspondencia durante "Residencia en la tierra,"* 1980 (letters; with Héctor Eandi).

BIBLIOGRAPHY

Méndez-Ramírez, Hugo. *Neruda Ekphrastic Experience: Mural Art and "Canto general."* Lewisburg: Bucknell University Press, 1999. This research focuses on the interplay between verbal and visual elements in Neruda's masterpiece *Canto general*. It demonstrates how mural art, especially that practiced in Mexico, became the source for Neruda's ekphrastic desire, in which his verbal art paints visual elements.

Orellana, Carlos, ed. *Los rostros de Neruda*. Santiago, Chile: Planeta, 1998. This collection of essays examines various aspects of the multifaceted poet. The editor collected testimonials from the poet's contemporaries: literary and critical writers, journalists and critics familiar with Neruda and his work. Like a meticulous sculptor, the editor carefully re-creates the face of Neruda. In Spanish.

Sayers Pedén, Margaret. Introduction to *Selected Odes of Pablo Neruda*, by Neruda and translated by Sayers Pedén. Berkeley: University of California Press, 2000. Sayers Pedén is among the most highly regarded translators of Latin American poetry. Here her introduction to the translations in this bilingual edition constitutes an excellent critical study as well as providing biographical and bibliographical information.

Kenneth A. Stackhouse;
bibliography updated by Carole A. Champagne

GÉRARD DE NERVAL

Gérard Labrunie
Born: Paris, France; May 22, 1808
Died: Paris, France; January 26, 1855

PRINCIPAL POETRY

Elégies nationales, 1826
Poésies allemandes, 1830 (translation)
Petits Châteaux de Bohème, 1853 (includes poetry and prose)
Les Chimères, 1854 (English translation, 1965; also known as *Chimeras*, 1866)
Fortune's Fool: Selected Poems, 1959

OTHER LITERARY FORMS

Gérard de Nerval tried his hand at drama, short fiction, and nonfiction. He wrote two dramas in collaboration with Alexandre Dumas, *père*. They are *Piquillo* (pb. 1837) and *Alchimiste* (pb. 1839). His other dramas include *Chariot d'enfant* (1850, with Joseph Méry), *L'Imagier de Haarlem* (pr. 1851), and a translation of

Johann Wolfgang von Goethe's *Faust* in 1827 and 1840. Among his nonfiction prose works are *Voyage en Orient* (1851; *Journey to the Orient*, 1972); *Les Illuminés* (1852), and *Aurélia* (1855; English translation, 1932). A collection of his stories came out as *Les Filles du feu* (1854; *Daughters of Fire*, 1922).

ACHIEVEMENTS

During his lifetime, Gérard de Nerval was generally regarded as an enthusiastic but harmless eccentric, a writer of some genius whose best and freshest productions were marred by occasional lapses into obscurity. Because of his bouts with madness—both manic-depressive psychosis (or, in modern psychological language, cyclothymic depression) and schizophrenia— he struck most of his contemporaries as an oddity, a poet sometimes pathetic yet never dangerous except to his own well-being. Around him numerous legends accumulated, most of them ludicrous. Some of the more absurd stories were given wider circulation by Champfleury in *Grandes Figures* (1861) and by Arsène Houssaye in *Confessions* (1885). In part as a result of such droll anecdotes, Nerval's reputation during the first half of the nineteenth century was that of a minor figure: a poet with close affinities with German Romanticism, a distinguished translator of Johann Wolfgang von Goethe's *Faust*, a moderately popular playwright and the author of sumptuously exotic travel literature, and a lyricist whose originality and vigor were evident but whose interests were too often attached to the curious and the extravagant. Later during the century, critics compared Nerval with Charles Baudelaire, treating both as psychologists of the aberrant. After the beginning of the twentieth century, commentators judged Nerval favorably in relation to the Symbolists, especially to Stéphane Mallarmé and Arthur Rimbaud. Still later, Nerval was appreciated as a forerunner of Guillaume Apollinaire and modernist experimentation. Since the 1920's, Nerval's achievements have been viewed independently of their connections with other writers or movements. Treated not as a precursor of greater talents but as a towering genius in his own right, Nerval has been examined as a seer, a mystic, a student of Hermetic doctrine and of alchemy, a poet of extraordinary complexity, resonance, and power. His most important works in prose and

poetry—*Petits Châteaux de Bohème, Aurélia,* and *Daughters of Fire*—are among the
glories of French literature.

BIOGRAPHY

Gérard de Nerval was born Gérard Labrunie, the son of Étienne Labrunie, a medical doctor, and of Marie-Antoinette Marguerite Laurent, daughter of a Paris draper. Nerval
did not change his name until 1831, when he
signed a letter "G. la Brunie de Nerval," taking the name from a property, Le Clos de
Nerval, belonging to his mother's family. The
name is also an anagram of his mother's
maiden name, Laurent. It is known that Nerval
hated his father, who served with Napoleon's
Grande Armée as a field surgeon and who
was, throughout the poet's life, an aloof, insensitive parent. Nerval's mother died when
the boy was only two years old, and Nerval
was sent to live with his granduncle, Antoine
Boucher, at Mortefontaine. These early years
Nerval later described as the happiest of his
life. He had free range of a library of occult
books and discussed philosophy with his
granduncle, who may have served as a model
for Père Dodu in Nerval's short story "Sylvie."
When Nerval's father returned from the front

Gérard de Nerval (Library of Congress)

in 1814, the boy joined him in Paris. In 1820, Nerval entered the Collège Charlemagne, where he began to exhibit a fondness for literary pursuits and began his lifelong friendship with the poet Théophile Gautier.

In November, 1827, Nerval published his translation
of Goethe's *Faust: Eine Tragödie* (1808), but under the
publication date of 1828. This work was well received in
Parisian literary circles, and Nerval became a disciple of
Victor Hugo and joined his *Cénacle Romantique.* In the
notorious dispute that followed the disruptive theatrical
opening (February 25, 1830) of Hugo's play *Hernani,*
however, Nerval sided with Gautier, and thereafter Nerval frequented Gautier's *petit cénacle.*

An inheritance from his maternal grandfather in 1834
allowed Nerval to give up his medical studies and pursue a literary career, much to his father's disapproval.
In the fall of that year, Nerval visited Italy (Florence,

Rome, and Naples), a trip that later proved invaluable
to his writing. Upon his return to Paris in 1834, he met
and fell in love with the actress Jenny Colon. In May
of 1834, he founded the theatrical review *Le Monde
dramatique,* dedicated to the glorification of Jenny Colon.
For a brief time, Nerval enjoyed a life of prosperity,
identifying himself with the "Bohème galante." When
the review failed in 1836, however, financial difficulties
forced Nerval to become a journalist, writing articles for
Le Figaro and *La Presse.* He visited Belgium with
Gautier in 1836 in an effort to forget his personal struggles for a time.

On October 31, 1837, Nerval's play *Piquillo* premiered in Paris with Jenny Colon in the lead role as
Silvia. The play was a success, and Nerval was encouraged to declare his love for her. On April 11, 1838, however, Jenny married the flutist Louis-Gabriel Leplus, an

event that left the poet bitterly disillusioned. During the summer of that year, he traveled to Germany with Alexandre Dumas, *père*, and from that time the two writers began a series of theatrical collaborations.

The next two years were ones of increasing mental instability and depression for Nerval. Though he published his translation of *Faust: Eine Tragödie, Zweyter Teil* (1833) in 1840, the strain of the work took its toll, and Nerval was hospitalized as a result of a nervous breakdown. The death of Jenny Colon in 1842 did nothing to restore his ailing spirits. In ill health and overcome with grief, he embarked in 1843 on a trip to Malta, Egypt, Syria, Cyprus, Constantinople, and Naples. He later published an account of his travels in *Journey to the Orient*. Nerval had discovered his psychological need to wander, a theme found in his major works.

Though his mental and physical health continued to deteriorate, Nerval struggled to support himself with his writing. Still hoping to establish himself in the theater, he wrote *Chariot d'enfant* with Joseph Méry, a production which premiered on May 13, 1850. In September, 1851, Nerval suffered an accident, followed by a serious nervous breakdown. Nerval believed that he would soon become incurably insane, a realization which made him increase his literary efforts. In 1852, he published *Les Illuminés*, a series of biographies on historical figures interested in mysteries of the occult and of alchemy. In 1853, he published a volume of nostalgic poems recalling a happier youth, *Petits Châteaux de Bohême*. In the summer of that year, Nerval published his best-known story, "Sylvie," followed by two other great works, *Daughters of Fire* and *Les Chimères*, in 1854. *Aurélia*, an account of his madness, appeared in 1855. Alone and destitute, Nerval hanged himself in an alley on January 26, 1855.

ANALYSIS

Théophile Gautier, who perhaps appreciated the fine qualities of Gérard de Nerval's character and art more than any other contemporary, once described his friend as an "apodal swallow." To Gautier, Nerval was

all wings and no feet: At most he had perceptible claws; these enabled him to alight, at least momentarily, just long enough to catch his breath, then go on . . . to soar

and move about in fluid realms with the joy and abandon of a being in his element.

Gautier's idealization of Nerval as an ethereal figure—a Shelleylike bird in flight who abjured the common terrestrial condition of humanity—is a valid judgment only to a limited degree. To be sure, a reader may approach Nerval on a superficial level as a poet of intense, vivid, direct intuition; a poet of dreams and visions; a creator of myths and fantastic personal symbolic constructs that reach into the archetypal imagination.

Certainly, most of Nerval's poetry, much of his prose poetry, and a portion of his dramatic work can be appreciated according to the qualities of Impressionism. His work has, on a simple level of perception, an evocative, dreamy, otherworldly, melancholy vein that resembles the Impressionism of otherwise dissimilar poets such as Edgar Allan Poe and Paul Verlaine. One can enjoy the seemingly imprecise but hauntingly evocative imagery of a familiar Nerval poem such as "Le Point noir" ("The Dark Smudge") as though the writer were merely inducing an impression of malign fate. Reading Nerval for his surface characteristics of hauntingly sonorous music, vague but unsettling imagery, and technically perfect mastery of verse forms, one can accept Gautier's early evaluation of the poet as a kind of bird-like spirit—or, to use Baudelaire's image of a poet idealized as an albatross ("L'Albatros"), a creature free in the air but confined and crippled on the crass Earth.

Moreover, a reader who approaches Nerval's basic themes without first investigating their intellectual context is likely to appreciate their surface qualities of authentic feeling and simplicity of expression. Nerval is always concerned with human values, no matter that he may choose exotic subjects or complex methods to express them. His work is nearly always confessional. Although in his poetry he rarely tends to be self-dramatizing, he often places his persona—his other self—at the center of the theme in order to examine the psychological insights of a human life. An early verse, "Épître première," at once expresses his artistic philosophy and predicts his fate; he will, despite madness under the aegis of the moon, serve humanity with a generous desire. In his poems as well as in much of his prose and drama, Nerval appeals directly—without a reader's need for critical exegesis—to the human heart: to its courage, its idealism, its love. Although Nerval's subjects often appear to be odd, exotic, or perverse, the poet treats the flowers of his imagination not as "evil," as does the great poet of the next generation, Baudelaire, but as fragrant symbols of a mysterious, arcane harmony in the universe.

Indeed, Nerval is best appreciated as a mystic and a seer, a poet whose surface qualities of vague dreaminess conceal an interior precision of image and ideas. Reading a popularly anthologized lyric such as "Fantaisie" ("Fantasy"), for example, one tends to dismiss the poem as a piece influenced by German Romanticism, especially by the *Märchen*-like songs of Heinrich Heine or Goethe. A closer reading, however, will show that the seemingly vague images are not merely decorative; they are rendered with precision, although their precise significance as personal symbol is not clear. Nevertheless, the "green slope gilded by the setting sun" and the stone castle are objects, not atmosphere, and the mysterious theme of déjà vu is intended to be psychological truth, not fairy tale.

GERMAN ROMANTICISM

To appreciate Nerval fully, one should understand the poet's relationship to German Romanticism without treating him exclusively as a Romantic—or, indeed, exclusively as a pre-Impressionist, pre-Symbolist, or pre-modernist. Although his affinities to poets such as Heine and Goethe (Romantics), Poe and Verlaine (Impressionists), and Mallarmé and Rimbaud (Symbolists) are obvious—as are his temperamental affinities to Baudelaire—Nerval is best compared to two poets whose productions are similarly visionary and, in some respects, arcane: William Blake and William Butler Yeats. Like Blake, Nerval was a seer who searched into the heart of mysteries to discover the correspondence of opposites; a follower of the eighteenth century mystic Emanuel Swedenborg; and an originator of complex myths and symbolic systems. Like Yeats, Nerval was a student of theosophy and an adept of the religions of the East. He believed in magic and the occult, communicated with revealers of the spirit world, and—using the phases of the moon and similar cosmic symbols—created a complex system of psychological and historical types of personalities.

ARCHETYPAL IMAGERY

In addition, Nerval cultivated dream visions, experimented with drugs such as hashish, and was a student of the Cabala, alchemy, ancient mystery religions, Illuminism, Orphism, Sabbean astral worship, and the secrets of the Egyptian pyramids. If his abstruse researches were merely incidental to his work, much of his thinking might be safely ignored as burdensome, esoteric, or irrelevant. Nerval, however, uses a great deal of his learning in his prose and poetry. An extremely careful writer, he placed layer upon layer of meaning, often mixing different systems that are not related historically into a single new system, within the texture of his poetic prose and his poetry. To ignore these layers of meaning is to neglect as well a great deal of Nerval's subtlety as an artist.

In *Aurélia*, for example, he used archetypal images that appear to emanate from the collective unconscious—among them the image of the *magna mater* (great mother). Included are manifestations of woman as loving, gentle, compassionate, noble-hearted; as vain, dissembling, inconstant; or as the dangerous fury who terrorizes a dreamer; or finally, as the temptress, the coquette. Also he includes, in various manifestations, the father archetype. In *Journey to the Orient*, the poet transmutes the legend of Solomon and Sheba from a biblical tale into a personal vision centering on the character of Adoniram, a "double" for the artist, the creator. In this book, Nerval exposes themes involving the story of Cain as well as the secrets of Hermetic lore and of the pyramids (Nerval actually visited the site of the Great Pyramid of Khufu, or Cheops, and descended into its depths).

SYMBOLISM AND HERMETICISM

Nerval's poetry is less obviously arcane than much of his symbolic prose; nevertheless, a careful student should understand that the poet uses language in a very special way. His constant endeavor was to express through symbolic language a unity that he perceived in the spiritual and the material elements of the universe. To grasp this language, a reader needs to know several concepts basic to Swedenborgian correspondence and Hermetic alchemy.

Nerval's research into these abstruse subjects began early in his life, notably from his interest in a tradition of thought known as Illuminism. This tradition affected writers from the middle of the eighteenth century until the end of the nineteenth century. Illuminists were fascinated with ancient Oriental manuscripts and with the tenets of Middle Eastern thinkers. Among the manuscripts that they studied were the *Corpus Hermeticum*, a collection of forty-two books attributed to Hermes Trismegistus, perhaps the most important source of alchemical knowledge of the period. To these books were added the works of Paracelsus and his disciples.

These doctrines were cultivated by members of various secret societies (Rosicrucians, Freemasons, Martinists) which flourished at the end of the eighteenth century, particularly in France and in Germany. By means of such secret societies, Nerval came to acquire knowledge and appreciation of alchemy, while his visionary application of alchemical principles can be traced to the works of Swedenborg. In his study of the *Corpus Hermeticum* and of the Cabala, Swedenborg had reached two conclusions that were to have a tremendous influence upon the literary world of the nineteenth century. The first of these conclusions was his idea of correspondence, the notion that every visible phenomenon has a direct opposite—upon which it depends—in the invisible and spiritual world. The second conclusion was his conception of a universal language in which these correspondences can best be expressed.

LES CHIMÈRES

Nerval's poetry reveals his obsession with creating a new language, one that will allow for a communication between the visible and the invisible, the sensible and the spiritual. Such a language would permit a correspondence between the two orders. A corollary of this belief is the principle of the identity of contraries or opposites. Thus, in *Les Chimères*, Nerval establishes a syncretism of religious beliefs based upon compatibilities. His object is to demonstrate the oneness of religious thought; to achieve this high purpose, he selects a special language, using the metaphors of alchemy principally but not exclusively, as a vehicle to redeem humanity.

A reader may wonder whether a poet so learned as Nerval actually believed in the esoteric doctrines of alchemy. Certainly he used these doctrines, extracting from their classical and medieval origins a philosophical rather than pseudoscientific content, in order to con-

struct his metaphors. In this sense, Nerval believed in alchemy as Blake believed in his visions and as Yeats believed in the symbolic constructs of his spiritual communicators. Nerval's poetry incorporates four basic alchemical principles: first, the theory of correspondence; second, the act of imagining, which can bring about corporeal transformations; third, meditation, or an inner dialogue with the invisible, which requires a "new language"; and finally, the identity of opposites, whereby every image elicits by definition its contrary. In this complex scheme, Mercury (quicksilver) becomes the symbol of alchemy: liquid metal, or the embodiment of a contradiction.

To appreciate how deeply interfused with the surface dreaminess of Nerval's verse are his symbolic constructs of alchemy, one can examine the cycle of twelve sonnets titled *Les Chimères*. The number twelve is crucial in the alchemical system, since it represents the *coniunctio tetraptiva*, or the dilemma of three and four—the chimera being the archetype of the triad. It should also be noted that the structure of the sonnet itself is representative of the problem of three and four, but in reverse. If the chimera represents the triad in the *coniunctio tetraptiva*, the four symbolizes the union of persons, and this is the underlying matrix of *Les Chimères*. By a process known as *henosis*, a tetrasomia or synthesis of opposites is produced to create a unity.

"EL DESDICHADO"

The first sonnet of *Les Chimères* is probably Nerval's best-known poem, "El desdichado" (the title, meaning the unhappy one), was borrowed from Sir Walter Scott's *Ivanhoe*, 1819). It focuses upon the descent into the abyss, the *nigredo* of the alchemist, or the opening stage of the process. The images used to describe this phase are all somber: images of death and of caves, and even of Hell (the Achéron and the evocation of Orpheus). More important, however, is Nerval's linking of these dark, demoniac images with traditionally positive images—the union of contraries being the functional principle in such expressions as "soleil noir" (black sun). The most powerful character in the poem, one who is there by implication and not by name, is Melusina, the absent-but-present feminine principle. Melusina also embodies the identity of contraries, possessing either the tail of a fish or that of a snake; sometimes she appears only as a snake. Her ability to metamorphose as well as to heal diseases and injuries makes her—in the mind of the alchemist and of the poet-seer—the feminine counterpart to Mercury. Thus, in "El desdichado," Nerval posits a synthesis of the medieval duality with the Greco-Roman duality, Hermes-Mercury.

"MYRTHO"

In the succeeding sonnet, "Myrtho," Nerval assesses the descent into the abyss. It is in this manner that one can achieve the light. Moreover, it is here that the black is an essential component of the gold: "Aux raisins noirs mêlés avec l'or de ta tresse" ("and black grapes mingled in your golden tresses"). In this descent into the interior world of the light, the poet-seer necessarily meets the sovereign of the underworld, Bacchus-Dionysus-Osiris. The final two lines announce the reconciliation of certain poetic visions: that of Vergil's neopaganism with the Illuminism of the eighteenth century. Like "El desdichado," then, "Myrtho" presents a unification of various systems of thought.

"HORUS"

The sonnet "Horus" concerns the Egyptian deity considered by the syncretists to be a prefiguration of Christ. Horus also symbolizes Hellenistic mysticism, providing a direct link with Hermes and, by association, with Hermes Trismegistus, the alchemist. Isis, Horus's mother, the symbol of nature's mysteries, is identified with Venus in the same manner that Hermes is linked with Osiris, leading to a form of Greco-Egyptian religious syncretism. In this system is to be found the "esprit nouveau," the result of which is a rainbow or the vision of colors, a necessary stage which precedes the appearance of gold in alchemy.

"ANTÉROS"

"Antéros" presents a vision of Hell, with Semitic overtones. To be of the race of Antéros (Antaeus) means to gather strength from the earth from which one has sprouted. This agrarian subtext is consistent with references to Cain, the keeper of the fields, and to Dagon, the Philistine agrarian god. The Satanic aspect is sustained in the mark of Cain and in the thrice-dipping into the Cocyte, one of the rivers of Tartarus. The sonnet projects the archetypal struggle of the vanquished giant who refuses defeat—here represented by the Amalekites, a nomadic tribe which was virtually exterminated by the Is-

raelites during the time of David. These pagans are associated with the race of Satan and Cain. "Antéros" ends with a metaphor of rebirth, that of sowing the dragon's teeth in order to create a new race of giants. In alchemical terms, the sowing of the divine seed (*germinis divi*) provides the continuity necessary for the continual process of transformation which involves death and rebirth, descent and resurrection. The baptism of Hell is the equivalent of the baptism at the holy font.

"DELFICA"

In "Delfica," Nerval includes the trees most often discussed by alchemists as symbols for the human body. Daphne, who was transformed into a tree, is the personification *par excellence* of the desired synthesis of man and nature. The lemons which carry the imprint of her teeth are the natural equivalents in tree code to the metallic gold. Just as the *lapis philosophorum* (the philosopher's stone) holds the key to the mysteries at its center, so, too, the grotto holds the dragon, sign of the danger of the penetration into the mysteries and also carrier of the all-important seed, or seminal material, which now lies dormant. Ancient beliefs, Nerval suggests, have been overcome by Christianity, yet like the anima of Daphne in the tree, they remain essentially intact, awaiting a revival.

"ARTÉMIS"

"Artémis" begins with an invocation to the mysteries: the number thirteen, an indivisible number, joining the basis of oneness and of the Trinity (which is always One). Thirteen is also the symbol of death in the Tarot (Arcane XIII). The sonnet centers upon the alchemical mystique of the rose; Nerval follows the tradition whereby the rose symbolizes the relationship between king and queen. More important, the rose provides the essential alchemical link with Christ. As such, the rose must be blood-colored in order to be identified with the Redeemer and the Cross. The final line indicates that the descent into the abyss is a necessary step in the making of a saint.

In alchemical writings, the philosopher's stone represents the *homo totus*, which will shed a bloody sweat. In this way, the stone prefigures the agony of Christ. Indeed, the Evangelist Luke says of Christ: ". . . and His sweat was as it were great drops falling down to the ground" (Luke 22:44). It should therefore come as no surprise that Nerval would follow "Artémis" with five sonnets dealing with Christ in the Garden of Gethsemene. In his final hours of agony, Nerval's Christ is truly human, doubting the existence of a supreme power. In the fifth sonnet of the series, he recalls the necessity of descent in order to ascend, the necessity of death in order to give life. Christ's death gives life to a new belief which spells death to the old gods, yet Nerval poses an interesting question: "Quel est ce nouveau dieu qu'on impose à la terre?" (who is this new god who is being imposed on the Earth?). The answer is reserved for the Almighty, who blessed the children of Adam ("les enfants du limon"). As already noted, the lemon is symbolic of the alchemical gold—that is, the quest for perfection and transcendence that Christ represents.

"VERS DORÉS"

In "Vers dorés" ("Golden Verses"), Nerval not only states his theory of correspondences but also offers his most compact statement concerning the role of alchemy in poetry. A new language is to be found—"À la matière même un verbe est attaché" ("Even with matter there's a built-in word")—and a Divine Spirit is present in the darkness, waiting to shed his light. The last two lines describe the poet-seer as having opened his third eye; thus, he is able to strip away the layers of stone (the *lapis*) and finally attain the "gold" of the alchemist. Nerval's *Les Chimères*, therefore, achieves a synthesis of various manifestations of contrary elements, each time through the use of personification. "Golden Verses" symbolizes the achievement of the *coniunctio*, the realization of a new form of poetic inspiration and performance.

OTHER MAJOR WORKS

SHORT FICTION: "Sylvie," 1853 (English translation, 1922); *Les Filles du feu*, 1854 (*Daughters of Fire*, 1922).

PLAYS: *Faust*, pb. 1827, enlarged pb. 1840 (translation of Johann Wolfgang von Goethe's play); *Piquillo*, pb. 1837 (with Alexandre Dumas, *père*); *Alchimiste*, pb. 1839 (with Dumas, *père*); *Chariot d'enfant*, pb. 1850 (with Joseph Méry); *L'Imagier de Harlem*, pr. 1851.

NONFICTION: *Voyage en Orient*, 1851 (*Journey to the Orient*, 1972); *Les Illuminés*, 1852; *Promenades et souvenirs*, 1854-1856; *Aurélia*, 1855 (English translation, 1932).

MISCELLANEOUS: *Selected Writings*, 1957.

BIBLIOGRAPHY

Knapp, Bettina L. *Gérard de Nerval: The Mystic's Dilemma*. Tuscaloosa: University of Alabama Press, 1980. A critical analysis of Nerval's work with bibliographic references and an index.

MacLennan, George. *Lucid Interval: Subjective Writing and Madness in History*. London: Leicester University Press, 1992. A history of literature and mental illness with particular attention to the work of Nerval. Includes bibliographical references and index.

Rinsler, Norma. *Gérard de Nerval*. London: Athlone Press, 1973. A biography of Nerval with bibliographic references and an index.

Tyers, Meryl. *Critical Fictions: Nerval's "Les Illuminés."* Oxford, England: Legenda, 1998. Provides the background for Nerval's publication of the collected volume *Les Illuminés* and an outline of the six previously published pieces collected to make up the volume. The contemporary critical reviews of Nerval's text and relevant scholarship up to the present day are analyzed.

*Leslie B. Mittleman;
bibliography updated by the editors*

MARGARET CAVENDISH, DUCHESS OF NEWCASTLE

Born: St. Johns Abbey, Colchester, Essex, England; 1623
Died: London, England; December 15, 1673

PRINCIPAL POETRY

Poems and Fancies, 1653
Philosophicall Fancies, 1653 (prose and verse; revised as *Philosophical and Physical Opinions*, 1655)
Natures Pictures, 1656 (prose and verse)
Plays Never Before Printed, 1668

Margaret Cavendish, duchess of Newcastle (© Bettmann/Corbis)

OTHER LITERARY FORMS

Margaret Cavendish, duchess of Newcastle, left many folio volumes in various prose genres. *Natures Pictures* (1656) contains a group of stories told around a winter fire; they are romantic and moralistic (disguises, abductions, wanderings, battles, reunions). The second part, a miscellaneous group of tales, has no framing device. *Grounds of Natural Philosophy* (1668) reworks her views regarding physics and medicine developed in *Philosophicall Fancies*. *Philosophical Letters* (1664) analyzes Thomas Hobbes, René Descartes, and Thomas More. Several romantic comedies, published in *Plays* (1662), have plot elements similar to the tales. The duchess herself appears in such figures as "Lady Contemplation" and "Lady Sanspariel." The duchess's most effective prose, and one of the century's finest biographical works, is *The Life of William Cavendish, Duke of Newcastle* (1667). Equally lively and clearly written is "A True Relation of the Birth, Breeding and Life of Margaret Cavendish, Duchess of Newcastle, Written by Herself," included in *Natures Pictures*. *The Worlds Olio* (1655) contains epistles on the branches of learning and the pleasures of reading, on the passions, fame, and educa-

tion. With *CCXI Sociable Letters* (1664), it contains many interesting observations on manners and literary taste.

ACHIEVEMENTS

As one of the first women who not only composed but also published their verses, the duchess anticipated the disdain that she would receive and so attempted to create a persona, as did other Cavalier poets, that would help readers understand what she was doing. She developed the concept of "fancy," and the "harmless mirth" it produced, arguing that it was a woman's as much as a man's pursuit. Her poems envision the world as guided by a benevolent goddess, Natura. They movingly express humanitarian sentiments and focus on responses by women to loss of love, misfortune, and death. She utilized many genres and themes of earlier seventeenth century poetry: the pastoral, the verse-treatise, the elegy, and the verse-narrative. She is at her best when she is guided by the traditional emblems and images of lyric and narrative verse.

BIOGRAPHY

Margaret (Lucas) Cavendish, duchess of Newcastle, was one of eight children afforded a privileged upbringing by her mother. Her favorite pastime was writing, for which she neglected her reading, her languages, and her spelling. She also enjoyed designing clothes and was known for her extravagance in dress as well as in her scientific opinions and her poetry. At nineteen, despite her great shyness, she became a maid of honor to Queen Henrietta Maria. In this capacity, she met William Cavendish, then Marquis of Newcastle. They married in 1645; he was thirty-three years her senior. The duke was a learned man, a patron of poets, and a virtuoso, a friend of René Descartes and Thomas Hobbes.

The duke and his lady lived happily at Welbeck Abbey after the Restoration, but during the Civil Wars and the Commonwealth the duke was in financial peril. He had left England after the battle of Marston Moor and spent most of the interregnum at Antwerp. The duchess, who met her husband at Paris, returned to London in 1652 to attempt the compounding of his estates. It was at that time that she resumed writing poetry. She continued in Holland, where the duke entertained many notable visitors in politics and the arts. The frontispiece of Lady Newcastle's *Natures Pictures* shows her and her husband, crowned with laurel, sitting at a table with the duke's sons and daughters. It provides a fair picture of the congenial literary readings and conversations that they shared.

In 1676, a commemorative volume of *Letters and Poems* in praise of Margaret Newcastle was published, with pieces by Thomas Shadwell, Henry More, George Etherege, and Jasper Mayne.

ANALYSIS

Seventeenth century volumes of poetry as diverse as George Herbert's *The Temple* (1633), Mildmay Fane's *Otia Sacra* (1648), and Robert Herrick's *Hesperides* (1648) have general but significant organizing principles. This is quite clearly the case with *Poems and Fancies*, despite its being very poorly printed by a craftsman who was puzzled by the state of the manuscript and was pressed to get the book out before the writer left England to rejoin her exiled husband. Margaret (writers so designate her not in a spirit of condescension but to distinguish her from her husband, Sir William) intersperses, throughout the book, transition pieces called "clasps" intended to join one section to the next. As for "Poems," these are verse-treatises on the atomistic structure of matter which establish the writer as a female virtuoso (one conversant in a disinterested, amateur way with the sciences and fine arts), followed by moral discourses including complaints about man's misuse of the world that God has placed under his stewardship; and descriptive pieces on, for example, dispositions to mirth and melancholy. Halfway through the work the heading "Fancies" ushers in verses on fairies and elegiac pieces. The "claspes" do more than divide the volume into sections. Their main function is to allow the duchess to explain her poetic temperament or cast of mind, her reasons for writing, her disdain for niceties of poetic style, and the primacy of the intellectual content of her own verses.

In her solitary apartment, where few were brave enough, in 1652, to visit the wife of a royalist general, she wrote quickly as the thoughts were generated in her original, thoroughly idiosyncratic, and nimble intellect. Some of her explanations are attempts to justify a woman's audacity in writing poetry. Lady Newcastle is primarily concerned, however, not with what others think of her but with contemporary notions of poetry, particularly philosophical verse, narratives, and lyrics. One must focus not only on her "claspes" but also on the prefatory matter to *Poems and Fancies* in order to understand the diverse body of poetry that she produced.

Commendatory poems by her husband and his brother Charles Cavendish (Margaret's companion in London in 1652) are on the surface fulsome praises but really "harmless mirth": lighthearted punning and sprightly humor. The cavalier and his lady do not take themselves so seriously as to pose as national heroes or great poets. For a fit audience of like-minded readers, affable modesty and whimsical self-deprecation mark the prefatory verses. In what other spirit could one take the duke's assertion that his wife's writings will set the ghosts of Edmund Spenser, William Shakespeare, and Ben Jonson into fits of jealous weeping? The duchess does indeed lay claim to fame, which she frankly desires for the variety of her fancies, her manifold curiosities about the workings of nature, and the scope of her subject matter. As a female writer, she is very much aware of her uniqueness. She notes that ordering fancies is a similar kind of economy to that which women need to run households, and that verse, being fiction, is recreative to the spirit, wholesomely entertaining, and ingenuous. One part of a poetess's contribution to her readers is in defeating male stereotypes regarding female propensities to idleness, gossip, and slander.

"FANCIES"

"Fancies" is an important word to the duchess; her usage of the word can be understood in relation to the Baconian contrast between imagination and reason. The former produced pleasant delusions, sprightly ingenuity, and alacrity of imaginings. Francis Bacon gave poetry faint praise, and the notion that fancy must be disciplined by judgment was a strong one. Lady Newcastle's own version of this dictum, stated in the "claspes," may be her emphasis on matter as opposed to niceties of style. In general, however, she is content with her fancies as a kind of self-improving, "harmless mirth," a magnanimous way for a studious and shy woman to pass the time. The duchess had a reputation (see Samuel Pepys and Dorothy Osbourne) for eccentricity and arrogance.

The prefatory materials in *Poems and Fancies*, however, suggest a writer who makes no great claims for her own poetic abilities. As with the Cavalier poets whose conventions she borrows and with whom she shares political and social as well as aesthetic values, a mind-muse analogy develops. The poetry provides recreation and reflects the amiable, benevolent disposition of the writer. In this spirit the duchess follows Robert Herrick and Mildmay Fane with a whimsical allusion to her book as her child. As an introduction, the conceit is in her case as apt as it is conventional.

ATOMISM

The duchess's treatment of atoms is somewhat indebted to Bacon's new rationalism and to the encyclopedic categorizing of the phenomenal world by Guillaume du Bartas and William Davenant. The latter's metaphors from applied and theoretical sciences are similar to some of Margaret's "similizing." Her diction and iambic pentameter rhymed couplets provide a sensible framework for discursive exposition, but she does not indulge in much analysis. Atomism is merely the trapping for fanciful description, which in itself is similar to du Bartas's quaint and fantastic compilations.

For example, she avers that plants are made up of branched atoms, with hooks that pull the tendrils upward from the roots. Healthy atoms are in tune with one another, like people dancing to harmonious music. Aged atoms slow down and finally move no more; this is the state of death. Sharp, arrow-like atoms make up fire; they can soar upward, while the atoms that cohere to form earth are flat and square, heavy and phlegmatic. Thus the duchess mixes an ancient notion (the four elements) with the modern, empirical one of Thomas Hobbes (a personal friend of the Newcastles with whom Sir William held lengthy discussions).

Lady Newcastle lived in the "divided and distinguished worlds" of which Sir Thomas Browne wrote. John Donne and John Milton lived there too, but while their inconsistencies involved seeing God's signatures in the real world (however empirically, up to a point, they were willing to observe it), the duchess's inconsistencies concern not nature and spirit, but nature and fancy. She ingenuously tells the reader that she has not read much Hobbes, Descartes, or Bacon, that her poems were written hastily and not revised to conform with what she read or recalled from her reading. She was fascinated with atomism, however, and was concerned with it throughout *Poems and Fancies*. In one place, she uses a "claspe" to explain that various atoms acting at cross-purposes within the human body are the work of mischievous fairies. The body's animal spirits can be similar tiny creatures working in nerves, muscles, and organs as the various races of humankind do in different parts of the earth, trafficking with one another through veins and arteries.

"A WORLD IN AN EARE-RING"

This leads to the duchess's version of the "metaphysical" metaphor of the body as a map and to other speculations bred of Renaissance skepticism. Her imagination is especially taken with microscopic convolutions of nature and with the perfections attainable within the smallest parameters of nature and art. Jonson and Herrick had similar interests. Although the duchess cannot match their perfections in imagery or verse rhythms, she shares their imaginative empathy. "A World in an Eare-Ring" supposes a universe suspended invisibly from a lady's ear. The poem envisions a grand panorama of mortal existence: great storms and their chaos, mountains, gardens and cities, and an entire cycle of life forms, all revolving around the center or hole in the ring.

PHILOSOPHICALL FANCIES

Lady Newcastle's atomism was undergoing revision as she was writing *Poems and Fancies*. In 1653, she published these revisions, alluded to on the last page of her first book, in a duodecimo volume titled *Philosophicall Fancies*, revised two years later as *Philosophical and Physical Opinions*. Here, in a mixture of prose and verse, she is concerned with matter and motion, the former being infinite while the latter is the agent which changes the form of matter. She also deals with causes of sunlight, diseases, tides, and God as first cause. Extravagant fancies regarding sublunary worlds different from earth and beyond human control predominate. She speculates that rational spirits might so change the laws of physics as to animate trees into deer and make mermaids of water lilies.

MORAL DISCOURSES

Lady Newcastle's moral discourses are dialogues between, for example, nature and man, wit and beauty, peace and war, and discourses on love, poverty, and humility. Some of her best poetry occurs here, concerned with faculty psychology, man's stewardship of God's creation, and the humanitarian and compassionate principles which underlie nobility. For the more discursive of these verses, her predecessors would be Samuel Daniel (*Musophilus*, 1599), Fulke Greville's treatises on fame, honor, and war, and George Chapman (*Euthymiae Raptus*, 1609). For the dramatic and narrative efforts, Edmund Spenser's didactic fables, Milton's *Il Penseroso* (1645), and perhaps George Wither's and Michael Drayton's works are analogues (not, it should be noted, sources). If indeed the duchess knew the work of these poets, it probably would have been by hearing them read rather than by close study. She was a sporadic reader, and even in childhood, she liked writing not only more than traditional feminine accomplishments such as deportment and snippets of foreign languages but also more than reading. Her widowed mother lovingly indulged these preferences.

"A DIALOGUE OF BIRDS"

Three of the moral discourses have considerable merit. "A Dialogue of Birds" has an effective dramatic framework: Various species talk of their experiences with humankind. They speak plainly and pathetically of their sufferings brought about by man's artful cruelties, not by nature's regime, however harsh. In fact, this poem, the one on the hare, and the fairy verses suggest the folk art which John Broadbent (in *Poets of the Seventeenth Century*, 1980) attributes to her and her husband. The poem is well organized, beginning with the lark's song and ending, after a horrific recital of suffering, with the birds settling their families in their nests, and finally singing a communal hymn, the birdsong softly fading as they fall asleep. The theme of the poem is art's perversion of nature, which is herself benevolent and informed by love. The birds pose the question of the root of man's viciousness; they have no answer, but portray—by citing their own mistreatment—human aggression hidden under universally accepted behavior which passes for custom and sport. With that, they turn from what they cannot prevent to practical concerns such as nest-building.

The rhetorical device at work here, *prosopopoeia*, was brought to perfection by Spenser, and Lady Newcastle uses it well.

"THE HUNTING OF THE HARE"

"The Hunting of the Hare" is successful in the same way. It is even more accurate in its detail of the animal's furtive movements and instinctual strategies for self-preservation. The poet's personification of the animal's innocence and despair as the hounds surround him incites pathos. The theme, once again, is man's willful ignorance of the suffering he causes and his prideful desecration of nature. Margaret's humanitarianism in these and other narratives is as revealing a part of her sensibility as are her introductory verses.

"A DIALOGUE BETWEEN MIRTH AND MELANCHOLY"

"A Dialogue Between Mirth and Melancholy" was noticed favorably in the eighteenth century (in a witty sketch in *The Connoisseur*, 1774), and in the nineteenth century by Benjamin Disraeli and Leigh Hunt. They appreciated the pastoral descriptions reminiscent of *L'Allegro* (1645) and *Il Penseroso*, but the most pervasive feature is the care with which the two states of mind are balanced against each other. Notably, the duchess, who loved retirement, lets melancholy have the last word. It is a "white" melancholy, like that which Herrick sometimes delineates, agreeable and clean. The pleasures of retirement allow sadness to be refined away by the duchess's guiding principle of the good life, fancy. In these verses she avoids the extravagances which mar so much of her work, including "The Hunting of the Stag," another humanitarian work, which is no sooner under way than a lengthy catalog of trees intrudes.

FAIRY POETRY

The duchess's fairy poetry constitutes a microcosm of all of her concerns. In a prose introduction she justifies the existence of fairies on the basis of recent scientific discoveries about invisible but potent natural forces. As usual, these speculations resolve themselves into fanciful explanations: If air moves ineluctably through walls, fairies can invisibly go where they will. In "The Fairy Queen" Margaret spends nearly the entire poem describing the habitat of fairies, which she places in the center of the earth. She brings in the elements, the movements of the earth, and the circulation of the waters. Her humanitarianism is also evident. In the microcosm of the fairies' world, the god of love is not Cupid but the goddess Natura, a female generative principle which gives Queen Mab control over the spirit world and extends motherly beneficence to all creatures. The duchess's interest in folklore and custom can best be seen in "The Pastime of the Queen of Fairies." This rings the changes on Hobgoblin's pranks and is very close to the speeches of William Shakespeare's Puck. Throughout all these verses one senses a preoccupation with miniature gem-like beauties, which only those with refined perceptions and respect for fancy can appreciate. The order of the universe can be seen in the order of minutest nature. The fairy verses in which some anthologists find the most attractive images (because of the succinctness with which they are stated) are in a collection of fragments, *Plays Never Before Printed* (1668).

The sources for all these poems are, in addition to Shakespeare, Michael Drayton and Herrick, writers who use this kind of pastoral without any didactic intentions, but for the ingenious play of the imagination. Newcastle's mushroom table with its dish of ant's eggs is from Herrick, as are the glowworm's eyes, used as lanterns, and snakeskin used as decoration. Mab's chariot made from a nutshell recalls Mercutio's speech in *Romeo and Juliet* (1594-1596). The differences between the duchess's verses and those of her great predecessors lie in their verbal music and their more striking juxtapositions of the familiarity of our world with the mysteriousness of the fairies' world.

ELEGIES AND FEMALE IMAGES

According to the Renaissance definition, an elegy need not be limited to verses on death; it could be any serious meditative poem. A large number of the duchess's poems might be so designated. In Margaret's elegiac and lyric verses, subjects are female: their beauty, their love, their griefs, their deaths. Some of these are given the general heading of "A Register of Mournful Verses." The two most ambitious deal with a "melting beauty" whose body turns to ice and melts into the funeral urn of her loved one, and with another "mourning beauty" from whose tears flowers with bowed heads grow, and for whom the stars become fellow mourners

lighting her way to the grave site. The gods transform her into a comet.

The imagery in the second of these elegies is effectively emblematic, although strained with macrocosm-microcosm analogies. The poem is well unified in its symbolic representation of universal gestures and attitudes of grief, and of grief's fateful consequences. In both poems one senses woman's isolation, and the psychological effects of the single emotion of black melancholy on the human mind. For this, Seneca is an exemplar, as Ovid is for the mysterious transformations of the women, which suggests in Margaret's work the principles of natural benevolence set forth in some of the dialogues. These and the duchess's other elegies, especially those for a bereaved mother and for her deceased daughter, would be well complemented by emblems. Her final elegy, on her brother, is in a similar vein, attempting emotional heightening with metaphoric emblems: Her heart is a sacrifice, her sighs are incense, her thoughts mourners. A mythic universality is attempted, or, more accurately, strained after. The opening and closing lines, however, are in an affecting plain style; their commonplaces about honor and fame do not spoil them.

SIMILITUDES

In her short lyrical pieces, Newcastle can focus more exclusively on her "similitudes." The effects are often bizarre; her formlessness and extravagance are all too evident. A sad lover's heart becomes meat for nature's dinner. If Dame Nature has any appetite left, Margaret presents her with a "bisque" made from a young female's broad forehead, rosy cheeks, white breasts, and swan-like neck. Another conceit involves "Similizing the Heart to a Harp, the Head to an Organ, the Tongue to a Lute, to make a consort of Musique." Another compares the world of the sea to an Arcadia in which the ocean is a country green, the mast a maypole, and the sailors shepherds.

The duchess's conceits often defy classification into Petrarchan, metaphysical, or plain (or eloquent) style. One wishes she were a bit more discreet, less spontaneously prolific, and perhaps a greater reader, like some lettered contemporaries: Lady Bedford; Lady Mary Wroth; Margaret Countess of Cumberland; Lady Falkland or her daughter-in-law, Letice Morison; or even Dorothy

Osbourne, who thought her mad for attempting to write, and especially to publish, poetry. Had she been only a patroness of writers, or a letter writer, however, she would not have been the self-possessed and courageous innovator that she was.

OTHER MAJOR WORKS

SHORT FICTION: *Natures Pictures*, 1656 (prose and verse).

PLAYS: *Plays*, pb. 1662; *Plays Never Before Printed*, pb. 1668.

NONFICTION: *The Worlds Olio*, 1655; *Philosophical Letters*, 1664; *CCXI Sociable Letters*, 1664; *The Life of William Cavendish, Duke of Newcastle*, 1667; *Grounds of Natural Philosophy*, 1668.

BIBLIOGRAPHY

Battigelli, Anna. *Margaret Cavendish and the Exiles of the Mind*. Lexington: University Press of Kentucky, 1998. Battigelli's meticulous scholarship brings Cavendish alive, creating a compelling portrait of her intellectual and creative life. Includes bibliographical references and index.

Blaydes, Sophia B. "Nature Is a Woman: The Duchess of Newcastle and Seventeenth Century Philosophy." In *Man, God, and Nature in the Enlightenment*, edited by Donald C. Mell, Theodore E. D. Braun, and Lucia M. Palmer. East Lansing, Mich.: Colleagues Press, 1988. Blaydes demonstrates how Cavendish went against the grain of male Enlightenment philosophy and established her own view of nature as a female. Contains a useful index and a bibliography.

Grant, Douglas. *Margaret the First: A Biography of Margaret Cavendish, Duchess of Newcastle, 1623-1673*. London: Hart-Davis, 1957. Still perhaps the best biography of Margaret Cavendish. Grant includes illustrations and a bibliography of the duchess's literary works.

Mendelson, Sarah Heller. *The Mental World of Stuart Women: Three Studies*. Amherst: University of Massachusetts Press, 1987. Mendelson discusses how seventeenth century society and customs in England affected the lives of three women: Aphra Behn, Mary Rich, Countess of Warwick, and Margaret Cavendish, duchess of Newcastle. Bibliography, index.

Paloma, Dolores. "Margaret Cavendish: Defining the Female Self." *Women's Studies* 7 (1980): 55-66. Paloma describes how Cavendish was one of the first women to write poetry, philosophy, and plays as freely as men did. Yet, in order to avoid serious censure, she had to work under the conceit that she was not a serious writer.

Perry, Henry Ten Eyck. *The First Duchess of Newcastle and Her Husband as Figures in Literary History*. Boston: Ginn, 1918. Perry's early study was reprinted in the late 1960's. It is a useful work that shows how, although the duchess and her husband pretended to be amateurs writing inconsequential verses, they deserve a place in the canon of important British poets.

Jay A. Gertzman;
bibliography updated by the editors

LORINE NIEDECKER

Born: Near Fort Atkinson, Wisconsin; May 12, 1903
Died: Near Fort Atkinson, Wisconsin; December 31, 1970

PRINCIPAL POETRY

New Goose, 1946
My Friend Tree, 1962
North Central, 1968
T&G: The Collected Poems, 1936-1966, 1968
My Life by Water: Collected Poems, 1936-1968, 1970 (enlargement of *T&G*)
Blue Chicory, 1976
The Granite Pail: The Selected Poems of Lorine Niedecker, 1985
From This Condensery: The Complete Writing of Lorine Niedecker, 1985
Harpischord and Salt Fish, 1991 (Jenny Penberthy, editor)

OTHER LITERARY FORMS

Although known primarily for her poetry, Lorine Niedecker also wrote radio plays, creative prose, and reviews. "As I Lay Dying" condenses and adapts William Faulkner's novel of the same title, and "Taste and Tenderness" centers on William, Henry, and Alice James. "Uncle," "Untitled," and "Switchboard Girl," local-color sketches, provide insight into Niedecker's family background, work experiences, and philosophy, and her reviews of the poetry of Louis Zukofsky and Cid Corman reveal Niedecker's poetics. Of her letters, which Zukofsky early praised as her best writing, her ten-year correspondence with Corman has been published, and her thirty-year correspondence with Zukofsky rests at the Humanities Research Center at the University of Texas, Austin.

ACHIEVEMENTS

Lorine Niedecker has proved that a twentieth century American writer does not have to travel far or have exotic experiences to be able to present her culture objectively and honestly. Although in her poetry, spring floods buckle her floors and breed water bugs under her hooked rugs, the waters also reminded her of life's constant flux and helped her avoid becoming static and rootbound. Relying primarily on the past, nature, and long-distance support from a few fellow poets, she overcame the fragmentation and materialism of which so many twentieth century artists complain and to which they often succumb. Sincerity, hard work, and isolation from fame have helped earn for her a reputation as the twentieth century's Emily Dickinson. In 1978, her home state recognized her achievements by awarding her the Notable Wisconsin Writers Award.

BIOGRAPHY

Born on May 12, 1903, on Blackhawk Island, near the Rock River and Lake Koshkonong, three miles from Fort Atkinson, Wisconsin, Lorine Niedecker, the only child of commercial fisherman Henry E. Niedecker and his swamp-bound housewife Theresa Daisy Kunz Niedecker, never grew far from her roots. Lorine Niedecker was educated in Fort Atkinson and Beloit, where she went to Beloit College to study literature from 1922 until 1924. Returning home because her mother was becoming increasingly deaf, Niedecker married Frank Hartwig in 1928, but the couple separated in 1930 when Hartwig defaulted on a loan and lost their house. Nie-

decker assisted in the Dwight Foster Public Library during this period. From 1928 until 1942, she worked in Madison for the Works Progress Administration's state guide as a writer and research editor, exploring the early history of her region. She began writing radio plays during the 1930's, her interest leading her in 1942 to a brief job as scriptwriter at station WHA in Madison. She returned that year to Blackhawk Island and in 1944 began work as a stenographer and proofreader at Hoard's Dairyman, publishers of a national journal, remaining there until 1950. Her mother, completely deaf, died in 1951, and her father, in 1954. Niedecker inherited two houses on Blackhawk Island and spent some time overseeing her property while living in a small cabin nearby, which she had built in 1947; then she scrubbed floors and cleaned the kitchen at the Fort Atkinson Memorial Hospital from 1957 until 1962. In mid-1960, she started keeping company with Harold Hein, a widowed dentist and amateur artist who spent his Christmas holidays in Florida and did not want to remarry. The couple spent most of their weekends together, driving north to Manitowish Waters in June, 1961, and reading together the Thomas Jefferson-John Adams correspondence. One of Niedecker's most valued gifts from Hein was a bird feeder, which attracted so many birds that the poet said she would have to hire a bird-sitter to keep it full of seeds while she was at work. During the fall of 1962, Hein visited Niedecker less often, and in spring, 1963, she met Albert Millen, a house painter from Milwaukee, to whom she was married on May 24, 1963, and with whom she moved to a run-down part of that city. When her husband retired, they built a two-and-a-half-room cabin on Blackhawk Island and spent most of their time there, although they traveled briefly to South Dakota and around Lake Superior. Niedecker died on December 31, 1970, where she was born.

Niedecker began writing early but published little until late in life. She mentions an ode to Lake Koshkonong written in high school, and her first published poem appeared in her high school annual, *The Tchogeerah*, in 1922. Her poems were printed in literary journals in 1928, and in 1933 several appeared in *Poetry*. In the early 1930's, she initiated correspondence with Louis Zukofsky, who would become one of her mentors and friends. She exchanged visits and gifts with the Zukofsky family and from Louis she learned about condensation, reliance on folk dialogue, rejection slips, and publication procedures. Her first book eventually appeared in 1946. In 1960, she began to correspond with Cid Corman, who published many of her poems in his influential magazine *Origin* and who recorded her only known poetry reading a few weeks before she died. In the late 1950's and into the 1960's, she wrote many poems to Zukofsky's violinist son, Paul, and finally, in the late 1960's, when she published three volumes of poetry, she began to be recognized by a wide audience. She left three finished manuscripts, which were included in her complete writings in 1985. All of her poems, most brief and many untitled, have been arranged chronologically in *From This Condensery* and divided into seven major sections: "Early Poems," "For Paul and Other Poems," "The Years Go By," "In Exchange for Haiku," "Home/ World," "North Central," and "Harpsichord and Salt Fish."

ANALYSIS

In her review of the poetry of Louis Zukofsky, Lorine Niedecker quotes William Carlos Williams: "You cannot express anything unless you invent how to express it. A poem is not a Freudian 'escape' (what childishness) but an adult release to knowledge, in the most practical, engineering manner." Niedecker used her poetry to invent herself, to discover her own wholeness. This quest for wholeness has been a persistent theme in the writing of American women since the time of Margaret Fuller. A glass cutter of words, Niedecker discards traditional poetic modes of expression *en masse*, yet selects those devices which best help her construct small stained-glass pieces, later combining some of these reflective objects into longer poems. She trims her glasslike achievements often, arranges them variously, and finally creates two outstanding large pieces: "Wintergreen Ridge" and "Paean to Place." Niedecker appropriates glass of many colors from several sources: the men and women whom she knew and read about, American society during her lifetime, nature, and art.

NIEDECKER'S FATHER

Of the men and women whom she knew, her father and mother engaged her most fully. In her early poems,

she depicts her father building and losing houses, rocking in his chair, seining to finance his daughter's education, and wondering about the meaning of life. In "For Paul," she recalls her father's description of a warm Thanksgiving Day when he helped seine twenty thousand pounds of buffalo fish by moonlight. Other times, his "hands glazed/ to the nets." In "The Years Go By," she recalls "mild Henry" as "absent" and describes him as a catalpa tree, serene, refusing "to see/ that the other woman, the hummer he shaded/ hotly cared/ for his purse petals falling—/ his mind in the air." Niedecker also pictures her father planting trees and burying "carp/ beneath the rose" after he lost his wife. She continues that "he opened his wine tank" to "bankers on high land," wanted "his only daughter/ to work in the bank" but had left her a "source/ to sustain her—/ a weedy speech." In "North Central," she again writes of the trees her father planted, "evenly following/ the road." She walks beside them on New Year's Day and each one speaks to her: "Peace." Niedecker's father learned the "coiled celery," "duckweed," and "pickerelweeds" of the swamp but "could not/ —like water bugs—/ stride surface tension/ He netted/ loneliness." He sat rocking at night "beside his shoes," "Roped not 'looped/ in the loop/ of her hair." Hard work, serenity, unhappiness in marriage, planting, swamp, rocking: These scattered details kaleidoscope into Niedecker's benediction for her father: Peace.

NIEDECKER'S MOTHER

Niedecker has more trouble coming to terms with her mother. The annual spring floods soak the floors, pump, washing machine, and lilacs of "the woman moored to this low shore by deafness," who has wasted her life in water. Niedecker's deaf mother contradicts herself, wishing she could hear, then complaining about "too much talk in the world." With "big blind ears" under "high" hair, a husband with "leaky boats," a writer daughter who "sits and floats," Niedecker's mother dies with "a thimble in her purse," her last words urging her daughter, "Wash the floors, Lorine!/ Wash clothes! Weed!" Daisy Niedecker parks uncharacteristically in "her burnished brown motorless automobile," "She who wheeled dirt for flowers" waiting to be buried in ground in which "She could have grown a good rutabaga." Daisy grew up in marsh land, Niedecker later explains, "married mild Henry/ and then her life was sand." Daisy, tall and thin, "took cold on her nerves," built the fires with the wood she chopped, helped rebuild a burned house, gave "boat" instead of birth to her daughter in the flooding spring, and philosophized: "Hatch, patch and scratch,/ that's all a woman's for/ but I didn't sink, I sewed and saved/ and now I'm on second floor."

Snow on branches later reminds Niedecker of the cotton that her mother "wore in her aching ears," her hard work, and her protectiveness. She calls her mother a "distrait wife," a "thorn apple bush,/ armed against life's raw push." Niedecker tells Kenneth Cox, however, that her mother had a "rhyming, happy" father and spoke "whole chunks of down-to-earth (o very earthy) magic." In "Wintergreen Ridge," which she considers her best poem, Niedecker remembers how her mother loved "closed gentians/ she herself/ so closed" and identifies with her in "Paean to Place," saying they both were born "in swale and swamp and sworn/ to water." A wealth of autobiographical material follows. Her father "sculled down" and saw her mother, who was playing the organ but who later stopped, turned "deaf/ and away." Daisy "knew boats/ and ropes," helped Henry "string out nets/ for tarring," and "could shoot." Niedecker mourns the fact that her mother could not hear canvasbacks take off and sora rails sing, and she wonders if she giggled when she was a girl. Her question underscores the somber light in which she sees her mother, the assonating *o*'s in "the woman moored to this low shore," and the following poem sustaining this sober mood:

> Hear
> where her snow-grave is
> the *You*
>   *ah you*
> of mourning doves

Her father, from upcountry, contemplating the stars, drawing fish from water, plants from land, rocking, lonely, wants his daughter to move to high ground. Her mother, from the swamp, enduring floods, protecting her family, closing gradually into total silence, ridicules her husband's "bright new car," declaring, "A hummingbird/ can't haul." Niedecker alternates between swamp and upland, but resides primarily in the former.

From this fragmented relationship, Niedecker must wrest her wholeness, which she does partly by observing other men and women from the present and the past. Her early poems depict her male contemporaries as J. Alfred Prufrock-like: posturing, ineffectual, directionless, out of touch with reality. Some play cards instead of chopping wood; one "strolls pale among zinnias." She later describes a prospective employer as "Keen and lovely," graceful, cultured, kind, but he does not hire her. She mentions the men who carefully build weapons to irradiate others; businessmen smoking cigarettes, leaving droppings/ larger, whiter than owls'," wearing time on their wrists, wool on their bodies, making money unscrupulously and demanding to be "jazzed" for which they pay in "nylons." She dislikes a "clean man," prefers one who falls while fishing in muddy water, "dries his last pay-check/ in the sun, smooths it out/ in *Leaves of Grass*." Niedecker mentions few modern examples of complete men.

GREAT MEN OF HISTORY

In the past she finds many men whom she admires: John James Audubon, Michel-Guillaume-Jean de Crève-coeur, Thomas Jefferson, John Adams, Michelangelo, William Morris, Charles Darwin, Carolus Linnaeus, Vincent van Gogh. Men who value the earth, the arts, solitude, exploration, plants, creation, equality, and humanity appeal to her. Poems on great men are sprinkled through her writing, ranging from an early short poem written from van Gogh's point of view to a long, late poem on Darwin. She compares Aeneas and Frédéric Chopin, observing that Aeneas "closed his piano/ to dig a well thru hard clay," whereas "Chopin left notes like drops of water." She ends this brief poem with Aeneas's words to Chopin: "O Frederic, think of me digging below/ the surface—we are of one pitch and flow." The high/low dichotomy which separated her parents is erased by these great men, who cooperate to bring harmony to the world. The examples supplied by great men also help Niedecker choose a partner from among her contemporaries, a man she chooses for "warmth."

Lacking models of great women from both present and past, Niedecker must create herself from within. She first deals with the female models which surround her. In her early poetry, she ridicules a lady wearing a leopard coat for being directionless and scorns women who demand only money from men and become slaves to fashion. She describes a woman who "hooks men like rugs," "covets the gold in her husband's teeth," and would "sell your eyes fried in deep grief." She rhymingly itemizes the "needs" of women: "washers and dryers, . . . bodice uplift, . . . deep-well cookers, . . . power shift." She describes an office girl who "carries her nylon hard-pointed/ breast uplift/ like parachutes/ half-pulled" which "collapse" at night among all of her material possessions.

GREAT WOMEN OF HISTORY

In contrast, she mentions in later poems famous women of the past. "Who was Mary Shelley?" she asks, who eloped, wrote her novel after Lord Byron and Percy Bysshe Shelley "talked the candle down," read Greek, Italian, and bore two children who died. Margaret Fuller "carried books/ and chrysanthemums/ to Boston/ into a cold storm." Abigail Smith, who according to her suitor John Adams had faults, such as hanging her head, reading, writing, thinking, and crossing her "Leggs/ while sitting," proved to be a faithful wife. Niedecker later writes that Abigail was an architect and artist, made cheese and raised chickens, talked as an equal with Jefferson, and wrote letters that both Adams and Jefferson appreciated.

In her early poems, Niedecker writes of refusing to admit excitement or pain, the former inconvenient and the latter too great. Writing to Zukofsky's son Paul, she tells how her feelings for the boy enable her to love more fully, and in "The Years Go By," she discusses, in a manner similar to Emily Dickinson's, the ebb and flow of sorrow. The central change in a woman's life, menopause, she describes as "hot fears" in "middle life" but says in "cool years . . . who'll remember/ flash to black?/ I gleamed?" Then she begins to look back at herself, examining a photograph and remembering her "young aloofness," her wish to stay "cool," the fact that she "couldn't bake." She also begins to express her discontent with her "black office," looking forward to her "three/ days of light: Saturday, Sunday,/ memory." In "Home/World," she says her life is "a wave-blurred/ portrait" and depicts herself as a "swamp/ as against a large pine-spread—." She becomes self-conscious: Out of ten thousand women dancing on skates, she is the only one who wears boots, she remarks. Much earlier she had praised the energy of women who could work, keep a house and children, go to church, and bowl, wondering what they would think if they knew how much energy she spent on her poetry. At the time of her marriage, she visits her family cemetery, recognizing and accepting that her family line ends with her: "but sonless/ see no/ hop/ clover boy to stop/ before me." The assonating *o*'s, which she reserves for special occasions, underscore the momentous solemnity of her recognition, the rhyming *e*'s focusing attention on her as an individual. Now she can speak of the peace her father's trees bring her and compare love to a leaf, all parts relating.

"PAEAN TO PLACE"

In "Paean to Place," about which she expressed excitement to Kenneth Cox in 1969 and stated that his questions about her background inspired the poem, she traces her life: a "solitary plover," a seven-year-old with only two dresses, a visitor to the grave of her grandfather who delighted her with folk and nursery rhymes. She recalls her love for the boy who played the violin and says,

> O my floating life
> Do not save love
> > for things
> > > Throw *things*
> > to the flood

She ends "Paean to Place" by describing the "sloughs and sluices" of her mind "with the persons/ on the edge."

She also felt herself to be part of American society. She expressed her concern for the social ills of her day repeatedly, discussing such topics as poverty, hunger, religion, electricity, consumerism, traffic speeding, commercialism, hunting, plumbing, private property, war, and the atom bomb. She opposed most modern conveniences and luxuries, pleased most with her "New-saved/clean-smelling house/ sweet cedar pink/ flesh tint" with a "Popcorn-can cover" over a hole in her wall "so the cold/ can't mouse in." She often describes *things* in terms of people and animals, maybe trying to lessen their otherness, and enjoyed such creative activities as hooking rugs, quilting, sewing, and cooking. She stresses that becoming involved with the material world leads one to wake up at night and say to oneself,

I'm pillowed and padded, pale and puffing
lifting household stuffing—
carpets, dishes
benches, fishes
I've spent my life in nothing.

NATURE

Rejecting materialism and those elements of society which thrive on it, Niedecker is especially appalled at people's desecration of nature. The "ten dead ducks' feathers/ on beer-can litter" will be covered by snow, but when man exterminated the carrier pigeon without cause, he destroyed "cobalt/ and carnelian." One of her most vehement protests involves the quiet muskrat who swims "as if already/ a woman's neck-piece." A second stanza juxtaposes the image of "Nazi wildmen/ wearing women."

Most of her nature poetry, however, exudes harmony and peace. She writes of wild swans, sandhill cranes, pheasants, pink flamingos, curlews, canvas-backs, mergansers, and warblers. Willows and poplars, cherry trees and maples, pines and catalpas dot her work. Flowers from the wild sunflower to the blue chicory to water lilies blossom, and she notes that "men are plants whose goodness grows/ out of the soil." She is especially attuned to the seasons. In winter, she watches chunks of ice swim swanlike down the river and in March notices her

> Bird feeder's
> snow-cap
> sliding
> off

April brings "little/ yellows" and frogs rattling in contrast to freight trains, whereas June is hot and sticky, "a lush/ Marshmushing, frog bickering/ moon pooling, green gripping." Waxwings stain berry branches red in July, while autumn nights force her to pull her curtains because the leaves have fallen, reminding Niedecker of tree toads and her starlight talks with a boy. October she considers to be the head of spring, which is in turn the body of the year. She notices small creatures: mites in rabbits' ears, dragonflies, gophers, crickets, and frogs which stop sounding because they have turned out their lights. Only occasionally does nature frighten her, as when she hears a muskrat eat frogs and mice outside her

door and when she describes a late fall weed stalk as a rapist. Generally, Niedecker presents nature as a cherished friend and often uses nature images to describe people. She also talks of multistratified rocks, lichens which can pulverize granite, and mosses and horsetails which outlived dinosaurs. People are composed of and interrelated with nature. The water lily exemplifies perfect order. In her longest poem, "Wintergreen Ridge," she calls wintergreen by its Indian name, pipsissewa, which literally means "breaks it into fragments." In no other part of life does Niedecker see the absence of fragments as in nature. Parts combine to make a whole, and her immersion in nature, evident throughout her poetry but especially in "Wintergreen Ridge" and "Paean to Place," helps her to recognize and to remember her own wholeness. As she wrote to Corman in 1969, "the lines of natural growth, of life, [were] unconsciously absorbed from foliage and flowers while growing up."

Niedecker drew on the life which surrounded her for her poetry, transforming life into art by filling her subconscious, leaving herself alone, then pulling out material for her poetry. The "lava" flowed only while she wrote; then came the discipline of forming and polishing her words. Her first collected poems show her awareness of the way her contemporaries have debased language, have defied slang and narrowed their vocabularies. She early recognizes her affinity for imagism and philosophy, describes her poetic inspiration rising like feathers and gas, and realizes that wealth for her is staying in one place and writing. She mentions several poets who have influenced her, showing what type of bird she would be if depicted by H. D., William Carlos Williams, Marianne Moore, Wallace Stevens, Louis Zukofsky, E. E. Cummings, and Charles Reznikoff. Bashō and Gerard Manley Hopkins also helped form her poetry. Intellectual influences include Plato, Marcus Aurelius, Gottfried Wilhelm Leibnitz, Emanuel Swedenborg, Ralph Waldo Emerson, and Henry David Thoreau. From these thinkers, she distilled mental rigor and a belief in the soul.

Niedecker, who created her poems from familiar people and surroundings, commented that she did not want her neighbors to know she wrote because she would lose some of her finest sources of language. She used both traditional and contemporary poetic devices to shape her work: rhyme of all types, varying rhythms, alliteration, assonance, consonance, juxtaposition. She experimented with both line and stanza length, revising, arranging, and rearranging her poems into different sequences. She took seriously her mother's final words to wash, scrub, and weed, and did just that to her poems, polishing them until they gleamed with meaning and clarity, compressing them until they yielded their intrinsic forms. Her work is alive because she grounded it thoroughly in life and because she encouraged it to grow and change as she did. Filled with fragments and whole poems, the work of Lorine Niedecker reminds one that wholeness is possible even amid a chaotic world.

OTHER MAJOR WORKS

NONFICTION: *Between Your House and Mine: The Letters of Lorine Niedecker to Cid Corman, 1960-1970*, 1986.

BIBLIOGRAPHY

Bertholf, Robert. "Lorine Niedecker: A Portrait of a Poet." *Parnassus: Poetry in Review* 12/13 (Winter/Spring, 1985): 227-235. Probably the best complete biographical sketch of Niedecker. Bertholf clearly places her in the context of the Objectivist poetry movement. Suitable for undergraduates as well as graduate students.

Crase, Douglas. "On Lorine Niedecker." *Raritan* 12, no. 2 (Fall, 1992): 47. As an appraisal of the commonwealth, Lorine Niedecker's poem "Lake Superior" extends a tradition that seems particularly American. The autobiographical elements of the poem are discussed.

Faranda, Lisa Pater, ed. *Between Your House and Mine: The Letters of Lorine Niedecker to Cid Corman, 1960-1970*. Durham, N.C.: Duke University Press, 1986. Faranda presents the letters written between Niedecker and poet Cid Corman, her literary executor. Provides insight into her literary acquaintances and her poetic influences. Includes index and bibliography.

Heller, Michael. *Conviction's Net of Branches: Essays on the Objectivist Poets and Poetry*. Carbondale: Southern Illinois University Press, 1985. Niedecker is considered an Objectivist poet. These essays shed light on the nature and convictions of the Objecti-

vists. Suitable for advanced undergraduate and graduate poetry students.

Middleton, Peter. "Folk Poetry and the American Avant-Garde: Placing Lorine Niedecker." *Journal of American Studies* 31 (August, 1997): 203-218. Suggests ordinary cultural acts of displacement are taken for granted by most writers and readers and describes how, for Niedecker, they represented highly conscious acts alien to her everyday world.

Penberthy, Jenny. *Niedecker and the Correspondence with Zukofsky, 1931-1970*. New York: Cambridge University Press, 1993. Explores the forty-year correspondence between Niedecker and Louis Zukofsky, which proved a collaborative enterprise of emotional and artistic significance for both. Reconstructs Niedecker's early years as a poet, looking at the influence of Surrealism on her work, and traces Zukofsky's impact on her work and her struggle for recognition. Includes bibliography and index.

_____, ed. *Lorine Niedecker: Woman and Poet*. Orono, Maine: National Poetry Foundation, 1996. Presents a collection of essays that greatly expands our understanding of Niedecker's reclusive life and her body of poetry that was largely neglected during her lifetime. Includes bibliography and index.

Perloff, Marjorie. "Recharging the Canon: Some Reflections on Feminist Poetics and the Avant-Garde." *American Poetry Review* 15 (July/August, 1986): 12-20. Perloff discusses how Niedecker and other women poets, such as Susan Howe, operate in the male-dominated world of poetry. She points out that Niedecker was the only woman in the Objectivist movement. As a result, she is rejected by the male poetry "establishment," yet, she is dismissed by feminists as "a male-identified woman poet."

Shelley Thrasher;
bibliography updated by the editors

JOHN FREDERICK NIMS

Born: Muskegon, Michigan; November 20, 1913
Died: Chicago, Illinois; January 19, 1999

PRINCIPAL POETRY

The Iron Pastoral, 1947

A Fountain in Kentucky and Other Poems, 1950

Knowledge of the Evening: Poems, 1950-1960, 1960

Of Flesh and Bone, 1967

Selected Poems, 1982

The Kiss: A Jambalaya, 1982

The Six-Cornered Snowflake and Other Poems, 1990

Zany in Denim, 1990

OTHER LITERARY FORMS

A distinguished translator, John Frederick Nims was most acclaimed for *The Poems of St. John of the Cross* (1959, revised 1968, 1979). He translated Euripides' *Andromache* for a volume in *The Complete Greek Tragedies* published by the University of Chicago Press (1959) and published a book of his translations from various languages, *Sappho to Valéry: Poems in Translation* (1971, revised 1979, 1990). His translations of *The Complete Poems of Michelangelo* appeared in 1998. Nims also edited a number of books, including *The Poem Itself* (with Stanley Burnshaw and others, 1960), *Ovid's Metamorphoses: The Arthur Golding Translation, 1567* (1965), and *James Shirley's "Love's Cruelty"* (1980). In 1974, he put his experience as poet, translator, and teacher to work in *Western Wind: An Introduction to Poetry*. Many of Nims's essays on poetry and translation have been collected in *A Local Habitation: Essays on Poetry* (1985).

ACHIEVEMENTS

John Frederick Nims made an important contribution to American letters through his multiple vocations as translator, critic, editor, and teacher, as well as poet. He deserves special praise for his translations, which are consistently remarkable for their sensitivity to the sound, form, and feeling of the originals. There is no way, of course, to measure his achievements as editor, scholar, and teacher, but it is safe to say that he brought the same care and hard work to these tasks as he did to his poems. He received a number of awards for his work, including the Harriet Monroe Memorial Prize (1942), the Guarantors' Prize (1943), and the Levinson Prize (1944), all from *Poetry* magazine; in 1974, he

received the Brandeis University Creative Arts Award; and in 1978, he was chosen Phi Beta Kappa Poet at Harvard University. Nims was also the recipient of grants and fellowships from the Fulbright Foundation (1952-1953), from the National Foundation for the Arts and Humanities (1967), from the Academy of Poets (1982), from the Institute of the Humanities at the University of Illinois (1983), and from the Guggenheim Foundation (1986). His poetry collection *Knowledge of the Evening* was nominated for a National Book Award. In 1991 he received the ten-thousand-dollar Aiken Taylor Award for Modern American Poetry, bestowed by the editors of *The Sewanee Review*, and in 1993 received the O. B. Hardison, Jr., Poetry Prize, awarded by the Folger Shakespeare Library.

His honors and awards aside, Nims was probably undervalued as a poet. If that is true, however, he was undervalued for the right reasons. For many years he labored against the grain of contemporary American poetry. His classic lyricism no doubt failed to move a good number of readers whose expectations of poetry were shaped largely by poets seeking to break with the traditions Nims cherished. His stature as a poet, then, must be measured more within the context and conventions of his own poems than by comparison with other poets, or in terms of the size of his audience. As Nims said,

> It would be comfortable to have a large audience, honestly won. But it would be shameful for the writer to say anything less well than he knows how simply to gain more readers. Any [established poet] could write something that would bring him a hundred readers for every one he has now. This would be a failure.

Nims may not have received the degree of recognition given to some of his contemporaries, but one thing is clear: His place in American poetry was "honestly won," and no poet can claim more than that.

BIOGRAPHY

Born in Muskegon, Michigan, John Frederick Nims attended a private high school in Chicago and spent two years at De Paul University before transferring to Notre Dame to take his bachelor of arts degree, with a double major in English and Latin, in 1937. After taking his master of arts degree from Notre Dame in 1939, he taught there until 1958, with periodic excursions abroad to teach at the University of Toronto (1945-1946), at Bocconi University in Milan (1952-1953), and at the University of Florence (1953-1954). While at Notre Dame, he did postgraduate work at the University of Chicago, and in 1945 he earned his Ph.D. in comparative literature, with an emphasis on the history and theory of Greek, Latin, French, and English tragedy; his special interest was the English stage of the sixteenth and seventeenth centuries.

After leaving Notre Dame, he taught at the University of Madrid (1958-1960), at Harvard University (1964, 1968-1969, and the summer of 1974), at the University of Illinois at Urbana (1961-1965), at the University of Florida at Gainesville (1973-1977), at Williams College (1975), and at the College of Charleston (1981). He taught, as well, at the Bread Loaf Writers' Conference (1958-1971) and at the Bread Loaf School of English (1965-1969). In 1945 he began a long association with the distinguished magazine *Poetry*, serving for some years as the magazine's principal editor. From 1965 until his retirement, between wanderings, he taught English at the University of Illinois at Chicago Circle as well. His renown as a scholar and a poet made his services as a judge of others' works desirable, and he served in that capacity for the National Book Awards (1969), the American Book Awards (1970, 1971), and the coveted Bollingen Prize (1987). He died in 1999, survived by his wife, a son, and two daughters. A few weeks before, he had sent to his editors revisions for a fourth edition of his acclaimed introduction to poetry, *Western Wind*.

Nims's formidable academic credentials might suggest a poet literary to the point of pedantry, but literary expertise and scholarship are only a part of the equipment that Nims brought to his poetry. In a review of Nims's second collection, *A Fountain in Kentucky*, Richard Wilbur described the "I" in Nims's poetry as "no disembodied spirit" and surely no celebrant of the erudite and esoteric. On the contrary, says Wilbur, his

> adventures are not extraordinary, and he lays claim to no out-of-the-way emotions. . . . He is a family man, and owns a cat and a dog. . . . Few poets so frankly ex-

ploit their day-by-day experiences. Few poets so cheerfully present us with a world so thoroughly mundane.

Wilbur's sketch is a good likeness of Nims the poet, husband, scholar, and father. Nims's poems make it plain that Bonnie Larkin, his wife of thirty-five years, and their five children were as much a source of inspiration as any of the considerable number of great authors in whose work he was so well-versed. When, in "Love Poem," he pays playful tribute to "My clumsiest dear, whose hands shipwreck vases,/ At whose quick touch all glasses chip and ring," he addresses no Helen, but a flesh-and-blood woman. When, in "The Masque of Blackness," Nims deals with the untimely death of a child, the death of his own son George is a haunting presence between the lines. In joy or sorrow, the sensitive father, the grateful husband, the wry and unpretentious teacher in Nims's poetry is, more often than not, Nims himself, trying to give words to that life—sweet, bitter, and salty—that he shared with his family, his students, and his readers.

ANALYSIS

"A poem," said John Frederick Nims (with help from Dylan Thomas), "should sing in its chains like the sea!" In an age that has witnessed a broadly based rejection of the apparent restrictions of traditional poetic forms and conventions, Nims made a career of "singing in his chains," of asserting that a poet can be both traditional and contemporary and that modern experience can find expression within the conventions of the past.

In a preface to his first published collection of poems in the 1944 anthology *Five Young American Poets*, Nims laid down some rules for himself. The poem, he insists, is "no mere meringue of sentiment. The emotion it holds is like blood in a man's body, hot and throbbing throughout, but fastened in tight channels, never seen." Imagery should be "sudden, true, and daring," diction "simple and intense," making use of whatever word best serves the poem, be it "from cathedral service or tavern riot." As to structure, the poem requires something "Mozartean . . . something stronger and shapelier than the Debussy tinkle and Wagnerian yowl to which the freer forms of poetry incline." Overseeing the whole delightful, demanding procedure is "a prodding 'Why?' . . . the poet's angel."

THE IRON PASTORAL

A survey of Nims's long career reveals these rules consistently at work; and in all that time, that same angel of wonder has never left his side. His first book-length collection proclaimed something of his intentions in its very title, *The Iron Pastoral*—a dull gleam of a word, suggestive of hardness and of subways, beside a graceful, comfortable word, evocative of ordered wilderness, of forest and field a bit greener than life. The book provides ample introduction to Nims's skill at ordering contemporary experience within traditional forms. In "Movie," the neon marquees of movie theaters blink on in iambic pentameter:

> Making a stately crossword of the night
> New stars are rising, *Gem* and *Regent*. Soon
> Great *Tivoli* takes the heaven, rose and white,
> Blanching Orion and the dappled moon.

In "Elevated," commuter trains run "Among the badland brick, the domes of tar,/ The mica prairie wheeling in the sun," gondolas in a town that "three stories up . . . is Venice," where "Flowers of the wash in highland vineyards shine." There is something at first a bit unsettling in hearing heroic quatrains and alexandrines singing in this context, something a little startling in the final image of "Colt Automatic": "at the belt a rare and terrible angel." Once one realizes, however, that William Shakespeare and John Milton would, no doubt, have gotten around to "crossword" and "quarterback," "fluoroscope" and "Florida," had they lived on a few centuries more, one can delight in Nims's rare devices.

It is no surprise that the sonnet has not escaped Nims's attention in *The Iron Pastoral*. In fact, he includes a brief sonnet sequence titled "Foto-Sonnets." Once again, Nims's title earns its keep: "Sonnet"— the verbal "snapshot" of another age, wed to a coy misspelling typical in a city of "ALL-NITE" diners and "WILE-U-WAIT" oil changes. In a skillful blend of Shakespeare, Petrarch, and Nims, these sonnets, like pictures in an album, preserve moments from a summer vacation in New England, mementos of Provincetown, of Cape Cod, and finally, of the return to the city, the tired travelers "wrapped in tatters of salt memory." There is a density to the poems of *The Iron Pastoral*, a weight of words that, at times, overburdens the

line, squeezing out articles in the bargain. More often than not, though, rereading reveals a richness that, at first reading, the eye might have taken for overindulgence and a careful flexing of the meter that first struck the ear as strain.

A FOUNTAIN IN KENTUCKY

In his next book, *A Fountain in Kentucky*, Nims worked further with the sonnet sequence. The result, "The Masque of Blackness," is one of his finest and most admired poems. Taking as its controlling metaphor the Shakespearean adage that "all the world's a stage," this narrative sequence of ten sonnets deals with the birth, brief life, and death of a child, as experienced by his parents. As the story unfolds, "in very dead of winter:/ A rumor of new breathing by late spring" places the parents in a world suddenly unreal, "since not yet real to the child," a world in which "Whether they shifted vases, turned a page/ All seemed last-minute touches on a stage." The child is born to the exultant cry, "Up with the drowsy curtain"; but the exultation is short-lived. This play, for all its glad beginnings, unfolds as tragedy. "One day they learned that sorrow wore old tweed,/ That lounging disaster spoke a soft hello." The doctors are all polite pessimism; it is their role. The mother must play hers as well, "her tight fingers round a rubber lamb/ She brought to show them all: See he can play." Perhaps the most poignant sonnet in the sequence is the eighth:

> Because someone was gone, they bought a dog,
> A collie pup, black, orange, flashy white.
> He gnawed on table legs, troubled the rug;
> His growls and pokings varied the empty night.

The sadness here is not so much in the new pet's inadequacy to the task of filling the void left in the bereaved couple's life, as in their awareness of that inadequacy. What could this creature do "in that house, with that shadow there?/ Oh nothing. They knew that." By the end of the elegy, they have learned hard lessons about this play, this life, and learned "from many-roped backstage." They have been no mere observers, however much they may wish they had been no more than that.

Throughout, "The Masque of Blackness" is marked by intensity, quantitative keenness of rhythm, and an effective use of momentum and pause within and between the lines. Like many of Nims's poems, it is preceded by an epigraph. Nims is accused by some critics of being too scholarly, too literary, in his poems, and this particular epigraph, an unidentified quotation from the opening stage directions of one of Ben Jonson's masques, may seem to support such an accusation. There is, upon further reflection, another way to look at the matter. "The Masque of Blackness" works extremely well for what it sets out to be—an elegy. There is, at times, a surreal, at times a mundane rightness to the imagery, and a psychological truth to the narrative, that are accessible to the average reader. The poem is moving in itself, although that is not to say that additional information might not make its effect still sharper. The epigraph is from Jonson's *Oberon, the Fairy Prince* (1611) an entertainment written to commemorate the installation as Prince of Wales of young Prince Henry, son of James I and Queen Anne. The prince himself appeared in the masque as a silent, unsmiling figure, "Oberon, the Faery Prince." The other masquers, in dance, poetry, and song, celebrate the virtues of this king-to-be. Less than two years later, the prince was dead of typhoid. A child is thus the central character in a play in which he has no lines; suddenly it is plain why Nims chose this particular epigraph. What may have seemed a mere literary ornament actually contributes to the emotional impact of the poem.

Further, Prince Henry, an intelligent lad, was a special favorite of Jonson, and the poet took some responsibility for the boy's literary education. Could this relationship have failed to remind Jonson of the death a few years earlier of his own eldest son? Taken in retrospect, the words from Jonson's elegy on his son, "Farewell, thou child of my right hand, and joy;/ My sinne was too much hope of thee, lov'd boy," are a haunting presence in the masque of *Oberon*, and, by extension, in Nims's "Masque of Blackness." If the reader learns that Nims wrote his sonnet sequence soon after the death of his own infant son, the poem's effect is only further heightened. To be able to place his own experience into a sort of constellation of reference with the death of a prince and a seventeenth century father's grief over his lost son, and to do it with skill and tact, redeems Nims from any charges of pedantry or inaccessibility.

KNOWLEDGE OF THE EVENING

In Nims's *Knowledge of the Evening*, there are poems of Europe and the Old World, steeped in history: "Florence," "Reflections in Venice," "Catullus," "A Frieze of Cupids." Nims, however, is less concerned with writing a poetic travelogue than he is with making the point, so aptly put by John Ciardi, that "Pompeii is everybody's home town, sooner or later." One lives with the past, whether or not one wants to, whether or not one knows it. Those who built the rooms in Nims's "Etruscan Tomb" knew it, back "when tombs were salons for living!/ Nothing had ended, that was sure." The bright paintings on the tomb walls, the rich furnishings, the "chuckle of jugs" and "crooning copper," are celebrated in the poem's refrain: "Oh alive and alive." The presence of the past is a theme that runs through much of Nims's work; it receives special emphasis in *Knowledge of the Evening*.

OF FLESH AND BONE

Of Flesh and Bone presents Nims at work with a fine, witty chisel, at the neglected art of the epigram. These poems, over sixty in all, are a tribute to his sense of classic brevity and concision, but, perhaps more important, they are also a tribute to his wry sense of humor. In a poem that must have given him considerable satisfaction, he answers the more iconoclastic members of the "Avant-Garde":

> "A dead tradition! Hollow shell!
> Outworn, outmoded—time it fell.
> Let's make it new. Rebel! Rebel!"
> Said cancer-cell to cancer-cell.

The "Philosopher," lost in hypothesis, comes in for some jibes: "He scowled at the barometer: 'Will it rain?'/ None heard, with all that pattering on the pane." That august figure, the "Visiting Poet," also receives a barb: "'The famous bard, he comes! The vision nears!'/ Now heaven protect your booze. Your wife. Your ears." These are playful poems and largely beyond comment, except to say that in each of them lies a hard kernel of homely truth.

THE KISS

The Kiss offers proof that Nims has paid as careful attention to the movements and conventions within his own work as to the larger tradition he gratefully accepts.

The book is subtitled *A Jambalaya*, the name of a spicy French Creole stew. The imagery is not wasted, for Nims has put together a well-seasoned mixture of traditional forms and new twists, of myth and science, of the ordinary and the fantastic, with, for good measure, a sprinkling of excellent translations. In short, the book is, indeed, a jambalaya of all that Nims has learned of the art of poetry. Further, the poems have one element in common—each is a variation on "the kiss," with its many implications, from the erotic to the metaphysical.

In "The Observatory Ode," Nims indulges in word-play and metric fireworks to commemorate Percival Lowell (brother of Amy), poet and astronomer, and discoverer of the planet Pluto, who:

> walked high ground, each long cold Arizona night,
> Grandeurs he'd jot: put folk on Mars, but guessed a
>   planet right,
> Scribbling dark sums and ciphers at white heat
> For his Pluto, lost. Till—there it swam!
> Swank, with his own P L for monogram.

The poem is an occasional piece, the Harvard Phi Betta Kappa poem for 1978. (Percival Lowell, Nims's note informs the reader, was Phi Beta Kappa Poet in 1889.) It ranges, however, far beyond that occasion to reflect upon the miracle of life here on this earth:

> Suppose we try
> —Now only suppose—to catch in a jar
> That palmful of dust, on bunsens burn till it flash,
> Could we, from that gas aglow, Construct the eventful
>   world we know,
> Or a toy of it, in the palm? Yet our world came so: we
>   are . . . dust of a dying star.

Despite protests, from Edgar Allan Poe and others, that scientific inquiry saps the magic from life, Nims proclaims that the more that is known about the cosmos the more wonderful a poem it becomes. The crystal spheres have nothing on the universe as man is coming to know it, "Heaven's gaudy trash," this universe, "*such stuff as dreams are made on . . ./* Yet stuff to thump, to call a spade a spade on." "No heat like this," says Nims, "No heat like science and poetry when they kiss." (Nims returned to the poetry of science in one of his last volumes, *The Six-Cornered Snowflake and Other Poems*, in 1990. In a sequence of twelve poems, each laid out in a hexag-

onal snowflake shape, Nims adopts the persona of the seventeenth century astronomer Johannes Kepler in order to utilize the study of nature as an illumination of the art of poetry.)

Not all the "kisses" in the collection are so all-encompassing, nor so suited to public occasions, as "The Observatory Ode." There is a translation from Plato: "That was my very soul that stole to the lips in our kissing./ Thinking to pass—poor thing!—over from me into you." There is the charming "Daughter, Age 4":

> Came traipsing to my bed today:
> No other gave so much
> Rough-and-tumble tenderness,
> Was such a flower to touch.

Nims's sense of humor is as wry as ever and transforms a linguistic discussion of "kiss" into an exercise in delight, as he pauses to

> think about *kiss*.
> Ugly word in the mouth, with its—ouch!—little
>   dental-pick *k*;
> Its vowel with no music at all, and that snake-hiss
>   of *s*'s.
> . . . Not a word the lips linger on lovingly,
> Although meant to mean: lingering lips.

Through more than forty poems, however, Nims lingers more than lovingly over that very word, over its various echoes. His wordplay is as brilliant as ever, but he balances his more exuberant effects with a lovely mellowness of tone and expression that is simple, muted, and intimate. In "A Summer Love," he is on potentially dangerous ground—an ice-cream cone at the end of a love affair, a sure-enough invitation to utter sentimentality. Yet the poem is so tactful, so calmly measured, that the result is anything but sentimental:

> So we part,
> no gift but this . . .
> Our melting present in a melting world . . .
> A thing not meant to last. Nor get us far.
> Call it a sort of rhyme for what we are.

Such simple, straightforward elegance puts to best use Nims's years of discipline and practice. This is lyricism, ripe, sure, "honestly won," anchored firmly in the present by the weight of the past, the "lively past" that, in Wilbur's words, the poet needs "as a means of viewing the present without provinciality and of saying much in little." Nims made very good use of that "lively past." In an era that witnessed a great deal of irreverence, if not open contempt, toward the traditions of English poetry, he and others like him—Wilbur, for example, and Howard Nemerov—persevered to make poetry not a "barbaric yawp" nor a "realistic" laundry list of human experience, but an ordered index of possibilities, a wondering "sort of rhyme for what we are."

OTHER MAJOR WORKS

NONFICTION: *Western Wind: An Introduction to Poetry*, 1974, 1983; *A Local Habitation: Essays on Poetry*, 1985.

TRANSLATIONS: *Andromache* in *The Complete Greek Tragedies*, 1959; *The Poems of St. John of the Cross*, 1959, 1968, 1979; *Sappho to Valéry: Poems in Translation*, 1971, 1979, 1990; *The Complete Poems of Michelangelo*, 1998.

EDITED TEXTS: *The Poem Itself*, 1960 (with Stanley Burnshaw and others); *Ovid's Metamorphoses: The Arthur Golding Translation, 1567*, 1965; *James Shirley's "Love's Cruelty,"* 1980; *The Harper Anthology of Poetry*, 1981.

BIBLIOGRAPHY

Ciardi, John. *Mid-Century American Poets*. New York: Twayne, 1950. Ciardi sets his article on Nims among fourteen others describing the lives and work of Ciardi's contemporaries in the middle of the twentieth century. This volume is one of the only biographical sketches available on Nims and so is extremely valuable to anyone studying him.

Epstein, Joseph. "John Frederick Nims and the Divine Silliness of Words." *Sewanee Review* 107, no. 3 (Summer, 1999): 476-478. In an article written shortly after Nims's death, Epstein describes how Nims gloried in the beauteous oddity of words and took great pleasure in food, friends, and quotidian pleasures.

Fulton, Alice. "On the Plains of Fancy." *Poetry* 159, no. 1 (October, 1991): 32. American plain style, by definition valuing the language of least resistance, has a rich tradition. Fulton examines the plain style

in "The Six-Cornered Snowflake" and "Zany in Denim" by Nims in addition to poems by Jennifer Atkinson, Michelle Boisseau, J. Allyn Rosser, and Maria Flook.

Kennedy, X. J. "John Nims and His Multitudes." *Harvard Review*, Spring, 1994. Poet Kennedy examines Nims's poetics from a temporal vantage point affording a perspective on the poet's full oeuvre.

Nims, John Frederick. *A Local Habitation: Essays on Poetry*. Ann Arbor: University of Michigan Press, 1985. Nims builds a clear picture of his philosophy of poetry in this collection of sixteen essays. He addresses both ancient and modern poets, from Ovid to Robert Frost. This book would be very helpful to any student of Nims's work.

Richard A. Eichwald,
updated by Leslie Ellen Jones

NOVALIS

Friedrich von Hardenberg

Born: Oberwiederstedt, Germany; May 2, 1772
Died: Weissenfels, Germany; March 25, 1801

PRINCIPAL POETRY

Hymnen an die Nacht, 1800 (*Hymns to the Night*, 1897, 1948)

Geistliche Lieder, 1802 (*Devotional Songs*, 1910)

OTHER LITERARY FORMS

The poetry alone does not even hint at the full scope of Novalis's literary activity or his encyclopedic interest in philosophy, science, politics, religion, and aesthetics. While two seminal collections of aphorisms–*Blütenstaub* (pollen) and *Glauben und Liebe* (faith and love)—were published in 1798, the bulk of his work was published posthumously. Among these writings are six neglected dialogues and a monologue from 1798-1799; the essay *Die Christenheit oder Europa* (*Christianity or Europe*, 1844), written in 1799 but first published fully in 1826; and two fragmentary novels, *Die Lehrlinge zu Sais*

(1802; *The Disciples at Sais*, 1903) and *Heinrich von Ofterdingen* (1802; *Henry of Ofterdingen*, 1842), begun in 1798 and 1799 respectively. As prototypes of the German Romantic novel, these two works comprise a variety of literary forms: didactic dialogues, poems, and literary fairy tales. Like so much of Novalis's work, these novels were first published by Ludwig Tieck and Friedrich von Schlegel in the 1802 edition of Novalis's writings. Insights into these literary works and into Novalis's poetics are provided by his theoretical notebooks and other papers, which include his philosophical and scientific studies and outlines and drafts of literary projects, as well as his letters, diaries, and professional scientific reports.

ACHIEVEMENTS

Novalis is perhaps best known as the creator of the "blue flower," the often trivialized symbol of Romantic longing, but his importance has a far more substantial basis than this. Within the German tradition, his Romanticism influenced important writers such as Joseph von Eichendorff, E. T. A. Hoffmann, and Hermann Hesse. As an innovative theorist and practitioner of the Romantic novel, Novalis prepared the way not only for the narrative strategies of Franz Kafka's prose, but also for the themes and structures of Thomas Mann's major novels. As the poet of *Hymns to the Night* and as a theorist of poetic language, Novalis set the Orphic tone for German Romantic poetry and the aesthetic agenda for German Symbolists such as Rainer Maria Rilke and Stefan George.

Novalis's impact outside Germany is no less consequential. His evocative imagery, the prose poems included in *Hymns to the Night*, and his view of poetic language as musical and autonomous make him a major precursor of the French Symbolist poets. Among them, Maurice Maeterlinck was especially drawn to Novalis's philosophy of nature, and he translated *The Disciples at Sais* in 1895. Later, Novalis's imaginative poetics not only inspired André Breton, one of the founders of French Surrealism, but also had an impact, less widely known, on Chilean Surrealism via the poets Rosamel del Valle and Humberto Díaz Casanueva. In the English-speaking world, Novalis was first praised in 1829 by Thomas Carlyle, whose enthusiasm spread ultimately to writers as diverse as Ralph Waldo Emerson, George Eliot, Edgar Allan Poe, Joseph Conrad, and George MacDonald.

In an anthology of poetry published in 1980, *News of the Universe: Poems of Twofold Consciousness*, the American poet Robert Bly justly lauded Novalis as a prime shaper of modern poetic consciousness. Such an evaluation offers hope that Novalis will continue to gain recognition as an internationally important forerunner of both modern poetry and literary theory, especially as more of his literary and theoretical works become accessible in translation.

BIOGRAPHY

Novalis was born Friedrich von Hardenberg, the first son of Heinrich Ulrich Erasmus von Hardenberg, a strict member of the pietistic *Herrnhut* sect, and Auguste Bernhardine von Bölzig. Throughout his life, Novalis attempted to reconcile the practical demands of his father with the poetic inspiration he claimed first to have received from his mother. Novalis's acquaintance with the popular poet Gottfried August Bürger in 1789 intensified his early literary aspirations, but encouraged by

Novalis (© Bettmann/Corbis)

his father to pursue an administrative career, Novalis began the study of law at the University of Jena in 1790. Although his lyric output during his stay in Jena seems to have abated, he soon found his poetic proclivities rekindled and redirected by the poet Friedrich Schiller, who was then a professor of history at the university. Under Schiller's spell, the young Novalis became more introspective and sought a solid foundation for his life and poetry. With this new outlook, he bowed to paternal pressure and transferred to the University of Leipzig in 1791. His experience there once again only strengthened his literary and philosophical interests, however, for it was in Leipzig that he began his friendship and fruitful intellectual exchange with Friedrich von Schlegel, the brilliant theorist of German Romanticism. Only after taking up studies in Wittenberg did he receive his law degree, in 1794.

After several carefree months with his family in Weissenfels, Novalis was apprenticed by his father to Coelestin August Just, the district director of Thuringia, who lived in Tennstedt. It was during his first months there that Hardenberg came to know the twelve-year-old Sophie von Kühn of nearby Grüningen, who revived his active poetic imagination and became a central figure in his new poetic attempts. Within a year they were engaged, but Sophie's serious illness led to her death in March, 1797. Sophie's death, followed by the loss of his brother Erasmus in April, shattered Novalis, and he turned inward to come to grips with the experience of death. This experience, certainly the most crucial of his life, helped him to articulate his mission to transcend the dual nature of existence through poetry. His confrontation with death did not weaken his will to live or cause him to flee from life, as is sometimes claimed; rather, it was a catalytic event that enabled him to reorient his life and focus his imaginative powers on the fusion of life and poetry.

With a new, clearly poetic mission before him, Novalis could commit himself to life; it was at this time that he assumed the pen name (meaning "preparer of new land") by which he is known. By the end of 1797, he had resumed his intense study of the Idealist philosophers Immanuel Kant and Johann Gottlieb Fichte. Novalis's interest in science grew also, and in December, he commenced studies at the Freiberg Mining Academy, which would later give him a career. In the next year, he not only published the philosophical aphorisms of *Blütenstaub* and *Glauben und Liebe*, but also attempted to articulate his own philosophical ideas in a novel, *The Disciples of Sais*. By December, 1798, his involvement in life embraced the domestic once again, and he became engaged to Julie von Charpentier.

Novalis had finally reconciled his poetic mission with the practical demands of life and career. During 1799, he not only worked on *Devotional Songs* and *Hymns to the Night*, which had grown out of the crisis of 1797, but also accepted an appointment to the directorate of the Saxon salt mines. Both his career and his literary endeavors flourished. In 1800, he worked on *Henry of Ofterdingen*, conducted a significant geological survey of Saxony, published *Hymns to the Night*, and wrote some of his best poems. Yet illness had overpowered Novalis's resolve to live and fulfill his poetic mission. On March 25, 1801, Novalis died in the family home in Weissenfels. A few days before his death, he had said to his brother Carl: "When I am well again, then you will finally learn what poetry is. In my head I have magnificent poems and songs." These died with him.

ANALYSIS

The late eighteenth century in Germany was a time of new beginnings. The gradual change from a feudal to a capitalistic society bestowed a new importance on the individual, as reflected in the philosophy of German Idealism, which emphasized the primacy of the subjective imagination. On the other hand, the weakening of the Holy Roman Empire gave rise to a new sense of German nationalism. German writers responded to these changes by seeking to initiate a new literary tradition, a new beginning that would free them from the tyranny of foreign taste and example. Understandably, in such a dynamic age, no single, unified movement emerged, and the literary pioneers—writers as diverse as Gotthold Ephraim Lessing, Friedrich Klopstock, and Christoph Martin Wieland—set out in many different directions. Nevertheless, by the end of the century, Friedrich von Schlegel would proclaim that he lived "not in hope but in the certainty of a new dawn of a new poetry."

Schlegel's optimism was based on his conviction that his contemporaries were on the verge of creating a new mythology, a new Romantic poetry in which the newly emerging self would examine its own depths and discover universal truths, ultimately achieving a synthesis of subject and object. Like the literature of the eighteenth century, the poetry of Novalis moved toward the realization of this Romantic goal. While in his early works he experimented with many styles, betraying his debt to various currents of the Enlightenment, he soon developed a personal Romantic voice and new mode of expression that marked the advent of a new poetic age. This development became more obvious after Sophie's death in 1797, but it is evident even in the poems of his literary apprenticeship (1788-1793). Indeed, many themes that preoccupied Novalis after the crisis of 1797 had already surfaced in his earliest poetry. The theme of death and the dual images of night and darkness, for example, find their initial expression in early poems, although at this stage his poetry was largely imitative. Only after his encounter with Schiller and his relationship with Sophie, which made him more introspective, did Novalis strike out on his own to record his own experiences and the changes that had taken place within himself. He was then able to create a consistent vision, a vision proclaiming the transforming power of love and raising personal experience to the level of mythology. In transforming his subjective experience into universal symbolism, Novalis created the Romantic mythology that Schlegel had proclaimed the *sine qua non* of the new poetic age. In his last poems, which envision the return to paradise brought on by the union of poetry and love, Novalis transcended his personal experience to create symbolic artifacts behind which the poet himself nearly disappears. In his lyric poetry, then, Novalis ultimately reveals himself not only as a pioneer of Romanticism but also as a precursor of Symbolism.

If Novalis's last poems are thematically consistent and anticipate the Symbolist movement, his early poems are endlessly diversified and echo the Enlightenment. In the poets of the eighteenth century, the young writer, searching for a poetic voice, found his models, limited only by his eclectic taste. Besides translations from classical poetry, Novalis composed serious political verse influenced by the work of Friedrich Stolberg and Karl Ramler, and in the bardic tradition of Klopstock; Rococo lyrics under the particular influence of Wieland; elegiac verse echoing Ludwig Christoph Heinrich Hölty and Schiller; and a spate of lyrics in the style of Bürger. The variety of these early attempts, the assorted literary models that they imitate, and the poems showing a young poet experimenting with traditional forms (such as the invented necrologues addressed to living family members) reveal a writer in quest of a suitable mode of expression.

"To a Falling Leaf"

While they do share some common concerns, many of which inform the later writings, the early poems lack the unified vision and unique perspective that would come later with Novalis's Romantic lyrics. Poems that foreshadow later developments also contrast significantly with the more mature poetry. The first version of the poem "An ein fallendes Blatt" ("To a Falling Leaf"), written in 1789, paints a melancholy scene in which the approach of winter storms is compared to the approach of death. The melancholy tone, however, is purposely undercut by a conclusion that affirms death as a joyous experience of the eternal that need not be feared. This view of death hints, perhaps, at the thanatopsis that Novalis would elaborate in *Hymns to the Night*, but it is merely a hint, for here the idea is actually no more than a common poetic cliché, and the poem as a whole lacks the visionary perspective that underlies the later works. This poem's persona, in fact, is barely visible at all, and his emotional response to death's coming at the end of the poem is expressed impersonally: "Oh happy . . ./ One need not then fear the storm/ That forbids us our earthly life." The persona and his climactic emotional exclamation vanish behind the anonymous "one," and death—which had been only indirectly introduced through a comparison—loses not only its sting, as the poet intended, but its poetic bite as well.

"Evening"

The poem "Der Abend" ("Evening"), probably written in the same year but in many ways a more suggestive and complex work, not only has a more directly involved and visible persona than "To a Falling Leaf," but also links death and night in anticipation of *Hymns to the Night*. This poem's persona, who stands in a sympathetic relationship to a thoroughly personified nature, perceives and responds to a serene evening by wishing that "the evening of my life" might be "more peaceful still than this/ Evening of the countryside." The lovely yet decidedly rational comparison of the soul to nature is still far removed from the Romantic identification of self and nature that can be found in Novalis's last poems—for example, in "Der Himmel war umzogen" ("The Heavens Were Covered"). Moreover, despite the reflective mood that nature inspires in the persona, this is not an introspective poem like those found among Novalis's first truly Romantic poems. "Evening" does not yet focus primarily on the poetic self but on the eighteenth century ideal of bucolic harmony. Similarly, the persona's final wish, that his "soul might slumber over to eternal peace" in the same way that the weary farmer "slumbers over" toward the next day, only tentatively prefigures the ideas and vocabulary of *Hymns to the Night*. The link between death and sleep remains, after all, an eighteenth century cliché, and its one-dimensional appearance here only lightly foreshadows Novalis's later and much more complex symbol of the eternal and truly visionary "holy sleep."

This poem, like "To a Falling Leaf," is still controlled by a rationalistic poetic consciousness. Simile, not symbol, is the rhetorical means of linking man and nature; subject and object are linked, not synthesized. This is the overriding technique of the early poems. The transcendent vision based on deep self-reflection and the unifying power of the imagination is not found here. The poet of "Evening" is one step closer to the Romantic poet of *Hymns to the Night* than the poet of "To a Falling Leaf," but the Romantic poet whose feelings, perceptions, and very self are the basis of Romantic expression steps forward only tentatively. Before he could free himself from his Enlightenment models, focus his vision, and become the very subject of his Romantic art, Novalis would first need to know himself.

"ON A SATURDAY EVENING"

The experience of love and death in his relationship with Sophie was the catalyst that would initiate important changes in Novalis's writings, the lens through which he would ultimately bring into sharper focus the themes and images that had been hinted at in the early poems. Initially, however, the experience led to self-

examination and the definition of a new, more Romantic voice. Much of the poetry from this period—and there is relatively little—records the changes that the Sophie-experience caused in Novalis, and it is, consequently, largely confessional, reflective poetry in which the poet himself becomes the subject.

In the poem "Am Sonnabend Abend" ("On a Saturday Evening"), for example, the persona expresses his astonishment at the transformation that has taken place within himself since his relationship with Sophie: "Am I still the one who yesterday morning/ Sang hymns to the god of frivolity. . . ." This confession suggests not only the changes that had affected a once frivolous university student but also those poetic changes that had occurred in the former poet of lighthearted Anacreontic verse. Earlier, in 1791, Novalis had expressed similar reservations about his lifestyle and youthful verse in "A Youth's Laments," a poem written under the maturing influence of Schiller, but it was only after Novalis had met Sophie that his inner reorientation became complete and the poet could begin anew.

"BEGINNING"

In the poem "Anfang" ("Beginning"), Novalis analyzes the nature of Sophie's effect on him and argues that his new state of mind is not "intoxication" (that is, illusion) but rather "higher consciousness," which Sophie as a mediator had revealed. This aptly titled poem is in several ways profoundly significant for Novalis's development as a Romantic poet. In the first place, its conclusion that higher consciousness not be mistaken for intoxication admits a new Romantic form of perception that is aggressively antirationalistic. Second, the characterization of Sophie, the embodiment of love, as a female mediator between visible and invisible worlds, not only marks the first use of this central Romantic image in Novalis's work but also signals the inception of a Romantic theory of Symbolism, which posits the fusion of the finite with the infinite. Finally, the intensely introspective persona, whose theme is his own consciousness ("the growth of a poet's mind," as William Wordsworth put it), places this poem directly into the Romantic tradition.

In "Beginning," Novalis's new vision, based on the higher consciousness inspired by Sophie, assumes a universal import transcending the initially personal experience. This is manifest in the last lines of the poem, where the private experience of the poet is superseded by a vision of humanity raised to a new level of existence:

> Someday mankind will be what Sophie
> Is to me now—perfected—moral grace—
> Then will its *higher consciousness*
> No longer be confused with the mist of wine.

THE STRANGER

The poems Novalis wrote in 1798 and 1799 in Freiberg after Sophie's death confirm this universalizing tendency. In fact, the relative paucity of poems written in the wake of the experience itself suggests that Novalis was not simply concerned with self-indulgent solipsistic effusions. (The one poem written shortly after Sophie's death in 1797, while Novalis was still in Tennstedt, is a humorous composition commemorating the Just family's purchase of a garden.) Similarly, it has been pointed out that Novalis probably chose the classical verse forms of the Freiberg poems as a more objective medium for his universal themes. One can also point to the objectifying perspective of the several poems that analyze the self from a point of view once removed. In both "Der Fremdling" ("The Stranger"), written in January, 1798, and "Der müde Fremdling ist verschwunden" ("The Weary Stranger Has Disappeared"), a fragment from one year later, Novalis—the stranger—analyzes his initial alienation after Sophie's death and then his self-rediscovery through a persona who "speaks . . . for him." This allows Novalis to remain in the introspective mode, making use of his experience, yet standing at an objective distance. As a consequence, the stranger symbolizes any individual who seeks the return of the paradise he has lost, "that heavenly land."

SELF-KNOWLEDGE

The major poems of the Freiberg period are inhabited by seekers who ultimately find themselves. Introspection leading to self-revelation is the goal and method of these poems, but the path inward does not lead to solipsism. Self-knowledge, as Novalis teaches in "Kenne dich selbst" ("Know Thyself"), results in a deep knowledge of nature's mysteries as well. Moreover, because his own path to self-knowledge, which had been prepared by the guiding spirit of love, led to higher consciousness, Novalis interprets his experience

as a symbol. He imbues his introspective poems with a universal significance, as in these lines from "Letzte Liebe" ("Last Love"):

> As the mother wakes her darling from slumber with a kiss,
> As he first sees her and comes to understand himself
> 　through her:
> So love with me—through love did I first experience the
> 　world,
> Find myself, and become what as a lover one becomes.

What *one*—anyone, not just Novalis—becomes when a lover, is a poet. The successful seeker of love and self-knowledge is called, like the poet addressed in "Der sterbende Genius" ("The Dying Genius"), to "sing the song of return," the myth of the return to paradise.

Having found himself again, Novalis defined for himself a Romantic mission: to transform his personal experience through poetry into a universal vision of love, which would lead others inward along the path to self-knowledge, higher consciousness, and rebirth: "Toward the East sing then the lofty song,/ Until the sun rises and ignites/ And opens for me the gates of the primeval world."

HYMNS TO THE NIGHT

In *Hymns to the Night*, the gates of eternity are opened not by the rising sun—the conventional symbol of rebirth—but by the fall of darkness and night. This poetic work is Novalis's "lofty song," "the song of return," the clearest and most complete fulfillment of his Romantic mission. In it, Novalis transforms his personal experience of Sophie's death—to be precise, his ostensibly mystical experience at her graveside on May 13, 1797—into a universalized vision of death and night as a realm of higher consciousness and eternal love.

Hymns to the Night was not merely an immediate emotional response to Sophie's death. Although he might have begun work on an early version in the fall of 1797, Novalis resumed serious work on the cycle only in late 1799 and early 1800, when he was well over his initial grief and actively involved in life. Moreover, the textual changes that he made between setting down that version in manuscript and publishing a still later prose version in the journal *Athenäum* in 1800 show a conscious effort to rise above personal experience and indicate that his goal was not autobiography but symbolism.

Unlike the fragmentary verse epic of 1789, *Orpheus*, which uses a classical myth to examine the theme of death, *Hymns to the Night* makes personal experience the basis of a broad symbolism utilizing elements of various mythological systems (including the theme of Orpheus). Although the first three hymns describe principally the poet's own experience of "the holy, ineffable, mysterious night"—his own Orphic descent to the realm of death—the work begins significantly with a more universal reference to all living creatures in the world of light. Among these stands "the magnificent stranger" who is man himself. As in the Freiberg poems, the stranger symbolizes the universal seeker of a lost paradise. From this broad context, it becomes clear that the persona, himself a stranger in the rational world of light, is representative and his experience symbolic. This universality is reinforced in the fourth hymn when, for example, the symbol of the Cross, which at first signifies Sophie's death and links her to Christ, is finally called "the victory banner of our race." The fifth hymn continues to broaden the significance of the poet's experience by restating his subjective development toward an understanding of death in terms of humankind's changing relationship to death in history. In the sixth and final hymn, subjective experience coalesces completely with the universal. Not only is the mediating beloved explicitly identified with Christ, but also the poet's individual voice is transformed into a universal "we" singing a communal hymn of praise. The stranger, who in the Freiberg poems had given up his voice to the poet who spoke for him, here lends his voice to the chorus of humankind.

DEVOTIONAL SONGS

Devotional Songs, also written during the years 1799 through 1800, were similarly intended to raise personal experience to the level of universal—if not entirely orthodox—religious symbolism. This is evident not only from the symbols that the poems share with *Hymns to the Night*—for example, the eroticism of Christ the beloved—but also from the shared communal context and implications. Novalis had tentatively planned these songs as part of "a new, spiritual hymnal"; in them, the Sophie-experience is so thoroughly transformed by virtue of the pervasive Christian imagery that many have been adopted (and sometimes adapted) for use in hymnals.

The songs, which are sometimes confessional, sometimes exhortative, are all informed by Novalis's self-conscious mission to reveal the role of love in the re-creation of the earth. The ninth song, for example, which proclaims the day of Resurrection to be "a festival of the world's rejuvenation," is more than a profession of religious faith in the coming of God's kingdom; it is a self-conscious profession of faith in the poet's mission to reveal that kingdom in man's midst:

> I say to each that he lives
> And has been resurrected
> That he hovers in our midst
> And is with us forever.
> I say to each and each says
> To his friends anon
> That soon everywhere
> The new kingdom of heaven will dawn.

In truly Romantic fashion, the voice of the prophet is first and foremost the voice of a poet, speaking out of his own experience but in the service of a still higher cause and announcing to all humankind the advent of a world renewed by love, which is made manifest in his words.

"THE POEM"

Novalis's last poems are almost exclusively concerned with the renewal of the universe and the return to the Golden Age; their vision is more explicitly secular and aesthetic than that which informs *Hymns to the Night* and *Devotional Songs*. Here, Novalis's belief that poetry itself can transform the world receives full expression, and many of these last works are indeed poems about poems, in which Novalis's personal experience is not the focus.

Such is the case in the significantly titled poem "Das Gedicht" ("The Poem"). The anonymous persona who speaks for humankind in its fallen state relates how "a lost page"—a poetic saga—inspires in the present a vision of the past Golden Age and keeps alive the hope for its return. Because it is able to unite past and future in the present and give form to the spirit of love, the poem itself temporarily re-creates the Golden Age. The paramount concern of "The Poem," then, is precisely what the title announces it to be: the poem—not simply the ancient saga and not even Novalis's poem in itself, but all poems, the poem per se. In its ability to unite subject and object, spirit and matter, every poem becomes a medium of higher consciousness and the salvation of the world.

"TO TIECK"

Once poetry becomes a major theme in Novalis's work, a new poetic voice emerges. The reflective persona that had spoken in the introspective poems of 1794 to 1799 is silenced. In "The Poem," for example, the reflective self is replaced by an essentially impersonal persona. This is no longer a case of a poet reflecting on himself but of poetry reflecting on itself. In the poem "An Tieck" ("To Tieck"), another anonymous persona narrates the tale of a child's discovery of an ancient book and an encounter with Jakob Boehme, which presage the coming of the Golden Age.

Despite the dedicatory title and autobiographical allusions in the poem (Tieck had introduced Novalis to Boehme's writings), the personal significance has been entirely transformed by the symbolism of the poem. The dominance of myth in these last poems precludes the need for a personal voice, as it does in the novel *Henry of Ofterdingen* of the same period. If early poems such as "To a Falling Leaf" resort to an anonymous voice because Novalis lacked experience, then the final poems do so because he succeeded in rising above his personal experience.

AUTONOMOUS LATE POEMS

The appearance of a first-person voice among the late poems does not contradict this conclusion. A number of poems in which the poet speaks in the first person were in fact intended for fictional characters in *Henry of Ofterdingen*. In some of these and in others not intended for the novel, the persona himself becomes part of an integrated mythos. Such poems are distinct from earlier reflective works such as "Beginning" and "Last Love."

Although the late poems also describe the changing consciousness of the persona, they do so in symbolic terms and not in the largely expository or intellectual manner of the earlier poems. Whereas the poet of "Beginning" simply states that Sophie has led him to higher consciousness, the speaker of "Es färbte sich die Wiese grün" ("The Meadow Turned Green") tells the story of his rebirth by *narrating* his experience of spring and love: During a walk deeper and deeper into the forest, the persona marvels uncomprehendingly at the transfor-

mation of nature; he then encounters a young girl and, hidden from the sun in deep shadows, suddenly understands intuitively the changes both in nature and within himself.

One can easily discern the same theme that dominated the Freiberg poems: The spirit of love, embodied by a female mediator, reveals the higher consciousness that leads to knowledge of self and of the external world. In this narrative plot, however, the theme has been thoroughly mythologized. The symbols which Novalis uses here and in all his late poems are autonomous, stripped of all but the most general personal relevance. The forest, the sun, the girl, springtime—all these derive their mythological significance from their shared archetypal context.

"The Meadow Turned Green" is autonomous, too, in that it reflects back upon itself. It is, after all, not merely a description of revelation and the path to higher consciousness; it is both the direct result of the poet's epiphany *and* the re-creation of it. The poem describes and mythologizes its own creation.

The process of objectifying and imbuing his personal experience with universal meaning that Novalis had begun in the poems of 1794 to 1799 was completed in his last poems, in which he totally transforms experience into myth, into symbols which have no fixed meanings outside themselves. This creation of a reflexive and fully autonomous poetry was a significant landmark on the road to nineteenth century symbolism. To reach this stage and to find his own poetic voice, it was not enough for Novalis that he free himself from Enlightenment models and create a poetry of the self. He also needed to rise above the self and to create a mythological poetry. For this, he needed a poetic voice that not only spoke from the core of his experience also spoke in the universal language of symbolism. In achieving this goal, Novalis fulfilled the Romantic ideal of becoming like God the Creator, whose creative voice echoes eternally throughout His autonomous creation while He hovers silently above.

OTHER MAJOR WORKS

LONG FICTION: *Die Lehrlinge zu Sais*, 1802 (*The Disciples at Sais*, 1903); *Heinrich von Ofterdingen*, 1802 (*Henry of Ofterdingen*, 1842).

NONFICTION: *Blütenstaub*, 1798; *Glauben und Liebe*, 1798; *Die Christenheit oder Europa*, 1826 (*Christianity or Europe*, 1844).

BIBLIOGRAPHY

Molnár, Géza von. *Romantic Vision, Ethical Context: Novalis and Artistic Autonomy.* Minneapolis: University of Minnesota Press, 1987. Highly philosophical approach to the life and work of Novalis. Discussion of his work involves detailed expositions of Novalis's interpretations of Kantian and Fichtean philosophy. Also examines Novalis's relationship with Sophie von Kuhn, his novel *Heinrich von Ofterdingen*, and his visionary poems *Hymns to the Night*. In addition, discusses Novalis's ideas in the light of their relevance to contemporary postmodern philosophical ideas and issues.

Neubauer, John. *Novalis.* Boston: Twayne, 1980. Excellent general introduction to Novalis, tailored to English-speaking readers. Interweaves the life and work to show the relationship between the two and also discusses Novalis both as a visionary and as a logical thinker. Includes useful discussions of Novalis's contributions to science, philosophy, the novel, poetry, politics, and religion. Makes a case for Novalis as one of the great early moderns, whose ideas are part of an intellectual and artistic heritage. Includes a bibliography and a chronology.

Newman, Gail M. *Locating the Romantic Subject.* Detroit: Wayne State University Press, 1997. Complex interpretation of the life and work of Novalis in light of the modern object-relations theory of British psychologist D. W. Winnicott. Particular emphasis on Novalis's major novel *Heinrich von Ofterdingen* as a psychoanalytic case study.

O'Brien, William Arctander. *Novalis: Signs of Revolution.* Durham, N.C.: Duke University Press, 1995. Examines both the life and the work of Novalis with the purpose of contradicting "the myth of Novalis" as a dreamy, death-obsessed mystic. Sees Novalis as the quintessential early German Romantic, an energetic and enthusiastic follower of the Revolution. Also explores the way in which Novalis's notebooks anticipate future trends in semi-otics and social action. Written to be accessible to people with little or no German, while retaining its usefulness for German scholars, this is an excellent book study for the general reader. A chapter called "The Making of Sophie" brings new perspectives to Novalis's profound experience with the young Sophie von Kuhn.

Donald P. Haase;
bibliography updated by Margaret Boe Birns

NAOMI SHIHAB NYE

Born: St. Louis, Missouri; March 12, 1952

PRINCIPAL POETRY
Different Ways to Pray, 1980
On the Edge of the Sky, 1981
Hugging the Jukebox, 1982
Yellow Glove, 1986
Invisible, 1987
Mint, 1992
Red Suitcase, 1994
Words Under the Words, 1995
Fuel, 1998

OTHER LITERARY FORMS

Naomi Shihab Nye has published many books for children, both poetry and fiction, including *Sitti's Secrets* (1994), *Habibi* (1997), and *What Have You Lost?* (2000). She has published a collection of essays, *Never in a Hurry* (1996), and edited several poetry anthologies, including *I Feel a Little Jumpy Around You* (1996; with Paul B. Janaeczko) and *The Tree Is Older than You Are: A Bilingual Gathering of Poems and Stories from Mexico with Paintings by Mexican Artists* (1995).

In addition to her work as a poet, Nye is a songwriter and singer who has recorded two albums, *Rootabag Roo* (1979) and *Lullaby Raft* (1981). Her work appears in *Modern Arabic Poetry* (1987), and she has translated into English the poems of Muhammad al-Maghut, *The Fan of Swords* (1991).

ACHIEVEMENTS

Naomi Shihab Nye's greatest contribution lies in her poetry, work that has been much honored. Both *Different Ways to Pray* and *Hugging the Jukebox* received the Voertman Award from the Texas Institute of Letters. *Hugging the Jukebox* was chosen by Josephine Miles as the National Poetry Series winner in 1982 and as one of the most notable books by the American Library Association. Her honors also include a 1997-1998 Guggenheim Fellowship, the I. B. Lavan Award from the Academy of American Poets, four Pushcart Prizes, and the Charity Randall Prize for Spoken Poetry with Galway Kinnell from the International Poetry Forum.

Nye has also received awards for her children's books: the Jane Addams Children's Book Award, the Judy Lopez Medal for children's literature, and the Texas Institute of Letters Best Book for Young Readers Award for *Habibi*.

BIOGRAPHY

Naomi Shihab Nye was born on March 12, 1952, in St. Louis, Missouri, the daughter of a Palestinian father, Aziz Shihab, and an American mother, Miriam Naomi Shihab. She spent her childhood in St. Louis, developing an interest in poetry at an early age; at seven, she had a poem published in *Wee Wisdom*, a children's magazine. From St. Louis, her family moved to Jerusalem, where she attended high school and absorbed many stories, impressions, and perceptions of the differences in cultures and the similarities among people. Many of her poems draw on her experiences with people she observed and family members she learned about or knew well. These experiences have been incorporated into her poems and her writing for children and young people.

From Jerusalem, the Nye family settled in San Antonio, Texas, where she completed her education, receiving her B.A. from Trinity University in 1974. She married her husband, Michael, a lawyer and photographer, in 1978. With their son, Madison Cloudfeather, born in 1986, they remained in San Antonio. The city's Mexican American culture has been important to Nye's work. She delights in observing and describing the daily activities of all the people she encounters. Her poems often catalogue the habits, concerns, and attitudes of various people and cultures. Her compassion for others and her appreciation of their individuality are the most outstanding characteristics of her poetry. Nye has traveled widely, gaining experiences that have enabled her to fill her poetic album with snapshots of people worldwide who simultaneously reveal both the unique and the universal qualities of humanity.

Teaching all over the United States, Nye has been the Holloway Lecturer at the University of California, a lecturer in poetry at the University of Texas at Austin, and a visiting writer at the University of Hawaii and the University of Alaska. She has traveled to conduct workshops with teachers and students of all ages in the Middle East and Asia with the United States Information Agency. Her poems show that she is at home in all cultures, from Madison Street in St. Louis to the jungle in Guatemala. In all places she looks for and finds connections between herself and others.

Often she appears as a spokesperson for poetry. She appeared in the series *The Language of Poetry*, an eight-part series on the Public Broadcasting System (PBS), in 1995 and was featured in another series, *The United States of Poetry*. She has also been recorded on National Public Radio and serves as poetry editor for *The Texas Observer*. Despite her busy schedule filled with reading, speaking, and teaching engagements, she urges readers in her poems and essays to take time to pause and savor their lives.

ANALYSIS

Naomi Shihab Nye, like earlier American poets Walt Whitman and Carl Sandburg before her, celebrates diverse people and their cultures. Today, the global village requires an inclusiveness that Nye affirms by describing Native and immigrant Americans as well as Pakistani, Japanese, Indian, and Central and South American people. While her poetic voice embraces, her content connects—with the earth, with all others. Her method depends on imagery, metaphor, and story.

Nye explores human attempts to grasp meaning and create a meaningful life. Describing ways people do this, she points out the beauty inherent in such everyday activities as Texas ladies shopping for peaches, or an Arab man making brooms "Thumb over thumb." Her poems demonstrate that heightened consciousness promotes new levels of awareness. They also show the meaningfulness of stories. They document people's conscious connections with others and the universality of cares, grief and joy, and behaviors. Her free-verse lyrics are full of images describing the ordinary perceived as extraordinary. Poetic stories become metaphors defining human lives.

DIFFERENT WAYS TO PRAY

In this first major collection, following several chapbooks, *Different Ways to Pray* explores the different ways people achieve self-awareness and revere the world. Poems document the new level of thinking and responding that results from getting to know oneself. The poem "Otto's Place" recounts the sense of completeness and satisfaction achieved as the speaker experiences a physical connection between her body and the earth. In a poem reminiscent of Theodore Roethke's "The Waking," "The Whole Self" analyzes the perceiver of actions and laments the accompanying loss of spontaneity. Recognizing there is no going back, the speaker exhorts herself to *"Dance!* The whole self was a current, a fragile cargo,/ a raft someone was paddling through the jungle,/ and I was there, waving, and I would be there at the other end."

"Different Ways to Pray" catalogs particular approaches: Whether one prays or is prayed for, kneeling, sitting, talking "with God as . . . with goats," central to prayer is a sense of connectedness. Other connections are celebrated. "Kindness" describes a state of being that, having experienced loss, finds comfort in giving. Giving in "Coming into Cuzco" is personified in a young woman who "handed me one perfect pink rose,/ because we had noticed each other, and that was all." In so doing, the young woman refreshed a tired and bewildered spirit. Another kind of connection occurs in "Walking Down Blanco Road at Midnight," where "a folding into the self . . . occurs/ when the lights are small on the horizon/ and no light is shining into the face." This collection ends with the poem "Words Under the Words," directed to the poet's Palestinian grandmother and expressing the hope that the spirit beneath words can be felt even if inadequately delivered, a hope, the poem implies, reflecting the prayerful hope of all people.

HUGGING THE JUKEBOX

This collection, published in 1982, continues earlier themes while placing particular focus on stories. "Hugging the Jukebox" reveals a young boy sent to live with his grandparents on a Caribbean island. At age six, he sings with great passion and with a large voice all the songs on the jukebox. Hugging the box and belting out songs, he leaves grandparents amazed and tourists spellbound. "For Lost and Found Brothers" celebrates the influence of people, known and unknown, and their stories, told and untold. The theme of this poem—stories of people feeling lost and the underlying connection of all people—develops motifs of the importance of stories and of the interconnectedness of all people, even of people yet unknown to one another.

Other poems reveal the way ordinary tasks assume significance. In "At the Seven-Mile Ranch, Comstock, Texas" the speaker, through solitary work on the ranch, becomes conversant with the land as if it were a friend: "The land walking beside you is your oldest friend,/ pleasantly silent, like already you've told the best stories." "Daily" demonstrates that ordinary tasks become sacred when accomplished with care and attention. With folding clothes, addressing an envelope, our "hands are churches that worship the world." In "The Trashpickers, Madison Street," trashpickers "murmur in a language soft as rags," and with their recovery of items from the trash, the discarded are reborn.

YELLOW GLOVE

In this collection, published in 1986, metaphors for the experience of our lives abound. In the title piece, "Yellow Glove," a child frets about a yellow glove identified by adults as valuable that is lost in a muddy, winter ditch. Surprisingly, the child finds it in the spring, now dirty and worn, refurbishes it, and puts it safely away. Later in life, the speaker ponders its significance in a world of "bankbooks and stereos," concluding that it is "Part of the difference between floating and going down."

The metaphor in "Dew" is that of wearing moccasins in the dew, a practice a Kickapoo grandmother suggests to make them fit. The metaphor in "The Use of Fiction," "a clear marble/ he [a boy] will hide in his sock drawer for months," refers to a truth—a new special bond—that is arrived at by a little lie. While Nye's work is usually optimistic, some pieces reflect another reality. "Hello" shows how a rat, real or metaphorical, can gnaw away at a special fruit. "No One Thinks of Tegucigalpa" laments the negligible care for the injustices and the poverty of lives that are a part of the world. "How bad is it to dress in a cold room? How small your own/ wish for a parcel of children? How remarkably invisible/ this tear?

RED SUITCASE

Continuing the exploration of stories is the operative metaphor of this collection, published in 1994. The metaphor that introduces the text draws on a Moroccan folk tale of a red suitcase with nothing but a blank sheet of paper inside. These poems capture stories that might have appeared on that sheet. In "How Palestinians Keep Warm," the speaker ruminates on how ancestors grounded themselves. "Choose one word and say it over/ and over, till it builds a fire inside your mouth." She wants to share this wisdom with babies and finds with only her thin shawl that she can do this best through stories.

"Travel Alarm" humorously advocates, in its story of a childish prank, the placing of priorities on loved ones and shared moments. "Arabic" reaffirms, through a bizarre story, the universality of human experience. An Arab complains that those who do not speak his language cannot share his pain, yet when the speaker "hailed a taxi by shouting *Pain!* . . . it stopped/ in every language and opened its doors."

FUEL

Poems in *Fuel* explore the subtle influences that shape lives. "Hidden" identifies the influence of the unspoken but significant name of someone. "Fuel" speaks to those apparently insignificant things in life that nourish people: a received look that is recognized, acknowledged, and fully accepted; the active listening response that emanates from a plant; the blue in the sky, recognized as a call. People are connected to others in ways they never see or know in "String," when at a certain time of day in a certain light, they connect with those they love who are far away, or they connect with their former selves. These connections are like knots in the string "giving us something to go by." One series explores the influence of the everyday, an approach first inspired in Nye by William Stafford, her mentor, and reflected in "Bill's Beans." Another series explores the mystery of things. Some transformed person writes on all the bus benches, *"NOTHING IS IMPOSSIBLE."* A little boy, in "One Boy Told Me," marvels, "Just think— no one has ever seen/ inside this peanut before!" The

first poem of this collection sums up the prevailing attitude of all the poems: "Muchas Gracias por Todo," thanks very much for everything.

WORDS UNDER THE WORDS

This 1995 compilation of three out-of-print collections, *Different Ways to Pray, Hugging the Jukebox*, and *Yellow Glove*, begins with an essay, "Loose Leaf," an extended prose poem describing Nye's perception of her life as poetry. She sees her life as a loose-leaf binder or a photo album, holding records of important incidents, like snapshots. The pages can be rearranged, the chronology is not important, and there are blank pages for the stories she has yet to know. This analogy speaks to her poetry as well as her life.

OTHER MAJOR WORKS

NONFICTION: *Never in a Hurry*, 1996.

TRANSLATIONS: *The Fan of Swords*, 1991 (of Muhammad al-Maghut's poetry).

CHILDREN'S LITERATURE: *This Same Sky: A Collection of Poems from Around the World*, 1992; *Benito's Dream Bottle*, 1994; *Sitti's Secrets*, 1994; *Lullaby Raft*, 1996; *Habibi*, 1997; *Come with Me: Poems for a Journey*, 2000; *What Have You Lost?*, 2000.

EDITED TEXTS: *The Tree Is Older than You Are: A Bilingual Gathering of Poems and Stories from Mexico with Paintings by Mexican Artists*, 1995; *I Feel a Little Jumpy Around You*, 1996 (with Paul B. Janaeczko); *The Space Between Our Foot Steps: Poems and Paintings from the Middle East*, 1998; *The Flag of Childhood: Poems of the Middle East*, 2002.

BIBLIOGRAPHY

Booth, Phillip. "Loners Whose Voices Move." Review of *Yellow Glove*, by Naomi Shihab Nye. *Georgia Review*, Spring, 1989, 161-178. This review provides a close reading and analysis of *Yellow Glove*. Booth points out Nye's humanity and attention to detail.

Colloff, Pamela. "The Texas Twenty, 1998: Naomi Shihab Nye—The Literature of the Examined Life." *Texas Monthly Magazine* 26, no. 9 (September, 1998): 111. This article, based on an interview with

Nye, includes quotes on her ideas, her inspirations, and her interests. It points out the importance to her of her mentor, William Stafford, and shows the value she has placed on her home in Texas as a place where her poetic voice could grow and be heard.

Kitchen, Judith. "Pensions." Review of *Fuel*, by Naomi Shihab Nye. *Georgia Review*, Summer, 1999, 381-384. This review provides insight into Nye's themes, recognizing that they convey the extraordinary in the ordinary and that while most poems are optimistic, some confront the realities of pain. Several poems in this collection, the reviewer points out, explore the suffering experienced by people in the Middle East.

Sparr, Lisa Russ. Introduction to *Texas Poetry in Concert: A Quartet*, by R. S. Gwynn, Jan Seale, Naomi Shihab Nye, and William Virgil Davis. Denton: North Texas University Press, 1990. The introduction to Nye's poetry in this anthology, collecting her poems along with three other Texas poets, provides a brief but valuable introduction pointing to the deep awareness of humanity evident in the selections.

Bernadette Flynn Low

O

JOYCE CAROL OATES

Born: Lockport, New York; June 16, 1938

PRINCIPAL POETRY

Women in Love, 1968
Anonymous Sins and Other Poems, 1969
Love and Its Derangements, 1970
Angel Fire, 1973
The Fabulous Beasts, 1975
Women Whose Lives Are Food, Men Whose Lives Are Money, 1978
Invisible Woman: New and Selected Poems, 1970-1982, 1982
The Luxury of Sin, 1984
The Time Traveler, 1989
Tenderness, 1996

OTHER LITERARY FORMS

Joyce Carol Oates is best known as the author of many novels, including *them* (1969), which won her the 1970 National Book Award. She is also a respected short-story writer, a playwright, and the author of several hundred critical articles.

ACHIEVEMENTS

Many of Joyce Carol Oates's short stories have been honored by inclusion in *The Best American Short Stories* and the *O. Henry Awards Anthology*; she won a National Book Award for the 1969 novel *them*. In addition, Oates is a member of the American Academy of Arts and Letters and has received both a Guggenheim Fellowship and a National Endowment for the Humanities grant.

BIOGRAPHY

Joyce Carol Oates was born into a rural working-class family in Lockport, a town in upper New York State along the Erie Canal. She is the oldest of three children, with a brother five years younger and a sister, thirteen years younger, who has been institutionalized with autism since early adolescence. Oates's early memories are of the maternal family farm, with chickens, pigs, and fruit trees. The economic depression of the 1930's kept her father, Frederic Oates, from schooling, but his talents in art and music and his capacity for joy and hard work had a profound influence on his daughter. He introduced her to the sport of boxing and the thrills of flying; as a child she saw the world of male violence from the ringside and felt the thrill of flight in an open-cockpit plane. The landscapes and people of her childhood and her parents' childhood are re-created in her literary work.

Oates was graduated Phi Beta Kappa and class valedictorian from Syracuse University in 1960 with majors in English and philosophy. She earned a master's degree in English literature at the University of Wisconsin at Madison, where, in 1961, she met and married Raymond Smith. After a period of graduate study in Texas, she moved to Detroit, where she taught at the University of Detroit. The inclusion of one of her stories in a prizewinning collection, Martha Foley's *Best American Short Stories*, prompted Oates to make the decision to become a professional writer. She continued to teach and write, moving from Detroit across the Detroit River to Windsor, Ontario, where she taught at the University of Windsor until 1978. Throughout this period, she read steadily and deeply, especially the works of William Faulkner, Franz Kafka, Friedrich Nietzsche, Thomas Mann, Henry David Thoreau, and Fyodor Dostoevski, and a favorite writer, D. H. Lawrence. She was profoundly influenced as a child by Lewis Carroll's *Alice's Adventures in Wonderland* (1865) and *Through the Looking-Glass and What Alice Found There* (1871) and the trust in instinctive, intuitive knowledge those books inspired.

In 1978, Oates and her husband settled in Princeton, New Jersey, where she began to teach at Princeton University. Her typical daily schedule would include morning writing from eight o'clock until early afternoon followed by relaxation, music (like her father, she plays the piano well), and, on some days, teaching. Her evenings are given to reading unless she is absorbed by her writing. With her husband, she edits *The Ontario Review*, a journal of new writing. She is a popular

Joyce Carol Oates

speaker at colleges throughout the United States, and at poetry readings, her enthusiasm and energy delight her audiences. She has become, like Honoré de Balzac in nineteenth century France, a "secretary to the nation," observing and re-creating her vision of post-World War II America in an astonishing outpouring of brilliant literary work.

ANALYSIS

The poetic chronicle of Joyce Carol Oates is so rich that no single study can do it justice. The poetry, for example, has humor, water imagery, and rhythmic effects, none of which could be discussed within the present thematic emphasis. Oates's poetry, however, forms a body of work on its own merits and does not need to be interpreted only as an adjunct to her novels and short stories, as critics have said. It pictures America and Americans in the second half of a violent and fascinating century while at the center of world power. Con-

fused, energetic, speeding and groping their way to understanding survival conditions, Americans see themselves mirrored in these poems. Their dramas, very often melodramas, seem outrageous until the reader examines a newspaper with stories more like fiction than fact.

Living in Detroit in the 1960's, Oates saw the heart of American life in the automobile manufacturer's boast, "What is good for General Motors is good for America." The city, though, erupted into riots, exposing its underside of poverty and rage. Perhaps these events triggered Oates's interest in the Great Depression of the 1930's, her parents' struggles, and photographs of poor people in the grip of economic forces they neither understood nor controlled. Attuned to the plight of helpless people, she observed rootlessness and frustration leading to family and civil violence. The smile of consumer society that gleams in advertising and movies covers a dark and dirty reality she cannot avoid. Her vision of America reveals a nation full of tragedy heading toward ever greater violence in public and private lives. With no religious message, but rather the stance of a witness, she reveals the difficulties of Americans trying to find love and peace in a culture that leads them toward death and destruction.

A future assessment of the place of poetry in the Oates canon may well increase its importance; such a reevaluation has happened with other major writers whose poetry was overlooked as the early readership more quickly perceived the message in prose. Poetry's compressed language releases its power more gradually, but intelligence and verbal brilliance combined with the "talk style" rhythm that is not yet much understood should bring a wider audience to these poems.

ASPECTS OF LOVE

The second half of the twentieth century seemed a magic time to Oates. With a sense of wonder, she observed the panorama of American lives: family patterns that veer from contentment to fear, hatred, and worse. Questions arise: How can one know what influence one has on another person? How can one know if the encounter means love? Why is love like a fall into an abyss? Also, love has a public and private nature. The constant movement in which Americans engage effaces the private nature of love. They see and feel others in motel rooms, airports, and gas stations as they travel and become veneer people, all smooth surface from which traces of their lives are wiped away easily. What happens to love between people under these conditions? How much of a relationship is need, and what does one have to offer? How do women and men survive? Oates's work addresses these questions and others like them.

DEATH

Many thinkers have compared love, sexual love as well as mystical love, to death. Oates's second great theme, related to the theme of loving, concerns the feelings of the living about dying. People can raise their hands against themselves in suicide, or diminish their lives by inhuman, mute behavior or by attacks on the human and material world around them; the death of human community happens in unlivable inner cities. As individuals, people experience the death of the ego or separate self-consciousness and entrance to a transcendental state. Transcendence can come to the artist and the mystic, and perhaps also in sex and violence. Like the poet D. H. Lawrence, whom she admires deeply, Oates questions the truth of being and nonbeing in her exploration of the boundaries and limitations in human life. The unconscious mind has much to do with the experience of life and fear of death. Dreams mediate the worlds human beings inhabit.

LANDSCAPE AND SETTING

A third feature of Oates's poetry is found in her eye for landscape and setting. Few poets can rival her ability to paint a memorable scene. The details glitter: highways, newspaper pages staining fingers with ink, a ripe pear, a rumpled bed, and a decaying city square become visions in the reader's mind. Ultimately, Oates's poetry displays a great love for the land and people to which she belongs—a gratitude for the "multitudinous stars" and forms around her. Behind the poetry lies a mind poised, certain, unafraid, and capable of communicating honestly the contours and colors of her time.

LOVE AND SEXUALITY

Like Rainer Maria Rilke, Lawrence, and other modernists, Oates sees love and sexuality as the center of being; the source of both physical and spiritual energy. This recognition does not make her a sentimental or ro-

mantic poet of love. Quite to the contrary, she expresses the difficulties, limitations, and ironies that love presents. Although love is the great transforming force that accompanies growth, it most often wears a tragic face. Her source for this bitter truth is the dark side of American family life: the frequency of divorce, the incidence of rape and murder, the homeless women and children. The modern poets she reveres—W. B. Yeats, Rilke, and Lawrence—share her view; their poetry celebrates the joy of sexuality but never omits the pain, despair, or sorrow of this fundamental experience. Rilke's mature poems "Love and Other Difficulties," for example, render the dark melancholy of love beautifully.

Love experiences certainly include joy, and Oates has written enchanting poems of intimacy. In the collection *Love and Its Derangements*, the poem "Loving" describes lovers cocooned in a balloon of gauze, breathed out and invisible, a warm sac that shelters the couple from the ordinary life of people in the street. An erotic poem, "In Hot May," tells of an influx of seeds blowing onto a brick floor. They "threaten/ to turn into voices or trees or human men" as they seek the surface of female skin. The poem "Sleeping Together" evokes the blurred calm rhythm of two bodies in harmony, "hips rocked by waves of sleep," all distinctions lost in an infinite light. Wave motions are symbolized by the stanza lines' indented pattern, which suggest regular and peaceful breathing.

Yet intimacy can jar the nerves. "What I Fear . . . " tells of sleeplessness when the lovers are alert, feeling separate, dull, and "newly derailed . . . In the silence after love." The fear of drowning in a merged identity assails the speaker in "Women in Love" from *Anonymous Sins and Other Poems*. "My arms pump/ high to keep/ from drowning." Love makes its way into a person's life, flowing like water, and, like water, can refresh and nourish or flood and destroy. The rhythm of moving from oneness to separation is depicted in the poem "Where the Shadow Is Darkest" from *Angel Fire*. The poem's lovers swing in and out of their unity, but where the shadow is darkest, they are merged.

COMING-OF-AGE AND WOMEN'S LIVES

Coming-of-age experiences of young women are an important part of Oates's vision; one of her finest novels, *Marya: A Life* (1986), captures the tumults, often violent, of this period of life. Falling in love provides the topic for a humorous poem "The Small Still Voice Behind the Great Romances." The young speaker is dominated by a need for drama, a sense that death must happen for life and growth to be possible. She wants to upset time, speed it up, "to see the reel run wild, the film/ torn off its track!—I needed to die/ so I fell in love." Death occurs in sexuality, and the poem concludes in wisdom: "I died only in moods/ and ascended again/ humanly." The speaker of "A Girl at the Center of Her Life" from *Anonymous Sins and Other Poems* experiences sex without love. In a field outside town, with a young man waiting for her in a car, she feels hate yet has no skill in confronting him. She fears the reaction of other people to her change. She is "A young girl, in terror not young,/ no colt now but a sore-jointed cow/ whose pores stutter for help, help."

Similar imagery of the small but furious voice of a woman standing in the center of a moment, wind or water at the speaker's feet, informs poetry in the voice of young married women. In "A Midwestern Song" a woman has recently left her family home for life with her husband. She is bored with love and "its anatomy" and cries out, "Why do they offer me nothing more? Is there/ nothing more?" Her imagination is alive, but her voice is mute. "A Young Wife," from *Angel Fire*, displays the emotions of a woman who circles "The two-and-a-half rooms of our marriage" like a fish in her scummy fish bowl, "barely living" and fearful of her childhood nightmares. She bumps her thighs against the new bedstead, and the bruised thighs appear as an image in "Domestic Miracles." In her new and unfamiliar surroundings, the speaker feels eternal, like clay artifacts discovered by an archaeologist. Her body knows that "something miraculous must happen."

FAMILY LIFE

Marriage, family life, and children are the outward signs of the great transformations love brings. Like many women poets, Oates has written a poem titled "Marriage." Not obscure and intimidating with learned references in the manner of Marianne Moore's famous poem or propositional and narrative in the style of Denise Levertov's, Oates's poem on marriage gives the voice of a woman who needs a partial escape as she grips her

skull "to stay put." She feels the heaviness of bodies. Yet the woman and her husband radiate light; they know how to love. The poem concludes with the beautifully rhythmic lines, "we touch and wander/ and draw together puzzled in the dark."

Many poets adopt an implausible voice—of a cat, a cow, or the spirit of a dead person. Oates imagines the voice of a human fetus three months before birth in "Foetal Song." As the poem begins, mother and child are in a car. The unborn infant guesses in his cave about the noises he hears: high heels pounding the floor, horns and drills in the street, jokes and arguments. The fetus likes to swim and feel comfortable. He knows the parents, months ago, agreed to let his life continue: "I am grateful,/ I am waiting for my turn."

Other poems talk about the beginnings of life that did not succeed. In "Unborn Child," the speaker meditates on an aborted fetus lost early in the life process—it has "no marks of identification." This unborn child can be forgotten as it returns to the flux of life and the cycles begin again. A more urgent tone sounds in "A Woman's Song." The insistent word "pounding" dominates the poem. As the pulse of life goes on—construction of bridges, fireman shooting water from hoses, truck wheels on the roadways—in the midst of all this vitality, "children fall in clots in water/ blood flushed safe to the river," and the river continues pounding under a highway overpass. In its uncompromising picture of water and the flushing of the unborn, this poem recalls "Dark Stream," a poem by the South African poet Ingrid Jonker. The fluidity of life matches in strength the pounding vitality of human action.

WOMEN WHOSE LIVES ARE FOOD, MEN WHOSE LIVES ARE MONEY

Oates satirizes lives that are empty of passion in "Women Whose Lives Are Food, Men Whose Lives Are Money," the title poem of her 1978 volume. The housewives live through days bounded by regular schedules: the garbage day, the shopping mall evening. The workmen husbands eat lunches from bags that they fold and put away over the weekend. Evenings they watch handsome strangers on television, fidget through the emotions they witness, yawn, and go to bed. Their children come home and see that nothing has changed. The poem summarizes such stasis in its conclusion:

"the relief of emptiness rains/ simple, terrible, routine/ at peace."

In the same volume, "Wealthy Lady" and "He Traveled by Jet First Class to Tangier" reveal in stream-of-consciousness style the fantasies and anxieties of a woman and man who have money to indulge themselves. The lady (as she sits making out checks at her eighteenth century writing desk) imagines herself smiling upon the many people who receive her charity. For a change of pace, she reviews her stock portfolio. Taking a pistol from the drawer, she imagines scenes: a lunch date, a visit to an art museum, perhaps also to a cemetery, and an adventure in the dangerous part of town; she will defend herself from attack by drawing the pistol. Finally returning to reality, she decides to cross off her list a church committee whose chairman eats indelicately. The traveling man's life is narrated in a catalog of airports, destinations, Kodak film stops, hotel room bookings (always the luxury suite), festivals, and competitive conversations. His litany of "I am only human, I am normal" reveals his obsession with self and his deep anxiety. These people have not learned to lose their egos for the contentments of love.

"MAKING AN END" AND "LIES LOVINGLY TOLD"

The poem "Making an End" from *Angel Fire* talks of male "hunger for blows that silence words." This insistence on a violent final solution (the "fifth act" of a tragedy) is "the deadliest of incantations/ the unsaying of love, love's urgency/ pronounced backward into silence. . . ." The reader feels a fear of apocalypse caused by masculine violence in place of words. The failure of politics is thus a moral failure in the exchange of blows for speech.

Similarly, in "Lies Lovingly Told" from *The Fabulous Beasts*, Oates treats the male-female configuration in political power terms. The poem revises the saying "Every woman loves a fascist" to "Every man adores/ the woman who adores/ the Fascist." The femme fatale, evil destroyer of a man's wife and children, is a creation of adolescent fantasy and must not be revised. In this fantasy, the man has no responsibility but has only to feel the woman's charms. Oates's moral assessment of love in her poetry traces an arc from delight to boredom to emptiness and, finally, to oppression and violence.

BEING AND NONBEING

As well as the polarities of love and hate, the polarities of life and death occupy a large place in Oates's poetry. Poems about accidents, near-death experiences, drownings, and suicides invite the reader to meditate with Oates on the nature of being and nonbeing. This interest in a major philosophical topic is unsurprising; Oates studied philosophy intently as a student. She earned a Phi Beta Kappa award in part by reading ancient Greek texts, and the ideas of Plato, Thales of Miletus, and Heraclitus of Ephesus, among others, contribute to her poems about the boundaries of existence.

Physical death is considered in the poem "Not-being" from *Women Whose Lives Are Food, Men Whose Lives Are Money*. Based on Plato's difficult work *Sophist*, the poem's message (spoken in the voice of a person who almost died but returned) is that Not-being is a kind of qualified Being. As the critic Thomas Chance explains,

> In their mutually exclusive sense, Being and Non-being are unknowable to us. They are objective *termini*, "located" at the outermost limits of our experience, and, like points on a compass, serve to reorient and direct our love and aspirations. Thus, only someone who "almost" died can inform us about an undifferentiated, perfect "consciousness" that recognizes no distinction between itself and its visible form on a mirror.

If one is upset or fearful about the change that will come to each, one needs to remember, as Plato said, that one can identify with the Being in one as the fixed point for one's soul's longing. Indeed, many of Oates's poems of death show physical death itself as a local and ordinary event, even a good event. The poems "Forgiveness of Sins," "Metamorphoses," "In Case of Accidental Death," "Seizure," and "The Survivor" all disavow the common fear and terror of death. Instead, Oates says, death is not the most difficult experience.

Where being and nonbeing are extreme limits of one consciousness, suicide is an impossibility. Yet however enigmatic it may be, suicide seems real. "On the Violence of Self-Death" asks if the suicide is blameless or guilty; this is a death willed by an unhappy adult that takes time to be prepared and is not like death by accident. It presents questions—perhaps a person fights as bravely for death as others do for life. "The Suicide" asks questions in a stark, breathless style, "Was he grateful? . . . Did he marvel? . . . Was that human?" The reader senses a life-loving mind trying to address the mystery of a suicide's mental state.

ARRESTED GROWTH, DIMINISHED LIVES

More complicated than physical death is the question of the life and death of the ego. "I die because I do not die" cries Saint Teresa of Avila. So long as she holds onto the individual ego, she will not be able to live fully. When one blocks the process of maturing into one's spiritual self, one's life remains stunted, ego-centered. Life events may bring one to the threshold of transcendence—beyond the ego—and one either pulls back or takes courage and accepts change. Oates sees the ego as a shadow of death between the universe and the individual.

The death or destruction of a personality—a death in the midst of life—takes the form for Oates of an arrested growth. Many years as a college teacher have made her familiar with both the usual patterns of growth in young lives and the blockage of normal growth.

A chilling poem from *Anonymous Sins*, "And So I Grew Up to Be Nineteen and to Murder," mentions nothing about murder in the poem itself. A boy with wealthy parents recounts the stages of his life. He is aware of class and race distinctions in his society, but he says he was "a good kid" eating his Cheerios for breakfast. At an expensive private school, he and a friend begin to steal things, and he worries about his height and his personality. A sense of emptiness invades him— even the telephone book cannot distinguish him; his name appears "fourteen separate times." The poet leaves the rest of his story to imagination; the reader must contemplate the poem's conclusion from the evidence of the title.

Stories of diminished lives range from the voice of a ten-year-old child in "Three Dances of Death" (about a child who is fat, lonely, and full of wonder at the adults dancing gaily in their home bomb shelter, which is decorated to resemble a night club) to the famous writer W. Somerset Maugham, whose words of bitterness or self-loathing are heard in the poem "'I can stand there in the corner. . . .'" He says, "I am a small man. I can stand there/ in the corner, and maybe Death will not see me." The way one looks at death, as confused children, young

adults, or aged and famous people, reveals much about one's sense of identity and self-esteem.

SOCIETAL HEALTH

A further dimension of being or nonbeing comes in the consideration of spiritual health in society at large. Each individual's tendency toward personal integration and maturity or blocked growth depends in part on the social environment. Like D. H. Lawrence and other modernists, Oates understands the materialistic, consumer-oriented society to be a huge obstacle to human spiritual growth. In its relentless pursuit of pleasure, American society is necessarily death-oriented, becoming saturated with desires and choking on overabundance. In the closing lines of "American Merchandise," Oates implies the threat of death from material bloat. After a catalog of the "goods" everyone enjoys, she says "Even now the great/ diesels are headed in your direction." The ninety-car, six-diesel-engine railroad caravans and eighteen-wheel, diesel-powered trucks can run over consumers in bringing them so much more than they need.

TRAVEL AND PLACE

Like William Carlos Williams, who displayed a consuming interest in the silk-manufacturing town of Paterson, New Jersey, Oates returns frequently in her poems to the area of upstate New York near Lockport, where she spent her childhood. Yet, unlike Williams, she is also a rover who takes the whole United States and its people as her subject. Her frequent travels by car provide the settings for her thoughts on the highways, people, and places she encounters. Some European and Pacific Ocean places figure in poems in *The Time Traveler*, but she writes principally of the deserts, seacoasts, and inland habitations of the United States. Her "town" might be called Detroit, the place where she lived and taught during the riots of the late 1960's and the automobile city crucial to America's direction in the twentieth century.

Two of Oates's poems are addressed specifically to Lockport: "City of Locks" from *Angel Fire* and "Locking Through" from *The Time Traveler*. Her frequent use of the idea of life "passing through us" may have been inspired by the very graphic passing through Lockport of the Erie Barge Canal, a once-vital Eastern commercial waterway. "Locking Through" describes the experience of dropping sixty feet on the artificial water-fall of the locks. "City of Locks" paints the city and its locks as a place of crude street names, sullen, foamy water, workmen repairing water damage, and cars full of shoppers. The city of Detroit becomes the quintessential urban scene. "In the Night" tells of sirens rising during the riots in the heart of the city. The speaker hears them from a distance and muses, fearfully, about the shudder-ing city. The poem recalls Denise Levertov's "Listening to Distant Guns," about the experience of hearing the guns of World War II from across the English Channel. Both poets felt the eerie contrast of battle noises and muted cries of unseen individuals.

Poems of "on the road" experiences are often dra-matic and narrative. "Whispering Glades" from *The Time Traveler* gives a stream of talk from an elderly woman, a displaced Northerner retired to a Florida mo-bile home. She complains to her vacationing grand-children about the flies and fleas, the worms that eat her marigolds, and her unhappy memories. "Playlet for Voices" speaks in a cacophony of small talk at a wake. The anxious hostess wants to please the guests, who arrive and depart in a flow of exclamations and ques-tions answered hastily. "Young Love, America" is a jazzy scene near a Pepsi vending machine. A young man and woman are flirting, playing at love; this scene could be drawn by Norman Rockwell in his characteris-tic realism-with-nostalgia style. Similarly, "An Ameri-can Tradition" evokes the rush to return gifts to the stores on the day after Christmas. In three stanzas, the poem describes a crowd waiting outside a K-Mart and entering in a rush as the doors open. The third stanza presents the mini-drama of a wife trying to return her husband's gift; he protests, she cries, and they leave. The poem combines the ingredients typical of Oates's "trav-elogue" poems: realistic, recognizable details and a fa-miliar moral point. American experiences teem through this poetry: rescues, near drownings, one's house be-ing robbed, music at a roller rink, a stuffed refrigerator in a kitchen, and always the noises of cars, trucks, jackhammers, trains, and airplanes. Oates looks into a landscape of heroism, crime, and ordinary human moti-vations. As she has stated, her purpose as a writer is to chronicle American life in all its breadth and depth and height.

OTHER MAJOR WORKS

LONG FICTION: *With Shuddering Fall*, 1964; *A Garden of Earthly Delights*, 1967; *Expensive People*, 1968; *them*, 1969; *Wonderland*, 1971; *Do With Me What You Will*, 1973; *The Assassins: A Book of Hours*, 1975; *Childwold*, 1976; *The Triumph of the Spider Monkey*, 1976; *Son of the Morning*, 1978; *Unholy Loves*, 1979; *Cybele*, 1979; *Bellefleur*, 1980; *Angel of Light*, 1981; *A Bloodsmoor Romance*, 1982; *Mys-teries of Winterthurn*, 1984; *Solstice*, 1985; *Marya: A Life*, 1986; *Lives of the Twins*, 1987 (as Rosamond Smith); *You Must Remember This*, 1987; *American Appetites*, 1989; *Soul/Mate*, 1989 (as Smith); *Because It Is Bitter, and Because It Is My Heart*, 1990; *I Lock My Door Upon Myself*, 1990; *The Rise of Life on Earth*, 1991; *Black Water*, 1992; *Snake Eyes*, 1992 (as Smith); *Foxfire: Confessions of a Girl Gang*, 1993; *What I Lived For*, 1994; *Zombie*, 1995; *You Can't Catch Me*, 1995 (as Smith); *We Were the Mulvaneys*, 1996; *First Love*, 1996; *Man Crazy*, 1997; *My Heart Laid Bare*, 1998; *Broke Heart Blues*, 1999; *Starr Bright Will Be with You Soon*, 1999 (as Smith); *Blonde*, 2000; *The Barrens* 2001 (as Smith); *Middle Age*, 2001; *Beasts*, 2002.

SHORT FICTION: *By the North Gate*, 1963; *Upon the Sweeping Flood*, 1966; *The Wheel of Love*, 1970; *Marriages and Infidelities*, 1972; *The Goddess and Other Women*, 1974; *The Hungry Ghosts*, 1974; *Where Are You Going, Where Have You Been?*, 1974; *The Poisoned Kiss*, 1975; *The Seduction*, 1975; *Cross-ing the Border*, 1976; *Night-Side*, 1977; *All the Good People I've Left Behind*, 1978; *The Lamb of Abyssalia*, 1979; *A Sentimental Education*, 1980; *Last Days*, 1984; *Raven's Wing*, 1986; *The Assignation*, 1988; *Heat and Ohter Stories*, 1991; *Where Is Here?*, 1992; *Haunted: Tales of the Grotesque*, 1994; *Will You Al-ways Love Me?*, 1994; *The Collector of Hearts*, 1998; *Faithless: Tales of Transgression*, 2001.

PLAYS: *Miracle Play*, pr. 1974; *Three Plays*, pb. 1980; *In Darkest America: Two Plays*, pb. 1991; *I Stand Before You Naked*, pb. 1991; *Twelve Plays*, pb. 1991; *The Perfectionist and Other Plays*, pb. 1995; *New Plays*, pb. 1998.

NONFICTION: *The Edge of Impossibility: Tragic Forms in Literature*, 1972; *The Hostile Sun: The Po-*

etry of D. H. Lawrence, 1973; *New Heaven, New Earth: The Visionary Experience in Literature*, 1974; *Contraries: Essays*, 1981; *The Profane Art: Essays and Reviews*, 1983; *On Boxing*, 1987; *(Woman) Writer: Occasions and Opportunities*, 1988; *George Bellows: American Artist*, 1995; *Where I've Been, and Where I'm Going: Essays, Reviews, and Prose*, 1999.

CHILDREN'S LITERATURE: *Come Meet Muffin*, 1998.

EDITED TEXTS: *Scenes from American Life: Contemporary Short Fiction*, 1972; *The Best American Short Stories 1979*, 1979 (with Shannon Ravenel); *Night Walks: A Bedside Companion*, 1982; *First Person Singular: Writers on Their Craft*, 1983; *The Best American Essays*, 1991; *The Oxford Book of American Short Stories*, 1992; *American Gothic Tales*, 1996; *Snapshots: Twentieth Century Mother-Daughter Fiction*, 2000 (with Janet Berliner).

BIBLIOGRAPHY

Bender, Eileen Teper. *Joyce Carol Oates: Artist in Residence*. Bloomington: Indiana University Press, 1987. Bender studies Oates as both artist and critic, the recorder of American mores and moral analyst. Her double consciousness applies to her position in the academic world and the world of feminist thought. The opening chapter and lengthy conclusion will help students of the poetry to understand Oates's "revisionist" art.

Grant, Mary Kathryn. *The Tragic Vision of Joyce Carol Oates*. Durham, N.C.: Duke University Press, 1978. Grant includes poetry in her excellent study of the Oatesian tragic vision of America. Topics that illuminate the poetry are violence (in Detroit, in cities, on the road), settings, personal power and powerlessness, and literary influence. Chapter 5, "The Tragic Vision," is particularly instructive about the sense of purpose in Oates's work—to awaken Americans to their common situation.

Johnson, Greg. *Invisible Writer: A Biography of Joyce Carol Oates*. New York: Dutton, 1998. Granted privileged access to Joyce Carol Oates's letters and journals, as well as extensive interviews with family, friends, colleagues, and Oates herself, biographer Greg Johnson examines the relationship between Oates's life and work in this fascinating exploration of a complex and gifted artist. Johnson reveals little-known facts about Oates's personal and family history and debunks many of the myths that have arisen about this brilliant, enigmatic woman.

Lercangée, Francine. *Joyce Carol Oates: An Annotated Bibliography*. New York: Garland, 1986. An ambitious and essential work that lists 423 poems by original publication and subsequent collection. A full table of contents is included for each collection of poems. Critical essays by Oates as well as criticism of her work by others receive careful and detailed annotation. The introduction by Bruce F. Michelson emphasizes her experiments in form. Several indices complete this useful reference work.

Pearlman, Mickey, and Katherine Usher Henderson. *Inter/View: Talks with America's Writing Women*. Lexington: University Press of Kentucky, 1990. Numerous interviews with Oates have been published, but this one, conducted by Mickey Pearlman, reveals topics germane to the poetry: class relations, gender relations, and the vital role of memory in her creativity. Oates talks about the biographers (whom Oates labels "pathographers") who ascribe sickness and deviance to women writers, conflating personal and professional lives in a very damaging way.

Stevens, Peter. "The Poetry of Joyce Carol Oates." In *Critical Essays on Joyce Carol Oates*, edited by Linda W. Wagner. Boston: G. K. Hall, 1979. A lengthy, detailed study of the first five collections of poems, from *Anonymous Sins* to *Women Whose Lives Are Food, Men Whose Lives Are Money*. Stevens relates themes and styles to the modernist aesthetic of D. H. Lawrence, Franz Kafka, and James Dickey and the psychic spirituality of Flannery O'Connor. He identifies major themes of modern meaninglessness, dualities of love, transcendence and limitation, and the shadow side of human existence. He finds a progression from early questioning in the poems to a declarative stance. An essential work.

Waller, G. F. *Dreaming America: Obsession and Transcendence in the Fiction of Joyce Carol Oates*. Baton Rouge: Louisiana State University Press, 1979. Although concerned mainly with the novels, this study will be useful to students of the poetry in its opening chapter, "The Obsessive Vision," and the second chapter, "The Phantasmagoria of American Personality." Both chapters are general and include mentions of poems from *Anonymous Sins*, *Angel Fire*, and *Love and Its Derangements*. The conclusion relies too heavily on the influence of D. H. Lawrence, but at the time the book was written such a view was natural. No index, but a very interesting bibliography of related sources, with names such as Victor Frankl, Paul Ricoeur, Paul Tillich, and Raymond Williams.

Doris Earnshaw;
bibliography updated by the editors

FRANK O'HARA

Born: Baltimore, Maryland; June 27, 1926
Died: Fire Island, New York; July 25, 1966

PRINCIPAL POETRY
A City Winter and Other Poems, 1952
Oranges, 1953
Meditations in an Emergency, 1957
Odes, 1960
Lunch Poems, 1964
Love Poems (Tentative Title), 1965
In Memory of My Feelings: A Selection of Poems,
    1967 (Bill Berkson, editor)
The Collected Poems of Frank O'Hara, 1971, 1995
    (Donald Allen, editor)
Selected Poems, 1974
Early Poems, 1946-1951, 1976
Poems Retrieved, 1951-1966, 1977

OTHER LITERARY FORMS
Frank O'Hara was always a poet, no matter what he wrote. His plays (published in *Selected Plays*, 1978), only a few of which are actually capable of being produced with any degree of dramatic effectiveness, are more often plays with words and visual effects than exploration of character or idea through dramatic con-

flict. Some juxtapose a vast variety of characters (from O'Hara's own friends to Benjamin Franklin, Marlene Dietrich, William Blake, and Generalissimo Franco), most with only a single short speech, with connections nonexistent outside of O'Hara's fertile imagination. Others of these short plays offer sustained characters speaking in non sequiturs or in monologues unheard by other characters. In one play, *Try! Try!* (written in 1950, first performed in 1951, rewritten in 1953), the monologues work in an interesting way, since there is a plot with a recognizable triangle of characters and actual dialogue, besides some poetic and psychologically suggestive monologues. Another produced play, *The General Returns from One Place to Another* (1964), uses verbal, visual, and dramatic means to satirize the American military abroad, particularly in the person of Douglas MacArthur.

O'Hara's prose has been collected in *Standing Still and Walking in New York* (1975, Donald Allen, editor). The volume consists chiefly of miscellaneous pieces on modern art and contains a small quantity of literary criticism as well.

Besides writing for *Art News*, O'Hara worked on the catalogs for various exhibits at the Museum of Modern Art, including those on contemporary American painters Jackson Pollock and Robert Motherwell. His art criticism tends to be impressionistic rather than technical, but it effectively conveys the essence of contemporary painting.

ACHIEVEMENTS
Other than the advent of the Beat movement at roughly the same time, probably the most exciting thing to happen to American poetry is the mid-twentieth century ascendance of vital and natural voices, with all the immediacy of actual human talk, through the work of the "New York Poets." Heading them were Frank O'Hara, John Ashbery, and Kenneth Koch, with O'Hara's voice being the dominant one. Drawing elements from Walt Whitman, William Carlos Williams, Gertrude Stein, French Surrealists such as Guillaume Apollinaire and Pierre Reverdy, and the Russian poets Vladimir Mayakovsky and Boris Pasternak, O'Hara shattered the prevailing poetic standards regarding language, form, and content and forged his own verse with tremendous vigor

and fire. He did not want to produce the sort of pristine, shapely work that could be found in scores of other volumes, admired by the literary establishment of New Critics for their traditional forms, metaphoric complexities, and mythic overtones. O'Hara rejected all of these familiar ingredients, writing in unfettered free verse, shifting images and metaphors wildly throughout a poem, and dealing with earthy subject matter or very personal experiences without any effort to make them seem universally significant. For his efforts, he received the National Book Award for Poetry for *The Collected Poems of Frank O'Hara* in 1972.

Most of O'Hara's poems flow, without any attempt to structure them formally, through the free association of his surrealistic poems, where one image or word leads to another, however logically unrelated, or through the simple recording of his actual activities, thoughts, and feelings on special occasion (or not-so-special ones). Because he was so keenly in tune with his feelings, such poems work splendidly in conveying the moods that generated them, especially through the marvelously vivid vocabulary which dances across his pages.

Not least among his achievements is his lively sense of humor, sometimes just a light tone that flavors much of his work as he playfully recounts his activities or observations, sometimes satiric views of various cultural and political icons (including the movies), sometimes raucous comedy full of delightful surprises, such as the sun appearing to chat with the poet abed or a vision of bugs walking through the apartment "carrying a little banner/ which says 'in search of lanolin.'"

Delight in words and experience, surprise at the variety of existence: These are the keynotes of O'Hara's poetry, which retains its freshness and appeal far beyond the attempts of so many others to imitate it.

BIOGRAPHY

Although born in Baltimore and reared in rural Massachusetts, Francis O'Hara discovered a more appropriate milieu first among fellow poets and aficionados of the other arts at Harvard (where he received his B.A. degree in English literature in 1950) and subsequently in New York City. In the meantime he had spent two years in the Navy in the South Pacific and a year at the University of Michigan, where he received his M.A. in 1951

and the Avery Hopwood Major Award in Poetry for a manuscript collection of poetry (his master's thesis). Once in New York, he rejoined fellow Harvard graduates John Ashbery and Kenneth Koch and involved himself in various arts in assorted capacities, while remaining, with the others, quite apart from the literary establishment of the day. He worked for the Museum of Modern Art, advancing from a staff position working on circulating exhibitions to an associate curatorship, selecting numerous exhibitions of contemporary American and Spanish artists and being responsible for the catalogs published in conjunction with the exhibits. He also wrote occasional articles and reviews for *Art News*, and had several plays performed. He adopted a very casual attitude toward his poetry, sending poems off to friends without keeping a copy, stuffing them in drawers, gathering material only under pressure from eager editors such as John Bernard Myers. He was intensely involved (whether as friend or lover) with many different and interesting women and men throughout these New York years until his death after a freak accident on Fire Island.

Frank O'Hara

ANALYSIS

To enter the world of Frank O'Hara is to abandon all familiar road maps, to give up hope for a straight and clear way through, for easily recognizable landmarks that indicate where one is going, where one has been. With "no revolver pointing the roadmarks," the reader is free to travel without preconceptions and without insistent points made by the poet. O'Hara's world is closer to Lewis Carroll's than to Robert Frost's, being constantly full of surprises, twists in the road, byways, sharp turns, cul-de-sacs, a grotesquerie of roadside attractions, and few places to stop or rest, so that one ends up nowhere near one's anticipated goal, perhaps not even at an ending at all but simply at a halt, like running out of gas. For that is how many O'Hara poems conclude—with neither a bang nor a whimper, but only a sudden cessation of the impetuous, rapid drive of words and images and feelings that has made up the poem. His poetry is exciting, startling, dizzying, frightening, overwhelming, demanding, involving, crude, elaborate, stark, disorderly, sexy, and sometimes very funny. As a poet crafting his art, O'Hara had as much gleeful fun—even when dealing with feelings considerably less than euphoric—as the liveliest child or the most daredevil racer.

O'Hara was the epitome of the New York poet: fast, frenzied, jazzy, upbeat, smart-aleck, shrewd, unzipped, down-to-earth, open, and full of action. Like his fellow New York poets (friends, some contemporaries, some followers or students from a workshop he offered), he thrived on the bustle of the city and participated in its multitude of activities. Far from being a poetic hermit in an ivory tower, he actively involved himself with people and with the other arts—notably with painters, but also with dancers and musicians. The kind of painting he favored was action painting, a style indigenous to New York and led by Jackson Pollock. Its random quality, abstractness, and emphasis on the process of painting rather than the static permanence demonstrated in a still life or a portrait all have their correspondences in O'Hara's poetry.

This poetry pulses with action of all sorts—sexual, mental, emotional, physical, natural, industrial, transportational—all the types of action, in fact, that make up America. Action itself is the subject of some of his poems, such as his self-styled "I do this I do that" poems.

The action of the poem may be expressed in vocabulary (colorful concrete nouns and vivid active verbs expressing dynamic movement); in syntax (whether conventional—using such devices as piled-up participial phrases, short sentences, and parataxis, though quite grammatically—or unconventional—omitting parts of a sentence or letting a single word or phrase serve two different but simultaneous functions in two adjacent syntactical units); in interjections ("Hey!," "Yeah!"); or in rapid shifts of subject, place, or time—from stanza to stanza, sentence to sentence, line to line, and even from one word or phrase to the next.

"MY HEAT"

"My Heat" provides evidence of all of these. The opening stanza is filled with verbs denoting vigorous action: four finite verbs ("committed," "fell off the balcony," "I'd force the port!/ Violate the piers"), one infinitive ("to refountain myself"), and two present participles ("jetting," "turning in air"). Unconventional syntax and punctuation give a sensation of dizziness fitting this turning and falling: The "if" clause seems to have two main verbs unseparated by a conjunction or comma, both with "I" as subject; then O'Hara does not set off what is presumably his main clause by a comma after the subordinate clause, so that the infinitive could be regarded as part of either the subordinate or the main clause. The verb's unfamiliarity ("refountain") also sharpens the reader's attention, as does the unclearness of its connection with the rest of the sentence. This main clause seems to end with the exclamation point after "port," yet the next word is another verb, presumably another main verb for the subject "I"—unless it is an imperative for the two vocatives ending the stanza ("you bores! you asses!"). Keeping readers alert, the very next word, "geology," at the beginning of the next stanza, not only has nothing to do with "the balcony," "the port," or "the piers," but also is punctuated by a question mark.

The punctuation is certainly not completely unorthodox, though it is surprising. What would give the traditional poetry reader more trouble are the rapid shifts in imagery, but this is part of O'Hara's point: the pleasure he takes in "jetting" from one image to whatever it suggests, the pleasure he takes in "jetting" such words and phrases from his typewriter—all as opposed to the "you" in this poem, who always seems a few steps behind poet "Frank," who proclaims, with another surprising but apt and active verb choice, "I've kayoed your popular cant/ I'd rather jet!"

A New Critic such as John Crowe Ransom would probably throw up his hands at the untidiness of O'Hara's metaphorical maneuverings. There is no clear one-to-one correspondence between tenors and vehicles here; there is certainly no single picture provided out of which the meaning derives, no identifiable incident which gives rise to the poetic expression. The meaning, rather, resides in the exuberant movement of the poem and its words, images which—in themselves and in their transformations throughout the poem—suggest the force of creativity as well as that of sexuality.

This poem is, in fact, only one of the most compressed treatments of sexuality among O'Hara's work, from the ejaculatory "jetting" of its opening line on to the final line: "'That's no furnace, that's my heart!'" The heat of passion is inflated to the power of a furnace. The diffuse jetting rampant throughout the poem amply reflects the exuberant sexuality—not a sexual desire directed at a single person and thus capable of being satisfied, but rather directed at no one in particular, an all-pervasive urge, reveling in the fact of sexuality and the pleasure of the sexual feeling itself. O'Hara's images are used not as specific metaphors—he mixes them too outrageously for that—but rather as evocations of the many flavors and feelings of sexuality (or, in other poems, whatever has motivated that poetic outburst): its sweetness and beauty in roses, its violence (in violating the piers), its power (as a volcano "to melt everyone into syrup"), its self-containment, its richness, even its humor ("laughing like an old bedspring," a simile that makes a believable aural comparison as well as fitting the sexual subject matter).

JOYFUL SEXUALITY, IMAGISTIC FERTILITY

O'Hara's eroticism is far from *fin de siècle* decadence, which hints at more than it tells; nor does it explicitly depict sexual acts, as in pornography. Rather, it revels in a joyous sexuality that fellow homosexual poet Walt Whitman would certainly recognize and appreciate. Only rarely does O'Hara depict an actual sexual act, as in "Twin spheres full of fur and noise/ rolling softly up my belly" for an act of fellatio. A lively choice

of images ("my mouth is full of suns") and abstractions ("that softness seems so anterior to that hardness"), with a climactic hint of Apollo's chariot of the sun, raises the experience to a mythic level, but not for long. O'Hara's poetry must constantly move, never rest, and of course the moment of sexual ecstasy dissolves, even as it is achieved: "It must be discovered soon and disappear."

Sex is not, however much it may appear so from these examples, O'Hara's only concern; like Whitman, he felt intense pleasure simply in living, and since sex represents the most intense form of physical pleasure, he naturally perceived a sexual quality in his relationship with living—in all its aspects—and hence with the rest of the world. He could penetrate the world—make an impact on it, enter its multifarious experiences—just as he could penetrate a lover; he could also be penetrated by experience, by the myriad sensory impressions all around him—just as a lover might penetrate him. This openness to both roles parallels his sexual orientation; his homosexuality, indicating openness to nonstandard sexual practice, may have a share in O'Hara's imagistic fertility, as he presents (in "Easter," for example) nonhuman and inanimate nature surging with sexuality ("it's the night like a love it all cruisy and nelly"; "the world booms its seven cunts/ like a river plunged upon and perishing"). Such images, which cannot be deciphered into metaphorical correspondences of tenor and vehicle with an "underlying" subject behind the metaphorical development, serve to suggest sexuality in O'Hara's more public poems (as contrasted with private poems such as "Twin spheres," written for his lover Vincent Warren) without having to be gender-specific.

In most of his poems the images shift constantly; the reader is meant to flow with the stream of O'Hara's free associations, which is often remarkably easy to do because of his vivid and emotionally evocative choice of nouns, verbs, and adjectives, even when the precise meaning of a passage remains indecipherable. "Savoy" shifts ground even more rapidly than "My Heat," yet it conveys a rich sequence of moods.

"SAVOY"

"Savoy" opens with a feeling of terror, although its cause is unclear. Like other O'Hara poems, it begins with an image which he proceeds to join to a simile—a logical enough poetic device—but the simile proceeds to take over as the poem's main concern. Yet O'Hara writes elsewhere, "How I hate subject matter!," and the reader realizes that actually neither simile nor its tenor is the subject of the poem. Looking at the extended so-called simile ("like a bespectacled carapaceous witch doctor of Rimini/ beautifying an adolescent tubbed in entrails of blue cement . . .") reveals that it is hardly to be apprehended in the manner of a Metaphysical conceit. What is a witch doctor doing in Rimini, on the Italian seacoast? How can anyone be beautified in a bath of "blue cement"? A few lines down, who is the "you" suddenly addressed? The rapid changes mirror those of a dream or nightmare, in which identities shift inexplicably. This is the method of surrealist poetry, which O'Hara brought into American poetry with a new force after it had flourished in Europe several decades earlier. O'Hara clearly indicates a romance with the word and whatever lively images it evokes rather than with its specific literal denotation. Even in describing terrors and dangers in "Savoy," O'Hara is having fun; the pleasure is in the movement of the poem, not in discerning its "meaning."

"I do this I do that" poems

His less surrealistic poems, however, which record his actions, are not hard to understand at all. Simple in form and structure, the "I do this I do that" poems, as he calls them in "Getting Up Ahead of Someone (Sun)," are, at their best, more than a mere transcription of the day's activities; they convey the quality of the poet's conscious mind and the shifting moods stirred by his activities. The most famous—and most moving—example of this sort of poem is "The Day Lady Died," which pays tribute to singer Billie Holiday upon her death but is hardly a standard elegy with explicit presentation of grief and concentration on praise for the deceased. Instead, O'Hara begins the poem—and carries on for the bulk of it—with an account of his movements, fairly random, around New York on a Friday afternoon. Suddenly he is caught short by "a NEW YORK POST with her face on it," and he is reminded of hearing Holiday ("Lady Day") sing "in the 5 SPOT," when "everyone and I stopped breathing." This last action (or rather lack of it) stunningly conveys the whole impact not only of

Holiday's art but also of her death and is especially effective in stopping movement and thought after such a bustling buildup. The rest of the poem does not prepare the reader for such a conclusion at all.

Most of his "I do this I do that" poems are much less serious, and often poke fun at himself or take a delightfully lighthearted approach to the addressee, a friend or a lover, and the particular relationship they share. In fact, O'Hara's humor is one of his most characteristic traits; however, his work is quite different from light verse because it rarely satirizes and certainly does not use rhyme and rhythm. Rather, it is based on surprise, giving his readers the unexpected, as his surrealist pieces do. Yet those are rarely comic because they so constantly shift ground that the reader has no solid base to stand on, a necessity if comic surprise is to hit with true effectiveness.

"Poem (Lana Turner has collapsed!)"

A true comic gem is "Poem (Lana Turner has collapsed!)," a delightful little poem that O'Hara wrote on the spur of the moment on a ferry to a poetry reading. Written in the conversational tone at which he was so adept, it enters the world of comedy with the very first line, with its hysterical exclamation point like a sensationalistic headline (as the poem later reveals it in fact to be). The reader knows not to take this as seriously as Lady Day's death, first because of the exclamation point, then because this announcement appears at the beginning of the poem rather than at its climax.

The second line continues the humorous tone with O'Hara's verb choice—"I was trotting along." The speaker is obviously not a horse, nor does this verb have the intensity of suggestion of those in "My Heat"; it merely gives the reader a funny sense of the light, frolicsome quality of the poet's movements. The humor continues—and builds—stylistically with the paratactic structure of short clauses joined by coordinating conjunctions, then in content with the poet's slight disagreement with his friend about the weather (whether it was raining and snowing or hailing), and further, with the surprising apparent shift in position of the "you," who at first appears to be with the speaker and then is seen as the goal he is walking toward. The poet notes the traffic "acting exactly like the sky," using the humorous idiom of very mild outrage ("isn't that exactly like so-and-so?"). Then comes the appearance of the head-line—to complete what now appears to be a flashback after the poem's opening line. The poet proceeds to as-sure the motion-picture star that she has no reason to collapse, there being no snow or rain in Hollywood; moreover, he refers to his own behavior at parties, where he himself has never collapsed. He concludes with an actual address to the actress—comically unpunctuated, although it encompasses an interjection, a vocative, and two short clauses not joined by conjunctions: "oh Lana Turner we love you get up." This last line suggests that all the motion-picture star needs here is reassurance of her fans' love and an affectionately authoritative encour-agement. O'Hara is implying that he cannot take this in-flated problem seriously, nor should anyone else; he is gently mocking the superhuman status accorded celebri-ties. Of course this is a poem simply to be enjoyed, hardly to be pondered seriously. Although O'Hara cer-tainly took poetry seriously, he also believed in enjoying it, as he did life.

Living in a throbbing city, he had countless experi-ences to enjoy, from attending films and ballet to walk-ing the streets (as in the poems just discussed) to meet-ing with a wide range of acquaintances, for a Coke, a trip to a museum, a party, or even sex. All these experi-ences are celebrated in his vital poetry, through which he has vividly conveyed not only a sense of the excitement of life but also a rich sense of himself as a living person: As with Walt Whitman, it is not a mere book one en-counters when reading O'Hara: "Who touches this touches a man."

OTHER MAJOR WORKS

PLAY: *Selected Plays*, pb. 1978.

NONFICTION: *Jackson Pollock*, 1959; *Robert Moth-erwell, with Selections from the Artist's Writings*, 1965; *Standing Still and Walking in New York*, 1975.

BIBLIOGRAPHY

Breslin, James E. B. "Frank O'Hara." In *From Modern to Contemporary: American Poetry, 1945-1965*. Chicago: University of Chicago Press, 1984. O'Hara's "lunch hour poems" demythologize city poetry, con-trasting him with T. S. Eliot and Allen Ginsberg. A

close analysis of "On Seeing Larry Rivers' *Washing-ton Crossing the Delaware* at the Museum of Mod-ern Art" is made with reference to the painting, which is included as an illustration. Complemented by footnotes and an index.

Feldman, Alan. *Frank O'Hara*. Boston: Twayne, 1979. This book introduces O'Hara as a New York poet. His language, style, and degrees of coherence are analyzed. Themes of "the self," varieties of feelings, and humor are examined in succeeding chapters. The conclusion is an assessment of O'Hara's influ-ence. Supplemented by a chronology, a select bibli-ography, and an index.

Gooch, Brad. *City Poet: The Life and Times of Frank O'Hara*. New York: HarperPerennial, 1994. Gooch's biography of O'Hara details his life from his Massa-chusetts Catholic boyhood, to Harvard, and to New York where his art criticism became seminal to the abstract expressionist painters and sculptors.

Holahan, Susan. "Frank O'Hara's Poetry." In *American Poetry Since 1960: Some Critical Perspectives*, ed-ited by Robert B. Shaw. Cheadle, England: Carcanet Press, 1973. O'Hara's poems are ceremonies of naming persons, places, and things in New York; they are gestures of art in a poetic rather than a phys-ical universe. His style is illustrated for its remark-able syntax, separating one perception from another. *In Memory of My Feelings* is analyzed as an echo of William Wordsworth.

Molesworth, Charles. "'The Clear Architecture of the Nerves': The Poetry of Frank O'Hara." In *The Fierce Embrace: A Study of Contemporary Ameri-can Poetry*. Columbia: University of Missouri Press, 1979. Placed in a context of plastic arts, O'Hara's poetry gains more than by comparing it with other poetry. Contains notes and an index.

Perloff, Marjorie. *Frank O'Hara: Poet Among Painters*. New York: George Braziller, 1977. Perloff analyzes O'Hara's "aesthetic of attention" and surveys the early poems. Her central chapter looks at his "poem-paintings," and then his "great period" is presented. The conclusion covers the 1960's and the relation-ship of his poetry to John Ashbery and Allen Ginsberg. Augmented by illustrations, notes, a bibliographical note, and an index.

Vendler, Helen. "Frank O'Hara: The Virtue of the Alterable." In *Part of Nature, Part of Us: Modern American Poets*. Cambridge, Mass.: Harvard University Press, 1980. This essay reviews O'Hara's work as a genre of overproduced conversation with an incapacity to be abstract and a discomfort with form. His poetry contrasted the appeal of film with the great reality of sex. O'Hara, however, proved in his late poetry that he could capture the rhythms of America better than most of his contemporaries.

Ward, Geoff. *Statutes of Liberty: The New York School of Poets*. New York: Palgrave, 2001. An acclaimed account of the New York school and its key figures: John Ashbery, Frank O'Hara, and James Schuyler and their growing influence on postmodern poetics.

*Scott Giantvalley;
bibliography updated by the editors*

JOHN OLDHAM

Born: Shipton Moyne, Gloucestershire, England; August 9, 1653

Died: Holm Pierrepont, near Nottingham, England; December 9, 1683

PRINCIPAL POETRY

A Satyr Against Vertue, 1679
Satyrs upon the Jesuits, 1681
Some New Pieces Never Before Publisht, 1681
Poems and Translations, 1683
Selected Poems, 1980 (Ken Robinson, editor)
The Poems of John Oldham, 1987 (Raman Seldon and Harold F. Brooks, editors)

OTHER LITERARY FORMS

John Oldham's literary output was restricted to verse and verse imitation. Nevertheless, his influence in these forms produced a shaping force in English literature.

ACHIEVEMENTS

As a notably influential although minor literary figure, John Oldham is probably less recognized for any single achievement of his own than for the way he helped to shape the development of seventeenth and eighteenth century verse satire. The two major phases of his brief literary career reflect two very different satiric styles: the harshness of Juvenalian invective and the more tempered voice of Horatian conversation. Although his *Satyrs upon the Jesuits*, the harshest of the Juvenalian satires, contains Oldham's most well-known and frequently anthologized pieces, his later satires reflect a comparatively moderate tone and are now recognized as his best poems. Among these, his "imitations" of such figures as Horace, Juvenal, and Nicholas Boileau were formative in establishing a loose form of verse translation in which the original appeared in a contemporary social and literary context.

Oldham's severity in his early satires looks back to the extreme style of sixteenth century satirists; his somewhat more tempered voice in the later verses looks forward to the moderation of John Dryden and Alexander Pope. When Oldham died at the age of thirty, he had already won a firm position for himself in the development of English literature. He failed, however, to produce a satire to rival those of the great satirists who followed him and who were indebted to his limited though influential literary achievement.

Although no complete edition of Oldham's poetry exists, several partial editions are available, notably the Centaur edition of 1960 and Ken Robinson's facsimile edition of 1980. *The Poems of John Oldham* (1987; Raman Seldon and Harold F. Brooks, editors), corrects errors found in the previous editions.

BIOGRAPHY

John Oldham was born in the English countryside on August 9, 1653, the son of a dissenting minister. He received a solid education both at home and in grammar school, entered St. Edmund's Hall, Oxford, when he was seventeen and took his bachelor's degree in May, 1674. Sometime during this period, Oldham wrote his first poem, a long Pindaric ode "To the Memory of My Dear Friend, Mr. Charles Morwent." By this time he had confirmed, at least to himself, a lifelong commitment to the writing of poetry.

Because it was impossible to make a living from one's pen without the aid of a literary patron, Oldham assumed the position of "usher" (assistant master) in Whitgift's school, Croyden, where he remained in employment from 1674 to 1677. Although the aspiring poet had written several poems since his first ode, it was during these years that he wrote his first verse satire, *A Satyr Against Vertue* (1679). It was also during the years at Croyden that Oldham was recognized by the more prominent Restoration wits, notably the earls of Rochester and Dorset, and Sir Charles Sedley.

As his poetic reputation grew, so did Oldham's dissatisfaction with his position at Whitgift's. Considering his tutoring duties to be little more than menial labor, in 1678 he accepted a position as a private tutor, which he kept until 1680 when he decided to move to London and become part of the literati of Restoration society. A year before the move to London, his *Satyrs upon the Jesuits* had been piratically printed, and Oldham's reputation as a promising young verse satirist was already established.

Not much is known of the time Oldham spent in London. He studied medicine for about a year, but then devoted himself wholly to poetry. He admitted to adopting the lifestyle of the Restoration town gentleman, engaging in drinking and debauchery, although he was quick to feel the pangs of conscience when reflecting on his excesses. During these three final years of his life, his health declined, and finally he retired to Nottinghamshire, residence of the young earl of Kingston, who offered the poet a comfortable home where he might pursue his literary career.

It was here that, free from the social and literary demands which London society placed on him, Oldham produced some of his finest satires and imitations. In 1683, however, only three years after he had moved to London in pursuit of literary fame, Oldham contracted smallpox. He died on December 9 of that year.

ANALYSIS

John Oldham's calling was not to the polite muse. Instead, he saw himself as inheriting the role of the poet who rails against the faults and vices of the age. His harsh Juvenalian satires and lively verse imitations were quick to attack what was wrong with society. Oldham's tone was rugged yet sharp; his poetic attitude was one of indignation. He mastered the art of the cankered muse, and left behind him some of the finest examples of vituperative verse satire.

The subjects, themes, and satirical approaches that Oldham adopted account for much of the bite in his work. Early in his career, when he wrote his most severe satires, Oldham typically addressed himself to issues which were either personally or socially repulsive to him. In *A Satyr Against Vertue*, for example, he rails against affected notions of virtue which "plague our happy state;" in the "Satire Addressed to a Friend" he complains about his own personal circumstances; and in his *Satyrs upon the Jesuits* he vents his indignation about a subject which aroused some of the most heated political and religious controversy of the age. Unlike many of his more witty contemporaries who were content to treat their subjects with humor and objectivity, Oldham focused directly on the victims of his satire—cursing them for their actions, condemning the society in which they thrived, and depicting them in the most offensive ways. While John Dryden or even the earl of Rochester might dexterously mix censure with praise, there is no mistaking the focus of Oldham's direct accusations.

Both personal and social circumstances might account for the severity of Oldham's satiric tone. His strong sense of individualism made him an unsuitable candidate for the system of patronage, and what he perceived as the declining position of literature in Restoration England only served to confirm his individualism. It is not surprising that Oldham wrote some of his best verses after he had left London and retired to the English countryside, detached from the environment of "hack" writers and commercial values. Yet it was that very society which gave him the subjects for his satires. Political disputes between Tories and Whigs, religious controversy between Catholics and Protestants, and what many perceived as the general decadent atmosphere of London society supplied him with his best materials.

SATYRS UPON THE JESUITS

Oldham's *Satyrs upon the Jesuits*, probably written shortly before his move to London, typifies the kind of invective and raillery for which he has become so famous. In the prologue, Oldham describes satire as his weapon and indignation as his muse; in each of the four satires, he adopts the perspective of a different speaker who functions as the vehicle of his satiric lashes. This satiric approach made it possible for him to focus directly on his victims and at the same time vary his tone so that the satire might remain consistent in its attack and yet flexible in its point of view. The ghost of Henry Garnet, a provincial of the Jesuits who was executed in 1606 for his role in the Gunpowder Plot, speaks in the first satire, urging the Jesuits to kill and plunder, to create another "inquisition." When Oldham speaks in his own voice in the second satire, he then vents his own rage against the Jesuits with the same vigor that "Garnet's Ghost" used to plot against king and nation. Perspective shifts again in the third satire, "Loyola's Will," where Oldham speaks through the voice of Ignatius Loyola himself, founder of the Jesuit order. Here St. Ignatius, pictured on his deathbed, passes on to his followers the "hidden rules" and "secrets" of villainy. In the final satire, the perspective is even more removed as the wooden image of St. Ignatius assumes the satiric voice, exposing its own worthlessness and the emptiness of Catholic ritual.

The Juvenalian rant of the *Satyrs upon the Jesuits* has its source not only in the different perspectives that Oldham adopted in each satire, constantly allowing him to shift the focus of his invective, but also in the details of each speaker's remarks. One of the most savage passages of "Garnet's Ghost," for example, is filled with specific instructions on how to murder priests, mothers, unborn children, infants, young virgins, the aged, and the crippled. In "Loyola's Will," readers are given a gruesome picture of the dying Jesuit leader as he "heaves" and "pants" on his deathbed. The picture becomes even more gruesome in the final satire where spiders and rats find "refuge" and "religious sanctuary" in the decaying body of Saint Ignatius. In depicting such scenes, Oldham was extending himself far beyond the lines of general religious satire: The Jesuits are not merely criticized; they are portrayed and condemned in vicious terms.

TRANSLATIONS AND IMITATIONS

Satyrs upon the Jesuits was Oldham's masterpiece in his harsh Juvenalian mode. His verse translations and imitations, however, which began to consume his poetic energies, were more temperate and moderate. Several critics believe that the very act of imitation helped to tame Oldham's sharp satiric voice. Even the last of the *Satyrs upon the Jesuits*, spoken from the perspective of a dead, wooden image, was modeled in part on one of Horace's satires and is more distant and mocking in its manner.

With the verse imitations, Oldham entered the most influential phase of his brief literary career. The refined Horatian style of the translations looked forward to the moderation of Dryden and Alexander Pope. Equally influential was the theory of imitation which Oldham practiced: Instead of translating the original in its own historical context, he rendered it in a contemporary English setting—at once making the classics more alive and immediate, and making his own contemporary verse more intellectually respectable. Again, both Dryden and Pope in their own imitations were to follow Oldham's practice.

Among Oldham's early imitations were "Bion's Lamentation for Adonis," which was his elegy on Rochester, and the renditions of two odes of Horace. His outstanding satiric imitations, of Horace, Juvenal, and Nicholas Boileau, were to follow in 1681 and 1682. The art of translation and imitation dominated this final phase of Oldham's career; even poems which were not strict imitations nevertheless drew on classical sources. "Spenser's Ghost" and "Satire Addressed to a Friend," two of his outstanding satires of this period, both draw on Juvenal's seventh satire. The three imitations generally considered to be Oldham's masterpieces are his renditions of Horace's ninth satire, first book (1681), Juvenal's third satire (1682), and Boileau's eighth satire (1682).

The conversational tone and comic subject of the Horatian imitation immediately distinguishes it from Oldham's earlier satiric invective. Instead of writing about plots and murder and villainy, Oldham's subject here is the poet's encounter with a bore whom he cannot manage to escape. The story is humorous, not vengeful; the "tedious chat" of the bore clearly contrasts with the bitter pleas of "Garnet's Ghost" and the deathbed speech of St. Ignatius. Contemporary social issues are satirized, but only mildly, at times almost with understatement. The Popish Plot, for example, which fired much of Oldham's invective in his *Satyrs upon the Jesuits*, becomes in the imitation a bothersome issue which the poet would just as soon dismiss. In his translation of Horace, Oldham was not only imitating the Horatian style, but adopting and perfecting a very different kind of satiric voice for himself.

The imitations of Juvenal and Boileau exemplify Oldham's mastery of this new satiric voice. Although the subject of each of these imitations is more serious than that of the Horatian piece, Oldham continues to treat his subject with a notably lighter tone. The criticism of London in his translation of Juvenal, for instance, describes the "nauseous town" as totally lacking any value or worth, but the details of the satire are often comic, especially in the portraits of the city's hairdressers, plotters, and courtiers. When Oldham describes England as the "common sewer" for France, his portraits of fops and their fashions are more often the object of humor than of indignation. The situation is much the same in his rendition of Boileau's eighth satire, which often exaggerates comedy to the point of absurdity. In this dispute between doctor and poet, man's position in the animal kingdom becomes a playful issue which Oldham easily exploits for his satiric purposes. Urbane conversation and pointed ridicule allow Oldham to treat the satire with humor: While the doctor defends, for example, man's serious position as "Lord of the Universe," the poet luxuriates in descriptions of tigers creating plots and factions, or "Whig and Tory lions" engaging in political disputes. The poet's final sustained comparison of man with an "ass" may not convince the doctor, but it makes Oldham's satire all the more engaging for its fine sense of wit.

VIGOROUS INVECTIVE

Despite this change in tone, Oldham never lost his ability to write fiercely vigorous invective. This ability was, after all, his distinguishing achievement as a satirist and is almost always apparent in the details of his verse. One passage in the Juvenal imitation, for example, portrays London society as enslaved to money. Oldham describes everything, from court favors to the consent of lovers, as the object of purchase. London becomes more than merely an "expensive town"; it is depicted as a society which thrives on a system of social prostitution. Another passage, in the Boileau imitation, relies on the intrusion of a notably harsh subject in the midst of comparatively light satire. As the poet proceeds to ridicule man by contrasting him with animals, he pauses to make an accusation that recalls the subject matter of *Satyrs upon the Jesuits:* the "trade of cutting throats" and the "arts" of warfare and murder. Although in his best imitations Oldham had learned to moderate his depiction of

the gruesome details of these arts, passages of this kind are reminders that he never entirely abandoned the cankered muse.

DRYDEN'S "TO THE MEMORY OF MR. OLDHAM"

John Oldham will be remembered for the invective of his *Satyrs upon the Jesuits* and his contributions to the art of verse imitation. He will probably be better remembered, however, as the subject of one of Dryden's finest poems, "To the Memory of Mr. Oldham." It is an appropriate memorial, for Dryden knew only too well both Oldham's shortcomings and his achievements. The harshness of Oldham's satire, Dryden says, was a "noble error," one which could not conceal what Dryden saw as Oldham's distinguishing qualities, the "wit" and "quickness" of his best verse. "To the Memory of Mr. Oldham" both praises the poet and laments his early death, reflecting the double poetic legacy which John Oldham left behind: the accomplishments of an outstanding satirist, and the promise of literary distinction which an untimely death prevented.

BIBLIOGRAPHY

Brooks, Harold F. "The Poetry of John Oldham." In *Restoration Literature: Critical Approaches*, edited by Harold Love. London: Methuen, 1972. Brooks discusses Oldham's poetry in terms of his life and his contemporaries, sources, and genres; no Oldham poem receives extended explication. The essay is, however, valuable in terms of providing information about Abraham Cowley's influence on Oldham and the evaluation of Oldham as a better satirist than Metaphysical poet.

Griffin, Julia. "John Oldham and the Smithfield Crickets." *Notes and Queries* 45, no. 1 (March, 1998): 64-65. An etymological study of Oldham's "Some New Pieces."

Hammond, Paul. *John Oldham and the Renewal of Classical Culture.* Cambridge, England: Cambridge University Press, 1983. In his revaluation of Oldham, Hammond uses the Rawlinson manuscripts to show how Oldham composed his best poems. Focuses on his subject's early indebtedness to Abraham Cowley and on the translations from Horace, Juvenal, and Nicolas Boileau. For Hammond, Oldham prepared the way for the work of Samuel Johnson, John Dryden, and Alexander Pope. The book contains a biographical chapter, a chronology, and a bibliography.

Malekin, Peter. *Liberty and Love: English Literature and Society, 1640-88*. New York: St. Martin's Press, 1981. In a chapter on the satirical aftermath of the Popish Plot, Malekin analyzes Oldham's religious satire, particularly his four satires directed at the Jesuits. For Malekin, Oldham's abusive and bitter satires, written in the Juvenalian manner, created emotional prejudice, but the lack of humor and subtlety dates and thereby weakens the poems.

Selden, Raman. "Oldham, Pope, and Restoration Satire." In *English Satire and the Satiric Tradition*, edited by Claude Rawson. Oxford, England: Basil Blackwell, 1984. Selden discusses Oldham's wide range of poetry (Rochesterian, Metaphysical, Ovidian, pastoral, and irony) and demonstrates, through parallel passages, Alexander Pope's extensive knowledge of Oldham's poetry. It is Oldham's rough wit that constitutes the Restoration strain in Pope's eighteenth century poetry.

_____. "Oldham's Versions of the Classics." In *Poetry and Drama, 1570-1700: Essays in Honour of Harold F. Brooks*, edited by Antony Chapman and Antony Hammond. London: Methuen, 1981. Selden describes Oldham as the most "adventurous of Augustan classicists" in his imitations of Roman satiric verse and love poetry. There are many comparisons not only between Oldham's poems and their sources but also between Oldham's versions and those of his contemporaries.

Ruth Salvaggio;
bibliography updated by the editors

SHARON OLDS

Born: San Francisco, California; November 19, 1942

PRINCIPAL POETRY

Satan Says, 1980
The Dead and the Living, 1984
The Gold Cell, 1987
The Sign of Saturn: Poems, 1980-1987, 1991
The Father, 1992
The Wellspring, 1995
Blood, Tin, Straw, 1999

OTHER LITERARY FORMS

Sharon Olds has published several articles, including "A Student's Memoir of Muriel Rukeyser" in *Poetry East* 16/17 (1985), and "A Small Memoir on Form" in *Poetry East* 20/21 (1986).

ACHIEVEMENTS

Sharon Olds has earned national honors for her poetry. In 1981 she won the San Francisco Poetry Center Award for *Satan Says*. Her second book, *The Dead and the Living*, won both the Lamont Poetry Selection (awarded by the Academy of American Poets) in 1984 and the National Book Critics Circle Award in 1985. *Blood, Tin, Straw* was awarded the Paterson Poetry Prize in 2000. She has been the recipient of a Guggenheim Foundation Fellowship, and selections of her poems have been translated into French, Italian, Chinese, Russian, and Estonian. Olds is among the most widely anthologized contemporary American poets, her work represented in more than one hundred collections. In a review of *The Gold Cell* (published in *Poet Lore*, Spring 1988), Roland Flint wrote: "What is Sharon Olds but our gifted and startling poet of the body?" For many, this is her primary distinction.

BIOGRAPHY

Born in San Francisco in 1942, Sharon Olds lived in her native city until the age of fifteen, when she was sent to a Massachusetts boarding school. Many of her poems focus on her difficult childhood, but in one interview she describes an outwardly placid youth: "I lived near a school for the blind and sang in an Episcopal church choir with girls from that school. In the summer I went to Girl Scout camp. On special campfire nights, I would stand behind a Ponderosa pine and recite, in a loud quavery voice, homemade verses that began, 'I am the spirit of the tree.'" Upon moving to Massachusetts, she became entranced with the seasons of New England.

Olds was graduated with distinction from Stanford University in 1964 and earned a Ph.D. in literature from Columbia University in 1972; her dissertation was on the prosody of Ralph Waldo Emerson's poems. She has taught poetry and poetry-writing at many institutions, including Sarah Lawrence College, New York University, Columbia University, and Brandeis University. For three years she was director of New York University's creative writing program, and she continues to teach in the graduate creative writing program there. In 1985 she founded the Golden Writers' Workshop at Goldwater Hospital for the severely handicapped in New York. She became an associate professor of English at New York University in 1992

Sharon Olds

and directed the graduate program in creative writing. In 1998 she received the Walt Whitman Citation of Merit from the New York State Writers Institute and was named New York State Poet Laureate for 1998-2000. She frequently contributes to such periodicals as *The New Yorker, Poetry, Atlantic Monthly, American Poetry Review, and Nation.*

ANALYSIS

Sharon Olds's signature poems are autobiographical lyrics, many of them charged with eroticism, violence, or both. She writes frequently about her sadistic father, her victimized mother, her unhappy sister and brother, her loving, lusty husband, and her son and daughter. The best of these poems are fluid, startling in their immediacy, and filled with remarks on the genitals of her family members. Her sometimes perversely comic poems about her beastly father conjure up a contemporary version of Sylvia Plath's famous "Daddy." Yet Olds's obsessive poems about her father—who, according to one poem, tied her to a chair and denied her food—are more blatantly autobiographical than Plath's. In the course of her several collections, Olds's family members evolve into flesh-and-blood characters whose significance lies in their particularity rather than their universality.

SATAN SAYS

In *Satan Says*, Olds sets forth the themes that also dominate her later work. The book is divided into four sections: "Daughter," "Woman," "Mother," and "Journey." All four sections assume a self-consciously female perspective. In the first section, the poet explores her own identity as defined by relationships with her parents and sister. In the second section, she writes mostly about her sexual coming of age and her relationship with her husband. The third section contains poems about her children and about the literally creative act of giving birth; there are also four related, third-person poems about "young mothers." The final section, "Journey," contains poems about all the different relationships explored in the book's first three parts.

The title poem beginning the collection announces the poet's aim in writing so explicitly about her family: "I'm trying to say what happened to us/ in the lost past." The poems in all of her books dwell at length on "what happened to us"—the poet and the people most important to her. Olds's poetry is about one woman's connections—physical, sexual, emotional—with family members and lovers of the past and present.

Sometimes Olds celebrates her connections, as a woman, with the whole world. Among the most high-spirited poems in the book, for example, is "The Language of the Brag." In this zesty feminist manifesto about childbirth, the poet proudly elbows aside Walt Whitman and Allen Ginsberg and proclaims that the most important accomplishment is "this giving birth, this glistening verb,/ and I am putting my proud American boast/ right here with the others." The last poem, "Prayer," celebrates womanhood in a more personal way. It identifies sex and childbirth as "the central meanings" in the poet's life. After an alternating consideration of these two acts, the poet entreats herself: "let me not forget:/ each action, each word/ taking its beginning from these." For Olds, determining her own identity always involves the recognition of the body and the powerful bonds characterizing intimate relationships of all kinds.

The poet's bond with her father is especially significant in *Satan Says* and in her later volumes. In "Love Fossil," for example, the father is a dinosaur—"massive, meaty, made of raw steak,/ he nibbled and guzzled, his jaw dripping weeds and bourbon,/ super sleazy extinct beast my heart dug for." In "That Year," he is the brute whom the poet's mother divorces so "there were no more/ tyings by the wrist to the chair,/ no more denial of food/ or the forcing of foods." The father in these poems is a riveting presence, a source of terror whom the poet's imagination has transformed into an object of sexual desire.

This transformation is seen clearly in one of the "Woman" poems, "The Sisters of Sexual Treasure," where the speaker describes her sister's and her own insatiable lust after they left home: "The men's bodies/ were like our father's body! The massive/ hocks, flanks, thighs, elegant/ knees, long tapered calves—." Such incestuous eroticism is simultaneously reverent and irreverent. The poet is both bad daughter and passionate woman, a self defined by the men who remind her of her father. Yet in recognizing this, in writing out the immoral fantasies of the "lost past," she assumes a surprising amount of power. She, not her lovers or her father, is in control. This is female lust, not patriarchal oppression, on a rampage.

Throughout her first three books, Olds conveys feelings of love through forthright descriptions of sex. She relishes men, their bodies, their ability to satisfy women sexually. Her depiction of sex as a means of healing and triumphing is one way she combats the memories of an unhappy childhood. In "First Night," she describes losing her virginity in terms of a biblical migration: "The inhabitants of my body began to/ get up in the dark, pack, and move." The poem reveals the extreme importance Olds places on sexual revelation: "By dawn the migrations were completed. The last/ edge of the blood bond dried,/ and like a newborn animal about to be imprinted/ I opened my eyes and saw your face."

THE DEAD AND THE LIVING

In *The Dead and the Living*, Olds continues to explore female sexuality, motherhood, and relationships with family members. Like her first book, this one is divided into thematic sections. The twenty poems in "Part One: Poems for the Dead" are divided into nine that are "public" and eleven that are "private." In "Part Two: Poems for the Living," the first fifteen poems are grouped as "The Family," the next eight as "Men," and the last nineteen as "The Children." The large number of poems about children shows Olds's growing interest in chronicling her children's young lives as well as her own life as a mother.

The "public" poems at the book's beginning deal with social issues and people outside the poet's immediate family. Among them are several poems based on photographs of strangers suffering, as well as a poem titled "The Death of Marilyn Monroe." These works signal an expanded focus for Olds, but they lack the cohesion and force of the "private" poems that return to the drama of her personal history. Although the latter poems deal with the same relationships that were central to *Satan Says*, they are more gracefully executed than those in the earlier volume. In "Miscarriage," for example, Olds recollects the realization, with her husband, "that we could/ botch something, you and I. All wrapped in/ purple it floated away, like a messenger/ put to death for bearing bad news." The poem not only brings together Olds's recurring themes of love, sex, and motherhood but also contains an element of mature reflection, tempered sadness. This maturity, seen in glimpses in *Satan Says*, flowers more fully in *The Dead and the Living*.

In this book Olds continues to write memorable poems about her father. In "Fate," she declares, "Finally I just gave up and became my father,/ his greased, defeated face shining toward/ anyone I looked at." She pictures herself taking on all of his characteristics—even "his sad/ sex dangling on his thigh, his stomach/ swollen and empty." The poem, which is surprisingly triumphant, shows how much the speaker has internalized her father and how much she believes his life has shaped her own: "I saw the whole world shining/ with the ecstasy of his grief, and I/ myself, he, I, shined." Another poem, "My Father's Breasts," evokes in eleven lines the speaker's enduring love for her father. Appropriating the feminine image of breasts on her father's behalf, she remembers his chest "as if I has spent/ hours, years, in that smell of black pepper and/ turned earth." The love and nostalgia in this poem are a stark counterpoint to the anger in "The Ideal Father," which portrays a father "who passed out, the one who would not/ speak for a week, slapped the glasses off a/ small girl's face." The multiple portraits of the father reveal an aggressive yet vulnerable man—and an equally aggressive, vulnerable daughter struggling to resolve, and perhaps exorcise, her passion for the man at the center of her life.

In the poems concluding *The Dead and the Living*, Olds turns her sometimes alarmingly steady gaze on her young son and daughter. In "Six-Year-Old Boy," she writes of her son as he sleeps on the back seat of the car, "his wiry limbs limp and supple/ except where his hard-on lifts his pajamas like the/ earth above the shoot of a bulb." In "Pajamas," she describes the little girl's pajamas on the floor: "You can almost see the hard/ halves of her young buttocks, the precise/ stem-mark of her sex." The speaker's evident fascination with her children's emerging sexuality—and her willingness to transform the subject into verse—may seem exploitative to some. Many readers, however, have been impressed by her willingness to explore a maternal eroticism not often articulated in verse.

After a series of alternating poems about her son and her daughter, the book ends with "The Couple," which portrays the children asleep in the back seat of a car. Though "enemies,/ rulers of separate countries," the two now look like a child bride and groom in the Middle Ages, who find unity only in sleep, "in the solitary/ power of the dream—the dream of ruling the world." Even this poem, which is not overtly sexual in its portrayal of the children, forces the reader to ac-

knowledge the sexuality lurking in their young, sleeping bodies.

THE GOLD CELL

In her third collection, *The Gold Cell*, Olds continues to write confessional, sometimes erotic poems about her family. Like the first two books, this one is divided into sections. The first part, similar to the beginning of *The Dead and the Living*, contains poems about public scenes and atrocities, including rape in "The Girl" and a baby found in a litter basket in "The Abandoned Newborn." The second part contains poems about the poet's childhood in San Francisco and about her father and mother. The third section consists of poems about sexuality, including "This," which describes the centrality of the speaker's body to her identity, and the witty "Topography," which describes lovemaking in terms of two maps pressed to each other. The last section returns to the subjects of childbirth and the poet's children.

In addition to its serious, "public" poems, the first section contains several audacious works—"The Pope's Penis," "Outside the Operating Room of the Sex-Change Doctor," and "The Solution." The first two of these poems hover between shock effect and subversive humor. Olds seems to delight in freely discussing penises; they are the totems of her verse. In "The Solution," a four-paragraph prose poem, she creates a darkly comic vision of sexuality gone wild. Single people go to huge "Sex Centers" in search of the ideal mate. Things get out of control; the whole country lines up for sexual gratification "in a huge wide belt like the Milky Way, and since they had to name it they named it, they called it the American Way." Olds's punning punch line neatly distills a wry social commentary. She mocks momentarily the overwhelming urge for sex that she celebrates so earnestly in other poems.

The family poems in the second section are among Olds's most graphic work. She metaphorically describes her father's cruel treatment of her brother in "Saturn," recollects her mother's incestuous behavior in "What if God," describes finding her father smeared with blood when she was thirteen in "History: 13," and remembers terrifying childhood drives with her father in "San Francisco." The section's last three poems, however, are loving tributes to her parents; in these, Olds moves beyond rage, fear, and eroticism toward reconciliation and acceptance.

The third section's poems about female love and sexuality begin with a young girl's perspective, move through remembrances of a young lover who died in a car crash, and end with several poems about mature love and sex. These poems are also graphic, sometimes amusing, sometimes poignant, but always written with force and conviction. Olds is at her most confident and sympathetic when writing about lovemaking. As in the concluding poem in *Satan Says*, sex remains one of the "central meanings" in her life and writing.

The poems concluding *The Gold Cell* are full of love and heightened awareness of the little things making up the poet's shared life with her son and daughter. In "When My Son Is Sick," "Gerbil Funeral," and "Liddy's Orange," Olds celebrates the homely, often unsung moments of a happy family's days together. The helpless love expressed in many of these poems contrasts with detailed imagery and sweetness of mood. Olds at least temporarily leaves eroticism behind and portrays her children as vessels of purity and goodness that she wishes fiercely to protect. Given her own traumatic childhood, the possessive love Olds expresses for her children carries a special poignancy, lending a strain of dark beauty to her powerful verse.

THE FATHER

The Father is perhaps Olds's riskiest volume in a high-risk career. Its narrow focus allows the reader little relief from a subject that is at once unpleasant and treated with frankness. The individual poems, as they accumulate, tell the story of a daughter's witnessing of her father's fatal bout with cancer. At the same time, they detail memories of an abusive relationship. The loving act of writing the poems involves a transformation of childhood pain and hatred into a vigil of chaotic emotions and finally to a transcendence of the old psychic scars.

THE WELLSPRING

Like several of her books, *The Wellspring* is a carefully devised sequence, almost a novel in verse. It tells of a woman's transit from birth through childhood, sexual awakening, maternity and parenthood, and mature conjugal relationship. As ever, emotional and physical accuracy make these poems soar and sting. Olds presents a

wider range of tones and feelings than in *The Father*, and the best poems in the collection are among the best she has ever done, though perhaps too many a bit below the level of intensity that her readers have grown to expect. The meticulously shaped arc of experience conveyed in the sequence is compelling and rich in wisdom.

BLOOD, TIN, STRAW

Blood, Tin, Straw reveals Olds writing with undiminished power as she moves further into middle age. Perhaps time's urgency has added even more heat to a style and imagination already characterized by heat waves of shock. Here her candor of sex and flesh are still present, but she has added to it a new strength and lyricism of metaphor and image. She seems to embrace the entire universe, from the microscopic to cosmic events like shooting stars or volcanic eruptions. The title, alluding to the *Wizard of Oz*, is provocative. It grows out of Olds's observation that Dorothy and her comrades are attacked with what they are made of: "what they/ were made of was to be used against them." So, too, are we all attacked, suggests Olds, when the very things we are made of (our flesh, our instincts) are not given due acknowledgment and respect by our society. So, too, is her poetry sometimes attacked for what it is made of. Her lyrical gifts ablaze, Olds continues to walk the thematic path and take the daring stances that have made her a major poetic force for more than two decades.

BIBLIOGRAPHY

Baker, David. *Heresy and the Ideal: On Contemporary Poetry.* Fayetteville: University of Arkansas Press, 2000. In a brief section on Olds, Baker explains why, though he admires dozens of her poems, he does not admire her books. *The Wellspring* in particular suffers from its structure and presents a whole that is less than the sum of its parts. He faults Olds, as well, for "sentimentality and exaggeration, even falsification."

Libby, Anthony. "Fathers and Daughters and Mothers and Poets." *The New York Times Book Review.* (March 22, 1987): 23. This brief review is an example of the ambivalent reaction Olds's poetry sometimes elicits. Libby finds Olds's frequent references to genitalia excessive and suggests that many of her poems are overdone, lacking control.

Matson, Susan. "Talking to Our Father: The Political and Mythical Appropriations of Adrienne Rich and Sharon Olds." *American Poetry Review* 18 (November/December, 1989): 35-41. Matson examines the rhetorical strategies Rich and Olds use in poems addressed to their fathers and argues that, in different ways, both poets triumph over the limitations women face in male-dominated families and cultures. The section on Olds focuses on several poems in *The Gold Cell.*

Mueller, Lisel. "Three Poets." *Poetry* 138, no. 3 (1981): 170-174. This review of *Satan Says* considers the book a significant debut but criticizes Olds's vehemence and her occasionally "uneasy metaphor."

Olds, Sharon. "Sharon Olds." Interview by Laurel Blossom. *Poets and Writers Magazine* (September/October, 1993): 30-32. In this wide-ranging interview, Olds discusses such issues as influences, her relationship to confessional poetry, and the spectrum of loyalty and betrayal. Comments on Robert Lowell, Muriel Rukeyser, and others.

Ostriker, Alicia. "American Poetry, Now Shaped by Women." *The New York Times Book Review.* (March 9, 1986): 1. Placing Olds at the vanguard of contemporary poetry, Ostriker suggests that a younger generation of women poets is following in the pioneering tradition of Sylvia Plath, Anne Sexton, and Adrienne Rich.

Scheponik, Peter C. "Olds's 'My Father Speaks to Me from the Dead.'" *The Explicator* 57, no. 1 (Fall, 1998): 59-62. Examines the way in which the speaker in this poem strives "to extract the emotional validation" from her father that he never offered during his life. The poem's power resides in the conflict between her father's philosophy and the speaker's emotional needs.

Wright, Carolyn. Review of *The Dead and the Living. The Iowa Review* 15, no. 1 (1985): 151-161. This review compares Olds's second volume to a successful book of short fiction. Although Wright believes that Olds sometimes overwrites or overexplains, she praises the book's focus on family and its "concern for the larger family of humanity."

Hilary Holladay,
updated by Philip K. Jason and Sarah Hilbert

MARY OLIVER

Born: Cleveland, Ohio; September 10, 1935

PRINCIPAL POETRY

No Voyage and Other Poems, 1963, expanded 1965
The River Styx, Ohio, and Other Poems, 1972
Sleeping in the Forest, 1978
The Night Traveler, 1978
Twelve Moons, 1979
American Primitive, 1983
Dream Work, 1986
Provincetown, 1987
House of Light, 1990
New and Selected Poems, 1992
White Pine, 1994
West Wind, 1997
The Leaf and the Cloud, 2000

OTHER LITERARY FORMS

Mary Oliver has written collections of essays: *Blue Pastures* (1995) and *Winter Hours* (1999). Although the essays are mainly prose meditations, some are written in poetic form. The subject matter is the creation of poetry, by Oliver herself or by poets who have influenced her. *Blue Pastures* celebrates the creative power of imagination, its capacity to reorder circumstances and to enter the natural world to find comfort, community, and joy. The meditations center on ponds, trees, animals, and seasons and on Romantic writers who looked to nature—Walt Whitman, John Keats, Percy Bysshe Shelley, William Blake, and Edna St. Vincent Millay, in whose house Oliver lived periodically for several years after college, serving as an assistant to Millay's sister.

Winter Hours takes up the same lines but offers essays and prose poems more sharply focused on the making of poems. Three essays consider the qualities that make powerful writing in the work of Edgar Allan Poe, Robert Frost, and Walt Whitman.

ACHIEVEMENTS

Mary Oliver is known for her graceful, passionate voice and her ability to discover deep, sustaining spiritual qualities in moments of encounter with nature. Her vision is ecstatic, arising from silence, darkness, deep pain, and questioning—a searching sensibility acutely aware and on the lookout everywhere for transformative moments. Her central subject is the difficult journey life is, and the capacity of the human imagination to discover energy, passion, compassion, and the light of conscious being in the very places where the difficult is encountered.

Acts of deep attention enable a crossing over into nature's consciousness for a time to revitalize bodily awareness. The poet imaginatively disappears into nature, merges with it, and reemerges transformed in experiential fire. Whitman is her great forebear, although instead of an ever-present "I" seeking a merging intimacy, Oliver seeks instead a dissolving oneness in which the reader displaces her in order to enter more directly the experience she renders. Ordinary diction and syntax coupled with startlingly fresh images fuse in a passion that seems ordinary yet extraordinarily tender and liquid.

Among Oliver's awards are the Shelley Memorial Award, an Achievement Award from the American Academy of Arts and Letters, the Lannan Award, a Guggenheim Fellowship, a National Endowment for the Arts Fellowship, the Pulitzer Prize for *American Primitive*, and the National Book Award for *New and Selected Poems*.

Mary Oliver (© Molly Malone Cook)

BIOGRAPHY

Mary Oliver's poetry bears witness to a difficult childhood, one in which she was particularly at odds with her father, a teacher who died without their being reconciled. Her childhood experience profoundly influenced her poetry, as the body of her work develops a journey of healing from the effects of trauma. In "Rage" she writes of a childhood incest scene, detailing its damaging and continuing effects on daily adult life. Her poetry is remarkable for its limited focus on herself as a personality while showing a path out of terror and sorrow to acceptance, safety, joy, and freedom.

Oliver attended Ohio State University for one year, then transferred to Vassar College, but left after a year. She has taught at several places: the Fine Arts Workshop in Provincetown, Massachusetts; Case Western Reserve

as Mather Visiting Professor; Sweet Briar College in Virginia as Banister Writer-in-Residence; and Bennington College in Vermont as Catherine Osgood Foster Chair for Distinguished Teaching. She has divided her time between residences in Vermont and Massachusetts.

ANALYSIS

Mary Oliver's presence in her poems is most often a clear-sighted moving of eye and mind while staying physically still. She disappears, in a sense, by projecting her sense and moral life onto precise and compelling images that draw the reader into the "I" as experiencer. Through the projection of sensibility in the scene of nature, she can be harsh but accepting and express responsibility for her own life. For example, in "Moccasin Flowers" the plant and human merge in spiritual ecstasy:

> But all my life—so far—
> I have loved best
>   how the flowers rise
>   and open, how

the pink lungs of their bodies
enter the fire of the world
and stand there shining
and willing—the one

thing they can do before
they shuffle forward
into the floor of darkness, they
become the trees.

In her characteristic step-down lines, which give a feel of graceful floating, Oliver expresses the nature and work of beings to be fully and joyfully in the world before they move on to their merging in death.

Although Oliver began writing in the midst of the confessional movement of Robert Lowell, Anne Sexton, and Sylvia Plath, she never took on a victim persona. To the contrary, all her effort has gone toward entering the deepest truths of what is within reach of human consciousness. Thus she embraces the totality, from our wild and animal nature—joyful and painful—to our storied and moral questionings. Most often looking to nature for experiential knowledge, she is deeply Romantic in the American vein, taking as her models Henry David Thoreau, Ralph Waldo Emerson, and Walt Whitman. The opening of "The Buddha's Last Instruction" puts succinctly her aim: "'Make of yourself a light.'" The closing line, "He looked into the faces of that frightened crowd," speaks of the terrifying difficulty of that journey. Between these lines, Oliver sees existence as a gift of "inexplicable value," and to see this fact, which is imaged in the sun, is to become oneself a light. The way of healing and spiritual awareness is through entering what nature knows.

NO VOYAGE AND OTHER POEMS AND TWELVE MOONS

The first six volumes of poetry, published over sixteen years, show the poet beginning with a lyrical "I" who is, like Whitman, awake, watching and listening to nature, simultaneously an individual person grounded in a scene of mythic resonance and "at ease in darkness" of creative natural life. In "Being Country Bred,"

Spring is still miles away, and yet I wake
Throughout the dark, listen, and throb with all
Her summoning explosions underground.

The dark underside of nature is the unconscious coming to light, bringing danger and the excitement of possibility. In "No Voyage," she refuses to leave her own identity, determining instead to stay and "make peace with the fact" of her grief.

The poems of the first two volumes are conventionally versified, and many are narrative-based vignettes of people from Oliver's childhood. "At Blackwater Pond," however, is a short nine-line lyric that presages her mature work. In a baptism-communion-resurrection scene, the poet dips her hands in water and drinks.

. . . It tastes
like stone, leaves, fire. It falls cold
into my body, waking the bones. I hear them
deep inside me, whispering
oh what is that beautiful thing
that just happened?

The mystery of ecstatic awakening precisely matches the flow of rapturous experience. The subject and technique develop further in *Twelve Moons*; for instance, "Mussels" with its short, step-down lines resisting, like the shelled animals, her grip. In "Sleeping in the Forest," the poet finds herself imaginatively transformed as she becomes a dark, fluid consciousness, one with the night's beings and businesses: "By morning/ I had vanished at least a dozen times/ into something better." James Wright's influence is evident (three poems are dedicated to him) in the leaving of the body in ecstatic moments to "break into blossom."

AMERICAN PRIMITIVE

With this volume, Oliver achieved a fully developed vision of return to the earth for healing and a reciprocal healing of the earth. The acute perceptiveness and radiant clarity presaged in some earlier poems arrives strong and sustained. Using nature and Native American themes, the body becomes firmly the locus of mind and spirit. Yet, there is a clear separation; Oliver is fully aware that boundaries can be crossed but must be crossed back again. Knowledge is brought back from the visions of nature.

Poems such as "Lightning" and "Vultures" acknowledge the journey into the other world as fearful and painful: Sorrow and death are part of nature, and the only way to heal is to accept this and go the difficult path straight through terror. "Mushrooms" accepts nature's poisonous aspects but engages respect versus fear as the helpful knowledge. "Egrets" traces the journey into the dark interior. The traveler is "hot and wounded" but comes suddenly to an empty pond out of which three egrets rise as "a shower/ of white fire!" She sees that they walk through each moment patiently, without fear "unruffled, sure/ by the laws/ of their faith not logic,/ they opened their wings/ softly and stepped/ over every dark thing." In "The Honey Tree," she boldly ascends into ecstatic joy of the body as a result of the difficult work of acceptance for her other poems. Ecstasy, she writes, results from so long hungering for freedom to be oneself unrestricted by pain of the pain. "Oh, anyone can see/ how I love myself at last!/ how I love the world!"

Yet there is mourning for beings who did not survive. "Ghosts" is an elegy for the plains buffalo. This long poem ends with a dream in which a cow tenderly attends her newborn calf like "any caring woman." In a characteristic prayerful image, the poet kneels and asks to become part of them. It is a gesture toward death, which so many of Oliver's poems make, expressing simultaneously sorrow and ecstasy balanced in empathic tenderness. In "University Hospital, Boston," she mourns a friend who is dying, and one she did not know who is gone suddenly from his bed.

DREAM WORK

Dream Work is the darkest of Oliver's work, as she goes back to consider and repair major losses. Continuing in the vein of *American Primitive* and the Deep Image poets, shamanist and other mythic vehicles are her major ways of entering the otherness of consciousness to understand and absorb the power she wants to incorporate while shedding what is outworn or harmful. There is a new probing of the personal and the political as she delves into the suffering human beings cause each other.

"Rage," "The Journey," and "A Visitor" revisit the effects of abusive childhood experience in order to name harm and reclaim active responsibility. Perhaps the best known of these poems is "Wild Geese," which honors the experience of "the soft animal of your body" as essential to moving out of blame, guilt, and isolation and back to connection with the world. Other poems, such as

"Stanley Kunitz," honor those she has learned from and express that learning is the result not of magic but of hard, patient digging, weeding, pruning, and "coaxing the new."

NEW AND SELECTED POEMS

This volume contains thirty new poems and generous selections from the twenty-year span of Oliver's poetry up to 1992. The volume makes Oliver appear to be more of a nature writer than she is, as the majority of poems selected are engagements with nature but are without their full context of the healing journey. The new poems find Oliver on the other side of pain, having resolved grief and moved past terror, so that she is able to cross with ease "that porous line/ where my own body was done with/ and the roots and the stems and the flowers/ began" ("White Flowers"). "Alligator Poem" relates a terrifying encounter with the animal while drinking on her knees. The lesson is in how the water "healed itself with a slow whisper" after the alligator has sunk out of sight, how she "saw the world as if for the second time/ the way it really is." She gathers a token of wild flowers to hold in her shaking hands—a gesture that is an emblem of her poetic enterprise, nature giving both dark and light, fear and comfort, death and life. She chooses to gather and hold life and beauty.

THE LEAF AND THE CLOUD

A long epigraph from John Ruskin's *Modern Painters* (1843-1860) explains the leaf as a veil between the darkness of natural being and humankind, and the cloud as a veil between God and humankind. The book is a single long poem, a seven-lyric sequence that progressively swells higher into ecstatic union with the world. Oliver writes the journey of a person who is sixty, who looks back on her painful childhood, buries her parents, but will not "give them the kiss of complicity" or "the responsibility for my life." She declares "glory is my work" and imaginatively becomes all creatures and parts of the earth, hunter as well as hunted. The poet is part of the world, its radiant witness, not separate: Words "sweet and electric, words flow from the brain/ and out the gate of the mouth."

Whitman is evident everywhere in voice, style, subject, and theme. The "I" ranges from the personal to the universal, gives bits of personal history to set the record down and then moves beyond them, lists objects of nature as divine life, declares prophetically, asks rhetorical questions, and embraces death as part of life.

OTHER MAJOR WORKS

NONFICTION: *A Poetry Handbook*, 1994; *Blue Pastures*, 1995; *Rules for the Dance: A Handbook for Writing and Reading Metrical Verse*, 1998; *Winter Hours*, 1999.

BIBLIOGRAPHY

Burton-Christie, Douglas. "Nature, Spirit, and Imagination in the Poetry of Mary Oliver." *Cross Currents* 46, no. 1 (Spring, 1996): 77-87. Examines Oliver's poetry as the work of spiritual attention and acceptance versus the will to change and domesticate.

Fast, Robin Riley. "Moore, Bishop, and Oliver: Thinking Back, Re-Seeing the Sea." *Twentieth Century Literature* 39, no. 3 (Fall, 1993): 364-379. Considers Oliver in the line of Marianne Moore's and Elizabeth Bishop's concern with death and the unconscious as background context for poetic imagination.

Graham, Vicki. "'Into the Body of Another': Mary Oliver and the Poetics of Becoming Other." *Papers on Language and Literature* 30, no. 4 (Fall, 1994): 352-372. An extensive treatment of Oliver as a postmodern feminist poet for whom, contrary to male Romantic poets, merging with consciousnesses regarded as other is a fuller apprehension of multiplicity instead of a loss of subjectivity.

McNew, Janet. "Mary Oliver and the Tradition of Romantic Nature Poetry." *Contemporary Literature* 30, no. 1 (Spring, 1990): 59-77. A fascinating treatment of Oliver's work as a feminist Romantic poet writing against the tradition of male Romantics, who imagined nature as feminine to be both desired and feared. Critiques mainline Romantic criticism as gender-biased.

Voros, Gyorgyi. "Exquisite Environments." *Parnassus: Poetry in Review* 21, nos. 1/2 (1996): 231-250. An omnibus review of three of Oliver's books and two by Gary Snyder, who is used to show what Oliver should be doing. An interesting perspective that understands Oliver's work narrowly as nature poetry only, the kind of opinion that Janet McNew critiques.

Rosemary Winslow

CHARLES OLSON

Born: Worcester, Massachusetts; December 27, 1910
Died: New York, New York; January 10, 1970

PRINCIPAL POETRY

Y & X, 1948
Letter for Melville 1951, 1951
This, 1952
In Cold Hell, in Thicket, 1953
The Maximus Poems 1-10, 1953
The Maximus Poems 11-22, 1956
O'Ryan 2 4 6 8 10, 1958 (expanded edition, *O'Ryan 12345678910*, 1965)
The Maximus Poems, 1960
The Distances, 1960
Charles Olson: Reading at Berkeley, 1966 (transcription)
The Maximus Poems, IV, V, VI, 1968
Archaeologist of Morning: The Collected Poems Outside the Maximus Series, 1970
The Maximus Poems, Volume 3, 1975
The Horses of the Sea, 1976
The Maximus Poems, 1983
The Collected Poems of Charles Olson: Excluding "The Maximus Poems," 1987
A Nation of Nothing but Poetry: Supplementary Poems, 1989

OTHER LITERARY FORMS

Charles Olson was a prolific essayist, espousing the essay form in order to advance his poetic concerns to a wider audience. His prose style can present as many difficulties as his poetry, however, difficulties to a large extent deliberately sought by Olson, who was concerned that his literary production not be consumed too easily in an era of speed-reading. With *Call Me Ishmael: A Study of Melville*, a book-length study of Herman Melville, published in 1947, Olson announced his intention to define America for his day, even as Melville had, Olson believed, for *his* time, in *Moby-Dick* (1851). Key essays published within four years of *Call Me Ishmael* include "The Human Universe" and the celebrated "Projective Verse," which, together with many others, may be found in one of several collections, namely *Human Universe and Other Essays* (1965), *Selected Writings of Charles Olson* (1966), *Pleistocene Man* (1968), *Causal Mythology* (1969), *The Special View of History* (1970), *Poetry and Truth: The Beloit Lectures and Poems* (1971), and *Additional Prose: A Bibliography on America, Proprioception, and Other Notes and Essays* (1974).

Olson's letters have also proved of much interest, and many are collected in *Mayan Letters* (1953), *Letters for "Origin," 1950-1956* (1969), and the series of volumes issuing from Black Sparrow Press of his correspondence with the poet Robert Creeley.

ACHIEVEMENTS

With his first poems and essays, Charles Olson caught the attention of readers ready, like himself, for a profound renaming of a present grown extremely ambiguous with the destruction of traditional values during World War II. This audience continued to grow and, with the publication in 1960 of Don Allen's anthology *The New American Poetry, 1945-1960*, a year that also saw the publication in one book of the first volume of *The Maximus Poems* and another book of poems, *The Distances*, he was widely hailed as a leader of a revolution in poetry. Olson's section in the Allen anthology came first and was the largest; the poetry conference held at the University of British Columbia in 1963, and another, held at the University of California at Berkeley in 1965, were dominated by his presence. He remained "center-stage" until his death in 1970, and since then, his contribution has received steadily increasing attention from the scholarly community, while his influence on younger poets has continued to spread.

Olson spoke through his art to a historical moment that had come unhinged, and the cogency with which he advocated "screwing the hinges back on the door of civilization" inspired a fervor of response. Poets, editors, teachers, and lay readers formed a kind of "Olson underground," a network that disseminated the kinds of information which Olson's project favored, and these were various indeed: the founding and the decline of early civilizations (Sumer, Egypt, Greece, the Maya), the pre-Socratics, the Tarot, psychedelic drugs, non-Euclidean geometry, the philosophy of Alfred North Whitehead, and documents of the European settlement of New England—a far from exhaustive list. For the most part, Olson shunned publicity and was therefore less known to the counterculture of the 1960's than was his fellow poet Allen Ginsberg, but there can be no doubt that Olson, both in his own person and through this network, helped instigate and name the cultural revolution then attempted.

Olson's poetry instructs, deliberately, as do his essays. In this respect, it is noteworthy that his career as a teacher spanned four decades, starting at Clark University in the 1930's and resuming (after an interim during which he worked first for the American Civil Liberties Union and then in the Office of War Information) at Black Mountain College in the late 1940's. Olson continued to teach at Black Mountain until the college closed in 1956; he moved on to the State University of New York at Buffalo in 1963, where he worked for three years, and concluded his teaching career at the University of Connecticut. A partial list of his distinguished students includes John Wieners, Edward Dorn, Michael Rumaker, Fielding Dawson, Joel Oppenheimer, and Jonathan Williams. While serving as rector of Black Mountain College, from 1951 to 1956, Olson turned it into a center of the literary arts and was responsible for the publication of the *Black Mountain Review* (edited by Creeley), which gave its name to the group of writers most often published therein.

Olson was the recipient of two Guggenheim grants, in 1939 to continue his work on his dissertation on Herman Melville and in 1948 to write about the interaction of racial groups during the settling of the American West; in 1952, he received a grant from the Wenner-Gren Foundation to study Mayan hieroglyphics in the Yucatan. (It is characteristic of Olson that he completed none of these projects within the guidelines proposed but instead transmuted them into poetic essays and poetry.) In 1965, he was awarded the Oscar Blumenthal-Charles Leviton Prize by *Poetry* magazine, possibly the most prestigious award he received for his poetry. His poetry was too radical, and his life too short, for further such acknowledgment to come his way during his lifetime.

BIOGRAPHY

Charles John Olson was born on December 27, 1910, in the central Massachusetts town of Worcester. His mother, Mary Hines, was of Irish immigrant stock; his father, also named Charles, was of Swedish origin. Olson's giant proportions (fully grown, he was to stand six feet, nine inches) obviously came from his father's side, the elder Olson having stood well over six feet tall himself, whereas the poet's mother was barely above five feet tall. Olson's father worked as a letter carrier, a career the poet was to take up at one point in his life. From 1915 until he left home, Olson spent part of each summer with his family in Gloucester, a small seaport of Massachusetts north of Boston; he would later live there and anchor his Maximus poems in this, to him, "root city." In 1928, he entered Wesleyan University, being graduated in 1932 and receiving his M.A. there the following year; his thesis, "The Growth of Herman Melville, Prose Writer and Poetic Thinker," led him to discover hitherto unknown portions of Melville's library, and this, in turn, led to his paper "Lear and Moby-Dick," written in the course of his doctoral studies at Harvard and published in *Twice-a-Year* in 1938. Between 1932 and 1939, Olson supported himself either by grants or by teaching: at Clark University from 1934 to 1936 and at Harvard from 1936 to 1939.

In 1939, awarded a Guggenheim Fellowship, Olson lived with his widowed mother in Gloucester, laying the groundwork for what was to become *Call Me Ishmael*. In 1940, he moved to New York City, working first as publicity director for the American Civil Liberties Union and then as chief of the Foreign Language Information Service of the Common Council for American Unity. During this period, Olson met and married Constance Wilcock. From 1942 to 1944, Olson served as associate chief of the Foreign Language Division of the Office of War Information, in Washington, D.C., and during Franklin D. Roosevelt's campaign for a fourth term in 1944, he served on the Democratic National Committee. The following year, he was offered high office in the new Democratic administration but chose instead to devote himself to writing, and, with the help of Ezra Pound, whom Olson often visited at St. Elizabeth's Hospital, he published *Call Me Ishmael* in 1947.

For the next ten years, Olson's life was to be closely associated with Black Mountain College, an experiment in education being carried on near Asheville, North Carolina, where he worked first as a lecturer and subsequently, starting in 1951, as rector. Olson during this period wrote his landmark essays on poetics and the poems that made up his book *The Distances*. Through Vincent Ferrini, a Gloucester poet, Olson met Robert Creeley, and a correspondence ensued that was to prove seminal to the movement in poetry known as "Black Mountain poetry" or "projective verse" (the latter from the Olson essay so titled). In 1954, Creeley came to teach at the college and edited the *Black Mountain Review*. Another poet, Robert Duncan—association with whom was to prove vital to Olson—also taught at Black Mountain during this time. Olson, meanwhile, had ended his first marriage (which produced one child, Katherine, born in 1951) and embarked on a second, to Elizabeth Kaiser, whom he met and married in 1954; their son, Charles Peter, was born in May of the following year.

As Black Mountain College was no longer proving fiscally viable, Olson closed it in 1956, the year that saw the publication of *The Maximus Poems 11-22* (*The Maximus Poems 1-10* had been issued in 1953). In 1957, Olson journeyed to San Francisco to read at the Museum of Art and The Poetry Center and to deliver in five lectures his "special view of history." Olson then settled with his wife and son in Gloucester, working on another volume of Maximus poems. The year 1960 was his *annus mirabilis:* He was included in the anthology *The New American Poetry, 1945-1960*, his Maximus poems were reissued as a single book, and his other poems were collected into the volume *The Distances*. Thenceforth Olson's star, in the ascendant throughout the previous decade, was much more visibly so, and he met his quickly growing audience at a number of venues, among these the Vancouver Poetry Conference (1963), the Festival of the Two Worlds in Spoleto, Italy (1965), the Berkeley Poetry Conference (1965), the Literary Colloquium of the Academy of Art in Berlin (1966), the International Poetry Festival in London (1967), and Beloit College (1968), where he delivered the lectures subsequently published as *Poetry and Truth*. Several collections of his essays were issued during this decade also. From 1963 to 1965, Olson served as visiting professor of English at the State University of New York at Buffalo; in 1969, he accepted a similar post at the University of Connecticut.

These years were marked, however, by dissipation and heartbreak. His wife died in an automobile accident in 1964; Olson's health began to fail, and, in 1969, cancer of the liver was diagnosed; he died in a New York City hospital on January 10, 1970.

ANALYSIS

Charles Olson's poetry is political in a profound, not superficial, sense; it does not spend time naming "current events," but rather, it devotes itself to defining "the dodges of discourse" that have enabled humanity (especially in the West) to withdraw from reality into increasingly abstract fictions of life. Olson came of age during the Great Depression and admired Roosevelt's New Deal, but with the death of the president in 1945 and the bombing of Hiroshima and Nagasaki, Olson lost faith in the possibilities for liberal democracy. Olson believed that it did not go wide enough or deep enough in the attempt to restore humanity's lost meaning—nor did it provide enough checks and balances against the corporate takeover of the world.

RESISTANCE

Olson encouraged a resistance based on knowledge from a range of sources which he endeavored, through his essays and his poems, to bring to common attention. "Resistance," in fact, is a key word here: One of his first essays bears that title, and often, Olson's stance reminds one of the Maquis and other "underground" pockets of resistance to the Fascists during World War II. His is a sort of intellectual commando operation bent on destroying, marshaling not yards or military arsenals but modes of thought (and therefore of action) that are out of kilter with current realities and "fascistic" in their ability to crush individual senses of value that would struggle toward a coherence—where the merely subjective might transcend itself and establish a vital community.

However sweeping Olson's proposals, in effect his program is reactive; such a reaction against the status quo was, as he saw it, the essential first step toward building a civilization that put people before profits. "When man is reduced to so much fat for soap, super-

phosphate for soil, fillings and shoes for sale," Olson wrote, the news of the Nazi death camps fresh in the minds of his audience as in his own, "he has, to begin again, one answer, one point of resistance only to such fragmentation, one organized ground. . . . It is his physiology he is forced to arrive at. . . . It is his body that is his answer."

This answer led Olson to ground his poetics in the physical breathing of the poet, the vital activity that registers the smallest fluctuations of thought and feeling. Language had become separated from being over the centuries of Western civilization, so that, for example, it became more important to carry out orders than to consider their often terrible consequences. In the words of Paul Christensen, "The denotational core of words must be rescued from neglect; logical classification and the principles of syntax must be suppressed and a new, unruly seizure of phenomena put in their place." Civilization, to the extent that it alienates one from one's experience of the actual earth and the life that arises therefrom, has failed, and it supplants with "slick pictures" the actual conditions of human lives.

DECONSTRUCTING AUTHORITY

Therefore, it has become necessary, Olson argues, to deconstruct the accepted authorities of Western thought, while seeking to preserve the thought of such persons who, throughout history, have warned against systems of ideation that debase human beings. In Olson's vision, one of the great villains is Aristotle; one of the heroes, Apollonius of Tyana. With Aristotle, "the two great means appear: logic and classification. And it is they," Olson continues in the essay "Human Universe," "that have so fastened themselves on habits of thought that action is interfered with, absolutely interfered with, I should say." Olson in this same passage points out: "The harmony of the universe, and I include man, is not logical, or better, is post-logical, as is the order of any created thing." As for classification,

What makes most acts—of living and of writing—unsatisfactory, is that the person and/or the writer satisfy themselves that they can only make a form . . . by selecting from the full content some face of it, or plane, some part. And at just this point, by just this act, they fall back on the dodges of discourse, and immediately, they lose me, I am no longer engaged, this is not what I know is the going-on. . . . It comes out a demonstration, a separating out, an act of classification, and so, a stopping.

"APOLLONIUS OF TYANA"

In "Apollonius of Tyana, a Dance, with Some Words, for Two Actors," Olson addresses the reader through the medium of a contemporary of Christ, Apollonius, and the play's one other character, Tyana, the place of his origin, as well as through himself, as narrator/commentator. This last tells how Apollonius "knows . . . that *his* job, at least, is to find out how to inform all people how best they can stick to the instant, which is both temporal and intense, which is both shape and law." Apollonius makes his way through the Mediterranean world of the first century C.E., which "is already the dispersed thing the West has been since," conducting "a wide investigation into the local, the occasional, what you might even call the ceremonial, but without . . . any assurance that he knows how to make objects firm, or how firm he is."

Apollonius, readers are told, learned from his journeyings

> that two ills were coming on man: (1) unity was crowding out diversity (man was getting too multiplied to stay clear by way of the old vision of himself, the humanist one, was getting too distracted to abide in his own knowing with any of his old confidence); and (2) unity as a goal (making Rome an empire, say) had, as its intellectual pole an equally mischievous concept, that of the universal—of the "universals" as Socrates and Christ equally had laid them down. Form . . . was suddenly swollen, was being taken as a thing larger a thing outside a thing above any particular, even any given man.

These descriptions of the confusions which beset Apollonius clearly apply to those Olson himself was encountering, and therefore readers look to find, in Apollonius's solutions, those of Olson. This part of the work, however, rings less convincingly: Olson makes some rhetorical flourishes, but in the end the reader is simply told that Apollonius has learned that he must "commit himself"; he has also learned that Tyana (surely a figure for Olson's Gloucester) is intimately connected with his endeavor.

PROBLEMS OF DISCOURSE

Olson's brilliance when specifying the major ills, and his vagueness when speaking to their cure, his inability to resolve the inherent contradictions between the latter and the former (how shall the individual make himself responsible for many of the elements in a society in whose false unity and swollen forms he himself is caught and of which he is a part?), all so clearly to be seen in this piece, persist throughout his canon. It is the problem he recognizes in Melville, who finds splendid embodiment for his society's evils in Ahab but who can never create a convincing hero. Large answers, the sweeping solution, evade Olson by the very nature of his method, which is to focus on particulars, even on "the blessing/ that difficulties are once more."

These difficulties include the obvious truth that Olson is trammeled at the outset by the very tricks of discourse he would overthrow: Witness, for example, his sweeping generalization, near the beginning of his essay "Human Universe": "We have lived long in a generalizing time, at least since 450 B.C." Again, and on the other hand, given that he is urgent about reeducating his contemporaries to eradicate society's evils before it is too late, his refusal to write in received forms was bound to delay dissemination of his message. Moreover, while he was embodying the difficulties and the particularities in highly difficult and particular forms, and thereby rendering these virtually inaccessible except by the slow "trickle-down" process which accompanies aesthetically responsible art, he was given, in both poem and essay, to assertion without supporting evidence—such is the nature of the intuitive perception he espoused, as against a stupefied insistence on proof—and thereby to alienating many more conventionally trained readers.

OPEN VERSE

That Olson could not accomplish his project was a result of its inherent impossibility; this failure, however, in no way erases the spellbinding body of his poetry. His magnificent embodiment and evocation of the dilemma in which he found himself remains as both consolation and exhortation. He gave a rationale for free (or, to use his own term, Open) verse, of which his own work is the most telling demonstration; he gave a scale and a scope to poetry which inspired and continue to inspire other poets and which make his own among the most compelling of all time. If his more general prescriptions regarding society—true as they still ring, particularly in their diagnostics—have been largely ineffectual against the momentum of social change (surely, from Olson's point of view, for the worse), his speculations, conjecture, and assertions concerning the practice of poetry stay valid, viable, and vital. Moreover, his insistence that the poet (as Percy Bysshe Shelley thought, a century and more before) be lawgiver to those of his day must be a salutary thorn in the side of any practitioner of the art.

"THE KINGFISHERS"

The power of Olson's finest poems stems from a double movement: The poet strives to fill his poem with the greatest variety of subject matter that he can; the poet strives to empty his poem of everything he has brought into it. The plethora of subject matter (information, often conflicting) is there to say that the world is absolutely fascinating—its details are fit matter for anyone's attention; the act of emptying these out is to say nothing is as important, as worthy of attention, as the moment about to come into being.

"The Kingfishers" is a case in point: A quick topic sentence ("What does not change/ is the will to change"; "As the dead prey upon us,/ they are the dead in ourselves"), broad enough in application, allows Olson to bring in all manner of materials by logical or intuitive association that somehow fit under its rubric: Meditation upon change leads, first, to a recalled cocktail party conversation that touched upon the passing of the fashion for kingfishers' feathers; this soon leads Olson to recall Mao Zedong's speech upon the success of his revolution; and, a dialectic having now been set up between West (tyrannized by its markets—"fashion"—and associated with a dying civilization) and East (Mao's revolution, source of the rising sun), the poem proceeds to "dance" (one of Olson's favorite terms, used to denote the poetic act), its details representing East/novelty/ uprising in among those representing West/stagnation/ descent, in a vocabulary variously encyclopedic, colloquial, hortatory, cybernetic, lyrical, prosaic. It is a collage, then, but one filled with movement, bearing out Olson's dictum "ONE PERCEPTION MUST IMMEDIATELY AND DIRECTLY LEAD TO A FURTHER PERCEPTION." Yet the poem ends: "shall you uncover honey/ where maggots are?// I hunt among stones," and

while to one reader this may suggest that the poet's weight is thrown on the side of those details which belong to the "East/novelty/uprising" sequence, to a reader who bears in mind that *all* these details now are of the past, it suggests that the poet opts for the present/future, which, being as yet all potential, is blank—as a stony landscape.

PROJECTIVE VERSE

Ends, however, are only tiny portions of their poems and cannot cancel the keen pleasure a reader may take in tracing meaning among such enigmatically juxtaposed blocks of constantly altering language, while being carried along at such various velocities. There are many striking formulations—often evidently stumbled on in the compositional process, which appears to unfold before the reader's very eyes (and ears); these often appear as good counsel ("In the midst of plenty, walk/ as close to/ bare// In the face of sweetness,/ piss"; "The nets of being/ are only eternal if you sleep as your hands/ ought to be busy"). Syntax—at times so filled with baffles and circumlocutions as to be more properly parataxis—brilliantly evokes the difficulties Olson would name, even court; nouns carry much of the freight, whereas adjectives are scarce (description Olson thought not projective, not able to break the circle of representation); verbs tend to be those of concealment and discovery and of social acts—talking, urging, hearing, permitting, obtaining, and the like. Because his notation favors the phrase over the sentence, in Olson's poetry words can appear to leap from the page, freed significantly of their usual subjections. Although on occasion Olson (an accomplished orator) segues into a Roman kind of rhetoric, for the most part he stays true to his aim, namely, to attack a universe of discourse with a poetry not only of particulars but also particulate in its construction. As indicated earlier, each of these elements helps constitute an intense dialectic whose synthesis occurs only as the abolition of its components: "It is undone business/ I speak of, this morning,/ with the sea/ stretching out/ from my feet."

THE MAXIMUS POEMS AND ARCHAEOLOGIST OF MORNING

While Olson's poetry appeared as a number of volumes during his lifetime, these are now contained in two texts: *The Maximus Poems* and *Archaeologist of Morn-*

ing (containing all of his non-Maximus poems). "Maximus" is the poetic figure Olson created to "speak" poems (sometimes called letters) to the people of Gloucester and, by extension, to any who would be people of "a coherence not even yet new"—persons of that vivid and imminent future which is the Grail to Olson's search and labor. Maximus knows the history of the geography of this seaport and, by extension, of both pre- and post-settlement New England; of the migratory movements of Europe and the ancient world; of other civilizations which, at some (usually early) stage, discovered the will to cohere, which Olson praised. He is to some degree based upon Maximus of Tyre, a maverick sage akin to Apollonius of Tyana from the second century C.E., although Olson appears not to have investigated this historical personage with much thoroughness, preferring, no doubt, not to disturb the introjected Maximus he was finding so fruitful.

The significance of the city of Gloucester in these poems is complex but has to do with a place loved so well that it repays its lover with a battery of guarantees and tokens, enabling him to withstand the greased slide of present culture, the suck of absentee ownership and built-in obsolescence. It is for Olson the place where, in William Wordsworth's terms, he first received those "intimations of immortality" that even in the beleaguered present can solace and hearten. In his attachment to its particulars, his heat for its physical reality, the reader is invited to discover feelings for some actual place or entity akin to that of the poet, thereby to be led to the commitment essential to an awakened sense of life and a practice of person equal "to the real itself."

OTHER MAJOR WORKS

SHORT FICTION: *Stocking Cap: A Story*, 1966.

PLAYS: *The Fiery Hunt and Other Plays*, pb. 1977.

NONFICTION: *Call Me Ishmael: A Study of Melville*, 1947; *Mayan Letters*, 1953; "Projective Verse," 1959; *Human Universe and Other Essays*, 1965; *Proprioception*, 1965; *Selected Writings of Charles Olson*, 1966; *Pleistocene Man*, 1968; *Causal Mythology*, 1969; *Letters for "Origin," 1950-1956*, 1969; *The Special View of History*, 1970; *On Black Mountain*, 1971; *Additional Prose: A Bibliography on America, Proprioception, and Other Notes and Es-*says, 1974; *Charles Olson and Ezra Pound: An Encounter at St. Elizabeth's*, 1975; *The Post Office*, 1975; *Muthologos: Collected Lectures and Interviews*, 1978-1979 (2 volumes); *Charles Olson and Robert Creeley: The Complete Correspondence*, 1980-1990 (8 volumes; George F. Butterick, editor); *Charles Olson and Cid Corman: Complete Correspondence, 1950-1964*, 1987 (2 volumes; George Evans, editor); *Letters for "Origin," 1950-1956*, 1989 (Albert Glover, editor); *Selected Letters, Charles Olson*, 2000 (Ralph Maud, editor).

MISCELLANEOUS: *Selected Writings of Charles Olson*, 1966; *Poetry and Truth: The Beloit Lectures and Poems*, 1971.

BIBLIOGRAPHY

Bollobás, Eniko. *Charles Olson*. New York: Twayne, 1992. An introductory biography and critical study of selected works by Olson. Includes bibliographical references and index.

Cech, John. *Charles Olson and Edward Dahlberg: A Portrait of a Friendship*. Victoria, B.C.: English Literary Studies, University of Victoria, 1982. Cech describes the relationship between these two longtime friends and writers. Provides background for students interested in literary movements of the time. Includes a bibliography.

Evans, George. "A Selection from the Correspondence: Charles Olson and Cid Corman, 1950." *Origin*, 5th ser. Vol. 1 (1983): 78-106. Evans presents the first 14 of 175 letters between Olson and Corman. In 1950, Corman was attempting to launch a new poetry magazine. He writes to Olson to persuade him to take the position of contributing editor. Interesting to all students of the Objectivist movement.

Heller, Michael. *Conviction's Net of Branches: Essays on the Objectivist Poets and Poetry*. Carbondale: Southern Illinois University Press, 1985. Corman was a major figure in the Objectivist poetry movement. These essays shed light on the nature and convictions of the Objectivists. Suitable for advanced undergraduate and graduate poetry students.

Maud, Ralph. *Charles Olson's Reading: A Biography*. Carbondale: Southern Illinois University Press, 1996. A narrative account of the life and work of Olson, focusing on the poet's lifelong reading material as a basis for understanding his work. Maud links the intellectual and poetic development of Olson's career to a catalog of his library, childhood books, and poetry by his contemporaries.

Olson, Charles, and Cid Corman. *Charles Olson and Cid Corman: Complete Correspondence, 1950-1964.* Edited by George Evans. 2 vols. Orono, Maine: National Poetry Foundation, 1987. Evans presents the 175 extant letters between the founder of *Origin* magazine and its contributing editor. They reveal that Olson was initially skeptical of Corman's aims, fearing that Corman was starting a magazine with too broad a scope to serve the needs of the Objectivist poets.

_____. *Letters for "Origin," 1950-1956.* Edited by Albert Glover. New York: Paragon House, 1989. Cid Corman founded *Origin* magazine as a forum for Objectivist poets, and he hired Charles Olson to be its contributing editor. Their letters discuss the struggles of the fledgling periodical and of the Objectivist poetic movement.

Rifkin, Libbie. *Career Moves: Olson, Creeley, Zukofsky, Berrigan, and the American Avant-Garde.* Madison: University of Wisconsin Press, 2000. Argues that antiestablishment poets of the 1950's and 1960's, including Olson, were just as bent on building their careers, reputations, and audiences as were more mainstream poets.

David Bromige;
bibliography updated by the editors

OMAR KHAYYÁM

Born: Nishapur, Persia; May 18, 1048(?)
Died: Nishapur, Persia; December 4, 1123(?)

PRINCIPAL POETRY

The *Rubáiyát* manuscripts were discovered after Omar Khayyám's death, in the early thirteenth century. Additional manuscripts were also found in the fourteenth and fifteenth centuries. In 1859, Edward FitzGer-

ald translated the verses, publishing *The Rubáiyát of Omar Khayyám.*

OTHER MAJOR WORKS

Some twelfth and thirteenth century commentators, writing half a century or more after Omar Khayyám's death, describe him as a poet writing in both Persian and Arabic, but, aside from the Persian *Rubáiyát* (meaning "quatrains"), only a few miscellaneous verses in Arabic and a Persian ode, all of doubtful authorship, have been attributed to him. Besides poetry, he wrote an important ground-breaking treatise on algebra, the scientific treatise *Mizan al-Hikma* (eleventh century; *The Measure of Philosophy*, 1941), an essay on Euclid's problems, another essay on the science of universals, and brief commentaries on such philosophical topics as free will and predestination, good and evil, and the meaning of existence. Some of his scientific and philosophical writings have been collected and translated into English by Swami Govinda Tirtha, *The Nectar of Grace: Omar Khayyám's Life and Works* (1941).

OTHER LITERARY FORMS

Omar Khayyám is remembered primarily for his *Rubáiyát.*

ACHIEVEMENTS

Omar Khayyám's contemporaries spoke of his mathematical, scientific, and scholarly achievements with immense respect, heaping upon him such epithets as Sage of the World, Philosopher of the Universe, Lord of the Wise Men, and Proof of the Truth—but none mentioned his poetic achievement. One reason for the omission is obvious: Omar Khayyám's quatrains were not published (at least by the regular mode then prevailing) during his lifetime, but only gradually came to light in various citations and manuscripts during the following centuries. Meanwhile, apparently, the quatrains were circulating, either orally or in clandestine written versions, with potent effect. So much may be gathered from the backhanded compliment of a successor, one Abu'l-Hasan Ali Qifti (1172-1248), a defender of the faith who wrote in *Tarikh al-Hukama* (thirteenth century) that the Sufis, a mystical Islamic sect, had been corrupted by Omar Khayyám's quatrains: ". . . these poems are like beautiful snakes, outwardly attractive, but inwardly poisonous and deadly to the Holy Law." Qifti's remarks indicate why the *Rubáiyát* could not be published during Omar Khayyám's lifetime, but, ironically, the religious critics' citation of offending quatrains was one way they were circulated and preserved.

Omar Khayyám's ranking alongside the snake in the Garden of Eden is certainly a tribute to his poetic power; nevertheless, the opposition of religious zealots and the embrace of the mystical Sufis finally did him in. As Persian poets with more substantial *divans* (collections) came to the fore—such as Rumi, Sa'di, Hāfez, and Jami—the amateur Omar Khayyám and his one hundred or so quatrains faded into obscurity. The dilution of his achievement through transmission (sometimes by unfriendly hands) and through eventual attribution to him of hundreds of repetitious, inferior quatrains did not help his reputation. Omar Khayyám continued to be thought a very minor poet until suddenly, in Victorian England, his *Rubáiyát* blazed forth again like a literary comet. The cause was Edward FitzGerald's English version, one of the most successful translations of all time, a translation which FitzGerald polished through five editions (the first published in 1859, the fifth in 1889). To the Pre-Raphaelites and others, the *Rubáiyát* gave expression to a whole sad *Weltanschauung*, and as such the work has continued through many editions and translations into the world's major languages. For some time after FitzGerald's translation, Omar Khayyám the poet remained without recognition in his own country, aside from illustrated editions of his quatrains produced for the tourist trade, but in recent decades Iranian literary scholars have also been giving him their serious attention.

For scholars of the *Rubáiyát*, simply establishing what Omar Khayyám wrote has been, and remains, the biggest problem. One theory is that he produced no quatrains at all, another that he produced thousands. There are numerous competing manuscripts (a few forged) from copyists. Comparing manuscripts endlessly, scholars conservatively accept no more than one hundred or so quatrains as authentic (though differing on which quatrains). Based on a fourteenth century manuscript considered as reliable as any, FitzGerald's translation (fifth edition) is used here for purposes of quotation.

Despite his limited production, Omar Khayyám was no literary lightweight, certainly not the shallow Epicurean condemned by early religious fanatics and sought after by modern sensualists. Worthy of Jean-Paul Sartre or Albert Camus, these thoughts have an amazingly modern flavor which is not merely the result of FitzGerald's translation. Although Qifti considered them venom, they are really the wine distilled from a life in the harsh desert soil of an old Muslim land. That such freethinking could proceed from the midst of such repressive conditions as those surrounding Omar Khayyám is one indication of his achievement, and certainly an encouragement to the human race. This freedom of tone gives the *Rubáiyát* a paradoxically uplifting quality despite Omar Khayyám's pessimism about the human condition.

BIOGRAPHY

Just as it is difficult (if not impossible) to say exactly what Omar Khayyám wrote, so also it is difficult, except in the broadest outline, to establish the facts of his life. The scanty information available on Omar Khayyám is embroidered by romantic legend, attempts to discredit him (or to show him repenting), and idle speculation. One source, for example, calls him inhospitable and bad-tempered, but this characterization is not borne out by other information. Another source maintains that Omar Khayyám believed in metempsychosis, then tells the following story to prove it: One day when Omar Khayyám and his students were walking about the college, they came across a donkey too stubborn to move with its load of bricks. Omar Khayyám explained that the donkey was inhabited by the soul of a former lecturer at the college, whose beard had transmigrated to the donkey's tail, and he got the donkey to move by improvising a quatrain on it. Such is the nature of most of the information on Omar Khayyám.

The poet's full name was Ghiyasoddin Abolfath Omar ibn Ebrahim Khayyámi, the name Khayyám meaning "tent-maker," probably referring to the trade of one of his ancestors. His family had lived in Nishapur for generations before he was born. After attending school at Nishapur, he continued his studies at Balkh, distinguishing himself especially in geometry and astronomy. Following his schooling, he worked for the magistrate of Samarkand, the ruler of Bokhara, and eventually the grand Sultan Malekshah (reigned 1072-1092). Among the projects he worked on were the construction of an observatory and the creation of a more accurate calendar.

During the first half of his life, Omar Khayyám's growing prominence and powerful patrons seem to have shielded him from the religious fanatics, while also attracting their attention. When Sultan Malekshah died, Omar Khayyám appears to have suffered setbacks. Apparently he had to leave Nishapur in 1095, staying away for several years, during which time he made his pilgrimage to Mecca and visited Baghdad. The ruler of the province which included Nishapur was Malekshah's son Sanjar, whom, the story goes, Omar Khayyám alienated with an offhand remark when Sanjar was a child. In 1117, Sanjar became sultan. It may have been from his own experience of political reverses that Omar Khayyám was speaking when, in the *Rubáiyát*, he advocated the simple life in the wilderness, "where name of Slave and Sultan is forgot."

ANALYSIS

A noteworthy coincidence in intellectual history is that Edward FitzGerald's translation of Omar Khayyám's *Rubáiyát* came out the same year as Charles Darwin's *On the Origin of Species by Means of Natural Selection* (1859). Despite their obvious differences, the two works show remarkable similarities: Both are inimical to religion and evince a thoroughgoing empiricism. Like Omar Khayyám, Darwin thought God was cruel, and both authors espouse a deterministic view of the world. Both authors had sharpened their minds through years of scientific investigation, enabling them to cut through the fat of human illusion to the heart of things. Taking their stand as rebels and empiricists, both authors were precursors of modern Existentialism, with its doctrine of the absurd. Sticklers for facts will point out that Omar Khayyám lived eight to nine centuries before Existentialism. Precisely. His quatrains had to wait all those centuries before they finally found a responsive audience in Victorian England, an alien society which nevertheless had much in common with the Muslim world in which Omar Khayyám lived.

If Darwin's *On the Origin of Species by Means of Natural Selection* marked the triumph of science over religion in the Christian world, the suppression of Khay-

yám's quatrains symbolized religion's triumph over science in the Muslim world. The centuries preceding Omar Khayyám had seen a great flowering of scientific achievement in Muslim lands, but by Omar Khayyám's time, religious reaction had set in. In near-hysteria over losing control, the religious authorities had hardened their attitudes, sometimes to the point of fanaticism. In Persia, the religious authorities regained control with the rise of the Seljuq rulers, nomadic Turks from central Asia only recently converted from barbarism. Both parties found a political alliance convenient. The pursuit of knowledge, except for knowledge with immediate practical applications, became suspect. Rationalism was attacked as a foreign import (from the Greeks), and the study of logic was banned; only those words and thoughts which ran within the circumscribed patterns set by the Koran and its interpreters were allowed—and even there, any ambiguity could be fatal. For example, the great religious scholar Abu Hamed Mohammed Ghazali, a friendly opponent and contemporary of Omar Khayyám (both taught at Nishapur for a time), was charged with apostasy and his books burned because he said "There cannot be anything better than what is," which he took as a statement of God's power but others took as a statement of God's weakness (he had also made enemies by favoring logic and by publicly criticizing another religious authority). Other religious leaders who misspoke were crucified or burned at the stake. Indeed, aside from powerful friends, only the factionalism of the fanatics themselves offered any precarious safety.

THE RUBA'I STANZA

In this repressive atmosphere, what mode of expression remained for the independent, rational thinker who wished to retain his sanity? For Omar Khayyám, it was apparently the quatrain (*ruba'i*), a literary form especially suited to guerrilla tactics. In quantitative meter (translated by FitzGerald as iambic pentameter), rhyming *aaba* and occasionally *aaaa*, the *ruba'i* is like a haiku or epigram—or, even better, a combination of haiku and epigram, of image and pointed, witty remark. The unrhymed third line causes the rhyming fourth line to fall with particular force. Each *ruba'i*, it should be stressed, is a separate poem, not a stanza in a longer work (in Persian, a collection of *rubáiyát* is arranged alphabetically, according to the final rhyming letter of each *ruba'i*). Thus, the *ruba'i* is not long enough to be taken too seriously; it can be delivered orally, perhaps as a humorous aside or innocuous rhyme; and it is easy to remember.

How Omar Khayyám safely transmitted his *rubáiyát* is unknown—whether individually and orally to trusted students and friends, or collected in circulating manuscripts, or in a secret manuscript discovered after his death—but their underground nature can be easily seen when they are compared with his public utterances. Treating many of the same issues as the quatrains, Omar Khayyám's philosophical commentaries are models of evasiveness: brief, vague, and noncommittal, sketching out the issues without taking a stand (unlike the quatrains, which assert heretical positions on everything from God to wine).

CRITIQUING GOD

Omar Khayyám's conception of God represents a critique of the orthodox idea of a personal God. From orthodox teachings, Omar Khayyám deduces a God who is either cruel or incompetent. Only a cruel God would make man weak, beset his path with sin, and then punish him for falling. Not even "a peevish Boy" would take such perverse delight in destroying his creation. From this point of view, men are only God's playthings: "a moving row/ Of Magic Shadow-shapes" presented "by the Master of the Show"; "helpless Pieces of the Game He plays/ Upon this Chequer-board"; the "Ball" that "the Player" tosses onto "the Field" and strikes with his mallet. Or, if this view seems too extreme, then God must at least be incompetent, a potter who mars his pots. In either case, God is placed in the position of needing man's forgiveness, rather than vice versa.

THE RUBÁIYÁT

If anyone is cruel or incompetent, it is the theologians, whose efforts to define God Omar Khayyám is really attacking. Their definitions tend to be circular: They define God in their own image. At other times, they contradict themselves by trying to reconcile a perfect Creator with an imperfect creation, or merely slip into wishful thinking. In the *Rubáiyát*, some of this mushy logic is exemplified in the conversation among the "Pots":

> Whereat some one of the loquacious Lot—
> I think a Súfi pipkin—waxing hot—

> "All this of Pot and Potter—Tell me then,
> Who is the Potter, pray, and who the Pot?"
> "Why," said another, "Some there are who tell
> Of one who threatens he will toss to Hell
> The luckless Pots he marred in making—Pish!
> He's a Good Fellow, and 'twill all be well."

None of this confusion stands up under the scrutiny of Omar Khayyám, who considers theological speculation a waste of time.

Instead, Omar Khayyám constructs an empirical worldview based strictly on available evidence. Admittedly, evidence is in short supply—"Into this Universe, and *Why* not knowing/ Nor *Whence*, like Water willy-nilly flowing...." Still, the Universe exists, hence a Creator. From what Omar Khayyám can see, however, the Creator pays little attention to humans, but is only an impersonal force rather like Fate:

> The Moving Finger writes; and, having writ,
> Moves on: nor all your Piety nor Wit
> Shall lure it back to cancel half a Line,
> Nor all your Tears wash out a Word of it.

There is no Heaven and no Hell (except of man's own making), hence no afterlife. All that remains is this life, wherein man's fate is defined by the limitations of his nature: "With Earth's first Clay They did the Last Man knead,/ And there of the Last Harvest sow'd the Seed...."

The salient facts of man's fate are a transitory life and a certain death, dust to dust. Death takes the good and the bad, the great and the small indifferently; all that remains of the departed is the dust beneath one's feet or the grass along the riverbank. Therefore, seek neither "the Glories of This World" nor "the Prophet's Paradise to come"; instead, "take the Cash, and let the Credit go," seize the day, live like the blooming rose:

> Come, fill the Cup, and in the fire of Spring
> Your Winter-garment of Repentence fling:
> The Bird of Time has but a little way
> To flutter—and the Bird is on the Wing.

Like any good teacher, Omar Khayyám instructs not only by his advice but also by his example. He confesses that he once spent his time in trifling scholarly pursuits—improving the calendar ("'Twas only striking from the Calendar/ Unborn To-morrow, and dead Yes-terday"), and conducting scientific and philosophical in-vestigations ("Of all that one should care to fathom, I/ Was never deep in anything but—Wine"). Eventually, however, Omar Khayyám repented such a sorry exis-tence and "made a Second Marriage": He "divorced old barren Reason" from his bed and "took the Daughter of the Vine to Spouse."

Whether or not Omar Khayyám found happiness with wine, his example and advice need not be taken lit-erally. In the *Rubáiyát*, wine is also important as a sym-bol, the central symbol wherein the two main lines of thought, the antireligious sentiment and the empiricism, converge. In traditional Islamic law, one sip of wine is worth eighty lashes, so Omar Khayyám's description of the tavern as a temple indicates his scorn for religious teachings, for the prohibitions and illusions which cut people off from seizing life while they can. It is also ap-propriate that what is prohibited by religion should, as so frequently happens, symbolize the heart's desire, for empiricism shows that, even if life is absurd, some peo-ple do not know any better than to be happy. In the *Rubáiyát*, wine symbolizes the possibility of seizing happiness, in whatever form. Happiness does not necessar-ily have to take the form of spending one's day in taverns:

> A book of Verses underneath the Bough,
> A jug of Wine, a Loaf of Bread—and Thou
> Beside me singing in the Wilderness—
> Oh, Wilderness were Paradise enow!

It is to be hoped that, with his wine, his Sákí (the girl who serves the wine), and his quatrains, Omar Khayyám did manage to find happiness even in old Persia.

OTHER MAJOR WORKS

NONFICTION: *Mizan al-Hikma*, eleventh century (*The Measure of Philosophy*, 1941); *The Nectar of Grace: Omar Khayyám's Life and Works*, 1941 (in-cludes *The Measure of Philosophy* and other essays).

BIBLIOGRAPHY

Dashti, Ali. *In Search of Omar Khayyám.* Translated from the Persian by L. P. Elwell-Sutton. New York: Columbia University Press, 1971. Intended for the general reader, this book gives a wide variety of in-formation helpful to students of the *Rubáiyát*. The lengthy introduction by Elwell-Sutton explains the difficulty of gathering a text actually authored by Omar Khayyám. Dashti then discusses Khayyám's reputation among his contemporaries, his character as it is revealed in his poetry, and his religious be-liefs. From this understanding, Dashti distinguishes the quatrains most likely to be authentic from those that are not and includes his own translations of both groups.

Dougan, Abdullah. *Who Is the Potter? A Commentary on the "Rubáiyát of Omar Khayyám."* Auckland, New Zealand: Gnostic Press, 1991. This book is based on tape-recorded comments made by Dougan on the *Rubáiyát* during meetings with students. Each quatrain is followed by Dougan's interpretation of its meaning and relevance to Sufi teaching. Al-though Dougan was not a trained scholar or literary critic, his mystical approach to the poem helps the reader to understand its essential seriousness, evi-dent in the religious and philosophical imagery and themes.

FitzGerald, Edward. *"Rubáiyát of Omar Khayyám": A Critical Edition.* Edited by Christopher Decker. Charlottesville: University Press of Virginia, 1997. This is a thorough and thoroughly reputable presen-tation of FitzGerald's treatment of the *Rubáiyát*. All four of FitzGerald's versions of the *Rubáiyát* are given, including his Latin translation, along with FitzGerald's original prefaces and notes. Decker's extensive introduction discusses the circumstances surrounding FitzGerald's publications of his transla-tions, and although the heart of this useful text is the *Rubáiyát*, most of Decker's attention is on FitzGer-ald himself and on his free translation of the poem.

Graves, Robert, and Omar Ali-Shah. *"The Rubaiyyat of Omar Khayaam": A New Translation with Critical Commentaries.* London: Cassell & Company, 1968. Two-thirds of this book is devoted to introductory material, notes, and bibliography. Graves attacks Edward FitzGerald's famous translation of the *Rubáiyát*, arguing that it led to a profound misunder-standing of the poem and the poet. Graves then of-fers his own translation as a more faithful rendering of the original poem. Ali-Shah's historical preface continues to denounce FitzGerald's treatment of the *Rubáiyát* and corrects misunderstandings of Sufi doctrine and Persian culture perpetrated by other translators and commentators.

Yogananda, Paramhansa. *"The Rubáiyát of Omar Khay-yám" Explained*. Edited by J. Donald Walters. Nevada City, Calif.: Crystal Clarity, 1994. Yogananda uses FitzGerald's first edition of the *Rubáiyát* as a springboard for his own contributions to an understanding of the poem. Each of FitzGerald's quatrains is followed by Yogananda's prose paraphrase, an interpretation of the quatrain, and an explanation of its imagery and thought. Both Yogananda and Walters often interject their own mystical musings into the explanations. Their efforts are an interesting balance to the work of scholars and critics who search for authentic manuscripts of the *Rubáiyát* and provide accurate, literal translations of them. This book may not be scholarly, but it gives a fresh treatment to the growing interest in Omar Khayyám and his poetry.

Harold Branam;
bibliography updated by Bernard E. Morris

MICHAEL ONDAATJE

Born: Colombo, Ceylon (now Sri Lanka); September 12, 1943

PRINCIPAL POETRY

The Dainty Monsters, 1967
The Man with Seven Toes, 1969
The Collected Works of Billy the Kid, 1970
Rat Jelly, 1973
Elimination Dance, 1978, revised 1980
There's a Trick with a Knife I'm Learning to Do: Poems, 1963-1978, 1979
Secular Love, 1984
The Cinnamon Peeler: Selected Poems, 1991
Handwriting, 1998

OTHER LITERARY FORMS

Michael Ondaatje has published several novels, a memoir about his childhood in Sri Lanka, and literary criticism. He has also transformed two of his works into plays: *The Collected Works of Billy the Kid* was produced in Stratford, Ontario, in 1973, in New York City in 1974, and in London in 1984; and *In the Skin of a Lion* was produced as a play in 1987. He is the editor of several anthologies of fiction and poetry as well.

Ondaatje has also exercised his writing talents in cinema, which has always fascinated him. After making *Sons of Captain Poetry* (1969), a short film about poet bp Nichol (Barrie Phillip Nichol), and *The Clinton Special* (1972), a longer documentary that explores the relationship between living and performing, he was invited by director Norman Jewison to join the Canadian Centre for Advanced Film Studies; there he wrote the script for *Love Clinic*, a short film.

ACHIEVEMENTS

Ondaatje has been the recipient of numerous literary honors, among them the Ralph Gustafson Award (1965), the Epstein Award (1966), the E. J. Pratt Medal (1966), President's Medal of the University of Western Ontario (1967), the Governor-General's Literary Award, awarded by the Canadian Council for the Arts (1971, 1980, 1992, 2000), the Canada-Australia Prize (1980), the Toronto Book Award (1988), the Trillium Award (1992), and the prestigious Booker McConnell Prize (1992), awarded by the British Book Trust for his novel *The English Patient* (1992)—the first Canadian to receive this coveted prize for the best literary work in the British Commonwealth.

Though his fiction has received the most critical attention, his poetry has won its share of accolades. He received the Chalmers Award for *The Collected Works of Billy the Kid* and the du Maurier Award for poetry. The year after *There's a Trick with a Knife I'm Learning to Do* was published and that *Coming Through Slaughter* was staged in Toronto, 1980, was the year in which he received the Canada-Australia Literary Prize.

BIOGRAPHY

Michael Ondaatje was born on a tea plantation in Colombo, Ceylon (now Sri Lanka). Philip Mervyn Ondaatje, his father, was descended from a wealthy family that can be traced back to 1600. By the time Ondaatje

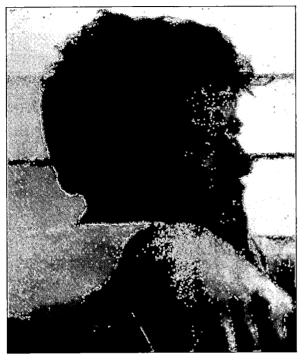

Michael Ondaatje (© Quentin Ondaatje)

was born, however, his father had sold most of the family's holdings; two years later (1945) his father and mother, Enid Doris Gratiaen, were divorced. His mother went to England and sent him to St. Thomas's College Boys' School in Colombo, a school modeled on English boarding schools. By 1952, his mother had earned enough money to bring him to England, where he continued his education at Dulwich College before he immigrated in 1962 to Lennoxville, Quebec, Canada. There he attended Bishop's University and won the President's Prize for English. After marrying Betty Jane Kimbark (Kim Jones) in 1964, he transferred to University College, University of Toronto, where he won the Ralph Gustafson Award and received a B.A. degree. While working on his M.A. degree at Queen's University in Kingston, he had some poems included in *New Wave Canada*, an anthology, tied for the E. J. Pratt Gold Medal for Poetry, and won the Norma Epstein Award for Poetry.

After receiving his M.A. and publishing *The Dainty Monsters*, he began teaching at the University of Western Ontario, but despite publishing a critical study of Leonard Cohen and the critically acclaimed *The Col-*

lected Works of Billy the Kid, Ondaatje was fired for lack of "academic" publications. He was then hired by the Glendon College English Department at York University. During the 1970's Ondaatje worked in film and translated some of his work to the stage. He received awards for both poetry (the Chalmers Award for *The Collected Works of Billy the Kid* and the du Maurier Award for poetry) and fiction (the *Books in Canada* First Novel Award for *Coming Through Slaughter*).

When Ondaatje served as a visiting professor at the University of Hawaii in 1981, he met Linda Spalding and separated from his wife. With Linda Spalding, he coedited *The Brick Reader* (1991). After that he published several volumes of verse, including *Secular Love, The Cinnamon Peeler: Selected Poems,* and *Handwriting*. It is his fiction, however, that has received the most critical recognition. The novel *The English Patient* established him as an international literary figure with much the same stature Margaret Atwood enjoys. The novel was adapted into an award-winning film in 1996.

ANALYSIS

Perhaps no other Canadian writer, with the exception of Margaret Atwood, has written well in such a variety of genres and received the international acclaim accorded Michael Ondaatje. This "international" reputation is hardly surprising, given his Sri Lankan heritage, his thoroughly "British" schooling, and the foreign teaching positions he has held. In fact, since *Coming Through Slaughter* and *The Collected Works of Billy the Kid* have distinctly American themes (the first about jazz man Buddy Bolden; the second about a Western cultural icon), there has been a tendency to deny Ondaatje Canadian status. Similarly, given the unconventional nature of the narrative in *Coming Through Slaughter* and the blending of poetry and prose in *The Collected Works of Billy the Kid* (which some critics have categorized as fiction or "other"), Ondaatje's writing tends to blur, if not to obscure, conventional distinctions between fiction and poetry.

THE DAINTY MONSTERS

The Dainty Monsters, Ondaatje's first volume of verse, contains many poems about animals and birds. "Description Is a Bird" is the first of eight poems in the collection. For the most part, humans are absent from these poems; the animals seem to serve as symbols but resist interpretation, leaving room for various responses. Douglas Barbour reads the poem as follows: "Love is a performance against solitude which demands discipline in the midst of apparent chaos." The birds' actions describe love. Barbour feels that poems like these, those that allow "closure," were omitted in later collections because "Ondaatje's restless imagination" found them "too confining."

THE COLLECTED WORKS OF BILLY THE KID

In 1970, three years after *The Dainty Monsters*, Ondaatje published *The Collected Works of Billy the Kid*, a hybrid book containing some lyric poems but also photographs, a fictional newspaper account, ballads, and selections from real documents. For Dennis Lee, "this polyphony introduces an exuberant flow into the book's movement, which carries a reader with ease through the discontinuities of the plot." In the book, civilization and nature are at odds, and Billy dehumanizes himself by becoming a killing machine. Constantly on edge, Billy is the outsider constrained by boundaries which he crosses or observes. The volume begins with an empty square that represents a picture of Billy, but the prose passage alludes to moving pictures. In fact, the book contains references and descriptions that suggest that Billy is a camera, observing angles and distances, or a motion picture camera, describing actions as one would write a screenplay:

> Garrett smiles, pokes his gun towards the door.
> The others melt and
> surround.
> All this I would have seen if I was on the roof looking.

As a filmmaker, Billy, like Ondaatje, is an artist; and in this volume, as in his other works, Ondaatje tends to resemble his protagonist.

"LETTERS AND OTHER WORLDS"

In "Letters and Other Worlds" (from *Rat Jelly*), which Stephen Scobie has described as "the greatest single poem in Canadian literature," Ondaatje attempts to come to terms with his absentee father, a recurrent figure in his work. The poem recounts his father's drinking bouts, his self-destructive behavior, and his self-imposed isolation in a room with bottles of liquor. The poem is at once amusing and tragic, like his father's life: "His early life was a terrifying comedy." Ondaatje jokes that his fa-

ther's "falling/ dead drunk onto the street" and stopping the Perahara procession was "a crucial/ turning point" that "led to Ceylon's independence in 1948" because his father was a "semi-official, and semi-white at that."

The last verse paragraph presents, through balancing imagery, the tenuous hold his father had on his life. In his room Ondaatje's father wrote apologies, "Letters in a clear hand of the most complete empathy." While his heart widened to accept "all manner of change in his children and friends," he "himself edged/ into the terrible acute hatred/ of his own privacy." Fearful (earlier Ondaatje writes, "My father's body was a globe of fear") of accepting and forgiving himself, "he balanced and fell."

"LIGHT"

Ondaatje often used mythology in his early poems, but in the later ones he tends to mythologize domesticity. Community becomes a major concern as he probes relationships with friends and family. In "Light" (from *There's a Trick with a Knife I'm Learning to Do*), dedicated to his mother, as he sits through a midnight summer storm, he sees the slides "re-shot from old minute photographs" projected on the wall. His relatives "stand/ complex ambiguous grainy," at several removes from reality. The complexity and ambiguity are reflected in memories of eccentric but endearing behavior (his Aunt Christie thought Harold MacMillan was "communicating with her through pictures in the newspapers"). The pictures, like the various pieces that comprise *The Collected Works of Billy the Kid*, are "fragments, all I remember"; but Ondaatje can see his family not only reflected in himself and in his children, but also "parade in my brain" and make connections between "expanding stories," partly of his creation, and "the grey grainy pictures." Like the trees around his house, they "Haven't moved an inch from me."

SECULAR LOVE

In *Secular Love* Ondaatje became more autobiographical, more intimate, and more confessional, in the manner of poets like Robert Lowell. The volume describes the disintegration of a marriage, a near mental breakdown, "Rock Bottom" (the title of one of the four sections), and recovery and new love. Although the poems are part of a whole and are, for the most part, interdependent, "To a Sad Daughter," which has been anthologized, stands on its own. It is a secular love poem-lecture to a daughter who is not what he "expected." She delights in violent sports, retreats into "purple moods," and finds his expression of "love" embarrassing, but he likes this behavior. Uncomfortable with the role of father and not good at giving advice, he nevertheless gives her a "lecture" which is poignant and life-affirming (perhaps the advice applies to his own life). Using myth, he advises her to listen to the song of the sirens, to not be fooled by anyone but herself, and to "break going out not in." The poem ends on a quasi-religious note ("suburban annunciation") and suggests that love may lie beneath a violent exterior: "Your goalie/ in his frightening mask/ dreams perhaps/ of gentleness."

HANDWRITING

In this volume of poetry Ondaatje turns his attention to Sri Lanka, to Sri Lankan culture, and to the writing process. The poem that begins "What we lost" best describes how Sri Lankan culture has deteriorated. In it the poet describes the loss of the "interior love poem," the "dates when the abandonment/ of certain principles occurred." The principles involve courtesy, the arts, and "Lyrics that rose/ from love/ back into the air." The nuances of human communication, the harmony between humans and nature, and the tie between nature and religion—"All this we burned or traded for power and wealth." In this volume Ondaatje addresses the political problems of Sri Lanka as he juxtaposes "men carrying recumbent Buddhas/ or men carrying mortars."

OTHER MAJOR WORKS

LONG FICTION: *Coming Through Slaughter*, 1976; *In the Skin of a Lion*, 1987; *The English Patient*, 1992; *Anil's Ghost*, 2000.

PLAYS: *The Collected Works of Billy the Kid*, pr. 1973 (adaptation of his poems); *In the Skin of a Lion*, pr. 1987 (adaptation of his novel).

NONFICTION: *Leonard Cohen*, 1970; *Claude Glass*, 1979; *The Roof*, 1982; *Running in the Family*, 1982.

EDITED TEXTS: *The Long Poem Anthology*, 1979; *From Ink Lake: Canadian Stories*, 1990; *The Brick Reader*, 1991 (with Linda Spalding); *The Faber Book of Contemporary Canadian Short Stories*, 1990; *An H in the Heart*, 1994 (with bp Nichol and George Bowering).

BIBLIOGRAPHY

Barbour, Douglas. *Michael Ondaatje*. New York: Twayne, 1993. Barbour's book contains an introductory biographical chapter, four chapters on Ondaatje's poetry, a chronology, and an annotated bibliography. Barbour discusses Ondaatje's fascination with history, his early literary debts to Wallace Stevens and Robert Lowell, and his later affinity with Ezra Pound in his longer literary works. For Barbour, Ondaatje moves from modernism to postmodernism with *Secular Love*, and Barbour uses Ondaatje's indeterminacy as evidence. *Secular Love* also, according to Barbour, contains a great number of autobiographical elements.

Heble, Ajay. "'The Widening Rise of Surprise': Containment and Transgression in the Poetry of Michael Ondaatje." *Wascana Review* 26 (Spring/Fall, 1991): 117-127. Heble examines the unexpected pairings, the jarring juxtapositions, and the abrupt shifts in tone in Ondaatje's poetry. His explication of "Letter and Other Worlds" is especially interesting since it deals with Ondaatje's father. In the poem Heble demonstrates how the poet transforms a bit of personal history, his father's drunken fall, into local mythology, a factor in the Home Rule movement. Using the line "My father's body was a globe of fear/ His body was a town we never knew," Heble shows how private body and public space coalesce.

Jewinski, Ed. *Michael Ondaatje: Express Yourself Beautifully*. Toronto: ECW Press, 1994. Jewinski's biography corrects some of the erroneous material, contributed by Ondaatje, that appeared in some reference works and traces Ondaatje's life through the publication of *The English Patient*. Jewinski maintains that Ondaatje's absent father (his parents divorced when he was two years old) affected all his writing: "In a way, he's never stopped writing to— and for—his father." Because Ondaatje has been a bit reclusive, Jewinski's book is quite valuable. He provides detailed information about Ondaatje's family and his problems with critics who charged him, because of his subject matter, with being "Americanized" and were prone to dismiss him as an ethnic writer. The book contains a chronology and a bibliography.

Scobie, Stephen. "Two Authors in Search of a Character: Michael Ondaatje and bpNichol." In *Poets and
Critics: Essays from "Canadian Literature," 1966-
1974*, edited by George Woodcock. Toronto: Oxford
University Press, 1974. Friends Ondaatje and Nichol
won Governor-General's Awards for their books on
Billy the Kid in the same year . Scobie compares the
two books and attributes Ondaatje's choice of subject matter to his love for Hollywood and Italian
Westerns. Scobie sees Ondaatje as creating a myth;
Nichol, as telling a joke. For Scobie, Billy the Kid is
outlaw as artist; Ondaatje is artist as outlaw.
Solecki, Sam, ed. *Spider Blue: Essays on Michael
Ondaatje*. Montreal: Vehicule Press, 1985. Roughly
a third of Solecki's book consists of eleven essays,
including two by Solecki, on Ondaatje's poetry covering his first volume through *Secular Love*. The
essays concern Ondaatje's ties to earlier writers and
traditions, his use of central concerns and myths,
and his *The Collected Works of Billy the Kid*, which
Solecki includes because it contains prose as well as
poetry, in a section on "The Longer Works." Solecki's
introduction notes the problem of placing the Sri
Lankan-born Ondaatje in a Canadian literary tradition. The book also contains two Solecki interviews
with Ondaatje, as well as a bibliography by Judith
Brady.

Thomas L. Erskine

GEORGE OPPEN

George Oppenheimer

Born: New Rochelle, New York; April 24, 1908
Died: Sunnyvale, California; July 7, 1984

PRINCIPAL POETRY

  Discrete Series, 1934
  The Materials, 1962
  This in Which, 1965
  Of Being Numerous, 1968
  Alpine, 1969
  Seascape: Needle's Eye, 1972

The Collected Poems of George Oppen, 1975
Primitive, 1978

OTHER LITERARY FORMS

In addition to his poetry, George Oppen published
several reviews and essays. Of these, two are central to
an understanding of his work: "The Mind's Own Place,"
published in *Kulchur*, in 1963, and "A Letter," published
in *Agenda*, in 1973. Oppen's many published interviews
and his extensive correspondence with both American
and British writers provide an in-depth look into Oppen's
poetics and his sense of poetry's place in the contemporary world; *The Selected Letters of George Oppen* was
published in 1990.

ACHIEVEMENTS

In a long and distinguished career, George Oppen
never wavered from that which Ezra Pound in 1934
noted of his work: its commitment to sustained seriousness, craftsmanship, and individual sensibility. Out of
this commitment, Oppen created one of the most moving
and complex bodies of poetry of the twentieth century.

Oppen was one of the original Objectivist poets; his
work can be associated with that of William Carlos Williams, Pound, and the Imagists. Yet more than any other
poet associated with that group, he was to develop a
radical poetics of contingency, a poetics as wary of
formalist assumptions about art as it is about naïve realism in poetry. His unique combining of imagery and
rhetoric, the breadth of his subject matter, and its nearly
populist strain have made his work extremely important
to younger poets.

In recent years, with the receipt of the Pulitzer Prize
for Poetry in 1969 and an award for his distinguished
contribution to poetry from the National Endowment for
the Arts and with increasing critical attention (much of it
contained in *George Oppen: Man and Poet*, published in
1981), Oppen's place in twentieth century poetry is beginning to be recognized as one of major significance.

BIOGRAPHY

George Oppen was born on April 24, 1908, in New
Rochelle, New York, into a moderately wealthy Jewish family. His father, George August Oppenheimer,
was a diamond merchant. Oppen's mother committed

suicide when he was four years old. His father remarried in 1917 and the next year moved his family to San Francisco, a city which has been both an inspiration and a resource for much of Oppen's poetry. In 1926, at Oregon State Universtiy, Corvallis, he met Mary Colby. They were married in 1927, the same year that the family shortened its name to Oppen. Of their relationship, Mary wrote that it was not simply love but the discovery that "we were in search of an aesthetic within which to live." For both, it meant distancing themselves from their pasts and striking out into new territory, both geographical and psychic. This departure was not so much a break with the past as a desire to obtain distance from and insight into it, for in this, as in all of their subsequent travels, the Oppens sought to live close to, and understand, ordinary working people.

Together, the Oppens hitchhiked to New York City, completing the last leg of the journey on a barge through the Erie Canal. In New York they met Louis Zukofsky and Charles Reznikoff, whose friendship and influence were to shape Oppen's poetry significantly over the years. These poets, with the encouragement of William Carlos Williams and Ezra Pound, formed themselves into the Objectivists, one of the most significant groupings in the field of twentieth century poetry, and began publishing one another's work.

In 1930, the Oppens traveled to France and Italy, meeting Pound and Constantin Brancusi; returning to the United States, the couple became involved in labor organizing and other left-wing political movements, an involvement which for Oppen ultimately led to a twenty-five-year hiatus from writing poetry. In 1940, they had a daughter, and two years later Oppen was fighting in the trenches of Europe with the Allied forces.

After the war and living in California, the Oppens were investigated by the FBI for their old left-wing politics. This situation led the Oppens to flee to Mexico during the McCarthy period, where Oppen began to write poetry again. This work, collected in *The Materials*, and touching on the themes of Oppen's past, his travels, and his sense of contemporary urban life, brought Oppen immediate recognition as a unique and powerful voice in contemporary poetry.

In 1960, the Oppens returned to the United States,

George Oppen (Ann Resor Laughlin, courtesy of New Directions Publishing Corp.)

living alternately in New York, San Francisco (where they eventually settled), and Maine, places which play a prominent role in Oppen's poetry. Oppen died in Sunnyvale, California, southeast of San Francisco, in 1984.

ANALYSIS

In one of George Oppen's poems, the poet is being driven around an island off the coast of Maine by a poor fisherman and his wife. The landscape, the lobster pots and fishing gear, the harbor, and the post office are noted, and the poet is, unaccountably, moved by a nearly metaphysical sense of passage. The experience is at once intimate and remote, and the poet is moved to exclaim to himself: "Difficult to know what one means/ —to be serious and to know what one means—." Such lines could be emblems for Oppen's entire career, for, of contemporary poets, none has more searchingly investigated through poetry the attempt to mean, to examine how language is used, and so to account for the very vocabulary of modernity.

For Oppen, inquiry is synonymous with expression. In a world of mass communication and of a debased language riddled with preconceptions about the nature of reality, the poet, according to Oppen, must begin in a completely new way; he must begin, as he says in one poem, "impoverished of tone of pose that common/ wealth of parlance." In Oppen, this is not so much a search for a language of innocence or novelty as it is a resolve against making use of certain historical or elegiac associations in language, a desire on the part of the poet not to be bewitched (as the philosopher Ludwig Wittgenstein warned) by conventional ways of speaking and of making poetry.

Oppen's entire body of work can be seen as a modern test of the poet's capacity to articulate. The terms of his poetry are the common meanings of words as they attempt to render the brute givens of the world of appearance. For this reason, Oppen has called his work "realist"; it is realist in the sense that it is "concerned with a fact (the world) which it did not create." In a way, the subject of all Oppen's poetry is the nature of this encounter, whether with the world or with others. The task for the poet is neither to beautify sentimentally nor to categorize such encounters but to render their living quality, to make the poet's relatedness to the facts into something felt. As Oppen acknowledges in one of his poems, "Perhaps one is himself/ Beyond the heart, the center of the thing/ and cannot praise it/ As he would want to."

DISCRETE SERIES

In all Oppen's work, there is an attempt to render the visual datum accurately and precisely; this is in keeping with the Imagist and Objectivist techniques at the root of Oppen's poetics. The aim of the technique, however, is more philosophical than literary; it is to establish the material otherness of the visual event. In the poems, objects and landscapes obtrude and reveal their existence as though seen for the first time. *Discrete Series*, Oppen's first book, is nearly procedural in its epistemological insistence on what is seen. The short lyrics which compose its contents are less like poems than they are the recording of eye movements across surfaces juxtaposed with snatches of statement and remembered lines from older poetry and fiction. The white space of the page surrounding these elements becomes a field of hesita-tions, advances, and reconsiderations, and the burden of meaning in the poem resides in the reader's recomposition of the fragmented elements. It is as though a crystal or prism had been interposed between poet and subject.

By the time Oppen had resumed writing poetry in the late 1950's, he had greatly modified his reliance on visual sense as a source of knowledge. One of the chief distinctions of his poetry remains its persuasive powers of registration, as in a poem written in the 1960's where "the north/ Looks out from its rock/ bulging into the fields," or from a poem of the 1970's where the sun moves "beyond the blunt/ towns of the coast . . . fishermen's/ tumbled tumbling headlands the needle silver/ water. . . ." Such imagery evokes the solidity and palpability of the world, and, at the same time, suggests its ungainliness and its obdurate self-referential quality which contrasts sharply with the usual visual clichés.

This sense of the visual, however, is for Oppen only one element in a dialectical occasion in which poetic truth resides neither in the object nor in the poet but in the interaction between the two. If, as Oppen would insist, the poet's ultimate aim is truth, then what is seen has the possibility of being a kind of measure: Seeing precedes its verbalization and therefore offers an opportunity for an open response to the world. This opportunity is hedged about with all one's conditioned reflexes, the material which the poet must work through to arrive at a sense of the real. It is through this struggle that Oppen's poetics, though they are concerned with ambiguity and paradox, strive for a clarity that is both immediate and complex. Oppen has described this as an attempt to write poetry which "cannot not be understood."

THE MATERIALS

This process can be seen at work in *The Materials*, the first of Oppen's major collections to be written and published after his twenty-year hiatus from the world of poetry. The book's underlying theme, carried through its forty poems, is clearly signaled in its epigraph from the philosopher Jacques Maritain, "We awake in the same moment to ourselves and to things." Oppen's "subjects" are these awakenings, which are capable of transcending the usual notions of self and society. In one of the book's major poems, "The Return," amid "the dim sound of the living" the impingement of the natural world becomes a moment in which "We cannot reconcile ourselves./ No one is reconciled, tho we spring/ From the ground together—." Nor is this estrangement eased by a sense of history or community; these are fictions in their way, and to look closely at them is to feel "The sense of that passage, is desertion, betrayal, that we are not innocent of loneliness." The poem ends with an image of the poet's old neighborhood "razed, whole blocks of a city gone," in which "the very ceremony of innocence" has been drowned.

In Oppen, such loss of innocence is not to be mourned; rather, it is the very beginning of a purer association between individuals and between the individual and the world, based on a language shorn of old, inauthentic mythologies. "Leviathan," the last poem in *The Materials*, insists that "Truth also is the pursuit of it," that "We must talk now. Fear/ is fear. But we abandon one another."

THIS IN WHICH

Oppen's next book, *This in Which*, is an exploration of the nature of such "talk." Here the poet's search is for a "substantial language of clarity, and of respect," based on a willingness to look fully, without illusion, at the human condition. It is "possible to use words," the poet says, "provided one treat them as enemies./ Not enemies—Ghosts which have run mad." Comparing modern consciousness to that of the primitive Mayans and their mythic view of life, "the poor savages of ghost and glitter," Oppen reminds the reader that it is necessary to examine squarely the "terror/ the unsightly/ silting sand of events." The critic Hugh Kenner, in discussing Oppen's method of stripping language of its historical associations, suggests that an apt motto for his work (and for that of the other Objectivist poets) might be "No myths." "Art," Oppen warns, "also is not good for us/ unless . . . it may rescue us/ as only the true/ might rescue us."

OF BEING NUMEROUS

These themes, the need for a demythologizing poetics and a language adequate to render the fullness of reality, are brought to culmination in *Of Being Numerous*, the book-length poem which many critics consider to be Oppen's masterpiece. *Of Being Numerous* is concerned with the deepest notions of community and the basis on which community might be established: what is meant by humanity, ethics, and love. The poem is, in a sense,

an interrogation of these terms, an attempt to discover whether they can truthfully be retained in the light of what humanity has become. For Oppen, the word "community" represents, in the present, an expression of the individual's psychic needs, of the effect of anxiety on contemporary life. Hence, in Oppen's view, the very notion of community is, at best, flawed and irrational. Humanity, the poem tells us, is "bewildered/ by the shipwreck/ of the singular"; thus, "we have chosen the meaning/ of being numerous." Given this situation, there is now only "a ferocious mumbling in public/ of rootless speech." Against this mumbling, Oppen seeks to set the truth-value of poetic speech. The poem attempts, not to lull one into another false sense of community, but to clear the air of bankrupt sentimentality about community and to genuinely reestablish it on a recognition of one another's essential aloneness. This is to discover, the poem continues, "Not truth, but each other." The poem's last word, "curious," overshadows the argument of the poem, for it is Oppen's intention to lead the reader to this understanding, not by rational means, but by the dynamics of aesthetic response. In such a response is to be found "our jubilation/ exalted and as old as that truthfulness/ which illumines speech."

SEASCAPE: NEEDLE'S EYE AND PRIMITIVE

Oppen's last work, beginning with *Seascape: Needle's Eye* and continuing through his final collection, *Primitive*, involves a radical departure from the poetry that had come before. In the earlier poems, especially in *Of Being Numerous*, Oppen created a restrained but rhetorically powerful amalgam of statement and imagery, a poetry which, like a Socratic dialogue, aimed at undermining conventional thought and attitude. In the later poems, the chaos and flux of life and the ever-partial mythologizing that language enacts are embodied in a troubled and moving voice that seems to embrace deeply the contingency and indeterminacy of life.

In these poems, syntax, punctuation, and rhythm are wrenched into a compelling new tone; words and phrases are enjambed and repeated, then modified into a poetic architecture which in its cadence expresses a new urgency, as in this excerpt from *Seascape: Needle's Eye*:

Pride in the sandspit wind this ether this other this
   element all

It is I or I believe
We are the beaks of the ragged birds
Tune of the ragged birds' beaks.

Such poetry seems at once immensely sophisticated and primordial; it is sophisticated inasmuch as behind its strange and powerful technique lies the history of the use and misuse of language. At the same time, it strikes the reader as a kind of first poetry, fashioned out of an unconditioned and open sense of life.

Such poems range across all the characteristic themes of poetry, love, death, politics, and being; yet the ambiguity of their claims, rather than diminishing them, adds a new, previously unheard richness to the verse. This richness is in the service not only of the present but also of history.

As Oppen notes in *Primitive*, harking back to the very beginning of his career and his insistence on the visual, "the tongues of appearance/ speak in the unchosen journey . . . the words out of that whirlwind his." In Oppen, this "unchosen journey" has been transformed into a powerful poetry of both collective and individual pain and loss, into a desire to make "a music more powerful," a music meant to redeem humanity "till other voices wake us or we drown."

OTHER MAJOR WORKS

NONFICTION: "The Mind's Own Place," 1963; "A Letter," 1973; *The Selected Letters of George Oppen*, 1990.

BIBLIOGRAPHY

Duplessis, Rachel Blau, ed. *The Selected Letters of George Oppen*. Durham, N.C.: Duke University Press, 1990. Oppen's correspondence provides a human face to a man whose poetry is known for its austerity and deep moral commitment. Includes bibliography and index.

Freeman, John, ed. *Not Comforts/But Visions: Essays on the Poetry of George Oppen*. Budleigh Salterton, Devon: Interim Press, 1984. This volume, intended to introduce Oppen to British readers, contains contributions by poets and critics. The essays survey Oppen's work rather than analyze the poems.

Hatlen, Burton. "Feminine Technologies: George Op-

pen Talks at Denise Levertov." *The American Poetry Review* 22, no. 3 (May, 1993): 9. Oppen wrote more than fifteen poems that in one way or another touch on women's distinctive experience and consciousness. Oppen's fascination and correspondence with poet Denise Levertov are examined.

_____, ed. *George Oppen, Man and Poet*. Orono, Maine: National Poetry Foundation, 1981. This homage dedicated to Oppen and his wife is an anthology of twenty-eight articles and two separate bibliographies, all but six published for the first time. The essays are well organized, and good bibliographies appear in notes. Two essays (by John Peck and Rachel Blau DuPlessis) give political and philosophical contexts to the poetry. Contains an index and two personal memoirs by Mary Oppen.

Ironwood 5 (1975). This special issue devoted to Oppen is really a celebratory bouquet. It contains, among other things, an "Introductory Note on Poetry" by Charles Tomlinson; seven poems by the poet; an interview, photographs, and memoirs by Charles Reznikoff and Mary Oppen ("France 1930-33"); and a critical essay by Rachel Blau DuPlessis ("What Do We Believe to Live With?"). Supplemented by a bibliography.

Ironwood 13 (Fall, 1985). This second special issue on the poet contains a number of excellent essays, memoirs, and appreciations. This volume contains more critical work than the first volume and a different selection of critics, poets, and scholars are presented.

Nicholls, Peter. "Of Being Ethical: Reflections on George Oppen." *Journal of American Studies* 31 (August, 1997): 153-170. Nicholls discusses why Oppen's work continues to occupy a marginal place in most literary histories, even though his work encapsulates some of the major shifts in American writing between high modernism and contemporary Language poetry.

Paideuma 10 (Spring, 1981). This journal, normally dedicated to Ezra Pound studies, is a memorial to George Oppen. It contains a collection of more than thirty appreciations, poems, explications, biographical sketches, and memorials, and it begins with Pound's preface to Oppen's *Discrete Series*. This, like the 1975 *Ironwood* special issue, is really a commemorative collection of material on the poet's life and work.

Tomlinson, Charles. *Some Americans: A Personal Record*. Berkeley: University of California Press, 1981. The British poet, Tomlinson, tells of his encounters with many major artists during the mid-twentieth century. Includes a character sketch of George and Mary Oppen.

Michael Heller;
bibliography updated by the editors

JOEL OPPENHEIMER

Born: Yonkers, New York; February 18, 1930
Died: Henniker, New Hampshire; October 11, 1988

PRINCIPAL POETRY
  The Dutiful Son, 1956
  The Love Bit and Other Poems, 1962
  In Time: Poems, 1962-1968, 1969
  On Occasion, 1973
  The Woman Poems, 1975
  Just Friends/Friends and Lovers: Poems, 1959-1962,
    1980
  At Fifty, 1982
  *Poetry, the Ecology of the Soul: Talks and Selected
    Poems*, 1983
  New Spaces: Poems, 1975-1983, 1985
  *Names and Local Habitations: Selected Earlier
    Poems, 1951-1972*, 1988
  The Collected Later Poems of Joel Oppenheimer,
    1997

OTHER LITERARY FORMS

In addition to writing book reviews and critiques, introductions and jacket blurbs, Joel Oppenheimer worked on the primary level as a printer and typographer. He was also a regular columnist for *The Village Voice* from 1969 to 1984.

Oppenheimer wrote several plays that have been performed Off-Off-Broadway: *The Great American Desert* (1961), *Miss Right* (1962), and *Like a Hill* (1963).

Oppenheimer's collection of short stories, *Pan's Eyes*, was published in 1974. Through the aficionado's eyes, he has viewed popular American culture in *The Wrong Season* (1973) and *Marilyn Lives!* (1981). *The Wrong Season* re-creates the year 1972 from the point of view of a disappointed New York Mets baseball fan. With interviews, photographs, personal narrative, and poems, *Marilyn Lives!* looks at the life of Marilyn Monroe.

ACHIEVEMENTS

For the first fifteen years of his writing career, Joel Oppenheimer worked, in the tradition of William Carlos Williams or Wallace Stevens, outside the university to support himself and his writing, mostly as a production manager for printing firms. Beginning in 1969, he became an active presence at various universities, teaching and giving poetry readings. His work was recognized by his appointments as director of the St. Mark's Poetry Project and the New York City Teachers and Writers Collaborative, as well as by such awards as the Creative Artists Public Service Fellowship (1971) and the National Endowment for the Humanities (1980). In addition, he held the poet-in-residence positions at the City College of New York and at New England College and visiting professorships at St. Andrews Presbyterian College in North Carolina and the Black Mountain II College at the State University of New York at Buffalo. In his own words, his achievement was that he "made poems and children much of his adult life, and also a living."

BIOGRAPHY

Joel Lester Oppenheimer was born in Yonkers, New York, a son of a leather goods retailer; he was the youngest of three boys. He went to Cornell University (1947-1948), wanting to become an architect, but—compromising with his mother—he enrolled in civil engineering. He left Cornell for the University of Chicago, where he stayed only briefly.

For the next three years (1950-1953), Oppenheimer attended Black Mountain College, enrolled as a painter/writer. Here he met and was influenced by such men as Robert Creeley, Charles Olson, Robert Duncan, and Jonathan Williams. Remembering his grandfather, who had founded a printing union, Oppenheimer tried to start his own press. He shortly abandoned it, however, after completing only one or two jobs.

Leaving Black Mountain, Oppenheimer worked in various print shops for the next fifteen years, mostly as a production person, mediating between advertisers' demands and the printer's experience. He worked first in Washington, D. C. (living in Olson's apartment); and later in Rochester, New Hampshire; Provincetown, Massachusetts; and New York City.

For two years beginning in 1966, Oppenheimer directed the Poetry Project at St. Mark's in the Bowery, followed by one year directing the New York City Teachers and Writers Collaborative. In 1969, he began writing for *The Village Voice*, and after teaching part-time at the City College of the City University of New York, in 1970 he was offered a part-time but untenured position as poet in residence. On leave from City College, he taught, again as poet in residence, at New England College in New Hampshire. He also taught poetry workshops and seminars at the State University of New York at Buffalo's "Black Mountain II Summer Arts Program." In 1982, Oppenheimer became associate professor of communications and poet in residence at New England College. He died in New Hampshire in 1988.

ANALYSIS

This "sports-loving Jewish intellectual/ writer" ("Dear Miss Monroe"), who "still grew up a jew in/ yonkers new york" admits at one moment that "finally i am through with it, with/ the american dream, a dream that ran through/ all my ancestors who fought here for you/ america" ("17-18 April, 1961"). Don't believe him. Joel Oppenheimer's own language and ideas give him away. His book *On Occasion* includes "Life," the poem, and "Life," a subsection of the collection. Two major sections are titled "Liberty" and "The Pursuit of Happiness."

Not only does the triumvirate of American independence reign throughout his work, but the language of his poetry also shows that he has not abandoned America. Instead of the Christmas jingle "not a creature was stirring, not even a mouse," he writes, "inside the/ window/ not even a/ football game not even/ a haiku disturbing/ us" ("Found Art"). He defines "contra naturam" as "the pot which boils while/ watched" ("The Zoom Lens"). Beginning "The Riddle," he asks, "what/ s gray and

comes in quarts"; answering, "is an elephant or my brain." His biblical allusions take the form of "it/ is very hot/ my sweat runneth over, even if/ my belly be not sheaved/ wheat" ("The Bye-Bye Happiness Swing"). He reaffirms or readjusts the platitudes "love *is* a/ many-splendored thing" ("Untitled") and "it's the world we live in/ we can't eat our cake or have it/ either" ("Four Photographs by Richard Kirstel"); and he haunts one with an echo of the now classic radio line, "who knows what shadows lurk in the hearts of old girl friends" ("Come On Baby"). As he exclaims in "Poem Written in the Light of Certain Events April 14th, 1967," "finally, i am here, goddamnit!/ i am american, goddamnit!"

POLITICAL POEMS

Only an American would take and insist on such liberties with language. Oppenheimer insists not only that one can take liberties with language, but also that it is language that gives us our liberty and freedom. He vehemently defends that right, to "defend that truth/ that is our inheritance" ("Poem in Defense of Children"). The fight is against those that would take it away—"the first amendment was here/ before mendel rivers or lbj" ("A Dab of Cornpone")—as well as against those who would equally damage individual freedom by manipulation and lies. Echoing Williams's complaint against T. S. Eliot, he rejects language that is not part of and does not express one's own experience: "there is the problem of words, how/ to sound like language, and/ one/ s self" ("The Great American Novel").

Oppenheimer's American heritage runs from Thomas Jefferson, through Davy Crockett and Andrew Jackson— "andy/ show them all. once/ a free man ruled the free" ("The 150th Anniversary of the Battle of New Orleans"). His other ancestors include such persons (and literary banners) as Walt Whitman (I sing of myself), William Carlos Williams ("no ideas but in things"), Ezra Pound ("make it new"), and Charles Olson ("form is but an extension of content"). His immediate kin he addresses in "The Excuse":

> dear god, dear olson, dear
> creeley, dear ginsberg, my
> teachers and makers, bring
> me again to light, keep
> me from lies. . . .

These influences are political and literary. Many of Oppenheimer's poems are politically directed, created in the protesting air of the late 1950's and 1960's. Oppenheimer, however, does not separate politics from life, from art, art from politics or life—"after all man is a/ political animal" ("The Innocent Breasts"). All directly affect how one lives, and how one says one wants to live—"we have forgotten/ we once carried a flag into battle that/ read don't/ tread on me" ("17-18 April, 1961").

Life, however, in these United States as he states in "17-18 April, 1961" has somehow found it

> . . . better to lie and hope not
> to get caught, than to behave honorably.
> well, this has been true of the world
> all along, but it was not supposed
> to be true of you, america

Oppenheimer finds that America has ignored the simple tenets of life, liberty, and the pursuit of happiness. Instead of honor and justice, his poem "Keeping It" expresses how one lives by fear and deception:

> the world we live in
> is not what we sing,
> and we are afraid we will
> fall prey to that we
> are most afraid of, the
> truth.

In the world that Oppenheimer perceives, truths about how man is created are no longer self evident: "we are all incapable/ it seems of living in that/ environment we were created/ for . . ." ("A Prayer"). In "Sirventes on a Sad Occasion" (1967), an old woman loses control of her bowels walking up the stairs to her apartment. She tries to hide the accident, feeling inadequate and inhuman for it. Oppenheimer can only ask, sadly, "this is a/ natural act, why will you/ fear me for it. . . ." Without these truths the world is unnatural, alien, often hostile.

Against such threats, one must preserve one's liberty. "The Surgeon in Spite of Himself" endures his fear because "master of my fate and captain/ of my soul, i know that i will." Liberty, built into the Declaration of Independence, is a fundamental need; Oppenheimer declares, in "A Treatise": "all that matters is/ the built-in mechanism/ of self-preservation."

Oppenheimer's poetry is filled with slogans: "to live my own life" and "to thine own self be true." These might be taken as mere egotistical or selfish desires. Oppenheimer might respond, "So what?" Liberty is necessary to make and define one's self; he insists on a voice, the personal voice and poetic voice being one and the same. Oppenheimer's ideal is the self-made man—Crockett, Jackson, Jefferson, his grandfather who began his own printing union—all men of action who looked to themselves and into themselves for freedoms: "freedoms you might only/ have, anyhow, if you look deep inside/ yourself where all freedom is to be/ found . . ." ("17-18 April, 1961").

Oppenheimer's poems, as one title specifically indicates, provide "Some Suggested Guidelines" as to how one can live freely in this world; and they encourage individual action. His advice starts, of course, with himself. "Notes Toward Lessons to Be Learned at Thirty" advises taking care of his body; it provides advice on coffee, cigarettes, fresh fruit, and "the loveliest ass in the world." "Sirventes Against Waiting" underscores three lessons: "you do what you can . . . what you have to . . . [and] what you want to." Oppenheimer's faith in America, then, comes down to a faith in the self. His declaration of independence is "the simple/ declaration of the/ faith a man must have,/ in his own balls, in/ his own heart" ("Keeping It").

LOVE POEMS

Not all of Oppenheimer's poems are political. Many are love poems—love that varies and that takes as many forms as do the women he invokes—Artemis, Persephone, Diana, Medusa, and Marilyn Monroe. *The Woman Poems* presents his fourfold synthesis of woman—Good Mother, Death Mother, Ecstasy or Dancing Mother, and Stone or Tooth Mother—all embodied in the mythical figure of Mother Goddess. As a true democrat, he loves and lusts after them all, equally. His poems, in addition, are filled with tenderness, affection, and hope—for friends, children, and parents. There is fighting and plain sex; there are elegies, celebrations of births and weddings, and blues. A poem in *New Spaces: Poems, 1975-1983* celebrates a marriage (and in the process touches on the relationship between art and life), nothing that people ask for poems as "blessing on their union"; he adds, "the wonder is/ we keep writing/ they keep getting married."

Oppenheimer's definition of happiness invokes the old-time notion of a little peace and quiet—"this much/ will a little quiet do,/ and peace, in our times" ("Modern Times")—and a little honesty and decency. Happiness is having one's own space, "asking for/ space to build our own perimeters/ in defense of such" ("Poem for Soho"). Happiness for Oppenheimer is not so much being happy as pursuing happiness. Happiness is the labors of Hercules, not their completion; or, more apt, the labors of love. It is the act of happiness, not the state, which seems more real. In fact, the last poem of *On Occasion* is "The Act":

> as i do
> it is as it is
> does as it does
> as i am it is
> is as is is as
> i do as i do
> as it does as it
> does as it is
> as is is

All active, simple verbs, "The Act" defines, blends with, but does not constrict, personal pronouns and direct objects. The act defines itself and oneself. "The Act" summarizes Oppenheimer's self and his world in language, idea, and act.

OTHER MAJOR WORKS

SHORT FICTION: *Pan's Eyes*, 1974.

PLAYS: *The Great American Desert*, pr. 1961, pb. 1966; *Miss Right*, pr. 1962; *Like a Hill*, pr. 1963.

NONFICTION: *The Wrong Season*, 1973; *Marilyn Lives!*, 1981.

BIBLIOGRAPHY

Beach, Christopher. "Interview with Joel Oppenheimer." *Sagetrieb* 7 (Fall, 1978): 89-130. An informative interview conducted ten years before the poet's death. Contains Oppenheimer's comments on his contemporaries and poetry in general, interspersed with personal detail. This lengthy document gives an excellent portrait of the poet. His personality surfaces as he reflects on topics and figures in American poetry.

Gilmore, Lyman. *Don't Touch the Poet: The Life and Times of Joel Oppenheimer.* Jersey City, N.J.: Talisman House, 1998. Gilmore has done an admirable job of balancing views about Joel Oppenheimer and goes beyond facade to show a man obsessed with magic, routine, and lists. Gilmore provides a very human view of the Black Mountain and Greenwich Village poetry world of the 1950's and 1960's.

Landrey, David W. "Simply Survival: David Budbill and Joel Oppenheimer." *Credences*, n.s. 1 (Fall/Winter, 1981/1982): 150-157. This article explores the two poets' shared quest for life, knowledge, and understanding, their different approaches to their work, and their shared need for a changed sense of self through poetry. Particularly significant is the discussion of Oppenheimer working from the inside out. Several themes are pointed out and short examples given.

Oppenheimer, Joel. *Poetry, the Ecology of the Soul: Talks and Selected Poems.* Edited by David Landrey and Dennis Maloney. Buffalo, N.Y.: White Plains Press, 1983. This excellent collection is preceded by an introductory appreciation by David Landrey. The volume contains a number of poems, three informative talks, and a bibliography of Oppenheimer's work. The lectures on the Black Mountain poets and on *The Woman Poems* are of particular importance because of what they reveal about the poet's craft.

Sylvester, William. "Joel Oppenheimer Talks About His Poetry." *Credences*, n.s. 3 (Fall, 1985): 69-76. This transcription of several conversations with Oppenheimer lets the poet speak for himself about his craft, his career, and his early influences from theater and film. It gives one a strong sense of who Oppenheimer was and what informed his thinking.

Thibodaux, David. *Joel Oppenheimer: An Introduction.* Columbia, S.C.: Camden House, 1986. This study provides an overview of Oppenheimer's work and examines closely his literary themes, including the significance of images, motifs, and symbols. Approximately half the book is devoted to poetry. The remainder discusses fiction, drama, and nonfiction prose. An excellent bibliography cites several useful journal articles on specific poems, interviews, and reviews.

Steven P. Schultz;
bibliography updated by the editors

GREGORY ORR

Born: Albany, New York; February 3, 1947

PRINCIPAL POETRY
  Burning the Empty Nests, 1973
  Gathering the Bones Together, 1975
  The Red House, 1980
  We Must Make a Kingdom of It, 1986
  New and Selected Poems, 1988
  City of Salt, 1995
  Orpheus and Eurydice: A Lyric Sequence, 2001

OTHER LITERARY FORMS

Gregory Orr's prose writings are all, nonetheless, about poetry. He has published a critical study, *Stanley Kunitz: An Introduction to the Poetry* (1985), and other works about poetry: *Richer Entanglements: Essays and Notes on Poetry and Poems* (1993) and *Poets Teaching Poets: Self and the World*, co-edited with Ellen Bryant Voigt (1996).

ACHIEVEMENTS

Gregory Orr has received a number of awards and fellowships for his poetry, beginning with a Discovery Award from the Poetry Center of the Young Men's-Young Women's Hebrew Association and the poets' prize from Academy of American Poets, both in 1970. He was a junior fellow of the Society of Fellows at the University of Michigan from 1972 to 1975, a Guggenheim fellow from 1977 to 1978, and a National Endowment for the Arts fellow in 1978-1979 and 1989-1990.

BIOGRAPHY

Gregory Orr's childhood in the Hudson River Valley was disrupted by two deaths. When he was twelve, he accidentally shot and killed his brother, a scene described in his sequence of seven short poems, "Gathering the Bones Together":

> A gun goes off,
> and the youngest brother
> falls to the ground.

> A boy with a rifle
> stands beside him, screaming.

When he was fourteen, his mother died in Haiti, a time recalled and reawakened in "Black Moon" and "Haitian Suite." Orr's early work, obsessed with grief and guilt, transforms these deaths into dream imagery, which may seem like an evasion, a looking-away, but which is actually an intensification. The porcelain face of "The Doll" is disfigured by a "bullet hole/ like a black mole" on its cheek. Orr's losses do not disappear: They leave behind shells, husks, evidence of their absence, like the doll he carries "in a glass jar," like the snails, "little death-swans," and like the coat his great-grandfather made from his favorite horse, "because when the horse died/ he wouldn't let it go" ("A House in the Country"). Orr's poems occupy a world "where the dead and half/ dead live together" ("Lullaby Elegy Dream").

The poems of his first three collections represent an exorcism (but not an exclusion) of his demons, a coming to terms with what he has seen and sensed as fate: "a lugged burden/ of the invisible and unforgiving dead." In the same poem ("On the Lawn at Ira's"), Orr admits that now he is "mostly/ happy, even . . . blessed among so many friends." The working-through of grief began at the very center, in dreams, but completed itself by breaking out of the cave of darkness into the light of everyday life.

Orr received a master of fine arts degree from Columbia University, eventually teaching at the University of Virginia, where he became director of the writing program. He settled in a farmhouse near Charlottesville, Virginia, with his wife Trisha and their two daughters.

ANALYSIS

Although the models for Gregory Orr's writing can be found in the Deep Image school of Robert Bly and the visionary lyrics of W. S. Merwin (as well as in the European poetry translated by these poets and others), Orr's poems have spoken with a distinctive voice from the beginning, compelled as much by inner necessity as by outside example. Several things characterize his poems: They are very brief; their diction is clipped; they are cleanly articulated; they thrive on imagery and rejoice in metaphor ("The water;/ a glass snake asleep in the pipes"); they revolve around dramatic situations; and they do not explain but break off quickly, so that one is left with a silence in which echoes of the poem reverberate.

Orr's concept of the image comes largely from Surrealism: a "variant of symbol." In a statement prepared for "The Inward Society," a symposium on Surrealism held at the University of Virginia (published in *Poetry East*, Spring, 1982), Orr remarked that

> Surrealism kept alive the poet's notion of the self as that which mediates between inner and outer worlds; as that which focuses and constellates perceptions of the world.

This mediation between the self and the world is central to Orr's work, which began its explorations and excavations in the interior, with dreams and the anxieties of the unconscious, but which later began to summon realistic scenes from his waking life.

A number of Orr's poems are parables: "The Ambassadors," the early sequence "The Adventures of the Stone," and "The Man in the Suit of Mirrors." As his work has become more realistic, this emblematic mode (close to allegory, with the same mechanical predictability) has receded. The later poems are more celebratory and undisguised, drawing on the resources of dream life to heighten the realism, which is now in the foreground. All Orr's work seeks to transcend his private griefs, but to accomplish that he must go deeper into the source of the pain. He must unmask what is hidden: "I stand at the sink/ washing dinner plates/ that are smooth as the masks/ my grief once wore" ("After the Guest"). Orr's poems, in the words of "The Bridge," continually call out: "Return to yourself."

MAPPING THE JOURNEY

Since the poems of Gregory Orr represent a symbolic journey, it is not surprising that maps are of central importance in his work. The opening poem of Orr's first book ends with "A moth lands on the toe of my boot./ Picking it up, I discover a map on its wings" ("When We Are Lost"). Dream and memory both offer maps to the lost wayfarer, clues to a mystery that neither the conscious nor the unconscious mind alone can apprehend completely. More and more, Orr's work has sought to bring these two worlds—of darkness and of light, roughly speaking—into consonance.

If his first three books can be said to constitute a trilogy, they resemble, in general outline, the three stages of Dante's *The Divine Comedy* (c. 1320): descent, purgation, and enlightenment. The poems attempt to become "accurate maps/ for the spirit's quest:/ always death at the center/ like Rome or some oasis/ toward which all paths tend" ("Song of the Invisible Corpse in the Field"). The poems of memory that dominate *The Red House* have not been ignited to consume the poems of dream and nightmare. Rather, the dream imagery heightens Orr's close observation of the outer world.

The titles of Orr's early poems usually furnish coordinates for the dream terrain that will follow: "When We Are Lost," "Lines Written in Dejection, Oklahoma," "Manhattan Island Poem." These down-to-earth titles, flat and explanatory, ground the poems in the electrical sense. They act as a kind of documentation, safe passage into an alien world.

"WASHING MY FACE"

The simple act referred to in the title "Washing My Face" leads to an illumination of the no-man's-land between dreaming and waking. The complete poem is only three lines long: "Last night's dreams disappear./ They are like the sink draining:/ a transparent rose swallowed by its stem." The poem is nearly a haiku, both in length and content, but its dependence on connectives ("They are like") keeps it in the Western Hemisphere. Each line elaborates on the line before it: statement, then simile, then metaphor. If the process should go on, it would become baroque, but Orr's inclination is always to stop while the poem is still uncluttered. The process depends upon clarity and quickness of metaphor.

The first two lines of the poem are flat declarations. They are joined by "like" because the comparison is an obvious and easy step. Metaphor demands more of a leap, and what comes in the final line is strong enough to electrify both statements. The rose may be an overworked symbol in itself, but its transparency (and unreality) brings back the full mystical force of the flower. Whereas T. S. Eliot's rose in *Four Quartets* (1943) blends into fire, Orr's dissolves into water. The clear rose being "swallowed by its stem" resembles a film run backwards; the natural process is reversed. It is both an apt comment on forgetfulness and a snapshot of a real sink draining: a picture, yet beyond a picture; a surreality.

"THE BEGINNING"

In "The Beginning," a poem from his first book, Orr writes that "you will make each journey many times," a prediction—or prophecy, or curse—that touches upon the importance of journeying in his poems and the even greater importance of obsession, the repetition of charms, the consultation of oracles. The locus of the earlier poems is a blank arena: the bareness of snow and "the way the word sinks into the deep snow of the page." The blankness extends indoors, into "empty rooms" with "bare walls." Even when a child's drawing becomes a window, the means of escape and the journey's starting point ("The Room"), the path merely adds distance to emptiness: "Far ahead in the valley, I saw the lights/ of a village, and always at my back I felt/ the white room swallowing what was past." The last image represents one of Orr's obsessions, an image out of the brothers Grimm, in which breadcrumbs (providing a trail back to the familiar world) are eaten by birds, the same "flock of sparrows" that is "eating your footprints" in "The Wooden Dancer."

"GATHERING THE BONES TOGETHER"

The fear of the past disappearing is countered by the persistence of memory that one finds in dreams, the tokens left behind as outward signs of an invisible presence. Orr's central poem, "Gathering the Bones Together," unites these two obsessions just as the poet confronts the greatest trauma of his life: the accidental killing of his brother.

The poem begins with an epigraph that is Orr's rethinking of an earlier poem, "The Sleeping Angel": "When all the rooms of the house/ fill with smoke, it's not enough/ to say an angel is sleeping on the chimney." Orr rejects the relatively easy myth of the sleeping angel in favor of examining the inner smoke. It is "not enough" to offer solutions that quell the greater mystery. The drama of the poem begins with the abandonment of costumes.

"A Night in the Barn" is the first section of the poem. A boy, referred to in the third person, "keeps watch/ from a pile of loose hay." He is guarding a "deer carcass (that) hangs from a rafter," a portent of what will follow. (In "Spring Floods," the dead brother is likened to a deer "high in a tree, wedged/ there by the flood.") The rustling of pigeons and the German shepherd that "snaps its

jaws in its sleep" create an ominous music, a mood of anxiety and dread. Between these descriptions of the night scene, the prophetic dream is revealed: the "death that is coming." Yet the vision narrows in the aftermath of death, the gathering of bones in an empty field. It is a sentence fit for the inferno, the reparations that the boy must pay to the dead, the impossible task of reassembling a skeleton and making the dry bones sing.

The accident, the killing, is set forth with complete simplicity in part two, which is untitled. Another deer has just been killed. On the way to retrieve the body, "a gun goes off."

In the third section, the point of view switches from third person to first. Although he is hiding, the boy feels compelled to reveal himself through speech. Already the events have been transformed through terror into nightmare images: the "glass well/ of my hands," in which the brother drowns. The leaves, "shaped like mouths" (an image that recalls Jean Cocteau's movie, *Blood of the Poet*, 1932), litter the ground outside: a silent chorus of grief and accusation. As though the world had been flooded, the leaves form a "black pool" in which snails glide like "little death swans." The water, following the dryness of the barn, immerses the boy in his guilt. The world has become alien and threatening. Nothing is more disturbing than the underwater silence, so different from the laughter and chattering just before the accident.

The water imagery is replaced by smoke in the poem's middle section. This smoke from an unseen fire has made everyone weep, has turned "people into shadows." It is, of course, smoke from the pyre, the imaginary bone-fire for the dead brother, and even after the funeral it remains in the pillows, to be smelled "when we lie down to sleep."

In the fifth section of the poem, the "glass well" becomes "a house of black glass" where the boy visits and talks with his dead brother. It is another world, separate from the familiar one, close to fairy tale and close to madness; the clarity of glass is turned into the "dark night of the soul." Yet the voice is naïve: "My father says he is dead,/ but what does that mean?" The disorientation of the boy is reinforced by the reference to "a child/ sleeping on a nest of bones" that follows. It is the same brother, yet it is not. The brother he visits is the ghost of the one he knew in life. The child he carries (like the one preserved in "The Doll") is the image of the brother in death, "a red, leafshaped/ scar on his cheek." The wound is like a leaf, which has already been likened to a mouth. The certainty of the boy's communion with the dead is offset by his uncertainty about the destination to which he is traveling, loaded down with the weight of his guilt and remorse.

"The Journey" is described in the penultimate section: "Each night, I knelt on a marble slab/ and scrubbed at the blood." This act of devotion and expiation is fruitless: the stain is too deep, the gravestone too permanent. When his own bones "begin to burn," the boy begins his journey, still ignorant of his destination and destiny. The slab remains under his feet, "a white road only as long as your body." The whiteness contrasts with the "house of black glass." Everything disappears in the course of the journey except this movable stretch of road, which is as inescapable as a shadow.

In "The Distance," the last section of the poem, a winter scene is recalled, when "a horse/ slipped on the ice" (another accident), "breaking its leg." The boy watched the carcass burn. The speaker says that, when he killed his brother, he "felt my own bones wrench from my body." When he walks beside the river, what he gathers are both his own bones and those of his dead brother, which "have become a bridge/ that arches toward the other shore": a passageway like the white road of the marble slab, yet offering a way to reconnect with all that has been lost, a way to "gather at the river" and to atone for the taking of life. The bridge, one of Orr's key images, recurs in another poem as "this bridge/ of poems: a thousand/ paper coffins/ laid end to end" ("Before We Met"). All the elements of the poem coalesce in this final section: animals, fire, water, bones, the road. The poem ends on the aspiration to unite the two shores, to span the moving waters.

"THE PROJECT"

This construction project is echoed and qualified by two poems later in the same volume. In "The Project," the speaker plans "to generate light/ with no outside source." The parable about this Thomas Alva Edison of the psyche goes on to elaborate, in terms resembling Franz Kafka, how this is to be accomplished in a burrow (which must be read as both a grave and

a kind of subway to the underworld). The speaker wants to capture the "faint light" given off by his body in the darkness. He supposes it comes from the bones (Orr's bridging material) but once the flesh is scraped away, "the light was gone too." The ending resembles Marco Polo's argument, in Italo Calvino's *Le città invisibili* (1972, *The Invisible Cities*), that without stones there can be no arch. Without the life of the flesh, in all its voluptuousness, there can be no life. Stripping everything down to the bare bones is not an act of renewal but of denial.

"THE BUILDERS"

In "The Builders," however, the feat is accomplished: A windowless hut is "filled with light," but it is the light given off by love. The couple, in quarrying the field of white stone and carrying it "strapped to our backs" (like the body of the dead brother in "Gathering the Bones Together"), have reclaimed the white stone of the grave slab for their rebuilding. The surroundings are still bleak, and the elements are the same, but the scene has been transformed by the love of the living. Instead of black windows, there are none at all, but this retreat is a necessary step toward self-forgiveness and eventual benediction.

THE RED HOUSE

This rapprochement is achieved in the main sequence of *The Red House*, assisted by an epigraph from William Wordsworth's *The Prelude* (1850). The close attention to physical detail, to the inner life of the ordinary, is new to Orr's work. The Haiti of his "Haitian Suite" springs to life in the exuberant images of a "flamboyant tree" and a girl who squats "to fill/ her calabash at the gurgling spring/ in the gully." Part of the impression is conveyed by the sound, musically more alive than before. The title of the collection suggests both the vivacity of new color and a grounding in domestic peace, the gift to be simple—as opposed to the restless participles of *Burning the Empty Nests* and *Gathering the Bones Together*. The images that predominate belong to the light:

> In the barn's huge gloom
> light falls through cracks
> the way swordblades
> pierce a magician's box.

The ecstasy of the passage which ends "Morning Song" comes from the awareness that the swords do not represent danger, but rather the magician's power to keep things whole.

The poems glory in the senses: "bluebottle flies . . ./ magnetized to the gleaming/ scales of a carp"; "his father's red car crossing/ the flats, dragging huge plumes of dust" (both from "The Ditch"). After the passage through "Gathering the Bones Together" the road leads clearly to this exultation. It may disappoint some of Orr's early disciples and devotees, but it is a necessary continuation of a journey that has turned out to be different from the repetitive, futile path of Sisyphus; Orr is fortunate to have come upon a new landscape, which is, in fact, the old one which had been lost through grief.

One of the side effects of the change has been a greater interest in other people. Love has cleared the way for this interest: "So many years/ before the soft key of your tongue/ unlocked my body" ("Before We Met"). Now the open door admits "Neighbors," such as Edith, with a "photo on the mantel:/ her Texas Ranger husband" and Christopher Augustinovich, who "jabbered about his youth/ in the Czar's army."

"The Drawing Lesson" introduces Mr. Knight and re-creates a realistic scene that leads, quite naturally, to something from another world:

> To loosen my wrists, he tried to teach me
> the bones: I was supposed to hold the two
> delicately-curved pieces of rosewood
> in one hand and clack them deftly together
> to music.

After so much emblematic use of "bones," it is a pleasant surprise to come upon the witty and frightening play on the word in this poem. More than anything else, this passage demonstrates the growing delicacy of Orr's poetry, which accompanies the affection he lavishes upon what he portrays.

Through this affection, and through the many songs that go into *The Red House*, Orr approaches the affirmations and discoveries of Rainer Maria Rilke, giving himself over into other beings, alive with "The 'new life' of freedom" mentioned in "Leaving the Asylum." This poem represents his coming to terms with the grief of his childhood, a litany that has released him:

> Hollow tree
> though I am, these things I cherish:
> the hum of my blood, busily safe
> in its hive of being; the delicate
> oily kiss my fingertips give
> everything they touch; and desire,
> a huge fish I drag with me
> through the wilderness:
> I love its glint among the dust and stones.

Light and music rise out of the desolation. The poems are free to become songs of celebration.

ORPHEUS AND EURYDICE

In a 1997 interview, Orr reflected that his 1995 book *City of Salt* had "close[d] the books on certain autobiographical themes." His next work, *Orpheus and Eurydice*, was a lyric sequence on the myth of the archetypal poet and musician whose attempt to retrieve his beloved wife from Hades fails when she unwittingly looks back to the underworld, breaking the condition of her release. Orr had begun to explore this myth in "Betrayals/Hades, Eurydice, Orpheus" in *City of Salt*, where he draws an explicit connection between Orpheus's song and memory:

> . . . What had he brought?
> Songs of anguish and desire—
> All she had gladly forgot.
> His words about the world
> were meant to lure her back,
> to hurt her into memory.

The longer sequence of *Orpheus and Eurydice* seems to show Orr acknowledging both the attraction and inspiration of death. Orr's Eurydice looks back deliberately, choosing to return to Hades where, it seems, she has found freedom in the release from her body's limitations. "How could he know how free I felt/ as I unwound the long bandage/ of my skin and stepped out?"

In the moment of crisis, as the couple approaches the upper world, the gaze that unites them is ultimately what pulls them apart. Eurydice sees Orpheus, silhouetted against the light of the world, as the "dark pupil/ of an eye that stared." From the opposite perspective, Orpheus admits that, in his moment of fear, "She was something between/ the abyss and me,/ something my eyes could cling to." When Eurydice turns to look back to the underworld—breaking the gaze between them—Orpheus is left with nothing to see—or touch—only his memories. Yet his memories will become the source of his poetry:

> Who knows? Maybe it would be simpler.
> When she was alive, her body
> confused him; he couldn't think
> clearly when she was close. Smells
> of her skin made him dizzy.
>
> Now, where she had been: only
> a gaping hole in the air,
> an emptiness he could fill with song.

OTHER MAJOR WORKS

NONFICTION: *Stanley Kunitz: An Introduction to the Poetry*, 1985; *Richer Entanglements: Essays and Notes on Poetry and Poems*, 1993.

EDITED TEXT: *Poets Teaching Poets: Self and the World*, 1996 (with Ellen Bryant Voigt).

BIBLIOGRAPHY

Glück, Louise. "On Gregory Orr's Poems." *The Iowa Review* 3 (Fall, 1973): 86-88. Glück examines the characteristic persona assumed in Orr's poetry, one of solitude of the narrator, inevitability of events, and ambiguity of experiences. This highly personal and compelling evaluation of Orr's poetry includes ruminations on the cinematic quality of his poems and their sense of necessity, irreversibility, and dream-logic.

Harris, Peter. "A Shelter, a Kingdom, a Half Promised Land: Three Poets in Mid-Career." *The Virginia Quarterly Review* 63 (Summer, 1987): 426-436. This enlightening essay examines Orr's distinct vision of psychic, surreal images. Harris studies the battle between abstraction and specific, familiar and metaphysical, body and soul, and hidden and known in Orr's work. *We Must Make a Kingdom of It* is the featured text, and stanzas of several poems are used to illustrate key points.

Kohl, Greg. "Transparency and Prophecy: Gregory Orr's 'Burning the Empty Nests.'" *The American Poetry Review* 14 (July/August, 1975): 40-42. Kohl

has a very specific and explicit agenda in his exploration of *Burning the Empty Nests:* He seeks to determine the influences of shamanistic experiences and techniques and identify the value of shamanism in dealing with personal and social experience as found in Orr's poetry. To this end, he is successful, but limits the appeal of his work to Orr's scholars.

Lazer, Hank. Review of *The Red House* by Gregory Orr. *The Iowa Review* 11 (Winter, 1981): 148-156. Lazer asserts that this work is Orr's finest due to its sophisticated exploration of two lyric modes: an expressionistic imagery inspired by Georg Trakl and the persuasive, lyrical tone of Theodore Roethke's greenhouse poems. Orr uses his distinct lyric voice to explore his obsession with grief, precipitated by the death of his mother and brother.

Lehman, David. "Politics." *Poetry* 122 (December, 1973): 178-180. Lehman addresses the lack of political references in Orr's first book of poetry, *Burning the Empty Nests*, explores the stark landscapes evoked by the poet, and analyzes Orr's tendency to "turn nature inside out." Acknowledging the influence of W. S. Merwin and Robert Bly on Orr's work, the author asserts Orr's poetry is unique, in part, due to the tension between his spare writing style and dense imagery.

Leo, John Robert. "Finding the Imagination." *Poetry* 128 (November, 1976): 106-108. This work examines the elements Orr unites in his poetry, such as text and illustration, surface and depth, child and adult, and nature and artifice. Also explored are the themes of "home," interior landscapes, and the primitive dream world. Leo defends Orr against critics who argue the poet's work has become increasingly fragmented and reductive.

Orr, Gregory. *Richer Entanglements: Essays and Notes on Poetry and Poems*. Ann Arbor: University of Michigan Press, 1993. One of the best resources on Orr's poetics, by the poet himself. Part of the University of Michigan Press's Poets on Poetry series.

John Drury,
updated by Leslie Ellen Jones

SIMON J. ORTIZ

Born: Albuquerque, New Mexico; May 27, 1941

PRINCIPAL POETRY

Naked in the Wind, 1971

Going for the Rain: Poems, 1976

A Good Journey, 1977

Fight Back: For the Sake of the People, for the Sake of the Land, 1980 (poetry and prose)

From Sand Creek: Rising in This Heart Which Is Our America, 1981

A Poem Is a Journey, 1981

Woven Stone, 1992

After and Before the Lightning, 1994

Telling and Showing Her: The Earth, the Land, 1995

OTHER LITERARY FORMS

Even before the publication of his first book of poetry in 1971, Simon J. Ortiz had begun to write short fiction, publishing his first short stories in the 1960's. "I've known 'story'—or stories—all my life," Ortiz observed in the preface to *Men on the Moon* (1999), a collection of his work in this genre. He has also edited several volumes devoted to the writing of Native American authors, most notably *Earth Power Coming: Short Fiction in Native American Literature* (1983) and *Speaking for the Generations: Native Writers on Writing* (1998), and has contributed to many books concerned with the heritage and cultural history of indigenous people, including *Toward a National Indian Literature* (1981) and *I Tell You Now: Autobiographical Essay by Native American Writers* (1987). *The People Shall Continue* (1977) is designed for young readers, as is *The Good Rainbow Road* (2001), a trilingual children's book.

Ortiz has made a number of recordings of his work and has appeared on radio programs and videos. *Nothing but the Truth: An Anthology of Native American Literature* (2001) contains an extensive contribution by Ortiz.

ACHIEVEMENTS

Simon J. Ortiz, along with Leslie Marmon Silko, N. Scott Momaday, and Louise Erdrich, was one of the people most directly responsible for the elevation of Native American literature to a position of prominence in American literary life during the 1970's. In his poems and short fiction, Ortiz draws on the vibrant styles and subjects of the oral tradition which has endured for millennia in Native American cultural communities and brings them into a contemporary context as a written record of a people's experience. His poetry, in conjunction with the stories that deal with a complementary range of psychic conditions, social considerations and geophysical phenomena, moves from an individual's encounters with life in the United States to the ways in which that person's life is presented as a reflection and representation of the cultural patterns and values of a clan or extended family within an ethnographic matrix.

Ortiz has remained closely connected to the increasingly complex and varied world of Native American writing since the initial publication of his own work, teaching at numerous institutions and editing and collecting the work of his peers. His efforts have been recognized with many awards, including a National Endowment for the Arts Discovery Award (1969), a White House Salute to an Honored Poet (1981), a Lifetime Achievement Award from the Native Writer's Circle of the Americas (1993), and the Wordcraft Circle Writer of the Year Award (1998).

BIOGRAPHY

Simon J. Ortiz grew up in the town known as McCartys on maps of New Mexico, but familiar to the people of the Laguna (or Aacqumeh) Pueblo, his community (or *hanoh*), as Deetseyamah in the Acoma language. Like most of the residents, he spoke the Acoma language at home and English at the McCartys Day School he attended, a place which Ortiz describes as carrying out a national policy designed to "sever ties to culture, family, and tribe," and to "make us into American white people." In spite of this, Ortiz recalls that "it was exciting, however, to go to school," and that "Reading was fun" because he "loved language and stories."

In 1954, when Ortiz was in the fifth grade, his family moved to Skull Valley in Arizona, where his father was employed by the Santa Fe railroad, and Ortiz became aware of a world beyond his local community. He and his younger sister and brothers were the only Native

Americans at the school, and his curiosity about the other students led him to "read voraciously just about anything I could get my hands on," authors ranging from H. G. Wells to Mark Twain. His first publication, a Mother's Day poem, appeared in the Skull Valley School newspaper.

At the St. Catherine's Indian School in Sante Fe, Ortiz was encouraged by nuns to read beyond the minimal grade requirements, and he began to keep a diary, which led to his lifelong habit of writing in a personal journal. Ortiz continued to write poetry and began to compose "brief, cursory passages" of description, character sketches, plot outlines, and other elements of fiction. When he transferred to Albuquerque Indian School closer to his family's home, Ortiz registered for a program in vocational training in order to "become employable," but at Grants High, an integrated school, he began to take his writing more seriously, seeing himself "as a writer later in life" and becoming "even more of a reader, heavily into recent and current poets and novelists," an eclectic grouping including Dylan Thomas, Sinclair Lewis, and Flannery O'Connor, as well as "a lot of the American and European classics."

While he took part in athletics and other school activities, Ortiz emphasizes that he "wanted to read and read and read and think." As a kind of pivotal point in his development as a writer, he cites a growing "awareness that our Acoma people and culture were in a fateful period in our destiny," and he resolved to direct himself as a writer to the preservation and presentation of his cultural heritage. His earliest fiction, which he concentrated on more than poetry, was about people struggling with poverty, social discrimination, and ethnic dispersion.

Unsure of how to become a writer, Ortiz went to work for Kerr-McGee, an energy corporation mining uranium, and began to develop characters modeled on the working men he met. The limits of their lives, and the restrictions that constrained members of the Acoma community, fed an anger that had been "seething for years," and Ortiz began drinking heavily to "exert the independence [he] wanted." He justified this by using the examples of Ernest Hemingway and Malcolm Lowry: He "believed in their greatness and in drinking as a part of that." Alcoholism did not prevent Ortiz from entering

Ft. Lewis College in 1961, serving in the U.S. Army from 1962 to 1965, then attending the University of New Mexico and winning a fellowship in the writing program at the University of Iowa, where he graduated with a master of fine arts degree in 1969.

His first book of poetry, *Naked in the Wind*, was published in 1971, and Ortiz worked as a newspaper editor for the National Indian Youth Council from 1970 to 1973. He underwent treatment for alcoholism during 1974 to 1975 but was able to begin a teaching career at San Diego State University in 1974, then at the College of Marin from 1976 to 1979 and at the University of New Mexico from 1979 to 1981. Ortiz published *Going for the Rain: Poems* with Harper and Row in 1976, marking his emergence as an important American writer.

After that, he remained very active in community affairs, serving as lieutenant governor of the Acoma Pueblo, while presenting his work at numerous conferences, university readings, and other literary gatherings throughout the North American continent. The strength and resonance of his writing has earned him the kind of respect that has given him the status of a wisdom figure or sage who, as he says, has worked to make "language familiar and accessible to others, bringing it within their grasp and comprehension."

ANALYSIS

Simon J. Ortiz has reiterated throughout his writing life that at the core of his poetry is the idea that "Indians always tell a story" because this is the "only way to continue." His concern for the survival of a cultural heritage that has been threatened with extinction and his deep grounding in the oral tradition that has enabled it to endure in spite of efforts at suppression provide the purpose and direction for his work. Ortiz identifies the oral tradition as the key to the "epic Acoma narrative of our development," an ongoing expression of the fundamental consciousness of the Aacqumeh *hanoh*. His poetry has been charged with the energy of a living language that draws on songs, chants, spoken tales, and intimate speech for sustenance, its essence which he has labored to capture and convey in written forms.

GOING FOR THE RAIN

Ortiz recalls that when he was working on the manuscript that was eventually published as two separate collections since "I was told 300-page first major poetry collections weren't a good idea," he came to the realization that the oral tradition was more than a "verbal-vocal manifestation in stories and songs." In the largest sense, it "evokes and expresses a belief system, and it is a specific activity that confirms and conveys that belief." Consequently, he structured his first substantial book of poems, *Going for the Rain*, as a narrative of discovery, a journey on the *heeyaanih* (road of life) in which the poetic voice presents a series of incidents that lead toward an understanding of the belief system at the center of the Aacqumeh community.

It is a book of origins, with seven poems exploring the mythic trickster/shape-shifter Coyote, an archetypal figure in Native American cultural history, as well as a record of geographic immersion, with poems located in many places in the United States, and a book of portraits where the poet describes his encounters with people within and outside First Nations settlements. The journey is divided into four sections, "Preparation," which is rooted in family life; "Leaving" and "Returning," a journal of life on the road; and "The Rain Falls," the last part a kind of summary of previous experience and a tentative presentation of a philosophic position that links metaphysical speculation with natural and ultranatural phenomena. Although not specifically identified, the book is patterned after an Acoma myth that involves a ceremonial trek in which the motion of the *schiwana* (or Cloud People) encourages the return of the rain, which is necessary for the continuing life of the *hanoh*.

The poet's voice is primarily conversational, often addressed to a specific person, sometimes turned inward as a dialogue placed within the narrative consciousness. Ortiz tends to focus on the small details of a person's existence, finding something vital in the familiar, as in the poem "21 August '71 Indian"

> Fire burns the thin shavings quickly
> and soon dies down under larger pieces.
> The red coals are weak, have to watch
> and put smaller pieces on next time.
> Get knife and splinter larger into smaller
> and feed the coals, being patient.
> Will have a late supper tonight;
> maybe the clouds will part some by then
> and let me see some stars.

A GOOD JOURNEY

The second part of Ortiz's initial manuscript was published in the following year, and he describes it as being based on "an awareness of heritage and culture," with "the poetry in the book styled as a storytelling narrative ranging from a contemporary rendering of older traditional stories to current experience." As Ortiz says in the preface, he writes so that he may have a "good journey" on his way home, and in a larger context, "Because Indians always tell a story." Ortiz has explained that he wanted to try to get something of the styles of the stories preserved in the oral tradition into print form, and he uses various devices, including multiple voices, direct address to the reader, quotations in several languages and intertextual commentary to produce some of the effect of oral performance. The are five parts to the journey of the title, beginning with "Telling," a section containing many versions of traditional stories, epitomized by the poem "And there is always one more story," whose title is a paradigm for the philosophical position that informs the narrative.

Further sections are titled "Notes for My Child," which picks up similar thoughts in "Going for the Rain; How Much He Remembered," which continues the idea of a travel journal; "Will Come Forth in Tongues of Fury," which focuses on political issues; and "I Tell You Know," which returns to family, community and the poet's universal beliefs. The appearance of Coyote in many poems suggests a correspondence of sorts between the legendary figure and aspects of the poet's own soul/spirit, with an ongoing dialogue between parties evolving through the book. A brief, cryptic poem, "How Much Coyote Remembered," states, "O, not too much./ And a whole lot./ Enough," an assertion of the vast span of time that constitutes the history of indigenous people on the North American continent which Ortiz is examining and rehearsing.

AFTER AND BEFORE THE LIGHTNING

Ortiz, operating in the largest conception of a "story," frequently combines what might be conventionally called poems with other rhetorical modes, and in *From Sand Creek*, he placed narrative commentaries on facing pages with poems about what he described as "an analysis of myself as an American, which is hemispheric, a U.S. citizen, which is national, and an Indian, which is spiritual and human." He employed a similar structural technique in a more complex manner in *After and Before the Lightning*, a version of a journal/memoir of the time he spent on the Rosebud Sioux Indian Reservation through a long, harsh winter season.

Completely integrating prose narratives with poetic sections in many forms—lyrics, chants, songs, meditations—Ortiz developed an account of physical and psychic survival that paralleled a personal journey across a frozen landscape ("bitter cold nights, and endless wind") with legendary tales of survival on frigid terrain and against the assaults of governmental agencies. Ortiz found this poetry connecting his life to existence, so that a direct confrontation with fierce elemental forces provided a test as well as a source of inspiration. "The vast and boundless cosmos," Ortiz writes, was "vividly present, immediate, and foremost as context on the prairie." Moving from the universal in the first section, "The Landscape: Prairie, Time, and Galaxy," with entries marked by dates beginning in November, then moving toward the quotidian in the next section, "Common Trials: Every Day," followed by a visionary time, "Buffalo Dawn Coming" and on toward a revival in "Near and Evident Signs of Spring" in April, Ortiz assembles an exploration of and a tribute to the "Lakota friends" whom he celebrates as "the true caretakers of their beautiful prairie land."

OTHER MAJOR WORKS

SHORT FICTION: *Howbah Indians*, 1978; *Fightin': New and Collected Short Stories*, 1983; *Men on the Moon*, 1999.

CHILDREN'S LITERATURE: *The People Shall Continue*, 1977; *The Good Rainbow Road*, 2001.

EDITED TEXTS: *A Ceremony of Brotherhood, 1680-1980*, 1981 (with Rudolfo A. Anaya); *Earth Power Coming: Short Fiction in Native American Literature*, 1983; *Speaking for the Generations: Native Writers on Writing*, 1998.

BIBLIOGRAPHY

Gingerich, William. "The Old Voices of Acoma: Simon Ortiz's Mythic Indigenism." *Southwest Review* 64, no. 1 (Winter, 1979): 18-30. An informative discussion of the ways in which Ortiz utilizes traditional materials from his community.

Lincoln, Kenneth. "Common Walls: The Poetry of Simon Ortiz." In *Native American Renaissance*. Berkeley: University of California Press, 1983. An illuminating overview of Ortiz's emergence as a poet.

Litz, A. Walton. "Simon J. Ortiz." In *The American Writers*, supp. 4, part 2. New York: Charles Scribner's Sons, 1996. A retrospective by an experienced critic that emphasizes Ortiz's early life as a key to his work.

Rader, Dean. "Luci Tapahonso and Simon Ortiz: Allegory, Symbol, Language, Poetry." *Southwest Review* 82, no. 2 (Spring, 1997): 75-92. Useful comparisons of the similarities in technique of two Native American writers.

Smith, Patricia Clark. "Coyote Ortiz: 'Canis Latrans Latrans' in the Poetry of Simon Ortiz." In *Studies in American Indian Literature*. New York: Modern Language Association Publications, 1983. A revealing study of the multiple appearances of the Coyote figure in Ortiz's poetry.

Studies in American Literature 8 (Summer/Fall, 1984). A special issue devoted to Ortiz's poetry, with a wide variety of viewpoints ranging from brief biographical notes and reminiscences to extended analytical examinations of the poetry and short fiction.

Wiget, Andrew. *Simon Ortiz*. Western Writers 74. Boise: Boise State University, 1986. A fundamental discussion of Ortiz' work to the mid-1980's, combining basic biographical information with sensible commentary on the poetry.

Leon Lewis

_____

BLAS DE OTERO

Born: Bilbao, Spain; March 15, 1916
Died: Majadahonda, Spain; June 29, 1979

PRINCIPAL POETRY

Cántico espiritual, 1942
Ángel fieramente humano, 1950
Redoble de consciencia, 1951

Pido la paz y la palabra, 1955

Ancia, 1958

Parler clair, 1959 (*En Castellano*, pb. in a French/
    Spanish ed.)

Esto no es un libro, 1963

Twenty Poems, 1964

Que trata de España, 1964

Expresión y reunión: A modo de antología, 1969,
    1981 (as *Blas de Otero: Expresión y reunión*)

Mientras, 1970

*Miguel Hernández and Blas de Otero: Selected
    Poems*, 1972

Todos mis sonetos, 1977

Poemas de amor, 1987

OTHER LITERARY FORMS

Blas de Otero experimented with progressively freer verse forms. An evolution began with the collection *Pido la paz y la palabra* (I ask for peace and the right to speak) and continued until his poetry approached prose. In their brevity, their imagery, and their dependence on sound effects, the pieces collected in his only full-length book of prose, *Historias fingidas y verdaderas* (1970), resemble poetry more than prose, as in "Andar" (walking): "And I saw the world as a sea churning with people, hanging on to one another as they went down; and the world just risen among broken tombs and inscriptions that lied."

As Geoffrey Barrow has noted, Otero's prose represents a further slackening of poetic convention rather than an abjuration of poetry. The first section of *Historias fingidas y verdaderas* (false and true history) includes fifty-six pieces in which Otero meditates on his own personality. The next section comprises his thoughts on Spain, its long and tangled history and how it could profit from the Socialist Revolution. The third section is devoted to speculation on the human condition in general. In contrast to the confidence that typified his writing of the previous decade, he raises doubts about the effectiveness of his role as a poet; it is now self-scrutiny rather than faith in the revolutionary potential of the majority that occupies him. Although no political theory of art emerges from his desultory observations, he attributes the social marginality he experiences as a poet to the *written* nature of the transference of his poetry. The secular millenarianism to which he subscribes, his belief in the imminent redemption of Spain and the world heralded by the Cuban Revolution, betokens the incontrovertible romanticism of his revolutionary stance.

ACHIEVEMENTS

During his lifetime, Blas de Otero certainly did not lack recognition and praise. He was hailed as one of the most virile poets Spain had produced since its civil war; Dámaso Alonso placed his sonnet "Hombre" (man) in the company of the sonnets of Francisco de Quevedo y Villegas; and the social and metaphysical concerns of his poetry have prompted comparisons to the work of Miguel de Unamuno y Jugo, William Blake, Arthur Rimbaud, Gerard Manley Hopkins, and Robert Lowell. Otero was awarded the Premio Boscan in 1950, and later the Premio de la Critica and the Premio Fastenrath from the Real Academia Española de la Lengua. His works have been translated into many languages, and criticism of his work has appeared in all of the major European languages.

Blas de Otero (© F. Catalá Roca)

BIOGRAPHY

Blas de Otero Muñoz was born in 1916 in the industrial city of Bilbao, Spain, that "dark lap" of his youth, a city "damp with rain and smoky with priests." His ancestry was Basque, and though he boasted of being a "universal Basque" and occasionally wrote poems to fellow Basques such as the poet Gabriel Aresti, his powerful love for Spain as a single entity precluded regional or ethnic partialities.

Otero was a laconic man who did not leave behind an abundance of biographical detail. "I write and am silent," he wrote in one of the most valuable autobiographical documents available, the poem "Biotz-Begietan"; when Otero was questioned on whether the poem were indeed autobiographical, he replied with one word: "Almost."

His early schooling in Bilbao was typically Basque: traditional, Catholic, and Jesuit in an environment of fear, severity, and intellectual repression that contributed to the distrust he felt toward priests and the Catholic Church. He began writing poetry at an early age; he tells the story of being struck at school by a priest who disliked some of his youthful verses. Although many of Otero's poetic anecdotes from childhood are painful, he speaks warmly of such things as the light of August streaming down upon the cherry trees of his grandmother's orchard, the happy days of his confused adolescence in Madrid, and the laughter of a youthful girlfriend nicknamed "Little Porcelain Jar." He was graduated from high school in Madrid, took a law degree at the University of Valladolid (although he never practiced law), and then began the study of literature at the University of Madrid. By the time he was nineteen, he had published several poems, including "Baladitas humildes" (humble little ballads) and "Cuerpo de Cristo, por mi amor llagado" ("body of Christ, by my love wounded"), in the *Revista de la Congregación (Kostkas) de Bilbao*. Then, the Spanish Civil War erupted, and Otero, apparently caught between shifting lines of battle, found himself fighting on one side and then the other. The postwar period was for Otero as painful as the war itself, and his desperate search for God, as it became more and more emotional, turned eventually into a desperate struggle with God. The poet who, in 1942, wrote, "oh beautiful God, oh flesh of my flesh and of my soul/ that, without You, would disappear like the fog," would write sarcastically in 1963, "What a shame there is not/ a god as excellent as they say."

Luis Romero describes Otero in 1946 as thin, ascetic-looking (although then not so much as he would later appear), ironic, a convincing polemicist, preoccupied, and looking more like a mystic or a philosopher than a poet. At this time, he lived on the Alameda Recalde in Bilbao with his widowed mother and an unmarried sister, of whom he rarely spoke. He earned his living as a tutor of private students, but this did not occupy much of his time.

Otero made his first trip outside Spain to Paris in 1951, where, according to his poem "Biotz-Begietan," he suffered "pangs of the spirit." Soon he became interested in Communism and for the rest of the 1950's was continuously preoccupied with leveling criticism at the Francisco Franco regime. If Otero lost interest in his search for God, he did not lose his sense of messianic purpose (his own life he called "Calvary," and he titled a poem about himself "Ecce Homo"), which he transferred to his search for brotherhood among men. Even after his commitment to Marxism, his literary work expresses a longing for revolution in primarily moral and religious terms.

From 1955 to 1958, Otero lived in Barcelona; in 1959, he participated in the homage for Antonio Machado at the Sorbonne in Paris, where he read his poem "Palabras reunidas para Antonio Machado" (words put together for Antonio Machado). In 1963, he traveled to the Soviet Union and to China and had insuperable difficulties with the Spanish censors. *En Castellano* (in plain words), which was published in Paris in 1959 (*Parler clair*), was still not available in Spain, so Otero decided to permit its bowdlerized publication; when it came out, more than a hundred poems were missing.

Otero spent three years in Cuba, from 1965 to 1968, and returned to Spain with the word *guajiro* (Cuban peasant) in his vocabulary and with images of *los yanquis* (yankees) taking unfair advantage of everyone in the Americas. Soon after his return to Spain, he had a malignant tumor removed, a fact to which he refers in his chilling "Cantar de amigo" ("friend's song"): "Where is Blas de Otero? He's in the operating room, with his/ eyes open . . . / Where is Blas de Otero? He is dead, with his eyes/ open." Throughout the 1970's, he continued assembling anthologies of his past work and writing new poetry which appeared primarily in magazines. In 1976, in ill health, he participated in commemorative services for Federico García Lorca at Fuentevaqueros. Apparently late in life, he was married to Sabina de la Cruz, who wrote the introduction to the posthumous edition of his anthology *Blas de Otero: Expresión y reunión*. Otero died in 1979 at his home in Majadahonda, outside Madrid.

ANALYSIS

Blas de Otero was fond of embedding his own name in his poems, and he did not shrink from acknowledging by name other poets whom he admired in his own work. The title *Ángel fieramente humano* (angel fiercely human) is admittedly taken from Luis de Góngora y Argote; *Esto no es un libro* (this is not a book) is from Walt Whitman; and *Historias fingidas y verdaderas* is from Miguel de Cervantes; Otero also makes ample use of epigraphs for his poems, taken from the Bible, popular Spanish songs, Saint John of the Cross, Antonio Machado ("A solitary heart is not a heart at all"), Francis Thompson, Augusto Ferrán, Rubén Darío ("Shall we be silent now in order to cry tomorrow"), and Luis de León.

Otero addresses poems to Machado, Quevedo, the Basque poet Aresti, Nobel Prize winner Vicente Aleixandre, the Turkish Communist poet Nazim Hikmet ("Considering how you have moved me/ at this time when tenderness is so difficult"), Paul Éluard, and Miguel Hernández, and recognizes by name as kindred spirits Pablo Neruda, the Bulgarian poet Nicolai Vaptzarov, Rafael Alberti, Cesar Vallejo, Gabriel Celaya, and León Felipe.

Similarly, he made no secret of his scorn for the idea that poetry, not accessible to everyone, is for the "immense minority," as advanced by Juan Ramón Jiménez; thus was inspired his own commitment to the "immense majority." Otero was also vocal in denying Unamuno's influence on his thinking, an idea put forth by the critic Emilio Alarcos Llorach, and his attitude toward Cervantes and his knight errant is complicated by his resentment that both of them helped to perpetuate the myth of idealism.

LANGUAGE AND STYLE

As regards Otero's style, he is partial to words that convey violence and passion (such as *rasgar*, "to tear"; *arrancar*, "to wrench") and derivative verbs and participles using the prefix *des-* (such as *desterrar*, "to drive away"; *desarraigar*, "to uproot"; *desgajar*, "to wrench off"), the violence of which presents a striking contrast to the more positive condition of the word without the prefix (*terra*, "land"; *arraigo*, "stability"; *gajo*, "branch"). He commonly adds the suffix *-azo* to nouns, thereby incorporating the strong Castilian *th* pronunciation (as in *trallazo*, "whiplash"; *zarpazo*, "thud"). Among colors, yellow (*amarillo*) appears the most frequently, redolent of aging and decay.

In contrast, when moments of violence and anger give way to resigned melancholy and "when roses spring forth from the wall of grief," some of Otero's favorite words are *paz* (peace), *luz* (light), the neologism *frondor* (the lushness of fronds), and the names of various birds and flowers. Generally, Otero adheres to a basic Spanish vocabulary, almost colloquial, and for the most part he avoids literary or unusual words. An exception is his delight in some of the more unusual designations for rugged terrain (such as *llambria, galayo, cantil*), whose very "difficulty" seems to mimic that which they denote.

Otero's conception of man as adrift in a vast abysmal ocean, straining to grasp some support, or as an island, floating with its flora of anxieties and its fauna of appetites, leads the poet to employ a full panoply of nautical terms, some of which are technical enough to sound awkward in English translation. The same is true of the poet's reliance on the imagery of directional winds, such as *cierzo* (cold northerly wind) and *galerna* (stormy northwest wind). The word *zafarrancho*, metaphorically "struggle," which Otero uses to sum up his life in a later poem, is another nautical term, originally referring to the drudgery of cleaning the deck of a ship.

Otero also creates new words, which he does by agglutination (as in the title "Españahogándose" / "Choking on Spain"), by blending (as in *Ancia*, composed of the first syllable of *Ángel fieramente humano* and the last syllable of *Redoble de consciencia*, "drumroll of conscience," which also suggests *ansia*, "anguish," one of the key words in Existential philosophy), and by analogy ("alángeles y arcángeles," where the former is created on the model of the latter to denote another type of angel). Another feature of Otero's style is his tendency to freshen clichés and lines from other poets by making slight changes. Thus, the idiom "cogido de la mano" (hand in hand) is converted to "cogidos de la muerte": "You and I, linked by death" instead of "You and I, hand in hand." Otero takes a line from Luis de León, "espaciosa y triste España" (sad and spacious Spain), and recasts it as "esta espaciosa y triste cárcel" (this sad and spacious prison). A famous line from Gustavo Adolfo Bécquer, "While there exists one beautiful woman,/ there will always be poetry," becomes for Otero "Where there is in the world/ one single word,/ there will be poetry."

"DÉJAME"

To inculcate an idea, Otero does not avoid repeating the same or near-synonymous words (for example, "doors, doors, and doors. And more doors"). He is also fond of enjambment, which serves to speed up the rhythm of some of his poems or, conversely, to slow down their progress, as it does in the following lines from "Déjame" (leave me), where it suggests the uneven, ill-defined quality of the poet's relationship with God:

> You do me harm, Lord. Take your hand
> from upon my head. Leave me with my vacancy,
> Leave me. For an abyss, with my own
> I have enough. Oh God, if you are human,
> take pity, remove your hand
> from my head. It does me no good. It makes me cold
> and scared.

Other noteworthy techniques operative in Otero's poetry are the hyphenation of words in such a way as to permit an ambivalence of meaning: frequent use of the rhetorical question and experimentation with unconventional punctuation.

WOMEN AND LOVE POETRY

Although Otero did not customarily write love poetry unmarred by the dark thoughts connected with one or another of his compulsive searches, he was not reluctant to name names, and he identifies in his poems a significant number of women important to him. In his earliest poems, he treats the desired woman as a virginal symbol and his potential union with her as a union of body and soul: "Mademoiselle Isabel," apparently his teacher of French as an adolescent, with her carnation-colored breasts and rose-colored body; "Little Porcelain Jar," who smelled of hyacinth; "La Monse" reclining in a field of yellow flowers. A special case is Tachia, nickname of Conchita Quintana, who, little more than a teenager when she befriended Otero, then in his thirties, gave the poet some of the happiest moments of his life. In fact, it was Tachia who helped the poet to realize the futility of his marathon bout with God, and it was she who invited him to concern himself instead with the brotherhood of humankind: "You said: Entwine your grief with mine,/ like a long and jubilant tress;/ immerse your dreams in my kind; push aside/ your thirst for God. My kingdom is of this world."

In later poems, this ethereal love becomes tainted by the tantalizing pain caused by the body of a woman, and Otero's imagery becomes less dainty: The poet lifts the warm skirts of one woman to find a shadow, fear, and a "silent hole," and he writes cheerlessly of the impoverished Laura, who has a "little accordion/ between her legs." In the relatively late "La palmatoria de cobre" ("the copper ferule"), Otero avails himself of the appellation "sister," borrowed from the biblical Song of Solomon to address the consoling female subject of his poem. The consolation of love with women, however, is not enough to provide the poet with a permanent distraction from his *Weltschmerz*. In fact, one of the only times he speaks of women generically is in the form of a savage diatribe, where women are characterized as "Cunning, calculating, liars/ lily-white in public, notorious with their masks."

CÁNTICO ESPIRITUAL

Otero destroyed hundreds of early poems, or so he claims in "Es a la inmensa mayoría" (to the immense majority). His attempts to maintain his faith in God after the horrors of the Spanish Civil War are the theme of his first published work, *Cántico espiritual* (spiritual canticle), written in homage to Saint John of the Cross on the occasion of the fourth centenary of his birth (1942). These homage poems, which establish the relationship of God and man as the product of a violent meditation ("I moan and clamor for You like a sin"), Otero never allowed to be reprinted, and in comparison to his later poems, they seem rather less spontaneous.

ÁNGEL FIERAMENTE HUMANO

For the next eight years, Otero published in the Basque literary magazine *Egan* and began to acquire a following. In 1950, *Ángel fieramente humano* appeared, dedicated to the "immense majority" and bringing into sharper focus Otero's personal quarrel with God and his conception of the vacancy and loneliness to which man is subjected in this life. The Existentialism of these poems recalls Søren Kierkegaard; Otero's views during this period were influenced by discussions among the young Basque intellectuals connected with *Egan*. Otero speaks of the terrible silence of God, a silence made to seem even more terrible in the wake of the unnecessary killing (twenty-three million, by Otero's count) in World War II. When the poet raises his hand, God, clearly the angry God of the Old Testament rather than the loving Jesus of the New, lops it off; when he raises his eyes toward God, God gouges them out. If man is an angel in the image of God, then his wings are like chains. Nevertheless, there are still to be found in this work vestiges of Otero's deep religious feeling, as in "Salmo por el hombre de hoy" ("Psalm for the Man of Today"), written as a prayer: "Raise us, O Lord, above death./ Extend and sustain our gaze/ so that it can learn henceforth to see You."

REDOBLE DE CONSCIENCIA

Otero's next collection, *Redoble de consciencia*, was devoted to the same theme and written mainly in free verse. The lament of Job that he was ever born serves as the epigraph of the sonnet "Tierra" (land), and St. John's observation that the soft hand of God can weigh heavily on the soul of man, serves to introduce "Déjame" (leave me). In the latter poem, Otero, equal in pride to God who made him, reaches the point of wishing he could kill God as God kills man; a godless abyss without hope is thus preferable to an abyss reigned over by an oppressive God who tantalizes with a hope that is unattainable.

PIDO LA PAZ Y LA PALABRA

In *Pido la paz y la palabra*, Otero, heeding the advice of Tachia, devoted himself to the working class in poems which J. M. Cohen has called monotonous in their anger. Such apparently self-indulgent lines as "I have seen few Calvaries like the one I have" and "I am a man literally beloved by all sorts of ruin" are relieved somewhat by subsequent pledges to offer his life "to the gods/ who live in the country of hope" and "to leap up to

the beautiful towers of peace," "sway other breezes," and "call at the doors of the world." One remarkable poem from this collection is "Hija de Yago" (daughter of Saint James), which depicts Spain on the map of Europe as its bloody heel which trod upon the face of a torpid America.

ANCIA

In 1958, Otero published *Ancia*, comprising a selection from *Ángel fieramente humano* and *Redoble de consciencia* as well as thirty-eight new poems, some of which were from the earlier periods of his life and among which is Otero's version of Matthew Arnold's "Dover Beach," a poem addressed to Tachia and titled "Paso a paso" (step by step). As the drum rolls from one side of Europe to the other, he begs his beloved to put death behind her; "The night is long, Tachia/ . . . Listen to the sound/ of daybreak/ opening its way step-by-step—between the dead."

EN CASTELLANO

En Castellano, which did not pass the Spanish censors and had to be published in France in a bilingual edition as *Parler clair* in 1959, contained Otero's most unconventional poetry to date. Here, Otero broke up his customary hendecasyllables by distributing the words of a single line over several lines or by introducing short lines of another measure. He was increasingly concerned with eliminating decorative rhetoric and achieving the most direct style possible. The collection includes this now-famous dictum: "Formerly I was—they say—an existentialist./ I say that I am a co-existentialist." Much of its content, however, was aimed at the Franco dictatorship and is of limited interest to the contemporary reader.

ESTO NO ES UN LIBRO

Esto no es un libro, so called because its poems deal with real people and places, was published in Puerto Rico in 1963. It is a thematic anthology containing poems from different periods of the poet's life as well as several poems he was forced to omit from *Que trata de España* (all about Spain), which was published in Barcelona the following year and is confined to expressing the beauty and the misery of Otero's native land. Although in this book he evokes memories by the mention of place-names (130 of them) or words for regional phenomena (such as *orvallo* and *sirimiri* for "rain"), and although many of the images are beautiful in their own right ("the mountains of Leon glitter/ like a blue sword/ waved in the mist"), Otero manages to insert social criticism into every poem, touching upon everything from consumerism and agrarian reform to Vietnam and the United Nations. If he rhapsodizes about "bright Catalonia," "pure Leon," and "Segovia of ancient gold," he ends the poem with a tweak of conscience about "fertile Extremadura,/ where people and bread/ are parted unjustly."

QUE TRATA DE ESPAÑA

The original, uncut edition of *Que trata de España*, published by Ruedo Ibérico in Paris in 1964, contains 155 poems, subdivided thematically into five parts: "El forzado" (he who is forced), "La palabra" (the word), "Cantares" (songs), "Geografía e historia" (geography and history), and "Verdad comun" (common truth). The first section depicts the poet as the child of a miserable and beautiful mother and stepmother who is Spain, a proud country soaked by centuries of fratricidal bloodletting and disdainful of science and progress. It is to the people that Otero speaks, a people broken and burned beneath the sun, hungry and illiterate in their millenarian wisdom and "hospitable and good,/ as the bread they do not have."

The second section reflects the poet's admiration for simple words, especially for the simple, vivid (albeit sometimes ungrammatical) speech and eloquent gestures of the Spanish peasants. By this time, Otero had begun to realize that his poetry was not reaching the working man for whom it was written, and in defense of his original premise he added to one of his poems an epigraph (author unidentified): "In the condition of *our hemisphere* poetry is for the majority not because of the number of its readers, but because of its theme."

Spain has a richer inheritance of epic poetry and folk ballads than does any other European country, with the possible exception of England, and it was in appreciation of this inheritance that Otero named his third section "Cantares." All the poems included here have some link with the folk poetry of Spain or with folk-inspired modern poetry, such as that of Federico García Lorca, and Otero's use of certain archaic variants of poetic words underscores this folk element. It is in this section that Otero launches a violent diatribe against the lie of literature and proffers the advice, "if you want to live peacefully,/ don't be corrupted by books."

In the fourth section, Otero paints more loving vignettes of Spain and probes deeply into the sad history of the country, invoking the aid of the painter Diego Rodriguez de Velázquez to forge an iron tongue on the anvil of truth; there is also a memorial poem to Machado and a collage poem on the death of Don Quixote. The final section attempts to join Spain with other countries of the world in a common hope for a better future: "we/ open our arms to life,/ we know/ another fall will come, heavy with gold,/ beautiful as a tractor in the wheat."

MIENTRAS

The collection *Mientras* (in the meantime), which the poet later wished to have incorporated into a larger work to be called "Hojas de Madrid con la galerna" (pages from Madrid with the northwest wind, contains poems written in Madrid after his return there from his three-year residence in Cuba and often shares metaphors, allusions, and symbols with the prose pieces of *Historias fingidas y verdaderas*, published the same year. The poems are characterized by the subjectivity and reflectiveness of a dying man who reviews and evaluates the facts of his life. In "Morir en Bilbao" (to die in Bilbao), he observes that although he loves Moscow as he does his right arm, he *is* Bilbao with his entire body in a way he can never be Moscow. The burden of being so peculiarly Spanish, however, is no longer as oppressive as it was in the earlier poems; the poet concedes that in part, his wishes for peace have been granted, and the subject of death no longer inspires defiance in him.

Whether Otero was struggling against the dreadful aloneness of man, as in his earlier work, or against the evils of war and political dictatorship, as he did in his later work, he plied his trade with subtlety and power. The justice he sought for Spain, "disheveled in its grief" under fascism, he grew to demand for citizens of the entire world, even if within a political framework as extreme in the other direction as the fascism that he loathed. His voice is sometimes sarcastic and often bitter, but it never quavers, and it is never without hope for a tomorrow better than today.

OTHER MAJOR WORKS

NONFICTION: *Historias fingidas y verdaderas*, 1970.

BIBLIOGRAPHY

Barrow, Geoffrey R. *The Satiric Vision of Blas de Otero.* Columbia: University of Missouri Press, 1988. A critical examination of de Otero's work. Includes bibliographic references and an index.

Cannon, Calvin, ed. *Modern Spanish Poems: Selections from the Poetry of Juan Ramón Jiménez, Antonio Machado, Federico García Lorca, and Blas de Otero.* New York: Macmillan, 1965. A collection of twentieth century Spanish poetry with commentary by the editor.

Debicki, Andrew Peter. *Spanish Poetry of the Twentieth Century: Modernity and Beyond.* Lexington: University Press of Kentucky, 1994. Debicki examines the sweep of modern Spanish verse, which he situates in the context of European modernity, tracing its trajectory from the Symbolists to the postmodernists.

Mellizo, Carlos, and Louise Salstad, eds. *Blas de Otero: Study of a Poet.* Laramie: University of Wyoming, 1980. A collection of critical essays in English and Spanish. Includes bibliographic references and an index.

Jack Shreve;
bibliography updated by the editors

OVID

Publius Ovidius Naso

Born: Sulmo, Roman Empire (now Sulmona, Italy); March 20, 43 B.C.E.

Died: Tomis on the Black Sea, Moesia (now Constanța, Romania); 17 C.E.

PRINCIPAL POETRY

Amores, c. 20 B.C.E. (English translation, 1597)

Ars amatoria, c. 2 B.C.E. (*Art of Love,* 1612)

Heroides, before 8 C.E. (English translation, 1567)

Medicamina faciei, before 8 C.E. (*Cosmetics,* 1859)

Remedia amoris, before 8 C.E. (*Cure for Love,* 1600)

Fasti, c. 8 C.E. (English translation, 1859)

Metamorphoses, c. 8 C.E. (English translation, 1567)

Epistulae ex Ponto, after 8 C.E. (*Letters from the Black Sea,* 1639)

Ibis, after 8 C.E. (English translation, 1859)

Tristia, after 8 C.E. (*Sorrows,* 1859)

OTHER LITERARY FORMS

Ovid composed a tragedy, *Medea* (before 8 C.E.), probably a rhetorical closet-drama in the manner of Seneca. Only two or three short fragments of this work remain.

ACHIEVEMENTS

Without any hostility toward Vergil, Ovid led Roman poetry away from the manner and technique of epic poems such as the *Aeneid* (29-19 B.C.E.). Ovid was a poet of great talent whose works cover a vast range of types, including love elegy, mytho-historical epic, handbooks on love, and a set of fictitious letters written by mythological heroines. He produced a voluminous body of poetry even though he had studied to be an advocate and government official.

Ovid's extensive influence began in his own lifetime. His poems were known throughout the Roman Empire, and they continued to be read through the Middle Ages. Ovid was a favorite author of the period of chivalry, and his works live again in Geoffrey Chaucer, Giovanni Boccaccio, Petrarch, and the whole circle of Italian Renaissance writers and painters, the *Metamorphoses* in particular providing many subjects for the artists. Later, Ovid was to influence Ludovico Ariosto, Desiderius Erasmus, Johann Wolfgang von Goethe, Pierre de Ronsard, Jean de La Fontaine, Jean-Baptiste Molière, Edmund Spenser, William Shakespeare, John Milton, William Congreve, and Lord Byron. Early American literature has preserved a retelling of some of his stories in Nathaniel Hawthorne's *Tanglewood Tales for Boys and Girls* (1853). Ovid was not profound—he had none of the vision and greatness of Vergil—but he remains one of the most skillful writers of verse and tellers of tales that the Western world has ever known.

BIOGRAPHY

Publius Ovidius Naso was born at Sulmo in the Pelignian territory of Italy on March 20, 43 B.C.E., of wealthy parents. They were not particularly generous with their son while they lived but left him a comfortable inheritance upon their death. Of equestrian, not aristocratic rank, but with good connections and great talents, Ovid was expected to devote himself to the duties of public life. At first, he studied law but had no interest in such a profession. He soon abandoned law in disgust and turned to rhetoric, studying at Rome under Arellius Fuscus and Porcius Latro. Then, according to the custom, he spent a short time in Athens; while he was in Greece, he took the opportunity to visit the renowned cities of Asia Minor. He returned to Rome at the age of twenty-three or twenty-four, and made a halfhearted beginning at a public career, holding such minor offices as triumvir and decemvir. The effort, however, was short-lived. He felt that he had neither the physical nor the mental stamina for a civic career, and he certainly lacked the interest. He finally abandoned politics and threw himself headlong into the life of a man-about-town. He joined the literary circle which included the love poets Aemilius Macer, Sextus Propertius, and Albius Tibullus. Ovid heard Horace recite and, although Ovid was not an intimate of Vergil, the two probably met.

Ovid soon made a name for himself, and before long his elegant poems were being recited in the salons and streets of Rome. His literary career falls into three clearly defined periods. The first is marked by the composition of the *Amores*, the *Heroides*, and the brilliant but calamitous trio, the *Art of Love*, the *Cure for Love*, and *Cosmetics*. The *Amores* was a collection of short elegiac poems, addressed to an imaginary mistress, Corinna; the *Heroides* purported to be letters from famous ladies of heroic times to their lovers. (There are twenty-one epistles, but only the first fourteen are beyond all doubt Ovid's own.) The *Art of Love*, one of the most elegant pieces of seduction in all literature, was published in 2 B.C.E., to be followed shortly after by *Cure for Love*, which may have been intended as a recantation, and by a treatise on *Cosmetics*.

The next ten years constitute the second phase of Ovid's literary career. During this period, Ovid turned from amorous compositions to serious themes. His interest in Greek and Roman literature and mythology now had free rein. He wrote the *Fasti*, a poetic calendar of astronomical data, embellished with references to the historical, political and social highlights of the Roman year. To this period also belongs the *Metamorphoses*, his great poem of transformations, and the greatest col-

lection of mythology in any literature. This monumental work had been completed but had not received the master's finishing polish, when, in 8 C.E., like a thunderbolt from a blue sky, an imperial decree banished Ovid from Rome forever.

This shattering calamity marked the commencement of the third and final period of Ovid's life. The rest of his extant poetry was written after his banishment and includes *Sorrows*, an autobiographical poem, and *Letters from the Black Sea*, letters written in an attempt to induce Augustus to change the location of his banishment. Besides these works, Ovid wrote, while in exile, the *Ibis*, a vicarious piece of learned abuse. The *Fasti* is by far the most important product of Ovid's banishment, although the first books were probably composed before his exile. It is a versified Roman calendar for the first six months of the year. Several other poems by Ovid are now lost.

His banishment is one of the great mysteries of literature, for no explanation was ever given (at least to the public), and Ovid himself refers to the cause in only the vaguest of terms. It was generally believed that the reason was the emperor's anger at the immorality of the *Art*

Ovid (Hulton Archive)

of Love. This is reasonable enough, because Augustus had tried very hard, even by legislation, to reduce the moral laxity prevailing in the capital. Ten years, however, had passed since the *Art of Love* was published, and it must be assumed that some more immediate cause had suddenly fanned the flames of this old resentment. Historians had not far to seek. The emperor's daughter, Julia, and his granddaughter (also named Julia) were both wanton and dissolute women, and their behavior in court circles had long been a source of anxiety, distress, and shame to Augustus. In the same year in which Ovid was banished, Augustus also banished his granddaughter from the court and the city of Rome. It has been surmised that Augustus knew (or suspected) that Ovid had been aware of some intrigues in the royal household involving the younger Julia which he neither prevented nor reported. In his autobiographical poem *Sorrows*, Ovid several times takes pains to deny any complicity. He says that he was merely an innocent witness of something he should not have seen and that the cause of his banishment was an error, not a crime.

The punishment, grievous though it was, was not as bad as it might have been. Ovid was banished, not exiled, and this apparently subtle distinction had tangible advantages, for he was allowed to retain not only his citizenship but also his property in Rome. Ovid's wife (his third—he had divorced the first two) did not accompany him. She remained in Rome at Ovid's request, possibly to look after his property and to endeavor to persuade her influential friends to intercede for her husband. This was the brighter side of Ovid's disaster. The rest was a refinement of cruelty. Ovid, the genial, friendly, pleasure-loving poet, was ordered to Tomis on the Black Sea, a barbarous town on the very frontiers of civilization, peopled by long-haired, uncouth Sarmatians, chilled by interminable frost and snow, constantly attacked by savages, and utterly devoid of any culture, literature, or even intelligent conversation.

In anger and despair at the downfall of his hopes, Ovid, on leaving Rome, burned the unrevised manuscript of his *Metamorphoses*. Some friends, however, had kept a copy, and thus the masterpiece was preserved.

For nearly ten years, Ovid lived out a miserable existence which was one long apologia for his life. He defended himself, excused himself, and explained himself.

He sorely missed the sights and sounds of Rome: They were always in his thoughts. One thing remained to him: the exercise of his poetic gift. He continued to pour out elegiac verses, but the sparkle had gone out of them. The lamp was burning low. Nine years of self-pity, self-reproach, abject self-abasement, prayers, tears, and, finally, total despair had taken their toll.

All this time, Ovid had never ceased to hope for a reprieve, but Augustus was unbending, and his successor Tiberius was equally adamant. Ovid bitterly realized that there is no pardon when a deity is offended. The gentle, self-indulgent spirit of the poet was broken. He pathetically pleaded that his ashes be brought home and that imperial malice not pursue him beyond the grave. In 17 C.E., Ovid, the playful singer of tender loves, was dead.

ANALYSIS

Ovid always maintained a decorous loyalty to language and sentiment in his poetry. He was not a propagandist but a man of letters, pure and simple. He produced mainly love poetry until he turned his attention to something on a larger scale, a quasi epic. His talents were not suited to long flights, such as the *Aeneid*. He was a thorough Alexandrian in that respect, as in his learning and high polish. It was with the poetry on amatory themes that Ovid first won his reputation, and he continued to work at them for some years, recasting and rearranging them.

AMORES

The existing poems of the *Amores* form three books containing, in all, forty-nine poems, none very long (they range from 18 to 114 lines). Most of them tell the story of the poet's relations with a certain Corinna. No one has ever succeeded in identifying her and a careful reading of these charming trifles reveals Corinna to be a fantasy figure, whom Ovid could adorn with all his taste and ingenuity.

Love poetry as a genre in Roman literature already existed and had been developed by a whole generation of poets before him. Ovid employed two aspects of the genre developed by earlier poets: the autobiographical mode of composition and the devising of transitions from one traditional motif to another. Ovid's strength, however, lies in grace, not depth. The major pleasures of the *Amores* are their verbal and metrical dexterity. These poems have an epigrammatical quality; verbal dexterity has sharpened a point to precision but no mental picture is evoked. The result is, at times, a slight incoherence, characteristic of poetry that concentrates more on effect than on expression. Ovid produces three effects in the *Amores:* neatness, ingenuity, and irony. Neatness is largely a matter of antithesis, balance, and contrast, both in thought and expression, supported often by verbal echoes. Ingenuity is evident in word order, brevity, compression, allusive periphrases, and deliberate ambiguity. Irony, often implied by antithesis, is enhanced by parentheses and asides. The diction is based on the stock amatory vocabulary, but Ovid does coin new words in moderation and skillfully manipulates different registers of diction against the poetic norm. Ovid calculates his effects with great precision and accuracy; imagery consequently plays a minor part in his poetry, in contrast to the various figures of balance and antithesis.

Like earlier Roman love poets, Ovid employs the autobiographical mode of composition. He does so not because he is trying to express inner feelings with the greatest attainable immediacy, but because, for Ovid, the autobiographical form has the advantage that characters and situation can be taken for granted; no explanation is needed. Ovid leaves little to the reader and only demands that he keep his sense of language and the subtle relationships of words at key pitch.

Ovid's love poetry is far easier to understand than that of his predecessors, because of his clearer transitions from one idea or emotion to another. Ovid's technique of composition is self-consciously concerned with the fine details of language and thought. This form encouraged him to use an extremely orderly, even rigidly logical process of exposition. Surprising leaps of thought and reversals of emotion are ruled out by a technique that leaves nothing unsaid that can be said.

The style of the *Amores* is not, of course, beyond criticism. Its brilliance is in a sense superficial; it lacks majesty and mystery; and it is too lucid to present real intellectual problems. Yet the *Amores* is not an entirely superficial work. The serious note in the poems on poetic immortality has long been recognized, and there is an underlying seriousness in Ovid's treatment of love and in his attitude to the Augustan regime. His attitude toward love is one of amused resignation, where the difficulties, follies, and deceptions of the lover are humorously magnified, cheerfully minimized, or positively welcomed. In a sense Ovid is offering an alternative and perhaps more practical approach to love than the shapeless idealism of other love poets and the negative stance of the moralists. The work is saved from mere triviality by the warm humanity and psychological truth which underlie its ironic approach. At only one point, when he discusses abortion, does Ovid's genial banter seem to descend to callousness.

The technique and spirit of the *Amores* are basically Alexandrian, although in some cases the setting is clearly Roman rather than Greek. It was, however, impossible for a Roman of the Augustan Age to detach himself from the political and social conditions of his time. The *Amores* inevitably reflects Ovid's attitude to the regime of Augustus and its ideals. In Ovid's choice of love rather than any higher theme for poetry and in his evident enthusiasm for the life of a lover, he is clearly flying in the face of Augustus's attempts to reform marriage. Ovid is flippant about religion, the military ideal, and Augustus himself, but toward politics he reveals indifference rather than any positive stance. The *Amores* seems to be apolitical and not exactly what Augustus had in mind for the Roman literary scene.

ART OF LOVE AND CURE FOR LOVE

The *Art of Love*, along with its companion piece, the *Cure for Love*, is an adaption of the elegiac tradition to the didactic poem, a genre with a clearly defined tradition which had in Vergil a distinguished recent practitioner. Superficially, the *Art of Love* is on a par with practical poems such as that on hunting by Ovid's contemporary Grattius, but the use of the didactic form for such an untraditional subject as love creates a light, even comic atmosphere. Ovid establishes his place in the higher poetic form of the tradition by using the standard introductory (*principio*), transitional (*adde quod*), and hortatory (*accipe*) formulas of Lucretius and Vergil, and by employing the traditional ship and chariot metaphors for the progress of the poem. Nevertheless, the *Art of Love* lacks the dedication to a patron which is common in more serious works.

The poem, in which Ovid denies the traditional divine inspiration and claims that his poem is based entirely on experience, announces his ironic approach to the genre. When Ovid refers to his literary predecessors, it is not in a spirit of reverence, but rather to show how cleverly he can twist their serious themes to his own lighthearted purposes. Lucretius's passage on the birth of civilization is adapted to prove the susceptibility of women to love, and Vergil's instructions on seasons and types of soil become, with a little modification, instructions on how to find and win women. Ovid's most interesting adaptation of the genre is his creation of a humorous persona for the mentor of love, thus underlining the element of burlesque. This persona makes extravagant claims for his powers, seeing himself as a prophet or a pilot of the chariot of love. Thus, between the sophisticated poet and his sophisticated readers there is a fictitious mentor and the equally fictitious students to whom the work is addressed. In other words, the whole work is an elaborate literary game.

The *Art of Love*, like the *Amores*, makes extensive use of the themes of love poetry, but there is an essential difference between the two. The setting of the didactic poem is unmistakably contemporary Rome. The *Amores*, although Roman in some details, is set in the shadowy half-Roman, half-Hellenistic world of elegy. This contemporary element of the *Art of Love* has two aspects. First, it presents many glimpses of the more private aspects of Roman life. Second, it can hardly avoid making at least an implicit comment on Augustan society and on the ideals of the regime. The ideas hinted at in the *Amores* are now expressed much more strongly. For example, there is one passage in which Ovid explicitly rejects the idealization of the past and of rustic simplicity. Instead, he prefers the splendor of contemporary Rome and the life of refinement. The main theme of the *Art of Love*, a manual of seduction and intrigue, is clearly in conflict with Augustus's attempts to encourage marriage. Ovid's claims that he is not writing for married women does nothing to disguise this fact.

There are other ways in which Ovid seems to show little respect for Augustus and for the symbols of his prestige. His budding program, his public spectacles, his foreign policy, and his cults of the gods are all either treated frivolously or at least debased by being set in a frivolous context. All of this does not turn Ovid into a political propagandist or imply that the main purpose

of the *Art of Love* was to criticize Augustus and his regime. What is clear is that Ovid's natural impudence, irreverence, and sense of the incongruous were not inhibited by any feeling of veneration for the ideals of Augustus. Ovid no doubt expected to delight many of his readers by his daring, and he was not concerned if he shocked others. He himself brushed off criticisms of the *Art of Love* in his *Cure for Love*, and in this he ultimately miscalculated. In the end, a jaded bureaucracy seized upon the subversive aspects of the work, although its original purpose was surely humorous rather than political.

The basic style of the *Art of Love* and the *Cure for Love* is the style of the *Amores*, characterized by neatness and wit. This style is perfectly suited to the persona of the mentor of love. The most significant stylistic developments in the *Art of Love* (apart from the adoption of didactic formulas and imagery) are the techniques of description and narrative, evident especially in the vignettes of Roman life and in the set-piece, mythological digressions. A careful analysis of the language of the descriptive passages (both of city life and in the many similes from nature) reveals an eye for detail and a sense of color and brightness, vigor and enjoyment, beauty and elegance. The narratives are technically accomplished; a single episode, the "Rape of the Sabines," includes the following devices: aphorism, wordplay, verbal repetition, antithesis, extended description with small details and hints of color and scent, similes from nature, focus on individuals, carefully varied rhythms, impudent reinterpretation of Roman history, and an aetiological conclusion. Here, undeniably, is the basis of the narrative style of the *Fasti* and of the *Metamorphoses*.

The final question is whether the *Art of Love* is anything more than a *jeu d'esprit*. It is right to emphasize that the main quality of these poems is wit and that their main appeal lies in their sophistication and ingenuity. As in the *Amores*, however, they are saved from triviality or mere frivolity by their underlying humanity and psychological insight. It has often been observed that Ovid draws on works of serious philosophy in framing his precepts: The instructions to women in book 3 of the *Art of Love* share certain principles with Cicero's *De officiis* (c. 43 B.C.E.; *On Duty*); and the advice in the *Cure for*

Love echoes that of Cicero's *Tusculanae disputationes* (c. 44 B.C.E.; *Tusculum Disputations*). The aim of these borrowings may have been partly to show how cleverly Ovid could adapt other works to his own purposes; but the passages do not read like parody, and the effect is to give a backbone of human understanding to the poems. There was a basic decency with which the game of seduction and deception was to be played and Ovid was not being entirely frivolous in his ideal of civilized life.

METAMORPHOSES

The course of Ovid's life allowed him only seven more creative years after the publication of his early works. This short span sufficed for the composition of the fifteen volumes of the *Metamorphoses*; only the final revision was lacking. It is, nevertheless, his masterpiece; it is one of the finest poems handed down from antiquity.

The writing of the *Metamorphoses* meant a new departure for Ovid in several respects, and his poetic powers were to be exercised in fields where he had little previous experience. For one thing, his poetry had moved, so far, only in the given and natural world. Now, he was to conquer the province of the fabulous and miraculous. In his previous works, Ovid had been expressing emotional experiences, but now he had to cultivate concreteness. Definite characters had to be portrayed, their stories told in appropriate settings, and sceneries devised to fit plots. Ovid met the challenge and his invention was more than equal to the task. The epic style had to be handled by an author who had been writing elegiacs. Finally, Ovid had to overcome somehow a serious defect of his intellect: his inability to order his material systematically and to develop his ideas consistently. He compensated for this weakness with an inexhaustible ingenuity in improvisation. Ovid is constantly luring the reader on from one story to the next, and yet he is always arresting him with the present tale.

The main subject of the epic is the transformation of human beings or gods into animals, plants, stones, or constellations. The theme of metamorphosis provides a sense of continuity, reinforced by Ovid's ability to link the stories into groups and to create ingenious transitions between one story or group of stories and the next. He chose the theme because the fantastic and utopian character of the stories appealed to him and because it gave him scope for displaying many varieties of insecure and fleeting identity, of a self divided or spilling over into another self. Separation from the self usually means death, but not in a metamorphosis; Ovid's mild disposition avoided crushing finales. This is best illustrated by the Myrrha story. Myrrha cannot live on after a hideous sin that she has committed. She prays to the gods for a harsh punishment, a change in shape, denying her both life and death. Ovid intercedes in his own narrative and is not ashamed to betray how much it moves him; he feels relieved that Myrrha's prayer is answered and that she does not have to die. When he has reported how she was transformed into a myrrh tree, and how her tears were to be known in all ages as precious grains of incense, he even characterizes the metamorphosis as an honor rather than as a punishment.

In general, the character of the *Metamorphoses* is romantic and sentimental. A great many stories are concerned with the human experience of love. The poem is remarkable for its wide range in this regard: Pyramus and Thisbe, Iphis and Anaxarete, Cephalus and Procris, Ceyx and Alcyone, Baucis and Philemon, Pygmalion, Myrrha, Io, Callisto. Indeed, one of the outstanding elements of the poem is the breadth of human sympathy which is obvious despite the unrealistic atmosphere and the rhetorical elements of Ovid's style. The story of Io, the woman loved by Zeus and transformed by him into a cow, is a good example. Why, in spite of the fantastic plot, is the reader moved by the tale to feel concern for the cow woman? Everyone can understand what it means to try to escape from his own self. There is much in Ovid's fables that can easily be divested of the miraculous and translated into some everyday occurrence.

Another theme employed by Ovid in the *Metamorphoses* is the interplay between otherness and sameness. He explored this new frontier of experience in a great number of stories. One of his best is the tale of the narcissus which once upon a time was a young man. At the age of sixteen, between boyhood and manhood, Narcissus aroused the love of both men and women, but tender though his beauty was, it made him arrogant and hard; his heart remained unmoved. His punishment was to fall in love with himself. In the secluded solitude of a lush meadow deep in the woods, he lay down at the edge of a pond to drink, and the calm water mirrored his shape.

Ovid describes at length the strong deception and enchantment with which Narcissus unwittingly desires himself. Then Ovid breaks into his narrative with a direct address. The poet, like an excited child in a theater who tries to help the hero, forgets his supposed aloofness and talks to his character in order to extricate him from error. Finally the truth dawns on Narcissus: "He is I." Narcissus longs for nothing but death, and he wastes away in physical and mental starvation. Self-love turns into self-destruction. When Narcissus is gone, his beauty is preserved by his metamorphosis into a flower as white and pink as he used to be, and as fine, proud, and useless as he was.

The *Metamorphoses* is too long and somewhat repetitious. The range of Ovid's creative imagination was great but not unlimited, and the poet overtaxed his inventive powers. After book 11, the epic changes its character and no longer is there a bounty of short, tender, sentimental fables. An ambition for grandeur develops, and Ovid begins to insert massive compositions, each devoted to a single subject. In the last four books, he competes with historical epic and recounts patriotic legends.

The style of the *Metamorphoses* is so rich and varied as to make generalization difficult. The essential qualities of Ovid's narrative style are speed and vividness. A lead-in is provided for each story by a swift transition, and little time is wasted in introducing the new characters. The scenic descriptions with which a number of stories begin contribute both to the vividness of the scene (with their typical pool, wood, cave, and pattern of light and shade) and to the atmosphere, but the apparently tranquil or innocent elements of the setting portend, and are even symbolic of, danger or sexuality. The narrative itself can be elliptical and syncopated, even abrupt; details are carefully selected and highlighted in what is almost a cinematic technique. Similes are carefully used to create vividness or to emphasize violence and emotion, but they are rarely developed at such a length as to distract from the stories. The final metamorphosis often comes as an abrupt conclusion, even though its details are described with curious fascination. The verse itself flows smoothly and easily; the diction is straightforward but never dull. Words are coined in moderation, and examples of archaism or vulgarism are rare.

Another important aspect of the style is its pervasive humor. Humor is notoriously difficult to analyze, but Ovid's sense of humor is implicit in his treatment of his material and is often underlined by asides and parentheses. It can frequently be seen in his humanization of the gods, his exploitation of the paradoxes of divine and human behavior, and his ironic attitude toward the credibility of his own stories. Ovid's literary humor is largely based on incongruity and exaggeration, together with an element of audacity.

At the end of his epic, Ovid boldly asserts that he will prove to be no less immortal or divine than the deified emperors. He has dared the supreme worldly power and predicts that the *Metamorphoses* will triumphantly survive. It did.

OTHER MAJOR WORKS
  PLAY: *Medea*, pr. before 8 C.E. (fragment).

BIBLIOGRAPHY
Anderson, William S. *Ovid: The Classical Heritage*. New York: Garland, 1995. This collection of essays examines Ovid's influence on Western literature and arts chronologically, from the first century Romans through the Middle Ages and Renaissance to the seventeenth, eighteenth, nineteenth, and twentieth centuries. Select bibliography.

Barchiesi, Alessandro. *The Poet and the Prince: Ovide and Augustan Discourse*. Berkeley: University of California Press, 1997. A scholarly assessment of Ovid's *Fasti* that examines pro-Augustan and anti-Augustan readings of the poem. Bibliography, index, index locorum.

Bate, Jonathan. *Shakespeare and Ovid*. New York: Oxford University Press, 1993. Ovid is as important to students of Renaissance, English Elizabethan, and Jacobean literature as he is in his own right, and the plays of Shakespeare are rife with references to him. This work focuses on Shakespeare's plays and sexual poetry as they refer to Ovid. Bibliography, index.

Boyd, Barbara Weiden. *Ovid's Literary Loves: Influence and Innovation in the "Amores."* Ann Arbor: University of Michigan Press, 1997. For the student of Ovid, analyzes influences on *Amores* in chapters titled "Reused Language: Genre and Influence in the

Interpretation of *Amores*," "Literary Means and Ends: Ovid's *Ludus Poeticus*," "Ovid's Visual Memory: Extended Similes in the *Amores*," "From Authenticity to Irony: Programmatic Poetry and Narrative Reversal in the *Amores*," "Ovid's Narrative of Poetic Immortality," and "*Legisse Voluptas:* Some Thoughts on the Future of Ovid's *Amores*." Bibliography, index locorum, general index.

Brown, Sarah Annes. *The "Metamorphoses" of Ovid: From Chaucer to Ted Hughes*. New York: St. Martin's Press, 1999. The principal source for much of what we know of Greco-Roman myth, the *Metamorphoses* has perhaps been Ovid's most important work down the ages. This work examines the influence of "Ovidianism" on poets from Geoffrey Chaucer to Hughes as well as musicians and painters.

Calabrese, Michael A. *Chaucer's Ovidian Arts of Love*. Gainesville: University Press of Florida, 1994. Love, particularly sexual love, is a central theme in Ovid, and its influence is rife in the works of Geoffrey Chaucer. One of the fullest studies of Ovid's influence on the English poet and his *Canterbury Tales* and *Troilus and Criseyde*.

Dalzell, Alexander. *The Criticism of Didactic Poetry: Essays on Lucretius, Virgil, and Ovid*. Toronto: University of Toronto Press, 1997. Five essays on didactic poetry by the well-known classics professor at the University of Toronto, one of which focus on Ovid's *Art of Love*. Bibliography.

Ovid. *After Ovid: New Metamorphoses*. A new translation of *Metamorphoses* Edited by Michael Hofmann and James Lasdun. New York: Farrar, Straus, and Giroux, 1995. Compiled by two young poets who asked forty-two of their seniors—including such writers and poets as Thom Gunn, Seamus Heaney, Paul Muldoon, Charles Tomlinson, and others—to contribute adaptations or translations of the stories. The result is a unique rendition of Ovid's work. Includes introduction, commentaries, index of translators, biographical notes.

_____. *The Poems of Exile*. Translated and introduced by Peter Green. New York: Viking Penguin, 1994. The introduction by Green provides commentary to accompany his translations of *Tristia* and *Epistulae ex Ponto*, written after Ovid was banished to Tomis on the Black Sea and was unsuccessfully attempting, through these poems, to flatter his way back into civilization. Index.

Reeson, James E. *Ovid, "Heroides" 11, 13, and 14: A Commentary*. Leiden, Netherlands: E. J. Brill, 2001. Close interpretation of these three verse epistles, introduced by an examination of Ovid's use of his sources and the epistle form.

Stapleton, M. L. *Harmful Eloquence: Ovid's "Amores" from Antiquity to Shakespeare*. Ann Arbor: University of Michigan Press, 1996. Looks at Ovid's early elegiac poetry and how it influenced literature from approximately 500 C.E. to 1600, seeing *Amores* as the model for love poetry of the Middle Ages and Renaissance. Chief among poets examined are the troubadours, Dante, Petrarch, and Shakespeare. Bibliography, index.

Williams, Gareth D. *Banished Voices: Readings in Ovid's Exile Poetry*. New York: Cambridge University Press, 1994. Examines the exile poetry in close readings that reveal the irony and hidden meanings of these poems, particularly the rift between Ovid's overt despair over his declining talents and the reality of the artistry of the poems. Bibliography, indexes of authors, passages cited, and words and themes.

Shelley P. Haley;
bibliography updated by the editors

_____

WILFRED OWEN

Born: Oswestry, England; March 18, 1893
Died: Sambre Canal, France; November 4, 1918

PRINCIPAL POETRY

Poems by Wilfred Owen, 1920 (Siegfreid Sassoon, editor)

The Poems of Wilfred Owen, 1931 (Edmund Blunden, editor)

The Collected Poems of Wilfred Owen, 1963 (C. Day Lewis, editor)

Wilfred Owen: War Poems and Others, 1973 (Dominic Hibberd, editor)

OTHER LITERARY FORMS

Like many of the poets and artists of his time, Wilfred Owen professed a strong interest in the theater and supposedly drafted a play while recovering from shell shock in Craiglockhart military hospital in 1917, although no manuscript has appeared. Owen's letters, which have been collected, deserve mention for two reasons. First, the style reflects both the poetic temper of the man and the adherence to detail reflective of an age of correspondence which will probably never return. Second, and perhaps more important, Owen's letters record the transitions typical of most British soldiers who survived on the front for a long time: from resolve to do the soldier's duty, to disgust, fear, and depression, to the solemn acceptance of fate that extended service produced. One is fascinated by Owen's attempt to depict his life on the front for his naïve family and friends, as well as his ability to do so in spite of censorship.

ACHIEVEMENTS

Many commentators have emphasized that Wilfred Owen exhibited more potential to continue and enlarge the craft of poetry than any of the soldier-poets of World War I. He was a technician, an innovator, a "poet's poet" long before he was a proud soldier, a horrified combatant, a victim. The kinds of criticisms applied to Rupert Brooke (immature, too much style and too little substance) or Siegfried Sassoon (limited, more propaganda than art) have little validity when it comes to Owen. Indeed, in spite of his early death and limited canon, several twentieth century poets (among them W. H. Auden and Stephen Spender) have publicly stated their admiration for Owen's work or have used or expanded his methods. A notable dissenting voice is that of William Butler Yeats, who shocked many writers and critics by excluding Owen's work from his *Oxford Book of Modern Verse* (1936). Yeats defended his decision in a famous venomous blast, writing to Dorothy Wellesley that Owen was "unworthy of the poet's corner of a country newspaper. He is all blood, dirt, and sucked sugar stick . . . (he calls poets, 'bards,' a girl a 'maid,' and talks about 'Titanic wars'). There is every excuse for him, but none for those who like him."

Owen's champions, however, far outnumber his detractors. It is true that all of his work, from earliest to lat-

Wilfred Owen (Library of Congress)

est, is characterized by a kind of romantic embellishment, an intensity that borders on parody. This was more of a problem early in his career; as he matured, he assimilated the devices of John Keats, Percy Bysshe Shelley, and Lord Byron (among others), creating effective juxtapositions and dramatic tensions. This change was perhaps a result of the sophisticated and shocking material he found in his war experience.

Shocking the war poems are. Certainly among the most descriptive and horrifying of their era, they continue to penetrate minds supposedly benumbed by exposure to the twentieth century. In what became the preface to his first published volume of poetry, Owen wrote: "Above all, I am not concerned with Poetry. My subject is War, and the pity of War. The Poetry is in the pity." Indeed it appears true; of the many horrifying experiences suffered by the artists who recorded their experience in World War I (Robert Graves, Sassoon, Isaac Rosenberg, Edward Thomas, Brooke, and others), it is Owen's cries which are the loudest and most anguished. Owen seems to have been more outraged than most by the lamentable tragedy of fine young men lost in the struggle. What is surprising, however, is that the resultant verse is never self-indulgent, self-pitying; rather, Owen was able to focus his vision outward. He concluded sadly in the preface previously cited that "all a poet can do today is warn." Owen's disgust with the war he experienced and despised is readily apparent, but it goes beyond immediacy and is elevated to prophecy as well.

Another of Owen's goals, through all the years of fighting and suffering, was to cling to his artistic voice, to expand his abilities, to become a better poet. He sought new ways to use language, and his mastery of alliteration, onomatopoeia, assonance, and dissonance have been often cited. Perhaps his most consistently brilliant device was the use of slant rhyme (or "half rhyme" or "pararhyme" as it has been called), the subtle and effective mixture of vowel dissonance and consonant assonance most often effectively employed at the end of his lines (for example, "cold" and "killed").

The effect of Owen's expert use of form (he was a master of sonnets and elegiac mood) and his fluency (both traditional and experimental) was to suggest a poet who would have been very much at home with modernism, but who never would have forgotten his literary heritage. In fact, an observation often made concerning the poetry of Thomas Hardy, that his was the soul of the nineteenth century anticipating twentieth century innovations, applies equally well to Wilfred Owen. That Owen was able to sustain his brilliance under the stress of battle makes the reader appreciate his achievement all the more.

BIOGRAPHY

Wilfred Edward Salter Owen was born in Oswestry, Shropshire, England, on March 18, 1893, the first child of Tom and Susan Owen. Owen's mother was a devout and cautious woman; his father was an active, rough-hewn, hardworking sort who was nostalgically attracted to the sea and those who sailed it. The early years of their marriage, and Owen's childhood, were sometimes difficult, characterized by several moves, frequent if not severe financial difficulties, and tensions produced by his parents' conflicting characters. Their union produced

four children. Owen's younger brother Harold became a successful artist and devoted much of his adult life to chronicling the life of his more famous war-poet brother.

Owen was sent to Birkenhead Institute for his first years of schooling; his father approved of the discipline for which the school was noted, but Owen probably profited most from an adoring teacher and early exposure to the pleasures of literature. He also showed a great interest in religious matters, much to the delight of his mother. In 1907, the family moved to Shrewsbury, where Owen enrolled in the technical school. There he read diligently and began to compose serious essays (some on politics, some on art theory) and put down his first attempts at verse.

Somewhat confused about his future after his matriculation examination at London University in 1911, Owen accepted an opportunity to become a lay assistant to the Vicar of Dunsden. His activities were many-faceted, from the intellectual (extensive reading and attending lectures) to the practical affairs of the parish (playing with children and assisting the poor). His poetry began to mature, not so much in its subject matter as in its increasing flexibility of language. For reasons that remain unclear, Owen became disenchanted with his commitment to the vicarage and left Dunsden. After a period of contemplation, during which he struggled with his health, he was offered, and he accepted, a post to teach English at the Berlitz School in Bordeaux. He enjoyed the experience and the climate was beneficial, even as the clouds of war gathered over Europe.

Because Owen was in France during the "exhilarating" first part of the war, a time when nationalism and enthusiasm for battle possessed young men like him in England, his wavering emotions regarding the conflict are understandable. He had left his job in late 1915 to assume a position as a private tutor to a well-to-do family in Merignac, France. His correspondence reveals a confused but honor-bound attitude toward his own responsibilities: appalled at the destruction and suffering so near by, confident and proud of his ability to serve, excited at the prospect of taking his gift for poetry into battle. He briefly investigated business opportunities, flirted with but rejected the idea of joining either the French Army or the Italian Cavalry, and in September, 1915, returned to England, where he enlisted with the Artists' Rifles.

During his training he sought not only to become a fine soldier but also to become familiar with many people active in literary circles of London. He met Harold Monro of *The Poetry Review* and lived briefly in a flat adjacent to the magazine's offices. Owen performed admirably as a soldier and claimed to enjoy his work, though he appeared uncomfortable, out of place with his peers. He was well liked, however, and in June, 1916, 2nd Lieutenant Owen was attached to the 5th Battalion of the Manchester Regiment.

After a few months of polishing, Owen was sent with thousands of his fellows to the front. The Somme offensive, begun in July, 1916, had been stalled tragically for several months, and war planners had determined to begin another push as the new year began. Immediately, Owen was struck by the difference between the grotesque reality of the war zone and the appallingly inaccurate depictions of the war at home. These sentiments, together with supportive vivid details, were relayed home regularly. Still, he took comfort in his devotion to duty and in writing, criticizing, and discussing poetry, pleasures which he never neglected.

Writing and fighting with distinction for six months, Owen showed signs of suffering from the strain and was finally sent to Craiglockhart military hospital, where he was diagnosed as suffering from neurasthenia, or shell shock. His stay there was to be crucial, not only for his health but for his poetic and intellectual development as well. Owen participated in many of the therapeutic activities offered by the hospital. Also at Craiglockhart was Siegfried Sassoon, the distinguished soldier, poet, and most recently a virulent antiwar spokesman. The two became friends and eventually Sassoon became audience and critic for the work which began to reveal Owen's growing artistry. Robert Graves, a friend of Sassoon and a regular visitor to the hospital, also encouraged Owen to continue his work. In December, Owen was dismissed and returned to London, where he pursued other contacts in the literary establishment. (Later, in 1920, Sassoon became responsible for collecting and publishing selections of Owen's poetry.)

In spite of his increasing disgust at the carnage of battle, amply evident in his poems of this time, Owen was compelled to return to the war, and during the summer of 1918 he was granted permission to cross to France. Participating in the heavy fighting preceding and during the armistice talks, Owen became a respected and competent soldier, winning the military cross. Invigorated artistically by his friendship with prominent writers during his recuperation, he sent poems and lively letters back to England. On November 4, 1918, one week before the armistice, Owen was killed while leading his troops across the Sambre Canal.

ANALYSIS

Wilfred Owen's most memorable, and often cited, works reveal several characteristic traits. Romantic imagery dominates his work, regardless of whether it is war-inspired. Owen was a passionate disciple of Keats; he made pilgrimages to Keats's shrines and felt a personal affinity for the great Romantic poet. There is also brutal realism in Owen's war descriptions. Had Owen not been there himself, the reader might be tempted to believe the verse exaggerated, such is its power. The poetry is also characterized by the sensual glorification of male beauty and bravery, and the hideous waste of wartime slaughter. Such elements have prompted a plentitude of conjecture about Owen's personal relationships; but the sentiment with which he glorifies male qualities in his early years, and the depth with which he expressed his concern for his fellows in his war years are not, in his case, cause for prurient speculation by the psychological critics. The simple fact concerning Owen's poetry is that he wrote about his comrades in ways that were never offensive and always eloquent.

"To POESY"

Innovations and experiments with the potential of language give Owen's best work a quality that is more of the modernistic than the Edwardian or Georgian temper. In spite of its strength and ferocity, however, there is an equally noticeable fragility. Owen's earliest extant attempts at poetry (according to Jon Stallworthy, it is probable that his first efforts were burned by his mother at his death, at the poet's request) reflect a somewhat awkward sentimentalism. He laboriously expresses his adoration for the muse in "To Poesy." The poem, an odd beginning for one who would later write that he was "not concerned with poetry," contains a variety of religious, erotic quest images (none very effective) designed to signify the "purer love" of his aesthetic principles. Also noticeable at this time in Owen's poetic infancy are poems and fragments which either imitate Keats or illustrate his exultant emotions after having visited locales associated with Keats's life and work. Again, the sentiments are apparent, if hardly laudable artistically, as in "SONNET, written at Teignmouth, on a Pilgrimage to Keats's House." Its sestet begins: "Eternally may sad waves wail his death,/ Choke in their grief 'mongst rocks where he has lain." Still, the young poet shows signs of searching for more sophisticated methods. A revealing fragment from an early manuscript shows that Owen had penciled in lines to attract attention to the interesting effect of half-rhymed words, "tomb, home," "thou, below," "spirit, inherit."

"DULCE ET DECORUM EST"

The effect which one experiences when turning from Owen's earlier works to his mature verse is dramatic indeed. "Bent double, like old beggars under sacks,/ Knock-kneed, coughing like hags, we cursed through sludge," begins "Dulce et Decorum Est," one of his most often cited depictions of the reality of war. An interesting juxtaposition established at the beginning is that of the simple exhaustion of the troops who "marched asleep . . . lame . . . blind . . . drunk with fatigue," and the nightmarish, almost surreal atmosphere of the battle, lighted by "haunting flares," pierced by the "hoots" of artillery fire, and pervaded by the sickening presence of gas. The soldier who has donned his gas mask looks through "misty panes" at thick green light, as if submerged in a "green sea." The nightmare is unrelieved by the passage of battle as the persona sees "in all my dreams," without relief, a comrade who was unable to survive the attack, who lurches grotesquely, "guttering, choking, drowning."

After witnessing these events, the reader is drawn more intimately into the scene, as the persona uses the second person, asking directly if "you too" could imagine witnessing eyes "writhing in his face" and blood that "gargles from froth-corrupted lungs." As Owen builds the intensity and visceral detail of his description, he is preparing the reader for the ironic and bitter conclusion which utilizes a tag from Horace (*Odes*, III. 2.13), familiar to schoolboys and used to glorify the war effort: *Dulce et decorum est pro patria mori* (it is sweet and honorable and proper to die for your country). For

Owen, and surely for most readers, however, the sentiments expressed in the phrase can now only be considered an "old lie" which cannot honestly be told to children anymore. Owen brilliantly half-rhymes in the last three lines the words "glory" (what children seek) and "mori" (what happens to them in war).

"STRANGE MEETING"

Another nightmare vision serves as the stimulus for a greatly admired work. "Strange Meeting" recounts a frightful reverie, an encounter between two soldiers in hell. Their confrontation, unified by dramatic dialogue, is inspired by the horrors of war, but it also serves as an occasion for Owen to comment on poetic principles and to prophesy (quite accurately and depressingly) on the nature of the new century.

Owen begins by describing his descent down "some profound dull tunnel," arriving at a shattered place where "encumbered sleepers groaned." He is surprised when one of these fellows jumps up; there is a moment of recognition not only between them but also of their mutual circumstance, standing "in Hell." Owen comforts his opposite in a dramatic understatement, suggesting that even *here*, dead, in hell, there "is no cause to mourn." Such was the gruesome reality above ground, alive, in battle. The stranger is in no mood to be assuaged, because he too had been a poet who ventured and strove for "the wildest beauty in the world." Thus, the poet's life is lost, but that loss is not to be lamented nearly as much as the loss of the truth he might have written, the "truth untold." The ultimate tragedy is not temporary, but lasting, as future generations will be unaware of the truth of war which the poet could have recorded. Instead of rejecting the past, those generations will embrace it, probably with devastating efficiency. Had he lived, the poet would also have battled, not with instruments of war, but with his "courage" and "wisdom." His would have been a war to dominate men's minds, fought when men wearied of bleeding and death, a soothing message of "truths that lie too deep for taint" that would have flowed from his "spirit."

Owen does not wish to end the poem at this abstract level, seeking instead to pull the reader back to the immediacy of war. Even though the setting is highly contrived, Owen provides a "surprise ending" which serves two purposes: to impress upon the reader the brutal in-

fighting characteristic of many World War I battles, and
to ridicule the notion of nationalism and emphasize the
common humanity of all the war's combatants. The
early "recognition," a foreshadowing device, had not
been between friends but between enemies, as the poet-
narrator had evidently slain the poet-prophet with a bayonet. Rather than continuing either the hostilities or the
discussion, the soldier who had been thus murdered offers a simpler, but more final and disturbing alternative:
"Let us sleep now. . . . "

"ARMS AND THE BOY"

In other poems Owen draws attention to the waste of
young men slaughtered. "Arms and the Boy" (an ironic
revision of the opening of Vergil's *Aeneid*, c. 29-19 B.C.E.,
"Arms and the Man I sing. . . .") is a three-stanza portrait
of youthful innocence confronting the awful mysteries
of the instruments of war. He emphasizes the apparent
discomfort as a boy tests a bayonet "keen with hunger
for flesh" and caresses a bullet which seeks "to nuzzle in
the hearts of lads." These gestures are not natural for
youngsters whose "teeth seem for laughing round an apple" (the immediate thought here is of a soldier's death-
grimace). Moreover, the human animal was not designed for battle; there are "no claws behind his fingers
supple." His appearance is of gentle, delicate demeanor,
a face framed with "curls," as opposed to the brutish nobility of animals which possess "talons" and "antlers."

"ANTHEM FOR DOOMED YOUTH"

Similar sentiments, now supported by religious imagery, are expressed in "Anthem for Doomed Youth," a
sonnet which illustrates Owen's fusion of the traditional
elegiac mood with the realities of modern warfare. The
opening question serves as an example: "What passing-
bells for these who die as cattle?" The answer is that the
only possible form of lamentation for the war dead is the
cacophonous sounds of war, "the stuttering rifle's rapid
rattle." Not only are religious ceremonies out of the
question, but they would also be a "mockery." Here
Owen shows the extent to which his disillusionment
with organized religion had gone. Instead of the glow of
holy candles, the poet finds light in "their eyes." They
will wear no "pall," but will be recognized and remembered through the "pallor of girl's brows." The essence
of this poem is that in such times as these, Christianity
seems incapable of providing its traditional comfort.

The memorial of the dead soldiers will not be "flowers"
but memories held by "patient minds." Their legacy,
sadly and not of their making, is but darkness, at "each
slow dusk drawing-down of blinds."

In a sense, Owen's poetic legacy can also inspire
darkness for the reader. His work is highly educational,
however, and thus valuable, especially when read in the
context of World War I and in contrast to that of some of
his fellow soldier-poets. The reader, ultimately grateful
for the work that Owen left, is intrigued by what he
might have become.

OTHER MAJOR WORKS

NONFICTION: *Collected Letters*, 1967 (Harold
Owen and John Bell, editors); *Selected Letters*, 1998
(John Bell, editor).

BIBLIOGRAPHY
Breen, Jennifer. *Wilfred Owen: Selected Poetry and
Prose*. London: Routledge, Chapman & Hall, 1988.
Breen does an excellent job of giving a brief analysis of Owen's major poems and supports her opinions by subjectively looking at his personal correspondence to gain insight for her analysis. This short
book is organized by a chronological table of contents and contains a limited bibliography.
Hibberd, Dominic. *Owen the Poet*. Athens: University
of Georgia Press, 1986. Presents Owen as a single
identity, not as a poet whose works are traditionally
studied as being either before the war or after.
Hibberd examines Owen's growth to "poethood,"
his imagination, and his understanding of himself,
and complements this approach with an exhaustive
bibliography and a concise index.
Lane, Arthur E. *An Adequate Response: The War Poetry of Wilfred Owen and Siegfried Sassoon*. Detroit:
Wayne State University Press, 1972. Analyzes Owen's
poetry from the aspect of the cataclysmal effect of
the war on the use of poetic language. Owen's influence from John Keats is considered as he replaces
traditional, figurative images with realistic scenes
from the battlefield and weaves them into his verses.
Owen, Wilfred. *Wilfred Owen: Collected Letters*. Harold Owen and John Bell, eds. London: Oxford University Press, 1967. Follows the life of Owen from

the time he was five until his death at the age of twenty-five, through his letters to his family and friends. While not providing critical analysis of his poetry, this fascinating collection gives the reader rare insight into the personality of this gifted poet. Supplemented by a complete index.

Purkis, John. *A Preface to Wilfred Owen*. London: Longman, 1999. A brief biographical and critical introduction to Owen and his work. Includes bibliographical references and index.

Simcox, Kenneth. *Wilfred Owen: Anthem for a Doomed Youth*. London: Woburn, 1987. Begins with Owen's interaction with his family, focusing on his influential mother. His religious background is highlighted as Simcox reviews the major issues in Owen's poetry, amply augmented with examples from his primary works. Supplemented by a comprehensive index.

Stallworthy, Jon, ed. *The Poems of Wilfred Owen*. New York: W. W. Norton, 1985. An intensive study into the chronological sequence of 103 poems and 12 fragments by Owen. Aims to offer factual footnotes to allow readers a more concise foundation to formulate their own explications.

_____. *Wilfred Owen*. New York: Oxford University Press, 1995. A full and sensitive illustrated biography of the short-lived poet and war hero. Appendices offer genealogies, fragments of previously unpublished poems, a bibliography of Owen's library, and index.

White, Gertrude. *Wilfred Owen*. New York: Twayne, 1969. White traces Owen's maturation as a poet from dreamy, romantic imagery to the harsh realities of World War I. Discusses his standing with other war poets and stresses that genre is more important than chronology in focusing on his development. Includes bibliography and index.

Robert Edward Graalman, Jr.;
bibliography updated by the editors

P

DAN PAGIS

Born: Radautsi, Romania; 1930
Died: Jerusalem, Israel; 1986

PRINCIPAL POETRY
Shaon ha-hol, 1959
Sheut mauheret, 1964
Gilgul, 1970
Poems by Dan Pagis, 1972
Moah, 1975
Points of Departure, 1981
Milim nirdafot, 1982
Shneim asar panim, 1984
Shirim aharonim, 1987
Variable Directions: The Selected Poetry of Dan Pagis, 1989
Col ha-shirim, 1991

OTHER LITERARY FORMS

Although Dan Pagis is internationally known as a poet, he has written a children's book in Hebrew, *ha-Beitzah she-hithapsah* (1973; the egg that tried to disguise itself). As a professor of medieval Hebrew literature at Hebrew University, he has published important studies on the aesthetics of medieval poetry, including expositions of Moses Ibn Ezra, Juda ha-Levi, Solomen Ibn Gabirol, and the other great poets of the eleventh and twelfth centuries who celebrated the colors and images of worldly existence in elegant, formal verse. Pagis's own poems, more understated and conversational than the medieval texts he studied, have been translated into Afrikaans, Czech, Danish, Dutch, Estonian, French, Hungarian, Italian, Japanese, Polish, Portuguese, Romanian, Serbo-Croatian, Swedish, Vietnamese, and Yiddish.

ACHIEVEMENTS

The first generation of Israeli poets often used a collective identity to write poetry of largely ideological content. Yet the reaction to previous ideological values that arose in the late 1950's and the 1960's has been described by Hebrew critic Shimon Sandbank as "the withdrawal from certainty." Poets Yehuda Amichai and Natan Zach were at the forefront of this avant-garde movement, a "new wave" that included Dan Pagis, Tuvia Ruebner, Dahlia Ravikovitch, and David Rokeah. These poets of the 1950's turned away from the socially minded national poets, believing in the poet as an individual and using understatement, irony, prosaic diction, and free verse to express their own views.

Most of all, the revolution in Hebrew verse that Pagis, Amichai, and Zach brought about was the perfection of a colloquial norm for Hebrew poetry. Pagis and Amichai especially made efforts to incorporate elements of classical Hebrew into the colloquial diction, with Pagis often calling upon a specific biblical or rabbinical text. His poems have appeared in major American magazines, including *The New Yorker* and *Tikkun*.

BIOGRAPHY

Dan Pagis was born in Radautsi, Romania, and was brought up in Bukovina speaking German in a Jewish home in what was once an eastern province of the Austro-Hungarian Empire. He spent three years in Nazi concentration camps, from which he escaped in 1944. After he arrived in Palestine in 1946, Pagis began to publish poetry in his newly acquired Hebrew within only three or four years, and he became a schoolteacher on a kibbutz.

He settled in Jerusalem in 1956, where he earned his Ph.D. from Hebrew University and became a professor of medieval Hebrew literature. Pagis also taught at the Jewish Theological Seminary in New York, Harvard, and the University of California at San Diego and Berkeley. During his life he was the foremost living authority on the poetics of Hebrew literature of the High Middle Ages and the Renaissance. He was married and had two children. Pagis died of cancer in Jerusalem in 1986.

ANALYSIS

Reflecting the geographic and linguistic displacements of his life, displacement is a governing concept in Dan Pagis's poetry, in the sense that to "displace" is to remove or put out of its proper place. Although there is a great deal of horror in his poetry, the historical record of that horror is so enormous that Pagis uses displacement to give it expression without the shrillness of hysteria or the bathos of melodrama. Instead, he cultivates a variety of distanced, ventriloquist voices that become authentic surrogates for his own voice. Dan Pagis survived one of the darkest events in human history and managed to set distance from it through the medium of his art. Yet Pagis is a playful poet as well, sometimes using humor and whimsy to transform the displacement of his life from a passively suffered fate into an imaginative reconstruction of reality.

POEMS BY DAN PAGIS

In this early selection of his poems, it is apparent why many discussions of Pagis's poems tend to pigeonhole him as a "poet of the Holocaust." The first poem is titled "The Last Ones," and the first-person speaker in the poem speaks for all the Jews left after the Holocaust. Ironically, he states that "For years I have appeared only here and there/ at the edges of this jungle." Yet, he is certain that "at this moment/ someone is tracking me. . . . Very close. Here." Yet, the poem ends with the line "There is no time to explain," indicating a collective consciousness that is still running in fear for its life.

A section of the book called "Testimony" contains six Holocaust poems, among them "Europe, Late," the brilliant "Written in Pencil in the Sealed Railway-Car," and the chilling "Draft of a Reparations Agreement." In "Europe, Late," the speaker betrays his innocence by asking what year it is, and the answer is "Thirty-nine and a half, still awfully early." He introduces the reader to the life of the party, dancing the tango and kissing the hand of an elegant woman, reassuring her "that everything will be all right." Yet the voice stops midsentence at the end of the poem, "No it could never happen here,/ don't worry so—you'll see—it could[.]"

Often Holocaust themes are placed in an archetypal perspective, as in the widely known poem "Written in Pencil in the Sealed Railway-Car." The speaker is "eve" traveling with her son "abel," and she means to leave a message for her other son. "If you see my other son/ cain son of man/ tell him i"; here the poem ends abruptly, leaving the reader to meditate on the nature of evil.

In "Draft of a Reparations Agreement," the speaker is again a collective voice, the voice of the perpetrators of the Holocaust. The agreement promises that "Every-

thing will be returned to its place,/ paragraph after paragraph," echoing the bureaucratic language in which the whole Nazi endeavor was carried out. In a kind of mordant displacement the draft writer promises "The scream back into the throat./ The gold teeth back to the gums." Also,

> . . . you will be covered with skin and sinews and you
>   will live,
> look, you will have your lives back,
> . . . .
> Here you are. Nothing is too late.

The exquisite irony exposes the absurdity of reparations as well as the lunacy of the speaker.

POINTS OF DEPARTURE

In this 1981 collection, Pagis's voice runs the gamut from horrifying to deceptively whimsical. In "End of the Questionnaire" he creates a questionnaire to be filled out posthumously, with questions including "number of galaxy and star,/ number of grave." "You have the right to appeal," the questionnaire informs the deceased. It ends with the command, "In the blank space below, state/ how long you have been awake and why you are surprised." Ironically, this poem provokes the reader to meditate on the great finality of death.

"The Beginning" is a poem about "the end of creation." Pagis envisions the end as "A time of war," when "distant fleets of steel are waiting." The shadow of the Holocaust hovers over all, as "High above the smoke and the odor of fat and skins hovers/ a yellow magnetic stain." The poet seems to be saying that the Holocaust is the beginning of the end, when "at the zero-hour/ the Great Bear, blazing, strides forth/ in heat."

In a charming cycle in which five poems are grouped under the heading "Bestiary," each poem is rich with humor and whimsy. In the first, "The Elephant," we find the pachyderm who ties on sixteen "marvelously accurate wristwatches" and "glides forth smoothly/ out of his elephant fate." Armchairs also become animals in this bestiary: "The slowest animals/ are the soft large-eared leather armchairs" that "multiply/ in the shade of potted philodendrons." Balloons also are animate, as they "fondle one another" and cluster at the ceiling, humbly accepting their limit. Yet what is playful suddenly becomes ominous, as

> The soul suddenly leaks out
> in a terrified whistle
> or explodes
> with a single pop.

The darkest poem in this group is the one titled "The Biped." Pagis points out that though he is related to other predatory animals, "he alone/ cooks animals, peppers them,/ he alone is clothed with animals," and he alone "protests/ against what is decreed." Yet what the poet finds strangest is that he "rides of his own free will/ on a motorcycle." "The Biped" becomes an existential comedy through this odd mixture of traits Pagis chooses to juxtapose, including the last three lines of the poem, which state "He has four limbs,/ two ears,/ a hundred hearts."

"BRAIN"

The highly intellectual poetry of Dan Pagis treats each subject in a style which seems most appropriate. In the poem "Brain," Pagis uses several different styles to illustrate the tortured life of this brain in exile, or, what the reader might imagine, Pagis himself. Typical of his later poetry, "Brain" is concerned with the ambivalence of the poet's experience of the world and employs images from the laboratory, popular culture, the Hebrew Bible, and medicine. The poem begins with a reference to religious life, although the "dark night of the soul" here becomes ironically "the dark night of the skull," during which "Brain" discovers "he" is born. In part 2, in a biblical reference, "Brain hovers upon the face of the deep," yet he is not a deity; when his eyes develop he discovers the world complete.

Brain first suspects that he is the whole universe, as an infant is aware only of itself, but then suspects he embodies millions of other brains, all "splitting off from him, betraying him from within." In a sudden shift of tone in part 4, Pagis gives us an image of Brain, looking exactly as one would picture him: "grayish-white convolutions,/ a bit oily, sliding back and forth." Brain sets out to explore the world and makes a friend, with whom he communicates over radio sets in the attic. He questions the friend to find out if they are alike, and when they become intimate Brain asks, "Tell me, do you know how to forget?"

When his life is half over, he finds his "bush of veins" enveloping him, snaring him, and in a fit of exis-

tential despair, Brain wonders why he ever spoke, to whom he spoke, and if there is anyone to listen to him. Part 9 is an encyclopedic entry describing the brain, and Brain is embarrassed by so much praise; he commands "Let there be darkness!" and closes the encyclopedia. Brain metamorphoses throughout the poem and starts to think about outer space.

Toward the end of this remarkable poem, Brain is receiving signals from light years away and makes contact with another world, which may be a heart. The discovery is cloaked in the language of science fiction; Brain is both a microcosm and a macrocosm, and he is astounded to find that

> There is a hidden circle somewhere
> whose center is everywhere
> and whose circumference is nowhere;
> . . . so near
> that he will never
> be able
> to see it.

With his new knowledge, his old sarcasm and jokes desert him, along with his fear. Finally, he achieves what he desires; "he no longer has to remember."

"INSTRUCTIONS FOR CROSSING THE BORDER"

The second line of this poem, "You are not allowed to remember," is typical of the preoccupation with memory that haunts this poet. The advice is positive, almost upbeat: "you are a man, you sit in the train./ Sit comfortably./ You've got a decent coat now." This is sinister advice, considering that the last line is a direct contradiction of the second: "Go. You are not allowed to forget." The voice is that of an official speaking, addressing "Imaginary man." It is a dehumanized voice, one that cannot recognize the man to whom it is speaking; the addressee is only present in the speaker's imagination. Although it is an early poem, using the stripped and spare vocabulary of his early work, "Instructions for Crossing the Border" forecasts the later "Brain" in its preoccupation with obliterating memory.

"HARVESTS"

This is another of Pagis's poems that starts with a deceptively benign image, that of "The prudent fieldmouse" who "hoards and hoards for the time of battle and siege." Other benign images follow until an ironic twist in the sixth line, "the fire revels in the wheat," hints at what is ahead. What waits, of course, is the hawk, against whom the mouse's prudence and marvelously tunneled home is no protection at all. To darken the image further, the hawk is both "sharp-eyed" and "punctual," implying that the time of the mouse's demise is determined and no matter how canny he is, the hawk will appear at the appointed time. "Harvests" is a small parable in which Pagis, typically, uses animals to make a statement about the human condition, similar to his whimsical poem "Experiment of the Maze."

OTHER MAJOR WORKS

NONFICTION: *The Poetry of David Vogel*, 1966, fourth edition, 1975; *The Poetry of Levi Ibn Altabban of Saragossa*, 1968; *Secular Poetry and Poetic Theory: Moses Ibn Ezra and His Contemporaries*, 1970; *Hindush u-mascoret be-shirat-ha-hol ha-'Ivrit, Sefarad ve-Italyah*, 1976.

CHILDREN'S LITERATURE: *ha-Beitzah she-hithapsah*, 1973.

BIBLIOGRAPHY

Alter, Robert. "Dan Pagis and the Poetry of Displacement." *Judaism* 45, no. 80 (Fall, 1996). This article places the poet among his peers, primarily Yehuda Amichai and Natan Zach, illuminating Pagis's similarities and differences.

Burnshaw, Stanley, T. Carmi, and Ezra Spicehandler, eds. *The Modern Hebrew Poem Itself*. New York: Holt, Rinehart and Winston, 1989. This book offers a stunning explication of Pagis's poem "The Log Book," as well as an "Afterword: Hebrew Poetry from 1965-1988," which provides an in-depth discussion of the literary world Pagis inhabited. It places Pagis securely in the poetic movement of his generation. Each poem is presented in the original Hebrew, in phonetic transcription, and in English translation.

Ezrahi, Sidra DeKoven. "Shattering Memories." *New Republic* 71, no.8 (February 25, 1991): 36. In this review of *Variable Directions*, Ezrahi compares Pagis with Paul Celan, whose work acquired canonical status in postwar Germany. Pagis's poetry never enjoyed the popularity that Celan's did, because Pagis's work decomposes cultural assumptions and public rhetoric.

Schwartz, Howard, and Anthony Rudolf. *Voices Within the Ark: The Modern Jewish Poets*. New York: Avon, 1980. This is a comprehensive anthology featuring poets in English translation from over thirty different languages, with an excellent introduction to the Hebrew section by Laya Firestone. Pagis's contemporaries are well represented also.

Sheila Golburgh Johnson

DOROTHY PARKER

Dorothy Rothschild
Born: West End, New Jersey; August 22, 1893
Died: New York, New York; June 7, 1967

PRINCIPAL POETRY

Enough Rope, 1926
Sunset Gun, 1928
Death and Taxes, 1931
Not So Deep as a Well, 1936

OTHER LITERARY FORMS

In addition to Dorothy Parker's verse—not serious "poetry," she claimed—her principal writings, identified by Alexander Woollcott as "a potent distillation of nectar and wormwood," are several collections of well-crafted short stories: *Laments for the Living* (1930), *After Such Pleasures* (1933), and *Here Lies: The Collected Stories* (1939). These stories focus on the superficial, pointless, barren lives of middle- and upper-class Manhattanite women of the flapper and early Depression times, unhappily dependent on men for their economic support and emotional sustenance. Parker also wrote witty drama reviews for *Vanity Fair* (1918-1920), *Ainslee's* (1920-1933), and *The New Yorker* (1931); and terse, tart book reviews for the *The New Yorker* (1927-1933) and *Esquire* (1959-1962). "Tonstant Weader Fwowed Up," her provoked, personal reaction to A. A. Milne's *The House at Pooh Corner* (1928), typifies her "delicate claws of. . . superb viciousness" (Woollcott). Parker's major plays are *The Coast of Illyria* (1949, with Ross Evans), about Charles and Mary Lamb's tortured lives, and *The Ladies of the Corridor* (1953, with Arnaud d'Usseau), three case histories of death-in-life among elderly women.

ACHIEVEMENTS

Dorothy Parker's poems, stories, and reviews, wise-cracking and wary, were the toast of New York in the 1920's and early 1930's. She presented a brittle, world-weary, cynically urban view of life appealing to pseudo-sophisticates—who, indeed, were the subjects of many of her writings. Her literary coterie, the verbally glib, self-promoting journalists of the Algonquin Round Table, were minor writers in relation to their major contemporaries, such as Ernest Hemingway, William Faulkner, and Eugene O'Neill, and later estimates see her work as flashy but not penetrating. Yet, although many of her characters seem superficial, her women being "self-absorbed snobs, her men philanderers, scoundrels, or subservient husbands" (Arthur F. Kinney, *Dorothy Parker*, 1978), Parker's stories have remained perennially popular. Critics have noted that the repeated themes of Parker's poetry and prose are ever contemporary: anxieties, social hypocrisy, waning or unequal love between the sexes, failures of human sympathy and communication.

A few poems and various *bons mots* continue to be anthologized ("Men seldom make passes/ At girls who wear glasses"), though since the advent of World War II, Parker's poetry, itself highly derivative, has had little or no influence on subsequent writers of verse, light or otherwise. Today, as the poetry of the contemporaries with whom she was most often compared, Elinor Wylie and Edna St. Vincent Millay, is being treated with renewed critical respect, Parker's reputation continues to languish. To call her, as Kinney does, "the most accomplished classical epigrammatist of her time" is praise of very limited scope. Some feminists perceive Parker as a kindred spirit in her concern for the chronic, debilitating, and also demeaning dependence of women upon their husbands or lovers.

BIOGRAPHY

Dorothy Rothschild Parker Campbell was the daughter of a prosperous Jewish clothier, Henry Rothschild (no relation to the banking family), and the Protestant

Eliza Marston, who died shortly after childbirth. Her childhood loneliness was exacerbated by her mixed religious ancestry and the fact that her hated stepmother sent her for some years to the Blessed Sacrament Convent school in West End, New Jersey. She later said she wanted to write her autobiography if only for the sake of calling it *Mongrel*, an epitomization of her self-image as "a mongrel that wanted to be a thoroughbred."

After a year (1911) at the fashionable Miss Dana's School in Morristown, New Jersey, Parker gradually developed as a writer. Her first job was to write fashion blurbs and drama criticism for *Vanity Fair* (1916-1920). She later wrote short stories for *The New Yorker*, irregularly from 1926 to 1955; Hollywood film scripts at intervals, 1934 to 1954; and *Esquire* book reviews, 1959 to 1962.

Through her associates at *Vanity Fair*, Parker, whose wisecracking wit and cynical demeanor epitomized for many the insouciant flapper spirit of the 1920's, became a charter member of the *bons vivants* of the Round Table at the Algonquin Hotel. Other founders include Robert

Dorothy Parker (Library of Congress)

Benchley, Robert Sherwood, Alexander Woollcott, Franklin P. Adams, and Harold Ross, who later established *The New Yorker*. Over daily lunches they exercised through endless wordplay the careful concern for precise and vivid (and, some would say, smart-alecky) language that characterized their writing. Parker's reputation for finesse as a punster caused more outrageous witticisms to be attributed to her than she deserved, though this quintessential response to Franklin P. Adams command to use "horticulture" in a sentence is authentic: "You can lead a horticulture but you can't make her think." At the Algonquin, Parker met many theater people and lesser literati to whom later critics attribute her downfall. Because the literary shallowness of her admirers led them to exaggerate her early reputation, and because Parker believed them, she failed to fulfill her early promise of developing into a serious writer of enduring distinction. From them she learned to value terse expression, and to engage in satiric repartee that culminated in the typical sardonic punch lines of her verse after 1920. From them, especially, she came fervently to believe in the importance of not being earnest.

Beneath the surface gaiety lay an unstable personal life reflected in Parker's continual heavy drinking. Her marriage to Edwin Pond Parker (1917 to 1928) was succeeded by two marriages to the bisexual actor-writer Alan Campbell. They were married from 1934 until 1947 and from 1950 until 1963, when Campbell died of an overdose of sleeping pills, just as Edwin Parker had done. Campbell, Lillian Hellman, and others nurtured Parker, but they could not control her drinking and her worsening writer's block that kept her from finishing many of her literary attempts during the last fifteen years. Her sad and bitter old age ("People ought to be one of two things, young or dead") was ended by a heart attack in her decrepit hotel room where she was found dead on June 7, 1967. Her acerbic self-assessment echoes the contemporary judgment of Parker as "a woman who outlived her time."

ANALYSIS

Dorothy Parker's slight reputation as a poet rests on three slender volumes of verse with funereal titles: *Enough Rope*, *Sunset Gun*, and *Death and Taxes*—collected in 1936 with five additional poems in *Not So Deep as a*

Well. Although her poems on the whole are highly restricted in scope and depth, her poetic techniques became somewhat more sophisticated and more effectively controlled during the decade when these books were published.

The major motifs of Parker's poems are love, loneliness, and death. Loneliness and death, however, are usually variations on the theme of romantic love—exploited or exploitative, betrayed, feigned, unrequited, abandoned, lost. Parker finds the relations between men and women disagreeable and duplicitous: "Scratch a lover and find a foe." In Parker's limited poetic world, women as epitomized by the narrative persona are doomed to perpetual emotional dependence on men, whose indifference, fickleness, and callousness drives them to the despair implied in the books' macabre titles. Love relationships, so fleeting and superficial, are based on appearance ("A curly mouth . . . long, tapered limbs") and "dust-bound trivia" ("The Searched Soul") that foreordain their failure. Lovers kiss—and invariably tell ("A Certain Lady"). If they swear that their passion is "infinite, undying," one or both are bound to be lying ("Unfortunate Coincidence"). Dalliance, not marriage, is the aim of the men, and sometimes of the women, for lovers are numerous, faceless, and somewhat interchangeable: "I always get them all mixed up" ("Pictures in the Smoke").

The narrative female persona from whose perspective nearly all the poems are presented plays one of two characteristic roles. In one role the rejected lover, dominated by her own grief and a sense of unworthiness, tries to cope with her own devastation. This penitent suppliant sometimes seeks a new love, wanting to give away her heart, "the wretched thing," "now to that lad, now to this." Otherwise, she dies, literally or figuratively. On occasion she lies "cool and quiet," finding the grave a tranquil antidote to the fever of unrequited love ("Testament"). At other times she returns as a ghost to haunt her lover "In April twilight's unsung melody" ("I Shall Come Back").

PARKER'S WITTY PERSONA

The other role, however, is the image most commonly associated with Dorothy Parker, the wisecracking wit of the Algonquin Round Table. This narrative persona, worldly-wise and weary, knows that it is always "just my luck to get One perfect rose" instead of "one perfect limousine." She knows, too, as a lover, "my strength and my weakness, gents" is to love only until her passion is reciprocated ("Ballade at Thirty-Five"). She realizes that, as a latent romantic, she is bound to be "spectacularly bored" with a constant lover ("On Being a Woman"), and to prefer inappropriately one who is "sudden and swift and strong" to a wealthy wooer—"Somebody ought to examine my head!" To cope, she undermines her sentiment with cynical punch lines, either one-liners or couplets: "I shudder at the thought of men . . . I'm due to fall in love again" ("Symptom Recital"). She relishes the calculated insult ("I turn to little words—so you, my dear/ Can spell them out") as much as the imagined injury: If she had a "shiny gun" she could have "a world of fun" shooting her antagonists ("Frustration").

These contrasting personae alternate poems in Parker's collections and the intermittent presence of the cynic undermines the credibility of the rejected lover. Once conditioned, readers expect a witty riposte or a slangy word ("Here's my strength and my weakness, gents") to shift the poem from seriousness to satire, as indeed it often does. Though anticipated, the slang startles, as in "Coda" ("For art is a form of catharsis/ And love is a permanent flop") and provokes laughter in hitherto serious contexts. Even if the author meant some of her poems to be taken seriously, as individually they might be (see "Transition"), the cynical persona and her attendant language establish the prevailing comic tone for Parker's collected verse. Thus Parker's poetic techniques reinforce the impression that her verse is primarily an exercise in verbal ingenuity rather than a presentation of authentic emotion or experience.

LIGHT LYRICS

Composed mostly of simple iambic quatrains or couplets, Parker's lyric poetry lacks the formal complexity, structural finesse and variations, and metaphorical ingenuity that add interest to much other poetry on the same themes, such as the love poetry of John Donne, William Shakespeare, John Keats, or Emily Dickinson. Kinney has favorably compared Parker's techniques and control of meter and line to Horace, Martial, Catullus, Heinrich Heine, and her contemporaries Elinor Wylie and Edna St. Vincent Millay. Although Parker may have read the classical authors, it seems likely that she learned their

techniques from the verse of her companion of the Algonquin Round Table, Adams, whose "Conning Tower" column in the *New York World* sported such whimsies as "Give me the balmy breezes! . . ./ Wind on my cheek and hair!/ And, while we're on the topic,/ Give me the air." Adams and Parker share control, compression, precise diction, and a fondness for puns—perhaps all that one can or should ask of light verse.

The difficulty is that the techniques and diction which make Parker's light verse comical and airy simply seem banal when applied to poetry that purports to be of greater seriousness. The imagery is predictable—stormy seas, softly dropping rain, withering flowers to denote an absent or lost lover; the rejected maiden "a-crying," or sleeping chastely, or mourning "whenever one drifted petal leaves the tree" for the dream that "lies dead here." Moreover, the language in some of the more serious poetry is too often self-consciously anachronistic: "what shallow boons suffice my heart" or uncomfortably poetic—"e're," "lay a-drying," "Little will I think. . . ."

One could apply to Parker's poetry the judgment that she herself applied to the performance of a famous actress, who ran "the gamut of emotions from A to B." Within that restricted compass, her comic verse succeeds where her more serious poetry fails.

OTHER MAJOR WORKS

SHORT FICTION: *Laments for the Living*, 1930; *After Such Pleasures*, 1933; *Here Lies: The Collected Stories*, 1939; *The Portable Dorothy Parker*, 1944; *The Penguin Dorothy Parker*, 1977.

PLAYS: *Nero*, pr. 1922 (with Robert Benchley); *Close Harmony*, pr. 1924 (with Elmer Rice); *The Coast of Illyria*, 1949 (with Ross Evans); *The Ladies of the Corridor*, pr., pb. 1953 (with Arnaud d'Usseau).

SCREENPLAYS: *Business Is Business*, 1925 (with George S. Kaufman); *Here Is My Heart*, 1934 (with Alan Campbell); *One Hour Late*, 1935 (with Campbell); *Mary Burns, Fugitive*, 1935; *Hands Across the Table*, 1935; *Paris in Spring*, 1935; *Big Broadcast of 1936*, 1935 (with Campbell); *Three Married Men*, 1936 (with Campbell); *Lady Be Careful*, 1936 (with Campbell and Harry Ruskin); *The Moon's Our Home*, 1936; *Suzy*, 1936 (with Campbell, Horace Jackson, and Lenore Coffee); *A Star Is Born*, 1937 (with Campbell and Robert Carson); *Woman Chases Man*, 1937 (with Joe Bigelow); *Sweethearts*, 1938 (with Campbell); *Crime Takes a Holiday*, 1938; *Trade Winds*, 1938 (with Campbell and Frank R. Adams); *Flight into Nowhere*, 1938; *Five Little Peppers and How They Grew*, 1939; *Weekend for Three*, 1941 (with Campbell); *The Little Foxes*, 1941; *Saboteur*, 1942 (with Campbell, Peter Viertel, and Joan Harrison); *A Gentle Gangster*, 1943; *Mr. Skeffington*, 1944; *Smash-Up: The Story of a Woman*, 1947 (with Frank Cavett); *The Fan*, 1949 (with Walter Reisch and Ross Evans); *Queen for a Day*, 1951; *A Star Is Born*, 1954.

BIBLIOGRAPHY

Cooper, Wyatt. "Remembering Dorothy Parker." *Esquire* 70 (July, 1968): 56-57, 61, 110-114. A rich and reliable portrait of Dorothy Parker in her last years that offers insight into her life and work and assesses her place in American literature.

Keats, John. *You Might as Well Live: The Life and Times of Dorothy Parker*. New York: Simon & Schuster, 1970. This standard, popular biography, thin in places, is based on extensive research. Some facts and interpretations have been amended or superseded. The literary judgments tend to be sparse and overwhelmingly adulatory. Contains a bibliography.

Kinney, Arthur F. *Dorothy Parker*. Rev. ed. Boston: Twayne, 1998. In this excellent study of Parker's life and work, Kinney incorporates facts recorded for the first time and provides the first full critical assessment of her writing. The author traces the sources of Parker's writing and assesses her final achievement in order to locate what he views as her significant and unique contribution to American literature. Kinney calls Parker the best epigrammatic American poet of her century. Contains a bibliography and extensive notes and references.

Labrie, Ross. "Dorothy Parker Revisited." *Canadian Review of American Studies* 7 (Spring, 1976): 48-56. Labrie discusses Parker as a product of the 1920's, with her mixture of wit and skepticism, her uneven taste, and her concern with the American myths of glamour and success. According to Labrie, Parker's writing is drawn toward vividness and candor but also toward an austerity of form.

MacDermott, Kathy. "Light Human and the Dark Underside of Wish Fulfillment: Conservative Anti-Realism." *Studies in Popular Culture* 10 (Spring, 1987): 37-53. In one of the few and excellent critical studies of Parker's work, MacDermott compares Parker's realism to that of Robert Charles Benchley, S. J. Perelman, and P. G. Wodehouse. Delves beneath the surface of Parker's work to reveal its essentially complex nature.

Melzer, Sondra. *The Rhetoric of Rage: Women in Dorothy Parker*. New York: Peter Lang, 1997. An exploration of the treatment of women from a contemporary feminist perspective that reveals Parker's use of humor to voice anger toward a patriarchal society. Melzer finds the parallels between the author's life and fiction and demonstrates how Parker lived her life in fiction and her fiction in life.

Pettit, Rhonda S. *A Gendered Collision: Sentimentalism and Modernism in Dorothy Parker's Poetry and Fiction*. Rutherford, N.J.: Fairleigh Dickinson University Press, 2000. Reappraises Parker's work from a feminist perspective, seeing it as a collision between nineteenth century decadence and twentieth century modernism.

*Lynn Z. Bloom;
bibliography updated by the editors*

NICANOR PARRA

Born: Chillán, Chile; September 5, 1914

PRINCIPAL POETRY

Cancionero sin nombre, 1937
Poemas y antipoemas, 1954 (*Poems and Antipoems*, 1967)
La cueca larga, 1958
Versos de salón, 1962
Canciones rusas, 1967
Obra gruesa, 1969
Los profesores, 1971
Emergency Poems, 1972
Artefactos, 1972

Antipoems: New and Selected, 1985
Nicanor Parra: Biografía emotiva, 1988
Poemas para combatir la calvicie: Muestra de antipoesia, 1993

OTHER LITERARY FORMS

Nicanor Parra and Pablo Neruda coauthored *Pablo Neruda y Nicanor Parra: Discursos* (1962; Pablo Neruda and Nicanor Parra: speeches), which celebrated the appointment of the latter as an honorary member of the faculty of the College of Philosophy and Education of the University of Chile. The volume includes the speech of presentation by Parra, in which he proffers his point of view regarding Neruda's work, and that of acceptance by Neruda. Parra has been active on an international scale in poetry readings, seminars, conferences, and informal gatherings. Many of his poems composed since the publication of *Cancionero sin nombre* (untitled songs) are available in English through the two bilingual volumes published by New Directions: *Poems and Antipoems* and *Emergency Poems*.

ACHIEVEMENTS

Nicanor Parra is the originator of the contemporary poetic movement in Latin America known as "antipoetry." The antipoet, as this Chilean calls himself, is the absolute antiromantic, debasing all, even himself, while producing verses that are aggressive, wounding, sarcastic, and irritating. He has plowed new terrain in Latin American poetry using a store of methods which traditional poetry rejects or ignores. Parra's work is attacked as boring, disturbing, crude, despairing, ignoble, inconclusive, petulant, and devoid of lyricism. The antipoet generally agrees with these points of criticism, but begs the reader to lay aside what amounts to a nostalgic defense of worn-out traditions and join him in a new experience. Parra has established himself firmly in a prominent position in Hispanic American literature, influencing both his defenders and detractors.

BIOGRAPHY

Nicanor Parra, one of eight children in a family plagued by economic insecurity, grew up in Chillán, in the south of Chile. His father was a schoolteacher whose irresponsibility and alcoholism placed considerable strain on the life and order of the family, which was held together by Parra's mother. Parra was in his early teens when his father died. The earlier antipathy he felt toward his father then turned toward his mother, and he left home. He began a process of identification with his father, toward whom he felt both attraction and repulsion, and to whom he attributes the basic elements of his inspiration for antipoetry.

During his youth, Parra composed occasional verses, so that when he went to the University of Chile in Santiago in 1933 he felt that he was a poet in addition to being a student of physics. He associated with the literary leaders at the student residence where he lived, and a year prior to being graduated in 1938, he had published his first volume of poetry, *Cancionero sin nombre*.

After completing studies in mathematics and physics at the Pedagogical Institute of the University, Parra taught for five years in secondary schools in Chile. Between 1943 and 1945, he studied advanced mechanics at Brown University in the United States. Returning home in 1948, he was named Director of the School of Engineering at the University of Chile. He spent two years in England studying cosmology at Oxford, and upon his return to South America he was appointed Professor of Theoretical Physics at the University of Chile.

The publication of Parra's second collection of poetry, *Poems and Antipoems*, formally introduced the antipoetry with which his name is associated. This new poetry shook the foundation of the theory of the genre in Latin America, winning for its author both condemnation and praise. In 1963, Parra visited the Soviet Union, where he supervised the translation into Spanish of an anthology of Soviet poets, and then traveled to the People's Republic of China. He visited Cuba in 1965 and the following year served as a visiting professor at Louisiana State University, later holding similar positions at New York University, Columbia, and Yale.

ANALYSIS

Nicanor Parra avoids the appearance of didacticism, claiming that he is not a preacher, that he is suspicious of doctrines, yet his purpose is to goad the reader with his corrosive verses, caustic irony, and black humor until the poet's response to human existence is shared. Satiric rather than political, antipoetry's sad, essentially moral-

Nicanor Parra (Andres Sanchez, courtesy of New Directions)

izing, verse of hopelessness contains a strange and infinite tenderness toward man in his fallen condition. Neither philosophical nor theoretical poetry, it is intended to be an experience which will elicit a reaction and simulate life itself.

In spite of the fact that he is a mathematician and a physicist, Parra does not consider life to be governed by a logical system of absolutes which, when harnessed, can direct man toward organization and progress. On the contrary, he believes that the poet's life is absurd and chaotic, and the world is in the process of destruction and decay. Man either accepts this fact, together with his own impotence, or he deceives himself by inventing philosophical theories, moral standards, and political ideologies to which he clings. Parra views his own role as that of obliging humanity to see the falsity of any system which deceives him into believing in these masks that hide the grotesque collective condition in a chaotic universe. Parra makes fun of love, marriage, religion, psychology, political revolutions, art, and other institutions of society. They are rejected as futile dogmas which attempt to ennoble or exalt man above the reality

of his insignificance. Poetry too comes under attack by this anarchist who claims he has orders to liquidate the genre. As the antipoet, he resists defining his own poetic structure, knowing that in such an event it too must be destroyed. Thus, he searches continually for new paths, his own evolution, a revolution.

The prefix notwithstanding, antipoetry, however unconventional, is poetry, and Parra himself willingly explains his concept of the form. It is, he says, traditional poetry enriched by Surrealism. As the word implies, the "antipoem" belongs to that tradition which rejects the established poetic order. In this case, it rebels against the sentimental idealism of Romanticism, the elegance and the superficiality of the *Modernistas*, and the irrationality of the vanguard movement. It is not a poetry of heroes, but of antiheroes, because man has nothing to sing to or celebrate. Everything is a problem, including the language.

Parra eschews what he considers the abuse of earlier poetic language in favor of a direct, prosaic communication using the familiar speech of everyday life. He desires to free poetry from the domination of figures and tropes destined to accommodate a select group of readers who want to enjoy an experience in poetry that is not possible in life itself. He has declared his intent to write poems which are experiences. He is hostile to metaphors, word games, or any evasive power in language which helps to transpose reality. Parra's task is to speak to everyone and be understood by all. The antipoet recreates or reproduces slang, jargon, clichés, colloquialisms, words of the street and gutter, television commercials, and graffiti. He does not create poetry; he selects and complies it. The genius of the language is sought in the culture of each country as reflected in the language of life. It is poetry not for literature's sake, but for man's sake. Its sentiments are the frustrations and hysteria of modern existence, not the anguish and nostalgia of Romanticism. Inasmuch as poetry is life, Parra also utilizes local or national peculiarities in language to underscore a specific social reality.

The destruction of the traditional poetic language is the first step in stimulating the reader to be torn from the sacred myths that soothe him. Parra avoids so-called poetic words or uses them in unfamiliar contexts (the moon, for example, is poison). His images astonish the reader with their irreverence, lack of modesty, grotesqueness, and ambiguity. They inherit the oneiric and unusual qualities of the Surrealists. Placed in the context of daily life, they equate the sublime with the ridiculous, the serious with the trivial, the poetic with the prosaic. Comic clichés and flat language are used by the protagonists in the antipoems to express their hurt and despair. The irony thus created by these simultaneous prosaic and tragic elements charges the work with humor and pathos. The reader laughs, though the protagonist, or antihero, suffers. The antihero's ineptitudes, failures, and foolishness are viewed with pity, scorn, and amusement. Parra's placement of familiar language and everyday failures in the life of the antihero, however, catches up with the reader and compounds the irony, reducing the initial distance between reader and protagonist. The reader becomes uncomfortable as this distance closes, his laughter not far from sadness.

The antihero in Parra's poetry is a rebel, disillusioned with all aspects of life, who suffers and is alone. He is a wanderer, distrustful and doubting, obsessed with suicide and death. Too insignificant, too ridiculous and nihilistic to be a tragic hero, he is merely the caricature of a hero. In need of communication, he undermines himself at every turn, belittling all of his efforts at self-expression. The grotesque inhabitants of the antipoetic world, comedians in an absurd play, unfulfilled in love and in their potentialities, suffer the passage of time, the agonizing problems of aging, and the inevitable confrontation with death. They are incapable of heroic gestures in any realm because their environment, habits, and nature make them ridiculous. The antipoet holds nothing sacred. The serious, the traumatic, is presented in a casual and burlesque fashion. Life is absurd and death is trivial.

The antihero's self-destruction and demoralization are simply mirrors of the malaise of contemporary society. Antipoetry views the world as a sewer in which man, reduced to the level of vermin, lives and multiplies. Any effort to alter the situation is destined to failure. Man nurtures his own importance and worth, a self-centered creature obsessed with the need to possess and to consume. Love is false, friendship insincere, and social justice neither exists nor is desired; the environment becomes more and more artificial at the expense of na-

ture and beauty. Political revolutions are deceits which benefit the new leaders but alter nothing. Love is viewed as an egotistical pursuit to fulfill sexual desire; spiritual bonds are denied. Although a few of Parra's poems present women as fragile, innocent beings who are invariably abused by man, the majority of the antipoet's female characters are aggressive rivals who threaten and humiliate him. Yet man, who fears woman, desires and seeks her as a sexual object. Finally, Parra mocks a corrupt Church, greedy, lascivious priests, a hypocritical pope, and an omni-impotent God.

CANCIONERO SIN NOMBRE

Parra's first collection of poems, *Cancionero sin nombre*, was inspired by the gypsy ballads of Federico García Lorca. The poems are stylized versions of traditional Spanish folkloric ballads, but in Parra's volume the action remains a dreamlike illusion without taking form. This volume had more attackers than defenders, and although some of the elements of his later work are evident, Parra himself calls this work a sin of his youth, better forgotten.

Parra attributes the roots of antipoetry to an independent response to human circumstances, not to any traditions in literature. Nevertheless, he recognizes those writers who have influenced his own literary development. After the publication of his first collection, Parra became enthusiastic about the poetry of Walt Whitman. He delighted in the metric freedom, the relaxed, loose, unconventional language, the narratives and descriptions, and the passionate vehemence which characterized Whitman's verse. When Parra returned to Chile from the United States in 1946, he came to know and appreciate the works of Franz Kafka. Kafka showed Parra the alienation and neurosis of modern culture, the comic deformation, the ironic treatment of the absurd in the human condition, the peculiar importance of atmosphere, the distortions and deformations which entrap the helpless protagonist. Parra was much more comfortable with Kafka's struggling protagonists than with Whitman's heroic vision of man. The Chilean's developing poetic style, new to the Spanish-speaking world, was antiromantic, antirhetorical, antiheroic, and antipoetic. His two-year stay in England beginning in 1949 crystallized this style into that of the antipoet. He was moved by the poetry of John Donne, W. H. Auden,

C. Day Lewis, Stephen Spender, and especially T. S. Eliot. Parra appreciated Eliot's radical transformation of poetic diction and his inclusion of prosaic and colloquial language in his poems. These English-language poets inspired Parra in their observation of contemporary man, his environment, politics, manners, and religion, and in the didactic opportunities they exploited in treating these themes.

LA CUECA LARGA AND VERSOS DE SALÓN

Parra's third collection, *La cueca larga* (the *cueca* is a native dance of Chile), exalts wine; written in the popular tradition of marginal literature, the book is anti-intellectual, vulgar, a frivolous contribution to Chilean folklore, akin to antipoetry in preference for the masses and its position on the periphery of established literature.

In *Versos de salón* (salon verses), Parra returned to the antipoetic technique, but with some significant differences. The ironic attack on the establishments of society remains (the collection should be titled "Antisalon Verses"), but these poems are shorter than the earlier ones. They are fragments whose images follow one another in rapid fashion and mirror the absurd chaos of the world. The reader, forced to experience this confusion at first hand, is left restless, searching for a meaning that is not to be found. The chaotic enumeration of the Surrealists, a favorite technique with Parra, abounds, while the anecdotal poetry of *Poems and Antipoems*, with its emphasis on dialogue, all but disappears. The sense of alienation is sharper, the bitterness and disillusion more deeply felt, the humor more pointed. The antihero changes from a victim into an odd creature who flings himself at the world in open confrontation. His introverted suffering is now a metaphysical despair.

CANCIONES RUSAS

Canciones rusas (Russian songs) was a product of the antipoet's visit to the Soviet Union. These poems are gentle, serene, lyrical, serious, a bit optimistic. The caustic spirit of the antipoet is not entirely absent, and the poet is not enthusiastic, but there is an expression of hope. The Soviet experience, not a political doctrine but a hope for underdeveloped nations symbolized by the progress of a people, is responsible for the change in tone. This is visual poetry, simple, stripped of images. The title notwithstanding, however, there is no music in these verses.

ADDRESSING SOCIAL ILLNESSES

In *Obra gruesa* (basic work), Parra returned once again to antipoetry. The Soviet Union is no longer an ideal, and hope for humankind is extinguished. This volume includes all the poetry Parra had published to 1969, with the exception of his first collection. *Los profesores* is a parody of the world of education, in which overly serious teachers fill the minds of their students with worthless information unrelated to human needs. Parra overwhelms the reader with lists of stifling questions, and the pedagogical idiom of the teachers contrasts with the picturesque colloquialisms of the students. *Emergency Poems* is a reprinting of the verses which appeared in "Straight Jacket," a section of *Obra gruesa* as well as thirty-one new poems. These titles both refer to symptoms of a social illness that is becoming epidemic. A state of emergency is declared (hence the title) as inflation, pollution, and crime increase; wars exist in crisis proportion while man is controlled by the very monsters he has invented to protect himself from reality. Society has placed man in a straight jacket, and the antihero, an old man, is reduced to waiting for death; the sum of his life equals zero. Parra's cynicism allows for no program of hope; the symptoms are not accompanied by a proposed remedy. The author uses himself as an example of the critical state of things. These poems enjoy a greater coherence than the author's most recent verses. Anecdotes again begin to appear. Parra's poetry becomes more aggressive and more social, with the appearance of a host of frustrated, unhappy characters, including beggars, drug addicts, and revolutionaries.

ARTEFACTOS

In *Artefactos*, Parra moved to a new poetic form. The antipoem had become fashionable in Latin America, and with the imitators came the risk that Parra's creation might become a mere formula. *Artefactos*, not in truth a book but a box of postcards on which each "artifact" appears, along with a brief illustration, approximates antipoetry in purpose and spirit. If some of the lines of poetry from the author's more recent collections were isolated from the poem, they would become artifacts. Indeed, Parra defines them as the result of the explosion of the antipoem, which became so filled with pathos it had to burst. The brief and self-sufficient artifact reduces the antipoem to its essential element, its strength resulting from its brevity and freedom from poetic context. Thus, the once complex antipoem has evolved into the most basic of fragments while still retaining its essence.

OTHER MAJOR WORKS

NONFICTION: *Pablo Neruda y Nicanor Parra: Discursos*, 1962 (with Pablo Neruda); *Discursos de sobremesa*, 1997; *Pablo Neruda and Nicanor Parra Face to Face*, 1997.

BIBLIOGRAPHY

Carrasco, Iván. *Para leer a Nicanor Parra*. Santiago, Chile: Editorial Cuarto Propio, 1999. An insightful analysis of the perception of Parra's work as antipoetry. An expert on Parra's work analyzes the evolution of his poetry from its rejection of thematic and syntactic structures to the development of a unique yet mutable voice that responds to its social and political environment. In Spanish.

Kauffmann, Ruth A. *Scribes of Their Times: The Poetic Works of Nicanor Parra, Ernesto Cardenal, Rosario Castellanos, and Decio Pignatari*. Thesis, University of Chicago. Ann Arbor, Mich.: UMI Dissertation Services, 1994. Little has been published in English on Parra, and this study places him in poetic context. Illustrations, bibliographical references.

Neruda, Pablo. *Pablo Neruda and Nicanor Parra Face to Face*. Lewiston, N.Y.: Edwing Mellen Press, 1997. This is a bilingual and critical edition of speeches by both Neruda and Parra on the occasion of Neruda's appointment to the University of Chile's faculty, with English translations and a useful introduction by Marlene Gottlieb. Bibliographical references.

Parra, Nicanor. *Antipoems: New and Selected*. Edited by David Unger, translated by Frank MacShane. New York: New Directions, 1985. This bilingual anthology focuses on representative antipoems in an attempt to demonstrate how Parra's poetry has revolutionized poetic expression globally as well as within the sphere of Latin American poetry. Notes by the editor enhance understanding for English-speaking readers.

Parrilla Sotomayor, Eduardo E. *Humorismo y sátira en la poesía de Nicanor Parra*. Madrid: Editorial Pliegos, 1997. This study identifies and discusses the el-ements of humor and satire in Parra's antipoetry. It analyzes the poet's technique as well as unique anti-rhetorical style and language that creates a direct link to contemporary Latin American society. In Spanish.

Sarabia, Rosa. *Poetas de la palabra hablada: Un estudio de la poesía hispanoaméricana contemporánea*. London: Tamesis, 1997. This study analyzes the oral nature of the literary production of several representative contemporary Latin American writers with roots in oral literature. In her chapter titled "Nicanor Parra: La antipoesía y sus políticas," the author explores the origins and consequences of antipoetry in its political and social milieus in contemporary Latin America, especially the *Cono Sur*, Chile, and Argentina.

Alfred W. Jensen;
bibliography updated by Carole A. Champagne

GIOVANNI PASCOLI

Born: San Mauro di Romagna, Kingdom of Sardinia (now Italy); December 31, 1855
Died: Bologna, Italy; April 6, 1912

PRINCIPAL POETRY

Myricae, 1891
Poemetti, 1897
Canti di Castelvecchio, 1903
Poemi conviviali, 1904 (*Convivial Poems*, Part I, 1979, Part II, 1981)
Primi poemetti, 1904
Odi e inni, 1906
Canzoni di Re Enzio, 1908-1909
Nuovi poemetti, 1909
Poemi italici, 1911
Inno a Torino, 1911
Poesie, 1912
Poemi del Risorgimento, 1913
Traduzioni e riduzioni, 1913
Ioannis Pascoli carmina recognoscenda curavit Maria Soror, 1914
The Poems of Giovanni Pascoli, 1923

The Poems of Giovanni Pascoli, 1927
Selected Poems of Giovanni Pascoli, 1938
Poesie con un profilo del Pascoli e un saggio di Gian-
*   franco Contini*, 1968 (4 volumes)

OTHER LITERARY FORMS

Giovanni Pascoli dabbled in Dante criticism, and between 1898 and 1902 he wrote *Minerva oscura* (1898;
dark Minerva), *Sotto il velame* (1900; under the veil), and
La mirabile visione (1902; the marvelous vision). His
assertion that *La divina commedia* (c. 1320; *The Divine
Comedy*) "is not a strong and living poetic organism, a
harmonious whole . . . but a great ocean, in which the
poetic moments are the pearls" was not well received,
although he did influence the views of the scholar Luigi
Pietrobono. Pascoli's critical essays are more revealing
of Pascoli himself than they are of the works that he attempts to interpret. In defense of Italian colonial activity
in Africa, Pascoli wrote the essay "La grande proletaria
s'e mossa" (the great proletariat has moved) in 1911.

In his famous essay "Il fanciullino" (the little boy),
written in 1897, Pascoli explains his theory of poetry,
derived from the story of the child who led the blind
poet Homer by the hand. A true poet, says Pascoli, listens to the child within him, to what the child sees and
perceives. The blind man's *fanciullino* strives not to become famous but only to be understood. In his endeavor
to present as many objects as a child sees in a world that
is always new and beautiful, Pascoli found fault with literary Italian, cramped by classical tradition and condemned to an extremely restricting "poetic" vocabulary,
and he invented words and borrowed many others from
the nonliterary dialects of Italy. Pascoli's devotion to the
child's perception ruled out much of what is generally
thought of as poetry (love poetry, for example, and meditative poetry), and was so limiting that criticism came
swiftly, from Benedetto Croce among others. Croce,
who emphasized ideas over the mere words that describe them, found Pascoli's valorization of childhood
particularly offensive and attacked Pascoli's poetry for
its sentimentality, affectation, and childish emotionalism, claiming that it seemed "to oscillate perpetually between a masterpiece and a mess."

Pascoli was active as a translator. He translated folk
and heroic ballads (Breton, Greek, Illyrian) from the anthologies of Vicomte Hersart de la Villemarqué, Franz
Passow, and Niccolò Tommaseo; sections of Homer's *Iliad* and the *Odyssey* (both c. 800 B.C.E.); and a wide
range of classical works. He rendered into Italian some
of the Latin poetry of Pope Leo XIII and several poems
by Victor Hugo, Eduard Bauernfeld, Friedrich Schiller,
and José Antonio Calcaño. In addition, Pascoli translated Percy Bysshe Shelley's "Time Long Past," Alfred,
Lord Tennyson's "Ulysses," and William Wordworth's
"We Are Seven," the latter a poem of special significance to Pascoli because of his own childhood experience with the death of family members.

ACHIEVEMENTS

As one of the nineteenth century triad (Giosuè Carducci, Gabriele D'Annunzio, and Giovanni Pascoli) of
Italian literary greats, in company with the other two tri-
ads of Italian literature (Dante, Petrarch, and Giovanni
Boccaccio; Alessandro Manzoni, Ugo Foscolo, and Giacomo Leopardi), Pascoli is one of the sacred nine included in every survey of literature course offered to
Italian students.

While not as assertive or outspoken as Carducci
or D'Annunzio, Pascoli was ultimately more influential than either. Some modern critics are offended by
his sentimentality, but other aspects of his poetry in
one way or another anticipated almost all Italian poetry that was to follow: the work of Guido Gozzano,
Sergio Corazzini, Marino Moretti, and that group of
poets known as the *crepuscolari*; F. T. Marinetti and
the Futurists; the hermeticism of Eugenio Montale;
and the religious poetry of Carlo Betocchi and Paolo
De Benedetti. By translating his sense of the mystery of life into images and sounds, he anticipated the
neutral, grayish tones of consciousness elaborated by
the *crepuscolari*. His use of onomatopoeia, when successful, pointed the way to Marinetti's less successful "tumbtumb" and the like. Umberto Saba was influenced by Pascoli's use of humble subject matter, as
were such local color poets as the Sicilians Lucio Pic-
colo and Giuseppe Villaroel. The tone of his *Myricae*
(tamarisks) poems, when uncluttered by sentimental excesses, even points in the direction of Italian realism, the
school of literature that came to be dominant after World
War II.

Pascoli greatly enlarged the basic store of Italian poetic vocabulary. Even some of the dialectal words he introduced into his poems were used by subsequent poets, as, for example *cedrina* ("lemon verbena"; compare with the standard Italian *limoncina*), used by both Gozzano and Montale. Pascoli's interest in the common people has been described as nothing less than a poetic revolution which shifted the thematic and linguistic focus from the bourgeois to the petit bourgeois. This "lowering" of poetic language is evident in Pascoli's easy recourse to dialect and common words as yet unconsecrated by literary usage. Pier Paolo Pasolini, who wrote his graduate thesis on Pascoli, found in this practice a point of departure for his own theories concerning the "reduction of poetic language."

Pascoli died in 1912 and was mourned throughout the entire Italian peninsula. His death was part of the inspiration for the moving pages of D'Annunzio's "La Contemplazione della morte" (the contemplation of death), the first canto of a prose poem trilogy.

BIOGRAPHY

Giovanni Pascoli was born in 1855 in the village of San Mauro di Romagna (later renamed San Mauro Pascoli) in what was then the papal state of Romagna, the fourth of ten children born to Ruggero and Caterina Vincenzi Alloccatelli Pascoli. He was a sensitive child, and he thrived in an idyllic family situation until the age of twelve, when his father was murdered. Ruggero Pascoli, the bailiff of the La Torre estate of the princely Torlonia family, was driving his carriage home on August 10, 1867, when someone fired a shot from behind a hedge; his dapple-gray mare ("La cavalla storna" of Pascoli's poem of that title) brought him home a corpse. The unexplained and unpunished crime marked Pascoli for life. His first volume of verse, *Myricae*, was dedicated to his father and includes a poem that describes the incident, "X agosto" ("The Tenth of August"). He wrote, "Reader, there were men who opened that tomb. And in it a whole flourishing family came to an end." Later, in the preface to *Canti di Castelvecchio* (songs of Castelvecchio), he added, "Other men, who remain unpunished and unknown, willed the death of a man not only innocent, but virtuous, sublime in his loyalty and goodness, and the death of his family. And I refuse. I refuse to let them be dead."

In 1868, the oldest Pascoli child, Margherita, died of typhoid at sixteen, and within a month, Pascoli's mother followed. Three years later, Luigi, Pascoli's next older brother, died of meningitis, and shortly after that Pascoli's fiancé died of tuberculosis. Five years later, his oldest brother, Giacomo, died and then Giacomo's two small children. At the age of twenty-one, Pascoli became the head of a family consisting of his two younger brothers and two younger sisters, the latter still in a convent school. He possessed such a thorough familiarity with death that the worlds of life and death assumed for him a kind of parity, and he always numbered both the living and the dead when he counted the members of his family.

Despite the disintegration of his family, Pascoli was able to continue his studies with the brothers of the Scolopi Order at Urbino; later, he attended high school at Rimini and Florence. In 1873, he entered a competition for a scholarship to study at the University of Bologna, and the judges, among whom was Giosuè Carducci, who later acted as Pascoli's mentor, awarded him first place. In 1879, he participated in a Socialist demonstration and spent three months in jail. As a result, he lost his scholarship, but he was able to regain it later. He took his degree in Greek literature in 1882 and went to teach at a *lycée* in far-off Matera in southern Italy, transferred to Massa in northern Tuscany, and then spent eight years at Leghorn. In 1895, he was able to purchase a comfortable home in the Serchio Valley among the Tuscan mountains at Castelvecchio di Barga, and set up a household with his devoted sister, Maria. This was to be his home for life. Here he always returned to spend summers and whatever other free time he had; here he entertained such friends as composer Giacomo Puccini and author Gabriele D'Annunzio; and here he shared his life with his dog Gulì, who often figures in his verse.

In 1895, Pascoli became a probationary teacher at the University of Bologna, and in 1897, he was appointed professor of Latin literature at Messina, in Sicily, where he remained until 1903. From there, he went on to Pisa and, in 1907, upon the death of Carducci, was invited to assume Carducci's chair in Italian literature at Bologna.

From 1891 to 1911, Pascoli entered his own Latin poems in the yearly *Certamen poeticum hoeufftianum* (a competition in memory of the Dutch scholar Jacob Hoeufft) at the Amsterdam Academy of Sciences, and in thirteen of these years he won the highest award.

Pascoli remained a bachelor. His health began to fail in 1908 after he developed a tumor, and four years later, as he feverishly strove to complete unfinished projects, he died. He was buried in a chapel next to his home at Castelvecchio. His sister Maria, his lifelong devoted companion was his literary executrix. The book Maria wrote about her brother, *Lungo la vita di Giovanni Pascoli* (1961; about the life of Giovanni Pascoli), appeared after her death in 1953.

Analysis

Much of Giovanni Pascoli's poetry is autobiographical and touches upon his family, his home, the simple maritime and peasant folk he knew, his patriotism, his pessimism, and his obsession with death. His was a child's world of small actualities, and he wrote tenderly of children themselves. Predictably, some of his work borders on, or even crosses over into, the realm of the unabashedly sentimental.

Unlike Carducci, who unequivocally rejected Christianity, Pascoli called it "the poetry of the universe," and kept a candle lit before the Virgin's picture above his hearth. His attitude toward the Christian religion has been characterized by Ruth Shepard Phelps as indulgent rather than devout; she points out that when his dead speak to him, as in "Il giorno dei morti" ("All Souls' Day"), they address him from the tomb and not from Heaven. Nevertheless, he does not shy away from traditionally Christian themes: "La buona novella" ("The Good News"), appropriately placed at the end of his Hellenic *Convivial Poems*, heralds the age of a new humanitarianism and spares pagan Rome, "drunk with blood," no embarrassing details. In his Latin poetry especially, persecuted Christians figure prominently, as does Christ Himself. In "Centurio," for example, an old centurion who has returned to Rome is surrounded by boys begging for tales of adventure; instead, he tells them of the four times he saw and heard One Whom he last saw nailed upon the Cross.

Pascoli's classical interests are evident throughout his work, but his devotion to Greece and Rome functions not so much as a proud material possession, as it was for Carducci, or as a means to self-aggrandizement, as it was for D'Annunzio, but more as a wistful vision of a lost Eden to be recovered by a strategy as simple as assembling and savoring in a single work those Italian words that clearly mirror their Greek and Latin origins. As much as he loved the classical heritage of Greece and Rome, he could write in "Il fanciullino": "In our literary style we have taken the Latins for our model, as they did the Greeks. This may have helped to give concreteness and dignity to our writings, but it has suffocated our poetry." Despite a few isolated attempts to pattern his verse on Greek and Latin cadences, Pascoli generally adheres to the prosody of Italian, excelling in his treatment of the traditional hendecasyllable.

Romantic love did not interest Pascoli (it is not love of beautiful women, he wrote in "Il fanciullino," that interests the child but rather tales of adventure: "bronze shields and war-chariots and distant journeys and storms at sea"), nor was he concerned with politics, his own psychology, or syllogistic reasoning. In place of romantic love, Pascoli substitutes love of nature and concerns himself with the entire gamut of natural phenomena, observing and interpreting their varying states with the touch of a master. This emphasis on the natural world sometimes involves a vein of mysticism, and, despite his avowal that philosophy is too adult a matter for poetry, such poems as "Il ciocco" ("The Blockhead"; literally, "the log") and "La vertigine" ("Vertigo") are philosophical poems of cosmic imagination.

Much of his verse follows the pattern of common speech in its simplicity, novelty, and hesitation, and could be rewritten as prose. His unconventional rhythms resemble in some respects the poetry of Alexander Pushkin and the sprung rhythm of Gerard Manley Hopkins. Pascoli enjoyed using familiar forms but felt equally comfortable with forms of his own invention. He used alliteration and assonance extensively. Characteristic of his syntax (regarded at the time as daringly modern) is his oxymoronic pairing of contradictory words or ideas, such as "glauco pallore" (greenish pallor) or "la Vergine Maria piange un sorriso" (the Virgin Mary weeps a smile).

Pascoli stands out in the Italian poetic tradition for the quality of his language and for the individual words which he savored with the delight of a lexicographer. He does not hesitate to identify the humbler things of life by their even humbler dialectal designations, and he makes bold use of archaic Italian words and Latinate borrowings for special effect, of the pidgin Italian of returning emigrants, of childlike expressions, and of onomatopoeia. In the preface to the second edition of *Canti di Castelvecchio*, Pascoli thought it necessary to add an apologia for his use of so many dialectal words, insisting that the peasants speaking their dialects "speak better than we do," with their crude and pithy utterances. Pascoli thus anticipated by half a century the more extreme indulgences of descriptive linguistics.

Birds are important in the poetry of Pascoli—not only the romantic species such as larks and nightingales, but also the more plebeian sparrows, wrens, kites, plovers, shrikes, robins, and finches. Pascoli rendered bird and animal sounds as he heard them, from the charming *ku kuof* of the turtledove, *uid uid* of the lark, and *tri tri* of the cricket to the ridiculous extremes of the *tellterelltellteretelltell* of the sparrow, the *zisteretetet* of the titmouse, and the *addio addio dio dio dio dio* of the nightingale. In the poem "Un ricordo" (a memory), a scene of great poignance, describing the last time his mother sees his father before the latter's murder, is staged against a backdrop of brooding turtledoves making *hu hu* sounds; even in recounting such a moment, Pascoli could not forgo his fondness for onomatopoeia.

MYRICAE

Pascoli began to write poetry before 1880, but his first collection of poems, called *Myricae*, patterned on the eclogues of Vergil and symbolic of the humbler forms of rural poetry, was not published until 1891. The poems portray the minute distinctions of form or sound or action that the poet liked to observe, and in *Myricae*, as later in the *Canti di Castelvecchio*, there is an intimation of death, as though the tragic mourning of the poet was always there behind every vision. In the preface to *Canti di Castelvecchio*, he justified this obsession with death: ". . . life without thought of death, this is to say, without religion, which is what distinguishes us from the animals, is a madness, either intermittent or continuous, either expressionless or tragic."

In the first poem in *Myricae*, "All Souls' Day," Pascoli envisions the dead members of his family speaking from

their graves one cold rainy night. The storm rages, the water streams down the crosses, and his father moans his ever-yearning words amid the rhythms of the pelting rain. Ruggero Pascoli forgives his unknown killer, adding that if the murderer has no children, he can never know what sorrow he has caused. He asks a blessing for his own surviving children, that they be granted the capacity to forget, because for him there is no forgetting, and no rest.

"Romagna" ("The Romagna"), dedicated to Pascoli's friend Severino Ferrari, who is addressed in the second line of the poem, is generally taken as one of the poems which most clearly reveals the influence of Carducci, but it already shows in tone and detail the individual route that Pascoli would take. Sunny Romagna, the scene of his happy childhood, is recalled: the farmhands eating lunch, the child taking refuge from the dazzling sun in the shade of a mimosa tree to read tales of chivalry. Then, one black day, all the Pascolis scatter like swallows, and "homeland" for the poet is now merely "where one lives."

In the epigrammatic "Morte e sole" ("Death and the Sun"), Pascoli plays with the irony that the sun, supposedly the source of light and life, while symbolic of enlightenment, is also a symbol and revelation of death. When the eye looks upon the sun, it does not see light but instead blackness, a void. Nicholas Perella observes that Pascoli has here taken François de La Rochefoucauld's maxim ("One cannot look fixedly upon either the sun or death") and, by emphasizing the blackness, has refashioned La Rochefoucauld's original intention into an existential joke.

POEMETTI

Pascoli's next work, *Poemetti* (minor poems) later incorporated in *Primi poemetti* (first minor poems) and *Nuovi poemetti* (new minor poems), shifts from the lyrical emphasis of *Myricae* to the short narrative. Modeled upon Homer and Vergil and championing the outdated position that an emphasis on agricultural interests produces a healthy society, the poems chronicle the seasonal activities of a peasant family. Pascoli is also concerned here for the plight of Italians forced to emigrate for economic reasons, and in a longer poem titled "Italy" (the original title is in English) he writes of a family returning to Italy from Cincinnati, Ohio; they speak a kind of pidgin Italian that incorporates many English words.

CANTI DI CASTELVECCHIO

Pascoli's next book of poetry, *Canti di Castelvecchio*, contains more autobiographical poems and is often viewed as the peak of his poetic achievement. It includes the classic "La cavalla storna" ("The Dapple-grey Mare"), written in *laisses* of rhymed hendecasyllabic couplets that many Italian schoolchildren have been required to memorize. Pascoli felt great affection for the mare that loyally drew her master's body to his home and who alone knew the identity of his murderer, and the poem recalls Pascoli's mother's attempt to extract an identification from the little mare by means of a sign or a sound. The poem "La voce" ("The Voice") was a product of Pascoli's dark and lean years after his expulsion from the university. One night, while crossing the river Reno, weeping bitterly because he feels he must commit suicide, he hears his mother address him by his childhood nickname, "Zvanì," and the mysterious message blocks his resolution to die, imbuing him instead with the courage to live. The sentimentality inherent in the poem is counteracted somewhat by Pascoli's grotesquely effective assertion that his mother cannot be speaking to him, for in reality "her mouth is full of earth."

CONVIVIAL POEMS

In *Convivial Poems*, named for the impressive but short-lived review *Convito* (1895-1907) of Adolfo De Bosis in which Pascoli first published some of the poems included in the collection, the poet directs his attention to those readers capable of appreciating the values of the classical world. He refers to the title in the opening line of the first selection, "Solon" ("Sad is a banquet without song, sad as/ a temple without the gold of votive gifts"), and proceeds to discuss the enduring nature of poetry. In "Anticlus" the poet attempts to convey the incomparable beauty of the Greek Helen, and in the "Poemi di Psiche" ("Poems of Psyche"), the pantheism of the first segment, "Psiche" ("Psyche"), stands in contrast to the immortality of the soul put forth in the second, "Il gufo" ("The Owl"), a retelling of the story of the death of Socrates. In "Alèxandros" ("Alexander the Great"), the great conqueror appears at the end of his career to lament that there is nothing more on earth for him to win ("Oh! happier was I when a longer road/ lay be-

fore me"). He concludes that it is better to be able to hope and dream ("the dream is the infinite shade of the Truth") than to possess material things.

The atmospheric effects of Pascoli's introspective poems invite comparison with the work of such poets as Thomas Hardy, Paul Verlaine, Stéphane Mallarmé, and Maurice Maeterlinck. Indeed, Pascoli is a difficult poet to translate precisely because much of his work depends more on atmosphere and vocabulary than on form and idea. Pascoli did Italian literature an inestimable service by extending the vocabulary of poetry beyond the bounds of tradition and by offering it the benefit of countless new and daring images and analogies. His influence on later writers has been so great that the large body of distinguished Italian poetry written during the twentieth century would probably have been far less impressive without his example and leadership.

OTHER MAJOR WORKS

NONFICTION: *Minerva oscura*, 1898; *Sotto il velame*, 1900; *La mirabile visione*, 1902; *Pensieri e discorsi*, 1907; *Scritti danteschi*, 1952; *Lettere a Maria Novaro e ad altri amici*, 1971.

EDITED TEXTS: *Epos*, 1897; *Lyra*, 1899; *Sul limitare*, 1900; *Fior da fiore*, 1902.

BIBLIOGRAPHY

Brand, Peter, and Lino Pertile, eds. *The Cambridge History of Italian Literature*. Rev. ed. New York: Cambridge University Press, 1999. Includes introductory information on Pascoli's life and work and pertinent historical background.

Donadoni, Eugenio. *A History of Italian Literature*. Translated by Richard Monges. New York: New York University Press, 1969. Contains introductory biographical and critical information on Pascoli's life and work.

LaValva, RosaMaria. *The Eternal Child: The Poetry and Poetics of Giovanni Pascoli*. Chapel Hill, N.C.: Annali d'Italianistica, 1999. A critical interpretation of Pascoli's "Il fanciullino" with the text of the poem in English and Italian. Includes bibliographical references and index.

Perugi, Maurizio. "The Pascoli-Anderton Correspondence." *Modern Language Review* 85, no. 3 (July,

1990): 595. An analysis of the correspondence between Isabella Anderton and Giovanni Pascoli, including the text of some of their letters.

_____. "Pascoli, Shelley, and Isabella Anderton, 'Gen-
tle Rotskettow.'" *Modern Language Review* 84, no.
1 (January, 1989): 50. A discussion of the English
attributes of Pascoli's work and the influence Percy
Bysshe Shelley had on Pascoli's poetry.

Phelps, Ruth Shepard. *Italian Silhouettes*. Freeport, N.Y.:
Books for Libraries Press, 1968. Provides brief his-
torical background to the works of Pascoli and other
Italian literature.

Jack Shreve;
bibliography updated by the editors

PIER PAOLO PASOLINI

Born: Bologna, Italy; March 5, 1922
Died: Ostia, Italy; November 2, 1975

PRINCIPAL POETRY

Poesie a Casarsa, 1942
La meglio gioventù, 1954
Le ceneri di Gramsci, 1957
L'usignolo della chiesa cattolica, 1958
La religione del mio tempo, 1961
Poesia in forma di rosa, 1964
Poesie, 1970
Trasumanar e organizzar, 1971
La nuova gioventù, 1975
Poems, 1982

OTHER LITERARY FORMS

Pier Paolo Pasolini was a critic, philologist, film director, playwright, translator, and novelist as well as a
poet. His first novel, *Ragazzi di vita* (1955; *The Ragazzi*,
1968), based on rigorous sociological, ethnographic,
and linguistic observation, chronicles the wasted street-
life of shantytown adolescents through dialogue, flashbacks, and direct intrusions by the author; Pasolini makes
original and abundant use of slang and street language.
Within three months after the book appeared, the prime

minister's office reported it to the public prosecutor in
Milan for its "pornographic content," and Pasolini was
brought to trial. Similar controversies recurred throughout Pasolini's career as a writer and film director.

ACHIEVEMENTS

Outside Italy, Pier Paolo Pasolini is better known as a
director of films than as a poet, and even within Italy, it
was not until nearly a decade after his death that his
poetic talent was fully appreciated. His poetry is considered the most important in Italy after Giuseppe
Ungaretti's generation and ranks with the work of Bertolt
Brecht and Pablo Neruda as among the most powerful
political poetry of the twentieth century. At the time of
Pasolini's early education, a triad of nineteenth century
poets (Giosuè Carducci, Giovanni Pascoli, Gabriele
D'Annunzio), fond of artificial language and classical
literary convention, ruled Italian letters; they were followed by the hermetic school of poetry (Umberto Saba,
Ungaretti, Eugenio Montale), which emphasized personal expression and symbolic density.

Both schools were disdainful of social commentary
in poetry. After the fiasco of Italian Fascism, however,
the politically responsive Neorealist was born in Italy,
and it was within the framework of Neorealism that
Pasolini worked. When *Le ceneri di Gramsci* (Gramsci's
ashes) appeared in 1957, it broke a long line of pure
lyric and hermetic poetry in Italy: The poet described his
own inner conflict between reason and instinct, between
nostalgia for the past and the need for a new order, using
a straightforward Italian diction free of the Latinate loft-
iness to which his poetic predecessors had necessarily
been bound.

BIOGRAPHY

Pier Paolo Pasolini was the first of two sons born to
Carlo Alberto and Susanna Colussi Pasolini. Carlo Alberto
Pasolini, though from an aristocratic Bolognese family,
was reduced to poverty and became a soldier. Until his
death in 1958, his life was a dream of military and Fascist ideals, and after his discharge from the military, he
became an alcoholic. It was rather with the petite bourgeoisie background of his mother's family of the Friuli
area (in the northeastern corner of Italy, bordered by
Austria and Yugoslavia) that the poet identified. Susanna

Colussi, who had inherited her Hebrew name from a great-grandmother who was a Polish Jew, was a schoolteacher and already thirty when Carlo Alberto Pasolini married her.

Carlo Alberto Pasolini's wife and two sons accompanied him wherever he was stationed in Northern Italy. The marriage was turbulent and marked by frequent temporary separations, and Susanna channeled all her love into her relationship with her sons, especially her older son. Indeed, the relationship between Pasolini and his mother, whom he would one day cast as the Virgin Mary in his film *Il vangelo secondo Matteo* (1964; *The Gospel According to St. Matthew*, released 1964), was animated by an unequivocally incestuous tension. When the two of them moved to Rome without Carlo Alberto in 1945, Susanna took a position as a maid to support her son's literary aspirations. The image of his "artless, eternally youthful mother" pervades all the poet's work.

In high school in Bologna, after his inevitable exposure to the poetry of Carducci, Pascoli, and D'Annunzio, one of Pasolini's teachers read to him a poem by Arthur Rimbaud. Later, Pasolini claimed that his conversion away from Fascism dated from that day; he also wrote that after Rimbaud, poetry was dead. William Shakespeare was another early discovery, and Pasolini's reading of Niccolò Tommaseo's compilation, *I canti del popolo greco* (1943; songs of the Greek people), did much to awaken Pasolini's appreciation of the folk culture of his mother's Friuli. Shakespeare, Tommaseo, and Carducci constituted Pasolini's personal triad, recognized as such in "La religione del mio tempo" (the religion of my time). He came early under the spell of the Provençal *trobar clus* as well, and he considered himself a disciple of the Spanish poet Antonio Machado.

In the winter of 1942-1943, Susanna moved back to Friuli to avoid the bombings in the larger cities. Most of the following year, which Pasolini called the most beautiful of his life, was spent there with his mother and brother. That September, he was drafted, but a week later, on the day of Italy's truce with the Allies, he escaped into a canal as his column of recruits was marched to a train en route to Germany. In April, 1944, his brother Guido went to the mountains to join the Osoppo-Friuli partisan division. He and some comrades were captured by the Communist Garibaldi Brigade, po-

litically tied to Marshal Tito's fighters and favoring the incorporation of Friuli into the emerging nation of Yugoslavia; the comrades were later slain. The death of Guido was deeply traumatic to Pasolini and embarrassing to him as the Communist he would soon become.

Pasolini taught briefly in a private school, became involved in the local politics of Friuli, wrote for the local newspapers, and at length established himself as a Communist. With his maturity in the 1940's, he began to feel increasing guilt for his homosexuality, guilt he dwelt upon in his unpublished diaries (written from 1945 to 1949), from which he later extracted the completed whole of *L'usignolo della chiesa cattolica* (the nightingale of the Catholic Church). Repeatedly, he writes of "being lost," of being dominated by the "slave penis." By 1949, Pasolini's participation in homosexual activities was such that attempts were made to blackmail him, and he was formally charged by the magistrate of San Vito al Tagliamento with corrupting minors and committing lewd acts in public. Before the *carabinieri* of Casarsa, by whom he was also summoned, he defended himself by invoking the name of André Gide, who had

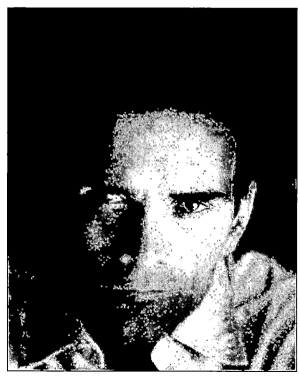

Pier Paolo Pasolini

won the Nobel Prize in Literature in 1947, and by describing his activities as an "erotic and literary experiment." Although Pasolini was acquitted in 1952, the fact that he did not deny the charge led the executive committee of the Communist Federation of Pordenone to expel him from the Italian Communist Party for moral and political unworthiness. It was a triple blow: Friuli had turned its back on him, his party had rejected him, and he had lost his teaching position. In a letter to a member of the Udine Federation, he declared his intention to remain a Communist and to persist in living for the sake of his mother, although another person might consider suicide. In the winter of 1949, he fled with her to Rome.

Pasolini's first few years in Rome were difficult, but the eternity and modernity of Rome captivated him, and he thrived on the sexual freedom that the metropolis afforded him. A teaching position was secured for him in 1951, and soon he was writing for *Il popolo di Roma, Il giornale* of Naples, and *Il lavoro* of Genoa. He cemented friendships with writers such as Giorgio Bassani, Alberto Moravia, Elsa Morante, Attilio Bertolucci, and Federico Fellini, whom he helped with the Roman dialect of Fellini's 1956 film *Le notti di Cabiria (The Nights of Cabiria*, released 1957). In 1952, Pasolini tied for second place and won 50,000 lire in the Quattro Arti contest in Naples for his article on Ungaretti.

The years from 1953 to 1961 were the most productive of Pasolini's career. He published two novels, two books of poetry, the critical essays collected in *Passione e ideologia* (1960; passion and ideology), and from 1955 to 1959 directed the literary magazine *Officina*. He wrote thirteen movie scripts, translated the *Oresteia* of Aeschylus, and directed and scripted his first film, *Accattone* (1961). Rome was alive in those years with intellectual creativity and political ferment, but as exciting as it was for Pasolini, it also took its toll on him. For the first time, he found himself getting involved with literary projects merely because he needed a public; he was plagued by litigation and by vicious journalistic attacks.

After his debut in the world of filmmaking, Pasolini's life changed course. His fertile mind seethed with new ideas, and the names of far-flung places began to appear in his work. In 1966, he made his first visit to New York, where he sought out young revolutionary blacks in Harlem and was mightily impressed by the potential he dis-

covered in the United States. Two years later, he was deeply disillusioned by the "tragedy-revolt" of the student riots of 1968; in his view, the youth, who had been cradled by the class struggle, had sold out to the bourgeoisie. Between 1970 and 1975, he made a successful and controversial trilogy of films–*Il decamerone* (released 1971; *The Decameron*, released 1975), *I racconti di Canterbury* (released 1972; *The Canterbury Tales*, released 1975), and *Il fiore belle mille e una notte* (released 1974; *The Arabian Nights*, released 1975)—based on his belief that the "last bastion of reality seemed to be the 'innocent' bodies, with the archaic, dark, vital violence of their sexual organs." In the *Corriere della Sera* of June 5, 1975, however, he repudiated this notion, claiming that "even the 'reality' of innocent bodies has been violated, manipulated, tampered with by the power of consumerism." Pasolini's polemics against the consumer society had become harangues, and the poet did not seem to have any cures to offer for the ills he so vehemently identified. His output in his last years was increasingly complex and contradictory.

The exact circumstances of Pasolini's death may never be clearly established. Late on the evening of November 1, 1975, Pasolini set off in his Alfa Romeo GT and picked up a street hustler named Giuseppe Pelosi. On the beach at Ostia, the two of them struggled, Pasolini was struck on the head with a board, and Pelosi subsequently ran over Pasolini with his own car. Because the boy was unmarked, however, and because he gave a confused testimony, there is some reason to believe that Pelosi was merely an agent for others who had more reason than he to eliminate Pasolini.

ANALYSIS

As a writer and as a man, Pier Paolo Pasolini was one of the most complex figures of twentieth century literature, and his life and work are replete with paradoxes. Despite his belief that his leftist poetry was different from all other poetry being written, he employed the hendecasyllable, the most widely used meter in all Italian verse in all periods, and the terza rima of Dante. He rebelled against Italy's long-entrenched cultural traditionalism yet declared himself a lover of tradition whom it pained to witness the disappearance of Italian peasant culture. He was a Marxist and at the same time did not abandon the Catholic Church; he condemned abortion and called on the Church to lead the fight away from the materialism that was gaining such a stranglehold on capitalistic societies everywhere. With his romantic spirit of identifying with the outcasts of the earth, Marxism came easily to him, but as an active, rather than a sublimated, homosexual, his Marxism demanded a morality that allowed for the individual. His religion was the liberation of the masses, yet he chose to focus not upon their struggle but rather upon their vindicated joy; and although he professed to love the common people, such people as individuals figure little in his poetry. His style in both his poetry and his films was stark and unsentimental, yet he could wax fulsome and self-indulgent when writing on the subject of his mother.

POESIE A CASARSA

To some extent, these contradictions were apparent in Pasolini's earliest, dialect poems. As a result of the breakup of the Roman Empire and the late emergence of Italy as a political entity, Italy inherited a multiplicity of dialects, substantially more varied than the dialects of most other Western European nations. Pasolini by nature felt attracted by the sound of his mother's dialect, Friulian, and, impressed by Paul Valéry's "hésitation prolongée entre le sens et le son," he opted for the sound element. He wrote his first volume of poetry, *Poesie a Casarsa* (poetry to Casarsa), in Friulian, publishing it privately in Bologna in 1942 and dedicating it to his father. When the slim volume of forty-six pages was reviewed, the review had to be printed in Switzerland, for dialect literature was very much anathema to the Fascist regime. In addition to the scandal implicit in using an Italian dialect for a literary endeavor, Pasolini's medium was a special, less recognized dialect within Friulian, distinct from the standardized jargon used by Friulian poets Ermes de Colloredo in the seventeenth century and Pietro Zorutti in the nineteenth century.

Pasolini consolidated *Poesie a Casarsa* with a group of Resistance poems known as "Il testamento Coran" (the Koran testament) and with several others written in Friulian, and published *La meglio gioventù* (the finest youth) in 1954. In all of these poems, the poet yearns for a recovery of moral health to be achieved through a reacquaintance with the peasant's world, and he treats the themes of nature, a boy's happiness with his mother,

and the exhilaration of the company of beautiful young men. In "Il dí la me muàrt" (the day of my death), for example, the poet tells of one who loved boys and "wrote/ poems of holiness/ believing that in this way/ his heart would become larger." In 1975, Pasolini made another consolidation and published *La nuova gioventù* (the new youth), in which he combined the poetry of *La meglio gioventù* with a reworked version of two parts of that book and with some new Italo-Friulian pieces composed in 1973-1974.

LE CENERI DI GRAMSCI

Le ceneri di Gramsci contains poems, dated carefully but not arranged in chronological order, that probe the poet's difficulties with a Marxism that in actual practice seeks to limit the expression of the individual spirit. The title poem, "Le ceneri di Gramsci" (Gramsci's ashes), takes its name from the words on Antonio Gramsci's grave in the English cemetery in Rome, not far from Percy Bysshe Shelley's. Gramsci, the Italian Marxist political philosopher whose works were written while he was imprisoned by the Fascists, had made loud charges that Italian literature was run by elitists more interested in eloquence and style than in people.

The first poems in *Le ceneri di Gramsci*, "L'Appennino" (Apennine) and "Il canto popolare" (the popular song), written during the poet's early days of residence in Rome, compare the grand Italy of the past with present conditions, in which major cities are besieged by hordes of impoverished immigrants from the poorer southern regions. It is in these poor people, however, living in pigsty encampments "between the shining modern churches and skyscrapers," that the poet's hope resides. In "Picasso," the poet focuses on the committed and socially responsive artist amid a decaying society, decreeing that "The way out/ . . . is by remaining/ inside the inferno with the cold/ determination to understand it," and not in Picasso's "idyll of white orangutans." "Le ceneri di Gramsci" (Gramsci's ashes), the central poem in the collection, probes the contrast between bourgeois society and Marxist commitment, between the ideal of freedom and the imperfect and irrational life as it is. Before Gramsci's grave and addressing him on a cloudy May day in a "scandal of self-contradiction," the poet declares himself to be "with you and against you." The poem is replete with the oxymorons which create a mood of excruciating tension.

"Récit" stems from the poet's outrage at the obscenity charges brought against him for *The Ragazzi*, while the last three poems in the volume, all written in 1956, in some way reflect the trauma of Khrushchev's anti-Stalin campaign, the revelation of Stalin's crimes, and the subsequent Soviet invasion of Hungary. In "Il pianto della scavatrice" (the tears of the excavator), the symbolic machine transforms the Earth and wails for change. This longest poem in the collection contains bright glimmers of hope, as the poet speaks glowingly of a Rome that taught him the grandeur of little things and taught him how to address another man without trembling—a Rome where the world became for him the subject "no longer of mystery but of history."

"Una polemica in versi" (a polemic in verse), clearly the result of the news of the Soviet invasion of Hungary, accuses the party of usurping the glory that rightfully belongs to the people and urges a hypothetical militant Communist to declare his error and his guilt. The poem ends with a panorama of the hopeful young characterized by "shameless generosity" against a backdrop of older people, aware of defeat and in various states of drunkenness, uncertainty, and disappointment.

The last poem in the volume, "Land of Work," stands in contrast to the first poem, "L'Appennino" (Apennine), in its less sanguine view of the potential of the poor. The Southern Italian peasants that the poet observes here belong more to the realm of the dead than to the living, and their prehistorical condition is underscored by a series of subhuman similes involving dogs, sheep, and other animals. Where there had been a hunger "taking the name of hope," now "every inner light, every act/ of conscience" seems to be a thing of yesterday. For once, the poet has no compassion to give: "You lose yourself in an inner paradise/ and even your pity is their enemy."

LA RELIGIONE DEL MIO TEMPO

La religione del mio tempo (the religion of my time) appeared the same year (1961) as Pasolini's first film, *Accattone*. The poet seems deliberately to abstain from direct political involvement here, but he is humiliated by the corruption of all attempts to renew society. For the first time, Pasolini experiments with epigrams, but often they do not rise above expressing a mere self-pity. Af-

rica, unsullied by the bourgeois taint, comes into view for the first time as the poet's "only alternative." There are poems of memory, poems of love for boys, and poems wherein little hope abides. In "To an Unborn Child," Pasolini grieves not at all for his "first and only child" who can never exist. In "To a Boy," a poem of praise for the inquisitiveness of young Bernardo Bertolucci, later to become a prominent film director in his own right, Pasolini concludes in the style of Giacomo Leopardi: "Ah, what you wish to know, young man/ will end up unasked, it will be lost unspoken." In "Sex, Consolation for Misery," he characterizes sex as "filthy and ferocious as an ancient mother," but concedes that "in the easiness of love/ one who is wretched can feel like a man." The title piece, "La religione del mio tempo" (the religion of my time), is the longest in the collection; in it, the poet isolates cowardice and its product, materialism ("All possessions are alike: whether/ industry or pasture, ship or pushcart"), as the disease and symptom plaguing modern society, and points an accusing finger at the "Vile disciples of a corrupted Jesus/ in the Vatican salons . . ./ strong over a people of serfs."

If there is any light in all this gloom, it shines forth from Susanna alone, and in an unusually self-indulgent "Appendice alla 'Religione': Uno luce" ("appendix to the 'religion': a light"), Pasolini celebrates her "poor sweet little bones" and longs for the day when they will be together in the Casarsa cemetery, where "passion/ keeps the bones of the other son/ still alive in frozen peace."

POESIA IN FORMA DI ROSA

Poesia in forma di rosa (poetry in the form of a rose), which appeared in 1964, is a poetic diary which includes Pasolini's description of the trial provoked by the episode titled "La Ricotta" in the film *Rogopag* (1962); Pasolini was charged with insulting the Church. Another section, "Worldly Poems," represents the diary he kept during the filming of *Mamma Roma* (1962); there is also a "Progetto di opere future" (plan for future works) and an account of his tours of Israel and Southern Italy while filming *The Gospel According to St. Matthew*. In the first part of the book, he employs the tercet, but in the rest he employs the loose hendecasyllable, rhythmic prose, and a geometric arrangement of words on the page. The poetry is imbued with Pasolini's sense of his own unidentifiable, obsessive error: "I who by the excess of my presence/ have never crossed the border between love/ for life and life." Ideology is a drug, and the moralists have made socialism as boring as Catholicism. When the poet cries that "only a bloodbath can save the world/ from its bourgeois dreams," the effect is immediately undone by: "This is what a prophet would shout/ who doesn't have/ the strength to kill a fly." His insistent pursuit of the consolation of sex with strangers is defended: "Better death/ than to renounce it"; the search, he claims, is for the "enchantment of the species" rather than for the perfect individual. Susanna is here as well, the object of his prayer in "Supplica a mia madre" ("prayer to my mother") requesting that she please not die and proclaiming that she is, as his readers well know, irreplaceable to him.

TRASUMANAR E ORGANIZZAR

In 1971, Pasolini published *Trasumanar e organizzar* (to transfigure and to organize). The volume consists of three parts: a private diary; a collection of lyrics written to Maria Callas, with whom Pasolini worked while filming *Medea* (1969; *Medea*, released 1970), and a section of wholly political poems. The collection also contains Pasolini's first elaboration in poetry of his frustrated relationship with his father, and his single serene love poem, written in 1969 to Nino Davoli, whom Pasolini had discovered in the Roman slums while preparing for *The Gospel According to St. Matthew*. Not all of the poems are dated, but most of them were written after 1968. The title refers to the polarity between the spiritual ascent and the institutionalization or organization of humankind, the thematic points between which Pasolini moves with alternating sarcasm and heartbreak. The title piece is a polemic against the Italian Communist Party; youth protest, in which he had placed so much hope, is now represented as the irrational behavior of unknowingly bourgeois children. The keynote of the collection is the contradictory, bewildering nature of contemporary reality and the poet's pathetic awareness that he can neither enter into that reality nor even claim a precise role in it: a fitting note for the conclusion of Pasolini's turbulent poetic career.

OTHER MAJOR WORKS

LONG FICTION: *Ragazzi di vita*, 1955 (*The Ragazzi*, 1968); *Una vita violenta*, 1959 (*A Violent Life*, 1968); *Teorema*, 1968 (*Theorem*, 1992).

SCREENPLAYS: *Accattone*, 1961; *Mamma Roma*, 1962; "La Ricotta," 1962; *Il vangelo secondo Matteo*, 1964 (*The Gospel According to St. Matthew*, released 1964); *Comizi d'amore*, released 1964; *Uccellacci e uccellini*, 1966; *Edipo re*, 1967 (*Oedipus Rex*, released 1967); *Teorema*, released 1968 (*Theorem*, released 1969); *Medea*, 1969 (*Medea*, released 1970); *Il decamerone*, released 1971 (*The Decameron*, released 1975); *I racconti di Canterbury*, released 1972 (*The Canterbury Tales*, released 1975); *Il fiore belle mille e una notte*, released 1974 (*The Arabian Nights*, released 1975); *Salò o le 120 giornate de Sodoma*, released 1975 (*Salò: Or, 120 Days of Sodom*, released 1975).

NONFICTION: *La poesia populare italiana*, 1960; *Passione e ideologia*, 1960; *Scritti corsari*, 1975; *Lettere luterane*, 1976 (*Lutheran Letters*, 1983); *The Letters of Pier Paolo Pasolini*, 1992.

EDITED TEXTS: *Poesia dialettale del novecento*, 1952; *Canzoniere italiano: Antologia della poesia popolare*, 1955.

MISCELLANEOUS: *Alì dagli occhi azzurri*, 1965; *Il padre selvaggio*, 1975 (*The Savage Father*, 1999); *La divina mimesis*, 1975 (*The Divine Mimesis*, 1980); *San Paolo*, 1977 (*Saint Paul*, 1980).

BIBLIOGRAPHY

Baranski, Zygmunt G., ed. *Pasolini Old and New: Surveys and Studies*. Dublin, Ireland: Four Courts Press, 1999. A collection of biographical and critical essays on Pasolini. Includes bibliographical references and indexes.

Gordon, Robert S. C. *Pasolini: Forms of Subjectivity*. New York: Oxford University Press, 1996. Gordon analyzes Pasolini's intensely charged, experimental essays, poetry, cinema, and narrative, and their shifting perspectives of subjectivity.

Pasolini, Pier Paolo. *The Letters of Pier Paolo Pasolini*. Edited by Nico Naldini. London: Quartet Books, 1992. A collection of Pasolini's correspondence translated into English that provides invaluable insight into his life and work.

Rohdie, Sam. *The Passion of Pier Paolo Pasolini*. Bloomington: Indiana University Press, 1995. A critical study that is primarily concerned with Pasolini's work in film, but provides valuable biographical information.

Rumble, Patrick and Bart Testa, eds. *Pier Paolo Pasolini: Contemporary Perspectives*. Buffalo, N.Y.: University of Toronto Press, 1994. A collection of essays that explore the work of Pasolini, his time with the Communist Party. From the 1990 conference, Pier Paolo Pasolini: Heretical Imperatives, held in Toronto.

Jack Shreve;
bibliography updated by the editors

LINDA PASTAN

Linda Olenik
Born: New York, New York; May 27, 1932

PRINCIPAL POETRY
  A Perfect Circle of Sun, 1971
  Aspects of Eve, 1975
  On the Way to the Zoo, 1975
  The Five Stages of Grief, 1978
  Selected Poems of Linda Pastan, 1979
  Even as We Sleep, 1980
  Setting the Table, 1980
  Waiting for My Life, 1981
  PM/AM: New and Selected Poems, 1982
  A Fraction of Darkness, 1985
  The Imperfect Paradise, 1988
  Heroes in Disguise, 1991
  An Early Afterlife, 1995
  Carnival Evening: New and Selected Poems, 1968-
    1998, 1998
  The Last Uncle, 2002

OTHER LITERARY FORMS
    Linda Pastan has written an autobiographical essay, "Roots," which appeared in a volume edited by William Heyen titled *American Poets in 1976* (1976).

ACHIEVEMENTS
    Since the appearance of Linda Pastan's first book, critics have praised the lucidity of her language, the freshness of her metaphors, and the consistency of her accomplishment. She has been appreciated as an artist of what she herself calls "dailiness"—contemporary domestic life. She has won a fellowship from the National Endowment for the Arts and a Maryland Arts Council grant, as well as several literary awards: *Mademoiselle*'s Dylan Thomas Poetry Award, the Alice Fay di Castagnola Award, the Bess Hokin Prize, and the Maurice English Award. *PM/AM* was nominated for an American Book Award in 1983. In 1991, Pastan was named Poet Laureate of Maryland, serving until 1995.

BIOGRAPHY
    Linda Pastan is the daughter of Jacob L. and Bess Schwartz Olenik. Her father, the son of Russian-Jewish immigrants, was a surgeon, and Pastan married a molecular biologist, Ira Pastan, in 1953. She earned a B.A. from Radcliffe College in 1954, an M.L.S. from Simmons College in 1955, and an M.A. from Brandeis University in 1957. The mother of three children—Stephen, Peter, and Rachel—and her husband reside in the Maryland countryside, near Potomac. She has been poetry editor of the literary magazine *Voyages*, has lectured at the Bread Loaf Writers' Conference in Vermont, and has taught graduate workshops in poetry at American University. From 1986 to 1989, Linda Pastan served on the governing board of the Associated Writing Programs. Although Pastan received recognition for her poetry while a student, winning *Mademoiselle*'s Dylan Thomas Award (winning against Sylvia Plath), she did not work regularly on her poetry for ten years and did not publish a collection until 1971. Since that time her books have appeared regularly, and she has received other prizes as well as critical praise in leading literary journals. Pastan has acknowledged the influence and support of the poet William Stafford and has been labeled a "Post-Confessional" poet, interested in sincerity as well as going beyond the personal.

ANALYSIS
    Like many American poets since Walt Whitman, Linda Pastan has made poetry from her experience, but she has been much less optimistic than the Whitman who wrote "Song of Myself" (1855), "Crossing Brooklyn Ferry" (1856), and "Passage to India" (1870).

Starting with her first book, published when she was nearly forty, Linda Pastan has seen the human individual as subject to such forces as genetics, mortality, gravity, climate, fate, and God. Not that the individual is powerless: in love her characters can choose to be wise or foolish, passionate or subdued, faithful or not; and Pastan thinks highly of artistic and domestic accomplishments. Unlike Whitman, however, she never suggests that the individual can transcend mortal limits.

A survey of Pastan's favorite metaphors suggests that most of their sources are autobiographical: her Jewish heritage, her childhood in New York City, her education and interest in literature, her medical knowledge stemming from her father's and husband's scientific interests, Greek and biblical mythology, a later interest in Asian culture, flora and fauna of her adult life in the Maryland countryside, the behavior of her offspring and husband, and vacations near the ocean. Yet to concentrate only on the origins of her imagery would be to ignore Pastan's vision and craft.

Starting with her first book, she tried various means of shaping material into poems and of arranging poems into collections. The four parts of *A Perfect Circle of Sun* conform to the seasons. *Aspects of Eve* alludes to the biblical story of Eden, and in this book Pastan relies more frequently on narratives, like "Folk Tale" and "Short Story," to present material in a more comprehensive, dramatic fashion. Elisabeth Kubler-Ross's description of the process of mourning underlies *The Five Stages of Grief*, and Pastan continues the quest for Kubler-Ross's final stage, acceptance, in *Waiting for My Life* and the new poems in *PM/AM*. The most compelling shaping principle in Pastan's poetry, however, is mythology—especially the story of Adam and Eve, with its emphasis on the Fall (see *Aspects of Eve* and *The Imperfect Paradise*), and the character of Penelope as depicted in Homer's *Odyssey* (c. 800 B.C.E.), legendary for her patience and domesticity. It is important to stress that the relationship between such myths and Pastan's own life is reciprocal: the myths help to frame her experience, but she also questions them, returning obsessively to meditate on their meaning and reinvent them—to tell them, that is, in her own way as a result of her experience.

It would therefore be inaccurate to suggest that Pastan has tucked her entire life into a pattern prescribed by any

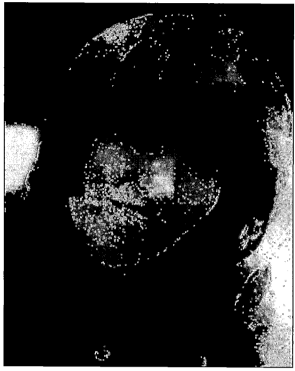

Linda Pastan (Courtesy of Linda Pastan)

single myth. Instead, one should place mythological allusions into the more comprehensive "story"—the interplay of Pastan's persona and the forces affecting her. "Persona" is an important concept: Pastan has acknowledged that her poems are not strictly or merely autobiography, calling "the poetic 'I' . . . more like a fraternal than an identical twin." What one finds in her poetry, then, is the tragic story of human limitation. She mentions many forces she cannot control. In "Last Will," she acknowledges that her children's only important inheritance is "in the genes," and in "balancing act: for N." she portrays the generations as acrobats "hooked together// by nerve/ and DNA." While hospitalized in "Accidents," she senses future accidents "waiting to happen." "On the Question of Free Will," one of her meditations on the Eden story, questions human freedom, hinting that "God's plan" may prevail.

WEATHER IMAGERY

Her most frequent metaphor for human vulnerability is the weather. As she says in "Hurricane Watch," "Some live in the storm's eye only./ I rise and fall/ with the barometer,/ holding on for my life." *A Perfect Circle of Sun* establishes the ambivalent vision of the annual cycle that applies to all of her work: Winter is both death and birth; the energy of spring can start growth or turn chaotic; summer, she says, is only winter in a "disguise of leaves"; and autumn is more a time for dirges than for harvest. Pastan's habitual and resourceful use of the weather reflects her sense of mortality. In "Hurricane Watch," the persona inhabits "a storm cellar/ of flesh," recalls "a blizzard of cells" in a microscope, and admits that "at times/ the hairs on my arm lift,/ as if in some incalculable wind." Her pessimism is such that she says "I read my palm as though it were a weather map/ and keep a hurricane watch/ all year." While fresh, lucid metaphors are essential to the success of this poem, Pastan's characteristic use of short lines is worth noting here suggesting her own tentativeness. Yet in the preceding line, "Some live in the storm's eye only," she lets a sentence about others run unbroken to its end, suggesting their greater courage.

TREE IMAGERY

As Pastan charts the seasons, she often refers to trees. In "Each Autumn," she writes, "We put our leaves in order,/ raking, burning, acknowledging,/ the persistence of time." In "After Agatha Christie," she implies her skepticism of summer by calling a tree's leaves "its false beard." Leaves ready to fall in "Consolations" are "scrolls bearing/ the old messages." "There is an age when you are most yourself," she remembers her father saying, and in "Something Above the Trees," which is written in a Malaysian form called *pantoum*, she wonders, "Was it something about the trees that made him speak?" The nearly unpunctuated poem "Family Tree" plays on the traditional *ubi sunt* theme by asking, "How many leaves/ has death undone . . . ?" Throughout this poem, Pastan chants the names of trees, and she finally declares that she will not drink to the New Year, in which her mother will die and her grandson be born. Instead, she broods on burned leaves' telling "the long story/ of smoke." In "Donatello's Magdalene," a fifteenth century wood sculpture of Mary Magdalene inspires one of Pastan's most inventive and anguished tree metaphors. After describing the sculpture, Pastan asks how many of its branches were "stripped/ and nailed/ to make each crucifix?" In this case, by alluding to the suffering and death of Jesus, Pastan adds a religious or mythic factor to her usual symbolic equation of trees with mortality.

SEA IMAGERY

The metaphors already discussed—weather and trees—play the roles, respectively, of agent and victim in Pastan's story of human limitation. Yet one natural metaphor—the sea—contains both roles. References to the sea enter her work in *Aspects of Eve*. Many later poems have coastal settings, usually with beaches, allowing Pastan to pit the individual against the awesome force of the ocean and introduce the impermanence of sand to characterize human life and relationships. Moreover, she often applies the verbs "to swim" and "to drown" to the human condition.

Pastan's most sustained metaphoric use of the sea occurs in the final four poems in the section of *The Imperfect Paradise* subtitled "Balancing Act." In "A Walk Before Breakfast," she dreams of an entire life like a vacation, "with the sea/ opening its chapters/ of water and light." "The Ordinary Weather of Summer," however, concludes pessimistically, with her imagining the last summer she and her husband will both be alive, when they walk up from the surf "on wobbly legs," "shaking the water out of our blinded eyes." "Erosion," the last poem of the group, expresses both optimism and pessimism. "We are slowly/ undermined," she declares, thinking of the slippage of sand, and adds, "The waves move their long row/ of scythes over the beach." Nonetheless, the sea appears "Implacably lovely," and the couple tries to stop the erosion. She has to admit, though, that "one day the sea will simply/ take us." The final stanza contains the most rewarding metaphors. Pastan allows, "We are made of water anyway," and says she has felt it "in the yielding/ of your flesh." She also thinks of her husband as sand, "moving slowly, slowly/ from under me."

Having acknowledged that the forces facing the individual are "implacable," Pastan still places considerable emphasis on human endeavor and accomplishment. Her people raise families, sustain professions, initiate projects and hobbies, love and hurt one another. In other words, though subject to the forces of creation, they are far from passive. Indeed, Pastan exerts herself metaphorically to depict human effectuality, even in the face of finally overpowering forces.

ART IMAGERY

One reliable metaphor of human accomplishment, often implicit, is art. Many of Pastan's poems have been inspired by works of art, and she frequently mentions her own reading and working at poems. One of her tenderest love poems, "Prosody 101," uses poetry itself as a metaphor. She begins by noting that she was taught that surprise, not regularity, was essential to poetry. (By writing the poem in blank verse, an unusual choice for her, Pastan can let the metrical pattern create rhythmic surprises.) Then, after describing surprises brought on by the weather, she relates a situation in which her husband startles her. He has acted so much like "a cold front" that she expects she might leave him, but he unexpectedly laughs and picks her up, making her feel young and alive—making her realize, "So this is Poetry."

Pastan has also dedicated a significant portion of her adult years to domestic concerns. In fact, the poems in the second part of *Waiting for My Life* depict her acceptance of "dailiness" as a vocation. In "Who Is It Accuses Us?" she angrily answers that domesticity is anything but safe. "You who risk no more than your own skins/ I tell you household Gods/ are jealous Gods," she declares, thinking of how they poison one's "secret wells/ with longing." Her autobiographical essay "Roots," in which she tells of postponing her career in poetry to raise her family, acknowledges the duties of home life as an important source of metaphor. She talks specifically of her identification with Penelope, Ulysses' wife in the *Odyssey*, who told her importunate suitors that she would choose a husband to replace the long-absent Ulysses when she finished a tapestry. Each day she worked on it, and each night tore out that day's work. Appropriately, throughout Pastan's poems one finds references to various types of needlecraft—lace, knitting, sewing—and two provocative meditations on the Penelope myth—"At the Loom" and "Rereading *The Odyssey* in Middle Age"—appear in *The Imperfect Paradise*. Images of closets, hallways, televisions, and entire houses also pervade Pastan's writing. Not surprisingly, kitchens supply some of the most compelling domestic metaphors. In "Soup," an angry persona likens her life to an "icebox . . . full/ of the homelier vegetables." A mellower view develops in "Meditation by the Stove," a poem that harkens to the traditional use of

kitchen fire to symbolize nurturing (as in many fairy tales, such as the Cinderella stories). Amid the baking of bread and looking after children, the persona acknowledges the disruptive presence of passion, but commits herself to domestic responsibility: "I have banked the fires of my body/ into a small domestic flame for others/ to warm their hands on for a while."

While there are references to her father's work as a surgeon, the primary male occupation in Pastan's poems is gardening—a passion belonging to her husband, which resonates with the story of the Garden of Eden. Pastan is alert to forsythias, locusts, lady slippers, bloodroot, milkweed, trillium, dandelions, onions, corn, and bees, as well as the work involved in tending plants. Her fine six-sonnet sequence "The Imperfect Paradise" contains the fullest portrayal of the gardener—devoted to spring, naming "everything in sight." His endeavors are such that he can seem godlike, destroying trees so that flowers flourish and carting off trapped squirrels so that birds can have the seed intended for them. Toward such activity Pastan's persona is often antagonistic. "In the Absence of Wings" portrays the gardener as her warden, holding her in his "maze of hawthorn and yew." Now that her children have grown, her father has died, and her writing of poems seems near an end, she wanders to a place where snow and flowers alternate. Still longing, she is like the mythical Daedalus before he invented the wax-and-feather wings that enabled him and his son Icarus to escape the power of King Midas: "The horizon is the thread/ I must tie to my wrist" "as I come/ to the vine-scrolled gatepost/ of the labyrinth."

TRAVEL IMAGERY

A final major metaphor of human endeavor—travel—is also ambiguous. More often than not, movement implies potentiality. Pastan writes of morning being "parked/ outside my window" in "Final," and in "To a Daughter Leaving Home," a girl's first tentative bicycle rides represent her maturation. Absence of movement represents failure. In "Waiting For My Life," for instance, the persona regrets her lack of initiative. She has stood at bus stops waiting for her life "to start," and even when she makes her way onto a bus she has no sense of direction or purpose. An even more frightening aspect of this metaphor lies in the fact that travel is not necessarily a matter of intention. The journey of life, especially progress toward death, is not merely one's own doing. "They seemed to all take off/ at once," Pastan writes in "Departures," referring to the deaths of several female relatives. The second stanza of "The Accident" may be the most eloquent passage on this theme. She imagines death as "an almost perfect ending": the icy road leading to a lamppost, the post being "a hidden exit . . . where the past/ and the future collide/ in one barbarous flash/ and only the body/ is nothing,/ disappearing at last/ into certainty."

BODILY MISFORTUNE

Pastan's discomfort with the fact that human efforts, regardless of their nature or immediate ends, lead finally to death makes her portrayal of the body highly distinctive. In "At the Gynecologist's," perhaps echoing Sylvia Plath's poem *Ariel* (1965), Pastan characterizes herself in the stirrups of the examining table as "galloping towards death/ with flowers of ether in my hair." The body is the focal point—even the battleground—in Pastan's story of human limitation. There is little celebrating of sensuality in her poems, in fact little visual description. Rather, she focuses on callouses, cramps, anesthesia, infection, rashes, scars, bruises, bandages, migraine, root canal surgery, bypass surgery, mammograms, X rays, EKG's, sonograms, insomnia, and (not surprisingly) hypochondria. The poem "Teeth" emphasizes physical decline and collapse, characterizing teeth as "rows of crumbling/ headstones."

If Pastan's concern lay only with perpetuating her youth or physical beauty, however, her poetry would lack its tragic dimension. Her real interest is moral, her preoccupation with bodily misfortune a reflection of her worry about her own failures. Yet her views are far from absurdist: She recognizes and values accomplishment. Her persona admits to "a nature always asking/ for the worst" and laments her "sins," "all my old faults," and various missed opportunities. Yet amid threatening forces, people can live admirable, even heroic lives. The often-praised early poem "Emily Dickinson," which links health and morality, praises Dickinson not for eccentricity but for "the sheer sanity/ of vision, the serious mischief/ of language, the economy of pain."

HUMAN LIMITATION

In Pastan's tragic story of human limitation, not only does the body journey toward death, but the self, as she says in "Low Tide," is "the passionate guest/ who would

inhabit this flesh," an entity—call it "soul"—eventually separate from the body. With age, medical charts become one's "only autobiography," she says in "Clinic." The human individual exists subject to forces—natural and perhaps supernatural—that surpass one's ability to control. Weather and the sea represent such forces, and trees reflect the individual's position in relation to them. The human being, however, has the freedom—or curse, if one recalls the Fall in Genesis—to exert oneself in significant ways. Thus, according to Pastan, we travel until, to quote "Clinic" again, "we stop/ being part of our bodies/ and start simply/ to inhabit them."

Poetry, then, is the preservative and fixative in the flux of time. Each Pastan poem is a spray of words and images drying before the colors further fade. Her poems have a decorum, a sense of quiet, but many suggest that hidden riots are about to break out, that each shedding oak or elm might suddenly become a Maypole. Such is the spirit of the title poem in *Carnival Evening*. In the long run, the distinction between dusk and festival diminishes, perhaps disappears.

BIBLIOGRAPHY

Franklin, Benjamin, V. "Theme and Structure in Linda Pastan's Poetry." *Poet Lore* 75 (Winter, 1981): 234-241. Summarizes Pastan's first four books and discusses the "fatalistic" nature of Pastan's vision, arguing that she is both "anguished" and "indomitable." She acknowledges frustration, but she is also a "realist who sees that proper understanding of one's realities is essential for living."

Gray, Richard. *American Poetry of the Twentieth Century*. London: Longman, 1990. While this book does not comment on Pastan, the chapter titled "Formalists and Confessionalists: American Poetry Since the Second World War" surveys poetry contemporary with and relevant to Pastan's. See the section titled "From Formalism to Freedom: A Progress of American Poetic Techniques Since the War."

Ingersoll, Earl G., et al. *The Post-Confessionals: Conversations with American Poets of the Eighties*. Rutherford, N.J.: Fairleigh Dickinson University Press, 1989. Stan Sanvel Rubin's "Introduction" provides a detailed definition of "The Post-Confessionals" and links Pastan with her contemporaries. "'Whatever Is at Hand': A Conversation with Linda Pastan," recorded in 1976 and updated in 1987, discusses Pastan's interest in mythology and science, the theme of death, and the influence of William Stafford, especially upon her writing habits.

Norvig, Gerda S. "Linda Pastan." In *Jewish American Women Writers*. Westport, Conn.: Greenwood Press, 1994. A solid overview of Pastan's career and accomplishment, paying special attention to the tension between the domestic and the transcendent in her work.

Pastan, Linda. "Roots." In *American Poets in 1976*, edited by William Heyen. Indianapolis: Bobbs-Merrill, 1976. Pastan charts her development from an early longing for escape, through an obsession with reading and then writing, into a difficult time when wifely duties precluded writing. Writing about Penelope gave Pastan a way out of her dilemma. In closing, she admits that "the road to discovery . . . loops backward."

_____. "Unbreakable Codes." In *Acts of Mind: Conversations with Contemporary Poets*, edited by Richard Jackson. Tuscaloosa: University of Alabama Press, 1983. In this 1979 interview, Pastan discusses her close involvement with nature. She explains that some of her metaphors create a sense of safety. She also tells how she organized her first books and stresses that there are only a few poetic themes of significance: aging, dying, passion, and identity.

Smith, Dave. "Some Recent American Poetry: Come All Ye Fair and Tender Ladies." *American Poetry Review* 11 (January/February, 1982): 36-46. In this unusually insightful review (of *Waiting for My Life*), Smith argues that Pastan's central theme is desire—an asking both of what people want and of what deserves their allegiance. He also notes the profundity and "innocence" in Pastan's telling of her main story—death.

Jay Paul,
updated by Philip K. Jason

BORIS PASTERNAK

Born: Moscow, Russia; February 10, 1890
Died: Peredelkino, U.S.S.R.; May 30, 1960

PRINCIPAL POETRY

Bliznets v tuchakh, 1914
Poverkh barierov, 1917 (*Above the Barriers*, 1959)
Sestra moia zhizn': Leto 1917 goda, 1922 (*My Sister, Life*, 1964; also as *Sister My Life*)
Temy i variatsii, 1923 (*Themes and Variations*, 1964)
Vysokaya bolezn', 1924 (*High Malady*, 1958)
Carousel: Verse for Children, 1925
Devyatsot pyaty god, 1926 (*The Year 1905*, 1989)
Lyutenant Shmidt, 1927 (*Lieutenant Schmidt*, 1992)
Spektorsky, 1931
Vtoroye rozhdeniye, 1932 (*Second Birth*, 1964)
Na rannikh poezdakh, 1943 (*On Early Trains*, 1964)
Zemnoy prostor, 1945 (*The Vastness of Earth*, 1964)
Kogda razgulyayetsa, 1959 (*When the Skies Clear*, 1964)
The Poetry of Boris Pasternak, 1917-1959, 1959
Poems, 1959
Poems, 1955-1959, 1960
In the Interlude: Poems, 1945-1960, 1962
Fifty Poems, 1963
The Poems of Doctor Zhivago, 1965
Stikhotvoreniya i poemy, 1965, 1976
The Poetry of Boris Pasternak, 1969
Selected Poems, 1983

OTHER LITERARY FORMS

Besides poetry, Boris Pasternak composed several pieces of short fiction. They include "Pisma iz Tuly" (1922; "Letters from Tula," 1945), "Detstvo Liuvers" (1923; "The Childhood of Liuvers," 1945), and *Rasskazy* (1925; short stories). He wrote two autobiographical works: *Okhrannaya gramota* (1931; *A Safe-Conduct*, 1949) and *Avtobiograficheskiy ocherk* (1958; *I Remember: Sketch for an Autobiography*, 1959). His novel *Doktor Zhivago* (*Doctor Zhivago*, 1958) was first published in Italy in 1957. An unfinished dramatic trilogy, *Slepaya krasavitsa* (*The Blind Beauty*, 1969), was published after his death, in 1969.

Among Pasternak's many translations into Russian are several of William Shakespeare's plays, including *Romeo and Juliet* (pr. 1595-1596) in 1943 and *Antony and Cleopatra* (pr. 1606-1607) in 1944. Most of these translations were published between 1940 and 1948. He also translated into Russian the works of several Geor-

Boris Pasternak, Nobel laureate in literature for 1958. (Hulton Archive)

gian lyric poets, especially those works of his friends Titian Tabidze and Paolo Iashvili. His translation of Johann Wolfgang von Goethe's *Faust* (1790, 1808, 1833) appeared in 1953, and Friedrich Schiller's *Maria Stuart* (1800) in 1957. Other authors whose works he translated include Heinrich von Kleist; George Gordon, Lord Byron; and John Keats.

The best English editions of Pasternak's prose works are found in *Selected Writings*—which includes the short prose works, *A Safe-Conduct*, and selected poems—translated by C. M. Bowra et al.; *I Remember: Sketch for an Autobiography*, translated with preface and notes by David Magarshack; and *Doctor Zhivago*, translated by Max Hayward and M. Harari, with the poems translated by Bernard G. Guerney.

ACHIEVEMENTS

Known in the West mainly as the author of *Doctor Zhivago*, Boris Pasternak established his reputation as a poet in the Soviet Union in 1922 with the publication of *My Sister, Life*. He is regarded as a "poet's poet," and his contemporary Anna Akhmatova referred to him simply as "the poet," as if there were no other in his time. Indeed, Pasternak ranks as one of the foremost Russian poets of the twentieth century, if not the greatest. At the turn of the century, Symbolism, as in the works of Andrey Bely and Aleksandr Blok, dominated Russian poetry, and in the years before the Revolution more daring innovation and verbal experimentation occurred in the Futurist movement, as in the poetry of Vladimir Mayakovsky and Sergei Esenin. Pasternak inherited from both movements and yet was a part of neither. Like the Symbolists, he is able to see life in images; like the Futurists, he uses daring verbal combinations, intricate sound patterns, and a relaxed conversational vocabulary. In his verses there is a simplicity and clarity that goes back to Alexander Pushkin, together with a freshness and originality that are timeless.

Pasternak's early poetry, especially *My Sister, Life*, is his most innovative and enigmatic. In these "rimes and riddles," as Robert Payne observes, Pasternak seemed to send the reader "in search of the key, until he realized that no key was necessary." Pasternak creates pure poetry, and the creation itself is the message. His poetry is music, like that of Paul Verlaine, whom he greatly admired; it is a search and a discovery, like Paul Valéry's; it is a perpetual celebration of the senses, as in Mikhail Lermontov; above all, it is a cosmic apotheosis of nature. It had a message of newness for the years of hope and optimism following the Revolution, and as Lydia Pasternak-Slater writes: "each reader discovered individually and for himself that these poems were the spontaneous outbursts of genius, of a 'poet' by the grace of God."

Pasternak was not a political poet. He seldom wrote of the Revolution or of reform. At first glance, he seems to be unaware of events, as he states in the poem "About These Verses": "Dear friends . . . what millennium is it out there?" A. Lezhnev states that these lines might be considered the epigraph of Pasternak's entire work. Yet the throbbing rhythm of *My Sister, Life* incarnates the Revolution, as *The Year 1905* sounds an ominous yet hopeful note, and as the poems of the 1940's speak of the desolation of the war years. Contemporary events are both present and absent in Pasternak's verse. Their absence angered Soviet officials, yet Joseph Stalin himself spared Pasternak.

Pasternak's greatest poetry, *The Poems of Doctor Zhivago* and the poems of his last years, sheds the excessive imagery and startling verbal play of his earlier works. It reaches a sublime simplicity in perhaps a single transparent image, and the music and the message are one. Such is "Winter Night," perhaps one of the greatest poems in all of Russian literature. Into these later works, Pasternak has injected a profound Christian symbolism, very much evident in the *The Poems of Doctor Zhivago*, more subtle in *When the Skies Clear*. Many of these poems have never appeared in an official Soviet edition, yet they are probably among the best-known modern poems in the entire world for their simplicity, universality, and lyricism.

BIOGRAPHY

Boris Leonidovich Pasternak was born in Moscow on February 10, 1890 (January 29, Old Style). He was the first and most illustrious of four children born to the painter Leonid Osipovich Pasternak and the pianist Rosa Isidorovna Kaufman. A close family relationship and a deeply cultured atmosphere marked his childhood. The influence of the Russian Orthodox religion came to this child of predominantly Jewish roots through his nurse Akulina Gavrilovna and was to reappear during his later years. Leonid Pasternak's literary associations, particularly with Leo Tolstoy and Rainer Maria Rilke, were to prove very important to Pasternak's development, although perhaps the most powerful influence on him was exerted by the composer Aleksandr Scriabin. Scriabin was his idol from 1903 to 1909, when Pasternak also began composing. Disillusioned in 1909, he abandoned the pursuit of a musical career and turned to philosophy. A trip to Marburg in 1912, then the philosophical center of Germany, where he was to study under Professor Hermann Cohen, seemed to be the ultimate fulfillment of his dreams. Then a sentimental crisis, Ida Vysofskaya's refusal of his proposal of marriage, led him to abandon philosophy and to turn to poetry—without, however, his losing altogether the musical gift and the philosophical preoccupations that are evident in his works.

Upon his return to Moscow, Pasternak became involved in literary circles and devoted himself completely to poetry. The wife of his early protector, the Lithuanian poet Jurgis Baltrushaitis, rightly warned him that he would later regret the publication of his first volume, pretentiously called *Bliznets v tuchakh* (a twin in the clouds). Its title suggested the Futurist movement, which Pasternak was unable to integrate into his work. Exempted from the draft because of a childhood leg injury, he tutored and worked at a chemical plant in the Urals from 1914 to 1917. The beauty of the Urals which so impressed him colors many of his works, from "The Childhood of Liuvers" to his poetry. When the Revolution broke out, he returned to Moscow enthusiastically, only to be disillusioned. This famous summer of 1917 is immortalized in the volume of poetry *My Sister, Life*, which was published in 1922, immediately assuring his reputation as a poet.

In 1922, Pasternak married Evgenia Vladimirovna Lourié, and their son Evgeny was born in 1923. The marriage, however, was not a happy one, and in 1930 he became enamored of Zinaïda Nikolaevna Neuhaus, whom he married in 1934. Their son Leonid was born in 1937. Although his second wife was to remain faithful to him until his death, their relationship was greatly strained by Pasternak's liaison with Olga Vsevolodovna Ivinskaya, which began in 1946. Ivinskaya showed a sensitive appreciation of Pasternak's literary works and aided him in much of his secretarial work. For her association with him, she was imprisoned and deported to Siberia twice, from 1949 until Stalin's death in 1953 and after Pasternak's death in 1960 until 1964. Pasternak himself was spared—miraculously, since the 1930's and 1940's saw the exile, death, or suicide of many of Russia's most gifted writers. Never hostile to the regime, he also never wrote according to the tenets of Socialist Realism and thus was in constant jeopardy.

During the difficult years of World War II and afterward, Pasternak supported himself and his family principally by translating, which he resumed later when he was unable to receive royalties from the West. After Stalin's death, he began working seriously on *Doctor Zhivago*, which he regarded as his most important work. Its refusal by the journal *Novy Mir* and subsequent publication in Italy by Petrinelli in 1957 placed him in a very dangerous position. When awarded the Nobel Prize in Literature in 1958, official pressures caused him to refuse. He died on May 30, 1960, at Peredelkino, the writers' village where he had spent almost all of his summers and many of his winters since 1936.

ANALYSIS

Although Boris Pasternak would refuse to equate music with poetry, his verse is inseparable from the music it embodies. D. L. Plank has studied the music of Pasternak in great detail and speaks of his "sound symbolism" and "phonetic metaphors." With its unusual rhythms and internal rhymes, alliteration, and evocative word patterns, Pasternak's poetry has a resonance that most translators have despaired of capturing. At all times he uses classical patterns and regular meters, never attempting the free verse of the Futurists, whose daring use of vocabulary, however, he does share. Perhaps one of the best examples of Pasternak's sound patterns is "Oars at Rest," brilliantly analyzed by Plank and Nils Nilsson.

It is not surprising that Pasternak's last work should be called *Zhivago*, which means "life," for his entire literary creation is a celebration of life. In *My Sister, Life*, he wrote: "In all my ways let me pierce through into the very essence. . . ." Although his sensitive nature suffered greatly during the personal and national upheavals in which he participated, he was basically positive and optimistic, a poet of hope and exultation. He frequently wrote of birth; one of his volumes of verse is titled *Second Birth*; the sight of the Urals for the first time is the vision of the great mountains in the pangs of childbirth and joy of new life. He frequently wrote of the change of seasons, implying life and death, growth and change. The religious poems of the Zhivago cycle lead to the Resurrection, the ultimate symbol of life and hope.

NATURE

Nature is the subject of the majority of Pasternak's poems. Poet Marina Tsvetayeva said: "We have written about nature, but Pasternak has written nature." Nature is the actor in his poems, the doer, the hero. Traditional roles are reversed: the garden comes into the house to meet the mirror ("Mirror"); "Dust gulps down the rain in pellets" ("Sultry Night"); young woods climb uphill to the summit ("Vision of Tiflis"). Pasternak became the river or the mountain or the snow. He captured nature on the move. For him, says Payne, "All that happened was eternally instantaneous."

Pasternak lived in a world of linden trees and grasses, lilacs and violets, herbs and nettles. They were personified and became the poet and time and life. "Today's day looks about with the eyes of anemones" ("You in the Wind . . ."); "The storm, like a priest, sets fire to the lilacs" ("Our Thunderstorm"). Lilacs and linden trees seemed to have a mysterious but definite significance for him. Most of nature entered his works through rain or snow. Marina Tsvetayeva said that the entire book *My Sister, Life* swims. The mere titles of the poems reveal this love of rain: "Rain," "Spring Rain," "The Weeping Garden." The same theme is evident in *When the Skies Clear*, but here snow dominates. There are blizzards, blinding snow, like the passing of the years, but also "Flowers covered with surprise;/ Corners where the crossroads rise," for Pasternak was essentially a poet of hope, and for him drenching rains and snowy winters were signs of life and growth.

LOVE

Life for Pasternak was inseparable from love. *My Sister, Life* evokes a tumultuous love affair. *Second Birth* is the story of his love for Zinaïda Nikolaevna, with regrets and admiration for Evgenia Vladimirovna. The poems of the Zhivago cycle probably refer to Ivinskaya in the person of Lara. Pasternak seldom wrote of love in explicit terms but used rhythm and metonomy: the sleepy breast, elbows, willows ("Oars at Rest"); crossed arms and legs ("Winter Night"). Like Stéphane Mallarmé, Pasternak frequently combined love and artistic creation, especially in his earlier works.

IMAGERY

Pasternak's early method is associative and linear. Many brief themes follow in rapid succession, with only a tenuous link, if any. Lezhnev observes that Pasternak, like an Impressionist painter, was a better colorist than draftsman. In the early works, images cascade and overwhelm one another and the reader. "Definition of Poetry" moves from the crescendo of a whistle to a ringing icicle to a duel between nightingales. Andrei Sinyavsky notes that for Pasternak, the poet does not compose or write images; he gathers them from nature. The young Pasternak was overwhelmed by all that he saw in nature, and his early works are saturated with such imagery.

SPIRITUALITY

The religious theme is barely present in Pasternak's earlier works, which seem like a pantheistic celebration of nature. Even in *When the Skies Clear*, man's creative power is seen in the might of the elements ("Wind"). In the Zhivago cycle, however, the spiritual element dominates, corresponding to a maturing and broadening of Pasternak's talent as well as to an inner conversion. This development has been interpreted as a poetic conversion to another set of images, but it is evident that Pasternak's values have moved to another sphere. He reaches a metaphysical and spiritual plane that uplifts the reader and draws him into an atmosphere of hope and immortality.

MY SISTER, LIFE

My Sister, Life (or *Sister My Life*, as Phillip Flayderman prefers in his translation) consists of fifty short lyrics written by Pasternak in a single burst of creative energy in the summer of 1917. It was his third volume of verse, and his first really great poetic achievement, immediately establishing his reputation. In it, Pasternak writes of life, love, and nature in a cosmic yet a very personal sense. The book is dedicated to Mikhail Lermontov, the great nineteenth century Russian poet whom Pasternak greatly admired, and the first poem recalls Lermontov's magnificent *Demon* (1841; *The Demon*, 1875). Pasternak himself states that in the summer of 1917, Lermontov was to him "the personification of creative adventure and discovery, the principle of everyday free poetical statement." The book is broken up by twelve subtitles, such as "Isn't It Time for the Birds to Sing," "Occupations of Philosophy," "An Attempt to Separate the Soul," and "Epilogue," which give only a slight indication of the contents of the respective sections.

The summer of 1917 was unlike any other in Pasternak's lifetime or in Russian history. It was the summer between the February and October revolutions, when Pasternak returned to Moscow, near which, at the family *dacha* at Molodi, he composed the poems of this cycle. There is scarcely an echo of revolutionary events in the whole volume, yet Pasternak calls it "A Book of the Revolution." Marina Tsvetayeva discerned "a few incontrovertible signs of 1917" in "The Sample," "Break-up," "The Militiaman's Whistle," "A Sultry Night," and the poem to Aleksandr Kerensky, "Spring Rain." Robert Payne sees the entire volume as poems "filled with the electric excitement of those days." The rhythm begins softly, as in "The Weeping Garden," and ends in stifling

heat and thunderstorms, as in "Summer," "A Momentary Thunderstorm Forever," and "At Home."

Many of the poems refer directly to a love affair: stormy, tumultuous, and at times tender. Pasternak does not reveal the person or the circumstances but simply portrays the emotional impact. He does this mostly through images of nature and sonorous evocations that defy translation. The significance of the images is intensely personal, and although the sensitive reader can feel the emotion and identify with it, he cannot interpret it. There are playful and sensual images ("Your lips were violets") as well as serious ones: "You handed me life from the shelf,/ And blew the dust away" ("Out of Superstition"). The love affair seems to end on a note of farewell, like a song that has been sung and a moment immortalized in poetry.

As is usual in Pasternak's early poetry, images of nature saturate each poem. Gardens (especially drenched in rain), lilac branches, summer storms, and starry skies run through most of the poems. Pasternak does not create them; he gathers them up from the universe in a net as a fisherman gathers his fish. He does not evoke them; he becomes the river or the storm or the rain. There is a cosmic quality about his nature imagery which excites and exalts. At the same time, Pasternak uses simple conversational language. He writes of mosquitoes and cafés and trolleys along with more exotic themes. The short prose work "The Childhood of Liuvers" has been considered to be a companion piece to *My Sister, Life* and thus helps to clarify some of the more enigmatic images which many critics, including Pasternak's sister Lydia, see as "too complicated, too cryptic, with too many escapes into the brilliance of sound and word."

If there is a philosophical message in these early works, it is the absolute value of freedom. Pasternak remains above political involvement and above conventional images. Like Lermontov, he seeks sensual freedom as well. He expresses freedom in language as he creates new melodies independent of ordinary vocabulary and syntax. Although Pasternak had not yet achieved the realism of Pushkin's imagery, with its universal application, his subjective boldness stands out in *My Sister, Life* as a new and fresh voice in Russian poetry.

HIGH MALADY

Pasternak's greatest achievement is in lyric poetry, but in the 1920's he attempted four longer poems of epic scope dealing with the Revolution. They are *High Malady*, *The Year 1905*, *Lieutenant Schmidt*, and *Spektorsky*—the latter was left unfinished. Although all of these poems have the narrative quality which Pasternak was to develop in his prose works, they are colored predominantly by his lyricism and emotional response.

High Malady is the only epic directly connected with the Revolution. It is a debate about the nature of poetry, "the high malady that is still called song," and Moscow under Bolshevik rule. Under the shadow of the siege of Troy, Pasternak speaks of the suffering in Moscow during the early 1920's: the cold winter, the lack of food, the imminence of death. Into this somber atmosphere he introduces Vladimir Lenin (Vladimir Ilich Ulyanov), whose "living voice pierced [us] with encircling flames like jagged lightning." He grows taller, his words are like the thrust of a sword, as alone "he ruled the tides of thought." Lenin is one with history and brings hope to the suffering people.

THE YEAR 1905

The Year 1905 is retrospective of twenty years, written by Pasternak in 1925 to 1926. As a young student, he had participated in some of the Moscow demonstrations in 1905, and the recollection remained with him all his life. The poem consists of six parts, of unequal lengths and varying meters. The first part, "Fathers," goes back to the roots of the Revolution in the 1880's, grouping together such diverse people as the anarchist Sergey Nechayev and the great novelist Fyodor Dostoevski. Part 2, "Childhood," is partially autobiographical and contains reminiscences of Pasternak's own student days, his father's study, and the music of Aleksandr Scriabin. Against a background of snow, Pasternak fuses and confuses events in both St. Petersburg (or Petrograd) and Moscow, as he is spiritually present in both. The third part, "Peasants and Factory Workers," short and perhaps the least successful, describes the Polish insurrection at Lodz.

"PRINCE POTEMKIN"

Part 4 describes the mutiny at sea aboard the *Prince Potemkin*. With classical overtones recalling Homer, Pasternak salutes the sea. With classical reticence, he avoids the direct description of violence. The hero, Afanasy Matushenko, is described in larger-than-life proportions, and as the section ends, the ship sails away

"like an orange-colored speck." Part 5, "The Students," tells of the funeral procession of Nikolai Baumann, killed by an agent of the secret police. In the tone of a lament, Pasternak writes: "The heavens slept plunged in a silver forest of chrysanthemums." The last part, "Moscow in December," speaks of the famous strike of the railwaymen. Pasternak himself was very moved by this event and, perhaps in memory of it, frequently used the image of railways in his poetry. The entire poem is powerful in its lyricism, but, as J. W. Dyck observes, it is too diffuse and lacks a central focus.

LIEUTENANT SCHMIDT

Lieutenant Schmidt remedies this problem by evoking a single subject. Lieutenant Schmidt was a historical personage who led a mutiny among the sailors at Sebastopol and almost single-handedly seized one battleship. Ten other ships had already joined him when he was captured and condemned. His famous "Testament," in which he speaks about cherishing his country's destiny and sees himself as "happy to have been chosen," is one of the most sublime parts of the entire poem.

SPEKTORSKY

Spektorsky was never completed, but Pasternak planned it as a novel in verse. It is highly autobiographical and tells of the unsuccessful love affair of Olga and Spektorsky and his later meeting with her while she was a revolutionary. A second love affair, with the poetess Maria Ilyna, is equally disappointing. The poem is also symbolic of the spiritual submission of the poet, not yet characteristic of Pasternak. It reflects independence in the face of any given ideology. The handling of plot in *Spektorsky* is unsure, but the poem does present a very modern character and shows the development of Pasternak's lyric gifts.

THE POEMS OF DOCTOR ZHIVAGO

Although the epic poems do not constitute the highest form of Pasternak's literary expression, they pleased the general public because of their accessibility. They also show the fusion of Pasternak's lyric and narrative skills, anticipating the achievement of *Doctor Zhivago*. In his *I Remember: Sketch for an Autobiography*, Pasternak describes *Doctor Zhivago* as "my chief and most important work, the only one I am not ashamed of and for which I can answer with the utmost confidence, a novel in prose with a supplement in verse." The essential connection between the poetry and prose is evident to the sensitive reader, for Pasternak intended the poems to constitute the seventeenth and final chapter of his work. Donald Davie, Dmitri Obolensky, and George Katkov, among others, have provided valuable commentaries in English which help to interpret the poems and show their link with the novel.

The Poems of Doctor Zhivago represents the most mature phase of Pasternak's poetry. The musical quality is important here, as in all of his works. The poems are inherently religious, a fact recognized by the editors of *Novy Mir*, who refused to print them. They speak of life and death, love and immortality, within a framework of the four seasons. The year begins in March, with a promise of spring, and ends with Holy Thursday and the hope of resurrection. The cycle begins and ends with Gethsemane and emphasizes the mission of Christ, of Hamlet, and of the poet "to do the will of him who sent me."

Obolensky divides the poems into three basic categories or themes: nature, love, and the author's views on the meaning and purpose of life. Although each of the twenty-five poems fits one of these categories better than the others, they overlap and the division is not absolute. The nature poems speak of all the seasons, but spring predominates: "March," "Spring Floods," "In Holy Week," "The Earth," and the religious poems that conclude the cycle. The nightingale, so frequent in Pasternak's poetry, is present here, and appears as the Robber-Nightingale of Russian folklore in "Spring Floods." The poems of spring point to the Resurrection, where "death finds its only vanquishing power."

The love poems are among the most intense in modern literature, yet they are remarkable for their restraint. The many women whom Pasternak knew and loved in his lifetime inspired the poems, yet there is a universality that applies to all human love, sublimated in the divine. The erotic "Intoxication," the tender "Meeting," and the mysterious "White Night" speak variously of the poet's passion. Perhaps the most successful is "Winter Night," which, by delicate repetitions of words and sounds (especially the letter *e*), by metonymic suggestions, and by the central image of the candle burning in a window, suggests the fateful passion and the consuming possession of love.

The love poems move imperceptibly into the religious cycle and form a part of it, underlining the deeply spiritual aspect of love and the ultimate meaning of life for Pasternak. "Christmas Star" introduces the series and recalls a medieval Russian icon and a Russian version of the Dutch *Adoration of the Magi* alluded to in *A Safe-Conduct*, Pasternak's first autobiography. "Daybreak" is addressed to Christ and emphasizes the importance of the New Testament to Pasternak, like a dawn in his own life. The other religious poems refer to the liturgical texts used in the Holy Week services in the Orthodox Church. They end with Christ in the Garden of Gethsemane and complete the cycle of death and resurrection, destruction and creation, sin and redemption—for Zhivago is a sinful man, yet one who has faith in life.

The Poems of Doctor Zhivago is a work of extraordinary simplicity. The use of religious imagery raises the poems above the purely personal symbols of *My Sister, Life*. Although Pasternak makes no effort to repeat the verbal brilliance and intricate sound patterns of his early years, the rhythm is clear and resonant. Each poem has a central focus around which the images converge. The cycle itself centers on the person of Hamlet, whom Pasternak considers to be a heroic figure, symbolizing Christ and, ultimately, resurrection. Pasternak's basic optimism, his celebration of life and exaltation of love, have their finest expression in this cycle of poems.

OTHER MAJOR WORKS

LONG FICTION: *Doktor Zhivago*, 1957 (*Doctor Zhivago*, 1958).

SHORT FICTION: "Pisma iz Tuly," 1922 ("Letters from Tula," 1945); "Deststvo Liuvers," 1923 ("The Childhood of Luvers," 1945); *Rasskazy*, 1925; *Sochineniya*, 1961 (*Collected Short Prose*, 1977).

PLAY: *Slepaya krasavitsa*, pb. 1969 (*The Blind Beauty*, 1969).

TRANSLATIONS: *Hamlet*, 1941 (of William Shakespeare); *Romeo i Juliet*, 1943 (of Shakespeare); *Antony i Cleopatra*, 1944 (of Shakespeare); *Othello*, 1945 (of Shakespeare); *King Lear*, 1949 (of Shakespeare); *Faust*, 1953 (of Johann Wolfgang von Goethe); *Maria Stuart*, 1957 (of Friedrich Schiller).

NONFICTION: *Pis'ma k gruzinskim*, n.d. (*Letters to Georgian Friends by Boris Pasternak*, 1968);

Okhrannaya gramota, 1931 (autobiography; *A Safe-Conduct*, 1945); *Avtobiograficheskiy ocherk*, 1958 (*I Remember: Sketch for an Autobiography*, 1959); *An Essay in Autobiography*, 1959; *Essays*, 1976; *The Correspondence of Boris Pasternak and Olga Frei-denberg, 1910-1954*, 1981; *Pasternak on Art and Creativity*, 1985.

MISCELLANEOUS: *Safe Conduct: An Early Autobi-ography and Other Works by Boris Pasternak*, 1949; *Sochinenii*, 1961; *Vozdushnye puti: Proza raz nykh let*, 1982; *The Voice of Prose*, 1986.

BIBLIOGRAPHY

Conquest, Robert. *The Pasternak Affair: Courage of Genius*. London: Collins and Harvill, 1961. An ac-count of Pasternak's conflict with the state upon his receipt of the Nobel Prize. Valuable information about Pasternak as a man and as a writer.

Erlich, Victor, ed. *Pasternak: A Collection of Critical Essays*. Englewood Cliffs, N.J.: Prentice-Hall, 1978. This skillfully arranged collection of essays covers all important facets of Pasternak's opus, with the emphasis on his poetry and *Doctor Zhivago*.

Fleishman, Lazar. *Boris Pasternak: The Poet and His Politics*. Cambridge, Mass.: Harvard University Press, 1990. An extensive study of Pasternak's life and works written under the oppressive political system and his ability to overcome all odds. Chapters on the *Doctor Zhivago* affair are especially poignant. A must for those who are interested in nonliterary in-fluences upon literary creations.

Gifford, Henry. *Boris Pasternak: A Critical Study*. New York: Cambridge University Press, 1977. Discussion of works written in various stages of Pasternak's life assessing his achievements as a poet, writer of prose fiction, and translator, with many keen critical re-marks. A chronological biography table and select bibliography.

Ivinskaya, Olga. *A Captive of Time*. New York: Double-day, 1978. Ivinskaya, the model for Lara in *Doctor Zhivago*, provides a wealth of information about Pasternak, his views and works, and the Russian lit-erary scene in the 1940's and 1950's.

Mallac, Guy de. *Boris Pasternak: His Life and Art*. Norman: University of Oklahoma Press, 1981. An extensive biography of Pasternak is followed by Mallac's interpretation of the most important fea-tures of Pasternak's works. A detailed chronology of his life, a large bibliography and copious illustra-tions.

Rowland, Mary F., and Paul Rowland. *Pasternak's "Doctor Zhivago."* Carbondale: Southern Illinois University Press, 1967. In this interpretation of *Doc-tor Zhivago*, the authors attempt to clarify allegor-ical, symbolic, and religious meanings. Although some interpretations are not proven, most of them are plausible, making for interesting reading.

Rudova, Larissa. *Understanding Boris Pasternak*. Co-lumbia: University of South Carolina Press, 1997. Presents Pasternak as more than the author of *Doc-tor Zhivago*. His poetic works defined his long ca-reer, and his cultural milieu shaped him. Rudova dis-cusses in detail the thematics, structure, and imagery that distinguish his work.

Sendich, Munir. *Boris Pasternak: A Reference Guide*. New York: Maxwell Macmillan International, 1994. This indispensable reference contains a bibliography of Pasternak editions with more than five hundred entries, a bibliography of criticism with more than one thousand entries, and essays on topics including Pasternak's poetics, relations with other artists, and influences.

Irma M. Kashuba; bibliography updated by Vasa D. Mihailovich and the editors

KENNETH PATCHEN

Born: Niles, Ohio; December 13, 1911
Died: Palo Alto, California; January 8, 1972

PRINCIPAL POETRY
Before the Brave, 1936
First Will and Testament, 1939
The Dark Kingdom, 1942
The Teeth of the Lion, 1942
Cloth of the Tempest, 1943
An Astonished Eye Looks Out of the Air, 1945

Outlaw of the Lowest Planet, 1946
Selected Poems of Kenneth Patchen, 1946, 1957,
    1964
Panels for the Walls of Heaven, 1946
Pictures of Life and Death, 1947
They Keep Riding Down All the Time, 1947
To Say If You Love Someone, 1948
Red Wine and Yellow Hair, 1949
Orchards, Thrones and Caravans, 1952
The Famous Boating Party and Other Poems in Prose,
    1954
Poems of Humor and Protest, 1954
Glory Never Guesses, 1955
A Surprise for the Bagpipe Player, 1956
Hurrah for Anything, 1957
When We Were Here Together, 1957
Poemscapes, 1958
Doubleheader, 1958
Because It Is, 1960
The Love Poems of Kenneth Patchen, 1960
Hallelujah Anyway, 1966
But Even So, 1968
The Collected Poems of Kenneth Patchen, 1968
Love and War Poems, 1968
There's Love All Day, 1970
Wonderings, 1971
In Quest of Candlelighters, 1972

OTHER LITERARY FORMS

Although mainly known as a poet, Kenneth Patchen, a dedicated experimentalist, rejected normal genre distinctions, participating in radical new forms of prose, concrete poetry, poetry-and-jazz, picture poems, and surrealistic tales and fables, as well as other innovations. His first published prose work, a short story titled "Bury Them in God," appeared in a 1939 collection by New Directions. Two years later, in 1941, he published his most celebrated prose work, a pacifist antinovel titled *The Journal of Albion Moonlight*. After that, his prose work began to appear irregularly between the publication of his numerous books of poetry.

ACHIEVEMENTS

An extremely prolific writer, Kenneth Patchen published roughly a book a year during his thirty-six-year writing career from 1936 to his death in 1972. Besides poetry, his artistic works consisted of prose and drama, silkscreen prints, paintings and drawings, hand-painted books, and even papier-mâché animal sculptures. Holding strongly to his belief in the "total artist," Patchen experimented with a wide variety of artistic forms, influencing a generation of poets with his creative energy.

Patchen also played a role in initiating the Poetry-and-Jazz movement in San Francisco during the 1950's. With Kenneth Rexroth and Lawrence Ferlinghetti, Patchen began reading his poetry to jazz accompaniment at the Cellar, a small club in San Francisco, in 1957. Patchen's own innovations in this area had begun six years earlier when he read and recorded his *Fables and Other Little Tales* (1953) to a jazz background. As early as 1945, in his novel *The Memoirs of a Shy Pornographer*, Patchen had presented a two page list of "the disks you'll have to get if you want a basic jazz library."

In addition to the Poetry-and-Jazz movement, Patchen made important contributions to at least three other

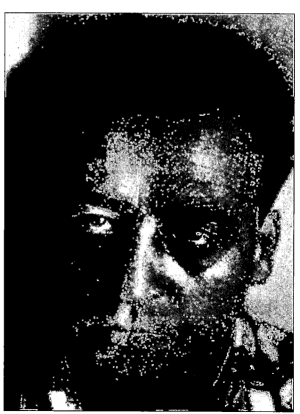

Kenneth Patchen

areas of poetic experimentation. First, in the 1950's, Patchen began to work with surrealistic fable and verse forms in such works as *Fables and Other Little Tales*, *Hurrah for Anything*, and *Because It Is*. Second, as an early experimenter in concrete poetry in this country— see, particularly, *Cloth of the Tempest, Sleepers Awake* (1946), and *Panels for the Walls of Heaven*—Patchen provided American poetry with a uniquely visual poetic form in which the poet is concerned with making an object to be perceived rather than merely read. Patchen's third contribution, also involving visual expression, is his fusion of painting and writing forms. Many of Patchen's books include self-painted covers, drawings printed with poems, and picture-poem posters. Such "painted books" as *The Dark Kingdom, Panels for the Walls of Heaven, Red Wine and Yellow Hair*, and *Poemscapes*, illustrate Patchen's impressive skill as a painter. Although he usually refused to exhibit his paintings, claiming that he preferred bookstores to art galleries, in 1969, a few years before his death, he finally conducted a one-man art show at the Corcoran Gallery in Washington, D.C.

Patchen received a Guggenheim Fellowship in 1936, the Shelley Memorial Award in 1953, and a cash award of ten thousand dollars in 1967 from the National Foundation of Arts and Humanities for his lifelong contribution to American Letters. A small but moving volume titled *Tribute to Kenneth Patchen* (1977), published after the poet's death, attests the great respect in which he was held by contemporaries, publishers, critics, and friends.

BIOGRAPHY

Kenneth Patchen was born into a working-class milieu in Ohio's industrial and mining area, an environment that helped to forge his reputation in the late 1930's and 1940's as a significant proletarian poet. His father, Wayne Patchen, had spent more than twenty-five years working in the steel mills, where both Patchen and his brother also worked for a time. As Larry R. Smith writes in his biography *Kenneth Patchen* (1978), "much like D. H. Lawrence's mining background in England, Patchen's roots in a hard working yet culturally wasted community of poor and semi-poor gave him an early sense of strength and violation." In his early childhood, the family moved to nearby Warren, Ohio, where Patchen

received most of his schooling. The town is located a few miles from Garretsville, the birthplace of Hart Crane.

In Warren, Patchen began writing poetry. He also spent two summers working in the steel mills with his brother and father to earn tuition money for his brief attendance at the University of Wisconsin in 1929. Following this successful year at the university, Patchen wandered around the United States and Canada, working at odd jobs, writing poetry, attending Columbia University for a while, and eventually meeting Miriam Oidemus, the daughter of Finnish immigrants, whom he was to marry in June, 1934, and with whom he would spend the rest of his life.

With the exception of a brief period in Santa Fe, New Mexico, and a short stay in Hollywood in 1937, the Patchens lived in and around Greenwich Village from 1934 to 1950. Although his marriage was happy, Patchen spent a good part of his life in intense physical pain caused by a serious back disability that began in 1937 when Patchen tried to separate the locked bumpers of two cars that had collided. In 1950, a writer's committee, consisting of such notables as T. S. Eliot, W. H. Auden, E. E. Cummings, Thornton Wilder, and William Carlos Williams, gave a series of readings to earn money for Patchen to have corrective surgery.

Finding a renewed sense of mobility after the surgery, Patchen and his wife moved to San Francisco where, in 1954, he befriended Kenneth Rexroth and Lawrence Ferlinghetti, with whom he collaborated in 1957, after a second spinal fusion, to create the Poetry-and-Jazz movement. By 1956, the Patchens were living in Palo Alto, at the southern end of San Francisco Bay, which was to become an important artistic center. In 1959, following a surgical mishap after prescribed exploratory surgery, further surgery was cancelled and Patchen returned to Palo Alto to a bedridden life of almost constant pain. The 1960's, despite his disability, were productive years for Patchen, resulting in such books as *Because It Is, Hallelujah Anyway, But Even So*, and his *Collected Poems*, as well as several recordings of his works and an exhibition of his art in Washington, D.C.

By the time of his death in January, 1972, Patchen had gained a sound reputation as one of America's most influential avant-garde poets and "painters of poems." His experimentation with new forms, whether poetic or paint-erly, as well as his insistence on living the life of the "total artist," despite excruciating pain and deteriorating health, points unmistakably toward a quality that made him the greatly respected artist he was: action even in the face of chaos and pain. "The one thing which Patchen can-not understand, will not tolerate, indeed," wrote Henry Miller, "is the refusal to act. . . . Confronted with excuses and explanations, he becomes a raging lion."

ANALYSIS

One way to trace the development of Kenneth Patchen's vast poetic output is to posit a shift from the emphasis upon class-consciousness and protest in the po-etry of the 1930's to 1940's to a later concern with a sense of wonder and with the spiritual and irrational side of ex-istence. Another and perhaps more compelling approach is to view the entire body of Patchen's work as both spir-itual and revolutionary, marked by the antiestablishment anger of the Old Testament prophets, who condemned the greed of the secular world while celebrating the coming of a just and sacred Kingdom of God.

BEFORE THE BRAVE

In his first book of poetry, *Before the Brave*, Patchen combines a vision of revolution with the wonder of the spiritual world. While lashing out angrily at the "sight-less old men in cathedrals of decay" ("Letter to the Old Men") and the police with "their heavy boots grinding into our faces . . ." ("A Letter to a Policeman in Kansas City"), he still confirms, in Whitmanesque terms, the ability of humanity to seize control of events:

> O be willing to wait no longer.
> Build men, not creeds, seed not soil—
> O raise the standards out of reach.
>
> new men new world new life.

In contrast to the world of the "culture-snob" and the emptiness of "civic pride," Patchen's prophetic voice calls out for a world of unity and wonder, for a "jangling eternity/ Of fellowship and spring where good and law/ Is thicker love and every day shall spawn a god."

FIRST WILL AND TESTAMENT

In another of his so-called protest books of the 1930's, *First Will and Testament*, Patchen again combines or

synthesizes the dual impulses of spiritual wonder and revolutionary zeal. In a poem called "A Revolutionary Prayer," he cries: "O great good God/ I do not know that this fistful of warm dirt/ Has any mineral that wills that the young die. . . ." Here the miner's son, Patchen, looks to the lesson of the ore that he, his father, and his brother had mined to confirm the injustice of war. Similarly, in "The Soldier and the Star," Patchen contrasts the grace, wonder, and wholeness of nature with the destruction of warfare. In the opening four lines he writes: "Rifle goes up:/ Does what a rifle does/ Star is very beautiful:/ Doing what a star does."

ANTIWAR POETRY

In all Patchen's poetry, life's energy and fruitfulness is contrasted with the mechanical, dead, and often violent world of the war makers and the ruling elite. Throughout his work runs a triple vision that serves to direct his ap-proach to the world. First is the painful reality of alien-ation and corruption, of a brutal, ruling monolith that forces people to move toward violence and control rather than growth and human fulfillment. In his earlier poetry this force often takes the form of an actual ruling class in the language of Marxist ideology, while in later works it appears as the nebulous darker side of human nature depicted by Mark Twain in his later works. Sec-ond is the need for humankind to become engaged in or committed to the fullness of life, unity, and social soli-darity. Third is the sense of wonder and imaginative power that opposes the brutal side of human nature.

The corruption and alienation that Patchen sees run-ning rampant in society are characterized largely by cap-italist greed and human violence. Although the first evil is emphasized in his earlier works, the second emerges and is stressed throughout his entire poetic career. "War is the lifeblood of capitalism; it is the body and soul of fascism," wrote Patchen in his novel, *The Journal of Albion Moonlight*, and it is mainly in his poetry that Patchen vividly depicts the bloody force of war. In such poems as "I DON'T WANT TO STARTLE YOU" and "Harrowed by These Apprehensions" (*First Will and Testament*), as well as in the later, more subtle antiwar works such as "In the Courtyard of Secret Life," from his 1957 book, *When We Were Here Together*, Patchen's pacifist sentiments, which he held his entire life, are powerfully expressed.

LOVE AS REDEMPTION

Faced with chaos, alienation, and violence, Patchen believed that the poet must not fall into apathy or bitterness but rather must adopt a worldview in which belief, love, and action are possible. In the face of nothingness, Patchen offers the richness of being; in the face of chaos, he offers unity and order; and in the face of despair and confusion, he offers belief. In the poem "No One Ever Works Alone," from *Panels for the Walls of Heaven*, Patchen further pursues his prophetic faith that a new order will soon sweep away the injustice and evil of the outmoded system. "O Speak Out!," urges Patchen, "Against the dead trash of their 'reality'/ Against 'the world as we see it.'/ Against 'what it is reasonable to believe.'"

Ultimately, for Patchen, the path that leads from destruction to unity is the path of love. "There is only one power that can save the world," writes Patchen in "The Way Men Live Is a Lie" (*An Astonished Eye Looks Out of the Air*), "and that is the power of love for all men everywhere." Though it is a rather prosaic statement, this affirmation illustrates the poet's unswerving belief in the need for commitment to and engagement in the energy of life as opposed to the forces of death that always threaten to engulf humanity. Love, both sexual and spiritual, is an important weapon in that struggle.

A SENSE OF WONDER

Apart from love, another element that maintains unity in life, and one that is particularly evident in Patchen's later books, is a sense of wonder, or, one might say, childlike amazement toward life. In a 1968 interview with Gene Detro, Patchen speakes of the absolute necessity of childlike wonder. Losing this sense, for Patchen, would be equivalent to death. In "O Fiery River" (*Cloth of the Tempest*), Patchen warns that "men have destroyed the roads of wonder,/ And their cities squat like black roads/ In the orchards of life."

For Patchen, as for such Romantic poets as William Blake and William Wordsworth, the most perfect paradigm for wonder is to be found in the innocence of the child. In describing the wonder that exists between two people in sexual union, for example, Patchen speaks of how coming to his beloved Miriam's "wonder" ("For Miriam") is "Like a boy finding a star in a haymow" (*The Teeth of the Lion*). Like Blake in his *Songs of Innocence* (1789), Patchen finds a kind of salvation from injustice and pain in the world of childlike wonder. "Children don't want to know," writes Patchen in "O What a Revolution," a prose poem from *The Famous Boating Party*, "They want to increase their enjoyment of not knowing." In "This Summer Day" (*An Astonished Eye Looks Out of the Air*), the child serves as a metaphor for both life and death. "O Death," writes Patchen, "must be this little girl/ Pushing her blue cart into the water," while "All Life must be this crowd of kids/ watching a hummingbird fly around itself."

As vividly as tanks and the "rustless gun" represent, for Patchen, the horror of history and the blind destructiveness of patriotism, the image of the child and childlike wonder (depicted often in collections of tales and verse such as *Fables and Other Little Tales*, *Hurrah for Anything*, and *But Even So*) represents the innocence, energy, and potential of life's richness. The critics who accuse Patchen of being a poet of dreary negativism ignore the fact that, throughout his poetry, Patchen offers a continuous prophecy of a world of wonder and delight that will inevitably shine through the universal darkness. As a revolutionary and a prophet, Kenneth Patchen was never far removed from the vision of humanity's enormous potential.

OTHER MAJOR WORKS

LONG FICTION: *The Journal of Albion Moonlight*, 1941; *The Memoirs of a Shy Pornographer*, 1945; *Sleepers Awake*, 1946; *See You in the Morning*, 1948.

SHORT FICTION: *Fables and Other Little Tales*, 1953; *Aflame and Afun of Walking Faces*, 1970.

PLAYS: *The City Wears a Slouch Hat*, pr. 1942 (radio play; music by John Cage); *Don't Look Now*, pr. 1959; *Patchen's Lost Plays*, pb. 1977.

BIBLIOGRAPHY

Morgan, Richard G. *Kenneth Patchen: A Collection of Essays*. New York: AMS Press, 1977. A comprehensive and diverse collection of articles and essays on Patchen, with a foreword by Miriam Patchen. From reviews and radio interviews to critical analyses, this is a must for all who are interested in this poet.

_____. *Kenneth Patchen: A Comprehensive Bibliography*. New York: Paul Appel, 1978. A comprehensive, annotated, descriptive bibliography of primary and secondary works. Essential for the Patchen scholar.

Nelson, Raymond. *Kenneth Patchen and American Mysticism*. Chapel Hill: University of North Carolina Press, 1984. A full-length and important literary criticism of Patchen that attempts to secure him a place among contemporary poets without the stigma of "cultist following." Discusses his major works and his leanings toward the mystical in his poetry. An appreciative study of Patchen that concedes, however, that his work is uneven.

Nin, Anais. *The Diary of Anais Nin, 1939-1944*. Vol. 3. New York: Harcourt Brace Jovanovich, 1969. Contains a short biographical sketch of Patchen during his New York days. Favorably analyzes his work *The Journal of Albion Moonlight*.

Smith, Larry R. *Kenneth Patchen*. Boston: Twayne, 1978. This study attempts to correct misunderstandings about Patchen by placing him in the context of his independence. Notes that his love poetry combines "hard realism with a visionary idealism." Discusses also his "poetry-jazz" form, which was one of his highest achievements.

_____. *Kenneth Patchen: Rebel Poet in America*. Huron, Ohio: Bottom Dog Press, 2000. An authorized biography of Patchen by Smith, who completed an earlier critical study of Patchen's works published by Twayne, and a video docudrama *Kenneth Patchen: An Art of Engagement* in 1989. Here this American rebel artist stands exposed as a person of great strength and perseverance. His and wife Miriam's story is one of the great love stories in American literature.

Donald E. Winters, Jr.;
bibliography updated by the editors

COVENTRY PATMORE

Born: Woodford, Essex, England; July 23, 1823
Died: Lymington, Hampshire, England; November 26, 1896

PRINCIPAL POETRY

Poems, 1844

Tamerton Church-Tower and Other Poems, 1853

The Betrothal, 1854

The Espousals, 1856

Faithful for Ever, 1860

The Victories of Love, 1862

The Angel in the House, 1863 (2 volumes; volume 1 includes *The Betrothal* and *The Espousals*, together known as *The Angel in the House*; volume 2 includes *Faithful for Ever* and *The Victories of Love*, together known as *The Victories of Love*)

Odes, 1868

The Unknown Eros and Other Odes, 1877, revised and enlarged 1878

Amelia, 1878

A Selection of Poems, 1931, 1948

The Poems of Coventry Patmore, 1949

OTHER LITERARY FORMS

Coventry Patmore's prose works include essays, a biography, numerous letters, and aphoristic collections. His *Essay on English Metrical Law* was published in 1857 (a critical edition was published in 1961). More than twenty years later he published his first book of prose, a biography of the poet Barry Cornwall titled *Bryan Waller Procter* (1877). He published an account of his success in managing his estate at Heron's Ghyll in *How I Managed and Improved My Estate* (1886). His major collections of prose are: *Principle in Art* (1889); *Religio Poetæ* (1893); and *Rod, Root, and Flower* (1895).

A five-volume edition of his *Works* was published in London in 1907. No edition of his letters exists, but many can be found in Basil Champneys's *Memoirs and Correspondence of Coventry Patmore* (1900) and in *Further Letters of Gerard Manley Hopkins* (1956, Claude C. Abbott, editor), the latter volume containing Patmore's correspondence with Hopkins.

ACHIEVEMENTS

Coventry Patmore has often been referred to as a man and a poet of contradictions, and his achievements—as both—are equally contradictory. He was one of the most popular of all Victorian poets. *The Angel in the House* had gone into a sixth edition by 1885, and by the time of his death in 1896 it had sold more than 250,000 copies. He was widely read throughout the British Empire as well as in the United States and other countries. He was also, however, one the most quickly forgotten of Victorian poets. His reputation went into eclipse in the late 1860's and early 1870's, enjoyed a brief revival in the late 1870's and early 1880's, and then fell into a critical and popular decline that has never been reversed.

BIOGRAPHY

Coventry Kersey Dighton Patmore's life falls roughly into four periods, the latter three of which correspond to his three marriages. The first period, up to his first marriage, was dominated by his father, Peter George Patmore. Peter Patmore was a man devoted to the arts, intent upon social climbing, and steadfast in his devotion to friends. His life, unfortunately, was beset with problems and scandals. Peter was the man to whom William Hazlitt wrote some of the letters later published in *Liber Amoris* (1823), letters in which the married Hazlitt confessed to a degrading love affair with a young girl. When the book was published, both author and recipients were critically condemned for, at least, a serious breach of taste. Two years earlier, in 1821, Peter had been a second in a duel during which his principal was killed, there being reason to believe that Peter's ignorance of the rules of dueling led to the death. In any event, he was condemned for his role in the affair and actually left the country to avoid prosecution. On his return, Peter married Eliza Robertson, a young Scotswoman of strict religious beliefs and practices.

Peter later speculated in railway shares, lost a great deal of money, and fled to the Continent, leaving the twenty-two-year-old Coventry and his siblings without support. Finally, in 1854, Peter published *My Friends and Acquaintances*, a book of memoirs that was poorly received and that managed to rekindle the flame of controversy surrounding the duel of years earlier. Peter died in the following year.

Despite his tumultuous life, Peter was a father who encouraged Coventry's poetic gifts early in life, insisting that his son publish his first volume of poems when he was only twenty-one. Peter had always encouraged

Coventry's love of literature, and the two often read and discussed various authors. Perhaps in response to his wife's stern religious beliefs, Peter offered his children no religious training, preferring to treat the Bible as merely a work in the body of literature for which he had much respect. Peter was concerned enough with Coventry's education, however, to send him to Paris in 1839 to improve his French. There Coventry fell in love with the daughter of Mrs. Gore, an English novelist who had a salon in the Place Vendôme. His love, however, was not reciprocated, and the bitterness of the affair became entangled with his bitterly anti-French sentiments, feelings that lasted most of his lifetime. While in Paris, Coventry began to explore the question of religious belief, seeking principles by which he could live and to which he could devote his work.

In 1842 Coventry visited Edinburgh and the home of his mother's family. There the religious questioning that had begun in Paris was intensified by a personal experience that brought him in contact with the Free Kirk piety and severity that surrounded him. This discomfiting episode became entangled with his anti-Scottish sentiment, also a feeling that lasted all his life.

For some time afterward, Patmore dabbled in reading, painting, and chemistry, conducting experiments in his own laboratory. He earned a meager living by translating and writing for the periodical reviews. In 1844, at the insistence of his father, he published his first volume, *The Poems of Coventry Patmore*. In 1846 he was given a post at the Library of the British Museum. Two years later he became engaged to Emily Augusta Andrews, the daughter of a Congregational minister. They were married in Hampstead in 1847.

The Patmores settled in Highgate, where they entertained such visitors as Robert Browning, Alfred, Lord Tennyson, Thomas Carlyle, and John Ruskin, not to mention Dante Gabriel Rossetti and others of the Pre-Raphaelite Brotherhood. They were very popular with their visitors and seemed to enjoy their "court" in this suburb of London.

Patmore continued his work at the British Museum, and Emily bore six children over the course of their marriage. From all that can be learned, this was indeed a happy marriage, one in which Emily felt the joys of love, home, and motherhood as much as Patmore reveled in being the "breadwinner," patron, and husband to such a family. One record of the marriage is, of course, *The Angel in the House*; the first two parts, *The Betrothal* and *The Espousals*, dealing with courtship and marriage, were published in 1854 and 1856. The second installment in this poem, titled *The Victories of Love*, was also published in two parts: *Faithful for Ever* in 1860 and *The Victories of Love* in 1862. This work anticipates and reflects the event that shattered the happiness of Patmore's fifteen years of marriage: In 1862 Emily died of tuberculosis.

Patmore never recovered from the death of his first wife. In spite of his two later marriages, it was to his first wife and marriage that he always looked when he sought inspiration. The emotional and spiritual completion—as well as the physical ecstacy—that he celebrated in *The Angel in the House* and later poems was never duplicated in his other unions.

For two years after Emily's death Patmore continued to work at the British Museum and sought to provide the warmth and guidance for his children that would have been given by Emily. In February, 1864, at the insistence of his friend Aubrey de Vere, he obtained a leave of absence and journeyed to Rome. There, the leanings he had felt even during his marriage to the stringently anti-Catholic Emily became irresistible and he converted to the Catholic Church, being received by a Jesuit, Father Cardella.

While in Rome, Patmore met his second wife, Marianne Byles. In a small comedy of errors, Patmore first proposed to her and then learned of her personal vow to become a nun. Thinking the vow irrevocable, he withdrew his proposal. When he learned that she could easily obtain a dispensation to revoke the vow, he proposed again, and was accepted. Then he learned that she was not, as he had first assumed, the poor traveling companion of a wealthy woman but was the wealthy heiress herself. Again, he withdrew to protect his freedom of idea and propriety. His friends, however, urged him to reconsider, and he agreed to the marriage. He returned to England before Mary (as she was known) to prepare his children for their new mother. In July, 1864, they were married.

This second marriage produced no children, but it provided Patmore with the opportunity to purchase an estate of four hundred acres near Uckfield in Sussex, known as Heron's Ghyll, into which his family and new wife moved in 1868; he had resigned from the British Museum in 1865. For six years, Patmore ran the estate successfully, surrounding himself with the comforts of the country and spending happy hours with his children and wife. He continued writing poetry and encouraged his wife in her literary project, a translation of St. Bernard's *On the Necessity of Loving God* (c. 1126-1141), which was later published. In 1874, Patmore sold Heron's Ghyll to the Duke of Norfolk for £27,000, realizing a profit of £8,500; he even published a pamphlet on his success as an estate manager. In 1875, the family moved to Hastings and remained there until 1891.

In 1877, Patmore published *The Unknown Eros*, a series of odes dealing primarily with the nature of human and divine love. In the same year he made a pilgrimage to Lourdes, after which he more fully devoted himself to the Blessed Virgin. In 1878, he published his final collection of poems, *Amelia*. After 1879 he wrote virtually no poetry, concentrating rather on expressing his difficult philosophy in prose.

Mary died in 1880. In 1881 Patmore married Harriet Robson, who had entered the household as a domestic during Mary's final illness. In 1882, Emily, Patmore's daughter, who had become a sister of the Society of the Holy Child Jesus, died. One year later, Henry, the youngest of the six children by Emily, died. In that same year, Harriet gave birth to a child, Francis Epiphanius, known as Piffie. Patmore, already sixty, greatly enjoyed the delights of the child—delights that helped to offset the grief he suffered at the death of so many of his loved ones.

In 1891, the Patmores moved to Lymington, where Patmore spent the remaining five years of his life in virtual seclusion. He made occasional trips to London, wrote reviews and columns for the *St. James's Gazette*, and continued writing prose, the first collection of which had been published in 1889 and the last of which would be published in 1895, a year before his death in 1896.

ANALYSIS

The reasons for the oddly varying extremes of Coventry Patmore's reputation are not hard to find. True to his contradictory nature, Patmore was a poet who could and did speak to the "common reader" in an intelligible manner, but he often spoke of mystical and esoteric subjects far beyond the grasp—or even concern—of that same reader. He gave his audience vignettes of domestic bliss—usually of the upper-middle-class variety—offering comfort in times that seemed to threaten the nuclear family and even the Empire's economic underpinnings, yet he included in these vignettes stark confrontations with emotional and spiritual absurdities intimately connected with the vicissitudes of love. Most significant, perhaps, he was able to couch profound psychological and emotional insights in apparently simple—and simplistic—aphorisms.

Patmore's poetry gained for him his great popularity, but his thoughts were often more adaptable to prose. It was in his poetry, however, that he was best able to reveal his artistry and his philosophy in a harmonious blend of lyrical beauty and rich perception. His poetry had for its subject one idea: love. In fact, at least ninety-five percent of his poems deal with love in one form or another. From his earliest musings to his last philosophical treatises in verse, he was preoccupied with the manifestations of divine and human love.

Patmore's early work betrayed his affinity with the Pre-Raphaelites in its overindulgence in description for description's sake, especially in the overabundant use of adjectives before nouns and in the awkward use of Nature as a substantive character. By the time Patmore wrote *The Angel in the House*, however, he had much better control of his language. His style underwent further change and refinement so that by the time of *The Unknown Eros* he had eliminated virtually all of the verbal "deadwood" from his work; even when the language fails in concision, it is usually because the thought attempted is, in itself, incommunicable. Along with control of style, Patmore gained control of emotion. His late poetry best reveals this control when he treats subjects that would easily lend themselves to the worst excesses of Victorian sentimentalism.

While not a systematic philosopher, Patmore was a profound and comprehensive thinker. He undertook to explain—as well as such a phenomenon could be explained—the very idea of Love, easily the most irrational, mysterious, and misunderstood of human emotions. He went even further and attempted to explain the love between God and human beings in terms of human love.

What Patmore attempted was *explanation* and not merely the ecstatic recounting of mystical experience. In order to explain, he believed that he first had to experience and then to know his subject (ironically, a very scientific attitude for someone who despised science). He used his life as such an experiment, and his poetry is his record of the results.

EARLY POEMS

Patmore began his poetic career, as did many of his contemporaries, under the influence of the burgeoning interest in the Middle Ages that had forced its way into many poems of the period. The poems in his first two volumes, published in 1844 and 1853, are filled with knights (both ancient and modern), long journeys on horseback through lush and wild countryside, and, of course, maidens and damsels in need of love or rescue. These early works are quite conventional and, frankly, dull. They attempt to deal with his favorite topic, love, but they stand too much in awe of the subject, afraid to assert with conviction any insight the young poet might have had. Rather, they present lovers meeting, wooing, wedding, and dying—and little else.

These poems are of interest, however, for what they reveal about Patmore's increasing poetic abilities. The earliest of them, especially, are filled with excesses of description that reflect the poet's immaturity and uncertainty. One example, from "The River," will suffice;

> The leafy summer-time is young;
> The yearling lambs are strong;
> The sunlight glances merrily;
> The trees are full of song;
> The valley-loving river flows
> Contentedly along.

It is significant to note that within six lines there are eight modifiers, words attempting to convey complete pictures in themselves but that, through their conventionality, become clichés. The diction fails to "paint" the kind of vivid word-picture the poet was aiming for. Between this early style and that of *The Angel in the House* there is a tremendous gap—and one that shows how far Patmore had progressed by the time he published his most popular poem.

"A LONDON FÊTE"

Of the early poems, however, one demands special attention. Titled "A London Fête," this work of forty-seven lines of four-stress iamb rhymed variously in open quatrains and couplets is unusual for Patmore. The subject is a hanging at Newgate, attended by a mob of curious and excited people. The poem is stark and realistic in its presentation of the bloodthirsty nature of the people "enjoying" this spectacle. Mothers jostle with other mothers to give their babes a good view; young girls tear their garments to provide themselves with rags to wave; sots yell out the doomed man's fate in Hell. The execution takes place, and the crowd releases a cry of joy. As they leave, one baby strings its doll to a stick, and the mother praises this "pretty trick." Two children catch and hang a cat. A pickpocket slinks off to ply his trade elsewhere. Two friends chat amicably. Two people, who fought over the best vantage point, leave to settle their score "with murderous faces."

The poem is an early revelation of Patmore's elitist politics. Throughout his life, he feared (even hated) the idea of democracy and its resultant "mob." The people depicted in this poem are that very mob: drunks, thieves, murderers, and, worst of all, mothers who do not know what is best for their children, or do not care. Although the poem gives voice to Patmore's political prejudices, it is extremely effective nevertheless. Its style is compact and journalistic; its impact is heightened by its one figure of speech: a simile comparing the howling mob to the mob of damned souls in Hell as they rejoice over the addition of another to their fold. The condemnation conveyed is so complete as to disallow any attempt at rebuttal, poetic or otherwise. What is unusual about the poem, in addition to its not being about love, is that it is concerned with one specific event treated as such and left to stand on its own. Later in his career, Patmore seemed unable to isolate and then reincorporate specific events in his poetry. In seeking the significance of the event, he sometimes felt obliged to introduce a prologue (or several) or to elaborate upon the event immediately upon his telling it. One of the faults of *The Angel in the House* is this insistence on commentary of occasionally excessive length. That fault, however, is nowhere to be found in this early, and quite moving, poem of political and social contempt.

THE ANGEL IN THE HOUSE

Patmore's popularity as a poet was achieved with the publication of *The Angel in the House*. This was to be his epic poem celebrating love, woman, home, and god in six books. He finished only four of them, published separately between 1854 and 1862: *The Betrothal, The Espousals, Faithful for Ever,* and *The Victories of Love,* collectively published together as *The Angel of the House* in 1863. The first two books concern a happy marriage between two true lovers; the second two books concern a marriage that begins without mutual love but ends in a state of shared happiness; the final two books, one can conjecture, would have dealt with a good marriage gone bad or a bad marriage that remained bad.

The Angel in the House (the title applies to the first two books, *The Betrothal* and *The Espousals,* as well as to all four) is the story of the courtship and marriage of Felix and Honoria. The poem begins with a prologue set on their eighth anniversary and ends on their tenth. The two books, with their twelve cantos each, cover, respectively, the betrothal and the marriage. The poem is Felix's gift to his wife, as a celebration of the bliss they have enjoyed and as a record of the emotions both felt throughout the course of their love and courtship. Each canto consists of a number of preludes (usually two, but no more than five) followed by an ode that contains the main "episode" or occurrence of that canto. These odes are divided into smaller numbered units. The rhyme is open quatrain and the meter is four-stress lines, usually iambic.

The cantos provide a roughly chronological account of the courtship and marriage; the chronologically arranged material falls within the odes, while the preludes range freely, dealing with any number of questions pertaining to Love but always applying them to the coming incident. How this schema works can be seen, for example, in Canto VI of Book I, "The Dean," in which Felix asks the Dean for his daughter's hand in marriage. The first prelude, "Perfect Love Rare," is a meditation on and apostrophe to Love as well as a lament that, indeed, perfect (that is, pure) love is a "privilege high" to be enjoyed by only the few who merit such reward. The poet goes on to add that

> A day [in Love's] delicious life
>   Though full of terrors, full of tears,
> Is better than of other life
>   A hundred thousand million years.

Thus, the opening prelude, through its conventional hyperbole, offers "evidence" of the rarity of perfect love (but, of course, hints that such rarity will be achieved in the coming match).

The next prelude, "Love Justified," is simply that, a justification of the poet's choice of a mate—as much choice, that is, as love allows. The poet concludes the prelude by claiming that his song will prove that "This little germ of nuptial love,/ . . ./ The root is . . ./ Of all our love to man and God." From the seeking of the rare in the first prelude, the poet carries his readers in the second into the realm of the earthly and attainable and offers a "logical" justification for the action.

The third prelude, "Love Serviceable," is an even more intense call to action. Here the poet asserts that the noble lover does not care about his own fate but only about the happiness of his beloved. His quest for her is, after all, to make her happy; failure in that quest would result in both his and her lack of fulfillment and joy. Thus, he must devote his full attention to obtaining his goal, for "He does not rightly love himself/ Who does not love another more." Another strong reason for taking action is offered in this prelude as the canto progresses to the ode containing the action.

There is, however, one final prelude, "A Riddle Solved," that reads:

> Kind souls, you wonder why, love you,
>   When you, you wonder why, love none.
>   We love, Fool, for the good we do,
> Not that which unto us is done!

The riddle thus solved by the altruistic nature of true love, the canto moves to the ode, divided into four parts. Felix is visiting the Dean's family. In the first part of the ode, the ladies leave to take tea outside. In the second part, the Dean and Felix make small talk over trifling matters. In the third part, Felix makes his plea for the daughter's hand. In the fourth part, the Dean, giving him his best wishes, sends him out to woo Honoria, who is having tea. Thus, the canto focuses on the act of Felix's seeking Honoria's hand but prefaces that act with observations on the rarity of perfect love, justifications for pursuing such a rare phenomenon, and insights into the nature of true love in such pursuit. The reader is, then, quite prepared for the act and its outcome by these philosophical probings that stand at the head of each canto.

The relationship among the preludes and between the preludes and odes is well handled by Patmore and provides much of the structural integrity of this long, thoughtful poem. By including such preludes, Patmore is able to take incidents with apparent meaning and amplify or alter such meaning to suit his didactic purpose. Usually behind such manipulation is the motive of revealing something to the readers that should have been quite obvious but was hidden by the mundaneness of the everyday occurrence. Such insight is one of the strengths of the poem.

The mundaneness of the subject matter, however, contributes to the poem's major flaw, and it is a significant one. Patmore was attempting to mold the everyday to the poetic and the poetic to the everyday. By further attempting to imitate the epic mode, he was forcing a gravity and significance upon his subject matter which it simply could not bear.

The poem's other principal fault—especially from a modern reader's point of view—is the philosophy upon which it is built, an extreme Victorian male chauvinism. Throughout the cantos there is constant reference to the most offensive stereotypes of women; they are foreign lands, whose customs can never be understood by men; they are frail children in need of paternalistic husbands; they are empty-headed vessels in need of men's intelligence; they are objects to be sought and possessed; they are long-suffering companions put on earth to please their men; they are parts in need of a whole. In fairness to Patmore, it must be admitted that he viewed man as equally incomplete and dependent upon woman for completion, but the poet insisted on basing his philosophy on "unequal equality," and, to echo George Orwell, man was "more equal than woman"—at least in Patmore's conservative worldview.

THE VICTORIES OF LOVE

This male chauvinism is also apparent in *The Victories of Love* (the title used to refer collectively to the third and fourth books of *The Angel in the House*, *Faithful for Ever* and *The Victories of Love*). The poem, written as a series of verse letters, is not as successful as its predecessor. It lacks a true emotional focus, its style is much less direct, and its structure is not as tightly controlled. The two books consist of nineteen and thirteen letters, respectively, written in four-stress couplets. The effect of such a scheme is monotony, which further undercuts the impact of the poem.

The "victories" of the title refer to the effort of the two lovers whose story is unfolded through the many letters. Frederick Graham, a cousin of Honoria, is deeply in love with her when she weds Felix (at the close of *The Angel in the House*). He embarks on a long sea voyage to try to overcome his passion, but, as his letters to his mother show, he is unable to do so. In desperation for "a change," he marries Jane, whom he does not really love, although she grows to love him. The remainder of the poem recounts their marriage, the births and deaths of some of their children, and their "victories" in establishing first respect, then concern, and finally love for each other. Unfortunately, Jane dies, leaving Frederick with a still-unabated passion for Honoria, a passion he again tries to lose by going to sea. He does, however, see his remaining child married to Honoria's (the subjects, perhaps, of the unwritten fifth and sixth books of the epic).

In this poem, Patmore attempts far too much. He tries to imitate prattling, gossipy old ladies in strictly rhymed couplets; he tries to convey genuine emotions regarding love and honor and felicity in verse letters; and he tries, again, to justify his view of women by placing too much of the philosophical burden on the shoulders of poor dying Jane, whose letters to her mother, mother-in-law, and husband just prior to her death do not escape the maudlin extremes that Patmore was usually able to avoid. Jane pleads with Frederick to accept that: "Image and glory of the man,/ As he of God, is woman. Can/ This holy, sweet proportion die/ Into a dull equality?" Perhaps Patmore himself realized the significant falling-off in effectiveness in these two books of his projected six and abandoned the idea of an epic on the Household of Love.

THE UNKNOWN EROS AND OTHER ODES

If *The Angel in the House* proved to be Patmore's most popular work, his final major volume of poetry, *The Unknown Eros and Other Odes*, has certainly proved to be his best collection. This volume, also published in two parts, consists of two books, the first containing a proem and twenty-four odes, the second eighteen odes. In these odes Patmore, loosening the hold of traditional prosody, uses a variety of meters and rhyme schemes to treat his favorite topic—Love—and his next-

favorite topic—the political and social decline of England and her empire. As a poet of analogies, Patmore saw the similarities in his love for Woman and for God and his love for his country. Likewise, he saw the decline and death of his beloved as a reflection of the decline and death of his beloved country, and vice versa. These analogies appear throughout the odes, both explicitly and implicitly. In fact, the poet boldly announces in the proem that it may be "England's parting soul that nerves [his] tongue" and gives him the impetus to break his years of silence with these odes designed to restore to his beloved (woman and country) some of the luster lost by either death or dying.

Part of the strength of these odes lies in their variety of subject and mode. Here Patmore's prosody, more relaxed and much more colloquial, comes closer to capturing the essence of speech he so vainly sought in his earlier works; these odes seem almost effortless in their flow and offer no resistance to the reader in terms of language. They may, however, continue to resist the reader in terms of the density of their thought, the political theories expounded, or the philosophical basis of the majority of the observations. In spite of such barriers, these odes succeed as no other of Patmore's poems do in their eloquence, their emotional impact, and their profundity.

The first twelve odes in the first book form a thematic unit on love and denial of love by death; the odes are probably based on Patmore's experience with his first wife, Emily. The first few odes focus on time and its passage. Beginning with the fifth ode, there is a distinct unit on his loss at the death of his wife, on his memory of her, on his fears and hopes, and on his remarriage. These poems are some of the finest Patmore wrote, containing emotions that manage to travel more than a century between then and now with grace and meaning. "The Azalea," "Departure," and, especially, "The Toys" show Patmore at his most mature and controlled; he is able, as few of his contemporaries were, to touch a poignant note lightly enough to allow the reverberations to have their full impact on the reader. There is moralizing here, and some preaching as well, but all is blended with a sensitivity unsurpassed in his other work, including his best prose. That sensitivity is well reflected in his superbly economical style; here is one example from "Eurydice," in which he addresses his lost mate:

Thee, whom en'n more than Heaven loved I have,
And yet have not been true
Even to thee,
I dreaming, night by night, seek now to see,
And, in a mortal sorrow, still pursue
Thro' sordid streets and lanes. . . .

Here, as in his earliest work, there is an abundance of modifiers; but now each one is charged with meaning, effectively holding readers before allowing them to move on to the next complementary and expansive link in an emotional chain.

True to his extremes, Patmore balances his best with some of his worst poetry in these odes. His political odes are not nearly as successful as the personal, nor are they, in themselves, good verse. They are marred by long-windedness, awkward lines, and, too often, repugnant ideas.

The second book of odes continues the mixture of personal and political observations but contains some of his most difficult work, the odes in which he uses the classical myths to expound his ideas on human and divine love. Some of them simply do not fulfill their intention, and most of the political odes are also unsuccessful. The personal poems, however, such as "The Child's Purchase," are generally very moving.

AMELIA AND LATER POEMS

After *The Unknown Eros and Other Odes*, Patmore wrote very few poems, and these are generally rather bland when they are not offensive. For example, *Amelia* returns to the theme of the sacrificing woman and has a young girl weep over the grave of her lover's former betrothed; that, however, is not enough: She actually takes the dead woman's ring and swears to wear it for *her* sake because "dear to maidens are their rivals dead." Here Patmore succeeds in straining—some would say rupturing—plausibility, as he does in "The Girl of All Periods," in which a "feminist" who smokes cigarettes and reads George Sand is "put in her place" by a few sly male compliments.

Patmore insisted that his poetry was not original, in meter or insight. He even abhorred the charge of "originality" when he heard it applied to himself. By this insistence on drawing from wells already much frequented, Patmore placed himself as a poet in a very vulnerable

position. Even profound insights can become monotonous if they are constantly delivered in simple aphorisms. To that temptation to be aphoristic, Patmore too often succumbed. It is unfortunate that so much of his best poetry and his best thought lie buried. Whether this arch-conservative Victorian poet's work will again be popularly read is open to question. What is certain is this: His works deserve attention.

OTHER MAJOR WORKS

NONFICTION: *Essay on English Metrical Law*, 1857; *Bryan Waller Procter*, 1877; *How I Managed and Improved My Estate*, 1886; *Principle in Art*, 1889; *Religio Poetæ*, 1893; *Rod, Root, and Flower*, 1895; *Memoirs and Correspondence of Coventry Patmore*, 1900 (Basil Champneys, editor).

BIBLIOGRAPHY

Anstruther, Ian. *Coventry Patmore's Angel: A Study of Coventry Patmore, His Wife Emily, and The Angel in the House*. London: Haggerston Press, 1992. A short biographical study of Patmore and his wife. Includes bibliographical references and index.

Crook, J. Mordaunt. "Coventry Patmore and the Aesthetics of Architecture." *Victorian Poetry* 34, no. 4 (Winter, 1996): 519-543. Crook discusses Patmore as an architectural critic of extraordinary power and perhaps the most eloquent expositor of architectural style.

Fisher, Benjamin F. "The Supernatural in Patmore's Poetry." *Victorian Poetry* 34, no. 4 (Winter, 1996): 544-557. An examination of supernaturalism in Patmore's work. Suggests that careful readers will discover ghosts, vampires, and hauntings recurring in Patmore's poetry.

Gosse, Edmund. *Coventry Patmore*. New York: Charles Scribner's Sons, 1905. The earliest book-length critical study published on Patmore, designed to complement the "official" biography of the Patmore family published by Basil Champneys. Full of anecdotes and personal accounts, it is nevertheless an important critical work on Patmore.

Oliver, E. J. *Coventry Patmore*. New York: Sheed & Ward, 1956. A short, accessible biography on Patmore suggested for the beginning reader. Discusses love as the focus of his life, his family, and his mystical leanings that put him at odds with clericalism. Examines the importance of place and background in his poems.

Reid, John Cowie. *Mind and Art of Coventry Patmore.* London: Routledge & Kegan Paul, 1957. This full-length study of Patmore explores the influences on Patmore and his thought, and his "doctrine" of love as expressed in his poems. Particularly noteworthy is the chapter on the odes, "The Unknown Eros and Other Odes." Includes an extensive bibliography.

Weinig, Mary Anthony. *Coventry Patmore.* Boston: Twayne, 1981. An appreciative introduction to Patmore, noting that his poems are "rooted in immediate experience of life and love and marriage." Contains strong critical commentary on *The Angel in the House* and *Faithful for Ever* (1860). Includes a separate section on his odes, which Weinig considers the best access to Patmore for the modern reader.

Richard F. Giles;
bibliography updated by the editors

CESARE PAVESE

Born: Santo Stefano Belbo, Italy; September 9, 1908
Died: Turin, Italy; August 27, 1950

PRINCIPAL POETRY

Lavorare stanca, 1936, expanded 1943 (*Hard Labor*, 1976)
La terra e la morte, 1947
Verrà la morte e avrà i tuoi occhi, 1951
Poesie edite e inedite, 1962
A Mania for Solitude: Selected Poems, 1930-1950, 1969

OTHER LITERARY FORMS

Cesare Pavese was primarily a novelist. He wrote nine novels, beginning with *Paesi tuoi* in 1941 (*The Harvesters*, 1961). His nonfiction *Dialoghi con Leucò* (1947; *Dialogues with Leucò*, 1966) and the novel *La luna e i falò* (1950; *The Moon and the Bonfire*, 1952) are

considered his masterpieces. Pavese is noted for dealing with classical myths and writing about characters from the countryside. R. W. Flint translated a selection of his fiction, and many of his works of fiction continue to be available in English.

Pavese was also a respected essayist. In his expanded edition of *Hard Labor*, published in 1943, he included two highly valued essays: "The Poet's Craft" and "Concerning Certain Poems Not Yet Written." His other essays were published posthumously as *La letteratura americana e altri saggi*, edited by Italo Calvino, in 1951. In 1970, they were translated in English by Edwin Fussell as *American Literature: Essays and Opinions*.

Pavese was also an accomplished translator of English works into Italian. He began with Sinclair Lewis's *Our Mr. Wrenn* in 1931. He went on to translate such authors as Herman Melville, James Joyce, Sherwood Anderson, and William Faulkner. His diaries and letters were also published.

ACHIEVEMENTS

Cesare Pavese was one of a group of writers to come to maturity during the mid-1930's. He is noted for his anti-fascist efforts and his commitment to other left-wing causes, and he was even imprisoned for his activities. His first volume of poetry, *Hard Labor*, published in 1936 and expanded in 1943, considered one of his major achievements, has been translated into English by such writers as Margaret Crosland and William Arrowsmith. Several poems were censored by the authorities, a testimony to Pavese's subversive political thinking. Pavese concentrated on prose in the years following World War II, but he returned to verse a few years before his death, first publishing a group of poems called *La terra e la morte* in a magazine. These poems have a stark, lyrical quality to them. In 1950, Cesare Pavese received the Strega Prize, Italy's greatest literary award.

BIOGRAPHY

Cesare Pavese was born to parents Eugenio and Consolina Pavese in 1908, at their family vacation spot in the Piedmont region of Italy. The family, which included an older daughter, lived in Turin. His father worked as a bailiff in the court system. When Cesare was six years old, his father died. He started writing poetry while still in secondary school. In 1923, Pavese entered the Liceo Massimo d'Azeglio to complete his high school studies. Agusto Monti became his teacher and mentor. In 1926, Pavese entered the University of Turin. It was here that he began his lifelong interest in American literature. He did his thesis work on Walt Whitman, getting a degree from the university in 1930. His mother died the same year. He also started work on a cycle on poems that would become part of *Hard Labor*.

To help support himself during his postgraduate years, Pavese translated Herman Melville's *Moby Dick* (1851), as well as works by James Joyce, John Dos Passos, and Sherwood Anderson. Pavese also joined anti-Fascist groups; in 1935, he was arrested for holding letters of a jailed anti-Fascist which he received from his girlfriend Tina Pizzardo, who was a member of the Communist Party. Pavese served seven months of a three-year sentence under house arrest and in exile.

His first book, *Hard Labor*, was published in 1936, but censors reduced the number of poems by four. Pavese would later publish this volume in a much larger edition. After his arrest, Pavese continued to write but stopped publishing for some time. His friend Guilio Einaudi restored a publishing company, and Pavese worked for and published most of his works with this publishing house. In 1941 and 1942, Pavese published two novels, as well as a translation of William Faulkner's *The Hamlet*. He left Turin in 1943, when the city fell under Nazi control. After the war, he returned to Turin and joined the Communist Party. After the war, Pavese published three books, *Feria d'agosto* (1946; *Summer Storm and Other Stories*, 1966), *La terra e la morte*, and *Dialogues with Leucò*, which is considered one of his masterpieces. In 1949, Pavese met and fell in love with the American actress Constance Dowling. Their affair lasted a year. Pavese was known as a troubled person. He seemed to embody the modern existentialist despair of his day. In August of 1950, despondent over a broken love affair, Pavese killed himself with an overdose of sleeping pills.

ANALYSIS

Though influenced by American writers such as Walt Whitman, Cesare Pavese's work is not particularly well known in the United States. Yet he has a worldwide rep-

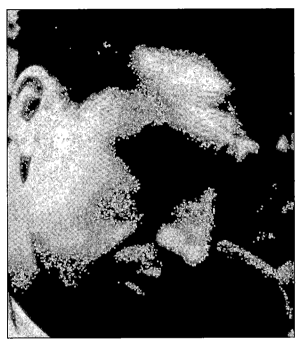

Cesare Pavese

utation and is a very important figure in twentieth century modern Italian literature. Pavese's work has influenced many modern poets, including Denise Levertov. Her volume *Life in the Forest* (1978) contains a section of poems inspired by Pavese's work.

HARD LABOR

Pavese once said of *Hard Labor* that it "might have saved a generation." For a volume in which he wished to speak to and for a generation, it is striking to note that one of its major themes is silence—and another solitude. It is a silence at times wished for, and freeing: "Here, in the dark, alone,/ my body rests and feels it is the one master of itself" (in "Mania di solitudine," "Passion for Solitude"); at other times it seems to crush the person who cannot escape it: "every day the silence of the lonely room/ closes on the rustle of movement, of every gesture, like air" (in "La voce," "The Voice"). In his early poem "Antenati" ("Ancestors"), Pavese strongly suggests that the inability to speak is passed down through generations of rough men: "I found out I had lived, before I was born,/ in tough, sturdy, independent men, masters of themselves./ None of them knew what to say, so they just kept quiet." The women in the family also endure a hard silence: "In our family women don't matter./ What I mean is, our women stay home/ and make children like me, and keep their mouths shut." They suffer their own hard labor.

In "Gente spaesata" ("Displaced People"), the natural landscape can induce a hypnotic silence between men: "We've seen too much of the sea./ Late afternoon—the colorless water stretches dully away, disappearing into air. My friend's staring at the sea,/ and I'm staring at him, and neither says a word." The antidote to the sea is the hills, which supplant the earlier barren landscape. In Pavese's words, almost like a drinking song or boast, the hills become fleshy and fertile, ripe for dreams—dreams of women. In such a dream landscape, imagined conversation is possible: "We could stroll through the vineyards and, maybe,/ meet with a couple of girls, dark brown, ripened by the sun,/ we could strike up a conversation, we could sample their grapes." A harsh landscape swirls with levels of talk: simple talk, drunken talk, imaginary talk—all transformed by the poet's language.

Though the individual suffers in silence, a kind of collective is available that unites these lonely, working people: "All he feels is the pavement, which other men have made—/ men with calloused hands, hands like his" (in "Lavorare stanca," "Hard Labor"). The old pastoral ode of a sheepherder following his flocks, has fallen away to reveal a flintier modern man—worn down but bearing up—in silence: if not a part of, at least within his or her community. In these kinds of poems the solitary wanderer is not the only person to hold dreams or to suffer dreams being crushed. Poems such as "Pensieri di Deola" ("Deola Thinking"), "La moglie del barcaiolo" ("The Boatman's Wife"), and "Atlantic Oil" show people beaten down, exhausted, by the world of work, by the necessity of getting by, which is the hard soil all men must cling to: "The long days work has left them dead" (in "Crepuscolo di sabbiatori," "Sand-Diggers' Twilight").

In "Atlantic Oil," a working mechanic is invited by the landscape to fall away into dreams: "And the story ends with the mechanic marrying the vineyard of his choice,/ and the girl that goes with it. He'll work outdoors in the sun." His heady dreams are contrasted with the knowledge of a drunken mechanic who sleeps in a ditch by the road. All these worlds will spiral down, "plunging in the valley below, down in the darkness."

Sometimes, memories of the past are all that are available, or fantasies of an imagined future with someone, a future that will never happen. The poems, despite their hard realities, contain romantic and lyric qualities that seem to hold out some hope of rescue. Usually it is an imagined woman who holds out the most hope for a man, as in "Paternità" ("Fatherhood"): "Every man,/ alone with a drink, will see her again. She'll always be there." Her permanent absence, her fleshly invisibility, ultimately creates longing and confusion and a return to silence in "Incontro" ("Encounter"): "I created her from the ground of everything/ I love the most, and I cannot understand her."

The poems in *Hard Labor* are often crafted with a long, prose-like line. The people in the city and countryside seem fresh from a young poet's developing vision, seem to take their inspiration from another solitary wanderer: Walt Whitman.

VERRÀ LA MORTE E AVRÀ I TUOI OCCHI

After a period of time when Pavese wrote only novels, he returned to verse. In the later poems, he uses a more spare line length. The poems are stark lyrics, often addressed directly to a "you." In 1945, he published in a magazine a group of nine poems called *La terra e la morte*. These poems were later collected in Pavese's posthumous volume *Verrà la morte e avrà i tuoi occhi* (death will come and it will have your eyes).

The later poems resonate with several of Pavese's familiar themes. The land and sea are ever-present, as is the quixotic search for a love that cannot be possessed. As always, silence pervades, and it assumes even darker forms, as in "La terre et la morte" ("Earth and Death"): "You are earth and death./ Your season is darkness/ and silence." In the series of love lyrics connected to the title poem, love becomes an open wound, a fatality, subsumed by silence:

Death will come, and it will have your eyes.
It will be like ending a vice, like seeing a dead face
emerge from the mirror,
like hearing closed lips speak.
We'll go down in silence.

A few months after these last poems were written, Cesare Pavese took his own life. He was only forty-one.

OTHER MAJOR WORKS

LONG FICTION: *Paesi tuoi*, 1941 (*The Harvesters*, 1961); *La spiaggia*, 1942 (*The Beach*, 1963); *Il compagno*, 1947 (*The Comrade*, 1959); *Il carcere*, 1949 (*The Political Prisoner*, 1959); *La casa in collina*, 1949 (*The House on the Hill*, 1956); *La bella estate*, 1949 (*The Beautiful Summer*, 1959); *Il diavolo sulle colline*, 1949 (*The Devil in the Hills*, 1954); *Tra donne sole*, 1949 (*Among Women Only*, 1953); *La luna e i falò*, 1950 (*The Moon and the Bonfire*, 1952); *Fuoco grande*, 1959 (with Bianca Garufi; *A Great Fire*, 1963).

SHORT FICTION: *Feria d'agosto*, 1946 (*Summer Storm and Other Stories*, 1966); *Notte di festa*, 1953 (*Festival Night and Other Stories*, 1964); *Racconti*, 1960; *Told in Confidence and Other Stories*, 1971; *Stories*, 1987.

NONFICTION: *Dialoghi con Leucò*, 1947 (*Dialogues with Leucò*, 1966); *La letteratura americana e altri saggi*, 1951 (Italo Calvino, editor; *American Literature: Essays and Opinions*, 1970); *Il mestiere di vivere: Diario, 1935-1950*, 1952 (*The Burning Brand: Diaries, 1935-1950*, 1961; also known as *The Business of Living*).

TRANSLATIONS: *Il nostro signor Wrenn*, 1931 (of Sinclair Lewis's *Our Mr. Wrenn*); *Moby-Dick*, 1932 (of Herman Melville's novel); *Riso nero*, 1932 (of Sherwood Anderson's *Dark Laughter*); *Uomini e topi*, 1938 (of John Steinbeck's *Of Mice and Men*); *Il borgo*, 1940 (of William Faulkner's *The Hamlet*).

BIBLIOGRAPHY

Arrowsmith, William. Introduction to *Hard Labor*. Baltimore, Md.: The Johns Hopkins University Press, 1976. Arrowmsith's introduction to Pavese's first volume of poetry is a wonderful look at Pavese's life, influence, and poetic achievement.

Biasin, Gian-Paolo. *The Smile of the Gods: A Thematic Study of Cesare Pavese's Works*. Translated by Yvonne Freccero. Ithaca, N.Y.: Cornell University Press, 1968. This critical study details Pavese's efforts in trying to modernize Italian literature and deal with American influences. Biasin looks at a major theme of Pavese's work and life: the failure of communication. The opening chapter focuses on Pavese's poetry.

O'Healy, Áine. *Cesare Pavese*. Boston: Twayne, 1988. This work provides a study, a biographical sketch, and a chronology of Pavese's life and work. The author seeks to correct the popular myths that have grown up around Pavese. She wants the critical attention to focus on his work.

Thompson, Doug. *Cesare Pavese: A Study of the Major Novels and Poems*. New York: Cambridge University Press, 1982. This critical study looks at Pavese's life and his major prose works and chronicles the development of his poetry from the early works to the last works of published and unpublished poems.

Williamson, Alan. "Pavese's Late Love Poems." *The American Poetry Review* 26, no. 5 (September/October, 1997). This article by a noted contemporary poet and critic looks at a few of Pavese's early poems from *Hard Labor* and compares them to a few late love poems, notably "La putana contadina" ("A Whore from the Country"). The article also addresses some of William Arrowsmith's translations of Pavese's poems.

Robert W. Scott

MIODRAG PAVLOVIĆ

Born: Novi Sad, Voyvodina, Serbia; November 28, 1928

PRINCIPAL POETRY

87 pesama, 1952
Stub sećanja, 1953
Oktave, 1957
Mleko iskoni, 1963
Velika Skitija, 1969
Nova Skitija, 1970
Hododarje, 1971
Svetli i tamni praznici, 1971
Velika Skitija i druge pesme, 1972
Zavetine, 1976
The Conqueror in Constantinopole: Poetry, 1976
Karike, 1977 (*Links*, 1989)

Pevanja na viru, 1977 (*Singing at the Whirlpool*, 1983)

Bekstva po Srbiji, 1979

Izabrane pesme, 1979

Vidovnica, 1979

Izabrana dela Miodraga Pavlovića, 1981 (4 volumes)

Divnoćudo, 1982

Nova pevanja na viru, 1983

The Slavs Beneath Parnassus: Selected Poems, 1985

Glas pod kamenom = A Voice Locked in Stone, 1985

Sledstvo, 1985

Bezazlenstva, 1989

Knjiga staroslovna, 1989

Ulazak u Kremonu, 1989

Cosmologia profanata, 1990

Esej o coveku, 1992

Pesme o detinjstvu i ratovima, 1992

Knjiga horizonta, 1993

Medustepenik: Pesme, 1994

Izabrane i nove pesme, 1946-1996, 1996

Nebo u pecini: Sa crtezima autora, 1996

Posvecenje pesme: Izbor iz poezije, 1996

Izvor: Poezija II, 2000

OTHER LITERARY FORMS

Miodrag Pavlović has published two books of short stories, *Most bez obala* (1956; a bridge without shores) and *Bitni ljudi: Price sa Uskrsnjeg ostrva* (1995; fundamental folk), and two books of short plays, *Igre bezimenih* (1963; the plays of the nameless), and *Koraci u podzemlju: Scensko prikazanje u dva dela* (1991; steps in the underworld). Although his stories and plays are not nearly as successful as his poetry, they illuminate his approach to other genres. More important are his essays on various aspects of literature in general and of Serbian and Yugoslav literature in particular; these are contained in *Rokovi poezije* (1958; the realm of poetry), *Osam pesnika* (1964; eight poets), and *Poetika modernog* (1978; modern poetry). Equally important is Pavlović's work on several anthologies, one of which, *Antologija srpskog pesništva, XIII-XX vek* (1964; an anthology of Serbian poetry, eighteenth to twentieth centuries), has continued to provoke animated discussion. He has also edited anthologies of Serbian lyric folk poetry, modern English po-

etry, and the poetry of European Romanticism. Finally, he has translated extensively from classical and modern literatures, especially German, English, French, and Italian.

ACHIEVEMENTS

Miodrag Pavlović is a powerful and significant poetic figure. Together with Vasko Popa and other poets, he was instrumental in bringing about the revolution in Serbian poetry in the early 1950's, when a more modernistic approach won over the more traditional and realistic one. He has written a great number of enduring poems; with his protest against the senselessness and injustice of existence, with his untiring quest for truth and for roots, with his elevation of Serbian poetry to a high level of technical excellence and spiritual richness, he has ploughed a deep furrow in Serbian, Yugoslav, and world poetry. Pavlović already has a large group of followers among younger poets, and he has been translated into many languages. In 1978 he was elected to the Serbian Academy of Sciences and Arts. When he has written his last verse, there is no doubt that critics will rank him as one of the most significant Serbian poets of the twentieth century.

BIOGRAPHY

Miodrag Pavlović was born in 1928 in Novi Sad, Voyvodina (later, Yugoslavia; now Serbia). He attended medical school at the University of Belgrade and, after he was graduated, practiced medicine for a short while. Soon, however, he abandoned medicine to devote all of his time to writing. He was briefly a director of the Theater of Belgrade and then was an editor in a leading Belgrade publishing house, Prosveta, from 1961 to 1984.

ANALYSIS

Miodrag Pavlović's first volume of poetry, *87 pesama* (87 poems), was one of those exceptional books that usher in a new era in literature. Together with Vasko Popa, Pavlović entered the scene at a crucial time in the history of contemporary Yugoslav literature—a time when World War II literature was decreasing in popularity and Yugoslav writers were once again becoming aware of the outside world. Of great significance is Pavlović's emphasis on a distinctly Anglo-Saxon way of conceiving, writing, and appreciating poetry. He was one of the first to heed the call for regeneration and to lead Serbian poetry away from Romanticism or pragmatic utilitarianism and toward a more disciplined, analytical, and intellectual approach.

In his essays on literature, especially on poetry, Pavlović reveals his thoughts, tastes, and preferences. Explaining the principles of selection which underlie his anthology of Serbian poetry, Pavlović has said that he chose poems that "speak about the fundamental questions of individual and collective existence, poems that either convey a thought or lead through their content directly to cognition." In the same book, he acknowledged that he had selected poems, not poets. This de-emphasis of personality is a reflection of T. S. Eliot's view that literature should be as depersonalized and unemotional as possible. A longtime student of Eliot and other English and American poets, Pavlović found it natural to implement their views and ideas in his poetry, adding, to be sure, his own approach.

87 PESAMA

Pavlović's significance as a poet is not, however, limited to the historical role that he has played. The purely artistic quality of his poetry, his many innovations, the

Miodrag Pavlović (Courtesy of Language Studies Centre, London School of Economics and Political Science)

influence he has exerted on younger poets—all of these add to his stature. The first poem in *87 pesama*, "Whirlwind," is almost a programmatic poem, fully indicative of Pavlović's early stage:

> I wake up
> over the bed a storm
> Ripe sour cherries fall
> into the mud
> In the boat
> dishevelled women
> wail
> The whirlwind
> of wicked fingernails
> chokes the dead
> Soon
> nothing will be known
> about that

Many recurring elements of Pavlović's poetry—elements which startled and even provoked some of his early readers—are present in "Whirlwind." This poem reveals the poet's anxiety and a certain revulsion against existence, undoubtedly caused in part by the horrors of the war. Similar images of anxiety, horror, despair can be found in other poems in this collection. Man is compared to an ant standing at the bottom of the cellar stairs, whose cry simply "does not reach." When someone nearby dies, "the world becomes lighter by a human brain" ("Requiem"). Corpses swim under the ground, and "lost days and dissipated suns drown in a river like dead clouds" ("The Damned Forest"). The collection is dominated by images of darkness, night, death, destruction, chaos, apocalypse: a skull, a funeral, a headless hen hanging by the leg from a cloud. The overwhelmingly bleak atmosphere is relieved only by the last poem, "Hope Should Be Found Again."

STUB SEĆANJA

This despairing mood of *87 pesama* is carried over to Pavlović's second collection, *Stub sećanja* (a pillar of memory). Skulls and heads without faces or hair reappear; cries are heard again. Yet, one feels that Pavlović is trying to escape the hopeless setting of his first book, embarking on a long quest for a meaning. It is not coincidental that the title of this collection refers to the power of memory, for it is in one's memory that the answers to life's riddles should be sought. Death is no longer the end of everything; rather, it is a key ("Variations on the Skull," IV). In the central poem of this book, "The Defense of Our City," the poet reiterates: "I have hopes for this city" ("this city" is a symbol of human existence).

OKTAVE

In Pavlović's third collection, *Oktave* (octaves), the poet continues his quest. He moves out of the city into nature's wide-open spaces; at the same time, he turns inward to the unconscious. The figure of a sleeping tiger whose head rests on the poet's shoulder symbolizes the potent forces of the unconscious, which reside in man like an animal. There are formal changes in this volume as well: Instead of brief poems consisting almost entirely of metaphors, images, and terse statements, there are long descriptive poems of eight stanzas, some of which rhyme—a rare occurrence in Pavlović's verse. Nevertheless, the central theme of these poems remains the merciless search for origin and identity: "On the ridge of the desert the chorus of stars is asking me:/ who are you?" ("Ulcinj").

MLEKO ISKONI

In order to answer such questions, Pavlović entered a new phase of development, a change that resulted in an entirely different kind of poetry. In *Mleko iskoni* (primeval milk), the poet turns to prehistoric times and Greek antiquity. Framed by poems about the creation and the end of the world, this cycle of fourteen poems depicts the downfall of the once-proud Greek civilization. Various witnesses of this downfall express their despair. Thus, Orestes laments: "On the bald earth/ another man stands/ and not a single god" ("Orestes on the Acropolis"). Odysseus complains: "Not even gods want to be born any more" ("Odysseus Speaks"). Pindar expresses doubt concerning the need for poetry: "I don't want to be a poet any more,/ heroes are buried" ("Pindar on a Stroll"). The decay has reached such proportions that "No one will join our secret society any more. . .,/ Eternity no longer has a form nor a substance./ No one will be accepted any more" ("Eleusinian Shadows").

Nevertheless, this cycle marks a significant departure from the pervasive despair of Pavlović's previous volumes. Here, he depicts the downfall of a mighty civilization in mythical terms. The dying Greek civilization is replaced in the poet's scheme with the advent of the Slavic tribes who had begun to settle in the north.

VELIKA SKITIJA AND NOVA SKITIJA

Pavlović devoted his next two books to these primitive but virile warriors and peasants who swooped down from the north and spread destruction in their wake, at the same time signaling a new beginning. *Velika Skitija* (great Scythia) and *Nova Skitija* (new Scythia) represent the high point in Pavlović's return to the past in his quest for the roots of his nation. Some of his best poems, such as "The Slavs Before Parnassus," "Epitaph of the Old Slavic Bard," "The Foundling," "The Song of the Bogomils," and "Dušan Before Constantinople," are to be found in these books. Touching upon the important events in the history of his people, the poet is at the same time searching for universal values and for the meaning of collective experience.

HODODARJE

The next stage in Pavlović's poetic wandering took him to Western European civilization. In *Hododarje* (sacrificial procession), he visits important places of this civilization—Amiens, Chartres, Rouen, Mainz, and so on. He also muses on the achievements of native figures such as Njegoš and Dis, visits some modern churches in the Balkans, and ends with a pilgrimage to Mount Athos. In all of these poems, he strives to find a connecting link among the Hellenic world, the Southern Slavs, and Western European civilization.

SVETLI I TAMNI PRAZNICI

With *Hododarje*, Pavlović completed a full circle: Starting from the modern city and moving back to primeval times, Greek antiquity, and the ancient Slavs, he returned to Western Europe, of which the modern big city of his youth is an integral part. A kind of synthesis of this circular quest and its findings can be found in *Svetli i tamni praznici* (bright and dark holidays), a book of poems with pronounced religious overtones. The emphasis on the Mother of God and the Savior, seen not in a conventional, church-oriented way but on the poet's own terms, seems to indicate that he has found unifying figures that give the road traveled by humanity an ultimate meaning. It may also indicate that the quest is over and that the tortuous wandering of Miodrag Pavlović as a poet has found a fruitful end. That this may be so is indicated by his later books of poetry. Lacking a unifying feature, these poems resemble in theme and form those of the various stages of his development. To be sure, new books take him to new places (Lepenski vir, for example, a newly discovered prehistoric site by the Danube in Serbia), but the discoveries seem to confirm the earlier findings; the difference is in degree, not in kind. Moreover, some of the latest poems reflect the poet's further development, so that when familiar motifs are repeated, they are offered in much more luxurious garb.

THE 1960'S

Pavlović's poetry of the 1960's established his international reputation and allowed him to travel widely. Visits to India and China allowed him to research the mythologies and oral traditions of Eastern cultures, which began to appear in his poems alongside his native South Slavic traditions in books such as *Bekstva po Srbiji* (1979; flights through Serbia) and *Divnoćudo* (1982; a divine miracle). The discovery in the 1970's of a Mesolithic archaeological site, Lepenski vir, inspired him to further explore the origins of human creativity in *Zavetine* (spells), *Links*, and *Nova pevanja na viru* (new singing at the whirlpool).

THE 1970'S AND 1980'S

His poetry throughout the 1970's and 1980's drew links between myth and poetry, tracing the unbroken connections from archaic life to the modern world. Beginning with *Pesme o detinjstvu i ratovima* (1992; poems about childhood and wars), Pavlović's poems began to become more intimate and biographical. The childhood of the title is his own; the war is World War II, although it foreshadows the events in Serbia at the end of the twentieth century.

This marks a distinct change in approach for Pavlović, whose previous poetry had been marked by a strong intellectualism. As mentioned, Pavlović has sought from the beginning to rid Serbian poetry of excessive Romanticism. He agrees with T. S. Eliot's view that poetry is not a turning loose of emotion but an escape from personality—provided one has a personality and emotions from which to escape. Though an intellectual and reflective poet, Pavlović is not devoid of emotion; he is an aloof but not an impassive observer, so that a certain cool passion emanates from his poems. If he were impassive, why would he raise his voice against the horrors of existence? Why would he search for explanations of life's riddles? Because he is against Romantic emotionalism and in favor of an intellectual approach to poetry,

he offers a rational solution: "The spark of reason,/ the most human of all humanities" ("A Cry Should Be Repeated"). Thus, in his efforts to depersonalize poetry, Pavlović keeps the individual in the background while interceding passionately on his behalf.

UNIVERSAL CONCERNS

Another feature of Pavlović's poetry is the universal scope that governs his entire outlook. Even when he speaks of geographically limited areas, such as ancient Greece, the old Slavic territories, the West, or his city, he always speaks for all humankind. All people have a common origin, and they still strive "toward the home of brotherly unity where our cradles are swaying/ . . . we seek the melody of our common lament in the moonlight" ("Idyll"). Such universality has given Pavlović's poetry a dimension which has greatly enhanced his appeal among poets and critics abroad.

FORM AND STYLE

Pavlović's poetry also demonstrates his technical mastery. The significance of his appearance in the early 1950's derived not only from new themes but also from formal innovations. Above all, his œuvre is characterized by a great variety of form, ranging from the sketchy, concise, almost laconic early poems to longer forms, and from the inner monologue and confessional style of the early poems to the narrative, descriptive, and dramatic verse of his later period.

Pavlović's language is rich, economical, precise, lapidary. He has a gift for striking metaphors, such as, "A skull/ the sword of nature/ the only raft on the black river" ("Variations on the Skull") and "Pieces of meat lie on the window/ from which the sinews hang down to the ground" ("Funeral"). Many of his images defy conventional logic: "two knives play on the piano" ("On the Death of a Hen"); "a rain of blood falls from the earth to the sky" ("Lament of Hector's Wife"). These predilections may reflect the influence of the prewar Surrealist poets, whom Pavlović knows well, although he is a strongly original poet who has assimilated all influences to his own purposes. Finally, Pavlović has enriched the language of Serbian poetry with many felicitous neologisms. It is his combination of thematic novelty, artistic boldness, and formal excellence that has made Miodrag Pavlović one of the most important and accomplished of contemporary Yugoslav poets.

OTHER MAJOR WORKS

SHORT FICTION: *Most bez obala*, 1956; *Bitni ljudi: Price sa Uskrsnjeg ostrva*, 1995.

PLAYS: *Igre bezimenih*, pb. 1963; *Koraci u podzemlju: Scensko prikazanje u dva dela*, pr. 1967.

NONFICTION: *Rokovi poezije*, 1958; *Osam pesnika*, 1964; *Dnevnik pene: Eseji*, 1972; *Poezija i kultura*, 1974; *Poetika modernog*, 1978; *Kina: Oko na putu*, 1983; *Prirodni oblik i lik: Likovni ogledi*, 1984; *Govor o nicem*, 1987; *Poetika zrtvenog obreda*, 1987; *Hram i preobrazenje: Jedna knjiga*, 1989; *Eseji o srpskim pesnicima*, 1992; *Ogledi o narodnoj i staroj srpskoj poeziji*, 1993; *Obredi poetickog zivota*, 1998.

EDITED TEXTS: *Antologija savremene engleske poezije*, 1956 (with Svetozar Brkić); *Antologija srpskog pesništva, XIII-XX vek*, 1964; *Pesništva evropskog romantizma*, 1969; *Nistitelji i svadbari*, 1979; *Antologija lirske narodne poezije*, 1982.

BIBLIOGRAPHY

Johnson, Bernard. Introduction and notes to *The Slavs Beneath Parnassus: Selected Poems*, by Miodrag Pavlović. St. Paul, Minn.: New Rivers Press, 1985. Johnson's introduction and notes on his translations of Pavlović's works offer rare biographical and critical information on the poet.

Mihailovich, Vasa D. "The Poetry of Miodrag Pavlović," in *Canadian Slavonic Papers* 20 (1978): 358-368. A critical analysis of selected poems by Pavlović.

Vasa D. Mihailovich
(including original translations);
bibliography updated by the editors

OCTAVIO PAZ

Born: Mexico City, Mexico; March 31, 1914
Died: Mexico City, Mexico; April 19, 1998

PRINCIPAL POETRY

Luna silvestre, 1933
Bajo tu clara sombra y otros poemas sobre España, 1937
Raíz del hombre, 1937
Entre la piedra y la flor, 1941
Libertad bajo palabra, 1949
¿Aguila o sol?, 1951 (*Eagle or Sun?*, 1970)
Semillas para un himno, 1954
Piedra de sol, 1957 (*Sun Stone*, 1963)
La estación violenta, 1958
Agua y viento, 1959
Libertad bajo palabra: Obra poética, 1935-1957, 1960, revised 1968
Salamandra, 1962
Selected Poems, 1963
Blanco, 1967 (English translation, 1971)
Discos visuales, 1968
Topoemas, 1968
La centena, 1969
Ladera este, 1969
Configurations, 1971
Renga: A Chain of Poems, 1971 (with Jacques Roubaud, Edoardo Sanguineti, and Charles Tomlinson)
Early Poems, 1935-1955, 1973
Pasado en claro, 1975 (*A Draft of Shadows and Other Poems*, 1979)
Vuelta, 1976
Poemas, 1979
Selected Poems, 1979
Airborn-Hijos del Aire, 1981 (with Charles Tomlinson)
The Collected Poems of Octavio Paz, 1957-1987, 1987
Arbol adentro, 1987 (*A Tree Within*, 1988)
Obra poética, 1935-1988, 1990
Stanzas for an Imaginary Garden, 1990 (limited ed.)
Viento, agua, piedra/Wind, Water, Stone, 1990 (limited ed.)
A Tale of Two Gardens: Poems from India, 1952-1995, 1997
"Snapshots," 1997

OTHER LITERARY FORMS

If Octavio Paz excels at poetry, he is no less respected for his writings in a multitude of other humanistic disciplines. Perhaps his best-known prose work is *El laberinto de la soledad: Vida y pensamiento de México*

(1950, rev. and enlarged ed., 1959; *The Labyrinth of Sol-itude: Life and Thought in Mexico*, 1961), which is a discussion of Mexican culture and the Mexican psyche. *El arco y la lira* (1956; *The Bow and the Lyre*, 1973) is an outstanding study in the field of poetics. His literary criticism includes *Los hijos del limo: Del romanticismo a la vanguardia* (1974; *Children of the Mire: Modern Poetry from Romanticism to the Avant-Garde*, 1974); the Charles Eliot Norton lectures for 1971-1972; *The Siren and the Seashell* (1976); and *Corriente alterna* (1967; *Alternating Current*, 1973). He has edited a number of important anthologies, including *Antología poética* (1956; *Anthology of Mexican Poetry*, 1958) and *New Poetry of Mexico* (1970), and he has written one short play.

ACHIEVEMENTS

Octavio Paz was Mexico's outstanding man of letters, the "leading exemplary intellectual of Latin America," as Ivar Ivask notes. His diverse output included poetry, literary criticism, philosophy, anthropology, art history, and cultural, social, and political commentary. As early as the mid-1960's, J. M. Cohen, in his influential study, *Poetry of This Age, 1908-1965*, cited Paz with Pablo Neruda as "two of the chief Spanish-American poets." Carlos Fuentes has described Paz as "certainly the greatest living poet of the Spanish language," while Kenneth Rexroth declared Paz to be "without any question the best poet in the Western Hemisphere. There is no writer in English who can compare with him." Although some may disagree with Rexroth, all agree that Paz was one of the finest poets of the twentieth century.

Paz's accomplishments have been recognized from the outset of his career. In 1944, he was awarded a Guggenheim Fellowship, which allowed him to study and travel in the United States. In 1963, he received the prestigious Belgian Grand Prix International de Poésie. He gave the Charles Eliot Norton lectures at Harvard during the 1971-1972 academic year. In 1977, three honors were bestowed on him: the Jerusalem Prize, the Premio National de Letras, and the Premio Crítico de Editores de España. The Golden Eagle Prize (Nice, France) followed a year later. The Ollin Yoliztli Prize, Mexico's richest literary honor, was conferred in 1980. The Miguel de Cervantes Prize, "the Spanish-speaking world's highest award," came in 1981. In 1982, Paz was the recipient of the Neustadt International Prize for Literature, one of the literary world's most important awards, often a prelude to the Nobel Prize. Indeed, just eight years later, Paz received the 1990 Nobel Prize in Literature. Other accolades included the German Book Trade Peace Prize (1984), the T. S. Eliot Award for Creative Writing (1987), and the Alexis de Tocqueville Prize (1989). The University of Mexico and Boston, Harvard, and New York Universities have conferred honorary degrees on Paz.

BIOGRAPHY

Octavio Paz was born on March 31, 1914, in Mexico City. His mother, Josephina Lozano, was of Spanish extraction, while the family of his father, Octavio, was both Mexican and Indian. Paz was a precocious youngster, influenced by his politically active grandfather, a journalist and writer, whose twelve-thousand-volume library provided the necessary material for his intellectual development. Paz's father was a lawyer who joined Emiliano Zapata during the 1910 Mexican Revolution and represented him in America. After secondary school, Paz studied from 1932 to 1937 at the National University of Mexico. In 1931, he founded *Barandal*, the first of his many journals. He also began to publish his poetry, and in 1933, *Luna silvestre*, his first collection, appeared; in the same year, he also founded his second journal, *Cuadernos del valle de Mexico*. In 1937, Paz attended a conference in Spain; after the conference, he decided to remain there for a year. His allegiance was, naturally, to the Republican cause during the Spanish Civil War. In 1938, he passed through Paris, where he met Alejo Carpentier and Robert Desnos; Paz's firsthand encounter with the Surrealists was particularly decisive, and their profound influence on his subsequent work cannot be overestimated.

In 1938, Paz returned to Mexico, where he worked with Spanish political refugees, wrote on political matters for *El popular*, and founded *Taller*. A fourth journal, *El hijo pródigo*, followed in 1943. For these literary periodicals he translated many French, German, and English works. Receipt of a Guggenheim Fellowship enabled him to spend the 1944-1945 academic year in the United States studying poetry. It was in the United States that he encountered the writings of T. S. Eliot, Ezra Pound, William Carlos Williams, Wallace Stevens, and E. E. Cummings, poets whose impact on Paz's work equaled that of the Surrealists some years before. When he ran out of money in New York in 1946, he decided to join the Mexican diplomatic service; he was sent to Paris, where he met Jean-Paul Sartre, Albert Camus, Jules Supervielle, and many other writers. During the next twenty-three years, his diplomatic work allowed him to spend extended periods in many countries, including Switzerland, the United States, Japan, and India. The Orient opened a new world to Paz, and after his first trip in 1952, his writings begin to display many Asian characteristics. He then returned to Mexico and spent the period from 1953 to 1958 writing in his usual prolific fashion.

In 1962, Paz was appointed Mexico's ambassador to India, and it was there that he met Marie-José Tramini, whom he married in 1964; they had one daughter. Although Paz's political interests had waned over the years, he resigned his ambassadorship in 1968 in protest against the Mexican government's overreaction to the student riots. During the 1970-1971 academic year, Paz was the Simón Bolívar Professor of Latin American Studies at Cambridge University, and during the following academic year he held the Charles Eliot Norton Professorship of Poetry at Harvard. He also taught at the universities of Texas, Pittsburgh, and California at San Diego. In 1971, he founded yet another journal, *Plural*, a political and literary review, which lasted until 1976, when he founded his last literary-cultural periodical, *Vuelta*. Early in 1982, King Juan Carlos of Spain presented Paz with the Miguel de Cervantes Prize, and some months later he received the Neustadt International Prize for Literature at the University of Oklahoma. The Nobel Prize in Literature followed in 1990. He died in Mexico City on April 19, 1998.

ANALYSIS

Any poet whose worldview has a chance to develop and mature over an extended period of time will create different types of poetry. T. S. Eliot, for example, began with short lyrics, moved toward longer and deeper pieces such as *The Waste Land* (1922), and concluded with the powerfully philosophical *Four Quartets* (1943). Eliot provides an especially germane analogue, since Octavio Paz was influenced by his work and is often compared to him thematically and stylistically; as J. M. Cohen has remarked, "With the exception of T. S. Eliot,

Octavio Paz, Nobel laureate in literature for 1990.
(© The Nobel Foundation)

Octavio Paz is the only contemporary poet capable of feeling his metaphysics, and calling them to life."

Paz, too, began his career writing short lyrics, advanced to longer, surrealistic pieces, reworked the prose poem, and finally, after more than a quarter of a century of creative activity, began to experiment with collagelike texts and assemblages which bear little relation to poetry as traditionally defined. Such experiments follow the logic of Paz's stylistic evolution; he has always been a self-conscious poet and he has written many poems about poetry and the nature of the creative process. Indeed, Paz's conception of poetry is philosophical: Poetry alone permits man to comprehend his place in the universe.

"POETRY"

In "Poesía" ("Poetry"), for example, Paz personifies this power of language to engage reality: "you burn my tongue with your lips, this pulp,/ and you awaken the rages, the delights,/ the endless anguish. . . ." The creative act is perceived as a struggle and the poet as a vehicle through whom words are spoken, comparable to a Greek oracle: "You rise from the furthest depth in me. . . ."

Paz's references to images as "babblings" and to "prophets of my eyes" confirm the implication of oracular utterance. The poet is a seer, and only his articulation can defeat the ubiquitous silence of the universe.

"THE BIRD"

It is silence against which Paz battled most consistently, beginning with his early lyric pieces. Silence can be neutral, but it also represents Camus's indifferent cosmos, offering neither help nor solace. "El Pájaro" ("The Bird") presents the neutral form of silence, a natural scene broken by a bird's song. Ironically, articulation is not a palliative; here, it merely reminds the poet of his mortality. There is the silence of lovers, the silence of solitude, and the silence of death—silences which can be broken only by the poet. Other thematic threads that run through Paz's poetry—recurring images and motifs such as light, lightning, women, transparency, mirrors, time, language, mysticism, cycles, the urban wasteland, and various mythic perceptions—all can be related to his conception of the nature of poetry.

"STARS AND CRICKET"

Many of Paz's poems fall within traditional lengths, ranging from roughly ten to thirty lines, but he has not hesitated to publish the briefest *haiku*-esque outbursts. Consider "Estrellas y grillo" ("Stars and Cricket") in its cryptic entirety:

> The sky's big.
> Up there, worlds scatter.
> Persistent,
> Unfazed by such a night,
> Cricket:
> Brace and bit.

SUN STONE

At the same time, Paz also experimented with the long poem: *Sun Stone* consists of 584 eleven-syllable lines of abstruse rumination:

> I search without finding, I write alone,
> there's no one here, and the day falls,
> the year falls, I fall with the moment,
> I fall to the depths, invisible path
> over mirrors repeating my shattered image. . . .

"INTERRUPTED ELEGY"

One of Paz's most moving poems is "Elegía inter-rumpida" ("Interrupted Elegy"), a philosophical description of a number of people whose deaths affected the poet. Each of the poem's five stanzas begins with the same incantation: "Now I remember the dead of my own house." From this point, Paz muses on first impressions, those who take their leave quickly, those who linger, those who are forgotten—and all of this in subdued, sparsely imagistic language. The poem itself is a metaphysical quest, and the dead whom it memorializes are brought to life. Despite the cathartic nature of the elegy, however, Paz's concluding couplet is despairing: "The world is a circular desert,/ heaven is closed and hell is empty."

EAGLE OR SUN?

Eagle or Sun?, a collection of short prose poems, the first book of its kind in Spanish, has been extremely influential. Part 1, "Trabajos del poeta" ("The Poet's Works"), consists of sixteen brief sections, each of which elaborates a narrative line, but usually in strongly imagistic and even surrealistic language. The surface concerns of these poems mask Paz's underlying interest: the poet's relationship with his creation. This is not allegory, which is read on one level and interpreted on another: Here, the reader perceives the two levels simultaneously. The ubiquitous silence is interrupted by a tapping ("it is the sound of horses' hooves galloping on a field of stone . . ."); these are the words appearing, demanding articulation. They pour out uncontrollably, this "vomit of words":

> The thistle whistles, bristles, buckles with chuckles. Broth of moths, charts of farts, all together, ball of syllables of waste matter, ball of snot splatter, ball of the viscera of syllable sibyls, chatter, deaf chatter. I flap, I swing, smashdunguided I flap.

Here, Paz conveys what it is like to be an artist, always at the mercy of competing inner voices, of spontaneous creative demands.

The second part of *Eagle or Sun?*, "Arenas movedizas" ("Shifting Sands"), consists of nine sections; each is a self-contained account couched in mundane, imageless prose with occasional dialogue interspersed. Some of the sections, such as "El ramo azul" ("The Blue Bouquet"), recall the manner of Jorge Luis Borges; others, such as "Un aprendizaje difícil" ("A Difficult Apprenticeship"), are Kafkaesque; still others, such as "Mi vida con la ola" ("My Life with the Wave"), have the flavor of André Breton: Together, they resemble a collection of very short stories more than they do a series of prose poems.

The concluding part of *Eagle or Sun?*, the title section, contains twenty-one pieces. Divided between investigations into the poetics of creation and metaphysical narratives—Paz thus attempts to combine the methodologies developed in parts 1 and 2—these pieces are abstract and are therefore less accessible than the earlier ones in the volume, but they are not meant to be hermetic conundrums. The opening sentences of "Mayúscula" ("Capital") exemplify this final mode:

> The screaming crest of dawn flames. First egg, first peck, decapitation and delight! Feathers fly, wings spread, sails swell, and wing-oars dip in the sunrise. Oh unreined light, first light rearing.

It is clear that *Eagle or Sun?* is a multifaceted volume, the three parts of which are tenuously connected only through their formal similarities, with each part functioning autonomously.

SURREALISTIC IMAGERY

One of the most pervasive stylistic elements in Paz's poetry is a finely controlled Surrealism. Unlike many programmatic Surrealists, Paz never allows his work to degenerate into a series of unrelated, bizarre images. Rather, he inserts potent incongruities into his lyric or metaphysical sequences, where they are most effective. Consider "Semillas para un himno" ("Seeds for a Psalm"), a relatively traditional fifty-four-line poem, imagistic to be sure, but in a subdued and striking fashion, as in the line "Even the blind decipher the whip's writing." This, however, is followed immediately by "Clusters of beggars are hanging from the cities." The power of this image—by far the most radical in the poem—derives precisely from the fact that it is not merely another in a string of bizarre, surreal tropes.

If surrealistic imagery is Paz's most pervasive rhetorical device, mythic experience is his favored structuring principle. Indeed, Paz believes that in the modern age, poetry has supplanted myth as a redemptive force, a revealer of truth as the poet perceives it. Rachel Phillips has observed that what she terms the mythic mode allows Paz "to clothe his epistemological anxieties in comfortingly familiar garb. . . ." This is certainly true for the tradi-

tional mythology with which most Western readers are acquainted, but many readers of Paz's work, even Latin Americans, will be confused and at times alienated by the complex indigenous Mexican myths that play such an important role in some of his poetry, especially in "Salamandra" ("Salamander") and the long and difficult *Sun Stone*, to which Cohen refers as "one of the last important poems to be published in the Western world. . . ." The same caveat obtains for Paz's poems that revolve around the history, philosophy, and myths of India.

BLANCO

Here and there throughout his œuvre, Paz has experimented with unusual poetic forms. Until the mid-1960's, this tendency was generally limited to eccentric page layout and syntactical sparsity; *Blanco* is the epitome of this phase. Here, the poem emerges from a multifaceted layout and, in its original publication, in the format of a scroll; one is reminded of *Un coup de dès jamais n'abolira le hasard* (1914; *Dice Thrown Never Will Annul Chance*, 1965) by Stéphane Mallarmé, a poet whose influence on Paz is often noted. An extremely complex poem with its three simultaneous lines, *Blanco* has met with a mixed critical response: Rachel Phillips calls it a masterpiece, while poet-translator Robert Bly regards the poem as a disaster.

DISCOS VISUALES AND RENGA

Paz followed *Blanco* with more extreme formal experiments. In *Discos visuales*, for example, sets of concentric and overlapping disks spin on axes; as the top disk revolves, different words appear in its little windows. One thus "creates" a variety of poems by turning the upper disk. Another of Paz's forays into the unconventional is the collaborative *Renga*, a poem in which the four stanzas of each section have been individually composed by four different poets in four different languages.

"SNAPSHOTS"

In 1997, a year before he died, Paz published "Snapshots" in a literary review. These eleven disconnected couplets are prosaic, metaphorical, surreal, and progressive. They are the desperate and sometimes depressing thoughts of an old man who may already be aware that he is ill: reminiscences, premonitions, and recollections scrupulously articulated indicate that Paz never stopped observing, thinking, and experimenting. This powerful echo of the past concludes,

'swarm of reflections on the page, yesterday confused
  with today, the seen,
entwined with the half-seen, inventions of memory,
  gaps of reason;

encounters, farewells, ghosts of the eye, incarnations
  of touch unnamed
presences, seeds of time: at the wrong time.

Paz's work is a fecund source of inspiration for his readers. His thematic and structural diversity, linguistic mastery, and philosophical commitment have produced an astonishing and replete body of poetry and prose. He drew upon both indigenous and international material in order to provide readers with a universally comprehensible message: plurality and diversity are positive objectives. The result is that Paz was the premiere man of letters in Mexico and Hispanic America and one of the outstanding literary and cultural figures of the twentieth century. Mario Vargas Llosa characterizes him as "one of the greatest poets that the Spanish-language world has produced," and Manuel Durán insists that "Paz is one of the best art critics of our century."

OTHER MAJOR WORKS

NONFICTION: *Voces de España*, 1938; *Laurel*, 1941; *El laberinto de la soledad: Vida y pensamiento de México*, 1950, rev. and enlarged 1959 (*The Labyrinth of Solitude: Life and Thought in Mexico*, 1961); *El arco y la lira*, 1956 (*The Bow and the Lyre*, 1973); *Las peras del olmo*, 1957; *Rufino Tamayo*, 1959 (*Rufino Tamayo: Myth and Magic*, 1979); *Magia de la risa*, 1962; *Cuatro poetas contemporáneos de Suecia*, 1963; *Cuadrivio*, 1965; *Poesia en movimiento*, 1966; *Puertas al campo*, 1966; *Remedios Varo*, 1966; *Claude Lévi-Strauss: O, El nuevo festín de Esopo*, 1967 (*Claude Lévi-Strauss: An Introduction*, 1970); *Corriente alterna*, 1967 (*Alternating Current*, 1973); *Marcel Duchamp*, 1968 (*Marcel Duchamp: Or, The Castle of Purity*, 1970); *Conjunciones y disyunciones*, 1969 (*Conjunctions and Disjunctions*, 1974); *México: La última década*, 1969; *Posdata*, 1970; *Las cosas en su sitio*, 1971; *Los signos en rotación y otros ensayos*, 1971; *Traducción: Literatura y literalidad*, 1971; *Apariencia desnuda: la obra de Marcel Duchamp*, 1973 (*Marcel Duchamp: Appear-ance Stripped Bare*, 1978); *El signo y el garabato*, 1973; *Solo a dos voces*, 1973; *La búsqueda del comienzo*, 1974; *Los hijos del limo: Del romanticismo a la vanguardia*, 1974 (*Children of the Mire: Modern Poetry from Romanticism to the Avant-Garde*, 1974); *El mono gramático*, 1974 (*The Monkey Grammarian*, 1981); *Teatro de signos/transparencias*, 1974; *Versiones y diversiones*, 1974; *The Siren and the Seashell*, 1976; *Xavier Villaurrutia en persona y en obra*, 1978; *In/mediaciones*, 1979; *México en la obra de Octavio Paz*, 1979, expanded 1987; *El ogro filantrópico: Historia y politica 1971-1978*, 1979; *Sor Juana Inés de la Cruz: O, Las trampas de la fé*, 1982 (*Sor Juana: Or, The Traps of Faith*, 1989); *Sombras de obras: Arte y literatura*, 1983; *Tiempo nublado*, 1983; *Hombres en su siglo y otros ensayos*, 1984; *One Earth, Four or Five Worlds*, 1985; *On Poets and Others*, 1986; *Convergences: Essays on Art and Literature*, 1987; *Primeras letras, 1931-1943*, 1988 (Enrico Mario Santi, editor); *Poesía, mito, revolución*, 1989; *La búscueda del presente/In Search of the Present: Nobel Lecture, 1990*, 1990; *La otra voz: Poesía y fin de siglo*, 1990 (*The Other Voice: Essays on Modern Poetry*, 1991); *Pequeña crónica de grandes días*, 1990; *Convergencias*, 1991; *Al paso*, 1992; *One Word to the Other*, 1992; *Essays on Mexican Art*, 1993; *Itinerario*, 1993 (*Itinerary: An Intellectual Journey*, 1999); *La llama doble: Amor y erotismo*, 1993 (*The Double Flame: Love and Eroticism*, 1995); *Un más allá erótico: Sade*, 1993 (*An Erotic Beyond: Sade*, 1998); *Vislumbres de la India*, 1995 (*In Light of India*, 1997).

EDITED TEXTS: *Antología poética*, 1956 (*Anthology of Mexican Poetry*, 1958; Samuel Beckett, translator); *New Poetry of Mexico*, 1970.

MISCELLANEOUS: *Lo mejor de Octavio Paz: El fuego de cada dia*, 1989; *Obras completas de Octavio Paz*, 1994; *Blanco*, 1995 (facsimiles of manuscript fragments and letters).

BIBLIOGRAPHY

Chantikian, Kosrof, ed. *Octavio Paz: Homage to the Poet*. San Francisco: Kosmos, 1980. A collection of addresses, critical essays, and lectures, with an introduction by the editor.

Chiles, Frances. *Octavio Paz: The Mythic Dimension.* New York: P. Lang, 1987. Discusses the use of myth in Paz's poetry.

Cohen, J. M. *Poetry of This Age: 1908-1965.* New York: Harper and Row, 1968. An important survey of mid-century modernism. Includes bibliography, index.

Durán, Manuel. "Remembering Octavio Paz." *World Literature Today* 73, no. 1 (Winter, 1999): 101-103. A reminiscence and critical commentary on Paz's work. Tributes, critical essays on, and an interview with Paz. (Reprinted with additions from *Books Abroad*, Autumn, 1972.)

Fein, John M. *Toward Octavio Paz: A Reading of His Major Poems, 1957-1986.* Lexington: University Press of Kentucky, 1986. A critical analysis of six of the longer works.

Hozven, Roberto, ed. *Otras voces: sobre la poesía y prosa de Octavio Paz.* Riverside, Calif.: University of California, 1996. A collection of critical essays in both English and Spanish. Includes bibliographical references.

Ivask, Ivar, ed. *The Perpetual Present: The Poetry and Prose of Octavio Paz.* Norman: University of Oklahoma Press, 1973. A compilation of critical essays on Paz and his poetics. Includes a biographical sketch and bibliography.

Phillips, Rachel. *The Poetic Modes of Octavio Paz.* New York: Oxford University Press, 1972. A monograph in the Oxford Modern Languages and Literature series. Includes bibliography.

Quiroga, José. *Understanding Octavio Paz.* Columbia, S.C.: University of South Carolina Press, 1999. A critical study of selected poems by Paz. Includes a bibliography of the author's works, an index, and bibliographical references.

Roman, Joseph. *Octavio Paz.* New York: Chelsea House, 1994. A brief introduction, presenting the poet's life and career. Suitable for young adults.

Underwood, Leticia Iliana. *Octavio Paz and the Language of Poetry: A Psycholinguistic Approach.* New York: P. Lang, 1992. Includes illustrations and bibliographical references.

Wilson, Jason. *Octavio Paz.* Boston: Twayne, 1986. A solid introduction in Twayne's World Authors Series. Bibliography, index.

_____. *Octavio Paz: A Study of His Poetics.* New York: Cambridge University Press, 1979. Brief, useful biographical and analytical study of Paz and his poetry. Encomiums, texts, and articles concerning Paz on the occasion of his receiving the Neustadt Prize.

World Literature Today 56, no. 4 (Autumn, 1982). Special Paz issue.

Robert Hauptman,
updated by Hauptman

MOLLY PEACOCK

Born: Buffalo, New York; June 30, 1947

PRINCIPAL POETRY

And Live Apart, 1980
Raw Heaven, 1984
Take Heart, 1989
Original Love: Poems, 1995

OTHER LITERARY FORMS

Although she is best known as a poet, Molly Peacock published a memoir, *Paradise, Piece by Piece* (1998), which gained a wide following for its straightforwardness in dealing with controversial issues and the vividness of its character portrayals, as well as for the laugh-out-loud humor that contrasts with and relieves the bleakness of some of its scenes. Also, Peacock is a poetry activist, helping through her books, presentations, and public activities to bring poetry back into the general culture. She has coedited two anthologies, *Poetry in Motion: One Hundred Poems from the Subways and Buses* (1996) and *The Private I: Privacy in a Public Age* (2001), essays on contemporary privacy issues. She has also written a handbook on poetry appreciation, *How to Read a Poem and Start a Poetry Circle* (1999).

ACHIEVEMENTS

Molly Peacock's work has been recognized by numerous honors and awards. When her first collection appeared in 1880, it was immediately acclaimed; her work over the years has won her multiple grants and honors, including a grant from the Lila Wallace/Woodrow Wilson Foundation (1994), a grant from the National Endowment for the Arts (1990), a grant from the New York Foundation for the Arts (1985), the Ingram Merrill Foundation Award (1981), and many others. She has served in numerous elected or appointed poetry posts, including a term as president of the Poetry Society of America.

BIOGRAPHY

Molly Peacock was born in Buffalo, New York, in 1947 into a working-class family in which signals were unclear and life was unpredictable. Her father, Edward Frank Peacock, was a charming but unreliable alcoholic, and her mother, Pauline Wright Peacock, was a churchgoing Baptist. As the first child, Molly found herself in the impossible situation of trying to bring order to their chaotic home and to nurture her younger sister. Summer visits with her grandmother in the country allowed her the peace and space to find her gift for writing, and she sent her grandmother her first work.

Writing was Peacock's key to control and escape. Putting her experiences into poetic patterns allowed Peacock to impose a sort of order on her life, and she continued to write as an undergraduate at the State University of New York at Binghamton. After receiving her B.A. magna cum laude, she continued to write as a fellow at the MacDowell Colony and then at the Johns Hopkins University, where she was a Danforth Fellow and received an M.A. in 1977. After receiving her degree she accepted several administrative positions before turning to a life as poet and teacher.

She has been writer-in-residence for the Delaware State Council on the Arts and has taught at Hofstra University, Columbia University, Friends Seminary, and elsewhere. Avoiding the usual tenured position of an academic poet in an M.F.A. program, Peacock decided instead to take short teaching engagements in widely different programs, allowing her to make of her career a continual discovery. She settled in New York and Toronto with her husband, Michael Groden.

ANALYSIS

Molly Peacock's unusual combination of form and content is unique in contemporary poetry. She allows her rhymes and rhythms to underscore rather than fully control the content, and her work serves as a counterexample for any theory that wishes to equate formalism and conservatism—poetic or political. Peacock's poems are blunt, direct, sensual, and sometimes shocking. She writes about sex, abuse, intimacies, and violations, often in sonnet form, making form seem as natural and real as her topics. The control exerted by form is sometimes almost invisible, but it is there, and the subtle poetic effect helps to center the reading. Moreover, she is a force for the democratizing of poetry and the reclamation of it from the elite. She has been active in the Poetry in Motion project, which placed poetry in public locations such as buses, and her handbook helps those who have more or less written off poetry as an enjoyable art form to appreciate it again.

Peacock is a strong voice for the practice and appreciation of formal poetry. She guides her own students gently into an attempt at form: "Start by just counting ten syllables," she tells them. After they have learned to do that, she finds it easier to lead them to subtleties of rhythm and language. By beginning with what is easy and natural in formal poetry, she is able to overcome prejudice against it and encourage skill in its use. She encourages a more feeling-based and participatory approach to poetry in her work and attempts to make readers more involved by inviting them to approach the poetry without academic preconceptions and heavy critical or theoretical paraphernalia.

Peacock's work shares related themes: that all life is interconnected, that the physical and the mental lives are really as one, that abuse ultimately either kills or toughens. Later poems show a preoccupation with transcendence and with the other end of the body-mind continuum: the spirit or soul. Indirectly but powerfully, Peacock's poetry teaches independence; more effectively than any therapist, it shows the many ways in which one may make choices, take action, and accept responsibility for one's acts. It goes on to demonstrate with sensuous intensity the rewards for doing these things.

Peacock's poems are often so physical that they seem like a blow—nothing is glossed over or romanticized, but her poetry is firmly rooted in the real soil of human passion. The wordplay and sheer joy of some poems are balanced by a certain grimness in others; her scope is wide. Animals populate Peacock's poetry, mostly live ones, glistening with a quirky, telling symbolism. These are beasts from a bestiary, elephants, squirrels, raccoons, birds, pets, and pests, animals whose pure vitality communicates itself to the poem even while their behavior comments on some element of human nature.

AND LIVE APART

Peacock's first poetry collection combines formalism with narrative to explore George Herbert's premise from the poem "Giddinesse," quoted as an epigraph, that "Surely if each one saw another's heart,/ There would be no commerce,/No sale or bargain passe: all would disperse,/And live apart." These poems explore the conflicts involved in the need for intimacy and the equally pressing need for independence and self-definition. The child's sentience and the mental energy needed to grow up are memorably evoked in poems such as the long "Alibis and Lullabies," which shows the speaker's journey to independence with its threats and gifts.

Peacock's gift for narrative and her ability to make connections that transmit messages are apparent in her first book. Delving into the muddy situations where love and repulsion meet, these poems set the stage for the more compact and more fully crafted poems of the next collection.

RAW HEAVEN

This second collection, from 1984, shows the full flowering of Peacock's craft. The poems are tighter than the earlier ones, as well as more direct; the forms are organic, melded to the themes. These poems focus on the carnal dimension of love—how awareness of love's "fleshiness" brings intensity as well as ambivalence. In this collection the sonnet is often a loose container for a tightly constructed reflection, even a philosophical argument. What may be Peacock's best-known sonnet, "The Lull" reflects on how it is necessary to accept the body, and that means the body's death as well as its life. This poem shows the flexibility and yet the precision of Peacock's use of form as two people view a dead possum:

> "That's disgusting." You said that. Dreams, brains, fur
> and guts: what we are. That's my bargain, the Pax
> Peacock, with the world. Look hard, life's soft. Life's
>   cache
> is flesh, flesh, and flesh.

The sonnet structure and content are welded, and the off-rhymes and missing syllables at the end serve to un-derscore the ironies in this poem about desire and death, and about the bargain the speaker must make to live in the world and accept it. Other poems focus on delight in the flesh and on the need to touch, as in the sonnet "Petting and Being a Pet," which concludes,

> We wish to be in the vast
> caress, both animal and hand. Like eyes make sense
> of seeing, touch makes being make sense.

TAKE HEART

Peacock's third collection explores deeply the wounds caused by abuse and again uses form in such a way as to keep the barest reins on emotion. This collection includes poems about abortion, abuse, and betrayal as well as many poems of nature, in which animals, stones, or leaves become vital symbols and the movement of the poem is controlled by form. "How I Come to You," the opening poem, begins, "Even a rock/ has insides./ Smash one and see/ how the shock/ reveals the rough/ dismantled gut/ of a thing once dense."

The "rockiness" of the self is underscored by the hard, jagged lines, and the poem serves as a good introduction to poems about the cut self and what is there. Peacock's use of formal patterns distances the subject matter and yet brings it back home; these poems are never self-indulgent but always invite the reader to enter and share, even to appropriate the experience. These poems also often have a sense of cosmic irony that causes a similar combination of distance and lure. "Good Girl" uses rhymed iambic pentameter to create a sonnet-like eighteen-line poem that makes a vivid contrast with Robert Frost's "The Silken Tent," showing the oppressiveness of a vision that perceives women as primarily useful, as some kind of support system whose beauty is wholly in service. In Peacock's poem the woman is told by others to "Hold up/ the tent that is the sky of your world at which/ you are the narrow central pole, good girl." Yet the speaker of the poem has different advice for the "good girl": "Sever/ yourself, poor false Atlas, poor "Atlesse," lie/ recumbent below the sky. Nothing falls down/ except you, luscious and limited on the ground."

Peacock's poem expresses a feminism that has appeal for a wide variety of readers.

ORIGINAL LOVE

Poems in this 1995 collection explore the gamut of love relationships—spousal, parent-child, human-nature, human-God. The love in the collection is truly "original"; the term suggests the adjectives "primal" or "basic", but the perspective is also new, rediscovered—original. The title suggests a theology founded in love rather than sin. In many ways these are positive poems demonstrating a voice that has defined itself. The book is divided into sections devoted to the various kinds of love. Some poems are amusing and may provide a jolt of recognition, such as "Have You Ever Faked an Orgasm?" Others are close readings of a difficult mother-daughter relationship, seen from the angle of the mother's death. Still others are metaphysical-exploratory, looking at directions spirituality may take outside the narrowly traditional. God is somewhere north of sex in this collection; nature, scrutinized and fully appreciated, turns into a transparent lens for glimpsing deity. Thus physical and spiritual life is a continuity and does not divide into antinomies of body and soul. "Prairie Prayer" catches these correspondences that become equivalents:

> The self, like land itself,
> beyond stamp or use
> in its unfarmed wealth,
> telescopes into the mind.

This is more meditative and less exuberant poetry, with a quieter charm. In general, the later poems are less obviously formally structured and more open. Peacock never abandons rhyme and rhythm, but some of these searching poems are so flexible that the reader may experience the effect of form without recognizing it. Peacock's later poems explore the spiritual dimension of life, without divorcing it from the physical; the metaphysical in her poetry is often reached in or through the physical. These poems suggest that personal freedom, however hard-won and justly valued, is not an end point but a beginning.

OTHER MAJOR WORKS

NONFICTION: *Paradise, Piece by Piece*, 1998 (memoir); *How to Read a Poem and Start a Poetry Circle*, 1999.

EDITED TEXTS: *Poetry in Motion: One Hundred Poems from the Subways and Buses*, 1996. *The Private I: Privacy in a Public Age*, 2001.

BIBLIOGRAPHY

Allen, Frank. Review of *Original Love*, by Molly Peacock. *Library Journal* 120 (February 15, 1995): 159. A brief but insightful review of *Original Love*.

Benfey, Christopher. Review of *Take Heart*, by Molly Peacock. *The New Republic* 201 (July 17-24, 1989): 31. A description and ambivalent judgment of *Take Heart*.

Muratori, Fred. "Traditional Form and the Living, Breathing American Poet." *New England Review* 9, no. 2 (Winter, 1985/1986): 219-241. Muratori discusses contemporary use of poetic forms and prosody by Peacock and others; uses poems from *Raw Heaven* as examples.

Peacock, Molly. "Peacock, Molly." In *Contemporary Authors, Autobiography Series*. Vol. 27. Detroit: Gale, 1995. A vivid first-person account of Peacock's life and her goals for herself and her art.

Phillips, Robert. "Poetry Chronicle: Some Versions of the Pastoral." *Hudson Review* 34, no. 3 (Autumn, 1981): 420-434. Peacock is discussed along with other contemporary nature poets.

Walzer, Kevin. *The Ghost of Tradition: Expansive Poetry and Postmodernism*. Ashland, Oreg.: Story Line Press, 1999. Analyzes Peacock's (and others') work in the context of the neoformalist movement. Especially useful for those interested in how Peacock uses form and for an understanding of contemporary formalist poetry in general.

Janet McCann

THE PEARL-POET

Born: England(?); fl. in latter half of the fourteenth century

PRINCIPAL POETRY
Pearl
Patience

Cleanness (Purity)
Sir Gawain and the Green Knight
Saint Erkenwald (attributed by some to the Pearl-
     Poet)

OTHER LITERARY FORMS

Even though the Pearl-Poet experimented with a variety of genres, he is best remembered for his four Middle English poems.

ACHIEVEMENTS

The work of the Pearl-Poet (also called the Gawain-Poet after his other major poem) was essentially lost until the nineteenth century. *Sir Gawain and the Green Knight* was first edited in 1839, to be followed twenty-five years later by the other three poems of the manuscript. Over the past hundred years, these poems (whose titles are modern, not found in the manuscript) have gained a secure place in Middle English poetry. Although attention has focused on *Pearl* and *Sir Gawain and the Green Knight*, considered masterpieces of their respective genres, the two verse homilies have more recently been the objects of much critical study as well.

A contemporary of Geoffrey Chaucer, the Pearl-Poet has often been compared to medieval England's most famous poet. Like Chaucer, he worked in a variety of genres and experimented with various verse forms. His poetry, like Chaucer's, shows a knowledge not only of the Bible and its commentaries but also of the new vernacular literature of the Continent. Again like Chaucer, he analyzes moral issues in narratives that create characters who are often unaware or confused by their situations. However, the Pearl-Poet must be judged apart from Chaucer, for he worked in a distinctly different poetic tradition, that of the Alliterative Revival, not Chaucer's French courtly style.

The poetry that flourished in northern and western England in the second half of the fourteenth century probably continued and modified (rather than reinvented) the Old English accentual and alliterative line. In contrast to the verse forms employed by Chaucer, which became the usual patterns of most English poetry after his time, the alliterative long line concentrates on stresses alone and does not count syllables. The unrhymed long lines of *Cleanness* and *Patience*, for exam-

ple, include four key stresses generally separated into two half lines by a caesura, the first three stresses falling on alliterating syllables. The pattern may be diagramed as follows: Á Á ns Á X́. These alliterative long lines (sometimes grouped in quatrains), skillfully developed by the Pearl-Poet, impart a surprisingly dramatic and active feeling to *Cleanness* and *Patience*. The alliterative tendency toward variation and realistic description prevents the verse homilies from disappearing into the mist of abstraction.

In *Sir Gawain and the Green Knight* the poet turns again to this traditional form, but arranges the lines in descriptive and narrative stanzas of varying length, rounded off by five shorter alliterating lines comprising a "bob and wheel," a device not unique to the poet but most skillfully employed by him. The one-stress line of the "bob" and the four three-stressed lines of the "wheel" rhyme *ababa*. These rhyming lines impart rhythmic variety to the poem and serve to sum up the major topic of the stanza and to emphasize key images and themes.

The mixture of alliteration and rhyme is more thorough in *Pearl*. Departing more freely from the tradition of the alliterative long line in the direction of the octosyllabic line of Chaucer's early poetry, *Pearl* is composed of 101 twelve-line stanzas, which resemble in both form and spirit the sonnet of later English poetry. Each stanza develops three rhymes in linked quatrains (*ababababbcbc*). These tightly structured stanzas are further grouped into twenty larger sections through the concluding repetition of key words and phrases forming a refrain for each stanza. The larger sections are also linked by concatenation, the device of repeating a key word from the final line of a previous stanza in the first line of a following stanza. These intricate poetic devices perfectly mirror the intricacy of the themes and arguments of the *Pearl*, a poem highly admired for its form and considered by Thorlac Turville-Petre in *The Alliterative Revival* to be "the finest of all the poems in rhyming alliterative stanzas."

In addition to the four poems that constitute the unique British Library manuscript, Cotton Nero A.x. (c. 1400), *Saint Erkenwald*, an alliterative poem describing the miraculous life of a seventh century bishop of London, has been attributed to the Pearl-Poet. Since 1882, scholars have argued that *Saint Erkenwald* shares a common diction, a similar style and dialect, and a peculiar phraseology with the poems of the Pearl-Poet. They further argue that *Saint Erkenwald* may be dated 1386, when the feast days of the bishop saint were given special status in London, thus making it contemporary with the Cotton Nero poems.

One modern editor of *Saint Erkenwald* (Clifford Peterson), however, has suggested an early fifteenth century date for the poem, which is extant only in a late fifteenth century manuscript. Scholarship, furthermore, has cast doubt on the attribution by showing that the common language is not unique to these poems and by arguing that the similar stylistic elements are best understood as reflecting the formulaic character of alliterative poetry. Therefore, it is best to limit the corpus of the Pearl-Poet to the four poems of the Cotton Nero manuscript.

BIOGRAPHY

As W. A. Davenport has aptly remarked, "Though the Gawain-poet may not have existed, it has proved necessary to invent him." Certainly, there is no external evidence to "prove" that the four poems found only in a single manuscript are by a single poet. It may be that the poems were crafted by a small school of poets working together closely at a court in the northwest Midlands during the late fourteenth century. As A. C. Spearing has argued, however, the principle of "Ockham's razor" suggests that it is more reasonable to postulate that the Pearl-Poet was a single poet of genius writing in a unique Middle English dialect (probably north Cheshire or south Lancashire, but with Scottish, French, and Scandinavian forms). The poems share to a remarkable extent imagery, diction, and stylistic features that cannot be entirely accounted for by a common alliterative tradition. More important, readers of the four poems are continually impressed by what Malcolm Andrew and Ronald Waldron, the poems' most recent editors, have called a "conviction of an individual poetic personality" and an "unbroken consistency of thought." The analysis of the four poems below will suggest, moreover, that they are thematically related.

Nevertheless, the Pearl-Poet remains unknown. The manuscript can help scholars locate him approximately in place and time, and the poems can provide clues to his interests and knowledge. Like other poets working in the Alliterative Revival, he perhaps was attached to the household of an aristocrat of the northwest Midlands. The manuscript (probably not in the poet's hand) includes twelve rough illustrations of the four poems (published in Charles Moorman's 1977 edition of the manuscript), suggesting to some that the poet may have had the support of a wealthy patron. Certainly, the poems reflect a familiar knowledge of court life, as well as an interest in contemporary religious issues, a thorough knowledge of the Vulgate Bible and its commentaries, and some awareness of French poetry and perhaps even the poetry of Dante Alighieri and Giovanni Boccaccio. Some scholars have argued that the descriptions, debates, and specialized diction of the poems suggest that the poet was trained as a priest or a lawyer, that he may have sailed or been, like Chaucer, on a diplomatic mission. Such arguments, however, deduced as they are from the four poems, provide little help in understanding his poetry.

Even more fruitless and really very misleading are the various attempts to identify the poet with certain historical figures of the late fourteenth century. These nominees have included the Oxford philosopher referred to by Geoffrey Chaucer in *Troilus and Criseyde* (1382), Ralph Strode; the poet Huchown of the Awle Ryale; and other names from the period, such as John Erghome, John Prat, and, most recently, Hugo de Mascy or John Massey or simply the "maister Massy" praised by Thomas Hoccleve. What readers would gain should such scholarly speculation finally attach a name to the Pearl-Poet is not clear, for modern interest in the poet is the result of interest in his superb poetry, and it is unlikely that the little which is known about these candidates for poetic fame will affect interpretations of the poems.

ANALYSIS

All four poems attributed to the Pearl-Poet reflect a great concern with establishing the distinctions between the temporal and sublunary viewpoint of human beings and the eternal and unvarying positions of God. This outlook is not uncommon in the art and thought of the later Middle Ages. It is the foundation of scholastic thought. Like scholasticism, furthermore, the arts were not content to establish only the distinctions between human and divine; they sought also to merge and synthesize the sacred and the secular. As long as the hierarchy of values was kept clear, allegiance to the divine and the human need not be in contradiction; it was possible to serve, for example, both the Virgin Mary and the courtly lady. However, if human sinfulness and obstinacy reversed the hierarchy, placing the earthly garden of delights above the promise of paradise regained, then the synthesis of earthly and divine was shattered and man was left to inherit the results of his folly.

The Pearl-Poet was thus an artist of his time not only in distinguishing between the earthly and the heavenly but also in showing how the two spheres could merge and interrelate. His greatness, however, lies in his sympathetic investigation of man's situation in the face of the divine. Man as creature is subordinate to his creator, and there is no room for doubt that man's rebelliousness is disastrous, because the Lord can become "wonder wroth." Yet, as Malcolm Andrew and Ronald Waldron conclude, the poet shares "a spirit of sympathetic identification with human frailty besides a zealous dedication to ideal virtue."

The distinctions between, yet juxtaposition of, human desires and divine standards are explored by the Pearl-Poet by concentrating on three ideals. These encompass a variety of social and Christian values, best summed up by the concepts of cleanness (understood as the divine requirement of purity in both body and soul), of truthfulness to duty and to God (and thus including loyalty, obedience, and faithfulness), and, finally, courtesy (a chivalric ideal given religious significance by the poet).

In three of the four poems, the poet creates a major character with whom readers sympathize yet who must come to learn of the differing values of humankind and the divine. In these poems, the major characters undergo a three-part mysterious journey: in *Patience*, a voyage in the belly of a whale; in *Pearl*, a visionary pilgrimage glimpsing the New Jerusalem; and in *Sir Gawain and the Green Knight*, a fantastic quest to meet an enchanted opponent. The characters face a divine or supernatural demand or challenge and are left quite befuddled, surprised, or overwhelmed by what they experience. More important, in each poem, the character is moved from a narrowly human and basically self-centered outlook to an awareness of man's essentially subordinate and often ignorant position in relation to the divine. Surprisingly, none of the characters has changed drastically by the end of the poems, although readers are left to assume that the new perspectives they have gained will lead to such change.

The fourth poem, *Cleanness*, also shares this three-part movement, but it presents not a journey of a single character to a mysterious or foreign land, but the history of humankind as outlined in the Old Testament and interpreted within the context of the New Testament. By concentrating on three key moments when the divine intervened in human history, the poem highlights the results of man's unwillingness to conform to the divine.

The four poems of the Pearl-Poet are of great artistic merit. In verse of great beauty, they include passages of vigorous narrative, realistic description, and dramatic intensity. They describe extremely violent situations as well as peaceful gardens, sailors as well as an enchanted green knight, the suffering of the dying as well as the joy of the saved. Drawing from a wide range of sources yet including much that is original, the poems are carefully crafted and structured. They are compelling not only for their presentation of deeply moral and human concerns, but also for their imaginative power.

PATIENCE

The Pearl-Poet's shortest and most simply structured poem, *Patience*, is a verse homily teaching the need for man to submit his will to God and to act faithfully and humbly. Like traditional medieval sermons, it establishes this theme in an introductory prologue and illustrates it in an exemplum, a narrative example intended to support the preacher's main argument. In the case of *Patience*, the narrative centers on the prophet Jonah. It is a dramatic expansion of the biblical account found in the Book of Jonah.

The poet's choice of Jonah may seem odd, since the usual Old Testament figure representing patience is Job. The poet may have felt that the best way to explore the virtue of patience (which might be viewed as rather passive and uninteresting) was through negative examples (as, again, in *Cleanness*). Certainly Jonah's sulking pride and abortive attempt to flee from the command of God serve as examples of what patience is not. It may also be that Jonah was selected because, although his human rationalizing and severely limited understanding of God's nature place him in conflict with the divine, he does ultimately accept the will of God. Finally, Jonah's figurative significance in medieval exegesis as an Old Testament type of Christ may be significant. As evident in numerous commentaries and sermons, and in popular literature, Jonah's three-day entombment within the belly of the whale typifies the death of Christ and his resurrection on the third day.

The association of Old Testament story with New Testament event is not unusual in medieval poetry. Medieval theology understood the Old Testament as prefiguring the New, and often interpreted the stories of the Jewish people as signifying Christian belief. The story of Jonah is thus told by the poet to exemplify the beatitudes preached by Christ in the Sermon on the Mount. These are recited in the prologue of *Patience*, and it is the last beatitude, interpreted as Christ's promise of heaven for those who endure patiently, that provides the poet's theme. The beatitudes certainly are classic examples of Christ's teaching that false earthly goals and aspirations are not to be confused with the true ideals of Heaven. Whereas man seeks riches, boldness, pleasure, and power, Christ praises poverty, meekness, purity, and patience. *Patience* tells how Jonah must come to recognize the distinction between human and divine in order to act truthfully and to obtain the mercy of God.

Although the four divisions of *Patience* in the manuscript accord with the four chapters of the biblical account, the poem's narrative actually moves in three parts: First, Jonah desperately attempts to avoid the command of God, rejects his role as prophet, and sets sail to escape the power of God; second, after being swallowed by the whale, he accepts his duty and faithfully obeys God and prophesies the destruction of Nineveh; finally, while sulking because Nineveh is not destroyed, he learns of God's grace, love, and mercy.

Jonah is at first the epitome of man's foolish opposition to God. The poet sympathetically imagines Jonah's motives for rejecting the prophetic mission and presents his fear as understandable; nevertheless, Jonah's flight from God, his attempt to hide, is obviously ridiculous. The God who created the world, the poet ironically comments, has no power over the sea! The power of the creator over his creation, however, becomes clear to all. Even the pagan sailors who at first pray to Diana and Neptune learn to worship the Hebrew God. At the height of the storm, Jonah, wakened from his unnatural sleep, recog-

nizes the Creator's power and identifies himself to the sailors as a follower of the world's Creator. From this point Jonah submits himself to the will of God and, in the belly of the whale, learns to act faithfully as a prophet.

He also prays for mercy, but it is not until the third part of the story, after Jonah has prophesied the destruction of Nineveh and its citizens actually repent, that the prophet of God learns the true nature of God's grace. Although now aware of the awesome power of God over his creation, Jonah remains earthbound in his attitudes. When Nineveh is saved, he feels humiliated. Again, rather than accepting God's will (the ultimate meaning of patience for the Pearl-Poet), Jonah reacts angrily, sulks childishly, and wishes he were dead. His wish does not come true, however, and through the remainder of the narrative Jonah learns that God not only controls but also loves his creatures.

Interestingly, in condemning what he does not understand, Jonah sets forth one of the major themes developed in the works of the Pearl-Poet: the bounty of God's grace. This grace is described in chivalric terms, as God's courtesy, and is linked to God's patience. Jonah prays for mercy in the belly of the whale, but now desires—because of his pride in preaching the very prophecy that he sought to avoid—that God turn against the repentant Nineveh and destroy the city. While the Lord patiently seeks to change him, Jonah's final attitude is not made clear, since the poet suddenly concludes with his epilogue urging patient acceptance of one's position and mission in life. The last lines of the narrative are the words of God, whose patience is displayed not only toward Nineveh but also toward Jonah. Thus, although the career of Jonah may be a negative example of patience, the courtesy of God reflected in his patience and grace becomes the positive representation of ideal patience.

CLEANNESS

The poet's much longer verse homily *Cleanness* (sometimes called *Purity*) also mixes negative and positive examples, although there is no doubt that the negative receives the bulk of his attention and that God's righteous wrath, rather than his patience, becomes most evident. Again, one of Christ's beatitudes provides the theme: "Blessed is he whose heart is clean for he shall look on the Lord." The promise to the blessed clean, however, is not developed as much as the threat of damnation for the unclean. In his prologue, for example, the poet concentrates on yet another New Testament passage, Christ's parable of the wedding feast. This rather harsh analogy comparing the kingdom of heaven to a king who has a guest thrown out of a wedding feast because he is improperly dressed receives a lengthy exposition, concluding with a list of the forms of uncleanness by which man hurls himself into the devil's throat.

In his conclusion, the poet notes that he has given three examples of how uncleanness drives the Lord to wrath. These three Old Testament examples are arranged in chronological order, thus establishing the poem's three-part movement through the history of salvation: from the destruction of the world by the Flood, through the annihilation of Sodom and Gomorrah by fire, and finally to the overpowering of "the bold Belshazzar." The three are linked by shorter Old Testament stories as well. The Flood is introduced by the fall of Lucifer and the angels, leading to the fall of Adam; the destruction of the two cities is preceded by the stories of Abraham and Lot and their two wives; and Belshazzar's feast is interwoven with the fall of Jerusalem under Nebuchadnezzar and his eventual conversion.

Like the story of Jonah, the Old Testament stories retold in *Cleanness* have typological significance in medieval theology. Each of the three major examples of God's wrath prefigures the Last Judgment. Combined with accounts of the fall of Lucifer and the origin of sin, this typological significance gives the poem a universal sweep from creation to doomsday, symbolically encompassing the entire Christian understanding of history. The emphasis, however, is on judgment, which is clearly the moral of the introductory parable of the wedding feast: "Many are called but few are chosen."

Judgment is particularly severe against the unclean, for the Lord of heaven "hates hell no more than them that are filthy." The concept of cleanness includes innocence, ceremonial propriety, decency and naturalness, physical cleanliness, and moral righteousness. Their opposites are encompassed by the concept of filth, which includes all manner of vices, sacrilege, sodomy, lust, and the arrogance of spirit that elevates man's earthly desires above God's requirement of truthfulness. God floods the world because sinfulness is out of control. Not only did man sin against nature, but devils copulated with human

beings, engendering a breed of violent giants as well. Similarly, the Sodomites practiced unnatural vices, filling a land that was once like paradise thick with filth so that it sunk into the earth under the weight of its own sins. The Lord is equally angered by blasphemy and sacrilege, as Belshazzar learns when he defiles the vessels of the temple in "unclean vanity."

Lack of truthfulness, although not arousing the violent wrath of God to the same extent as lack of cleanness, is represented in the minor exempla of the poem. The stories of Lucifer and Adam exemplify the results of disobedience. Sarah's mocking the word of God when told she would bear a child reflects human lack of faith, for she prefers worldly reason to divine wisdom. Lot's wife is turned into a pillar of salt for two faults, the results of her "mistruth." She disobeyed a direct command not to look at the doomed Sodom, and she set salted food before the two angels, thus angering the Lord for her ritual uncleanness. King Zedekiah and the Jewish nation were similarly found untruthful; they proved disloyal to their duties as God's chosen people and blasphemously worshiped idols.

The minor examples suggest that the lack of truthfulness is the cause of the uncleanness that ultimately leads to humankind's doom. They also expand the concept of filth beyond sexual misconduct to include the improper relationship between the natural and the supernatural, leading to unnatural perversion and sacrilege. Thus, the sexual intercourse of fallen angels and sinful human beings is punished by the flood because it represents unnaturalness on a cosmic scale. The Sodomite attempt to attack sexually the two angels visiting Lot is the most villainous example of their sacrilege. Although Lot's attempt to shift their lust from the angels to his two virgin daughters seems horrible, it is an attempt to keep the city's perversion on a human scale. Belshazzar's profanation of the sacred vessels consecrated to God is the final example of man's blasphemous desire to overturn the proper relationship between the human and the divine.

This long series of Old Testament stories linking untruthfulness to uncleanness is, luckily, broken by a few representatives of truth and cleanness: Noah, Abraham, Lot in his hospitality, the prophet Daniel, and Nebuchadnezzar after his conversion. This right relationship between man and God evident in truth and cleanness is, furthermore, described by the poet in terms of courtesy. After the flood, for example, God promises never to send another universal deluge and establishes man once again as he was before the fall—as ruler over the earth. This new covenant between God and Noah is described by the poet as spoken in courteous words. As in *Patience*, the Pearl-Poet understands God's mercy and grace as reflecting divine courtesy. Early in the Introduction to *Cleanness*, for example, he couples the need for purity with courtesy. Similarly, when explaining how the divine became human, the poet notes that Christ came in both cleanness and courtesy, accepting and healing all who "called on that courtesy and claimed his grace." Here, then, is the key to the right relationship between the human and the divine.

PEARL

Less overtly didactic than *Cleanness* and *Patience*, *Pearl* sets forth its main ideas by creating two characters: a dreamer who mourns the loss of a pearl and a beautiful young girl who speaks in a dream from the vantage of heaven. The dreamer, who narrates the poem in the first person, is earthbound in his outlook, mourning and complaining, like Jonah in *Patience*, against his fate. He rather foolishly debates theological issues with the visionary maiden, who speaks with divine wisdom. This relationship between a naïve narrator and an authority figure representing truthfulness is typical of the poem's genre: the dream vision. Such is evident in the early but highly influential *The Consolation of Philosophy* by the sixth century philosopher Anicius Manlius Severinus Boethius, as well as in the fourteenth century masterpiece of the genre, William Langland's *The Vision of William Concerning Piers the Plowman*. The human dreamer, schooled by the agent of the divine, is also a feature of the New Testament Book of Revelation, the poem's most important source. However, the rather passive role of John during his apocalyptic visions is avoided by the poet. *Pearl*, as A. C. Spearing and others have noted, presents its teachings by means of "a dramatic encounter."

Unfortunately, attention has been diverted from analysis of this dramatic encounter by the scholarly arguments attempting to identify the meaning of the lost pearl. According to some scholars, the lost pearl represents the poet's daughter (and the poem thus is an elegy in her

memory), who died at a "young and tender age" before she was two. Postulating such an occurrence may help explain the dreamer's mourning at the beginning of the poem, but the problem with reading the poem as an elegy is that it identifies the foolish narrator with the poet and equates the dream's fiction with historical and biographical events about which nothing is known. Certainly it is not the case, as A. C. Cawley writes in the introduction to his edition of the poem, that "there would be no poem" if the poet's daughter had not died—or that the poet in *Pearl* "was recording an actual vision he had experienced."

On the other hand, rejecting the naïve biographical reading of the poem as an elegy for the poet's daughter need not imply that those who argue that the poem is an allegory are closer to the truth. This reading interprets the pearl as representing some Christian concept or ideal that has been lost or misunderstood. Identifications, all with limitations, include the purified soul, virginity and innocence, the grace of God, and even the Eucharist. However, *Pearl* is not a consistent allegory in the tradition of *Everyman* or John Bunyan's *The Pilgrim's Progress*. Its characters and objects are not static but dynamic, symbols that shift as the dreamer gains fuller self-knowledge and greater awareness of the divine.

The growth in the dreamer's knowledge takes place as the poem moves through three settings. The narrator at first describes a beautiful garden, luxurious in its growth. This ideal earthly garden is nevertheless timebound. In August at the height of the season, it blooms with flowers and natural beauty, but the garden is subject to change and all will decay. It is here that the narrator has lost his pearl, here that he comes to mourn, mortally wounded by his loss, and here that he falls asleep, his spirit setting forth on a marvelous adventure while his body remains in the garden. At this point, the pearl is to be understood as a lost jewel, "pleasant for a prince," perfect, round, radiant, smooth, and without spot. The narrator's grief over the loss of this precious but earthly object, however, is to be judged as excessive. The narrator seems vaguely aware of his problem, since he refers to his "wretched will," but he must learn to put his treasure in heavenly, not earthly, things.

The second setting is introduced immediately. Now the dreamer finds himself in another garden, even more radiant and dazzling than the first. The dreamer is in a garden that is beyond change, a beautiful setting that makes him forget all grief. This is the Earthly Paradise lost by Adam for his sin and reached by Dante near the conclusion of his ascension through Purgatory in *The Divine Comedy* (a possible source for *Pearl*). Here, the dreamer comes to a river which he cannot cross and on the far bank sees a beautiful, gleaming maiden dressed in white. She is associated with the pearl by her appearance and purity and by the fact that she is adorned with pearls. Whether or not this association implies an elegiac reading of the poem, it is clear that the maiden (and thus the pearl) represents the beauty, perfection, and eternity of the soul beyond the ravages of place and time. The maiden identifies herself as the bride of Christ, a traditional symbol for the righteous soul, derived from Revelation 19:7-9. Her status as bride and her position in Heaven will become the main focus of her debate with the dreamer.

The poem's third setting, the New Jerusalem, is described by the pearl maiden and only glimpsed by the dreamer. This setting is clearly beyond the reach of the dreamer as long as he lives, at least in this world. When he foolishly attempts to cross the river separating the earthly paradise where he stands from the New Jerusalem whence the pearl maiden speaks, he is startled from his dream and awakes to find himself in the very garden where he fell asleep. However, this third setting, along with the maiden's discussion of Christ's parable of the pearl of great price, provides yet another significance of the pearl—Heaven itself. The maiden's advice to the dreamer is to forsake the mad world and purchase Heaven, the spotless and matchless pearl. He is, she scolds, too concerned with his earthly jewel.

The close associations of the pearl with smoothness and with roundness, whiteness, and brightness are extended in the poem so that the pearl comes to symbolize perfection and purity. The traditional symbolic significance of the circle and sphere as representing the soul and eternity is also developed in the poem, both in its imagery and in its symmetrical structure, with each stanza linked by concatenation from beginning to end. This linking device has been compared to a chain and to a rosary. The poem's final line, furthermore, echoes its first, the 101 stanzas implying not only the completion of a full circle but also the beginning of another. The

whole suggests eternity. The centrality of the number twelve, traditionally the apocalyptic number, is also appropriate; it appears repeatedly in the Book of Revelation. Thus, the image of the pearl, the vision of Heaven, and the poem itself merge into one. As Thorlac Turville-Petre concludes, "Heaven, the pearl and the poem are all constructed with the same flawless circularity, an idea which reflects the words at the beginning and the end of the Apocalypse: 'I am Alpha and Omega, the beginning and the end, saith the Lord.'"

Thematically the poem is also concerned with Heaven and its perfect nature, order, and ideals. Much of *Pearl* develops a debate between the pearl maiden and the obtuse earthbound dreamer. As in *Cleanness*, a parable of Christ is at the center of the poem's teaching. The parable of the workers in the vineyard is particularly suitable, because it represents sharply the distinction between man's sense of worth and reward based on reason and a general sense of fairness and God's loving gifts of mercy and grace tendered equally to all. Christ tells how the owner of the vineyard pays those workers who labored for only an hour the same amount as those who labored all day. This apparent unfairness elicits protests and grumbling from the latter, and the dreamer foolishly allies himself with them by similarly complaining to the pearl maiden. The expectation of earth is simply not met in Heaven. The parable makes the point cogently: The last will be first and the first last.

From the divine perspective, no man is worthy of Heaven. Salvation is a gift of God. This gift is an example, the pearl maiden argues, of God's courtesy. Thus, although the ideals of cleanness and truthfulness remain important in *Pearl*, the poet here concentrates on the ideal of courtesy as his basis for exploring the nature of Heaven. God is portrayed as a noble and courteous chieftain, and the Virgin Mary is known not only as the Queen of Heaven—her traditional title—but also Queen of Courtesy. All the righteous become, in fact, kings and queens, members of the chivalric court of equals because they are members of Christ's body through courtesy. The poem thus expands the traditionally social virtues of the chivalric ideal into a religious concept with a wide range of applications. In addition to the usual sense of the term to signify good breeding, proper speech, kind manners, and unhesitating generosity, in *Pearl* courtesy connotes as well the freely given grace of God and the loving relationship between man and the divine lost on earth through sin but available in Heaven.

SIR GAWAIN AND THE GREEN KNIGHT

As a romance in the chivalric tradition dealing with knights of renown and beautiful courtly ladies, *Sir Gawain and the Green Knight* quite naturally also examines the ideal of courtesy. It is not discussed as a characteristic of Heaven, for the romance limits its focus to earthly heroes and events, although they may be superhuman and altogether marvelous. Courtesy is examined as a characteristic of the Arthurian court and especially of Gawain, the nephew of King Arthur, a favorite of the charming ladies of court, and the epitome of chivalry. His character does, however, merge secular ideals with religious devotion. This merger is evident in his elaborate shield, described and explained at length by the poet. Decorated with a pentangle, the "endless knot" suggesting eternal ideals, the shield reflects not only Gawain's bravery, generosity, truthfulness, cleanness, and courtesy, but also his devotion to the five wounds of Christ and the five joys of the Virgin. Yet, through the mysterious challenge of the Green Knight, Gawain and the chivalric ideas he represents are both tested severely. When the requirements of courtesy come into conflict with truthfulness and cleanness, even the perfect knight may fail.

Although the poem is generally divided into four parts, the testing of the knight takes place as the hero moves through three locales. At first Gawain is portrayed at the Arthurian court, feasting over Christmas and celebrating the New Year with King Arthur, the knights of the Round Table, and Queen Guinevere. Here he is tested in his duty as a knight when the reputation of Camelot is threatened. Acting courteously and bravely, he accepts the challenge of the Green Knight, whom he beheads—only to be told by the enchanted figure that Gawain's turn for the return blow will come in a year and a day. As J. A. Burrow notes, this test of courage in combat is the easiest for Gawain to pass, for it involves an obvious knightly virtue—truthfulness to his word— in conflict with the desire for life, and brave knights often face such challenges successfully.

The hero's second locale is the court of Bertilak at Hautdesert, where a year later Gawain rests on his journey to meet the unknown Green Knight. Here, Gawain is welcomed in a chivalric court and undergoes a much more subtle test. At this court the ideals of truthfulness and cleanness come into conflict with the demands of courtesy. Burrow sees Gawain here as "subjected to one of the most complex and elaborately contrived test situations in all medieval literature." After agreeing with Bertilak to exchange each evening whatever he gains during the day, Gawain is tempted by Bertilak's beautiful wife. She approaches him in bed for three mornings, calling on his reputation as a courtly lover. Gawain must overcome this threat to cleanness and loyalty to his host while remaining courteous to the lady. This he accomplishes through his great talent for gentle speech. Each morning the lady settles for a kiss from Gawain, which he passes on to his host each evening. The host, who has spent his days hunting, similarly gives Gawain his winnings. On the third morning, however, apparently successful in turning back the lady's sexual advances, Gawain accepts a green girdle from her. That evening he does not give it to Bertilak, ostensibly because he would be discourteous in revealing the lady's gift, but also because the green girdle's magical powers will protect him when he faces the Green Knight the following day. Thus, in one decision, Gawain fails the test of truthfulness by breaking his word to Bertilak, and the test of bravery by carrying an enchanted girdle to the Green Chapel.

Finally, Gawain journeys to the poem's third locale, the Green Chapel. Here he meets the Green Knight, who three times swings his axe over the bowed head of Gawain. The third time, he nicks the skin, symbolizing Gawain's failure at Hautdesert in his third temptation. The Green Knight now reveals himself as Bertilak and explains that he has known all along of his wife's morning rendezvous with Gawain. The whole adventure, Gawain discovers, has been instigated by the enchantress, Morgan le Fey, as a means of testing Arthur's court. Although Bertilak praises Gawain's performance under this test, the hero himself is humiliated and angry. He has failed the test of bravery and truthfulness and now, in an antifeminist harangue, he also reveals his lack of courtesy.

Like *Pearl*, *Sir Gawain and the Green Knight*, after 101 stanzas, ends where it begins. Recalling the introduction, the poem returns to Camelot. Gawain, however, has been changed by his experience, and although the knights and ladies of the round table—along with many modern readers—believe he has acted as honorably as can be expected of any mortal, Gawain takes his failure very seriously.

The poet has shown that earthly virtues alone, even those of the greatest knight, fail. Human values and societies are by definition sinful and subject to the ravages of time and weaknesses of the flesh. Thus, the poet introduces the Arthurian court with references to the fall of Troy, war, and betrayal. Furthermore, the ideal societies of Camelot and Hautdesert represent vulnerable and artificial islands of civilization surrounded by wild nature and affected by the changing seasons. By the end of the poem the dominant symbol of Gawain's character has been changed. Instead of the pentangle, he is now associated with the green girdle, which he wears as a penitential reminder of his failure.

Gawain's marvelous adventure is narrated in the third person, but the point of view is generally limited to Gawain's perceptions of events. The result is a masterful story with suspense and awe in which the reader, surprised like the hero by the unfolding plot, sympathizes with the hero's bewilderment. As Larry Benson and other scholars have shown, the plot artistically combines several traditional romance and folklore motifs into a seamless whole. Like *Pearl*, it is symmetrically structured: It counterpositions the two courts, two feasts, two journeys of the knight, and his two symbols, and it balances the three temptations of Gawain with Bertilak's three hunting expeditions and the three blows of the axe at the Green Chapel. Also like *Pearl*, it includes descriptions of great natural beauty, and, like *Patience*, it creates a character overwhelmed by the supernatural. Like *Cleanness*, *Sir Gawain and the Green Knight* relates a narrative of strange visitors and violent deeds in vigorous and forceful verse filled with realistic details. It shares with the other poems of the Cotton Nero manuscript many stylistic and thematic features, and remains the greatest work of the Pearl-Poet.

BIBLIOGRAPHY

Blanch, Robert J., and Julian N. Wasserman. *From "Pearl" to "Gawain": Forme to Fynisment*. Wasserman. Gainesville: University Press of Florida, 1995. Presents the thesis that works within the Pearl manuscript not only share a common author but are connected and intersect in fundamental ways. Explores interrelated themes such as language, covenants, miracles, and the role of the intrusive narrator. Includes bibliography and index.

Brewer, Derek, and Jonathan Gibson, eds. *A Companion to the Gawain-Poet*. Arthurian Studies 38. Rochester, N.Y.: Boydell & Brewer, 1999. A collection of original analysis by an international group of medievalists. Explores a range of topics including theories of authorship, the historical and social background to the poems, the role of chivalry, and the representation of women. Includes illustrations and maps, and bibliography and index.

Conley, John, ed. *The Middle English "Pearl": Critical Essays*. Notre Dame, Ind.: University of Notre Dame Press, 1970. The twenty essays in this volume, published originally since the 1940's, represent a variety of critical approaches and include general interpretations of the poem as well as more specialized studies. Middle English and foreign-language quotations are followed by modern translations.

DeVries, David N. "*Unde Dicitur*: Observations on the Poetic Distinctions of the Pearl-Poet." *The Chaucer Review* 35, no. 1 (2000): 115-132. DeVries explores the way that the Middle English poem "Pearl" happens and what it does to the language in which it happens. The Middle English poet was able to wrench out of the recalcitrant facts of grief and the limitations of language a difficult and marvelous "vineyard" of a poem whose power continues to resonate through the centuries.

Gardner, John, ed. *The Complete Works of the Gawain-Poet*. Chicago: University of Chicago Press, 1965. Gardner's long introduction discusses what is known about the poet in question. Describes conventions and traditions in the poems, analyzes the poems themselves, and offers notes on versification and form. Gardner's own modern verse translations of the poet's works, including *Saint Erkenwald*, compose the body of this volume.

Howard, Donald R., and Christian Zacher, eds. *Critical Studies of Sir Gawain and the Green Knight*. Notre Dame, Ind.: University of Notre Dame Press, 1968. This collection of twenty-three essays includes two essays of introduction and background followed by discussions of critical issues, style and technique, characters and setting, and interpretations. Quotations are in Middle English with Middle English alphabet characters.

Moorman, Charles. *The Pearl-Poet.* New York: Twayne, 1968. This volume is an excellent introduction to the anonymous writer of *Pearl, Patience, Purity,* and *Sir Gawain and the Green Knight.* Biographical information is by necessity replaced by more general information about the fourteenth century. Includes a chapter that examines each poem in turn, a chronology, and an annotated bibliography.

Spearing, A. C. *The Gawain-Poet: A Critical Study.* Cambridge, England: Cambridge University Press, 1970. After a brief discussion of the Middle Ages, the alliterative tradition, and the question of authorship, this book devotes one chapter to each of the four poems attributed to the poet. The extensive quotations from the poetry have not been modernized, although only modern alphabet letters are used.

Richard Kenneth Emmerson;
bibliography updated by the editors

CHARLES-PIERRE PÉGUY

Born: Orléans, France; January 7, 1873
Died: Near Villeroy, France; September 5, 1914

PRINCIPAL POETRY

Jeanne d'Arc, 1897 (as Marcel and Pierre Baudouin)

La Chanson du roi Dagobert, 1903

Le Mystère de la charité de Jeanne d'Arc, 1910 (*The Mystery of the Charity of Joan of Arc,* 1950)

Le Porche du mystère de la deuxième vertu, 1911 (*The Portico of the Mystery of the Second Virtue,* 1970)

"Châteaux de Loire," 1912 ("Chateaux of the Loire")

Le Mystère des saints innocents, 1912 (*The Mystery of the Holy Innocents and Other Poems,* 1956)

La Tapisserie de sainte Geneviève et de Jeanne d'Arc, 1912

"Les Sept contre Thèbes," 1912 ("Seven Against Thebes")

Ève, 1913

Sainte Geneviève, patronne de Paris, 1913

"Les Sept contre Paris," 1913 ("Seven Against Paris")

La Tapisserie de Notre-Dame, 1913

Quatrains, 1939

Œuvres poétiques complètes, 1941

God Speaks: Religious Poetry, 1945

OTHER LITERARY FORMS

Most of Charles-Pierre Péguy's prose falls into the category of journalism. His articles, which first appeared in *La Revue socialiste* (1897) and *La Revue blanche* (1899), are currently available in *Notes politiques et sociales* (1957). Other prose works by Péguy have been collected in *Œuvres en prose I, 1898-1908* (1959) and *Œuvres en prose II, 1909-1941* (1961), both edited by Marcel Péguy. Gallimard has also published the *Œuvres complètes* (1917-1955) in twenty volumes, including *Deuxième Élégie XXX, L'Esprit de système, Un Poète m'a dit, Par ce demi-clair matin, Situations,* and *La Thèse,* all posthumous publications or fragments. *Les Œuvres posthumes de Charles Péguy* (1969) was edited by Jacques Viard.

Very few of these works have been translated into English in their entirety. Selections from Péguy's prose are available in *Basic Verities: Prose and Poetry* (1943), *Men and Saints: Prose and Poetry* (1944), and *God Speaks: Religious Poetry.* In *Temporal and Eternal* (1958), translated by Alexander Dru, there are selections from *Notre Jeunesse* (1910; our youth), *Clio* (1917, 1955), and *Deuxième Élégie XXX.* Péguy's correspondence is published in *Lettres à André Bourgeois* (1950). Marcel Péguy has edited a volume of selected correspondence titled *Lettres et entretiens* (1927).

ACHIEVEMENTS

Charles-Pierre Péguy, the militant journalist, the unswerving Socialist, the ardent defender of Alfred Dreyfus, was a writer who might be unknown to the world at large and even to France today if it were not for his poetry. In the last four years of his life, having "found the faith anew," he turned to poetry as a medium of expression. This intensely personal verse, in colloquial but correct French, in which God speaks with men as if He were one of them, touches the reader with its simplicity.

Péguy is able to personify hope as a little child in *The Portico of the Mystery of the Second Virtue*; God himself is taken off guard by the unassuming courage of this girl who can change the world. Péguy sees hope in the possibility of beginning anew: "Le premier jour est le plus beau jour" (the first day is the most beautiful day). His Joan of Arc is also a defenseless child who nevertheless believes in action: One must not save, but spend, oneself. Thus, Péguy offers a message of simple heroism, much needed in prewar France and still appealing two wars later.

Péguy extols France, perhaps a bit too much when the God of the Holy Innocents says that the French are His favorite people. Péguy weaves a rich tapestry of French heroes and saints, most of whom are drawn from the Middle Ages: King Dagobert, Saint Genevieve, Joan of Arc, Saint Louis, Jean de Joinville. Perhaps the only

Charles-Pierre Péguy

nonmedieval heroes admitted are Pierre Corneille, Jules Michelet, and Victor Hugo. The cathedrals of France, Notre Dame de Paris and Chartres, are woven into the tapestry, itself a cathedral with its images of porches, mysteries, and saints. With a profound sense of history, a theme that always fascinated Péguy, the ship of the ages approaches Paris, bearing France's sins and virtues, victories and failures, from the day when the Île-de-France was first inhabited by the Romans.

All of Péguy's poetry is deeply religious, in contrast to his Socialist prose. A nonpracticing Catholic convert who claimed that he had never left the Church, Péguy puzzled his many friends and has continued to fascinate critics—among them Pie Duployé, who has dedicated a sizable volume to the question of Péguy's religion. The faith which informs Péguy's poetry is universal; it touches believer and nonbeliever alike, for it is moral without being dogmatic, uncompromising but gentle. Deeply rooted in the soil of France yet revealing a profound understanding of universal human concerns, Péguy's poetry has found a small but devoted audience.

BIOGRAPHY

Charles-Pierre Péguy was born at Orléans in the Faubourg Bourgogne on January 7, 1873, the only son of a poor working woman who was to lose her husband within a few months. Péguy was always proud to be a member of a hardworking family, and he regarded France's peasants and workmen as her greatest strength. He grew up under the care of his mother and grandmother, attending local schools. He was able to attend the *lycée* at Orléans in 1885 because of a scholarship and because of the new system of public education which he was later to extol. Higher education even became possible; thus, he attended both the Lycée Lakanal at Sceaux in 1891 and the École Normale Supérieure in 1894, which was eventually to deny him the *agrégation*. For this, as well as for its adherence to the values of the modern world, Péguy was to immortalize the school as "l'école dite normale, autrefois supérieure" (called normal, formerly superior). Around 1895, he became attracted to socialism, not in the Marxist sense but rather in the idealistic tradition of the early nineteenth century—the tradition of Pierre Proudhon and Pierre Leroux, as Jacques Viard has demonstrated. Péguy founded a Socialist group, and at the turn of the century actively supported Dreyfus for idealistic reasons, "so that France will not be in the state of mortal sin." Yet when, in Péguy's view, other Socialist leaders began to use Dreyfus for their own ends, when what he originally envisioned as "mystique" degenerated into "politique," Péguy went his own way. In 1900, he founded his *Cahiers de la quinzaine*, "pour dire bêtement la vérité bête . . ." (to tell the stark truth starkly).

Several years earlier, in 1896, Péguy's best friend, Marcel Baudouin, had died, yet Péguy kept his memory alive. Indeed, Péguy's first poetic work, *Jeanne d'Arc* (Joan of Arc), a long drama in blank verse, was published by "Georges Bellais" (a pseudonym for Péguy) under the names "Marcel and Pierre Baudouin" (also pseudonyms for Péguy) in 1897. All of his subsequent works (with the exception of two posthumously published works) were first published by Péguy himself in the *Cahiers de la quinzaine* (1900-1914). He married Marcel's sister, Charlotte-Françoise, in 1897. They had four children and were to remain faithful to each other, though not always happy. Péguy's main work was his *Cahiers de la quinzaine*, by no means lucrative, for he had a talent for antagonizing his subscribers through the uncompromising honesty of many of the articles he printed, which were nevertheless of the highest literary quality.

In 1908, Péguy surprised his friend Joseph Lotte by declaring, "J'ai retrouvé la foi" (I have returned to the faith). Perhaps, however, because of Péguy's civil marriage and his wife's anti-Catholic convictions, he did not practice his religion or have his children baptized. The whole tenor of his work, however, changed at this time, becoming more reflective, often mystical. His best prose works, such as *Clio, Notre Jeunesse,* and *L'Argent* (1913; money), and most of his poetry date from his conversion. In 1912-1913, he made several pilgrimages to Chartres for the cure of his sick child Marcel, immortalizing the experience in his poem, "Présentation de la Beauce à Notre-Dame de Chartres." Indeed, the Chartres pilgrimage has been reestablished in France as a result of Péguy's inspiration.

Péguy's last years were troubled by spiritual and emotional uncertainties. He derived particular help and consolation from his friendship with Henri Bergson, whose lectures at the Collège de France Péguy attended faithfully. At the outbreak of World War I in August, 1914, Péguy—then forty-one years old—immediately enlisted as a lieutenant in the infantry. Killed near Villeroy on September 5, 1914, by a bullet in the forehead, Péguy became the model of those heroic soldiers who died for their country. Ironically, during World War II, a bullet was to strike the forehead of the bust erected in front of his birthplace, 48 rue Bourgogne.

ANALYSIS

Like that of his contemporary, Paul Claudel, Charles-Pierre Péguy's style recalls the Psalms, yet Péguy has none of Claudel's triumphant exuberance. Péguy's verse has been called a "piétinement": It is plodding, a step-by-step advancement, like a pilgrimage to Chartres or a Corpus Christi procession. Péguy says that it is not important to arrive but simply to go. His verse is repetitive, yet the reiterations serve to emphasize, to clarify, and to articulate his thought.

Péguy's three *tapisseries* (tapestries) are written in four-line rhymed stanzas in the traditional Alexandrine, while the *Quatrains* and *La Chanson du roi Dagobert* are ballads with a very folkloristic air. All the rest of Péguy's major poems are written in free verse. Péguy's free verse is idiosyncratic, ranging from brief lines consisting of only a word or two to proselike paragraphs; some stanzas are only a line long, while others continue for pages. In his first work, the dramatic poem *Jeanne d'Arc*, Péguy baffled the printers by leaving entire pages blank, without any explanation.

Péguy is known for his use of contrasts and paradoxes. The most important of these in his poetry are the polarities spiritual and physical, aging and newness, and temporal and eternal. The theme of aging and newness, which is not peculiar to his poetry, is also basic to his later prose, especially *Clio*. Clio, the Greek Muse of history, is a symbol of aging, as are Ève, deadwood, and paper. Péguy sees newness in the Virgin Mary, the medieval world, Joan of Arc, and hope, the second theological virtue. These elements are characterized by powerlessness and abandonment and are symbolized also by the dawn, the first bud of April, the first day of creation, or fresh springs of water, all suggesting originality, spontaneity, and a freshness of vision. Péguy infinitely prefers this attitude to one of conformity and habit, symbolically connected with aging and decay.

In contrasting the spiritual and the physical, Péguy does not use the word *charnel* (physical) in its usual sexual connotation, but simply to insist that a human being is composed of both body and soul. He imagines the soul and the body as a horse hitched to a plow, with the soul pulling the body but the two closely united. The temporal and the eternal are also contrasted throughout Péguy's work. Among his favorite symbols for the temporal is Ève, while the Virgin Mary represents the eternal, yet here again he prefers to integrate them into a single concept, the human condition. He also refuses to dichotomize the secular and the sacred. These ideas echo the Bergsonian philosophy of time and duration that was very popular in Péguy's day—a philosophy which Péguy learned from Bergson himself.

Péguy's first poetic works were dramatic, and much of his verse maintains a dramatic orientation. The *mystères* are essentially dialogues; in them, God speaks in a very human tone. Throughout his verse, Péguy assumes an intimacy with God, Christ, and the saints. Péguy recounts biblical events with a sense of immediacy and personal involvement, and he frequently addresses the Virgin Mary in a tone that recalls medieval courtly love poems or the confidence of a small child in his mother.

Péguy's poetic universe is peopled largely by women, a point which has attracted the attention of many critics. Only in the *Quatrains* is there any indication of romantic love. These women do not represent the typical feminine image in literature, nor are they the "eternal feminine" of wisdom and beauty; they are, rather, symbols of Péguy's ideals.

Open to all nations and races, and particularly sympathetic to the oppressed, Péguy nevertheless insisted on the importance of the "race" (his conception of race was essentially nationalistic) embodied in France. Its fundamental unit, Péguy believed, was the parish, and his choice of images suggests the rural France of a bygone—indeed, a mythical—era in which the Church and the French nation were mystically united. In Péguy's imagery, France is a garden and the French people are God's gardeners. "La Beauce" is the "océan des blés" (ocean of wheat) over which shines the Star of the Sea, the Virgin of Chartres. Nothing is as great as plowing the fields, says Péguy, as he mentions each tool by name. The rhythm of the seasons and the centuries suggests the

presence of the eternal in the temporal and the temporal in the eternal. Thus, Péguy's poetry, disconcerting and sometimes tedious, moves into a cosmic dimension, making him truly a poet of the twentieth century.

JEANNE D'ARC AND THE MYSTERY OF THE CHARITY OF JOAN OF ARC

Of all Péguy's poetic subjects, Joan of Arc seems to have fascinated him the most. Two works are completely devoted to her: *Jeanne d'Arc*, a "drama in three plays," and *The Mystery of the Charity of Joan of Arc*, and she plays a considerable role in seven others. For Péguy, the ardent Socialist, she was in 1897 the heroine of the new Socialist city, but his bulky *Jeanne d'Arc* was unbelievable, unsalable, and unstageable. This first verse play has three parts: "Domrémy," "Les Batailles" (the battles), and "Rouen." The first part, "Domrémy," was the source for *The Mystery of the Charity of Joan of Arc* in 1910.

The Mystery of the Charity of Joan of Arc is dedicated to all who wish to remedy evil in the world, a major preoccupation of Péguy, especially after 1908, when he transferred Socialist problems to a spiritual level. The work contains three characters: Madame Gervaise, Hauviette, and Jeannette. Madame Gervaise is a twenty-five-year-old Franciscan nun who has evolved from the stereotyped religious figure of the *Jeanne d'Arc* of 1897, in which she had retired to a convent for her individual salvation. Here, she is a mature woman who recognizes the involvement of everyone in the problem of evil and who frequently represents the traditional Catholic viewpoint. Her dialogues with Jeannette are almost monologues, for Jeannette prefers to pray rather than to engage in dialogue.

In her dialogue with Hauviette, Jeannette's extraordinary vocation comes to light. Jeannette is unhappy because people suffer. She wants to relieve their misery, as she expresses in her "Our Father," a prayer that might be Péguy's own. She is especially concerned about the problem of eternal damnation, an enigma which haunted Péguy throughout his life. Jeannette articulates the need of a saint who will succeed and faintly sees her own vocation in these words.

Jeannette is called not only to liberate France but also to participate with Christ in saving the world, for Péguy places great emphasis on human and divine cooperation. This is perhaps the reason for the lengthy account of the

Passion of Christ which occupies almost half of the play. At the end of the Passion, Jeannette asks whom one must save and how. She learns that she must save everyone, in imitation of Christ, by prayer and suffering. Jeannette also asks for a sign—namely, the safety of Mont Saint-Michel. She receives it and welcomes it in a glorious hymn of praise. In one of several unpublished conclusions, Jeannette receives her vocation to save France in words that echo the call of the prophets in the Old Testament. Why Péguy never published these conclusions is not clear. Perhaps he wished to emphasize Jeannette's agony; perhaps, too, he meant the next two *mystères* as a response to her dilemma.

THE PORTICO OF THE MYSTERY OF THE SECOND VIRTUE

Written between June, 1910, and 1911, *The Portico of the Mystery of the Second Virtue*, the second of the *mystères*, was published in the *Cahiers de la quinzaine* on September 24, 1911. A lengthy work, it occupies 140 pages in the Pléiade edition and contains Péguy's most important poetic themes. Romain Rolland called it Péguy's best work, and with the *The Mystery of the Holy Innocents*, Pie Duployé considers it Péguy's most authentically religious poem. Surprisingly, neither poem attracted great attention at the time of its publication.

The Portico of the Mystery of the Second Virtue is Péguy's poem of abandonment, in the spirit of the "little way" of Saint Thérèse of Lisieux, as Marjorie Villiers observes (*Charles Péguy: A Study in Integrity*, 1965). It is his most overtly autobiographical work, containing references to Péguy's (then) three children, to their ages, names, and patron saints, to the illness of his son, Marcel, and to his own reconciliation with God. It is very biblical and rests more on the parables of the Lost Sheep and the Prodigal Son, and on the Book of Wisdom, than on the catechism which Péguy recalled from his boyhood days at St. Aignan. The prayers to the Virgin Mary echo the Hail Mary and the famous litanies.

As in all of Péguy's works, the digressions here are many and mysterious, yet he never loses sight of the central theme, hope, personified as a powerless little child who is powerful in her nothingness. Here, and in *The Mystery of the Holy Innocents*, Hope returns like a refrain, continuing to amaze God, who narrates the poem through the person of Madame Gervaise. Péguy

contrasts Hope with her grown sisters, Faith and Charity, who do not astound God. Christ came to Earth, however, to make hope possible, to give the lost sheep a second chance, to allow men to transmit His message to one another and to share in His creative work. The poem ends with a beautiful celebration of night and sleep, the virtue of a confident child and the sign of the triumph of hope.

THE MYSTERY OF THE HOLY INNOCENTS

The Mystery of the Holy Innocents, written in 1912 and published on March 24 of the same year, returns to many themes already treated in the preceding work: the three theological virtues (faith, hope, and charity) and a beautiful hymn to night that again evokes the burial of Christ, freedom, and abandonment. Péguy announced its theme as paradise, a thread which runs through the poem and serves as its conclusion. The title *The Mystery of the Holy Innocents*, referring to the unbaptized Jewish victims of Herod's jealousy, may suggest Péguy's own unbaptized children. He mentions the Holy Innocents only at the end of the poem, along with a beautiful eulogy of childhood and children.

Again in this poem God speaks, commenting on His love of night and His astonishment at hope. He prefers the person who does not calculate for tomorrow. He loves especially the French people, builders of cathedrals and leaders of Crusades, worthy descendants of Saint Louis and champions of freedom. Madame Gervaise gives an instruction on prayer, especially the "Our Father," as an example of trust and hope. Péguy also develops his favorite parable, that of the Prodigal Son, a subject which he had intended for a fourth *mystère* but which never grew beyond a few pages. His portrayal of hope as the youngest of the family suggests the story of Benjamin, the youngest of Jacob's sons. Thus, Madame Gervaise and Jeannette relate the biblical narrative of Joseph and his brothers, with a sympathy for the Jewish people habitual in Péguy. In Péguy's narrative, the Old Testament story of Joseph and his brothers represents the temporal, while the New Testament, from which the story of the Prodigal Son is taken, represents the eternal. Here, as elsewhere in his poetry, Péguy attempts to integrate the two concepts.

LA TAPISSERIE DE SAINTE GENEVIÈVE ET DE JEANNE D'ARC

In addition to the *mystères*, Péguy wrote several *tapisseries*. He defined a *tapisserie* as a lengthy succession of stanzas on the same theme, frequently following the same rhyme scheme as well; many of the stanzas begin with the same line. The first of Péguy's three *tapisseries*, *La Tapisserie de sainte Geneviève et de Jeanne d'Arc*, published December 1, 1912, was planned as a novena beginning on the feast of Saint Genevieve, January 3, 1913. It is dedicated to the Patrons of Paris and France, Saint Genevieve and Saint Jeanne d'Arc respectively, and it contains nine poems of varying length, with several sonnets among them.

Péguy calls upon Saint Genevieve, the shepherdess, to guard the flock of Paris in the twentieth century as she defended the city against the Huns in her own day. In poems 4 and 5, Péguy compares Saint Genevieve and Jeanne d'Arc. In Poem 8, the longest of the series, he compares the weapons of Christ with those of Satan, which are sometimes identical. In poems 8 and 9, Jeanne is not named, but it is evident that the poems refer to her. She takes part in a battle and like Christ is led to death at the end of the last poem. Jeanne here is not the anguished Jeannette of *The Mystery of the Charity of Joan of Arc*, but rather the victorious leader of the French forces and the courageous martyr of the fifteenth century.

LA TAPISSERIE DE NOTRE-DAME

The second tapestry, *La Tapisserie de Notre-Dame*, consists of five poems, four short ones dedicated to Notre-Dame de Paris and one longer one, "Présentation de la Beauce à Notre-Dame de Chartres." Perhaps the richest in images among all the *tapisseries*, these poems depend on the symbol of a ship, and the Virgin Mary as the Star of the Sea. Mary becomes the refuge of sinners, for she will obtain forgiveness from her Son for the sins that weigh down the boat. "Présentation de la Beauce," rhythmic and melodic, eventually loses its effect. Despite its excessive length, however, it is a sensitive portrayal of pilgrims wending their way through the fertile wheat fields to pay homage to the heavenly Queen.

ÈVE

In its conception, *Ève*, the last of Péguy's *tapisseries*, was his most ambitious work. Unfinished at his death, it already ran to some nine thousand lines, including a "suite" discovered after his death. It is a dense and difficult work, brilliantly studied by Joseph Barbier, Albert Béguin, Jean Onimus, and other scholars.

Péguy defined its subject as salvation. He begins with Ève's expulsion from the earthly paradise, a place he describes with great poetic beauty. It echoes the harmonious city that he had created in his early Socialist works, a utopia modeled on Plato's *Republic*. Péguy sees Ève as the mother of humanity, as the representative of all women, responsible for their change in status. He muses on the human condition, the intransigence of the sinner, and the solitude of man without God. He evokes the ancient world, which Christ was to inherit, and Judgment Day. Perhaps the most popular lines of Péguy's entire oeuvre appear in the middle of the poem, in the otherwise tedious monologue addressed to Ève. These lines refer to soldiers who have died for country in a just war: "Heureux ceux qui sont morts pour la terre charnelle. . . ." (Happy are they who have died for this land of flesh). This was soon to become Péguy's epitaph, for he was to die for his country in September, 1914.

OTHER MAJOR WORKS

NONFICTION: *Notre Jeunesse*, 1910; *L'Argent*, 1913; *Clio*, 1917.

MISCELLANEOUS: *Œuvres complètes*, 1917-1955 (20 volumes); *Basic Verities: Prose and Poetry*, 1943; *Men and Saints: Prose and Poetry*, 1944; *Les Œuvres posthumes de Charles Péguy*, 1969.

BIBLIOGRAPHY

Aronowicz, Annette. *Jews and Christians on Time and Eternity: Charles Péguy's "Portrait of Bernard-Lazare."* Stanford, Calif.: Stanford University Press, 1988. An insightful book which explains clearly Péguy's deep sympathy for Jews and his strong opposition to anti-Semitism. Aronowicz argues persuasively that there is a unity in Péguy's writings from his period as a socialist activist to his religious writings composed after his return to Catholicism in 1908.

Contosta, David. "Charles Péguy: Critic of the Modern World." *American Benedictine Review* 32, no. 2 (June, 1981): 177-188. A thoughtful essay which examines the theological reasons for Péguy's opposition to economic practices which permitted the exploitation of ordinary people.

Humes, Joy. *Two Against Time: A Study of the Very Present Worlds of Paul Claudel and Charles Péguy.*

Chapel Hill: University of North Carolina Press, 1978. A clearly written book which describes the profound differences between Claudel and Péguy, who were the most important Catholic poets in France during the early twentieth century.

St. Aubyn, F. C. *Charles Péguy.* Boston: Twayne, 1977. Albeit somewhat old, this book remains the best introduction to the rich diversity of Péguy's life and works. This book contains an annotated bibliography of his works and important critical studies on his writings.

Savard, John. "The Pedagogy of Péguy." *The Chesterton Review* 19, no. 3 (August, 1993): 357-379. An essay which compares masterful uses of paradox by Péguy and the English Catholic writer G. K. Chesterton. Savard argues that through paradoxical arguments both writers lead their readers to deal with complex moral issues.

Schmitt, Hans A. *Charles Péguy: The Decline of an Idealist.* Baton Rouge: Louisiana State University Press, 1967. A biography of Péguy by an accomplished historian of modern Europe. Includes bibliographic references.

Villiers, Marjorie. *Charles Péguy: A Study in Integrity.* London: Collins, 1965. This well-researched book remains the only biography in English of Péguy.

Irma M. Kashuba;
bibliography updated by Edmund J. Campion

NIKOS PENTZIKIS

Born: Thessaloníki, Greece; October 30, 1908

PRINCIPAL POETRY
Ikones, 1944
Anakomidhi, 1961
Paleotera piimata ke neotera, 1980 (includes *Ikones* and prose pieces)
Psile e perispomene, 1995

OTHER LITERARY FORMS
Nikos Pentzikis might be called the odd case of modern Greek literature, for he combines in his poetry as well as in the much larger body of his prose a restless and inquisitive spirit typical of the modern era with a kind of pre-Renaissance, more particularly Byzantine, religious mysticism. The young hero of his first novel, *Andreas Dhimakoudhis*, published in 1935, suffers from unrequited love and commits suicide. This death is symbolic of Pentzikis's own early disappointments in love, the "death" of his sentimental self. His second book, *O pethamenos ke i anastasi* (wr. 1938, pb. 1944; the dead man and the resurrection), a stream-of-consciousness narrative, deals again with a young man (unnamed this time, but an obvious persona of his creator), who, though he regains his trust in life, regains it at the level of myth. He upholds the religious traditions of his country and accepts a metaphysical explanation of the world while returning and developing his sense of the concrete, his love for the world of shapes and colors. From that time on, Pentzikis cultivated his metaphysical and physical certainties in the parallel activities of writing and painting.

Pentzikis's love of the concrete is particularly evident in his book *Pragmatognosia* (1950; knowledge of things), which deals mostly with the realities of Thessaloníki, his native town, and in two works in diary form, *Simiosis ekato imeron* (1973; notes of one hundred days) and *Arhion* (1974; filing cabinet). These idiosyncratic works catalog dry data of all kinds, from skin diseases to bus fares and theater tickets (the writer sorts out and reorders cartons of souvenirs); they also rework religious information from old Greek Orthodox texts. The methodology behind these as well as other, stylistically more traditional works, such as *Arhitektoniki tis skorpias zois* (1963; architecture of the scattered life), *Mitera Thessaloniki* (1970; *Mother Salonika*, 1998), *Sinodhia* (1970; retinue), and *Omilimata* (1972; homilies), is based upon the so-called "copying" memory. Pentzikis spurns self-consciously aesthetic writing, which he finds hubristic. Instead, he favors an itemized record of reality as a fitting homage to God for the world which is His handicraft. The beautiful and the ugly, the banal and the exalted—all must find a place in Pentzikis's work, under the unifying veil of Christian myth, especially its Greek Orthodox version.

Pentzikis's later narrative method also incorporates a system of numerology. He writes or paints in clustered units of words, both religious and secular, that are ordered by their numerical values as defined by ancient Pythagorean and Neoplatonic tenets. The method is mechanical but true to his belief that a writer cannot rely entirely on his own mind but must have some external reference hallowed by time and practice.

ACHIEVEMENTS

Nikos Pentzikis's principal achievement is to have survived at all as a writer, to have persisted in his own idiosyncratic ways of seeing the world and so registering it in his poetry and prose. In his unswerving commitment to an utterly individual metaphysical vision only tangentially shaped by the currents of his time, Pentzikis shares affinities with Elias Canetti and Jorge Luis Borges.

In the context of modern Greek letters, Pentzikis has successfully integrated national and personal memory with the stuff of his everyday experience, producing prose narratives and poems which explore both the human condition and the nature of writing. In the words of the distinguished translator Kimon Friar, Pentzikis's texts are

> a dizzying depository of words that are demotic, purist, formal, colloquial, archaic, modern, medieval, ecclesiastical, obsolete, scientific—all strung together in an eccentric syntax of his own devising. By flying beyond convention and good taste, by concentrating on things and not on rhythms or cadences or composition, he has evolved an inner style of his own, a "nonstyle" that is the man.

BIOGRAPHY

Nikos Ghavril Pentzikis was born in Thessaloniki, Greece, on October 30, 1908. Pentzikis's father operated a successful pharmaceutical business; his sister, Zoe Karelli (née Hrisoule Pentzikis), became a poet and translator, an active figure on the Greek literary scene. Pentzikis completed his elementary schooling at home and, beginning in 1919, attended a regular high school. Two years later, he was writing his first poems. Between 1926 and 1929, while studying pharmacology in Paris and Strasbourg, he read extensively in literature, particularly the Symbolists. Returning to his native city to take charge of the family business (his father had died in 1927), Pentzikis published some of his writings, but dissatisfied with the reaction they provoked, he burned them.

Pentzikis's first book, *Andreas Dhimakoudhis*, reflected his student days in France and his emotional, restless nature. His second publication in book form, *O pethamenos ke i anastasi*, marked his return to, and conscious acceptance of, the traditions of his native land, particularly the traditions of the Greek Orthodox Church. This reconciliation was also evident in his collection of poems *Ikones* (icons). The war years, although difficult for Pentzikis, were also formative for his subsequent literary production and rich in contacts with other Greek writers. Between 1945 and 1947, he issued— with the help of others—the literary journal *Kohlias*, an avant-garde publication that welcomed both original material and translations.

By 1950, Pentzikis had achieved a measure of stability in his life. Married in 1948, he was professionally secure as the representative in northern Greece of Geigy, the Swiss pharmaceutical company. Both his prose work *Pragmatognosia* and the poems which he wrote and published in the late 1940's and throughout the 1950's exuded a new self-confidence, celebrating the concrete realities of his land, his native city, and the religious and folk traditions of his people. During this period, Pentzikis was also active as a painter. He began to concentrate on his own work and rarely translated or reviewed the work of others. An exception, in 1960, was his brief but incisive article on the poet George Seferis, a man and a writer very dissimilar to himself.

In the 1960's, Pentzikis continued to write and paint and began lecturing and giving interviews about his work. In 1970, he published no fewer than three books, to which he added three more between 1972 and 1974. Since 1976, he has been producing revised and expanded editions of his earlier works and has also been painting steadily. Having retired with a pension from Geigy, he devotes all of his time to his literary and artistic work, which continues to be controversial and is still rejected by many readers and critics for its apparent shapelessness. For Pentzikis, however, this is his *askissi*, his own way of practicing the solitary, virtually monastic life of the visionary artist. It must be noted that, over the years, Pentzikis has managed to enlarge, albeit slightly, the circle of his readers and admirers. A small but growing readership has discovered the wisdom and the flashes of genius sometimes obscured by the forbidding surface of his work.

ANALYSIS

Poetry is often a substitute or corrective for life. Nikos Pentzikis rounded out his first collection of poems, *Ikones*, during the difficult years of World War II. His family's diminished status and his own disappointments had already induced him to find solace in Christianity, particularly in the Greek Orthodox faith, and not, like so many other men of his generation, in political engagement. If life seemed absurd, he would espouse the Christian myth, whose special kind of absurdity harked back to Tertullian's early declaration of faith: "Credo quia absurdum" ("I believe because it is absurd").

Pentzikis's poems, however, proved that being a Greek Orthodox writer did not necessarily mean the conventional repetition of religious formulas and articles of faith. He shunned such abstractions and aimed, instead, for the concrete. In long, flowing verses which one could compare to deep breaths, he named all objects that had set his senses in motion, even the most humble, in order to place in relief the universal sympathy that governs them. He copied or reaffirmed objective reality in a way that helped him dissolve or forget his ego. The "I" became "we" or remained "I" in relation to others, not in isolation from them.

IKONES

Ikones comprises responses to old letters, photos, and other souvenirs stored in a carton. (Much of Pentzikis's work has taken its inspiration from the miscellaneous contents of such cartons.) The Greek title, *Ikones*, is ambiguous; it might mean "images," "pictures," or "icons" proper (that is, Byzantine religious paintings). In his introduction to the collection, Pentzikis stated that all but the last poem had been written while he was looking at a number of photos of sculptures from the Louvre. He then took great care to list all of those items, filling nearly a page, but not before he expressed some thoughts that made the list more meaningful. He believed that he should get down to basics, that his reactions to the world should be unclouded by emotions and thoughts which tend to compartmentalize and distort reality. The *Ikones* are not self-contained poems, based more or less on mood or offering a particular message; they are rather stages in a process, tentative attempts at developing an objective relationship with the world:

By dying I myself become an object, a statue of life,
a replica like the face which I now hold before me
admiring it, as the artist of the Renaissance admired
a vertebra of the human body. The truth of the human
body's life with all its possible variations excels
over any idea.

Working with a pile of mementos in front of him, Pentzikis both challenged and surrendered to his memory. He was deliberate when he extracted from memory its secrets, but he also found in memory an escape from actuality—in the case of *Ikones*, the actuality of war and personal failure. The dual mechanism of memory is clear in "Dhidhahi," (instruction), the first poem of the volume. The impatient and heavily charged lines of this poem suggest the struggle waged by the observing mind with its memories. These, like roses pressed between the pages of an old book, preserve enough of their fragrance to interfere with the mind's resolution to break out into a state of pure essence, an indivisible objective reality.

The poetry of *Ikones* is much more angular than mere summaries or descriptions of it can show. In its convolutions, one discerns Pentzikis's constant and insistent search for a rhythm. He looked for a pattern, a method of living that would honor both the complexity and the simplicity of life. This search is more explicit in the sixth poem (which, like all of the poems in the volume except the first and the last, is untitled):

> I must not fail anything
> more of the components of being
> in the matrix that is being put together
> the beautiful in simple forms
> simplicity and complicated structure
> progressing all the time

This is the flow, the vital flow—often undercut or reversed by its own rashness but also persistent—of the subject to the object. As Pentzikis writes in the fourth poem, "the object has its own value/ if I love life I should not subdue it/ its not coming to see me does not matter."

The last poem in *Ikones*, "Rapsodhia skeseon" (rhapsody of relationships), comprises more than five hundred lines. In a brief note appended to the poem, Pentzikis informed his readers that its composition had been bracketed by two deaths, that of a cousin of his mother and that of an old lady who used to clean his drugstore. One death heralded the poem and another underscored it. The poem itself also contains visions of death, among which is a recollection of the funeral of Pentzikis's own father. Dryly descriptive scenes alternate with meditative passages in which the experience of death is revaluated in the light of religion.

THE MIDDLE POEMS

Between 1949 and 1953, Pentzikis published in successive issues of the journal *Morfes* a series of poems which one might call his "middle poems," because they fall between *Ikones* and the later series of poems, *Anakomidhi* (transferal of relics) and were given no general name. The "middle poems" are more lyric and topical than the poems of *Ikones*; they tell stories and evoke legends associated mostly with Greek Macedonia, describing various geographical areas and combining reality with myth in an effort to enlarge upon the central theme by means of concrete detail.

The poem "Topoghrafia" (topography) is in free verse, but the lines are grouped in quatrains. As its title promises, the poem provides an exact topographical and historical description of a particular spot in Thessaloníki, but the description ends on a sentimental note which is the secret core of the poem. Here, Pentzikis confounds the reader's expectations. He might have started with the image of the sitting girl, the poet's beloved, and then located or described the surrounding landscape outward. Instead, he progresses from the borders to the center of the scene, through allusions to the life and martyrdom of Saint Demetrius, Thessaloniki's patron saint. Thus, the image of the sitting girl at the end of the poem comes as a revelation. It is a lyric image, but the sentiments it evokes have been colored and deepened by the girl's precise placement in a space hallowed by time.

In the much longer poem "Symvan" (event), a group of soldiers on leave visit a country chapel. One of the soldiers narrates an old story of the miraculous rescue of Thessaloniki by Saint Demetrius from a hostile invasion from the north. The soldiers gain a vision of the city not as a group of buildings but as a living person. The past comes alive, and the present becomes meaningful. Pentzikis uses the same method in the poem "Messa ston paleo nao" (in the old church), in which he describes the interior of a church while musing on the faith which motivated the church's builders.

Not all of these "middle poems," however, structure and control the poet's feelings around some historical or topographical reality. In the poem "Strophil" ("Turn," or "Turning Point"), exclamation seems to be the dominant note:

> I want to sing of you, flowers of the earth
> as I plunge my hand in the past of the race
> through heaps of fallen dead leaves
> to the stem that raises its head high.
> The head that will be reaped at some moment
> to the most heartfelt satisfaction of God
> reading it we are able to die
> serene in our intimacy with another life.

The message is similar to that of a number of the "middle poems"—indeed, of Pentzikis's entire oeuvre: The "other" life, the truer life, can be gained via death. The manner of this particular poem, however, is unusually lyric, like a dance. It expresses no doubts; Pentzikis lets himself go on simple faith.

ANAKOMIDHI

In the later series of poems, *Anakomidhi*, Pentzikis reverted to a looser and more abstract form. He no longer grouped lines in stanzas of four lines each but ran them consecutively. The poems collected in *Anakomidhi* are very much like pieces of prose, but they are also dense and allusive. They reminded Pentzikis's readers of *Ikones*, with which they are linked by the introductory poem, "Horos kimitiriou" (space of cemetery). This poem was written in the late 1940's, while the other thirteen poems in the collection—twelve of them numbered with Greek numerals and the thirteenth entitled "Sinanastrofi sinehis" (constant association)—were written in 1960 and 1961 in response to the transferal of the remains of Pentzikis's mother.

The spade which unearths the bones of the dead mixes deeply buried memories and feelings with the soil. The poems are like bones, so to speak, suddenly exposed to light together with the contents of the grave. Images, thoughts, impressions, and sentiments jostle against one another and at the same time struggle to cohere. All of the poems in *Anakomidhi* are transpositions of *things* into poetry, avenues of traffic between the present and the past, between life and what is wrongly thought to be dead and gone.

A similar rhythm can be felt throughout Pentzikis's verse as he moves up into the realm of myth and down into the world of doubt and despair, the world of perishable things, which he rediscovers and embraces only in the light of myth. Thus, for Pentzikis, a human being is insignificant, a particle of dust or a "garbage can," but also a vehicle of memory and a reflection of the Godhead.

OTHER MAJOR WORKS

LONG FICTION: *Andreas Dhimakoudhis*, 1935; *O pethamenos ke i anastasi*, wr. 1938, pb. 1944.

NONFICTION: *Pragmatognosia*, 1950; *Arhitektoniki tis skorpias zois*, 1963; *Mitera Thessaloniki*, 1970 (*Mother Salonika*, 1998); *Sinodhia*, 1970; *Omilimata*, 1972; *Simiosis ekato imeron*, 1973; *Arhion*, 1974; *Pros ekklesiasmo*, 1986.

BIBLIOGRAPHY

Friar, Kimon. *Modern Greek Poetry*. New York: Simon and Schuster, 1973. Translations of Greek poetry in English with some commentary on the biographical and historical backgrounds of the poets.

Thaniel, George. *Homage to Byzantium: The Life and Work of Nikos Gabriel Pentzikis*. St. Paul, Minn.: North Central, 1983. A critical study of Pentzikis's work. Includes bibliographic references and an index.

George Thaniel;
bibliography updated by the editors

SAINT-JOHN PERSE

Alexis Saint-Léger Léger
Born: Guadeloupe, French Antilles; May 31, 1887
Died: Giens, France; September 20, 1975

PRINCIPAL POETRY

Éloges, 1911 (English translation, 1944)
Amitié du prince, 1924 (*Friendship of the Prince*, 1944)
Anabase, 1924 (*Anabasis*, 1930)
Exil, 1942 (*Exile*, 1949)
Pluies, 1943 (*Rains*, 1949)

Éloges and Other Poems, 1944 (includes *Éloges* and *Friendship of the Prince*)
Neiges, 1944 (*Snows*, 1949)
Vents, 1946 (*Winds*, 1953)
Exile and Other Poems, 1949 (includes *Exile, Rains, and Snows*)
Amers, 1957 (*Seamarks*, 1958)
Chronique, 1960 (English translation, 1961)
Oiseaux, 1962 (*Birds*, 1966)
St.-John Perse: Collected Poems, 1971, 1982

OTHER LITERARY FORMS

Some 440 pages of the Pléiade edition of Saint-John Perse's *Œuvres complètes*, an edition supervised by the poet himself, are given to letters. Perse's letters provide the reader not only with a wealth of details about his life but also with comments about his poems and political and cultural events during more than half a century. In Perse's letters to his family and to literary figures such as André Gide, Paul Claudel, Jacques Rivière, Archibald MacLeish, Allen Tate, and T. S. Eliot, one can find clues to the duality of Saint-John Perse the poet and Alexis Saint-Léger Léger the diplomat. An English translation of these letters by Arthur Knodel, *St.-John Perse: Letters* (1979), gives them the same emphasis as Gide's or Claudel's journals.

Perse's Nobel Prize acceptance speech, "Poésie" ("On Poetry"), delivered in Stockholm on December 10, 1960, and his address "Pour Dante" ("Dante"), delivered in Florence on April 20, 1965, to mark the seventh centenary of Dante Alighieri's birth, are available in *St. John Perse: Collected Poems*, a bilingual edition. Perse's manuscripts, his annotated personal library, his notebooks on ornithology, several scrapbooks with clippings, and other documents have all been gathered by the Saint-John Perse Foundation in Aix-en-Provence, France.

ACHIEVEMENTS

Saint-John Perse is a "poet's poet." Although he won international recognition with the Nobel Prize in Literature in 1960, preceded by the Grand Prix National des Lettres and the Grand Prix International de Poésie in 1959, his readership has remained small. Poets as diverse as T. S. Eliot and Czesław Miłosz have paid him tribute; it is in the tributes of Perse's fellow poets that one finds the measure of his work, rather than in the standard literary histories of his age, for he remained aloof from fashionable movements of the century.

Indeed, Perse is characterized above all by a self-conscious detachment. During his diplomatic career, from 1914 to 1940, he maintained a sharp division between his public and his poetic persona. In these years, he published only two works, *Anabasis* and *Friendship of the Prince*. His choice of a partly English pseudonym emphasized his aloof stance.

Perse's exile to the United States in 1941 marked the end of his political career but the revival of his poetic creation. *Exile*, his first poem written in the United States, was first published in French in *Poetry* magazine in 1941. Although Perse never wrote in English, his poems were always published in the United States in bilingual editions and followed by numerous articles and reviews by American critics. Perse disdained literary factions and did not give public readings of his works. He twice refused the Norton Chair of Poetry at Harvard, in 1946 and 1952, but he was officially recognized by the American Academy and the National Institute of Arts and Letters in 1950, when he received the Award of Merit medal for poetry.

In his poetry, Perse maintained distance by seldom including place-names or markers of any kind that would locate his work in a specific place or time. In Perse's conception, the poet's task, like the scientist's, is to explore the universe, the elements, and human consciousness. The distinguishing quality of Perse's poetry is its universality, its endeavor to celebrate the cosmos and humankind beyond the limits of the personal, beyond the literary currents of the time. In this conception, poetry is not a re-creation or a transcription of reality; rather, poetry *is* reality, continually in flux, with all its tensions and its complexity. Perse's long poems, free from a specific form or traditional meter, and his symphonic compositions, with echoes and variations of the same phrase, achieve a musical quality seldom surpassed by his contemporaries.

BIOGRAPHY

Marie-René Alexis Saint-Léger Léger (who later shortened his name to Alexis Léger and chose the

pseudonym Saint-John Perse) was born on May 31, 1887, on a small island near Pointe-à-Pitre in Guadeloupe. His parents were both of French descent and came from families of plantation owners and naval officers established in the islands since the seventeenth and eighteenth centuries. Perse spent his childhood in Guadeloupe, where his father was a lawyer. The young poet and his sisters were brought up on family plantations among servants, private tutors, and plantation workers. It was not until the age of nine that Perse started school. In 1899, a few years later, earthquakes, the Spanish-American War, and an economic crisis compelled the family to leave for France, where they settled in Pau. In 1904, Perse began studying law, science, literature, and medicine at the University of Bordeaux. He wrote his first poems there, and between 1904 and 1914 he met a number of writers, among them Francis Jammes, Paul Claudel, Paul Valéry, André Gide, and Jacques Rivière. After his military service in 1905 and 1906, Perse divided his time between traveling and studying political science, music, and philosophy; he soon extended his circle of friends to include Erik Satie and Igor Stravinsky.

Perse spent the years from 1916 to 1921 in Peking, where he wrote *Anabasis*. After serving in the Ministry of Foreign Affairs, he was promoted in 1933 to secretary general, a position that he held until 1940, when the war and the Vichy government forced him to leave for England and, shortly after, for the United States. It was Archibald MacLeish who encouraged him to accept an appointment at the Library of Congress. In 1942, he published *Exile* and became known officially as Saint-John Perse. He spent the following seventeen years in the United States, where his voluntary exile provided him with an endless array of new scenery, including rare species of birds and plants that he painstakingly detailed in his notebooks. In 1946, he published *Winds*, followed by *Seamarks* in 1957; in the latter year, he returned to France, where he continued to spend most of his summers. In 1958, he married Dorothy Milburn Russell in Washington, D. C. Limited editions of his last two major works, *Chronique* and *Birds*, were illustrated with color etchings by Georges Braque. Although the years that followed his Nobel Prize in 1960 were rich in translations, new editions, and tributes, Perse's publications af-

Saint-John Perse, Nobel laureate in literature for 1960.
(© The Nobel Foundation)

ter *Birds* were limited to a few short poems. He spent his last years in France at the Presqu'île de Giens, where he died in 1975 at the age of eighty-eight.

ANALYSIS

When asked why he wrote, Saint-John Perse always had the same answer: "to live better." For him, poetry was a way of life, not self-centered but open to the world. In his work, the universe predominates over the self, and very little space is left in the texts for the poet's own life and feelings. Perse recorded details of travels and carefully described the flora and fauna that he encountered; these details constitute the only "autobiographical" elements in his *Œuvres complètes*. Perse was a close observer of nature, often compared to the Swedish botanist Carolus Linnaeus, Henry David Thoreau, and Walt Whitman. He was not only a scientist who named things but also a thinker and wanderer. The constant tension be-

tween the microcosm and the macrocosm, the precise words for small details, provided Perse with a means to stop, to reverse, or to capture what the Romantics cried for: the passage of time. Few poets have been so at ease with the concept of time and space; for Perse, these concepts are not limited by nihilism or religion. Perse rejected the alternatives represented by Jean-Paul Sartre and Paul Claudel: Neither man nor God is the center of his vision. There is only the universe and the beyond, the symbiosis of man and the elements. Perse goes beyond traditional spatiotemporal limits. He is everywhere and nowhere in particular; in his sweeping vision, time and space merge in one eternal movement.

This universality was recognized by the Swedish Academy, which awarded Perse the Nobel Prize for "the soaring flight and the evocative imagery of his poetry, which in a visionary fashion reflects the conditions of our time." Perse's oeuvre leaves an impression of wholeness. He saw his poems as "one long uninterrupted phrase," as if they belonged to the same mold or flow.

ÉLOGES

In Perse's first collection, *Éloges*, one can find the roots of his later, more solemn, longer poems: the mysterious forces of the elements, the insistent presence of the sea, the celebration of life as well as the yearning for other shores, for a place *outre-mer* (beyond the sea) and *outre-songe* (beyond the dream). The figure dominating Perse's works has no proper name; "Navigator" and "Poet" together provide enigmatic suggestions of anonymity and leadership.

Perse's manuscripts, with their lists of variations and echoes of other poems or lines, sometimes more than half a century apart, show that the final version of a given poem was often highly condensed, frequently a synthesis of passages written at different times. His œuvre is characterized by an unusual consistency of style and vision; a complex network of recurring motifs provides an inner structure that belies the prosaic "formlessness" of his verse.

ANABASIS

Anabasis, Perse's first major poem, recounts an expedition through the desert, the symbol of man's march through time and space and through consciousness. Although it was written in China in a Daoist temple in the Gobi desert, it echoes the *Anabasis* (c. fourth century

B.C.E.) of the Greek historian Xenophon, describing the retreat of a mercenary force of ten thousand Greeks after the failure of an expedition organized by Cyrus the Younger against his older brother Artaxerxes. Emphasizing the literal meaning of "anabasis," an expedition beyond geographical boundaries (in this case, both inland and inward, toward the essence of Being), Perse sets his poem outside a particular time and place. In addition to the narrative and epic aspects of the poem, it is perhaps this very movement of the expedition and march that has inspired composers such as Alan Hovhaness and Paul Bowles in their musical transcriptions of passages from *Anabasis*. They were preceded by the Swedish composer Karl-Birger Blomdahl, a disciple of Paul Hindemith and Béla Bartók, who composed an oratorio using the original French version of the poem. Blomdahl saw *Anabasis* as an "uninterrupted dialogue" and compared the work to a Byzantine mosaic. This fragmented aspect of some of the more elliptical and condensed passages in *Anabasis* perhaps results from the fact that the published poem was the condensed version of an original poem four times as long.

This epic poem has ten cantos framed by two songs in which the birth of a colt, the passage of a stranger, and the "feminine" soul are related parts of Perse's main network of motifs. In the first group of cantos, the stranger reappears, contemplating his land. Through the figure of the stranger, Perse explores the conflict between the restless urge to conquer new lands and the civilizing impulse to build a city. Tracing a cycle of exploration, achievement, and renewed restlessness, the poem conveys the movement of human history.

SEAMARKS

Seamarks, Perse's longest poem, recalls classical Greek drama with its imagery, its chorus and altar, the sea being the theatrical arena where man and woman celebrate life. In French, the title *Amers* also suggests a fusion of "sea" (*mer*) and "love" (*amour*). The poem's four parts are divided in turn into cantos of uneven length. In the first part, "Invocation," ritual preparation for the celebration of the sea is accompanied by ritual preparation for the poem, unifying reality and poetry. The second part, "Strophe," or "movement of the chorus around the altar," introduces the different groups and individuals confronting the sea for "questioning, entreaty,

imprecation, initiation, appeal, or celebration." The second part ends with a very long canto, "Étroits sont les vaisseaux . . ." ("Narrow Are the Vessels . . ."), the high point of the poem, which celebrates the physical and psychological union of man and woman. They are navigating on a ship as narrow as a couch, and the woman's body has the shape of a vessel; thus, the sea, which seems to protect and "bear" the lovers, becomes feminine and a synonym for love.

In the third part, "Choeur" ("Chorus"), one collective voice exalts the sea on behalf of humankind, and the procession from the city to the shore led by the poet is, according to Perse, the "image of humanity marching towards its highest destiny." In the concluding fourth part, "Dédicace" ("Dedication"), it is noon; the drama is over, and the poet removes his mask, after having brought his people to the highest point in time and space, where man is immortal. One finds the same ascension and defiance of death in Perse's next poem, *Chronique*, which is the "chronicle" of the earth, of man, and of the poet himself in pursuit of nomadism toward higher elevations and a "higher sea," beyond death.

BIRDS

Perse's last major poem, *Birds*, is more a meditation on art and on poetry than a continuation of the cosmic cycle of *Anabasis, Seamarks*, and *Chronique*. The limited first edition of the poem was illustrated with twelve lithographs by Georges Braque; the references to Braque's birds were added after Perse had already written most of the poem. They add a new dimension to the bird in flight, now caught on the canvas, where it continues to live, not as a visual image but as a living part of reality. The descriptive, the technical, and the metaphysical passages of the poem, although very different from one another, all convey the movement of the bird in flight—on the canvas, in the air, and in poetry.

The poem is divided into thirteen parts, the first part introducing the migratory bird, which searches for "an uninterrupted summer," as do the painter and the poet. The asceticism and the "combustion" of his flight have a symbolic import, reinforced in the last part, in which the bird's wings are like a cross. Part 2 presents a very technical description of the anatomy of the bird compared to the structure of a ship, as was the woman in *Seamarks*. It is followed in parts 3 through 7 by the description of the bird perceived by Braque's eye, like the eye of a bird of prey, and painted on the canvas, where it continues to live and fly in its metamorphoses throughout the successive stages of the painting. The finished painting is like the launching of a ship, and the needle of the nautical compass, shaped as a bird, now becomes the symbol for direction and equilibrium. In parts 8 through 10, the bird, defying the seasons, night, and gravity, continues its migration, searching for eternity and "the expanse of Being." In parts 11 and 12, Perse returns to Braque, but only to give a long list of legendary or historical birds that are different from Braque's anonymous birds on the canvas. Thus, the bird becomes the poet's sacred messenger and a symbol for the nomadism of his poetic creation.

Perse's epic vision of the universe informs his entire œuvre—a timeless vision that will endure when many celebrated poems, tied too closely to their time and place, have faded into oblivion.

OTHER MAJOR WORKS
NONFICTION: *St.-John Perse: Letters*, 1979.
MISCELLANEOUS: *Œuvres complètes*, 1972 (includes poetry and letters).

BIBLIOGRAPHY
Baker, Peter. *Obdurate Brilliance: Exteriority and the Modern Long Poem*. Gainesville: University of Florida Press, 1991. Critical interpretation of some of Perse's works with an introduction to the history of American poetry in the twentieth century. Includes bibliographical references and index.
Knodel, Arthur. *Saint-John Perse*. Edinburgh: Edinburgh University Press, 1966. Critical analysis of selected works by Perse. Includes bibliographic references.
Kopenhagen-Urian, Judith. "Delicious Abyss: The Biblical Darkness in the Poetry of Saint-John Perse." *Comparative Literature Studies* 36, no. 3 (1999): 195-208. Kopenhagen-Urian examines Saint-John Perse's oxymoron "delicious abyss" in relation to four functions observed in Perse's use of the Bible: the contrasting perspective, the structured allusion, the repeated motif, and the "collage."
Sterling, Richard L. *The Prose Works of Saint-John Perse*. New York: P. Lang, 1994. A critical study of

the prose works of Perse that is intended to give a fuller understanding of his poetry. Includes bibliographical references and index.

Marie-Noëlle D. Little;
bibliography updated by the editors

PERSIUS

Aulus Persius Flaccus

Born: Volaterrae, Etruria (now Volterra, Italy); December 4, 34 C.E.
Died: Campania; November 24, 62 C.E.

PRINCIPAL POETRY
Saturae, first century (*Satires*, 1616)

OTHER LITERARY FORMS
Persius is remembered only for his satires.

ACHIEVEMENTS
Modern critics slight Persius for lacking the *felicitas* of Horace and the *indignatio* of Juvenal; ancients were apparently satisfied to allow him to occupy his own space. The *Life of Persius* reports that Lucan, upon hearing a reading of the satires, cried that these were true poetry while he himself was composing trifles. Persius clearly influenced Juvenal, although Juvenal chooses not to mention him by name. Martial and Quintilian, however, single him out for praise, emphasizing that Persius wrote only one book. Quintilian also cites him often for lexical or grammatical illustrations.

That the satires are preserved in several manuscripts is evidence of their continuing popularity in the Middle Ages. Persius's luster began to tarnish when modern critics decided that the difficulties of his language did not repay their efforts, but interest in his work is currently being revived by new studies and commentaries, and he should regain some measure of his former status. He is, indeed, not Horace or Juvenal. Persius has his own distinct style and persona. He is worth reading not only for his place in the tradition of Roman satire but also for the use to which he put the genre: an exhortation to moral goodness.

BIOGRAPHY

Most of the information about Aulus Persius Flaccus comes from the anonymous *Life of Persius* attached to various manuscripts. Persius belonged to the equestrian order; he was of distinguished Etruscan lineage and prosperous circumstances. His father died when he was six, and a stepfather died within a few years of marriage to his mother. At twelve, Persius went to Rome to study with the grammarian Remmius Palaemon and the rhetorician Verginius Flavus. When he was sixteen, he attached himself to Lucius Annaeus Cornutus, author, teacher, and freedman from the house of the Annaei, to which the Senecas and Lucan belonged. In satire 5, Persius describes Cornutus's acceptance of him in terms which properly refer to a father's acknowledging a child; Cornutus, however, was more mentor than parent. Persius credits Cornutus with "sowing his ears with Cleanthean fruit"—that is, with inculcating in him the Stoic way of life. He was a relative of the famed Arriae, the elder of whom showed her condemned husband how to die by stabbing herself. The younger Arria was the wife of the Stoic, Thrasea Paetus, himself condemned by Nero in 66 C.E. Persius was cherished by Thrasea, sharing with him an earnest adherence to Stoicism.

Very little biographical material can be gleaned from Persius's satires apart from the relationship with Cornutus and his friendship with a certain Macrinus and the poet Caesius Bassus, addressed in satires 2 and 6, respectively. In satire 3, someone tells an anecdote of his school days when he put oil on his eyes to appear ill and so to avoid a recitation to be attended by his father and his father's friends. Persius is sometimes assumed to be the speaker. If so, the anecdote is a fiction, because Persius's father, and probably also his stepfather, would have been dead. The passage more naturally belongs to the primary voice of the satire, one of Persius's companions who is urging him to virtue. The *Life of Persius* calls him temperate and chaste, a man of the gentlest character, of maidenly modesty, fine reputation, and exemplary devotion to his mother, sister, and aunt. This description has prejudiced many against him and has influenced the interpretation of the satires, especially of the obscenity present in satires 1 and 4. Persius makes few references to women and no specific ones to his female relatives. Unbiased reading of the satires themselves provides no justification for the labels "priggish" and "cloistered," which are often associated with him.

Persius died from some kind of stomach ailment before he turned twenty-eight. His very early poetic attempts and some verses about the elder Arria were suppressed by Cornutus, who also shortened the last poem to make it appear finished. The *Life of Persius* says he wrote "both rarely and slowly." Six hundred fifty lines in six satires and fourteen lines of prologue are left. These were published by Bassus and were popular immediately and for several hundred years after Persius's death.

ANALYSIS

Any evaluation of Persius's poetry must begin with satire 5, which presents Cornutus's supposed judgment of Persius's proper manner and goals of composition:

> You follow the words of the toga, skillful at striking juxtaposition . . . expert at scraping pale morals and at pinning down fault with the humor worthy of a gentleman.

Like the rest of Persius's language, these words involve controversy and present problems of interpretation; nevertheless, they clearly assert the place of Persius within the satiric tradition. His role is to criticize moral failings with humor. Again, at the end of the programmatic first satire, when he associates himself with Lucilius, inventor of satire, and with Horace, his great predecessor in the genre, the terms of the association are criticism and humor.

WIT, HUMOR, AND VISUAL IMAGES

While Stoicism and the Stoic sage provide the standard against which others are criticized, Persius's claim to humor is usually denied. His humor is most apparent when seen against a Ciceronian background. The *ingenuo ludo* (humor worthy of a free man) can be traced back to Cicero. In the *Orator* and *De Oratore*, Cicero treats sources of laughter for the orator, divided into wit and humor. Wit is based on words and is suitable for attacking or responding to attack; humor is based on substance of thought or facts and is displayed in sustained narration and caricature. Although examples from all the Ciceronian categories can be found in Persius's satires, various kinds of verbal ambiguities and vivid scene painting in narration are the most important for appreciating his wit and humor. When Persius describes a scene, it requires visualization, because the picture is more humorous than the words themselves.

The visual aspect of Persius's art is pertinent also to his use of other poets, especially Horace. In *Lines of Enquiry: Studies in Latin Poetry*, Niall Rudd shows that Persius knew Horace by heart and that association of visual images accounts for the pattern of his imitation of Horace. This imitation—or rather, the extensive use of Horatian vocabulary—has obfuscated modern interpretation and commentary. The language of Persius is Horatian but the thought is not, and a case can be made that Persius considered that he was, if not outstripping, at least challenging Horace with his own words.

Apart from his Horatian language, Persius presented other difficulties caused to a large degree by frequent neologisms, use of metaphor, and "striking juxtapositions." Horace had named his satires *Sermones* (conversations) and had affected an easy conversational manner, frequently expressed in dialogue. Persius's conversational style and dialogues are of another sort. The conversation follows its own flow, almost in a stream of consciousness; respondents or adversaries appear and disappear with disconcerting abruptness; nevertheless, the satires are coherent and their meanings are clear.

SATIRE I

All except satire 1 are primarily explications of Stoic doctrine. Satire 1 is an extended joke, based on the Ovidian story of King Midas, whose ears Apollo changed into those of an ass because he could not distinguish good music from bad. In satire 1, Persius separates himself from his literary milieu and sets himself within the satiric tradition, content with only a few discriminating readers. The joke is established in the eighth line. Persius does not care if he has no readers; one should not seek standards outside himself, for "who at Rome does not—." The conclusion comes in line 121: "Who does not have ass's ears?" Between lines eight and 121, the diminutive *auriculae*, the word for "ears," is put to curious uses. The goal of contemporary poetry, and even forensic oratory, is to offer sexual titillation to the audience. Persius first says this straightforwardly by having the poems enter the loin and scratch the internal organs. Then by repetition of *auriculis*, he equates the parts of the word; that is, *auri-* (ear) equals *-culis* (buttocks). Si-

multaneously, he establishes the ears as hungry and poetry as food. Through these two perversions of poetry, as sexual stimulus and as food, Persius disparages other poets and their audiences. By contrast, the ear of his reader will be whole (*aure*) and clean (*vaporata*).

SATIRE 2

In most of the other satires, the humor is more spice than substance, used to relieve the seriousness of the message. Nominally, satire 2 is a birthday poem to Persius's friend Macrinus, otherwise unknown. In fact, the poem is about prayer: the wicked or foolish things people pray for, habits of life counterproductive to their prayers, imputation to the gods of their own venal character. Persius acknowledges that there is a proper use of externals while denying the efficacy of gold in supplication. From petitioners, the gods desire a soul disposed to what is just and right, pure recesses of the mind, and a heart steeped in noble virtue. With such a nature, one can offer a sacrifice of grain.

SATIRE 3

The whole of satire 3 is ironic. Persius is making fun of himself. He sets the scene, speaks near the beginning and end, and falls asleep in the middle. The premise is that he was carousing the previous night and so has overslept. He is awakened by a friend who sees the drinking as a clear sign that Persius has taken the first step on the path to moral degradation. A lecture is, therefore, in order. The lecture most resembles that given by the worried parent of a college student in a similar condition. The friend appeals to his sense of guilt and shame; he points out all the advantages Persius had that were not available to himself; he provides negative examples of similar behavior; he wonders what will become of him. The premise allows for a presentation of Stoic teaching, and most of what there is, is couched in medical metaphor. The passage, however, is straightforward Stocism:

> Wretches, learn and understand the causes of things: what we are and what life we are born to live; what ranking has been given or where and from where the bend around the goal is easy; what the limit is for silver; what it is right to pray for; what use harsh money has; how much it is fitting to bestow on country and dear kin; whom god has bidden you to be; and in what part of the human sphere you have been placed.

What some centurion would say to all of this abruptly ends the sermonizing. For Persius, the centurion is the prototype of the unphilosophical man; his speech, an example of illiberal humor, is a caricature of philosophers which is apt, occasions laughter, and is funny.

The satire ends with the proposal that Persius is afflicted by the disturbing passions of avarice, lust, fear, and anger, such that even mad Orestes would judge him mad. Single references to madness at the beginning and in the middle of the poem, together with this one to Orestes, suggest that the whole satire illustrates the Stoic paradox that all fools are impious.

SATIRE 4

In satire 4, the level of irony and ambiguity is such that the politician as male prostitute has been named the dominant metaphor. In fact, the whole satire contains seemingly innocent words which have also sexual or, at least, genital connotations. The problem in concentrating on the double meanings is that on the sexual level, the poem is not coherent. Persius seems to be simply teasing.

Although there is no attempt to make the scene Athenian, the reader is asked to pretend that Socrates is talking to Alcibiades. The message of the satire is serious: know yourself; have internal standards before applying external ones; see your own faults before criticizing others. The satire is, however, structured in terms of sucking and spitting: Socrates sucked hemlock, Alcibiades should suck hellebore, the miser sucks flat vinegar; the stranger spits out abuse against Alcibiades, Alcibiades should spit back what he is not. A carefully constructed image of Alcibiades the precocious politician is destroyed by a reference to his "vaunting his tail to the flattering rabble."

Two caricatures illustrate the observation that no one tries to descend into himself but each looks at the pack on the back in front. Alcibiades prompts the ridicule of Vettidius, but if he should sun himself, some stranger would make fun of him. Exaggeration makes both characterizations humorous, but unrelenting obscenity combines with the exaggeration in the tirade against Alcibiades.

At the end, Socrates alludes to the passions of avarice, lust, and ambition. If Alcibiades is influenced by these, "for nothing would he give his thirsty ears to the people." The final verse is haunting: "Live with yourself; know how damaged your furniture is."

SATIRE 5

Satire 5 is a discussion of the nature of freedom. For this, Persius needs a serious style and so begins by identifying with bards of epic and tragedy who require a hundred voices for their subjects. Persius cannot sustain the level, and the conceit of the hundred voices deteriorates, becoming in turn a hundred mouths, tongues, and, finally, throats into which are heaped globs of hearty song. Cornutus corrects Persius: for him the words of the toga and the moderate style, plebeian meals and not the heads and feet of Mycenaean banquets.

Persius first defines freedom by implication. He, as a legally free Roman citizen, subjected himself to Cornutus. This subjection to Cornutus represents subjection to reason; his "mind is constrained by reason and labors to be conquered." Paradoxically, such a subjection to reason is almost a definition of Stoic freedom, as a comparison with a later section of the satire shows. Only the wise man is free. As Persius "labors to be conquered" by reason, others are conquered by such passions as avarice, gluttony, athletics, gambling, and lust. They realize too late that they have wasted their lives.

Such a sequence of thought leads to the dramatic, open introduction of the discussion: "There is need for freedom." The freedom desired is not the legal freedom possessed by Persius, granted to slaves by masters and Praetors. The real masters are those within, the passions mentioned briefly before. Now Persius offers longer illustrations of these masters. One slave to passion is torn between Avarice and Luxury, both of whom address him. Avarice's appeal is urgent; that of Luxury, sensuous. A scene from comedy shows a slave to love. Ambition makes an aedile sponsor an extravagant Floralia. Superstition provokes adherence to foreign cults whose most conspicuous features are held up for ridicule. The litany and the satire are abruptly ended by the laughter of another centurion.

SATIRE 6

The sixth satire is the least humorous and perhaps the least successful of the collection. It is addressed to Bassus, the poet and friend who published Persius's work after his untimely death. Bassus and Persius are spending the winter at their respective country estates. As in satire 2, the address to the friend is only the preface to another subject, here the proper use of wealth.

Persius's treatment can be seen as an answer to questions posed indirectly in satire 3: What use does money have? How much should one bestow on country and kin? For his part, Persius claims a middle course. He does not envy others who are richer; he will be neither miserly nor lavish; he will live within his means and, when necessary, share his resources with less fortunate friends. Such a way of life calls forth a voice suggesting that Persius's heir will resent the diminution of his inheritance and that importation of Greek philosophy is responsible for such heretical attitudes. The heir himself is summoned. If he is displeased, Persius will leave his money to a beggar, since, ultimately, all are related. He refuses to deprive himself now for the pleasures of some future prodigal. The avarice of the heir must be satisfied by his own efforts, but such avarice knows no limits.

In all the satires on Stoic themes, Persius seeks an unobtrusive pretext for his message. Although based on Stoic doctrine, the calls to virtue have almost universal applicability and are not weighed down by specific references to time or circumstances. Such a universality makes Persius profitable reading in any age.

BIBLIOGRAPHY

Anderson, William, ed. *Essays on Roman Satire.* Princeton, N.J.: Princeton University Press, 1982. The essays "Part vs. Whole in Persius' Fifth Satire" and "Persius and the Rejection of Society" are useful to students of Persius.

Bramble, J. C. *Persius and the Programmatic Satire: A Study in Form and Imagery.* Cambridge, England: Cambridge University Press, 1974. After a brief study of Satire 5, Bramble focuses on Satire 1 with a close analysis of how the satire form best suits the thematic material.

Coffey, Michael. *Roman Satire.* 2d ed. Bristol, England: Bristol Classical Press, 1989. Contains a concise chapter on Persius in the context of Roman letters and the genre, as well as his influence on later Latin satirists.

Harvey, R. A. *Commentary on Persius.* Leiden, Netherlands: E. J. Brill, 1981. Provides an overview of each satire, then close commentary on the texts line by line, clarifying words and phrases and explaining the cultural context of references or allusions. Includes a history of editions.

Hooley, D. M. *The Knotted Thong: Structures of Mimesis in Persius.* Ann Arbor: University of Michigan Press, 1997. A monographic treatment of "allusive artistry" in Persius's satires, especially his use of Horace. Hooley treats this use of mimesis in a thematic rather than systematic and comprehensive way, producing an admittedly exploratory rather than definitive work.

Morford, Mark. *Persius.* Boston: Twayne, 1984. A brief biography and critical overview of Persius and his six satires, in the publisher's World Authors series. The biography is quite concise, but the treatment of Persius's works is detailed as both criticism and commentary.

Rudd, Niall. *Lines of Enquiry: Studies in Latin Poetry.* New York: Cambridge University Press, 1976. Under the rubric "Imitation," Rudd delineates the "associative process" at work in specific and closely studied examples drawn from several satires. English translations of quoted passages.

Carrie Cowherd;
bibliography updated by Joseph P. Byrne

FERNANDO PESSOA

Born: Lisbon, Portugal; June 13, 1888
Died: Lisbon, Portugal; November 30, 1935

PRINCIPAL POETRY

Thirty-five Sonnets, 1918 (as Alexander Search)
English Poems I-III, 1921 (3 volumes; as Alexander Search)
Mensagem, 1934
Obras completas, 1942-1956
Sixty Portuguese Poems, 1971
Selected Poems, 1971
The Poems of Fernando Pessoa, 1986

OTHER LITERARY FORMS

In addition to his verse, Fernando Pessoa published many critical essays and polemical tracts during the course of his career. Most of these were published in the many Portuguese journals with which he was associated, or as short-run pamphlets for particular occasions. He also accumulated a large body of nonliterary writing of a speculative, philosophical nature that was never intended to be published during his lifetime. Moreover, Pessoa was a prolific letter writer, and he left a large body of uncollected correspondence containing some of his clearest and most detailed commentary on his own work. The vast bulk of this material is now available in the following posthumous collections: *Páginas de doutrina estética*, 1946; *Páginas de estética e de teoria e crítica literárias*, 1966; *Páginas íntimas e de auto-interpretação*, 1966; *Textos filosóficos*, 1968; *Cartas a Armando Côrtes-Rodrigues*, 1945; and *Cartas a João Gaspar Simões*, 1957.

ACHIEVEMENTS

Although very little of Fernando Pessoa's work was collected and published in book form during his lifetime, his poetry—appearing mainly in small literary journals that he founded, supported, or helped to edit himself—has come to be considered an important expression of the modern sensibility. Today Pessoa is considered to be a major poet of the twentieth century—and, in the opinion of many of his countrymen, the greatest of all Portuguese poets since Luís de Camões.

This is evident in the increasing influence that his posthumously published work has had on the modern Portuguese tradition in poetry—in which he has come to be considered the seminal figure—as well as in his effect on the work of such prominent later poets as José Régio and João Gaspar Simões, and, finally, in the works of his many admirers among poets writing in Spanish, English, and many other languages.

Pessoa's preoccupations—the introspective, philosophical nature of his poetry, the epistemological doubts that it expresses, and the anxiety-ridden existential atmosphere that pervades his work—are not provincial but universal in character, and they convey the central concerns found in the work of countless modern writers. Among the recurring themes of Pessoa's work is a persistent concern with understanding the essential nature of the self and its difficulties when subjected to the contingencies of life. Like many other modern writers, Pessoa sought to discover through his writing the psy-

Fernando Pessoa (Centro de Turismo de Portugal)

chological truth about the artist's identity: Who is the artist, and what is his or her role among all the fictional selves that inhabit the work? These two concerns are clearly expressed in the reflexive nature of Pessoa's work, where the "I" is constantly turning back upon itself, asking: Who is speaking? and Who is speaking now?

Until 1942, when Pessoa's work began to be published in collected form, his reputation was based mainly on his early poems in English. These were published under the pseudonym Alexander Search and were written mostly between 1903 and 1905, although not published in collected form until a decade later. Otherwise, there was the collection *Mensagem* (message), the only volume of Pessoa's Portuguese verse published before his death, assembled and submitted to a poetry contest sponsored by the Portuguese Secretariat of National Propaganda in 1934. Neither of these two volumes, however, is representative of the poet's best work, for the verse written in English is imitative, while the poetry of *Mensagem* is fervently nationalistic and hence deliberately provincial. The remainder of his work was known only to the small readerships of short-lived Portuguese literary journals such as *A Águia, A Renascença,*

Orpheu, Centauro, Exílio, Portugal futurista, Contemporânea, Athena, and *Presença,* in which the majority of his published work—both poetry and prose—appeared between 1912 and 1928.

BIOGRAPHY

Fernando António Nogueira Pessoa was born in Lisbon, Portugal, on June 13, 1888. After the early death of his father, Joaoquim de Seabra Pessoa, in 1893, and the subsequent remarriage of his mother, Maria Madalena Pinheiro Nogueira, to Commandante João Miguel Rosa, the newly appointed Portuguese consul to Durban, South Africa, Pessoa and his mother left Portugal for South Africa in December of 1894. Here, Pessoa received his education in English. From 1894 until August of 1905, when he returned to Lisbon to attend the university there, Pessoa was developing the skills which were later to have such an important effect upon his career: his bilingual abilities in Portuguese and English and his interest in business and international commerce, which led to a lifelong career as a commercial translator in Lisbon. This position gave Pessoa the flexibility of movement and the leisure necessary to participate in his literary activities, which consisted of the founding and editing of numerous literary journals whose purpose, it became increasingly clear, was to further the development of an indigenous, innovative, modern Portuguese literature.

This developing literary nationalism is evident in the change from Pessoa's early poetry, written in English between 1905 and 1909, to the appearance in that year of his first verse in Portuguese. That early work in Portuguese is clearly reflected in *Mensagem,* much of which was written long before its publication in 1934. It was, however, with the development of his "heteronyms" (three distinct pseudonymous personalities, each with a different style), which first appeared in 1914 and were later widely employed in the many poems he published in small magazines, that the mature work that contributed to his growing international reputation came into being.

This fame, however, was late in coming. Pessoa rarely left Lisbon after his return from South Africa in 1905, and he never left Portugal again. When he died on November 30, 1935, in Lisbon—a victim of alcoholism at the age of forty-seven—he was virtually unknown outside his own country, and to those Portuguese readers who did know him, his greatest accomplishment was thought to be his allegorical collection of nationalistic poems, *Mensagem.* Pessoa's real fame, however, was to come later—through the work of his surrogate selves, of heteronyms (as later critics described them), when the posthumous publication of his complete works, beginning in 1942, revealed the large body of Pessoa's work that had been published under the names Álvaro de Campos, Alberto Caeiro, and Ricardo Reis.

ANALYSIS

During several decades of intense and sustained critical interest, initiated by João Gaspar Simões's *Vida e obra de Fernando Pessoa* (1950; life and works of Fernando Pessoa), Fernando Pessoa's status as a poet has been transformed from that of a literary oddity—combining an intense nationalistic provincialism with an affinity for the faddish avant-garde literary movements of the early twentieth century—into that of a major figure in modern European literature. His poetry is now seen by many critics to express—in both content and form—the deepest concerns of the modern age. Ronald W. Sousa, his "rediscoverer," expresses this new perception of Pessoa's work in *The Rediscoverers:*

> Pessoa's writing . . . while not "philosophical" in a strict sense, nonetheless not only treats in practical application the systematic intellectual problems of the day but also does so at a level of abstraction and in a mode of presentation that approach many of the formal properties of traditional philosophy.

This modernist sensibility is characterized by two strong emphases in Pessoa's work: the assertion of the relative or subjective nature of the interior psychological world of the self, and the epistemological reduction of the external world of objects and persons to the status of concrete phenomenological data that exist in a wholly different order of reality from that of the reflecting mind. For this reason, Pessoa's work has come, in recent years, to be associated with the work of two better-known writers: Jorge Luis Borges and Alain Robbe-Grillet.

In the stories and parables of Borges, such as "Borges y yo," ("Borges and I"), "Las ruinas circulares" ("The Circular Ruins"), and "De alguien a nadie" ("From Someone to No One"), one finds an intense questioning of the reality of the self which explores in a more self-conscious, didactic way the identical questions of existence that Pessoa considers in his "Passos da cruz" ("Stations of the Cross"). There, the narrator is the incarnate Christ, Jesus, who reveals his bewilderment in the course of a confusing series of events.

"STATIONS OF THE CROSS"

"Stations of the Cross," written under Pessoa's own name, consists of a series of fourteen sonnets that retell the story of Christ's Passion from the perspective of the suffering victim. In this work, Pessoa's literary kinship with Robbe-Grillet is made evident, for, like the central characters of Robbe-Grillet's New Novels (*nouveaux romans*)—*Les Gommes* (1953; *The Erasers*, 1964) and *Le Voyeur* (1955; *The Voyeur*, 1958)—the speaker of the "Stations of the Cross" sequence is plagued by a split in consciousness that finds him acting out a role in a drama of whose ultimate purpose he is not consciously aware. This epistemological dilemma is well illustrated in sonnet 6, where Jesus speculates on his role in history: "I come from afar and bear in my profile,/ If only in remote and misty form,/ The profile of another being." The puzzled speaker, reflecting on the role into which he has been cast unaware (unlike the biblical account of Christ's Passion, in which He is granted foreknowledge), concludes: "I am myself the loss I suffered." Like Borges's narrators, this speaker seems intended to be a figure representing modern man's existential bewilderment.

MENSAGEM

Also included in Pessoa's orthonymic poetry (that part of his work published under his own name) are the fervently nationalistic poems of *Mensagem*. These poems constitute the only collection of his poems in Portuguese published during his lifetime. Fortunately, the collection was put together shortly before his death, so that the volume contains work spanning nearly the entire period during which he wrote verse in Portuguese. It would be a mistake, however, to see this collection as representative of his work. For one thing, the collection is dominated by a tone of intense longing for the restoration of Portugal's once-illustrious past. Furthermore, as Sousa has shown in his work on Pessoa, the volume has an elaborate, systematic, symbolic structure (not characteristic of Pessoa's other work) which gives it the thematic unity of a sustained political allegory. Sometimes

the nostalgia of *Mensagem* is expressed as a generalized attitude, as in his reminiscence of an unidentified sea explorer in "Mar Português" ("Portuguese Sea"). At other times, Pessoa speaks through the personage of a historical figure such as the sixteenth century king of Portugal Dom Sebastian, who is elevated to the status of a legendary hero in the poem bearing his name: "Mad, yes, mad, because I sought a greatness/ Not in the gift of Fate./ I could not contain the certainty I felt."

This concern with the relativity of the self goes beyond being merely a theme of much of Pessoa's best poetry; it is also expressed in the very manner of its presentation. The writer now known as Fernando Pessoa wrote much of his mature work under the assumed identity of a series of three "heteronyms," for each of which Pessoa created not only a biographical background but also a distinctive style.

ÁLVARO DE CAMPOS: "IN THE TERROR OF THE NIGHT"

The first of the three heteronyms that Pessoa adopted was Álvaro de Campos, whose writing was characterized by the use of long verse lines of uneven length, informal, colloquial diction, and the organic forms of free verse. This style is illustrated in the long, overlapping lines of a poem such as "Na noite terrível" ("In the Terror of the Night"), a poetic meditation on a common existential theme—the creation of oneself by one's own actions. As in much of Pessoa's work, the poem is pervaded by a tone of elegiac regret: "In the terror of the night—the stuff all nights are made of,/ . . . I remember what I did and could have done with life,/ . . . I'd be different now, and perhaps the universe itself/ Would be subtly induced to be different too." This poem exhibits Campos's tendency to mold entire lines—and at times entire poems—around subtle variations of key words. In the example above, this is done with the noun "night," the verb "to do," and the adjective "different," where Pessoa carefully retains their grammatical functions consistently throughout the passage. Another characteristic of Campos's style illustrated in the poem is the use of the paradoxes, oxymorons, and *non sequiturs* that has frequently led critics to compare his style to that of the French Surrealists.

"TOBACCO-SHOP"

The surreal quality of Campos's work is best seen in "Tabacaria" ("Tobacco-Shop"), in which verbal irrationality is used to create a subtly ironic form of black humor reminiscent of the best poetry of Benjamin Péret, the master comedian of the French Surrealist movement. The speaker of this poem, self-characterized as a metaphysical "genius," sits dreaming in a garret, out of which he observes a little tobacco shop far below in the street. He finally concludes that dreams and fantasies are man's only certainty, though they can never have more than an accidental correspondence with the external world.

ALBERTO CAEIRO: "IF, AFTER I DIE"

Pessoa's second major Portuguese heteronym, Alberto Caeiro, which he employed from time to time between 1914 and 1920 (when he "killed him off" at the tragically young age of twenty-six), is predominantly a nature poet. As Caeiro himself says in a poem titled "If, After I Die":

I am easy to describe.
I lived like mad.
I loved things without sentimentality.
I never had a desire I could not fulfil, because I never
    went blind.
. . . And by the way, I was the only Nature poet.

This epitaph illustrates well Caeiro's simple, colloquial style, which has been described by many critics as essentially prosaic. In creating an informal style for Caeiro which imitates the structure and content of ordinary speech, Pessoa eschews traditional poetic devices such as elevated diction, figures of speech, meter, rhyme, and predictable stanzaic patterns, and employs rhetorical locutions that call attention to the poems as conversation.

"THE KEEPER OF FLOCKS" AND "I'M A SHEPHERD"

These qualities of Caeiro's style are best illustrated in his most famous work, a series of forty-nine brief poems collectively titled "O guardador de rebanhos" ("The Keeper of Flocks"). There are also, however, other characteristic elements of Caeiro's work. One of the most important of these is what critics have called the "antimetaphysical" nature of his thought. As Peter Rickard, one of Pessoa's recent translators, puts it:

Fundamental to his worldview is the idea that in the world around us, all is surface: things are precisely what they seem, there is no hidden meaning anywhere.

This attitude of calm, naturalistic objectivity toward the world is prominent in poems such as "Sou um guardador de rebanhos" ("I'm a Shepherd"):

I'm a shepherd.
My sheep are my thoughts.
And my thoughts are all sensations.
I think with my eyes and ears
And with my hands and feet
And with my nose and mouth.
And so on a warm day,
. . . I feel my whole body lying full-length in reality,
I know the truth and I'm happy.

Some critics see in Caeiro's thought a foreshadowing of Existentialism's assertion of the primacy of existence over essence—where man's immediate physical experience in the world is valued above the rational productions of his reflecting consciousness.

RICARDO REIS

It was Pessoa's third major Portuguese heteronym, Ricardo Reis, that served him longest. Works by Reis appeared from 1914, the first year of Pessoa's adoption of the heteronyms, until 1935, the year of his death. Under this guise, Pessoa produced some skillful imitations of Latin poetry, writing a series of Horatian odes the style of which is characterized by archaic, formal diction and the use of free verse. Reis's odes, like those of Horace, are governed by classical conventions which constrain not only the language of the poem but its theme as well. As Pessoa later said of Reis's classicism in a letter to one of his friends: "He writes better than I do, but with a purism which I consider excessive."

Equally important, however, is Reis's attitude toward the world, for in many ways his resigned attitude of detachment from life is the psychological converse of Caeiro's engagement with it. This important contrast in attitude is succinctly characterized by F. E. G. Quintanilha, one of Pessoa's translators:

In opposition to Caeiro's constant discovery of things . . . Reis assumes a stoic and epicurean attitude towards Existence. As he assumes that he can learn nothing more, he shuts himself up in his world and accepts life and destiny with resignation.

"THE ROSES OF THE GARDENS OF ADONIS"

These attitudes and techniques are well illustrated in

one of Reis's best odes, "As rosas amo dos jardins do Adónis" ("The Roses of the Gardens of Adonis"), which illustrates a number of characteristic elements: The elevated poetic diction, the Latinate syntax, the perfect strophic form, the use of conventional symbolism drawn from mythology—even the name by which the beloved is addressed is a poetic convention. Yet the imitative nature of this ode is not limited to its style, form, or content. The didactic conclusion that the speaker reaches at the end of the poem expresses the *carpe diem* (seize the day) theme common in classical poetry:

> Like them, let us make of our lives *one day*—
> Voluntarily, Lydia, unknowing
> That there is night before and after
> The little that we last.

As Pessoa himself suggested, this degree of imitative purity cannot help but strike the modern reader as "excessive," however skillfully it might be accomplished.

CREATING SELVES

Pessoa's attempt to resolve the epistemological doubts that have plagued the artist in the modern age led him to consider the essential nature of the self, which constituted for him the core of the problem. He concluded that the self is multiple, that it contains many conflicting potentialities. To prove the truth of this proposition, he created the heteronyms, giving each of them a distinctive personality which was reflected in the work they wrote. To Álvaro de Campos, he gave a painful awareness of the reflexive nature of thought and language; he granted Alberto Caeiro an absolute, almost inhuman, objectivity; he provided Ricardo Reis with a stoic detachment. Each of these selves is thoroughly consistent within itself yet is challenged by the equal though quite different reality of the other two.

Perhaps Pessoa's greatest challenge, however, is not to the reader but to the modern artist himself. To the question of the relation of the author to the fiction that he creates, Pessoa's work provides a clear answer. The mere existence of the heteronyms suggests that the author himself is as much a fiction as the work he creates. To assume that a poem signed Fernando Pessoa is somehow more honest or authentic than one signed by a heteronym—who, after all, is just a name, not someone who really lived—would be to ignore the radical critique of thinking about literature and reality that his accomplishment clearly represents.

OTHER MAJOR WORKS

NONFICTION: *Cartas a Armando Côrtes-Rodrigues*, 1945; *Páginas de doutrina estética*, 1946; *Cartas a João Gaspar Simões*, 1957; *Páginas de estética e de teoria e crítica literárias*, 1966; *Páginas íntimas e de auto-interpretação*, 1966; *Textos filosóficos*, 1968; *Always Astonished: Selected Prose*, 1988; *The Selected Prose of Fernando Pessoa*, 2001.

BIBLIOGRAPHY

Monteiro, George. *Fernando Pessoa and Nineteenth-Century Anglo-American Literature*. Lexington: University Press of Kentucky, 2000. The critic searches for the poet's literary influences rooted in the English language. His European models and precursors included John Keats, Lord Byron, and Elizabeth Barrett Browning. Edgar Allen Poe was the most influential of his American models, along with Nathaniel Hawthorne and Walt Whitman. The critic traces elements of influence in Pessoa's work as he identifies the poet's own legacy of influence.

Sadlier, Darlene J. *An Introduction to Fernando Pessoa: Modernism and the Paradoxes of Authorship*. Gainesville: University Press of Florida, 1998. This study focuses on the diminished value of authorship in twentieth century literature and the modernist pursuit of source. This vision is consistent with Pessoa's personae as his heteronyms relate their literary creation to source. This study also explores links between Pessoa's heteronomous writings and his literary predecessors. The critic seeks to broaden an understanding of European modernism by demonstrating that Pessoa's authorship was a mimetic textual performance.

Sousa, Ronald W. *The Rediscoverers: Major Writers in the Portuguese Literature of National Regeneration*. University Park: Pennsylvania State University Press, 1981. Addresses Pessoa in the context of Portuguese literature and the modern age. Bibliography.

Zenith, Richard. *Fernando Pessoa and Co.* New York: Grove Press, 1998. This excellent translation of Pessoa's work is manifested through his various personae, enabling the reader to comprehend the corpus of poetry in an organized presentation. The poet's heteronyms served to distance his art from his person. Alberto Caeiro, Ricardo Reis, and Álvaro de Campos attribute stylistic variations and personalities to impersonal entities. Zenith demonstrates that even the poetry that Pessoa wrote under his own name was not personal. The poet identified "Pessoa" as an "orthonym" made up of sub-personalities. Zenith captures the complexity of this evolutionary process in his English translations.

Steven E. Colburn;
bibliography updated by Carole A. Champagne

SÁNDOR PETŐFI

Born: Kiskőrös, Hungary; January 1, 1823
Died: Segesvár, Hungary; July 31, 1849

PRINCIPAL POETRY

A helység-kalapácsa, 1844 (*The Hammer of the Village*, 1873)
Versek, 1842-1844, 1844 (*Poems, 1842-1844*, 1972)
Cipruslombok Etelke sírjáról, 1845 (*Cypress Leaves from the Tomb of Etelke*, 1972)
János Vitéz, 1845 (*Janos the Hero*, 1920)
Szerelem gyöngyei, 1845 (*Pearls of Love*, 1972)
Versek II, 1845 (*Poems II*, 1972)
Felhok, 1846 (*Clouds*, 1972)
Összes költeményei, 1847, 1848 (*Collected Poems*, 1972)
"Széchy Mária," 1847
Az apostol, 1848 (*The Apostle: A Narrative Poem*, 1961)
Sixty Poems, 1948
Sándor Petőfi: His Entire Poetic Works, 1972

OTHER LITERARY FORMS

Sándor Petőfi wrote several short narrative pieces for the fashion magazines and periodicals of his day. "A szökevények" (the runaways) was published in the *Pesti Divatlap* in 1845. The following year, his melodramatic novella *A hóhér kötele* (*The Hangman's Rope*, 1973) was published in the same magazine. In 1847, he published two tales in *Életképek:* "A nagyapa" (the grandfather) and "A fakó leány s a pej legény" (the pale girl and the ruddy boy). "Zöld Marci," a drama written in 1845, was destroyed by the author when it was not picked up for theatrical production; the bombastic *Tigris és hiéna* (tiger and hyena) was withdrawn from production but published in 1847. The most valuable prose Petőfi wrote was the personal essay and brief diary entries relating to the events of March, 1848. "Úti jegyzetek" (journal notes) was serialized in *Életképek* in 1845; in 1847, *Hazánk* published his "Úti levelek Kerényi Frigyeshez" (travel notes to Frigyes Kerényi). *Lapok Petőfi Sándor naplójából* (pages from the diary of Sándor Petőfi) appeared in 1848. In addition, his letters, published in the 1960 *Petőfi Sándor összes prózai muvei és levelezése* (complete prose works and correspondence of Sándor Petőfi), provide good examples of his easy prose style. Early in his career Petőfi earned some money doing translations of works by such authors as Charles de Bernard, George James, and William Shakespeare. In 1848, Petőfi's translation of Shakespeare's *Coriolanus* (1607-1608) appeared. He also began a translation of *Romeo and Juliet* but died before finishing it.

ACHIEVEMENTS

Sándor Petőfi has been called Hungary's greatest lyric poet. He made the folk song a medium for the expression of much of the national feeling of the nineteenth century, establishing a new voice and introducing new themes into Hungarian poetry. Building on past traditions, he revitalized Hungarian poetry. Though a revolutionary, he did not break with all tradition, but rather sought a return to native values. Choosing folk poetry as his model, he endorsed its values of realism, immediacy, and simplicity. He also exploited to the fullest its ability to present psychological states through natural and concrete images, with an immediacy that had an impact beyond the poetic sphere.

Petőfi's poetry is the "poetry of Hungarian life, of the Hungarian people," according to Zsolt Beöty. Yet, although Petőfi drew on popular traditions, he did so with the conscious art of a cultivated poet. This combination of Romantic style and realistic roots gives his poetry a freshness and sincerity that has made him popular both in Hungary and abroad. More important, it has assured him a place in the development of Hungarian lyricism.

Petőfi's impact, however, goes beyond Hungary. He appeals to the emotions yet maintains a distance: His themes seldom lose their universality. For Petőfi, the revolutionary ideal of the nineteenth century applied equally to politics and poetics. Folk orientation and nationalism were equally an organic part of his poetry, and his revolutionary ideals were unthinkable without a popular-national input. Thus, he both mirrors and creates a new world, a new type of man, and a new society. He is an iconoclast and revolutionary only when he perceives existing values and systems as denying the basic value of human life. His endorsement of conventional values of family, home, and a just social order can only be understood in this context.

Style and form, matter and manner were never separate for Petőfi. A consummate craftsman and a conscious developer of the style and vocabulary of mid-nineteenth century Hungarian poetry, he knew that in helping to create and enrich the new poetic language, he was bringing poetry to the masses. In exploring the language, he made poetic what had been commonplace.

Following in the footsteps of the great Hungarian language reformers and poets of the late eighteenth and early nineteenth centuries, Petőfi expanded the scope of poetry in both theme and language. Like William Wordsworth and Robert Burns in English literature, he placed emphasis on everyday themes and the common man. It would be unfair to the earlier molders of Hungarian poetry, from Mihály Csokonai Vitéz through Károly Kisfaludi, Dániel Berzsenyi, and Mihály Vörösmarty, to minimize their influence on Petőfi. To a great extent, they created a modern Hungarian poetic medium no longer restricted by the limitations of language. Simultaneously, they created a poetic language and encouraged the taste of the public for native themes and native styles. Classical and modern European influences had been absorbed and naturalized by these men. The German influence, strong for both political and demographic reasons, had also been greatly reduced. The intellectual and cultural milieu, in fact, changed so dramatically in these years that German-language theaters and publications were becoming Hungarian in language

as well as sentiment. For example, *Hazánk* (homeland), a periodical to which Petőfi contributed regularly, was called, until 1846, *Vaterland*.

As a poet of a many-faceted national consciousness, Petőfi was always committed to the simple folk, to the common man. He did not categorically support the unlettered peasant in favor of the clerk, nor did he condemn the class hierarchy of earlier times without cause. He did condemn, however, inequity and petrified institutions that did not allow for the free play of talent. He endorsed human values above all.

BIOGRAPHY

Sándor Petőfi was born on January 1, 1823, in Kiskörös—a town located on the Hungarian plain—to István Petrovics, innkeeper and butcher, and his wife, Mária Hruz. Petőfi's father's family, in spite of the Serbian name (which Petőfi was to change when he chose poetry as his vocation), had lived in Hungary for generations. His mother, Slovak by birth, came from the Hungarian highlands in the north. Such an ethnic mix was not unusual, and the young man grew up in what he himself considered the "most Magyar" area of all Hungary, the region called Kis Kúnság (Little Cumania) on the Great Plains. Much of his poetry celebrates the people and the landscape of this region: Though not the first to do so, he was more successful than earlier poets in capturing the moods of the region known as the Alföld (lowlands).

Petőfi's father was wealthy and, desiring his sons to be successful, he determined to educate them. The young Petőfi was sent to a succession of schools that were designed to give him a good liberal education in both Hungarian and German, among them the lower gymnasium (high school) at Aszód, from which he was graduated valedictorian. He was active in various literary clubs and, through the zeal of several nationalistic teachers, became acquainted with the prominent authors of the eighteenth century: Dániel Berzsenyi, József Gvadányi, and Mihály Csokonai Vitéz, as well as the popular poets of the day, Mihály Vörösmarty and József Bajza.

The year spent at Selmec, in the upper division of the gymnasium, was marred by his father's financial troubles and by Petőfi's personal clashes with one of his teachers. As a result of these pressures, he yielded to his penchant for the theater and on February 15, 1839, when he was barely sixteen, ran away with a group of touring players.

Petőfi's decision to become an actor was not made lightly, for he knew the value of an education, and he made every effort to complete his studies later. The years that followed were particularly hard ones. Petőfi roamed much of the country, traveling mostly on foot. He took advantage of the hospitality offered at the farms and manor houses and thus he came to know a wide spectrum of society. On these travels, he also developed his appreciation for nature, uniting his love for it with the objectivity of one who lives close to it. Since acting could not provide him a living, Petőfi decided to join the army, but he was soon discharged for reasons of ill health. In the months following, he became friends with Mór Jókai, later a prominent novelist but at that point a student at Pápa. Petőfi, determined to complete his studies, attended classes there. He joined the literary society and gained recognition as a poet: "A borozo" (the wine drinker), his first published poem, appeared in the prestigious *Athenaeum* in May, 1842, and he also won the society's annual festival.

Petőfi, then nineteen, considered himself a poet; he was determined that this would be his vocation. He planned to finish his studies, to become a professional man able to support himself and to help his parents and also to pursue his chief love, poetry. When a promised position as tutor fell through, however, he was once more forced to leave school and to make his living as an actor, or doing whatever odd jobs (translating, copying) he found. In the winter of 1843-1844, ill and stranded in Debrecen, he copied 108 of his poems, determined to take them to Vörösmarty for an opinion. If the verdict was favorable, Petőfi would remain a poet and somehow earn his living by his pen; if not, he would give up poetry forever. The venture succeeded, and this volume, *Poems, 1842-1844*, firmly established his reputation.

A subscription by the nationalistic literary society Nemzeti Kör provided Petőfi with some funds, and on July 1, 1844, he accepted a position as assistant editor of the *Pesti Divatlap*. From this time on, he earned his living chiefly with his pen. Besides submitting shorter pieces to a variety of journals, he published two heroic poems and a cycle of love lyrics. In March of 1845, he left the *Pesti Divatlap* to tour northern Hungary. A rival journal,

Életképek, published the series of prose letters, "Journal Notes," in which Petőfi reported his impressions of the people and scenes he encountered. Two more volumes of poetry, *Pearls of Love* and *Poems II*, appeared. Although he became increasingly dedicated to *Életképek*, Petőfi continued to publish in a variety of journals.

In 1846, while campaigning for better remuneration for literary contributors to journals—founding the Society of Ten and even leading a brief strike—Petőfi published another volume of poetry, *Clouds*, and a novella, *The Hangman's Rope*. In the fall, he took a trip to eastern Hungary, intending to publish a second series of travel reports. Early in the trip, however, he met Júlia Szendrey, and the travelogue, as well as his life, changed dramatically. He fell in love with her almost at their first meeting. They were engaged and, despite parental opposition, gained a grudging approval and were married a year later. Júlia was to provide the inspiration for Petőfi's best love lyrics. Sharing his political and national convictions, she encouraged his involvement in politics, even in the campaigns of 1848 and 1849. Petőfi's "Úti levelek Kerényi Frigyeshez" (travel notes to Frigyes Kerényi) thus became more than an account of the customs and sights of Transylvania and the eastern part of the country; they show the development of the relationship between Petőfi and Júlia, their courtship and marriage.

The year 1846 also marked the beginning of Petőfi's friendship with János Arany. Petőfi had been drawn to Arany when the latter won a literary prize with his epic, *Toldi* (1847). Feeling that they were kindred spirits, Petőfi wrote immediately—and also composed a poem in praise of the then-unknown man from Nagyszalonta. Later, after they met, their friendship deepened and, with it, Arany's influence on the younger man. Arany helped form the objective vein in Petőfi's poetry. Thus, the influence of a worthy mentor who could rein the excesses of his emotions helped Petőfi attain the perfection of the poems he wrote between 1846 and 1849.

Finally, Petőfi also achieved a measure of financial independence through a contract signed in August of 1846 with the publisher Gustáv Emich for the publication of his *Collected Poems*. This relationship assured Petőfi a regular, if modest, income and gave him a friend and adviser who would stand him in good stead in his last, troubled years.

After his marriage and brief honeymoon at Koltó, the hunting castle lent to him by Count Teleki, Petőfi and his wife returned to Pest in November of 1847. Several poems commemorate the weeks at Koltó, including "Szeptember végen" (at the end of September), regarded by many critics as one of the masterpieces of world literature. In Pest, too, Petőfi continued to write, contributing to various journals. His poetry of this period included political themes, and he became increasingly involved in the liberal movements that were sweeping the city. While the seat neither of the Diet nor of the King, Buda and Pest were still regarded by many Hungarians as the rightful center of the country. There was agitation to have the capital returned from Pozsony, now that the reason for its move, the presence of the Turks, no longer existed. Social, legal, and economic reforms were sought, and the cessation of certain military measures, such as the special occupation status of Transylvania and parts of the southeastern region of the country; simply, the Hungarian people desired the reunion of their artificially divided country.

As one of the leaders of the young radicals, Petőfi took part in these political activities, which were to culminate in the demonstrations of March 15, 1848. He had written his "Nemzeti dal" (national ode) the previous day for a national demonstration against Austria. During the day, when his poem, along with the formal demands expressed in the Twelve Points, was printed and distributed without the censor's approval as an affirmation of freedom of the press, Petőfi was in the forefront, reciting the ode several times for the gathering crowds. Through a series of negotiations, acceptance in principle of the program of reform was won. The revolution—as yet a peaceful internal reform—had begun.

When both public safety and national security seemed threatened by the invitations of the Croatian army of Count Josef Jellačić and similar guerrilla bands, Petőfi became a member of the Nemzetor (national guard), which he was to commemorate in one of his poems. He joined the staff of the *Életképek*, which had been edited by his friend Mór Jókai since April, 1848. He published his diary on the events of March and April, 1848, a lively if fragmented account of his activities and thoughts in those days, and also a translation of William Shakespeare's *Coriolanus*. In September, he undertook a re-

cruiting tour, and in October, he joined the regular army. The War of Independence was in full force by this time, relations between the Hungarians and the Habsburgs having deteriorated completely. Even the fact that Júlia was expecting the couple's first child in December did not allow Petőfi to draw back from the struggle he had so often advocated in his poems.

Commissioned as a captain in the army on October 15, 1848, Petőfi was assigned to Debrecen. He had difficulties with the discipline and procedures of army life, however, until transferred to the command of General József Bem, a Polish patriot and skillful general who was winning the Transylvanian campaign. Through the first half of 1849, Petőfi participated in the Transylvanian campaigns, visiting his wife and son whenever a lull in the fighting or his adjutants' duties allowed. On July 31, 1849, he took part in the Battle of Segesvár and was killed by Cossack forces of the Russian army, which had come to aid the Austrians according to the agreements of the Holy Alliance. Petőfi's body was never found, because he was buried, according to eyewitnesses, in a mass grave. This fact, however, was not known until much later, and many rumors of his living in exile, in hiding, or in a Siberian labor camp were circulated in the 1850's, proof of the people's reluctance to accept his death. His widow's remarriage was severely criticized, though eventually the poet's death had to be accepted. His poetry, however, continues to live.

ANALYSIS

Antal Szerb remarked in his 1934 work, *Magyar irodalomtörténet* (history of Hungarian literature), "Petőfi is a biographical poet. There is no break between the experience and its poetic expression." Sándor Petőfi's poetry, although best analyzed from a biographical perspective, is not autobiographical; its themes and topics span a surprisingly broad range for a career compressed into such a few years.

THE HUNGARIAN TRADITION

In the early poems, written from 1842 to 1844, Petőfi had already established his distinctive style and some of his favorite themes. Although he was influenced both by classical poets (especially Horace) and by foreign poets of his own era—Friedrich Schiller, Heinrich Heine, the Hungarian-born Austrian poet Nikolas Lenau, and probably the English poets Lord Byron and Percy Bysshe Shelley—Petőfi believed that Hungarian poetry must free itself of its dependence on foreign rules of prosody in order to reflect native meters and patterns.

In this, he was not the first: The tradition of medieval verse and song had survived and had been revived by previous generations of poets; the seventeenth century epic of Miklós Zrinyi had continued to inspire poets; the folk song, too, had been cultivated by earlier poets, notably Csokonai in the late eighteenth century and Kisfaludi in the early nineteenth century. What was new in Petőfi's approach was his conscious effort to establish a poetic style that put native meters and current speech at the center of his art. Proof of his success is found not only in the immense and ongoing popularity of his poetry among all classes of the population, but also in the recognition accorded him by János Arany, who was later to define the "Hungarian national meter" chiefly on the basis of a study of Petőfi's use of native rhythms.

Petőfi's early poems were written primarily in the folk-song style. In subject, they ranged from Anacreontics to love lyrics to personal and meditative poems. The love poems are light and playful exercises without great emotional commitment, but they present the people and locale Petőfi was later to make his own: the *puszta*, its people, plants, and animals. In "Egri hangok" (sounds of Eger), however, the Anacreontic is used for a serious and patriotic purpose, anticipating Petőfi's later use of this genre.

The poem grew out of a personal experience: Walking from Debrecen to Pest in February of 1844, in his gamble to be recognized as a poet or to abandon this vocation, he was welcomed by the students of the college. The poem opens with a quiet winter scene: On the ground, there is snow; in the skies, clouds; but for the poet everything is fine, because he is among friends in a warm room, drinking the fine wines of Eger. The mood is not rowdy but serene and content. Juxtaposing natural imagery and emotion in a manner reminiscent of folk song, he states: "If my good spirits would have seeds:/ I'd sow them above the snow,/ And when they sprout, a forest of roses/ Would crown winter." The mood here, however, only sets the stage for the patriotic sentiment that is the poem's real purpose. Petőfi moves on to consider the historical associations of the city of Eger, the

scene of one of the more memorable sieges of the Turkish wars; thus, he examines the decline of Hungary as a nation. He does not dwell long on nostalgia, however, but turns back to the good mood of the opening scenes to predict a bright future for the country.

THE FAMILY

Petőfi's early poems about his family reveal the emotional depth of his best work. They are full of intense yet controlled feeling, but the setting, the style, and the diction remain simple; a realistic note is never lacking. Contemplating a reunion with the mother he has not seen for some time, he rehearses various greetings, only to find that in the moment of reunion he "hangs on her lips—wordlessly,/ Like the fruit on the tree."

The felicitous choice of image and metaphor is one of the greatest attractions of Petőfi's poetry. "Egy estém otthon" (one evening at home) and "István öcsémhez" (to my younger brother, István) reflect the same love and tender concern for his parents. The emotions are deep, yet their expression is restrained: He sees his father's love manifest in the grudging approval bestowed on his "profession" and his mother's love manifest in her incessant questions. Objective in his assessment of his father's inability to understand him, he knows that the bond between them is no less strong. His own emotions are described in a minor key, coming as a comment in the last line of the quatrain, a line that has the effect of a "tag," because it has fewer stresses than the other three.

THE HAMMER OF THE VILLAGE

Petőfi's two heroic poems use the same devices to comment on society—albeit in a light and entertaining manner. *The Hammer of the Village*, written in mock-heroic style, satirizes both society and the Romantic epic tradition, which by this time had become degraded and commonplace. Using a mixture of colloquialism and slang, the parody is peopled with simple villagers who are presented in epic terms. The characters themselves behave unaffectedly and naturally; it is the narrator who assumes the epic pose and invests their jealousies and Sunday-afternoon amusements with a mock grandeur. Thus, Petőfi shows his ability to use the heroic style, though he debunks certain excesses in the heroic mode then fashionable, presenting the life he knows best; he does this not by ridiculing simple folk but by debunking pretentiousness. Though popular, the poem understandably failed to gain the critical approval of the journal editors, whose main offerings were often in the very vein satirized by Petőfi.

JÁNOS THE HERO

In contrast, *János the Hero* received both critical and popular support. It has served as the basis of an operetta and has often been printed as a children's book—especially in foreign translations. Yet much more than a fairy tale cast in folk-epic style, the work has several levels of meaning and explores many topics of deep concern for the poet and his society.

The hero and his lover, his adventures, his values, and his way of thinking are all part of the folktale tradition. The epic is augmented by more recent historical material: the Turkish wars and Austrian campaigns, events that mingle in the imagination of the villagers who have fought Austria's wars for generations and who fought the Turks for generations before that. The characterization, however, remains realistically rooted in the village. The French king, the Turkish pasha, even the giant are recognizable types. The hero, János, remains unaffected and unspoiled, but he is never unsophisticated. His naïveté is not stupidity; he is one to whom worldly glory has less appeal than do his love for Iluska and his desire to be reunited with her.

The style of the poem reinforces this "obvious" level: It is written in the Hungarian Alexandrine, a ten- to eleven-syllable line divided by a caesura into two and two, or two and three, measures. The language is simple and natural, but, as in the folk song, the actual scene is merged with the psychological world of the tale. The similes and metaphors of the poem reflect the method of the folk song and thus extend the richness of meaning found in each statement. The use of the devices goes beyond their traditional application in folk song. Through the pairing of natural phenomena and the protagonist's state of mind, a higher level of meaning is suggested: The adventures of János become symbolic of the struggle between good and evil. Iluska becomes the ideal for which he strives as well as the force that keeps him from straying from the moral path; he does not take the robbers' wealth to enrich himself, nor does he accept the French throne and the hand of the princess. Helping the weak and unfortunate, he continues to battle oppression, whether in the form of an unjust master or the Turks or

giants and witches who rule over the forces of darkness.

The images used by the lovers upon their parting illustrate these principles quite well: János asks Iluska to remember him in these words: "If you see a dry stalk driven by the wind/ Let your exiled lover come to your mind." His words are echoed by Iluska's answer: "If you see a broken flower flung on the highway/ Let your fading lover come to your mind." The cosmic connections are suggested, yet nothing inappropriate on the literal level is said. Furthermore, the dry stalk is an appropriate symbol for the grief-stricken and aimlessly wandering János. The faded flower as a symbol of the grieving girl becomes a mystical metaphor for her; in the concluding scenes, János regains Iluska when he throws the rose he had plucked from her grave into the Waters of Life.

The realism of the folk song and the quality of Hungarian village life are not restricted to the description of character or to the imagery. The setting, particularly when János is within the boundaries of Hungary, is that of the Hungarian plain. He walks across the level, almost barren land, stops by a sweep well, and encounters shepherds, bandits, and peddlers, as might any wanderer crossing these regions. These touches and János's realistic actions—such as eating the last of the bacon that he had carried with him for the journey, using the brim of his felt hat for a cup and a mole's mound for a pillow, and turning his sheepskin cloak inside out to ward off the rain—reaffirm the hero's basic humanity. He is *not* the passive Romantic traveler in the mold of Heine or of Byron. He never becomes a mere observer; instead, he naturally assumes an active role and instinctively takes charge of his own life and of events around him. Even in the more mythical setting of the second half of the poem, his sense of purpose does not waver.

The years 1845 and 1846 were intensely emotional ones for Petőfi, and many of his works of this period suffer from a lack of objectivity and of emotional distancing. Love, revenge, and patriotism, a struggle between national priorities, the gulf between the rich and the poor—all sought a voice. The simple lyric of the traditional folk song was not yet strong enough to carry the message, and Petőfi sought a suitable medium of expression. In this time of experimentation, he found in the drama of the Hungarian people an objective correlative for his own emotions.

CLOUDS

The collection *Clouds* contains occasional poems in the world-weary mood of the previous year, but new forms and a new language show that to a great extent Petőfi had mastered the conflicting impulses of the earlier works. The best poems lash out against injustice, or they are patriotic poems that become increasingly militant in tone. In "A Csárda romjai" (the ruins of the Csárda), Petőfi takes a familiar landmark of the arid, deserted lowlands and makes it a metaphor for the decline of the country. The poem opens as a paean to these plains, the poet's favorite landscape because they remind him of freedom; in succeeding stanzas, he seems to digress from the objective scene into sentimentality. He stops himself, however, before this train of thought goes too far; inasmuch as it is the ruin before him that has inspired these thoughts, the poem is also returned to the concrete scene. The ruin is of stone—a rarity here—so he seeks an explanation, which is soon given: A village or city once stood here, but the Turks destroyed it and left only a half-ruined church. A parenthetical expression brings the poem back to the idea of lost liberty ("Poor Hungary, my poor homeland,/ How many different chains you have already worn"), and the narrative is then resumed.

In time, an inn was built from the church, but those who once lodged there are now long dead. The inn has lost its roof, and its door and window are indistinguishable; all that remains is the sweep of the well, on top of which a lone eagle sits, meditating on mutability. In the final four lines, the scene is expanded to encompass the entire horizon, which serves to give it an optimistic and magical tone. The melancholy scene is bathed in sunshine and surrounded by natural beauty. The parallelism between the decline of the nation and the slow ruin of the church-inn has been established, and a note of optimism for the nation's future has been introduced, but precise development of this idea is only suggested. The point is not belabored.

"A NÉGY-ÖKRÖS SZEKÉR"

The poems of these years showed great variety; not all are in the meditative-patriotic vein. In "A négy-ökrös szekér" (the ox cart), for example, Petőfi returned to a more personal theme: a nighttime ride in an oxcart. The poem is set in the country; the speaker is on a visit home.

With a group of young friends, he returns to the next village in an oxcart to prolong the party. The magic of the evening is suggested in the second stanza—"The merchant breeze moved over the nearby leas/ And brought sweet scents from the grasses"—but the refrain anchors the scene in reality: "Down the highway, pulling the cart,/ The four oxen plodded slowly." The poem remains a retelling of the evening, although a pensive note is introduced when the poet turns to his companion, urging that they choose a star "which will lead us back/ To the happy memories of former times." The poem then closes with the calm notes of the refrain.

"TÜNDÉRÁLOM"

The culmination of this process of revaluation and poetic development comes in "Tündérálom" (fairy dream). This lyric-psychological confession is written in iambic pentameter and eight-line stanzas with a rhyme scheme of *abcbbdbd* so that the *b* rhyme subtly connects the two halves. Its real theme, despite the poet's explicit statement that he has here conjured up "first love," is the search for happiness. As such, the poem fits Petőfi's preoccupations in 1845 and 1846. Although many of the trappings of Romanticism are found in the poem, the longing for an unattainable ideal is given its own expression. It is almost impossible to trace specific influences, yet the poem expresses some of the quintessential notions of the Romantic movement without ever quite losing touch with reality.

The poem owes its success partly to its images, through which the everyday world is constantly brought into contact with the ethereal without disturbing it in the slightest:

> I'm a boatman on a wild, storm-tossed river;
> The waves toss, the light boat shakes,
> It shakes like the cradle that is rocked
> By the violent hands of an angry nurse.
> Fate, the angry nurse of my life.
> You toss and turn my boat,
> You, who like a storm drove on me
> Peace-disturbing passions.

Throughout, the ambiguity between realistic phenomena and magical manifestations is maintained: The dreamer seems to imagine the latter, but the former are asserted. Thus, the mysterious sounds he hears are identified as a swan's song, and, as he leaps from a mountain peak into the sky to gain his ideal, he falls back to awake to a lovely yet earthly maiden. Thus, the idyll is again returned to reality.

The ambiguity can be sustained so successfully because it is the imagery that creates the mood, and Petőfi's sure handling of imagery never allows it to get out of control. The description of the progress of the idyll illustrates this well:

> Dusk approached. On golden clouds
> The sun settled behind the violet mountains;
> A pale fog covered this dry sea,
> The endlessly stretching plain.
> The cliff on which we stood glowed red
> From the last rays, like a purple pillow
> On a throne. But truly, this was a throne
> And we on it the youthful royal couple of happiness.

In a sense, this poem was for Petőfi the swan song of the purely internal lyric. Appropriately, it exhibits the best qualities of his subjective, Romantic early verse. It is melodious, and it unfolds the story in a series of rich and sensuous images. The objective world is completely subordinated to the imaginative one, but it is not ignored. Symbols abound, but they are suggestive, not didactic. The girl in the poem is Imagination and Inspiration; she is the ideal goal of those starting their careers. When she is lost, the ideal is lost, but Petőfi suggests in the closing lines that such an ideal can be held for only a moment. It must give way to reality; thus, it is not lost, only changed. The impractical dreams of youth are supplanted by the practical programs of adulthood which will implement these goals.

"LEVÉL VÁRADY ANTALHOZ"

Two more poems of this fertile period deserve mention: "Levél Várady Antalhoz" (letter to Antal Várady) and "Dalaim" (my songs). Each of these poems serves as an *ars poetica*. In the former, Petőfi states that the beauty of nature has revived him and cured him of his world-weariness, and he affirms his commitment to social and political causes. The six stanzas of "Dalaim" are a masterful expression of the variety of themes and moods found in Petőfi's poetry, from the landscape poetry of his homeland to joy, love, Anacreontics, patriotism, and the desire to free his homeland of foreign rule,

as well as to the fiery rage that makes his songs "Lightning flashes of/ his angry soul."

"DALAIM"

"Dalaim," like "Tündérálom" (fairy dream), serves as a transition to the final, mature phase of Petőfi's poetry, characterized by a harmonious fusion of the often divergent trends identified so far in his poetry. Personal experiences and national events play as important a part in the formation of this style as do the experimentations of his earlier years. Structure and mood, internal and external scenes merge as his themes become more complex and his subjects more serious. "Naïve realism" is supplanted by a deeper realism, and the personal point of view is gradually replaced by a conscious spokesman for the Hungarian people. The intense emotions of Petőfi's mature poems continue to be expressed in a restrained style, and even the deep love poetry addressed to his wife finds expression in a controlled style that continues to reflect the Hungarian folk song and the European traditions that influenced him at the beginning of his career.

"RESZKET A BOKOR, MERT"

The objective lyric style that marks the best of Petőfi's poetry had two inspirations. One was his wife, Júlia Szendrey; the other was his friend and fellow poet János Arany. Though Petőfi's love for Júlia was deep and passionate, the poetry in which he celebrates that love is both objective and universal.

The poems of his courtship and marriage show a progression from an emphasis on physical beauty to a desire for spiritual identification. The style remains that of the folk song and the direct personal lyric, but the imagery brings a wealth of associations to bear on the relationship. Most prominent are images of blessedness and fulfillment. In "Reszket a bokor, mert" (the bush trembles, because), the intensity of feeling is almost too much for the classic folk-song pattern, yet the poet retains the delicate balance between form and content. Written shortly after their meeting, before Petőfi had a firm commitment from Júlia, the poem is essentially a question posed through a range of associations: "The bush trembles, for/ A little bird alighted there./ My soul trembles, for/ You came to mind." In the following lines, the balance between the exterior, natural scene and the interior, psychological one is maintained. The beloved is likened to a diamond—pure, clear, and precious—and to a rose. This latter image receives emphasis and gains freshness as Petőfi uses the word *rozsaszálam*—that is, a single, long-stemmed rose. To the usual associations, grace and slenderness are added, along with the suggestion of something individual, unique.

The last stanza poses a question: Does Júlia still love him in the cold of winter, as she had loved him in the warmth of summer? Through the reference to the seasons, Petőfi not only retains the parallelism on which the poem is built but also refers to the actual moment from which the poem springs. All of this, even the gentle note of resignation in these lines, leads to the statement: "If you no longer love me/ May God bless you,/ But if you do still love me,/ May He bless you a thousandfold." Júlia's answer was, "A thousand times," and from that time on, Petőfi seems to have had no doubt that her commitment to him was as complete as his to her.

"Szeptember végen"

The poems continue to chronicle the events and emotions of the courtship, marriage, and honeymoon. "Szeptember végen" (at the end of September) records a day of meditative peace touched by melancholy. The images raise it to extraordinary heights, and the skillful use of meter and mood, image and meaning makes it a masterpiece. It unites the virtues of folk poetry and the gentle philosophy of Petőfi's peaceful moments in an eternal tribute to his wife. Its three stanzas of eight lines each, written in dactylic tetrameter, a relatively slow and descending cadence, are meditative yet grand, suggesting that the poet's soliloquy is not merely a personal matter. The images reflect the scene at Koltó in the foothills of the eastern Carpathians and the autumn setting with its associations of death. The atmosphere created again depends on the union of the natural and the psychological. The poet addresses his wife, calling her attention to the contrast between summer in the garden and the snow already on the mountaintops. He, too, feels this contrast:

> The rays of summer are still flaming in my young heart,
> And in it still lives spring in its glory,
> But see, gray mingles with my dark hair;
> The hoarfrost of winter has smitten my head.

A line that rivals François Villon's "Où sont les neiges d'antan?" (Where are the snows of yesteryear?) introduces the next stanza: "The flower fades, life fleets away." This line gently leads the poem to the next topic, the brevity of life and the poet's premonition that he will precede his wife to the grave. Will she mourn him, or will she soon forget their love?

The gradual movement of the poem, revealing the manner in which one emotion fades into another, enables the poet to escape excesses of sentimentality and melancholy in spite of the topic. As always, realistic touches help bring the reader to accept the closing lines. On one level, the poem is a metaphysical statement concerning the enduring reality of love. On another, it is a deeply felt personal declaration of love set in a specific time and place. The poet's control of his material enables him to assert, without a trace of the maudlin, that life has no more durability than a flower, that permanence is to be found only in the love that endures beyond the grave. The themes of love, nature, and death are united in such a way that not one of them is slighted, not one of them is vague and impersonal.

"Rózsabokor a domboldalon"

Though his married years were also years of increasingly greater involvement in public affairs and politics, Petőfi continued to write beautiful love poems to his wife. In "Rózsabokor a domboldalon" (rosebush on the hillside), he returns to the happy, carefree tones of the folk song as he compares his wife's leaning on him to the wild rosebush hugging the hillsides. "Minek nevezzelek?" (what shall I name you?) also uses a lighter style, as the poet seeks to explain just what his wife means to him. A catalog of her ethereal charms and spiritual qualities tumbles forth, for he cannot summarize her essence in a word. The directness of his approach, as well as the seeming paradoxes in which the description is couched, again invites the reader to go beyond the surface to think about the thesis of the poem.

"Szeretlek, kedvesem"

Shortly before his death, Petőfi wrote "Szeretlek, kedvesem" (I love you, my dear). Again, there is what seems to be a breathless profession of love as Petőfi lists the ways in which he loves Júlia. The eighty lines of the poem constitute essentially one sentence. Its form, free verse in lines ranging from two to four measures, reflects this quality. The message is not frivolous, however, for he succeeds in conveying a depth of love that excludes all other feelings yet encompasses all. Theirs is a fully mutual relationship, as he states in the last line, for he has learned all he knows of love from her.

"BOLOND ISTÓK"

In Petőfi's objective poetry of the time, also, the mood of these years of married happiness is seen. The verse narrative "Bolond Istók" (crazy Steve) reflects this mood in its story of a wandering hero who finds a haven and a loving wife through his dedication and service. The objectivity and restrained style of the poem balance the hardships of the student with the sentimental overtones of the grandfather, who is disillusioned with his son. Even the romantic flight of the granddaughter to escape a marriage her father wishes to force on her is spared sentimentality. Tongue-in-cheek hyperbole is often the key: The deserted farm "seems to be still in the throes of the Tatar raids," and the old housekeeper and host seem about as civil as Tamburlaine's forces when Istók first comes upon them. The young man's optimism serves to offset this mood and also to introduce the new theme: the arrival of the granddaughter, whose plea for help is to bring hope and new life to the old farmstead. In time, he marries the girl, and in due course a cradle is rocked by the hearth. The cycle of life reasserts itself over the disruption caused by evil.

Other poems, such as "A vídor" (the wanderer), "A kisbéres" (the hired man), and "A téli esték" (winter evenings), return to the theme of domestic bliss, as do two prose works written during this period: *Életképek:* "A nagyapa" (the grandfather) and "A fakó leány s a pej legény" (the pale girl and the ruddy boy).

JÁNOS ARANY

Petőfi's friendship with János Arany also reinforced the objective orientation of his poetry. The two men shared many of the same goals, though they did not always agree on the methods to be followed in achieving them. Poetically, too, they differed, yet the friendship was fruitful for both. In the years following their first exchange of letters, their correspondence ranged from their common concern with creating a national poetry, to their families, to a general exchange of information and ideas. The naturally more reserved as well as more pessimistic Arany was often shaken out of his soberness by the playful letters of Petőfi.

The two friends, occasionally joined by others, undertook several projects together. As a result of their col-laborative efforts, Petőfi wrote "Széchy Mária" (1847) and began his translation of Shakespeare. It was in Petőfi's genre and landscape poems, however, that the influence of Arany's calmer, more objective style seems to have borne the richest fruit.

PATRIOTIC POEMS

Nationalism, a sense of commitment to and concern for the Hungarian people, and patriotism, a commitment to the political institutions of a free and independent Hungarian nation, are themes found throughout Petőfi's poetry. Often, these concerns appear in an oblique way. Increasingly, after March 15, 1848, however, they became open topics of his poetry while continuing to influence the other genres in the same indirect fashion as earlier. As early as 1846, in "Egy gondolat bánt engement" (one thought troubles me), Petőfi had expressed a desire to die on the battlefield in defense of liberty. The next year, he stated the obligation of the poet to sacrifice personal feelings in the interests of patriotic and human duty in "A XIX: Század költői" (the poets of the nineteenth century). After the events of March, 1848, Petőfi plunged into these responsibilities fully; it is perhaps this which gives his poetry the masculine quality not captured by Western European poets of his time: He calls for action with the conviction of one who is ready to be the first to die in battle. These sentiments are skillfully stated in "Ha férfi vagy, légy férfi" (if you are a man, then be one)—a poetic declaration of principles in which didacticism does not detract from poetic value.

A sense of responsibility to his wife and family did not interfere with Petőfi's commitment to his people; if anything, it contributed to the commitment. Júlia shared his sentiments and supported her husband, and he considered her his partner in his work. "Feleségem és kardom" (my wife and my sword) must be read in conjunction with "Ha férfi vagy, légy férfi" for it balances the picture. His wife, an equal partner, will tie the sword on her husband's waist and send them off together, if necessary. Her heroism is to be admired no less than bravery on the battlefield.

In the early years, Petőfi's patriotic poetry had some nostalgic moments. By 1846, however, he had moved beyond the glorification of the past to the criticism of the present and suggestions for reforms. He called on poets to be active in bringing about reforms, and urged his readers to take pride in Hungarian traditions. In "Magyar vagyok" (I am a Hungarian), he stated his unequivocal loyalty; "Erdélyben" (in Transylvania) shows the dedication to this eastern region of Hungary that had preserved Hungarian traditions and language in the trying years of the Turkish wars and the Austrian Partition—a dedication echoed by Hungarian poets today.

"NEMZETI DAL"

The events of March 15, which were to transform not only Petőfi's life but also the history of his country, seemed to crown with success the efforts of the reformers. Petőfi's "Nemzeti dal" (national ode) inspired the demonstrators, and the Twelve Points made clear to everyone the goals they were espousing. The spirited call to arms in the refrain—"By the God of the Magyars,/ We swear/ We swear that captives/ We'll no longer be!"—became the rallying cry of the nation. In the poem, nostalgia for the past is united with faith in the future, and the urgency and immediacy of the situation are emphasized in the words that virtually leap at the listener: "Up Magyar, the country calls!/ Here's the time, now or never!/ Shall we be free or captives ever?/ This the question you must answer!" In contrast to the direct address here, the refrain is in a collective mode. A dialogue is thus established, with the poet calling on his audience to respond and prompting their response through the oath phrased in the refrain.

In the six stanzas of this poem, Petőfi chides his countrymen for enduring servitude. It is time for the sword to replace the chain, he urges, so that the Hungarian name will again be great and future generations will bless them. The language and the images are as direct as the tone, and throughout, the poet emphasizes the need for heroic action regardless of the consequences. Understandably, the poem had great impact. If Petőfi had made only this contribution to the independence movement, he would have been remembered, but he did much more.

The Revolution that had begun peacefully, and seemed, at first, to accomplish its goals through legal reform, escalated into war when Hungarian territory was invaded, first by the Croatian armies of Jellačić, who had Imperial support, and later by Austrian forces, as the Chan-

cery consolidated around the new King, Franz Joseph. National minorities within the country were urged by the Austrian government to attack the Hungarians, and some did. Others, notably the German towns, remained neutral or espoused the Hungarian cause. As the war became an open struggle between the Hungarian Ministry and the Habsburgs, Hungarian leader Lajos Kossuth was able to force a final break with Austria, and the Habsburgs were formally deprived of their position as monarchs of Hungary. Petőfi became increasingly involved in both the political and the military events, seeing a break with Austria and the establishment of a Republic as the only means of achieving social reform. Of the nearly 150 short lyrics he wrote in 1848 and 1849, almost all deal with the political and military turmoil in Hungary. Some are antimonarchist or anti-Habsburg; some chide the nationalities for turning on the land that gave them shelter earlier; and an increasing number glorify national virtues and ancient constitutional rights that had long been ignored by the monarchs.

WAR POEMS

Petőfi was not sanguine, however, and hopeful poems such as "1848" alternate with ones that express bitter disappointment, such as "Európa csendes, ujra csendes" ("Europe is quiet, is quiet again"). He saw that Europe had given up its democratic ideals, and no hope of support was left. Yet, he did not speak of Hungary's cause as a hopeless if glorious one. Even the combined forces of Austria and Russia were no match for his poetic belief in victory, expressed in "Bizony mondom, hogy gyoz most a magyar" ("truly I say, now the Hungarians will win").

Though they constitute a relatively small percentage of his poetic work, Petőfi's war poems deserve attention. For the most part, they are spirited, upbeat marches or a lively mixture of narrative and lyric moods, emphasizing the dedication and heroism of the soldiers. They do not glorify war for its own sake, but rather emphasize the patriotic reason for the combat. "Bordal" (wine song) returns to a traditional genre to urge all men to defend their homeland, "draining blood and life" from anyone who seeks to destroy it just as they "empty the glass of wine."

Petőfi's confidence in the ultimate triumph of his cause, if not on the battlefield or in the treaty rooms then at least in the judgment of history, can be sensed in one of the last battle songs he wrote, "Csatában" (in battle). This poem is also notable for the personal involvement of the poet. He begins the poem by re-creating a battle in vivid natural images and giving it a cosmic frame:

> Wrath on the earth,
> Wrath in the sky!
> The red of spilt blood and
> The red rays of the sun!
> The setting sun glows
> In such a wild purple!
> Forward, soldiers,
> Forward, Magyars!

Through such images and a wonderfully effective onomatopoeia, the whole universe seems to become involved in the strife. The poet's own involvement, symbolic of the involvement of the nation, is signaled in the change in the refrain from "Forward" to "Follow me."

Shortly after composing this poem, Petőfi died on the fateful battlefield of Segesvár. Within weeks, the Hungarian Resistance was also over, but Petőfi lives on in legend and in his poetry.

LEGACY

Petőfi's short poetic career established him as a poet of the first rank. The variety of themes and styles he handled with success is amazing; even the less powerful lyrics of his early years have enriched Hungarian literature and music, many of them having been set to music and passing into the modern "folk-song" repertory. His early fame and his fame abroad rested on both his republican sentiments and his romantic early death. Early translations into German were followed by English versions based on the German. His popularity grew with the worldwide interest in the Hungarian Revolution of 1848 and its brutal suppression; it also waned as political realities changed. The Petőfi behind the legend was neglected even in Hungary for a long time; abroad, he is still mostly known as a revolutionary hero, not as a poet. Translations, prepared with enthusiasm but lack of knowledge or skill, seldom do him justice. In Hungary, the most talented of his contemporaries recognized his talents independent of his political views. Today, there is general agreement about his position as

a central figure in Hungarian literature and in the development of the Hungarian lyric. His republican, nationalistic, and patriotic ideas are also recognized; they are an essential part of the poet who spoke from the heart of his generation, who spoke for his people, and who spoke for the masses and indeed to give all classes of society a voice. He was truly a poet of national consciousness.

OTHER MAJOR WORKS

LONG FICTION: *A hóhér kötele*, 1846 (novella; *The Hangman's Rope*, 1973).

SHORT FICTION: "A szökevények," 1845; "A fakó leány s a pej legény," 1847; "A nagyapa," 1847.

PLAYS: *Tigris és hiéna*, pb. 1847; *Coriolanus*, pb. 1848 (translation of William Shakespeare's play).

NONFICTION: "Úti jegyzetek," 1845; "Úti levelek Kerényi Frigyeshez," 1847; *Lapok Petőfi Sándor naplójából*, 1848; *Petőfi Sándor összes prózai muvei és levelezése*, 1960; *Petőfi Sándor by Himself*, 1973; *Rebel or Revolutionary? Sándor Petőfi as Revealed by His Diary, Letters, Notes, Pamphlets, and Poems*, 1974.

MISCELLANEOUS: *Works of Sándor Petőfi*, 1973.

BIBLIOGRAPHY

Basa, Enikő Molnár. *Sándor Petőfi*. Boston: Twayne, 1980. An introductory biography and critical study of selected works by Petőfi. Includes bibliographic references.

Curwen, Henry. *Sorrow and Song: Studies of Literary Struggle*. London: H. S. King, 1875. Volume 1 includes a biography of Petőfi. Invaluable for its near-contemporary insights.

Illyés, Gyula. *Petőfi*. Translated by G. F. Cushing. Budapest, Hungary: Corvina, 1973. An exhaustive biography and critical examination of the life and works of Petőfi.

Jones, David Mervyn. *Five Hungarian Writers*. Oxford, England: Clarendon Press, 1966. A collection of biographical studies of influential Hungarian writers including Petőfi.

Enikő Molnár Basa
(including original translations);
bibliography updated by the editors

PETRARCH

Francesco Petrarca

Born: Arezzo, Italy; July 20, 1304
Died: Arquà, Italy; July 18, 1374

PRINCIPAL POETRY

Epistolae metricae, 1363 (*Metrical Letters*, 1958)
Bucolicum carmen, 1364 (*Eclogues*, 1974)
Africa, 1396 (English translation, 1977)
Rerum vulgarium fragmenta, 1470 (also known as *Canzoniere*; *Rhymes*, 1976)
Trionfi, 1470 (*Tryumphs*, 1565; *Triumphs*, 1962)
Rime disperse, 1826 (also known as *Estravaganti*; *Excluded Rhymes*, 1976)

OTHER LITERARY FORMS

Petrarch's other writings, except for some prayers in Latin hexameters, are all in Latin prose and consist of epistles, biographies, a collection of exempla, autobiographical works, psalms, orations, invectives, assorted treatises, and even a guidebook to the Holy Land, which he never visited and knew only through the eyes and books of others. Ironically, although the author believed that he would achieve lasting fame because of his Latin compositions, he is remembered today largely for his vernacular poetry. Contemporary scholars do study his Latin works, but primarily to gain insight into his Italian poems. A knowledge of his classically inspired writings, however, is essential to anyone who would understand the cultural milieu that led to the birth of the Renaissance in Italy.

ACHIEVEMENTS

Two words sum up Petrarch's profound historical legacy: Petrarchianism and Humanism. The first stands for the widespread influence of the author's vernacular poetry, especially his love sonnets but also *Triumphs*, on Western European culture from the late fourteenth century to the mid-seventeenth century. It refers to the imitation in literature and the representation in art of the themes and images so carefully crafted in Petrarch's Italian verse: in literature, for example, the expression of the lover's torment through the use of antithesis, oxymo-

ron, hyperbole, and other appropriate rhetorical figures, or the description of the beloved as an ideal yet real lady with golden hair, ivory skin, and pearl teeth; in art, the reproduction of *Triumphs* on canvas and wedding chests and in other media, such as woodcuts, enamels, tapestries, and stained glass, as well as in pageants, ballets, and theatricals. The second term, with a capital *H*, refers to the intellectual and cultural movement that derived from the study of classical literature and civilization during the late Middle Ages and that was one of the main factors contributing to the rise of the Renaissance. Petrarch is commonly called the "Father of Humanism" because his intense interest in antiquity led him to be the first in modern times to collect ancient manuscripts, compose letters to great Roman and Greek figures of the past, imitate Cicero in his prose and Vergil in his epic poetry, and examine classical writings in their own context, with waning regard for accrued medieval traditions and superstitions. Early fifteenth century Italian Humanists, such as Coluccio Salutati and Leonardo Bruni, were followers of Petrarch and saw him as the enlightened initiator of a new age, the epoch now known as the Renaissance. In reality, although Petrarch does embody many of the qualities of a "Renaissance man" because of his well-rounded nature and varied accomplishments, he is neither wholly in the Renaissance nor entirely in the Middle Ages. Rather, he is a transitional or pivotal figure. His vernacular amorous poetry, with its emphasis on the unreciprocated love for an idealized woman, is in many ways only a culmination of the Provençal troubadour tradition; his *Triumphs*, written in Dante's *terza rima*, could hardly be more medieval; and his psalms and autobiographical dialogues mirror the Middle Ages' confessional literature. Yet the genres and classical style of most of his Latin compositions, his anti-Scholastic attitudes, and his love of secular learning for its moral and civic teachings clearly place him in what would become the mainstream of the Renaissance cultural tradition.

BIOGRAPHY

Francesco Petrarca was born in Arezzo, Italy, on July 20, 1304, the oldest child of Pietro di Parenzo, an exiled Florentine notary. Di Parenzo, more commonly called Ser Petracco ("Ser" indicates a notary), was a White Guelph and, like Dante, had been exiled from Florence and its territory in 1302. (Petrarch later formed his own surname by ingeniously reworking Petracco into an elegant Latinate form.) Early in 1305, Petrarch's mother, Eletta Canigiani, took her son to her father-in-law's home in Incisa, north of Arezzo and in Florentine territory. There, she and Petrarch lived until 1311, when her husband moved them to the independent state of Pisa. In 1312, the family moved to Carpentras, in Provence, to be near the papal seat, which Clement V had moved to Avignon in 1309. In Carpentras, Petrarch began his study of the *trivium* with Convenevole da Prato and continued his studies there until 1316, when, at the tender age of twelve, he was sent to the University of Montpellier to study law. In 1320, he and his younger brother Gherardo, of whom he was very fond, moved to Bologna to continue their legal studies. Petrarch, however, never completed the work for his degree because of his many varied interests. Upon the death of his father in 1326, he abandoned forever his pursuit of law and returned with his brother to Avignon. There, the two of them began ecclesiastical careers in order to improve their financial situations. Petrarch received the tonsure, but he never went further than the minor orders. Gherardo, on the other hand, later became a Carthusian monk.

On Good Friday, 1327, Petrarch saw a woman in the Church of Santa Chiara in Avignon and fell in love with her. The poet identifies her only as Laura, except once when he calls her "Laureta"; her exact identity has never been definitively established. While many critics believe her to be Laura de Noves, who married Hugues de Sade in 1325, others question her very existence. Whatever the case, the figure of Laura, ever reluctant to return the poet's love, is the inspiration or motivation for most of Petrarch's Italian poetry. He even records her death from the plague on April 6, 1348, in his precious copy of Vergil, an indication of the reality and depth of his devotion to her.

In 1330, Petrarch entered the service of Cardinal Giovanni Colonna and remained under that family's patronage for almost two decades. Petrarch soon became, as he characterized himself, a *peregrinus ubique* (pilgrim everywhere). In 1333, he traveled through northern France, Flanders, and Germany. He visited Paris, where Dionigi da Borgo San Sepolcro gave him a copy of Saint Augustine's *Confessions* (c. 397); Liège, where he dis-

covered two new orations by Cicero; and Aachen, where he visited the tomb of Charlemagne. In 1336, he climbed Mount Ventoux with his brother. At the top, he read from his copy of the *Confessions* a passage on the vanity of man. He meditated at length on what he had read, and the experience marked the beginning of the serious introspection which characterized the rest of his life. From the top of the mountain he also looked down on Italy and felt a strong desire to return to his native country. This he accomplished in a trip to Rome, where he visited Giacomo Colonna toward the end of that year.

Petrarch returned to Avignon in 1337, desirous of solitude, which he found fifteen miles away, in Vaucluse, a valley which afforded him a quiet place to study and write. In that same year his first illegitimate child, Giovanni, was born. The mother is unknown, and the son died from the plague in 1361. By Petrarch's midthirties, he was well-known in Italy and France for his Latin verse, and in 1340, he received letters from the Senate in Rome and the University of Paris offering him the poet laureate's crown. He chose to receive the honor

Petrarch (Library of Congress)

in Rome and left the next year for Naples, where King Robert examined him on various questions and proclaimed him worthy of the prize. On Easter Sunday, 1341, he accepted the laurel crown in Rome and delivered a coronation speech on the nature of poetry. It was the first time that such a ceremony had been held since classical times, and it dramatized the significance that the literary models of antiquity were assuming. From Rome, he traveled to Pisa, then to Parma, where he spent about a year working on his epic *Africa*.

In 1342, Petrarch was back in Avignon, where the following year his illegitimate daughter Francesca was born. In October, 1343, he traveled again in Italy, this time as ambassador of the new pope, Clement VI, to the new queen, Joan I. In December, he left Naples, disgusted with the corruption of the court, and went to Parma, where his stay was cut short by the outbreak of war. He escaped through enemy lines and visited Modena, Bologna, and Verona before returning to Avignon by the end of 1345. Soon after arriving in Avignon, he retired to Vaucluse, where he spent all of 1346. In the summer of 1347, he learned that Cola di Rienzo had been elected tribune of Rome. Delighted with the election, Petrarch wrote him a congratulatory Latin eclogue in which he rebuffed all the Roman nobles, including members of the Colonna family, who were hostile to the tribune. At this time, he became entirely independent of Colonna patronage. In November, he headed toward Rome, but in Genoa he learned of the despotic actions of the tribune and decided to interrupt his trip. He selected Parma as his main residence but traveled around Italy at will for three years. In the autumn of 1350, on his way to Rome for the Jubilee, he stopped in Florence, where he visited Giovanni Boccaccio. They met again in Padua in April of the following year. In June, 1351, Petrarch was back in Vaucluse, whence he traveled back and forth to Avignon in hope of papal assistance. The death of Clement VI and the election of Innocent VI to the Papacy in December, 1352, caused Petrarch to lose all hope of support from the Papacy, as Pope Innocent suspected him of necromancy. Petrarch bid his brother farewell for the last time in April of the next year and left in May for Italy.

Back in his native land, Petrarch accepted an offer from the Visconti family to live in Milan, where he remained for eight years (1353-1361). In June, 1361, he left Milan because of the spread of the plague and traveled to Padua, where he was a guest of Francesco da Carrara. In early 1362, he returned to Milan, but because of renewed danger from the plague, he was back in Padua in the spring. In September, he went to Venice, where he remained until 1368, alternating his sojourn there with repeated trips to Padua, Milan, and Pavia. In 1363, Boccaccio paid him a visit in Venice that lasted for a few months. In 1368, Petrarch moved to Padua and from there, in 1370, to nearby Arquà with his daughter Francesca and her family. He spent his final years in Padua and in Arquà, where he died during the night on July 18, 1374.

ANALYSIS

Francesco Petrarca, known in English as Petrarch, was both an Italian and a Latin poet, and any analysis of his poetry must take into consideration both aspects of his career. Petrarch revised continually and extensively most of his compositions; the exact chronology of his works, therefore, whether poetry or prose, is difficult to establish. His first book in Italian is *Canzoniere*, poems written and revised between 1336 and 1374 but not printed until 1470, almost a full century after his death. Any "publication" prior to that date refers, more precisely, to the circulation of a manuscript. The earliest edition of Petrarch's collected Latin works dates from 1496; his complete works, including Italian verse, titled *Opera quae extant omnia*, were first published in Basel in 1554 and later reprinted there in 1581. No modern edition of the complete works exists, although a national edition has been in progress since 1926.

While he longed to be remembered, as has been indicated, for his prodigious production in Latin, the smaller body of his Italian verse has been much more widely appreciated since the end of the fifteenth century. In both cases, however, his compositions have been widely influential because of the basic principle of imitation which he endorsed and which the Renaissance accepted as canon. Petrarch believed in the necessity of imitating the great Latin authors in order to produce works of lasting significance. His adherence to this doctrine in the bulk of his poetry and prose established the precedent for *imitatio* which later Humanists refined. Curiously, the subsequent refinement of the principle led to compositions that were much more Ciceronian, in terms of correct grammar and pure style, than Petrarch ever achieved in his own prose. This fact may account for the declining interest in his Latin prose after the fifteenth century. In his Italian poetry, Petrarch himself was not concerned with the imitation per se of preceding traditions as much as with the application of the best of those traditions, such as certain images found in the troubadour lyrics, to a real model: Laura. In the early sixteenth century, however, Pietro Bembo cited Petrarch's Italian lyrics as the best model for those who would write vernacular poetry. With the flourishing of the printing press at the same time as the cardinal's endorsement, Petrarch's Italian poems, already outstanding for their lyric quality and psychological insights, became destined to serve as models and to achieve prominence in the literature of the Western world.

RHYMES

Drawing on a literary-historical examination of the past, Petrarch's Latin writings, as critic Aldo Bernardo has emphasized, "contain a virile and noble view of mankind [and] exalt the achievements of ancient heroes and thinkers as indications of the heights that man can attain." Petrarch discovered in the classical era examples of moral and civic virtue capable of instructing modern man, who, with the additional light of Christianity, could then surpass the accomplishments of pagan antiquity. Petrarch also shows the boundaries or limitations of paganism, with its bent for the things of this world, such as earthly fame and glory. The tension caused by attempting to balance the appeal of this world's attractions with the Christian's hope of a better life hereafter finds its ultimate expression in the poet's Italian lyrics.

In the collected *Rhymes*, Laura is both a *figura Christi* and a *figura Daphnae*, a symbol of Christ's purity and Daphne's sensuality. More than a study of Laura, however, the poems constitute a keen analysis of the poet's struggle to keep the attractions of this world in proper perspective. For the Christian, the eternal happiness of the next life should outshine the fleeting pleasure of this world; for Petrarch, this knowledge simply compounded his internal conflicts, as he struggled to bring his passions and desire for worldly renown under control and to submit to God. As in Saint Augustine's *Confessions*, the final word of the *Rhymes* is "peace," something that Petrarch's revered saint achieved but of which the poet claims only to have caught glimpses.

The Latin inscription at the head of the Vatican holograph of Petrarch's collected Italian poems is *Rerum vulgarium fragmenta* (fragments of vernacular rhymes). This title emphasizes the nonunitary nature of the collection of 366 lyrics. First, the poems, although mostly sonnets, include a variety of types and may be divided into the following categories: sonnets, canzones, sestinas, ballads, and madrigals. The total number corresponds to the maximum number of days in a year and makes the collection a sort of breviary. Second, the poems treat many topics in addition to the poet's love for Laura, including the themes of friendship, papal corruption, and patriotism. Petrarch continually reordered the poems from 1336 until his death, but the criteria for their final ordering are unclear. Except for the universally accepted grouping of a few sonnets either according to shared themes (such as poems 41 through 43, dealing with Laura's departure for an unknown place, and poems 136 through 138, treating the corruption of the Church in Avignon) or in order to juxtapose one idea to another (such as poems 61 and 62, expressing respectively the exaltation of love and reason), no single organizational principle, such as a meaningful chronology, has been established. Because of the blank pages which separate poems 263 and 264 in Vatican manuscript 3195, a two-part division of the overall framework has traditionally been made. The first 263 poems, which depict Laura as a real woman who moves, talks, laughs, cries, and travels, are usually designated "In vita di madonna Laura" (in the lifetime of Laura). The last 103 poems, which present Laura as a more ethereal being whose carnal presence is not felt, then receive the label "In morte di madonna Laura" (after the death of Laura). Although the headings are not original to Petrarch, they seem generally appropriate.

The true subject of the poems in which Laura appears, either in person or more often in the form of a conceit, such as the laurel tree or the dawn (*l'aurora*, in Italian), is not really Laura. Rather, it is the love of Petrarch for Laura. The *Rhymes* are the intimate story of the poet's emotions, perceptions, feelings, and changing moods produced by the sight or memory of his beloved. The actual descriptions of Laura, whose hair is always blonde like gold and whose skin is white like snow or ivory, are not nearly as significant as the depictions of the poet's melancholic or exalted states as he contemplates her beauty or ruminates over his unreciprocated love. Closely connected with the repeated motif of one-sided love are the themes of the transitoriness of time, the brevity of life, and the vanity of earthly objects and honors.

Two famous canzones, "Spirito gentil" ("Noble Spirit") and "Italia mia" ("My Italy"), best exemplify the category of patriotic or political poems in the *Rhymes*. The first poem was probably written either to Cola di Rienzo in 1347, when he attempted to reinstate the Roman Republic, or to Bosone de' Raffaelli da Gubbio, a Roman senator. It pleads with the "noble spirit" to call Rome's erring citizens back to her ancient path of virtue and glory. Rivalries should be put away and a sense of national pride engendered to wake Italy from her lethargy. "My Italy" constitutes an eloquent plea for peace and is addressed to Italy's warring lords; the most famous section, "Ancient Valor Is Not Yet Dead in Italic Hearts," was chosen by Machiavelli to conclude *Il principe* (1532; *The Prince*). The sonnet sequence previously referred to, poems 136 through 138, represents possibly the most colorful and violent depiction of the corruption of the Church, but references to the papal court at Avignon as "Babylon" occur throughout the *Rhymes*. The best-known poems of friendship treat members of the Colonna family: "Gloriosa columna" ("Glorious Column") and "Rottalè l'alta colonna" ("Broken Is the High Column"). Whatever the theme, all Petrarch's vernacular rhymes are characterized by a sensitivity to beautiful images and sounds which is almost without parallel in the history of Italian versification. In addition, the poet perfected the sonnet form.

TRIUMPHS

Begun in 1351 or 1352 and revised between 1356 and 1374, *Triumphs* was never completed by Petrarch. Like Dante's *La divina commedia* (c. 1320; *The Divine Comedy*), Petrarch's *Triumphs* is an allegorical poem written in interlocking rhymed tercets. Its main divisions are six in number and relate the following story: "Triumphus amoris" ("Triumph of Love"), in four chapters, has Love—in a chariot and surrounded by classical figures—appear to the poet in a dream; as the poet observes the spectacle, Laura appears and he falls in love with her; thus enslaved, he follows the chariot to Cy-

prus, where Love's triumph is celebrated. "Triumphus pudicitiae" ("Triumph of Chastity"), in one chapter, shows Love vainly attempting to imprison Laura, who—armed with her virtues—succeeds in taking Love prisoner; then, surrounded by a court of ladies famous for their virtue, Laura ultimately celebrates her triumph in the temple of Chastity in Rome, where Love is left a prisoner. "Triumphus mortis" ("Triumph of Death"), in two chapters, has Laura die without suffering and then visit Petrarch in a dream, at which time she reveals that she always loved him. "Triumphus famae" ("Triumph of Fame"), in three chapters, has Fame arrive as Death leads Laura away; surrounded by famous literati, Fame explains that she has the power to take a man from the grave and give him life again. "Triumphus temporis" ("Triumph of Time"), in one chapter, shows the Sun, envious of Fame, accelerating time so that the poet will realize that Fame is like snow on the mountain and that Time triumphs over her. Finally, "Triumphus aeternitatis" ("Triumph of Eternity"), in one chapter, depicts the poet's realization that everything in the world passes away; as the poet turns his thoughts to God, he sees a new world, more beautiful and outside time and space; there the righteous triumph, and there the poet hopes to see Laura.

The individual triumphs are successive until the sixth and final one, which provides a vision of the future. The allegorical meaning of the poem points to the necessity of man's looking to God for the ultimate fulfillment of his aspirations. The tone of the work, therefore, is undoubtedly medieval and reminiscent of Dante. Although Petrarch claimed in a letter to Boccaccio that he had never read *The Divine Comedy*, his allegorical poem, with its many Dantean echoes and allusions, including borrowed phrasing, stands as proof that he knew Dante's work very well. Unfortunately, the lyric quality of the unfinished poem fails to match that of the *Rhymes*. This is true for at least two reasons: First, the catalogs of characters are almost interminable and serve to break up the poetic rhythm almost before it is established; second, the allegorical frame, too obvious even from the brief summary provided, is so heavy as to be oppressive. Nevertheless, this composition, although vastly inferior to the collected lyrics, exerted a dramatic influence on Renaissance art because of the esteem in which its author was held. The representation of its processionals in all the major and most of the minor artistic media was an essential part of the phenomenon of Petrarchianism.

AFRICA

Petrarch believed that *Africa*, his epic poem composed in Latin hexameters and divided into nine books, was his most promising work. He began writing the poem in 1338 or 1339, reworking and revising it during the next thirty-five years but never finishing it. Because it was never completed, it was never more than promising. Part of it was presented to King Robert in Naples prior to Petrarch's receiving the crown of poet laureate, but the poem never circulated during the author's lifetime. After his death, friends circulated it, and it was poorly received. In truth, the poem has never enjoyed critical acclaim or approval, except for rare passages such as the tragic love story of Masinissa and Sophonisba. The epic hero is Scipio Africanus; the sources upon which the poem is based include Cicero's "Somnium Scipionis" ("Dream of Scipio") at the end of *De republica* (c. 52 B.C.E.) and Livy's history.

The story begins with an account of Scipio's dream of his deceased father, who died gloriously in the Roman defeat of the Carthaginians in Spain. The father carries Scipio to Heaven, where the son sees a vision of the rise and fall of their beloved Rome and learns that to follow virtue is the duty of man on Earth. His father assures him of victory over Hannibal in the upcoming African campaign and promises him lasting fame because of a poet to be born in the distant future—a not-too-subtle reference to Petrarch himself. The poem, regrettably, is almost completely lacking in both subtlety and dramatic tension. Scipio, brimming with virtue, foils his ally Masinissa's illicit love affair and proves himself an unbelievable character. The outcome of the battle is known before it begins: Hannibal will be defeated, and Scipio will return to Rome victorious. On the voyage home, the conquering general and his friend Ennius discuss the nature of poetry. The latter relates a dream he had of Homer, in which a young poet of great genius figures prominently; the future poet of renown sits in an enclosed valley (read Petrarch seated in Vaucluse). The epic, with its initial and final dream sequences in which Petrarch enjoys a conspicuous place, strikes most critics as too self-congratulatory and ill conceived from beginning to end. As Thomas Bergin has stated, the poem lacks a reading public, "for a reader of Latin epics will want to read true Latin epics and not late medieval imitations."

ECLOGUES

Petrarch's Latin eclogues number twelve, one for each month of the year. As was common in the tradition of Roman and medieval pastoral poems, the bucolic setting disguises quite contemporary events. The pastors or shepherds in a faraway idyllic landscape parallel people close at hand; rustic dialogues find their analogue in contemporary issues. In brief, Petrarch's compositions are a series of allegories placed in rural settings. The themes have all been encountered before: the Roman revolution of Cola di Rienzo, the poet's love for Laura, his coronation in Rome, the corruption of the Church, the conflict in Petrarch between worldliness and spirituality, the death of King Robert, the usefulness of sacred and secular poetry, the destructiveness of the Black Death, and the poet's decision to leave the service of the Colonna family. The eclogues, although neither notably influential nor necessarily inferior, testify to Petrarch's ability to compose countless variations on any number of themes, many of which are notably personal. His life provided almost as much source material for his work as his scholarly studies did. Most of the eclogues were composed between 1346 and 1348, with the definitive version completed in 1364.

METRICAL LETTERS

The *Metrical Letters* make up a collection of sixty-six epistles in Latin hexameters, subdivided into three books. Petrarch dedicated the collection to his friend Marco Barbato di Sulmona, who was chancellor to King Robert. Beginning in 1350, the poet reorganized the letters during a period of more than a decade, completing his task in 1363. The subjects treated range from personal confessions and descriptions of autobiographical happenings to political exhortations and stirring praises for Italy. In purpose, these varied and unequal epistles are not unlike the prose letters found in four other Petrarchan collections. Their intent is to present the poet as he wished to be remembered by posterity. Consequently, they are not filled with spontaneous comments and casual observations, no matter how they may appear at first glance. Every comment and every observation is calculated; this is especially true in those letters which have been carefully rewritten in hexameters. Petrarch's desire, from the first letter to the last, is to interpret for future readers the events of his life, to analyze the results of his studies, and to speculate on the significance of his work. What may have started as another exercise in introspection quickly evolved into a new form of autobiography: an epistolary account revised through time with the reader constantly in mind.

OTHER MAJOR WORKS

NONFICTION: *Rerum familiarium libri*, wr. 1325-1366 (English translation, 1975-1985, also known as *Books on Personal Matters*); *Collatio laureationes*, 1341 (*Coronation Oath*, 1955); *Psalmi penitentiales*, 1342-1347; *Rerum memorandum libri*, 1343-1345; *De vita solitaria*, 1346 (*The Life of Solitude*, 1924); *De viris illustribus*, 1351-1353 (later reorganized as *Quorundam virorum illustrium epithoma*, with a preface by Petrarch, completed by Lombardo della Seta); *Secretum meum*, or *De secreto conflictu curarum mearum*, 1353-1358 (*My Secret*, 1911); *Invectivarum contra quendam magni status hominen sed nullius scientiae aut virtutis*, 1355; *Itinerarium Syriacum*, or *Itinerarium breve de Ianua*, 1358; *Sine nomine*, 1359-1360 (*Book Without a Name*, 1973); *Senilium rerum libri*, wr. 1361-1374 (*Letters of Old Age*, 1966); *Rerum familiarium libri xxiv*, 1364-1366 (*Books on Personal Matters*, 1975); *De remediis utriusque fortunae*, 1366 (*Physicke Against Fortune*, 1597; also as *On Remedies for Good and Bad Fortunes*, 1966); *De sui ipsius et multorum ignorantia*, 1367 (*On His Own Ignorance and That of Many*, 1948); *Posteritati*, 1370-1372 (*Epistle to Posterity*, 1966); *Invectiva contra eum qui maledixit Italiae*, 1373; *De otio religioso*, 1376; *Miscellaneous Letters*, 1966.

MISCELLANEOUS: *Opera quae extant omnia*, 1554, 1581.

BIBLIOGRAPHY

Bishop, Morris. *Petrarch and His World.* Bloomington: Indiana University Press, 1963. Standard biographical treatment in one volume. Excellent introduction to his life, social contexts, and major works.

Bloom, Harold, ed. *Petrarch.* New York: Chelsea House, 1989. Well-chosen collection of eight previously published essays by major scholars including Bernardo, Durling, and Scaglione.

Boyle, Marjorie O'Rourke. *Petrarch's Genius: Pentimento and Prophecy.* Berkeley: University of California Press, 1991. Boyle rejects literal interpretations of Petrarch's "poetics of idolatry," seeing his obsession in rhetorical terms and as an expression of his "frustrated self."

Braden, Gordon. *Petrarchan Love and the Continental Renaissance.* New Haven, Conn.: Yale University Press, 1999. Sticking close to the works themselves, Braden studies Petrarch's poems and their effects on the likes of Giovanni Boccaccio, Pietro Bembo, Pierre de Ronsard, and Garcilaso de la Vega. He emphasizes the continuity of subject matter and the poets' "creative narcissism."

Jones, Frederic J. *The Structure of Petrarch's "Canzoniere": A Chronological, Psychological, and Stylistic Analysis.* Rochester, N.Y.: Boydell & Brewer, 1995. Studies the psychological evolution of Part I of *Canzoniere* through the lens of "catastrophe theory" (applied to Petrarch's relationship with the living Laura).

Mazzotta, Giuseppe. *The Worlds of Petrarch.* Durham, N.C.: Duke University Press, 1993. Mazzotta synthesizes the major elements of and influences on Petrarch's character (humanism, spirituality, history, rhetoric, antiquity, and love) and explores this "unity of parts" in his poetry.

Sturm-Maddox, Sara. *Petrarch's Laurels.* University Park: Pennsylvania State University, 1999. The relationship between Petrarch's concerns for love and for glory is encased in that of "Laura" and "the laurel." This study of their relationship in his poetry examines the conflicts, metamorphoses, and parallels that entwine the two.

Trinkaus, Charles. *The Poet as Philosopher: Petrarch and the Formation of Renaissance Consciousness.* New Haven, Conn.: Yale University Press, 1979. Trinkaus explores the impact of Petrarch's poetic mentality on his humanistic works and of both on the emergence of the modern concept of self.

Madison U. Sowell;
bibliography updated by Joseph P. Byrne

MARGE PIERCY

Born: Detroit, Michigan; March 31, 1936

PRINCIPAL POETRY

Breaking Camp, 1968
Hard Loving, 1969
Four-Telling, 1971 (with Bob Hershon, Emmett
    Jarrett, and Dick Lourie)
To Be of Use, 1973
Living in the Open, 1976
The Twelve-Spoked Wheel Flashing, 1978
The Moon Is Always Female, 1980
*Circles on the Water: Selected Poems of Marge
    Piercy*, 1982
Stone, Paper, Knife, 1983
My Mother's Body, 1985
Available Light, 1988
Mars and Her Children, 1992
Eight Chambers of the Heart, 1995
What Are Big Girls Made Of?: Poems, 1997
Early Grrrl: The Early Poems of Marge Piercy,
    1999 (also known as *Written in Bone: The
    Early Poems of Marge Piercy*, 1998)
*The Art of Blessing the Day: Poems with a Jewish
    Theme*, 1999

OTHER LITERARY FORMS

Marge Piercy published many novels, which span a
wide range of genres from historical and political to
science fiction and feminist utopian themes. Her fiction
has appeared in an array of periodicals, including *The
Transatlantic Review, Works in Progress*, and the *New
England Review*. Various translations of her work appear
in more than a dozen foreign-language editions. In addition, her poetry was featured on several recordings during the 1970's.

Piercy has experimented with drama as well: *The
Last White Class: A Play About Neighborhood Terror*,
written with Ira Wood, was produced in 1978. Her nonfiction includes a calendar publication, *The Earth Shines
Secretly: A Book of Days* (1990). She has written essays,
has edited an anthology, and has had her own work appear in more than 150 anthologies. She maintains a Web
site devoted to her work and current interests. Her manuscript collection and archives are housed in the University of Michigan Harlan Hatcher Graduate Library.

ACHIEVEMENTS

Marge Piercy's attainments are as numerous as her
publications. She was the first person in her family to attend college and earned a scholarship to the University
of Michigan. As an undergraduate, she won Hopwood
Awards for original student writing, the first for poetry
and fiction in 1956 and the second for poetry the following year. She later received a fellowship to Northwestern
University, where she earned a master's degree. Her poetry was occasionally printed during the 1960's, but she
wrote six novels before finding a publisher who would
accept her work; *Going Down Fast* was her first success.
She was a founding member of the Students for a Democratic Society (SDS) and the North America Congress
on Latin America (NACLA). Piercy has earned numerous literary awards, including a National Endowment
for the Arts award in 1978, the Sheaffer Eaton-PEN
New England Award for Literary Excellence in 1989,
the Arthur C. Clarke Award for best science fiction
novel in the United Kingdom in 1992 and 1993, and the
Shalom Center's Brit ha-Dorot Award in 1992.

BIOGRAPHY

Marge Piercy was born and raised in Detroit, Michigan, and lived with her parents in a working-class neighborhood. Her Welsh father, Robert, repaired heavy machinery for the Westinghouse Corporation. Her mother,
Bert Bernice Bunnin, was the daughter of Jewish immigrants from Russia. Piercy had one sibling, her half-
brother Grant. Piercy was raised in the Jewish tradition
by her grandmother and mother. Her 1999 publication
*The Art of Blessing the Day: Poems with a Jewish
Theme* reflects that connection to her Jewish roots.

Political activism was a part of Piercy's family history. Her maternal grandfather, a labor organizer, was
killed while attempting to unionize bakery workers.
During adolescence, Piercy had a stormy relationship
with her mother, but later said her mother made her a
poet. Storytelling was a part of what Piercy termed her
"family culture." Her Jewish heritage, the poverty of her
childhood, and a bout with German measles and rheu-

matic fever that left her a thin and sickly child, set Piercy apart from other children. In her loneliness, she turned to books and cats. Later, she became an avid storyteller, inventing elaborate action plots that helped her establish relationships with the neighborhood boys during her junior high school years.

After graduation from a Detroit high school, Piercy entered the University of Michigan on an academic scholarship. She performed well scholastically, motivated by her native curiosity and intelligence. Yet she rejected the cultural conformity of the 1950's. Her views on sexuality and politics were outside the social mainstream. Her semiautobiographical novel *Braided Lives* (1982) recounts the conflicts of her 1950's university experience.

Piercy completed a master's degree at Northwestern University in 1958 and later married Michel Schiff, a Jewish physicist. The couple settled in France but later returned to the United States. Eventually they separated, and Piercy moved to Chicago. She held several part-time positions, ranging from secretary to college instructor, began working in the Civil Rights movement, and continued to write. Piercy called those Chicago years the most difficult of her life. Her friends and allies in leftist causes were not supportive of her role as a writer. Publishers rejected her manuscripts for being too radical, too feminist, or too political. In addition, she sought to create what she termed "valid art," a poetic voice authentic to her experience. However, during the 1960's the accepted academic poetry was more elaborate and formal, employing literary allusions far removed from the colloquial style Piercy preferred. Thus, only a few of her poems had been published by 1970.

She married Robert Shapiro in 1962. During the 1960's, Piercy joined the Ann Arbor chapter of Voice, a movement mounting opposition to the Vietnam War. She became a founding member of the Students for a Democratic Society (SDS) and later worked with a leftist organization, the North America Congress on Latin America (NACLA), which researched the activities of the Central Intelligence Agency (CIA) and its connection to other social and political power structures within the United States. However, Piercy did not find support for her writing efforts until she joined the women's movement.

Eventually, the stress of urban living, participation in violent protests, and respiratory complications resulting from Piercy's long-term smoking prompted her relocation to Cape Cod, Massachusetts, in 1970. The move benefited Piercy's health and creativity, but her relationship with Shapiro gradually deteriorated. After their divorce, Piercy married Ira Wood. She and Wood settled in a small cottage in Wellfleet, Massachusetts. The couple founded the Leapfrog Press in 1997, publishing poetry, fiction, and nonfiction. Beginning in the 1990's, they taught writing workshops. Piercy's years on the Cape are responsible for her love for nature and gardening—interests reflected in her poetry. She has supported herself through her writing, poetry readings, and occasional university appointments as a visiting professor or writer in residence.

ANALYSIS

In an interview with Michelle Gerise Godwin, Marge Piercy characterized herself as "blatantly sexual and raunchy"—a "stubborn" and "stupidly persistent" writer who kept creating even when no one seemed to understand her poems and novels. The worldly vision of her poetry encompasses politics, feminism, love, nature, and religion: "I don't really differentiate between writing a

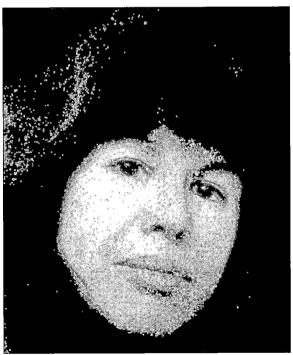

Marge Piercy

love poem or a poem about a blue heron, or a poem about a demonstration or a poem about a Jewish holiday. To me, it's all one vision." Piercy says she exorcises her desire for autobiography in her poetry. Her poetry collections reflect phases of her life beginning in the late 1960's. Her verse mirrors her interest in women, their bodies, social functions, and unrealized potential.

CIRCLES ON THE WATER

Circles on the Water includes poems from Piercy's earlier collections, ranging from the political works in *Breaking Camp* (1968) and *Hard Loving* (1969) to the personal poems contained in *Living in the Open* (1976) and *The Moon Is Always Female* (1980). *Circles on the Water* contains several poems that are often anthologized. Three popular works, "Barbie Doll," "What's That Smell in the Kitchen?," and "A Work of Artifice," ridicule the conventional roles of women in American society. "Barbie Doll" (1969) introduces the "girlchild . . . born as usual" who plays with dolls, lipstick, and miniature household appliances. However, at puberty a classmate says, "You have a big nose and fat legs." The girl must process contradictory messages—to "play coy" but "come on hearty." Piercy characterizes the child's dilemma in the simile "Her good nature wore out/ like a fan belt." The poem ends with unemotional violence. The girl cuts off her offending nose and legs and achieves ultimate perfection in a casket at the undertaker's hand.

In "A Work of Artifice" (1973), Piercy compares women to bonsai trees. The twenty-four lines are clipped short like bonsai branches. Each contains only three to five words. A tree capable of towering eighty feet is pruned to nine inches. The gardener croons, "It is your nature/ to be small and cozy,/ domestic and weak." The last eight lines expand the metaphor to other dwarfed creatures with "bound feet," "crippled" brains, "hair in curlers," and hands "you/ love to touch." Thus, a dominant society of gardeners keeps women in check with their careful pruning.

The comic satire of "What's That Smell in the Kitchen?" (1982) launches a protest against women's domestic lives. The poem opens with a unified objection, "All over America women are burning dinners," and closes with the battle cry, "Burning dinner is not incompetence but war." Again Piercy uses simile to compare life to everyday objects: "Carbonized despair presses like a clinker/ from a barbecue against the back of her eyes." The American housewife is moved by the anger that "sputters in her brainpan." Piercy objects to the ways in which American society has stunted women's potential. These poems assert that women are more than dolls and household accoutrements.

AVAILABLE LIGHT

In the 1988 publication *Available Light*, Piercy in her fifties confronts midlife issues—aging, childhood memory, menopause, and technology. The title poem explores the poet's past and present with the wisdom and experience that come with middle age. At fifty, she declares she knows herself and can forgive her dead parents for what they could not see in life through their limited "light" and knowledge. Piercy classifies as a religious poem "How Divine Is Forgiving," which examines humankind's need to forgive. The collection also includes "Wellfleet Sabbath," a meditative verse set in Piercy's seaside home near Cape Cod. The speaker metaphorically unites the welcoming of the Sabbath with the beauty of nature: "The great doors of the sabbath are swinging/ open over the ocean." At day's end "the Shekinah/ comes on the short strong wings of the seaside/ sparrow." The collection exhibits the reflective dimension of Piercy's poetry.

EARLY GRRRL

Piercy's 1999 publication *Early Grrrl* contains poems previously unpublished. "Grrrl" is a designation adopted by third-generation feminists who use music, film, and "zines" (underground newsletters and publications) to voice their sexuality, humor, and rage. Piercy frequents "grrrl" Web sites and reads their publications. She says she identifies with the term "grrrl" and understands their anger: "I relate to the grrrls of today. . . . We are all trained to feel inferior as girls and as women." One work in the volume, "the well preserved man" (1998), compares the fossilized corpse of a bog man exhumed fully intact (with teeth, toenails, and stomach contents) to a woman rejected. The man was "fed and then killed" perhaps as a sacrifice to a "god or goddess/ for fertility, good weather,/ an end to a plague, who knows?" The contemporary woman, likewise, realizes as she dines with her companion that she is to be "terminated." The speaker confesses, "I could not eat my last meal./ I kept running to the ladies room." She is "Sacrificed/ to a woman with more to offer up." At the close of the poem, the women retreats to her bed as if entering the grave like the bog man, but she endures:

> How astonished I was to survive,
>
> to find I was intact and hungry.
> All that happened was I knew the story
> now and I grew long nails and teeth.

Another *Early Grrrl* poem, "The Name of That Country Is Lonesome" (1998), exposes the growing disconnection of persons who use modern technology to escape human contact: "Who can be bothered with friends?" the speaker asks. Friends have needs, a desire to talk: "Leave the answering machine on." Fear and convenience replace companionship:

> Talk only to the television set.
> It tells you just what to buy
>
> So you won't feel lonely
> any longer, so you won't feel
> inadequate, bored, so you can
> almost imagine yourself alive.

The anxiety of contemporary life drives individuals to sacrifice human warmth for the isolated safety of machinery.

THE ART OF BLESSING THE DAY

In *The Art of Blessing the Day: Poems with a Jewish Theme*, Piercy includes contemplative verse. "Apple Sauce for Eve" portrays the Garden of Eden saga in feminist terms. Women are in search of the world's secrets, the speaker explains, and praises Eve for her thirst for knowledge: "We are all products of that first experiment,/ for if death was the worm in that apple,/ the seeds were freedom and the flowering of choice." Other poems in the collection are more personal. In "Snow-flakes, My Mother Called Them," Piercy describes how her grandmother and mother taught her the art of paper-cuts. The folded paper opened to reveal "intricate birds, trees, . . ./ . . . moons, flowers." The speaker had forgotten the artwork until she received one in a thank you note: "A woman sent me a papercut/ to thank me for a poem, and then/ in my hand I felt a piece of past/ materialize." The poem considers memories of pain and pleasure united in retrospect. Piercy admits her composi-

tions derive from her recollections, visions, and need to communicate. The poems in this collection express Piercy's persistent themes. The direct language and forthright tone of her verse declare her interests in family, marriage, daily life, history, politics, and faith.

OTHER MAJOR WORKS

LONG FICTION: *Going Down Fast*, 1969; *Dance the Eagle to Sleep*, 1970; *Small Changes*, 1973; *Woman on the Edge of Time*, 1976; *The High Cost of Living*, 1978; *Vida*, 1980; *Braided Lives*, 1982; *Fly Away Home*, 1984; *Gone to Soldiers*, 1987; *Summer People*, 1989; *He, She, and It*, 1991; *The Longings of Women*, 1994; *City of Darkness, City of Light*, 1996; *Storm Tide*, 1998 (with Ira Wood); *Three Women*, 1999.

PLAY: *The Last White Class: A Play About Neighborhood Terror*, pr. 1978 (with Ira Wood).

NONFICTION: *Parti-Colored Blocks for a Quilt: Poets on Poetry*, 1982; *The Earth Shines Secretly: A Book of Days*, 1990; *So You Want to Write: How to Master the Craft of Fiction and the Personal Narrative*, 2001 (with Ira Wood); *Sleeping with Cats: A Memoir*, 2002.

EDITED TEXT: *Early Ripening: American Women's Poetry Now*, 1987.

BIBLIOGRAPHY

Godwin, Michelle Gerise. "Marge Piercy." *The Progressive* 65, no. 1 (2001): 27-30. Godwin describes her encounter with Marge Piercy at a poetry reading for the Worcester Women's History Conference. The interview contains the author's impressions as well as Piercy's commentary on her life and work.

Robinson, Lillian S., ed. *Modern Women Writers*. Vol. 3. New York: Continuum, 1996. This reference volume provides an overview of eight critical articles relating to Piercy's works from 1970 to 1985. The entry includes excerpts from essays by Jean Rosenbaum and Margaret Atwood.

Rodden, John. "A Harsh Day's Light: An Interview with Marge Piercy." *The Kenyon Review* 20, no. 2 (1998): 132-143. Rodden recounts his visit to Piercy's home in Wellfleet, Massachusetts. He relates Piercy's conversation about her past and her art, including comments concerning particular works.

Wainer, Nora R. "Women Writers of the Left: Le Sueur, Piercy, and Lessing." *Against the Current* 3, no. 3 (1985): 17-21. Wainer discusses ways in which women writers are noted as feminists and ignored for their politics. Her focus is the radicalism of Piercy's novels *Small Changes*, *Vida*, and *Braided Lives* in conjunction with the themes of Meridel Le Sueur and Doris Lessing.

Walker, Sue, and Eugenia Hamner, eds. *Ways of Knowing: Essays on Marge Piercy.* Mobile: Negative Capability Press, 1992. The collection includes thirteen perceptive essays discussing Piercy's poetry and fiction. An extensive bibliography details the author's publications, and includes comprehensive lists of reviews and critical essays related to Piercy's work.

Paula M. Miller

PINDAR

Born: Cynoscephalae, near Thebes, Boeotia, Greece; c. 518 B.C.E.

Died: Argos, Greece; c. 438 B.C.E.

PRINCIPAL POETRY

Epinikia, 498-446 B.C.E. (*Odes*, 1656)

OTHER LITERARY FORMS

Pindar is remembered only for his poetic achievement.

ACHIEVEMENTS

Pindar's victory odes are among the greatest achievements of ancient Greek poetry, but they are also probably the most consistently misunderstood. Composing in a genre (*epinikion*) and mode (choral lyric poetry) foreign even to later Greek audiences, Pindar stands alone as the chief archaic Greek poet whose works survive in any bulk. The archaic age itself—that period from the time of Homer in the eighth century to the rise of classical literature in fifth century Athens—is relatively obscure. The events, manners, and traditions of the period were not those of later times, so that it is hard to extrapolate from

literary activity at Athens when analyzing the work of Pindar a generation earlier. The additional difficulty of having little to compare with Pindar's work in his own genre (only some poems by his contemporaries Bacchylides and Simonides) means that any assessment of his achievement is necessarily limited. What comparison one can make shows Pindar to have a distinctive style, complex and exciting. So highly compressed is the style, in fact, that the general opinion of Pindaric odes, from antiquity on, can be summed up in the remark of the English poet Abraham Cowley: "If a man should undertake to translate Pindar word for word, it would be thought that one madman had translated another." Yet Cowley is only one among a number of poets who have been fascinated by Pindar, in whom they have found a model for "inspired" verse (Pierre de Ronsard and Friedrich Hölderlin are among the great poets deeply influenced by Pindar). Even Horace, the astute transposer of old Greek lyric verse into Roman poetry, failed to get beyond the fixation on Pindaric style, which later led to Pindar's image as that of a rather wild, raving, "natural" bard:

> Rushing down like a mountain stream
> Which rains have swollen over its known banks,
> Unmeasurable Pindar boils and flows, deep mouth. . . .

Pindar's legacy, then, has little to do with his real achievement. His imitators dwelt on style; divorced from the context and conventions of the poetry, this style is bound to seem odd at best and at worst, incomprehensible. In his own terms, however, Pindar might best be judged by determining whether he has achieved what he set out to do. In that case, he has been a successful composer of *epinikia*, because he has fulfilled the promise that lies behind this genre: He preserves the names and victories (often otherwise unknown) of fifth century aristocrats who desired the prestige of Pindar's poetry to commemorate their participation in the Panhellenic games. Pindar, like the epic poet Homer before him, conferred immortality on heroic deeds, this being the ideology behind his poetry as expressed in *Nemean Ode* 7:

> . . . if a man succeeds in an exploit, he casts
> a delightful theme upon the streams of the Muses
> for great deeds of strength, if they lack songs,
> are sunk in deep obscurity.

BIOGRAPHY

Little is known about Pindar beyond what has been recorded by ancient scholars in elucidating the circumstances of composition for various poems. This produces a sort of lifelong itinerary around the Greek world rather than a clear biography of the poet. Clearly, his life was spent in aristocratic circles. He was born into a socially superior family having connections with the Aegid clan, a far-flung kinship group that included members of the Spartan ruling elite. Ancient tradition records that Pindar went to Athens for schooling in the art of choral poetry; the district of Boeotia was apparently backward in such matters (as Pindar implies, referring to the old insult "Boeotian sow," that his poetry has cast aside). Pindar's first recorded poem, *Pythian Ode* 10, was written when he was about twenty and performed in Thessaly for an aristocratic patron.

Pindar performs his poetry before an audience. (Library of Congress)

Pindar's later life was ruled by this pattern. He traveled throughout the Greek world at the invitation of local tyrants, self-made absolute rulers (not despots, as implied by the modern sense of the word) who were at that time in the process of replacing hereditary kings as the supreme authority in the Greek city-states. They needed the prestige that an internationally known poet such as Pindar could bring to their accomplishments—not only athletic, but military and political as well. Pindar was not the first poet to be patronized by tyrants: The sixth century poet Ibycus and, later, Simonides and Bacchylides also celebrated the deeds of these wealthy and powerful men. All, including Pindar, were certainly paid for their efforts, in money and lavish hospitality.

Pindar would either write a choral ode for his patrons, then oversee its performance, or send a poem with instructions for the accompanying song and dance, while he himself remained in Thebes. Pindar seems, at times, to have accompanied the victor from the games to his hometown, where the ode would then be performed at festival occasions. It is even possible that a few odes were actually composed extempore at the games. These compositions survive, it appears, because the aristocratic patron families handed down manuscripts as treasured heirlooms. The Alexandrian scholars Zenodotus and Aristophanes helped to collect Pindar's poetry in the third century B.C.E.

Further, acquaintance with one aristocratic family often led to commissions from others. Thus, after celebrating the victory of Xenocrates at Delphi in 490 B.C.E., Pindar became known to the family and, in 476 B.C.E., was invited to compose *epinikia* for Xenocrates' brother Theron and for Hieron, another tyrant, in Sicily. In such a fashion, Pindar's patrons came to include aristocrats in Sparta, Rhodes, Corinth, Cyrene, and Athens. His international reputation is reflected in the geographical distribution of the *epinikia:* Only five of the surviving forty-five poems are addressed to victors from Pindar's home state of Thebes; fifteen are for Sicilians and eleven for victors from the island of Aegina, for which Pindar had a special affection.

The patron-poet bond, however, based as it was on traditional Panhellenic codes of behavior, led to conflicts for Pindar when the political situation during the years of the Persian invasions of 490 B.C.E. and 480

B.C.E. polarized the Greek city-states. Pindar tended to identify his patrons' families with their homelands. In praising Athens, then, as he did in *Nemean Ode 2*, the poet risked offending the citizens of Aegina, with whom Athens was at war during the decade after Marathon in 490 B.C.E. Similarly, his continuing affirmations of support for the Theban oligarchy, even when it joined with the Persians against most of the other Greek states, posed problems of loyalty. Nevertheless Pindar, in most instances, was able to reconcile his conflicting affiliations by an appeal to the common Greek ideals and myths; references to both occur frequently in the *epinikia*. Once, however, shortly after the Persians were repulsed, the jealous rivalry between Thebes and Athens did affect Pindar, resulting in the levy of a heavy fine on the poet by the Thebans after he praised Athens in a dithyramb, calling it "defense of Greece, Athens renowned, divine citadel," and recalling the Athenian naval victory over the Persians at Salamis in 480 B.C.E.

Although Pindar fascinates historians because of the unusual perspectives he offers on the turbulent events of the fifth century B.C.E., to look to his poetry for reasoned historical judgments would be as much in vain as it would be to seek therein a coherent picture of his life. His poetry was not meant to be either biography or chronicle, but rather a celebration of a series of victorious moments, which, by their semisacred nature, move personal and political history into the background.

ANALYSIS

Of the seventeen books representing Pindar's vast production in a variety of poetic genres, only four books of one genre, the victory odes (*epinikia*), survived antiquity intact. These odes are named for the periodic Panhellenic festival games held at Olympia (the Olympian odes), Delphi (the Pythian odes), Nemea (Nemeans), and Corinth (Isthmians).

FRAGMENTS

The remaining books of Pindar survive as several hundred fragments, some of them only a line long. As was usual in Greek archaic poetry, his compositions were most often meant for public performance, and the now lost books were arranged by third century B.C.E. editors according to the social occasions for which the poems were written: *encomia* (praise poems), *threnoi*

(dirges), hymns, *paians* (hymns to Apollo), dithyrambs (to Dionysus), *hyporchemata* (dance songs), *parthenia* (maiden songs), and *prosodia* (processionals). While the modern reader might regret the loss of the huge mass of verse Pindar wrote, the fragments of these other genres make it clear that the Pindaric style known from the *epinikia* is representative of his works as a whole.

THE GREEK GAMES

To understand the *epinikia* requires an appreciation of both their occasional nature and the nature of those occasions for which they were written. The most prestigious games—Olympian, Pythian, Nemean, and Isthmian—occurred at regular intervals and united the independent Greek city-states as few other traditions, with the exception of Homeric poetry, could. So important were these Panhellenic athletic and musical contests that a sacred truce prevailed whenever they were held. To their local communities, victors became heroes; although their immediate reward at the games consisted only of a wreath of laurel leaves, their later perquisites very often included free meals at public expense, statues, coins with their imprint, and inscriptions. In this context, poetry was yet another reward for victory.

In many ways, Pindar's odes mimic the rituals they celebrate. For example, just as a sacred herald would proclaim the victor, the event won, the city and father of the winner in footraces, wrestling, boxing, pancratium, pentathlon, or chariot, horse, or mule races, so Pindar was obliged to include these details in the program of his poem for the victor. The *epinikia* are thus amplified announcements of the event. Pindar, on the other hand, also associates himself with the athletic victor and the poem with a feat of skill (in Pindar, *sophia*, "skill," is used with respect to both poetry and other forms of wisdom, including the knowledge which trainers impart to athletes): "Let someone dig me a wide jumping pit . . . there's a spring in my knees," exclaims the poet as he embarks on one song of praise. This extended metaphor implies that the victory provides an opportunity for Pindar to compete in performance with the victor, as he attempts to produce a poem as perfect as the feat that it commemorates.

ODES AS PERFORMANCE ART

Performance was central to the *epinikia*, so that the text of each poem in fact represents only a third of Pindar's work. That each poem was sung and danced by a trained chorus explains much about the form of the compositions: usually a repeated series of strophe, antistrophe, and epode, representing dance instructions (literally, "turn," "counterturn," and "added song"—all performed while standing in place). Gestures probably highlighted the often tersely narrated myths which Pindar employs. Perhaps most important, the poet could use the chorus, as in Greek tragedy, to reflect upon the greater implications of the hero's victory for the city-state, which the chorus personifies. Since archaic Greek ethical thought constantly reminds one that wealth, good fortune, and all types of victory are threatened by jealous gods (as one author writes, "The tallest trees are struck by lightning"), the danger of the victor's newly acquired status must be kept before his eyes by his lesser fellow citizens, the chorus: Again, as in Greek tragedy, the chorus warns. Finally, the presence of the chorus means that the "I" which appears commonly in the *epinikia* should not be taken as equivalent to the poetic self. It is more often a sort of shorthand for the opinion of the chorus; it can also simply be a device for making transitions within the poem, from praise to narrative myth to gnomic utterances, as will be illustrated shortly.

RITUAL FUNCTION OF THE ODES

Thus, the ode both incorporates the heroic athlete into the community (by warning of excess in good fortune) and distances him from it (by praise). In Pindar's hands, the poetry of victory also integrates the past with the present, as the poet draws on local mythological examples in comparing the celebrated athlete with the city-state's earlier heroic figures. Again, both praise and warning are served by the myth: The victor is like Achilles or Heracles or Pelops, Pindar says; he should avoid being like Ixion or the ungrateful Tantalus. In this, Pindar's use of myths, though idiosyncratic and innovative in details that he considers sacrilegious, fairly represents the outlook of much archaic Greek poetry from Homer on; it is conventional and traditional. As Frank Nisetich explains in *Pindar's Victory Songs*, "to see the general behind the particular, to grasp one thing by contrast with its opposite, to trace human vicissitudes to the will of the gods and explain, appreciate, or find the right response to a present situation through reference to myth or proverb"—these purposes represent the dominant forms of style in archaic poetry; they are certainly Pindar's.

PYTHIAN ODE 10

In his earliest surviving *epinikion*, Pindar constructs the poem in the manner in which he will become adept: Praise of a victor precedes and follows a mythical narrative, which is in some way related to his topic. In *Pythian Ode* 10 (498 B.C.E.), the victor Hippokleas has won a race for boys: Both his name and the event are mentioned in the first series of strophe-antistrophe epode. The poem begins, however, with a bit of complex mythological genealogy, in the fashion Pindar sometimes follows: "Lacedaemon is happy, Thessaly is blest; both have their kings descended from one father, Heracles. . . ." This reference to the kinship bonds of Spartan and Thessalian royal houses ends suddenly, with a transition question in the first person, another Pindaric device: "Why am I declaiming in this way?" Pindar answers that he was commissioned to write; yet he includes Pytho (that is, Delphi, home of Apollo's sacred shrine and site of the Pythian games) as his inspiration. The appearance of spontaneity is important to Pindar, and he often downplays, as here, the more mercantile aspects of his craft in favor of the almost mystical lure of the games and their ideals and the effect victory has on him, compelling his praises.

In the first counterturn of this ode, Pindar typically uses a gnomic statement to direct attention to a new topic—in this case, from the victor to the victor's father. The statement here acknowledges the role of the gods in bringing human deeds to fulfillment; with them, the victor's father "has found all the happiness our mortal race can come to." A contrast immediately follows: the happy race which mortals cannot reach, the mythical Hyperboreans, who live (as their name denotes) beyond the North Wind, feasting and singing continually, freed from the fear of death. Pindar works his way into describing them by reference to the Gorgon slayer, Perseus, who is said to have dined with this race. Is this relevant? Contemporary notions of a poem's unity would probably reject the detail; here, the aesthetics of archaic Greek poetry differ. In social context, Perseus's myth is exactly right for the occasion, since he was the great-grandfather of Heracles, the mythical progenitor of the very family Pindar is praising (and of the rulers of Sparta, mentioned earlier). Poetically, Perseus fills the role of the praiseworthy athlete, corresponding to his descendant in real life. As the victor has returned from Delphi northward to his Thessalian home, so Perseus, in the myth, once moved north to the celebrations of the immortal race; Pindar makes the comparison implicit and complimentary. The poem's conclusion contains more praise, this time of Hippokleas's beauty; a warning ("there is no telling what will be a year from now"); and an affirmation of the social bond between patron and poet, expressed in athletic imagery (the patron Thorax has "yoked the chariot of the Muses").

Already in *Pythian Ode* 10, the imagery is Pindaric by being animated—that is, a static image (counterturn two: one cannot reach the Hyperboreans on a *ship*) becomes part of the "piloting" of the poem by Pindar: "Stay the oar now," says the poet as he steers clear of a digression in the third epode. The poem, after being a ship, immediately becomes a bee, digressively flitting; his song is honey, the poet says; then the poem is a chariot; finally, the ship image returns at the end of the poem, when Pindar praises Thorax's brothers: "In their hands belongs the piloting of cities. . . ."

OLYMPIAN ODE 1

A highly developed, rapidly shifting scheme of imagery is characteristic of Pindar. *Olympian Ode* 1 (476 B.C.E.), one of his finest and most difficult compositions, shows the technique in abundance, illustrating how Pindar can redouble the messages of gnomic utterance and myth by the way in which he chooses and structures images. Consider, for example, the constellation of images which opens the poem in symphonic fashion:

> Water is preeminent and gold, like a fire
> burning in the night, outshines all possessions
> that magnify men's pride. But if, my soul,
> you yearn to celebrate great games,
> look no further for another star shining
> through the deserted ether brighter than the sun,
> or for a contest mightier than Olympia. . . .

Water and fire will recur in the myth that Pindar proceeds to tell (how Pelops was allegedly cut and boiled in a pot); gold and the sun echo each other within this passage, as primary elements, one by day, one by night. Beyond this, however, the arrangement of images is itself a contest: Pindar names the "victor" substances in each sphere, and the contest of Olympia wins. There are few

more exciting collocations of imagery that enacts its subject.

Mention of the Olympian victor (Hieron), his horse, and his kingly status brings Pindar shortly to tell of "Pelops's land"—Olympia itself—and thus of the myth of Pelops. Here one notes a characteristically Pindaric way of retelling the old story: He claims that the received version is wrong, that the gods could never have chopped up the boy and consumed him; this, says Pindar, is a myth concocted by jealous neighbors upon the boy's disappearance to become cup-bearer of Zeus, a great favor to the boy's family. Pindar typically does not tell the story in straightforward manner, even when not revising the myth; here he also backtracks to tell of the misfortunes of Tantalus, Pelops's father, which caused Pelops to be cast out of Olympus, the home of Zeus, back into the world of men. Then Pindar leaps ahead to Pelops's marriage to Hippodameia; as in *Pythian Ode* 10, the young hero of myth, striving against obscurity, becomes an ideal image of the young athlete-king for whom the poem is performed. As Pelops won a chariot race to win his bride, so Hieron wins fame by victory in a horse race.

Finally, Pindar ends *Olympian Ode* 1 with another redoubling of imagery within the poem: Pelops had prayed to Poseidon to win the strength for a victory; thus, in conclusion, Pindar prays for a double boon (again, victor and poet are united): that Hieron win another victory with the gods' favor, and that he himself "consort with victors, conspicuous for my skill among Greeks everywhere." This is indicative of growing confidence in his art.

PYTHIAN ODE 8

Pindar's last datable poem, *Pythian Ode* 8 (446 B.C.E.), shows the effects of controlled compression of myth, in a format reminiscent of the ending of *Olympian Ode* 1; this time, the entire poem is a prayer. It opens with an address to *Hesychia* (Peace); at turn four, Pindar prays to Apollo to help in the singing of the song; next, the gods in general are invoked to "look with unjealous eyes" upon the fortunes of the victor's father (again, the warning motif occurs); finally, the poem ends with invocations of Aegina, the nymph who gave her name to the island home of the victor, and to Zeus and several heroes of the city-state, that they guide the island's fate. Evident here is a significant aspect of Pindar's mature art. The myth itself is expressed in direct quotation of a mythical figure: Amphiarus, a prophet and soldier, is given oracular words of wise counsel, ostensibly to the second wave of invaders against Thebes (his son among them), but clearly intended to remind the athletic victor of aristocratic ideals. The prophet is quoted as saying that "the spirit of the fathers lives in their sons"; Pindar himself has often said the same thing, but here he makes it more dramatic by placing the sentiment in a hero's mouth.

Pythian Ode 8, represents the most concise statement of Pindar's ideas on his own art, while at the same time showing him distancing himself from the moralizing maxims inherent in the genre. Thus, he claims, after narrating the Amphiarus myth, to have actually met the hero's son, Alcman, and to have received a true prophecy from him. Pindar says elsewhere, in a poetic fragment, that he is "prophet of the Muses"; here he dramatizes that status. Because he can foretell the future, he can make the victor fly ahead into that time on the "wings of devising." In the end, he foresees that his poetic/athletic ideal—for it is one notion—will survive. The expression of his confidence can serve as the capstone to Pindar's lifework: "What is someone? What is no one? Man: A shadow's dream. But when god-given glory comes, a bright light shines upon us and our life is sweet...."

BIBLIOGRAPHY

Carne-Ross, D. S. *Pindar.* New Haven, Conn.: Yale University Press, 1985. A critical treatment of a dozen victory odes, for the general reader with no knowledge of Greek.

Crotty, Kevin. *Song and Action: The Victory Odes of Pindar.* Baltimore, Md.: The Johns Hopkins University Press, 1982. Studies the genre of the victory ode as a subject and form, and Pindar as a poet of genius working within a traditional genre.

Fitzgerald, William. *Agonistic Poetry: The Pindaric Mode in Pindar, Horace, Hoelderlin, and the English Ode.* Berkeley: University of California Press, 1987. Examines Pindar's poetry and its reception as a study in comparative literature.

Kurke, Leslie. *The Traffic in Praise: Pindar and the Politics of Social Economy.* Ithaca, N.Y.: Cornell University Press, 1991. Wrestling with the broad question, what is value?, Kurke studies the poems in terms of their social dimensions: the influences of the society on the poetry.

Mullen, William. *Choreia: Pindar and Dance.* Princeton, N.J.: Princeton University Press, 1982. Explores both direct and indirect relationships of Pindar's poems to contemporary communal dance as expression.

Nagy, Gregory. *Pindar's Homer: Lyric Possession of an Epic Past.* Baltimore, Md.: The Johns Hopkins University Press, 1990. Pindar's work is a centerpiece in this detailed study of allusion in form and content in late archaic lyric poetry.

Newman, John K., and Frances Stickney Newman. *Pindar's Art: Its Tradition and Aims.* Munich: Weidmann, 1984. After a review of major interpreters, the Newmans provide a close and technical study of the vocabulary and structure of Pindar's poems, especially his use of repetition and elements of the comic.

Race, William H. *Pindar.* Boston: Twayne, 1986. A brief biography and overview of the major and minor works of Pindar for the general reader.

_____. *Style and Rhetoric in Pindar's Odes.* Atlanta, Ga.: Scholars Press, 1990. A technical study of the rhetorical aspects and elements of the odes, and the purposes for Pindar's uses of them.

Rutherford, Ian. *Pindar's Paeans: A Reading of the Fragments with a Survey of the Genre.* New York: Oxford University Press, 2001. The paean, or sacred hymn to Apollo, had a central place in the song-dance culture of classical Greece. The most celebrated examples of the genre in antiquity were Pindar's paeans. These became known to twentieth century scholars thanks to the discovery of papyrus fragments. Rutherford offers a comprehensive reevaluation of the poems. It includes the Greek text and translation of all the paeans of Pindar with a supplement comprising fragments from poems of uncertain genres. Ian Rutherford accompanies each fragment with an interpretation regarding issues of religion, performance, and genre.

Richard Peter Martin;
bibliography updated by Joseph P. Byrne

Robert Pinsky

Born: Long Branch, New Jersey; October 20, 1940

Principal poetry
Sadness and Happiness, 1975
An Explanation of America, 1979
History of My Heart, 1984
The Want Bone, 1990
*The Figured Wheel: New and Collected Poems,
  1966-1996*, 1996
Jersey Rain, 2000

Other literary forms

Mindwheel (1984) is a kind of metanovel: an interactive electronic computer game in the form of a novel. Robert Pinsky has also written two volumes poetry criticism: *The Situation of Poetry* (1976) and *Poetry and the World* (1988). He has translated *The Separate Notebooks*, by Czesław Miłosc (1983), and *The Inferno of Dante* (1994). *The Sounds of Poetry* (1998) helps readers and other poets understand and appreciate the acoustic dimension of poetry.

Achievements

Robert Pinsky has won many literary and academic awards, including Woodrow Wilson fellowships in 1962 and 1966 and a Fulbright Award in 1965, a year he also won the Stegner Fellowship in Poetry. The National Endowment for the Humanities awarded him a fellowship in 1974, and in 1979 he won the Oscar Blumenthal Prize for Poetry. In 1980 he won three significant awards: the American Academy and Institute of Arts and Letters Award, the Saxifrage Prize, and a Guggenheim Foundation Fellowship. In 1984 he garnered a National Endowment for the Arts Fellowship, and in 1985 he won the William Carlos Williams Prize, which is awarded by the Poetry Society of America. In 1988 he was a nominee for the National Book Critics Circle Award in Criticism. His Dante translation received the *Los Angeles Times* Book Prize and the Harold Morton Landon Translation Award. *The Figured Wheel* won the 1997 Lenore Marshall Poetry Prize and was a Pulitzer Prize nominee. He also received the Shelley Memorial Award from the Po-

etry Society of America. Pinsky served as poet laureate of the United States for three years beginning in 1997. In that year he was elected to the American Academy of Arts and Sciences.

Biography

Robert Pinsky was born in 1940, in the coastal town of Long Branch, New Jersey, a locale that figures prominently in many of his nostalgic and autobiographical poems. Pinsky completed his undergraduate studies at Rutgers University, then moved to the West Coast to undertake graduate studies at Stanford University, where he came under the powerful influence of the critic and poet Yvor Winters. After taking a Ph.D. in English at Stanford, Pinsky taught at Wellesley College for several years before becoming a faculty member at the University of California at Berkeley and later at Boston University in the graduate creative writing program. From 1979 to 1986 he was poetry editor for *The New Republic*. After his tenure as Poet Laureate of the United States ended in 1997, Pinsky became poetry editor for the Internet magazine *Slate*.

Analysis

Like many of the creative writers in the second half of the twentieth century, Robert Pinsky is closely identified with a university and may be accurately described as a major poet-critic. As a graduate student, Pinsky was charmed and influenced profoundly by the work of Yvor Winters, one of the most important poet-critics of the twentieth century and a man who is memorialized as the "old Man" in Pinsky's long poem "Essay on Psychiatrists," which appears in his first volume of poetry, *Sadness and Happiness*. From Winters, Pinsky learned the virtues of clarity in thought and diction as well as a rigorous attention to poetic meter and other details of craftsmanship. Even in the freest of his free verse, the reader will detect no slackness or raggedy edges in the lines of Robert Pinsky: a quiet elegance and reassuring feeling of control seem to guide all of his poetic compositions.

Under the influence of Winters, Pinsky developed a fondness for certain poets such as Fulke Greville, Robert Herrick, Thomas Hardy, Robert Bridges, and Wallace Stevens. While at Stanford, Pinsky became especially interested in the nineteenth century English Romantic poets, an enthusiasm that resulted in a dissertation on the work of Walter Savage Landor and a lifelong passion for the great odes of John Keats. Pinsky's first published work, in fact, was not a book of poetry but his dissertation on Landor, which appeared under the title *Landor's Poetry* (1968). In that work, Pinsky began to sketch out the architecture of his critical beliefs, key ideas that would be fully examined in his two other important books of criticism: *The Situation of Poetry* and *Poetry and the World*.

To some extent, all of Pinsky's critical theories trace their roots to his close reading and analysis of Landor's poetry. Pinsky develops the notion that all great poetry (classical, modern, or contemporary) possesses three unmistakable characteristics: the expression of universal sentiments (love and death, for example), the use of history, and the use of mythology, not merely as decoration but as a true archetype or universal symbol (as in the work of Carl Jung).

In *The Situation of Poetry*, Pinsky began to refine and clarify his critical thinking, a process that undoubtedly contributed to the growth of his poetic craftsmanship. Pinsky began to move toward statements that suggest the

Robert Pinsky

social responsibilities of poetry and the necessity of having poetry that is humanly comprehensible, with real people and real ideas at its center. That general theory does not imply the desirability of a simplistic or merely didactic kind of poetry, but Pinsky does insist that poetry have a human center and that relationships, memory, and personal experience become the touchstones of this kind of poetry. Too much modern poetry, he believes, is unnecessarily pretentious, intent on creating a cool, non-involved attitude. This kind of poetry is the sort that comes from creative writing programs and writing workshops at their worst, a sort of ready-made poetry that relies on superficial effects such as surrealism without making important statements. For that reason, famous poets such as Charles Simic and May Swenson fall short of the mark, in Pinsky's estimation. He admires a poetry that does not shrink from making abstract statements about life, a poetry that relies heavily on discursive statement, proportion (in thought and formal arrangement), and naturalness (appropriateness of language).

At first sight, Pinsky seems to be a reductionist, wanting to weed out any poets who do not fit his tidy definition. Actually, his program is generous and expansive, more in keeping with the spirit of two great American poets who also lived in the state of New Jersey, Walt Whitman and William Carlos Williams. What Pinsky wants, finally, is a poetry firmly based in human experience, as he explains in a chapter titled "Conventions of Wonder": "The poem, new or old, should be able to help us, if only to help us by delivering the relief that something has been understood, or even seen, well." Poetry, then, is the ultimate form of knowledge, and for Pinsky himself that knowledge will come through poems about his father, his daughter, and his hometown. Personal poems are the key to universal poetry in this view, and for that reason Pinsky is particularly impressed by the poetry of John Keats, Wallace Stevens, T. S. Eliot, Robert Creeley, A. R. Ammons, Frank O'Hara, Louise Bogan, and, to a lesser degree, Sylvia Plath and John Ashbery. Bad poets are those who show marks of insincerity, or of self-conscious flaunting of an adopted poetic identity or persona. Their verse sounds like an echo of the English literature classroom; among them would be poets such as Robert Lowell, Theodore Roethke, and John Berryman.

These heterogeneous groupings of good and bad poets suggest that Pinsky is a complex thinker, and that his distinctions depend upon the ultimate effect of poems rather than upon their particular verse forms or metrical patterns. What the poet has to say about human experience counts more in the long run than how it is said. This complex grouping also prepares the reader for Pinsky's third book of poetry criticism, *Poetry and the World*, an especially well-written critical analysis in which a kind of wholeness or inclusiveness becomes the sought-after ideal, a goal that incorporates all the varieties of Pinsky's taste (from Keats to Creeley). Pinsky's admiration for the poet Elizabeth Bishop is based on the duality of her approach, her ability to remain in the world and yet simultaneously transcend it. Pinsky admires Robert Frost, William Carlos Williams, Jean Toomer, Philip Levine, and John Ashbery because they are also in and out of the everyday material world in their poetry. Also, they use a kind of metalanguage or "heteroglossia"—that is, a contrasting mixture of ordinary Anglo-Saxon or American speech and Latinate words or exotic diction. Their poetry results in a realistic complexity that mirrors the actual way Americans speak and think at representative points during the twentieth century.

SADNESS AND HAPPINESS

The first poem of Pinsky's *Sadness and Happiness* serves as a kind of illustration of his desire to espouse a human-centered poetry and proves that Pinsky is the rarest of all critics: one who actually practices what he preaches. That opening poem, significantly titled "Poem About People," offers the reader a catalog of ordinary American types, such as gray-haired women in sneakers, buying their weekly supply of soda pop, beefsteaks, ice cream, melons, and soap at the local supermarket, and young male workers in green work pants and white T-shirts that cannot conceal bulging beer bellies. Between all these types there is a gulf of emptiness, the realm of dark spaces that can be filled only with love and tenderness, a recognition that in spite of unlovable aspects each human being absolutely requires love. This poem makes a great pronouncement on the need for compassion in all human undertakings (one of Pinsky's consistent themes), for without this compassion life would be intolerable. It is also unthinkable that human beings could, indeed, be human without the potential for com-

passion and love to fill the dark spaces that surround them. That love may be impossible to attain for some, but it is the fundamentally unifying dream of the human spirit. It is significant that the poem unifies all the contrary states of human life, which is why Pinsky includes Nazi and Jewish elements in the poem and why Pinsky, himself a product of Jewish tradition, wishes "to feel briefly like Jesus."

This theme of human compassion can be expressed on the most elemental plane as well. The poet need not feel cosmic love for the human race but merely a sympathetic appreciation for the tedium and occasional boredom inherent in the ordinary passage of time, what the church fathers during the medieval age called *taedium vitae*. In "Waiting," Pinsky composes a kind of minimalist poem that takes the form of a list or string of images (air, a rake handle, the stone of a peach, a dirty Band-Aid, junk in a garage) that become odd little markers of time slipping by, things unimportant in themselves but remembered simply because they create the texture of life as it is lived. These inconsequential minutiae help to create a sense of expectancy, a quickening desire for something better in life.

Perhaps that lack of fulfillment explains why the poet symbolizes this inescapable tedium in the act of watching trains go by, a kind of hypnotic involvement that goes on and on without any great conclusion—a fitting symbol for the everyday, the quotidian. Finally, by beginning and ending the poem with this image of watching trains, the poet suggests a kind of circular entrapment, as if human life can be summarized in this sad but touching gesture. What keeps the poem above the plane of triviality on the one hand and cynicism on the other is Pinsky's careful handling of the tone, which is unvaryingly compassionate without ever descending to pity or sarcasm.

In the title poem of this volume, "Sadness and Happiness," Pinsky meditates on the great mood swings that define the human condition, the fundamental peaks and valleys of the human emotional condition, beginning with another image of unfulfilled desire, this time symbolized not by watching a train but by shopping for a new house. Pinsky opens this long poem (of thirteen parts) with the image of a short-changed American family visiting model homes every Sunday in a futile and desperate attempt to realize their impossible dream. Then he shifts abruptly to a sexual image of *post coitum triste* (or depression after love) to suggest sadness and happiness in a more immediate and personal way. In fact, his successes and failures as a lover and poet become one of the major themes in the poem. He admits that his primary problem is a comic-tragic self-awareness, a kind of egotism that makes him see himself as a star of the film of his life, in which he is grotesquely transformed into medieval knight, blues singer, and jazz musician. The comic absurdity of all these roles, including the additional one of Petrarchan love poet, makes him confess his shame and pride. There is a grotesque quality, after all, about a film star, "tripping over his lance, quill, phallic/ symbol or saxophone." Later in the poem, this same line of imagery returns when he sees himself (again comically) as a kind of "Jewish-American Shakespeare"—or even Longfellow. Perhaps another role he might play is that of the worn-out old jazz musician whose outpourings consist no longer of melodious notes but of repugnant phlegm and vomit, caused by excessive consumption of cheap wine and gin. Yet as the poem draws to its conclusion, Pinsky becomes lyrical and serious, noting that somehow his eyes have learned to have visionary experiences, to see beyond the here and now, to appreciate and feel gratitude for the unmediated beauty of young women and even small triumphs such as the perfect home run he hit during a sandlot game (an image that has stayed with him ever since it occurred).

Sadness and happiness, then, are always juxtaposed in this unpredictable drama called human life, and they can take on unusual dimensions, as when "Sadness and Happiness" becomes the name of a bedtime game Pinsky, the loving father, plays with his young daughters, who must tell him one happy and one sad thing that occurred on that particular day. In so doing, they are like the poet and the artist because they are organizing life itself—the most difficult and the most rewarding of all accomplishments.

The final sections of *Sadness and Happiness*, titled "The Street of Furthest Memory" and "Essay on Psychiatrists," constitute some of Pinsky's most important writing. In the poems that make up these subsections of the larger book, he offers some of his truest observations about his life as a poet, exploring all the roots of his being, adopting a manner that is clinically precise but tenderly nostalgic and touchingly autobiographical. In ef-

fect, these sections could be seen as touchstones of his own poetic theories, proofs of a very special kind that poetry can be abstract and personal, rational and emotional, all at the same time.

Perhaps the key to achieving this marvelous yoking of private and public sentiments is the recognition of place and hometown in American life. Within a country as mobile and shifting as the United States, a sense of roots becomes a precious tool for aesthetic and personal introspection. To be denied roots is to be denied identity, as the writer Alex Haley demonstrated in his great saga *Roots* (1976).

LONG BRANCH POEMS

For Pinsky the locus of all the deep emotions summed up by the term "nostalgia" is the community of Long Branch, New Jersey, a seaside settlement with resemblances to the more famous Atlantic City (decaying neighborhoods, ethnic enclaves, and dilapidated boardwalks along the beach). In "Salt Water," a splendid nostalgic essay that Pinsky tellingly includes with the critical essays in *Poetry and the World*, he describes Long Branch as a place famous for having been visited by Abraham Lincoln and painted by Winslow Homer, and also celebrated for having produced the renowned literary critic M. H. Abrams and the controversial novelist-essayist Norman Mailer. Yet Long Branch is also the location of cheap bars and honky-tonks, burned buildings, junkyards, and various underworld hideaways, including one used by mobster Vito Genovese.

For Pinsky, it is the private, personalized history of Long Branch that matters most, a complicated narrative web made of countless strands and details, such as the details in the poem "To My Father." Pinsky's father, Milford, was an optician, and his shop is evoked by such details as glass dust, broken spectacles, and lenses in every possible dimension and shape, all in the service of showing Pinsky's filial affection. "To My Father" occurs in an earlier section of the book ("Persons"), suggesting how pervasive and obsessive these images are for the poet. "The Street of Furthest Memory," which is the title poem of the Long Branch section, fills in more of the details, offering a panorama of tar-paper shacks, cheap luncheonettes, awnings flapping in the rain—images that somehow are still filled with sweetness for the poet because they are endowed with the wonder of childhood, in much the same way as William Wordsworth endowed the Lake District of England with all his sense of childhood enthusiasm.

In "Pleasure Pier" Pinsky is transported to the arcades and carnival atmosphere of his boyhood, the fake Oriental facades, the pinball machines, the boat ride, the Fun House, and the imaginary scene in which he dies dramatically, having rescued the girl of his dreams from flames that even in retrospect feel all too real. Another imaginative reconstruction occurs in "The Destruction of Long Branch," in which the poet imagines himself burying the Long Branch of his numinous childhood under miles and miles of artificial turf rather than have it buried under the squalor and decay that seem to be its inexorable fate.

The last of the Long Branch poems, and one of the most successful, is "The Beach Women," a work that perfectly captures the mores of the 1950's with references to best-selling books by John O'Hara, Herman Wouk, and Grace Metalious and allusions to cultural icons such as oval sunglasses, *Time* magazine, sweatshirts, and floppy dungarees. The poem creates a focal point on the beach where rich women come to pick up their young lovers, while young Bob Pinsky, clerking at the drugstore, admires their tanned bodies and painted nails and is reduced to selling them

— Perfume and lipstick, aspirins, throat lozenges and Tums,
   Tampax, newspapers and paperback books—brave stays
   Against boredom, discomfort, death and old age.

Sadness and Happiness concludes with one of Pinsky's most quoted and celebrated works, a long twenty-one-part poem called "Essay on Psychiatrists," in which the word "essay" is employed in its eighteenth century sense of the discursive treatment of a subject. Pinsky offers no plodding essay in prose form to the reader but, rather, a series of twenty-one closely interlocking poems that deal with the role of therapy in the modern world, the history of madness, the role of logic and reason, and the theories of Pinsky's mentor, Yvor Winters. The poem shifts in mood from serious to whimsical and back again, always offering Pinsky's sharp insights on the human condition. In section VII, "Historical (*The Bacchae*)," Pinsky treats the idea of madness and loss of control in the context of Greek mythology. He firmly

connects the myth to the realities of modern life, including a group of actors in Cambridge, Massachusetts, who perform the ancient play of Euripides in which the worshipers of Bacchus are whipped into an insane frenzy and tear limbs from living creatures. In the midst of the sea of chaos stands the figure of Pentheus, a rock of stability, whom Pinsky admires for "reason . . . good sense and reflective dignity." It is clear that Pentheus serves here as a tidy summation of Pinsky's personal and aesthetic ideals. Pinsky later dismisses many of the patients of psychiatrists in a rather whimsical way because they miss the seriousness of the whole enterprise, primarily because they view psychiatry as another consumer product, a small part of trendy lives fashioned around Ann Landers, designer glassware, and Marimekko drapes.

Later in the poem Pinsky quotes his literary idol Walter Savage Landor, who once undertook an imaginary conversation with Fulke Greville and Sir Philip Sidney, great thinkers whom Pinsky regards as his own psychiatrists because they taught him that truth never appears in a pure or undiluted form. In this recognition, the poet believes, lies his own sanity.

In section XX, "Peroration, Concerning Genius," Pinsky offers a brilliant and moving portrait of his pipe-smoking mentor, Yvor Winters, delivering a magnificent lecture on madness in English poetry. Winters expounds on his theory that around the middle of the eighteenth century, at the same time as the rise of capitalism and the scientific method, the logical underpinnings of Western intellectual life collapsed. The result was catastrophic for the practice of poetry, because poets were still on the scene, and they were filled "With emotions and experiences, and no way/ To examine them. At this time, poets and men/ Of genius began to go mad." A list of madmen follows, including such notables as the poets Thomas Gray, William Collins, Christopher Smart, William Blake, and Samuel Taylor Coleridge, and their modern counterparts, Hart Crane and Ezra Pound. This passage is one of the revealing moments in Pinsky's published writing because it offers the formative conditions and catalysts for his own work—his desire to escape the crudeness of capitalism and science, while insisting on logic and reason as ways of warding off the great wave of madness that tends to overwhelm any poet working in the post-industrial age. Like his mentor, Pinsky believes that only wisdom can arm the poet against attacks of madness. Temporary, faddish, or clever speech is not enough; one needs the highest forms of poetry to survive this onslaught, because poetry, finally, offers truth.

AN EXPLANATION OF AMERICA

In *An Explanation of America*, Pinsky addresses his daughter, using her as a focal point for his meditations on American culture and social history in much the same way that he used his father and the town of Long Branch to anchor his thoughts about growing up and discovering one's identifying roots. *An Explanation of America*, despite its somewhat grandiose title, is in fact a collection of a dozen poems, three groups of four, each group with a proper subtitle. In part 1, "Its Many Fragments," Pinsky is at his most personal, writing persuasively and passionately about his daughter, her habits, and her idiosyncrasies. For example, she chooses the *nom de plume* Karen Owens and under this disguise reveals her innermost thoughts about childhood in an "Essay On Kids." In games she does not choose the conventionally desirable parts such as Mother or Princess but prefers instead to be cast as Bad Guy, Clown, or Dragon. Although talkative, and good at spelling, she exhibits a somewhat wobbly penmanship: "you cannot form two letters/ Alike or on a line." Besides, she still sucks her thumb. Like any doting father, however, he loves her for her gazing eyes full of "liberty and independence."

Liberty and independence are highly resonant words in the vocabulary of patriotism, but Pinsky bewails what Americans have made of those patriotic opportunities in "From the Surface," a poem that depicts the sleaziness that all too often typifies contemporary American life. The poem begins with a shocking image of a scene from an X-rated film, which is followed by a dizzying sequence of other images of day-to-day life, including cars crashing, people dressed up as Disney cartoon animals, a collie, a pipe and slippers, tennis rackets, two people kissing on Valentine's Day, a napalmed child from the Vietnam War, a hippie restaurant—all the good and bad that make up the visible surface of America, a documentary of what Americans are and what they dream as opposed to what they should be.

One of the goals Americans might desire is a nation in which everyone took voting seriously again, Pinsky explains to his daughter in "Local Politics" (although he realizes that she may not actually read this poem or any of the others in the book). A utopian America would be one, Pinsky insists, in which citizens no longer view the critical act of democracy, voting, as a necessary evil.

In "Countries and Explanations," voting becomes a way of protecting the many places that make up the United States, the ground in which the roots of identity will thrive. These places include the rutabaga farms of northern Michigan and better-known places such as Levittown, Union City, Boston, Harlem, and Pinsky's own Long Branch. These sites were all once part of a nation before the United States became a country "of different people living in different places."

This preoccupation with place continues in part 2, "Its Great Emptiness," which evokes the vastness of scale and simplicity of effect that define the American prairie. Almost like Walt Whitman or Carl Sandburg, Pinsky sees the prairie and its settlers in broad, epic terms, and he narrates a brief story of Swedish and German immigrants who harvest the grain until there is a horrible accident in which a man is chewed up by the threshing machine. Events such as this provide a starting point for a true mythology of American workers and immigrants. Instead, Pinsky notes in "Bad Dreams," Americans tend to read and interpret their experiences in terms of European or foreign models, as if they had no proper sense of identity. In "Horace, Epistulae, I, xvi," his poetic comment on Horace's first epistle, Pinsky also notes that unless Americans can break away from the shackles of their self-imposed materialism, they can never discover their own identity. A similar fate awaited the ancient Romans, he implies.

Pinsky believes that a glorious American union is possible in real political terms, because he sees the process already underway at the level of language, specifically in the unifying effects of American names, which nevertheless preserve a distinct racial and ethnic flavor. These names may be French, Spanish, Scottish, Italian, or German in origin. A "Yankee" is just a *jankel* or Dutchman, after all. Thus the Germanic Mr. Diehl could hire boys with Italian surnames to work for him. America is a patchwork quilt of names, including eagles, elks, moose, and masons. Pinsky ends this magnificent poetic meditation by echoing Robert Frost's "The Gift Outright," when he concludes that America is "so large, and strangely broken, and unforeseen." It is in that "unforeseen" that all the promise and potential lie, waiting to be tapped.

HISTORY OF MY HEART

If *Sadness and Happiness* was directed toward Pinsky's father and *An Explanation of America* toward his daughter, then *History of My Heart* is addressed to his mother, whose powerful will and even stronger imagination created the matrix in which young Robert thrived. The title poem narrates his mother's imaginary memory of seeing Fats Waller and two girlfriends when she was still a girl and worked at Macy's during school vacations. This magical moment is replayed on a more pedestrian scale by young Robert at a Christmas party, dancing erotically with his girlfriend, then going out into the snow, just like Fats Waller. His mother gives him his name not only in the legal sense but in a physical one, too, since she has a printer make up a lead slug with the twelve letters of his name (ROBERT PINSKY) reversed on their surface. In the end of his adolescence, all of her claims upon him, except perhaps her claim as a catalyst for his imagination, prove powerless. Robert goes off into his own world, playing his saxophone, and, like adolescents everywhere, tries desperately to attract the notice of the world. That, he concludes, is the history of his heart, since the saxophone player-poet is still craving the attention of an audience.

THE WANT BONE

In *The Want Bone*, Pinsky returns to the themes and interests expressed in *Landor's Poetry* and *Sadness and Happiness*, especially the great theme of compassion based on a deep sympathy for human needs and desires (as symbolized by the "want bone") and the use of religious symbolism and mythology (especially his use of apocryphal material loosely based on the life of Christ). This apocryphal material figures prominently in the first poem of the collection, "From the Childhood of Jesus." In this bizarre and arresting tale, Jesus is depicted as a precocious five-year-old boy who apparently violates the Sabbath by fashioning twelve clay sparrows and by damming the river to make a little pool from which the birds might drink. A self-righteous Jew immediately complains to Joseph about the boy's apparent profanation of the holy day, but Jesus claps his hands, and the clay birds miraculously flutter their wings and fly away.

The son of Annas the scribe appears and destroys Jesus' dam. Jesus curses him, and the son of Annas begins to wither and die. The poem ends with the boy Jesus crying himself to sleep as the twelve birds fly continually throughout the night.

In this rewriting, retelling, or reinventing of scriptures, Pinsky is putting his theories about religious symbolism and mythology into practice. Clearly, he seeks to emphasize in this paradoxical tale that sympathy (or faith) is what Jesus will require in his mission on earth, and that his powers of creation are, indeed, godlike even if he chooses to curse the nonbeliever. Most important in the tale are the birds that have taken off and will not land—until they become the twelve chosen apostles.

"The Want Bone," the title poem of the collection, is a generous and complex work of art, enticing and subtle, a poem that manages in sixteen lines to compress the whole history of human desire—and perhaps the history of life itself—in a brilliant sequence of fresh and startling images. Like all of Pinsky's poetry and criticism, "The Want Bone" enshrines the great qualities of balance (the word "O" is positioned at the very center and end of the poem), clarity of language and imagery (images such as "the tongue of the waves"), precise diction ("swale," "gash," "etched," and "pickled"), and precision of thought (a movement, a kind of zoological and historical evolution from the waves of the ocean to the rapacious mouth of the shark, whose jaw provides the literal "want bone" of the title). Finally, like all of Pinsky's work, "The Want Bone" is a supremely human utterance, not merely because it is the product of a human artist but also because its meaning is fundamentally human, a celebration of human desire, an evocation of all the "wanting" that may never be fulfilled. The "O" is thus a great zero of emptiness and frustration and simultaneously a resounding "O" of exultation and unalloyed joy—a perfect symbol for the mysterious complexity that Pinsky manages to discover again in the best of his poetry. As the bleached jaw of the shark seems to sing, so, too, may the poet say to the world: "But O I love you."

THE FIGURED WHEEL

The Figured Wheel brought together Pinsky's four previous volumes plus more than twenty new poems and a generous representation of his translations. This three-hundred-page collection made clear that Pinsky, still then only in his mid-fifties, had been a commanding figure in American poetry for a quarter century. It shows the remarkable range of his interests, intelligence, and craft. Never a fashionable poet or a trendsetter, Pinsky has nevertheless brought a distinctive, highly intelligent voice to the great poetic feast of his era.

JERSEY RAIN

Jersey Rain reveals an unusually lyrical—even musical—Pinsky. A slim and subtle volume, its poems radiate around the symbolic suggestiveness of the book's presiding central figure, the Roman god Hermes, at once messenger, trickster, and inventor of instruments. Alternately erudite, personal, witty, and reverent, the poems in *Jersey Rain* step beyond the boundaries of collected volume into fresh territory. In "Ode to Meaning," Pinsky defines the spirit he serves: "You not in the words, not even/ Between the words, but a torsion,/ A cleavage, a stirring."

OTHER MAJOR WORKS

LONG FICTION: *Mindwheel*, 1984 (computerized novel).

NONFICTION: *Landor's Poetry*, 1968 (dissertation); *The Situation of Poetry*, 1976; *Poetry and the World*, 1988; *Image and Text: A Dialogue with Robert Pinsky and Michael Mazur*, 1994; *The Sounds of Poetry: A Brief Guide*, 1998.

TRANSLATIONS: *The Separate Notebooks*, 1983 (of Czesław Miłosz); *The Inferno of Dante*, 1994.

EDITED TEXTS: *The Handbook of Heartbreak: 101 Poems of Lost Love and Sorrow*, 1998; *Americans' Favorite Poems: The Favorite Poem Project Anthology*, 2000 (with Maggie Dietz); *Poems to Read: A New Favorite Poem Project Anthology*, 2002 (with Dietz).

BIBLIOGRAPHY

Glück, Louise. "Story Tellers." *American Poetry Review* (July/August, 1997): 9-12. Glück explores the narrative impulse in Pinsky's work through comparisons with the poems of Stephen Dobyns. She attends to how each poet's work is involved with time and history.

Lehman, David, ed. *Ecstatic Occasions, Expedient Forms: Sixty-five Leading Contemporary Poets Select and Comment on Their Poems*. New York: Macmillan, 1987. Lehman's concept appears to be superficial, but the choices of poems and the quality of the author's commentaries are exceptional throughout. Pinsky explicates "The Want Bone" with candor and shares his enthusiasm for the use of the word "O." His remarks are incisive and revealing.

Longenbach, James. "Robert Pinksy and the Language of Our Time." *Salmagundi* 103 (Summer, 1994): 155-177. Longenbach argues that Pinsky's originality in vision and in poetic diction can be understood by taking seriously his acknowledged indebtedness to and affinities with other writers.

Molesworth, Charles. "Proving Irony by Compassion: The Poetry of Robert Pinsky." *The Hollins Critic* 21 (December, 1984): 1-18. Molesworth is a distinguished critic, and his interpretations here are well worth the time of any interested reader. He deals with three major topics, generously illustrating all: Pinsky's use of discursive poetry, the role of irony in his work, and the all-important theme of compassion.

Parini, Jay. "Explaining America: The Poetry of Robert Pinsky." *Chicago Review* 33 (Summer, 1981): 16-26. Parini has written widely on the subject of contemporary poetry, and this short study gives an excellent account of the connection between Pinsky's critical theories and the volume *An Explanation of America*.

Pinsky, Robert. Interview by Adam J. Sorkin. *Contemporary Literature* 25 (Spring, 1984): 1-14. Although one might have wished for an even longer interview, this intelligent and wide-ranging interview, if read sensitively, can give abundant insight into the role of certain autobiographical elements in Pinsky's poetry, such as his hometown of Long Branch and the influence of Yvor Winters, his mentor.

Pollitt, Katha. "World of Wonders." *The New York Times Book Review* 18 (August 1996): 9. Addressing *The Figured Wheel*, Pollitt praises Pinsky's unique contribution in probing the human experience through poems that give both intellectual and sensual pleasure.

Tangorra, Joanne. "New Software from Synapse Takes Poetic License." *Publishers Weekly* 227 (April 19, 1985): 50. Even though Tangorra's piece is relatively brief, it offers an intriguing glimpse at another side of Pinsky's creative expression—his electronic novel-game *Mindwheel,* the construction of which provides some fascinating clues about how Pinsky's mind works and about how he organizes material in more traditional formats, such as those of poetry.

Daniel L. Guillory,
updated by Philip K. Jason

SYLVIA PLATH

Born: Boston, Massachusetts; October 27, 1932
Died: London, England; February 11, 1963

PRINCIPAL POETRY
  The Colossus and Other Poems, 1960
  Three Women, 1962
  Ariel, 1965
  Uncollected Poems, 1965
  Crossing the Water, 1971
  Winter Trees, 1971
  Fiesta Melons, 1971
  Crystal Gazer, 1971
  Lyonesse, 1971
  Pursuit, 1973
  The Collected Poems, 1981
  Selected Poems, 1985

OTHER LITERARY FORMS
    Sylvia Plath was a prolific writer of poetry and prose. Her first publication was a short story, "Sunday at the Mintons'," which appeared in *Mademoiselle* in 1952. Throughout the remainder of her life, her stories and prose sketches appeared almost yearly in various journals and magazines. Ted Hughes edited a selection of these prose works, *Johnny Panic and the Bible of Dreams* (1977, 1979). Plath's extensive diaries and journals were also edited by Hughes; they were published as *The Journals of Sylvia Plath* in 1982. Her mother has edited a collection of letters written by Plath to her between 1950 and 1963, *Letters Home* (1975). Plath's work in other forms included a poetic drama, *Three Women,* that was aired on the BBC on August 19, 1962; an autobiographical novel, *The Bell Jar,* published under the pseudonym "Victoria Lucas" (1963); and a popular children's book, *The Bed Book* (1976).

ACHIEVEMENTS
    Sylvia Plath's poetry, like that of Hart Crane, will be read, studied, and known for two reasons: for its intrinsic merit, and for its bearing on her suicide. In spite of efforts to disentangle her poetry from her life and death, Plath's reputation and impact have fluctuated with public interest in her suicide. Almost immediately after her death, she was adopted by many members of the feminist movement as an emblem of the female in a male-dominated world; her death was lamented, condemned, criticized, and analyzed as a symbolic gesture as well as an inevitable consequence of her socialization. Explanations for her acute mental anguish were often subsumed in larger arguments about her archetypal sacrifice.
    With the publication of *The Bell Jar* and the posthumous collections of poetry, however, her audience grew in diversity and appreciation. *The Collected Poems* (1981) was awarded the Pulitzer Prize for Poetry in 1982. While she never lost her value to the feminist movement, she gained other sympathetic readers who attempted to place her in a social and cultural context that would help to explain—although certainly not definitively—her artistic success and her decision to end her life.
    It is not difficult to understand why Plath has won the respect of a wider audience. Her poems transcend ideology. Vivid, immediate re-creations of mental collapse, they are remnants of a psyche torn by severely conflicting forces. Yet Plath's poems are not merely re-creations of nightmares; were they only that, they would hardly be distinguishable from reams of psychological case histories. Plath's great achievement was her ability to transform the experience into art without losing its nightmarish immediacy.
    To retain that immediacy, Plath sometimes exceeded what many readers consider "good taste" or "aesthetic appropriateness"; she has even been convicted of trivializing universal suffering to the level of

Sylvia Plath in 1955. (Eric Stahlbert, Sophia Smith Collection, Smith College)

individual "bitchiness." The texture of her poetry demands closer scrutiny than such judgments permit, for Plath was one of the few poets to adhere to Theodor Adorno's dictum: "To write lyric poetry after Auschwitz is barbaric." In one sense, Plath redefined *lyric* by using that mode in a unique way. Plath's Auschwitz was personal but no less terrifying to her than was the horror of the German death camps to the millions who died there and the millions who learned of them later. For Plath, as for the inmates of Auschwitz, survival became paramount, but her Nazis were deep in her own psyche and her poetry became a kind of prayer, a ritual to remind her of her identity in a world gone mad. As a record of such experiences, Plath's poetry is unexcelled in any tradition.

BIOGRAPHY

Few poets demand that we know as much about their lives as Sylvia Plath does. Her intensely personal poetry was often rooted in everyday experiences, the knowledge of which can often open obscure references or cryptic images to fuller meaning for the reader.

Plath's father, Otto, was reared in the German town of Grabow and emigrated to the United States at the age of fifteen. He spoke German, Polish, and French, and later majored in classical languages at Northwestern University. In 1928 he received his Doctor of Science degree in applied biology from Harvard University. He taught at Boston University, where he met Aurelia Schober, whom he married in January, 1932. In 1934 his doctoral thesis was published by Macmillan as *Bumblebees and Their Ways*, and he became recognized as an authority on this subject. Beginning about 1935, Otto's health declined; he stubbornly refused any kind of medical treatment, assuming his illness to be lung cancer. When, in August, 1940, he stubbed his toe and suffered immediate complications, he submitted to medical examination. He was diagnosed as suffering from diabetes mellitus, a disease he could possibly have conquered had he sought treatment earlier. The condition of his toe worsened, however, and on October 12 his leg was amputated. He died on November 5 from a pulmonary embolus.

Plath's mother had also been a teacher—of English and German. At Otto's request, she gave up her career and devoted her time to housekeeping. Of Austrian ancestry, she too spoke German as a child and took great interest in Otto's scientific research and writing as well as in her own reading and in the teaching of her children.

Plath's early years were spent near the sea in her native Massachusetts, where she passed much of her time with her younger brother, Warren, exploring the beaches near their home. A very bright student, she consistently received high grades in virtually all of her subjects, and won many awards.

In September, 1950, Plath began her freshman year at Smith College in Massachusetts, the recipient of a scholarship. She continued her brilliant academic record, and at the end of her third year she was named guest managing editor of *Mademoiselle* and given a month's "working vacation" in New York. In August, 1953, after returning from New York, she suffered a nervous breakdown and attempted suicide. She was hospitalized and given shock treatments and psychotherapy. She returned to Smith for her senior year in February, 1954.

Plath won a full scholarship to study German at Harvard in the summer of 1954. She returned to Smith in

September; in January, 1955, she submitted her English honors thesis, "The Magic Mirror: A Study of the Double in Two of Dostoevsky's Novels," and graduated summa cum laude in June. She won a Fulbright Fellowship to study at Newnham College, Cambridge University, and sailed for England in September.

After one semester of study, she briefly toured London and then went to Paris to spend the Christmas break. Back in Cambridge, she met Ted Hughes at a party on February 25, 1956. They were married on June 16 in London. That summer she and Hughes toured France and Spain. She was awarded a second year on her Fulbright; Hughes began teaching at a secondary school. She completed her year of study, and, in 1957, she submitted her manuscript of poetry, "Two Lovers and a Beachcomber," for the English tripos and M.A. degree at Newnham College. In June, 1957, she and Hughes sailed for the United States, where she would be an instructor in freshman English at Smith College. She enjoyed her teaching and was regarded as an excellent instructor, but the strain of grading essays led her to abandon the academic world after one year. She and Hughes remained in Boston for the following year, both trying to earn a living by writing and part-time work. In the spring of 1959 Hughes was given a Guggenheim fellowship; meanwhile, Plath was attending Robert Lowell's seminars on poetry at Boston University.

In December of 1959 the couple returned to England, settling in London after a brief visit to Hughes's Yorkshire home. Plath was pregnant with her first child, and it was during these months in early spring that she learned of the acceptance by William Heinemann of her first book of poems, *The Colossus*, for publication in the fall. On April 1, Plath gave birth to her daughter, Frieda. Her book was published in October, to generally favorable reviews.

In February, 1961, Plath suffered a miscarriage, and in March she underwent an appendectomy. That summer, Plath and Hughes purchased a house in Croton, Devon, and went to France for a brief vacation. In August they moved into their house in Devon, and in November Plath was given a grant to enable her to work on *The Bell Jar.*

On January 17, 1962, Plath gave birth to her second child, Nicholas. Within a period of ten days in April she composed six poems, a sign of her growing desire to fit into the village life of Croton and of her returning poetic voice.

In June, Plath's mother arrived from the United States and remained until August. In July, Plath learned of Hughes's affair with Assia Gutman. On September 11, Plath and Hughes journeyed to Ireland; almost immediately Hughes left Plath and went to London to live with Gutman. Plath returned alone to Devon, where, with her children, she attempted to rebuild her life. She wrote extensively: twenty-three poems in October, ten in November. She decided, however, that she could not face another winter in Devon, so she found a flat in London and moved there with her children in the middle of December.

That winter proved to be one of the worst on record, and life in the flat became intolerable. The children were ill, the weather was cold, there was little heat, the pipes had frozen, and Plath was suffering extremes of depression over her separation from Hughes. On January 14, 1963, *The Bell Jar* was published to only lukewarm reviews. Plath's mood worsened. On February 11, 1963, she committed suicide in the kitchen of her flat.

ANALYSIS

In many ways, Sylvia Plath as a poet defies categorization. She has been variously described as a lyricist, a confessionalist, a symbolist, an imagist, and a mere diarist, but none of these terms can adequately convey the richness of approach and content of her work. Perhaps the proper way to identify Plath is not through a process of exclusive labeling but through inclusion and synthesis. All of these terms aptly describe the various modes of discourse that work effectively in her poetry and her prose.

She was definitely a lyricist, capable of creating great verbal beauty to match feelings of peace and tranquillity. Her lyricism can range from a simple but effective evocation of a Spanish sunrise ("Southern Sunrise") in which adjectives and metaphors balance finely against the simple intent of the word-picture, to a very Hopkinsian ode for her beloved ("Ode for Ted"), in which a blending of delicacy of emotion with startling diction is achieved. Even toward the end of her tortured life, she was able to return to this mode in a few of her last poems, the finest of which is "Nick and the Candle-stick," in which transcending not only the usual maudlin and mawkish treatment of maternal love but her own emotional plight as well, she is able to re-create a moment of genuine tenderness that emerges from her wholly realistic viewing of herself and her young son. This lyrical trait was not restricted to whole poems; quite often in the midst of utter frustration and despair Plath creates images or sounds of great beauty.

Plath's poetry is largely confessional, even when it is lyrical. Most of her confessional poetry, however, is not at all lyrical. Especially in her last years, she used this mode frequently, personally, and often viciously. She seldom bothered to create a persona through whom she could project feelings; rather, she simply expressed her feelings in open, exposed, even raw ways, leaving her self equally exposed. One such poem is "The Jailer," written after her separation from Hughes. The focus is the authorial "I," which occurs twelve times (together with the pronouns *my* and *me*, which occur thirteen times) within the poem's forty-five lines. This thinly disguised persona imagines herself captive of her lover/husband (the jailer of the title), who has not only drugged her but also raped her; she has become, in her degradation, a "Lever of his wet dreams." She then imagines herself to be Prometheus; she has been dropped from great heights to be smashed and consumed by the "beaks of birds." She then projects herself in the role of a black woman being burned by her captor with his cigarettes. Then she sees herself as a starved prisoner, her ribs showing after her meals of only "Lies and smiles." Then she sees herself as persecuted by him because of her rather frail religious belief (her "church of burnt matchsticks"). She is killed in several ways: "Hung, starved, burned, hooked." In her impotence to wish him the harm she feels he deserves, she retreats to slanders against his sexuality, making him impotent as well. She is paralyzed: unable to attain freedom through his death (by her wishes) and unable to escape her own imagination and her own psyche's fears. She ends the poem by unconsciously revealing her worst fear: "What would the light/ Do without eyes to knife, what would he/ Do, do, do without me?" She seems reconciled to the pain and suffering that awareness brings, but, by repeating "do" three times, she shows that she cannot face her aware-

ness that her lover has already assumed another active role, that he is performing on his new victim the same deeds he performed on her. Written only four months before her death, this poem shows Plath at both her strongest and her weakest. She is in command of the poetic form and language, but the emotions running through the words are in control of her. This same phenomenon occurs in many of Plath's other confessional poems, but especially in "Daddy," perhaps her most infamous poem. There she also seems able to control the artistic expression within the demands of the poem, but she ultimately resorts to "screaming" at her father, who is transformed into a "Panzer-man," a "Fascist," and a "bastard."

Plath used many symbols throughout her poetry, some assuming the value of motifs. While her mode was not, in the strictest literary sense of the word, symbolic, she frequently resorted to symbols as primary conveyors of meaning, especially in some of her most personal and most obscure poems. The moon held a special fascination for her, and it recurs throughout her entire poetic output. Colors—especially white—take on greater significance with each appearance. In the same manner, trees become larger and more significant in her later poems. Fetuses and corpses, although less often used, are two prominent symbols in her poetry. Animals move in and out of symbolic meaning in both her poetry and prose. The sea is second only to the moon as one of her favorite symbols. Other recurring symbols include: bees, spheres (skulls, balloons, wombs, heads), mirrors, flowers, and physical wounds. This is only a partial list, and the meaning of each of these symbols in any particular context is governed by many factors; but the mere repetition shows that Plath allowed them to assume special value in her own mind and imbued them with special meaning in her poems.

Plath was also capable of creating Imagistic poems, word-pictures intended to evoke a specific emotional response. Using an economy of words and an artist's eye (Plath did sketch and draw for a brief period), she could present a picture from her travels in Spain ("Fiesta Melons"), ships tied up at a wharf in winter ("A Winter Ship"), or a beach scene in which her eye is attracted by an incongruous figure ("Man in Black").

Perhaps Plath's greatest talent lay in her ability to transform everyday experiences—the kind that would be appropriate entries in a diary—into poems. Her poetry is a journal, recording not only full-fledged experiences but also acute perceptions and a wide range of moods. One such poem based on an everyday happening is "Medallion," in which the persona tells of discovering a dead snake. In fact, if the lines of the poem were simply punctuated as prose, the piece would have very much the appearance of a diary entry. This style in no way lessens the value of the piece as poetry. It is, indeed, one of Plath's most successful works because it is elegantly easy and colloquial, exemplifying one more mode of expression in which the poet excelled.

As Plath developed as a poet, she attempted to fuse these various modes, so that, by the end of her life, she was writing poems that combined any number of symbols and images into a quasilyrical confessional poem. What remains constant throughout her life and the various modes in which she wrote, however, is the rooting of the poem in her own experience. If Plath is to be faulted, this quality is perhaps her greatest weakness: She was not able to project her personae a great distance from herself. Plath was aware of this limitation (she once wrote: "I shall perish if I can write about no one but myself"), and she attempted to turn it into an advantage. She tried to turn her personal experiences and feelings into a vision. Her vision was in no way comprehensive, nor did it ever receive any systematic expression in prose, but it did govern many of her finest creations, especially in her later poetry, and it does account for the "lapses of taste" that many readers find annoying in her.

"MARY'S SONG"

One of her last poems will serve as an example of how this vision both limited and freed Plath's expression. "Mary's Song" is a complex of religious imagery and the language of war, combined to express feelings of persecution, betrayal, impending destruction, and, at the same time, defiant hope. The poem is very personal, even though its language works to drown the personal voice. An everyday, ordinary scene—a Sunday dinner in preparation, a lamb cooking in its own fat—suddenly provokes violent associations. It is the Sunday lamb whose fat sacrifices its opacity. The fire catches the poet's attention—fire that crystallizes window panes, that cooks the lamb, that burned the heretics, that burned

the Jews in Poland. The poet re-creates the associations as they occurred to her, as it was prompted by this everyday event of cooking. Her vision of the world—bleak, realistic, pessimistic—demands that the associations follow each other and that the poem then turn on the poet herself, which it does. The victims of the fire do not die, she says, implying that the process has somehow transformed them, purified them. She, however, is left to live, to have the ashes of these victims settle on her eye and in her mouth, forcing her to do a psychic penance, during which she sees the smokestacks of the ovens in Poland as a kind of Calvary. The final stanza returns the poet to her immediate plight: Her own heart is a holocaust through which she must travel; it too has been victimized by fathers, mothers, husbands, men, gods. She ends by turning to her own child—her golden child—and lamenting that he too will be "killed and eat[en]" by this same world.

This poem shows how Plath's vision worked to take a moment in her day and, rather than merely entering it mechanically in her journal, transform it into a statement on suffering. The horror of death by fire for heretics and Jews in Poland is no less intense, she says, because her horror—a heart that is a holocaust—is as real as theirs was; nor is her horror any the less horrible because other victims' horror was so great or so real. Plath's vision works to encapsulate this statement with its corollary in virtually all of her later confessional pieces.

While Plath's vision remained, unfortunately for her, fairly consistent, the personae through whom she expressed that vision often varied widely. In some poems there is no reason to assume the presence of any persona; powerful, sometimes psychotic emotions brush aside any obstacle between Plath and her reader. This shortened distance can be seen in such poems as "The Disquieting Muses," "On the Decline of Oracles," "Full Fathom Five," "Lesbos," and "Lady Lazarus," all poems written with a specific person in mind as both the subject of the poem and the object of the feeling, usually anger, expressed therein. In these works, Plath does little to create a mask behind which she could create feelings analogous to her own. Rather, she simply charges frontally and attacks whoever she feels has somehow wronged her. As a result of too much frontal assault and too little consideration for the poetic mode, some of these poems are not as successful as those in which she is at least in control of the poetic medium.

On the other hand, Plath could at times be a bit too detached from her persona, trying to force personal sentiment into a statement intended to have universal significance. One example of this kind of distancing is "Maudlin," a poem rooted in Plath's experience but one which attempts to moralize without sufficiently providing the moral, or literal, groundwork. Its cryptic images—a sleep-talking virgin, "Faggot-bearing Jack," and "Fish-tailed girls"—drive the reader to hunt for clues outside the poem, weakening the basis for the moralizing that takes place in the last two lines. The poem seems to be based on a birth that Plath witnessed during one of her visits to a hospital with a medical student. The "sleep-talking virgin" is the expectant mother (thus Plath indulged her love of dark and comic irony), rambling on in her drug-induced stupor. "Jack" is the child, reluctant to emerge from the mother (hence, "in his crackless egg"), a male bearing a "faggot" (a penis). He finally emerges with his "claret hogshead" (the placenta) to take his place with the dominant sex in the world ("he kings it"). This scene is behind the poem, but it can't be reconstructed from the poem itself: The reader must turn to *The Bell Jar* and other prose. Without an understanding of this scene—knowledge of what is literally occurring—the reader is not only unprepared for the moral at the end of the poem, but is also unwilling to accept such a pat bit of overt sermonizing, especially after pondering the cryptic clues. The poet simply warns her readers, especially women, that such pain as the mother suffers in childbirth results from the loss of the maidenhead. "Maudlin" is one of the few poems by Plath that actually needs less distance between the poet and her persona; it stands as an example of the other extreme to which Plath occasionally went, confusing her readers in an attempt to "depersonalize" her poems. A similar poem is "Among the Narcissi," about her ailing neighbor in Devon: It lacks the presence of the persona, it lacks a perspective, and it lacks a reason for its stark diction.

"BY CANDLELIGHT"

Such failures, however, were not typical: Few of her poems suffer from excessive detachment. Rather,

her recurring struggle was against uncontrolled subjectivity and self-dramatization. Two poems written in October, 1962, demonstrate the difficulties Plath faced when her poetic persona was simply herself, and her poetry less an act of communication than a private rite of exorcism. The first poem, "By Candlelight," presents a winter night's scene of a mother and her young son. The first stanza represents the exterior environment as threatening to break through the windows and overwhelm the two characters in cold and darkness. The next stanza focuses on the reality given the child by the light that fights the darkness (the candlelight of the title). The next stanza presents the awakening of the child and the poet's gazing on a brass figure supporting the candle. That figure is the focus of the final stanza, in which the little Atlas figure becomes the child's sole heirloom, his sole protection "when the sky falls." The poem is Plath's lamentation on her inadequacy, as a mother, as a human being, and as a poet, to ward off the world that threatens to break through the window. Her perception is made graphic and horrifying, as the surroundings take on an autonomy beyond human control. The tone of this poem is submissive, not even rebellious; the poet writes as therapy for her wounded self, as justification for resorting to words when all else fails.

"NICK AND THE CANDLESTICK"

"Nick and the Candlestick," written five days later, reveals changes in the poet's psyche that make the poem more assertive and alter its tone. Even the very beginning of the poem reflects this change of tone: "I am a miner." At least now the poet has assumed some sort of active role, she is doing something other than resorting to mere words to ward off mortality. She does, in fact, assume the role of a target, a lightning rod to attract the overwhelming forces toward her and away from the child. Even her small gestures—decorating their "cave" with rugs and roses and other Victoriana—have taken on great significance as acts to ward off the reality outside the window. The poet is able to end on a note of strengthened resignation, almost challenging the world to hurl its worst at her, for her child has been transformed by her into her own messiah, "the baby in the barn." The process by which this quasireligious transformation and salvation has occurred accounts for the major differences in tone in these two poems; but, again, without reference to Plath's life, the reader cannot be expected to grasp this process.

The tonal fluctuation and the inconsistent and varied personae in Plath's poems are rooted in her personality, which is capable of adopting numerous, almost infinite, masks. Plath played at many roles in her life: wronged daughter, brilliant student, coy lover, settled housewife, poet of promise, and mentally disturbed woman. Her life reflects her constant attempt to integrate these masks into what she could consider her identity—an irreproachable and independent psyche that needed no justification for its existence. Her life was spent in pursuit of this identity. She attempted to reassemble her shattered selves after her first suicide attempt, to exorcise selves that seemed to her too horrible, and to invent selves that she felt she should possess. Her poetry overwhelms its readers with its thematic consistency, drafted into this battle by Plath to help her survive another day, to continue the war against a world that seemed always on the verge of undoing the little progress she had made. Her personae were created from her and by her, but they were also created *for* her, with a very specific intent: survival of the self as an integrated whole.

In her quest for survival, Plath uncannily resembled Hedda Gabler, the title character of the 1890 Henrik Ibsen play. Like Hedda, Plath viewed the feminine self as a product created and manipulated by traditions and bindings far beyond the control of the individual woman. Also like Hedda, Plath felt that by rejecting the traditional demands placed on women, she could take one step toward assertion of an independent self. Plath's reactions to these traditional demands can be seen in "All the Death Dears," "The Ghost's Leavetaking," and "Magi," but the bulk of her poetry deals not so much with rejection of demands as with the whole process of establishing and maintaining identity. Masks, roles, charades, lies, and veils all enter Plath's quest and all recur throughout her poems.

"CHANNEL CROSSING"

In "Channel Crossing," an early poem, Plath uses the excitement of a storm at sea to suspend temporarily the identity of the persona, who reassumes her identity when the poem ends and she picks up her luggage. Identity is depicted as a fragile, dispensable entity. The na-

ture of identity is also a theme in "The Lady and the Earthenware Head," in which the head is a tangible mask, a physically separate self that the persona seeks unsuccessfully to destroy. Here, instead of fragility, Plath emphasizes the oppressive durability of a prefabricated self. Identity's endurance, if it violates one's personal sense of self, is a terrible burden. That quality is displayed in "The Bee Meeting." Here the persona is a naked, vulnerable self that assumes identity only when the villagers surrounding her recognize her need for clothing, give her the clothing, and respond to the new self. The poem ends with the implication that her *perceived* identity will prove to be permanent, despite any efforts she might make to alter these perceptions. Identity becomes a matter of perception, as is clearly stated in "Black Rook in Rainy Weather." In this poem the persona concedes to the artist's perception the very power to establish the artist's identity. The dynamic of power between perceived and perceiver is finely balanced in this poem. In "A Birthday Present," the balance is tipped by the duplicity of veils and what they hide in identities that are established within personal relationships.

"DADDY" AND "LADY LAZARUS"

Toward the end of her life Plath's concern with identity became defensively rebellious. In "Daddy," she openly declares her rebellion, severing the demands and ties of tradition that so strangled her earlier in her life and in her poetry. She adopts several methods to achieve her end of freedom: name-calling, new identities, scorn, humiliation, and transfer of aggression. Her freedom rings false, however; the ties are still there. "Lady Lazarus" reveals Plath's awareness of the lingering ties and stands as an encapsulation of her whole life's quest for identity—from passivity, to passive resistance, to active resistance, and finally to the violently imagined destruction of those people who first gave and then shattered her self: men. This poem contains meaning within meaning and exposes much about Plath's feelings on *where* her identity arose. She saw herself as a product of a male society, molded by males to suit their particular whims or needs. Her contact with females in this context led inevitably to conflict and competition. This duality in her self was never overcome, never expelled, or, worse, never understood. Having failed to manipulate her manipulators, she tried to find identity by destroying her creators. Set free from the basis she had always known even if she despised it, she had nowhere else to go but to the destruction of the self as well.

"WORDS"

Plath realized this quandary. In "Words," a poem written ten days before her death, she looked back:

> Years later I
> Encounter them on the road—
> Words dry and riderless,
> The indefatigable hoof-taps.
> While
> From the bottom of the pool, fixed stars
> Govern a life.

The words with which she had striven to create a self—a meaningful self that would integrate her various sides in a harmonious whole and not merely reflect "daddy's girl," "mommy's girl," "big sister," "sorority Sue," or "Mrs. Hughes"—these words had turned "dry and riderless." They too had failed her, just as her family, friends, husband, and her own self had failed her. She had sought identity in traditional places—parents, school, marriage, and work—but had not found enough strands to weave her various selves together. She had sought identity in unorthodox places—the mind, writing, Devon, and hope—but even these failed her.

Plath finally conceded her failure to create a self that would satisfy her and the world about her. She reviewed a life that she had tried to end earlier. Even then she had been forced to regroup, forced to continue inhaling and exhaling. The truth of the real world that had threatened to overwhelm her collection of masks throughout her life had finally yielded to her on one point. She asked ten days before her death: "Once one has seen God, what is the remedy?" The perfection of death that had haunted her throughout her life seemed the only answer. Her final act was her ultimate affirmation of self in a world that would not let her or her words assume their holistic role.

OTHER MAJOR WORKS

LONG FICTION: *The Bell Jar*, 1963.

NONFICTION: *Letters Home*, 1975; *The Journals of Sylvia Plath*, 1982 (Ted Hughes and Frances McCul-lough, editors); *The Unabridged Journals of Sylvia Plath, 1950-1962*, 2000 (Karen V. Kukil, editor).

CHILDREN'S LITERATURE: *The Bed Book*, 1976.

SHORT FICTION: *Johnny Panic and the Bible of Dreams*, 1977, 1979 (prose sketches).

BIBLIOGRAPHY

Alexander, Paul. *Rough Magic: A Biography of Sylvia Plath.* New York: Da Capo Press, 1999. Using interviews and extensive archival research, Alexander probes the events of Plath's life with a compassionate view of this fiercely talented, deeply troubled artist. Includes thirty-six photos.

Axelrod, Steven Gould. *Sylvia Plath: The Wound and the Cure of Words.* Baltimore: The Johns Hopkins University Press, 1990. Calling his book a "biography of the imagination," Axelrod makes sophisticated use of psychoanalysis, feminist and other recent critical theory, and biographies of the poet to interpret her life and work, including not only her major poems but her letters and journals as well. Supplemented by an extensive bibliography of primary and secondary sources.

Britzolakis, Christina. *Sylvia Plath and the Theatre of Mourning.* New York: Clarendon Press, 1999. A closely sustained study arguing that Plath developed a theatrical conception of the speaking subject. Britzolakis relates Plath's texts both to their historical moment and to contemporary debates about language, gender, and subjectivity.

Bundtzen, Lynda. *Plath's Incarnations: Woman and the Creative Process.* Ann Arbor: University of Michigan Press, 1983. The critic's approach is shaped by the "current feminist awareness of the difficulties peculiar to being a woman and an artist." Bundtzen probes the reasons for Plath's suicide and takes issue with earlier works on the poet, such as Butscher's biography. Includes extensive notes and an index.

Butscher, Edward. *Sylvia Plath: Method and Madness.* New York: Seabury Press, 1976. The first critical biography of Plath by a poet. Based on extensive interviews with Plath's friends and colleagues, although without the cooperation of Plath's family or estate, Butscher defines the poet's life and art in controversial terms, calling her the "bitch goddess," a term he takes from D. H. Lawrence to describe "fierce ambition and ruthless pursuit of success."

Hall, Caroline King Barnard. *Sylvia Plath*. New York: Twayne, 1998. A critical introduction to the life and work of Plath. Hall identifies remaining puzzles that face Plath scholarship, particularly those rearrangements and deletions made by Ted Hughes, her husband. Hall also relates Plath to the women's movement. She raises interesting questions about the relationship between the life and the art.

Newman, Charles, ed. *The Art of Sylvia Plath*. Bloomington: Indiana University Press, 1970. An early but still valuable collection of criticism, with seven major articles on Plath's poetry and fiction, a section of reminiscences, and another of short reviews. Includes Plath's pen drawings, an annotated checklist of criticism, and a bibliography of her poetry.

Stevenson, Anne. *Bitter Fame: A Life of Sylvia Plath*. Boston: Houghton Mifflin, 1990. Written with the cooperation of the executor of Plath's estate, Stevenson's book presents a rather harsh view of the poet and a defense of her husband, poet Ted Hughes. Stevenson, a fine poet, presents several provocative readings of Plath's poetry. Her book should be read in conjunction with Linda Wagner-Martin's biography.

Wagner, Erica. *Ariel's Gift*. New York: W. W. Norton, 2001. The literary editor of the London *Times* comments on the destructive relationship of Ted Hughes with Sylvia Plath and as revealed through Hughes's *Birthday Letters*, his poetry cycle dedicated to Plath. Bibliography, index of works by Hughes and Plath, general index.

Wagner-Martin, Linda. *Sylvia Plath: A Biography*. New York: St. Martin's Press, 1987. A more detached and sympathetic biography than Butscher's and Stevenson's accounts. Presents Plath as a feminist in a broad sense of the term and concentrates on the poet's identity as a writer. Based on nearly two hundred interviews and limited cooperation from the Plath estate, Wagner-Martin presents the most balanced view of Plath.

Richard F. Giles;
bibliography updated by the editors

STANLEY PLUMLY

Born: Barnesville, Ohio; May 23, 1939

PRINCIPAL POETRY
In the Outer Dark, 1970
How the Plains Indians Got Horses, 1973
Giraffe, 1973
Out-of-the-Body Travel, 1976
Summer Celestial, 1983
Boy on the Step, 1989
The Marriage in the Trees, 1997
Now That My Father Lies Down Beside Me: New and Selected Poems, 1970-2000, 2000

OTHER LITERARY FORMS

Throughout the 1970's, Stanley Plumly contributed critical essays and book reviews to *The American Poetry Review*. His best-known essay, "Chapter and Verse," appeared in two parts in the January and May, 1978, issues.

ACHIEVEMENTS

In his essay "Chapter and Verse," Stanley Plumly explains his belief that the direction of contemporary American poetry is away from a strict reliance on imagery and toward a stronger emphasis on rhetoric, on the centrality of the poem's voice and the speaker's attitude. His own poems stand as strong examples of this aesthetic. For his first book, *In the Outer Dark*, Plumly received the Delmore Schwartz Memorial Award. In 1973-1974, he received a Guggenheim Fellowship. He received National Endowment for the Arts grants in 1977 and 1983; a National Book Critics Circle Award nomination and William Carlos William Award, both for *Out-of-the-Body Travel*; a nomination for the Lenore Marchall Poetry Prize, Ac4ademy of American Poets in 1998; and an Ingram-Merrill Foundation fellowship.

BIOGRAPHY

Stanley Ross Plumly was born in 1939 in the small Quaker town of Barnesville, Ohio, and grew up in the lumber and farming regions of Ohio and Virginia. After receiving his B.A. degree from Wilmington College,

Plumly attended Ohio University, where he studied writing and literature with Wayne Dodd and where he received an M.A.

Plumly has taught writing at Louisiana State University, Ohio University, the University of Iowa, Princeton, Columbia, and the University of Michigan. He served as the editor of *Ohio Review*, 1970-75, and *Iowa Review*, 1976-78. In 1979, he joined the faculty of the University of Houston, directing and teaching in the writing program there until 1985, when he moved to the University of Maryland at College Park.

ANALYSIS

T. S. Eliot said that writing poems is a way of escaping personality. Stanley Plumly holds a similar view. Only when one abandons an intense internal focus, Plumly believes, can one see the outer world clearly. Such a clarity typifies Plumly's own poetry. This freeing oneself of the confines of personality allows one to absorb the outer world more fully, a world that Plumly's poems reveal to be mysterious.

For Plumly, such an escape from personality does not mean, however, a poetry that is impersonal. On the contrary, in his own poetry Plumly establishes a very intimate voice. His "out-of-the-body travel" allows him to understand nature, the outer world, more clearly, but he can also understand his own distinctive place in the natural world. He is able to stand apart from and observe himself at the same time.

GIRAFFE

The poems in *Giraffe* clearly exemplify this concern with escaping personality. In this volume, Plumly repudiates confessional poetry because it allows the poet to indulge in his or her own psychological struggles and leads nowhere. The poet, Plumly suggests, must enter the world outside himself, no matter how dark, foreign, or foreboding, and live in it. In the transcendental tradition of Ralph Waldo Emerson or Hart Crane, Plumly sees entry into the outer world as a means by which one can intuit a sense of his or her own place in the natural order of things, thereby realizing a more harmonious existence with nature.

This focus on nature is often manifested in poems whose subjects are animals, plants, or trees. Horses, for example, appear in several poems, particularly in *Gi-*

raffe, where they represent a kind of sacred, spiritual union with nature. Plumly's examination of the natural world also points to his admiration for his fellow Ohio poet, James Wright. Like Wright, Plumly aims to see the natural world anew and, through fresh imagery, to make it live in his poems.

Another important similarity to Wright's work is Plumly's spare style, which follows Wright's ideal of a reliance on the "pure, clear word." The diction in Plumly's poems is direct but quiet, and the resonating emotive quality of the language often leans toward lyricism.

Plumly's poetry, however, is distinguished stylistically in several ways. The poems most often begin in an intense state of emotion and move toward an understanding of those feelings. Thus, a poem's forcefulness often depends on the strength of its closure, and it is this strength in particular which contributes to Plumly's individual style. The poems build toward a final moment of epiphany in which often contradictory emotions are condensed into a single clarifying image, as in "Wrong Side of the River" (*Out-of-the-Body Travel*). In this poem two people try to communicate from opposite banks of the river:

> . . . you began shouting and I didn't
> want you to think I understood.
> So I did nothing but stand still,
> thinking that's what to do on the wrong side
> of the river. After a while you did too.
> We stood like that for a long time. Then
> I raised a hand, as if to be called on,
> and you raised a hand, as if to the same question.

In this example, Plumly depends in the last two lines, as he often does, on repetition, and on the strong cadence that results from it. The chantlike effect makes the poem's emotional resonance all the more powerful.

As this passage suggests, Plumly is concerned with questions that are common to everyone. In many of the poems these are questions of loyalties to and relationships with parents, or questions about why certain childhood memories remain so strong and recur so often. In Plumly's major collections, several poems center on a father-son relationship. In the earlier volumes, *In the Outer Dark* and *Giraffe*, the son has difficulty accepting the father's death because the father-son relationship in life had been incomplete. The son resents the father's passing and cannot let go of his father because an understanding between the two had not been achieved. In *Out-of-the-Body Travel*, however, the son has become more forgiving of the father for dying before a mutual understanding between them had been reached.

Many of the poems, particularly those whose subject is the father or another relative, also focus on the steadfastness of early memories. These poems reflect Plumly's belief in the shaping importance of early experiences. In "This Poem" (*Out-of-the-Body Travel*) he writes: "The first voice I ever heard/ I still hear, like the small talk in a daydream." These lines also illustrate Plumly's notion that traveling out of oneself enables one to turn back and look more clearly *at* oneself and to understand in retrospect the experiences that contributed to forming one's individuality. It is also by so doing that one sees one's similarities to others in the world.

IN THE OUTER DARK

The poems comprising *In the Outer Dark*, as the title suggests, are about outer darkness, but they are also about inner light, the power of the imagination and the feeling mind to illuminate. The poems are rich with contrasting images of light and dark. Inextricably caught up in the imagery and ideas of light and dark are the related subjects of time and space. Plumly considers the dark in "Now the Sidewise Easing into Night" as the embodiment of space. In this poem the dark has walls; it measures distance. Light, on the other hand, connotes openness, the physical and metaphysical sense of infinite possibility. In "All the Miles of a Dream," for example, men travel across snowy fields toward light: "The light sat in the window// and was the only direction/ all the miles of a dream/ can offer three men moving across such spaces."

The title poem reflects a similar concern for coming to terms with the complexities of time and space. In this poem, people move toward one elusive center at which they never arrive. As suggested by the title of another poem, "Arriving at the Point of Departure," time propels people in such a way that their arrival points are also their points of departure. Plumly sees poetry, however, as a vehicle that can stop time and allow people to reflect on a single moment. In "Rilkean Autumn," he writes:

Tomorrow the pump will freeze.
But today, thought, in the held moment,
sucked to a single drop,
still wags at the lip of the tap.

Such held moments for Plumly often depend on the absence of ego, and it is in such moments that the imagination sees beyond the confines of personality. Furthermore, many poems, such as "Chinese Jar," suggest that only when the outer world seems darkest and most silent does one's inner spirit become most active, most fully engaged. This creates a compelling tension in the poems. The held moment, the narrated experience, appears still, while the poem's emotion, the feeling discovered from the moment, resonates with powerful intensity. These moments are most often memories: digging potatoes with his father, driving in the car with his mother, listening to the wind in Kansas. In silence and darkness, then, Plumly suggests, the spirit recharges itself by transcending the self and entering more directly into the moment. This in turn enables one to perceive finally and more fully the significance of a moment.

Understanding the significance of one's memories, a dominant concern throughout all three volumes, is especially important in *In the Outer Dark*. Several poems speak of the son's inability to accept the finality of his father's death. "My father," writes Plumly in "Arriving at the Point of Departure," "breaks down into the slightest memory at random." The title, then, also describes memory as that point of both departure and arrival. The experiences that shape people also return to them as memory throughout life, or as reminders, Plumly suggests, of who they are.

Stylistically, the poems in this volume reflect Plumly's thematic concerns of time and space. The poems narrate experiences that happen sequentially in time but also capture those experiences completely in one moment, the moment of each poem itself. Consequently, the emotions of a poem come to the reader whole and distilled with the poem's closure.

HOW THE PLAINS INDIANS GOT HORSES AND GIRAFFE

Ten poems in *Giraffe* were published earlier in 1973 in a chapbook titled *How the Plains Indians Got Horses*. As both titles suggest, many of the poems have animals as subjects, but more important, the poems in *Giraffe* are about how man can learn from animals to become more fully a part of the natural world. Again, the lesson is to center on transcendence of self in order to identify one's proper place in the order of nature—to achieve harmony with the outer world. As the last few lines of "Mile of the Animal" indicate, animals achieve such harmony because they have "the distance beyond the body." Addressing an anonymous animal, Plumly writes: "Your mind throws down its perfect shadow/ at your feet. You begin to walk,/ away from yourself, not simply out of the dark." Similarly, in the title poem "Giraffe," the giraffe, a shy, gawky creature, is described lovingly as embodying that harmony in which it is unafraid to

> stand still
> in a camouflage of kind
> in a rare daylight
> for hours,
> the leaves spilling
> one break of sun
> into another,
> listening to the lions.

Horses, the subjects of several poems in this volume, also exemplify this compatibility with nature. In "How the Plains Indians Got Horses," a horse is described in majestic terms, as more than human. An Indian chief, tired and hungry, sees a horse for the first time, and at the end of the poem he

> rise[s] from [his] body
> as from the ground
> onto this other, second of itself, horse
> and rider.

In the prose passage by Franz Kafka, titled by Plumly "The Wish to Be a Red Indian," which ends the book, a rider becomes one with his horse, leaning into the wind and giving up his spurs and reins as unnecessary. He allows the horse to carry him where it will, and he hardly notices "when the horse's neck and head would be already gone." The union with nature is accomplished. The journey through life, Plumly suggests, is a similar kind of travel, in which acceptance and appreciation of the new and unknown landscapes beyond and outside the self can make the person whole, at one with the world.

For this reason Plumly thinks the ability to move beyond the self is essential. Movement inward, as Plumly shows in the poem "Jarrell," about Randall Jarrell's continual progression toward suicide, is unhealthy. The confessional poets, Plumly implies, perhaps best represented by Jarrell, John Berryman, and Sylvia Plath, exemplify this illness. Because of their preoccupation with self, they are unable to participate in those out-of-the-self activities that Plumly believes feed and fulfill the human spirit.

The language and tone of the poems in *Giraffe* reveal the mind of an observer who has traveled beyond the self and is in awe of the natural world, as if seeing it for the first time. The images and the uniqueness of the similes, such as the giraffe who "bends like a bow/ over the water," convey Plumly's admiration for the animals. The language and tone also bring to mind the poems of James Wright's *The Branch Will Not Break* (1963), especially the well-known poem "The Blessing," in which the poem's speaker says, upon realizing the horses' harmony of power and gentleness and how much a part of their world he is, that "if [he] stepped out of [his] body [he] would break/ into blossom." The poems in *Giraffe* resonate with a similar kind of joy, a spiritual fullness that comes from the deliberate projection of the self into the natural world.

OUT-OF-THE-BODY TRAVEL

The poems in *Out-of-the-Body Travel* examine more closely the ability of the past to inform the present, to shape personality, and to determine how one perceives the world. Although the poems in this volume continue to focus on a movement out of the self, the self, through memory, receives added emphasis. The powerful relationships of father and son, the subject of several poems in this volume as well, exemplify this concern. In the title poem, for example, the narrator realizes that, although his relationship with his father has been troublesome, certain retained associations with his father have influenced his perceptions of the world. The narrator recalls his father playing the violin, slaughtering a bull, and laying his hand on his (the son's) feverish forehead. Each of these memories associated with the father represents a kind of travel from the body. The son comes to understand, through memory, how his father contributed to shaping his own concept of transcending the self.

Similarly, in the long poem "For Esther," the son comes to understand how his mother also contributed to shaping the same concept. In this poem, the speaker remembers his childhood love of watching the trains and playing along the tracks. Afraid for him, however, his mother cautioned him away from the tracks. The narrator was thus caught between his desire to participate in the world, to hop a train, perhaps, or simply to play along the tracks regardless of the danger, and his mother's "orders" to be only an observer, to watch the trains from a distance. The strong details of the poem suggest that the narrator has learned from his mother another, perhaps better, way to travel: "It's what we hear all night,/ between Troy and anywhere, what you meant// to tell me, out of the body, out of the body travel."

The ties to one's past, the poems in *Out-of-the-Body Travel* assert, are strong, and the images convey this strength. In "The Tree," for example, a family tree's roots and branches are described as "inlaid" into a man until "the man's whole back, root and stem [are] veins." Similarly, in "Iron Lung" the strength of the past entraps the poem's persona in the same way that an iron lung entraps, although, in this poem, it is largely through dreams that the past does its entrapping. As with several poems in this volume and the two earlier ones, the strength of the past shows itself in the son's feelings of being victimized by the sins of the father. "Iron Lung" ends, however, with the son's realization that dreams may end in daylight—the iron lung lifted:

> Once there was a machine for breathing.
> It would embrace the body and make a kind of love.
> And when it was finished it would rise
> like nothing at all above the earth
> to drift through the daylight silence.

The poems in *Out-of-the-Body Travel* perhaps represent Plumly's greatest strides in establishing a unique voice. His imagery in this volume is inventive, apt, and beautiful. In the poem "Rainbow," for example, he describes a standard poetic subject, a sunset, but in a striking new way: "Taking its time/ through each of the seven vertebrae of light/ the sun comes down"; at the end of the poem, "It looks as if the whole sky is going down on one wing."

SUMMER CELESTIAL

The poems in *Summer Celestial* continue Plumly's explorations of memory and of the relationships that it mysteriously captures. In the poem "Virginia Beach," he writes: "Sometimes when you love someone/ you think of pain—how to forgive/ what is almost past memory." The poems describe nature and landscapes in Plumly's typically graceful way. In "Chinese Tallow," he writes of a tree quite unlike the family tree of "The Tree" in *Out-of-the-Body Travel*—he wants to see it "large with the rain inside it"; he wants to "wake in a room bright with small dark leaves." Again in this volume there is the play between the inner world and the outer world of nature, between imagination and sensory details. The tone of *Summer Celestial* is generally more hopeful than that of the previous volume; emphasis is more on characters and the events in which they are involved than on the inner life of the poet himself.

THE MARRIAGE IN THE TREES

Plumly's lyric poetry sustains its melancholy air in *The Marriage in the Trees:* trees are "gothic with winter," a neighbor seems "boiled at birth/ in anger," and the streets harbor characters out of Fellini ("Dwarf with Violin"). This is a longer book than his previous collections and contains thirty-nine poems, some of which also display Plumly's developing sense of humor. He uses metaphors to explore nature in human terms and feels that other living things possess an unknowable wisdom that humans can only appreciate intuitively.

NOW THAT MY FATHER LIES DOWN BESIDE ME

Plumly culls works from six past collections to include in his volume titled *Now That My Father Lies Down Beside Me.* Poems that explore his rural childhood, relationship with his parents, and influential literary figures make appearances here, while his newer work focused intently on nature, especially trees and birds. "Souls of Suicides as Birds" and "Cedar Waxwing on Scarlet Firethorn" link birdsong to human grief in an elated swoon: "before the trees-/ to be alive in secret, this is what/ we wanted, and here, as when we die what/ lives is fluted on the air." A pre-modernist style dominates the collection, which displays a range of blank and metrical verse, and is encompassed with a hushed, elegiac tone.

OTHER MAJOR WORKS

NONFICTION: "Chapter and Verse," 1978.

EDITED TEXT: *The New Bread Loaf Anthology of Contemporary American Poetry*, 1999 (with Michael Collier).

BIBLIOGRAPHY

Dodd, Wayne. "Stanley Plumly." *The Ohio Review* 25 (1980): 33-57. An excellent, probing, and wide-ranging interview in which the poet discusses the characteristics of American poetry, the nature of lyric poetry, the synesthetic qualities of poetry, and aspects of the narrative. Plumly also discusses his views of his own writing style, his approach to storytelling, and poets who have influenced his work.

Heyen, William. *American Poets in 1976*. Indianapolis: Bobbs-Merrill, 1976. Plumly discusses his poems, "The Iron Lung," "Now That My Father Lies Down Beside Me," and "Horse in the Cage," as well as those found in his book, *Out-of-the-Body-Travel*. The poet comments on the inspiration and real-life events that precipitated his works, the practical and aesthetic issues related to the poems, and the writers who have influenced his distinct poetic voice.

Plumly, Stanley. "Stanley Plumly: An Interview." Interview by David Biespiel and Rose Solari. The American Poetry Review 24, no. 3 (May/June 1995):43. Plumly discusses the creative act, his poems, and the influence of other artists such as John Keats on his work. On his own work, Plumly believes that his early poems were not as demonstrative and open in feeling and content as later works.

Stanton, Maura. "On Stanley Plumly's Poems." *The Iowa Review* 3 (Fall, 1973): 92-93. Stanton views the imagery of the body and its state of sleep and death in Plumly's work. References to these images are noted and discussed in "Dreamsong," "In Sleep," and "Light." The issues that emerge include the meaning of escape from the body, the "other" of objective reality, the memory and reality, and the literal and metaphorical death.

Stitt, Peter. "On Stanley Plumly." *The American Poetry Review* 9 (March/April, 1980): 16-17. An in-depth examination of Plumly's book, *Out-of-the-Body Travel*, and the theme that recurs in many of his po-ems: the death of his father. Stitt explores the various technical and stylistic methods used by Plumly to explore this subject with enduring spirituality rather than pathos and self-pity. Stitt also celebrates Plumly's verbal, lyrical, and figurative density.

Wyatt, David. "Working the Field." *The Southern Review* 36, no. 4 (Autumn 2000): 874-880. In-depth review of *Now My Father Lies Down Beside Me: New and Selected Poems, 1970-2000*.

Young, Vernon. "A Belated Visit." *Parnassus: Poetry in Review* 8 (Fall/Winter, 1979): 297-311. Young deals with the broad issues raised by Plumly's poetry such as diction problems, reconstruction of reality, the religious and ritualistic connotations of his language, and the purge of suffering. Young points to the shortcomings of Plumly's poems as well as his strengths to provide an uncommonly balanced assessment of the poet's work.

Nance Van Winckel,
updated by Philip K. Jason and Sarah Hilbert

EDGAR ALLAN POE

Born: Boston, Massachusetts; January 19, 1809
Died: Baltimore, Maryland; October 7, 1849

PRINCIPAL POETRY

Tamerlane and Other Poems, 1827
Al Aaraaf, Tamerlane, and Minor Poems, 1829
Poems, 1831
The Raven and Other Poems, 1845
Eureka: A Prose Poem, 1848
Poe: Complete Poems, 1959
Poems, 1969 (Volume 1 of *Collected Works*)

OTHER LITERARY FORMS

Edgar Allan Poe wrote several major essays of literary criticism, in addition to numerous book reviews for magazines. Especially important are his reviews of Nathaniel Hawthorne, containing Poe's theory of short fiction, and his reviews of the works of English and American poets, which explain much of his theory of the poetic imagination. Poe's philosophical speculations are found in his book-length *Eureka: A Prose Poem* (1848) and in his "Marginalia." In the former he attempts no less than a complete theory of God and the universe. Although he was untrained in science, some of his ideas about the nature of space and time clearly anticipate significant discoveries in twentieth century theoretical physics. He was one of the founders of the short story, and today's "category fiction" owes two of its most popular and enduring types to Poe: the detective story and the story of "Gothic" horror. He also wrote a verse drama, *Politian* (pb. 1835-1836), and a novella, *The Narrative of Arthur Gordon Pym* (1838).

ACHIEVEMENTS

Edgar Allan Poe is regarded as an important and influential figure in American literature. He established basic principles for analyzing poetry which have subsequently been modified but never abandoned. Before Poe, American critics saw their job as protecting the public from European decadence and revolutionary ideas. Poe maintained that the critic should rather protect readers from bad poetry and remind poets to live up to their potential. He was also among the first to introduce theoretical considerations into book reviewing. He believed that the critic must judge poetry by a definite body of standards rather than by the vague and impressionistic criteria so often resorted to by his contemporaries. He pioneered in insisting that a poem is an aesthetic object and that its existence can be justified solely on aesthetic grounds. He was also concerned with making poetry accessible to a wide public, something which often irritated his fellow reviewers.

Poe was one of the first American poets to be famous in his own lifetime, and has remained, with Robert Frost and Walt Whitman, one of America's three best-known poets. His command of the entire range of technical devices available to the poet, especially of sound effects, remains unsurpassed. While his subject matter is narrow and sometimes idiosyncratic, he has written some of the finest lyrics and descriptive poems in the language. Poe's poetry was never completely ignored in nineteenth century America, but it was in France after 1850 that he was most admired. His theory and practice had an enormous influence on French—and later on British and

Edgar Allan Poe (Library of Congress)

American—poetry, particularly on the Symbolist movement of the later nineteenth century. The Symbolists admired Poe's conception of ideal beauty, his use of atmosphere, his command of the musical qualities of language, and his notion of the poem as a rationally constructed work. Perhaps most important, he influenced the symbolists, and through them much of twentieth century poetry, with his insistence that art is an appropriate instrument for dealing with the subjective and the transcendent in human life. The list of great artists who acknowledged him as an important influence on their work would have to include the poets T. S. Eliot, William Butler Yeats, Dante Gabriel Rossetti, and Charles Baudelaire; the dramatists August Strindberg and George Bernard Shaw; and the composers Claude Debussy, Maurice Ravel, Serge Prokofiev, Alban Berg, and Igor Stravinsky.

BIOGRAPHY

Edgar Allan Poe was born to parents who were professional actors. Poe always believed that he inherited his talents as a reciter of verse especially from his mother, and it is not farfetched to see his lifelong concern for the effect of the poem on the reader as an outgrowth of this early exposure to the stage. One of the most important events of his early life was the death of his mother when he was not yet three, and his poetry bears the imprint of his various attempts to find an ideal woman adequate to her memory. Since his father abandoned the family about this time and probably died shortly thereafter, young Edgar was taken into the family of John Allan, a merchant from Richmond, Virginia. It was from Allan that Poe took his middle name. From 1815 to 1820 the family lived in England, where Poe acquired much of his early education as well as his first exposure to the Gothic style which figures so prominently in the atmosphere and settings of his work. Back in Richmond, Poe studied the Classics in several schools, and entered the University of Virginia, where he seems to have impressed his teachers and fellow students with his knowledge of languages. He ran up large gambling debts which Allan refused to pay, however, forcing Poe to drop out of school. Thus began an estrangement from Allan which lasted until Allan's death six years later. At eighteen Poe enlisted in the United States Army, rising within two years to the rank of sergeant-major. Already at eighteen he had managed to have a slim volume of verse published, followed by another when he was twenty. At about that time he requested (with Allan's approval) a discharge from the Army so that he could apply to West Point. He entered the Academy in 1830 and did well, but when Allan again refused him necessary financial support he felt that he had no choice but to get himself expelled in order to find a job. He left West Point with enough material for a third volume of poetry, which appeared that year (1831) when he was still only twenty-two.

Poe now set himself to making a career in the world of professional letters, which he pursued with mixed success until his death eighteen years later. His financial circumstances were often desperate as he moved from one eastern city to another looking for work as a writer or editor of literary magazines. In 1836 he married his cousin, Virginia Clemm, and in 1839 received his first job as an editor. In 1841 he became editor of *Graham's Magazine:* the first of two periodicals whose circulation he increased dramatically while in charge. Yet sometimes erratic behavior and frequent problems with alcohol cost him jobs even when his actual performance was

adequate. The journalistic world of the 1830's and 1840's was characterized by fiercely polemical writing, full of vituperation and personal attacks—a style which Poe practiced with great zest and ability. Despite his attacks in print on his fellow writers, some of them aided him in times of unemployment and stress.

In 1842 Poe's young wife burst a blood vessel, and her deteriorating health over the next five years added greatly to the anxiety caused by lack of money. Poe's mother-in-law was an important source of strength to the couple during these years. Amazingly, he was able to turn out dozens of first-rate poems, reviews, and stories for the magazines even while fighting off problems of health and finances. The publication of his poem "The Raven" in 1845 made him famous, enabling him to begin earning good money as a public reciter of poetry. When Virginia finally died in 1847, Poe himself became desperately ill, and even after recovering he never regained his old resiliency. In 1848 he became engaged to one of several women whom he was seeing, Mrs. Sarah Whitman, who attempted with some success to help him conquer his problems with drinking. In what was to be the last year of his life he felt more secure with Mrs. Whitman, with a regular income from lecturing and writing, and with his popularity in Richmond society. In the early fall of 1849, on his way to Philadelphia to help a woman edit her poems, he stopped off in Baltimore and began drinking. He was found senseless in a polling place and taken to a hospital, where he died a few days later on October 7 at the age of forty.

ANALYSIS

The poetry of Edgar Allan Poe cannot be understood adequately apart from his concepts of the role of the poet and of poetry in human life. Probably few poets have followed their own theories more completely than Poe did, and his great popularity with all sorts of readers is due in large part to his consistency in producing certain universally appealing effects. A Poe setting, atmosphere, or situation is instantly recognizable. Specific poems of his have so passed into the common literary heritage that readers with only the slightest acquaintance with his work can quote lines and phrases from such poems as "Annabel Lee" and "The Raven." Yet the very ease with which bits of Poe can be absorbed tends to obscure the fact that all of his poetry is based on carefully thought-out principles of artistic creativity. Poe contended that the poet must be concerned above all with the effects to be produced on the reader. Further, only certain effects are proper to poetry. Poetry must take beauty as its sole province, leaving logic and truth to prose. The poet must do everything in his power to create an intense impression of beauty, marshaling verse form, imagery, rhythm, rhyme, and subject matter in this effort. By "beauty" Poe meant something quite specific: the pleasurable excitement of the soul as it reaches for a perfection beyond this earth. This yearning for an unattainable, supernal beauty means that the subject matter of poetry will almost inevitably be melancholy. Logic and reason as we ordinarily think of them cannot be the poet's concern because ultimate beauty can be grasped, if at all, only aesthetically, not rationally. The universe itself is essentially a work of art, not a logical construct to be analyzed.

The task of poetry, then, is to induce a state of mind in the reader corresponding to the exaltation felt by the soul as it explores the limits of perception in search of ideal beauty. Further, since the intense excitement thus produced cannot be sustained over long periods, a poem by definition must be rather brief: One of Poe's best-known principles is that a long poem is a contradiction in terms. As the poet seeks appropriate images for ideal beauty, he should avoid the concrete, ordinary objects of everyday life, since these are corporeal, not spiritual, and therefore impede the mind's progress toward perfection. The realms of dream, fantasy, the subconscious, and glimpses of life after death are what the poet will find most congenial. These realms cannot be represented directly in language, since they cannot be grasped directly by human beings. Nevertheless, poetry can approach them more nearly than can other kinds of writing because it depends on powers of suggestion, of intuitive imagining, of rhythmical effects which bring the soul some sense of what ideal beauty must be. The poet becomes a careful calculator of effects. Nothing must be allowed into the poem which violates the unity of impression which the poet desires to create in the reader. Brevity will aid here, also, since a very long poem would, according to Poe, dilute and finally destroy the unity of impression for which the poet strives.

"SONNET—TO SCIENCE"

In his poetry, Poe returns again and again to a few basic themes, and to explore the subtle variations he weaves on his themes is one of the principal pleasures of reading his verse. Poe's first important treatment of the poet's relation to the world is found in his "Sonnet—To Science," published when he was twenty. It is an important question for Poe because, according to his theory, the poet will find much in the world that is a barrier to the attainment of ideal beauty. This poem begins by seeming to hail science, but its purpose is actually the reverse, as quickly becomes apparent. Like time itself, the speaker says, science alters everything without regard for human feeling. It peers into every corner of our lives, preying especially upon the poet's heart. In a series of effective rhetorical questions, the speaker demands to know how the poet can love science when it deprives the imagination of inspiration, destroys the power of myth, and prevents him from soaring into worlds of ideal beauty. For Poe, "science" was synonymous with "logic" and "truth"—all representing an approach to reality by means of consecutive reasoning, attention to material objects, and mathematical calculation. The poet should shun such ways of thinking, for the very nature of his activity emphasizes the indefinite, the ideal, the symbolic. Even by protesting, as he does in this poem, the dominance of science in the world, Poe seems to wish not to alter the situation so much as to declare that the poetic and scientific ways of viewing reality are irreconcilable.

"ROMANCE"

Another very important poem, "Romance," provides a version of this position in more personal terms and makes its point through imagery more than through argument. In "Romance" (titled "Preface" in some collections) the contrast is not between poetry and science but between the ideal world of the imagination and the painful world of everyday reality. In the first of two richly suggestive stanzas, he shows us romance as a "painted paroquet." The speaker sees only the reflection of this beautiful bird in the water of "some shadowy lake." Yet it had been a familiar sight to him because it had taught him his alphabet when he was a child in "the wild wood." Through the bird's being visible only by reflection, Poe may be saying that poetry cannot communicate truth directly, but only as truth is comprehended in the beautiful. The second stanza contrasts dramatically with the first. If the childhood years of immersion in Romance may be imaged as a colorful paroquet, the adult period of almost unceasing "tumult" and "unquiet" are figured as "eternal Condor years." Now as an adult the speaker has no time for the idle concerns of every day—he must always be watching for the return of the Condor. He concludes this contrast of images by saying that even when an hour of calm is allowed him and he returns briefly to the beauties of Romance, his conscience would reproach him did not his heart "tremble with the strings." The poem "Romance" represents Poe's version of a familiar Romantic myth: The years of childhood with their heightened imaginative vision are in many ways preferable to the adult's dependence on fact and reason. For Poe specifically, these early years were more attractive because he identified them with a type of poetry which most nearly approached ideal beauty. "Romance" is almost unmatched in the Poe canon for the way the subtle variations in the rhyme scheme (*aabbcdcdee* and *deedeffgfgf*) and the regular iambic tetrameter rhythm unobtrusively reinforce the emotional impact of the poem.

BEAUTY, LOVE, AND LOSS

Poe may be better known for his poems of longing for a lost love than for those on any other subject. He works various modulations on the theme. The woman may personify the pure classical beauty of ancient Greece and Rome ("To Helen"), or she may represent some version of the popular nineteenth century theme of the sleeping beauty who may never awaken ("The Sleeper"). The speaker in the poem may be a surviving husband or lover ("Annabel Lee"), or he may himself be dead or recovering from a brush with death ("For Annie"). The poem may be totally taken up with longing for the lost love ("To One in Paradise"), or her loss may provide an excuse to treat another subject (such as the relationship of body and soul, in "Ulalume"). Finally, the poem may be an intensely personal monologue, like several already named, or it may take the form of a dialogue or brief drama where two speakers debate how the dead should be mourned ("Lenore").

Whatever the mode of treatment, Poe's poetry (as well as his stories) makes clear that the death of a beautiful woman was for him the supremely interesting sub-

ject, since, if ideal beauty is ultimately unattainable, it follows that the most appropriate tone of a poem is melancholy, and certainly there can be no subject more melancholy than the loss of beauty through death.

The autobiographical element in this mixture must be noticed, whatever cautions have to be added in interpreting its appearance in an art form. Poe lost his mother as a young child, and was not close to his stepmother. At fifteen, an older woman whom he loved as a combination of mother and romantic lover died (she was the mother of a friend), and his age undoubtedly made the loss all the more traumatic for him. He watched his wife die a horrible death from tuberculosis, and during the last two years of his life he was declaring his love to several women almost simultaneously. One of these women was widowed from a man whom she had married years before instead of Poe himself.

It will not do, of course, to assume that the sole or even chief explanation of these poems' meaning is the frequency with which Poe himself experienced such loss. The importance of any theme in a writer's work is not how it reflects the events of his life, but what meaning it has for him in the work itself. In Poe's case the meaning centers on the ways in which the loss can be made to embody the effects of yearning, for supernal beauty: thus the frequency in these particular poems of memories, dreams, prophetic visions of the future, and of other expressions of the need to transcend earthly concerns and achieve illumination (however partial) in an imagined land of perfect beauty and truth. Very often the lost woman inhabits a kind of twilight zone, and the speaker in the poem, acting as mourner, guards her memory here on earth while re-creating the effects of the realm of spiritualized beauty which the beloved now presumably inhabits.

"ULALUME"

The poem which most fully reveals Poe's typical treatment of this theme is "Ulalume," written near the end of his life. Readers new to Poe often do not notice that he wrote "Ulalume" to be recited aloud (as he did "Annabel Lee" and "The Bells"). This device undoubtedly explains the somewhat obvious repetition of certain words, especially rhyme words, and the great emphasis on regularity of rhythm found in the poem. Readers keeping the circumstances of the composition of this poem in mind will be less likely to regard its versification as overdone; or, alternatively, they will not be as likely to ignore the narrative thread for the musical effects.

It is autumn of a particularly important year, the speaker's "most immemorial" year. He wanders with his Soul through a semireal, semi-imaginary landscape characterized by gloominess, but also by images of titanic struggle. As he so often does, Poe here provides a vivid *sense* of spiritual extremity without identifying its cause. He is more interested, especially at the beginning, in emotional effect than in analysis, since his initial need is to transport the reader to another level of consciousness. Neither the speaker nor his Soul notes the time of year, however, because they are concentrating so intensely on their inward gloom. The strange landscape through which they travel affects them like the music of Auber or the magic colors in the paintings of Robert Weir. Poe knew that his contemporaries would recognize the artists to whom he referred; thus he could call in his aid his readers' awareness of certain musical and painterly effects to complement the aural effects of the recited words.

As the night advances, two brilliant lights appear in the sky: One is Diana, the Moon, and the other is Venus. (In Poe's poetry, the Moon is always "colder" and "more distant" than Venus, probably because the haziness of Venus in the sky could more easily symbolize the vague outlines of ideal beauty.) Here, Venus observes sympathetically that the speaker yet mourns the loss of someone, so the goddess of love has risen in the sky to lead the mourner to a "Lethean peace of the skies." The Soul mistrusts Venus, but the speaker urges them to go on, guided by "this tremulous light." This seems to be a variation on Poe's favorite idea that the realm of ideal beauty will somehow be a better guide, a surer inspiration for human beings, than will the transient beauties of this world. The speaker therefore pacifies his Soul with soothing words, and they proceed on "to the end of the vista" (a line emphasizing Poe's concern that his readers see this landscape as one in a painting), where they find a tomb. On the door is written the name of his lost love: Ulalume. The speaker now remembers that it was on this very night of the previous fall that he journeyed here—not with his Soul

but with the body of his beloved. "What demon has tempted me" to come here again? he wonders. He can offer only a tentative answer: that the spirits guarding this place have some greater secret than this to hide. They have therefore created this "spectre of a planet" (Venus) to mislead earthly beings.

If this secret is the nature of the Soul's existence in the realm of ideal beauty, as seems likely, then "Ulalume" offers one of Poe's last comments on the difficulty of reaching that realm. Thus the poem ends not with an answer but with a question. The ultimate human tragedy would be to have to give up hope of ever finding ideal beauty. Even the Soul as companion on the quest is not sufficient guarantee of finding it, for the Soul fears confronting the truth. Poe's poems on the loss of a beautiful woman are important, then, not only for their articulation of the theme of ideal beauty, but also for the theme of the imaginary landscape which embodies and controls the means of the search.

IMAGINARY LANDSCAPES

Poe always maintained that objects do not lend themselves readily to the metamorphosis that the artist wishes to impose on them. Therefore he should not represent the objects themselves in his work, but the ideas and feelings they inspire. Poe further believed that words can evoke mental states without referring directly to phenomena. Thus an imaginary landscape is superior to an actual one because the artist can create a total, unified effect without being hindered by unmalleable objects. It is in the imaginary landscapes of Poe's poetry that readers will recognize the closest connections to his fiction. Several poems featuring such landscapes, in fact, such as "The Haunted Palace" and "The Conqueror Worm," were originally parts of short stories. These poems tend to be of two kinds: those that look backward in time to a shadowy memory of primal innocence, and those that look forward to an apocalypse which will substitute for this sad earthly existence a higher, purer one.

"THE CITY IN THE SEA"

One of Poe's most successful poems on the latter theme is his "The City in the Sea" because of its concise descriptive power and marriage of sound and meaning. At the opening of the poem, Death occupies a throne in a strange city lying somewhere "within the dim West." Here the souls of the dead abide. The city resembles "nothing that is ours," and it is surrounded by "melancholy waters." The sun does not shine on this city: Its light comes from out of the sea. It is a lurid light, revealing buildings suspended in air, with Death surveying all from his "proud tower." The sea around the city, like a "wilderness of glass," is "hideously serene." And yet the city is not completely removed from time and motion, for the speaker detects faint movement, a redder glow to the water, a "breathing" of time. He foresees that when this motion increases sufficiently, the city will sink into the waters, and even Hell itself shall bow to it.

Poe seems to mean that Death shall at last itself be conquered. In an earlier version of this poem, Poe shows Death as being forced to find other worlds whose inhabitants he can hope to control—perhaps representing Poe's wish that we will somehow be able to break down the barriers that separate us from the eternal. A paraphrase cannot do justice to the compact energy and power of this poem. There are, in fact, less successful poems by Poe which make his argument on this point more explicit. In "Dreamland," for instance, the speaker is able to pass through the strange landscape of postmortal existence, although he can behold it "but through darkened glasses." It is a place where those who have suffered most in this life may find surcease.

"THE HAUNTED PALACE"

The other theme in the imaginary landscape poems is one of looking not forward to the apocalypse but backward to the primordial innocence first treated by Poe in a different way in "Romance." This group of poems is very important in Poe's total output for its working out of one of his key ideas: that the outline of the poet's life may serve as a model to explain the meaning of all our earthly existence.

Poe's most concise and successful poem on this theme is "The Haunted Palace." There was once, in "the greenest of our valleys," a beautiful palace, guarded by good angels. The valley was perpetually fair, under the dominion of "Thought." At that time, travelers could see in the windows of this palace spirits "moving musically" to the laws of harmony. The ruler of this realm was surrounded by beings who carried out his will in "voices of surpassing beauty." Evil, however, invaded the palace and the valley, destroying their perfection; their ideal beauty is now but a "dim-remembered story." Travelers

through this valley now see in the windows of the palace forms that move to discordant sounds, while, "like a ghastly rapid river," a hideous throng continually rushes out.

"The Haunted Palace" is one of Poe's most explicitly allegorical poems. The images on which the poem depends form a system of symbols which add up to something like the following: As an infant, the poet enjoyed psychic integrity, unified consciousness, and harmony with nature. Time, however, betrayed him; rational language and philosophy estranged him from his visionary self. As an adult, a captive of the everyday world, he longs continually for his former condition when he had unbroken communion with ideal beauty and universal truth. So different is his fallen state from his former one that he can only touch his visionary self through reverie and dream. The only escape from the now hideous palace and its discord is death, and the dying are only too eager to rush out of the palace as quickly as they can.

IDEAL BEAUTY

Ultimately, then, Poe's poems on the imaginary landscape are part of the same fabric as those on the poet in the world and those on the loss of a beautiful woman. Ideal beauty can be conveniently represented as a beautiful woman whose death signifies loss of the original psychic integrity and innocence, as the beautiful bird whose reflection brings us all we know of truth but is replaced by the terrifying condor, and as the palace haunted by pure mind and perfect harmony and the valley forever green, until it is invaded by discord and mere logic.

To read the poetry of Edgar Allan Poe is to enter a world at times so bizarre that some have dismissed it as juvenile fantasy, absurd posturing, or sound without sense. Admirers of Poe are wisest if they acknowledge in his poetry a little of each of these elements. His accomplishments in lyric and descriptive poetry, however, are very impressive. His command of vivid images and subtle rhythms and sound effects (particularly alliteration and assonance) raises his subjects to a level of keen interest for a very wide range of readers. The very regularity of his lines and stanzas makes them easier to remember than those of many other poets. His psychological insight, especially into the abnormal subconscious, is unmatched, at least in nineteenth century poetry.

Although his essay "The Philosophy of Composition" makes demonstrably untrue claims concerning his composition of "The Raven," its importance (as the French were the first to recognize) is that it taught poets the importance of unity, coherence, structure, and economy; of knowing how something will affect a reader; of the dullness and insipidity of didactic verse. Poets as well as readers of poetry will always read Poe to benefit from these not inconsiderable accomplishments.

OTHER MAJOR WORKS

LONG FICTION: *The Narrative of Arthur Gordon Pym*, 1838.

SHORT FICTION: *Tales of the Grotesque and Arabesque*, 1840; *The Prose Romances of Edgar Allan Poe*, 1843; *Tales*, 1845; *The Short Fiction of Edgar Allan Poe*, 1976 (Stuart and Susan Levine, editors).

PLAY: *Politian*, pb. 1835-1836.

NONFICTION: *The Letters of Edgar Allan Poe*, 1948; *Literary Criticism of Edgar Allan Poe*, 1965; *Essays and Reviews*, 1984.

MISCELLANEOUS: *The Complete Works of Edgar Allan Poe*, 1902 (17 volumes); *Collected Works of Edgar Allan Poe*, 1969, 1978 (3 volumes).

BIBLIOGRAPHY

Buranelli, Vincent. *Edgar Allan Poe*. 2d ed. Boston: Twayne, 1977. A thematic approach that deals with Poe's poetry and prose, the history of his reputation, recent critical attitudes, and the permanence of Poe's best work, which Buranelli analyzes as a "retreat" from and "return to reality." The notes and select annotated bibliography provide a good introduction to Poe's scholarship and criticism.

Carlson, Eric W., ed. *Critical Essays on Edgar Allan Poe*. Boston: G. K. Hall, 1987. An extensive, heavily documented introduction surveys the essays in this volume, which is divided into three sections: "Poe's contemporaries," "Creative Writers on Poe," and "Modern Criticism." Each contains important commentary on the poems and is easily located in the detailed index.

Hoffman, Daniel. *Poe Poe Poe Poe Poe Poe Poe*. Baton Rouge: Louisiana State University Press, 1998. A perceptive, if sometimes overly ingenious, study of Poe's personality and work. As the title suggests, Hoffman finds many Poes, a man and artist of many masks. He traces the coherence of the poet's work through the unity of his images.

Kennedy, J. Gerald. *A Historical Guide to Edgar Allan Poe*. New York: Oxford University Press, 2001. Considers the tensions between Poe's otherworldly settings and his representations of violence, delivers a capsule biography situating Poe in his historical context, and addresses topics such as Poe and the American publishing industry, Poe's sensationalism, his relationships to gender constructions, and Poe and American privacy. Bibliographic essay, chronology of Poe's life, bibliography, illustrations, index.

Peeples, Scott. *Edgar Allan Poe Revisited*. New York: Twayne, 1998. An introductory critical study of selected works and a short biography of Poe. Includes bibliographical references and index.

Quinn, Arthur Hobson. *Edgar Allan Poe: A Critical Biography*. Baltimore: Johns Hopkins University Press, 1998. The first comprehensive biography to correct errors in earlier treatments of Poe's life and work, this informative but dry biography is indispensable for a thorough, reliable account of the poet's development.

Regan, Robert, ed. *Poe: A Collection of Critical Essays*. Englewood Cliffs, N.J.: Prentice-Hall, 1967. Introduction focuses on Poe's reputation. Poe's poetry is slighted, but the general essays on his art, especially by Floyd Stovall and Richard Wilbur, are essential reading. Includes select bibliography.

Sova, Dawn B. *Edgar Allan Poe, A to Z*. New York: Facts On File, 2001. A reference encyclopedia consisting of two thousand short entries, alphabetically arranged, on all aspects of Poe, his times, his life, and his works. Bibliographical references, index.

Symons, Julian. *The Tell-Tale Heart: The Life and World of Edgar Allan Poe*. New York: Harper & Row, 1978. A short biography of Poe. Although Symons concedes that his biography is not a work of "original scholarship," he provides the best short life of Poe, with a chapter on his poetry, a succinct, annotated bibliography, and an index.

Walker, I. M., ed. *Edgar Allan Poe: The Critical Heritage*. London: Routledge & Kegan Paul, 1986. The introduction is an in-depth description and analysis of the critical reception of each of Poe's books from 1827 to 1848. Walker includes the important reviews of *Poems* and *The Raven and Other Poems*, general estimates, obituary notices, reviews of his collected works, and "views from abroad."

Mark Minor;
bibliography updated by the editors

POLIZIANO

Angelo Ambrogini
Born: Montepulciano, Italy; July 14, 1454
Died: Florence, Italy; September 28, 1494

PRINCIPAL POETRY
Manta, 1482
Rusticus, 1483
Ambra, 1485
Nutricia, 1491 (the four previous works are collectively known as *Sylvae*)
Stanze cominciate per la giostra del magnifico Giuliano de' Medici, 1518 (commonly known as *Stanze*; *The Stanze of Angelo Poliziano*, 1979)
Rime, 1814

OTHER LITERARY FORMS

Poliziano was a great scholar, a professor, critic, and translator of Greek into Latin, as well as a great poet. At age sixteen, he won the title of *Homericus juvenis* (Homeric youth) by translating books 2 through 5 of the *Iliad* (c. 800 B.C.E.) into Latin hexameters. His translations of the *Enchiridion* (c. 120 C.E.) of Epictetus, the *Histories* (c. 200 C.E.) of Herodian, the *Eroticus* (c. first century C.E.) of Plutarch, the *Charmides* (fourth century B.C.E.) of Plato, the *Problemata* (c. 200 C.E.) of Alexander Aprodisias, and works by Galen and Hippocrates delighted his contemporaries with their stylistic grace. His love of philology, as seen in his *Miscellaneorum centuria prima* (1489), which treats the origins of classic institutions and ceremonies, the significance of fables, words and their uses, and even spelling, made him one of the founders of

modern textual criticism. He was also interested in jurisprudence and composed a recension of the *Pandects* (sixth century C.E.) of Justinian, which, though not a milestone in juristic erudition, gave impetus to further criticism of the scholarly code. Twelve volumes of his letters, written to Lorenzo de' Medici, Marsilio Ficino, and a wide range of other friends and contemporaries, were published in Paris in about 1512. Near the end of his life, Poliziano wrote to King John II of Portugal, tendering him the thanks of the civilized world for dragging from secular darkness into the light of day new worlds and offering his services to record these great voyages.

ACHIEVEMENTS

Poliziano is important in Italian letters both as an interpreter of Italian humanism and as the most significant writer in the language between Giovanni Boccaccio and Ludovico Ariosto. Poliziano mastered the art of Italian versification and gave to the octave a new capacity for expression that would be utilized in the following centuries by Ariosto, Torquato Tasso, and Giambattista Marino. In Poliziano, to quote John Addington Symonds, "Faustus, the genius of the Middle Ages, had wedded Helen, the vision of the ancient world."

BIOGRAPHY

Poliziano was born Angelo Ambrogini in the Tuscan town of Montepulciano, the Latin name of which, Mons Politianus, was the source of the appellation by which the poet is known. His father, Benedetto Ambrogini, a capable bourgeois jurist, was murdered for championing the cause of Piero de' Medici in Montepulciano, whereupon the ten-year-old Poliziano was sent to Florence to seek consolation in his studies. He studied Latin under Cristoforo Landino, who was remarkable for instilling in his pupil the notion that the Tuscan vernacular was in no way inferior to Latin and that, like Latin, it ought to be subject to rules of grammar and rhetoric. Poliziano studied Greek under Giovanni Argyropulos, Andronicus Callistos, Demetrius Chalcondyles, and Marsilio Ficino; and he also studied Hebrew. At sixteen, he began writing epigrams in Greek; at seventeen, he was writing essays on Greek versification; and at eighteen, he published an edition of Catullus. By 1473, Poliziano was in the service of Lorenzo de' Medici, the ruler of Florence and the chief patron of the arts in Italy. To provide Poliziano with an income, Lorenzo appointed him secular prior of the College of San Giovanni. Poliziano obtained the degree of Doctor of Civil Law, took clerical orders, and was appointed to the canonry of the Cathedral of Florence. In 1475, Lorenzo made him tutor to his sons Piero (who succeeded his father for a brief time) and Giovanni (later Pope Leo X), but his wife, Clarice Orsini, who was pious and conventional, preferred a religious education for her sons rather than the secular one Poliziano offered, and she lobbied for his removal as tutor.

Following the tradition set by Pulci, who wrote a tribute in octaves to Lorenzo's tournament held in 1469, Poliziano wrote a celebration of the tournament of Lorenzo's brother Giuliano, held on January 28, 1475, in honor of the latter's beloved, Simonetta Cattaneo, the wife of Marco Vespucci. The undertaking, however, was ill-starred. First, Simonetta died (April 26, 1476), and she had to be changed from the heroine of book 1 of the *Stanze* to her role as resurrected Fortune in book 2. Exactly two years later, on April 26, 1478, Giuliano was murdered at Mass by members of the Pazzi family, who hoped to murder both Medici brothers and thus wrest Florence from Medici control. This second calamity robbed the poem of its hero, and Poliziano never progressed beyond the first stanzas of the second canto. Instead, he wrote a prose memorial in Latin against the Pazzi conspiracy, titled *Conjurationis pactianae commentarium* (1478).

In 1479, Poliziano was dismissed from the Medici household; after six months of wandering in northern Italy, he was finally readmitted to Lorenzo's favor, but Poliziano was never to regain his position as sole tutor to the Medici children. At the Court of Mantua in 1480, in only two days according to his own boast, he wrote his *Orfeo*, the first secular play in Italian. There is, however, a great deal of uncertainty as to the date of the play's composition, and other sources date the work as early as 1471. In 1480, Poliziano was made professor of Greek and Latin literature at the University of Florence, and he continued to hold that position until his death.

Poliziano was not involved in public affairs, and his private life seems to have been uneventful. He did not marry; judging from his Greek epigrams on the youth Chrysocomus, it is possible that the homosexual senti-

ments he placed in the mouth of Orfeo were really his own. In one of Poliziano's *canzoni a ballo*, he pokes light fun at a priest who has a pig stolen from him and then hears the confession of the thief but cannot press charges. Poliziano's comparison of his own situation to that of the priest, "Woe, by what a grief I'm hit;/ I can never speak of it!/ I too suffer like the priest," may be a reference to his homosexuality.

Poliziano's letters reveal how much he enjoyed the rustic pleasures of his villa at Fiesole in the neighborhood of his friends Count Giovanni Pico della Mirandola at Querceto and Marsilio Ficino at Montevecchio. Away from Florence but still close enough to enjoy its panorama, the solitude which he could savor at Fiesole was "beyond all price." He expatiates on this pleasure in the *Rusticus:* "Give unto me the life of a tranquil scholar, amongst the pleasures of the open fields; for serious thought in hours of study, give me my books; I ask but for moderate wealth, well-earned without weary toil, but I desire no Bishop's mitre nor triple tiara to rest as a burden upon my brow."

Poliziano's devotion to Lorenzo was steadfast, and he was at his patron's bedside when Lorenzo died on April 8, 1492; in a Latin monody written after Lorenzo's

Poliziano (© Corbis)

death, Poliziano cried, "Oh that my head were waters and mine eyes a fountain of tears, that I might weep day and night!" He survived his friend and patron by only two years; influenced by the spiritual revival of Girolamo Savonarola, Poliziano was buried as a penitent in the cowl of a Dominican friar.

ANALYSIS

Although the subject matter of Poliziano's poetry has not traveled well into modern times, he has never lost his place in literary history; both his name and his rather unattractive face, with its prominent aquiline nose, are familiar to those who have studied the Italian Renaissance. He was considered the foremost scholar of his day; Erasmus called him a "miracle of nature," and Pietro Bembo, who succeeded him as arbiter of Italian letters, called him the "master of the Ausonian lyre." The enthusiasm with which he applied himself to his teaching of Homer and Vergil drew students from all over Europe, who took his humanistic learning back to their homelands. Among his non-Italian students were the German Johann Reuchlin, the Englishmen William Grocyn and Thomas Linacre, and the Portuguese Arias Barbosa. Linacre, a physician under whom Erasmus studied, introduced the first secular study of Greek at Oxford, and Arias Barbosa introduced the study of Greek at Salamanca. Luigi Pulci, an older poet whose *Giostra* (c. 1470) had set a precedent for the *Stanze* of Poliziano, was in turn aided by Poliziano in the composition of Pulci's parody of the French epic, the *Morgante maggiore* (1483), which work is concluded with a good word for Pulci's "Angel" from Montepulciano. Outside Italy, Poliziano's Italian verse directly influenced the poetry of Juan Boscán in Spain half a century later.

It seems likely that passages in Poliziano's *Stanze* inspired as many as three of Sandro Botticelli's paintings: *The Birth of Venus* (1484), *Primavera* (1478), and *Venus and Mars* (1477). According to Giorgio Vasari and Condivi, Poliziano advised the young Michelangelo on classical subjects. It has also been suggested that Poliziano's version of the myth of Polyphemus and Galatea in the *Stanze* provided the model for Raphael's frescoes in the Villa Farnesina in Rome.

The best of Poliziano's Latin odes on the death of Lorenzo were set to music by Heinrich Isaac, who had succeeded Antonio Squarcialupi as organist at the Medici Court in 1475. George Chapman used a passage from the *Ambra* in the dedication of his translation of the *Odyssey* in 1615, and he reworked the ode on the death of Albiera degli Albizzi into his "Epicede or Funerall Song" on the death of Henry, Prince of Wales (1612).

ORFEO

Poliziano's idyllic *Orfeo* is the earliest secular play in Italian literature and marks the beginning of that characteristic Renaissance genre of the dramatic mythological pastoral that would culminate in Tasso's *Aminta* (1581; English translation, 1591). Because the playlet was also accompanied by music, now unfortunately lost, it is seen as a forerunner of modern opera, and because of the author's attempts to individualize the psychology of his characters, it is deemed important in the evolution of the tragicomedy as well.

Although Poliziano's *Orfeo* is technically more a dramatic work than it is a poem, it is actually better poetry than it is drama. As drama, it is flawed and illogical; as poetry, according to John Addington Symonds, "the very words evaporate and lose themselves in floods of sound." Its hero, Orpheus, who represents Renaissance Italy, is a lover of art and beauty who dares to invade the dark depths of Hades in search of his lost lover, Eurydice. *Orfeo* is a short work of only 454 lines, written mostly in octaves, but also containing one passage in *terza rima*, two *ballate*, two *canzonette*, and two bits of Latin verse. The first third of the play is pastoral; the middle third, in which Orpheus pleads passionately before Pluto in Hades for the release of his lady, is the most lyrical:

> Therefore the nymph I love is left for you
> When Nature leads her deathward in due time:
> But now you've cropped the tendrils as they grew,
> The grapes unripe, while yet the sap did climb:
> Who reaps the young blades wet with April dew,
> Nor waits till summer hath o'erpassed her prime?
> Give back, give back my hope one little day!
> Nor for a gift, but for a loan I pray.

The last third culminates in the brutal murder of the hero. When Orpheus turns to look at Eurydice before the stipulated time, she disappears, and the embittered lover launches into a wild lament: "And since my fate hath wrought me wrong so sore,/ I swear I'll never love a woman more." He proceeds to decry the man who mopes and moans for a woman's love, and then declares that, after all, it is the love of males that is "sweetest, softest, best." He invokes the names of gods who have loved boys, and then is silenced by an indignant maenad who invites her followers to slay the slanderous Orpheus for his insult to their sex. They tear him limb from limb and soak the forest in his blood; after boasting of their deed, the maenads join in the drunken *ballata* that concludes the playlet. This final song, which resembles the *trionfo* in form and its spirit of recklessness, appears to be Poliziano's own contribution to the Orphic legend. It was indeed a remarkable innovation; neither the Greek nor the Roman maenads were characterized to this extent by drunkenness or lust for drink.

STANZE

If Poliziano adapted classical material to contemporary form in *Orfeo*, in the *Stanze*, he dressed contemporary material in classical style. Despite its complete title, *Stanze cominciate per la giostra del magnifico Giuliano de' Medici* (stanzas begun for the tournament of the magnificent Giuliano de' Medici), the poem offers no details of the joust itself: The subject disappears beneath the strata of decoration. While there is little that is original in the poem, which might accurately be called a collage of snippets taken from such authors as Statius, Claudian, Theocritus, Euripides, Ovid, Vergil, and Petrarch, its sheer ornamentation is lush and impressive.

The poem addresses three of the most fervent interests of the fifteenth century Italian public: the love of classical literature, the search for artistic beauty, and the enjoyment and appreciation of nature. As the narrative begins, Giuliano is indifferent to love while amorous nymphs sigh over him. He prefers instead to ride his Sicilian steed, and as a simple hunter untroubled by other passions, he often makes his home in the forest, protecting "his face from the rays of the sun with a garland/ of pine or green beech." He has no sympathy for frenzied lovers; love, he reasons, is but the result of lust and sloth. Cupid decides to challenge the young man's indifference and sends a white doe to lure him to a flowery glade under the shadow of gnarled beech trees, where he is smitten by the nymph identified as Simonetta. The fair-skinned, white-garmented Simonetta is ornamented with roses, flowers, and grass, and there are ringlets of her golden hair upon her "humbly proud" forehead. When Giuliano asks what friendly star makes him worthy of a sight so beautiful, Simonetta demurs, answering that she is not what he is searching for, that she is not worthy of an altar, and that furthermore she is already married.

Cupid reports the success of his mission to his mother, Venus, and there ensues a lengthy description of the realm of Venus on the island of Cyprus, a "realm where every Grace delights, where Beauty/ weaves a garland of flowers about her hair,/ where lascivious Zephyr flies behind Flora and/ decks the green grass with flowers." It was this passage (octave 68) that inspired Botticelli's painting *Primavera*, which itself may have served as a kind of frontispiece to Poliziano's *Stanze*. Here, in the realm of Venus, on the doors of her palace, "splendid with gems and with such/ carvings that all other works would be crude and lifeless in comparison," there is one carving of "a young woman not with human countenance/ carried on a conch shell, wafted to shore by playful zephyrs." These lines (octave 99) were probably the source of Botticelli's masterpiece, *The Birth of Venus*.

Venus decides to provoke Giuliano to hold a tournament in honor of his new lady, and the second canto of the *Stanze* begins triumphantly with wonderful dreams and prophecies of the glory to be achieved by Giuliano in the tournament, for which the entire first canto had been an introduction. The death of the actual Simonetta, however, required the conversion of the nymph bearing her name to a personified Fortune, who governs Giuliano's life in a different capacity. After discussing the futility of tears in the face of this disaster, the poet proffers this bit of realistic advice: "Blessed is/ he who frees his thoughts from her [Fortune] and encloses/ himself completely within his own virtue." The work breaks off abruptly at the end of octave 46; the political murder of the actual Giuliano robbed the poet of his hero.

RISPETTI AND STRAMBOTTO RHYMES

In the decade from 1470 to 1480, Poliziano used Italian for many of his lyrics. He wrote as many as two hundred *rispetti*, eight-line or occasionally six-line love poems rhyming alternately and followed by a concluding couplet with a new rhyme, that are called *strambotti* elsewhere in Italian literature. The *strambotto* may in its origin reflect an original link with folk dance. The poems of Poliziano are not quite folk songs, and although unhampered by erudite language, their accomplished phraseology and carefully selected metaphors are obviously the work of a master. Their expression aspires to a collective rather than a personal essence. Here, instead of the *contadino* willing to mortgage heaven for his *dama*, there is the scholar-courtier dabbling at love as a pastime and imitating "the gold of the heart with the baser material of fine rhetoric" (Symonds). Less generous than Symonds's judgment is the appraisal of Francesco De Sanctis. He finds even less originality in the *rispetti* of Poliziano than is found in the *Stanze*, and De Sanctis further charges the poet with haste and inattentiveness, lamenting the lack of the personal and subjective touch achieved in similar works by Petrarch. In Poliziano, the same ideas are repeated with only slight variation: The catalog of folk themes was small, and Poliziano did little to make it larger. These few popular ideas move in a circle around the most uncomplicated of situations, such as the beauty of the lover, jealousy, leave-taking, waiting, hope, provocation, despair and thoughts of death, avowals of love and crushing rejections.

CANZONETTE

The best of Poliziano's Italian lyrics are his thirty or so dance songs in the *ballata* form, sometimes classed variously as *canzoni a ballo* or *canzonette*, written in ottava rima but longer and more sophisticated than the *rispetti*. They certainly fail as poetry if judged by Matthew Arnold's definition of poetry as a "criticism of life," but Symonds has made a valiant attempt to coax modern readers to a sympathetic appreciation of these curiously time-bound lyrics. If, proposes Symonds, one transports oneself back to Florence on a summer night, as Prince Lorenzo wanders in the streets with Poliziano, his singing-boys joining hands with beautiful workshop girls and apprentice lads and marble carvers, one can appreciate such lines as these:

> For when the full rose quits her tender sheath,
> When she is sweetest and most fair to see,
> This is the time to place her in thy wreath,
> Before her beauty and her freshness flee.
> Gather ye therefore roses with great glee,
> Sweet girls, or ere their perfume pass away.

These lines are from Poliziano's dance song "I' mi trovai fanciulle un bel mattino" ("I Went A-Roaming, Maidens, One Bright Day"). The title recurs five times as the refrain between four stanzas that describe the violets and the lilies of the landscape, relate the poet's discovery of the incomparable roses and the rapture that their perfume induces in him, and culminate with the poet's instinct to pluck the blooming flowers before they fade and are lost, ending with the *carpe diem* lesson of the stanza quoted above.

"OH, WELCOME MAY" AND "MY BRUNETTE"

Another May song is "Ben venga maggio" ("Oh, Welcome May"), which in addition to its now clichéd topos, suffers a further indignity in its transference to modern English: The loss of sonority and cadence when its refrain word, *maggio*, becomes the lackluster monosyllable *May*. The mirth and exuberance of the original do, however, survive in translation: "With rose and lily crowned,/ and your lips a thirst,/ Love, laughing, comes a ground./ Welcome him to your feast./ Who will, of you, be first/ to give him buds of May?" The birds and flowers of this poem are not merely a backdrop but rather an integral part of the whole exhilarating ritual. Every word contributes to the enthralling gaiety.

The Tuscan peasants' songs of Maying and wooing were those most often reworked by Poliziano when he wrote in Italian. Of his wooing songs, the best is "La brunettina mia" ("My Brunette"), a poem which Symonds judged untranslatable. The brunette of the title is a village beauty who bathes her face in the fountain and wears upon her hair a wreath of wild flowers. She is a blossoming branch of thorn in spring; her breasts are May roses, her lips are strawberries. It should be noted, however, that Poliziano's modern editor, Giosuè Carducci, concluded that this poem was in fact not written by Poliziano.

STREET SONGS

Departing from the aristocratic tradition of poetry that dictates restraint and decorum, Poliziano, like Lorenzo, wrote *canti carnascialeschi*, street songs that could be satirical, gibing, or even ribald and to which Savonarola accordingly took exception. It was precisely the disrespectful tone of such poems that typified to the patriot-priest Savonarola the decadence of his age.

GREEK EPIGRAMS AND LATIN POEMS

Poliziano's output in Greek was limited to fifty-seven epigrams that appeared in his *Opera omnia* (1498). Poliziano's Greek vocabulary is "unexceptionable" and "simple"; he writes in the ordinary dialect of the epigrammatic poets as well as in Doric. Thematically, Poliziano follows the ancient practice of reworking familiar ideas; his epigram on Chalcondyles, for example, was modeled on Plato's epigram in praise of Aristophanes. Six of the epigrams, written about 1492, praise the scholarly Alessandra Scala, "whose immortal beauty could not be the effect of art but only of simple nature." There are also the Doric couplets on two beautiful boys and the love sonnet to the youth Chrysocomus.

Poliziano's poems in Latin were among the most accomplished written since antiquity. His use of Latin was more original than his use of Greek; rather than merely culling phrases from classical works, he trusted his own ear, which did, however, cause him to mix dictions from different periods. In addition to composing Latin poems in established forms such as elegy, epigram, satire, and idyll, he struck out in a new direction and poured forth torrents of hexameters that testified to his remarkable intellectual energy. About one hundred epigrams in Latin by Poliziano have survived, many of which are addressed to Lorenzo and other heads of state and to his friends; some are epitaphs, such as the one for Fra Lippo Lippi and Squarcialupi; and some are inscriptions, such as the one for the bust of Giotto by Benedetto da Maiano. Others are harangues against humanist rivals and still others are love poems. Among Poliziano's longer Latin poems are odes and elegies on, for example, the death of Lorenzo and the death of Albiera degli Albizzi, a young and lovely lady soon to have been married.

Written during the decade from 1480 to 1490 and based on Poliziano's lectures at the University of Florence were four pieces collectively titled *Sylvae*. Poliziano borrowed the title from Statius; the poems combine classical scholarship with great poetic skill. The *Manta* is a panegyric of Vergil. The *Rusticus* celebrates the joys of country life and prefaces the study of the bucolic poets, primarily Hesiod and Vergil. The *Ambra*, from the name of Lorenzo's favorite villa, contains an idyllic description of the Tuscan landscape and a eulogy of Homer.

The *Nutricia* is a general introduction to the study of ancient and modern poetry, from the legendary and real poets of Greece and Rome to Dante Alighieri, Petrarch, Giovanni Boccaccio, and Guido Cavalcanti, closing with a characterization of some of Lorenzo's poems. Poliziano's brief dismissal in this work of the great triad of Greek tragedians is quaintly revealing of how little fifteenth century Italians valued the drama of ancient Greece.

Poliziano, the most brilliant classical scholar of his age, was a true philologist in the etymological sense of the word; he loved learning, and his scholarly writings are remarkably free of the pedantry that had marred and unnecessarily complicated such writing before his example. Poliziano was charged with the fire of his classical studies, and he saw no contradiction in rendering the poetic offshoots of his glorious lore in the lowly vernacular. Despite his vast learning, the diction of his vernacular poetry is down-to-earth and uncomplicated, and if he was accused of composing his Latin verses "with more heat than art," it was because he actually responded to his craft as an ancient rather than as an imitator.

OTHER MAJOR WORKS

PLAY: *Orfeo*, pr. 1480 (English translation, 1879; also known as *Orpheus*)

NONFICTION: *Miscellaneorum centuria prima*, 1489 (commonly known as *Miscellanea*); *Conjurationis pactianae commentarium*, 1498.

MISCELLANEOUS: *Opera omnia*, 1498.

BIBLIOGRAPHY

Brand, Peter, and Lino Pertile, eds. *The Cambridge History of Italian Literature*. Rev. ed. New York: Cambridge University Press, 1999. Includes introductory information on Poliziano's life and work, and pertinent historical background.

D'Amico, John F. *Theory and Practice in Renaissance Textual Criticism: Beatus Rhenanus Between Conjecture and History*. Berkeley: University of California Press, 1988. The first chapter gives a short account of Poliziano's achievements.

Donadoni, Eugenio. *A History of Italian Literature*. Translated by Richard Monges. New York: New York University Press, 1969. Contains introductory biographical and critical information on Poliziano's life and work.

Godman, Peter. *From Poliziano to Machiavelli: Florentine Humanism in the High Renaissance.* Princeton, N.J.: Princeton University Press, 1998. Godman presents an intellectual history of Florentine humanism from the lifetime of Poliziano in the later fifteenth century to the death of Niccolo Machiavelli in 1527. Making use of unpublished and rare sources, Godman traces the development of philological and official humanism.

Grafton, Anthony. *Defenders of the Text: The Traditions of Scholarship in an Age of Science, 1450-1800.* Cambridge, Mass.: Harvard University Press, 1991. In chapter 2 Grafton summarizes Poliziano's innovations as a classical scholar.

Jack Shreve;
bibliography updated by the editors

FRANCIS PONGE

Born: Montpellier, France; March 27, 1899
Died: Le Bar-sur-Loup, France; August 6, 1988

PRINCIPAL POETRY

Douze Petits Écrits, 1926
Le Parti pris des choses, 1942 (*Taking the Side of Things,* 1972; also known as *The Nature of Things,* 1995)
Le Carnet du bois de pins, 1947
Proêmes, 1948
La Seine, 1950
La Rage de l'expression, 1952
Le Grand Recueil, 1961 (3 volumes: *Lyres, Méthodes,* and *Pièces*)
Tome premier, 1965
Le Savon, 1967 (*Soap,* 1969)
Nouveau Recueil, 1967
La Fabrique du Pré, 1971 (*The Making of the Pré,* 1979)
Things, 1971

The Voice of Things, 1972 (includes *Taking the Side of Things* and selected other poems and essays)
Comment une figue de paroles et pourquoi, 1977
L'Écrit Beaubourg, 1977
The Sun Placed in the Abyss, 1977
Selected Poems, 1994

OTHER LITERARY FORMS

Although Francis Ponge did admit to writing poetry, he was reluctant to call his works poems, inventing instead other names for them, such as "prétextes," "définitions-descriptions," and "proêmes." Most of his works are generally classified as prose poems, ranging from a few sentences in length to those which are book length, such as *Soap.* Certain of his texts, however, are not readily classifiable. Commentary on the act of writing poetry is a feature of many of Ponge's works; the transcripts of his conversations with Philippe Sollers, for example, are prose texts *about* poetry, while a work such as "Le carnet du bois de pins" ("The Notebook of the Pine Woods") is clearly a poetic piece which also features a level of meta-commentary about the act of writing. There are, however, other works, many of them contained in a volume titled *Méthodes,* that are basically theoretical works expounding Ponge's aesthetic, but whose structural and poetic qualities effectively blur the distinction between theoretical work and literary text. Ponge's interest in the creation of the literary text as process is evidenced by two of his other works, *The Making of the Pré* and *Comment une figue de paroles et pourquoi* (how a fig of words and why). In each of these two works, a comparatively short poem is preceded by the notes, doodles, dictionary definitions, preliminary drafts, and the like which chronicle the various stages of evolution toward the finished poem. Also worthy of mention, as constituting a separate literary form, are Ponge's works of art criticism, which have been collected in the volume *L'Atelier contemporain* (the contemporary workshop), published in 1977.

ACHIEVEMENTS

During the first thirty-five years of Francis Ponge's career, he was known only within limited artistic circles. His reputation grew slowly, and in 1956, *La Nouvelle Revue française* devoted an entire issue to his work. In

1959, Ponge received a prize for his poem "La Figue (séche)" ("The [Dried] Fig"). In that year, he also received the medal of the French Legion of Honor. Between 1965 and 1971, he lectured extensively in the United States, Canada, and Great Britain, and in 1966-1967 he was a visiting professor at Columbia University. He received the Ingram Merrill Foundation Award for 1972 and the Books Abroad/Neustadt International Prize for Literature in 1974. In 1975, at the prestigious international colloquium at Cerisy-la-Salle, his oeuvre was the subject of study by a distinguished group of his literary colleagues (the proceedings of this conference were published in 1977).

BIOGRAPHY

Francis Ponge was born on March 27, 1899, in the city of Montpellier, in the south of France. His father was a bank manager, and his Protestant parents provided him with a secure and loving middle-class upbringing. His childhood in this Mediterranean environment often brought him in contact with the remains of Roman architecture and monuments with their Latin inscriptions; his early awareness of France's cultural and linguistic links with classical civilization is everywhere evident in his poetry.

In 1909, the Ponge family moved to Normandy, where Ponge attended secondary school. He studied Greek and Latin and grew to love their precision; this classical training taught him to appreciate the historical depth of the French language. His study of the natural sciences familiarized him with the scientific method and developed in him the habit of careful observation and the minute recording of details which characterize his poetry. He also excelled in philosophy, taking top honors for his *baccalauréate* essay, titled "L'Art de penser par soi-même" (the art of thinking for oneself).

In 1916, Ponge entered a *lycée* in Paris to prepare himself for university study. In 1917, he began reading philosophy at the Sorbonne and law at the École de Droit. His tastes in philosophy led him to study Arthur Schopenhauer, John Locke, and Benedict de Spinoza, rather than currently popular figures, such as the vitalist Henri Bergson. In 1918, and again in the following year, his hopes for admission to the École Normale Supérieure were blocked by a traumatic inability to speak during crucial oral examinations. This unhappy failure may have been symptomatic of some greater emotional disturbance during that period of his life, or, as some critics have suggested, it may have been caused by a fear of being unable to express himself orally in a precise manner. In any case, there appears to be a connection between these events and the development of Ponge's restrained, meticulous poetic style.

Ponge's awareness of social and political problems was heightened by the chaotic events of World War I and the Russian Revolution. Ponge was becoming thoroughly disgusted with what he perceived to be the weakness and corruption of a society lacking strong moral principles. In April, 1918, he joined the army. The indignities he suffered as a common soldier serving in an army that rewarded mediocre performance and crushed the individual's spirit only compounded his negative feelings about the deficiencies of French society.

Demobilized in 1919, Ponge spent the next three or four years on the edges of Left Bank literary circles. During this time, he published some poems and made a few important contacts with critics and editors. He judged the

Francis Ponge

Parisian literary world to be generally snobbish and affected, however, and refused to play the role of attentive young disciple which might have gained for him greater exposure. Preferring to work alone, he began to search for his own aesthetic voice that would express the spirit of revolt he felt against social and literary decadence.

Whether because of his Protestant upbringing, his parental influence, his education, or certain other factors, even at a young age Ponge had exhibited a marked strength of character and independence, high ideals, and a belief in the individual's responsibility for his own actions. These traits influenced his literary and political development. Throughout his adult life, he was attracted to various political, literary, and philosophical movements because of affinities with certain of their beliefs; his refusal to adopt completely any system of beliefs but his own, however, made most of these alliances rather brief. He associated himself with the Surrealists because of their spirit of literary and linguistic revolt, but he was uncomfortable with their undisciplined approach to composition and the excessive hermeticism of some Surrealist writings. Ponge joined the French Communist Party in 1937 because he saw it as the only viable means of improving living and working conditions for French workers, but his inability to accept the dogmatism of the Party and its doctrinaire attitudes toward art eventually led him to resign. His beliefs about the limitations and moral imperatives governing humankind's actions in the world have much in common with those of Albert Camus and other Existentialist writers, although Ponge's ultimate view of the human condition is more optimistic than Camus's. Aspects of Ponge's philosophy and aesthetics can be labeled materialist, mechanist, phenomenological, Stoic, and Epicurean, but Ponge's individualism resists categorization.

After the death of his father in 1923, Ponge's mother came to live with him in Paris. With the exception of an interlude in 1927 when a small inheritance allowed him to live comfortably and write full-time, Ponge was almost constantly plagued by financial difficulties for the next twenty years of his life. A succession of minor jobs with publishing houses and insurance companies, punctuated by periods of unemployment, often left him with no more than twenty minutes a day to devote to his writing.

Ponge's association with the Surrealist movement came in the late 1920's. He met André Breton and other prominent Surrealists, participated in some of their less extravagant activities, and followed their literary experiments with interest. His involvement with them was brief, however. He discovered that he wished to marry, and not wanting to offend his fiancé's middle-class family by continuing to affiliate with an artistic movement so thoroughly disliked by the French bourgeoisie, he abandoned his lukewarm connections with the Surrealists. He accepted an appropriately respectable job with the publishing firm Messageries Hachette in 1931. He and Odette Chabanel were married in that same year, and their daughter Armande was born in 1935.

The drudgery and demeaning nature of his "respectable" job inspired great sympathy in Ponge for his fellow workers. A desire to see the quality of life improved for all workers, as well as a growing concern about fascism, led him to become a labor union official in 1936 and a member of the Communist Party in 1937. His role as a union activist resulted in his losing his position in 1937.

Unemployed for a time, Ponge subsequently worked for an insurance firm until he joined the army in 1939. Demobilized in 1940 after the fall of France, he was active in the Resistance movement in the south of France, both as a journalist and in the underground. He continued to write poetry, and his first major collection of poems, *Taking the Side of Things*, was published in 1942.

Returning to Paris after the Liberation in 1944, Ponge became the literary and art editor for *Action*, a communist weekly newspaper. This brought him into stimulating contact with the work of such literary and artistic figures as Louis Aragon, Paul Éluard, Albert Camus, René Char, Pablo Picasso, Georges Braque, and Jean Dubuffet. In 1944, Jean-Paul Sartre drew attention to Ponge; his essay on *Taking the Side of Things* was influential in introducing Ponge to the French literary public.

Ponge became increasingly irritated with the dogmatic attitudes of both *Action* and the Communist Party, and by 1947 he had resigned his editorship and allowed his membership in the Communist Party to lapse. For the next few years, Ponge found little employment, and he and his family were reduced to extreme poverty. His literary work was becoming better known, but in spite of occasional publications and speaking engagements, he was from time to time forced to sell personal possessions in order to pay his debts. Not until 1952, when he was fifty-three years of age, was Ponge to know a fair degree of financial security; in that year, he was offered a teaching position at the Alliance Française in Paris, which he held until he reached retirement age. Subsequently, he lived and wrote in Provence, with occasional visits abroad as a visiting professor or guest lecturer, until his death in 1988.

Most of Ponge's literary recognition came late in his career, although essays by Sartre and Camus helped to generate some early interest in his work. In the 1960's, the *Tel Quel* group, headed by Philippe Sollers, and exponents of the French New Novel such as Alain Robbe-Grillet, discovered their kinship with Ponge's aesthetic and linguistic explorations. Ponge finally seems to have a secure place in the mainstream of contemporary French literature.

ANALYSIS

The title of Francis Ponge's first major book of poems epitomizes his aesthetic philosophy and poetic style. Usually translated as *Taking the Side of Things*, it announces both Ponge's preference for things over ideas and his desire to correct what he believes is a human anthropocentric conception of the universe. Ponge disapproves of the human tendency to regard abstract ideas as absolutes rather than as linguistic constructs whose truth is only relative. He is also unhappy with commonplace cultural notions which deem certain subjects unworthy of poetic consideration. Rejecting such assumptions, Ponge has adopted an ironic anti-intellectualism by devoting his literary endeavors to the defense of the concrete things of the world. As subjects for his poems, he chooses ordinary objects encountered in daily life that are often taken for granted. He perceives them as relegated to a kind of second-class citizenship by their inability to express themselves, and he sympathetically imagines them as pleading with him to speak for them.

Ponge has thus designated himself as the advocate of things. In his poems, he declines to describe the object as though it were a human being, and he resists the lure of lyric excess which might tempt him to forget his self-appointed task. Choosing an object such as a door, a pebble, a loaf of bread, or a bar of soap, he observes it

with the concentration of a scientist. He avoids preconceived ideas and linguistic formulas unless he can transform them to offer the reader fresh insights into the nature of the object or the functioning of language. He seeks not to render the object from a human point of view, but rather to find a literary form whose structure, density, and character will be the verbal equivalent of the object.

Ponge has labeled his works *définitions-descriptions*, a term he invented to describe a literary form that would combine the functions of encyclopedias, etymological dictionaries, and dictionaries of synonyms, rhymes, and analogous words. Whereas the traditional dictionary definition uses words devoid of connotation to describe each object, Ponge chooses words with greater affective content for his descriptions; the object is evoked repeatedly by words whose sound, spelling, etymology, or secondary meanings reflect and echo the object.

For Ponge, the ideal result of this faithful attention to the object will be a literary text which has as much material solidity as the object it represents. Although manifestly not the same as the object itself, this kind of poetic formulation has characteristics similar to those of the object. The words which make up the poetic text are thus to be reckoned with as material presences, not as transparent signs which are to be transcended in search of the "real" object to which they refer. In addition, each object poem will have its own unique structure; Ponge avoids established literary forms because they require the poet to make compromises. In Ponge's view, for example, the requirements of the sonnet's structure might cause a poet to reject that word that best reveals the object's essence because it does not satisfy the requirements of meter or rhyme.

An insistence upon the irreducible materiality of language is central to Ponge's approach to poetry. He speaks of words as objects which are "strangely concrete, with two dimensions, for the eye and the ear, and the third is perhaps something like their meaning." Language has an often startling ability to reveal the essential characteristics of the things it describes, but careless use of language devalues it, allowing historically acquired meanings to be lost. With a rigor which is classical in its insistence on proportion and in its rejection of subjective emotionalism, Ponge seeks forms so apt that they will resist the ravages of time, much, as he has suggested, as the Roman inscriptions of his beloved Provence have weathered the centuries.

"ESCARGOTS"

For Ponge, the ability to use language is not a reason to elevate man to a position of superiority in the world. He does not often refer to human beings in his poetry of objects, fearing that he cannot be objective; Ponge's object lessons, however, reveal that he holds man to be neither more nor less important than any other part in the mechanistic workings of the universe. In a poem titled "Escargots" (snails), Ponge contrasts the snail's evanescent secretion, its "silvery wake" of slime, to its enduring shell. He then draws the analogy to man's own "secretions"—his mundane, everyday language, which will disappear as quickly as does the snail's trail—and man's literary creations, which, fashioned with care, can be as lasting as the snail's shell. Ponge admires the snail, whose art is an inherent product of its life and whose modest shell will endure as a monument even after the snail is gone. Its shell is perfectly proportioned to the snail and is eminently suited to its nature. The analogous conclusion, for Ponge, is that language is man's essential property and that it is his ethical duty to use it as deliberately as possible, so that what he produces is as perfectly suited to man as the shell is to the snail.

"LE CYCLE DES SAISONS"

Ponge views the entire world as expressive, although most of its objects have severely limited vocabularies. In "Le Cycle des saisons" (the cycle of the seasons), for example, trees manifest their exuberance in an eloquent profusion of "words"—that is, their leaves. Because each tree "utters" the same leaf again and again, however, the trees can only repeat their single-word vocabulary. Since humans represent the sole creatures whose language enables them to speak about, and on behalf of, other things, they can, like Ponge, use their talent so that the poetic "monuments" they leave behind dignify not only humanity, but also the objects which so faithfully serve it.

EQUIVALENCE

Ponge's belief that the poem should perfectly suit its object-subject has led him to formulate a compositional ideal which he calls *adéquation*, best translated from its Latin components—*ad* (to) and *aequus* (equal)—as "equivalence." A perfect realization of this ideal results

in a poem with almost magical qualities; its words, while remaining true to language's own laws of syntax, so perfectly conjure up the object they describe that the poem becomes the verbal equivalent of the object. Ponge attempts to achieve *adéquation* through the use of various compositional techniques: the creation of forms that are tailor-made for their subjects, the frequent use of word associations, the exploration of etymologies, the innovative and often humorous use of figurative language, the coining of puns and portmanteau words, and the enlistment of typography in support of a poetic idea.

FITTING FORM TO OBJECT

Ponge attempts to fit the form of the poem to the object it describes, both on the level of overall structure and on the level of syntax. "L'Huître" (the oyster), for example, has three sections. The first describes the outward appearance of the oyster, stressing its obstinate refusal to reveal its inner self. The second section uses a metaphor that describes the shell's contents as a separate world whose sky is a hard mother-of-pearl *firmament*. Finally, a single sentence refers to that rarity, the pearl, as a *formule* ("tiny form," but also "formula"). This mimetic approach to form is not without its humorous side; the "Ode inachevée à la boue" (unfinished ode to mud) is as formless as the substance it describes, covering several pages and finally trailing off in mid-sentence. In *Soap*, words froth and bubble and proliferate in imitation of the effervescence of soap and include such airy coinages as *ebullescence* (ebullience). In "Le Papillon" (the butterfly), soft fricative and plosive sounds abound, and the poem's breathless manner cleverly mimics the whimsical and erratic flight of the butterfly: "Dès lors, le papillon erratique ne se pose plus qu'au hasard de sa course, ou tout comme" ("From then on, the erratic butterfly no longer alights except by chance in its flight, or just about").

"LE MIMOSA" AND "PLUIE"

Sometimes Ponge's poems present an intentional air of formlessness. Composed of numerous short sections with labels such as "Variant" and "Other," these alternative versions approach the same subject from slightly different points of view in a manner reminiscent of the multiple perspectives of Cubist art. For example, in "Le Mimosa" (the mimosa), Ponge subtly demonstrates the process of poetic creation by catching the reader off guard with a mélange of false starts and complaints about how difficult it is to capture the essence of the mimosa in words. The effect of all of this "beating around the bush" is a poem that simultaneously communicates a great deal both about the elusive fragility of flowers and about the mysterious nature of the creative process.

However winding the linguistic route through a typical Ponge poem may be, the end is reached when, after having led the reader on a thorough search of all the levels and relations of meaning, the object of the poem is present in the reader's consciousness with an unprecedented, harmonious clarity. For example, "Pluie" (rain) ends its detailed description of a shower with the brief phrase "il a plu" (it has rained). Here, the rain, which first appeared in the poem as an object (noun), is finally seen as a process (verb); and, as is indicated by the use of the past tense, one which is not finished. Ponge avoids the simple past tense, more common in literary texts but clearly connoting finality. Instead he uses the present-perfect tense, which in French indicates the strong link between this past action and the present time; in this line resonates the memory of all that has transpired in the poem. Furthermore, since *plu* is the past participle of the verb *plaire* (to please) as well as of the verb *pleuvoir* (to rain), an additional interpretation of this last line is, "It has been pleasing"—a modest judgment on the part of the poet with which most readers would concur.

ETYMOLOGIES, PUNS, AND PORTMANTEAU WORDS

Ponge maintains that language contains truths about the essential nature of the objects it is capable of describing, if only writers are willing to work hard enough to find these truths. Once the inherent harmony between language and the objects of the world is struck, the poet will find that the words intertwine to form a network of secondary meanings and serendipitous etymologies.

In an essay on his creative method, Ponge gives an illustration of the inherent ability of language to form metonymical links that illuminate the world with sudden insights: Once, when writing in Algeria, the word *sacripant* (roguish) continually occurred to him as an adjective descriptive of the harsh red color of the Sahel at the foot of the Atlas mountains. Curious about the etymology of the word, he traced it to the name of Ludovico Ariosto's characters. He then discovered to his

delight that this name, Sacripant, was linked to that of Rodomont—a king of Algeria, whose name (red mountain) furnished Ponge with the sort of felicitous coincidence in which his poems abound.

Sometimes Ponge puns on words in such a way that their literal meaning is revealed in a fresh and unexpected manner. In "L'Orange" (the orange), Ponge describes a squeezed orange; in a play on the French *pression* (pressing or squeezing), he portrays the orange as having undergone an ordeal of "expression" and of having submitted to a forced "oppression." In yet another punning excursion, Ponge compares the "aspirations" of the squeezed orange to regain its "countenance" (an allusion not only to its shape or disposition, but also to its contents) to those of a sponge; he remarks that, whereas the sponge will soak up any liquid, even dirty water, "l'orange a meilleur goût"—"the orange has better taste." These and other clever plays on words seem particularly apt as they are applied to the orange. The reader comes away glad that Ponge has tried to render it "aussi rondement que possible"—as loyally, as ardently as possible (which *rondement* ordinarily means in French)—but in the case of the orange, also adding a further layer of meaning, in that *rondement* is a word originally derived from that roundness so descriptive of an orange.

Such puns are typical of Ponge's playful approach to words. He is also very sensitive to the ability of word associations to trigger poetic observations and to create stylistic unity. In "La Huître" (the oyster), the circumflex and -*tre* ending of the poem's title inspire Ponge's use of the French suffix -*âtre*, as in *blanchâtre* (whitish), *verdâtre* (greenish), *noirâtre* (blackish), and *opiniâtrement* (obstinately). In "Le Pain" (the loaf of bread), Ponge compares the crusty surface of the loaf to the raised surface of a relief map or a globe. This novel view of the loaf's surface suddenly yields a panoramic impression of the geography of Earth, thus trading on an imaginative link between the words *pain* (bread) and *panoramique* (panoramic), which appear in the first lines of the poem.

Ponge is not above inventing etymologies for words when it suits his purpose. His discussion of "L'Ustensile" (the utensil) is a product of his imaginative conjecture that *ustensile* is derived from a combination of the words *utile* (useful) and *ostensible* (ostensible); this latter word refers to the fact that a utensil is usually hung in plain sight on the kitchen wall, ready to be of service.

Ponge also delights in creating portmanteau words in the manner of Lewis Carroll. Describing the change of seasons in "La Fin de l'automne" (the end of autumn), Ponge pictures a marshy, rain-drenched bit of earth as a *grenouillerie*, a "frog-preserve," characterized by an *amphibiguïté salubre*—a "salubrious amphibiguity." This latter phrase suggests an ambiguous region—neither lake nor dry land—that is inhabited by amphibians, and a rainy season of autumn becoming winter that affords its creatures a healthy period for cleansing reflection before the onset of spring.

VISUAL POETRY

Ponge is fascinated by the graphic possibilities of the written word. Although he has created at least one visual poem, "L'Araignée mise au mur" (the spider placed on the wall), that is reminiscent of Guillaume Apollinaire's *Calligrammes*, Ponge does not ordinarily write purely concrete poetry; the dominant role of language in his poems is always that of a verbal rather than a graphic medium. Nevertheless, he is intrigued by the ability of the shapes of the letters of the alphabet to participate in the process of symbolization. In an essay from *Méthodes* titled "Proclamation et petit four" (proclamation and petit four), Ponge points out that the modern reader's acquaintance with poetry is almost exclusively an acquaintance with the printed page; only infrequently does one hear poetry spoken aloud. He thus finds it appropriate to explore the link between the subject of the poem and the poem's typography. In this same essay, he expresses the hope that readers of his poem "L'Abricot" (the apricot) will be aware of the resemblance between the *a* in "apricot" and the fruit itself. Other links between typography and meaning are made explicit in the poems themselves. In "La Chèvre" (the goat), Ponge sees the goat's little beard in the accent mark in its name; his poem "La Cruche" (the pitcher) begins with the observation that its *u* is as hollow as the container it describes; and in "Notes prises pour un oiseau" (notes taken for a bird), Ponge sees the silhouette of the resting bird in the *s* of *oiseau*. The role of typography as an active participant in Ponge's poems ranges from a minor one in which the

letters in the object's name are shown to illustrate certain of its qualities, to poems inspired almost entirely by typographical observations. "Le 14 juillet" (July 14, or Bastille Day) is generated from the characters of its title, whose letters and numbers are transformed into French citizens carrying flags and wielding weapons in a miniature reenactment of the drama of the French Revolution.

Although Ponge's various compositional techniques have seemed contrived to some readers, at their most apt, woven together into a tightly composed prose poem, these techniques approach Ponge's ideal of "equivalence." This sense of focus and unity is perhaps strongest in Ponge's shorter poems, in which virtually every word is linked to every other word through etymology, assonance, visual links, or word associations. The Pongian poem at its best delights the reader, bringing to light unnoticed qualities of the object it describes; it inspires, as well, a deep understanding of the expressive potential of language. In a Ponge poem, language becomes another kind of object, whose profoundly established connections to the things of the world reveal much about that world.

Ponge has conceded that human involvement can never be eliminated from the process of writing about things, yet he firmly relegates man to the role of a simple participant in a functioning system. This view is very much in keeping with current trends in French scholarship, which increasingly portray man as a product of the cultural structures into which he is born rather than as their master.

LEGACY

Although predicated on the notion of "equivalence"—an aesthetic ideal difficult if not impossible to achieve—Ponge's approach to poetry is yet a pragmatic one, based both upon careful observation of his object-subjects and upon diligent mining of the language for the insights it provides. Ponge asserts that the resistance posed by a centuries-old system of structures such as language actually helps him to write better poetry. The poet's commitment to a meticulous use of language prevents the annexation or the taking for granted of objects by human beings and, at the same time, furnishes insights into human behavior.

Like Albert Camus, Ponge has acknowledged the impossibility of attaining philosophical absolutes and recognizes the absurdity of the human condition. Like Stéphane Mallarmé, he has endeavored to develop a poetic language capable of a perfect rather than an approximate rendering of the world. Unlike these two writers, however, Ponge is not greatly distressed by the realization that such efforts are doomed to fall short of perfection. Refusing to be conquered by a daunting quest for absolutes, he adopts a pragmatic and ultimately optimistic attitude toward human potential. For Ponge, man's dignity is to be found in the faithful performance of his duty to strive for proportion and perfection in the use of that most uniquely human of all human attributes—language. There is a kind of heroism or sainthood in accepting time and again the challenge to find in language a perfect equivalent for the things of the world; in striving to meet this challenge to the best of his ability, man perfects himself morally. Ponge invites man to learn a lesson from the snail, whose patient work of construction is necessary to his existence and is perfectly suited to—and is a perfect expression of—his nature. In a like manner, human nobility or sainthood is attained by perfecting one's self, by knowing and accepting one's limitations and by obeying one's own nature. "Perfect yourself morally," Ponge advises, "and you will produce beautiful poetry."

OTHER MAJOR WORKS

NONFICTION: *Méthodes*, 1961; *Pour un Malherbe*, 1965; *Entretiens de Francis Ponge avec Philippe Sollers*, 1970; *L'Atelier contemporain*, 1977.

BIBLIOGRAPHY

Andrews, Chris. *Poetry and Cosmogony*. Atlanta, Ga.: Rodopi, 1999. Andrews analyzes references to science and to the creation of the universe in the works of Raymond Queneau and Ponge. Includes bibliographical references and index.

Higgins, Ian. *Francis Ponge*. London: Athlone Press, 1979. Critical assessment of Ponge's oeuvre. Includes bibliographic references.

Meadows, Patrick Alan. *Francis Ponge and the Nature of Things: From Ancient Atomism to a Modern Poetics*. Lewisburg, Pa.: Bucknell University Press, 1997. Critical interpretation of Ponge's works. Includes bibliographical references and index.

Minahen, Charles D. *Figuring Things: Char, Ponge, and Poetry in the Twentieth Century*. Lexington, Ky.: French Forum, 1994. A collection of critical essays on the poetic works of René Char and Ponge. Includes bibliographical references.

Puchek, Peter. *Rewriting Creation: Myth, Gender, and History*. New York: Peter Lang, 2001. Critical interpretation of the works of selected twentieth century poets including Ponge. Includes bibliographical references and index.

Sorrell, Martin. *Francis Ponge*. Boston: Twayne, 1981. An introductory biography and critical analysis of selected works. Includes bibliographic references.

Janet L. Solberg
(including original translations);
bibliography updated by the editors

MARIE PONSOT

Born: New York, New York; 1921

PRINCIPAL POETRY

True Minds, 1956
Admit Impediment, 1981
The Green Dark, 1988
The Bird Catcher, 1998

OTHER LITERARY FORMS

Marie Ponsot has also gained recognition for her translations of children's books from the French. She has translated roughly forty books, focusing primarily on fairy tales.

ACHIEVEMENTS

Marie Ponsot's poetry has merited several honors, including a creative writing grant from the National Endowment for the Arts, the Delmore Schwartz Memorial Prize, and the Eunice Tietjens Prize from *Poetry* magazine. She has also received the Modern Language Association's Shaughnessy Medal. For her collection of poetry *The Bird Catcher*, she received the National Book

Critics Circle Award and was a finalist for the 1999 Lenore Marshall Poetry Prize.

BIOGRAPHY

Marie (Birmingham) Ponsot was born in Queens, New York. Her father, William, was a partner in a wine importing company. Her mother, Marie (Candee), was a schoolteacher. Marie Ponsot began publishing as a child, in *The Brooklyn Eagle*. Graduating with her bachelor of arts degree from St. Joseph's College for Women in Brooklyn, Ponsot then attended Columbia University, receiving a master's degree with a concentration in seventeenth century literature. She has often spoken of how the early influence that her parents provided stimulated her love of literature.

After World War II, Ponsot went to Paris for postgraduate studies, where she met artist and painter Claude Ponsot. They were married in 1948. Together they had seven children, one daughter and six sons. They divorced in 1970. Marie Ponsot met Beat poet and publisher Lawrence Ferlinghetti while they were fellow passengers on a boat. He published her first collection, *True Minds*, through City Lights Books in San Francisco in 1958.

Ponsot has had an extensive teaching career. When her second collection was published, she was an English professor at Queens. She has also taught in graduate programs at Beijing United University, New York's YMHA Poetry Center, New York University, and Columbia University.

ANALYSIS

Ponsot's use of her personal experiences never degenerates into the maudlin. Nor does she invoke the circumstances of her life simply for dramatic effect. In *Strange Good Fortune* (2001), poet David Wojahn suggests that such writing is misleading and dishonest, warning against writing talk-show poetry that aches for attention and headlines:

> For a poem of invective to work as it should, a writer must in most cases be especially careful to counterbalance the development of his/her argument with structural or formal devices which sharpen and underscore the writer's conviction and rage.

The strength of Ponsot's work is in how carefully she weaves her poems, utilizing formal structural and sonic devices to sustain her argument. For example, when Ponsot speaks with anger about her divorce, her poems use traditional forms and fixed rhyme schemes to give the impression of a struggle between restraint and strong emotion. The emotion never sweeps away the poem, nor does the structure ever seem merely incidental or decorative. Both form and sense work together to create an organic whole.

TRUE MINDS

Lawrence Ferlinghetti published *True Minds*, Ponsot's first collection, just after he published Allen Ginsberg's *Howl* (1956). Based on Ferlinghetti's choice, the public expected that Ponsot's work would follow in Ginsberg's Beat style, and therefore greeted Ponsot's measured, formal verses with a profound silence. Although she continued to publish individual poems in magazines and journals, twenty-five years would pass before the publication of her second book.

A slim collection, *True Minds* presents a metaphysical meditation within the context of her life experiences. The sonnet form underscores the spiritual stance that characterizes much of Ponsot's work. The poem "Espousal" echoes the vibrance of Gerard Manley Hopkins's ecstatic poems. This sonnet uses four stanzas of three lines, employing an *abc* rhyme scheme in each stanza. The sonnet ends with a couplet using *bc*. This interlocking echoes the images, which also repeat, describing a link between the spiritual and physical worlds:

> And the cut-out sun-circle plunges, down it dives;
> And fire blazes at the earth's jewel-runneled core.

Ponsot takes liberties with the basic requirements of the form—the five-stress line with its regular rhyme scheme. The resulting poem celebrates the freshness of love as well as its connection to the natural world. This is a poem of young love that seems indestructible.

A poem of foreboding, "The Given Grave Grown Green" questions the assumption that love can endure, as if the poet foresees her future divorce. This is a poem of change. The poet experiences change occurring all around her. Wondering about where she finds herself in the midst of such change, addressing the person who has been the agent of such turmoil, she finally says:

You can watch from your closed window
How true false love has grown.

These lines mirror the contradiction inherent in the title. A grave is green only because of growth above it, not life within it. Likewise, what is true about love in this poem is that the love has become false.

ADMIT IMPEDIMENT

Ponsot's second collection provides a fuller exploration of the themes found in *True Minds*. Both collections take their titles from Shakespeare's Sonnet 116, which begins, "Let me not to the marriage of true minds/ Admit impediments." Divided into four sections, the second collection opens with "For a Divorce," one of the longer poems gathered here. It is a dark poem, whose irregular stanzaic patterns lead the reader through the emotional intricacies that attend a divorce. This poem catalogs the pain of the divorce and the specific areas of brokenness, recalling the various images of the marriage itself. The short, strong lines emphasize the full-stop of the relationship, the sounds within the lines almost jarring at times. The poet concludes:

> Deaths except for amoeba articulate
> life into lives, separate, named, new.
> Not all sworn faith dies. Ours did.

This is an angry poem whose emotion is carefully controlled for vivid effect. While the poet attempts to avoid blame (the lines previously quoted are as close as she comes to specific details about the cause of the break), she achieves a level of clarity for the reader's consideration by beginning her poem with nearly all of Shakespeare's Sonnet 116. Although she does not quote Shakespeare's final two lines, their sense is implied throughout this collection:

> If this be error, and upon me prov'd
> I never writ, nor no man ever lov'd.

THE GREEN DARK

Ponsot's third collection weaves mythic elements into the fabric of her poems, along with her accustomed biographical references, resulting in poems in which dream and reality share space. "Take Time, Take Place" is a long meditation in several parts. In Part I, the poet

longs for the fantasy of passionate love but realizes that such love is inaccessible, saying, "Sleep take it. Awake I like a drier wine." Part II takes a different turn. Even the use of language becomes more grounded in day-to-day expression, as Ponsot uses "wd" for "would," as "The landscape I have left behind/ waits for me."

The poems in parts I and II use irregular line lengths and slant rhymes, which give the poem an exploratory, testing sense of experience, as if the poet would invite the reader on a journey whose end is uncertain. Part III, however, is quite different. Comprising seven sonnets and ending with a five-line stanza, this section questions the assumptions of the first two parts. Beginning with "Fantasies dampen the pang of cherishing/ goods and chances lost or left behind," these poems challenge the easy redemption which fantasy alone can bring.

Each sonnet ends with a line that is repeated as the first line of the next sonnet, albeit sometimes slightly altered. The poet searches for signs, for the "hard sun of memory," which would enable her to enter the world of her fancy, but then realizes:

> Such grace. It names the saving world I might seize
> but am too locked in time to see: unless
> we are what our imagination frees.

What the imagination frees is the human capacity to feel joy, even after a great pain has occurred. The bird that has flown throughout this poem becomes the unifying symbol of "thick experience." The poems that Ponsot crafts with such precision emphasize the idea that, as a poet, she is free to construct a world that encourages her selfhood and to leave any world that denies her the right to grow.

THE BIRD CATCHER

Winner of the National Book Critics Circle Award for the best collection of poetry published in 1998, *The Bird Catcher* continues to probe Ponsot's fascination with poetic forms, using them to shape the expression of the emotive thrust in each poem. Likewise, the poet reviews the concerns that preoccupied her earlier work. Crafted in four sections, the book begins with a poem "To the Muse of Doorways Edges Verges," which sets the creative tone. The "gentle visitor" in the doorway is someone whose visits are "irregular," as the poet makes her welcome. These visits, however, contain a nervy edge of warning:

She smiles. She speaks up, some.
Each word ravishes,
bright with the sciences
she practices
in the music business.

"One day, when you're not dumb,
you must come
to my place," she says,
and vanishes.

Twenty-five years elapsed between the publication of Ponsot's first and second books; meanwhile, she experienced marriage, the birth of her children, and her subsequent divorce. Tillie Olsen's book *Silences* (1978) elaborates on the lives of women writers who fall silent for significant periods of their career, as did Ponsot. It would perhaps be accurate to read "dumb" as "mute," not as a reference to intelligence. The poet shows herself at the edge of an awakening, a rebirth into the world of her own words. This is the "place" to which the muse calls her.

The first section, "For My Old Self," contains poems that focus on her life as a wife and mother. The poet's use of forms becomes, at times, playful, as if concealing a more serious tone which is pervasive. "Trois Petits Tours et Puis . . ." speaks of conflicting ways in which the husband and wife interpret the world. Each seems unable to recognize the gift that is present in the spouse, until, finally, the inevitable break occurs. The sonnet uses a varied rhyme scheme and an irregular stanzaic pattern. The first stanza contains five lines, the second, seven, and the third, two. The final stanza summarizes the outcome:

His map omits her. His snapshots go to friends.
A fresh music fills her house, a fresh air.

For both, the end of this relationship is the beginning of another life. In each poem in which Ponsot discusses the breakdown of her marriage, she avoids a self-pitying stance that could undermine the vitality of her work. Instead, the poet affirms her own ability to continue—not merely to endure, but to flourish.

In the second section, "Separate, in the Swim," the poem "The Border" begins with a young girl's idealized vision of what marriage is. A flower girl for Dorothea's wedding, the girl practices walking so that she can gracefully present herself holding the flowers. Her grandmother tells her that she should not worry, as everyone will be looking at the bride. She then starts to blow bubbles, allowing them to float over the pansies into the bridal-wreath bush before they vanish. Her understanding is at once naïve and chilling:

Getting married is like that.
Getting married is not like that.

The poem is both an affirmation and a warning, as if the poet were speaking to herself as a young, newly married woman.

Other sections explore mythology, women who find themselves in situations that are conflicting, almost dream-states. In "Persephone, Packing," the poet wonders whether the duality of Persephone's life—and by extension the poet's life—is actually a dream. She ponders whether life above or below is real. Again, the poet examines the institution of marriage, especially in this case, in which Persephone has been taken against her will. How much of a woman's will must be sacrificed for the sake of the union is a question that Ponsot asks in her poetry, with no easy answers.

The final poem, "Even," uses jagged lines and enjambment to follow the story of Adam and Eve, who finally comes to understand her position in the world. The poem refers to Noah and his wife, suddenly freed from danger. The poet then draws a parallel between modern women, including herself, and the need for a new way of being.

OTHER MAJOR WORKS

NONFICTION: *Beat Not the Poor Desk*, 1982 (with Rosemary Deen); *The Common Sense: What to Write, How to Write It, and Why*, 1985 (with Deen).

TRANSLATIONS: *Fables of La Fontaine*, 1957; *Cinderella and Other Stories of Charles Perrault*, 1957; *The Fairy Tale Book*, 1958; *Once Upon a Time Stories*, 1959; *Old One Toe*, 1959; *My First Picture Encyclopedia*, 1959; *Russian Fairy Tales*, 1961; *Tales of India*, 1961; *Mick and the "P-105,"* 1961; *Bemba*, 1962; *Pour toi*, 1966; *Chinese Fairy Tales*, 1973; *Golden Book of Fairy Tales*, 1999; *The Snow Queen and Other Tales*, 2001; *Love and Folly: Selected Fables and Tales of La Fontaine*, 2001.

BIBLIOGRAPHY

Seaman, Donna. Review of *The Bird Catcher.* *Booklist* 94, no. 11 (February 1, 1998): 894. The reviewer celebrates the poet's use of homonyms and varied rhyme schemes, as well as linguistic and philosophical paradoxes.

Smith, Dinitia. "Recognition at Last for Poet of Elegant Complexity." *The New York Times*, April 13, 1999, p. E1. The review provides an extensive analysis of the precision of word choice and the complexity of syntax that Ponsot employs in her poetry. The reviewer finds that the rhetorical patterns are well thought out, and that Ponsot pays particular attention to the fixed forms such as the villanelle, the sestina, and the tritina.

West, Phil. "In with the Old, in with the New." *The Austin Chronicle* 18, no. 8 (October 26, 1998). The poet uses innovative forms such as the tritina to provide a new spin on the language. Her voice is steadied and precise, shaped in a straightforward way through her use of fixed forms such as the sestina, villanelle, and sonnet.

Willis, Mary-Sherman. "Diving into It: *The Bird Catcher*, by Marie Ponsot." *Poet Lore* 94, no. 4 (Winter, 2000). This cogent review discusses the poet's use of biographical elements in her work. The reviewer shows how the full life that Ponsot led has shaped these poems, which are ultimately life-affirming. The reviewer finds that the general theme is one of movement, of buoyancy and danger, of leaving the shore and returning.

Martha Modena Vertreace-Doody

VASKO POPA

Born: Grebenac, Yugoslavia; July 29, 1922
Died: Belgrade, Yugoslavia; January 5, 1991

PRINCIPAL POETRY

Kora, 1953 (*Bark*, 1978)
Nepočin-polje, 1956 (*Unrest-Field*, 1978)
Sporedno nebo, 1968 (*Secondary Heaven*, 1978)
Selected Poems, 1969
The Little Box, 1970
Uspravna zemlja, 1972 (*Earth Erect*, 1973)
Vučja so, 1975 (*Wolf Salt*, 1978)
Živo meso, 1975 (*Raw Flesh*, 1978)
Kuća nasred druma, 1975
Collected Poems, 1943-1976, 1978 (includes *Bark, Unrest-Field, Secondary Heaven, Earth Erect, Wolf Salt, Raw Flesh*, and selections from *Kuća nasred druma*)
The Blackbird's Field, 1979
Homage to the Lame Wolf: Selected Poems, 1956-1975, 1979
Ponoćno sunce: Zbornik pesničkih snovidenja, 1979
Rez, 1981 (*The Cut*, 1986)

OTHER LITERARY FORMS

In addition to poetry, Vasko Popa published *Urnebesnik: Zbornik pesničkog humora* (1960), a selection of Serbian wit and humor, and *Od zlata jabuka* (1966; *The Golden Apple*, 1980), a collection of folk poems, tales, proverbs, riddles, and curses, which Popa selected from the vast body of Yugoslav folk literature.

ACHIEVEMENTS

When Vasko Popa's first book of verse appeared in 1953, it was rejected by many readers and critics who did not believe that Yugoslav poetry was in need of modernization. In the struggle against traditional forms and themes, Popa's poetry, like that of Miodrag Pavlović, played a prominent role and contributed decisively to the victory of the modernists. Since then, he has gained steadily in stature and popularity; today, he is considered by many to be the preeminent contemporary Yugoslav poet.

Popa's contributions are manifold. He not only has helped rejuvenate Serbian and Yugoslav poetry but also has brought it to the level of world poetry—one of the few Yugoslav poets to do so. His profound interest in finding the primeval roots of his nation's culture; his creation of myths for modern times; his probings into the deepest recesses of the subconscious; his gift for striking visions, images, and metaphors; and his highly accomplished, seemingly effortless poetic skill—he has brought all of these elements to contemporary Yugoslav poetry. Popa's wrestling with fundamental human problems—death, fate, the meaning of life, love—makes his poetry universal and enduring. Uncompromising when his poetic freedom is questioned, determined to reconfirm the superiority of poetry, and captivated by his craft almost to the exclusion of all other concerns, he is a poet's poet, whose place at the top of all Serbian and Yugoslav literature seems assured.

BIOGRAPHY

Vasko Popa was born on July 29, 1922, in Grebenac, a village near Bela Crkva in the Banat region of Yugoslavia. He studied literature at the universities of Belgrade, Bucharest, and Vienna and was graduated from Belgrade in 1949. He settled in Belgrade, working as an editor in various publishing houses, chiefly Nolit, one of the largest publishers in Yugoslavia, from which he retired in 1982. Popa began to publish poetry in 1951, and his first book appeared in 1953. He has traveled widely and is highly respected outside his native land. He has received numerous literary awards, and his poems have been translated into many languages.

Vasko Popa (© Lufti Özkök)

ANALYSIS

Vasko Popa's poetry displays many unique features. From the very first, he showed a predilection for objects, for specifics rather than generalities, for the concrete rather than the abstract. As if to restore the equilibrium disturbed in his early manhood during the war, he felt a need to call everything by its proper name, to relegate each object to its appointed place.

BARK

Among his first poems, which appear in *Bark*, are those titled simply "Chair," "Plate," and "Paper." In such poems, he attempts to penetrate the outer shell of objects, arriving at their core. One gets the impression that he stares persistently at an inanimate object until it appears to breathe and to move. In one of his finest poems, "The Quartz Pebble," he extols the magnificent beauty of a stone in its seeming immobility and indifference to its surroundings ("headless limbless"). Soon, however, the smooth white stone begins to move "with the shameless march of time," holding everything "in its passionate/ Internal embrace." Thus, the essential traits of the quartz pebble are illuminated in a very few lines. Al-

though not a living being, it moves, breathes, smiles, and shows passion. (This poem first appeared in *Bark* and was repeated and expanded into a cycle in Popa's second collection, *Unrest-Field.*) The secret of Popa's propensity for things lies in the fact that they are *not* merely things for him but beings, which only the sixth sense, or the inner eye, of a poet can discern.

Popa's dead world pulsates with a weird life that is more intense than that of living beings in the familiar world. Speaking of a cigarette in "In the Ashtray," he calls it "a tiny sun/ With a yellow tobacco hair" being extinguished in an ashtray while "the blood of a cheap lipstick suckles/ The dead stumps of stubs." In "On the Hat Stand," "collars have bitten through the necks of hanging emptiness." "In a Smile" describes a scene where "Blue-eyed distances/ Have coiled up into a ball." The culmination of this anthropomorphism is found in the cycle "Spisak" ("List"). In addition to the quartz stone mentioned above, this cycle comprises a duck that "will never learn/ How to walk/ As she knows/ How to plough mirrors"; a horse that has eight legs and drags the whole earth behind him; a pig that runs joyfully toward "the yellow gate," only to feel the "savage wild knife in her throat"; a dandelion that is "A yellow eye of loneliness/ On the sidewalk edge/ At the end of the world"; and a chestnut tree that "lives on the adventures/ Of his unreachable roots." A dinner plate is "A yawn of free lips/ Above the horizon of hunger." Popa's obsession with things reveals not only his uncanny ability to see the world from their perspective but also his intention to speak through natural symbols, to present graphically the mysterious nature of human destiny.

UNREST-FIELD

Popa's closeness to things was undoubtedly accentuated by the war experience of his impressionable years, when the language spoken around him was blunt, terse, bloody, and final. From this experience stem two haunting cycles of poems in *Unrest-Field*, "Igre" ("Games") and "Kost kosti" ("One Bone to Another"). "Games" is Popa's response to the frightening games of war. The poems of this cycle resemble an eerie pantomime of creatures beyond the natural and comprehensible, for Popa's "games" defy logical explanation, symbolically reflecting the cruelty, grotesqueness, and fatuity of human existence. In "The Seducer," one person fondles a chair leg until it gives him "the glad"; another kisses a keyhole while a third person gapes at them, turning his head until it falls off. In "The Chase," people bite arms and legs off one another and bury them like dogs, while others sniff around, searching for buried limbs; whoever finds his own is entitled to the next bite.

Even more drastic is the cycle "One Bone to Another." By stripping human beings to their bones and allowing the bones to express the feelings of their former bodies, Popa speaks the subterranean language of life beyond the grave. This *danse macabre* suggests the life that was or might have been. When, in the first section (the poem "At the Beginning") one bone says to another, "We've got away from the flesh," the stage is set for a new existence entirely different from the human, yet the bones proceed to emulate their former "owners": "It's marvelous sunbathing naked," "Let's love each other just the two of us"; "Then we'll . . ./ Go on growing as we please." Soon, flesh commences to grow back on them, "As if everything were beginning again/ With a more horrible beginning" ("In the Moonlight"). They have no place to go: "What shall we do there/ There long awaiting us/ There eagerly expecting us/ No one and his wife nothing" ("Before the End"). Finally, they devour each other: "Why have you swallowed me/ I can't see myself any more . . ./ All is an ugly dream of dust" ("At the End"). Again, the application to human conditions is all too obvious.

In these bleak conditions, Popa assails his nemesis— his fate or death—head-on, demanding the return of his "little rags": the minimum requirements for existence. He calls his nemesis a "monster"; he threatens it ("Flee monster . . ./ We're not meant for each other") and challenges it to a show-down, trying all the while to build an immunity against adversity, albeit unsuccessfully. It is a valiant protest just the same, capable of restoring one's dignity ("I've wiped your face off my face/ Ripped your shadow off my shadow"). Thus, Popa can even be called an optimist, despite the macabre atmosphere of his world.

In such an atmosphere, the love experience, too, undergoes a Popa-esque metamorphosis. In the cycle "Daleko u nama" ("Far Within Us"), from *Bark*, Popa tries to save his love from a nightmarish dream:

> Horror on the ocean of tea in the cup
> Rust taking a hold
> On the edges of our laughter
> A snake coiled in the depths of the mirror . . .
> Murky passages flow
> From our eyelashes down our faces—
> With a fierce red-hot wire
> Anger hems up our thoughts . . .
> The venomous rain of eternity
> Bites us greedily

In such moments of acute danger, the poet expresses unabashed tenderness: "The streets of your glances/ Have no ending/ The swallows from your eyes/ Do not migrate south"; "I would steal you from silence/ I would clothe you in songs." Even the hours of fear ("The pillars supporting heaven crumble/ The bench with us slowly/ Falls into the void"), of parting ("Only in sleep/ we walk the same paths"), of threatening loss ("I go/ From one side of my head to the other/ Where are you?") are only temporary. In Popa's world, love seems to be the only power capable of overcoming the adversities of fate and death.

SECONDARY HEAVEN

From the small, seemingly insignificant objects of his early verse, Popa has moved to the larger arena of his native land and from there to the universe itself, in the collection *Secondary Heaven*. In Popa's cosmology, the sun rules in his empire, but his rule is marred by the struggle between the forces of darkness and light. Popa uses this allegory to suggest his worldview and to treat complex human problems in an oblique fashion.

Secondary Heaven begins with a symbol of emptiness in the form of zero: "Once upon a time there was a number/ Pure and round like a sun/ But alone very much alone." No matter how much the zero adds or multiplies itself, the result remains zero. The forces of light, represented by King Sun, are engaged in a battle against the world of nothingness (zero). Tragically, the heir to King Sun, Prince Sun, is a blind bastard led by two crippled rays. Hope seems betrayed, and the chances of the forces of light are slim, yet the struggle goes on. This is the bare outline of *Secondary Heaven*. Popa's allegory should be seen not as a metaphysical or mythological interpretation of reality but rather as a reflection of man's fate in a celestial mirror. The force of the poet's idiom, the familiar simplicity, the use of old legends and folklore, and the original humor and charming irony make his collection a great achievement. Above all, it shows that Popa's poetic thought has come full circle. By way of the universe, he has reached his final destination—his own self.

WOLF SALT, RAW FLESH, AND KUĆA NASRED DRUMA

Of Popa's later collections, *Wolf Salt* is centered on the myth of a wolf as an old Slavic symbol of vitality, not of evil and destruction. The wolf is depicted as a benign creature, lame yet possessing indestructible tenacity, symbolizing the vitality of the Serbian people. He is connected with the Serbian historical and legendary figure St. Sava, who is his shepherd. Popa's characteristic terseness and directness of expression add to the exceptional quality of this book, making it one of the best in his entire opus. *Raw Flesh* represents a slight departure from Popa's customary manner, in that it is more personal and realistic. The poet returns to his native region, evokes memories of his childhood, and even names names. Although the poems have a realistic surface, they resonate with ancient myths, popular beliefs, and superstitions, all indicating the depth of Popa's immersion in the soul of his people. These poems seem somewhat lighter than his usual poetry, as if to show another, less somber side of the poet. *Kuća nasred druma* (the house on the highroad) is a heterogeneous collection lacking a tight cyclical unity, but even here one can perceive a potentially unifying subject matter that may eventually lead to the further development of this cycle and possibly give birth to other cycles.

Stylistically, Popa's poetry is marked by several distinct characteristics. Rather than composing individual, self-contained poems, he generally works in cycles of poems dealing with the same subject matter and written in the same vein. In turn, these cycles are related to one another; for this reason, Popa frequently changes the order of cycles in new editions, where they acquire new pertinence.

TERSE VERSE, HUMOR, IRONY

Perhaps the most conspicuous feature of Popa's verse is its terseness. His poetry is often aphoristic, and his language is reduced to a bare minimum. When he wants to underscore the maddening intensity and chaos of a battle, he describes a river turning and twisting, unable to find its shores again. The agility of a horse is illustrated by its eight legs—the impression one gets when observing a galloping horse. Popa always uses fewer rather than more words, to the point of being cryptic and difficult to fathom at times.

There is also a certain playfulness in Popa's poetry, connected with his aforementioned predilection for games and pantomime amid the horrors of war. It can be good-natured fun (a picture of a donkey that cannot be seen for its large ears), often turning, however, into the nervous, biting humor of a sensitive man dissatisfied with his world. Not infrequently, Popa's humor takes a mordant, even macabre twist, but more often he laughs at the absurdity, the tragicomedy, of human life. In his most exalted poetry, in *Secondary Heaven*, the old sun stopped "Three paces from the top of heaven . . ./ And went back to his rising/ (So as not to die in our sight)"; similarly, two lame rays lead a blind sun, and "morning is out somewhere seeking his fortune." Such humor is hard to separate from the irony with which Popa's worldview is suffused.

His irony, too, assumes various forms. The most noticeable is his almost chatty approach to problems facing his creatures or things. At a crucial moment, when a solution is expected, the poet half jestingly quips, "What shall I tell you?" meaning, "Oh, what's the use!" His ironic attitude arises for the most part from his awareness that he is locked in a losing battle with his old nemesis, although he stubbornly refuses to admit defeat.

LANGUAGE AND IDIOM

Popa's language requires a study in itself. No other Yugoslav poet (save perhaps Laza Kostić or Momčilo Nastasijević) has shown such originality and resourcefulness—indeed, virtuosity—of language. Particularly notable is Popa's ability to distill the existing lexicon, to select the *mot juste*, and even to coin words. Striking also is the deceptive simplicity of Popa's idiom—deceptive because his "simple" expressions often harbor a variety of meanings, depending on the context. That is why he is both easy and difficult to translate. His language also reveals elements of folk speech, evident also in other aspects of his poetry, especially in *Secondary Heaven:*

> A transparent dove in the head
> In the dove a clay coffer
> In the coffer a dead sea
> In the sea a blessed moon

A stanza such as this (from "A Dove in the Head") resembles a folk poem or riddle in both content and form. Popa's poetry abounds in similar examples.

Popa's prosody is idiosyncratic: He eschews rhyme and strict meter, but he also avoids free verse. His lines are roughly metric, by no means following a regular pattern yet possessing a strong underlying rhythm.

INFLUENCES

There is no critical consensus concerning the extent to which Popa has been influenced by other poets, in part because the uniqueness and elemental power of his poetry belie any simple notion of imitation. Early in his career, Popa was attracted by the Surrealists, whose Yugoslav offshoot was very strong between the two wars, but he refused to follow their prescriptions blindly, believing that each period brings its own problems and solutions. Another source of influence is Momčilo Nastasijević, one of the most unusual and enigmatic of modern Yugoslav poets. This dark genius, creating his art outside, and often against,

the mainstream of Yugoslav poetry between the two wars, has always attracted Popa, even when Nastasijević was almost a forgotten poet. As a matter of fact, Popa has edited Nastasijević's collected works. How much direct influence Nastasijević has exercised on Popa is indeed difficult to ascertain, because both poets have followed the dictates of their own strong personalities; that there has been some influence, however, is beyond doubt. Other poets mentioned as influences on Popa are Léon-Gontran Damas, Francis Ponge, and even Rainer Maria Rilke.

Popa's own influence on contemporary Yugoslav poetry is just as difficult to establish. At the beginning of his career, he was shunned by the established poets; today, younger poets do not show clearly what they have learned from him, their reverence for him notwithstanding; his forceful originality and unconventional style are difficult to imitate without the appearance of mere copying. Like many great poets, he remains a poetic world unto himself and without legitimate offspring. (This does not mean that he is not emulated or that he has had no direct influence upon his fellow poets.) As for his possible influence on foreign poets, he has begun to be known to the outside world only recently: It is too early to tell.

OTHER MAJOR WORKS

SHORT FICTION: *Urnebesnik: Zbornik pesničkog humora*, 1960 (selection of Serbian wit and humor); *Od zlata jabuka*, 1966 (*The Golden Apple*, 1980).

BIBLIOGRAPHY

Alexander, Ronelle. *The Structure of Vasko Popa's Poetry*. Columbus, Ohio: Slavica Publishers, 1985. A critical analysis of Popa's linguistic technique in selected works. Includes bibliographic references.

Lekic, Anita. *The Quest for Roots: The Poetry of Vasko Popa*. New York: P. Lang, 1993. Lekic's study of Popa and his work provides the complex background where Popa's imagination and metaphysics have their beginnings. Includes bibliographical references and index.

Mihailovich, Vasa D. "Vasko Popa: The Poetry of Things in a Void." in *Books Abroad* 53 (1969): 24-29. A basic introduction to the themes in Popa's poetry.

Vasa D. Mihailovich;
bibliography updated by the editors

ALEXANDER POPE

Born: London, England; May 21, 1688
Died: Twickenham, England; May 30, 1744

PRINCIPAL POETRY
Pastorals, 1709
An Essay on Criticism, 1711
The Rape of the Lock, 1712, 1714
Windsor Forest, 1713
The Works of Mr. Alexander Pope, 1717 (first collected edition including "Elegy to the Memory of an Unfortunate Lady" and *Eloisa to Abelard*)
Cytherea, 1723
The Dunciad, 1728-1743
Moral Essays, 1731-1735
Imitations of Horace, 1733-1737
An Essay on Man, 1733-1734
Epistle to Dr. Arbuthnot, 1735
One Thousand Seven Hundred and Thirty-Eight, 1738
Epilogue to the Satires, 1738
The Twickenham Edition of the Poems of Alexander Pope, 1939-1967 (11 volumes; John Butt, general editor)

OTHER LITERARY FORMS
Apart from original poetry, Alexander Pope's works include an edition of William Shakespeare, translations of the *Iliad* (1715-1720) and the *Odyssey* (1725-1726), an edition of his personal correspondence, and a prose satire titled *Peri Bathos: Or, The Art of Sinking in Poetry* (1727). Pope's edition of Shakespeare is chiefly of interest for the response which it brought from Lewis Theobald, a rival editor of Shakespeare's plays. Although not always unjust in his criticisms, Theobald did overlook some of the genuine excellences of Pope's edition, especially Pope's penetrating introduction. (It must be admitted, however, that even this is vitiated at times by Pope's inability to appreciate Shakespeare's so-called deviations from the eighteenth century notion of "correctness.") The translations from Homer are not strictly literal, but are rather adaptations of Homer's genius to the conventions and expectations of Augustan sensibil-

ity. Still, they are regarded as the most readable and eloquent versions of Homer to come out of the eighteenth century, notwithstanding the numerous instances of periphrasis (the substitution of a phrase such as "finny prey" for "fish") which belie the vigor of the original.

Pope's edition of his own letters is among the most notorious of his publications. By allowing several of his letters to be published without his apparent permission, Pope was able to bring out an ostensibly "correct" version of his private correspondence, the chief purpose of which was to present him in a favorable light to posterity. Understandably, the letters are rather too self-conscious and artificial for modern tastes.

Peri Bathos is a hilarious instructional booklet detailing all the elements that are necessary to produce poetry which is vulgar, tautological, florid, and inane. One other composition of Pope surely deserves mention: an essay contributed to *The Guardian* on the aesthetics of gardening. Pope had a decisive influence on the development of eighteenth century taste in gardens. In opposition to the rigid formalities which characterized the landscaping of the period, Pope held that gardens should be arranged in a more natural manner.

ACHIEVEMENTS
Alexander Pope's position in the history of English poetry has been, at times, a subject of acrimonious debate. In his own day, Pope's achievement was frequently obfuscated by the numerous political controversies which surrounded his name. Although he finally emerged, in the estimation of the eighteenth century, as the greatest English poet since John Milton, his reputation soon reached its lowest ebb, during the Romantic and Victorian periods; he was derided by Thomas De Quincey as an author of "moldy commonplaces" and demoted by Matthew Arnold to the position of being a "classic of [English] prose." Even in Edith Sitwell's generally favorable study (1930), Pope is appreciated for achieving, in certain poems, a richness of imagery "almost" as lush as that of John Keats. In short, it was not until recently that the balance was redressed. Pope is now recognized as one of the consummate craftsmen of the English language.

Responding to and expressing the fundamental aesthetic tenets of the Augustan age, Pope cannot be fully appreciated or understood without some awareness of the neoclassical assumptions which undergird his compositions. Pope's audience was more homogeneous than Shakespeare's and less enthusiastic (in Samuel Johnson's meaning of that term) than Milton's. As a result, he eschews the dramatic intensity and colloquial richness of the former and bypasses the mythopoeic passion and religious afflatus of the latter. (It must be remembered, however, that the Miltonic allusions in, say, *The Rape of the Lock* are not intended to derogate Milton, but to expose, by sheer force of contrast, the small-mindedness of eighteenth century society.)

Sophisticated allusion, verbal brilliance, the promulgation of moral and aesthetic standards—these are the components of Pope's poetic art. The audience for which Pope wrote was small, urban, and keenly intelligent, capable of appreciating a high degree of technical virtuosity in its poets. These poets were not expected to indulge in lyrical effusions on the subject of their private griefs or to thrust forward their own personal speculations on the end and aim of human existence. On the contrary, their purpose was to crystallize in language conspicuous for its clarity, balance, and poise, the cultural standards, aesthetic ideals, and moral certitudes which they could presume to hold in common with a sensitive and educated audience. As Pope's career progressed, these ideals seemed increasingly remote from the political and literary arenas where he was forced to contend; hence, his later poetry—especially *The Dunciad*—reveals a growing rift between Pope and his public. On the whole, however, Pope's is a public voice which distills in witty and unforgettable couplets the values of self-control, civic virtue, uncorrupted taste, critical intelligence, and spiritual humility.

As a youth, Pope was exhorted by William Walsh, a former member of John Dryden's literary circle, to pursue "correctness" in his compositions. Pope's career as a poet witnesses to the assiduity with which he acted on Walsh's advice. No poet has brought to the rhyming couplet an equivalent degree of perfection or given to the form, distinguished by its technical difficulty, a greater suppleness and elasticity in the expression of various moods and situations. From the farcical brilliance of *The Rape of the Lock* and the passionate intensities of *Eloisa to Abelard* to the dignified discursiveness of *An Essay*

Alexander Pope (Library of Congress)

on Man and the nervous energy of *The Dunciad*, Pope attains a perfect balance between thought and expression, between verbal wit and the felt rendering of experience.

BIOGRAPHY

The two most important elements in Alexander Pope's life were his being born a Catholic and his contracting, during his twelfth year, a severe tubercular infection from which he never fully recovered. Because of his Catholicism, Pope was compelled to live outside of London and was not allowed to enroll in a formal university program. Because of his illness, Pope attained a height of only four and a half feet, suffered from migraine headaches, was obliged to wear several pairs of hose and an elaborate harness to compensate for the slightness of his legs and the curvature of his spine, and was subject to frequent and caustic ridicule by critics, such as John Dennis, who directed their rancor at his physical deformities as much as at his poetic efforts. Pope's physical ailments and the acrimony with which political and literary pundits attacked both his person and his work should never be forgotten in evaluating, say, the optimistic faith of *An Essay on Man* or the acidulous satire of *The Dunciad*. The affirmations of the former poem were not written out of ignorance of human suffering, and the vituperations of the latter poem cannot be understood apart from the contumely which Pope suffered at the hands of his adversaries—Lady Mary Wortley Montague, Lord Hervey, John Dennis, Joseph Addison, and Lewis Theobald, to name a few. Pope's reference in *Epistle to Dr. Arbuthnot* to "this long disease, my life," is no literary confabulation but an accurate description of his sufferings.

There were, however, compensations. In the library of his father, a wealthy linen merchant who retired to a vast estate at Binfield in 1700, Pope acquired a profound, if desultory, knowledge of English history and letters. In his youth he was, moreover, the special favorite of William Wycherley, who encouraged the publication of Pope's *Pastorals* in Jacob Tonson's *Miscellany* (1709). In 1713, Pope was to find companionship and support in "The Scriblerus Club," a Tory brotherhood which included among its principal members Jonathan Swift, John Gay, and John Arbuthnot. Together, they inveighed against the scientific rationalism and aggressive commercialism which, they believed, threatened the survival of humanistic values in the first half of the eighteenth century. It is important to remember that the political climate of Pope's day was such that poetic compositions were less frequently evaluated on their intrinsic merits than on the sponsorship which they were accorded by either Tory or Whig. Thus Pope's literary career was plagued at its inception by mean-spirited attacks from henchmen of the political and literary establishment.

Pope's masterful translation of the *Iliad*, from which he earned £9,000, enabled him to retire in 1719 with his mother (for whom he scrupulously cared until the end of her life) to Twickenham: a neoclassical villa designed in part by Pope himself, where he was able to indulge his love of gardening and to escape from the contumacious atmosphere of literary London. Here, in the companionship of Swift, Gay, Viscount Boling-

broke, and Arbuthnot, Pope was granted some respite from the venomous attacks upon his person and character, the history of which virtually makes up the rest of his recorded biography. Apart from a deep attachment to Martha Blount, a Catholic neighbor sympathetic to Pope's aspirations and literary ideals, his life was a constant endeavor to stem the materialistic current of his times by iterating in polished and penetrating couplets a theocentric humanism which espoused the virtues of self-discipline, the recognition of metaphysical values, and the need for standards of measure and restraint.

ANALYSIS

Alexander Pope's poetry is an unmistakable challenge to the post-Romantic sensibilities of the twentieth century reader. John Stuart Mill's dictum that "eloquence is *heard*, poetry is overheard," seems entirely contradicted by the public and topical voice which characterizes the epistles, satires, and philosophic exordiums of Pope. The language of introspective reverie which poets, from the nineteenth century on, cultivate in lonely self-communion among the bowers of a refined aestheticism could not be further removed from the racy, tough, and contentious idiom of Pope. That is not to say that Pope's language is devoid of sculptured phrases or chiseled locutions; on the contrary, his compositions are exquisitely wrought and develop with an inevitability that makes Pope, after William Shakespeare, the most quoted poet in the English language. Following the translation of the *Iliad*, however, Pope's works became increasingly didactic and satirical in nature and engaged in topical assaults on the foibles, idiosyncrasies, and shortcomings that characterized the literary and political arena during the reigns of Anne and George II. The astonishing thing is that these topical satires of literary hacks long since forgotten and social customs consigned to oblivion, touch, time and again, upon that which is enduring and universal in the moral being of humanity. The literary battles and political machinations which gave occasion to Pope's vitriolic utterances may be forgotten, but the integrity with which Pope affirmed the centrality of letters, the tempering spirit of humanism, the need for standards, and the cultivation of reverence as indispensable ingredients of a just and balanced society, retains its relevance in the broken world of the twentieth century.

Like Vergil, Pope began as a writer of pastorals; his first poems, composed when he was sixteen, are delicate evocations of an idyllic world of shepherds and shepherdesses poised among settings reminiscent of François Boucher and Jean Fragonard. These highly stylized exercises won for him the accolades of contemporary critics and gave him the confidence to essay the next task which tradition prescribed for the developing poet: the epic. Pope's translation of the *Iliad*, the first books of which appeared in 1715, was a watershed in his poetic career. Though Pope had already written poems which prefigure his later orientation as a satirist, it was the publication of the *Iliad* that triggered the wholly irrational and unexpected assault upon Pope's life, family, writings, and physiognomy by his political enemies and rivals to poetic fame. These attacks diverted Pope from the musings of *Windsor Forest*, the perorations of *An Essay on Criticism*, and the witticisms of *The Rape of the Lock*, and obliged him, to paraphrase a Nobel laureate, "to grab his century by the throat." After 1719, Pope's career is notable for the increasing venom of his pen and the sustained brilliance of his polemic.

AN ESSAY ON CRITICISM

Pope's first important utterance gives us direct access to the critical values of the Augustans and remains the best and most compendious statement of a poetic tradition which extends from Horace to Nicolas Boileau. Indeed, as a distillation of neoclassical attitudes, Pope's *An Essay on Criticism* is without a peer. The critical assumptions on which the poem is based could not be further removed from the splintered aesthetics and boneless relativism of the present: As a statement of poetic intention and practice, it provides a necessary corrective to the farrago of contradictions which characterize the contemporary critical scene. Pope vigorously attacks the notion that taste is a purely subjective matter, arguing that a deterioration in aesthetic values is both a symptom and a portent of a general disequilibrium in the moral being of the individual and the political fabric of society. The poem's controlling symbol is the sun—an emblem of universal reason and light whose rays are an expression of the original creative word, or *logos*. Individual taste is evaluated from the perspective of this light-

giving word, which is identified in the poem as "Unerring Nature, still divinely bright,/ One clear, unchanged, and universal light." Though individual judgments may differ, they may and should be regulated—as watches by the sun—in accordance with objective standards of value and taste. Thus, the rules which govern the composition of poetry are not arbitrary inventions, but expressions of the natural law of measure and restraint: "Those Rules of old discovered, not devised/ Are nature still, but Nature methodized;/ Nature, like Liberty, is but restrained/ By the same laws which first herself ordained."

The first duty of a poet and a critic, then, is to recognize the law of human limit, and to balance individual judgments by constant and circumspect reference to a hierarchy of inherited values. Pope does not recommend the self-abnegation of the poet in the face of his predecessors, but rather his need to adapt to his own time those values which inform ancients and moderns alike and which are of continued relevance because their source is eternal and their origin beyond the vagaries of individual taste. Still, Pope maintains that the success of a composition must be estimated by the value and significance of the poet's purpose and the artistic integrity with which that purpose is fulfilled, rather than by arbitrary and invidious comparisons between works of antithetical spirit and intention. In this regard, "Pegasus, a near way to take,/ May boldly deviate from the common track;/ From vulgar bounds with brave disorder part,/ And snatch a grace beyond the reach of art."

There is, however, one important qualification to this expansionist poetics: Namely, that although the poet's deviations may elude the letter of aesthetic law, they must not violate the spirit of that law: "Moderns, beware! or if you must offend/ Against the precept ne'er transgress its end." As Pope argues at the opening of Part II of *An Essay on Criticism*, the poet and the critic must never allow themselves to become victims of pride or to equate the spark of their peculiar talents or insights with the all-embracing splendors of the eternal *logos*. Poets and critics of lesser rank, according to Pope, allow their obsession with the parts of a composition to take precedence over their comprehension of its total design. An efflorescence of decorative detail in a poet and a pedantic and small-minded preoccupation with minutiae in a critic are unmistakable indications of debilitated sensibility and false judgment: "But true Expression, like th' unchanging Sun,/ Clears and improves whate'er it shines upon." To value sound over sense, expression over content, nuance over theme, is to sacrifice instruction to delight and to worship the dead letter at the expense of the living spirit.

Furthermore, the prosody of a poetic composition should be judged by the following criteria: "'Tis not enough no harshness gives offence,/ The sound must seem an echo to the sense." Pope crystallizes this point in a series of couplets rich in verbal pyrotechnics. The lines sing, strain, limp, or lilt in accordance with the action described:

> Soft is the strain when Zephyr gently blows,
> And the smooth stream in smoother numbers flows:
> But when loud surges lash the sounding shore,
> The hoarse, rough verse should like the torrent roar:
> When Ajax strives some rock's vast weight to throw,
> The line too labours, and the words move slow;
> Not so, when swift Camilla scours the plain,
> Flies o'er th' unbending corn, and skims along the main.

Here, as so often, the restraint of the couplet inspires Pope to rhythmic feats which make a game of art and bear witness to his own adage: "The winged courser, like the generous horse/ Shows most true mettle when you check his force."

After attacking the patronage system and the proclivity of critics to celebrate poets of superior social rank while denigrating those genuine talents who arouse jealousy and spite, Pope goes on to affirm that, in their ultimate issues, literary, social, and moral values are mutually interdependent. A vacillating and fickle critic inconstant in his service to the muse is thus compared to a degenerate amorist who abandons the lawful embraces of his wife for the specious thrills of a strumpet. Constipated scribblers who "Strain out the last droppings of their sense/ And rhyme with all the rage of Impotence," and Restoration rakes who combine "Dulness with Obscenity . . ./ As shameful sure as Impotence in love," underscore Pope's sense that larger issues of decorum, decency, and health are involved in questions of literary tact. For Pope, the authentic poet and critic is honest and circumspect, capable of elasticity in his judgment but constrained by nature and common sense. He does not neglect the rigors of composition in a false straining for effect nor abandon moral and metaphysical principles in order to flatter public taste. Pope never deserted the values adduced in *An Essay on Criticism* and the poem may be profitably used as a yardstick to measure the underlying integrity of Pope's poetic vision and the vigilance with which he applied it to the literary and cultural aberrations of his age.

An Essay on Criticism was followed by *Windsor Forest* and *The Rape of the Lock*; the former poem is an expression of unity in diversity in which the ecological balance of Windsor Forest is perceived as analogous to the balanced and harmonious development of the British realm following the Peace of Utrecht. Pope's perception of a concordant cosmic design maintained by the mutual subservience of antagonistic forces adumbrates the more compelling philosophic arguments of *An Essay on Man*.

THE RAPE OF THE LOCK

Pope's most brilliant achievement in his early work is, of course, *The Rape of the Lock*. Its sophisticated humor and virtuoso technique are unsurpassed. In this genial spoof of a society abandoned to the pursuit of spurious values, Pope avoids the extreme indignation of his later satires. Instead, he takes an impish delight in the conventions and rituals which are the object of his gentle mockery. Though Belinda and the Baron may be self-regarding fools, the poet obviously relishes their behavior.

The poem itself derives from an actual quarrel between Arabella Fermour and her suitor, Lord Petre. At the request of his friend, John Caryll, Pope undertook the poem, hoping, through his raillery, to laugh the young beau and belle into common sense. Not surprisingly, the tempers of Miss Fermour and Lord Petre were not mollified when, in consequence of Pope's poem, their misadventures became the talk of the town.

Pope's principal strategy in this mock-epic is to stand the conventions of epic poetry on their heads. By counterpointing the dramatic situations and epic conventions of Homer, Vergil, and Milton with the fatuities of a vain coquette and a foppish lord, Pope exposes the pretensions and trivialities of the eighteenth century upper class. Hence, the battle for Troy, Latium, or Heaven becomes a bathetic war between the sexes; the celestial powers of the *Iliad* or *Paradise Lost* (1667) are reduced to diminutive sylphs; and the ferocious appetites of the Homeric warrior are replaced by the pampered palates of a degenerate aristocracy. As in *An Essay on Criticism*, the controlling metaphor is the sun. Belinda's propensity to arrogate to herself the divine attributes of that celestial orb reflects the expansive self-conceit permeating her entire culture. As they are over and over in Belinda's world, the finite preoccupations of pleasure, seduction, flirtation, and gossip are accorded an infinite status. The worship of these things becomes, in consequence, obsessional and demonic. Thus the sylphs who whisper in Belinda's ear on the eve of her molestation by the Baron recall the seductive whispers of Milton's Satan in the ear of the sleeping Eve. Moreover, as Belinda sits before her boudoir mirror and allows herself to be transformed by the ministrations of her attendant sylphs, the religious connotations of Pope's imagery underscore the debasement of true worship into self-worship through "the sacred rites of Pride." Still, Pope's condemnation of Belinda's world is not unequivocal: The radiance, iridescence, and bejeweled splendor of this perfumed society retain a vestige of that divine light which the society caricatures or distorts.

In the last analysis, however, Belinda's chastity is not a positive virtue but an expression of vanity. Her aloofness is a deliberate and insulting challenge to her suitors, whose numbers swell as she remains unfixed and flirtatious. Nowhere is this more apparent than in Belinda's outcry in Canto IV, after the Baron has successfully clipped and stolen a lock of her hair: "Oh hadst thou, cruel! been content to seize/ Hairs less in sight, or any hairs but these!" Belinda is not consciously aware of the comic and lewd implications of her statement, but Pope's cruel joke is definitely intended at her expense. Belinda's unconscious preference for a private seduction over a public insult—that the Baron should have seized "hairs less in sight"—reveals how virtue and chastity remain for her largely a matter of appearance. With the exception of Clarissa, who councils Belinda to exercise restraint, humility, and humor, the moral spinelessness of this society—its appalling indifference to standards and its inability to discriminate between the trivial and the tragic—is epitomized in Pope's use of the couplet and in his juxtaposition of incongruous images. For example,

Belinda's cries at the Baron's violation of her lock are described as follows: "Not louder shrieks to pitying heaven are cast,/ When husbands, or when lap dogs breathe their last;/ Or when rich China vessels fallen from high/ In glittering dust, and painted fragments lie!" The deaths of husbands and of lap dogs, the breaking of china, and the loss of virginity are reduced to the same level.

The poem ends in a mock apotheosis. In the midst of the fracas between Belinda and the Baron, the pilfered lock ascends comet-like to the starry heavens to assume its place among the other constellations. Pope concludes with a poignant reminder of mortality and an implicit plea for Belinda to attain fulfillment in marriage and love: "For, after all the murders of your eye,/ When after millions slain, yourself shall die;/ When those fair suns shall set, as set they must,/ And all those tresses shall be laid in dust,/ This Lock, the Muse shall consecrate to fame,/ And midst the stars inscribe Belinda's name."

ELOISA TO ABELARD

Following *The Rape of the Lock*, Pope's efforts were directed toward a mode of composition with which he is not usually identified: the elegiac verses "Elegy to the Memory of an Unfortunate Lady" and the romantic psychodrama, *Eloisa to Abelard*. The "Elegy" is, perhaps, only partially successful; its chief interest lies in the poet's vacillation between a Christian and a Stoic understanding of the lady's death. *Eloisa to Abelard* is another matter altogether. G. Wilson Knight claims that it "is certainly Pope's greatest human poem and probably the greatest short love poem in our language"—a judgment from which few critics are likely to dissociate themselves.

In the form of an epistle to her beloved and banished Abelard, Pope's Eloisa dramatically expresses the psychological tensions which threaten her reason and divide her soul. Confined to a monastery (ironically founded by Abelard), she receives, at length, a letter from her former lover that reawakens her suppressed passion. The recrudescence of these feelings not only threatens her stability, but also, in her own estimation, endangers her soul; and her situation is rendered even more poignant by the fact that Abelard, having been castrated by henchmen in the employ of her outraged uncle, can neither respond to nor share in her struggles against the flesh. Here the couplet is used not only ironically to counterpose discordant images, as in *The Rape of the Lock*, but also to reflect, in balanced antitheses, the very struggles of Eloisa's soul. In the extravagance of her affliction, Eloisa takes on the attributes of a Shelleyan heroine, preferring damnation with Abelard to redemption without him: "In seas of flame my plunging soul is drowned,/ While altars blaze, and angels tremble round." Even as she submits to the decrees of Heaven and composes herself to meet her maker, she erotically mingles her love for Abelard with her struggle for salvation: "Thou Abelard! the last sad office pay,/ And smooth my passage to the realms of day,/ See my lips tremble, and my eyeballs roll,/ Suck my last breath, and catch my flying soul!" *Eloisa to Abelard* belies the notion that Pope was incapable of composing in the pathetic mode. As Lord Byron observed, "If you search for passion, where is it to be found stronger than in *Eloisa to Abelard*."

Between *Eloisa to Abelard* and *An Essay on Man*, Pope composed a preliminary version of *The Dunciad* (1728), but it was not until 1742 that the poem appeared in its final form.

AN ESSAY ON MAN

Pope's principal achievements from 1731 to 1737 were *An Essay on Man* and associated ethical epistles. These moral essays encompass a variety of subjects: two addresses, to the Earl of Burlington and Lord Bathurst, respectively, on the uses of riches; a study of the Ruling Passion in the development of individual character, addressed to Lord Cobham; and an epistle to Martha Blount on the hypocrisy of women in sophisticated society. The key to each of these studies of the foibles and idiosyncrasies of human character is provided by *An Essay on Man*—Pope's most celebrated poem during his own lifetime and the chief source of his international fame. The poem deserves close study. As a synthesis of eighteenth century apologetic thought on the nature of man, the existence of evil, and the harmony of the creation, it is unsurpassed. Apart from its creedal assertions—which are considerable and not to be dismissed as glib rationalizations or "moldy commonplaces," as Thomas De Quincey would have it—the poem's chief merit lies in Pope's ability to express in taut and pellucid couplets the fundamentals of a religion derived from natural law. In a word, it exemplifies Pope's dictum that "True Wit is Nature to advantage dress'd/ What oft was thought but ne'er so well expressed."

Although Pope's ontology is based on reason and observation as opposed to dogma or revelation, the poem does not deny metaphysical axioms. On the contrary, it continually approximates to "some sphere unknown." The recognition of this metaphysical "sphere" is elaborated in language which is purged of sectarian or denominational accretions, reflecting Pope's belief in a natural illumination or "way" vouchsafed to all men irrespective of particular creeds, forms of worship, or varieties of belief. In short, it is an eighteenth century *tao* which reflects and transcends the thought and expression of the period. Pope's poem is intended to develop in the reader a capacity to recognize the interdependencies of all things; to attune himself or herself in thought and action, to the whole of creation; and to accept, in humility and reverence, an appointed place in the cosmic design.

The first epistle is chiefly concerned with demonstrating that the human place in the scheme of creation is providentially ordained. Pope claims that apparent human limitations are blessings in disguise: If people were possessed of prescience greater than that with which divine wisdom has endowed them, they would pose a threat to cosmic order—that "great chain, that draws all to agree"—and attempt to make themselves the center of the universe. This would be in direct opposition to ". . . the first Almighty Cause," that "Acts not by partial, but by general laws." Although human limitations tax people sorely and the apparent indifference of the universe offends one's sense of justice, it is precisely those limitations which allow for humanity being in existence at all and permit them to develop, through interaction with others, conscious senses of identity. If natural laws were suspended every time a person is threatened by their operation, the world would turn topsy-turvy and the order of both the universe and human society would fall into chaos. Hence, "The general Order, since the whole began,/ Is kept in Nature, and is kept in Man." Furthermore, if man were granted access to the divine plan and made privy to the Creator's will, his stature as a being midway between the Infinite and nothing would be destroyed. Pope reasons: "If nature thundered in his opening ears,/ And stunned him with the music of the spheres,/ How would he wish that Heaven had left him still/ The whispering Zephyr and the purling rill?" To be sure, humans, through an act of faith, must develop the capacity to perceive the infinite in and through the finite, but to cherish the illusion that, in their present state, they are or should be equal to the "Mind of All" is to "invert the laws/ Of Order" and to sin "against th' Eternal Cause."

Pope cautions that humankind should not expect more from life than it is capable of providing and that they should look to death for the fulfillment of that hope which has been implanted in them as a sign of their transcendent destiny. This is to comport oneself authentically to the divine will: "Hope humbly then, with trembling pinions soar,/ Wait the greater teacher Death, and God adore./ What future bliss, he gives not thee to know/ But gives that Hope to be thy blessing now." In the last analysis, true happiness is a consequence of one's adjustment to that "stupendous whole,/ Whose body Nature is, and God the soul." From this proceeds the recognition that "All nature is but art, unknown to thee,/ All Chance, Direction, which thou canst not see,/ All Discord, Harmony, not understood;/ All partial Evil, universal Good."

For Pope, as it is in great things so it is in small. As a microcosm of the universe, man's internal being reflects those same polarities and tensions which, held in harmonious balance, sustain and animate the cosmic scheme. Just as nature may deviate from that balance in eruptions, earthquakes, and cosmic catastrophes, so human equilibrium may itself be usurped by the dominance of a particular passion or impulse. Pope argues, however, that the human mental constitution, despite its precarious balance, witnesses to the ingenuity of its Maker. Reason, by itself, is not enough to activate, kindle, and inspire our existence. Without the promptings of passion, humanity would sink into a contemplative torpor. Thus, "Two Principles in human nature reign;/ Self-love, to urge, and Reason, to restrain." In the elaboration of these mental categories, Pope strikingly anticipates Sigmund Freud. Pope's "self-love" and "Reason" are roughly equivalent to Freud's "Id" and "Super-Ego."

Like Freud, Pope recognizes that "Self-Love"—the id, or pleasure-principle—is the source of those instinc-

tual urges which give vitality and movement to our lives. He also affirms that "Reason"—the Superego, or reality-principle—is necessary to direct those urges into socially acceptable channels and to keep them from becoming self-destructive. To expunge these passions altogether would destroy the human organism and rob life of its daring and splendor. Thus, "Love, Hope, and Joy, fair pleasure's smiling train,/ Hate, Fear, and Grief, the family of pain,/ These mixed with art, and to due bounds confined,/ Make and maintain the balance of the mind:/ The lights and shades, whose well-accorded strife/ Gives all the strength and color of our life." Moreover, each person possesses "One Master Passion" which gives his life impetus and direction. Without that passion his life would proceed without tremor, but his potential for virtue and creation would be severely diminished.

Like Freud, Pope here posits a theory of sublimation which recognizes that all virtues and achievements are transformations of subliminal and potentially destructive energies: "Nor Virtue, male or female, can we name,/ But what will grow on Pride, or grow on shame./ Thus Nature gives us (let it check our pride)/ The virtue nearest to our vice allied." Hence, lust, restrained and harmonized by Reason, becomes love: Spleen becomes honesty; envy, emulation; avarice, prudence; and idleness or sloth—as Friedrich Nietzsche himself observed—philosophy. Finally, "Even mean Self-love becomes, by force divine,/ The scale to measure others' wants by thine./ See, and confess, one comfort still must rise,/ 'Tis this, Though Man's a fool, yet God is wise."

After examining, in Epistle II, the internal economy of human nature, Pope next scrutinizes the relationship between the individual and society. Not surprisingly, Pope's perception of society as an association of countervailing forces parallels his remarks on human psychology and cosmic order. Just as virtue is a product of sublimated vice, so human institutions—families, religious organizations, political bodies—are a product of human weakness. If man is born needy and deficient, that is not an argument against divine dispensation; on the contrary, it is precisely those deficiencies that necessitate the formation of a society based on mutual solicitude and love. In this way, self-love imperceptibly yields to social love—a love which is directly inspired by our need for and reliance on one another. The image that Pope uses to characterize this movement from self-love to social love and, finally, to cosmic love, is that of a pebble dropped in a peaceful lake: "Self-love but serves the virtuous mind to wake,/ As the small pebble stirs the peaceful lake;/ The center moved, a circle straight succeeds,/ Another still, and still another spreads;/ Friend, parent, neighbor, first it will embrace;/ His country next; and next all human race." At length, these spreading circles, and widening arcs of worship encompass the whole of Being and reflect, in miniature, the love of God for his creation. As Maynard Mack observes: "The controlling theme of *An Essay on Man* is the theme of constructive renunciation. By renouncing the exterior false paradises, man finds the true one within. By acknowledging his weakness, he learns his strengths. By subordinating himself to the whole, he finds his real importance in it."

Although it is important to estimate Pope's achievement in *An Essay on Man* in terms of his stated purpose, there is perhaps one legitimate criticism to which the poem gives rise: Pope's failure to recognize and express the intense spiritual struggle involved in accepting one's place in the divine plan. To be sure, Pope's response to those who would question God's justice is not dissimilar from the response accorded Job: "Where was thou when the foundations of the world were laid?" Unlike the Hebrew poet, however, Pope fails to dramatize the efforts of the individual to adhere to the divine will. Pope seems to regard all questionings of or disputations with Providence as manifestations of human pride. In this way Pope vitiates the existential validity of his doctrines and devalues man's struggle to bring his will and intelligence into conformity with the Creator. As one critic remarks: "The wisdom that teaches us not to weep cannot dry our tears, still less can it draw them forth." In the final analysis, however, *An Essay on Man* is a compelling and thoughtful theodicy. As a poetry of statement it comes as close as any statement or assertion can to justifying and explaining the cosmic order. If it leaves the existential dimension of that order out of account, it must be remembered that Pope's intention is to "vindicate the ways of God to Man" through argument and persuasion rather than to *justify* those ways through drama or personal testimony.

EPISTLE TO DR. ARBUTHNOT

The next phase of Pope's career is characterized by rage and indignation at a literary and social milieu in which intellectual blankness and moral bankruptcy are the accepted standard. Pope's voice becomes increasingly apocalyptic as he contemplates, with derision and dismay, the opportunistic secularism of the Augustan age. In the Horatian satires and epistles Pope expresses his outrage at the moral breakdown in the court of George II and the brutalizing cynicism in the administration of Robert Walpole, where "Not to be corrupted is the shame."

From an aesthetic point of view, the most interesting of these Horatian diatribes is *Epistle to Dr. Arbuthnot*. Again Pope astonishes us with the expressive capabilities of the rhyming couplet. By using enjambment and an almost syncopated rhythm to resist the couplet's natural tendency to fall into balanced antitheses with neatly placed caesuras in the middle of a line, Pope is able to capture the idiomatic flavor of a living conversation. One can hear Pope's labored breathing as he slams the door on those flatterers and careerists who have pursued him to the very threshold of Twickenham: "Shut, shut the door, good John!, fatigued I said,/ Tie up the Knocker, say I'm sick, I'm dead./ The Dog Star rages! nay 'tis past a doubt,/ All Bedlam, or Parnassus, is let out." The poem is not merely an attack on Pope's detractors—Atticus (Addison), Bufo (The Earl of Halifax), and Sporus (Lord Hervey)—but a withering indictment of a literary establishment which pursues reputation, influence, fashion, and power to the neglect of truth.

THE DUNCIAD

The ultimate expression of Pope's outrage at a world which ravages the principles of order adduced in *An Essay on Man* and subverts the disciplined training of the moral sensibility and character to curry favor is, of course, *The Dunciad*. Like *The Rape of the Lock*, *The Dunciad* is a mock-epic; but unlike its predecessor the satire here is scathing to the last degree. In its first version, Pope's principal antagonist was Lewis Theobald, a humorless and dry-as-dust pedant who is chiefly remembered for having pilloried Pope's edition of Shakespeare. In the final version, Theobald is replaced by Colly Cibber, a negligible drudge who, according to

Pope, achieved the position of poet laureate through flattery and the propitiation of Dullness. As the King of Dunces, Cibber presides over a factious following of dilettantes and poetasters. In Book IV, the reign of Dullness shakes the very foundations of civilization as chaos supplants cosmos, and moral order is overthrown. Educators, scientists, lawyers, politicians, pedants, and versifiers are all subjected to the withering scorn of Pope's pen. Each has allowed the allures of self-advertisement to compromise the disinterested search for value and truth. In short, *The Dunciad* is a vision of cultural fragmentation and breakdown in which the holistic vision of *An Essay on Man* deteriorates into the deconstructionism, the intellectual madness and lawlessness of those who only "See Nature in some partial narrow shape,/ And let the Author of the whole escape." The arts and sciences, perverted from their true function, become soulless self-reflections of man's skill: "Art after art goes out and All is Night,/ Lo! thy dread empire, CHAOS! is restored,/ Light dies before thy uncreating word./ Thy hand, great Anarch! lets the curtain fall;/ And universal Darkness buries All."

The Dunciad is a trenchant and corrosive probing of the moral, political, and cultural decay of a society controlled by self-important publicists, crass careerists, and opportunistic power-brokers. It is perhaps regrettable that Pope felt the need to encrust this poem with tedious and obscure references to the intellectual disloyalists of his day. Even so, the cumbersome and tortuous inventory of malodorous statesmen and maleficent critics is arguably at one with the poem's substance; the burden which they impose on the reader is a verbal equivalent to their stifling effect on a society from which every vestige of the spirit has been systematically expunged. Moreover, it is important to remember that these references are themselves a parody of "bookful blockheads ignorantly read/ With loads of learned lumber in their head." As Austin Warren observes apropos of Pope's dunces: "The context provides the categories which are permanent, while the proper names are annually replaceable."

Viewed as a whole, Pope's achievement is astonishing in its range and diversity. As the guardian and interpreter of a spiritual tradition distilled from the collective wisdom of Western culture, Pope articulates a "coherent romanticism," as it has been termed by G. Wilson Knight, which has as immediate a bearing on the fractured world of the twentieth century as it had on the refractory world of the Augustans. For those who believe that the preservation of humanistic letters and the survival of spiritual values are inextricably intertwined, Pope's poetry will continue to carry urgency and command attention.

OTHER MAJOR WORKS

NONFICTION: *An Essay on Criticism*, 1711; *Peri Bathos: Or, The Art of Sinking in Poetry*, 1727; *Mr. Pope's Literary Correspondence*, 1735-1737; *The Correspondence of Alexander Pope*, 1956 (5 volumes; G. Sherburn, editor); *The Literary Criticism of Alexander Pope*, 1965.

EDITED TEXT: *Works of Shakespear*, 1723-1725 (6 volumes).

TRANSLATIONS: *The Iliad of Homer*, 1715-1720; *The Odyssey of Homer*, 1725-1726.

MISCELLANEOUS: *The Works of Mr. Alexander Pope*, 1717-1741.

BIBLIOGRAPHY

Baines, Paul. *The Complete Critical Guide to Alexander Pope*. New York: Routledge, 2000. An introduction that offers basic information on the author's life, contexts, and works. Outlines the major critical issues surrounding Pope's works, from the time they were written to the present.

Damrosch, Leopold, Jr. *The Imaginative World of Alexander Pope*. Berkeley: University of California Press, 1987. Damrosch's book is highly recommended for its success in the "imaginative recovery" of Pope, his work, and his world. This is a full and rich treatment, covering a wide range of topics and providing social, political, scientific, and religious contexts within which to read Pope's work.

Erskine-Hill, Howard, ed. *Alexander Pope: World and Word*. New York: Oxford University Press, 1998. A collection of essays that take a fresh textual approach to Pope's achievement. The contributors focus on topics and issues important to Pope but rarely discussed, including his relation to slavery and the non-sexual relation between female and male.

Hammond, Brean S. *Pope*. Atlantic Highlands, N.J.: Humanities Press, 1986. This is an excellent entry in the Harvester New Readings series, and is particularly recommended for its willingness to bring the most recent critical approaches to bear on Pope. Hammond's five chapters are thematically organized, dealing in turn with Pope's life, his politics, his "ideology," his writing career, and his attitudes toward women. A bibliography follows the text.

Mack, Maynard. *Alexander Pope*. New York: W. W. Norton, 1985. Mack's grand and elegant work immediately—and rightfully—took its place as the "definitive" biography of Pope. Bringing to his task a lifetime of distinguished scholarship, Mack paints a complex, fully dimensioned portrait of Pope while managing at the same time an especially rich recreation of English society during the period known as the "Age of Pope."

Pollak, Ellen. *The Poetics of Sexual Myth: Gender and Ideology in the Verse of Swift and Pope*. Chicago: University of Chicago Press, 1985. An important "revisionist" reading of Pope's views of women. Difficult, but highly rewarding.

Rogers, Pat. *An Introduction to Pope*. London: Methuen, 1975. This excellent introduction to Pope and his work is accessible, stylish, and full of textual and contextual insights. A scholar of great erudition, Rogers is particularly adept at providing readings of individual poems against a bright background of Pope's career and age. A useful reading list follows the text.

Rumbold, Valerie. *Women's Place in Pope's World*. Cambridge, England: Cambridge University Press, 1989. Although Pope has long been celebrated for his sympathetic portraits of women, critics like Rumbold have taken long and close looks at Pope's highly complex attitudes toward the "opposite sex." Rumbold's work is very successful at examining the social roles open to women in the generally oppressive, restricted world of eighteenth century England.

Weinbrot, Howard. *Alexander Pope and the Traditions of Formal Verse Satire*. Princeton, N.J.: Princeton University Press, 1982. Pope's greatest achievements as a poet were in the genre of satire, and he and his contemporaries were very aware of the rich satiric traditions bequeathed them by such classical predecessors as Horace, Juvenal, and Persius. Weinbrot thoroughly examines these traditions and considers their influence on Pope and the satiric enterprise in general in early eighteenth century England.

> *Stephen I. Gurney;*
> *bibliography updated by the editors*

EZRA POUND

Born: Hailey, Idaho; October 30, 1885
Died: Venice, Italy; November 1, 1972

PRINCIPAL POETRY
A Lume Spento, 1908
A Quinzaine for This Yule, 1908
Personae, 1909
Exultations, 1909
Provença, 1910
Canzoni, 1911
Ripostes, 1912
Lustra, 1916
Quia Pauper Amavi, 1919
Hugh Selwyn Mauberley, 1920
Umbra, 1920
Poems, 1918-1921, 1921
Indiscretions, 1923
A Draft of XVI Cantos, 1925
Personae: The Collected Poems of Ezra Pound, 1926
A Draft of the Cantos XVII-XXVII, 1928
Selected Poems, 1928
A Draft of XXX Cantos, 1930
Eleven New Cantos XXXI-XLI, 1934
Alfred Venison's Poems: Social Credit Themes, 1935
The Fifth Decad of Cantos, 1937
Cantos LII-LXXI, 1940
A Selection of Poems, 1940
The Pisan Cantos, 1948
The Cantos of Ezra Pound, 1948
Selected Poems, 1949

The Translations of Ezra Pound, 1953
Section: Rock-Drill 85-95 de los cantares, 1955
Thrones: 96-109 de los cantares, 1959
Drafts and Fragments of Cantos CX-CXVII, 1968
Selected Cantos, 1970
The Cantos of Ezra Pound I-CXVII, 1970
Selected Poems, 1908-1959, 1975
Collected Early Poems, 1976 (Michael J. King,
  editor)

OTHER LITERARY FORMS

Ezra Pound was the most influential translator of poetry in the twentieth century. He translated, sometimes
with assistance, from Greek, Latin, Provençal, Italian,
French, German, Old English, Chinese, and Japanese.
The Translations of Ezra Pound (1953) contains most of
his poetic translations; there are also two separate books
of Chinese translations, *The Classic Anthology Defined
by Confucius* (or *The Confucian Odes*, 1954) and *Confucius* (1969), which gathers together in one volume
Pound's translations of *The Analects*, the *Chung Yung*
(*The Unwobbling Pivot*), and the *Ta Hio* (*The Great Digest*).

Pound wrote a great deal of criticism. His music criticism has been collected in *Ezra Pound and Music: The
Complete Criticism* (1977); the best of his art criticism
is found in *Gaudier-Brzeska: A Memoir* (1916) and his
miscellaneous pieces have been brought together in *Ezra
Pound and the Visual Arts* (1980). More important than
either of these was his literary criticism, which, though
more the notes of a working poet than a systematic body
of doctrine, influenced many of the important poets of
the century. *Literary Essays* (1954) and *ABC of Reading*
(1934) contain the best of Pound's formal criticism,
though the informal criticism found in *The Letters of
Ezra Pound, 1907-1941* (1950) is at least as interesting.

Pound's translations and criticism have aroused controversy, but nothing in comparison with that aroused by
his writings on social, political, and economic questions.
These include *ABC of Economics* (1933), *Jefferson and/
or Mussolini* (1935), *Guide to Kulchur* (1938), and *Impact: Essays on Ignorance and the Decline of American
Civilization* (1960). Pound's *Selected Prose, 1909-1965*
(1973) includes a generous sampling of his writing in
this area.

It testifies to the diversity of Pound's interests that
even this account far from exhausts Pound's work in
other forms. He composed an opera, *The Testament of
François Villon* (1926); one of his first books, *The Spirit
of Romance* (1910), was an extended discussion of medieval literature; he translated Confucius into Italian as
well as English; and his contributions to periodicals
number in the thousands.

ACHIEVEMENTS

There is more disagreement over Ezra Pound's
achievements than over those of any other modern poet.
There can be no disagreement, however, over Pound's
extraordinary importance in the literary history of the
twentieth century. Such importance derives in large measure from the close relationship that he enjoyed with so
many of the twentieth century's leading writers. While
serving as W. B. Yeats's secretary (from 1913 to 1915),
he introduced Yeats to Japanese No drama, which served

Ezra Pound (Boris De Rachewiltz, courtesy of New Directions)

as a model for Yeats's subsequent plays for dancers. In the same period, he discovered, promoted, and found publishers for James Joyce and T. S. Eliot. Later, in 1922, he edited Eliot's masterpiece, *The Waste Land*, into final form. In 1914, he and Wyndham Lewis founded the Vorticist movement and the short-lived but seminal magazine *Blast*. During these years, he was actively involved with some of the most exciting literary journals of the period, including *Poetry, The Egoist, The Little Review,* and *The Dial.*

In the 1920's, as he began to write the long poem that would occupy him for fifty years, the *Cantos,* his pace of activity as a promoter of other writers declined. Nevertheless, he was an important influence on several generations of American poets, from his contemporaries William Carlos Williams and Marianne Moore to E. E. Cummings, Louis Zukofsky, Charles Olson, and others. It is no exaggeration to say that the literary history of the twentieth century is unthinkable without Pound.

Pound's work as a translator was as multifarious and stimulating as his activities on behalf of other writers. With Pound's Chinese translations in mind, Eliot in his introduction to Pound's *Selected Poems* called Pound "the inventor of Chinese poetry for our time." His versions of Sextus Propertius, Arnaut Daniel, and Guido Cavalcanti have done a great deal to increase interest in these poets. More important, Pound's example has redefined the art of translation and has influenced several generations of poets. The enormous importance of translation in contemporary poetry can largely be traced to Pound's groundbreaking work. Nevertheless, his translations have also been attacked as hopelessly inaccurate; his scholarship has been said to be nonexistent; and it must be granted that Pound's translations, in attempting to catch the spirit of the original, often do great violence to the letter.

The achievement of Pound's early verse (that written between 1908 and 1920) is, to put it simply, that he created, with Eliot, the modern poetic idiom in English and American poetry. Breaking free from the Victorian style in which he had begun, he began to write concise, laconic, austere poems in free verse, in which the line was the chief unit of composition. This style is usually called Imagism, a useful term as long as one remembers that Pound was the instigator of the style and movement, not

simply one among equals. The best-known Imagist poem is Pound's famous two-line poem, "In a Station of the Metro" (1913), but Pound quickly outgrew the tight, haiku-like style of his Imagist period (1912-1914), applying its concision and characteristically elliptical juxtapositions in longer, more complex, and more substantial poems.

This change quickly bore fruit in *Homage to Sextus Propertius* (first published in *Quia Pauper Amavi,* 1919), a kind of translation whose problematic status as a translation has diverted critical attention from its substance, and *Hugh Selwyn Mauberley,* one of the classics of modernism. Even before completing the dense, witty *Hugh Selwyn Mauberley,* Pound had begun what was to be the work of a lifetime, the *Cantos.* He first published sections from the *Cantos* in 1917; the poem was left unfinished at his death in 1972. The *Cantos* has been praised as the greatest long poem of the twentieth century, but it has also been vigorously attacked or simply dismissed without comment. For a number of reasons, the achievement of the *Cantos* remains a matter of great controversy and may not be settled soon.

Pound was awarded the Bollingen Prize in 1949. In 1963, he was the recipient of the Academy of American Poets Fellowship along with Allen Tate.

BIOGRAPHY

It seems appropriate that Ezra Loomis Pound should have been born on the frontier (in Hailey, Idaho, in 1885) and then moved to Philadelphia at the age of two, to be reared in the suburb of Wyncote until his education at the University of Pennsylvania Hamilton College (Ph.B. 1905, and M.A. 1906). Pound, though always presenting himself as the ultimate American, kept moving east, in search of culture, in a voyage that would lead him to England, then to France, finally to Italy, and in spirit all the way to China.

After his education in romance languages and philology—what today would be called comparative literature—he took a teaching position at Wabash College in Crawfordsville, Indiana. Given his scholarly bent, he might easily have become a teacher and a scholar, but a scandal involving Pound's offering a night's hospitality to a destitute woman ended his career at Wabash and, as it was to turn out, his academic career as well.

He left for Venice in 1908, published his first book of poems there, *A Lume Spento*, and then went to London, where he was to spend the next twelve years remaking literature. Tiring of London after World War I, he moved to Paris in 1921; in 1924 he moved again, to the lovely Italian seaside town of Rapallo. In his twenty years of residence there, he became increasingly enamored of the policies of Italy's Fascist ruler, Benito Mussolini. When war broke out between Italy and the United States in 1941, Pound stayed in Italy, either unable or unwilling to return home (the record is not entirely clear), and broadcast on Rome Radio throughout the war. In July, 1943, he was indicted for treason for his talks; in 1945 he was taken into custody by the American Army. Though returned to Washington for trial and in some danger of being executed for treason, Pound was never tried. He pleaded unfitness to stand trial by reason of insanity—he had suffered a complete break down from his harsh treatment after his capture in Italy—and was sent to Saint Elizabeth's Hospital, where he was to remain until 1958. Finally, after a worldwide campaign on Pound's behalf, the indictment against him was dismissed. He immediately left for Italy and spent the remaining years of his life there, mostly in Venice. Deeply scarred by his experiences, convinced that his political activities had been a mistake, and unable to finish the *Cantos*, Pound refused to speak throughout most of the last ten years of his life.

ANALYSIS

In 1926, Ezra Pound took the title of his third collection of verse, *Personae*, as the title for his collected shorter poems, which complicated his bibliography but afforded his readers a valuable cue. *Persona* in Latin means "mask," and in the 1909 volume *Personae*, there are a number of poems in which Pound takes on the persona, the mask, of an earlier poet and speaks in his voice. By calling his collected shorter poems *Personae*, Pound indicates that this device of the persona, far from being confined to a single volume, is central to his poetry.

Thus Pound's personality is not directly expressed in his poetry; it is found almost nowhere in his work. This clashes strongly with the Romantic notion that poetry is the expression of a poet's personality. One could say

that, for Pound, poetry is the expression of someone else's personality. Pound's choice of personae, however, is never haphazard and his own sensibility and voice come through in the choice of the persona. In Pound's best works, the mask that the poet assumes is a perfect fit: The original speaker is rendered so expertly that readers can take the poem as their own and see Pound as merely a poetic midwife; yet the reader can also view the poem as Pound's through and through and see the original speaker as a mask that Pound has donned for the occasion.

It should be easy to see how this poetic of the persona is also a poetic of translation, and much of the fascination to be found in Pound's early work lies in watching him attempt to bring "translation" and "original composition" together. Poets from the time of Ovid to that of Samuel Johnson would not have seen these as distinct categories, but Romanticism, in its insistence that poetry was what could not be translated, separated what Johnson would have seen as one activity into two very different ones. Pound's early work preserves this Romantic dichotomy even though attempting to transcend it: He translated Cavalcanti and Arnaut Daniel, and wrote poems using Cino da Pistoia and Bertran de Born as personae.

Pound's choice of these Provençal and early Italian poets indicates the indebtedness of his early work to the Victorian poets Robert Browning and Dante Gabriel Rossetti. Pound's notion of the persona owes much to Browning's choice of Cino and Bertran as personae. Rossetti's translations of the early Italian poets helped to direct Pound's interest in these poets and, though Pound wanted to translate Cavalcanti employing a modern idiom, a look at his Cavalcanti translations reveals how much he was still caught in Rossetti's idiom as late as 1912. Nevertheless, though his early work did derive from Browning and Rossetti, his aim was always to go beyond them. He was not a dramatic poet, having none of Browning's interest in rendering a dramatic situation; nor was he, really, a translator, with the translator's self-effacement. He wanted to write translations which were original compositions; he wanted to put Browning and Rossetti together.

He succeeded in such a project only when he moved away from the Provençal and early Italian material with which he had worked from 1909 to 1912. In 1913, he reworked a group of poems from H. A. Giles's *History of Chinese Literature*, "After Ch'u Yuan," "Liu Ch'e," "Fan-piece, for her Imperial Lord," and "Ts'ai Chi'h." Impressed by the quality of these translations (or rather re-translations), Mary Fenollosa got in touch with Pound and asked him if he would be interested in editing her husband's manuscripts. Ernest Fenollosa, an important Orientalist and long-time resident of Japan, had left rough manuscript translations of Chinese poetry and Japanese drama. Pound agreed, and in 1915 the first fruits of Pound's work appeared: *Cathay: Translations by Ezra Pound for the Most Part from the Chinese of Rihaku, from the Notes of the Late Ernest Fenollosa and the Decipherings of the Professors Mori and Ariga*, a book of translations from the Chinese.

CATHAY AND HOMAGE TO SEXTUS PROPERTIUS

It was with the publication of *Cathay* that Pound became a major poet and began to write the kind of poetry he had long wanted to write. The poems in *Cathay* are far more than beautiful translations, though they are that. Pound selected, translated, and published these poems—in 1915—as an indirect way of writing about Europe in the midst of World War I. In other words, Pound *translated* poems about war, exile, parting, and loss as a way of writing "war poetry." This was not, however, immediately recognized; the poems were regarded simply as translations and readers missed or ignored the implicit relation between the world of the poems and the world of the translator.

Pound's first extended poem, *Homage to Sextus Propertius*, was called an homage in order to make Pound's presence in the poem clear. It works in the same way that *Cathay* does: It is a translation of Propertius, a very lively if not overly accurate one; but here too translation and original composition fuse. Pound is interested in Propertius because he sees an extraordinary parallel between Propertius's times and his own and between their respective situations. Both, according to Pound, are ironic sensualists surrounded by an imbecilic empire, and the thrust of Pound's poem is to assert a parallel between Propertius's Rome and Pound's London. Despite the title, Pound's intention of using Propertius to make his own statement was not grasped and the

Homage to Sextus Propertius has never received its due as Pound's most important poem before the *Cantos*. It was attacked by classicists as a horrible mistranslation, and in places it is. Perhaps the most notorious phrase in the poem is Pound's reference to "a frigidaire patent." Pound put in such phrases deliberately to signal to the reader that this poem is about the London of frigidaire patents, not simply about Rome. Instead, these phrases were seen as Pound's crude attempt to modernize his idiom, and so what should have provided valuable clues to Pound's intention were rejected as tasteless excrescences.

Cathay and the *Homage to Sextus Propertius* thus represent the main line of Pound's development toward the *Cantos* because they combine his poetic of the persona with an indirect way of commenting on the present by means of implicit parallels with the past. Pound's reconciliation of the split between translation and original composition in these poems, however, was beyond his audience. Even the most sophisticated of his readers did not get the point, and it is only with the perspective offered by the *Cantos*, which work in the mode of *Cathay* and the *Homage to Sextus Propertius*, that one can see the return to the present implicit in these works. In the wake of the stormy reception of the *Homage to Sextus Propertius*, Pound wrote *Hugh Selwyn Mauberley*, which presents virtually the same perceptions about London as the *Homage to Sextus Propertius*, but with the subtle temporal loop between Rome and London replaced by an ironic persona, Hugh Selwyn Mauberley. Mauberley's relation to Pound is problematic: He shares certain traits with him, yet the poem is only tangentially autobiographical. It is perhaps most accurate to say that Mauberley is a self that Pound sloughed off, or the kind of figure that Pound might have become had he stayed in England. Mauberley, though fighting the stupidity and crassness he stayed in English literary life, will not win that fight, and, the reader feels, he knows it. The dominant mood of *Hugh Selwyn Mauberley* is a resigned acceptance of lesser hopes and aspirations. Written just after World War I, it clearly expresses Pound's disillusionment with the course of history and with the state of English civilization. For these reasons, it is often referred to as Pound's farewell to London. It is also Pound's farewell to poems using a persona alone, without the more complicated temporal loops of *Cathay* and *Homage to Sextus Propertius*, and his farewell to the short, independent poem. After 1920, aside from a few stray political poems written in the 1930's, Pound's work in poetry was confined to the *Cantos*, a massive, sprawling eight-hundred-page poem that dwarfs the early poetry discussed so far.

CANTOS

Pound had always wanted to write a long poem, in this, as in other ways, remaining faithful to the traditional model of the poetic career. According to this model, he actually began his "epic" very early, for sections of the *Cantos* began to appear as early as 1917, though the first section to be published in book form, *A Draft of XVI Cantos*, did not appear until 1925. The last section of the *Cantos* to be published, *Drafts and Fragments of Cantos CX-CXVII*, came out in 1968, fully fifty-one years after the first, and it marked not the completion of the poem but its abandonment, as Pound at the age of eighty-two realized that he could not finish it.

This circumstance makes discussion of the *Cantos* extraordinarily difficult. Perhaps the difficulty is best expressed by asking a simple question: Does one refer to the poem in the singular or the plural? That in turn leads to another question, involving one's critical approach to the work: Is it one long, unified poem, or is it a collection of separate parts? It is not easy to describe what unifies the poem, aside from Pound's claim that it is one poem. The first canto begins with a translation of Homer, the second with a few lines about Robert Browning's *Sordello*, and the third with an autobiographical reminiscence of being a young and poor traveler in Venice. The poem freely moves across all times and all places and all languages as well, as phrases in most of the major European languages and hundreds of Chinese ideograms dot the text. A majority of the cantos have explicit sources outside the poem, and clues to such source material are to be found within the poem. Cantos VIII-XI, for example, constitute a detailed portrait of Sigismundo Malatesta, the fifteenth century ruler of the Italian city of Rimini; Cantos LIII-LXI summarize twenty-five hundred years of Chinese history. Nevertheless, the kind of material included changes considerably in the course of the poem, so this does not really tie it together either. The *Cantos*, in short, are probably

more complicated than poems written since the Renaissance.

The reader's difficulty in subsuming all these materials under one unifying scheme should not, however, blind one to the fact that Pound hoped that the reader would be able to discover such a design. He did set out to write a unified poem, even if he took unprecedented risks in doing so. What complicates the issue is that his ideas about the structure of the poem changed, which should come as no great surprise, given the fifty-odd years that the poem occupied him. To make sense of the *Cantos*, therefore, one must approach them historically, precisely as a poem written across fifty years. The *Cantos* do not have the unified structure of, say, *The Divine Comedy* (c. 1320); there is no shortcut through them, no helpful map or schema. Nevertheless, they are hardly 117 different poems, for the various cantos are integrated by a web of interconnections and they must be read with an attentive eye for what brings them together.

This summary may make one wonder, why bother? Certainly, though the *Cantos* are Pound's most important work, no reader should begin with them. Only a reader convinced of the value of the earlier work ventures into the *Cantos*; but many of those who do find the work totally compelling. Such readers fall into a number of (not necessarily distinct) categories. First, there are those who are held by the beauty and majesty of Pound's language. Even those who consider the *Cantos* a jumble in formal terms concede that certain passages are among the most impressive poetry of the twentieth century. Consequently, Pound has been the poet's poet; his has been the greatest single poetic influence on his own contemporaries and on the poetry of today. The second group of "Poundians" are those who find Pound's ideas compelling. They are the readers that Pound hoped to have, for the *Cantos* constitute perhaps the most ambitious didactic poem of the twentieth century. Although this group forms a distinct minority, many who cannot accept Pound's ideas still feel that his very attempt to write such an intellectually ambitious poem is worthy of praise. Pound single-handedly made it again possible to include serious intellectual and political matters in poetry. Moreover, the *Cantos* is a fascinating intellectual argosy, no matter what one's opinions of Pound's ideas may be. Readers who fall under his spell learn about Chinese history and the Chinese language, early Italian poetry, and hundreds of other things. Thus, the *Cantos*, whatever their difficulties, have their rewards.

What follows cannot under the circumstances be a deep reading, but a brief overview of the *Cantos* may prove helpful to the reader curious about this strange but fascinating work. The 115 cantos available in the collected edition are customarily divided into four sections: Cantos I-XXX are known as the Early Cantos; Cantos XXXI-LXXI are the Middle Cantos; Cantos LXXIV-LXXXIV are *The Pisan Cantos*; and Cantos LXXXV-CXVII are the Later Cantos. These sections are further subdivided. Certain sections have been titled by Pound himself: Cantos LXXXV-XCV are known as *Rock-Drill* and Cantos XCVI-CIX are known as *Thrones*, the titles under which these sections were originally published. Other sections have acquired titles by convention: Cantos VIII-XI are the Malatesta Cantos; Cantos LII-LXI the Chinese History Cantos; Cantos LXII-LXXI the Adams Cantos. Although material in every section escapes any ready classification, the *Cantos* in any given section tend to gather around one common theme.

EARLY CANTOS

The theme of the Early Cantos is the Renaissance, as the two longest sequences in this section are about Sigismundo Malatesta and sixteenth century Venice. The one feature of the *Cantos* that never changes is that they are always, no matter how indirectly or obliquely, really about the present. The implicit return to the present in the Early Cantos is that Pound is wondering whether his own era can fulfill its potential to be a new Renaissance. It has the turbulence of Malatesta's time; has it the brilliance? Toward the end of the 1920's and the Early Cantos, Pound grows less optimistic about contemporary culture and more interested in the economic and political conditions that allow art to flourish. In an implicit contrast with Malatesta's support for the arts treated in the Malatesta Cantos, the Venetian Cantos relate how Titian failed to paint works the government had commissioned, in effect defrauding the state.

MIDDLE CANTOS

This change in Pound's focus and vision prepares the reader for the new direction taken by the Middle Cantos. The cultural and artistic material of the Early Cantos is replaced by political and economic material. Cantos XXXI-LXXI present a series of images of good and bad rulers and good and bad banks: mostly good rulers—Thomas Jefferson, John Adams, Martin Van Buren, Duke Pietro Leopoldo of Tuscany—and bad banks. For Pound there has been only one good bank in history, the Monte dei Paschi Bank in Siena, and modern banking practices are responsible for the growing disorder of the modern world. History for Pound at this point is a Manichaean struggle between the forces of order and disorder, and Cantos LII-LXI summarize twenty-five hundred years of Chinese history because this struggle between order and disorder can be seen most clearly there. According to Pound, the forces of order are the Confucians, and the ideas of Confucius are the most reliable guide to the creation of political order.

None of this would have excited much interest or controversy in itself, but Pound, as always, applies his vision to the present. The implicit thrust of the Middle Cantos is that Benito Mussolini, the Fascist ruler of Italy, is the modern embodiment of the Confucian will to order; the forces of disorder are modern banks and speculative capitalists. This perception led Pound toward anti-Semitism, as he identified the Jews with the usurious banking practices he deplored. Pound, as has already been discussed, attempted to put these political ideas into action as well as putting them in his poem. The resulting personal consequences and the collapse of Mussolini's regime in 1945 were obviously catastrophic for Pound, as his thirteen years in an insane asylum attest. The artistic consequences were disastrous as well, for the contemporary political implications of the *Cantos* were rendered hopelessly out of date and exposed as absurd. Mussolini had obviously not proved to be the twentieth century's Great Emperor; Pound's poem was in praise of a murderous buffoon.

This turn of events doomed Pound's poem to be unfinished and unfinishable, at least in the sense of having a single, articulated direction and structure. What resulted, however, was paradoxically the most brilliant section of the poem. Pound, writing in a prison camp, with all action blocked, no prospect beyond incarceration or execution, his beloved Italy and much of the rest of Europe in ruins, his political vision and his poem in a similar state of ruin, could not continue to write the Confucian epic of the Middle Cantos. Forced into a fresh start, he wrote *The Pisan Cantos*, Cantos LXXIV-LXXXIV, which are in sharp contrast to what has come before in a number of respects.

THE PISAN CANTOS

First of all, *The Pisan Cantos* mark at least a temporary abandonment of the ordering and definition of universals so prominent in the Middle Cantos. This modification has broad implications, as Pound's formal imperative to order particulars had been linked to his Confucian politics of order. No longer is he exclusively concerned with defining what constitutes a good or a bad bank, or a good or a bad ruler. There is a new willingness on Pound's part to stay with the fragment or detail, to respect its concreteness, rather than to align it with other details for the purpose of defining a generality.

In *The Pisan Cantos*, consequently, Pound comes to accept a new measure of disorder, and this allows him to open the poem to new kinds of material. He includes elements that resist generalization, such as details from nature, snippets of conversation he overhears in the detention camp, personal memories, particularly of his first years in London, and selected images and passages of poetry. These details are set out page after page, in a bewildering if dazzling array, in many languages and on every conceivable subject, without any apparent plan or order. In the earlier cantos, one canto might be set in Homeric Greece and the next in Renaissance Greece, but in *The Pisan Cantos* this kind of juxtaposition occurs on the level of the line: A quotation from Mencius will follow a detail about how olive trees look in the wind, details about economics will follow a line of conversation overheard by Pound in the camp. In these cantos, Pound feels free to include whatever he wants, and he freely moves from particular to particular by means of haiku-like juxtapositions.

This change ought to make *The Pisan Cantos* the most baffling and unrewarding section of the *Cantos* but, mysteriously, precisely the opposite is true. When, earlier in the *Cantos*, Pound puts a canto about the Renaissance next to one about Confucius, the reader feels that the juxtaposition must be significant and he is likely

to feel at a loss if—as is often the case—no apparent reason for such a juxtaposition emerges. In *The Pisan Cantos*, however, there are so many such juxtapositions to grasp that the reader should not be expected—at a first reading, at any rate—to puzzle over every one. In other words, both poet and reader adopt (or need to adopt) a more relaxed attitude about both content and sequence in *The Pisan Cantos*. Pound no longer attempts to order his materials; instead, he proceeds confident that it is ordered. That confidence is justified by the entirety of *The Pisan Cantos* as, despite the open, fluid style, these cantos do organize themselves around certain themes. To put it more precisely, the reader, attentive to certain repetitions, discovers the organizing themes of the sequence. The reader does in a sense have to put the poem together, but the elements are there to work with. At the end of the first Pisan canto, Canto LXXIV, Pound turns to the reader and asks whether he has seen that the fragments are parts of a whole. Alluding to the rose pattern formed when a field of iron filings is touched by a magnet's field of force, he asks, "Hast' ou seen the rose in the steel dust?"

It is natural that different readers will have different answers to this question. Pound's analogy is inexact because he has not transformed the shape of the fragments already included in the pages of his poem. He can at most transform the way they are seen. *The Pisan Cantos* are nevertheless universally considered to be the best section of the *Cantos*, so one may conclude that Pound is not alone in seeing a rose in their steel dust.

LATER CANTOS

Critics divide much more sharply on the Later Cantos. In *Rock-Drill* and *Thrones*, though continuing in the more open style achieved in *The Pisan Cantos*, Pound returns to promoting his views on order, and anyone is likely to protest who regards with pleasure the personal turn taken in *The Pisan Cantos*. Nevertheless, although these cantos do not maintain the high level of achievement of *The Pisan Cantos*, *Rock-Drill* in particular is much more interesting than the Middle Cantos. Pound maintains much the same views on society, but he recognizes that he will not see his ideals realized in his lifetime and this lessens his messianic intensity. It also leads him into extended lyric passages that move away from his social and political concerns.

At times in these Late Cantos, therefore, Pound is a prophet who will, he hopes, be justified by history, and at other times, like Stephen Dedalus in *Ulysses* (1922), history for him is a nightmare from which he is trying to awake.

DRAFTS AND FRAGMENTS OF CANTOS CX-CXVII

By the wonderful yet terrible *Drafts and Fragments of Cantos CX-CXVII*, the mood of nightmare dominates. By this time, the history from which he wishes to awake is in large part the history of his own poem. The publication of *Drafts and Fragments of Cantos CX-CXVII* in 1968 marked Pound's formal abandonment of the poem four years before his death. This abandonment seems to have been an act very close to despair. Cantos CXVI and CXVII contain confessions of failure similar to those found in a number of Pound's late statements and interviews. He not only felt that his political activities and his anti-Semitism had been stupid and shallow, but he also felt that the *Cantos* were a failure. In formal terms, he was certainly right. As he says in Cantos CXVI, he could not make it cohere. Yet he does not stop there. He continues, "it coheres all right/ even if my notes do not cohere." Just as *The Pisan Cantos* began in tragedy but ended in triumph, here Pound abandons the poem in an act of humility that somehow goes a long way toward redeeming what has come before. These notes, these CXVII cantos, may not be the coherent structure Pound had hoped for, but Pound is confident that the order he sought to express is out there. He invites the reader to go beyond him to grasp it, to find that it does cohere.

Whether or not to do this is, of course, up to the reader, and different readers, as has been emphasized here, respond and will continue to respond to this invitation in radically different ways. For some, it does cohere, and Pound is the greatest English-language poet of the twentieth century. For others, it simply fails to cohere, and Pound is not worth the bother. For still others, the patterns of coherence are so overwhelmingly totalitarian that Pound should be condemned—not even discussed lest his ideas infect others. The truth, as always, lies somewhere in between, but much of the interest of Pound is that it does not lie comfortably in between.

OTHER MAJOR WORKS

NONFICTION: *The Spirit of Romance*, 1910; *Gaudier-Brzeska: A Memoir*, 1916; *The Chinese Written Character as a Medium for Poetry*, 1920 (editor); *Instigations of Ezra Pound, Together with an Essay on the Chinese Written Character by Ernest Fenollosa*, 1920; *Antheil and the Treatise on Harmony*, 1924; *Imaginary Letters*, 1930; *How to Read*, 1931; *ABC of Economics*, 1933; *ABC of Reading*, 1934; *Make It New*, 1934; *Social Credit: An Impact*, 1935; *Jefferson and/or Mussolini*, 1935; *Polite Essays*, 1937; *Guide to Kulchur*, 1938; *Orientamenti*, 1938; *What Is Money For?*, 1939; *Carta da Visita*, 1942 (*A Visiting Card*, 1952); *Introduzione alla natura economica degli S.U.A.*, 1944 (*An Introduction to the Economic Nature of the United States*, 1950); *L'America, Roosevelt, e le cause della guerra presente*, 1944 (*America, Roosevelt, and the Causes of the Present War*, 1951); *Orro e lavoro*, 1944 (*Gold and Work*, 1952); *"If This Be Treason . . .,"* 1948; *The Letters of Ezra Pound, 1907-1941*, 1950; *Lavoro ed usura*, 1954; *Literary Essays*, 1954; *Impact: Essays on Ignorance and the Decline of American Civilization*, 1960; *Nuova economia editoriale*, 1962; *Patria Mia and the Treatise on Harmony*, 1962; *Pound/Joyce: The Letters of Ezra Pound to James Joyce*, 1967; *Selected Prose, 1909-1965*, 1973; *Ezra Pound and Music: The Complete Criticism*, 1977; *"Ezra Pound Speaking": Radio Speeches of World War II*, 1978; *Letters to Ibbotson, 1935-1952*, 1979; *Ezra Pound and the Visual Arts*, 1980; *From Syria: The Worksheets, Proofs, and Text*, 1981; *Pound/Ford: The Story of a Literary Friendship*, 1982; *Ezra Pound and Dorothy Shakespear: Their Letters, 1909-1914*, 1984; *The Letters of Ezra Pound and Wyndham Lewis*, 1985.

TRANSLATIONS: *The Sonnets and Ballate of Guido Cavalcanti*, 1912; *Cathay: Translations by Ezra Pound for the Most Part from the Chinese of Rihaku, from the Notes of the Late Ernest Fenollosa and the Decipherings of the Professors Mori and Ariga*, 1915; *'Noh' or Accomplishment*, 1916 (with Ernest Fenollosa); *The Natural Philosophy of Love*, 1922 (of Remy de Gourmont's work); *The Testament of François Villon*, 1926 (translation into opera); *Rime*,

1932 (of Guido Cavalcanti's poetry); *Homage to Sextus Propertius*, 1934; *Digest of the Analects*, 1937 (of Confucius's work); *Italy's Policy of Social Economics, 1930-1940*, 1941 (of Odon Por's work); *Confucius: The Unwobbling Pivot and the Great Digest*, 1947; *The Translations of Ezra Pound*, 1953; *The Classic Anthology Defined by Confucius*, 1954 (*The Confucian Odes*); *Women of Trachis*, 1956 (of Sophocles' play); *Love Poems of Ancient Egypt*, 1964; *Confucius*, 1969.

EDITED TEXTS: *Des Imagistes: An Anthology*, 1914; *Catholic Anthology 1914-1915*, 1915; *Active Anthology*, 1933; *Confucius to Cummings: An Anthology of Poetry*, 1964 (with Marcella Spann).

BIBLIOGRAPHY

Froula, Christine. *A Guide to Ezra Pound's Selected Poems*. New York: New Directions, 1983. A competent and useful companion to the poems that serves as an aid to the reader's understanding of Pound's experimental style and is a good accompaniment to his early work. Includes a select bibliography and an index.

Heymann, David. *Ezra Pound: The Last Rower*. New York: Viking Press, 1976. Offers a detailed look at the case for treason which the United States brought against Pound at the end of World War II. By presenting a careful examination of Pound's political and economic beliefs, Heymann attempts to reconcile the poet's life and work. Supplemented by letters, photographs, and an index.

Kenner, Hugh. *The Poetry of Ezra Pound*. London: Faber & Faber, 1951. Rev. ed. Lincoln: University of Nebraska Press, 1985. This classic examination and exposition of Pound's poetry addresses and clarifies most of the obvious misunderstandings that have occurred to those not familiar with his work. This volume does not attempt to be a critical study. Includes a new preface by the author and a foreword by James Laughlin. Complemented by a select bibliography and an index.

Knapp, James F. *Ezra Pound*. Boston: Twayne, 1979. One of the Twayne United States Author series, this volume offers a good, basic introduction to, and an overview of, Pound's work. Augmented by a select bibliography and an index.

Laughlin, James. *Pound as Wuz: Essays and Lectures on Ezra Pound*. Saint Paul, Minn.: Graywolf Press, 1987. A substantial biographical portrait of Pound composed of a collection of recent biographical and critical pieces written by Laughlin, one of Pound's closest friends and literary associates. Supplemented by a select bibliography and an index.

Pound, Ezra. *Ezra and Dorothy Pound: Letters in Captivity*. Edited and annotated by Omar Pound and Robert Spoo. New York: Oxford University Press, 1999. A collection of letters that capture the most traumatic experience of Ezra Pound's life, when he was incarcerated at the end of World War II and indicted for treason. Contains previously unpublished correspondence between the poet and his wife combined with military and FBI documents and previously unknown photographs.

Stock, Noel, ed. *Ezra Pound Perspectives: Essays in Honor of His Eightieth Birthday*. Chicago: H. Regnery, 1965. Contains essays and tributes from a wide range of Pound's contemporaries including Ernest Hemingway, Conrad Aiken, Allen Tate, and Wyndham Lewis. Includes an introduction by Stock. Complemented by illustrations.

_____. *The Life of Ezra Pound*. 1970. Rev. ed. San Francisco: North Point Press, 1982. Follows Pound from his birth in Idaho through his years abroad in England and Italy, to his arrest for treason, his return to the United States, his incarceration in Saint Elizabeth's Hospital, and finally, to his return to Italy. Includes bibliographical references, photographs, and an index.

Surette, Leon. *Pound in Purgatory: From Economic Radicalism to Anti-Semitism*. Urbana: University of Illinois Press, 1999. Surette demonstrates that Pound was not a lifelong anti-Semite and consistently ignored or resisted anti-Semitic comments until after 1931. As the world spiraled toward war, Pound gradually succumbed to a paranoid belief in a Jewish conspiracy. Surette shows how this belief fostered the virulent anti-Semitism that pervades Pound's work from this time forward.

Reed Way Dasenbrock;
bibliography updated by the editors